University Centre at
Blackburn
College

Telephone: 01254 292165

Please return this book on or before the last date shown

CARE ACT MANUAL

by

Tim Spencer-Lane

Second Edition

SWEET & MAXWELL

Published in 2015 by Thomson Reuters (Professional) UK Limited trading as
Sweet & Maxwell, Friars House, 160 Blackfriars Road, London, SE1 8EZ
(Registered in England & Wales, Company No. 1679046. Registered Office and
address for service: 1 Mark Square, Leonard Street, London, EC2A 4EG)

For further information on our products and services, visit
http://www.sweetandmaxwell.co.uk

Printed in the United Kingdom by Hobbs the Printers Ltd, Totton, Hampshire

No natural forests were destroyed to make this product;
only farmed timber was used and re-planted.

A CIP catalogue record for this book
is available from the British Library.

ISBN 978-0-414-05088-4

CONTENTS

CARE ACT 2014

(2014 c.23)

INTRODUCTION

An act to make provision to reform the law relating to care and support for **I1–001** adults and the law relating to support for carers; to make provision about safeguarding adults from abuse or neglect; to make provision about care standards; to establish and make provision about Health Education England; to establish and make provision about the Health Research Authority; to make provision about integrating care and support with health services; and for connected purposes.

[14 May 2014]

BE IT ENACTED by the Queen's most Excellent Majesty, by and with the advice and consent of the Lords Spiritual and Temporal, and Commons, in this present Parliament assembled, and by the authority of the same, as follows:

BACKGROUND TO THE ACT

The Care Act 2014 (the "Care Act") is predominantly about adult care and support, **I1–002** which is the focus of this book. Part 1 brings in long-awaited and fundamental reform. It was introduced following five years of, what the Government described as, "one of the most collaborative processes ever used to develop legislation".[1] The Care Act represents the biggest change in the law governing care and support in England since the National Assistance Act 1948. It not only consolidates and streamlines into a single statute 60 years of piecemeal legislation, but also places personalisation on a statutory footing, introduces a national eligibility threshold and creates the framework for a capped costs system.

The Care Act is likely to touch the lives of everyone. At some point, most of us will need care and support, either for ourselves or for a friend or family member. In 2013–14, a total of 1.27 million people in England were supported by the provision of adult social care services from local authorities.[2] It is estimated that local authority net spend on adult social care in 2014-15 was £14.4 billion.[3] Only a small proportion of social care is publicly funded. Many people will arrange and pay for their own services, or receive support informally from unpaid relatives, friends and neighbours. Many others will have unmet care and support needs. The overall numbers are likely to continue to grow. Baroness Bakewell has referred to a "change in human society on a Darwinian scale; for the first time in history the human race will be living substantially longer than ever before".[4] With population aging, many people will live longer and fitter lives—but the number of people with dementia and additional health problems will also increase. The number of people aged 65—and who are

---

[1] *Hansard* (House of Commons), 10 March 2014, Vol.577, col.85 (Norman Lamb MP).
[2] Health and Social Care Information Centre, *Community Care Statistics, Social Services Activity in England—2013–14 (2014).*
[3] Comptroller and Auditor General, *Care Act First-phase Reforms*, Session 2015–16, HC 83, p.4.
[4] *Hansard* (House of Lords), 21 May 2013, Vol.745, col.769.

in need—is expected to rise by over 40 per cent between 2005 and 2020.[1] Moreover, advances in medicine are enabling more young disabled people to reach adulthood, and more adults to live longer with multiple and complex needs. The Government estimates that in the next 20 years 1.4 million more people are likely to need care and support.[2]

The Care Act is divided into five parts and eight schedules. The reform of the care and support system is dealt with in Pt 1 (ss.1 to 80) and Schs 1 to 4. Part 2 (ss.81 to 95) amends the Health and Social Care Act 2008 by giving new powers to the Care Quality Commission to regulate health and social care provision. It provides the Government's legislative response to the Francis Inquiry into the failings at Mid-Staffordshire Hospital. Part 3 of the Care Act (ss.96 to 120 and Schs 5 to 8) makes changes to the Trust Special Administration regime and establishes Health Education England and the Health Research Authority as statutory non-departmental public bodies. The Better Care Fund (which aims to ensure that every area establishes a pooled budget for integrated health and social care) and additional safeguards in respect of the dissemination of information by the Health and Social Care Information Centre are provided for in Pt 4 (ss.121 to 122). The final part of the Act (ss.123 to 129) contains technical matters including consequential amendments and territorial extent. The Care Act applies to England, except for cross-border provisions in relation to care and support and the Health Research Authority's co-operation duties.

The following factors can be said to have driven the process that cumulated in the passing of the Care Act: the inadequacy of the previous legislative framework, the Law Commission's review, demographic trends and funding crisis, the Commission on Funding Care and Support, and safeguarding failings.

THE PREVIOUS LEGISLATIVE FRAMEWORK

I1–003   The inadequacy of the previous adult social care legal framework had been the subject of criticism for many years, most notably by Professor Luke Clements and Pauline Thompson in their influential publication *Community Care and the Law.*[3] There had also been judicial criticism from Mr Justice Scott Baker (as he was then) who described the complexity of the law in the following terms:

> "Community care legislation has grown piecemeal through numerous statutes over the last half century. There are many statutes aimed at different targets whose provisions are drawn in differing language. Each Act contains its own duties and powers. Specific duties have to be distinguished from target or general duties and duties from discretions. Sometimes a local authority has several ways in which it can meet an obligation. Some provisions overlap with others and the inter-relationship is not always easy."[4]

The previous statutory framework dated back to the National Assistance Act 1948, one of the key Beveridge measures that helped to establish the post World War II welfare state put in place by the Labour Government.[5] The 1948 Act formally abolished the Poor Law that since 1601 had been administered by local authorities. Part 3 placed a strong duty of last resort on authorities to provide residential care, which was "designed to assist the poorest and most needy members of society, at rock bottom".[6] It also provided a general duty to

---

[1] Comptroller and Auditor General, *Care Act First-phase Reforms*, Session 2015–16, HC 83, p.17.

[2] *Hansard* (House of Commons), 11 March 2014, Vol.577, col.280 (Jeremy Hunt MP).

[3] L. Clements and P. Thompson, *Community Care and the Law*, 5th edn (London: Legal Action Group, 2011).

[4] *A v Lambeth LBC* [2001] EWHC Admin 376; [2001] 2 F.L.R. 1201 at [24].

[5] The other measures were the Education Act 1944, the National Health Service Act 1946 and the Children Act 1948. Their purpose was to fight, what Sir William Beveridge had called, the "five giants on the road to reconstruction"—want, disease, ignorance, squalor and idleness. See Sir William Beveridge, "Social Insurance and Allied Services: Report", November 1942, Cmd.6404.

[6] *R. v Royal London Borough of Kensington and Chelsea Ex p Kujtim* [1999] 4 All E.R. 161; (1999) 2 CCLR 340 at 355A.

provide a broad swathe of welfare services for disabled people in the community. However, the 1948 Act retained certain features of the Poor Law such as the eligibility and means tests, and a heavy legal emphasis upon institutional care, while establishing less certain and limited rights to community and domiciliary services. However, the 1948 Act would remain the bedrock of adult social care provision for the next 65 years.

The statutory framework remained largely unchanged for two decades until s.45 of the Health Services and Public Health Act 1968 was enacted, which gave local authorities a power to provide services "promoting the welfare of older people". This was a response to concern that some older people were ineligible for welfare services under the National Assistance Act 1948 because they did not fall within the relevant definition of disability. Section 45 did not, however, amend the 1948 Act. Therefore, both Acts enabled the same (or similar) services to be provided in respect of overlapping categories of persons. This approach would become a defining characteristic of the previous legislative framework.

The Chronically Sick and Disabled Persons Act 1970 was the first major reform of adult social care law post-1948, and has been described as a "fundamental Bill of Rights for disabled people".[1] Originally a Private Member's Bill sponsored by Alf Morris MP, its civil rights agenda was in marked contrast to the notion of social care as a service of last resort articulated by the National Assistance Act 1948. Section 2(1) of the 1970 Act aimed to bolster the weak duty in the 1948 Act to provide non-residential services, with a strong and specific duty, amenable to enforcement by individual disabled people. It was the strength of this duty that made the 1970 Act the focus of many judicial review cases.[2] However, the 1970 Act did not amend the 1948 Act but instead was a "gateway" legal duty that augmented the 1948 Act.[3]

The National Health Service Act 1977[4] extended the remit of adult social care by giving **I1–004** local authorities a power to provide services for the prevention of illness, and for the care and after-care of people suffering from illness.[5] It also established a duty to provide services for people with a mental disorder, and a duty to provide home help and a power to provide laundry services. These reforms were again a response to concerns that certain groups were ineligible for services under the National Assistance Act 1948, but the legislation did not amend the 1948 Act but created parallel duties and powers. Moreover, the groups of people eligible for assistance under the 1977 Act (and the services that could be provided) overlapped with the previous legislation.

Section 117 of the Mental Health Act 1983 added a further nuance to the legal framework. It placed a strong duty on health and social services to provide after-care services to certain former psychiatric patients. This duty remains in force and is discussed in more detail in paras 1–725 to 1–733 below.

The Disabled Persons (Services, Consultation and Representation) Act 1986—like the Chronically Sick and Disabled Persons Act 1970—originated as a Private Member's Bill and was based on a disability rights agenda.[6] Amongst other matters, the 1986 Act aimed to close what was considered to be a lacuna in the 1970 Act, whereby local authorities were required to provide welfare services to disabled people but not required first to carry out an assessment. However, it did not amend the 1970 Act but created a separate assessment regime on top of the existing legislative provisions. The 1986 Act was passed despite Government opposition, and some of its provisions—such as a right to advocacy for disabled people and a statutory right to a care plan—were never implemented.

---

[1] *Hansard* (House of Lords), 19 April 2000, Vol.612, col.745 (Lord Hunt).
[2] For example, *R. v Gloucestershire CC Ex p Barry* [1997] A.C. 584 and *R. (Mcdonald) v Royal Borough of Kensington and Chelsea* [2011] UKSC 33; (2011) 14 CCLR 341.
[3] *R. v Powys County Council Ex p Hambridge* [1998] 1 F.L.R. 643 at 650.
[4] This was consolidated by the National Health Service Act 2006.
[5] National Health Service Act 1977 Sch.8 para.2(1).
[6] Sponsored by Tom Clarke MP.

The National Health Service and Community Care Act 1990 was the first major government-initiated reform of adult social care law post-1948. It established a central right to a community care assessment and, under the care management process, made local authorities responsible for assessing and arranging packages of care from the public, private and voluntary sectors. This was a significant recasting of the relationship between the public and private sectors. Local authorities moved away from the role of exclusive service provider and were instructed to develop a "mixed economy of care making use of voluntary, not for profit and private providers whenever this was most cost-effective".[1] The consumerist and managerial principles of the 1990 Act sat uneasily alongside the notion of the welfare state contained in the National Assistance Act 1948. Although attempting to give coherence to the previous legal framework, the 1990 Act did not consolidate nor alter the access and entitlements to services contained in previous Acts.

I1–005 The rights of carers had been ignored by almost all of the previous legislation. It was left to a Private Member's Bill, sponsored by Malcolm Wicks MP, to begin to redress this imbalance. The Carers (Recognition and Services) Act 1995 provided that, when a local authority carried out a community care assessment, a carer could request an assessment of their own ability to provide care to that individual. Even though the duty interlocked with the National Health Service and Community Care Act 1990, it did not amend this statute but instead added a parallel legal entitlement to a carer's assessment. It also existed alongside s.8 of the Disabled Persons (Services, Consultation and Representation) Act 1986, which already required local authorities to have regard to the ability of a carer to continue to provide care when deciding which services to provide to a disabled person.

Following on from the 1995 Act, the Carers and Disabled Children Act 2000 gave carers a further right to request an assessment. But unlike the 1995 Act, it did not require that a community care assessment was also taking place. This aimed to address a flaw in the 1995 Act whereby a carer's assessment could not take place where the cared-for person refused a community care assessment. The 1995 Act and 2000 Act existed in parallel, and each had to be read and understood in conjunction with the other. Both Acts were later amended substantively by the Carers (Equal Opportunities) Act 2004 which had again originated as a Private Member's Bill[2] and provided a number of new rights for carers, including a requirement that a carer's assessment must take into account whether the carer wishes to work or undertake education, training or any leisure activity. In doing so, it moved away from a focus on supporting the caring role and instead emphasised the need to address social exclusion.

The personalisation agenda was recognised for the first time in statute by the Community Care (Direct Payments) Act 1996. This Act empowered local authorities to make direct payments to people with care and support needs in order that they could arrange their own services. This was largely a response to the rise of the disability rights and independent living movements in the 1990s that criticised the care management system as disabling and disempowering, and sought greater control.[3] The 1996 Act was superseded by the Health and Social Care Act 2001, which, amongst other matters, introduced a qualified duty on local authorities to provide direct payments and widened the groups of people who are eligible to receive them (see para.1–342 below). However, the statutory recognition of personalisation was short lived. The growth of personalisation—including the provision of personal budgets and self-assessments—was achieved largely through guidance, circulars and policy statements rather than any reforms to the underlying statutory framework. This led to friction and uncertainty when personalisation came up against this framework.

---

[1] *YL v Birmingham City Council* [2007] UKHL 27; [2008] 1 A.C. 95 at [51], per Baroness Hale.
[2] Sponsored by Dr Hywel Francis MP.
[3] See, for example, J. Morris, *Independent Lives? Community Care and Disabled People* (1993) and C. Barnes and G. Mercer, *Independent Futures: Creating User-led Disability Services in a Disabling Society* (2006).

THE LAW COMMISSION REVIEW

The process that cumulated in the passing of the Care Act began with a three-year review **I1–006** of adult social care undertaken by the Law Commission of England and Wales.[1] In 2010 the Commission undertook a public consultation on its next programme of law reform. In its written submission, the Law Society suggested the need for a review of adult social care, describing the legal framework as one which frequently baffled social care workers, service users, informal carers and lawyers alike, and being in urgent need of reform.[2] A separate proposal was also submitted by the parents of two disabled boys (then aged 19 and 15) who had experienced over the years major issues and protracted legal battles with their local authorities. In particular they highlighted that the process for the transfer of care packages from one local authority to another was confused and inconsistent, and pointed to the inadequacy of the system for challenging local authority decision-making. They argued for the introduction of an expert tribunal system using the special educational needs tribunals as a model.[3] The review of adult social care was announced in 2008 as part of the Law Commission's Tenth Programme of Law Reform.[4]

The scoping report

In November 2008, the Law Commission published its scoping report, "Adult Social **I1–007** Care", which set out the key areas that it considered should form part of the review. It stated that:

> "Adult social care law remains a confusing patchwork of conflicting statutes enacted over a period of 60 years. Some of these statutes reflect the disparate and shifting philosophical, political and socio-economic concerns of various post-war governments. Other statutes were originally Private Member's Bills and represent an altogether different agenda of civil rights for disabled people and their carers. The law has also developed with an inconsistent regard for previous legislation: some statutes amend or repeal previous legislation; others repeat or seek to augment previous law; and others can be categorised as stand-alone or parallel Acts of Parliament."[5]

However, the need for law reform did not arise solely because of an inadequate legal structure. The Commission also identified more fundamental reasons for reform, and in particular it criticised adult social care law for perpetuating outdated and discriminatory concepts. For example, it contrasted the strong duty to provide residential care to older and disabled people, with the less-certain rights to community and home-based care provision contained in the National Assistance Act 1948. This legal emphasis on institutionalised care, it argued, reflected the principles of the Poor Law and commonly held attitudes of the 1940s. In addition, the Commission pointed to s.29(1) of the National Assistance Act 1948, which contained the principal definition of a disabled person for the purposes of community care law, and included a cross heading describing the content of the section as: "welfare arrangements for blind, deaf, dumb and crippled persons, etc". Section 29 went on to describe those who are potentially eligible for welfare services as persons aged 18 years or over who are:

> ". . . blind, deaf or dumb, or who suffer from mental disorder of any description and other persons aged 18 or over who are substantially and permanently handicapped by illness, injury, or congenital deformity or such other disabilities as may be prescribed by the Minister."

---

[1] The Law Commission is a non-political independent body, set up by Parliament in 1965 to keep all of the law of England and Wales under review, and to recommend reform where it is needed.
[2] Email from Tim Spencer-Lane (then Policy Adviser (Mental Health and Disability) to the Law Society) to the Law Commission (13 March 2007).
[3] Email from Michael and Henrietta Spink to the Law Commission (16 March 2007).
[4] Law Commission, *Tenth Programme of Law Reform* (2008), Law Com No.311, p.10.
[5] Law Commission, *Adult Social Care: Scoping Report* (26 November 2008), para.2.1.

This definition was widely accepted as being "out of date, offensive and does not provide a useful starting point for enabling disabled people to fulfil their roles as citizens".[1] The Commission argued that the outdated and discriminatory nature of the law might also filter through into types of care and support that are provided:

> "If, for example, services are being designed for people who are 'substantially and permanently handicapped by illness, injury, or congenital deformity', then they are more likely to be based on assumptions of dependency and deficiency rather than providing disabled people with access to full citizenship".[2]

The scoping report also identified areas of the law that were difficult to reconcile with the European Convention on Human Rights. A key example being s.47 of the National Assistance Act 1948, which enabled the removal of certain people from their homes to a place of safety for the purpose of securing necessary care and attention. It was argued that the range of persons who could be detained under this power extended beyond the categories authorised under art.5(1)(e) and the limited ability of people to challenge the use of this power and seek a review might breach art.5(4).[3] This is discussed in further detail at para.1–507 below. Finally, the Commission concluded that the legal framework had generated inefficiency, since negotiating complex and outdated law "takes longer and requires more resources". It argued that a clearer and more cohesive legal framework would lead to "less time being spent on law and litigation".[4]

The Government approved a substantive law reform project on most of the areas identified in the scoping report. The one area it did not want the review to cover was the system for complaining about, and seeking redress for, failures in decision-making and service provision by local authorities.[5]

Public consultation and final report

I1–008   On 24 February 2010, the Law Commission published its consultation paper which set out 57 provisional proposals and 25 consultation questions on the reform of adult social care law.[6] This was followed by a four-month public consultation. The stated aim was to create:

> ". . . an effective legal framework that can accommodate current and future policies, while also maintaining the core entitlements and obligations that have been established over the past 60 years".[7]

Underpinning the consultation paper was the proposal for a single statute for adult social care in England and Wales, and the repeal of the vast majority of existing legislation, most notably the National Assistance Act 1948 and the Chronically Sick and Disabled Persons Act 1970. The proposed statute would provide a new legal framework for those with care and support needs, carer's rights to support and safeguarding adults from harm.

Members of the Commission attended 72 consultation events across England and Wales. These included meetings with service users, carers, local authorities, individual social workers, health staff, academics, safeguarding boards, lawyers, service providers, charities and campaigning organisations. The Commission received 231 written responses to the

---

[1] Prime Minister's Strategy Unit, *Improving the Life Chances of Disabled People* (2005), p.73.

[2] Law Commission, *Adult Social Care: Scoping Report* (26 November 2008), para.2.32.

[3] Law Commission, *Adult Social Care: Scoping Report* (26 November 2008), para.4.301.

[4] Law Commission, *Adult Social Care: Scoping Report* (26 November 2008), para.3.2.

[5] Law Commission, *Better law for disabled people, older people and carers—reforming adult social care legislation*, Press release, 26 November 2008.

[6] Law Commission, *Adult Social Care: A Consultation Paper*, Law Commission Consultation Paper No.192 (2010).

[7] Law Commission, *Adult Social Care: A Consultation Paper*, Law Commission Consultation Paper No.192 (2010), para.1.2.

consultation paper, from a range of different individuals and organisations. The consultation analysis was published on 31 March 2011.[1]

The Commission's final report was laid in Parliament and published in May 2011. It contained 76 recommendations for the reform of adult social care.[2] The Commission remained of the view that the existing legal framework urgently needed to be consolidated and simplified, which it argued would be best achieved by a unified adult social care statute. It noted that this could be achieved by separate statutes in England and in Wales, or a single statute covering both countries—but concluded that the issue had been settled in practice by the introduction of Pt 4 of the Government of Wales Act 2006 which had given the National Assembly for Wales the power to legislate on social care matters. It therefore recommended there should be single and consistent statutes for each of England and Wales, and that in Wales this should be implemented by means of an Act of the National Assembly. The new statutes were the first level of a new three level structure for adult social care, and would set out the core duties and powers of local authorities. The second level would be regulations made by the Government to provide more detail where necessary and to allow for developments of policy in the future. The third level would consist of a code of practice for adult social care.[3]

The Law Commission's recommendations contained in its final report are discussed in detail throughout this book. They included:

- an overarching statutory principle to promote individual well-being which would apply to all decisions under the legislation;
- giving carers new legal rights to assessments and services;
- placing duties on local authorities and the NHS to work together;
- a new single eligibility framework for residential and non-residential services;
- a duty to investigate cases where people with care and support needs and their carers are at risk of harm; and
- a requirement to establish Adult Safeguarding Boards in every local authority area.

The Law Commission argued that it was recommending "the most far reaching reforms of adult social care law seen for over 60 years".[4]

DEMOGRAPHIC TRENDS AND FUNDING CRISIS

The need for a new adult social care system was also driven by fundamental demo- **I1–009** graphic changes. Population projections by the Office of National Statistics indicate that the UK population is ageing rapidly, with the average (median) age rising from 39.7 years in 2010 to 39.9 years in 2020 and 42.2 years by 2035.[5] As the population ages, the numbers in the oldest age groups will increase the fastest. In 2010, there were 1.4 million people in the UK aged 85 and over; this number is projected to increase to 1.9 million by 2020 and to 3.5 million by 2035, more than doubling over 25 years.[6] It is acknowledged widely that an ageing population presents economic and social opportunities, and that many people will lead longer and fitter lives. But it will also lead to increased costs since, as people get older, they are more likely to need care and support. The Government expects 600,000 more older people to have care and support needs in the next 20 years.[7]

---

[1] Law Commission, *Adult Social Care: Consultation Analysis* (31 March 2011).

[2] Law Commission, *Adult Social Care*, Law Com No.326 (2011).

[3] Law Commission, *Adult Social Care*, Law Com No.326 (2011), paras 3.1 to 3.34.

[4] Law Commission, "Law Commission recommends radical overhaul of adult social care law", Press release, 11 May 2011.

[5] Office for National Statistics, *National Population Projections, 2010-Based Statistical Bulletin* (26 October 2011).

[6] Office for National Statistics, *National Population Projections, 2010-Based Statistical Bulletin* (26 October 2011).

[7] Department of Health, *Caring For Our Future: Reforming Care and Support: Impact Assessments Summary Document* (July 2012), para.20.

Demographic trends also mean that the proportion of older people in the population is growing, compared to the proportion of working age adults (known as the "dependency ratio"). In 2012 there were around five people aged under 65 for every person aged over 64. By 2060, there is likely to be just three people aged under 65 for every person aged over 65.[1] This may have a significant impact on for example the provision of informal care. However, the use of the old age dependency ratio has been criticised since it is a static measure based on how many people are aged over 65 compared to the remainder, and assumes wrongly that all older people are dependent.[2]

Medical advances also mean that the life expectancy of disabled people is rising. It is now possible for people who develop severe and complex health and social care needs at a younger age (including disabled children) to live longer. Between 2002 and 2041, the number of disabled people is expected to double.[3] This will lead to increased demand for health and social care. It is expected for example that the number of adults with learning disabilities who require some form of support will increase between 3.2 per cent and 7.9 per cent per year.[4]

The impact of demographic trends has led rising concern about the future affordability of care and support. In England around 1.1 per cent of GDP is spent on adult care and support, which is expected to rise to 1.25 per cent by 2025–26.[5] The costs of supporting the health and social care needs of older people are also increasing and expectations of the quality of care and support that people want are rising. To meet the demographic pressures, it is estimated that an additional £400 million a year of public expenditure is required; but this would only maintain existing expenditure levels, in other words "that is just to stand still".[6] The Government predicts that by 2028 there will be a funding gap of over £6 billion in adult social care.[7]

I1–010 Concerns about the future affordability of care and support also need to be set in the context of the post-2007 economic downturn and cuts to public services. In 2012–13, 26 per cent fewer people aged over 65 were receiving publicly funded social care, along with 24 per cent fewer disabled people, compared to 2008–09, the year in which the global financial crisis struck. The decline has been sharpest (30 per cent) amongst those receiving care and support at home.[8] In Parliament, during the passage of the Care Bill, it was pointed out that in order to cope with the funding cuts, a number of local authorities have raised the eligibility bar for access to services, and accordingly:

". . . despite growing numbers of older people, fewer people are now being helped because their needs are assessed as moderate, not substantial, even though earlier support can prevent the need for higher costs later."[9]

---

[1] Department of Health, *Caring For Our Future: Reforming Care and Support: Impact Assessments Summary Document* (July 2012), para.21.

[2] Commission on the Future of Health and Social Care in England, *A New Settlement for Health and Social Care: Interim Report*, King's Fund (2014), pp.25 to 28.

[3] R. Hancock and others, *Paying for Long-Term Care for Older People in the UK: Modelling and Distributional Effects of a Range of Options* (2007).

[4] Department of Health, *Caring For Our Future: Reforming Care and Support: Impact Assessments Summary Document* (July 2012), para.20.

[5] Department of Health, *Caring for Our Future: Consultation on Reforming What and How People Pay for their Care and Support* (2013), para.12.

[6] *Hansard* (House of Commons: Public Bill Committee, 23 January 2014 (AM): Ninth Sitting, col.351 (Meg Munn MP) and *Hansard* (House of Commons), 10 March 2014, Vol.577, col.83 (Grahame M. Morris MP).

[7] HM Government, *The Case for Change: Why England Needs a New Care and Support System* (May 2008), p.24.

[8] Commission on the Future of Health and Social Care in England, *A New Settlement for Health and Social Care: Interim Report*, King's Fund (2014), p.5.

[9] *Hansard* (House of Lords), 3 July 2013, Vol.746, col.1244 (Lord Best).

The combined effect of the demographic trends and funding crisis on adult social care has for some time pointed towards an urgent need to establish a new funding system, as well as a more effective legal structure. Social care funding reform was not a new issue, and had been the subject of many previous reviews and reports.[1] But what had changed by 2014 was the political consensus over the urgent need for reform.

COMMISSION ON FUNDING CARE AND SUPPORT

In July 2010, the Commission on Funding Care and Support, chaired by the economist **I1–011** Sir Andrew Dilnot, was given the task by the Government of making recommendations on how "to achieve an affordable and sustainable funding system" for care and support for all adults in England, "both in the home and in other settings". In particular, it was asked to examine three issues:

- "how best to meet the costs of care and support as a partnership between individuals and the state";
- "how people could choose to protect their assets, especially their homes, against the costs"; and
- "how both now and in the future public funding for the care and support system can be best used to meet care and support needs".[2]

In December 2010, the Commission launched a call for evidence and received over 250 responses. It also undertook a programme of research that included a literature review of public opinion research, deliberate research on funding options and trade-offs people were willing to make, and economic modelling and analysis of the impact of the various funding models. The Commission reported in July 2011, and concluded that:

"The adult social care funding system conceived in 1948 is not fit for purpose in the 21st century and is in urgent need of reform . . . The current system does not encourage or reward saving, and is poorly understood. People are not prepared, which often leads to poor outcomes and considerable distress."[3]

The Commission put forward a limited liability model whereby, in addition to the current means-tested assistance system, the state would pick up the cost of care for people who met a maximum financial contribution. It claimed that "everyone would benefit from knowing that, if they ended up having to face these costs, they would be covered". By removing the fear and uncertainty inherent in the current system, the Commission argued that people would be encouraged to make preparations for the future and in particular the reforms would "create a new space for financial products, which could support people in making their individual contributions".[4] In total, the Commission made 10 recommendations:

1. a cap on an adult's lifetime contribution to their care costs set at between £25,000 and £50,000 (with £35,000 put forward as the "most appropriate and fair figure") with an improved national deferred payment scheme;
2. an increase in the upper means test threshold for state support from £23,250 to £100,000;
3. free state support for those who enter adulthood with care and support needs;
4. the retention of universal disability benefits for people of all ages;
5. a standard, fixed, amount paid towards general living costs, such as food and accommodation, by those in residential care;

---

[1] See, for example, King's Fund, *Securing Good Care for Older People: Taking a Long-Term View* (2006).

[2] Commission on Funding of Care and Support, *Fairer Care Funding: The Report of the Commission on Funding of Care and Support: Volume I* (2011), p.9.

[3] Commission on Funding of Care and Support, *Fairer Care Funding: The Report of the Commission on Funding of Care and Support: Volume I* (July 2011), p.11.

[4] Commission on *Funding of Care and Support, Fairer Care Funding: The Report of the Commission on Funding of Care and Support: Volume I* (July 2011), p.20.

6. national eligibility criteria for service entitlement across England, and portability of assessments;
7. a government awareness campaign to inform people of the new system and encourage them to plan ahead for their later life;
8. a statutory duty on local authorities to provide information, advice and assistance services in their areas;
9. new legal rights to assessments and services, as recommended by the Law Commission; and
10. a review of the scope for improving the integration of adult social care with other services in the wider care and support system.

The Commission also concluded that, in the short-term, it was reasonable for a minimum eligibility threshold to be set nationally at "substantial" under the current system. It estimated that the recommended new funding system would cost from around £1.3 billion for a cap of £50,000 to £2.2 billion for a cap of £25,000. The cap on care costs and extended availability of means-tested state support are considered in detail at paras 1–164 to 1–168 and 1–181 to 1–197 below.

Safeguarding failings

I1–012   A number of adult safeguarding scandals in the years leading up to the publication of the Care Bill (and during the passage of the Bill through Parliament) reinforced the need for a new statutory framework. In particular, the events led to increased scrutiny of long-term institutional care provided by hospitals and care homes. This began in May 2011 when a BBC Panorama broadcast "Undercover Care: the Abuse Exposed" showed staff at Winterbourne View Hospital in South Gloucestershire mistreating and assaulting adults with learning disabilities and autism. The abuse included water-based punishment, the use of illegal and dangerous methods of restraint, needless suffering of patients and the transgression of professional boundaries. Moreover, whistleblowing concerns had been ignored by the managers of Winterbourne View, and by the Care Quality Commission. Winterbourne View Hospital was a private facility which catered mostly for patients detained under the Mental Health Act 1983. The Serious Case Review, commissioned by South Gloucestershire's Safeguarding Adults Board, detailed a litany of failings by the Hospital, its owners (Castlebeck Care (Teeside) Ltd), NHS commissioners, the local authority, police and regulators. It concluded that the apparatus of oversight across sectors was "unequal to the task of uncovering the fact and extent of abuses and crimes at Winterbourne View".[1] As a result of the programme, Winterbourne View Hospital closed and following a police investigation nine support workers and two learning disability nurses were convicted under the Mental Health Act 1983 of ill-treating patients. Six were imprisoned and five received suspended sentences. In March 2013, following a second Panorama programme, Castlebeck Care (Teeside) Ltd went into administration.

In Wales, an investigation by Gwent police started in 2005—known as Operation Jasmine—uncovered instances of historic neglect and abuse in care homes, and was the biggest investigation into care home abuse ever undertaken in the UK. There were 103 alleged victims of care home abuse and neglect (including 63 deaths), however only three convictions were secured for wilful neglect by carers. Moreover, charges brought against the care home owner did not directly relate to poor care for residents in his homes, but instead to breaches of health and safety legislation and false accounting. In 2013, the Welsh Government announced a review of Operation Jasmine.[2] The final report

---

[1] M. Flynn, *South Gloucestershire Safeguarding Adults Board: Winterbourne View Hospital: A Serious Case Review* (2012) p.143.

[2] See Action on Elder Abuse, *Operation Jasmine: An Example of Why We Need a New Law on Ill-treatment or Neglecting Adults* (2013); *Hansard* (House of Lords), 22 July 2013, Vol.747, col.1101 (Lord Touhig); *Hansard* (House of Commons), 16 December 2013, Vol.572, col.530 (Nick Smith MP).

was published in 2015 which included a series of lessons to be learnt.[1] The period leading up to the Care Bill also saw one of the worst hospital care scandals of recent times. An estimated 400–1,200 patients are believed to have died between January 2005 and March 2009 as a result of poor care at Stafford hospital. The standard of care provided by the Mid Staffordshire NHS Foundation Trust was the subject of several investigations and reports, culminating in a public inquiry. The final report of the public inquiry was published on 6 February 2013 (known as the Francis Report).[2] The events that led to these inquiries were summed up in the following terms by the Prime Minister:

> "What happened at Mid Staffordshire NHS Foundation Trust between 2005 and 2009 was not just wrong; it was truly dreadful. Hundreds of people suffered from the most appalling neglect and mistreatment. There were patients so desperate for water that they were drinking from dirty flower vases. Many were given the wrong medication, treated roughly or left to wet themselves and then lie in urine for days, and relatives were ignored or even reproached when they pointed out even the most basic things that could have saved their loved ones from horrific pain or even death. We can only begin to imagine the suffering endured by those whose trust in our health system was betrayed at their most vulnerable moment."[3]

The report states that external organisations failed to prevent the scandal in two ways: first, none of them "appreciated the scale of the difficulties" and second, none of the organisations "did anything effective to stop" the failings. Consequently:

> "The system as a whole failed in its most essential duty—to protect patients from unacceptable risks of harm and from unacceptable, and in some cases, inhumane, treatment that should never be tolerated in any hospital".[4]

Following the Francis Report, the Keogh Report into high mortality rates in NHS hospital trusts, and concerns about maternity services at Morcombe Bay NHS Foundation Trust raised further concerns about the poor quality of in-patient care.[5]

The effect of these safeguarding failings are most evident in the adult safeguarding provisions in the Care Act, which are contained mainly in ss.42 to 47 (as well as Pt 2 of the Act which implements the Government response to the Francis Report).

DRAFT CARE AND SUPPORT BILL

To take forward the reform of adult social care law, in July 2012 the Government published a White Paper Caring for our Future, a draft Care and Support Bill, its formal response to the Law Commission's report, and a progress report on the reform of the funding of adult social care.[6] In the foreword to the draft Care and Support Bill, Andrew Lansley, the then Health Secretary, and Paul Burstow, the then Minister for Care Services, said that **I1–013**

---

[1] M Flynn, *In Search of Accountability: A Review of the Neglect of Older People Living in Care Homes Investigated as Operation Jasmine* (2015).

[2] R. Francis, "Report of the Mid Staffordshire NHS Foundation Trust Public Inquiry—Executive Summary", 2013, HC 898.

[3] *Hansard* (House of Commons), 6 February 2013, Vol.558, col.279.

[4] R. Francis, "Report of the Mid Staffordshire NHS Foundation Trust Public Inquiry—Executive Summary", 2013, HC 898, pp.7–8.

[5] B. Keogh, "Review into the Quality of Care and Treatment Provided by 14 Hospital Trusts in England: Overview Report", 16 July 2013); and Care Quality Commission, "University Hospitals of Morecambe Bay NHS Foundation Trust Investigation Follow-Up Report", September 2013.

[6] HM Government, *Caring for Our Future: Reforming Care and Support* (TSO, July 2012) Cmd 8378, Department of Health, *Draft Care and Support Bill* (TSO, July 2012) Cm.8386, Department of Health, *Reforming the Law for Adult Care and Support: The Government's Response to Law Commission Report 326 on Adult Social Care* (TSO, July 2012), Cm.8379, and Department of Health, *Caring for our Future: Progress Report on Funding Reform* (TSO, July 2012) Cm.8381.

the draft Bill represented "an historic reform of care and support legislation". They added that:

> "For over 60 years, social care law has been anchored in the post-war period, looking back to the Poor Law for its principles. Whilst other areas have moved forward with modern times and expectations of public services, care and support law has been left unreformed; a web of complicated, overlapping requirements which have led to confusion, challenge and frustration".

They went on to state that the draft Bill:

> ". . . consolidates provisions from over a dozen different Acts into a single, modern framework for care and support. It is intended to do more than bring those Acts together; it achieves a fundamental reform of the way the law works. It places the well-being, needs and goals of people at the centre of the legislation to create care and support which fits around the individual and works for them. It provides a new focus on preventing and reducing needs, and putting people in control of their care and support. For the first time, it brings carers into the heart of the law, on a par with those for whom they care."[1]

The Government accepted the vast majority of the Law Commission's recommendations. The Law Commission estimated that out of its 76 recommendations, 66 had been taken forward.[2] The draft Bill, however, contained no clauses regarding funding reform. The Government progress report stated that the principles of the model set out by the Commission on Funding Care and Support were the "right basis for any new funding model" and that "protecting people against very high costs would provide peace of mind and enable them to plan and prepare for their future care needs". But it said that more time was needed to consider the costs and other key implications.[3]

The draft Bill was subject to a three-month public consultation. Its central elements included:

- a duty on local authorities to promote individual well-being;
- general duties on local authorities to provide information and advice, prevention services, and shape the market for care and support services;
- duties on local authorities to promote co-operation and integrate services;
- a new assessment and eligibility system for people with care and support needs, and a similar system for carers;
- new statutory duties to provide a personal budget and a care and support plan to all service users;
- provisions to encourage continuity of care when a service user moves between local authority areas and when a child transitions to adult services; and
- a new statutory framework for adult safeguarding, setting out the responsibilities of local authorities and their partners, and creating Safeguarding Adults Boards in every area.

Joint Committee on the draft Care and Support Bill

I1–014   It was also decided that the draft Bill should receive pre-legislative scrutiny by a joint committee of both Houses of Parliament. This Committee (the Joint Committee) was chaired by the former Minister for Care Services Paul Burstow MP and constituted on 22 November 2012. It held a total of 16 meetings. In response to its call for written evidence, it received 143 submissions. It also held 17 evidence sessions during which it

---

[1] Department of Health, *Draft Care and Support Bill* (TSO, July 2012) Cm.8386, p.4.
[2] House of Lords House of Commons Joint Committee on the Draft Care and Support Bill, *Draft Care and Support Bill, Session 2012–13, Oral Evidence* (2013), p.78, Q83 (Frances Patterson QC).
[3] HM Government, *Caring for our Future: Progress Report on Funding Reform* (July 2012), Cm.8381, p.37.

took oral evidence from 61 persons, including the relevant Government Ministers. The Joint Committee was also able to consider the views given in response to the Government's consultation on the draft Care and Support Bill, in addition to those replying to the Committee's call for evidence.

The Joint Committee's report was published in March 2013 and made 107 recommendations in total (93 of which related to care and support).[1] It stated that:

"The draft Bill represents a major reform of the legal framework governing the provision of adult care and support in England. It goes further than just a consolidation by establishing in law, for the first time, that well-being is the guiding principle of decision-making in care and support. It significantly extends the rights of adult carers, and it places greater emphasis on prevention."[2]

The report went on to say that:

"The draft Bill has been widely welcomed. That does not mean that it cannot be improved. There are gaps, risks of unintended consequences and further opportunities to realise the Government's White Paper vision."[3]

The joint Committee's recommendations in respect of care and support are discussed in detail throughout this book. In summary, its key recommendations included the following:

- the Government should launch a national awareness campaign about what the national care and support offer is, how people can plan and prepare for their care needs, and what their rights to care and support are;
- the Secretary of State should be bound by the well-being duty when designing and setting a national eligibility threshold;
- the boundary between free NHS services and means-tested care and support should be amended to ensure that more people in residential care do not fall into the means tested system;
- the advice made available to those navigating their way through the care and support system should include advice on housing options and on personal finances;
- the rules should make it easier for local authorities and the NHS to pool budgets and to commission services together, and the Secretary of State should have the ability to mandate joint budgets and joint commissioning in certain circumstances;
- the Government must address the position of young carers who will be left with reduced rights in "rump legislation";
- guidance should be issued to rule out unacceptable commissioning practices such as contracting care by the minute;
- the responsibilities of local authorities to prevent abuse and neglect should be made explicit;
- all care providers (whether from the private or voluntary sector) should be subject to the same legal obligations as the local authority itself, including the Human Rights Act 1998; and
- where abuse has taken place there should be corporate criminal responsibility, with organisations and key individuals held to account.

As noted above, when the Joint Committee began its work the Government had not confirmed its policy on funding reform. However, on 11 February 2013 Jeremy Hunt, the Health Secretary, announced to the House of Commons that the Government had decided

---

[1] House of Lords House of Commons Joint Committee on the *Draft Care and Support Bill, Draft Care and Support Bill Report, Session 2012–13* (TSO, March 2013) HL paper 143, HC 822.

[2] House of Lords House of Commons Joint Committee on the Draft Care and Support Bill, *Draft Care and Support Bill Report, Session 2012–13* (TSO, March 2013) HL paper 143, HC 822, p.3.

[3] House of Lords House of Commons Joint Committee on the Draft Care and Support Bill, *Draft Care and Support Bill Report, Session 2012–13* (TSO, March 2013) HL paper 143, HC 822, p.3.

to accept the main recommendations of the Commission on Funding Care and Support.[1] This announcement came shortly before the Joint Committee published its final report.

The Joint Committee noted that this delay had hampered its ability to "test the draft Bill's compatibility with a capped costs system".[2]

The Care Bill 2013–2014

I1–015 On 8 May 2013 it was announced in the Queen's Speech that "legislation will be introduced to reform the way long-term care is paid for, to ensure the elderly do not have to sell their homes to meet their care bills".[3] The next day, Earl Howe (Parliamentary Under Secretary of State at the Department of Health) introduced the Care Bill in the House of Lords. At the same time the Government published *The Care Bill Explained*, which set out its response to the public consultation on the draft Bill and the Joint Committee's report.[4] At second reading in the House of Lords, the Government stated:

> "The Bill represents the most significant reform of care and support legislation in more than 60 years. The foundations of social law are based on principles that are no longer relevant in today's society. This long-awaited Bill implements the recommendations of the Law Commission's excellent three-year review, begun under the previous Administration, to pull together over a dozen different Acts into a single, modern framework."[5]

As well as the Law Commission's recommendations, the Bill gave effect to a new funding system based on the model recommended by the Commission on the Funding of Care and Support. It also brought forward reforms which reflected Government policies that had been set out in *Caring for our Future*, the outcome of its public consultation on the draft Bill and many of the recommendations of the Joint Committee in its report. The key provisions contained in Part 1 of the Bill included the following:

- the general responsibilities of local authorities, including to provide care and support aimed at preventing or delaying needs;
- the process of assessments, charging, capping the costs of care, establishing entitlements to care and support, care planning, and the provision of care and support;
- the responsibilities of local authorities and other partners in relation to the safeguarding of adults, including a new requirement to establish Safeguarding Adults Boards in every area;
- the Care Quality Commission's new role of monitoring the financial position and sustainability of the most difficult to replace providers in England, and local authorities' responsibilities for ensuring continuity of care where a provider sustains business failure and ceases to provide a service; and
- the transition for young people between children's and adult care by giving local authorities powers to assess children, young carers and parent carers.

The Care Bill received widespread support in the House of Lords. For example, Baroness Campbell, an independent peer and renowned disability rights campaigner, referred to the Bill as "the culmination of more than 25 years' work by the Independent Living Movement of disabled people".[6] She went on to say of the Care Bill:

---

[1] *Hansard* (House of Commons), 11 February 2013, Vol.558, col.592.
[2] House of Lords House of Commons Joint Committee on the Draft Care and Support Bill, *Draft Care and Support Bill Report, Session 2012–13* (TSO, March 2013) HL paper 143, HC 822, para.18.
[3] *Hansard* (House of Lords), 8 May 2013, Vol.745, col.2.
[4] Department of Health, *The Care Bill explained—including a response to consultation and pre-legislative scrutiny on the draft Care and Support Bill* (TSO, May 2013) Cm.8627.
[5] *Hansard* (House of Lords), 21 May 2013, Vol.745, col.746 (Earl Howe).
[6] *Hansard* (House of Lords), 21 May 2013, Vol.745, col.755.

"It represents a sea change in the values and attitudes embodied in the legislative framework for adult social care. It treats people requiring support as citizens first and foremost, with rights and entitlements stemming not only from this Bill but from the Human

Rights Act, the Equality Act, and international agreements, such as the UN Convention on the Rights of Persons with Disabilities."[1]

Baroness Tyler, the Liberal Democrat peer, referred to the Bill as "a landmark piece of legislation, addressing one of the key social policy issues of our time",[2] and the Labour peer Baroness Pitkeathley described the Care Bill as the "most significant development" in the history of the carers movement.[3]

On behalf of the opposition, Baroness Wheeler welcomed the consolidation of adult **I1–016** social care law, but also raised concerns that the aims of the legislation would not be met as a result of Government cuts to local authority budgets. She also argued that the proposals on social care funding did not go far enough and the Bill needed to go further in the integration of health and social care. There was also criticism of Pt 2 of the Bill and what was described as "a partial response to the recommendations of the Francis Report".[4]

A significant number of Government amendments were made to the Bill in the House of Lords, in particular a duty on the Secretary of State to have regard to the well-being duty when issuing guidance and making regulations (see para.1–775 below) and new rights to independent advocacy (see para.1–665 below). In addition, a non-Government amendment tabled by Lord Low was passed during Report Stage, to extend the definition of public authorities for the purposes of the Human Rights Act 1998 to include all regulated providers of care and support, whether or not the care and support has been arranged by a local authority. In effect, all care and support providers who are regulated by the Care Quality Commission would be required to act in a way which is compatible with the European Convention on Human Rights. This amendment is discussed in more detail at paras 1–715 to 1–720 below.

However, the consensual atmosphere that had dominated proceedings in the House of Lords altered radically when the Bill went to the House of Commons. For instance, the then Secretary of State for Health, Jeremy Hunt MP, made the following opening statement at second reading (referring to Pt 2 of the Bill):

"In recent years, we have heard of patients being left in their own excrement at Mid Staffs, of patients left unchecked on trolleys for hours on end at Tameside, and of blood on the curtains and catheters on the floor at Basildon. All are issues that could and should have been dealt with by the last Government. Tragically, those problems were swept under the carpet, with devastating consequences for families across the country."[5]

This speech was condemned as "churlish", "partisan", "disagreeable", and "political knockabout" by various opposition MPs.[6] But none of the main parties came out of the debate with much credit. There was very little talk of landmark legislation amongst opposition MPs, many of whom rounded on the Bill for lacking ambition,[7] representing a "wasted opportunity",[8] and being "inadequate".[9] The Labour Party tabled an amendment to decline to give the Bill a second reading, claiming this was a "reasoned amendment",

---

[1] *Hansard* (House of Lords), 21 May 2013, Vol.745, col.756.
[2] *Hansard* (House of Lords), 21 May 2013, Vol.745, cols 763 to 764.
[3] *Hansard* (House of Lords), 3 July 2013, Vol.746, col.1311.
[4] *Hansard* (House of Lords), 21 May 2013, Vol.745, cols 749 to 753.
[5] *Hansard* (House of Commons), 16 December 2013, Vol.572, col.487.
[6] *Hansard* (House of Commons), 16 December 2013, Vol.572, col.539 (Anne McGuire MP) and *Hansard* (House of Commons), 16 December 2013, Vol.572, col.554 (Grahame M. Morris MP).
[7] *Hansard* (House of Commons), 16 December 2013, Vol.572, col.511 (Hazel Blears MP).
[8] *Hansard* (House of Commons), 16 December 2013, Vol.572, col.517 (Barbara Keeley MP).
[9] *Hansard* (House of Commons), 16 December 2013, Vol.572, col.558 (Sharon Hodgson MP).

motivated by concerns that the Bill was an inadequate response to the scale of the funding crisis facing social care.[1] The Shadow Health Secretary stated:

> "We will not oppose the Bill, in the sense that we will not vote against it on Second Reading, but it contains measures to which we simply cannot give a clear endorsement".[2]

This led to accusations that the amendment precipitated the debate "going down into the gutter of partisan politics".[3] The Labour amendment was defeated by 231 to 289 votes.[4]

There were fewer amendments made to the Bill in the House of Commons, compared to the House of Lords. Most of the Government amendments were of a technical nature. However, a major amendment came at Committee stage when the Government introduced a regulation-making power to provide for appeals of decisions under Pt 1 of the Bill (see paras 1–196 to 1–197 below). In addition, a Government deleted the clause that had been inserted by the House of Lords to extend the remit of the Human Rights Act 1998.

At third reading in the House of Commons, the final word on the Care Bill came from Paul Burstow MP who said of the new legislation:

> "it replaces 60 years of piecemeal, dog's breakfast legislation. In place of that it will put a system focused on promoting the well-being and quality of life of the individual. It provides a foundational set of changes . . . My 18 years in this place have been about campaigning for the changes that the [Care Act] brings about. I have seen countless Green Papers and heard countless promises of reform. This legislation brings that reform home and delivers change—change that I hope all Members will support, because it is for the good of our constituents that we are here and the [Care Act] delivers a lot of good."[5]

At "ping pong"[6] in the House of Lords, the Government offered an amendment to extend the remit of the Human Rights Act 1998 to regulated care providers when providing care and support arranged or funded in whole or in part by local authorities. Whilst this did not go as far as the original amendment in the House of Lords, it was welcomed and passed by peers. This amendment was also agreed by the House of Commons.

The Bill received Royal Assent on 14 May 2015.

Implementation of the Act

I1–017   Most of the provisions of the Care Act came into force on 1 April 2015, including the statutory guidance and regulations. Some reforms were due to be implemented from 1 April 2016, including the cap on care costs system, the duty on local authorities under s.18(3) of the Care Act to meet the eligible needs of self-funders in care homes and an appeals system for care and support. However, the Department of Health has announced that these reforms will be delayed until April 2020.[7] The statutory guidance discusses the transition to the new legal framework in Ch.23.

The Act had been phased in so that service users prior to 1 April 2015 will continue to receive services under the old community care law, until the local authority completes a new review of that person's case, at which point the Care Act will apply. But reviews are required to take place before 1 April 2016. If the person has not had a review by this date they are treated as eligible under the Care Act.[8]

---

[1] *Hansard* (House of Commons), 16 December 2013, Vol.572, col.494 (Andy Burnham MP).

[2] *Hansard* (House of Commons), 16 December 2013, Vol.572, col.495 (Andy Burnham MP).

[3] *Hansard* (House of Commons), 16 December 2013, Vol.572, col.495 (Andrew George MP).

[4] *Hansard* (House of Commons), 16 December 2013, Vol.572, cols 581 to 585.

[5] *Hansard* (House of Commons), 11 March 2014, Vol.577, col.290.

[6] Before a Bill receives Royal Assent it must be passed in its final form by both the House of Commons and the Lords. This process is commonly known as "ping pong".

[7] *House of Commons Written Answers and Statements Daily Report*, Cap on Care Costs: Written Statement—HCWS145, 20 July 2015, pp.162 to 164 (Alastair Burt MP).

[8] Care Act 2014 (Transitional Provision) Order 2015 (SI 2015/995).

The Care Act 2014 and Children and Families Act 2014 (Consequential Amendments) Order 2015 provided that 60 years' worth of community care legislation—such as the National Assistance Act 1948, the Chronically Sick and Disabled Persons Act 1970 and the National Health Service and Community Care Act 1990—ceased to apply in England from 1 April 2015 (or at least ceased to apply in full). This order also provided that community care legislation will continue to apply in Wales until 1 April 2016, when the Social Services and Well-being (Wales) Act 2014 comes into force. The duty to assess under s.47 of the National Health Service and Community Care Act 1990 will continue to apply in England for the purposes of after-care services under s.117 of the Mental Health Act 1983. Also, the Chronically Sick and Disabled Persons Act 1970 will continue to apply to disabled children in England.[1]

Do local authorities need to consult?

When considering how they intend to discharge functions under the Care Act, local auth- **I1–018**
orities will need to decide whether or not to carry out a local consultation process. The Local Government Association has advised that the following questions should be considered:

1. is there a statutory duty to perform the function? If so, it is less likely that local consultation will be necessary. Where there is a power, or where there is discretion in how to implement a duty, then it is more likely to be necessary to consult;
2. is anything actually changing? Where the exercise of the function represents no change from the previous position, it is less likely that consultation will be necessary;
3. to what extent are people affected? The need to consult may be triggered where the proposals are expected to impact negatively on people with care and support needs, and carers; and
4. has the authority committed to consultations in the past? If there is an expectation or previous commitment to consult on certain matters, there may be a duty to consult.[2]

Difficulties may arise where the effect of the proposal would be to impact positively on people. The Local Government Association suggests that in such cases it may not be necessary to consult. However, it is submitted that there may still be a need to consult, particularly where people are likely to argue that the local authority should go further than it is proposing.

In addition, Cornerstone Barristers has produced guidance on consulting on changes to local practice under the Care Act.[3] This is not statutory guidance but it has been produced with the approval of the Department of Health (see 1–770 below).

Post-legislative scrutiny of the Act

The Government has confirmed that it will conduct post-legislative scrutiny of the Care **I1–019**
Act, which it had committed to do across the board for all new Acts. This will be undertaken between three and five years after Royal Assent.[4] The scrutiny process will be undertaken by the Department of Health as the relevant Government Department, and is likely to involve a review by a select committee, such as the Health Committee.

In addition, s.71 requires the Secretary of State every five years to review and report on the level of the cap on care costs, of daily living costs to be disregarded for the purposes of the cap, and the threshold for the financial assessment (see para.1–690 below).

---

[1] Care Act 2014 and Children and Families Act 2014 (Consequential Amendments) Order 2015 (SI 2015/914).
[2] Local Government Association, *Do Councils Need to Consult Locally?* (2015).
[3] Cornerstone Barristers, *Consulting on Changes to Local Practice under the Care Act 2014* (February 2015).
[4] *Hansard* (House of Lords), 14 October 2013, Vol.748, cols 287 to 288 (Earl Howe).

Territorial extent of the Act

I1–020   Part 1 of the Care Act applies to local authorities in England only. This is because social care is a devolved matter for Scotland, Wales and Northern Ireland. The Welsh National Assembly has passed its own legislation, the Social Services and Well-being (Wales) Act 2014. This Act includes many of the same provisions contained in the Care Act, but also includes important differences (not least of which is the fact that it extends to children and families, as well as adult social care).

Some elements of Pt 1 of the Care Act also apply in Scotland, Wales and Northern Ireland. These are the provisions on cross-border placements (s.39(8) and Sch.1), certain provisions on provider failure (ss.49 to 52) and the Human Rights Act provision (s.73).

CARE ACT 2014

(2014 c.23)

ARRANGEMENT OF SECTIONS

19

PART 1

CARE AND SUPPORT

GENERAL RESPONSIBILITIES OF LOCAL AUTHORITIES

GENERAL NOTE

Sections 1 to 7 place a number of general duties (also known as target duties) on local **1–001** authorities. In broad terms, statutory duties imposed on public authorities can be divided into two categories: general duties and specific duties. General duties are not expressed as being owed to any specific individual but rather towards the relevant population as a whole. The courts allow public authorities considerable discretion in determining how to implement its general duties and therefore such duties are difficult to enforce. A notable example of a general duty is s.17 of the Children Act 1989 which requires local authorities to promote the welfare of children in need and their families. Section 17 does not impose a mandatory duty to take specific steps to meet the needs of any one child regardless of resources, but sets out general requirements on how local authorities should approach the provision of services in their area taken as a whole.[1] In contrast, specific duties place strong obligations upon public authorities in respect of an individual. For example, s.117 of the Mental Health Act 1983 requires NHS and local social services authorities to provide after-care services to certain former psychiatric patients, and once eligibility is established an enforceable individual duty arises.[2] Some specific duties are qualified in some way, for example a duty to provide "necessary" services or "take reasonable steps" to achieve a particular objective, in which case the local authority can take into account, amongst other things, its overall financial resources.[3]

Promoting individual well-being

1.—(1) The general duty of a local authority, in exercising a function under this **1–002** Part in the case of an individual, is to promote that individual's well-being.

(2) "Well-being", in relation to an individual, means that individual's well-being so far as relating to any of the following—

(a) personal dignity (including treatment of the individual with respect);

(b) physical and mental health and emotional well-being;

(c) protection from abuse and neglect;

(d) control by the individual over day-to-day life (including over care and support, or support, provided to the individual and the way in which it is provided);

(e) participation in work, education, training or recreation;

(f) social and economic well-being;

(g) domestic, family and personal relationships;

(h) suitability of living accommodation;

(i) the individual's contribution to society.

(3) In exercising a function under this Part in the case of an individual, a local authority must have regard to the following matters in particular—

(a) the importance of beginning with the assumption that the individual is best-placed to judge the individual's well-being;

---

[1] *R. (G) v Barnet London Borough Council* [2003] UKHL 57; [2004] 2 A.C. 208.

[2] *R. v Ealing Health Authority Ex p Fox* [1993] 1 W.L.R. 373.

[3] Prior to the Care Act, the duty under s.2(1) of the Chronically Sick and Disabled Persons Act 1970 was an example of a specific individual duty which required local authorities to provide welfare services where this is "necessary".

(b) the individual's views, wishes, feelings and beliefs;

(c) the importance of preventing or delaying the development of needs for care and support or needs for support and the importance of reducing needs of either kind that already exist;

(d) the need to ensure that decisions about the individual are made having regard to all the individual's circumstances (and are not based only on the individual's age or appearance or any condition of the individual's or aspect of the individual's behaviour which might lead others to make unjustified assumptions about the individual's well-being);

(e) the importance of the individual participating as fully as possible in decisions relating to the exercise of the function concerned and being provided with the information and support necessary to enable the individual to participate;

(f) the importance of achieving a balance between the individual's wellbeing and that of any friends or relatives who are involved in caring for the individual;

(g) the need to protect people from abuse and neglect;

(h) the need to ensure that any restriction on the individual's rights or freedom of action that is involved in the exercise of the function is kept to the minimum necessary for achieving the purpose for which the function is being exercised.

(4) "Local authority" means—

(a) a county council in England,

(b) a district council for an area in England for which there is no county council,

(c) a London borough council, or

(d) the Common Council of the City of London.

GENERAL NOTE

1–003 Contemporary health and social care legislation often includes a statement of fundamental principles upon which the legislation is based, as an initial point of reference. The main examples are the Children Act 1989, Adoption and Children Act 2002 and Mental Capacity Act 2005. There are also numerous examples of principles in similar statutes in other jurisdictions, especially Scotland, Canada and Australia.[1] Decision-makers are normally required to consider the statutory principles when a decision or action is being made under the relevant legislation.

At an early stage of its review of adult social care, the Law Commission observed that none of the various community care statutes that were in force at the time contained an explicit statement of principles. This did not mean that legal principles were not in force. But instead those principles needed to be discerned from a range of statutory and non-statutory guidance and other supporting documents. The Commission argued that a coherent set of overarching statutory principles would help to guide decision-makers acting under the legislation, provide a clear statement of the legislation's purpose, perform an important educational function and give prominence to existing principles that already exist but are not consistently recognised or applied.[2] In making the case for statutory

---

[1] See, for example, the Adult Support and Protection (Scotland) Act 2007; Mental Health (Care and Treatment) (Scotland) Act 2003; Adults with Incapacity (Scotland) Act 2000; Long-Term Care Homes Act 2007 (Canada); Long-Term Care Act 2000 (Canada); Aged Care Act 1997 (Australia); and Family Law Act 1975 (Australia).

[2] Law Commission, *Adult Social Care: Scoping Report* (26 November 2008), paras 4.2 to 4.15 and Law Commission, *Adult Social Care: A Consultation Paper*, Consultation Paper No.192 (2010), paras 3.5 to 3.13.

principles, the Law Commission was influenced in particular by the perceived success of the welfare principle of the Children Act 1989 and the best interests principle of the Mental Capacity Act 2005.

The Law Commission's consultation paper considered two approaches to statutory principles. The first was to provide a list of principles, each of which would be of equal status and should be considered alongside and in conjunction with one another. Practitioners would be required to have regard to each of the principles when making a decision. This is the approach to statutory principles adopted for example in s.1 of the Family Law Act 1996. The precise list of principles put forward by the Law Commission for consultation were choice and control, person-centred planning, that a person's needs should be viewed broadly, the need to remove or reduce future need, independent living, an assumption of home-based living, dignity in care and the need to safeguard adults at risk of abuse and neglect. The second approach was for the statute to establish an overarching principle which sets out the primary purpose of adult social care and is given primary over all other principles. The overarching principle would be supported by a checklist of factors that should be considered and weighed against each other. This is the approach adopted by s.1 of the Children Act and ss.1(5) and 4 of the Mental Capacity Act 2005.[1]

In its final report the Law Commission opted for the second approach. It was noted that while the National Health Service Act 2006 defines the central purpose of health services in England as securing improvement in physical and mental health, and in the prevention, diagnosis and treatment of illness—there is no equivalent statement in law that defines the purpose of adult social care. The Commission concluded that the new statute should set out the primary "well-being principle" which establishes clearly in law that the overarching purpose of adult social care is to promote or contribute to the well-being of the individual. In effect, individual well-being must be the basis for all decisions made and actions carried out under the statute. This principle would apply to both an adult with care and support needs and an adult carer.[2]

The Law Commission's recommendation was heavily influenced by consultation responses from the Association of Directors of Adult Social Services, Social Care Institute for Excellence and Local Government Association. All three organisations argued that the statute could be built around a single organising principle that adult social care should "promote or contribute to the well-being of the individual and support people to be active citizens". It was suggested that with the exception of some people who lack capacity, an adult would be presumed the best judge of their own well-being and that common elements of well-being would include personal identity; autonomy and self-determination; dignity, privacy and respect; physical and mental health; security and freedom from abuse; and economic and social inclusion.[3]

The Law Commission rejected the limb of the proposal that referred to supporting people **1–004** to be active citizens on the basis that it was not sufficiently precise to be capable of operating in legislation. But it retained the central well-being element. Rather than defining well-being, the Law Commission recommended that the statute should set out a broad list of outcomes to which the well-being principle must be directed—namely:

- health and emotional well-being;
- protection from harm;
- education, training and recreation;
- the contribution made to society; and
- securing rights and entitlements.[4]

---

[1] Law Commission, *Adult Social Care: A Consultation Paper*, paras 3.1 to 3.53.
[2] Law Commission, *Adult Social Care*, Law Com No.326 (2011), paras 2.1 to 2.9 and 4.1 to 4.37.
[3] Law Commission, *Adult Social Care: Consultation Analysis* (31 March 2011), paras 3.228 to 3.230.
[4] Law Commission, *Adult Social Care*, paras 8.2 to 8.25.

The Law Commission argued that the inclusion of a list of broad outcomes would ensure that the legislation would be future proofed against developments in social care service provision and would not be service-led, thereby allowing for personalised services. This approach was influenced by the Government of Wales Act 2006, which although used for a very different purpose, provided a similar list of outcomes that "well-being" must address.[1] The 2006 Act was in turn based on the outcomes listed in s.10 of the Children Act 2004.

Furthermore, the Law Commission recommended that the statute should set out a checklist of factors which must be considered before a decision is made in relation to an individual. In effect, a decision-maker must:

- assume that the person is the best judge of their own well-being, except in cases where they lack capacity to make the relevant decision;
- follow the individual's views, wishes and feelings wherever practicable and appropriate;
- ensure that decisions are based upon the individual circumstances of the person and not merely on the person's age or appearance, or a condition or aspect of their behaviour which might lead others to make unjustified assumptions;
- give individuals the opportunity to be involved, as far as is practicable in the circumstances, in assessments, planning developing and reviewing their care and support;
- achieve a balance with the well-being of others, if this is relevant and practicable;
- safeguard adults wherever practicable from abuse and neglect; and
- use the least restrictive solution where it is necessary to interfere with the individual's rights and freedom of action wherever that is practicable.[2]

The Government accepted the Law Commission's approach.[3] In its response to the Joint Committee, the Government confirmed that individual well-being is central to the new Act:

"Clause 1 of the Bill creates a new statutory principle designed to embed individual well-being as the driving force behind care and support. The first clause of the Bill sets the context for all the provisions which follow: that the well-being of the individual is paramount and that local authorities must promote the individual's well-being in all decisions made with and about them. 'Well-being' is described in terms of the most important outcomes for people who use care and support for carers. This principle is intended to establish what the Law Commission called a '*single unifying purpose around which adult social care is organised*'."[4]

Section 1 of the Act sets out the general duty to promote individual well-being, which governs how local authorities must carry out their care and support functions under the Care Act. In some areas—particularly the well-being outcomes in s.1(2)—the Government has added detail to the Law Commission's scheme. The well-being duty is discussed in Ch.1 of the statutory guidance.

During second reading in the House of Commons, Stephen Dorrell MP—the chair of the Health Select Committee—made the following observation about s.1:

"The reason I welcome the Bill is that it begins to look at health and care from a different point of view from the one with which those of us who have participated in health and care debates in this Chamber over a long period are familiar. When a Bill comes before the House, it usually starts off by describing the function of one bit of the bureaucracy—

---

[1] Government of Wales Act 2006 Sch.5 Pt 1 field 15.

[2] Law Commission, *Adult Social Care*, paras 4.22 to 4.37.

[3] Department of Health, *Reforming the Law for Adult Care and Support: The Government's Response to Law Commission Report 326 on Adult Social Care* (TSO, July), Cm.8379, paras 3.5 to 3.14.

[4] Department of Health, *The Care Bill explained—including a response to consultation and pre-legislative scrutiny on the draft Care and Support Bill*, para.23.

perhaps creating a strategic health authority or re-creating a different bit of the bureaucracy somewhere else on the landscape. This Bill starts in a quite different place. Clause 1 talks about the "well-being" of individuals and suggests that if we are to build a health and care system that meets the needs of patients and users for the 21st century, we should, instead of thinking of it as a bureaucracy planned from the top down, think about the service that is delivered to individuals who rely on these services. Clause 1 talks about the needs of individuals, and later clauses place an obligation on local authorities to do needs assessments for those individuals".[1]

To WHOM DOES THE WELL-BEING DUTY APPLY?

The Joint Committee had criticised the draft Care and Support Bill for failing to clarify **1–005** that the well-being principle applies to carers as well as adults with care and support needs. The main concern was that the draft Bill had referred to the well-being principle applying "in relation to an adult" but elsewhere the draft Bill had differentiated between an adult and a carer.[2] The Government accepted this point, and revised the clause by removing the references to "an adult" and referring instead to "an individual".[3]

As well as adults with care and support needs and adult carers, the well-being principle applies to children, in relation to the functions set out in ss.58 to 66.

The Secretary of State must also have regard to the well-being principle when issuing guidance or regulations (see s.78(3)).

The well-being principle however does not apply to the NHS. During Committee stage in the House of Commons, there was an attempt to amend the Bill to extend the well-being duty to any health service body when exercising any function jointly with one or more local authorities. The Government argued this was unnecessary for three reasons:

"First, the NHS already has a number of duties related to promoting well-being; most notably, in the NHS constitution, about taking a patient-centred approach, promoting equality and understanding the priorities, needs and abilities of patients . . . I cannot imagine a situation in practice in which the duty to promote individual well-being in the Bill would apply to a local authority, but the NHS, performing similar functions, would be able to ignore the same considerations. That could not conceivably be the case, particularly given the existing duties on the NHS."

Secondly,

". . . where a local authority and the NHS seek to do things together, there is a duty through the Bill on the local authority to focus all of its attention on the well-being principle. For it to be satisfied that the outcome from that joint work met the well-being of the individual, it would have to ensure, in co-operation with the NHS body, that it had achieved that objective."

Thirdly, the Government argued that the amendment would only impose the well-being principle on joint functions and, in legal terms, there are few such functions in the Bill.[4]

The well-being principle applies specifically when the local authority performs an activity or task, or makes a decision, in relation to a person. The statutory guidance also emphasises that the principle should also be considered by the local authority "when it

---

[1] *Hansard* (House of Commons), 16 December 2013, Vol.572, cols 507 to 508.
[2] House of Lords House of Commons Joint Committee on the Draft Care and Support Bill, *Draft Care and Support Bill, Report, Session 2012–13*, paras 75 to 79.
[3] Department of Health, *The Care Bill explained—including a response to consultation and pre-legislative scrutiny on the draft Care and Support Bill*, para.24.
[4] *Hansard* (House of Commons: Public Bill Committee), 9 January 2014 (AM): First Sitting, cols 21 to 23 (Norman Lamb MP).

undertakes broader, strategic functions, such as planning, which are not in relation to one individual".[1]

1–006   The well-being principle is framed as a general duty (see above at 1–001). It is therefore not intended to be directly enforceable as an individual right. The explanatory notes confirm that it carries "indirect legal weight, where a local authority's failure to follow the principle may be challenged through judicial review".[2]   This point was also made by the Law Commission in its oral evidence to the Joint Committee:

> "Of course there is the scope for challenging decisions that have been made on an individual basis; that will be by way of judicial review. As part of that there is the issue about how the well-being principle feeds in. It does feed in, in our view, because that is part of the context in which an individual decision is made. It may be that the decision is flawed because either the well-being principle has been ignored or it might have been wrongly interpreted in a way that is flawed legally, so it has a role to play."[3]

The Law Commission went on to give the following example:

> "Say you were challenging an individual decision and saying, 'You have mis-assessed my needs' or, 'You are not providing services that meet my needs adequately'; in that situation the well-being principle would have a hard-edged impact because the local authority decision-maker, who made those decisions, should have been exercising its functions to promote your wellbeing."[4]

The statutory guidance emphasises that s.1 does not require a specific course of action:

> "Neither these principles, nor the requirement to promote well-being, require the local authority to undertake any particular action. The steps a local authority should take will depend entirely on the circumstances. The principles as a whole are not intended to specify the activities which should take place. Instead, their purpose is to set common expectations for how local authorities should approach and engage with people."[5]

1–007   "Well-being" is not defined precisely. However, this subsection provides guidance on the interpretation of the general duty in subs.(1). It lists a set of broad outcomes or areas to which the well-being principle must be directed. The outcomes are "not a series of requirements, but serve as a description to aid decision-making".[6]   The statutory guidance states that promoting well-being "involves actively seeking improvements" in the aspects of well-being.[7]   The list is based on (but also expands significantly) the Law Commission's recommended list of well-being outcomes and similar provisions in the Government of Wales Act 2006 and Children Act 2004 (see para.1–004 above). The interpretation of each outcome is largely self-explanatory. At report stage in the House of Lords, the Government explained its approach to the drafting of the list in subs.(2):

---

[1] Department of Health, *Care and Support Statutory Guidance* (2014), para.1.13.
[2] Bill 123–EN 2013–2014, Explanatory Notes to the Bill, para.40.
[3] House of Lords House of Commons Joint Committee on the Draft Care and Support Bill, *Draft Care and Support Bill, Session 2012–13, Oral Evidence* (2013), p.84, Q90 (Frances Patterson QC).
[4] House of Lords House of Commons Joint Committee on the Draft Care and Support Bill, *Draft Care and Support Bill, Session 2012–13, Oral Evidence* (2013), p.86, Q96 (Richard Percival).
[5] Department of Health, *Care and Support Statutory Guidance* (2014), para.1.17.
[6] Care Act 2014: Explanatory Notes para.58.
[7] Department of Health, *Care and Support Statutory Guidance* (2014), para.1.7.

"It is framed in terms of high level principles. It is not designed to exclude any form of well-being whatever. It is designed to look at the person holistically and to ensure that no aspect of well-being is overlooked."[1]

The list of outcomes is cross-referenced in the following provisions of the Care Act:

- the needs assessment must consider the impact of the adult's needs on the matters specified in the list—see s.9(4)(a);
- the carer's assessment must consider the impact of the carer's needs on the matters specified in the list—see s.10(5)(c);
- needs will only meet the eligibility criteria if there is, or is likely to be, a significant impact on the adult's or carer's well-being as set out in s.1(2) —see Care and Support (Eligibility Criteria) Regulations 2015 (SI 2015/313) regs 2(c) and 3(c);
- the child's needs assessment must consider the impact on the matters specified in the list of what the child's needs are likely to become after they become 18—see s.59(1)(a);
- the child's carer's assessment must consider the impact on the matters specified in the list of what the child's needs are likely to become after they become 18—see s.61(1)(c); and
- the young carer's assessment must consider the impact on the matters specified in the list of what the young carer's needs are likely to become after they become 18—see s.64(1)(c).

This may mean that in some circumstances the outcomes may cystilise into more directly enforceable provisions—particularly when they are linked directly to the operation of the eligibility criteria (see A1–274).

PERSONAL DIGNITY (INCLUDING TREATMENT OF THE INDIVIDUAL WITH RESPECT). The Law **1–008** Commission had originally concluded that dignity was too imprecise to be expressed as a statutory principle.[2] However, the Joint Committee argued that dignity was no less precise than some of the other factors listed, and recommended its inclusion.[3] The Government accepted this.[4]

In the original version of the Care Bill, introduced in the House of Lords, a reference to personal dignity was included, but only at the end of the first outcome and after the references to physical and mental health and emotional well-being.[5] However, concerns were raised by Lord Bichard that personal dignity did not stand out "boldly enough" in cl.1 of the Bill, and its impact was therefore diminished. He also contended that "dignity and respect" encapsulated the fundamentals of good care.[6] Moreover, Baroness Tyler argued that:

"dignity and respect are absolutely fundamental pillars of well-being, which is why I would like to see these words spelt out in the Bill. Well-being is unattainable without dignity and respect as central components".[7]

In response, the Government tabled an amendment in the House of Lords to provide that personal dignity was included as a separate and self-contained outcome at the beginning of the list, and added the adjunct wording "including treatment of the individual with

---

[1] *Hansard* (House of Lords), 9 October 2013, Vol.748, col.87 (Earl Howe).
[2] Law Commission, *Adult Social Care*, para.4.35.
[3] House of Lords House of Commons Joint Committee on the *Draft Care and Support Bill, Draft Care and Support Bill Report, Session 2012–13*, para.70.
[4] Department of Health, *The Care Bill explained—including a response to consultation and pre-legislative scrutiny on the draft Care and Support Bill*, para.24.
[5] Care Bill (HL Bill 001 2013–2014, as introduced) cl.1(2)(a).
[6] *Hansard* (House of Lords), 3 July 2013, Vol.746, col.1263.
[7] *Hansard* (House of Lords), 3 July 2013, Vol.746, col.1269.

respect". In doing so, Earl Howe explained that the intention behind the amendment was to "give greater emphasis to personal dignity and respect as components of well-being".[1]

In recent years there has been a proliferation of reports, circulars, guidance and toolkits on dignity in care. The dignity in care campaign was launched by the Department of Health in 2006 and is now hosted by the Social Care Institutive for Excellence. The *Dignity in Care Guide* identifies eight main factors that promote dignity in care: choice and control, communication, eating and nutritional care, pain management, personal hygiene, practical assistance, privacy and social inclusion.[2]

Dignity in care has, however, proved a difficult concept to define, often because it is subjective and will differ from one person to another. The Social Care Institute for Excellence's guide is based on the following definition:

> "A state, quality or manner worthy of esteem or respect; and (by extension) self-respect. Dignity in care, therefore, means the kind of care, in any setting, which supports and promotes, and does not undermine, a person's self-respect regardless of any difference. Or, as one person receiving care put it more briefly, 'Being treated like I was somebody.' "[3]

The Care Quality Commission requires service providers to treat service users with dignity and respect as part of its registration regulations. In order to comply with this requirement, service providers must ensure the privacy of the service user; support the autonomy, independence, and involvement in the community of the service user; and have due regard to any protected characteristic (as set out in s.4 of the Equality Act 2010) of the service user.[4]

The principle of dignity has also been applied and developed by the courts, mainly in the context of art.3 and art.8 of the European Convention on Human Rights. In *R. (A) v East Sussex CC*, Mr Justice Munby (as he was then) described the concept of dignity in the following terms:

> "The recognition and protection of human dignity is one of the core values—in truth the core value—of our society . . . The invocation of the dignity of the patient in the form of declaration habitually used when the court is exercising its inherent declaratory jurisdiction in relation to the gravely ill or dying is not some meaningless incantation designed to comfort the living or to assuage the consciences of those involved in making life or death decisions: it is a solemn affirmation of the law's and of society's recognition of our humanity and of human dignity as something fundamental."[5]

In this case it was held that severely disabled people are entitled to an "enhanced degree of protection" when human dignity is at stake and in order to achieve this, it may be necessary to treat the disabled person differently because "their situation is significantly different from that of the able-bodied".[6] The judgment also explicitly recognised the art.8 rights of disabled people to participate in the life of the community and to have "access to essential economic and social activities and to an appropriate range of recreational and cultural activities" and that:

> "This is matched by the positive obligation on the State to take appropriate measures designed to ensure to the greatest extent feasible that a disabled person is not "so circumscribed and isolated as to be deprived of the possibility of developing his personality."[7]

---

[1] *Hansard* (House of Lords), 9 October 2013, Vol.748, cols 85 to 86 (Earl Howe).
[2] Social Care Institutive for Excellence, *Dignity in Care Guide* (Published June 2010/Updated May 2013), SCIE Guide 15.
[3] Social Care Institutive for Excellence, *Dignity in Care Guide* (Published June 2010/Updated May 2013), SCIE Guide 15.
[4] Health and Social Care Act 2008 (Regulated Activities) Regulations 2014 (SI 2014/2936), reg.10.
[5] *R. (A) v East Sussex CC* [2003] EWHC 167 (Admin); (2003) 6 CCLR 194 at [33].
[6] *R. (A) v East Sussex CC* [2003] EWHC 167 (Admin); (2003) 6 CCLR 194 at [93].
[7] *R. (A) v East Sussex CC* [2003] EWHC 167 (Admin); (2003) 6 CCLR 194 at [99].

In *R. (Bernard) v Enfield LBC* Mr Justice Sullivan considered that art.8 obliged councils to take positive measures to enable the claimants, a severely disabled woman and her husband who was also her carer, "to enjoy, as far as possible, a normal private and family life".[1] Their house was inaccessible to wheelchair use and not adapted to the needs of a disabled person and it was held that the council's failure to provide suitably adapted accommodation services was incompatible with art.8. This was because such accommodation "would have not merely facilitated the normal incidents of family life" but would have also secured Mrs Bernard's "physical and psychological integrity" because:

> "She would no longer have been housebound, confined to a shower chair for most of the day, lacking privacy in the most undignified of circumstances, but would have been able to operate again as part of her family and as a person in her own right, rather than being a burden, wholly dependent upon the rest of her family. In short, it would have restored her dignity as a human being."[2]

The Charter of Fundamental Rights of the European Union states that dignity must be protected by all public authorities, and the United Nations Convention on the Rights of Persons with Disabilities describes its purpose as "to promote respect for their inherent dignity".[3] It has also been argued that human dignity should be granted regardless of whether or not the individual wants their dignity respected or, indeed, whether they deserve it, because "dignity is not an earned characteristic, and it is equally ascribed to all human beings, irrespective of their external moral and physical attributes".[4] However, there are limits to the concept of dignity. Baroness Hale has pointed out that "dignity can so often be used on both sides of an argument", particularly in arguments concerning assisted suicide, abortion or stem cell research; and that it "may have to be balanced against other rights, or against the interests of the community as a whole, and then . . . begins to lose its universal quality".[5]

The concept of dignity was considered in *McDonald v United Kingdom*. This case concerned a disabled woman who was not incontinent, but due to a small bladder needed to urinate two or three times a night, and due to her disability needed assistance to reach her commode. The local authority had withdrawn the provision of a night-time carer and instead had provided her with incontinence pads, thereby reducing the cost of care at night. It was argued that the offer of pads was an affront to her dignity. The Supreme Court upheld the local authority's decision. Lord Brown concluded that the authority had respected her dignity and autonomy by allowing her to choose the details of her care package within its overall assessment of her needs, such as the particular hours of care attendance.[6] However, Baroness Hale in a dissenting judgment argued that the local authority's decision was irrational and that the concept of dignity would require that disabled people enjoy the same access to toilet facilities as non-disabled people.[7] The European Court of Human Rights agreed with Baroness Hale's general assessment that considerations of human dignity were engaged when someone who could control her bodily functions was obliged to behave as if she could not. It held that there had been a violation of art.8 (right to respect for private and family life) of the European Convention on Human Rights in respect of the initial period during which the person

---

[1] *R. (Bernard) v Enfield LBC* [2002] EWHC 2282 (Admin); (2002) 5 CCLR 577 at [31].
[2] *R. (Bernard) v Enfield LBC* [2002] EWHC 2282 (Admin); (2002) 5 CCLR 577 at [33].
[3] Charter of Fundamental Rights of the European Union 2000 and United Nations Convention on the Rights of Persons with Disabilities, art.1.
[4] H. Mountfield and R. Singh, *The Value of Dignity* (2004), cited by B. Hale, "Dignity", 31 *Journal of Social welfare and Family Law* 101, 104.
[5] B. Hale, "Dignity", (2009) 31 *Journal of Social Welfare and Family Law* 101, 106 to 107.
[6] *R. (McDonald) v Royal Borough of Kensington and Chelsea* [2011] UKSC 33; (2011) 14 CCLR 341 at [19].
[7] *R. (McDonald) v Royal Borough of Kensington and Chelsea* [2011] UKSC 33; (2011) 14 CCLR 341 at [78].

had been assessed as being in need of assistance to use the commode at night. This was because the local authority had been in breach of its statutory duty to provide care in accordance with its own assessment of need, and therefore the interference with her private life had not been in "accordance with the law" as required by para.2 of art.8. But the Court also held that the complaint concerning the period afterwards (when a re-assessment had taken place) was inadmissible as manifestly ill-founded because the State had considerable discretion when it came to decisions concerning the allocation of scarce resources and, as such, the interference with the person's rights had been "necessary in a democratic society".[1]

1–009 PHYSICAL AND MENTAL HEALTH. The Law Commission argued that well-being must include health and emotional well-being because "it is important that service provision should aim to secure both physical health (for example, through gym membership or a commode) and mental health (for example, through counselling)".[2] The Government confirmed that the reference to "health" is intended to ensure that local authorities work in tandem with health services.[3]

1–010 EMOTIONAL WELL-BEING. The Government confirmed in the House of Lords that emotional well-being incorporates consideration of pets.[4]

1–011 SPIRITUAL WELL-BEING. The Government faced a concerted attempt in the House of Lords at both committee and report stage to include express reference to spiritual well-being. This was led by Baroness Barker in support of the right of Christian Scientists to have their beliefs respected, in particular their right to refuse treatment.[5] At committee stage the Government argued that emotional well-being incorporates the concept of spiritual well-being and that therefore any express reference was unnecessary.[6] At report stage, Earl Howe set out in detail the Government's position:

> "I emphasise now, that the Government recognise the importance of spiritual well-being as a concept and understand the particular significance that it can have for some people, especially at the end of their life. We would absolutely not want an approach that excluded spiritual well-being from consideration where that was clearly of consequence to the individual concerned. However, it is important to understand that that is not the approach which the Bill sets out. The factors included in Clause 1(2) contain high-level matters which should be interpreted broadly to fit the individual case. Spiritual well-being should be considered where it is relevant to the person's overall well-being. Moreover, spiritual well-being is likely to be closely related to other matters, such as emotional well-being, which are listed in the clause.
>
> In addition, local authorities must also consider the person's views, wishes and feelings, as set out in Clause 1(3)(b). This provides a further clear direction to local authorities to have regard to personal matters, which could well include beliefs or other views that would promote an individual's spiritual well-being. Although it is not explicitly mentioned, spiritual well-being is nevertheless accounted for."[7]

---

[1] *McDonald v United Kingdom* (20 May 2014) Application no.4241/12.
[2] Law Commission, *Adult Social Care*, para.8.24.
[3] *Hansard* (House of Lords), 3 July 2013, Vol.746, col.1272 (Earl Howe).
[4] *Hansard* (House of Lords), 3 July 2013, Vol.746, col.1272 (Earl Howe).
[5] *Hansard* (House of Lords), 3 July 2013, Vol.746, cols 1263 to 1264; *Hansard* (House of Lords), 9 October 2013, Vol.748, col.84.
[6] *Hansard* (House of Lords), 3 July 2013, Vol.746, col.1272 (Earl Howe).
[7] *Hansard* (House of Lords), 9 October 2013, Vol.748, col.86 (Earl Howe).

PROTECTION FROM ABUSE AND NEGLECT.   This emphasises that safeguarding may be a **1–012** relevant consideration when making any care and support decision, and not just decisions under ss.42 to 47 of the Care Act. Safeguarding is also included in the well-being checklist under subs.(3) – see discussion below at 1–030.

CONTROL BY THE INDIVIDUAL OVER DAY-TO-DAY LIFE (INCLUDING OVER CARE AND SUPPORT, **1–013** OR SUPPORT, PROVIDED TO THE INDIVIDUAL AND THE WAY IN WHICH IT IS PROVIDED).   Subsection (2)(d) refers to control but not to choice. In the House of Commons, during Committee stage, the Government argued that "if one is in control of one's life and can control one's day-to-day living, that necessarily involves the concept of being able to choose what one wants to do." It therefore felt that an express reference to choice was unnecessary.[1]

The principles of choice and control have been central to various adult social care policy documents issued over the past 20 years. For example, the 1989 White Paper, *Caring for People*, identified one of the three key intentions behind the proposals that led to the National Health Service and Community Care Act 1990 as being to "give people a greater individual say in how they live their lives and the services they need to help them do so", and the 2009 Green Paper, *Shaping the Future of Care Together* stated that one of the six aspects of a National Care Service should be to ensure that people have "much greater choice over how and where [they] receive support".[2]

The principles of choice and control over care and support are evident in many areas of the Act such as supported self-assessments (s.12(1)(e)), personal budgets (s.26), the choice of accommodation provisions (s.30) and direct payments (ss.31 to 33).

The courts have considered the principles of choice and control through the requirement, in statutory guidance, that a person's preference must be considered when undertaking an assessment and the care and support planning process. This is considered at para.1–268 below.

PARTICIPATION IN WORK, EDUCATION, TRAINING OR RECREATION.   The Law Commission **1–014** argued that adult social care services have an important role to play in addressing peoples' education, training and recreation needs, for example by providing a day centre or funding to attend evening courses or football matches. Amongst other matters, it emphasises the art.8 rights of disabled people to participate in the life of the community and to have "access to essential economic and social activities and to an appropriate range of recreational and cultural activities".[3] The Commission also argued that this outcome is particularly important to carers because it replicated the amendments to carers' legislation introduced by the Carers (Equal Opportunities) Act 2004 (see para.1–121).[4]

During Committee stage in the House of Commons, the Government rejected as unnecessary an amendment which would have provided for "full and equal access" to work, education, training or recreation on the basis that this is implicit in the concept of "participation" in those areas, as well as in the reference to social and economic well-being (in subs.(2)(f)). Moreover, it argued that the phrase "equal access" would add nothing to existing equalities legislation.[5]

---

[1] *Hansard* (House of Commons: Public Bill Committee), 9 January 2014 (PM): Second Sitting, col.37 (Norman Lamb MP).

[2] Department of Health and Department of Social Security, *Caring For People: Community Care in the Next Decade and Beyond* (1989), Cm.849, para.1.8; HM Government, *Shaping the Future of Care Together* (2009) Cm.7673, p.57.

[3] *R. (A) v East Sussex CC* [2003] EWHC 167 (Admin); (2003) 6 CCLR 194 at [99]. Also, see discussion of *R. (A) v East Sussex CC* at para.1–008 above, and discussion of *R. v Haringey LBC Ex p Norton* at para.1–026 below.

[4] Law Commission, *Adult Social Care*, paras 8.22, 8.24 and 8.31.

[5] *Hansard* (House of Commons: Public Bill Committee), 9 January 2014 (PM): Second Sitting, col.37 (Norman Lamb MP).

1–015 SOCIAL AND ECONOMIC WELL-BEING. The Law Commission had rejected the inclusion of a specific outcome based on social and economic well-being because it was not sufficiently precise and added little to the other outcomes.[1] However, this was not accepted by the Government.

Aspects of social well-being might include the quality of a person's relationships with others and preventing disruptive behaviour, violence and bullying. Economic well-being would include support with accessing employment and training opportunities. Social and emotional well-being is influenced by a range of factors, including interventions at an individual level and society at large. As a result, activities concerning individual well-being may only form one element of a broader, multi-agency strategy.

During Committee stage in the House of Commons, the Government argued that the reference to social well-being (alongside the reference to the individual's contribution to society in subs.(2)(i)) encapsulated "cultural, public and community life".[2]

1–016 DOMESTIC, FAMILY AND PERSONAL RELATIONSHIPS. The Joint Committee accepted that this outcome would include parenting.[3]

1–017 SUITABILITY OF LIVING ACCOMMODATION. The draft Care and Support Bill contained no reference to housing. The Joint Committee had recommended that the list of well-being outcomes should include the availability of "safe and settled" accommodation. It argued that the quality of housing is of such importance that a local authority should always have it in mind when considering the well-being of the individual. This included supporting people to live independently in an accessible home which can be adapted to fit their needs.[4] The Government accepted the Joint Committee's recommendation and added this subsection.[5]

During Committee stage in the House of Commons, the Government argued that the suitability of living accommodation (along with the concept of control over day-to-day life in subs.(2)(d)) "naturally also encompass[es] choice of living accommodation".[6]

1–018 THE INDIVIDUAL'S CONTRIBUTION TO SOCIETY. The Law Commission concluded that the outcomes must recognise the important role played by social care services in helping service users to take part in society, for example through the provision of communicator guides for deafblind people and providing assistance with transport.[7]

During Committee stage in the House of Commons, the Government rejected an amendment to this subsection which would have added "and their participation and inclusion as equal and valued citizens". It argued that this concept was already captured by the subsection, as well as by the reference to social and economic well-being in subs.(2)(f).[8]

1–019 INDEPENDENT LIVING. The right to independent living is enshrined in art.19 of the United Nations Convention on the Rights of Persons with Disabilities. It provides that:

---

[1] Law Commission, *Adult Social Care*, para.8.24.
[2] *Hansard* (House of Commons: Public Bill Committee), 9 January 2014 (PM): Second Sitting, col.38 (Norman Lamb MP).
[3] House of Lords House of Commons Joint Committee on the Draft Care and Support Bill, *Draft Care and Support Bill Report, Session 2012–13*, para.72.
[4] House of Lords House of Commons Joint Committee on the Draft Care and Support Bill, *Draft Care and Support Bill Report, Session 2012–13*, para.74.
[5] Department of Health, *The Care Bill explained—including a response to consultation and pre-legislative scrutiny on the draft Care and Support Bill* (TSO, July), Cm.8386, para.24.
[6] *Hansard* (House of Commons: Public Bill Committee), 9 January 2014 (PM): Second Sitting, col.38 (Norman Lamb MP).
[7] Law Commission, *Adult Social Care*, para.8.24.
[8] *Hansard* (House of Commons: Public Bill Committee), 9 January 2014 (PM): Second Sitting, col.38 (Norman Lamb MP).

"States Parties to the present Convention recognise the equal right of all persons with disabilities to live in the community, with choices equal to others, and shall take effective and appropriate measures to facilitate full enjoyment by persons with disabilities of this right and their full inclusion and participation in the community, including by ensuring that:

a) Persons with disabilities have the opportunity to choose their place of residence and where and with whom they live on an equal basis with others and are not obliged to live in a particular living arrangement;

b) Persons with disabilities have access to a range of in-home, residential and other community support services, including personal assistance necessary to support living and inclusion in the community, and to prevent isolation or segregation from the community;

c) Community services and facilities for the general population are available on an equal basis to persons with disabilities and are responsive to their needs."

It has been pointed out that adult social care is a particularly important policy area in terms of independent living as adult social care policy is a key delivery mechanism for the support that many disabled people need to go about their daily lives.[1] Despite the UK having ratified the Convention, independent living does not currently exist as a free-standing, justiciable right in UK law. The status of the Convention is discussed at para.1–704.

The Law Commission had considered whether independent living, as well as a presumption of home-based care, should be included in the well-being principle. However, it concluded that both concepts were too imprecise to be expressed as statutory principles. In particular the Commission noted that the concept of independent living was cast in general terms and went beyond adult social care to cover matters such as discrimination and human rights law. The Commission also felt that its inclusion as a statutory principle (as opposed to a hard edged legal right) would not necessarily add anything, and in this sense independent living was already covered adequately by arts 8 and 19 of the Convention. In relation to a presumption of home-based care, the Commission concluded that "the key issue should be the person's wishes and feelings, and in effect this principle could skew choice in one particular direction".[2]

During Committee stage in the House of Commons, there was an attempt to amend the Bill to add independent living to the well-being principle. The Government argued that this was unnecessary:

"The precise term 'independent living' is not easy to define. It is often associated, as we heard, with article 19 of the UN convention, as is the case in amendment 58, but it is not actually defined there. We have focused on reflecting in the Bill the outcomes and rights in article 19 of the UN convention that are relevant to care and support, which means the substance of article 19, rather than the phrase 'independent living', which is not actually defined in that article. For instance, clause 1 deals with such things as control, the suitability of living accommodation, contribution to society and, crucially, requiring local authorities to consider each person's views, wishes and feelings. We think that this language is clearer and that it focuses on the outcomes that people want to achieve."[3]

---

[1] House of Lords House of Commons Joint Committee on Human Rights, *Implementation of the Right of Disabled People to Independent Living: Twenty-third Report of Session 2010–12* (1 March) HL Paper 257, HC 1074, para.163.

[2] Law Commission, *Adult Social Care*, paras 4.35 to 4.36.

[3] *Hansard* (House of Commons: Public Bill Committee), 9 January 2014 (PM): Second Sitting, col.37 (Norman Lamb MP).

In the subsequent division the amendment was defeated by 12 to 10 votes.[1]

This issue was also raised by the Joint Committee on Human Rights. In its *Independent Living* Report, the Joint Committee had made a series of recommendations in relation to adult social care, and concluded that a freestanding right to independent living should be expressly included in any forthcoming legislation on adult social care.[2] Its report on the Care Bill contained similar recommendations. The Joint Committee expressed disappointment that the Government had not taken the opportunity to provide for a free-standing right to independent living that could be directly enforced in domestic law. It called on the Government to amend the Bill to introduce such a right or to at least amend the well-being principle to include an express reference to the right to independent living.[3]

1–020   In *K v LBX* the Court of Appeal rejected the proposition that in cases of incapacity, there is a legal presumption that adults should be assisted to have the greatest control possible over the way they live their lives. But any pre-determination that independent living would be bound to be less beneficial for the person than living with their family, has also been described as unhelpful.[4] The Court held that—in respect of a person who lacked capacity to decide where to live, and where an order had been made authorising a trial placement in a supported living facility—the maintenance of care with the family was not the starting point for an assessment of that person's best interests. Instead s.4 of the Mental Capacity Act 2005 required a balancing exercise and the decision-maker is required to take into account all relevant circumstances. But it is of "great importance" that regard must be had to art.8 of the European Convention on Human Rights.[5] See also para.1–268 below on the significance of the person's wishes and feelings during the care planning process.

The statutory guidance emphasises that the concept of independent living is a core part of the well-being principle, and points to the inclusion of matters such as control by the individual of their day-to-day life, suitability of living accommodation, contribution to society and the need to consider each person's views, wishes, feelings and beliefs.[6] It sets out that:

> "The well-being principle is intended to cover the key components of independent living, as expressed in the UN Convention on the Rights of People with Disabilities (in particular, art.19 of the Convention). Supporting people to live as independently as possible, for as long as possible, is a guiding principle of the Care Act. The language used in the Act is intended to be clearer, and focus on the outcomes that truly matter to people, rather than using the relatively abstract term 'independent living'."[7]

Subsection (3)

1–021   This is a list of factors, which local authorities must consider when exercising any function about an adult, under Pt 1 of the Act. The list is also discussed in para.1.14 of the statutory guidance. The listed factors direct local authorities on a number of issues that they must consider in complying with the general well-being principle. These factors are not intended to operate as legal rules but instead, for example, direct the decision-maker to consider a particular point or establish certain assumptions, which are either phrased in mandatory terms but contain general caveats, or are broadly worded to give decision-makers sufficient flexibility. This flexibility allows resources to be taken into account

---

[1] *Hansard* (House of Commons: Public Bill Committee), 9 January 2014 (PM): Second Sitting, cols 38 to 39.

[2] House of Lords House of Commons Joint Committee on Human Rights, *Implementation of the Right of Disabled People to Independent Living: Twenty-third Report of Session 2010–12* (1 March) HL Paper 257, HC 1074, para.65.

[3] House of Lords House of Commons Joint Committee on Human Rights, *Legislative Scrutiny: Care Bill: Eleventh Report of Session 2013–14* (27 January 2014) HL Paper 121, HC 1027, paras 34 to 35.

[4] *K v LBX* [2012] EWCA Civ 79; (2012) 15 CCLR 112 at [50].

[5] *K v LBX* [2012] EWCA Civ 79; (2012) 15 CCLR 112 at [52] and [54].

[6] Department of Health, *Care and Support Statutory Guidance* (2014), para.1.18.

[7] Department of Health, *Care and Support Statutory Guidance* (2014), para.1.19.

where appropriate. Thus, resources would be relevant to *how* the well-being principle is applied, not whether it is applied at all. For instance, a decision-maker may have a number of options available that could meet an individual's assessed needs, and would in most circumstances be entitled to take resources into account when making this decision—so long as the decision promoted the person's well-being.

The list of factors is "not in order of importance, and the weight afforded to each will differ according to the circumstances of the individual case". Moreover, the list is not exhaustive. There may be other factors not listed which are relevant to the well-being of an individual, and which should be considered by decision-makers.[1]

It had been suggested to the Joint Committee that the checklist should include a reference to having regard to the United Nations Convention on the Rights of Persons with Disabilities. The Joint Committee rejected this on the basis that the Convention's obligations are cast in very general terms, many of which have nothing to do with social care.[2] There were also suggestions that there should be an explicit reference to having regard to human rights legislation. This had been rejected by the Law Commission on the basis that it would simply repeat unnecessarily the provisions of the Human Rights Act 1998.[3] This view was supported by the Joint Committee.[4]

MUST HAVE REGARD TO. A duty to have regard has been described by the courts as a **1–022** "strong obligation" but it should not be interpreted to mean "shall follow slavishly" and proper regard must be paid to other relevant factors.[5] As noted under para.1–006 above, a failure to have regard or have proper regard to the matters listed could be used in a judicial review of a local authority decision.

It is submitted that decision-makers should be able to explain how they have had regard to the list when acting or making decisions under the Act, and record the reasons for any departure. It is possible that the courts may adopt a similar approach to that taken to the duty to have "due regard" under the Equality Act 2010 (see 1-060 below). However, the Government suggested during the passage of the Care Act that the duty to have "due regard"—which would require "appropriate and conscious consideration"—was a stronger duty than having regard.[6] See also discussion under para.1–066 below.

THE IMPORTANCE OF BEGINNING WITH THE ASSUMPTION THAT THE INDIVIDUAL IS BEST- **1–023** PLACED TO JUDGE THE INDIVIDUAL'S WELL-BEING. This establishes an assumption that people are the best judges of their own well-being and therefore provides that the starting point for decision-makers is always the views of the individual concerned. This assumption can be overridden only if there are good reasons to do so. For example, there may be safeguarding concerns or resource considerations which lead the decision-maker to conclude that an alternative decision or action is necessary to secure or promote the person's well-being, or the person may lack capacity to judge his or her well-being and did not express any views at a previous time when he or she had capacity.

---

[1] Care Act 2014: Explanatory Notes para.60.
[2] House of Lords House of Commons Joint Committee on the Draft Care and Support Bill, *Draft Care and Support Bill Report, Session 2012–13*, para.72.
[3] Law Commission, *Adult Social Care*, para.4.37.
[4] House of Lords House of Commons Joint Committee on the Draft Care and Support Bill, *Draft Care and Support Bill Report, Session 2012–13*, para.73.
[5] *A-Wear Ltd v Commissioner of Valuation for Northern Ireland* [2003] R.A. 217 at [28].
[6] *Hansard* (House of Lords), 22 July 2013, Vol.747, col.1079. This was in the context of discussing s.37 and the continuity of care provisions of the Care Act.

1–024   THE INDIVIDUAL'S VIEWS, WISHES, FEELINGS AND BELIEFS.   To some extent this principle will overlap with the assumption that people are the best judges of their own well-being. If this assumption applies then it is more likely to follow that decision-makers will consider the person's views, wishes, feelings and beliefs, and follow them wherever practical and appropriate.

The views, wishes, feelings and beliefs of a service user and carer will always be a significant factor to which decision-makers and the courts must pay close regard. This will apply in circumstances where the person lacks the relevant decision-making capacity and where they retain decision-making capacity. The significance of a person's views, wishes, feelings and beliefs in respect of the care planning process is discussed at para.1–268 below.

The need to consider a person's ascertainable past and present wishes and feelings is recognised expressly in s.4(6)(a) the Mental Capacity Act 2005 as an important aspect of the best interests principle. The person's wishes and feelings can be expressed orally, in writing or through behaviour. The past and present wishes and feelings set out in an advance statement are treated as indicative of the person's past wishes and feelings, and in written form as relevant written statements, which must be considered when determining whether any proposed treatment is in the incapacitated person's best interests.

The importance attached to a person's wishes and feelings will be "case-specific and fact specific".[1]   Decision-makers may be faced with the task of balancing a person's views, wishes, feelings and beliefs against a contrary course of action that is believed to be in his or her best interests. In *R. (Wilkinson) v Broadmoor Special Hospital Authority*, Lady Justice Hale (as she was then) stated that:

> "The wishes and feelings of the incapacitated person will be an important element in determining what is, or is not, in his best interests. Where he is actively opposed to a course of action, the benefits which it holds for him will have to be carefully weighed against the disadvantages of going against his wishes, especially if force is required to do this."[2]

The statutory guidance also emphasises the importance of taking views, feelings or beliefs (including religious beliefs) into account, especially where the person has expressed views in the past but no longer has capacity to make decisions.[3]

1–025   THE IMPORTANCE OF PREVENTING OR DELAYING THE DEVELOPMENT OF NEEDS FOR CARE AND SUPPORT OR NEEDS FOR SUPPORT AND THE IMPORTANCE OF REDUCING NEEDS OF EITHER KIND THAT ALREADY EXIST.   The statutory guidance explains that "effective interventions at the right time can stop needs from escalating, and help people maintain their independence for longer".[4]   See discussion under para.1–033 below.

1–026   THE NEED TO ENSURE THAT DECISIONS ABOUT THE INDIVIDUAL ARE MADE HAVING REGARD TO ALL THE INDIVIDUAL'S CIRCUMSTANCES (AND ARE NOT BASED ONLY ON THE INDIVIDUAL'S AGE OR APPEARANCE OR ANY CONDITION OF THE INDIVIDUAL'S OR ASPECT OF THE INDIVIDUAL'S BEHAVIOUR WHICH MIGHT LEAD OTHERS TO MAKE UNJUSTIFIED ASSUMPTIONS ABOUT THE INDIVIDUAL'S WELL-BEING).   Government guidance has long stressed the need for local authorities to consider a wide range of needs and circumstances when conducting an assessment and any subsequent care and support planning (including specialist assessments).[5]

---

[1] *ITW v Z* [2009] EWCOP 2525 (Fam) at [35].
[2] *R. (Wilkinson) v Broadmoor Special Hospital Authority* [2001] EWCA Civ 1545; [2002] 1 W.L.R. 419 at [64].
[3] Department of Health, *Care and Support Statutory Guidance* (2014), para.1.14.
[4] Department of Health, *Care and Support Statutory Guidance* (2014), para.1.14.
[5] For example, Department of Health Social Services Inspectorate and Scottish Office Social Work Services Group, *Care Management and Assessment: Practitioners' Guide* (1991) and Department of Health, *Single Assessment Process: Guidance for Implementation* (2002), Annexes E and F.

The courts have been prepared to intervene where the scope of the assessment has been restricted for policy or financial reasons. In *R. v Haringey LBC Ex p Norton* the court rejected the local authority's submission that, while it could meet the person's personal care needs, it did not need to provide for their social, recreational and leisure needs on the basis that it was "forced to make decisions based upon prioritising need and working within existing resources".[1] It was held that:

> "The care package which should have been assessed by the respondent had to be a multi-faceted package. This applicant has been able to overcome or at least to live with some of the most awful characteristics of his illness by the social intercourse achieved in recreational facilities such as the playing of bridge, swimming etc. A re-assessed care package should have comprehended such matters and should not have discriminated in the manner that it did."[2]

The courts have also been critical of local authorities whose assessments have failed to take into account the views of the person's general practitioner,[3] a comprehensive social work assessment report,[4] and the needs of a person for a holiday.[5]

Of course, this does not mean that all needs assessments must be comprehensive. In general terms, the type and level of the assessment will be proportionate to the level and complexity of the person's need and therefore simple needs will require less investigation than more complex ones.[6] However, the assessment process must ensure that, as far as practicable, all relevant information is collected and taken into account when decisions about the provision of services are made.

The second element of this principle (unjustified assumptions) dovetails with the requirement in s.2(3) of the Mental Capacity Act 2005 that a lack of capacity cannot be established merely by reference to a person's age, appearance, condition or behaviour. The need to avoid unjustified assumptions is also an important aspect of the time and function specific element of mental capacity assessments.

In adult social care, the need to avoid unjustified assumptions is often associated with the **1–027** concept of person-centred planning. A 2008 Department of Health circular described person-centred planning as placing the individual "firmly in the centre in identifying what is personally important to deliver his or her outcomes" and enabling people to "design the support or care arrangements that best suit their specific needs".[7] This approach is often contrasted with the so-called traditional model of service provision, whereby professionals decide care packages by reference to pre-commissioned services and focus on the person's deficits and negative behaviours, viewing them as passive recipients of care. Person-centred planning was adopted as Government policy in the 2001 White Paper on learning disability, *Valuing People*.[8] Subsequent Department of Health guidance and policy statements continued to promote a person-centred approach to assessments and care planning and support.[9]

The courts have considered the requirement that local authorities must assess and re-assess peoples' needs individually. For example, it has been held that:

---

[1] *R. v Haringey LBC Ex p Norton* (1997–98) 1 CCLR 168 at 172(F).
[2] *R. v Haringey LBC Ex p Norton* (1997–98) 1 CCLR 168 at 181(B).
[3] *R. v Birmingham City Council Ex p Killigrew* (1999) 3 CCLR 109.
[4] *R. (Goldsmith) v Wandsworth LBC* [2004] EWCA Civ 1170; (2004) 7 CCLR 472.
[5] *R. v North Yorkshire CC Ex p Hargreaves* (1997–98) 1 CCLR 104.
[6] Department of Health and Social Services Inspectorate and Scottish Office Social Work Services Group, *Care Management and Assessment: Practitioners' Guide* (1991), para.3.3.
[7] LAC(DH)(2008)1, *Transforming Social Care*, para.17.
[8] Department of health, *Valuing People: A New Strategy for Learning Disability for the 21st Century* (2001), Cm.5086.
[9] For example, Department of Health, *Single Assessment Process: Guidance for Implementation* (2002), Annex A, HM Government and others, *Putting People First: A Shared Vision and Commitment to the Transformation of Adult Social Care* (2007), p.3 and LAC(DH)(2008)1, *Transforming Social Care*, Annex B, para.10.

- local authorities are not entitled to make blanket decisions to cut services, merely because of a reduction in revenues, without any individual re-assessments of the people affected. In such cases, assessments must be "needs-led by reference to the particular needs of a particular disabled person"[1] ; and
- the obligation to carry out an individual assessment of needs is not satisfied by writing letters to those affected or potentially affected by cuts in service provision for reasons of financial stringency and simply offering them a re-assessment.[2]

1–028 THE IMPORTANCE OF THE INDIVIDUAL PARTICIPATING AS FULLY AS POSSIBLE IN DECISIONS RELATING TO THE EXERCISE OF THE FUNCTION CONCERNED AND BEING PROVIDED WITH THE IN-FORMATION AND SUPPORT NECESSARY TO ENABLE THE INDIVIDUAL TO PARTICIPATE. This provides that service users and carers must be given the opportunity to be involved, as far as possible in the circumstances, in assessments, planning, developing and reviewing their care and support. It also recognises that advocacy, information and advice are sometimes needed in order to make full participation meaningful. This principle is consistent with ss.1(3) and 4(4) of the Mental Capacity Act 2005.

However, in some cases full participation may not always be applicable or welcome. There will be cases where people do not want to participate: for example, Solicitors for the Elderly has pointed to cases of "people being forced to accept a direct payment, where they do not have the desire or energy to arrange their own care". Similarly, the Royal Institute for Blind People and Guide Dogs has argued that people should be able to choose to have traditional services, delivered in the traditional way.[3]

1–029 THE IMPORTANCE OF ACHIEVING A BALANCE BETWEEN THE INDIVIDUAL'S WELL-BEING AND THAT OF ANY FRIENDS OR RELATIVES WHO ARE INVOLVED IN CARING FOR THE INDIVIDUAL. This principle requires the decision-maker to achieve some balancing of the well-being of the person with care and support needs, against that of any carer. The Law Commission argued that the well-being principle should apply to both carers and adults needing care and recognised this may cause practice difficulties in individual cases where decisions may impact on both a carer and an adult needing care and support. In such cases the Law Commission suggested:

> "As a general rule the well-being principle relates to the subject of the decision. If there are competing interests, such as those of the carer, these would only be relevant insofar as they related to the well-being of the subject of the decision."[4]

The Commission went on to suggest that in cases where it has been assessed that the well-being of the individual and the carer is incompatible, then this principle requires the decision-maker to seek a solution that balances the well-being of both parties. For example, if a person with dementia wants to remain living at home (and it is agreed that this would promote their well-being) and their carer wants them to move into a care home (and it is agreed that this would promote their well-being) then the solution that balances the well-being of both parties may be the provision of respite care on a regular basis.[5]

This principle can also be interpreted as an acknowledgement, in part, of "relational autonomy" approaches which highlight how interdependence and caring relationships can enable autonomy. These are often contrasted to liberal individualist accounts of autonomy based on the rational and responsible contractor.[6] The statutory guidance states that:

---

[1] *R. v Islington LBC Ex p McMillan* (1995) 1 CCLR 7; 16(F) by McCowan LJ.
[2] *R. v Gloucestershire CC Ex p Radar* (1998) 1 CCLR 476.
[3] Law Commission, *Adult Social Care: Consultation Analysis* (31 March 2011), paras 3.50 to 3.51.
[4] Law Commission, *Adult Social Care*, para.4.32.
[5] Law Commission, *Adult Social Care*, para.4.32.
[6] See, for example, L.Series (2015), "Relationships, Autonomy and Legal Capacity: Mental Capacity and Support Paradigms" in International Journal of Law and Psychiatry 2015, Vol.40, p.80.

"People should be considered in the context of their families and support networks, not just as isolated individuals with needs. Local authorities should take into account the impact of an individual's need on those who support them, and take steps to help others access information or support."[1]

THE NEED TO PROTECT PEOPLE FROM ABUSE AND NEGLECT. The Law Commission argued **1–030** that it is vital that well-being is provided through protecting people from abuse and neglect. For example, local authorities may need to apply for appointeeship under social security legislation or deputyship under the Mental Capacity Act 2005 where a service user is being financially abused.[2] The Commission argued that safeguarding relates to the prevention of abuse and neglect, and therefore has a broad focus that extends to all aspects of a person's general welfare and not just intervention when it is suspected that abuse may have occurred. In other words, safeguarding, seen in the round, is properly part of the general approach to be taken to assessment and the delivery of services.[3]

In the current policy environment of personalisation, which emphasises the importance of individuals exercising choice and control, it may be particularly important to recognise that some people may need safeguarding from abuse and neglect. For example, it has been argued that, in the field of learning disabilities, preventing substantial harm and premature death must take precedence over promoting health choices:

". . . in matters of health, which are not within the experience of adults with learning disabilities, the duty of care should override misplaced respect for "choices". The latter have been a distracting detour in service provision and are permitting the abdication of decision-making responsibility."[4]

It has also been suggested that one of the "unanticipated consequences" of the empowering ethos of the Mental Capacity Act 2005 has been to leave vulnerable adults at risk of harm, in some cases leading to their deaths, after having disengaged from services, and where that decision to disengage had not been sufficiently examined by health and social care professionals.[5]

Of course, it is not always the case that the exercise of choice and control will be incompatible with the need to safeguard those at risk. In many cases, these principles will reinforce each other. In other cases it will be necessary to come down on the side of either choice and control, or safeguarding from abuse and neglect. This often difficult balance was acknowledged by Mr Justice Munby (as he was then) in *Local Authority X v MM* in the following terms:

"The fact is that all life involves risk, and the young, the elderly and the vulnerable, are exposed to additional risks and to risks they are less well equipped than others to cope with. But just as wise parents resist the temptation to keep their children metaphorically wrapped up in cotton wool, so too we must avoid the temptation always to put the physical health and safety of the elderly and the vulnerable before everything else. Often it will be appropriate to do so, but not always. Physical health and safety can sometimes be bought at too high a price in happiness and emotional welfare. The emphasis must be on sensible risk appraisal, not striving to avoid all risk, whatever the price, but instead seeking a proper balance and being willing to tolerate manageable or acceptable risks as the price appropriately to be paid in order to achieve some other good—in particular to

---

[1] Department of Health, *Care and Support Statutory Guidance* (2014), para.1.14.
[2] Law Commission, *Adult Social Care*, para.8.24.
[3] Law Commission, *Adult Social Care*, para.9.2.
[4] M. Flynn and others, "Warning: Health 'Choices' Can Kill", (2003) 5 *The Journal of Adult Protection*, pp.30–34.
[5] House of Lords Select Committee on the Mental Capacity Act, *Mental Capacity Act 2005: Post Legislative Scrutiny* (2014) HL Paper 139, para.61.

achieve the vital good of the elderly or vulnerable person's *happiness*. What good is it making someone safer if it merely makes them miserable?"[1]

This case involved the court making declarations where a woman had the capacity to consent to sexual relations, but lacked capacity to make decisions with respect to contact and residence, which included contact with the person with whom she had a sexual relationship. The judgment went on to note that if a person falls just above or below the borderline of capacity:

"The more weight must in principle be attached to her wishes and feelings, because the greater the distress, the humiliation and indeed it may even be the anger she is likely to feel the better she is able to appreciate that others are taking on her behalf decisions about matters which vitally affect her—matters, it may be, as here, of an intensely private and personal nature."[2]

On the other hand, the serious case review into the case of Stephen Hoskin, a man with learning disabilities who was tortured and murdered in 2006, recommended that health and social services in Cornwall should "review the implications of acceding to people's 'choice' if the latter is not to be construed as abandonment". In particular, the review noted that Steven Hoskin had been able to exercise his choice to terminate contact with adult social care services without any investigation, even though this decision may have been made on the basis of inadequate or inappropriate information or as a result of coercion from third parties.[3]

Safeguarding is also included as a well-being "outcome" in subs.(2)—see para.1–012 above. However, it is not referred to in the eligibility criteria (see A1–274). See also para.1–346 below on safeguarding and personal budgets.

1–031   THE NEED TO ENSURE THAT ANY RESTRICTION ON THE INDIVIDUAL'S RIGHTS OR FREEDOM OF ACTION THAT IS INVOLVED IN THE EXERCISE OF THE FUNCTION IS KEPT TO THE MINIMUM NECESS-ARY FOR ACHIEVING THE PURPOSE FOR WHICH THE FUNCTION IS BEING EXERCISED.   Statutory principles which require decision-makers to consider the least restrictive course of action are apparent in s.1(6) of the Mental Capacity Act 2005 and to a more limited extent, in s.1(5) of the Children Act 1989. The Law Commission's final report concluded that the inclusion of a similar principle in the adult social care statute:

". . . will be an important way of reminding local authorities, especially when undertaking adult protection interventions, of the need to approach such action with sensitivity and a proper appreciation of the limited extent of their powers, as well as helping to alleviate the fears of service users and carers that they will be the subject of coercive action. It also reflects the fact that some decisions by local authorities will necessarily be more restrictive of a person's rights and freedoms than alternative courses of action; for example, a care home placement may be more restrictive than a home-based care package."[4]

The Commission went on to warn that this principle should not be implemented in a way which undermines the views, wishes and feelings principle, and that it must not suggest that a local authority can impose restrictions where it cannot. But the Commission acknowledged that:

"However, there is scope for the principles in the checklist to pull in different directions. For instance, following the views and wishes of the person concerned may not accord with the safeguarding principle, and in such cases decision-makers would need to

---

[1] *Local Authority X v MM* [2007] EWHC 2003 (Fam); (2008) 11 CCLR 119 at [120].
[2] *Local Authority X v MM* [2007] EWHC 2003 (Fam); (2008) 11 CCLR 119 at [124].
[3] Cornwall Adult Protection Committee, *The Murder of Steven Hoskin: A Serious Case Review, Executive Summary* (2007), para.5.13.
[4] Law Commission, *Adult Social Care*, para.4.31.

achieve the appropriate balance in light of the circumstances of the case. The single uni-fying purpose of the individual factors in the checklist would be their relationship with the overarching well-being principle."[1]

In arguing that this principle must not suggest that a local authority can impose restric-tions where it cannot, the Commission had in mind the following comments of Mr Justice Munby (as he was then) in *A Local Authority v A*:

"People in the situation of A and C, together with their carers, look to the State—to a local authority—for the support, the assistance and the provision of the services to which the law, giving effect to the underlying principles of the Welfare State, entitles them. They do not seek to be 'controlled' by the State or by the local authority. And it is not for the State in the guise of a local authority to seek to exercise such control. The State, the local authority, is the servant of those in need of its support and assistance, not their master."[2]

Preventing needs for care and support

2.—(1) A local authority must provide or arrange for the provision of services, **1–032** facilities or resources, or take other steps, which it considers will—
  (a) contribute towards preventing or delaying the development by adults in its area of needs for care and support;
  (b) contribute towards preventing or delaying the development by carers in its area of needs for support;
  (c) reduce the needs for care and support of adults in its area;
  (d) reduce the needs for support of carers in its area.
  (2) In performing that duty, a local authority must have regard to—
  (a) the importance of identifying services, facilities and resources already available in the authority's area and the extent to which the authority could involve or make use of them in performing that duty;
  (b) the importance of identifying adults in the authority's area with needs for care and support which are not being met (by the authority or otherwise);
  (c) the importance of identifying carers in the authority's area with needs for support which are not being met (by the authority or otherwise).
  (3) Regulations may—
  (a) permit a local authority to make a charge for providing or arranging for the provision of services, facilities or resources, or for taking other steps, under this section;
  (b) prohibit a local authority from making a charge it would otherwise be per-mitted to make by virtue of paragraph (a).
  (4) The regulations may in particular (in reliance on section 125(7)) make pro-vision by reference to services, facilities or resources which—
  (a) are of a specified type;
  (b) are provided in specified circumstances;
  (c) are provided to an adult of a specified description;
  (d) are provided for a specified period only.
  (5) A charge under the regulations may cover only the cost that the local auth-ority incurs in providing or arranging for the provision of the service, facility or resource or for taking the other step.

---

[1] Law Commission, *Adult Social Care*, para.4.32.
[2] *A Local Authority v A* [2010] EWHC 978 (Fam); (2010) 13 CCLR 404 at [52].

(6) In cases where a local authority performs the duty under subsection (1) jointly with one or more other local authorities in relation to the authorities' combined area—

(a) references in this section to a local authority are to be read as references to the authorities acting jointly, and

(b) references in this section to a local authority's area are to be read as references to the combined area.

(7) Sections 21 (exception for persons subject to immigration control), 22 (exception for provision of health services) and 23 (exception for provision of housing etc.) apply in relation to the duty under subsection (1), but with the modifications set out in those sections.

(8) "Adult" means a person aged 18 or over.

GENERAL NOTE

1–033   Prevention can be described as early interventions that prevent or defer the need for more costly intensive support. Prevention services can be provided to prevent harm before it occurs or needs from developing; ensure prompt interventions when difficulties start to emerge; and reduce or delay care needs that have begun to intensify. They are made up of a continuum of services "from intermediate services at the top end of the spectrum to 'low-level' interventions and community care services supporting social inclusion at the other".[1] Examples of the latter include befriending, social skills training, employment support, grab rails and social groups. This approach is often contrasted with models of social care that focus resources on people with the highest levels of need. The statutory guidance divides prevention into three general approaches—primary (aimed at those who currently have no particular health or care needs), secondary (for those who have an increased risk of developing needs) and tertiary (aimed at minimising the effect of disability or deterioration). It also distinguishes between reablement (services in the home to help people live independently), rehabilitation (services to help people regain or relearn capabilities) and intermediate care (short-term support when a person leaves hospital or is at risk of being admitted).[2]

The drive towards prevention services is said to reflect changing demographic patterns, with active older people becoming a focus for policy attention, and the need to reduce expenditure on care services.[3] In recent years, prevention services have been identified as a policy priority for Governments.[4] In the House of Commons, during the Committee stage of the Care Bill, prevention was described as the "holy grail of health and social care policy".[5]

Section 2 places a general duty (see para.1–001) on local authorities to take steps, including providing and arranging for services, which are intended to prevent, reduce or delay needs for care and support for all local people including adults and carers. In the House of Lords Committee, the Government stated:

---

[1] B. Hudson and M. Henwood, *Prevention, Personalisation and Prioritisation in Social Care: Squaring the Circle? A Report Commissioned by CSCI for the Review of Eligibility Criteria* (2008), para.2.1.

[2] Department of Health, *Care and Support Statutory Guidance* (2014), paras 2.5 to 2.15.

[3] For example, HM Government, *Opportunity Age: Meeting the Challenges of Ageing in the 21st Century* (2005) and D Wanless, *Securing Our Future: Taking a Long-term View* (2002).

[4] For example, Department of Health, *Independence, Well-being and Choice: Our Vision for the Future of Social Care for Adults in England* (2005) Cm 6499, para.5.9, HM Government, *Our Health, Our Care, Our say: A New Direction for Community Services* (2006) Cm 6737, paras 2.80 to 2.83, LAC(DH)(2008)1, *Transforming Social Care*, Annex B, para.10, and *Shaping the Future of Care Together* (2009) Cm 7673, pp.50 to 53.

[5] *Hansard* (House of Commons: Public Bill Committee), 9 January 2014 (PM): Second Sitting, col.34 (Liz Kendall MP).

"Preventing and delaying needs from arising, or reducing them where they exist, is a central part of local authorities' modern responsibilities for care and support. Adopting preventive approaches can reduce needs in the longer term, saving public money and improving outcomes. There has never before been a clear legal duty that reflects this priority and establishes prevention as part of the core local authority responsibility."[1]

During his oral evidence session with the Joint Committee, the Minister of State for Care and Support, Norman Lamb MP, argued that the introduction of a capped costs system could reinforce the aim of this duty. He expressed the hope that a cap:

"encourages people to come forward early to have the assessment as to whether their care needs meet the threshold for the clock to start. The more the local authority can do to have the early conversation with people to help them build their own resilience and to give advice and support about what the family can do—and the more the community can do to maintain independence and slow down any deterioration of condition—the better."[2]

This view was supported by the Joint Committee which stated that "realising the 'public health' benefit from introducing a capped costs system" could result in "significant quality of life gains by helping to engage more people in maintaining their health and well-being, with a positive impact on demand for long-term care".[3]

During the second reading of the Care Bill in the House of Commons the Government confirmed that the s.2 prevention duty is a universal obligation and will "have no relation to the criteria for eligibility".[4] This was confirmed at Committee stage.[5] The statutory guidance confirms that the local authority is not required to provide a care and support plan where it only takes steps under s.2, but it should consider "which aspects of the plan should be provided in these circumstances" and provide necessary information to enable the person to understand:

- what needs the person has or may develop, and why the intervention or other action is proposed in their regard;
- what the expected outcome for the action proposed is, and any relevant timescale in which those outcomes are expected; and
- what is proposed to take place at the end of the measure (for instance, whether an assessment of need or a carer's assessment will be carried out at that point).[6]

The guidance goes on to state that "the person concerned must agree to the provision of any service or other step proposed by the local authority". Where the person refuses but continues to appear to have needs, the local authority must proceed to offer the individual an assessment.[7]

There are other provisions in the Act which are intended to reinforce the prevention duty, for example:

- prevention is mentioned in s.1(3)(c) as part of the well-being principle;

---

[1] *Hansard* (House of Lords), 3 July 2013, Vol.746, col.1299 (Earl Howe).
[2] House of Lords House of Commons Joint Committee on the Draft Care and Support Bill, *Draft Care and Support Bill, Session 2012–13, Oral Evidence* (2013), p.310, Q238.
[3] House of Lords House of Commons Joint Committee on the Draft Care and Support Bill, *Draft Care and Support Bill Report, Session 2012–13*, para.147.
[4] *Hansard* (House of Commons), 16 December 2013, Vol.572, col.529.
[5] *Hansard* (House of Commons: Public Bill Committee), 9 January 2014 (PM): Second Sitting, col.49 (Norman Lamb MP).
[6] Department of Health, *Care and Support Statutory Guidance* (2014), para.2.45.
[7] Department of Health, *Care and Support Statutory Guidance* (2014), para.2.46.

- the duty to ensure the integration of care and support and health services applies where this would ensure the prevention or delay of needs under s.3(1)(b);
- sections 13(5)(b) and 24(2)(b)(ii) provide that following an assessment, if there is no duty to meet the adult's needs, the local authority must give them information and advice about prevention; and
- the care and support plan, and the support plan, must include information and advice about prevention (s.25(1)(f)).

Section 116 and 116A of the Local Government and Public Involvement Act 2007 require a local authority and each of its partner clinical commissioning groups to prepare a joint strategic needs assessment and joint health and well-being strategy which should include any needs that can be met by the local authority exercising its functions under this section. The link between joint strategic needs assessments and prevention is also discussed in paras 2.29 to 2.31 of the statutory guidance.

Subsection (1)

1–034 "Arranging for" may include commissioning from others. The statutory guidance emphasises that local authorities should develop a local approach to prevention. Some types of prevention may be provided by the authority itself, others may be provided in partnership with other local agencies (e.g. rehabilitation or falls clinics provided jointly with the local NHS), and further types may be best provided by other organisations e.g. specialist housing providers or some carers' services.[1] The guidance goes on to state that:

"Where the local authority does not provide such types of preventative support itself, it should have mechanisms in place for identifying existing and new services, maintaining contact with providers over time, and helping people to access them."[2]

Subsection (2)

1–035 This provision requires that local authorities must have regard to how they could make the best use of community facilities to prevent, delay and reduce needs for care and support; and to have regard to identifying adults and carers in their area who have unmet needs for care and support, when providing or arranging for preventative services under this section. See also paras 2.37 to 2.40 of the statutory guidance.

The Joint Committee was concerned that this provision referred only to the importance of identifying those who already have unmet needs, and recommended that it should be extended to include those who do not yet have needs, but may be at risk of developing such needs, and those who already have needs, but for whom prevention of deterioration might delay an increase in their needs.[3] The Department of Health agreed with the principle of local authorities engaging at an early stage with adults who may have future needs or whose needs are at risk of deteriorating. But it argued that the well-being principle (s.1), the prevention duty (s.2) and provision of information and advice (s.4) "taken together ensure that all adults can benefit from preventative interventions". The Department also questioned how the Joint Committee's recommended approach would be carried out in practice and "there may be unintended consequences and cost burdens to local authorities".[4]

At Committee stage in the House of Commons, the Government clarified that "the importance of identifying suitable living accommodation" is covered by s.2(2)(a) which requires local authorities to identify services, facilities and resources in performing the

---

[1] Department of Health, *Care and Support Statutory Guidance* (2014), paras 2.23 to 2.24.

[2] Department of Health, *Care and Support Statutory Guidance* (2014), para.2.27.

[3] House of Lords House of Commons Joint Committee on the *Draft Care and Support Bill, Draft Care and Support Bill Report, Session 2012–13*, para.145.

[4] Department of Health, *The Care Bill explained—including a response to consultation and pre-legislative scrutiny on the draft Care and Support Bill* (TSO, July 2012), Cm.8386, p.66.

s.2 duty.[1] Housing to support prevention of needs is discussed in paras 15.60 to 15.64 of the statutory guidance.

The meaning of "have regard to" is discussed at 1–022 above. It should be noted that the s.2 duty is not a duty to have regard to the listed factors, but to have regard to "the importance of" those factors. This is likely to give local authorities even greater discretion in how this duty is achieved.

Subsections (3), (4) and (5)

These subsections provide for regulations to be made which specify when a local auth- **1–036** ority can charge for prevention services. During the passage of the Care Bill through the House of Lords, the Government explained its intention:

". . . certain services will be provided free of charge, and regulations will set out which types of prevention services must be provided free of charge. Regulations will also set out which types of prevention services local authorities can charge for. It will then be for local authorities to decide whether they charge for such services. This will maintain the current position, where charging for preventive services is determined locally, in accordance with local requirements."[2]

Subsection (3)(b) allows regulations to prohibit charging where subs.(3)(a) would otherwise allow this. The explanatory notes explain:

"This is to allow for local authorities to continue to charge for some preventative services as they do now (for example subsidised leisure services), and to enable local authorities to broaden access to services that can prevent, delay or reduce needs for care and support, that may fall outside of traditional models of care and support, to a wider range of adults and carers in their area."[3]

Subsection (5) provides that any charge made under these regulations can cover only the cost to the local authority of providing or arranging the service.

The relevant regulations are the Care and Support (Preventing Needs for Care and Support) Regulations 2014 (SI 2014/2673). They are reproduced and discussed at A1– 153 to A1–158 below. These provide that a charge must not reduce the adult's income to below the minimum income guarantee, and that a carer must not be charged for prevention services which consists of provision made directly to the adult needing care (reg.3).

The regulations also provide that local authorities cannot make a charge for community equipment (aids and minor adaptations) and intermediate care and reablement support services, and services provided to an adult suffering from variant Creutzfeldt-Jakob disease (regs 4 and 5). Charging for preventative support is discussed in paras 2.54 to 2.62 of the statutory guidance. In particular it advises that a financial assessment for prevention services is likely to be "disproportionate", and that alternatives should be considered such as a light-touch assessment. In any event, a local authority should not charge more than it costs to provide or arrange for the service facility or resource.[4]

Charging for services following an assessment—including entitlements to free intermediate care for a specified period and minor aids and adaptations up to a certain cost— is covered by separate regulations made under s.14 (The Care and Support (Charging and Assessment of Resources) Regulations 2014 (SI 2014/2672)).

Subsection (6)

This acknowledges that a local authority may take steps to prevent, reduce or delay needs **1–037** for care and support together with one or more other local authorities.

---

[1] *Hansard* (House of Commons: Public Bill Committee), 9 January 2014 (PM): Second Sitting, col.49 (Norman Lamb MP).
[2] *Hansard* (House of Lords), 14 October 2013, Vol.748, col.278 (Earl Howe).
[3] Bill 123–EN 2013–2014, Explanatory Notes to the Bill, para.40.
[4] Department of Health, *Care and Support Statutory Guidance* (2014), paras 2.57 to 2.58.

Promoting integration of care and support with health services, etc.

1–038   **3.**—(1) A local authority must exercise its functions under this Part with a view to ensuring the integration of care and support provision with health provision and health-related provision where it considers that this would—

(a) promote the well-being of adults in its area with needs for care and support and the well-being of carers in its area,

(b) contribute to the prevention or delay of the development by adults in its area of needs for care and support or the development by carers in its area of needs for support, or

(c) improve the quality of care and support for adults, and of support for carers, provided in its area (including the outcomes that are achieved from such provision).

(2) "Care and support provision" means—

(a) provision to meet adults' needs for care and support,

(b) provision to meet carers' needs for support, and

(c) provision of services, facilities or resources, or the taking of other steps, under section 2.

(3) "Health provision" means provision of health services as part of the health service.

(4) "Health-related provision" means provision of services which may have an effect on the health of individuals but which are not—

(a) health services provided as part of the health service, or

(b) services provided in the exercise of social services functions (as defined by section 1A of the Local Authority Social Services Act 1970).

(5) For the purposes of this section, the provision of housing is health-related provision.

(6) In section 13N of the National Health Service Act 2006 (duty of NHS Commissioning Board to promote integration), at the end insert—

"(5) For the purposes of this section, the provision of housing accommodation is a health-related service."

(7) In section 14Z1 of that Act (duty of clinical commissioning groups to promote integration), at the end insert—

"(4) For the purposes of this section, the provision of housing accommodation is a health-related service."

GENERAL NOTE

1–039   As discussed at para.1–249 below, the division of health and social care provision dates back to the inception of the NHS. The 1948 settlement established the NHS as a comprehensive service which was open to all and free at the point of use, and in contrast social care is often targeted towards those with high needs and means tested. In broad terms the NHS is paid for through general taxation and operates with a ring-fenced budget, while local authorities are responsible for raising money to fund some social care provisions and the social care budget is not ring-fenced.

This section places a duty on local authorities to carry out their responsibilities under Pt 1 of the Care Act with the aim of integrating services with those provided by the NHS and other health-related services. As a general duty, s.3 does not specify how local authorities must ensure integration. This is left to the local authority. Indeed, integration can mean many things, including joint commissioning for one or more services, single assessments, sharing data, the delivery of care through generic teams and single locations where people can access therapeutic services, nursing or social care. However, it is important to emphasise that this is not legal integration. The distinct powers and duties under the Care Act and the National Health Service Act 2006 remain distinct. Promoting integration is discussed in paras 4.88 to 4.92 and 15.3 to 15.14 of the statutory guidance.

Section 3 is intended to reflect the similar integration duties placed on NHS England by s.13N and clinical commissioning groups by s.14Z1 of the National Health Service Act 2006. Also, under s.75 of the 2006 Act the Secretary of State can make provision for local authorities and NHS bodies to enter into partnership arrangements in relation to certain functions. The specific provision for these arrangements is set out in the NHS Bodies and Local Authorities Partnership Arrangements Regulations 2000 (SI 2000/617), which includes powers to pool budgets and undertake joint or lead commissioning. The Care Act also amends the 2006 Act to provide for the Better Care Fund (previously referred to as the Integration Transformation Fund).[1] The Fund was announced as part of the 2013 spending round and provides for £3.8 billion funding in 2015/16 to be spent locally on health and care through pooled budget arrangements under s.75 of the 2006 Act. The aim is to ensure that every area establishes a pooled budget for integrated health and social care. However, concerns were raised during the passage of the Care Bill through Parliament that the Fund is not new money but has been "top-sliced" from other budgets, primarily the NHS.[2] The Government rejected claims that as a result of the fund local authorities will face a choice between implementing the legislation and investigating in integrated services, arguing that this was a "false choice" and that the reforms were "part of the same agenda".[3] The implementation of local Better Care Funds began on 1 April 2015.[4]

There are other provisions in the Care Act which are intended to reinforce the s.3 integration duty, for example:

- s.1(2)(b) makes it clear that the well-being principle incorporates physical and mental health. Local authorities must therefore already consider a person's health when exercising any functions under Pt 1; and
- s.12(1)(f) and (g) provide that regulations may set out when a local authority must consult someone with expertise before undertaking an assessment and may also set out conditions around co-operation with the NHS, by specifying the circumstances in which the local authority must refer the adult concerned for an assessment of eligibility for NHS continuing health care.

During the passage of the Care Bill, at report stage in the House of Lords, the Government pointed to the links between s.3 and the s.6 duty to co-operate:

". . . it is incontrovertible that local authorities and relevant partners must co-operate in order to ensure both integration and safe and timely transfers of care; indeed, the Bill already requires this. [Section 6] requires that local authorities and relevant partners co-operate with one another where relevant to care and support. [Section 6(6)] of this clause sets out some key examples of when this duty should be used. There can be no question that this duty would also apply to promoting integration. With respect to integration, [s.3] requires local authorities to promote integration while carrying out their care and support functions. Consequently, this applies to [s.6]. Further, the co-operation duty requires the relevant partners, including NHS bodies and local authorities, to co-operate with one another in the exercise of their respective functions. Such co-operation is inexorably linked to the integration duty."[5]

---

[1] Care Act 2014 s.121. This amends ss.223B of the National Health Service Act 2006, and inserts s.223GA into the 2006 Act.

[2] *Hansard* (House of Commons: Public Bill Committee), 4 February 2014: Fifteenth Sitting, cols 573 to 583.

[3] *Hansard* (House of Commons), 10 March 2014, Vol.577, col.87 (Norman Lamb MP).

[4] See, Department of Health and Department for Communities and Local Government, *Better Care Fund: Policy Framework* (December 2014).

[5] *Hansard* (House of Lords), 9 October 2013, Vol.748, col.107 (Earl Howe).

1–040   Section 116B of the Local Government and Public Involvement in Health Act 2007 requires local authorities and clinical commissioning groups to have regard to the relevant joint strategic needs assessment and joint health and well-being strategy in exercising any of their functions. This includes their duties to co-operate and promote integration. See paras 15.8 to 15.10 of the statutory guidance.

The Department of Health rejected the Joint Committee's recommendation that the s.3 integration duty should apply to housing provision as well as health and health-related provision, and should include a particular emphasis on the adequacy of housing provision on discharge from hospital:

> "Whilst we agree with those who said that housing should be included as one example of a 'health-related service', we have not sought further to be prescriptive about how and when local authorities (including housing authorities) should integrate. Instead, we want to encourage local authorities to innovate and make decisions according to the needs [sic] the people in their area."[1]

Similarly, the Department did not agree with the Joint Committee that s.3 should include a power to prescribe groups of people or services that should be subject to joint commissioning and joint budgets, because "we want commissioners to have autonomy and flexibility as to how they work together to secure services to deliver improved outcomes for patients and their families".[2]

During Committee stage in the House of Commons, there was an attempt to amend the Bill to extend the duty to integrate services to NHS bodies. The Government argued this was unnecessary given that ss.13N and 14Z1 of the National Health Service Act 2006 already place duties to promote integration on NHS England and clinical commissioning groups, and s.195 of the 2012 Act places a duty on health and well-being boards (which include a representative on the relevant clinical commissioning group) to promote integrated working when that would promote health and well-being.[3]

1–041   The Government also rejected an amendment which would place a duty on all housing providers to ensure integration:

> "Extending the duty in that way would be an additional and unnecessary burden on the private sector and, in a sense, it would be impossible for the private sector to achieve because it simply does not have control over integrating health and care . . . The measure would also be unworkable because, in so far as housing providers are private landlords, they do not have any public or statutory functions to provide care and support or health provision. Accordingly, it is not in their power to ensure the integration of such services. Rather, the duty to promote integration needs to be imposed on the local authorities and NHS bodies, working together with housing providers and other health-related providers, as is currently proposed in the Bill."[4]

In 2013 the King's Fund established the Commission on the Future of Health and Social Care in England to consider whether the health and social care systems could be better aligned to meet the needs of patients and service-users. Its final report published in 2014 recommended a single ring-fenced budget for health and social care, with a single local commissioner (with Attendance Allowance brought within the health and social care system). Under this scheme, lower levels of need would be met through a cash payment called "care and support allowance". For higher levels of need, all care would be free at the point

---

[1] Department of Health, *The Care Bill explained—including a response to consultation and pre-legislative scrutiny on the draft Care and Support Bill* (TSO, July 2012) Cm.8386, para.33.

[2] Department of Health, *The Care Bill explained—including a response to consultation and pre-legislative scrutiny on the draft Care and Support Bill* (TSO, July 2012) Cm.8386, para.34.

[3] *Hansard* (House of Commons: Public Bill Committee), 9 January 2014 (AM): First Sitting, col.25 (Norman Lamb MP).

[4] *Hansard* (House of Commons: Public Bill Committee), 9 January 2014 (PM): Second Sitting, col.56 (Norman Lamb MP).

of use, although still subject to an assessment of what those needs are and how they should be met. The Commission also recommended that work be undertaken to explore whether Health and Well-being Boards could evolve into a single commissioner for health and social care, and that all care home residents should pay accommodation costs (including those currently eligible for NHS continuing health care). The proposed new scheme would be funded through a range of measures including (in the short-term) a revamped prescription charge, National Insurance contributions when people work on past the state pension age and an increase in the rate of National Insurance for those aged over 40, and (in the longer term) new wealth taxes.[1]

Subsection (1)

The integration duty applies where the local authority considers that integration of services would promote the well-being of adults with care and support needs (including carers), contribute to the prevention or delay of developing care needs, or improve the quality of care in the local authority's area. The Joint Committee argued that the inclusion of the words "where it considers that this would" gave too much latitude to local authorities.[2] The Government however stated that: **1–042**

> "The words 'it considers that' are permissive rather than restrictive of the circumstances in which the local authority will be under a duty to promote integration. They reflect the intention that decisions about integrating the provision of services should be made locally by the local authority. Local authorities are not able to unreasonably decide that integrating the provision of services would not promote well-being, contribute to the delay and prevention of needs, or improve quality of care and support."[3]

Subsection (4)

"Health-related provision" includes any service that may have an effect on the health of individuals that is not provided as part of the health service or local authority social services. In the House of Lords, during the committee stage of the Bill, the Government confirmed that this is intended to include housing, thus creating a clear duty on both local authorities and the NHS to promote integration between care and support, health and housing.[4] The statutory guidance also emphasises the need to involve housing in strategic planning.[5] **1–043**

Subsections (6) and (7)

These subsections were added by Government amendment in the House of Lords. They were in response to general concerns in the House of Lords, particularly from Lord Best, that the Bill gave insufficient prominence to the link between health, social care and housing.[6] The subsections amend the integration duties placed on NHS England by s.13N and clinical commissioning groups by s.14Z1 of the National Health Service Act 2006, by clarifying that housing is a health-related service. The Government explained its intention behind these amendments: **1–044**

> ". . . both local authorities and the NHS are required to promote integration between care and support, health and housing. This makes the importance of housing explicit

---

[1] Commission on the Future of Health and Social Care in England, *A New Settlement for Health and Social Care: Final Report* (King's Fund, 2014).

[2] House of Lords House of Commons Joint Committee on the Draft Care and Support Bill, *Draft Care and Support Bill Report, Session 2012–13*, para.125.

[3] Department of Health, *The Care Bill explained—including a response to consultation and pre-legislative scrutiny on the draft Care and Support Bill* (TSO, July 2012) Cm.8386, p.64.

[4] *Hansard* (House of Lords), 9 July 2013, Vol.747, col.195 (Earl Howe).

[5] Department of Health, Care and Support Statutory Guidance (2014), para.15.7.

[6] *Hansard* (House of Lords), 9 July 2013, Vol.747, cols 173 to 187; *Hansard* (House of Lords), 9 October 2013, Vol.748, cols 101 to 103.

not only in the integration duty in this Bill but in the comparable duties on the NHS in the 2006 Act."[1]

Providing information and advice

1–045   **4.**—(1) A local authority must establish and maintain a service for providing people in its area with information and advice relating to care and support for adults and support for carers.

(2) The service must provide information and advice on the following matters in particular—

    (a) the system provided for by this Part and how the system operates in the authority's area,

    (b) the choice of types of care and support, and the choice of providers, available to those who are in the authority's area,

    (c) how to access the care and support that is available,

    (d) how to access independent financial advice on matters relevant to the meeting of needs for care and support, and

    (e) how to raise concerns about the safety or well-being of an adult who has needs for care and support.

(3) In providing information and advice under this section, a local authority must in particular—

    (a) have regard to the importance of identifying adults in the authority's area who would be likely to benefit from financial advice on matters relevant to the meeting of needs for care and support, and

    (b) seek to ensure that what it provides is sufficient to enable adults—

        (i) to identify matters that are or might be relevant to their personal financial position that could be affected by the system provided for by this Part,

        (ii) to make plans for meeting needs for care and support that might arise, and

        (iii) to understand the different ways in which they may access independent financial advice on matters relevant to the meeting of needs for care and support.

(4) Information and advice provided under this section must be accessible to, and proportionate to the needs of, those for whom it is being provided.

(5) "Independent financial advice" means financial advice provided by a person who is independent of the local authority in question.

(6) In cases where a local authority performs the duty under subsection (1) jointly with one or more other local authorities by establishing and maintaining a service for their combined area—

    (a) references in this section to a local authority are to be read as references to the authorities acting jointly, and

    (b) references in this section to a local authority's area are to be read as references to the combined area.

GENERAL NOTE

1–046   This replaces and expands the duty in s.1 of the Chronically Sick and Disabled Persons Act 1970, by requiring local authorities to provide an information and advice service in relation to care and support for adults, and support for carers. This is a general duty and

---

[1] *Hansard* (House of Lords), 9 October 2013, Vol.748, cols 106 to 107 (Earl Howe).

concerns were raised in the House of Lords report stage that the legislation does not set any measure for whether anyone actually receives or understands the information and advice.

"You can easily see a situation in which local authorities can, at least technically, fulfil a duty to provide advice and information without providing much of it, or knowing how many people are reached by it and how many of those reached understand it and the implications it has for them." [1]

In response to a question on this from Lord Hunt, the Government stated that individuals might be able to bring legal proceedings on the basis that an authority's failure to comply with such a duty has adversely affected them. It was also suggested that the Care Quality Commission may have a role to play through its power to review local authority commissioning practices in certain circumstances. [2]

Information is not the same as advice—although the line between them can be blurred in places. In broad terms, "information" is just data that is left to the individual to interpret and base decisions upon. "Advice" includes telling the person what should prudently and sensibly be done in the relevant context. The Joint Committee pointed to concerns that local authorities are not well placed to offer impartial advice (as opposed to information) and, for example, are more reluctant to promote and even engage with private companies than third sector providers. It argued that advice services should be provided at arm's length, and not by the local authority itself. [3] This is catered for, but not required, by subs.(1). The local authority itself is not required to provide advice. The obligation is to "establish and maintain a service". Therefore other organisations may provide advice on the local authority's behalf, such as Citizens Advice Bureau and welfare benefits advice services. The section also refers expressly in a number of places to independent financial advice (see para.1–047 below).

During Committee stage in the House of Commons the Government also stated that advice and information can be provided effectively "only by the local authority working together with health organisations" and confirmed that the duty to promote integration of care and support with health services in s.3 is applicable to information and advice services under s.4. [4] This is confirmed by the statutory guidance. [5]

In Parliament the Government faced attempts to amend the Care Bill to require a public awareness campaign on the implications of the funding reforms. In part, this was rejected on the basis that local authorities are already under a duty to provide information and advice on care and support under s.4 which will need to include information on the capped costs system. This is discussed at para.1–166 below.

INDEPENDENT FINANCIAL ADVICE

Subsections (2)(d), (3)(b)(iii) and (5) include express references to "independent finan- **1–047** cial advice". "Independent" means independent of the local authority. These subsections were inserted into the Care Bill during its Parliamentary passage as a result of Government amendments. A recommendation from the Joint Committee and responses from the public consultation had highlighted the need for such advice particularly in view of the reforms on care and support funding, the availability of deferred payments and an increasing use of

[1] *Hansard* (House of Lords), 9 October 2013, Vol.748, col.128 (Lord Sharkey).

[2] *Hansard* (House of Lords), 9 October 2013, Vol.748, cols 122 to 123 (Earl Howe).

[3] House of Lords House of Commons Joint Committee on the Draft Care and Support Bill, *Draft Care and Support Bill Report, Session 2012–13*, para.85.

[4] *Hansard* (House of Commons: Public Bill Committee), 9 January 2014 (PM): Second Sitting, col.65 (Norman Lamb MP).

[5] Department of Health, *Care and Support Statutory Guidance* (2014), para.3.57.

direct payments.[1] The Government explained that the intention behind the amendments was to provide a:

"clear and unambiguous statement that the information and advice service must cover how a person can access independent financial advice on matters relevant to the meeting of needs for care and support."[2]

The Joint Committee had also recommended that local authority services should recommend financial advisers only if they are regulated by the Financial Services Authority (now the Financial Conduct Authority).[3] However, the Government's response stated that:

" . . . while sympathetic to the Joint Committee's argument, the clause covers a service for broad range of needs. Some people may require financial advice on the welfare benefits available, while others may require detailed advice on financial products such as equity release. This level of detail is most appropriately covered within guidance. For example guidance will emphasise the importance of access to an independent, regulated financial advice for anybody considering the deferred payment arrangements."[4]

During committee stage in the House of Lords, further arguments were put to the Government about the importance of securing access to regulated financial advice. In response the Government stated that:

"The fact that an organisation or individual is regulated is in itself no guarantee that the person has knowledge or experience of wider care and support issues; for example, housing or other care-related options. All this makes the adult's choice of an adviser a vital aspect. The local authority should advise about the importance of independent regulated advice and signpost the adult to offer a choice of where they can obtain the best and most relevant advice."[5]

But in response to the concerns raised in the House of Lords, the Government amended subs.(3) at report stage. First, subs.(3)(a) was added to make it clear that local authorities must have regard to the importance of identifying individuals who would be likely to benefit from financial advice. The intention is to encourage "a more active role for local authorities to consider whether people would benefit from financial advice".[6] Secondly, s.(3)(b)(iii) was added which provides that local authorities must seek to ensure that adults understand how to access information and advice on the range of financial options available to them. The Government explained:

"There are various options for people who could benefit from financial advice relating to care and support, both regulated and non-regulated. Our amendments highlight the importance of ensuring that people understand how to access the variety of advice available independently from local authorities. They mean that local authorities must seek to ensure that adults understand how to access the different financial advice available to them, thereby supporting people to make informed choices."[7]

1–048 However, the Government was at pains to emphasise that it would not be appropriate to require local authorities to make direct referrals:

---

[1] Department of Health, *The Care Bill explained—including a response to consultation and pre-legislative scrutiny on the draft Care and Support Bill* (TSO, July 2012) Cm.8386, para.36.

[2] *Hansard* (House of Lords), 9 October 2013, Vol.748, col.121 (Earl Howe).

[3] House of Lords House of Commons Joint Committee on the Draft Care and Support Bill, *Draft Care and Support Bill Report, Session 2012–13*, para.91.

[4] Department of Health, *The Care Bill explained—including a response to consultation and pre-legislative scrutiny on the draft Care and Support Bill* (2013), p.61.

[5] *Hansard* (House of Lords), 9 July 2013, Vol.747, col.217 (Earl Howe).

[6] *Hansard* (House of Lords), 9 October 2013, Vol.748, col.120 (Earl Howe).

[7] *Hansard* (House of Lords), 9 October 2013, Vol.748, cols 120 to 121 (Earl Howe).

"For the most part, local authorities do not possess the necessary expertise, and there is a risk that a referral leading to poor advice could bring a significant burden of accountability on to the local authority."[1]

This response was criticised by a number of members of the House of Lords for providing that "the perfect gets in the way of the good" and "deferring to a risk adverse culture at the expense of the public interest".[2]

At report stage in the House of Lords, the Government rejected an amendment which would have required regulations to specify when a local authority must refer an adult to a regulated financial adviser:

"We agree that, in some instances where someone is considering a financial product such as a care annuity, financial advice should be regulated through the Financial Conduct Authority. However, there are many sources of valuable financial advice that do not need to be regulated and can be provided free of charge—such as advice on managing money from the citizens advice bureau or from the Money Advice Service. In addition, the fact that financial advice is regulated does not mean that it is appropriate for care and support purposes."[3]

The Government also repeated its concerns about direct referrals:

". . . it would be inappropriate to require local authorities to make direct referrals where, for the most part, they do not possess the necessary expertise to judge between advisers. Requiring them to do so would present a significant burden and could result in a local authority making an unnecessary or inappropriate referral. There is the further risk that a referral leading to poor advice could be seen as the fault of the local authority, a point he acknowledged, bringing yet more of a burden of responsibility in increased disputes, and even legal challenge. We believe that the decision to take up financial advice, of whatever form, and the choice of adviser, should belong to the individual and not to the local authority."[4]

A Government initiated review of financial products to help people to pay for their care and support, concluded that the local authority should consider what information and advice might be beneficial to individuals depending on personal circumstances and help people understand how to access it. This would apply to both generic advice (such as from the Money Advice Service and Citizens Advice Bureau) as well as advice from regulated financial providers. It was argued that paid for financial advice is suitable for some but not all individuals. This advice should be weighted towards those most likely to benefit, such as self-funders whose asset mix and liability for care costs means that they face the most complex decisions and have the most to gain from advice.[5]

The statutory guidance discusses financial information and advice in paras 3.36 to 3.51. In particular it considers facilitating access to independent financial information and advice, and states that:

"Local authorities should make people aware which independent services may charge for the information and advice they provide. Local authorities should be able to actively describe the general benefits of independent information and advice and be able to explain the reasons why it may be beneficial for a person to take independent financial advice based on what is known of their circumstances to an individual." [6]

It also states that:

---

[1] *Hansard* (House of Lords), 9 October 2013, Vol.748, cols 120 to 121(Earl Howe).
[2] *Hansard* (House of Lords), 9 October 2013, Vol.748, cols 130 (Lord Deben) and *Hansard* (House of Lords), 9 October 2013, Vol.748, cols 134(Lord Hunt).
[3] *Hansard* (House of Lords), 9 October 2013, Vol.748, col.135 (Earl Howe).
[4] *Hansard* (House of Lords), 9 October 2013, Vol.748, col.136 (Earl Howe).
[5] Department of Health, *Review of Care Products—Key Messages* (21 January 2014).
[6] Department of Health, *Care and Support Statutory Guidance* (2014), para.3.50.

"Where a person may be considering taking regulated financial advice local authorities are not required or encouraged to make a direct referral to one individual independent financial adviser, but they should actively help and direct a person to a choice of advisers regulated by the Financial Conduct Authority with the appropriate qualifications and accreditation. The local authority should ensure that they do this on a transparent basis."[1]

The statutory guidance sets out the minimum information that should be given by a local authority to a person who may benefit from or be eligible for a deferred payment agreement. This includes suggesting that the person "may want to consider taking independent financial advice (including flagging the existence of regulated financial advice)".[2] Providing information and advice in the context of transition assessments is discussed in paras 16.54 to 16.55.

Practice guidance has also been produced on facilitating access to independent information and advice. Amongst other matters, it emphasises that only regulated financial advisers can give regulated financial advice (for instance care fees planning and tax planning) and recommend regulated financial products, and that local authorities should not stray into such areas. It also identifies factors and customer profile types that may determine who would benefit from independent information and advice (examples of factors include moving into permanent care and becoming a carer and trying to balance this role with work). The guidance suggests that directing a person to a choice of regulated advisers means it is the person's decision to choose who they seek advice from and will limit the local authority's liability.[3]

ADVOCACY

1–049   The Government had argued that this section enabled the provision of advocacy, but that since information and advice must be "proportionate" to a person's needs, this is best judged on a case-by-case basis.[4] However, following pressure in the House of Lords the Government introduced a separate duty to provide advocacy support (see ss.68 and 69).

Subsection (1)
1–050   As discussed at 1–046 above, the local authority itself is not required to provide the information and advice service. The obligation is to "establish and maintain a service". The statutory guidance states that in order to fulfil its s.4 duty:

"a local authority is likely to need to go further than providing information and advice directly (though direct provision will be important) by working to ensure the coherence, sufficiency, availability and accessibility of information and advice relating to care and support across the local authority area."[5]

It also sets out that in some circumstances impartially provided information and advice will be needed and local authorities should consider "when this might most effectively be provided by an independent source rather than by the local authority itself". The guidance suggests that independent information and advice will be particularly important when people wish to question, challenge or appeal the decisions of the local authority or other statutory body. It further suggests that people should be directed to "appropriate independent information and advice" when they are entering into a legal agreement with a local authority or other third party, such as a deferred payment agreement or committing to a

---

[1] Department of Health, *Care and Support Statutory Guidance* (2014), para.3.51.
[2] Department of Health, *Care and Support Statutory Guidance* (2014), para.9.26.
[3] Department of Health and others, *Practice Guidance to Support Local Authorities to Facilitate Access to Independent Financial Information and Advice under the Care Act 2014* (March 2015).
[4] Department of Health, *The Care Bill explained—including a response to consultation and pre-legislative scrutiny on the draft Care and Support Bill* (TSO, July 2012), Cm.8386, para.39.
[5] Department of Health, *Care and Support Statutory Guidance* (2014), para.3.3. See also para.3.14.

top-up.[1] The guidance also sets out the expectation that local authorities should develop a plan for information and advice services which includes all relevant stakeholders and considers the need to signpost people to independent sources of information and advice – including national helplines and websites.[2]

The duty is owed to all people in the local authority's area and not just those who have care and support needs. Therefore information and advice should be available to assist people who do not yet have care and support needs but want to plan ahead for a time in the future when they may have such needs. This is confirmed by subs.(3)(b)(ii) and in paras 3.15 to 3.17 of the statutory guidance.

Whilst the duty is owed to people in the area, there is no requirement that the care and support services, which the information relates to, must also be based physically in the local authority's area. See also subs.(2)(b) which provides only that the care and support must be "available" to the local population, which must be read alongside subs.(4) which states that the information and advice provided must be proportionate to the needs of those for whom it is being provided. Therefore, the information and advice service "should, where it is reasonable, also cover care and support services that, while physically provided outside the authority's area, are usually available to its local population".[3]

The duty to establish and maintain an information and advice service is distinct from the duty to meet eligible needs. A person's eligible needs may be met by the provision of information and advice following an individual assessment. However, local authorities:

> "cannot fulfil their universal information and advice duty simply by meeting eligible needs, and nor would information and advice always be an appropriate way of meeting eligible needs".[4]

Subsection (2)

This sets out the general requirements for an information and advice service. Five par- **1–051** ticular matters are listed on which the local authority's service must provide information and advice:

- the system and how it operates;
- the choice of types of care and support, and of providers;
- how to access the care and support that is available;
- how to access independent financial advice; and
- how to raise concerns about the safety of an adult.

The statutory guidance discusses these matters in paras 3.23 to 3.24. This list is not exhaustive. Subject to subss.(3) and (4) it is for local authorities to determine the precise scope and manner of the information and advice they will offer.

The Joint Committee recommended that the list should include:

- ways in which people can contribute to the design of services, where none are available to meet their needs;
- local housing options, including specialist housing, accessible housing and adaptations;
- any relevant charging arrangements for care and support in the local authority's area; obtaining independent financial advice on the options for paying for care and support; and
- where such advice can be found.[5]

---

[1] Department of Health, *Care and Support Statutory Guidance* (2014), paras 3.22 and 3.64.

[2] Department of Health, *Care and Support Statutory Guidance (2014)*, paras 3.55 to 3.69.

[3] Care Act 2014, Explanatory Notes para.69.

[4] Department of Health, *Care and Support Statutory Guidance* (2014), para.3.4.

[5] House of Lords House of Commons Joint Committee on the Draft Care and Support Bill, *Draft Care and Support Bill Report, Session 2012–13*, para.92.

However, the Government did not consider it necessary to be so specific on the face of the legislation, as this section is intended to set a broad framework on which guidance will provide further detail.[1]

During Committee stage in the House of Commons the Government rejected amendments to specify that information and advice should be provided on the choice of available housing options. It stated that:

> "We do not consider it appropriate to provide a comprehensive list of what the information and advice duty is intended to cover, not only because the list would change over time, but because anything left off the list may look less important. We intend the detail to be covered in more depth in guidance . . . We will make it clear that information and advice should cover and draw together the wider housing options that might be available through general or specialist housing, such as extra care housing and support living, as well as adapted housing and home adaptations."[2]

The Joint Committee recommended that local authorities should be placed under a statutory duty to take steps to empower individuals to understand what abuse is, and how to protect themselves from it, whether by seeking help or otherwise.[3] In response, the Government pointed to various provisions in the legislation that stress the provision of information, advice and support in all situations—including s.4(2)(e) which places a duty on local authorities to provide information and advice on how to raise concerns about the safety and well-being of an adult who has needs for care and support.[4] The statutory guidance makes clear that the s.4 duty should include information and advice on matters such as housing, health services, employment services, understanding abuse and neglect, and other areas.[5] It also specifically discusses integrating information and advice on housing (see paras 15.65 to 15.68), and on employment and welfare (see paras 15.69 to 15.72).

See para.1–047 above for discussion about the reference to "independent financial advice" in subs.(2)(d).

Subsection (3)

1–052   As noted above (see paras 1–047—1–048), subs.(3)(a) was added during the passage of the Care Bill through Parliament to make it clear that local authorities must have regard to the importance of identifying individuals who would be likely to benefit from financial advice. Local authorities must also provide sufficient information and advice to enable adults to consider the financial aspects of meeting their care and support needs and to make plans for how they might meet any future needs. This should cover what people are likely to pay towards their care and support needs, potential benefits and financial entitlements, and other options to help them pay for care and support, such as deferred payment arrangements. The statutory guidance discusses financial information and advice in paras 3.36 to 3.51.

Subsection (3)(b)(iii) was also added during the passage of the Care Bill and provides that local authorities must seek to ensure that adults understand how to access independent advice on the range of financial options available to them. This supports subs.(2)(d) which refers to the need to provide information and advice on how to access independent financial advice. See discussion above at paras 1–047—1–048. The meaning of independent

---

[1] Department of Health, *The Care Bill explained—including a response to consultation and pre-legislative scrutiny on the draft Care and Support Bill* (TSO, July 2012) Cm.8386, para.37.

[2] *Hansard* (House of Commons: Public Bill Committee), 9 January 2014 (PM): Second Sitting, col.64 (Norman Lamb MP).

[3] House of Lords House of Commons Joint Committee on the Draft Care and Support Bill, *Draft Care and Support Bill Report, Session 2012–13*, paras 148 to 149.

[4] Department of Health, *The Care Bill explained—including a response to consultation and pre-legislative scrutiny on the draft Care and Support Bill*, pp.66 to 67.

[5] Department of Health, *Care and Support Statutory Guidance* (2014), paras 3.24, 3.53 and 3.54.

financial advice is clarified in subs.(5). See also paras 3.37 to 3.38 and 3.50 to 3.51 of the statutory guidance.

Subsection (4)

Information and advice should be accessible to all and provided in a proportionate man- **1–053** ner to meet individual circumstances and needs. The reference to accessibility was not included in the draft Care and Support Bill but was added to the Care Bill in response to particular concerns that online information might not be appropriate for everyone, such as those who are not information technology literate or do have access to the internet.[1] In particular, the Joint Committee had pointed out that there are over five million households without internet access.[2] During Committee stage in the House of Commons, the Government also confirmed that the service must be "accessible and available to all people in the local authority's area, regardless of whether they have eligible care needs".[3] Accessibility of information and advice is discussed in paras 3.27 to 2.31 of the statutory guidance.

The reference to proportionality is intended to emphasise the need for flexibility. The Department of Health stated that "for example, this could mean a simple leaflet in some circumstances, a face-to-face conversation in others, or at the other end of the spectrum, it could mean more intensive, long-term access to advocacy".[4] Proportionality of information and advice is discussed in paras 3.32 to 2.35 of the statutory guidance.

In the House of Lords, there was an attempt by Baroness Greengross to amend this subsection to provide that local authorities would also have a duty to "facilitate access" to the service. In effect, local authorities would be required to "have a proactive strategy to reach out to those in their area who would benefit from such information and advice, recognising that not everybody will request it and may not proactively approach the local authority".[5] The need for a proactive duty was explained in the following terms:

"Research for *Which?* has shown that often the problem is that people do not know what they need to know. One carer said, 'It's a chicken and egg process—before you can find the answer you've got to know that you've got a question that needs answering.' People also need information and advice at key pinch points; we know this. This amendment would ensure that local authorities consider these when designing their information and advice strategies. For example, people often see their general practitioner as a focal point for information and advice about care, and while the GP may not always be in the best position to give this advice, local authorities can proactively engage with GPs and other health services in their area in order to ensure access to information and advice about care for those who would otherwise slip under the radar."[6]

The Government argued that the amendment was unnecessary because the intended effect of subs.(4) was to facilitate access:

"Local authorities will have to meet the information needs of all groups, including those who often find it most difficult to access information, such as those with sensory impairments, people from BME backgrounds, people who are socially isolated or who have complex conditions."[7]

---

[1] Department of Health, *The Care Bill explained—including a response to consultation and pre-legislative scrutiny on the draft Care and Support Bill* (TSO, July 2012) Cm.8386, para.38.

[2] House of Lords House of Commons Joint Committee on the Draft Care and Support Bill, *Draft Care and Support Bill Report, Session 2012–13*, para.69.

[3] *Hansard* (House of Commons: Public Bill Committee), 9 January 2014 (PM): Second Sitting, col.64 (Norman Lamb MP).

[4] Department of Health, *The Care Bill explained—including a response to consultation and pre-legislative scrutiny on the draft Care and Support Bill* (TSO, July 2012) Cm.8386, para.39.

[5] *Hansard* (House of Lords), 9 October 2013, Vol.748, col.114.

[6] *Hansard* (House of Lords), 9 October 2013, Vol.748, col.114.

[7] *Hansard* (House of Lords), 9 October 2013, Vol.748, col.120 (Earl Howe).

It went on to say:

"'Accessible and proportionate'—the words that we use in the Bill—also mean ensuring that information and advice are available in the right format, in the right places and at the right time. A vital aspect of this is making them available face to face and one to one, by phone, through leaflets and posters as well as online. When appropriate and most effective, that advice should be given directly by a qualified social worker. There will be other occasions when information and advice are best and most appropriately provided by others." [1]

During Committee stage in the House of Commons the Government rejected an amendment which would have required the information and advice service to be of a good standard and that where appropriate it should be delivered through suitably trained individuals. The Government argued that subs.(4) already states that the information and advice provided by local authorities needs to be proportionate and accessible to the needs of the recipient and "in some cases, the needs of the recipient may be such that that can be achieved only if the person delivering the information and advice is appropriately trained". Moreover, it was argued that general public law principles mean that "local authorities must look to meet their duties to an appropriate standard". [2] The statutory guidance states that the local authority should take account of information standards published by the Information Standards Board for Health and Social Care under the provisions of the Health and Social Care Act 2012. [3]

Subsection (5)

1–054   This was added to the Care Bill by the Government in the House of Lords in response to "the potential confusion, particularly in the financial services industry, over the term 'independent financial advice'. The amendment clarifies that the term means "financial advice independent of the local authority". [4]

The Government also stated that:

"Very few regulated financial advisers currently have a qualification or expert knowledge of care and support, though we hope that this sector will develop over the coming months and years. In this context, the term 'independent financial advice' covers both regulated and non-regulated advice." [5]

Independent financial advice is discussed at para.1–047 above.

Promoting diversity and quality in provision of services

1–055   **5.**—(1) A local authority must promote the efficient and effective operation of a market in services for meeting care and support needs with a view to ensuring that any person in its area wishing to access services in the market—

(a) has a variety of providers to choose from who (taken together) provide a variety of services;

(b) has a variety of high quality services to choose from;

(c) has sufficient information to make an informed decision about how to meet the needs in question.

---

[1] *Hansard* (House of Lords), 9 October 2013, Vol.748, col.120 (Earl Howe).
[2] *Hansard* (House of Commons: Public Bill Committee), 9 January 2014 (PM): Second Sitting, col.64 (Norman Lamb MP).
[3] Department of Health, *Care and Support Statutory Guidance* (2014), para.3.18.
[4] *Hansard* (House of Lords), 9 October 2013, Vol.748, col.121 (Earl Howe).
[5] *Hansard* (House of Lords), 9 October 2013, Vol.748, col.136 (Earl Howe).

(2) In performing that duty, a local authority must have regard to the following matters in particular—

(a) the need to ensure that the authority has, and makes available, information about the providers of services for meeting care and support needs and the types of services they provide;

(b) the need to ensure that it is aware of current and likely future demand for such services and to consider how providers might meet that demand;

(c) the importance of enabling adults with needs for care and support, and carers with needs for support, who wish to do so to participate in work, education or training;

(d) the importance of ensuring the sustainability of the market (in circumstances where it is operating effectively as well as in circumstances where it is not);

(e) the importance of fostering continuous improvement in the quality of such services and the efficiency and effectiveness with which such services are provided and of encouraging innovation in their provision;

(f) the importance of fostering a workforce whose members are able to ensure the delivery of high quality services (because, for example, they have relevant skills and appropriate working conditions).

(3) In having regard to the matters mentioned in subsection (2)(b), a local authority must also have regard to the need to ensure that sufficient services are available for meeting the needs for care and support of adults in its area and the needs for support of carers in its area.

(4) In arranging for the provision by persons other than it of services for meeting care and support needs, a local authority must have regard to the importance of promoting the well-being of adults in its area with needs for care and support and the well-being of carers in its area.

(5) In meeting an adult's needs for care and support or a carer's needs for support, a local authority must have regard to its duty under subsection (1).

(6) In cases where a local authority performs the duty under subsection (1) jointly with one or more other local authorities in relation to persons who are in the authorities' combined area—

(a) references in this section to a local authority are to be read as references to the authorities acting jointly, and

(b) references in this section to a local authority's area are to be read as references to the combined area.

(7) "Services for meeting care and support needs" means—

(a) services for meeting adults' needs for care and support, and

(b) services for meeting carers' needs for support.

(8) The references in subsection (7) to services for meeting needs include a reference to services, facilities or resources the purpose of which is to contribute towards preventing or delaying the development of those needs.

GENERAL NOTE

According to the Government, s.5 marks "the first time that local authorities' responsi- **1–056** bilities to promote the market in local care and support services has been captured in law".[1] A duty is placed on local authorities to promote an effective and efficient market of care and support services for local people. This role is often referred to as "market shaping". In

---

[1] *Hansard* (House of Lords), 9 July 2013, Vol.747, col.246 (Earl Howe).

undertaking this duty, local authorities will need to have regard to commissioning frameworks, such as the *Adult Social Care Outcomes Framework* and *Making it Real*.[1] In addition, a range of general resources have been produced.[2] The duty is discussed in Ch.4 of the statutory guidance. The guidance also discusses the need to promote a local market that offers age appropriate local services and resources (in the context of the transition to adult services) in paras 16.58 to 16.60.

The need to shape or manage the market is a reflection of the diminishing role of local authorities in direct service provision. Only five per cent of home-care services were delivered by the private sector in 1993, but by 2011 this figure had risen to 81 per cent.[3] Around 90 per cent of care home provision for older people is supplied by the independent sector, that is, voluntary and for-profit organisations. However, three-fifths of this provision is commissioned by local authorities under contract with providers. The remaining two-fifths is bought privately by self-funders.[4]

The meaning of "have regard to" is discussed at 1–022 above.

COMMISSIONING SERVICES AND THE COSTS OF CARE

1–057   The market shaping duty is linked directly to the commissioning decisions of local authorities. The Joint Committee received oral evidence on this subject from care providers which was summarised in the following terms by its chair, Paul Burstow MP:

> "There was a real sense of alienation and anger about what many in the room on that occasion saw as long-standing problems and a long-standing dysfunction in the commissioning relationship. This was not just a concern of private providers; it was echoed by the charitable sector . . . The concern is long standing. Commissioning has in practice turned out to be crude procurement. It is not a genuine process of determining the level of need and the range of options to meet that need, and having proper conversations in advance of procurement with potential providers."[5]

The Joint Committee recommended that the legislation should include a requirement that local authorities properly take into account the actual cost of care when setting the rates they are prepared to pay providers. In addition it recommended that an independent adjudicator was necessary to settle disputes between local authorities and providers over the cost of care.[6] The Government accepted the first of these recommendations and subsequently amended s.28 to provide that the personal budget is the amount it will cost to meet the needs identified in the care and support plan.[7] During the Parliamentary passage of the Care Bill, the Government also argued that subs.(2)(d) makes clear that local authorities should not set prices that risk undercutting the stability of the market as a whole.[8]

However, the Government's response to the Joint Committee did not accept the case for an independent adjudicator on the basis that this would impose "disproportionate

[1] Department of Health, *Adult Social Care Outcomes Framework 2015/16 (November 2014) and Think Local, Act Personal, Making it Real: Marking Progress Towards Personalised, Community-based Support* (2012). See also Department of Health, *Care and Support Statutory Guidance* (2014), para.4.14.

[2] For example, Health Services Management Centre, (University of Birmingham), *Commissioning for Better Outcomes: A Route Map* (2014). A comprehensive list of resources on market shaping and commissioning can be found on the Local Government Association's website.

[3] UK Homecare Association, *An Overview of the UK Domiciliary Care Sector* (2012).

[4] J. Forder and S. Allan, *Competition in the Care Homes Market* (August 2011).

[5] *Hansard* (House of Commons: Public Bill Committee), 14 January 2014 (AM): Third Sitting, col.87.

[6] House of Lords House of Commons Joint Committee on the Draft Care and Support Bill, *Draft Care and Support Bill Report, Session 2012–13*, paras 113 and 114.

[7] Department of Health, *The Care Bill explained—including a response to consultation and pre-legislative scrutiny on the draft Care and Support Bill* (TSO, July 2012) Cm.8386, p.63.

[8] *Hansard* (House of Commons: Public Bill Committee), 14 January 2014 (AM): Third Sitting, col.90 (Norman Lamb MP).

burdens".[1] In Parliament, amendments were tabled which aimed to establish an independent adjudicator, and in rejecting these amendments the Government expanded on its objections. For example, in the House of Lords, Earl Howe stated that:

"it is our view that any disputes arising as part of a contractual negotiation must be resolved through that process. Appointing or establishing a new independent adjudicator would be likely to add unnecessary cost and bureaucracy to the process of commissioning. We also believe that it will be likely to increase disputes by providing a means of challenge which would soon become a standard process".[2]

In the House of Commons, the Government argued that the cost of any adjudication system would have to come out of money available for care, and moreover:

"Appointing or establishing a new independent arbitrator would add cost and bureaucracy to the commissioning process. It would be most likely to increase the risk of disputes, and might lead to participants in a dispute feeling absolved of a responsibility to negotiate and compromise. It could also mean issues becoming protracted by requiring more time for resolution, inevitably risking the continuity of care and support."[3]

At report stage, the Government also rejected a nationally set formula that would lead to standard rates of "tariff prices" for care and support, on the basis that this was best left to "local negotiations in the open market".[4]

In Parliament it was suggested that as a consequence of local authorities underpaying for care, self-funders subsidise the people in care homes who are paid for by the local authority. This is discussed at para.1–320 under s.28 (Independent Personal Budget).

The courts have been reluctant to pass judgment on the level of fees paid to care providers, and instead focus on the procedure for the setting of fees. But in *Abbeyfield Newcastle Upon Tyne Society Ltd v Newcastle City Council* the High Court took the unusual step of setting the fee that the local authority should have paid a care home provider. This case concerned a provider which had refused to sign up to the council's proposed new terms when its existing contract expired, but continued to support council-funded residents under individual "user agreements", with the fee set in accordance with the previous contract. The court decided that a "reasonable price" must be paid as an implied term of the user agreements, and rejected the council's view that the reasonable price was the same as the "market price" paid to the other providers that had accepted the council's rate.[5]

In October 2014, the Local Government Ombudsman (in sharing lessons from one of its investigation reports) advised local authorities that they cannot significantly change contractual funding arrangements for current care home residents because they alter the way they commission care. The investigation concerned a council which had established a "Quality Framework system". Care home providers were required to demonstrate that they met certain standards in order to be included in the framework and receive an enhanced fee. Not all care homes that met the standards were included in the framework but applicants were ranked depending on their evaluated scores and only higher scoring care homes were included. A man complained that as a result of this policy his mother—who was 80 and had dementia—had to pay significant additional costs every week to remain in the home she had lived in for the past three years. The care home had been excluded from the framework, despite meeting the set criteria. As a result, the council reduced its fee and there was a shortfall in the amount paid to the care home, which the

---

[1] Department of Health, *The Care Bill explained—including a response to consultation and pre-legislative scrutiny on the draft Care and Support Bill* (TSO, July 2012) Cm.8386, para.46.

[2] *Hansard* (House of Lords), 9 July 2013, Vol.747, col.249 (Earl Howe).

[3] *Hansard* (House of Commons: Public Bill Committee), 14 January 2014 (AM): Third Sitting, cols 89 and 90 (Norman Lamb MP).

[4] *Hansard* (House of Commons), 10 March 2014, Vol.577, col.88 (Norman Lamb MP).

[5] *Abbeyfield Newcastle Upon Tyne Society Ltd v Newcastle City Council* [2014] EWHC 2437 (Ch) at [39].

family had to make up. The Ombudsman concluded that residents and families had a legitimate and reasonable expectation that the council would meet the contractual payments that had been agreed on admission, unless there was a change to care needs.[1]

The statutory guidance discusses securing supply in the market and its quality and value for money in paras 4.93 to 4.108.

15 MINUTE CARE VISITS AND WORKFORCE TERMS AND CONDITIONS

1–058   As well as the cost of care, the Joint Committee raised concern about "unacceptable commissioning practices" such as 10 to 15-minute home care appointments. It recommended that the Government should ensure that they have the necessary statutory authority to make regulations or issue guidance on such matters.[2] The Government agreed to addresses this in guidance.[3]

However, the issue was raised again in Parliament. Research by Leonard Cheshire Disability—published just before the issue was being considered in the House of Lords— found that 60 per cent of local authorities commission 15 minute visits and the number has risen by 15 per cent in the past five years. Some local authorities delivered more than three-quarters of their care visits in 15 minutes and 15 per cent of councils delivered more than a quarter of all of their care visits in 15 minutes or less.[4] At report stage in the House of Lords, Baroness Meacher tabled an amendment which would have provided that commissioning must adhere to specific "minimum quality standards and requirements" as regulations may prescribe; the aim was to ensure that home visits are not normally commissioned for less than 30 minutes.[5] In the response, the Government argued that s.5:

". . . requires local authorities to promote a market in high-quality services and specifically requires authorities to consider this duty when arranging services to meet people's needs. This would make it very difficult for local authorities to commission services in 15-minute slots where doing so undermines the quality of those services."[6]

However, it went on to argue that "central prescription risks prohibiting practices that may, in some circumstances, be consistent with high-quality care", and argued that in some cases 15-minute homecare visits could be appropriate (for instance for helping people to take medication).[7] The Government went on to point to the limitations of law reform:

"Local authorities that commission such services are palpably failing in their duty to meet people's needs. That they still commission such services demonstrates the fact that the underlying problems here are cultural and cannot simply be legislated away. Banning specific poor practices will only lead to other poor practices emerging. Instead, I strongly believe that we need to work with authorities to enhance commissioners' understanding of the effects of their commissioning decisions on individuals' well-being and of how they can commission more effectively."[8]

The statutory guidance encourages local authorities to adopt an outcomes-based approach which involves changing the way services are bought "from units of provision

---

[1] Local Government Ombudsman, *Investigation into a compliant against Tameside Metropolitcan Borough Council* (24 September 2014) Ref no. 12 019 862.

[2] House of Lords House of Commons Joint Committee on the Draft Care and Support Bill, *Draft Care and Support Bill Report, Session 2012–13*, para.117.

[3] Department of Health, *The Care Bill explained—including a response to consultation and pre-legislative scrutiny on the draft Care and Support Bill*, para.44.

[4] Leonard Cheshire Disability, *Ending 15-Minute Care* (October 2013).

[5] *Hansard* (House of Lords), 9 October 2013, Vol.748, cols 148 to 150.

[6] *Hansard* (House of Lords), 9 October 2013, Vol.748, col.157 (Earl Howe).

[7] *Hansard* (House of Lords), 9 October 2013, Vol.748, col.159 (Earl Howe).

[8] *Hansard* (House of Lords), 9 October 2013, Vol.748, col.159 (Earl Howe).

to meet a specified need (for example, hours of care provided) to what is required to ensure specified measurable outcomes for people are met".[1] It goes on to state:

". . . short home-care visits of 15 minutes or less are not appropriate for people who need support with intimate care needs, though such visits may be appropriate for checking someone has returned home safely from visiting a day centre, or whether medication has been taken (but not the administration of medicine) or where they are requested as a matter of personal choice." [2]

As well as 15-minute care visits, concerns were also raised in Parliament about commissioning service providers who use questionable employment practices, in particular zero hours contracts with exclusivity and no guarantees of working.[3] The Government announced that in response to the Cavendish review, the guidance on commissioning practices will explicitly require local authorities to have regard to ensuring that provider organisations adhere to minimum wage legislation, including the payment of travel time between social care visits. It also amended the Health and Social Care Act 2008 to enable specific bodies to provide training standards for groups of workers, initially focusing on health care assistants and social care support workers (see s.94 of the Care Act). This will form the core of the new care certificate.[4]

The statutory guidance sets out that local authorities should consider how to encourage workforce training and development, and have evidence concerning staff remuneration, which must at least comply with national minimum wage legislation and include time spent between visits. It also emphasises that these matters should be secured through contract terms, conditions and fee levels.[5] The guidance goes on to state that:

". . . where a provider has previously been in breach of national minimum wage legislation, a local authority should consider every legal means of excluding them from the tendering process unless they have evidence that the provider's policies and practice have changed to ensure permanent compliance."[6]

Under s.234 of the Health and Social Care Act 2012 the Secretary of State may require the National Institute for Clinical Excellence (NICE) to develop standards in relation to the provision of social care services in England. It has already issued standards on autism and the mental well-being of older people in care homes.[7] In order to address concerns about the standards of care commissioned, the Joint Committee recommended that the market shaping duty should be amended to make an explicit link to both "the essential standards of quality and safety and to NICE quality standards".[8] The Government responded that there will be a range of ways in which local authorities can determine quality, including compliance with NICE standards, but it did not intend to stipulate the process in legislation.[9]

---

[1] Department of Health, *Care and Support Statutory Guidance* (2014), para.4.16.

[2] Department of Health, *Care and Support Statutory Guidance* (2014), para.4.100.

[3] *Hansard* (House of Lords), 9 October 2013, Vol.748, cols 148 to 157.

[4] *Hansard* (House of Commons), 10 March 2014, Vol.577, col.88 (Norman Lamb MP). See, Department of Health, *Cavendish Review: An Independent Review into Healthcare Assistants and Support Workers in the NHS and Social Care Settings* (July 2013).

[5] Department of Health, *Care and Support Statutory Guidance* (2014), paras 4.30 to 4.32.

[6] Department of Health, *Care and Support Statutory Guidance* (2014), para.4.102.

[7] National Institute for Clinical Excellence, *Autism* (January 2014) NICE Quality Standard 51 and National Institute for Clinical Excellence, *Mental Well-being of Older People in Care Homes* (December 2013) NICE Quality Standard 51.

[8] House of Lords House of Commons Joint Committee on the Draft Care and Support Bill, *Draft Care and Support Bill Report, Session 2012–13*, para.116.

[9] Department of Health, *The Care Bill explained—including a response to consultation and pre-legislative scrutiny on the draft Care and Support Bill*, p.63.

OVERSEEING LOCAL AUTHORITY COMMISSIONING

1–059   The Care Act removes the role of the Care Quality Commission in routinely assessing the quality of commissioning.[1] However, the Government has stated that the results of its inspections and intelligence monitoring of providers will highlight commissioning issues at national, regional and local level which will help to promote improvement amongst clinical commissioning groups and local authorities.[2]

At Committee Stage in the House of Lords, Lord Patel had tabled an amendment which would have placed a duty on NHS England to scrutinise the commissioning plans of local authorities for adult social care services to ensure that they are upholding the safety and care of vulnerable people, and the efficient and effective operation of a market. In particular, he pointed to the situation at Winterbourne View and Southern Cross where the commissioning systems and process were found wanting.[3] Lord Hunt also tabled an amendment to require the Care Quality Commission to periodically review and assess the standards of employment in health and social care, with particular emphasis on workforce conditions.[4]

As a result of this pressure, the Government introduced subss.(2)(f) and (4)—see below. It also introduced an amendment to make it clear that the Care Quality Commission may, with approval from both Secretaries of State of the Department of Health and Department for Communities and Local Government, undertake a special review of local authority commissioning of adult social services in cases of systematic failure. Subsequent to any such review, the Care Quality Commission could issue an improvement notice in the event of a non-substantial failing and recommend special measures to the Secretary of State in the event of substantial failings.[5]

In response to a parliamentary question which asked if the Care Quality Commission would inspect local authority commissioning of care services where no specific complaint had been made, the Parliamentary Under-Secretary (Department for Communities and Local Government) stated:

"Intervention in the activities of locally accountable councils should only be considered where a last resort. I am not aware of any evidence that would constitute the kinds of exceptional circumstances that would warrant deployment of this power. Indeed it is arguable that local councils have been very effective in procuring care services and local taxpayers will thank them for having kept care costs under control. Even where there is evidence of poor commissioning practice by particular councils, the Government expects councils collectively, through the Local Government Association, to take the lead in improving poor performance. The Association has developed a programme of peer support available to councils, which includes mentoring and peer challenges."[6]

COMMISSIONING DECISIONS AND PROCEDURAL REQUIREMENTS

1–060   The courts have put down important markers for local councils who are seeking to reduce costs through commissioning decisions. In particular, the courts have emphasised the

---

[1] Care Act s.91 (this replaces the previous duty in s.46 of the Health and Social Care Act 2008).
[2] Department of Health, *Introducing Fundamental Standards: Consultation on Proposals to change CQC Registration Requirements* (January 2014), p.14.
[3] *Hansard* (House of Lords), 22 July 2013, Vol.747, col.1137.
[4] *Hansard* (House of Lords), 9 October 2013, Vol.748, col.155.
[5] Care Act s.91 (which amends s.46 of the Health and Social Care Act 2008); *Hansard* (House of Lords), 9 October 2013, Vol.748, col.160 (Earl Howe).
[6] *House of Commons Written Answers and Statements Daily Report*, Care Quality Commission: Written Question – 221242, 9 February 2015, pp.31 to 32 (Kris Hopkins MP).

importance of following statutory guidance[1] and carrying out adequate consultation[2]. In *R(Moseley) v London Borough of Haringey* the Supreme Court considered the duties on a local authority when consulting on proposed cuts. In this case the local authority's consultation exercise was held to be unlawful primarily on the basis that its consultation materials failed to recognise the existence of alternatives to its proposed method of responding to cuts by central government, which was to cut council tax relief.[3]

The courts have also emphasised the importance of complying with the general public sector equality duty. Section 149 of the Equality Act 2010 establishes the public sector equality duty, requiring a public authority (including local authorities) in the exercise of its functions to have due regard to the need to:

- eliminate discrimination, harassment, victimisation and any other conduct prohibited by the 2010 Act;
- advance equality of opportunity between persons who share a relevant protected characteristic and persons who do not share it; and
- foster good relations between persons who share a relevant protected characteristic and persons who do not share it.

The s.149 duty does not require an authority to take any particular steps or to achieve any specific result or goal. For this reason s.149 has been described as a "process duty"—that is, "questions of lawfulness concern the degree to which public authorities are able to account for having shown 'due regard' and not in respect of the resulting degree of equality or inequality".[4] The courts have stressed that the public sector equality duty must be exercised in substance, with rigour and with an open mind. In other words, it is not a question of "ticking boxes". Moreover, the duty to consider the impact of a policy on people with protected characteristics is a continuing one.[5] A number of cases have established that in any case where the decision may affect large numbers of disabled people, the necessary due regard to the needs of disabled people under the public sector equality duty is very high.[6]

Subsection (1)

This requires each local authority to promote an efficient and effective market of care **1–061** and support services for people in its area. In particular, local authorities must ensure that people can choose from a variety of service providers and services and a variety of high quality services, and ensure people have sufficient information to make an informed decision about how to meet their needs. Ensuring choice is discussed in paras 4.37 to 4.49 of the statutory guidance. Amongst other matters, it sets out that where a local authority develops approved lists and frameworks to limit the number of providers, it "must consider how to ensure that there is still a reasonable choice for people who need care and support".[7] The use of approved lists is discussed further at para.1–268 below.

The equivalent duty in the draft Care and Support Bill to promote diversity and quality in provision of services only applied to those services located in the local authority's area.

---

[1] See, for example, *R. (JM) v Isle of Wight Council* [2011] EWHC 2911 (Admin) and *R. (Sefton Care Association) v Sefton Council* [2011] EWHC 2676 (Admin).

[2] See, for example, *R. v Devon CC Ex parte Baker* [1995] 1 All E.R.73, *R. (Sefton Care Association) v Sefton Council* [2011] EWHC 2676 (Admin) and *R. (LH) v Shropshire Council* [2014] EWCA Civ 404.

[3] *R (Moseley) v Haringey LBC* [2014] UKSC 56.

[4] House of Lords House of Commons Joint Committee on Human Rights, *Implementation of the Right of Disabled People to Independent Living: Twenty-third Report of Session 2010–12* (1 March 2012) HL Paper 257, HC 1074, para.62.

[5] *R. (Brown) v Secretary of State for Work and Pensions*, [2008] EWHC 3158 (Admin); para.96 and *R. (D) v Worcestershire CC* [2013] EWHC 2490 (Admin).

[6] See, for example, *R. (W) v Birmingham Council* [2011] EWHC 1147 (Admin) and *R. (JM) v Isle of Wight Council* [2011] EWHC 2911 (Admin).

[7] Department of Health, *Care and Support Statutory Guidance* (2014), para.4.39.

This was criticised at consultation for not addressing access to services outside a local authority's area.[1] The subsection therefore now states that the duty relates to services that people in the area use, as opposed to only services that are located in the area.

At Committee stage in the House of Commons the Government rejected attempts to specify in the Bill the types of organisations that make up a diverse range of providers "as they will vary, depending on the specific conditions and communities in a local authority area" and this could "exclude new future types of organisation that might evolve, potentially in response to moves to integrate health and social care and, critically, in response to the personalisation of services".[2] It did confirm however that local authorities will have to consider advocacy services alongside other services when implementing s.5.[3]

As noted above, the requirement to ensure high-quality services was viewed by Government as sufficient to ensure that 15-minute care visits should not be commissioned routinely. See para.1–058 above.

Also as noted above, in the House of Commons the Government confirmed that it would expect the Care Quality Commission's power to conduct thematic inspections to be used "where commissioning practices put the quality of care at risk".[4] See para.1–059 above.

Subsection (2)

1–062   The following factors must be considered by a local authority when exercising this duty:

- having and making available information about service providers and the types of services they provide;
- current and likely future demands for services, and how providers might meet that demand;
- enabling service users and carers to participate in work, education or training, where they wish to do so;
- ensuring market sustainability—when the market is operating effectively and when it is not;
- fostering continuous improvement in the quality, efficiency and effectiveness of services, and encouraging innovation;
- fostering a workforce that can deliver high quality services.

Local authorities are required to "have regard to" (rather than achieve) the listed objectives. The meaning of "have regard to" is discussed at 1–022 above. The list is not exhaustive.

The Joint Committee recommended that this list should be amended to put beyond doubt that local authorities must involve service providers, service users and carers in market shaping activity.[5] However, the Government argued this change was not necessary because subs.(2)(b) requires local authorities to have regard to "the need to ensure it is aware of current and likely future demand for such services and to consider how providers might meet such demand" which could not be achieved without proper engagement with service users, carers and providers. It also stated this will be made clear in guidance.[6] In addition, it was argued—in response to an amendment tabled at Committee stage in the House of

---

[1]   Department of Health, *The Care Bill explained—including a response to consultation and pre-legislative scrutiny on the draft Care and Support Bill*, para.42.

[2]   *Hansard* (House of Commons: Public Bill Committee), 9 January 2014 (PM): Second Sitting, col.78 (Norman Lamb MP).

[3]   *Hansard* (House of Commons: Public Bill Committee), 14 January 2014 (AM): Third Sitting, col.86 (Norman Lamb MP).

[4]   *Hansard* (House of Commons: Public Bill Committee), 14 January 2014 (AM): Third Sitting, col.90 (Norman Lamb MP).

[5]   House of Lords House of Commons Joint Committee on the Draft Care and Support Bill, *Draft Care and Support Bill Report, Session 2012–13*, para.108.

[6]   Department of Health, *The Care Bill explained—including a response to consultation and pre-legislative scrutiny on the draft Care and Support Bill*, pp.62 to 63.

Commons—that the requirement in subs.(2)(e) to foster innovation and improvement, could not be achieved without such engagement.[1]

The meaning of "have regard to" in the context of ensuring sufficiency of services is discussed at para.1–066 below—see also para.1–022 above for a general discussion of the meaning of "have regard to".

CURRENT AND LIKELY FUTURE DEMAND

Subsection (2)(b) requires local authorities to have regard to current and future demand **1–063** for services. Assessing demand is likely to be based on joint strategic needs assessments. Section 116 of the Local Government and Public Involvement in Health Act 2007 requires local authorities and clinical commissioning groups to assess and address the current and future health and social care needs of the area through joint strategic needs assessments and joint health and well-being strategies. Taken together, these are intended to inform commissioning of local health and care services by local authorities, clinical commissioning groups and the NHS Commissioning Board. In addition, the national support programme "Developing Care Markets for Quality and Choice" aims to help local authorities produce a market position statement, which summarises current and future need for services and sets out their commissioning intentions.[2] The statutory guidance discusses developing local strategies in paras 4.51 to 4.67.

As noted above, the Government argued that this subsection ensures that in order to fulfil the market shaping duty, local authorities are required to engage with the adults using services, carers, and providers (see para.1–062 above).

ENSURING THE SUSTAINABILITY OF THE MARKET

Subsection 2(d) provides that local authorities must have regard to the importance of **1–064** ensuring the sustainability of the market. The Government's intention was explained in the following terms during the passage of the Care Bill:

"[Local authorities] should not act in a way which might risk the sustainability of the market . . . local authorities that set unreasonable or undeliverable prices which undercut the financial sustainability of the provider market would therefore not be fulfilling this duty. However, it is important to emphasise that the normal and effective operation of any market includes some providers entering and exiting the market. The Government do not wish to prevent exit, or require local authorities to prevent exit. It would not, therefore, be appropriate for local authorities to promote the sustainability of individual providers rather than the market in general."[3]

As noted above, the Government also argued that subs.(2)(d) makes clear that local authorities should not set processes that risk undercutting the stability of the market as a whole (see para.1–057 and 1–062 above). The Government went on to assert that providers have a "clear responsibility", in this respect, as they participate in negotiations over local fees.[4] Supporting sustainability is discussed in paras 4.33 to 4.36 of the statutory guidance. Amongst other matters the guidance states that the development of a Market Position

---

[1] *Hansard* (House of Commons: Public Bill Committee), 9 January 2014 (PM): Second Sitting, col.78 (Norman Lamb MP).
[2] For example, Department of Health and Institute of Public Care, *Developing Care Markets for Quality and Choice Programme: A Briefing Paper* (September 2012).
[3] *Hansard* (House of Lords), 9 July 2013, Vol.747, col.247 (Earl Howe).
[4] *Hansard* (House of Commons: Public Bill Committee), 14 January 2014 (AM): Third Sitting, col.90 (Norman Lamb MP).

Statement should be central to this process and to facilitating the development of the market.[1]

FOSTERING A WORKFORCE ABLE TO DELIVER HIGH QUALITY SERVICES

1–065   This requires local authorities to consider through their commissioning decisions the importance of fostering a workforce able to deliver high-quality services when shaping local markets because, for example, they have relevant skills and appropriate working conditions. It was introduced as a Government amendment in the House of Lords (see discussion above on unacceptable commissioning practices at para.1–058 above). Earl Howe, in explaining the amendment, stated that:

> "This amendment is, of course, not just about local authority commissioning practices but more widely about how the local authority can work with the market in its area, including with providers from which it does not commission services, to foster a high-quality workforce. This reflects our strong belief that the characteristics of the workforce, including opportunities for learning and skills development, have a direct relationship with the quality of the care that individuals receive. Improving the capability of the workforce through continued skills development and appropriate working conditions is therefore a key component of market shaping."[2]

As noted above, the Government argued that this subsection ensures that in order to fulfil the market shaping duty, local authorities are required to engage with the adults using services, their carers, and providers (see paras 1–058 and 1–062 above). Promoting quality is discussed in paras 4.21 to 4.32 of the statutory guidance.

Subsection (3)

1–066   This requires that when having regard to current and likely future demand for services, local authorities must also consider the need to ensure that sufficient services are available. This subsection was added in response to a recommendation by the Joint Committee that the market shaping duty should be amended to provide for an obligation on local authorities not only to develop a local market but also to monitor the match between supply and demand in their areas to and report publicly on the sufficiency of care and support services.[3] However, the Government decided not to require local authorities to publish an assessment of the sufficiency of services, as this would create a "disproportionate burden on local authorities".[4]

The Government argued that local authorities can only ensure the availability of sufficient services by working in partnership with providers. It would not be appropriate to require local authorities to ensure sufficiency of services independently since "this could lead to local authorities finding themselves forced into providing services where a market had not developed otherwise".[5]

In the House of Lords there was some criticism of the wording "have regard to . . . the need to ensure" that sufficient services are available. Baroness Meacher tabled an amendment to require local authorities to ensure such services are available.[6] In response the Government explained the meaning of "having regard to" in this context:

---

[1] Department of Health, *Care and Support Statutory Guidance* (2014), paras 4.34, 4.55 and 4.81 to 4.87.

[2] *Hansard* (House of Lords), 9 October 2013, Vol.748, col.160 (Earl Howe).

[3] House of Lords House of Commons Joint Committee on the Draft Care and Support Bill, *Draft Care and Support Bill Report, Session 2012–13*, para.107.

[4] Department of Health, *The Care Bill explained—including a response to consultation and pre-legislative scrutiny on the draft Care and Support Bill*, para.43.

[5] *Hansard* (House of Lords), 9 October 2013, Vol.748, col.157 (Earl Howe).

[6] *Hansard* (House of Lords), 9 October 2013, Vol.748, col.150.

"Where that duty is present, it is not something that local authorities are able to ignore. In other words, if they have to have regard to a particular thing, that is not something they can disregard. Rather, the clause as drafted is intended to recognise, as I have said, that sufficiency of services can be achieved by local authorities only when working with providers and not by local authorities alone."[1]

The statutory guidance discusses understanding the market and gaining knowledge of current and future needs in paras 4.68 to 4.78.

Subsection (4)

This subsection was introduced as a Government amendment during the House of Lords **1–067** report stage of the Care Bill. It aimed to address concerns that the Bill did not go far enough in relation to poor local authority commissioning practices. It requires local authorities, when commissioning services, to consider the effect of their commissioning decisions on the well-being of the people using those services.

"This goes a long way towards achieving the objective we all share of tackling poor commissioning practices while maintaining local authorities' ability to decide the most appropriate approach to commissioning services for the people in their area, and acknowledging that the underlying issues here are cultural and cannot be tackled by legislation alone . . . Moreover, our approach is also holistic of commissioning for all types of care and support, not merely focused on one area: that is, not just on personal care."[2]

Subsection (5)

The local authority must have regard to its market shaping duty when either providing or **1–068** arranging services to meet the care and support needs of adults with care needs and carers. The explanatory notes explain that this is because local authorities' commissioning practices affect the local market of providers.[3]

Subsection (6)

This provides that local authorities may work together to exercise the market shaping **1–069** duty. The explanatory notes state that "local authorities might want, for example, to consider the sustainability and diversity of provision across their borders, in order to promote a flexible and responsive market for their local communities".[4]

Co-operating generally

6.—(1) A local authority must co-operate with each of its relevant partners, and **1–070** each relevant partner must co-operate with the authority, in the exercise of—

    (a) their respective functions relating to adults with needs for care and support,

    (b) their respective functions relating to carers, and

    (c) functions of theirs the exercise of which is relevant to functions referred to in paragraph (a) or (b).

    (2) A local authority must co-operate, in the exercise of its functions under this Part, with such other persons as it considers appropriate who exercise functions, or are engaged in activities, in the authority's area relating to adults with needs for care and support or relating to carers.

    (3) The following are examples of persons with whom a local authority may consider it appropriate to co-operate for the purposes of subsection (2)—

---

[1] *Hansard* (House of Lords), 9 October 2013, Vol.748, col.157 (Earl Howe).
[2] *Hansard* (House of Lords), 9 October 2013, Vol.748, col.158 (Earl Howe).
[3] Care Act 2014: Explanatory Notes para.77.
[4] Care Act 2014: Explanatory Notes para.78.

(a) a person who provides services to meet adults' needs for care and support, services to meet carers' needs for support or services, facilities or resources of the kind referred to in section 2(1);

(b) a person who provides primary medical services, primary dental services, primary ophthalmic services, pharmaceutical services or local pharmaceutical services under the National Health Service Act 2006;

(c) a person in whom a hospital in England is vested which is not a health service hospital as defined by that Act;

(d) a private registered provider of social housing.

(4) A local authority must make arrangements for ensuring co-operation between—

(a) the officers of the authority who exercise the authority's functions relating to adults with needs for care and support or its functions relating to carers,

(b) the officers of the authority who exercise the authority's functions relating to housing (in so far as the exercise of those functions is relevant to functions referred to in paragraph (a)),

(c) the Director of Children's Services at the authority (in so far as the exercise of functions by that officer is relevant to the functions referred to in paragraph (a)), and

(d) the authority's director of public health (see section 73A of the National Health Service Act 2006).

(5) The references in subsections (1) and (4)(a) to a local authority's functions include a reference to the authority's functions under sections 58 to 65 (transition for children with needs etc.).

(6) The duties under subsections (1) to (4) are to be performed for the following purposes in particular—

(a) promoting the well-being of adults with needs for care and support and of carers in the authority's area,

(b) improving the quality of care and support for adults and support for carers provided in the authority's area (including the outcomes that are achieved from such provision),

(c) smoothing the transition to the system provided for by this Part for persons in relation to whom functions under sections 58 to 65 are exercisable,

(d) protecting adults with needs for care and support who are experiencing, or are at risk of, abuse or neglect, and

(e) identifying lessons to be learned from cases where adults with needs for care and support have experienced serious abuse or neglect and applying those lessons to future cases.

(7) Each of the following is a relevant partner of a local authority—

(a) where the authority is a county council for an area for which there are district councils, each district council;

(b) any local authority, or district council for an area in England for which there is a county council, with which the authority agrees it would be appropriate to co-operate under this section;

(c) each NHS body in the authority's area;

(d) the Minister of the Crown exercising functions in relation to social security, employment and training, so far as those functions are exercisable in relation to England;

(e) the chief officer of police for a police area the whole or part of which is in the authority's area;

(f) the Minister of the Crown exercising functions in relation to prisons, so far as those functions are exercisable in relation to England;

(g) a relevant provider of probation services in the authority's area;

(h) such person, or a person of such description, as regulations may specify.

(8) The reference to an NHS body in a local authority's area is a reference to—

(a) the National Health Service Commissioning Board, so far as its functions are exercisable in relation to the authority's area,

(b) a clinical commissioning group the whole or part of whose area is in the authority's area, or

(c) an NHS trust or NHS foundation trust which provides services in the authority's area.

(9) "Prison" has the same meaning as in the Prison Act 1952 (see section 53(1) of that Act).

(10) "Relevant provider of probation services" has the meaning given by section 325 of the Criminal Justice Act 2003.

GENERAL NOTE

Adult social care does not exist in a vacuum. Those with care and support needs are often **1–071** in contact with a range of different agencies and professionals, such as GPs, nurses, the police and housing workers. Often the same service or similar types of services can be provided by many different organisations, including health, housing and voluntary agencies. In recent years, there has been increasing policy emphasis on achieving greater co-operation between social services departments and other organisations. The positive reasons for co-operation include the need to simplify the process for assessment and the provision of services, and to avoid duplication. A number of high-profile cases have also provided vivid reminders of the potential tragic consequences when vulnerable adults fall between services.[1] Statute law can be used as a vehicle to encourage greater co-operation. Section 6 is an example of such a provision, and was recommended by the Law Commission.[2] Other examples of similar duties to co-operate include s.82 of the National Health Service Act 2006 and s.10 of the Children Act 2004.

It is important, however, to recognise the limitations of legal duties to co-operate. The extent of co-operation between agencies will depend on a wide range of factors, such as resources, local policies and personal relationships. Many of these issues apply irrespective of the legal position. Therefore, the law is only one factor in ensuring greater co-operation between different agencies.

Section 6 is a general duty (see para.1–001 above) and does not specify what precise actions constitute co-operation. This is likely to mean that the duty will be difficult to enforce and it will be left to the local authority and the relevant partner to decide how, and to what extent, the duty is implemented. It is likely that a court would only find a breach of the duty in limited circumstances, such as where there has been an express refusal by the local authorities to co-operate on unreasonable grounds. However, s.6 is supplemented by a more specific duty in s.7.

The explanatory notes explain that s.6:

". . . does not require the local authority to take any specific steps to cooperate with relevant external partners, but there are a number of other powers which local authorities may use to promote joint working. For example, local authorities may share information with other partners, or provide staff, services or other resources to partners to improve

---

[1] See, for example, M. Flynn, "The Murder of Steven Hoskin: A Serious Case Review—Executive Summary, Adult Protection Committee, Cornwall" (2007) and Independent Police Complaints Commission, "Report into the Contact Between Fiona Pilkington and Leicestershire Constabulary 2004–2007" (2009).

[2] Law Commission, *Adult Social Care*, paras 11.135 to 11.139.

cooperation. Under section 75 of the National Health Service Act 2006, a local authority may also contribute to a 'pooled budget' with an NHS body —a shared fund out of which payments can be made to meet agreed priorities."[1]

The s.6 duty to co-operate is discussed in paras 15.15 to 15.24 of the statutory guidance. Some of the ways of co-operating for the purposes of s.6 will be the same as those which can be undertaken to promote integration under s.3, such as pooled budgets and joint commissioning (see para.1–039 above). The statutory guidance discusses co-operation between professionals and organisations (including joint assessments) in the context of transition assessments in paras 16.40 to 16.49.

Section 116B of the Local Government and Public Involvement in Health Act 2007 requires local authorities and clinical commissioning groups to have regard to the relevant joint strategic needs assessment and joint health and well-being strategy in exercising any of their functions. This includes their duties to co-operate and promote integration. See paras 15.8 to 15.10 of the statutory guidance.

The Children and Families Act 2014 includes a right for those with special educational needs to an Education, Health and Care Plan up until the age of 25. During the passage of the Care Bill in the House of Lords, the Government explained how s.6 of the Care Act would impact in such cases:

". . . when a young person over the age of 18 has an [Education, Health and Care Plan under the Children and Families Act 2014], and as such the care part of that plan is provided under [the Care Act], we would expect co-operation between adult and children's services in relation to any review of the plan under [section 6(6)(a) and (b)]. Such co-operation for those under 18 who are in transition is provided for by [section 6(6)(c)]. This would include co-operation with the preparation, maintenance and review of the [Education, Health and Care Plan] as provided for by the [the Children and Families Act], in respect of children. Guidance can ensure that this is clear."[2]

This is confirmed in paras 16.64 to 16.65 of the statutory guidance.

Subsection (1)

1–072   Local authorities and their "relevant partners" (listed in subs.(7)) are required to co-operate with each other in the exercise of their respective care and support functions. Subsection (5) confirms that the duty extends to when a local authority is undertaking its responsibilities under ss.58 to 65 in relation to transition for children with needs to adult care and support. The explanatory notes explain that "this duty does not confer any new functions but relates to co-operation in the exercise of the respective partners' pre-existing functions relevant to adults with care and support needs and support for carers and children in transition".[3]

Subsection (2)

1–073   The duty of the local authority to co-operate with its partners extends to any other person or body who the authority considers appropriate. An illustrate list is provided in subs.(3). However subs.(2) does not require this person or body to co-operate in return.

Subsection (3)

1–074   This subsection provides a non-exhaustive list of the types of "other persons" that local authorities would be expected to co-operate with, and includes certain providers of health, care and support, and housing services. This was added as a Government amendment to the Care Bill at report stage in the House of Lords in response to arguments that the legislation should clarify that local authorities are required to co-operate with providers of services, in

[1] Care Act 2014: Explanatory Notes para.83.
[2] *Hansard* (House of Lords), 22 July 2013, Vol.747, col.1156 (Earl Howe).
[3] Care Act 2014: Explanatory Notes para.79.

particular providers of housing services. However, these bodies could not be added as "relevant partners", because public law is limited in the extent to which it can place duties on such private bodies.[1]

The list consists of:

- social care providers;
- NHS service providers of primary medical services, primary dental services, primary ophthalmic services, and pharmaceutical services;
- independent hospitals; and
- private social housing providers.

The statutory guidance states that in these cases, the local authority should "consider what degree of co-operation is required, and what mechanisms it may have in place to ensure mutual co-operation (for example, via contractual means)".[2] Working with welfare and employment services is specifically discussed in paras 15.69 to 15.72 of the guidance.

Subsection (4)

The Law Commission recommended that the duty to co-operate must promote co-operation internally between social services and other departments, such as children's services, in unitary authorities and London Boroughs, housing departments.[3] Consequently, subs.(4) requires the local authority to ensure such internal co-operation. These officers are employees of the local authority, and are not therefore included in the list of external partners in subs.(7).[4] The inclusion of public health authorities was included to reflect local authorities' new responsibilities under the Health and Social Care Act 2012. Ensuring co-operation within local authorities is discussed in paras 15.23 to 15.24 of the statutory guidance.

1–075

Subsection (6)

This sets out five aims of co-operation between partners:

1–076

- promoting well-being;
- improving the quality of care and support;
- smoothing the transition to adults services for children;
- protecting from abuse and neglect; and
- identifying and learning lessons in cases of serious abuse or neglect.

However, the purposes of co-operation are not limited to these matters alone. These aims apply to co-operation between the local authority and its relevant partners (subs.(1)), co-operation between a local authority and any other person or body who the authority considers appropriate (subs.(2)) and internal co-operation between local authority officers (subs.(4)).

At report stage in the House of Lords the Government rejected an amendment which would have required co-operation to ensure that a post discharge plan is initiated upon admission to hospital. In response the Government argued:

> "There can be no question that this duty would apply also to ensuring safe and timely discharges, and we do not see the need to add further detail to such broadly worded provisions."[5]

---

[1] *Hansard* (House of Lords), 9 October 2013, Vol.748, col.107 (Earl Howe).
[2] Department of Health, *Care and Support Statutory Guidance* (2014), para.15.22.
[3] Law Commission, Adult Social Care, para.11.138.
[4] Care Act 2014: Explanatory Notes, para.81.
[5] *Hansard* (House of Lords), 9 October 2013, Vol.748, col.168 (Earl Howe).

Subsection (7)

1–077   The Law Commission recommended that the duty to co-operate must be precise about which organisations are included, and that as a minimum it should cover health services, the police, other local authorities and any other persons or bodies the authority consider appropriate.[1]   Consequently, subs.(7) provides the following list of the relevant partners for the purposes of the duties in ss.6 and 7:

- district councils (in the case of a county council) and local authorities;
- NHS bodies;
- social security;
- police;
- prisons; and
- probation services.

All of the relevant partners listed are public bodies with relevant care and support and carer's functions at a local level. The duty operates at the level of public law and cannot be made enforceable against purely private bodies.[2] The list can be extended through regulations. The statutory guidance discusses relevant partners in para.15.21.

The Joint Committee recommended that the list of relevant partners should be extended to cover registered housing providers, including housing associations and registered social landlords.[3] The Government argued that co-operation with these bodies is better achieved through commissioning and contractual means, as well as through the market shaping duty in s.5.[4] The Government also rejected the inclusion of care and support providers in the list.[5] In the House of Lords, it explained that public law cannot create an enforceable legal duty on private, independent or voluntary providers to require co-operation.[6]

Similarly, at Committee Stage in the House of Commons the Government rejected an amendment that would specify housing providers as a relevant partner of local authorities. It stated that section 6:

". . . includes the requirement for a local authority to ensure co-operation in delivering services relevant to care and support and to work co-operatively to ensure that services are joined-up. That includes private registered providers of social housing. Public law is limited on the extent to which it may place duties on private bodies. Extending the list to other housing providers would include private housing providers, such as private landlords, where they are providing housing to individuals, under entirely private contractual arrangements, which would extend the duty beyond those with whom the local authority holds a contractual duty."[7]

Co-operating in specific cases

1–078   **7.**—(1) Where a local authority requests the co-operation of a relevant partner, or of a local authority which is not one of its relevant partners, in the exercise of a function under this Part in the case of an individual with needs for care and support

---

[1] Law Commission, *Adult Social Care*, para.11.138.

[2] Law Commission, *Adult Social Care*, para.11.138.

[3] House of Lords House of Commons Joint Committee on the Draft Care and Support Bill, *Draft Care and Support Bill Report, Session 2012–13*, para.119.

[4] Department of Health, *The Care Bill explained—including a response to consultation and pre-legislative scrutiny on the draft Care and Support Bill*, para.50.

[5] Department of Health, *The Care Bill explained—including a response to consultation and pre-legislative scrutiny on the draft Care and Support Bill*, para.49.

[6] *Hansard* (House of Lords), 9 July 2013, Vol.747, col.196.

[7] *Hansard* (House of Commons: Public Bill Committee), 9 January 2014 (PM): Second Sitting, col.56 (Norman Lamb MP).

or in the case of a carer, a carer of a child or a young carer, the partner or authority must comply with the request unless it considers that doing so—

(a) would be incompatible with its own duties, or

(b) would otherwise have an adverse effect on the exercise of its functions.

(2) Where a relevant partner of a local authority, or a local authority which is not one of its relevant partners, requests the co-operation of the local authority in its exercise of a function in the case of an individual with needs for care and support or in the case of a carer, a carer of a child or a young carer, the local authority must comply with the request unless it considers that doing so—

(a) would be incompatible with its own duties, or

(b) would otherwise have an adverse effect on the exercise of its functions.

(3) A person who decides not to comply with a request under subsection (1) or (2) must give the person who made the request written reasons for the decision.

(4) "Relevant partner", in relation to a local authority, has the same meaning as in section 6.

(5) "Carer of a child" means a person who is a carer for the purposes of section 60.

GENERAL NOTE

This section supplements the general duty to co-operate in s.6 with a specific duty and is **1–079** based on a Law Commission recommendation.[1] Prior to the Care Act, the main provision in adult social care aimed at ensuring co-operation had been s.47(3) of the National Health Service and Community Care Act 1990. Section 47(3) provided that where a community care assessment disclosed a possible housing or medical need, the local authority must notify the relevant housing or health authority and invite them to assist, to such extent as is reasonable in the circumstances, in the making of the assessment. The Law Commission concluded that s.47(4) was weakened by the absence of any requirement that the invited authority respond to an invitation to assist. In contrast, the equivalent duty in s.27 of the Children Act 1989 enables a local authority to request the help of another organisation and specify the action in question, and the requested authority must comply with the request "if it is compatible with their own statutory or other duties and obligations, and does not unduly prejudice the discharge of any of their functions". A similar approach is adopted in s.322 of the Education Act 1996. The Law Commission originally consulted on a proposal based on these provisions.[2] But in its final report the Commission went further and recommended that the duty should be strengthened by the inclusion of a requirement to give written reasons if the requested body refused to co-operate. It also recommended that the duty should also be reciprocal and require the social services authority to give due regard to requests to co-operate from other bodies and give written reasons if it decides not to co-operate.[3]

The explanatory notes state that s.7:

". . . is intended to be used by local authorities or partners where co-operation is needed in the case of an individual who has needs for care and support. The duty is not limited to specific circumstances, but could be used, for example, when a child is preparing to move from children's to adult services; in adult safeguarding enquiries; when an adult requires an assessment for NHS continuing health care; or, when an adult is moving between areas and requires a new needs assessment."[4]

---

[1] Law Commission, *Adult Social Care*, paras 11.135 to 11.139.

[2] Law Commission, *Adult Social Care: A Consultation Paper*, Consultation Paper No.192 (2010), paras 11.81 to 11.92.

[3] Law Commission, *Adult Social Care*, para.11.139.

[4] Care Act 2014: Explanatory Notes para.84.

It is notable that whereas s.47(3) of the National Health Service and Community Care Act 1990 required local authorities to notify the relevant housing or health authority, s.7 of the Care Act is a power to require co-operation.

During the passage of the Care Bill in the House of Lords, the Government introduced amendments to s.7 to put beyond doubt its intention that the duty applies in relation to children undergoing transition from children's to adult services. These amendments replaced the reference to "adults" with "individuals" and expanded the description of carers.[1]

Duties to co-operate do not mean that local authorities can avoid their responsibilities by "passing the buck" to another body, rather that they can ask a partner to use its powers to help them discharge theirs.[2] The courts have been keen when considering duties to co-operate to emphasise the separate responsibilities or the relevant bodies. See, for example, the following observation on s.27 of the Children Act 1989 which has similarities in its wording to s.7:

> "Section 27 imposes a duty of co-operation . . . but co-operation is one thing; the preservation of the separation of powers between public authorities is another. Nothing in section 27 as a whole, or in section 27(2), in particular, enlarges or otherwise amends the powers or duties of the requested authorities under other statutes. Moreover, the duty to co-operate is not unlimited. On the contrary, section 27(2) guarantees the separation of the functions of the different public authorities. Section 27(2) expressly provides that the request must be compatible with the requested authority's own statutory or other duties and obligations, and that the request must not unduly prejudice the discharge of any of their functions. These provisions indicate that Parliament intended that the requesting local authority and the requested authority should co-operate in exercising their respective and different functions, under the relevant statutory schemes. Parliament did not, however, intend that the nature or scope of those respective functions of the requesting local authority and the requested authority should change, as a result of the imposition of a duty to co-operate."[3]

The statutory guidance discusses s.7 of the Care Act in paras 15.25 to 15.28.

Subsection (1)

1–080   A local authority may request co-operation from a relevant partner in relation to the case of an individual adult or carer, and the relevant partner must co-operate as requested, unless doing so would be incompatible with the relevant partner's own functions or duties or otherwise have an adverse effect on the exercise of its functions.

In Parliament, the Government confirmed that the s.7 duty could be used where a local authority or one of its relevant partners requires the co-operation of the other to obtain information relevant to care and support functions.[4]

1–081   INCOMPATIBLE WITH ITS OWN DUTIES. In *R. (T) v Haringey LBC*—which concerned responsibility for services to ensure that a child's tracheotomy tube was suctioned and remained in place—the local authority had invoked the co-operation provisions of s.27 of the Children Act 1989 in an attempt to require the NHS Primary Care Trust to provide additional respite care.[5] It was held that the local authority could not invoke s.27 because the nature of the disputed care did not fall within the scope of the Children Act 1989. In other words, the local authority had no function in respect of which it could seek co-operation. But in any event s.27 could not be used by social services authorities to evade their

---

[1] *Hansard* (House of Lords), 9 July 2013, Vol.747, col.251.

[2] *R. (G) v Southwark LBC* [2009] UKHL 26; [2009] 1 W.L.R. 1299 at [33].

[3] Mr Anthony Lester QC, approved by Lord Templeman in *R. v Northavon District Council Ex parte Smith* [1994] 3 W.L.R. 403; [1994] 2 A.C. 402.

[4] *Hansard* (House of Commons: Public Bill Committee), 14 January 2014 (PM): Third Sitting, col.94 (Norman Lamb MP).

[5] *R. (T) v Haringey LBC* [2005] EWHC 2235 (Admin); (2006) 9 CCLR 58.

responsibilities and to compel other authorities to do what they did not consider to be their duty. The level of care being proposed by the Trust was sufficient and within its discretionary judgement and did not breach the European Convention on Human Rights.

Subsection (1) does not expressly provide for an information gateway for example if a request is made to pass personal, sensitive or confidential information. This omission is likely to be because any disclosure of information would not need to go beyond that currently permitted by law.

ADVERSE EFFECT. The term "adverse effect" would appear to be a lower threshold for a **1–082** refusal to co-operate than "unduly prejudice" contained in s.27 of the Children Act 1989. The latter would only apply if the requested action prejudiced the discharge of functions in a way which was unnecessary or unreasonable in all the circumstances of the case. In contrast, a mere adverse effect does not require these additional considerations.

Subsection (2)
This creates the same duty as subs.(1) but in reverse, with the request made by the rel- **1–083** evant partner to the local authority.

Subsection (3)
If either the local authority, or the relevant partner, decides not to co-operate after receiv- **1–084** ing a request under subss.(1) or (2), they must write to the other person setting out their reasons for not doing so. The explanatory notes state:

> "Local authorities and their relevant partners must respond to requests to co-operate under their general public law duties to act reasonably, and failure to respond within a reasonable time frame could be subject to judicial review."[1]

This is confirmed in the statutory guidance.[2] However, the courts have emphasised that legal action is unlikely to be effective in achieving the necessary co-operation because "by its very nature; it incites opposition and entrenched and inflexible positions rather than the goodwill which is necessary to make such provisions work effectively".[3]

It is likely that, as well as the requesting authority, an adult with care and support needs or a carer might have standing to bring a judicial review claim.[4]

MEETING NEEDS FOR CARE ETC.

How to meet needs
   8.—(1) The following are examples of what may be provided to meet needs **1–085** under sections 18 to 20—
   (a) accommodation in a care home or in premises of some other type;
   (b) care and support at home or in the community;
   (c) counselling and other types of social work;
   (d) goods and facilities;
   (e) information, advice and advocacy.
   (2) The following are examples of the ways in which a local authority may meet needs under sections 18 to 20—
   (a) by arranging for a person other than it to provide a service;

---

[1] Care Act 2014: Explanatory Notes para.86.
[2] Department of Health, *Care and Support Statutory Guidance* (2014), para.15.28.
[3] *R. (T) v Haringey LBC* [2005] EWHC 2235 (Admin); (2006) 9 CCLR 58 at [100], per Mr Justice Ouseley, commenting on *R. v Northavon District Council Ex p Smith* [1994] 3 W.L.R. 403; [1994] 2 A.C. 410G–H.
[4] *R. (C) v Hackney LBC* [2014] EWHC 3670 (Admin).

    (b) by itself providing a service;

    (c) by making direct payments.

    (3) "Care home" has the meaning given by section 3 of the Care Standards Act 2000.

GENERAL NOTE

1–086   Prior to the introduction of the Care Act, the generic legal term "community care services" was used to describe the range of care and support that could be provided to meet the needs of older and disabled people.[1] Community care services were defined by reference to various and often detailed lists of services which appeared in different statutes and in approvals and directions. For example, s.2(1) of the Chronically Sick and Disabled Persons Act 1970 set out a list of "welfare services" which included practical assistance in the home, recreational facilities outside the home and the provision of or assistance in obtaining a wireless and a television. The Law Commission criticised this overarching structure on the basis that the various lists often duplicated each other and that some of the categories had become outdated, convoluted and confusing in places. In its consultation paper, it proposed the consolidation of the lists into a single short and broad list of services which would be set out on the face of the statute. It argued that this would allow the definition of services to evolve and remain up-to-date, whilst also maintaining some degree of clarity and certainty.[2] However, several consultees criticised this approach for being service-led and put forward an alternative approach, based on outcomes rather than services. Under an outcomes-based approach, the relevant services are not defined by reference to what they are, but rather the outcomes they must achieve for the person concerned. The Commission was persuaded to alter its approach and opted for a hybrid definition which incorporated both a list of services and outcomes. Thus it recommended that the statute should provide a broad list of services, and the purpose or aims of those services would be defined by reference to the outcomes to which the well-being principle must be directed in s.1(2). The Commission also concluded that the list of services in the hybrid definition must be as clear and straightforward as possible and include the minimum number of categories. Given the range of services that can be provided by social services authorities, including personalised services and self-directed support, it also considered that the list should be illustrative and non-exhaustive. The final recommendation was:

- residential accommodation;
- community and home-based services;
- advice, social work, counselling and advocacy services; and
- financial or other assistance.[3]

Section 8 implements the Law Commission's approach. It is intended to provide some indication of the range of what a local authority can do to meet an adult's needs, but also recognises that care and support needs will be specific to the individual concerned and there are many ways in which local authorities can meet such needs. The Government described its intention during the Committee stage of the Care Bill in the House of Commons:

"[Section 8] ensures that there are no legal barriers on the types of care and support that can be provided. Instead, [section 8] sets out a list of examples of how care and support needs can be met. This approach and the use of illustrations is intended to act as a signal

---

[1] National Health Services and Community Care Act 1990 s.46(3).

[2] Law Commission, *Adult Social Care: A Consultation Paper*, Consultation Paper No.192 (2010), paras 9.2 to 9.34.

[3] Law Commission, *Adult Social Care*, paras 8.2 to 8.24.

that in a modern care and support system, we should be thinking about more than just the traditional ways of meeting care and support needs, such as placing someone in a residential home or making domiciliary care visits."[1]

The list must be read in conjunction with the outcomes set out in s.1(2).

It is also not correct to state that there are no legal barriers to the types of services that can be provided. The prohibitions on the provision of care and support are contained in ss.22 and 23.

The statutory guidance discusses the s.8 list briefly in paras 10.11 to 10.14. It also explains that "meeting needs" is an important concept under the Act and is intended to move away from the previous terminology of "providing services" and be broader than a duty to provide or arrange a particular service.[2]

CARERS SERVICES

The list in s.8 is a radical departure from previous social care legislation since it applies **1–087** to carers' services, as well as services for adults with care and support needs. Prior to the Care Act, adult social care legislation did not define the types of services that could be provided to carers. Instead, each local authority was given discretion to provide any services that it "sees fit to provide" and that will "in the local authority's view help the carer care for the person cared for".[3]

The Law Commission concluded that there were compelling arguments for a consistent approach to the definition of carers' services and the definition of community care services. This was argued not only on the basis of clarity and certainty, but because it would encourage a broad assessment of carers' needs. In effect, it would underline the fact that, as well as considering the caring role, support can be provided to meet a broad range of needs and outcomes including to ensure a life outside of caring.[4]

Subsection (1)

The list contains five broad categories to indicate the types of care and support that could **1–088** be arranged or provided to meet the needs of both adults needing care and carers:

- accommodation in a care home or in premises of some other type;
- care and support at home or in the community;
- counselling and other types of social work;
- goods and facilities; and
- information, advice and advocacy.

The explanatory notes state that:

"This is not intended to be a definition of care and support or an exhaustive list, but to give a partial description for clarity. Local authorities may arrange or provide for any combination or type of service to meet needs, other than those services which they are prohibited from providing because they fall their outside their care and support functions (see sections 22 and 23)."[5]

In a written note to the Joint Committee, the Department of Health confirmed that holidays, travel, assistance to take advantage of educational facilities, and home adaptations are intended to be covered by s.8. The Joint Committee had been urged by respondents

---

[1] *Hansard* (House of Commons: Public Bill Committee), 14 January 2014 (AM): Third Sitting, col.95 (Norman Lamb MP).
[2] Department of Health, *Care and Support Statutory Guidance* (2014), para.6.2.
[3] Carers and Disabled Children Act 2000 s.2(2).
[4] Law Commission, *Adult Social Care*, paras 8.25 to 8.31.
[5] Care Act 2014: Explanatory Notes para.88.

to make recommendations to add to this list, but it concluded that "so long as the list is short, it is clear that it is illustrative only." Moreover, it felt that the longer the list was, "the more likely it is to be interpreted as not including matters unconnected to those in the list."[1]

1–089   ACCOMMODATION IN A CARE HOME OR IN PREMISES OF SOME OTHER TYPE.   Residential care remains a major aspect of adult social care provision. Out of the 1.3 million people receiving services in 2012–13, 209,000 received residential care and 87,000 received nursing care.[2] In law, different rules apply to residential and non-residential services, for example on ordinary residence and charging for services.

Subsection (1)(a) is clear that accommodation can include ordinary housing, as well as registered care homes and supported living.

1–090   ADVOCACY.   Subsection (1)(e) includes "advocacy" as an example of what a local authority may provide to meet an adult's or carer's needs. The Government has confirmed that advocacy can also be provided at an earlier stage in accordance with the s.4 duty to provide an information and advice service, and in particular the requirement to ensure that information provided is accessible to, and proportionate to the needs of, those for whom it is being provided (s.4(4)) (see para.1–049 above). In addition, there is a specific right to advocacy under ss.67 and 68.

Subsection (2)

1–091   This subsection confirms that in meeting any adult's needs, a local authority may provide a service itself or arrange for a service to be provided by another organisation. The local authority may also make a direct payment in lieu of a service (as detailed in ss.31 to 33), or undertake any combination of these approaches.

In the previous legal framework there was an express prohibition against the provision of money, other than through direct payments.[3] This has not been retained in the Care Act.

Subsection (3)

1–092   This subsection defines care home for the purposes of subs.(1)(a) by reference to s.3 of the Care Standards Act 2000. Section 3 provides that an establishment is a care home if it provides accommodation, together with nursing or personal care, for any of the following persons.

- persons who are or have been ill;
- persons who have or have had a mental disorder;
- persons who are disabled or infirm; and
- persons who are or have been dependent on alcohol or drugs.

An establishment in England is not a care home if it is a hospital (within the meaning of the National Health Service Act 2006), or a children's home, or if it is of a description excepted by regulations.

The fact that accommodation is provided by lease or licence does not mean that an establishment ceases to be a care home. The crucial consideration is whether the establishment provide accommodation together with nursing or personal care, which is a question of fact.

---

[1] House of Lords House of Commons Joint Committee on the Draft Care and Support Bill *Draft Care and Support Bill Report, Session 2012–13*, para.168.

[2] Health and Social Care Information Centre, *Community Care Statistics: Social Services Activity, England 2012–13* (2013).

[3] National Assistance Act 1948 s.29(6) and Health Services and Public Health Act 1968 s.45(4)(a).

The fact that a relationship is one of lessor and lessee could be an indication of a situation where an establishment does not provide both accommodation and care, but is not determinative.[1]

ASSESSING NEEDS

GENERAL NOTE

An assessment of need has always been central to social care. It operates both as the gate- **1–093** way to the provision of care and support, and as a "critical intervention in its own right which can help people to understand their situation and the needs they have, to reduce or delay the onset of greater needs, and to access support when they require it".[2] The right to an assessment of need is therefore regarded as a significant and valued legal entitlement. Adult social care is one of the few areas of law that contains express duties to assess. In contrast, the Children Act 1989 contains no such express provision, and the duty to assessment is implied by virtue of s.17.[3] Moreover, Mr Justice Scott Baker (as he then was) in *R. v Bristol CC Ex p Penfold* has observed that:

"Even if there is no hope from the resource point of view of meeting any needs identified in the assessment, the assessment may serve a useful purpose in identifying for the local authority unmet needs which will help it to plan for the future. Without assessment this could not be done."[4]

However, during the passage of the Care Bill in the House of Commons, concerns were raised about the role of assessments in social care. For instance, John McDonnell MP said:

"I do not know what other Members find in their constituencies, but I find that the process of assessment can be extremely difficult—first, getting an appropriate person who can do the assessment, then getting that appropriately skilled person to do the assessment, and then the bizarre continual re-assessment after re-assessment that amounts almost to harassment. Some people with severe disabilities—with permanent conditions who, to get a cure, would need a trip to Lourdes, to be frank—get re-assessed time and again. That becomes worrying for them, and some individuals can lose some element of their benefit through this process."[5]

Others warned that assessments may divert resources from service provision. For example, Meg Munn MP said:

"In my experience there seems to be a tendency of wanting to assess people and then reassess them, rather than putting effort into providing services for them. If we quantified the time that goes into assessment as opposed to provision, I think we would see some way in which we could shift some of these very scarce resources into helping people properly."[6]

The Law Commission recognised the importance of the right to an assessment, but at the same time sought to rebalance the centrality of assessments to adult social care. This was a response to two main pressures. First, it was concerned that the legal framework had created an *assessment industry* whereby social workers were required to assess all cases that

---

[1] *R. (Moore) v Care Standards Tribunal [2005]* EWCA Civ 627; (2005) 8 CCLR 354.

[2] Department of Health, *Care and Support Statutory Guidance* (2014), para.6.2.

[3] The courts have held that s.17 when read together with the relevant statutory guidance imposes a duty to assess, see *R. v London Borough Council of Lambeth Ex p K* [2000] 3 CCLR 141 at 144. See also *R. (G) v Barnet LBC* [2003] UKHL 57; [2004] 2 A.C. 208 at [32].

[4] *R. v Bristol CC Ex p Penfold* (1997–98) 1 CCLR 315 at 322(I), by Mr Justice Scott Baker.

[5] *Hansard* (House of Commons), 16 December 2013, Vol.572, cols 566 to 567.

[6] *Hansard* (House of Commons), 16 December 2013, Vol.572, col.567. For a similar point made about carer's assessments, see *Hansard* (House of Commons), 16 December 2013, Vol.572, col.552 (Dr Sarah Wollaston MP).

came to their attention—even when an assessment was inappropriate or unnecessary—and often leaving little time to devote to providing or arranging care and support. Second, at consultation, advocates of personalisation put forward a broad conception of local authority responsibilities in which authorities have a wider role in ensuring that there is a full range of universal services available within their area—which can be accessed without an assessment—to support people to maintain their independence and well-being, and to reduce or delay the need for more targeted social care interventions. The Law Commission's final report contemplates that there should be two levels at which care and support, broadly conceived, could be provided: at a universal level and a more targeted level. At the first level it recommended new duties on local authorities to provide information, advice and assistance, as well as to shape and stimulate the local market for services. Access to universal services, including advice, assistance and brokerage, would not depend on assessment. The second level would continue to be addressed though a right to an assessment, but two reforms sought to ensure that assessments are not carried out in inappropriately. First, regulations would require that a proportionate assessment must be carried out so that even if someone is within the requirement for an assessment, the process need not be overly bureaucratic. Second, the statute should codify the right of refusal of assessment and allow people to self-divert themselves away from assessment, while still taking advantage of universal services and advice and assistance.[1]

The Government accepted all of the Law Commission's recommendations in this area. In particular it recognised the need to rebalance adult social care away from being assessment driven:

> ". . . assessments will remain an integral part of the reformed care and support system. However, rather than acting primarily as a gateway to the adult receiving care and support, the future system will place more emphasis on supporting people to identify their needs; understand the options available to them; plan for meeting care and support needs, and reduce or delay needs where that is possible."[2]

The Care Act therefore implements the Law Commission's two-level structure. The first level is evident in ss.2 to 6 which set out the general responsibilities of local authorities including preventing needs for care and support, the provision of information, and market shaping. The second level is contained in ss.9 to 13 which allow for individual assessments—and include provisions for the refusal of an assessment and proportionate assessments.

In recognising the need to achieve this rebalance, the Government was not just responding to the Law Commission report but also the implications of its funding reforms. From April 2020, the assessment will also be the first stage of the process which establishes whether or not a person has eligible needs, and therefore whether their care and support costs will count toward the new cap on an individual's financial contributions towards the cost of care (see s.15). In effect, people and their families will have a significant economic interest in establishing that they have eligible needs because that is when the meter starts ticking for them getting free care and support. The Department of Health analysis estimates that, as a result of the reforms, around 500,000 more people with eligible care needs could make contact with their local authority when the cap is implemented.[3]

Challenging assessments

It has long been recognised that claimants face a heavy burden to establish that an assessment is unlawful. Decisions of fact are normally left to public bodies to determine and the remedy of judicial review is limited to unreasonable or irrational decisions (see discussion at 1–701 below). Notwithstanding this high hurdle, some challenges to assessments have

---

[1] Law Commission, *Adult Social Care*, paras 5.3 to 5.16.
[2] *Hansard* (House of Lords), 9 July 2013, Vol.747, col.262 (Earl Howe).
[3] Department of Health, *Caring for our Future: Consultation on Reforming What and How People Pay for their Care and Support* (2013), para.60.

been successful. These have included assessments that failed to give sufficient weight to relevant material (for example, the opinions of the GP, nurse and care provider) and relied excessively on the non-expert view of a social worker in the face of expert evidence to the contrary.[1]

ASSESSING NEEDS

Assessment of an adult's needs for care and support

9.—(1) Where it appears to a local authority that an adult may have needs for **1–094** care and support, the authority must assess—

(a) whether the adult does have needs for care and support, and

(b) if the adult does, what those needs are.

(2) An assessment under subsection (1) is referred to in this Part as a "needs assessment".

(3) The duty to carry out a needs assessment applies regardless of the authority's view of—

(a) the level of the adult's needs for care and support, or

(b) the level of the adult's financial resources.

(4) A needs assessment must include an assessment of—

(a) the impact of the adult's needs for care and support on the matters specified in section 1(2),

(b) the outcomes that the adult wishes to achieve in day-to-day life, and

(c) whether, and if so to what extent, the provision of care and support could contribute to the achievement of those outcomes.

(5) A local authority, in carrying out a needs assessment, must involve—

(a) the adult,

(b) any carer that the adult has, and

(c) any person whom the adult asks the authority to involve or, where the adult lacks capacity to ask the authority to do that, any person who appears to the authority to be interested in the adult's welfare.

(6) When carrying out a needs assessment, a local authority must also consider—

(a) whether, and if so to what extent, matters other than the provision of care and support could contribute to the achievement of the outcomes that the adult wishes to achieve in day-to-day life, and

(b) whether the adult would benefit from the provision of anything under section 2 or 4 or of anything which might be available in the community.

(7) This section is subject to section 11(1) to (4) (refusal by adult of assessment).

GENERAL NOTE

This section requires a local authority to carry out an assessment of an adult's needs for **1–095** care and support (known as a "needs assessment"). It is the mechanism by which local authorities determine whether a person has "eligible needs" and whether there is a duty or a power to meet the person's needs. The section replaces and largely seeks to replicate the express duty to assess in s.47(1) of the National Health Service and Community Care Act 1990 (see para.1–099 below). The Law Commission recommended that the new duty to

---

[1] See, for example *Clarke v London Borough of Sutton* [2015] EWHC 1081 (Admin).

assess should be based on s.47, which was accepted by the Government.[1] The s.9 assessment duty also replaces the implied assessment duties in previous legislation, such as s.2 of the Chronically Sick and Disabled Persons Act 1970, s.4 of the Disabled Persons (Services, Consultation and Representation) Act 1986 and s.47(2) of the National Health Service and Community Care Act 1990.

WHAT IS A CARE AND SUPPORT NEED?

1–096   In *R. v Gloucestershire CC Ex p Barry*, which concerned s.2 of the Chronically Sick and Disabled Persons Act 1970, Lord Lloyd made the following observation about a need:

> "The word 'need' like most English words has different shades of meaning. You can say to an overworked Q.C. at the end of a busy term 'You look as though you need a holiday.' The word 'need' in section 2 is not used in that sense; which is not to say that there may not be disabled people living in very restricted circumstances who may not *need* a holiday in the sense which Parliament intended. To need is not the same as to want. 'Need' is the lack of what is essential for the ordinary business of living."[2]

In *R. (M) v Slough Borough Council*, Baroness Hale considered the meaning of the words "care and attention" which had appeared in s.21 of the National Assistance Act 1948 and related to the provision of residential care. Although the Care Act repeals the 1948 Act, the judgment continues to provide useful guidance generally about the nature of a social care need:

> "I remain of the view . . . that the natural and ordinary meaning of the words 'care and attention' in this context is 'looking after'. Looking after means doing something for the person being cared for which he cannot or should not be expected to do for himself: it might be household tasks which an old person can no longer perform or can only perform with great difficulty; it might be protection from risks which a mentally disabled person cannot perceive; it might be personal care, such as feeding, washing or toileting. This is not an exhaustive list. The provision of medical care is expressly excluded."[3]

In the same case, Lord Neuberger observed that a "need" is a flexible word, and plainly means "more than merely 'want'", but it falls short of 'cannot survive without'".[4] He went on to say that:

> "I do not consider that 'care and attention' can extend to accommodation, food or money alone (or, indeed, together) without more. As a matter of ordinary language, "care and attention" does not, of itself, involve the mere provision of physical things, even things as important as a roof over one's head, cash, or sustenance. Of course, if a person has no home or money, or, even more, if he has no access to food, he may soon become in need of care and attention, but, as already explained, that is beside the point."[5]

The concept of a care and support need must also be interpreted in the light of the prohibitions on the provision of services contained in ss.21 to 23 of the Care Act.

In order to identify a social care need, the courts have noted the role of the social work professional. For example, Lord Lloyd in *Barry* noted that the assessment of needs "against contemporary standards" is left to "the professional judgment of the social worker concerned, just as the need for a bypass operation is left to the professional judgment of the

---

[1] Law Commission, *Adult Social Care*, para.5.23 and Department of Health, *Reforming the Law for Adult Care and Support: The Government's Response to Law Commission Report 326 on Adult Social Care* (TSO, July 2012), Cm.8379, paras 5.5 to 5.8.

[2] *R. v Gloucestershire CC Ex p Barry* [1997] A.C. 584; [1997] 2 W.L.R. 459 at 598.

[3] *R. (M) v Slough Borough Council* [2008] UKHL 52; 11 CCLR 743 at [33].

[4] *R. (M) v Slough Borough Council* [2008] UKHL 52; 11 CCLR 743 at [54].

[5] *R. (M) v Slough Borough Council* [2008] UKHL 52; 11 CCLR 743 at [56].

heart specialist".[1] Similarly, Lady Justice Hale (as she was then) observed in *R. (Wahid) v Tower Hamlets LBC* that "need is a relative concept which trained and experienced social workers are much better equipped to assess than are lawyers and courts provided that they act rationally".[2] The importance of professional judgement in identifying needs has also been recognised by Series and Clements:

"An 'assessment' is a standard tool in social welfare law—be it to determine the need for a heart operation, a judicial review, special educational support and so on. It is the need that has to be the focus of attention—the fact that one heart operation may use more blood than another, or one judicial review takes longer than another is a secondary issue—the need is what we value and the price follows. In assessing the eligibility of a need, we have to rely on professionals (surgeons, judges, social workers)—Michael Lipsky's (1989) 'street-level bureaucrats'—because the nature of their role 'calls for human judgment that cannot be programmed and for which machines cannot substitute' (p.162). Legal obligations of this nature are unruly things: necessitating social workers and home visits; discretion and 'dirty work' (Twigg 2000)—personal care, soiled bedding and disordered spreadsheets."[3]

The statutory guidance links the concept of a need to the "challenges and difficulties" the person faces "because of their condition(s)" and includes an example of where an adult expresses a need regarding their physical condition and mobility.[4] This is consistent with the approach taken in the Care and Support (Eligibility Criteria) Regulations 2015 (SI 2015/313) which provide that needs meet the eligibility criteria only if they arise from or are related to a physical or mental impairment or illness (see A1–274).

HEALTH AND HOUSING NEEDS

The Joint Committee recommended that the legislation should retain s.47(3) of the **1–097** National Health Service and Community Care Act 1990 which had stated that if it appears to a local authority when undertaking an assessment that the person being assessed has a health or housing need, then it is obliged to bring this need to the attention of the relevant health or housing authority, invite them to assist in the assessment, and take into account any services likely to be made available by that authority.[5] The Government argued that this was provided adequately for by duty to promote integration between local authorities and health services (s.3), the duties to co-operate (ss.6 and 7) and the local authority duty to refer adults for an assessment of eligibility for NHS continuing health care (s.12(1)(g)).[6]

The courts have emphasised that social workers should include non-social care needs in their assessments. In *R. (Wahid) v Tower Hamlets LBC* the Court of Appeal held that the local authority was entitled to conclude that the claimant—who had a history of mental illness and lived with his family in overcrowded accommodation—although needed better accommodation, did not have an unmet social care need for more extensive accommodation. He therefore fell to be housed under the Housing Act 1996 rather than social care legislation. The Court commented:

"It would be sad indeed if social workers were, consciously or unconsciously, deterred from identifying needs which properly fall within the province of other services by the fear that they might thereby be taken to be identifying a need for accommodation

---

[1] *R. v Gloucestershire CC Ex p Barry* [1997] A.C. 584; [1997] 2 W.L.R. 459 at 598.

[2] *R. (Wahid) v Tower Hamlets LBC* [2002] EWCA Civ 287; (2002) 5 CCLR 239 at [33].

[3] L. Series and L. Clements, "Putting the Cart Before the Horse: Resource Allocation Systems and Community Care", (2013) 35 *Journal of Social Welfare and Family Law* 207.

[4] Department of Health, *Care and Support Statutory Guidance* (2014), para.6.14.

[5] House of Lords House of Commons Joint Committee on the Draft Care and Support Bill, *Draft Care and Support Bill Report, Session 2012–13*, para.176.

[6] Department of Health, *The Care Bill explained—including a response to consultation and pre-legislative scrutiny on the draft Care and Support Bill*, p.68.

provided by social services. Social workers have traditionally been their clients' strongest advocates with the other agencies of the welfare state. We would be doing those clients no favours if social workers were inhibited in continuing that honourable tradition by the fear that responsibilities which properly lay with others might thereby be laid at social services' door.[1] "

CARER BLIND ASSESSMENTS

1-098   A carer blind assessment provides that when conducting the needs assessment and eligibility determination, the local authority will assess the totality of the adult's needs, regardless of whether a carer is currently meeting any of them. The Law Commission argued that case law prior to the Care Act had established that a need which is being met or could be met by a third party (such as a carer, a disabled facilities grant, or some other service) can nonetheless be an eligible need. Whether the local authority must provide services to meet the need, or whether that need could be met by a carer (or other third party) is properly a matter to be decided at the care planning stage and recorded in the care plan.[2] It recommended that the legislation should make this position clear.[3]

In broad terms this approach is reflected in the Care Act. A local authority should consider all needs when undertaking an assessment, irrespective of whether or not they are being met by the carer. Therefore, it does not follow that just because a carer is currently meeting a person's needs, those needs cannot be eligible needs. Nor does it mean that the need should be considered in isolation without considering the carer's contribution to meeting that need. Rather, as part of the assessment of needs, the local authority should consider if and how the needs are being met and whether this is appropriate. The question of whether a carer is able and willing to meet an eligible need is relevant at the care planning stage. Section 18(7) provides that the duty to meet eligible needs does not apply to such of the adult's needs as are being met by a carer. This approach is confirmed in the statutory guidance:

> "During the assessment, local authorities must consider all of the adult's care and support needs, regardless of any support being provided by a carer. Where the adult has a carer, information on the care that they are providing can be captured during assessment, but it must not influence the eligibility determination. After the eligibility determination has been reached, if the needs are eligible or the local authority otherwise intends to meet them, the care which a carer is providing can be taken into account during the care and support planning stage. The local authority is not required to meet any needs which are being met by a carer who is willing and able to do so, but it should record where that is the case. This ensures that the entirety of the adult's needs are identified and the local authority can respond appropriately if the carer feels unable or unwilling to carry out some or all of the caring they were previously providing."[4]

The guidance goes on to state that:

> "Authorities must only take consideration of whether the adult has a carer, or what needs may be met by a carer after the eligibility determination when a care and support plan is prepared. The determination must be based solely on the adult's needs and if an adult does have a carer, the care they are providing will be taken into account when considering whether the needs must be met. Local authorities are not required to meet any eligible needs which are being met by a carer, but those needs should be recognised and recorded as eligible during the assessment process. This is to ensure that should there be a

[1]   *R. (Wahid) v Tower Hamlets LBC* [2002] EWCA Civ 287; (2002) 5 CCLR 239 at [35].

[2]   See, for example, *R. (Spink) v Wandsworth LBC* [2005] EWCA Civ 302; [2005] 1 W.L.R. 2884 and *R. v Sefton Metropolitan Borough Council Ex p Help the Aged* (1997–98) 1 CCLR 57.

[3]   Law Commission, *Adult Social Care*, paras 5.100 to 5.102.

[4]   Department of Health, *Care and Support Statutory Guidance* (2014), para.6.15. See also para.10.26.

breakdown in the caring relationship, the needs are already identified as eligible, and therefore local authorities must take steps to meet them without further assessment.[1]

Subsection (1)

In order to trigger the duty to assess in s.9(1), it must appear to the local authority that an **1–099** adult may have needs for care and support. This wording closely follows that of the previous assessment duty in s.47(1) of the National Health Service and Community Care Act 1990. There have been some minor drafting amendments to reflect the different context of the Care Act. But in substance the duty remains the same, and it is therefore likely that much of the judicial interpretation of s.47(1) will be carried across to s.9(1). Certainly the express intention of the Law Commission was that the legal effect of s.47(1) should remain undisturbed in the new legal framework.[2]

This subsection retains the low threshold for a needs assessment. This is confirmed by subs.(3) which sets out that the assessment duty applies to those with relatively low levels of need and those that have the finances to fund their own care ("self-funders").

In addition, the assessment duty requires only that the adult must "appear" to have needs for care and support. Therefore it is not necessary in law for the person to request the assessment, formally or otherwise. However, in practice a formal request may be taken as an appearance of need and so will trigger the local authority's duty to undertake an assessment. Furthermore, the duty cannot be discharged by writing to the person to ask for a reply if they want an assessment.[3]

The reference is to care and support that the adult "may have needs for". Consequently, the local authority does not have to be certain that the person has an actual need, and there is also no requirement that the need must be urgent or pressing.

Like the previous s.47(1) National Health Service and Community Care Act 1990 duty, subs.(1) cannot be read as being subject to the local authority's "actual, practical ability to arrange services". Therefore a local authority cannot refuse an assessment on the basis that it does not have in place arrangements to provide services which the individual is likely to need.[4] Similarly, an assessment cannot be refused on the basis that the individual has no prospect of being awarded services because of constraints on local authority resources.[5]

The duty to assess is also not conditional on the adult being ordinarily resident in the local authority's area. The courts have recognised that theoretically this means that persons up and down the country may seek assessments from authorities with which they have no practical connection. Nonetheless, while the local authority may be obliged to assess, it "would be entitled to have regard to another authority's potential or actual responsibilities in deciding whether any action is necessary".[6] It may also be appropriate for the local authority in such a case to undertake a joint assessment with the home local authority or delegate the assessment to the home local authority under s.79. In order to ensure the co-operation of the home local authority, a specific request to co-operate could be issued under s.7 if necessary.

THE OBJECTIVE OF THE NEEDS ASSESSMENT

Subsection (1) provides that assessments should not be service-led and must focus on **1–100** needs alone. The objective of the needs assessment is twofold: to determine whether the person has care and support needs and what those needs may be. The Care Act clearly delineates between the needs assessment and decisions about service provision. The s.9 duty does not contain any reference to the care and support that might be provided following

---

[1] Department of Health, *Care and Support Statutory Guidance* (2014), para.6.119.
[2] Law Commission, *Adult Social Care*, para.5.23.
[3] *R. v Gloucestershire CC Ex p RADAR* (1997–98) 1 CCLR 476.
[4] *R. v Berkshire CC Ex p P* (1997–98) 1 CCLR 141 at 146(E)–(I).
[5] *R. v Bristol CC Ex p Penfold* (1997–98) 1 CCLR 315 at 322(K).
[6] *R. v Berkshire CC Ex p P* (1998) 1 CCLR 141 at 148(K)–149(A).

an assessment; how needs can be met is set out separately in s.8. Only once needs have been identified should they be evaluated against an eligibility framework and a decision made about whether the person is entitled to care and support.

Therefore, it is misleading to state that, for example, a person has a need for a day centre, since it conflates the need with the service. Instead, it would be accurate to say that a person has a need based on, for example, social isolation or lack of structured daytime activities that could be met through the provision of a placement at a day centre. The confusion that can arise in this respect was demonstrated in *R. (McDonald) v Royal Borough of Kensington and Chelsea.*[1] The claimant, Ms McDonald, was not incontinent but due to a small bladder needed to urinate two or three times a night, and due to physical disability needed assistance to reach her commode. She was originally assessed as being in need of assistance to use the commode at night. When the case was first decided by the High Court, it was held that the need should not be read literally but instead it was permissible to examine its underlying rationale and treat it as a need for safe urination at night.[2] However, the Court of Appeal overruled this first instance judgment since it was not open to the judge to disregard the deliberately chosen language of the assessment. But the local authority had in the meantime re-assessed Ms McDonald's needs as being "night-time toileting needs" and "a need to be safe from falling and injuring herself". The Court held this to be a lawful re-assessment of need and therefore the local authority was entitled to meet these needs by withdrawing night-time support and providing pads.[3] This conclusion was endorsed by the Supreme Court. However, Baroness Hale in a dissenting judgment argued that the "the need for help to get to the lavatory or commode is so different from the need for protection from uncontrollable bodily functions that it is irrational to confuse the two, and meet the one need in the way that is appropriate to the other".[4] The European Court of Human Rights agreed with Baroness Hale's general assessment that considerations of human dignity were engaged when someone who could control her bodily functions was obliged to behave as if she could not. The Court held that there had been a violation of art.8 (right to respect for private and family life) of the European Convention on Human Rights in respect of the initial period during which Ms McDonald had been assessed as being in need of assistance to use the commode at night. This was because the local authority had been in breach of its statutory duty to provide care in accordance with its own assessment of need, and therefore the interference with Ms McDonald's private life had not been in "accordance with the law" as required by para.2 of art.8.[5]

The statutory guidance discusses the purpose of the needs assessment in paras 6.9 to 6.12. In broad terms it stresses that the assessment should be outcomes-focused and person-centred.

Subsection (3)

1–101   As noted above (see para.1–099 above), subs.(3) confirms the low threshold for a needs assessment by stating that the duty to carry out a needs assessment applies regardless of the authority's view of the level of the adult's needs for care and support, or the level of the adult's financial resources. This is because the assessment duty in subs.(1) does not specify any level of care and support needs, all that is required to trigger the duty is the appearance of need. Therefore, the duty is triggered even by relatively low levels of needs and where the person is unlikely to be eligible for care and support. This is confirmed by subs.(3)(a).

Moreover, the resources of the individual are not relevant to the decision whether or not to carry out an assessment. This is particularly pertinent for self-funders. As noted above,

---

[1] *R. (McDonald) v Royal Borough of Kensington and Chelsea* [2011] UKSC 33; (2011) 14 CCLR 341.
[2] *R. (McDonald) v Royal Borough of Kensington and Chelsea* [2009] EWHC 1582 (Admin).
[3] *R. (McDonald) v Royal Borough of Kensington and Chelsea* [2010] EWCA Civ 1109; (2010) 13 CCLR 664.
[4] *R. (McDonald) v Royal Borough of Kensington and Chelsea* [2011] UKSC 33; (2011) 14 CCLR 341 at [75].
[5] *McDonald v United Kingdom* (20 May 2014) Application no.4241/12.

under the new funding arrangements it will be in the interests of self-funders to seek an assessment to establish whether or not their needs are eligible and therefore whether their care costs will count towards the cap. The assessment duty is therefore clear that a self-funder who appears to be in need of services will be eligible for an assessment, regardless of the fact that they may have to pay for any service that is provided as a result of that assessment. This is confirmed expressly by subs.(3)(b). The duty also applies regardless of whether the self-funder wishes to arrange care and support for themselves rather than this being undertaken by the local authority

Subsection (4)

    This subsection sets out three matters which must always be addressed by an assessment. **1–102** In broad terms the aim is to ensure that the needs assessment includes a focus on outcomes—both the outcomes to which the well-being principle is addressed and the outcomes identified by the person themselves. This is not an exhaustive list of all matters that an assessment can address.

    First, there must be an assessment of the impact of the adult's needs on their well-being. Section 1(2) defines well-being, in relation to an individual, as relating to any of the following:

- personal dignity (including treatment of the individual with respect);
- physical and mental health and emotional dignity;
- protection from abuse and neglect;
- control by the individual over day-to-day life (including over care and support, or support, provided to the individual and the way in which it is provided);
- participation in work, education, training or recreation;
- social and economic well-being;
- domestic, family and personal relationships;
- suitability of living accommodation; and
- the individual's contribution to society.

    Second, there must be an assessment of the outcomes that the adult wishes to achieve in day-to-day life. Outcomes describe the goals identified by the person being assessed. The need for a focus on outcomes was recommended by the Law Commission which had criticised the use of assessments that focus on the person's problems and perceived deficits and are thereby disabling for the person concerned and fail to support independence.[1]

    Third, there must be an assessment of whether, and if so to what extent, the provision of care and support could contribute to the achievement of the person's outcomes.

Subsection (5)

    In carrying out a needs assessment a local authority is required to involve the adult, any **1–103** carer they may have, and anyone else the adult may ask to be involved in the needs assessment. The adult could ask for a friend or partner to be involved, for example, or ask for their GP or a district nurse to be contacted to provide information relevant to their needs.[2] Where a person lacks capacity to ask, the local authority must also involve any person who appears to be interested in the individual's welfare. The explanatory notes state that the intention is to "allow the adult to set the outcomes they wish to achieve and to be fully involved throughout the assessment process". The notes also point out that the person may be eligible for the support of an advocate under s.67 if the adult would otherwise face difficulty in being involved in the process, for example due to communication problems, and they do not have anyone to support them.[3] The statutory guidance discusses supporting the person to be involved in the assessment in paras 6.30 to 6.32.

---

[1] Law Commission, *Adult Social Care*, paras 5.53 to 5.58.
[2] Department of Health, *Care and Support Statutory Guidance* (2014), para.6.11.
[3] Care Act 2014: Explanatory Notes para.93.

WHAT DOES INVOLVE MEAN?

1–104   The local authority is required to involve the relevant person when undertaking a number of functions under the Care Act. These are:

- carrying out a needs assessment (s.9(5)(a) and (b));
- carrying out a carer's assessment (s.10(7)(a));
- preparing a care and support plan (s.25(3)(a) and (b));
- preparing a support plan (s.25(4)(a) and (b));
- revising a care and support plan (s.27(2)(b)(i) and (ii));
- revising a support plan (s.27(3)(b)(i) and (ii));
- carrying out a child's needs assessment (s.59(2)(a) and (b));
- carrying out child's carer's assessment (s.61(3)(a)); and
- carrying out young carer's assessment (s.64(3)(a) and (b)).

In the draft Care and Support Bill the equivalent requirement in cl.9(5) was to "consult". The requirement was altered by the Government to meet the concerns of "those who felt local authorities should be required to actively involve people, not just consult them, in the assessment process".[1]   As noted above, the explanatory notes confirm the Government's intention to ensure that the adult is "fully involved" throughout the assessment process.[2]

However, the courts have struggled to discern a difference between "consult" and "involve". For example, the High Court has concluded that the difference is minimal; both terms did not entail a right to be party to the making of any decisions, and being involved means no more than informed and able to express a view.[3]   This case as a whole related to the different context of NHS planning and strategic decision-making, which did not involve a requirement to involve individuals but rather the public in general. Nevertheless, the discussion on the legal meaning of the term involve is likely to be highly relevant to the interpretation of subs.(5).

Involving a person may involve providing them with an advocate. The right to advocacy in s.67(1) of the Care Act expressly applies where a local authority is required by the relevant provision to involve the individual in the exercise of a function. This includes when carrying out a needs assessment (see s.67(3)). The statutory guidance confirms that "supported decision-making" must be carried out if the person is unable to request the assessment or struggles to express their needs, as well as a capacity assessment.[4]   The concept of supported decision-making is discussed at para.1–270.

WHEN SHOULD A PERSON NOT BE INVOLVED?

1–105   Normally duties to consult or involve people in decision-making are subject to certain caveats. For example, the Community Care Assessment Directions 2004 (which subs.(5) replaced) required that when conducting a needs assessment, the local authority must consult any carer where "appropriate". However, subs.(5) contains no such caveats. On the face of it, a carer and any other person who the adult asks to be involved must be involved even if this is not possible or viewed as inappropriate. In other places the Care Act does state that the duty to involve or consult only arises where it is "feasible" to do so. The main examples are when a local authority is reviewing an independent personal budget (see s.28(5)) when the NHS body is consulting a carer before it gives an assessment notice

---

[1] Department of Health, *The Care Bill explained—including a response to consultation and pre-legislative scrutiny on the draft Care and Support Bill* (TSO, July 2012) Cm.8386, para.54.
[2] Care Act 2014: Explanatory Notes para.93.
[3] *Smith v North Eastern Derbyshire Primary Care Trust* [2006] EWHC 1138 (Admin); [2006] ACD 75 at [4].
[4] Department of Health, *Care and Support Statutory Guidance* (2014), para.6.9.

under the delayed discharge regime (see Sch.3 para.1(4)(b)). This suggests that the absence of a similar caveat in subs.(5) was deliberate.

The Law Commission argued that any duty to consult in this regard would have to make some allowance for the very rare case where such consultation or involvement was realistically impossible. This might be because the person implacably refuses engagement, or it would involve serious risk to the assessor, or consultation with a carer might cause the cared-for person considerable emotional distress, or visa versa. But the Commission's intention was that the test should set a high threshold and make it clear that such cases would be rare and exceptional. It anticipated a test of something higher than "reasonable practicability". The Commission also felt that the code of practice would be valuable in indicating the kind of situation envisaged.[1] However, this test has not been stated on the face of the Care Act.

Nevertheless, the local authority will need to consider the adult's rights to private life under art.8 of the European Convention on Human Rights. This will be particularly important where, for example, the adult does not want the person to be involved or the person is in an abusive relationship with the adult. In a case where the statutory obligation to involve the person would constitute an interference with the adult's art.8(1) rights, it is submitted that the local authority will need to consider whether involvement is justified and proportionate in the particular circumstances of the case. In a small number of cases, therefore, it is possible that art.8(1) will preclude any active involvement of the person in the assessment or require the authority to consider whether the person could be involved in such a way that does not infringe art.8(1). It is also possible that such cases will trigger the duty to make safeguarding enquiries under s.42—where the requirement to "involve" does not apply.

In involving other people, local authorities will need to consider data protection law, such as adult's art.8(1) rights particularly when the adult in question lacks capacity to consent to the disclosure of information. In *Z v Finland* the European Court of Human Rights stated:

> "In this connection, the Court will take into account that the protection of personal data, not least medical data, is of fundamental importance to a person's enjoyment of his or her right to respect for private and family life as guaranteed by art. 8 of the Convention. Respecting the confidentiality of health data is a vital principle in the legal systems of all the Contracting Parties to the Convention. It is crucial not only to respect the sense of privacy of a patient but also to preserve his or her confidence in the medical profession and in the health services in general. Without such protection, those in need of medical assistance may be deterred from revealing such information of a personal and intimate nature as may be necessary in order to receive appropriate treatment and, even, from seeking such assistance, thereby endangering their own health and, in the case of transmissible diseases, that of the community . . . The domestic law must therefore afford appropriate safeguards to prevent any such communication or disclosure of personal health data as may be inconsistent with the guarantees in art.8 of the Convention . . .".[2]

The duty to involve the adult in the needs assessment also needs to be considered alongside the right to refuse an assessment under s.11 (see 1–126 below). In most cases the adult will have consented to the assessment, but in some cases the assessment will need to proceed in the face of a refusal (namely if the person lacks capacity or there are safeguarding concerns). Ensuring the involvement of the person may be challenging in these circumstances and may require assertive attempts to engage the adult, for example through advocacy support or the offer of a supported self-assessment (see below). In the face of outright refusal to engage, the authority will need to document clearly all its attempts to involve the adult.

---

[1] Law Commission, *Adult Social Care*, para.5.74.
[2] *Z v Finland* [1997] 25 EHRR 371 at [95].

SELF-ASSESSMENT

1–106   One way of involving the adult is through self-assessment. The term self-assessment can indicate a range of options giving individuals a varying degree of control over their assessment. Self-assessments can be co-produced with the local authority or they can be "pure", in the sense that the entire assessment process is carried out by the individual with minimum involvement by the local authority.

Section 9(1) places a duty on the *local authority* to assess. Therefore a "pure" self-assessment—in the sense that the local authority intends to rely on a self-assessment alone to assess a person's needs without any validation or review of the assessment—would require a delegation of the assessment duty to the person in accordance with s.79.

However, s.79(6) provides that anything done (or failed to be done) by the third party in carrying out any function delegated to them is treated as done (or not done) by the local authority itself. This means that the delegation of the assessment does not absolve the local authority from ultimate responsibility for ensuring the function is carried out properly and in accordance with all relevant statutory obligations.

A co-produced self-assessment—where the local authority retains sufficient control to be able to satisfy themselves that the assessment is adequate and appropriate to identify the person's needs—does not require the use of delegation since it is consistent with s.9(1).[1]

However, s.12(1)(e) requires the Government to make regulations which specify circumstances in which the adult to whom the assessment relates may carry out the assessment jointly with the local authority. The relevant regulations refer to such an assessment as a "supported self-assessment".[2]   The establishment of a separate provision under s.12(1)(e) suggests that a supported self-assessment means something more than the local authority involving the service user in order to inform its own assessment for the purposes of s.9(5). The statutory guidance describes supported self-assessments in the following terms:

"A supported self-assessment is an assessment carried out jointly by the adult with care and support needs or carer and the local authority. It places the individual in control of the assessment process to a point where they themselves complete their assessment form. Whilst it is the person filling in the assessment form, the duty to assess the person's needs, and in doing so ensure that they are accurate and complete, remains with the local authority".[3]

The legal framework for supported self-assessments is discussed below at paras 1–141 and A1–189.

PEOPLE WHO LACK CAPACITY

1–107   Subsection (5)(c) provides that where the person lacks capacity to ask the local authority to involve a person in the assessment, the authority must consult any person who appears to be interested in the adult's welfare. Therefore the relevant test of capacity is the ability to identify or ask for any specific person or people in general to be involved in the assessment.

The Joint Committee recommended that in the case of a person lacking capacity the list of those who must be consulted should include those concerned for the person's care and well-being in accordance with s.4(7)(b) of the Mental Capacity Act 2005.[4]   The Government originally rejected this recommendation arguing that the 2005 Act already requires local authorities to consult those persons listed in s.4 of that Act and there is no need to reproduce this requirement in the legislation.[5]

---

[1]   *R. v Commission for Racial Equality Ex p Cottrell and Rothon* [1980] 1 W.L.R. 1580.
[2]   Care and Support (Assessment) Regulations 2014 (SI 2014/2827), reg.2.
[3]   Department of Health, *Care and Support Statutory Guidance* (2014) para.6.44.
[4]   House of Lords House of Commons Joint Committee on the Draft Care and Support Bill, *Draft Care and Support Bill Report, Session 2012–13*, para.179.
[5]   Department of Health, *The Care Bill explained—including a response to consultation and pre-legislative scrutiny on the draft Care and Support Bill*, pp.68 to 69.

However, subs.(5)(c) does now refer to any person who appears to be interested in the individual's welfare. This would appear to be a wider obligation than that contained in s.4 of the 2005 Act which is to "take into account" their views (rather than "involve" them) and only applies if it is practical and appropriate to consult them.

Subsection (6)

This subsection requires that in parallel with the needs assessment, the local authority **1–108** must consider other matters that could contribute to achieving the person's outcomes, and the provision of prevention or information and advice services.

OTHER MATTERS THAT COULD CONTRIBUTE TO ACHIEVING THE PERSON'S OUTCOMES

Under subs.(6)(a) the local authority must *also* consider when carrying out an assessment **1–109** whether, and if so to what extent, other matters could contribute to the achievement of the person's outcomes. According to the explanatory notes "this might include the adult's own capabilities and what they may be able to do themselves to achieve those outcomes".[1] During the passage of the Care Bill through the House of Commons the Government explained that:

> "The assessment that we are legislating for here is not just a question of 'Do you pass or fail a eligibility test?' It has a much richer purpose than that, which is to identify what can be done to reduce the deterioration of a condition and what can be done to help an individual and their family to support themselves."[2]

The origins of subs.(6)(a) can be traced back to the Joint Committee's recommendation that legislation should include a provision to "support people planning to achieve well-being within their own resources". The intention was to "frame assessment as a discussion about the additional support people may need to maintain or achieve well-being".[3] In response, the Government inserted this provision into subs.(4) as one of the matters that must always be addressed by an assessment. This was one of a number of revisions that were introduced to reflect a more "asset-based" approach to prevention in both assessment and planning; for instance s.12(1)(c) provides that local authorities can be required to carry out assessments in a proportionate way that reflects the needs of the individual.[4]

However, this provision was criticised in the House of Lords for blurring the distinction between an assessment being about what the needs are and how needs can be met other than through the provision of services before any decision about eligibility has been made.[5] The Government in response explained that its purpose is not to suggest that support from friends and family should replace more formal types of care and support:

> "However, it recognises that in order to make the connections to the variety of support available in the community, the local authority should consider how these matters, along with more formal care and support provision, could be of benefit in achieving the adult's outcomes."[6]

To address these concerns the Government amended the Bill to remove the requirement **1–110** to assess the adult's capabilities and other matters as part of the needs assessment. Instead it

---

[1] Care Act 2014: Explanatory Notes para.94.

[2] *Hansard* (House of Commons: Public Bill Committee), 14 January 2014 (AM): Third Sitting, col.114 (Norman Lamb MP).

[3] House of Lords House of Commons Joint Committee on the Draft Care and Support Bill, *Draft Care and Support Bill Report, Session 2012–13*, para.173.

[4] Department of Health, *The Care Bill explained—including a response to consultation and pre-legislative scrutiny on the draft Care and Support Bill*, para.56.

[5] *Hansard* (House of Lords), 9 July 2013, Vol.747, col.260 (Baroness Wheeler).

[6] *Hansard* (House of Lords), 9 July 2013, Vol.747, col.263 (Earl Howe).

added a subs.(6)(a) which provides for a consideration of such matters to happen separate to, but alongside, the needs assessment. The intention is that:

"Local authorities should have a discussion with adults or carers in parallel to the assessment, considering how their own capabilities and any other matters can help to achieve the outcomes they want to achieve on a daily basis."[1]

Baroness Pitkeathley welcomed the amendments, stating:

"Disability and carers' organisations have very serious concerns that the original wording would lead to local authorities making assumptions about what families could provide without conducting a thorough assessment of a person's needs and then carefully considering how those needs could best be met, particularly taking into consideration the family's willingness to provide that care."[2]

However, she queried whether the wording "might be available in the community" would lead local authorities to view community services as an automatic alternative to statutory services and therefore create a further barrier for those in need of statutory support. In particular she argued that local authorities should not look to families and carers "to provide more care as a get out clause, if you like, from providing statutory services".[3] In response, the Government confirmed that the intention "is not to place extra responsibilities on carers and families, nor to delay local authorities in providing statutory services" and committed to make this clear in guidance.[4] The statutory guidance confirms that—when considering a person's own capabilities and the role of support from family and others—local authorities should not assume that others are willing or able to take up caring roles, and should consider how supporting the adult can prevent a young carer from undertaking inappropriate or excessive care and support responsibilities.[5] Considering the person's strengths and capabilities is further discussed in paras 6.63 to 6.64 of the statutory guidance. This includes a statement that:

"Any suggestion that support could be available from family and friends should be considered in light of their appropriateness, willingness and ability to provide any additional support and the impact on them of doing so. It must also be based on the agreement of the adult or carer in question."[6]

PREVENTION OR INFORMATION AND ADVICE SERVICES

1–111   Under subs.(6)(b) the local authority must consider whether the person would benefit from its prevention or information and advice services (provided under ss.2 or 4), or anything else that might be available in the community. The explanatory notes suggest that, for example, the local authority might consider "it would benefit the adult to undergo a reablement programme, and this could take place in parallel with the assessment process".[7] Similar to subs.(6)(a), this subsection was added by the Government at report stage in the House of Lords. It was included as a response to concerns that the assessment process was insufficiently supportive of the focus of the Bill on the prevention of need. This requires a local authority to consider at the time of the assessment if any universal services available locally, whether provided by the local authority under s.2 or s.4 or by another organisation would be of benefit to the person. The original version of the Care Bill, as introduced in the House of Lords, provided that such a consideration took place only

[1] *Hansard* (House of Lords), 14 October 2013, Vol.748, col.270 (Earl Howe).
[2] *Hansard* (House of Lords), 14 October 2013, Vol.748, col.271.
[3] *Hansard* (House of Lords), 14 October 2013, Vol.748, cols 271 to 272.
[4] *Hansard* (House of Lords), 14 October 2013, Vol.748, col.278 (Earl Howe).
[5] Department of Health, *Care and Support Statutory Guidance* (2014), paras 2.48 to 2.51.
[6] Department of Health, *Care and Support Statutory Guidance* (2014) para.6.64.
[7] Care Act 2014: Explanatory Notes para.95.

after the eligibility determination (in s.13).[1] This was replaced by subs.(6)(b). According to the Government:

> "This would support situations where, for example, a local authority might decide to defer the final eligibility determination until the person or carer has taken part in a preventive service, such as a reablement programme".[2]

In response to a question from Lord Low on whether an assessment will be deemed necessary where preventive services may be of benefit, even if someone is unlikely to be eligible, the Government (referring to the amendments which introduced subs.(6)(b)) stated:

> "The duty to assess in [section 9] is independent of the provisions on prevention. Amendments 33 and 45 make it clear that preventive services should be considered during the assessment rather than having to wait for the eligibility determination. This will mean that people can be advised during the assessment on their preventive needs, whether or not they have eligible needs."[3]

The statutory guidance confirms that the need to consider prevention applies "regardless of whether, in fact, the adult or carer is assessed as having any care and support needs or support needs". This is to ensure that as part of the assessment process, "the local authority considers the capacity of the person to manage their needs or achieve the outcomes which matter to them", and "allows for access to preventative support before a decision is made on whether the person has eligible needs". The guidance also emphasises the need to provide information and advice on prevention.[4]

The statutory guidance goes on to suggest prevention should be considered in parallel with the needs assessment, and that:

> "The local authority may 'pause' the assessment process to allow time for the benefits of such activities to be realised, so that the final assessment of need (and determination of eligibility) is based on the remaining needs which have not been met through such interventions. For example, if the local authority believes that a person may benefit from a short-term reablement service which is available locally, it may put that in place and complete the assessment following the provision of that service."[5]

Assessment of a carer's needs for support

10.—(1) Where it appears to a local authority that a carer may have needs for **1–112** support (whether currently or in the future), the authority must assess—

    (a) whether the carer does have needs for support (or is likely to do so in the future), and

    (b) if the carer does, what those needs are (or are likely to be in the future).

    (2) An assessment under subsection (1) is referred to in this Part as a "carer's assessment".

    (3) "Carer" means an adult who provides or intends to provide care for another adult (an "adult needing care"); but see subsections (9) and (10).

    (4) The duty to carry out a carer's assessment applies regardless of the authority's view of—

    (a) the level of the carer's needs for support, or

    (b) the level of the carer's financial resources or of those of the adult needing care.

---

[1] Care Bill (HL Bill 001 2013–2014, as introduced) cl.13(2)(b).

[2] *Hansard* (House of Lords), 14 October 2013, Vol.748, col.270 (Earl Howe).

[3] *Hansard* (House of Lords), 14 October 2013, Vol.748, col.278 (Earl Howe).

[4] Department of Health, *Care and Support Statutory Guidance* (2014), paras 2.47 and 2.52 to 2.53.

[5] Department of Health, *Care and Support Statutory Guidance* (2014), paras 6.61 and 6.62.

(5) A carer's assessment must include an assessment of—

(a) whether the carer is able, and is likely to continue to be able, to provide care for the adult needing care,

(b) whether the carer is willing, and is likely to continue to be willing, to do so,

(c) the impact of the carer's needs for support on the matters specified in section 1(2),

(d) the outcomes that the carer wishes to achieve in day-to-day life, and

(e) whether, and if so to what extent, the provision of support could contribute to the achievement of those outcomes.

(6) A local authority, in carrying out a carer's assessment, must have regard to—

(a) whether the carer works or wishes to do so, and

(b) whether the carer is participating in or wishes to participate in education, training or recreation.

(7) A local authority, in carrying out a carer's assessment, must involve—

(a) the carer, and

(b) any person whom the carer asks the authority to involve.

(8) When carrying out a carer's assessment, a local authority must also consider—

(a) whether, and if so to what extent, matters other than the provision of support could contribute to the achievement of the outcomes that the carer wishes to achieve in day-to-day life, and

(b) whether the carer would benefit from the provision of anything under section 2 or 4 or of anything which might be available in the community.

(9) An adult is not to be regarded as a carer if the adult provides or intends to provide care—

(a) under or by virtue of a contract, or

(b) as voluntary work.

(10) But in a case where the local authority considers that the relationship between the adult needing care and the adult providing or intending to provide care is such that it would be appropriate for the latter to be regarded as a carer, that adult is to be regarded as such (and subsection (9) is therefore to be ignored in that case).

(11) The references in this section to providing care include a reference to providing practical or emotional support.

(12) This section is subject to section 11(5) to (7) (refusal by carer of assessment).

GENERAL NOTE

1–113   The 2011 census found that 5.4 million people in England were providing unpaid care, and a third of those were providing 20 or more hours of care a week (an increase of 5 per cent on 2001 figures).[1] Research shows that the general health of carers deteriorates incrementally with the increasing hours of care provided. Many carers feel forced to give up work, or reduce their working hours, and find it difficult to return to the labour market. The vast majority of carers are not in contact with social care services.[2] Professor Luke Clements has contrasted the emergence of the "carer's movement" over the last 50

---

[1] Office for National Statistics, *2011 Census: Key Statistics for England and Wales, March 2011* (2012).

[2] A summary of the research is provided in HM Government, *Carers Strategy: Second National Action Plan 2014–2016* (October 2014) pp.9 to 11.

years with that of the suffragettes, disabled people's movement, and LGBT rights cam-paign. He argues that a tipping point has been reached whereby the key social and political ingredients are in place for carers to become a protected group for the purposes of discrimination law and for caring to be recognised formally as a human right. He also argues that the Care Act is a "distraction" in this respect and fails to address the severe disadvantages that carers experience.[1]

Prior to the Care Act, the rights of carers to a separate assessment, or to have their needs taken into account in the assessment of the adult needing care, were set out in a range of legislation. During the passage of the Care Bill through Parliament, this legislation was described as "a mishmash of relic semi-serviceable carers' Acts".[2]

The main provisions governing carer's assessments were the Carers (Recognition and Services) Act 1995 and Carers and Disabled Children Act 2000. Both of these Acts placed a duty on a local authority to assess a carer if they provided a substantial amount of care on a regular basis and formally requested an assessment.[3] The Law Commission was critical of these criteria. First, it argued that the substantial and regular test for an assessment was put-ting the cart before the horse, because a local authority would not know how much care was being provided until it had completed the assessment. Secondly, the Commission pointed out that the request mechanism was underused, which in part was because many carers did not identify themselves as being carers, but instead saw themselves as, for example, the per-son's husband, wife, brother sister or friend. In effect, such carers were excluded from the assessment duty. The Commission concluded that in principle there was no convincing reason why the threshold for a carer's assessment should not be the same as the threshold for a needs assessment. However, it recognised the practical concerns that lowering the threshold for a carer's assessment may lead to an increase in workload. The Commission argued this was unlikely because its consultation had indicated that many local authorities were not applying the high legal threshold and were simply assessing carers when they found them or undertaking assessments under the guise of initial pre-assessments to deter-mine if the criteria were met. In effect, local authorities were already doing what the new law would require them to do. It therefore recommended that the duty to assess a carer should apply to where it appears to a local authority that a carer may have needs for support, or will have upon commencing the caring role.[4]

The Government accepted the Law Commission's recommendations for carer's assess-ments.[5] Section 10 creates a single duty to assess carers. It requires a local authority to carry out an assessment, known as a "carer's assessment", where it appears that a carer may have needs for support at that time, or in the future. The statutory guidance does not discuss carers separately, although it does contain individual carer sections throughout (see 1–231 below). Carer's assessments are discussed in paras 6.16 to 6.19 of the statutory guidance.

There were 400,000 carer assessments carried out in 2010–11. The Government's impact assessment stated that the number of assessments of carers receiving an assessment under the Care Act would increase by between 230,000 to 250,000.[6] The duty to assess a carer replaces existing duties in relation to the assessment of adult carers in the Carers (Recognition and Services) Act 1995 and the Carers and Disabled Children Act 2000.

The language of the Care Act distinguishes between carers who have needs for "sup-port", while cared-for people have needs for "care and support".

---

[1] Luke Clements, "Caring as A Human Right? The Pauline Thompson Memorial Lecture 2014" (2014), 4(4) *Elder Law Journal* 375.

[2] *Hansard* (House of Lords), 21 May 2013, Vol.745, col.766 (Baroness Tyler).

[3] Carers (Recognition and Services) Act 1995 s.1(1) and Carers and Disabled Children Act 2000 s.1(1).

[4] Law Commission, *Adult Social Care*, paras 7.10 to 7.28.

[5] Department of Health, *Reforming the Law for Adult Care and Support: The Government's Response to Law Commission Report 326 on Adult Social Care* (TSO, July 2012), Cm.8379, paras 7.4 to 7.7.

[6] Department of Health, Impact Assessment: Care and Support Legal Reform (Pt 1 of the Care Bill: IA No 6107, paras 3.35 and 3.31.

IDENTIFICATION OF CARERS

1–114   The Care Act places great emphasis on carer's assessment, but less on the identification of carers. In the House of Commons there was a concerted attempt to amend the Bill to require various public bodies (particularly the NHS) to identify and support carers. Research by Macmillan Cancer Support claimed that 70 per cent of carers of people with cancer come into contact with health professionals but only 5 per cent of that group receives a carer's assessment. Moreover only one in three of those surveyed had even heard of a carer's assessment.[1] At second reading this research, and the importance of identifying carers, was raised separately by three opposition MPs.[2]

During Committee stage in the House of Commons there was an attempt to amend the Bill to require co-operation between local authorities and NHS bodies in relation to identifying carers and promoting their well-being. The Government however argued this was unnecessary given that:

- section 6 already requires NHS bodies and local authorities to co-operate with each other when exercising their respective functions relevant to care and support, including those relating to carers;
- there are existing duties under the Health Act 2009 on promoting and safeguarding the health and well-being of patients, which would cover patients who are carers; and
- changes to GPs contracts will mean that people aged over 75 will have a named GP responsible for their care, which will include identifying carers.

The Minister also agreed to consider whether the statutory guidance might usefully refer to the identification and support of carers as an example of co-operation, in addition to the specific duties that already exist in the Care Act in this regard.[3]

At Report Stage, Liz Kendall MP tabled an amendment to require the NHS to identify and promote the health of carers. The Government confirmed that the guidance will "absolutely reinforce the importance of co-operation between the NHS and local authorities on local authorities' duty to identify carers". It also confirmed that NHS England was developing an action plan for identifying and supporting carers, and that a plan for out-of-hours hospital care will be published which will emphasise the importance of GPs "identifying and supporting carers by directing them to information, advice and support".[4] The amendment was put to a vote and defeated by 269 to 212 votes.[5]

At Committee stage Liz Kendall MP tabled amendments which would have required schools and universities to identify and have a policy in place to help young carers. However, the Government argued that a legislative approach "is not in keep with the Government's drive to reduce burdens on schools and free them from central prescription".[6] It also pointed to Government policy initiatives and support already being provided in schools and universities.[7]

---

[1] Macmillan Cancer Research, "More than a Million" (2012).

[2] *Hansard* (House of Commons), 16 December 2013, Vol.572, cols 519 to 520 (Barbara Keeley MP), 524 (Meg Munn MP) 556 (Sharon Hodgson MP).

[3] *Hansard* (House of Commons: Public Bill Committee), 9 January 2014: First Sitting (AM), cols 21 to 25 (Norman Lamb MP).

[4] *Hansard* (House of Commons), 10 March 2014, Vol.577, col.89 (Norman Lamb MP). The plans referred to are: *NHS England, NHS England's Commitment to Carers* (April 2014); and Department of Health, *Transforming Primary Care: Safe, Proactive, Personalised Care for Those who Need it Most* (April 2014).

[5] *Hansard* (House of Commons), 10 March 2014, Vol.577, cols 97 to 101.

[6] *Hansard* (House of Commons: Public Bill Committee), 4 February 2014: Fifteenth Sitting, col.590 (Norman Lamb MP).

[7] *Hansard* (House of Commons: Public Bill Committee), 4 February 2014: Fifteenth Sitting, cols 590 to 591 (Norman Lamb MP).

Subsection (1)

In order to trigger the duty to assess in subs.(1), it must appear to the local authority that a **1–115** carer may have needs for support (whether currently or in the future). There is no requirement to request an assessment or for the carer to be providing, or intending to provide a substantial amount of care on a regular basis. The wording of subs.10(1) follows that of the duty to assess an adult needing support in s.9(1). Therefore, subs.10(1) similarly establishes a low threshold for a carer's assessment. In particular the duty applies when it "appears" that a carer "may" have needs for support. This means that most of the points made in para.1–099 above in relation to the low threshold for a needs assessment, will also apply to a carer's assessment. In particular, the duty will apply:

- irrespective of whether a formal request for an assessment has been made by the carer (although a formal request may be taken as evidence of the appearance of need);
- where the carer has relatively low levels of need for support or has the finances to fund their own support (this is confirmed by subs.(4));
- in cases where the local authority is not certain that the carer has an actual need; and
- whether or not the local authority has in place arrangements to provide services which the carer is likely to need, or thinks that the carer has no prospect of being awarded services.

The assessment duty is also triggered not just on the basis of apparent current needs but also possible future need. Therefore, eligibility for an assessment will arise where a carer intends to start providing care and will have needs for support upon doing so, but has not yet started caring. This situation may arise, for example, where the carer decides to leave their employment to start caring full-time.

THE OBJECTIVE OF THE CARER'S ASSESSMENT

Subsection (1) provides that carer's assessments should not be service-led and must **1–116** focus on needs alone. The objective of the assessment is twofold: to determine whether a carer has support needs either currently or, possibly, in the future and what those needs may be. The Care Act clearly delineates between the carer's assessment and decisions about service provision. The s.10 duty does not contain any reference to the support that might be provided following an assessment; how needs can be met is set out separately in s.8. Only once needs have been identified should they be evaluated against an eligibility framework and a decision made about whether the carer is entitled to support. The statutory guidance also emphasises that the assessment must consider the sustainability of the caring relationship and the outcomes the carer wants to achieve.[1]

See para.1–100 above, for further discussion about needs led assessments.

NHS CONTINUING HEALTH CARE

During the passage of the Care Bill, at Committee stage in the House of Commons, the **1–117** Government rejected an attempt to amend this section to impose a specific duty on the local authority to assess the ability of a carer to provide, or to continue to provide, care of an individual who is being assessed for NHS continuing health care in the community. In doing so it argued that:

"We propose to remove the existing requirement that a carer should be providing, or intend to provide, substantial care on a regular basis. Instead, the local authority will be required to offer a carer's assessment where there may be a need for support. That is the only bar that needs to be cleared—a very low one. Where the person whom the

---

[1] Department of Health, *Care and Support Statutory Guidance* (2014), paras 6.18 to 6.19.

carer supports is being assessed for NHS continuing care and wishes their care to be delivered in the community, the local authority is likely to regard the carer as needing to be supported. A carer's assessment would then be triggered."[1]

In addition, if a carer is identified in the course of an NHS continuing health care assessment, the *National Framework for NHS Continuing Health Care and NHS-funded Nursing Care* provides that the clinical commissioning group should:

- inform such carers about their entitlement to have their needs as carer assessed; and
- where appropriate, advise the carers either to contact the local authority or, with their permission, refer them to the local authority for an assessment.[2]

Subsection (3)

1–118   A carer is defined as an adult who provides or intends to provide care for another adult. Subsection (11) makes clear that care includes the provision of practical or emotional support.

Young carers (defined as carers aged under 18 caring for an adult) and child's carers (defined as an adult, including a parent, who has needs for support as a result of caring for a child) are excluded from this duty. As a result of amendments introduced by the Children and Families Act 2014 both groups now have express rights to assessments under the Children Act 1989. In addition, ss.61 to 66 of the Care Act give both groups rights to transition assessments. The position of young carers and child's carers is considered in more detail under ss.60 to 66 below.

Subsection (4)

1–119   This confirms the low threshold for a carer's assessment by stating that the duty to carry out a carer's assessment applies regardless of the authority's view of the level of the carer's needs for support, or the level of the carer's financial resources or those of the adult needing care. This is because the assessment duty in subs.(1) does not specify any level of support needs, all that is required to trigger the duty is the appearance of need. Therefore, the assessment duty is triggered where the carer has relatively low levels of need for support or has the finances to fund their own support.

Subsection (5)

1–120   This subsection sets out five matters which must always be addressed by a carer's assessment. This is not an exhaustive list of all matters that an assessment can address.

These matters include the carer's ability and willingness to provide care, both now and in the future. The policy guidance on the equivalent provision in the Carers and Disabled Children Act 2000 emphasised that consideration should be given to the carer's attitudes and mental capabilities and not just their physical ability—for example, some may feel under a moral obligation to provide care or "defeated, trapped, or depressed".[3] The implication is that caring is not a legal obligation but only to be done by those "able and willing".

In cases where the carer is unable or unwilling to continue to provide, very serious consequences may arise. In *R. (Hughes) v Liverpool City Council*, the court expressed the view that the shortcomings of the local authority in failing to provide services to meet a severely disabled man's eligible needs would have amounted to a breach of his right to private and family life under art.8 of the European Convention on Human Rights, but for the substantial

---

[1] *Hansard* (House of Commons: Public Bill Committee), 14 January 2014 (AM): Third Sitting, col.106.

[2] Department of Health, *The National Framework for NHS Continuing Healthcare and NHS-funded Nursing Care* (2012), para.54.

[3] Department of Health, *Carers and Disabled Persons Act 2000 and Carers (Equal Opportunities) Act 2004: Combined Policy Guidance (2005)*, para.43.

amount of care provided by his mother. In his general observations, Mr Justice Mitting suggested a potential breach of human rights will arise if "for example, his mother is unable to continue to provide the care that she does owing to her own difficulties, and her efforts are not adequately substituted by Liverpool".[1]

This subsection also provides that there must be an assessment of the impact of the carer's needs on their well-being. Section 1(2) defines well-being, in relation to an individual, as relating to any of the following:

- personal dignity (including the treatment of the individual with respect);
- physical and mental health and emotional dignity;
- protection from abuse and neglect;
- control by the individual over day-to-day life (including over care and support, or support, provided to the individual and the way in which it is provided);
- participation in work, education, training or recreation;
- social and economic well-being;
- domestic, family and personal relationships;
- suitability of living accommodation; and
- the individual's contribution to society.

In addition, the assessment should include a focus on outcomes—both the outcomes to which the well-being principle is addressed and the outcomes identified by the carer themselves.

Subsection (6)

In carrying out the assessment the local authority must also have regard to whether a **1–121** carer works or wishes to work, or participate in, or would like to participate in, education, training or recreation. This subsection replaces and largely consolidates the previous existing requirements of the Carers (Recognition and Services) Act 1995 and Carers and Disabled Children Act 2000. This aspect of the assessment is a crucial element of the carer's ability and willingness to care under subs.(5) and the implication is that local authorities must not, for example, assume a willingness to give up work in order to care.

The statutory guidance discusses considering education, training and employment needs in para.15.73.

Subsection (7)

The local authority must involve the carer and any other person nominated by the carer, **1–122** when carrying out a carer's assessment. See discussion at paras 1–104 to 1–105 above in respect of the meaning of involve and when involvement might not be appropriate.

The person with care and support needs is not involved automatically in the carer's assessment, but only if they are nominated by the carer.

Involving a person may involve providing them with an advocate. The right to advocacy in s.68 of the Care Act expressly applies to this subsection (see s.68(3)(b)).

Subsection (8)

This provision is explained in paras 1–108 to 1–110 above. **1–123**

Subsections (9) and (10)

Prior to the Care Act, the Carers (Recognition and Services) Act 1995 and Carers and **1–124** Disabled Children Act 2000 excluded from the definition of a carer (and thus eligibility for a carer's assessment) someone who provides or will provide the care in question by virtue of a contract of employment or other contract with any person, or as a volunteer for a voluntary organisation.

---

[1] *R. (Hughes) v Liverpool City Council* [2005] EWHC 428 (Admin); (2005) 8 CCLR 243 at [37]–[38].

In its consultation paper, the Law Commission proposed that these exclusions should be maintained. However, it also felt that certain categories of carers who receive payment for the care they provide should not be excluded from the definition of a carer. These were:

- a previously unpaid carer who now receives payment for their services through direct payments received by the cared-for person;
- a carer who is paid for some but not all of the care they provide; and
- a carer where the local authority believes the caring relationship is not principally a commercial one.

It argued that carers in these situations are often in a different position—with different relationships and personal dynamics at play—than an ordinary paid or volunteer care worker, and so should not be automatically excluded from accessing a carer's assessment.

The standard, but not only, situation envisaged was where someone had been an unpaid family carer, and was now receiving some payment from the cared-for person's direct payment.[1]

Consultation however persuaded the Law Commission that retaining the first two limbs in the form proposed could have resource implications, and might cause the duplication of effort by the local authority. Some local authorities argued that they would end up paying twice for carers: once for a direct payment to the cared-for person to pay the carer for care and secondly for a carer's assessment—with the potential for a third, if a carer is found to have eligible needs for services. Nonetheless, the Commission recommended that something based on the third limb would be useful provided it is recast as a power to assess. This would enable the local authority to control any significant adverse resource implications. In addition, it felt that the reference to commercial should be expanded to include an equivalent relationship between an external volunteer and the cared-for person.[2]

This recommendation has largely been taken forward in the subss. (8) and (9). The definition of a carer is subject to the proviso that those who care on a contractual or volunteering basis are not considered to be carers for the purposes of the Act. However, if the local authority thinks it is appropriate for such an individual (even if there is a contractual or volunteering element to the relationship) to be treated as a carer, then the adult is regarded as a carer and the duty to assess may apply. The statutory guidance suggests that if an adult provides care under contract or as part of voluntary work "they should not normally be regarded as a carer". But it goes on to state that where the adult is also providing care for the same adult outside of those arrangements, the local authority must "consider whether to carry out a carer's assessment for that part of the care they are not providing on a contractual or voluntary basis".[3]

Refusal of assessment

1–125   **11.**—(1) Where an adult refuses a needs assessment, the local authority concerned is not required to carry out the assessment (and s.9(1) does not apply in the adult's case).

(2) But the local authority may not rely on subsection (1) (and so must carry out a needs assessment) if—

(a)   the adult lacks capacity to refuse the assessment and the authority is satisfied that carrying out the assessment would be in the adult's best interests, or

(b)   the adult is experiencing, or is at risk of, abuse or neglect.

(3) Where, having refused a needs assessment, an adult requests the assessment, section 9(1) applies in the adult's case (and subsection (1) above does not).

[1] Law Commission, *Adult Social Care: A Consultation Paper*, Law Commission Consultation Paper No.192 (2010), paras 5.30 to 5.36.
[2] Law Commission, *Adult Social Care*, paras 7.34 to 7.41.
[3] Department of Health, *Care and Support Statutory Guidance* (2014), paras 6.16 to 6.17.

(4) Where an adult has refused a needs assessment and the local authority concerned thinks that the adult's needs or circumstances have changed, section 9(1) applies in the adult's case (but subject to further refusal as mentioned in subsection (1) above).

(5) Where a carer refuses a carer's assessment, the local authority concerned is not required to carry out the assessment (and section 10(1) does not apply in the carer's case).

(6) Where, having refused a carer's assessment, a carer requests the assessment, section 10(1) applies in the carer's case (and subsection (5) above does not).

(7) Where a carer has refused a carer's assessment and the local authority concerned thinks that the needs or circumstances of the carer or the adult needing care have changed, section 10(1) applies in the carer's case (but subject to further refusal as mentioned in subsection (5) above).

GENERAL NOTE

The Law Commission originally consulted on whether the statute should provide a right **1–126** for people with care and support needs to have an assessment on request. Section 4 of the Disabled Person (Services, Consultation and Representation) Act 1986 had provided that a local authority must decide whether the needs of a disabled person call for the provision of services under s.2(1) of the Chronically Sick and Disabled Persons Act 1970, if requested to do so by the disabled person, their representative or any carer. However, the Commission's final report rejected this option for a number of reasons, including that a request mechanism was overly bureaucratic and procedurally difficult, and might obscure the core duty to assess based on the appearance of need.[1]

Instead, the Law Commission considered whether the statute could clarify the legal effect of a refusal to be assessed or a failure to co-operate with an assessment. The previous core assessment duty in s.47(1) of the National Health Service and Community Care Act 1990 had required an assessment to be carried out when it appeared to the local authority that a person to whom they may provide community care services was in need of such services. The consent or agreement of the person assessed was not required, and lack of it did not, on the face of it, affect the mandatory nature of the duty. The Commission's analysis of the available case law (albeit in the different context of the Children Act 1989) concluded that where the refusal to engage with or consent to an assessment arose from or was part of the reason for social services being involved, then refusal should not be final.[2] It was also noted that in respect of service provision, a "persistent and unequivocal refusal" to accept the service in question means that a local authority is entitled to treat its duty as discharged.[3]

The Law Commission argued that there would be two advantages to clarifying this matter. In the first place, it would settle an obscure issue in the law, in such a way as to promote desirable outcomes: that is, perseverance with an assessment where necessary and efficient avoidance of the task when it is not. Secondly, it would facilitate the more expansive vision of the local authority's role suggested by personalisation, without undermining important legal rights. In other words, codifying the refusal of assessment would allow people to self-divert themselves away from assessment, while still taking advantage of universal services and advice and assistance. The Commission's recommendation was that a local authority should be able to accept a person's refusal to have an assessment (or the refusal of someone else with appropriate authority for the person), unless the person lacks capacity in some

---

[1] Law Commission, *Adult Social Care*, paras 5.24 to 5.35.

[2] For example, *R. (J) v Caerphilly County Borough Council* [2005] EWHC 586 (Admin); (2005) 8 CCLR 225 at [55].

[3] *R. v Royal Borough of Kensington and Chelsea Ex p Kujtim* (1999) 2 CCLR 340 at [32].

respect relevant to the assessment or there are safeguarding concerns. It also recommended that the same duty should be applied to carers.[1]

The Government accepted this recommendation, which has been implemented by s.11 (except in respect of carers where there is no power to override the refusal—see subs.(5)). In Parliament, during the passage of the Care Bill, the Government provided a further justification for this section:

> "The [section] also protects the interests of the local authority. Owing to the nature of care and support services, it would be extremely difficult and completely inappropriate to force care and support upon someone who did not wish to receive it."[2]

The statutory guidance refers to s.11 in paras 6.20 to 6.21.

Subsection (1)

1–127   This provides that where an adult has refused a needs assessment, the local authority does not need to carry out the assessment. There is no requirement in respect of the format of a refusal of an assessment. It can be written or verbal. However, the reference is to where an adult "refuses"—rather than to, for example, a reasonable belief that the adult has refused. This indicates that where the person uses a form of words that are ambiguous but nonetheless suggests that they do not want the assessment (for example "I do not like assessments"), the local authority may need to get a formal confirmation that the assessment has been refused. Similarly, the adult's refusal simply to engage in an assessment may not necessarily mean that the duty to assess has been discharged. The challenges of involving an adult who refuses to engage in an assessment are discussed at para.1–105 above.

Subsection (1) only impacts on the duty to assess. The social services authority would still have a power to assess, should it appear to be desirable for some other reason. This might apply for example where the lack of capacity is not clear-cut (see below).

This subsection does not apply to a carer's assessment, which is dealt with separately under subs.(5).

Subsection (2)

1–128   This subsection provides for two situations where the refusal of a needs assessment can be overridden: the adult lacks capacity to refuse the assessment and carrying out the assessment is in their best interests, or the person is experiencing or at risk of abuse or neglect.

ADULT WHO LACKS CAPACITY TO REFUSE THE ASSESSMENT

1–129   A refusal of an assessment would not discharge the local authority's duty if the adult lacks capacity to make this decision and carrying out the assessment is in their best interests. However, in many such cases the lack of capacity will not be clear-cut and can only be established by an assessment of capacity (which presumably they are also likely to refuse). In such cases the local authority may need to persist until the capacity or lack of capacity of the person can been confirmed—or exercise its power to assess (see above).

Section 1(2) of the Mental Capacity Act 2005 provides that a person must be assumed to have capacity unless it is established that they lack capacity. In legal proceedings the burden of proof will fall on the person who asserts that capacity is lacking. As a matter of last resort, if there was evidence to suggest the presumption might be rebutted, the Court of Protection can obtain jurisdiction over a person by ordering them to undergo a capacity assessment.

---

[1] Law Commission, *Adult Social Care*, paras 5.36 to 5.52 and 7.25.
[2] *Hansard* (House of Commons: Public Bill Committee), 14 January 2014 (AM): Third Sitting, col.107 (Norman Lamb MP).

THE ADULT IS EXPERIENCING OR AT RISK OF ABUSE OR NEGLECT

A refusal of an assessment would not discharge the local authority's duty in cases of **1–130** abuse and neglect. This includes current and future abuse and neglect. Most such cases would trigger the local authority's duty to make safeguarding enquiries under s.42. The exceptions would be cases where the adult is able to safeguard themselves for the purposes of s.42(1)(c).

The wording of this subsection points towards the decision-maker being certain that the adult is experiencing or at risk of abuse or neglect. It does not rely expressly on, for example, a reasonable belief or a suspicion of these matters. However, as in the case of a lack of capacity, such cases are often not clear-cut. In such cases the local authority may need to persist until the existence of abuse or neglect can been confirmed or ruled out—or exercise its power to assess (see above). Alternatively, the duty to undertake a safeguarding enquiry under s.42 (which is based on a reasonable belief of abuse or neglect) may be triggered. The relationship between the duty to assess and the safeguarding duty is discussed at para.1–475 below.

The meaning of abuse and neglect is considered in paras 1–483 to 1–484 below.

CAN A REFUSAL BE TAKEN AT FACE VALUE?

The principles in s.1 of the Mental Capacity Act 2005 provide for an assumption of **1–131** capacity and that a person should not be treated as lacking capacity merely on the basis of an unwise decision. Research has suggested that these principles have been interpreted in practice as a requirement to withhold support where people have capacity and are reluctant to engage with services. For example, Brown and Marchant (referring to their study of best interests decision-making in complex cases) found that:

> "A third of the cases involved people and/or carers who shrank from making decisions, avoiding or withdrawing contact with agencies. This highlighted a raft of cases where service refusal was a central issue. The early stages of the process suggested that decision-making should be thought of as a process requiring active support rather than a hands-off approach until this could not be maintained. Timely intervention might have prevented painful choices later because by the time signals had grown loud enough to be heard, some of the issues had become confrontational and options had closed down."[1]

In some cases services may need to persist in the face of an apparent refusal. The refusal may for example have serious implications for others or be generated by one or more of a number of complicated factors, such as fear of social services intervention, co-dependency, lack of full information and mental or physical frailty. There may be a need to at least attempt to build-up a relationship and gain the trust of the adult before the refusal can be taken as final.

It is submitted that in respect of subs.(1) as a minimum, the local authority will need to be clear that:

- the refusal was the person's true position and intention;
- the person has capacity to make this decision;
- there was no undue influence by a third party;
- the person has all relevant information and knows all available options; and
- the person was not experiencing any abuse of neglect.[2]

---

[1] H. Brown and L. Marchant, "Using the Mental Capacity Act in Complex Cases" (2013) 18 *Tizard Learning Disability Review 2.*
[2] See, for example, *Re Z* [2004] EWHC 2817 (Fam); [2005] 1 W.L.R. 959 at [19].

However, in practice if the person refuses to assist in the assessment, it will be difficult to complete an assessment or to develop any form of relationship.

Subsections (3) and (4)

1–132   The refusal of assessment is not final. There are two mechanisms for re-triggering the duty to assess. Under subs.(3) the person themselves may abrogate their refusal by requesting an assessment. This allows them to simply change their minds as to the desirability of an assessment, and for that change of mind to re-engage the statutory duty. Assuming they still satisfy the criteria for an assessment, then for all practical purposes this amounts to a right to an assessment on request.

The second mechanism is set out in subs.(4), which provides that the local authority may override the refusal if it thinks that the adult's needs or circumstances have changed. However, this is subject to further refusal. Therefore, it is likely that the local authority will only take such action if more information had come to light, which raised concerns about capacity or safeguarding such as to override the refusal.

Subsection (5)

1–133   As noted above the Law Commission recommended that the same right that is given to people with care and support needs to refuse an assessment should apply to carers. In other words, there should be a right to refuse that could only be overridden in the face of an incapacitous refusal or if there are underlying safeguarding concerns. However, subs.(5) provides that the refusal by a carer of a carer's assessment would, in all cases, discharge the local authority's duty to assess. This would apply even if the carer lacked capacity to make this decision or in cases of abuse and neglect.

In part this omission is likely to be because if a carer lacked capacity to refuse the assessment, they should be treated as a person with care and support needs and assessed under subs.(1). However, this would not deal adequately with a situation where a carer who lacked capacity to refuse the assessment is both able and willing to provide the care (see s.10(5)). It might be possible that if the carer lacked capacity to refuse an assessment, another person could agree on their behalf if an assessment was considered to be in the carer's best interests, in accordance with ss.1(5) and 4 of the Mental Capacity Act 2005.

If the carer was experiencing, or was at risk of, abuse and neglect, but refused an assessment, then the local authority may need to consider an application for the exercise of the inherent jurisdiction of the High Court (see para.1–460 below). This can be used to put protective measures in place in relation to vulnerable adults who do not fall within the Mental Capacity Act 2005 but whose autonomy may have been compromised through constraint, coercion, undue influence or other vitiating factor. In the case of *DL v A Local Authority* the inherent jurisdiction was invoked in order to protect two elderly parents who lacked capacity as a result of undue influence brought to bear upon them by their son. The subsequent appeal on a point of law, confirmed the availability of the inherent jurisdiction in such cases.[1]

Other possible options may include the use of the criminal law or a civil injunction under the Anti-Social Behaviour, Crime and Policing Act 2014 (see para.1–462 below).

It is also possible that the local authority's duty to make safeguarding enquiries under s.42 may still be relevant if a carer is experiencing abuse or neglect and refuses an assessment. In some cases the carer may have some level of care and support needs (even a relatively low level) which may trigger the s.42 duty (assuming the other criteria are met). The consequences could also be caught in the needs assessment of the adult needing care. Where a carer is perpetrating, or at risk of perpetrating, abuse or neglect, but refused an assessment, then the issues could be dealt with by the s.42 enquiry in relation to the adult needing care.

---

[1]   *DL v A Local Authority* [2011] EWHC 1022 (Fam) and *DL v A Local Authority* [2012] EWCA Civ 253.

It is submitted that the European Convention on Human Rights may require a response from a local authority if a carer refuses an assessment, but their needs may require the provision of services either to the cared-for person or the carer themselves. Under the Convention, a local authority has a positive duty to take reasonable action to prevent a person for whom it is responsible from being subjected to inhuman or degrading treatment and to ensure respect for private home and family life under arts 3 and 8 respectively.[1]

Subsections (6) and (7)

The duty to assess a carer can be re-triggered following a refusal if the carer requests the assessment or if the local authority thinks the needs or circumstances have changed (unless the carer continues to refuse). **1–134**

Assessments under sections 9 and 10: further provision

12.—(1) Regulations must make further provision about carrying out a needs or carer's assessment; the regulations may, in particular— **1–135**

  (a) require the local authority, in carrying out the assessment, to have regard to the needs of the family of the adult to whom the assessment relates;

  (b) specify other matters to which the local authority must have regard in carrying out the assessment (including, in particular, the matters to which it must have regard in seeking to ensure that the assessment is carried out in an appropriate and proportionate manner);

  (c) specify steps that the local authority must take for the purpose of ensuring that the assessment is carried out in an appropriate and proportionate manner;

  (d) specify circumstances in which the assessment may or must be carried out by a person (whether or not an officer of the authority) who has expertise in a specified matter or is of such other description as is specified, jointly with or on behalf of the local authority;

  (e) specify circumstances in which the adult to whom the assessment relates may carry out the assessment jointly with the local authority;

  (f) specify circumstances in which the local authority must, before carrying out the assessment or when doing so, consult a person who has expertise in a specified matter or is of such other description as is specified;

  (g) specify circumstances in which the local authority must refer the adult concerned for an assessment of eligibility for NHS continuing healthcare.

(2) The regulations may include provision for facilitating the carrying out of a needs or carer's assessment in circumstances specified under subsection (1)(d) or (e); they may, for example, give the local authority power to provide the person carrying out the assessment—

  (a) in the case of a needs assessment, with information about the adult to whom the assessment relates;

  (b) in the case of a carer's assessment, with information about the carer to whom the assessment relates and about the adult needing care;

  (c) in either case, with whatever resources, or with access to whatever facilities, the authority thinks will be required to carry out the assessment.

(3) The local authority must give a written record of a needs assessment to—

  (a) the adult to whom the assessment relates,

  (b) any carer that the adult has, if the adult asks the authority to do so, and

---

[1] See for example, *R. (Hughes) v Liverpool City Council* [2005] EWHC 428 (Admin); (2005) 8 CCLR 243 discussed above at para.1–120.

(c) any other person to whom the adult asks the authority to give a copy.

(4) The local authority must give a written record of a carer's assessment to—

(a) the carer to whom the assessment relates,

(b) the adult needing care, if the carer asks the authority to do so, and

(c) any other person to whom the carer asks the authority to give a copy.

(5) A local authority may combine a needs or carer's assessment with an assessment it is carrying out (whether or not under this Part) in relation to another person only if the adult to whom the needs or carer's assessment relates agrees and—

(a) where the combination would include an assessment relating to another adult, that other adult agrees;

(b) where the combination would include an assessment relating to a child (including a young carer), the consent condition is met in relation to the child.

(6) The consent condition is met in relation to a child if—

(a) the child has capacity or is competent to agree to the assessments being combined and does so agree, or

(b) the child lacks capacity or is not competent so to agree but the local authority is satisfied that combining the assessments would be in the child's best interests.

(7) Where a local authority is carrying out a needs or carer's assessment, and there is some other assessment being or about to be carried out in relation to the adult to whom the assessment relates or in relation to a relevant person, the local authority may carry out that other assessment—

(a) on behalf of or jointly with the body responsible for carrying it out, or

(b) if that body has arranged to carry out the other assessment jointly with another person, jointly with that body and the other person.

(8) A reference to a needs or carer's assessment includes a reference to a needs or carer's assessment (as the case may be) which forms part of a combined assessment under subsection (5).

(9) A reference to an assessment includes a reference to part of an assessment.

(10) "NHS continuing health care" is to be construed in accordance with standing rules under section 6E of the National Health Service Act 2006.

(11) A person is a "relevant person", in relation to a needs or carer's assessment, if it would be reasonable to combine an assessment relating to that person with the needs or carer's assessment (as mentioned in subsection (5)).

GENERAL NOTE

1–136   Prior to the Care Act, most of the detail about how an assessment should be conducted was spread out in a plethora of guidance (both statutory and non-statutory). This detail included information which should be provided about the assessment process, when consultation should take place with other professionals, and when an assessment must be conducted by a registered social worker.[1] The Law Commission argued that the framework for conducting an assessment caused confusion, lacked transparency, and led to inconsistent practice since leaving detail mainly to guidance meant that it was often treated as

---

[1] For example, Department of Health Social Services Inspectorate and Scottish Office Social Work Services Group, *Care Management and Assessment: Practitioners' Guide* (1991), Department of Health, *Single Assessment Process: Guidance for Implementation* (2002) and Department of Health, *Prioritising Need in the Context of Putting People First: A Whole System Approach to Eligibility for Social Care: Guidance on Eligibility Criteria for Adult Social Care, England 2010* (2010),

optional. Given the centrality of the assessment process to adult social care, the Commission argued that the process for an assessment must be clear and enforceable, and recommended that in the future it should be specified in regulations. These regulations would apply to both needs assessments and carer's assessment. On certain key matters the Law Commission felt that the Secretary of State should be required to make regulations. These matters were:

- that assessments must be proportionate to the needs of the individual;
- the circumstances in which a specialist assessment must be arranged;
- a requirement that all needs must be considered in the assessment, irrespective of whether the need can or is being met by a third party (such as a carer); and
- that needs assessments must take into account the outcome of any carer's assessment.

On other matters the Secretary of State would be given powers to make regulations.[1]

In broad terms, s.12 implements the Law Commission's recommendations. The Secretary of State is required to make regulations about how a needs assessment or a carer's assessment is to be carried out. However, there is discretion over the content of those regulations. In its response to the Law Commission, the Government stated its general approach in this respect:

"Regulations are intended to ensure clarity and consistent practice, but should cover only the key elements of assessment. It is a core principle of the Government's approach to regulations that they should not be overly prescriptive. Local authorities must be able to adopt a proportionate and flexible approach to assessment and regulations and guidance should not undermine professional judgement."[2]

The relevant regulations issued under s.12 are the Care and Support (Assessment) Regulations 2014 (SI 2014/2827). They are reproduced and discussed in para.A1–187. By virtue of s.65(1), the regulations also make provision for child needs assessments, child's carer's assessments and young carer assessments. Transition assessments are discussed at para.1–158 below. Any regulations made under s.12(1) and (2) are subject to the negative procedure in Parliament. This means that they will come into force unless Parliament passes a resolution annulling the regulations. In contrast, the affirmative procedure regulations to be laid before, and approved by resolution, of each House of Parliament (see para.1–161 below).

In addition, s.12 places a duty on local authorities to provide a written record of the assessment, and establishes a power to undertake joint assessments.

Subsection (1)

This subsection requires the Secretary of State to make assessment regulations and provides that the regulations may in particular make provision about seven matters: **1–137**

- a requirement to have regard to the needs of the family;
- other matters which must be taken into account (in particular, matters which will ensure the assessment is appropriate and proportionate);
- steps that will ensure the assessment is appropriate and proportionate;
- circumstances in which the assessment may or must be carried out by an expert or other person;
- circumstances in which the adult may carry out the assessment jointly with the local authority;
- circumstances in which an expert or other person must be consulted; and

---

[1] Law Commission, *Adult Social Care*, paras 5.59 to 5.105, 7.33, and 7.42 to 7.56.
[2] Department of Health, *Reforming the Law for Adult Care and Support: The Government's Response to Law Commission Report 326 on Adult Social Care* (TSO, July 2012), Cm.8379, para.5.10.

- circumstances in which the adult must be referred for NHS continuing health care.

As noted above, ss.(1) has been given effect by the Care and Support (Assessment) Regulations 2014 (SI 2014/2827). As well as the matters listed above, the regulations also contain requirements to give the person being assessed information about the assessment process—or to their parents in certain cases (regs. 3(4) and (5), and 4(2)). See para.A1–187 below.

THE NEEDS OF THE FAMILY

1–138   The Joint Committee felt it was unclear whether the reference to the "needs of the family" gave sufficient prominence to the need to prevent any children from undertaking inappropriate levels of caring. It recommended that subs.(1) should be amended to make clear that local authorities, when carrying out a needs or carer's assessment, must have regard to the need to prevent any children from undertaking inappropriate caring responsibilities.[1]   In response the Government confirmed its intention to set this out in the regulations and guidance "within the wider context of a whole family approach to assessment—which importantly would not be just limited to young carers".[2]

Regulation 4 of the Care and Support (Assessment) Regulations 2014 (SI 2014/2827) provides that a local authority carrying out an assessment must consider the impact of the needs of the individual to whom the assessment relates on any person who is involved in caring for the individual and any person the local authority considers to be relevant. It also contains specific provision where a child is involved in providing care to any individual. This regulation is discussed at para.A1–191 below. The statutory guidance covers the "whole family approach" in relation to assessments at paras 6.65 to 6.73.

APPROPRIATE AND PROPORTIONATE ASSESSMENTS

1–139   Subsections (1)(b) and (1)(c) both mention appropriate and proportionate assessments. The regulations can specify matters to which assessments must have regard and steps that must be undertaken to ensure appropriate and proportionate assessments. Regulation 3 of the Care and Support (Assessment) Regulations 2014 (SI 2014/2827) provides that a local authority must carry out an assessment in a manner which is appropriate and proportionate to the person's needs and circumstances and ensures that they are able to participate in the process as effectively as possible. This regulation is discussed at para.A1–190 below. The authority must also have regard to the individual's wishes and preferences, the outcomes they seek from the assessment and the severity and overall extent of their needs. The regulation also states that in the case of a person with fluctuating needs, the local authority must take into account the individual's circumstances "over such period as it considers necessary to establish accurately the individual's level of needs". The statutory guidance discusses appropriate and proportionate assessments in paras 6.2, 6.28, 6.35 to 6.43.

It is important to note that proportionality does not automatically equate to minimalism: where a person has complex or multiple needs, a proportionate assessment may mean an in-depth and comprehensive exploration of their needs. Conversely, a proportionate assessment for other people may mean a brief conversation. In some instances, a telephone assessment may be sufficient and proportionate; for example, when people call social services with low-level needs and request a simple service, the initial contact may be sufficient to deal with this situation, whilst in other instances, a face-to-face assessment will be essential. The statutory guidance recognises that:

---

[1] House of Lords House of Commons Joint Committee on the Draft Care and Support Bill, *Draft Care and Support Bill Report, Session 2012–13*, para.182.

[2] Department of Health, *The Care Bill explained—including a response to consultation and pre-legislative scrutiny on the draft Care and Support Bill*, p.69.

"Where appropriate, an assessment may be carried out over the phone or online. In adopting such approaches, local authorities should consider whether the proposed means of carrying out the assessment poses any challenges or risks for certain groups, particularly when assuring itself that it has fulfilled its duties around safeguarding, independent advocacy, and assessing mental capacity. Where there is concern about a person's capacity to make a decision, for example as a result of a mental impairment such as those with dementia, acquired brain injury, learning disabilities or mental health needs, a face-to-face assessment should be arranged."[1]

The statutory guidance also provides a non-exhaustive list of the different types of assessment that could be utilised in this respect.[2]

A PERSON WHO HAS EXPERTISE AND OTHER SPECIFIED PERSON

Subsections (1)(d) and (1)(f) both mention a person who has expertise in a specified mat- **1–140** ter or a person of such other description as is specified. The regulations may provide that an assessment must be carried out by any such person or that the local authority must consult them before or during an assessment.

The Law Commission argued that in some cases a specialist assessment should always be required. At a minimum, it recommended that the requirement for a specialist assessment of deafblind people, contained at that time in statutory guidance, should be elevated to the regulations. This guidance required that in the case of a deafblind person, local authorities must ensure "a specialist assessment is arranged, to be carried out by a specifically trained experienced person/team equipped to assess the needs of a deafblind person".[3] The Commission also felt that a specialist assessment may be needed in other cases, such as for people with severe and enduring mental health problems, people with borderline mental capacity or those with dual diagnoses.[4]

The draft Care and Support Bill 2012 included a provision enabling the Secretary of State to make regulations to specify the circumstances in which a person with expertise in a specified matter must carry out an assessment on behalf of the authority. However, this was dropped from the Care Bill introduced in the House of Lords, which instead only referred to consulting someone with the relevant experience. This omission was criticised by Lord Low during committee stage in the House of Lords.[5] In response the Government amended the Bill to provide for regulations to specify when an expert must carry out an assessment for complex needs, as well as when an expert may carry out an assessment. A further amendment provided that as well as being required to consult an expert, local authorities may also be required to consult any other person "of such other description as specified". The Government set out its intention in the following terms:

". . . we will require assessors who are trained but may not have experience of carrying out an assessment for a specific condition to consult a person with experience in that area. For example, an assessor who normally assesses older people who is asked to assess a person with learning disabilities would have to consult a person with experience in that condition."[6]

The Government also said:

". . . through the powers in [s.12], we will require local authorities to ensure that assessors have the appropriate training to carry out the assessment. We have listened to the

---

[1] Department of Health, *Care and Support Statutory Guidance* (2014), para.6.28.
[2] Department of Health, *Care and Support Statutory Guidance* (2014), para.6.3.
[3] LAC(DH)(2009)6, *Social Care for Deafblind Children and Adults*, para.22.
[4] Law Commission, *Adult Social Care*, paras 5.85 to 5.86.
[5] *Hansard* (House of Lords), 16 July 2013, Vol.747, col.667.
[6] *Hansard* (House of Lords), 14 October 2013, Vol.747, col.270 (Earl Howe).

concerns of adults who use care and support, and to their carers. They are right to say that assessors should receive appropriate training."[1]

The Government also confirmed that the regulations will require specialist assessments of deafblind people and will consult on what further groups or circumstances the power should apply to.[2]

In the House of Commons, during the passage of the Care Bill, Robert Buckland MP pointed out that assessments for adults with autism must be covered by these regulations because that will reinforce the obligation already placed by the Autism Act 2009 and the statutory guidance to train those who carry out needs assessments.[3] See para.1–771 below for further discussion on the 2009 Act.

Regulation 5(1) of the Care and Support (Assessment) Regulations 2014 (SI 2014/2827) require local authorities to ensure that any person carrying out the assessment (other than in the case of a supported self-assessment) has the skills, knowledge and competence to carry out the assessment in question, and is appropriately trained. Regulation 5(2) requires local authorities when carrying out an assessment to consult a person who has:

"expertise in relation to the condition or other circumstances of the individual whose needs are being assessed in any case where it considers that the needs of the individual concerned require it to do so".

Such consultation may take place before, or during, the assessment. These provisions are discussed at para.A1–192 below.

Regulation 6 provides that any assessment relating to a deafblind person must be carried out by a person who has specific training and expertise relating to individuals who are deafblind (defined as an individual who has "combined sight and hearing impairment which causes difficulties with communication, access to information and mobility"). This regulation is discussed at para.A1–193 below. Further instruction on such assessments can be found in the policy guidance on care and support for deafblind children and adults.[4]

The statutory guidance discusses the training and expertise of assessors, and the assessments of deafblind people, in paras 6.85 to 6.97.

JOINT ASSESSMENTS WITH THE PERSON BEING ASSESSED

1–141   Subsection (1)(e) enables the regulations to specify circumstances in which the adult to whom the assessment relates may carry out the assessment jointly with the local authority. Regulation 2 of the Care and Support (Assessment) Regulations 2014 (SI 2014/2827) refers to such an assessment as a "supported self-assessment". It includes a duty to carry out a supported self-assessment if an adult wishes to have, and has the capacity to take part in, such an assessment. There is also a power to carry out a supported self-assessment where the local authority is carrying out a child's needs assessment or a young carer's assessment and certain other criteria apply. This regulation is discussed at A1–189 below. The statutory guidance discusses supported self-assessments in paras 6.44 to 6.53. See also para.1–106 above on self-assessment.

---

[1] *Hansard* (House of Lords), 14 October 2013, Vol.747, col.278 (Earl Howe).

[2] *Hansard* (House of Commons: Public Bill Committee), 14 January 2014 (PM): Fourth Sitting, col.120 (Norman Lamb MP).

[3] *Hansard* (House of Commons), 16 December 2013, Vol.572, col.548. The guidance being referred to was Department of Health, *Implementing 'Fulfilling and Rewarding Lives': Statutory Guidance for Local Authorities and NHS Organisations to Support Implementation of the Autism Strategy* (2010), pp.15 and 17. This guidance has since been updated, see para.1–771.

[4] Department of Health, *Care and Support for Deafblind Children and Adults Policy Guidance* (December 2014).

REFERRALS FOR NHS CONTINUING HEALTH CARE

Subsection (1)(g) enables the regulations to specify circumstances in which the local **1–142** authority must refer the adult for an assessment of eligibility for NHS continuing health care.

This included in the Care Bill as part of the Government's response to the Joint Committee's recommendation that the legislation should retain the effect of s.47(3) of the National Health Service and Community Care Act 1990. Section 47(3) had provided that if it appears to a local authority when undertaking an assessment that a person has a health or housing need or other relevant need, it must bring this need to the attention of the relevant health or housing authority, invite them to assist in the assessment, and take into account any services likely to be made available by that authority.[1]

Regulation 7 of the Care and Support (Assessment) Regulations 2014 (SI 2014/2827) provide that where a local authority is carrying out a needs assessment and it appears that a person may be eligible for NHS continuing health care, the authority must notify the relevant Clinical Commissioning Group. In the case of a child's needs assessment, the same requirement applies where it appears that the child may, after becoming 18, be eligible for NHS continuing health care. This regulation is discussed at A1–194 below. The statutory guidance discusses referrals for NHS continuing health care in paras 6.80 to 6.83. NHS continuing health care is discussed at para.1–251 below.

TIMESCALES FOR ASSESSMENTS

The matters set out in subs.(1) are just illustrative examples of how the assessment regu- **1–143** lations could be used. It is possible that they could be used for other matters, such as timescales for assessments. The Law Commission noted concerns about delays by local authorities in commencing and finishing assessments. However, during its consultation, the importance of adopting an iterative approach to assessments was emphasised, where assessments are seen as an on-going process and not a one-off event. Nevertheless, the Law Commission felt that the statute should leave open the possibility of timescales in regulations. For example, this could cater for certain non-emergency assessments where it may be appropriate to prescribe timescales for commencing or completing an assessment in the regulations, in the interests of clarity and certainty.[2] The Government did not include timescales in the regulations. The statutory guidance states that:

"An assessment should be carried out over an appropriate and reasonable timescale taking into account the urgency of needs and a consideration of any fluctuation in those needs. Local authorities should inform the individual of an indicative timescale over which their assessment will be conducted and keep the person informed throughout the assessment process."[3]

The reference to fluctuation of needs reflects reg.3(3) of the Care and Support (Assessment) Regulations 2014 (SI 2014/2827) which states that in the case of a person with fluctuating needs, the local authority must take into account the individual's circumstances "over such period as it considers necessary to establish accurately the individual's level of needs". See para.A1–190 below.

The Local Government Ombudsman has stated that they normally consider that it is reasonable for an assessment to be carried out between four and six dates from the date of the original request.[4]

---

[1] House of Lords House of Commons Joint Committee on the Draft Care and Support Bill, *Draft Care and Support Bill Report, Session 2012–13*, para.176 and Department of Health, *The Care Bill explained—including a response to consultation and pre-legislative scrutiny on the draft Care and Support Bill*, para.57.

[2] Law Commission, *Adult Social Care*, paras 5.88 to 5.94.

[3] Department of Health, *Care and Support Statutory Guidance* (2014), para.6.29.

[4] Local Government Ombudsman, *Fact Sheet A4: Complaints about councils that conduct community care assessments* (2011).

Subsection (2)

1–144   In facilitating the carrying out of an assessment, the regulations may give the local authority power to provide the person carrying out the assessment with:

- information about the adult in the case of a needs assessment;
- information about the carer in the case of a carer's assessment, and the adult needing care; and
- resources, or access to facilities, that will be required to carry out the assessment.

The Care and Support (Assessment) Regulations 2014 (SI 2014/2827) give local authorities powers to provide assessors with such information in respect of supported self-assessments (reg.2(5)) and assessments of deafblind people (reg.6(2)). See paras A1–189 and A1–193 below.

Subsections (3) and (4)

1–145   The local authority must give a written record of the assessment to:

- the adult in the case of a needs assessment—plus (following a request by the adult) their carer and any other person; and
- the carer in the case of a carer's assessment—plus (following a request by the carer) the adult needing care and any other person.

The record of the assessment is not the same as the written record of the determination following the assessment of whether the person has needs which meet the eligibility criteria. The duty to provide a written record of the determination is dealt with separately under s.13(2). There is also a separate requirement to provide advice in writing for people whose needs do not meet the eligibility criteria under s.13(5) below.

Subsections (3) and (4) (and s.13(2)) were added by the Government in response to the Joint Committee recommendation that the legislation must put beyond doubt that a resource allocation system cannot include a blanket policy of reducing a person's personal budget or notional cost on the basis of the presence of a carer, without the carer's knowledge or consent.[1] The Government argued that these provisions will ensure there is an ability to challenge any incorrect assumptions about carers' input.[2]

There are no requirements for the format or content of the record, other than for it being in writing. However, the Equality Act 2010 may be relevant to the performance of this duty and if necessary, the explanation should be provided in alternative formats and using different methods of communication, as well as being in writing.

Subsections (3) and (4) do not specify or indicate how much detail should be provided in the record of the assessment. The extent of the detail is likely to depend upon the specific circumstances of the individual case, and may for example need to be proportionate to the extent and depth of the relevant person's needs and the assessment undertaken. Therefore, in some cases involving a simple contact assessment the legal of detail will be necessarily limited and straightforward, compared to the record of a comprehensive or specialist assessment.

It is submitted that if the person lacks capacity to ask for, or consent to, a copy being given to others, then the record may only be given to other persons if this is in the assessed person's best interests in accordance with s.4 of the Mental Capacity Act 2005.

---

[1] House of Lords House of Commons Joint Committee on the Draft Care and Support Bill, *Draft Care and Support Bill Report, Session 2012–13*, para.7.

[2] Department of Health, *The Care Bill explained—including a response to consultation and pre-legislative scrutiny on the draft Care and Support Bill*, p.57.

Subsections (5) and (6)

These subsections were added by the Government at report stage in the House of Lords in **1–146** response to concerns that the legislation needed to make clear links with the Children and Families Act 2014 (which at the time was also being considered by Parliament). They ensure that a local authority can combine an adult's assessment with any other assessment it is carrying out under the Care Act or other legislation as long as the individual or individuals being assessed agree. In Parliament, the Government confirmed that these subsections enable, for example, the local authority to carry out a needs assessment with a young carer's assessment.[1] The statutory guidance discusses combining needs and carer's assessments in para.6.74.

In the case of a child, subs.(6) provides that the child must have capacity or competence to consent to the assessments being combined and agrees, or if the child lacks capacity or competence the local authority must be satisfied that this is in the child's best interests. There is no similar provision for an adult. However, it is submitted that if the adult lacks capacity to consent to their assessment being combined, the local authority cannot combine the assessments unless this is in the person's best interests in accordance with s.4 of the Mental Capacity Act 2005

Some of those presenting evidence to the Joint Committee argued that the possibility of combining a needs and carer's assessment under this subsection may cause the person who needs care and support to "lose their individual identity and to lose control of the support they need". Nevertheless, the Joint Committee supported this provision, particularly to underpin whole-family assessment, and argued that the requirement for agreement of the adult needing care and of the carer provided sufficient protection for the adult.[2]

Subsection (7)

A needs assessment or a carer's assessment may be carried out jointly with an external **1–147** body or person when that body or person is carrying out an assessment of the individual or carer. Alternatively the local authority could carry out the other assessment on behalf of the body or person. The explanatory notes state that:

> "For example, if a local authority is carrying out a carer's assessment, and an NHS body is carrying out a continuing health care assessment of the person he or she is caring for, the local authority could jointly carry out the continuing health care assessment jointly with the NHS body."[3]

This implements the Law Commission's recommendation that the statute should also make clear that a local authority is able to carry out an assessment for care and support at the same time as another assessment is carried out.[4] Integrated assessments are discussed in the statutory guidance at paras 6.75 to 6.79. In particular the guidance emphasises the importance of linking together care and support plans "to set out a single, shared care pathway, for example when following the Care Programme Approach", and that where an assessment involves a body from outside of the local authority, the local authority should provide any resources or facilities which may be required to carry out the assessment.[5] The use of strategic planning to ensure combined assessments is discussed in para.15.14.

RELEVANT PERSON

The Care Bill was amended at report stage in the House of Lords to provide for the con- **1–148** cept of a relevant person. The Government stated that:

---

[1] *Hansard* (House of Lords), 14 October 2013, Vol.747, cols 270 to 271 (Earl Howe).
[2] House of Lords House of Commons Joint Committee on the Draft Care and Support Bill, *Draft Care and Support Bill Report, Session 2012–13*, para.184.
[3] Care Act 2014: Explanatory Notes para.109.
[4] Law Commission, *Adult Social Care*, paras 5.125 to 5.132.
[5] Department of Health, *Care and Support Statutory Guidance* (2014), paras 6.78 to 6.79.

"This allows the authority to carry out a needs or carer's assessment jointly with another assessment being carried out by another body, whether of that person or a person relevant to the situation, as long as the individual or individuals being assessed agree."[1]

The eligibility criteria

1–149 **13.**—(1) Where a local authority is satisfied on the basis of a needs or carer's assessment that an adult has needs for care and support or that a carer has needs for support, it must determine whether any of the needs meet the eligibility criteria (see subsection (7)).

(2) Having made a determination under subsection (1), the local authority must give the adult concerned a written record of the determination and the reasons for it.

(3) Where at least some of an adult's needs for care and support meet the eligibility criteria, the local authority must—

(a) consider what could be done to meet those needs that do,

(b) ascertain whether the adult wants to have those needs met by the local authority in accordance with this Part, and

(c) establish whether the adult is ordinarily resident in the local authority's area.

(4) Where at least some of a carer's needs for support meet the eligibility criteria, the local authority must—

(a) consider what could be done to meet those needs that do, and

(b) establish whether the adult needing care is ordinarily resident in the local authority's area.

(5) Where none of the needs of the adult concerned meet the eligibility criteria, the local authority must give him or her written advice and information about—

(a) what can be done to meet or reduce the needs;

(b) what can be done to prevent or delay the development of needs for care and support, or the development of needs for support, in the future.

(6) Regulations may make provision about the making of the determination under subsection (1).

(7) Needs meet the eligibility criteria if—

(a) they are of a description specified in regulations, or

(b) they form part of a combination of needs of a description so specified.

(8) The regulations may, in particular, describe needs by reference to—

(a) the effect that the needs have on the adult concerned;

(b) the adult's circumstances.

GENERAL NOTE

1–150 Prior to the Care Act, eligibility for adult social care was determined by two parallel schemes. First, s.21 of the National Assistance Act 1948 placed a duty on local authorities to provide residential accommodation for adults "who by reason of age, illness, disability or any other circumstance are in need of care and attention which is not otherwise available to them."[2] Secondly, eligibility for non-residential care was assessed against eligibility criteria contained in statutory guidance.[3] The guidance set out an *eligibility framework*—

---

[1] *Hansard* (House of Lords), 14 October 2013, Vol.747, col.271 (Earl Howe).

[2] LAC(93)10, Appendix 1.

[3] Originally LAC(2002)13, *Fair Access to Care Services: Guidance on Eligibility Criteria for Adult Social Care*, which was replaced by Department of Health, *Prioritising Need in the Context of Putting People First: A Whole System Approach to Eligibility for Social Care: Guidance on Eligibility Criteria for Adult Social Care, England 2010* (2010).

consisting of four bands (critical, substantial, moderate and low)—which local authorities were required to assess needs against. Each local authority had to specify which of these four bands it would provide services to meet (known as the *eligibility criteria*). A local authority could have regard to its resources (amongst other issues) when setting its eligibility criteria.[1] But if a person's needs fell within the local authority's eligibility criteria, the guidance provided that the local authority must meet those needs.

The Law Commission made three main criticisms of this framework. First, it was overly complex and there was no reason in principle why residential accommodation should be treated differently in respect of eligibility to other forms of care and support. Second, it was unacceptable that one of the most fundamental decisions in social care—whether or not a person is eligible for non-residential services—had been left to guidance, albeit statutory guidance. In making this argument the Commission had in mind reports of local authorities considering the introduction of so-called "super-critical thresholds" by setting eligibility criteria higher than critical needs, which had been the highest band in the previous statutory guidance. Finally, the Commission argued that carers should not be prevented from being able to establish entitlements for services. Local authorities at that time had a power to provide carers' services but not an express duty.

The Law Commission therefore recommended that the new statute should establish a single eligibility system for all forms of care and support (including residential accommodation and carers' services). The Secretary of State should be required to make regulations prescribing the eligibility framework (such as the four existing bands—or some different system). This could be used to implement a national eligibility threshold, or to allow local authorities to continue to set their own eligibility thresholds. But importantly, the eligibility framework would no longer be left to guidance. However, the Law Commission also concluded that if s.21 of the National Assistance Act 1948 was repealed, there was a possibility that some people might lose their entitlement to residential accommodation. The particular group that the Commission had in mind were asylum seekers and those people ineligible under housing legislation who had relatively low social care needs but who did not have access to accommodation in which those needs could be met. Section 21 had provided a duty of last resort for such people, and the Commission therefore recommended that s.21 should be retained in the new scheme as a long-stop legal duty, available only to those who fall below the local authority eligibility criteria.[2]

The Care Act implements most of the Law Commission's recommended eligibility scheme. In particular the Government agreed that the eligibility criteria must be specified in regulations and not left to guidance. During the passage of the Care Bill through the House of Commons the Government rejected an attempt to set the criteria in primary legislation, arguing that any future changes would as a result be "cumbersome and time consuming".[3] The relevant regulations issued under s.13(7) and (8) are the Care and Support (Eligibility Criteria) Regulations 2015 (SI 2015/313). The regulations establish eligibility criteria for adults with care and support needs and for carers. They are reproduced and discussed in paras A1–272—A1–275. The statutory guidance discusses eligibility at paras 6.100 to 6.140.

However, s.21 has not been retained. The Government argued that retaining s.21 would be "anomalous with our overall approach, and perpetuate the same divisions we intend to remove" and therefore it proposed to deal with these cases through the eligibility regulations:

" . . . so that individuals in the scope of these existing duties continue to be eligible for care and support, and in effect are 'mainstreamed' into the core processes for the provision of care and support".[4]

---

[1] *R. v Gloucestershire CC Ex p Barry* [1997] A.C. 584.

[2] Law Commission, *Adult Social Care*, paras 6.2 to 6.32 and 7.57 to 7.75.

[3] *Hansard* (House of Commons: Public Bill Committee), 14 January 2014 (PM): Fourth Sitting, col.145 (Norman Lamb MP).

[4] Department of Health, *Reforming the Law for Adult Care and Support: The Government's Response to Law Commission Report 326 on Adult Social Care* (TSO, July 2012), Cm.8379, para.6.17.

In its consultation on the draft regulations the Government asked if the new eligibility criteria would cover cases provided for under s.21. The majority of respondents (who were mainly local authorities) agreed that the new regulations and the powers in s.19 of the Act would ensure that such people would continue to be eligible for care and support.[1]

For carers, this will be the first time that local authorities have been required to meet eligible needs. Prior to the Care Act, local authorities had a power but not a duty to provide services to carers. In exercising this power, authorities were at liberty to apply an eligibility framework and criteria. Practice guidance to the Carers and Disabled Children Act 2000 advised that local authorities should implement an eligibility framework based on the extent of the risk to the sustainability of the caring role. This advice was cross referenced in the Prioritising Need statutory guidance—and the eligibility framework for carers was reproduced—but the guidance did not comment on whether this should be adopted by local authorities.

The costs in relation to the new legal framework for carers (including extended rights to assessment and entitlement to support) are expected to generate new costs rising to £175 million per year.

NATIONAL ELIGIBILITY CRITERIA

1–151   As noted previously, prior to the Care Act, local authorities had been able to set their own eligibility criteria for non-residential services. This system had been criticised for producing local variations in eligibility for care and support (referred to as the postcode lottery) and fears that people may lose their care and support if eligible needs are reclassified locally. Plans for nationally consistent eligibility criteria for social care were first put forward by Gordon Brown's Labour Government in 2010.[2] In the 2012 White Paper *Caring for Our Future* the Coalition Government made a commitment to introduce a national minimum eligibility threshold.[3] The Joint Committee recommended that the Government should put this beyond doubt by making this policy explicit in the legislation.[4] The Government agreed and stated that it would amend this provision to make clear its intention to introduce a national minimum eligibility threshold.[5] Consequently, the express reference to locally determined eligibility criteria in the draft Care and Support Bill has been removed.[6] However, see also the further commentary under subs.7 at para.1–160 on this point. In contrast, the Law Commission had recommended that the legislation should be future proofed by enabling the development of a national minimum eligibility threshold or allowing local authorities to set their own minimum thresholds.[7] The Government's intentions were explained in the House of Lords:

> "The system of locally-determined eligibility for care and support has been confusing to people for too long. It has been seen as an unfair system under which different levels of needs are met on the basis of where somebody lives. The changes we are bringing forward will mean that people's entitlements to care and support will be much clearer and fairer and will reduce variation in access between local authorities."[8]

---

[1] Department of Health, *Response to the Consultation on draft Regulations and Guidance for Implementation of Part 1 of the Care Act 2014* (2014) Cm 8955, p.23.
[2] *Building the National Care Service* (2010) Cm.7854, p.14.
[3] HM Government, *Caring for Our Future: Reforming Care and Support* (TSO, July 2012), Cmd 8378, p.32.
[4] House of Lords House of Commons Joint Committee on the Draft Care and Support Bill, *Draft Care and Support Bill Report, Session 2012–13*, para.191.
[5] Department of Health, *The Care Bill explained—including a response to consultation and pre-legislative scrutiny on the draft Care and Support Bill*, para.53 and pp.69 to 70.
[6] Draft Care and Support Bill (TSO, July 2012) Cmd 8386, cl.13(3)(b).
[7] Law Commission, *Adult Social Care*, para.6.17.
[8] *Hansard* (House of Lords), 16 July 2013, Vol.747, col.683 (Earl Howe).

One of the main arguments for a national eligibility threshold is consistency. However, it is likely that some differentiation in local implementation will remain. For example, the quality of assessment and availability of certain types of care and support may vary between different local authorities. The Government accepted that local authorities will need to be required to train assessors to ensure that assessments are carried out properly, and that guidance is necessary to reduce variation.[1]

The national eligibility criteria set a minimum threshold for needs which local authorities must meet. All local authorities in England must comply with this national threshold. Authorities can also decide to meet needs that fall below this threshold if they choose to do so.[2]

THE CARE AND SUPPORT (ELIGIBILITY CRITERIA) REGULATIONS 2015   **1–152**

As noted above, the national eligibility criteria for adults with care and support needs and carers are set out in the Care and Support (Eligibility Criteria) Regulations 2015 (SI 2015/313). They are reproduced and discussed in detail in paras A1–272 to A1–275. The following provides a general overview of the new criteria for adults with care and support needs, and for carers with support needs.

Overview of the eligibility criteria for adults with care and support needs

Following an assessment, local authorities must decide whether an adult's needs are sufficient to meet the eligibility criteria. This involves addressing three cumulative questions. If the adult's needs meet the eligibility criteria then in most cases the local authority must provide or arrange services to meet those needs. The main additional stipulation is that the adult must be ordinarily resident in the local authority's area. The eligibility criteria below are national, and apply to every local authority in England.

First, the adult's needs must arise from or be related to a physical or mental impairment or illness,

Secondly, as a result the adult must be unable to achieve two or more outcomes from the list below:

(a) managing and maintaining nutrition;
(b) maintaining personal hygiene;
(c) managing toilet needs;
(d) being appropriately clothed;
(e) being able to make use of the adult's home safely;
(f) maintaining a habitable home environment;
(g) developing and maintaining family or other personal relationships;
(h) accessing and engaging in work, training, education or volunteering;
(i) making use of necessary facilities or services in the local community including public transport, and recreational facilities or services; and
(j) carrying out any caring responsibilities the adult has for a child.

Finally, as a consequence there must be (or is likely to be) a "significant impact" on the adult's well-being. The meaning of well-being is contained in s.1(2) of the Care Act. This defines well-being, in relation to an individual, as relating to any of the following:

(a) personal dignity (including the treatment of the individual with respect);
(b) physical and mental health and emotional dignity;
(c) protection from abuse and neglect;
(d) control by the individual over day-to-day life (including over care and support, or support, provided to the individual and the way in which it is provided);

---

[1] *Hansard* (House of Lords), 16 July 2013, Vol.747, col.685 (Earl Howe).
[2] Department of Health, *Care and Support Statutory Guidance* (2014) para.6.100.

(e) participation in work, education, training or recreation;

(f) social and economic well-being;

(g) domestic, family and personal relationships;

(h) suitability of living accommodation; and

(i) the individual's contribution to society.

Overview of the eligibility criteria for carers with support needs

Following an assessment, local authorities must decide whether a carer's needs are sufficient to meet the eligibility criteria. This involves addressing three cumulative questions. If the carer's needs meet the eligibility criteria then in most cases the local authority must provide or arrange services to meet those needs. The main additional stipulation is that the adult needing care must be ordinarily resident in the local authority's area. The eligibility criteria below are national, and apply to every local authority in England.

First, the carer's needs must be due to providing necessary care for an adult;

Secondly, as a result the carer's physical or mental health must be (or is at risk of) deteriorating, or they are unable to achieve one or more of the following specified outcomes:

(a) carrying out any caring responsibilities the carer has for a child;

(b) providing care to other persons for whom the carer provides care;

(c) maintaining a habitable home environment in the carer's home (whether or not this is also the home of the adult needing care);

(d) managing and maintaining nutrition;

(e) developing and maintaining family or other personal relationships;

(f) engaging in work, training, education or volunteering;

(g) making use of necessary facilities or services in the local community, including recreational facilities or services; and

(h) engaging in recreational activities.

Finally, as a consequence there must be (or is likely to be) a "significant impact" on the carer's well-being. The meaning of well-being is contained in section 1(2) of the Care Act. This defines well-being, in relation to an individual, as relating to any of the following:

(a) personal dignity (including the treatment of the individual with respect);

(b) physical and mental health and emotional dignity;

(c) protection from abuse and neglect;

(d) control by the individual over day-to-day life (including over care and support, or support, provided to the individual and the way in which it is provided);

(e) participation in work, education, training or recreation;

(f) social and economic well-being;

(g) domestic, family and personal relationships;

(h) suitability of living accommodation; and

(i) the individual's contribution to society.

THE SIGNIFICANCE OF ARTICLE 8

1–153   Article 8 of the European Convention of Human Rights provides for a right to respect for private and family life. In some circumstances it can impose a positive obligation on a public authority to provide assistance if the claimant can establish "a direct and immediate link between the measures sought by an applicant and the latter's private life",[1] and "a special link between the situation complained of and the particular needs of [the applicant's] private life".[2] However, even in such cases the jurisprudence establishes a wide margin of

---

[1] *Botta v Italy* (1998) 26 EHRR 241 at [34] and [35].

[2] *Sentges v The Netherlands* (2003) 7 CCLR 400 at 405.

appreciation particularly where the issues involve "an assessment of the priorities in the context of the allocation of limited state resources".[1]

A positive obligation was found in the case of *R. (Bernard) v Enfield LBC*.[2] The claimants there were husband and wife. They had six children. The wife was severely disabled and confined to a wheelchair. In breach of their duty under s.21(1)(a) of the National Assistance Act 1948, the local authority failed for some 20 months to provide the family with accommodation suited to her disability. The wife was doubly incontinent and, because there was no wheelchair access to the lavatory, was forced to defecate and urinate on the living-room floor. And she was unable to play any part in looking after her six children. Mr Justice Sullivan described the art.8 case as "not finely balanced" and awarded £10,000 damages.[3]

The leading domestic case on the positive obligation to provide care and support under art.8 is *Anufrijeva v Southwark LBC* which concerned three separate asylum-seekers, one complaining of a local authority's failure to provide accommodation to meet special needs, the other two of maladministration and delay in the handling of their asylum applications.[4] All three failed in their claims. The court concluded that *Bernard* had been rightly decided, but that:

"We find it hard to conceive . . . of a situation in which the predicament of an individual will be such that article 8 requires him to be provided with welfare support, where his predicament is not sufficiently severe to engage article 3. Article 8 may more readily be engaged where a family unit is involved. Where the welfare of children is at stake, article 8 may require the provision of welfare support in a manner which enables family life to continue."[5]

This high threshold was demonstrated in *R. (McDonald) v Royal Borough of Kensington and Chelsea* where the Supreme Court held that the local authority's decision to provide a service user with incontinence pads (even though she was not incontinent but due to a small bladder needed to urinate two or three times a night, and due to physical disability needed assistance to reach her commode) did not interfere with her art.8 rights.[6] The European Court of Human Rights concluded that considerations of human dignity were engaged when someone who could control her bodily functions was obliged to behave as if she could not. However, except for an initial period where the local authority had failed to meet the assessed need, the Court held that the complaint was inadmissible as manifestly ill-founded because the State had considerable discretion when it came to decisions concerning the allocation of scarce resources and, as such, the interference with Ms McDonald's rights had been "necessary in a democratic society" in accordance with art.8.[7]

Subsection (1)

Where a local authority has completed a needs assessment or a carer's assessment, it **1–154** must determine whether on the basis of the assessment, any of the needs it has identified meet the eligibility criteria, as specified in the regulations (see subs.(7)). This subsection must be read alongside ss.18 and 20, which provide that the local authority must meet the adult's and carer's needs that fall within the eligibility criteria—provided that certain additional criteria are also satisfied. Therefore the local authority's first task following an assessment is to determine eligible needs, which is the first step towards deciding if the authority must meet those needs.

---

[1] *Sentges v The Netherlands* (2003) 7 CCLR 400 at 405.

[2] *R. (Bernard) v Enfield LBC* [2002] EWHC 2282 (Admin).

[3] *R. (Bernard) v Enfield LBC* [2002] EWHC 2282 (Admin) at [31].

[4] *Anufrijeva v Southwark LBC* [2004] Q.B. 1124; [2003] EWCA Civ 1406.

[5] *Anufrijeva v Southwark LBC* [2004] Q.B. 1124; [2003] EWCA Civ 1406 at [33].

[6] *R. (McDonald) v Royal Borough of Kensington and Chelsea* [2011] UKSC 33; (2011) 14 CCLR 341 at [19].

[7] *McDonald v United Kingdom* (20 May 2014) Application no.4241/12.

Subsection (2)

1–155   Everyone who has undergone an assessment must be given a written record of the decision and the reasons for it, whether their needs are eligible or not. The Equality Act 2010 may be relevant to the performance of this duty and if necessary, the record should be provided in alternative formats and using different methods of communication, as well as being in writing.

Subsection (2) does not specify or indicate how much detail should be provided in the written record. The extent of the detail is likely to depend upon the specific circumstances of the individual case. For example, where the person has relatively low-level needs and is not seeking direct local authority support, the record may be relatively straightforward and brief, compared to the record provided to someone whose needs fall only just below the national eligibility threshold.

The duty to provide a record of the decision and reasons for it, is in addition to the requirements to provide a written record of the assessment under s.12(3) and (4), and to provide advice in writing for people whose needs do not meet the eligibility criteria (see subs.(5) below). However, unlike s.12(3) and (4), there is no requirement to give a copy of the record to any other person.

In the original version of the Care Bill, as introduced in the House of Lords, this subsection had also contained a requirement that local authorities must consider whether the person would benefit from prevention services under s.2 or information and advice provided under s.4. However, this provision was removed by the Government and it now appears in s.9(6) to provide that such consideration must take place at the time of assessment and not after the eligibility determination. See paras 1–108 to 1–110 for further discussion on the background to this change.

Subsection (3)

1–156   If the needs assessment identifies that one or more of the adult's needs meet the eligibility criteria, the local authority is required to make three determinations.

First, it must consider what could be done to meet those needs. There could be a range of care and support that could be provided to meet the relevant need (for example, see s.8).

Second, the local authority must ascertain whether the adult wants to have their needs met by the local authority. From 2020, individuals who do not want the local authority to meet their needs or who choose not to undergo the financial assessment must be provided with an independent personal budget (see s.28) and a care account (see s.29). In effect a person can merely record their eligible care costs for the purposes of progressing towards the new cap on care costs. This duty is not replicated for carers in subs.(4), as they are not eligible for a cap on costs.

Third, the local authority must establish whether the adult is ordinarily resident in the local authority's area (see discussion at paras 1–430 to 1–431 below). If the person is so resident (or if they are of no settled residence), there may be a duty to meet those needs (s.18). Otherwise the local authority may have a power to meet those needs.

Subsections (4)

1–157   If the carer's assessment identifies that one or more of the carer's needs meet the eligibility criteria, the local authority is required to make two determinations.

First, it must consider what could be done to meet those needs. There could be a range of support that could be provided to meet the relevant needs.

Second, the local authority must establish whether the adult needing care (not the carer) is ordinarily resident in the local authority's area (see discussion at para.1–432 below). If the person is so resident (or if they are of no settled residence), there may be a duty to meet those needs (s.18). Otherwise the local authority has a power to meet those needs.

In contrast to subs.(3), there is no express requirement to ascertain whether the carer wants to have their needs met by the local authority. This is because carers will not be eligible for a cap on costs, and therefore there will be no requirement to provide an independent personal budget to a carer who does not want the local authority to meet their needs.

Subsection (5)

Where the individual or carer's needs do not meet the eligibility criteria, the local auth- **1–158** ority must provide them with advice and information in writing on what services are available in the community to meet the needs they do have and to prevent or delay their need for care and support.

There are no requirements for the format or content of the advice, other than for it being in writing. However, the Equality Act 2010 may be relevant to the performance of this duty and if necessary, the explanation should be provided in alternative formats and using different methods of communication, as well as being in writing.

Subsection (5) does not specify or indicate how much detail should be provided when giving the information and advice. The extent of the detail is likely to depend upon the specific circumstances of the individual case, and may for example need to be proportionate to the extent and depth of the relevant person's needs and the assessment undertaken. Therefore, in some cases where the person has low-level needs, the information and advice may be relatively straightforward and brief, compared to someone whose needs fall only just below the national eligibility threshold.

Subsection (6)

This enables (but does not require) the Government to make regulations about how a **1–159** local authority must go about determining under subs.(1) whether the person's needs meet the eligibility criteria. It will therefore enable an eligibility framework to be issued and allow the Government to specify which needs are eligible.

Regulations under subs.(6) are subject to the negative procedure in Parliament, and therefore will come into force unless Parliament passes a resolution annulling the regulations. At Committee stage in the House of Commons, the Government resisted an amendment which would have made the regulations subject to the affirmative procedure (under which they would need to be approved by resolution of each House of Parliament, see para.1–161 below). The Government argued that in practice it is unlikely that regulations under this subsection would be disaggregated from regulations under subs.(7) (which are subject to the affirmative procedure). But anyway such regulations under subs.(6), if ever used on their own, would be "solely for procedural matters around making the eligibility determination, which would not affect the threshold itself".[1] The Government won the subsequent division by 12 votes to 9.[2]

Subsection (7)

This specifies that a person's needs will meet the eligibility criteria if they are of a **1–160** description specified in regulations. In effect, the regulations must prescribe the minimum level of needs that local authorities must meet, subject to the further criteria and conditions set out in ss.18 and 20. Local authorities can decide to arrange services to meet needs at a lower level (see ss.19 and 20(7)).

As noted above at para.1–152, in response to the Joint Committee, the Government agreed to amend the legislation to make clear its intention to introduce a national minimum eligibility threshold. However, subs.(7) does not expressly rule out the possibility of the regulations allowing local authorities to set their own minimum thresholds—if Government policy on this matter changes.

The Joint Committee also suggested that the Government should consider whether the regulation-making power in subs.(7) provides an opportunity to establish criteria that

---

[1] *Hansard* (House of Commons: Public Bill Committee), 14 January 2014 (PM): Fourth Sitting, col.148 (Norman Lamb MP).

[2] *Hansard* (House of Commons: Public Bill Committee), 14 January 2014 (PM): Fourth Sitting, col.150.

would clarify the boundary between eligibility for local authority funded care and support, and NHS funded continuing health care.[1] In its response the Government confirmed that the power will not be used in this way and that the process for establishing eligibility for NHS continuing health care will continue to be governed by the *National Framework for NHS Continuing Health Care and NHS-funded Nursing Care* and the National Health Service Commissioning Board and Clinical Commissioning Groups (Responsibilities and Standing Rules) Regulations 2012 (SI 2012/2996).[2]

THE AFFIRMATIVE PROCEDURE

1–161   Section 125(4)(a) provides that regulations made under subs.(7) are subject to the affirmative procedure. This means they must be laid before, and approved by resolution, of each House of Parliament. The Government emphasised this point in Parliament. The power to set regulations on eligibility, it argued, is one of the most important in the Act and for this reason has been made subject to the affirmative procedure.[3] Regulations are also considered by the Secondary Legislation Scrutiny Committee on Statutory Instruments and the Joint Committee on Statutory Instruments.

However, for the opposition, Lord Hunt offered a more sceptical view of the Parliamentary scrutiny given under the affirmative procedure:

> "We usually have a debate of about one hour; the conventions allow us to defeat a statutory instrument on very few occasions, and there is no opportunity to amend those regulations."[4]

The Government rejected putting the eligibility criteria on the face of the statute on the basis of flexibility:

> "We are not proposing to amend the national eligibility criteria on a regular basis. However, we need the ability to amend the regulations if it is shown that the criteria need to change at some point in the future. Of course, we would consult fully before making any such change."[5]

Subsection (8)

1–162   This clarifies that the regulations may, in particular, describe needs by reference to the effect that they have on the adult concerned and the adult's circumstances.

The original explanatory notes for the Care Bill as introduced in the House of Lords, stated that:

> "These powers will enable regulations to provide that people in specific circumstances may be treated as meeting the eligibility criteria, when their level of need otherwise might not do so. For example, this might apply in the case of a person who lacks accommodation, and currently has care and support needs which do not meet the eligibility criteria, but whose condition will continue to deteriorate unless appropriate care and support is provided. In such circumstances, the local authority may have to provide care and support including accommodation if it is not otherwise available to the person. The intention is that the power will enable the eligibility regulations to replicate the effect of provisions currently are set out in s.21(1)(a) National Assistance Act 1948."[6]

---

[1] House of Lords House of Commons Joint Committee on the Draft Care and Support Bill, *Draft Care and Support Bill Report, Session 2012–13*, para.191.
[2] Department of Health, *The Care Bill explained—including a response to consultation and pre-legislative scrutiny on the draft Care and Support Bill*, p.70.
[3] *Hansard* (House of Lords), 16 July 2013, Vol.747, col.683 (Earl Howe).
[4] *Hansard* (House of Lords), 16 July 2013, Vol.747, col.682.
[5] *Hansard* (House of Lords), 16 July 2013, Vol.747, col.683 (Earl Howe).
[6] HL Bill 001 2013–2014, Explanatory Notes to the Bill, para.87.

This was not repeated in the final explanatory notes. However, since the wording of this **1–163** subsection is not altered it is submitted that this explanation (if not the policy intention) remains valid.

CHARGING AND ASSESSING FINANCIAL RESOURCES

GENERAL NOTE

The background to the establishment of the Commission on Funding Care and Support, **1–164** chaired by the economist Sir Andrew Dilnot—and the recommendations contained in the Commission's report, published in 2011—are set out in para.I1–011 above.

The Commission identified that everybody faced a high degree of uncertainty over the future costs of social care. Moreover, people were exposed to potentially very high care costs:

> "Around one in 10 people, at age 65, face future lifetime care costs of more than £100,000. Younger adults with care needs face significantly higher lifetime costs. As a result, in paying for care, some people can lose the majority of their income and assets. In particular, those entering residential care are often forced to sell their homes—this is widely regarded by the public as unfair."[1]

The Commission noted that the state did not offer protection beyond the means-tested system and there were no financial products on the market to help people prepare in advance for future costs of care. Social care was therefore described as "the only major area in which everyone faces significant financial risk, but no one is able to protect themselves against it."[2] In other words, people were faced with a very significant risk that they could do little to avoid or mitigate. This made it impossible for people to plan and make provision to pay for care with any certainty. Furthermore, a person with modest wealth and no savings or other investments may go on to lose everything because financial support was only available to people with assets less than £23,250 (in the case of residential care). As a result, many people were not able to access the type of care and support that they wanted, and people who could afford to save or invest proactively towards the costs of their care had little or no incentive to do so.

The Commission accepted that individuals should take responsibility for their own costs up to a certain point, but after this point the state should pay. It was not considered reasonable or fair for all of a person's wealth to be at risk. This model was based on a partnership between the individual and the state where the responsibility for care costs is shared. The Commission explained:

> "We see our proposals as a type of social insurance policy, with an 'excess' that people will need to cover themselves. We are proposing that risks are pooled, so that the cost of an individual with very high care needs is shared across the population."[3]

At the heart of the Commission's report were recommendations for a cap on care costs and extended availability of means-tested state support:

> "The capped cost model sets the maximum contribution that anyone will need to make towards their care costs over their lifetime. For those who are less able to afford this contribution, the means test ensures that the state helps them so they will not have to pay the full amount."[4]

---

[1] Commission on Funding of Care and Support, *Fairer Care Funding: The Report of the Commission on Funding of Care and Support: Volume I* (July 2011), p.12.

[2] Commission on Funding of Care and Support, *Fairer Care Funding: The Report of the Commission on Funding of Care and Support: Volume I* (July 2011), p.16.

[3] Commission on Funding of Care and Support, *Fairer Care Funding: The Report of the Commission on Funding of Care and Support: Volume I* (July 2011), p.35.

[4] Commission on Funding of Care and Support, *Fairer Care Funding: The Report of the Commission on Funding of Care and Support: Volume I* (July 2011), p.30.

1–165   The Commission looked at the costs and benefits of different approaches, including providing free social care funded from taxation. But it concluded that free care was not a "resilient proposal"—costing £4.75 billion in 2016–17, with that escalating over time owing to demographic change—and that the best way to provide a fair and sustainable system was to put a cap on care costs:

> "Experience in other countries, such as Germany and Japan, which have recently reformed their social care funding models, demonstrates the vulnerability of a free care system to a changing economic and political environment. In both of these countries, social care costs rose more quickly than had been predicted or governments were willing to sustain, and both governments adjusted their systems—by making them less generous—to control these costs. This then went some way to undermining the promise of free care as people were still exposed to significant costs."[1]

The Commission's recommendations of a cap on care costs and extended availability of means-tested state support form the basis of ss.14 to 17 of the Care Act. The Department of Health in accepting the case put to it by the Commission stated that:

> "The cap and extended means-test, define a clear and fair partnership between individuals and the government, with shared responsibility for care costs. People will still have responsibility for their initial care costs, but if they are unlucky enough to need a lot of care, they will not face catastrophic costs."[2]

The capped costs system was due to come into effect on 1 April 2016. However, the Department of Health has announced that these reforms will be delayed until April 2020.[3]

PUBLIC AWARENESS CAMPAIGNS

1–166   The Commission on Funding Care and Support placed significant importance on engaging the public with the realities of a means-tested adult social care system. As the Commission stated:

> "There is very poor understanding of how the adult social care system currently works and how much it can potentially cost. Many people live under the false impression that social care will be free if they need it. If people are confused over how the system works and the costs that they potentially face, they will not prepare appropriately for the future."[4]

The chief aim was to encourage people to plan for the future in a better way than at present. The idea of a capped costs system was seen as particularly important as providing a clear monetary incentive for greater involvement. The Commission's report viewed communication to be central to the success of the entire scheme. It made two recommendations in this area. The first was "to encourage people to plan ahead for their later life we recommend that the Government invests in an awareness campaign". The second was that "the Government should develop a major new information and advice strategy to help when care needs arise".[5]

---

[1] Commission on Funding of Care and Support, *Fairer Care Funding: Analysis and Evidence Supporting the Recommendations of the Commission on Funding of Care and Support: Volume II* (July 2011), pp.117 to 118.

[2] Department of Health, *Policy Statement on Care and Support Funding Reform and Legislative Requirements* (2013), para.18.

[3] *House of Commons Written Answers and Statements Daily Report*, Cap on Care Costs: Written Statement—HCWS145, 20 July 2015, pp.162 to 164 (Alastair Burt MP).

[4] Commission on Funding of Care and Support, *Fairer Care Funding: The Report of the Commission on Funding of Care and Support: Volume I* (July 2011), p.42.

[5] Commission on Funding of Care and Support, *Fairer Care Funding: The Report of the Commission on Funding of Care and Support: Volume I* (July 2011), p.6.

This was also raised during the passage of the Care Bill, in the House of Lords, when Lord Lipsey tabled an amendment to require the Secretary of State to ensure through public awareness campaigns that there is a high level of public awareness and understanding of the terms and implications of the cap on care costs.[1] In response the Government said that a specific duty in the legislation is not necessary since local authorities are already under a duty to provide information and advice on care and support under s.4 which will need to include information on the capped costs system. But it accepted that local awareness-raising may not be enough and that the Department of Health has an important role to play at national level.[2] These arguments were repeated by the Government in the House of Commons at Committee stage. It stated that the Department of Health "will co-ordinate the message to ensure that a simple, coherent campaign can be delivered nationally and locally" and confirmed that it was engaging with the voluntary sector, care providers and the financial services industry. The Government also accepted that a public awareness campaign "is something that obviously should happen with a major reform, but legislating for it would be inappropriate".[3]

THE DEVELOPMENT OF FINANCIAL PRODUCTS

The role of the financial services industry—and in particular the development of finan- **1–167** cial products—is seen as key to achieving the funding reforms. The Commission on Funding Care and Support found that although the industry already provides some products (such as care annuities), it should play a larger role and pointed to possible developments in pensions, insurance and housing equity. It felt that by capping care costs and therefore the overall risk that people face, new financial products could develop to support people in making their contribution.[4] A subsequent Government initiated review—undertaken by major firms and trade associations—argued that a range of products needed to be developed that could be used individually or in combination. It concluded that the products needed to extend and develop the existing market for care annuities and add flexibility to existing products including, retirement annuity, equity release and protection products such as health, life and illness. The review also found in order to create the demand for such products, better awareness and advice was required, as well as stability in how care is funded. It also recommended that the Government should explore if disincentives could be removed by excluding specialised care products (in full or part) from means testing.[5]

In announcing the delay to the implementation of the capped costs system, the Government noted that the private insurance market had not developed as expected.[6]

CRITICISM OF THE NEW FUNDING SYSTEM

The reforms—based on the system put forward by the Commission on Funding Care and **1–168** Support—have not been without their critics. It has been pointed out that the focus of the Commission was not on the chronic underfunding of social care, but on the impact that the charging arrangements have on self-funders.[7] During the passage of the Care Bill through the House of Lords, Lord Campbell-Savours argued that the new funding system:

---

[1] *Hansard* (House of Lords), 9 October 2013, Vol.748, cols 127 to 129.
[2] *Hansard* (House of Lords), 9 October 2013, Vol.748, col.134 (Earl Howe).
[3] *Hansard* (House of Commons: Public Bill Committee), 9 January 2014: Second Sitting (PM), col.66 (Norman Lamb MP).
[4] Commission on Funding of Care and Support, *Fairer Care Funding: The Report of the Commission on Funding of Care and Support: Volume I* (July 2011), pp.39 to 40.
[5] Department of Health, *Review of Care Products—Key Messages* (21 January 2014).
[6] *House of Commons Written Answers and Statements Daily Report*, Cap on Care Costs: Written Statement – HCWS145, 20 July 2015, pp 162 to 164 (Alastair Burt MP).
[7] See, for example, P Thompson "The 'Dilnot' Proposals: Behind the Headlines" [2011] *Eld LJ* 389.

". . . will simply transfer money from those without to those with, and has been introduced to appease—I repeat: to appease—the demands of those who insist on passing
inherited wealth from one generation to another, a most ignoble way of proceeding."[1]

In response the Government claimed that the majority of state support arising from these
reforms will be provided to the approximately 40 per cent of older people with the lowest
income and wealth.[2]

The reforms also came under attack in the House of Commons where the Shadow
Secretary of State for Health claimed that the cap was being paid for by "the restriction
of eligibility for care, and the removal of care from some people who are already receiving
it".[3] Previously, he had told MPs his party saw four problems with the new system:

"First, it fails the fairness test. We will only have a durable solution if it can answer this
question: will it help every person and every couple to protect what they have worked
for, whatever their wealth and savings? I am afraid that the answer is no.

Secondly, the plan is at best a partial solution. With this decision, the Government have
prioritised the funding of a cap on care costs with new money, over and above addressing
the crisis in council care budgets . . . In practice, it will mean that vulnerable people will
continue to face rising charges, as councils put up fees to cope with the growing shortfall
in their budgets, making it more likely that those people will, in time, have to pay right up
to the new £75,000 cap. To many people, that will not feel like progress . . .

The third problem is that this package disguises yet another coalition U-turn, this time on
inheritance tax . . . It is ironic, I must say. In 2007, a flagship pledge was made to
increase the inheritance tax threshold to £1 million. Just eight weeks ago, the
Chancellor said that he would increase the threshold in two years' time. What has happened in the past two months to make him change his mind? Is not this the quickest
coalition U-turn yet? The irony will not be lost on people that the Government are
now increasing death taxes to pay for their plan. The Secretary of State has also said
the rest will be made up from national insurance. Does he think it is fair to ask the working age population to pay for something else, rather than older people?

Finally, the proposal fails to meet the scale of the challenge of the ageing society. It will
not lead to more integration of care. Instead, it will entrench the separation between two
separate systems: a free-at-the-point-of-use NHS and charged-for social care. Would it
not have made more sense, rather than developing these piecemeal plans in isolation,
to have set them out as part of a single vision for a sustainable health and care system
in the 21st century? The Secretary of State has made progress, but he has missed an
opportunity to produce a long-term plan that is fair to everyone and built on cross-
party consensus. He has settled for a timid solution when what older people needed
was a far bigger and bolder response.[4] "

The funding reforms will also have considerable resource implications for the public sector. It is likely that many more people will come into contact with their local authority – for
instance, people will want to be assessed to start progressing towards the cap and more
people will qualify for help as a result of the extension to means-tested support. In response,
the Government has claimed that the reforms provide a "significant opportunity for them to
access information and advice, and support to maintain their independence, remain active
and connected in their communities and stay healthier for longer".[5] However, in

---

[1] *Hansard* (House of Lords), 16 July 2013, Vol.747, col.700.
[2] *Hansard* (House of Lords), 16 July 2013, Vol.747, col.710 (Earl Howe).
[3] *Hansard* (House of Commons), 11 March 2014, Vol.577, col.284 (Andy Burnham MP).
[4] *Hansard* (House of Commons), 11 February 2013, Vol.558, cols 595 to 596.
[5] Department of Health, *The Care Act 2014: Consultation on draft regulations and guidance to
implement the cap on care costs and policy proposals for a new appeals system for care and support*
(2015), para.2.18.

announcing the delay to the implementation of the capped costs system, the Government noted that the proposals would add £6 billion to public sector spending over the next 5 years and "a time of consolidation is not the right moment to be implementing expensive new commitments such as this".[1]

See 1–182 below for specific criticisms of the capped costs system.

Power of local authority to charge

14.—(1) A local authority—   **1–169**

(a) may make a charge for meeting needs under sections 18 to 20, and

(b) where it is meeting needs because Condition 2 in section 18 or Condition 2 or 4 in section 20 is met, may make a charge (in addition to the charge it makes under paragraph (a)) for putting in place the arrangements for meeting those needs.

(2) The power to make a charge under subsection (1) for meeting needs under section 18 is subject to section 15.

(3) The power to make a charge under subsection (1) for meeting a carer's needs for support under section 20 by providing care and support to the adult needing care may not be exercised so as to charge the carer.

(4) A charge under subsection (1)(a) may cover only the cost that the local authority incurs in meeting the needs to which the charge applies.

(5) Regulations may make provision about the exercise of the power to make a charge under subsection (1).

(6) Regulations may prohibit a local authority from making a charge under subsection (1); and the regulations may (in reliance on section 125(7)) prohibit a local authority from doing so where, for example, the care and support or the support—

(a) is of a specified type;

(b) is provided in specified circumstances;

(c) is provided to an adult of a specified description;

(d) is provided for a specified period only.

(7) A local authority may not make a charge under subsection (1) if the income of the adult concerned would, after deduction of the amount of the charge, fall below such amount as is specified in regulations; and the regulations may in particular (in reliance on section 125(7)) specify—

(a) different amounts for different descriptions of care and support;

(b) different amounts for different descriptions of support.

(8) Regulations under subsection (7) may make provision as to cases or circumstances in which an adult is to be treated as having income that would, or as having income that would not, fall below the amount specified in the regulations if a charge were to be made.

GENERAL NOTE

Unlike the NHS, social care is not a free, universal service. Local authorities have been **1–170** able to charge for services since the inception of the welfare state. As Paul Burstow MP explained during the second reading of the Care Bill in the House of Commons:

"Social care in this country today is not free. That is the nasty little secret that families discover when they are tipped into crisis and have to negotiate with their local authority

---

[1] *House of Commons Written Answers and Statements Daily Report*, Cap on Care Costs: Written Statement – HCWS145, 20 July 2015, pp.162 to 164 (Alastair Burt MP).

over whether they will have access to any means-tested support. Most people do not know that, and it comes as a shock and creates anger and dismay in many families."[1]

The contrast with the NHS is marked. The NHS is largely free at the point of use, which means "almost no-one has to worry about medical Bills. Thanks to the NHS, health care bankrupts no-body. Social care, by contrast can consume large amounts of an individual's or a family's income and resources".[2]

Prior to the implementation of the Care Act, local authorities were required to charge for the provision of residential accommodation,[3] while charging for non-residential services (including carers' services) was discretionary.[4] The law also provided that the following services must be provided free of charge:

- intermediate care and community equipment (aids and minor adaptations) services[5];
- non-residential services to people with Creuzfeldt Jacob Disease[6];
- advice about services or an assessment[7]; and
- after-care services under s.117 of the Mental Health Act 1983.[8]

The Law Commission's remit was confined to simplifying the law, rather than changing who and how much people should pay for services. It concluded that the various legal provisions on charging for services—which as noted above were spread out across statute law, guidance and case law—should be rolled into a single statutory provision. In order to achieve this, three options were considered. The first was to replicate the existing framework by setting out a duty to charge for residential accommodation, alongside a power to charge for non-residential services. However, this was rejected on the basis that it would not cater for future changes in Government policy. The second was to establish a general power to charge for all services. Whilst this represented a formal change in the law—the removal of the duty to charge for residential accommodation—the Commission considered that in practice local authorities would continue to charge for this service. However, this option was also rejected because the then Government's policy was that residents placed by local authorities must be charged for accommodation. Instead, the Commission recommended that, in order to cater for future changes in policy, the Secretary of State should have a regulation-making power to require or authorise local authorities to charge for residential and non-residential services.[9]

1–171 The Law Commission also recommended that the new statute should give the Secretary of State a regulation-making power to require that any services should be provided free of charge. This was based on a similar power contained in s.15 of the Community Care (Delayed Discharge etc) Act 2003. But whereas the legal provisions on free care had previously been contained mainly in case law and statutory guidance, the Commission argued that in future they must all be included in the regulations—with the stated expectation that the regulations must include as a minimum all the existing free services.[10]

---

[1] *Hansard* (House of Commons), 16 December 2013, Vol.572, col.527.
[2] Commission on the Future of Health and Social Care in England, *A New Settlement for Health and Social Care: Interim Report* (King's Fund, 2014), p.7.
[3] National Assistance Act 1948 s.22(1).
[4] Health Services and Social Security Adjudications Act 1983 s.17.
[5] Community Care (Delayed Discharge etc) Act (Qualifying Services) (England) Regulations 2003 (SI 2003/1196).
[6] Department of Health, *Fairer Charging Policies for Home Care and Other Non-Residential Social Services* (2003), para.75.
[7] Department of Health, *Fairer Charging Policies for Home Care and Other Non-Residential Social Services* (2003), para.8.
[8] *R. (Stennett) v Manchester City Council* [2002] UKHL 34; [2002] 2 A.C. 1127.
[9] Law Commission, *Adult Social Care: A Consultation Paper*, Consultation Paper No.192 (2010), paras 10.19 to 10.13 and Law Commission, *Adult Social Care*, paras 8.83 to 8.88.
[10] Law Commission, *Adult Social Care*, paras 8.89 to 8.92.

The Government accepted the Law Commission's recommendation for a single over-arching charging system (including a regulation-making power to specify services that must be provided for free).[1] However, by the time the draft Care and Support Bill had been published, Government policy on the duty to charge for residential care had changed and it was accepted that charging for all forms of care and support should be discretionary. Therefore, s.14 gives local authorities a power to charge for care and support (subject to certain exemptions). Where the local authority does charge, the section also provides for regulations to make about how the local authority must exercise its discretion. The relevant regulations are the Care and Support (Charging and Assessment of Resources) Regulations 2014 (SI 2014/2672). They are reproduced and discussed at para.A1–123 below.

In order to make a charge, the local authority will normally undertake a financial assessment of the person concerned. This assessment is provided for under s.17. In broad terms the financial assessment will follow the eligibility determination and the local authority decision whether or not it will meet the person's needs. The financial assessment may in practice run parallel to the needs assessment, but according to the statutory guidance "it must never influence an assessment of needs". Local authorities must inform individuals that "a financial assessment will determine whether or not they pay towards their care and support, but this must have no bearing on the assessment process itself".[2]

During the Government's consultation on the draft Care and Support Bill, some felt that using the word "impose" in relation to charging was inappropriately strong. The Government accepted this and changed the language used in s.14 to refer instead to making a charge.[3]

According to the statutory guidance, the "overarching principle" that should be applied to the charging framework is that "people should only be required to pay what they can afford". The following principles should therefore be taken into account by local authorities:

- ensure that people are not charged more than it is reasonably practicable for them to pay;
- be comprehensive, to reduce variation in the way people are assessed and charged;
- be clear and transparent, so people know what they will be charged;
- promote well-being, social inclusion, and support the vision of personalisation, independence, choice and control;
- support carers to look after their own health and well-being and to care effectively and safely;
- be person-focused, reflecting the variety of care and caring journeys and the variety of options available to meet their needs;
- apply the charging rules equally so those with similar needs or services are treated the same and minimise anomalies between different care settings;
- encourage and enable those who wish to stay in or take up employment, education or training or plan for the future costs of meeting their needs to do so; and
- be sustainable for local authorities in the long-term.[4]

CHARGING CARERS

Section 14 provides that local authorities can charge for services provided directly to **1–172** carers. The ability to charge has been available since 2000, but in practice very few authorities have exercised this power. This reflects the significant value and cost effectiveness

---

[1] Department of Health, *Reforming the Law for Adult Care and Support: The Government's Response to Law Commission Report 326 on Adult Social Care* (TSO, July 2012), Cm.8379, para.8.27.

[2] Department of Health, *Care and Support Statutory Guidance* (2014) para.6.12.

[3] Department of Health, *The Care Bill explained—including a response to consultation and pre-legislative scrutiny on the draft Care and Support Bill* (TSO, July 2012) Cm.8386, para.68.

[4] Department of Health, *Care and Support Statutory Guidance* (2014), para.8.2.

of supporting carers. As Baroness Pitkeathley stated in the House of Lords during the passage of the Care Bill:

"Carers already contribute a huge amount, often at great personal cost, as caring has a negative impact on their finances, health and well-being, and opportunities to engage in work and education. I make no apology for repeating the figure that I have quoted many times in your Lordships' House—Carers UK has calculated that the contribution of carers is worth £119 billion a year in savings to the Exchequer. Charging a carer for support to meet their needs, often in order to help them continue in caring, risks being counterproductive by preventing carers accessing services and may even discourage carers seeking support. As a result, the adoption of charging policies would result in additional costs to local authorities.[1]

Moreover, it was pointed out that under the capped costs system, any support provided by a carer will not count towards the cap and therefore reduce the amount that the public will have to contribute.[2] An amendment was tabled by Baroness Pitkeathley at report stage to remove charging for carers altogether.[3] However, the Government resisted this and stated:

"We remain of the view that local authorities should retain the power that they have now to charge carers for support provided directly to them. Many local authorities do not impose charges on carers because they, of course, recognise the valuable contribution that carers make to society. However, some may choose to impose a nominal fee to cover a proportion of the costs of providing a particular form of support for carers— for example, a relaxation class or gym membership—and we do not think it appropriate to remove that discretion and flexibility. Indeed, removing the ability to charge even a small amount could result in the withdrawal of such services altogether.[4]

The Government has also argued that in some circumstances where local authorities place a nominal charge on carers' services as a nudge for people to take up the service, and allow it to be provided.[5] This appears to be based on the view that charging carers for a service such as a therapy session acts as an incentive because a fee would help to ensure the service was of a high quality and presumably more worth taking a break for. However, organisations representing carers have challenged this view. For example, the Carer's Trust argued that in its experience:

". . . charging carers for support, is more likely to prevent them from accessing services and may even discourage carers from seeking support, rather than the opposite. Further, we believe that widespread adoption of charging policies would result in additional costs to local authorities and that this has been demonstrated by impact assessments undertaken by local authorities considering charging carers for support."[6]

The statutory guidance confirms that while a local authority has a power to charge the carer for support, it "must not charge a carer for care and support provided directly to the person they care for under any circumstances".[7] It goes on to say that in many cases charging a carer for support would be a "false economy":

"When deciding whether to charge, and in determining what an appropriate charge is, a local authority should consider how it wishes to express the way it values carers within its local community as partners in care, and recognise the significant contribution carers

---

[1] *Hansard* (House of Lords), 9 October 2013, Vol.748, cols 90 to 91.
[2] *Hansard* (House of Lords), 9 October 2013, Vol.748, col.91.
[3] *Hansard* (House of Lords), 9 October 2013, Vol.748, cols 91 to 92.
[4] *Hansard* (House of Lords), 9 October 2013, Vol.748, col.97.
[5] Department of Health, *Caring for Our Future: Consultation on Reforming What and How People Pay for their Care and Support* (2013), para.92.
[6] Carers Trust, *Caring for Our Future: Consultation on Reforming What and How People Pay for their Care and Support: Carers Trust Response* (October 2013), para.5.4.
[7] Department of Health, *Care and Support Statutory Guidance* (2014), para.8.49.

make. Carers help to maintain the health and well-being of the person they care for, support this person's independence and enable them to stay in their own homes for longer. In many cases of course, carers voluntarily meet eligible needs that the local authority would otherwise be required to meet. Local authorities should consider carefully the likely impact of any charges on carers, particularly in terms of their willingness and ability to continue their caring responsibilities." [1]

The statutory guidance further warns that "excessive charges" are likely to lead to carers refusing support, which in turn will lead to "carer breakdown and local authorities having to meet more eligible needs of people currently cared for voluntarily". It also suggests that charging may not be proportionate "when light touch carers assessments are undertaken for small scale help" and there is a risk that financial assessments might become "the most costly part of the process". [2]

Where the carer is being charged, local authorities must do so in accordance with the non-residential charging rules and will normally carry out a financial assessment. The statutory guidance notes that it may be more likely that the carer and local authority will agree that a full financial assessment would be disproportionate as carers often face significantly lower charges. In such cases, a local authority "may choose to treat a carer as if a financial assessment has been carried out". [3]

In addition, the Association of Directors of Adult Social Services has produced a factsheet for local authorities to use in considering whether to put in place a policy of charging carers. [4] This is not statutory guidance but it has been produced with the approval of the Department of Health (see 1–770 below).

Subsection (1)
Subsection (1)(a) sets out the local authority power to charge for care and support. The **1–173** power applies to care and support being provided following a needs assessment or a carer's assessment. A charge can be made whether or not the person has eligible needs or whether the local authority is exercising a discretion to provide services. However, the local authority may not charge for any type of care and support specified in the regulations under subs.(6). There is a separate power under s.2(3) of the Care Act to make regulations to enable local authorities to charge for prevention services.

A local authority cannot recover any administrative fee relating to arranging support, subject to one exception. Subsection (1)(b) provides that a local authority can charge a fee for arranging the provision of care and support. This fee will only apply where an adult has resources above the financial limit and:

- the adult has eligible needs but does not qualify for financial support from the local authority, and they have requested that the local authority arrange the care and support that they require on their behalf (s.18(3)—condition 2);
- a carer has eligible needs but does not qualify for financial support from the local authority, and they have requested that the local authority arrange the support that they require on their behalf (s.20(3)—condition 2);
- a carer's needs involve providing care and support to the adult needing care and the adult does not qualify for financial support from the local authority, and they have requested that the local authority arrange the care and support that they require on their behalf (s.20(5)—condition 4).

---

[1] Department of Health, *Care and Support Statutory Guidance* (2014), para.8.50.
[2] Department of Health, *Care and Support Statutory Guidance* (2014), paras 8.51 to 8.52.
[3] Department of Health, *Care and Support Statutory Guidance* (2014), paras 8.53 to 8.54.
[4] Association of Directors of Adult Social Services, *The Economic Case for Investment in Carers* (March 2015).

So, for instance, the arrangement fee cannot be made where an adult with eligible needs has resources above the financial limit and has their care and support arranged by a local authority because they lack capacity and do not have anyone to represent them (s.18 (condition 3)).

The Care and Support (Charging and Assessment of Resources) Regulations 2014 (SI 2014/2672) specify that the fee to arrange a person's care must be limited to what it costs the local authority to do so (reg 5)—see para.A1–128 below. The statutory guidance emphasises that people must be made aware that they might be liable to pay the arrangement fee. It also states that the arrangement fee should take into account "the cost of negotiating and/or managing the contract with a provider and cover any administration costs incurred".[1] As noted at para.1–126 below, the Government has announced that section 18(3) will be implemented in 2015/16 in relation to non-residential care and support only. During this period, local authorities will have discretion to arrange care homes for self-funders. The statutory guidance makes clear that where the local authority is exercising this discretion it must not charge an arrangement fee.[2] It also suggests that it may be appropriate to charge a flat fee for arranging care.[3]

Related administration fees can also be charged where an adult has a deferred payment agreement (see s.35(1)(b)).

During the passage of the Care Bill through Parliament, the Government confirmed that nothing in subs.(1) gives local authorities a power to charge for carrying out a need's or carer's assessment in any circumstances.[4] The statutory guidance sets out that, as well as assessments, care planning and financial assessments may not be charged for.[5]

Subsection (2)

1–174   The power to charge is subject to s.15 which stipulates that the local authority cannot charge an adult for meeting needs if the adult has reached the cap on care costs. However, the local authority can still require such a person to pay a contribution to daily living costs in residential care (see para.1–202 below). As noted earlier, the introduction of the capped costs system has been delayed until 2020.

Subsection (3)

1–175   Meeting a carer's needs may involve providing care and support to the cared-for person, rather than direct to the carer (for instance, respite or replacement care, in order to allow the carer to have a break). Under the previous legislation, services provided to the cared-for person in order to meet the needs of the carer could not include services "of an intimate nature".[6] This served to prevent carers being charged for respite care which included personal care.

Subsection (3) replaces this provision and provides that the carer cannot be charged for any care and support provided to the person being cared for. This would include services of an intimate nature provided to the person being cared for. If the local authority exercises its power under s.15(1)(a) in such cases, it could only charge the adult needing care.

At the report stage in the House of Lords, Baroness Pitkeathley argued that subs.(3) still leaves open the issue of how a practitioner decides to whom the service is provided and thus potentially charged, and tabled an amendment to reintroduce into the Bill a provision which confirmed that services provided to a disabled person to meet the needs of a carer cannot include services of an intimate nature.[7] In response the Government stated:

---

[1] Department of Health, *Care and Support Statutory Guidance* (2014), paras 8.57 to 8.58.
[2] Department of Health, *Care and Support Statutory Guidance* (2014), para.8.58.
[3] Department of Health, *Care and Support Statutory Guidance* (2014), para.8.59.
[4] *Hansard* (House of Commons: Public Bill Committee), 14 January 2014 (PM): Fourth Sitting, col.154 (Norman Lamb MP).
[5] Department of Health, *Care and Support Statutory Guidance* (2014), paras 8.14 and 8.59.
[6] Carers and Disabled Children Act 2000 s.2(3)
[7] *Hansard* (House of Lords), 9 October 2013, Vol.748, col.92.

"This would create a legal barrier that could significantly hinder the provision of a much-needed type of support to carers. Let me provide one example. It may be appropriate to meet a carer's needs by providing a service direct to the person cared for. If some type of replacement care is provided to allow the carer to take a break from caring, it may look like home care delivered to the adult needing care, even though it is provided to meet a carer's needs. The amendment would seriously limit the ability of local authorities to make such arrangements because it would provide that the care workers could carry out some activities, but not others of an "intimate nature". That could leave a situation where the care worker was able to sit with an adult needing care but not take them to the toilet. That is likely to lead only to confusion, I suggest. We accept that clarity is needed about when a type of support should be considered to be provided directly to the carer, and when to the adult needing care. We will produce guidance on this matter, but we cannot support an amendment that sets such an inflexible rule in primary legislation. I also reassure noble Lords that the Bill is already very clear that carers should not be charged for any form of support that is provided directly to the person needing care. [Section 14(3)] makes it absolutely clear that local authorities cannot charge carers for services provided to the person being cared for. This would include services of an intimate nature."[1]

Carers' personal budgets are discussed in paras 11.36 to 11.46 of the statutory guidance. Amongst other matters, the guidance acknowledges that, as a result of s.14(3), decisions on which services are provided to meet a carer's needs and which are provided to meet the needs of the adult for whom they care, will impact on which personal budget includes the costs of meeting those needs. It advises that such decisions should be made as part of the care planning process and that joint personal budgets may be of benefit.[2]

The statutory guidance also sets out that in some circumstances "replacement care" (also known as respite care) which is being provided in the form of a home care service to the person needing care that enables the carer to take a break, must be charged to the cared-for person, not the carer. The guidance specifically mentions regular replacement care overnight and longer periods of replacement care in this respect. The principle of charging the cared-for person for respite care also applies even if the adult needing care does not have eligible needs and does not have their own personal budget (but where the carer has eligible needs and a personal budget).[3] See discussion at para.1–304 below.

Subsection (4)

This provides that where the local authority is exercising its power to charge for care and support under subs.(1)(a), it may not charge a person more than what it costs it to provide or arrange the care and support. This does not apply to the arrangement fee under subs.(1)(b) but as noted above, the regulations include a similar requirement. **1–176**

Subsection (6)

The power to charge extends to all types of care and support, unless regulations state that the specific service must be provided free. Subsection (6) gives examples of how regulations might define the provision of care and support to be provided free of charge. These regulations will replace those made under s.15 of the Community Care (Delayed Discharges etc) Act 2003. During the passage of the Care Bill through Parliament, the Government confirmed on a number of occasions its intention to maintain the existing entitlements (free of charge) to aids, minor adaptations and intermediate care in the regulations.[4] **1–177**

---

[1] *Hansard* (House of Lords), 9 October 2013, Vol.748, cols 97 to 98.
[2] Department of Health, *Care and Support Statutory Guidance* (2014), paras 11.36 to 11.37.
[3] Department of Health, *Care and Support Statutory Guidance* (2014), paras 11.39 and 11.45 to 11.46.
[4] For example, *Hansard* (House of Lords), 16 July 2013, Vol.747, col.695 (Earl Howe) and Hansard (House of Lords), 14 October 2013, Vol.748, col.278 (Earl Howe).

This subsection provides that the regulations may in particular specify different charges for different descriptions of care and support, and support. This was added as a Government amendment at report stage in the House of Lords due to concerns that in places the Bill had not been sufficiently flexible:

"Currently, local authorities are free to set their own charging policies for non-residential care. The intention was to create a more consistent framework for charging across local authorities. However, there was uncertainty whether the regulation-making powers as drafted would have allowed local authorities to contribute towards the care and support costs of people who have resources above the financial limits. A rule which prohibits local authorities from making any contribution towards the care costs of such people would restrict the ability of local authorities to use different arrangements when these would best meet local needs. For example, local authorities sometimes subsidise services such as telecare. We wish to allow this to continue and do not want to require local authorities to charge people the full cost of these services."[1]

In the House of Commons, during Committee stage, the Government confirmed that "specific cases" could include the category of terminally ill persons.[2] See also paras 1–228 to 1–229 below.

The Care and Support (Charging and Assessment of Resources) Regulations 2014 (SI 2014/2672) provide that local authorities cannot make a charge for community equipment (aids and minor adaptations) and intermediate care and reablement support services, and cannot be where the care and support is provided to an adult, under ss.18, 19 or 20 of the Act, suffering from variant Creutzfeldt-Jakob disease (regs 3 and 4). See paras A1–126 to A1–127 below.

Subsection (7)

1–178 Previously, s.17(3) of the Health Services and Social Security Adjudications Act 1983 provided that if a local authority exercised its power to charge for a non-residential service, it could not require the person to pay more than what is "reasonably practical" for them to pay. The Joint Committee on the draft Care and Support Bill argued that the courts and the Local Government Ombudsman had found this requirement to be of value in cases concerning the level of such charges, and expressed concern that the "combination of a general discretionary power and an open ended regulation making power could have unintended consequences and lead to charging creeping into more areas". It recommended that this section should make clear that where charges are imposed they should be limited to what it is "reasonably practicable" for the person to pay.[3] The Government however argued that such a change was unnecessary because subs.(7) provides for regulations to set an amount below which a person's income cannot fall after paying any charges, which creates "a stronger protection for people's income than limiting charging to what is 'reasonably practicable'".[4]

At Committee stage in the House of Commons, Paul Burstow MP— who had been the chair of the Joint Committee—tabled an amendment which would have reinserted the test of "reasonably practical". In response, the Minster argued:

"To reiterate, regulations will set a specific amount of money that people must always be left with after charging to ensure that they can afford those charges. That is, in my view, a stronger and clearer protection than a provision based on what the local authority considers to be 'reasonably practicable'. The risk—I speak as an ex-lawyer—is that what

---

[1] *Hansard* (House of Lords), 14 October 2013, Vol.748, col.281 (Earl Howe).

[2] *Hansard* (House of Commons: Public Bill Committee), 16 January 2014 (PM): Sixth Sitting, col.204 (Norman Lamb MP).

[3] House of Lords House of Commons Joint Committee on the Draft Care and Support Bill, *Draft Care and Support Bill Report, Session 2012–13*, para.196.

[4] Department of Health, *The Care Bill explained—including a response to consultation and pre-legislative scrutiny on the draft Care and Support Bill*, para.69.

is interpreted as reasonably practicable by one official and one local authority may be different from what is interpreted by another official or authority. Having a sum of money that the individual must be left with after all charges seems to be a stronger protection."[1]

Therefore, the Government argued that setting a clear amount beyond which a person's income cannot be reduced provides stronger protection.

Regulation 7 of the Care and Support (Charging and Assessment of Resources) Regulations 2014 (SI 2014/2672) sets out the minimum income for adults and carers whose needs are being met otherwise than by care home accommodation (see para.A1–130 below).

Subsection (8)

This provides that regulations under subs.(7) may specify cases or circumstances where a **1–179** person should be regarded as having or not having income that would fall below the amount specified in the regulations if a charge were to be made. The Government introduced this as an amendment at report stage in the House of Lords in order to take into account circumstances in which a financial assessment has not taken place or a local authority considers that a full assessment is unnecessary (see also s.17(13)).[2] The explanatory notes provide the following example:

". . . in a case where a local authority would make a notional charge, regulations could ensure that a person who receives a certain welfare benefit is automatically exempt from that charge. This helps protect the person's income while giving greater flexibility to the local authority not to have to carry out a financial assessment where the care package is of low value."[3]

Cap on care costs

15.—(1) A local authority may not make a charge under section 14 for meeting **1–180** an adult's needs under section 18 if the total of the costs accrued in meeting the adult's eligible needs after the commencement of this section exceeds the cap on care costs.

(2) The reference to costs accrued in meeting eligible needs is a reference—

(a) in so far as the local authority met those needs, to the cost to the local authority of having done so (as reckoned from the costs specified in the personal budget for meeting those needs (see section 26));

(b) in so far as another local authority met the needs, to the cost to that other local authority of having done so (as reckoned from the costs so specified for meeting those needs);

(c) in so far as a person other than a local authority met the needs, to what the cost of doing so would have been to the local authority which would otherwise have done so (as reckoned from the costs specified in the independent personal budget for meeting those needs (see section 28).

(3) An adult's needs are "eligible needs" if, at the time they were met—

(a) they met the eligibility criteria,

(b) they were not being met by a carer, and

(c) the adult was ordinarily resident or present in the area of a local authority.

---

[1] *Hansard* (House of Commons: Public Bill Committee), 14 January 2014 (PM): Fourth Sitting, col.156 (Norman Lamb MP).

[2] *Hansard* (House of Lords), 14 October 2013, Vol.748, col.281 (Earl Howe).

[3] Care Act 2014: Explanatory Notes para.123.

(4) The "cap on care costs" is the amount specified as such in regulations; and the regulations may in particular (in reliance on section 125(7))—

(a) specify different amounts for persons of different age groups;

(b) specify zero as the amount for persons of a specified description.

(5) The total of the costs accrued in meeting an adult's eligible needs after the commencement of this section (as referred to in subsection (1)) is referred to in this Part as the adult's "accrued costs".

(6) Where the costs accrued include daily living costs, the amount attributable to the daily living costs is to be disregarded in working out for the purposes of subsection (1) the total of the costs accrued in meeting an adult's eligible needs after the commencement of this section.

(7) Where the cost to a local authority of meeting an adult's needs under section 18 includes daily living costs, and the accrued costs exceed the cap on care costs (with the result that subsection (1) applies), the local authority may nonetheless make a charge to cover the amount attributable to those daily living costs.

(8) For the purposes of this Part, the amount attributable to an adult's daily living costs is the amount specified in, or determined in accordance with, regulations.

GENERAL NOTE

1–181   As noted previously, the 2011 report of the Commission on the Funding of Care and Support concluded that the adult social care funding system in England was "not fit for purpose" and needed urgent and lasting reform.[1] Its key recommendation was the introduction of a cap on the lifetime contribution to adult social care costs that any individual needs to make. As set out at paras 1–164 to 1–165 above, the Commission's proposal to introduce a capped costs system aimed to address the difficulties caused when people face the risk of very high and unpredictable care costs. In particular it was felt that if the public knows that their liabilities would be capped, the development of insurance products to cover the remaining costs below the care cap would become feasible. The Commission summed up its case for a cap in the following words:

"We think the best way to reform the adult social care funding system is for the state to step in and take responsibility for the area of greatest unpredictable risk. This approach means that individuals would need to take responsibility for their own costs up to a certain point but, after this, the state would pay. We see our proposals as a type of social insurance policy, with a significant 'excess' that people will need to cover themselves. A minority of people would reach the level at which the state steps in—these would be those with the highest care needs over the course of their lifetime. However, everyone would benefit from knowing that, if they ended up having to face these costs, they would be covered. We believe that by removing the fear and uncertainty inherent in the current system, people would be encouraged to make sensible preparations for the future. The approach would create a new space for financial products, which could support people in making their individual contributions".[2]

The report suggested that the cap should be set at between £25,000 and £50,000 for older people. For those who reach adulthood with an eligible care and support need or who develop one before the age of 40 should have their cap set at zero (which means they have in effect met the cap). After the age of 40, the cap should increase up to retirement age. This could rise at £10,000 per decade—so a 40-year-old could be expected to have

---

[1] Commission on Funding of Care and Support, *Fairer Care Funding: The Report of the Commission on Funding of Care and Support: Volume 1* (July 2011), p.24.

[2] Commission on Funding of Care and Support, *Fairer Care Funding: The Report of the Commission on Funding of Care and Support: Volume I* (July 2011), p.20.

a cap of £10,000; a 50-year-old, £20,000; a 60-year-old, £30,000; and a 65-year old, £35,000. The Commission also said the cap should inflate over time so that every generation gets a fair deal.[1]

In February 2013, the Government confirmed that it planned to introduce a capped costs system.[2] Originally it was intended that this reform would be introduced from 1 April 2016. However, the Department of Health has announced that the cap on care costs system will be delayed until April 2020.[3] In particular it was noted that the proposals were expected to add £6 billion to public sector spending over the next five years and "a time of consolidation is not the right moment to be implementing expensive new commitments such as this".[4]

Section 15 provides for a limit on the amount that adults can be required to pay towards eligible care costs over their lifetime. Eligible care costs are the costs of meeting eligible needs that a local authority would meet under s.18. These costs are either specified in a personal budget (s.26) where the local authority is meeting the person's needs, or in an independent personal budget (s.28) where the person has decided that they do not want the local authority to meet their needs. Most of the detail of the care cap will be set out in regulations which are subject to the affirmative procedure in Parliament (s.125(4)(b)). The affirmative procedure is discussed at para.1–161 above under s.13(7).

In the House of Lords the Government stated:

"The clauses on the capped costs system represent a significant step forward, ending decades of uncertainty, with the introduction of a clear system that fairly shares costs. For the first time, people will be protected from spiralling costs and will no longer have to fear that their home will be sold while they are in a care home."[5]

In its consultation on the draft regulations and guidance to implement the cap on care costs, the Government confirmed that the tiered cap approach, proposed by the Commission, will not be introduced. Instead it was proposed that there will be a zero cap for people who develop care and support needs up to the age of 25, and a cap of £72,000 for people of all other ages.[6] However, this document was published before the delay to the funding reforms was announced. It is possible that new proposals will be developed before 2020.

The funding provisions are expected to be commenced in April 2020, and eligible care costs will only start counting towards the cap from the date of commencement of the sections. It has been estimated that the reforms will generate an extra 332,245 assessments and 259,308 care reviews in the first year, costing £255.1 million.[7] The Government had made available £146 million to support implementation of the reforms.[8]

What will and will not count towards the cap

In general terms, the costs that will count towards the cap are the costs to the local authority of meeting the person's eligible needs as specified in the personal budget or independent personal budget.

---

[1] Commission on Funding of Care and Support, *Fairer Care Funding: The Report of the Commission on Funding of Care and Support: Volume I* (July 2011), p.24.

[2] *Hansard* (House of Commons), 11 February 2013, Vol.558, col.592 (Jeremy Hunt MP).

[3] *House of Commons Written Answers and Statements Daily Report*, Cap on Care Costs: Written Statement – HCWS145, 20 July 2015, pp.162 to 164 (Alastair Burt MP).

[4] *House of Commons Written Answers and Statements Daily Report*, Cap on Care Costs: Written Statement—HCWS145, 20 July 2015, pp.162 to 164 (Alastair Burt MP).

[5] *Hansard* (House of Lords), 16 July 2013, Vol.747, col.709 (Earl Howe).

[6] Department of Health, *The Care Act 2014: Consultation on draft regulations and guidance to implement the cap on care costs and policy proposals for a new appeals system for care and support* (2015), para.6.15.

[7] Department of Health, *Social Care Funding Reform Impact Assessment: IA No 9531* (2015).

[8] LAC(DH)(2015) 2: *Care and Support: Getting Ready for the Cap on care Costs – Funding to Support Implementation.*

The following costs will not count towards the cap:

- costs of meeting eligible care and support needs incurred before 1 April 2020;
- costs of meeting non-eligible needs;
- daily living costs (for care home residents these are the costs at the level set in the regulations);
- "top-up payments" the person or a third party chooses to make, for example for a preferred choice of accommodation;
- costs of services not included in the personal budget such as prevention and reablement services;
- interest or fees charged under a deferred payment agreement;
- needs which are being met, and will continue to be met, by a carer;
- NHS-funded nursing care and continuing health care; and
- after-care under s.117 of the Mental Health Act.

The personal budget may include the above and other sources of funding that do not count towards the cap. For instance the personal budget may include the costs of meeting non-eligible needs or it may be pooled with that of another person or carer. Only the cost of meeting the person's eligible needs will count towards the cap and so this cost will need to be distinguished clearly within the personal budget.

The younger adult zero cap

According to the most recent Government proposals, there will be a zero cap for people who develop care and support needs up to the age of 25. The policy justification for the zero cap is that young adults are less likely to have been in employment and built up any assets. However, this has raised questions about the inequality that could arise if the young person did have significant assets for example due to an inheritance. Moreover, it has been pointed out that a young person may have needs for a short period of time at the age of 18 and thus acquire a zero cap, and still be entitled to free care if they subsequently develop unconnected needs, for example as an older person with dementia.

CRITICISM OF A CAPPED COSTS SYSTEM

1–182   There have been various criticisms of the proposed cap on care costs system. For example, during the passage of the Care Bill through the House of Lords, Lord Lipsey argued that it will be complex for local authorities to administer:

> "That is because, to implement the Dilnot report, it is necessary to track each individual from the time the meter starts ticking to see exactly what they are spending on care or, rather worse, to see exactly what a local authority thinks it should be providing in spending on care for each individual—a sort of abstract concept that has to be turned into a concrete figure."[1]

He went on to suggest that the implementation costs could be between £300 million and £500 million "before money is handed out to people", with most being spent on administration rather than meeting people's needs, and argued that the Commission's scheme was too complex for ordinary members of the public to understand.[2] Lord Hunt raised concerns that the reforms will fail to generate an insurance market since private companies may struggle to know how much their liability will be.[3]

The Commission on the Future of Health and Social Care in England, established by the King's Fund, suggested that individuals are likely to incur higher costs than the £72,000 cap implies, for several reasons. First, the cap only applies to eligible needs, which will be set at

---

[1] *Hansard* (House of Lords), 16 July 2013, Vol.747, col.698.
[2] *Hansard* (House of Lords), 16 July 2013, Vol.747, col.698 (Lord Lipsey)
[3] *Hansard* (House of Lords), 16 July 2013, Vol.747, col.701 (Lord Hunt).

substantial and above, and not the costs of meeting moderate needs and below. In addition, the costs will only be based on what the local authority would pay for that level of care, which in many cases will be lower than the amount individual self-funders currently pay. It also claimed that the reforms do not address the key issue of equity, such as why conditions like dementia are viewed largely as a social care issue and heavily means tested, even though its impact can be at least as devastating as cancer.[1]

It is possible that the system will lead to increased tension between local authorities, on the one hand, and those with care and support needs and their families on the other. Under the capped costs system there is a significant financial incentive for those with care and support needs and their families to establish, at the earliest stage possible, eligible needs since at that point the meter will start to tick towards the person's cap. The assessment decisions of local authorities will have significant financial implications for many people, and it is likely that authorities will face an increase in challenges if they determine that a person's needs fall below the eligibility threshold or over the level of a person's personal budget. There may also be a risk that people will try to stay in the community inappropriately in order to reach the cap before moving into residential care in order to avoid the value of their property from ever being included in their financial assessment.

In the House of Lords, Lord Lipsey put forward an alternative capping system based on the number of years a person has been receiving care at a substantial level.[2] The origins of the proposed amendment were a proposal in the minority report to the 1999 Royal Commission on Long Term Care.[3] Under this scheme, once a person has been assessed as having substantial care needs or the equivalent under a new system the clock starts ticking and after five years the person no longer has to pay the cost of their care.[4] The Commission on the Funding of Care and Support had considered this option and accepted that using years rather than costs would be easier to administer and simpler to understand. However, it felt that to adopt this approach would disadvantage those with more intensive care needs, who over a given period of time could spend significantly more on care than those with less intensive needs, so that "what we might gain in simplicity it would lose in fairness".[5] For these reasons the Government also rejected the amendment.[6]

APPROACHING THE CAP ON CARE COSTS

It is expected that people who are progressing towards the cap on care costs will have **1–183** regular contact with their local authority, either as part of calculating their personal budget (ss.26 and 28), or through the regular statement of their care account (s.29). To ensure people know when they will reach the cap, it was proposed that regulations should require local authorities to inform them. Specifically, the draft regulations would require local authorities to notify a person – whose care account indicates that they are likely to reach the cap within 18 months of an annual statement being issued—of the date they are expected to reach the cap and provide information about what will happen when they reach the cap. Where a person is in a care home and top-up payments are being made for a preferred choice of accommodation, the local authority would be expected to be clear that if the person wishes to remain in the accommodation they (or a third party)

---

[1] Commission on the Future of Health and Social Care in England, *A New Settlement for Health and Social Care: Interim Report* (King's Fund, 2014), p.8.

[2] *Hansard* (House of Lords), 16 July, 2013, Vol.747 cols 697 to 703.

[3] Royal Commission on Long Term Care, *With Respect to Old Age: Long Term Care—Rights and Responsibilities* (TSO, March 1999), Cm.4192-I, Note of Dissent.

[4] Royal Commission on Long Term Care, *With Respect to Old Age: Long Term Care—Rights and Responsibilities* (TSO, March 1999), Cm.4192-I, Note of Dissent, para.70.

[5] Commission on Funding of Care and Support, *Fairer Care Funding: Analysis and Evidence Supporting the Recommendations of the Commission on Funding of Care and Support: Volume II* (July 2011), p.56.

[6] *Hansard* (House of Lords), 16 July 2013, Vol.747, cols 701 to 702 (Earl Howe).

would continue to be responsible for meeting those costs or the person could move to accommodation within the cost of their personal budget.[1] It was also proposed that the statutory guidance should set out that, at an "appropriate time" before the cap is reached, local authorities should have an accurate overview of the person's finances and consider whether a new financial assessment is necessary, and prepare to provide a revised personal budget for when the cap is reached. In addition, if direct payments are being provided the local authority should establish whether the person wants to maintain their contract with their existing care provider themselves or choose to ask the local authority to assume responsibility for contracting.[2] However, these proposals were published before the delay to the funding reforms was announced. It is possible that revised plans will be developed before 2020.

REACHING THE CAP ON CARE COSTS

1–184   When a person reaches the cap, the local authority becomes responsible for meeting the person's eligible needs and paying the cost of the care to meet those needs. The Government has provided the following explanation of what should happen once a person reaches the cap:

> "In many cases a person will already be having some or all of their eligible needs met by the local authority. Once they reach the cap, the local authority will already be under a duty to meet their eligible needs. Their current arrangements at that time should continue if nothing else has changed. In practice, the only difference may be the local authority contributes more to the cost of meeting their care and support needs. Where a person has been arranging and paying for their own care and support whilst progressing towards the cap, they will have an independent personal budget and a care account. When the total of their accrued costs reaches the cap, the [Care Act] obliges the local authority to meet their eligible needs.
>
> The effect of this duty will be to put the person in the same position as people for whom the local authority is already arranging care and support; this means that the local authority must prepare a care and support plan (including a personal budget), and will be subject to on-going duties to keep this plan under review."[3]

The Government has stated that a local authority will not be required to carry out a new needs assessment of the person unless their needs or other circumstances have changed. The local authority will not be able to charge the person for the cost of meeting their eligible needs as defined in the personal budget, but may need to carry out a financial assessment to determine any charges for daily living costs when the person is in a care home.[4]

The Government expects that the transition for these people should be managed in a proportionate way. For instance, it will not always be necessary to undertake a detailed care and support planning process, when a person in a care home which is meeting their needs wishes to stay there. It may also not be necessary for the local authority to take on contracts with care providers, and the person may wish to retain this control personally, and receive a direct payment equivalent to the cost of meeting their eligible needs.[5]

---

[1] Department of Health, The Care Act 2014: *Consultation on draft regulations and guidance to implement the cap on care costs and policy proposals for a new appeals system for care and support* (2015), paras 3.13 and 3.15.

[2] Department of Health, The Care Act 2014: *Consultation on draft regulations and guidance to implement the cap on care costs and policy proposals for a new appeals system for care and support* (2015), paras 10.32 and 10.34.

[3] Department of Health, *Caring for Our Future: Consultation on Reforming What and How People Pay for their Care and Support* (2013), paras 253 to 254.

[4] Department of Health, *Caring for Our Future: Consultation on Reforming What and How People Pay for their Care and Support* (2013), para.255.

[5] Department of Health, *Caring for Our Future: Consultation on Reforming What and How People Pay for their Care and Support* (2013), paras 256 to 257.

During the passage of the Care Bill through the House of Lords, Lord Lipsey raised concerns about the position of a person who is self-funding and in a home where the fee exceeds what the local authority will pay. When they reach the cap it is likely that the state will only pay up to its limit and the person then must either opt out of the funding system altogether and continue to pay for their care in full or they must move to the cheaper home (which for some older people, it was pointed out, can have fatal consequences).[1] In response, the Government acknowledged that it would be "undesirable for a person to spend their life savings on residential care and late in life be faced with the prospect of having to move to alternative accommodation purely on affordability grounds". But this needed to be balanced against the impact of extending top-up payments, namely that if individuals purchase more expensive care, this could ultimately reduce local authorities' income from charges. However, the Government promised to consider this matter further through the consultation on funding reform.[2]

In addition, the Government stated:

"It may be appropriate for the local authority to meet any additional cost, for example, where moving the person receiving care and support would adversely affect their health. However, where paying the higher cost might limit the local authority's ability to support other individuals with care and support needs, the person may have to move to less expensive accommodation. In making any decisions, the local authority has to consider the exercise of its duty to promote that individual's well-being."[3]

The Government has also stated that as people near the cap, the local authority must have an understanding of the person's preferences for how their eligible needs are met. Moreover, the person should have a clear understanding of what the local authority would pay towards their care after the cap and what their continued contribution would be if they continued to receive the same care and support.[4] By virtue of subs.(7) a local authority may charge for daily living costs once the person has reached their cap.

Subsection (1)

This sets out that local authorities cannot charge for eligible care costs once the amount **1–185** of a person's accrued care costs reach the level of the cap. The cap only comes into effect when this section is implemented—which is expected to be in April 2020. Therefore the costs of care will only count toward the cap after this date.

Subsection (2)

"Costs accrued in meeting eligible needs" is defined by this subsection as meaning those **1–186** costs that the local authority would incur if it, or another local authority, were to meet the person's needs itself, or, in the case of a person who has an independent personal budget under s.28, what the cost to the local authority of meeting the person's needs would be.

The total cost of meeting all people's eligible needs will count towards the cap—rather than their financial contribution. Therefore, an individual's payments are added to those made by the local authority when measuring progress towards the cap. In effect, this will mean that many people who fall within the means test will face a lower cap than people outside of it. For example, many older people getting financial support towards the costs of meeting their eligible needs will reach the cap without paying out the whole £72,000 themselves.

In the House of Commons the opposition raised concerns that the cap will be based on the standard rate that local authorities pay for a care home place:

[1] *Hansard* (House of Lords), 16 July 2013, Vol.747, col.736 (Earl Howe).
[2] *Hansard* (House of Lords), 16 July 2013, Vol.747, col.734.
[3] *Hansard* (House of Lords), 16 July 2013, Vol.747, col.734.
[4] Department of Health, *Caring for Our Future: Consultation on Reforming What and How People Pay for their Care and Support* (2013), para.257.

"It is estimated that in 2016–17, when the cap is due to start, the average council rate for residential care will be £522 a week, and the average price of a care home place will be £610 a week. That is because self-funders pay more than councils. However, that will not be taken into account when the cap is calculated.[1]

This issue is also discussed at s.18(3) (see para.1–218 below) and s.28 (see para.1–320 below). As noted above, the implementation of the cap on care costs has now been delayed until 2020.

When the new system is introduced, it is not yet clear whether or not the cost of adaptations will count towards the cap. Significant disability-related works could result in the maximum being reached almost immediately and encourage people to seek such work being undertaken.

Subsection (3)

1–187   This subsection defines "eligible needs" as those that meet the eligibility criteria and are not being met by a carer. Adults must also be ordinary resident, or present in the local authority area to have eligible needs.

In the House of Lords Baroness Pitkeathley argued that it was unfair that carers were expected to provide unpaid care and that the cost of caring should not count towards the care account within the cap arrangement.[2] In response, the Government stated:

"Local authority assessments take the support provided by carers into account in determining the care package. We are clear that the care package should count towards the cap, because that should ensure that all people receive the support that they need. We have heard from the care and support sector that the cap will provide carers, as well as care users, with the financial support to help them decide on the right care for them to help provide, and to reassure them that their families will not face catastrophic care costs."[3]

Section 15(3)(b) also confirms that the local authority is not under a duty to meet any of the adult's eligible needs which are being met at that time by a carer.

Subsection (4)

1–188   This provides for the level of the cap to be set in regulations, and includes power to set the cap at different amounts for people of different ages. This will allow the cap to be set at different levels for working age adults, and includes the possibility of setting the cap at zero for specified categories of person. The most recent proposals in this respect are discussed at para.1–181 above.

By virtue of s.125(4)(b) regulations made under this subsection are subject to the affirmative procedure in Parliament (except those which vary the cap made under s.16(1)). The affirmative procedure is discussed at para.1–161 above.

Subsection (6)

1–189   Subsection (6) ensures that progress towards the cap will not include people's contribution towards their daily living costs.

See below at para.1–202 for further discussion on daily living costs.

Subsection (7)

1–190   A local authority may continue to charge for the daily living costs once the adult has reached the cap. It is proposed that the same means test will apply after people reach the cap on care costs to determine what proportion of £230 per week they can afford to contribute towards their daily living costs.

---

[1] *Hansard* (House of Commons), 16 December 2013, Vol.572, col.501 (Andy Burham MP).

[2] *Hansard* (House of Lords), 9 October 2013, Vol.748, cols 91 to 92.

[3] *Hansard* (House of Lords), 9 October 2013, Vol.748, col.97 (Earl Howe).

See below at para.1–202 for further discussion on daily living costs.

Subsection (8)
This provides a regulation making power to set the amount that will be considered as **1–191** representing an adult's daily living costs. The first use of this power is subject to the affirmative procedure in Parliament (see s.125(4)(c)). The affirmative procedure is discussed at para.1–161 above.
See below at para.1–202 for further discussion on daily living costs.

Cap on care costs: annual adjustment

16.—(1) Where it appears to the Secretary of State that the level of average **1–192** earnings in England is different at the end of a review period from what it was at the beginning of that period, the Secretary of State must make regulations under section 15(4) to vary the cap on care costs by the percentage increase or decrease by which that level has changed.

(2) If a variation is made under subsection (1), each adult's accrued costs are to be varied by the same percentage with effect from when the variation itself takes effect (and local authorities must accordingly ensure that care accounts and other records reflect the variation).

(3) The "level of average earnings in England" means the amount which represents the average annual earnings in England estimated in such manner as the Secretary of State thinks fit.

(4) "Review period" means—
(a) the period of 12 months beginning with the day on which section 15 comes into force, and
(b) each subsequent period of 12 months.

(5) The duty under subsection (1) does not restrict the exercise of the power to make regulations under section 15(4).

GENERAL NOTE
The Commission on Funding of Care and Support noted that "the care and support sys- **1–193** tem is constantly evolving, responding to demographic, social, economic, legal, technological and political change". In order to ensure that its proposed reforms form the basis of a "long-term, stable settlement", the Commission wanted to provide sufficient levers so that the Government can respond to different political and fiscal pressures. These levers include the overall level of the cap. The Commission recommended that it is uprated yearly on the same basis as the basic state pension. This was aimed to ensure that the real value of the cap remains constant. Furthermore, it suggested that the Government might set up an independent body to review, periodically, the overall level of the cap. This would "not only help the financial services sector design and price products, but also help individuals and families in their financial planning".[1]
The Government accepted the recommendation on yearly uprates. Section 16 therefore places a duty on the Secretary of State to make annual adjustments in order to ensure that the level of the cap and an adult's accrued costs in their care account (see s.29) keep pace with inflation. In addition s.71 requires a five yearly review of the level of the cap and the means test threshold. However, the Government rejected the establishment of an independent advisory body arguing that this was unnecessary because experts will be involved in assessing how external factors such as demographic change and healthy life expectancy are affecting affordability and the benefits of the capped costs system. Moreover, the Government felt that the creation of a standing independent committee could send out a

---

[1] Commission on Funding of Care and Support, *Fairer Care Funding: The Report of the Commission on Funding of Care and Support: Volume I* (July 2011), pp.77 to 78.

message that the system will be subject to constant change— resulting in fewer people planning and preparing on the basis of the reforms.[1]

In the House of Lords, the Government also rejected amendments to require the annual adjustment to be made in line with average care costs. It argued that there is no nationally recognised measure for care costs inflation and moreover it would be unnecessary to develop such a measure, because:

". . . a robust proxy already exists. Average earnings is one element of the measures used to determine the state pension and therefore represent changes in people's ability to pay. Earnings is a national statistic certified as compliant with the code of practice for official statistics. In addition, care costs and average earnings are related since labour is a substantial proportion of the cost of care. The latest Laing & Buisson market survey states that, 'in the longer term, fees are inevitably driven by costs . . . the major cost item is payroll'."[2]

See para.1–200 below in respect of uprating the lower and upper means test thresholds.

Subsection (2)

1–194   When the level of the cap is adjusted, the extent of a person's progress towards the cap will be maintained. The explanatory notes state that this subsection "ensures that an adult's accrued costs are adjusted by the same measure as the cap, so that if someone was previously 50 per cent of the way towards the cap, then they will remain so after adjustment."[3]

Subsection (3)

1–195   "Average earnings" for the purposes of this section is defined as average annual earnings in England as estimated by the Secretary of State.

Subsection (4)

1–196   This requires adjustment to be considered annually following commencement of the section. The Government has also stated that the Act does not prohibit adjustments at other times following commencement. As noted previously, the capped costs system is due to be implemented in April 2020.[4]

Subsection (5)

1–197   The power to set the level of the costs cap in s.15 is not restricted by the annual adjustment.

Assessment of financial resources

1–198   **17.**—(1) Where a local authority, having made a determination under section 13(1), thinks that, if it were to meet an adult's needs for care and support, it would charge the adult under section 14(1) for meeting at least some of the needs, it must assess—

    (a) the level of the adult's financial resources, and

    (b) the amount (if any) which the adult would be likely to be able to pay towards the cost of meeting the needs for care and support.

    (2) Where a local authority thinks that, in meeting an adult's needs for care and support, it would make a charge under section 15(7), it must assess—

    (a) the level of the adult's financial resources, and

---

[1] *Hansard* (House of Lords), 16 July 2013, Vol.747, col.710 (Earl Howe).

[2] *Hansard* (House of Lords), 16 July 2013, Vol.747, col.710 (Earl Howe).

[3] Care Act 2014: Explanatory Notes para.132.

[4] Department of Health, *The Care Act 2014: Consultation on draft regulations and guidance to implement the cap on care costs and policy proposals for a new appeals system for care and support* (2015), para.3.17.

(b) the amount (if any) which the adult would be likely to be able to pay towards the amount attributable to the adult's daily living costs.

(3) Where a local authority, having made a determination under section 13(1), thinks that, if it were to meet a carer's needs for support, it would charge the carer under section 14(1) for meeting at least some of the needs, it must assess—

(a) the level of the carer's financial resources, and

(b) the amount (if any) which the carer would be likely to be able to pay towards the cost of meeting the needs for support.

(4) Where a local authority, having made a determination under section 13(1), thinks that, if it were to meet a carer's needs for support, it would charge the adult needing care under section 14(1) for meeting at least some of the needs, it must assess—

(a) the level of the financial resources of the adult needing care, and

(b) the amount (if any) which the adult needing care would be likely to be able to pay towards the cost of meeting the carer's needs for support.

(5) An assessment under this section is referred to in this Part as a "financial assessment".

(6) A local authority, having carried out a financial assessment, must give a written record of the assessment to the adult to whom it relates.

(7) Regulations must make provision about the carrying out of a financial assessment.

(8) The regulations must make provision as to cases or circumstances in which, if the financial resources of an adult who has needs for care and support (whether in terms of income, capital or a combination of both) exceed a specified level, a local authority is not permitted to, or may (but need not)—

(a) in a case where the adult's accrued costs do not exceed the cap on care costs, pay towards the cost of the provision of care and support for the adult;

(b) in a case where the adult's accrued costs exceed the cap on care costs, pay towards the amount attributable to the adult's daily living costs.

(9) The regulations must make provision as to cases or circumstances in which, if the financial resources of a carer who has needs for support or of the adult needing care (whether in terms of income, capital or a combination of both) exceed a specified level, a local authority is not permitted to, or may (but need not), pay towards the cost of the provision of support for the carer.

(10) The level specified for the purposes of subsections (8) and (9) is referred to in this Part as "the financial limit"; and the regulations may in particular (in reliance on section 125(7)) specify—

(a) different levels for different descriptions of care and support;

(b) different levels for different descriptions of support.

(11) The regulations must make provision for—

(a) calculating income;

(b) calculating capital.

(12) The regulations may make provision—

(a) for treating, or not treating, amounts of a specified type as income or as capital;

(b) as to cases or circumstances in which an adult is to be treated as having, or as not having, financial resources above the financial limit.

(13) The regulations may make provision as to cases or circumstances in which a local authority is to be treated as—

(a) having carried out a financial assessment in an adult's case, and

    (b) being satisfied on that basis that the adult's financial resources exceed, or that they do not exceed, the financial limit.

GENERAL NOTE

1–199   Section 17 provides that where a local authority exercises its discretion to charge, it must carry out a financial assessment of a person's resources. The financial assessment determines the contribution by the individual and their local authority towards the cost of the care. The amount that the individual must pay, based on the financial assessment, must be included in the personal budget statement (see s.29(1)(b)).

Prior to the Care Act, the charging rules for residential care were set out in regulations (supported by statutory guidance), and applied uniformly across all local authorities.[1] For non-residential care, there was statutory guidance but local authorities had flexibility to design their own charging rules.[2] The Commission on Funding of Care and Support noted that this led to variation in the charging rules for non-residential care across England.[3]

As noted above at para.1–170, the Law Commission argued that the legal provisions on charging for services should be rolled into a single statutory provision. It also recommended that the vast majority of the detail on charging (such as the financial assessment) should be set out in regulations and supported by guidance.[4] This approach was accepted by the Government.[5] The relevant regulations are the Care and Support (Charging and Assessment of Resources) Regulations 2014 (SI 2014/2672). They are reproduced and discussed at para.A1–123. The statutory guidance considers financial assessments at paras 8.15 to 8.26, and Annexes B and C.

CAPITAL LIMITS

1–200   Only people with capital below a certain level (the upper capital limit) qualify for financial help to meet their care and support needs. The Commission on Funding of Care and Support criticised the £23,250 upper limit as being unfair and for failing to encourage people to plan and save for the future. Given the significant increase in the value of people's homes over recent decades, most home owners would be excluded automatically from any financial support for care in a care home, even if they had very little income. The Commission recommended that the upper threshold within the residential care means test should be raised to £100,000 (in 2010–11 prices). The upper limit level appears to have been based on the assertion that median housing wealth among single people over 65 who own property is around £160,000. The intention was to remove the cliff edge between being a self-funder and being supported by the local authority, whereby a small change in a person's capital results in a significant change in what they pay for care. In other words, the Commission hoped to ensure that more people are eligible for state support and avoid the risk of losing all their assets before they reach the cap—in particular those of more modest means whose savings have been accumulated in their home.[6]

In February 2013, the Government confirmed that it would introduce an extended means test and that the threshold will be increased at a level equivalent to that recommended by

[1] The National Assistance (Assessment of Resources) Regulations 1992 (SI 1992/2977) and Department of Health, *Charging for Residential Accommodation Guide (CRAG)* (April 2014).

[2] Department of Health, *Fairer Charging Policies for Home Care and other Non-Residential Social Services: Guidance for Councils with Social Services Responsibilities* (June 2013).

[3] Commission on Funding of Care and Support, *Fairer Care Funding: The Report of the Commission on Funding of Care and Support: Volume I* (July 2011), p.15.

[4] Law Commission, *Adult Social Care*, para.8.83 to 8.88.

[5] Department of Health, *Reforming the Law for Adult Care and Support: The Government's Response to Law Commission Report 326 on Adult Social Care* (TSO, July 2012), Cm.8379, para.8.27.

[6] Commission on Funding of Care and Support, *Fairer Care Funding: The Report of the Commission on Funding of Care and Support: Volume I* (July 2011), pp.27 to 28 and 35.

the Commission.[1] The Government has proposed that the upper capital limit will be increased to £118,000 for people in residential care whose home has been taken into account in their financial assessment. In all other cases, the upper capital limit will be £27,000. This includes people in residential care whose home has been disregarded from the financial assessment (for example, where an eligible relative such as a spouse continues to reside in the property). It was proposed that the lower capital limit will be increased from £14,250 to £17,000. If a person's assets are less than this amount then they will only be required to contribute towards their care costs from their income. It is estimated that in the first year alone, up to 23,000 additional people will receive support with their care costs.[2] It should be noted that these proposals were published before the delay to the funding reforms was announced. It is possible that revised plans will be developed before 2020. Until the funding reforms are introduced, the £23,250 upper threshold and £14,250 lower threshold will remain in place.

The Government intends to amend the statutory guidance to clarify that local authorities have discretion to set their own capital limits in relation to adults receiving support in locations other than care homes, provided they are no lower that £23,250 for the higher limit and £14,250 for the lower limit.[3]

The Joint Committee on the draft Care and Support Bill recommended that the legislation must provide for automatic uprating of the lower and upper means test thresholds using a defined measure specified in regulations, which are subject to the affirmative procedure.[4] In its response the Government argued that:

"The means test thresholds and tariff income are currently set using the negative procedure and this has been the case for many years. We are committed to annually uprating the means test threshold, but do not agree that we need to change the basis on which the regulations are made in order for our intentions on the threshold or tariff income to be clear."[5]

TARIFF INCOME Means tested support is available on a sliding scale and tariff income is **1–201** used to determine what contribution a person is asked to make towards their care costs from their assets (in addition to a contribution from their income). The calculation of a person's contribution from their assets in all care settings is set out in reg.25 of the Care and Support (Charging and Assessment of Resources) Regulations 2014 (SI 2014/2672)—see para.A1–148 below. This provides that people must contribute £1 per week for every £250 in assets which fall between the lower limit and the relevant upper limit (see above). People must be left with a minimum amount of income after charges. In care homes this is known as the Personal Expenses Allowance (reg.6) an in all other settings the Minimum Income Guarantee (reg.7).

Part 5 of, and Sch.2 to, the Care and Support (Charging and Assessment of Resources) Regulations 2014 (SI 2014/2672) make provision for the treatment and calculation of capital, and the capital sums which must be disregarded by the local authority (see paras A1–141 to A1–148, and A1–158.).

[1] *Hansard* (House of Commons), 11 February 2013, Vol.558, col.593 (Jeremy Hunt MP).
[2] Department of Health, *The Care Act 2014: Consultation on draft regulations and guidance to implement the cap on care costs and policy proposals for a new appeals system for care and support* (2015), para.13.
[3] Department of Health, *Update on the Final Orders under the Care Act 2014* (2015) para.25.
[4] House of Lords House of Commons Joint Committee on the Draft Care and Support Bill, *Draft Care and Support Bill Report, Session 2012–13*, para.38.
[5] Department of Health, *The Care Bill explained—including a response to consultation and pre-legislative scrutiny on the draft Care and Support Bill*, p.56.

DAILY LIVING COSTS

1–202   People receiving residential care remain responsible for their daily living costs (such as food and lighting) if they can afford to pay them. The Commission on Funding Care and Support recommended that living costs should be set at between £135 and £190 a week.[1] In 2013 the Government announced its intention that—in line with other local authority benefits such as pensions, attendance allowance and disability living allowance/ personal independence payment—the contribution to daily living costs will be set at a national level of £12,000, or approximately £230 per week (the equivalent of around £10,000 in 2010/11 prices). The person would be left with a defined minimum amount to cover appropriate expenses relevant to each care setting (with annual adjustments applied), and any income they earn will be retained.[2]   This is known as the personal expenses allowance. The policy justification was explained by the Government in the House of Lords:

> "When living at home, people pay for their food and heating from their income. It is right that people should continue to contribute towards these costs in residential care. The personal expenses allowance reflects the fact that for most people these costs represent a large proportion of their income, but it allows people to retain some of their income for other uses."[3]

Section 15(6) ensures that progress towards the cap will not include people's contribution towards their general living costs. Section 15(8) provides a power for Government to set the amount that will be considered as representing an adult's daily living costs.

It is expected that the same means test will apply after people reach the cap on care costs to determine what proportion of £230 per week they can afford to contribute towards their daily living costs.

The Government has set out that calculating a person's daily living costs is not intended to be a "precise science" and local authorities and providers are not required to calculate actual costs for each person in a care home progressing towards the cap. The amount is a "notional contribution" set in regulations at £230 per week.[4]

It has been announced that the introduction of the funding reforms (including the national level for daily living costs) will be delayed until April 2020.[5]   The proposals, set out above, were published before the delay was announced. It is possible that revised plans will be developed before 2020.

REFUSAL OF A FINANCIAL ASSESSMENT

1–203   Section 17 must be read alongside s.13(3)(b) of the Care Act which provides that the local authority must ascertain whether an adult with eligible needs wants to have their needs met by the local authority. This enables a person to refuse a financial assessment. If the adult refuses a financial assessment they are normally charged the full cost of their care and support. When the capped costs system is introduced, the person who has refused their financial assessment must be provided with an independent personal budget

---

[1] Commission on Funding of Care and Support, *Fairer Care Funding: The Report of the Commission on Funding of Care and Support: Volume I* (July 2011), p.34.
[2] Department of Health, *Caring for Our Future: Consultation on Reforming What and How People Pay for their Care and Support* (2013), paras 128 to 130.
[3] *Hansard* (House of Lords), 16 July 2013, Vol.747, col.730 (Earl Howe).
[4] Department of Health, *The Care Act 2014: Consultation on draft regulations and guidance to implement the cap on care costs and policy proposals for a new appeals system for care and support* (2015), para.10.13.
[5] *House of Commons Written Answers and Statements Daily Report*, Cap on Care Costs: Written Statement – HCWS145, 20 July 2015, pp.162 to 164 (Alastair Burt MP).

(see s.28) and a care account (see s.29). In effect a person can merely record their eligible care costs for the purposes of progressing towards the new cap.

Subsections (1) to (4)

These subsections require a local authority to carry out a financial assessment if it has **1–204** decided to charge for a particular service under its power in s.14(1). This applies in respect of:

- an adult with needs for care and support (subs.(1));
- a carer with needs for support (subs.(3)); and
- a carer with needs for support where the authority would charge the adult needing care for meeting those needs (subs.(4)).

The assessment must take place after an assessment has been completed and a decision made as to whether or not the person has eligible needs under s.13(1). The aim of the financial assessment is to determine the level of the adult's financial resources, and any amount they would be likely to pay towards the cost of meeting their needs for care and support.

Following the introduction of the funding reforms, a financial assessment must be carried out where the local authority exercises its power to charge under s.15(7) for the daily living costs once the adult has reached the cap (see para.1–190 above).

Where a person lacks capacity, they still may be assessed as being able to contribute towards the cost of their care. The charging rules also apply to people in prisons.

Section 17 does not specify how often a financial assessment should be reviewed. However, since the person's personal budget (which includes the amount that a person must pay towards their care costs, based on the financial assessment—see s.26(1)(b))— forms part of the care and support plan, or support plan (s.25(1)(e)) it is submitted that the financial assessment must be reviewed in accordance with section 27 of the Act. In other words, the local authority must keep under review generally the financial assessment and respond to a reasonable request for a review. The statutory guidance states that local authorities must "regularly" re-assess a person's ability to pay charges to take into account changes to their resources, and that this is likely to be on an annual basis but may vary according to individual circumstances. Moreover, a re-assessment must also take place if "there is a change in circumstances or at the request of the person".[1]

Subsection (6)

This requires a local authority to provide people with a written record of their financial **1–205** assessment. This subsection was not included in the draft Care and Support Bill but was added to the Care Bill following consultation on the draft Bill.[2]

There are no requirements for the format or content of the record, other than for it being in writing. However, the Equality Act 2010 may be relevant to the performance of this duty and if necessary, the record should be provided in alternative formats and using different methods of communication, as well as being in writing.

Subsection (6) does not specify or indicate how much detail should be provided in the written record of the financial assessment. The extent of the detail is likely to depend upon the specific circumstances of the individual case, and may for example need to be proportionate to the extent and depth of the person's financial circumstances and the assessment undertaken. Therefore, in some cases a person being provided with simple and shorter term support and whose financial assessment is relatively straightforward may require a less detailed record, compared to the record of a person being provided with expensive residential care whose finances are complex.

---

[1] Department of Health, *Care and Support Statutory Guidance* (2014), para.8.17.
[2] Department of Health, *The Care Bill explained—including a response to consultation and pre-legislative scrutiny on the draft Care and Support Bill*, para.70.

Subsection (7)

1–206   This requires the Secretary of State to make regulations in relation to financial assessments.

In the House of Commons, during the passage of the Care Bill, the Government rejected an amendment which would require regulations made under subs.(7) to be subject to affirmative resolution, arguing this would be "bureaucratic, unnecessary and time consuming". Moreover, since these regulations will need to be updated annually, The Government argued that the amendment could "seriously compromise the ability to keep provisions up to date" and to provide them to local authorities "with sufficient notice in advance of implementation".[1]

Subsections (8) and (9)

1–207   The regulations made under subs.(7) must set the maximum amount of financial resource an adult may have, above which a local authority is not permitted to contribute towards an individual's care and support costs, and daily living costs—or cases where local authorities do have the power to be more generous and contribute to the costs of an adult with resources above the financial limit.

A similar requirement is made in respect of carers (subs.(9)).

The Care and Support (Charging and Assessment of Resources) Regulations 2014 (SI 2014/2672) specify that if the financial resources of an adult who is provided with accommodation in a care home (a permanent resident) exceed £23,250 (in terms of capital), the local authority is not permitted to pay towards the cost of the provision of that accommodation. In any other case where the financial limit exceeds £23,250 (in terms of capital), the authority may (but need not) pay towards the cost of care and support (reg.12).

Subsection (10)

1–208   This clarifies that the regulation-making power to set a financial limit allows for different financial limits to be set for different types of care and support, or support in the case of carers.

Subsection (12)

1–209   The regulations may make provision for treating or not treating certain types of income as capital, and cases or circumstances in which an adult is to be treated as having, or as not having, financial resources above the financial limit.

Subsection (13)

1–210   The regulations may set rules where the local authority need not carry out a full financial assessment and whether, in these circumstances, the individual needing care and support is entitled to local authority support. According to the explanatory notes, this would allow for "less detailed financial assessments to be carried out in some situations", and could "enable the local authority to meet the needs of people who do not wish to have a full financial assessment, if the authority considers this necessary".[2]

The Government introduced this as an amendment at report stage in the House of Lords and explained its intention in the following terms:

"We wish to encourage people to undertake financial assessments because this will enable local authorities to charge them a fair contribution towards their care costs. However, we recognise that some people are likely to refuse to undergo a financial assessment; for example, someone may be unwilling to allow the local authority to access their financial information. In order best to promote these people's well-being, it may be appropriate for local authorities to arrange care on their behalf. The local

---

[1] *Hansard* (House of Commons: Public Bill Committee), 16 January 2014 (AM): Fifth Sitting, col.177 (Norman Lamb MP).
[2] Care Act 2014: Explanatory Notes para.136.

authority would be able to charge individuals the full cost of this care and any arrangement fee.

These amendments will therefore allow regulations to enable local authorities to broker care on behalf of people who do not wish to undergo a financial assessment. The regulations will also make provision for light-touch financial assessments where a full financial assessment would not be proportionate, such as for low-cost care packages, in particular for carers. Regulations and guidance will be designed to ensure that such assessments are used appropriately."[1]

The Care and Support (Charging and Assessment of Resources) Regulations 2014 (SI 2014/2672) set out the circumstances when a local authority is to be treated as having carried out a financial assessment in an adults case and being satisfied on that basis that their resources exceed or do not exceed the financial limit (reg.10). This includes where the authority, with the consent of the adult, has not carried out a financial assessment but is satisfied from the evidence available that their resources do not exceed the financial limit because the adult is in receipt of income support (see para.A1–333 below).

DUTIES AND POWERS TO MEET NEEDS

Duty to meet needs for care and support

18.—(1) A local authority, having made a determination under section 13(1), **1–211** must meet the adult's needs for care and support which meet the eligibility criteria if—

  (a) the adult is ordinarily resident in the authority's area or is present in its area but of no settled residence,
  (b) the adult's accrued costs do not exceed the cap on care costs, and
  (c) there is no charge under section 14 for meeting the needs or, in so far as there is, condition 1, 2 or 3 is met.

  (2) Condition 1 is met if the local authority is satisfied on the basis of the financial assessment it carried out that the adult's financial resources are at or below the financial limit.

  (3) Condition 2 is met if—

  (a) the local authority is satisfied on the basis of the financial assessment it carried out that the adult's financial resources are above the financial limit, but
  (b) the adult nonetheless asks the authority to meet the adult's needs.

  (4) Condition 3 is met if—

  (a) the adult lacks capacity to arrange for the provision of care and support, but
  (b) there is no person authorised to do so under the Mental Capacity Act 2005 or otherwise in a position to do so on the adult's behalf.

  (5) A local authority, having made a determination under section 13(1), must meet the adult's needs for care and support which meet the eligibility criteria if—

  (a) the adult is ordinarily resident in the authority's area or is present in its area but of no settled residence, and
  (b) the adult's accrued costs exceed the cap on care costs.

  (6) The reference in subsection (1) to there being no charge under section 14 for meeting an adult's needs for care and support is a reference to there being no such charge because—

  (a) the authority is prohibited by regulations under section 14 from making such a charge, or

---

[1] *Hansard* (House of Lords), 14 October 2013, Vol.748, cols 281 to 282 (Earl Howe).

(b) the authority is entitled to make such a charge but decides not to do so.

(7) The duties under subsections (1) and (5) do not apply to such of the adult's needs as are being met by a carer.

GENERAL NOTE

1–212   Prior to the Care Act, adult social care law contained several statutory duties to provide services. The formula adopted by most of these duties was to entitle a specific group or different groups of individuals with care and support needs to be provided with certain services. Such groups included disabled people, people with a mental disorder and those suffering from illness. However, most of the duties covered the same or similar services and the categories of individuals also overlapped. In addition, the degree of enforceability of each of these duties varied. So, for example, the duty to provide residential accommodation under s.21(1) of the National Assistance Act 1948 was a strong individually enforceable duty which provided limited scope for local authorities to take into account the availability of resources.[1]   Duties such as s.2(1) of the Chronically Sick and Disabled Persons Act 1970 to provide certain "welfare services" gave local authorities greater ability to have regard to resources or other factors in deciding whether a duty is owed.[2] Some of the other duties were general duties and therefore difficult to enforce.[3] In addition to the legislative framework, eligibility for non-residential care was assessed against eligibility criteria contained in statutory guidance.[4] Local authorities were required to apply this guidance when determining eligibility for non-residential services and could only deviate from it if there was good reason to do.[5]

Furthermore, ordinary residence was also an important aspect of establishing eligibility for services. Some local authority duties to provide community care services were conditional upon the individual concerned being ordinarily resident in the authority's area, or of no settled residence but present in the authority's area (for example, welfare services under s.29(1) of the National Assistance Act 1948). If the person was not ordinarily resident, then either the duty might be downgraded to a mere discretion or there may be no power to provide those services at all. In contrast, some duties to provide community care services applied irrespective of ordinary residence (such as those under the National Health Service Act 2006).

The Law Commission concluded that the legal framework for determining eligibility was convoluted, baffling and inadequate. It recommended that all of the existing duties needed to be consolidated into a single duty to meet eligible needs. The Commission also recognised the importance of retaining the existing strong individually enforceable entitlements to community care services. It therefore recommended that the wording of the duty must make it clear that the duty is an individual duty enforceable through judicial review.[6] In addition the Commission recommended that the concept of ordinary residence should apply to all forms of care and support. In effect a local authority should have a duty to provide services to those ordinarily resident in its area (subject to its eligibility criteria)—or of no settled residence but is in urgent need of accommodation—and a power to provide services for people not ordinarily resident or of no settled residence.[7]

In broad terms, s.18 implements the Law Commission's recommendations. It sets out the circumstances in which a local authority is obliged to meet an adult's eligible needs and is,

---

[1] *R. v Sefton Metropolitan Borough Council Ex p Help the Aged* (1997–98) 1 CCLR 57.

[2] *R. v Gloucestershire City Council Ex p Barry* [1997] A.C. 584.

[3] For example, National Assistance Act 1948 s.29.

[4] Originally LAC(2002)13, Fair Access to Care Services: Guidance on Eligibility Criteria for Adult Social Care, which was replaced by Department of Health, *Prioritising Need in the Context of Putting People First: A Whole System Approach to Eligibility for Social Care: Guidance on Eligibility Criteria for Adult Social Care, England 2010* (2010).

[5] *R. v Islington LBC Ex p Rixon* (1997–98) 1 CCLR 119.

[6] Law Commission, *Adult Social Care*, paras 6.2 to 6.12.

[7] Law Commission, *Adult Social Care*, paras 10.1 to 10.11.

therefore, the principal means through which individual entitlement to care and support is established (the equivalent for carers is provided for in s.20). The effect of s.18 is to create a strong and enforceable duty that is owed to the individual. If the adult has eligible needs (this would be decided using the eligibility framework set out in regulations made under s.13) *and* meets the other criteria specified in s.18, then the local authority must meet those needs and other factors—such as the availability of resources—are not relevant to this duty.

Whilst the Law Commission had envisaged that a local authority's duty to meet eligible needs would be subject only to the ordinary residence provisions, the Government has added to the criteria—in part to take into account the implications of its funding reforms. The net effect is that the s.18 duty is owed to any individual with eligible needs who is ordinarily resident in the local authority's area (or of no settled residence but is present in the authority's area), subject to two exceptions. These exceptions apply when the local authority is exercising its discretion to charge for a service. The first is when the person is a self-funder and does not want the authority to meet their needs. The second exception is where the person lacks capacity and there is a person authorised or in a position to arrange the relevant care and support.

The s.18 duty applies to all forms of care and support (including residential accommodation), and replaces the previous community care duties, including s.21(1) of the National Assistance Act 1948 and s.2(1) of the Chronically Sick and Disabled Persons Act 1970.

The ability of an individual to challenge the local authority decision under s.18 is considered at paras 1–699 to 1–702 below. See also para 1–153 above for a discussion on art.8 and positive obligations to provide assistance. **1–213**

Subsections (1)

This sets out the preconditions that trigger the local authority's duty to meet an adult's needs for care and support. First, a person's needs must meet the eligibility criteria set out in regulations under s.13. Secondly, the adult must be ordinarily resident in the local authority area, or has no settled residence in any area, but is living in the local authority area at that time. This is to ensure that "a single local authority can be identified as responsible for meeting that person's needs".[1] See discussion at paras 1–430 to 1–431 below in respect of ordinary residence and no settled residence. **1–214**

Thirdly, if the local authority does not charge for a type of care and support, or regulations provide that it is to be provided for free, there is a duty to meet needs regardless of the person's finances.

If the local authority does charge, the adult's financial circumstances are taken into account and one of the three conditions in subss.(2) to (4) must be met.

Finally, the local authority must meet an adult's eligible care and support needs if the person's care costs have reached the cap (see subs.(5)). As noted earlier, the introduction of the capped costs system has been delayed until 2020. The circumstances in which the local authority does not or may not charge are set out in subs.(6).

Subsection (2)

Condition 1 provides that if the local authority does charge, and the adult's financial resources are assessed as being at or below the financial limit set in regulations (under s.17), the duty to meet eligible needs is triggered. **1–215**

The explanatory notes state that:

"In other words, the adult does not have sufficient financial resources to be able to pay the charge which is assessed as due, although they may be required to make a contribution. The amount of resources required will depend on the type of care and support,

---

[1] *Hansard* (House of Commons: Public Bill Committee), 16 January 2014 (AM): Fifth Sitting, col.183 (Norman Lamb MP).

and will be calculated following a financial assessment carried out by the local authority (under s.17)."[1]

Subsection (3)

1–216   Condition 2 provides that if the local authority does charge, and the adult's financial resources are assessed as being above the financial limit set in regulations (under s.17), the duty to meet eligible needs is triggered if the adult requests that the local authority meets their needs. During the passage of the Care Bill, the Government described this as "an important and groundbreaking new right" for self-funders to ask the local authority to arrange care and support on their behalf.[2]

Section 14(1)(b) provides that a local authority can charge a fee for arranging the provision of care and support in such cases.

Regulation 3 of the Care Act 2014 (Commencement No.4) Order 2015 (SI 2015/993(C.68) has delayed the implementation of section 18(3) insofar as it creates a duty to meet needs by providing or arranging care home accommodation. Where the person asks the local authority to meet their eligible needs, and it is anticipated that their needs will be met by a care home placement, then the local authority may choose to meet their needs, but is not required to do so. In other cases, where the needs are to be met by care and support of some other type, the local authority must meet those eligible needs. Originally it was intended that the duty on local authorities under s.18(3) to meet the eligible needs of self-funders in care homes would be implemented on 1 April 2016. However, the Department of Health has announced that this reform (along with the other financial reforms) will be delayed until April 2020.[3]

The Government confirmed in Parliament that where the adult lacks capacity to make the request, it may be made by someone else acting on their behalf. It argued that this was the effect of the Mental Capacity Act 2005 and it was not therefore necessary to set this out in subs.(3).[4] This is also stated in the explanatory notes.[5] The person making the request on behalf of the incapacitated adult could only do so if this were in the adult's best interests under the Mental Capacity Act 2005. The person or another interested party, or the local authority could then arrange for the payment of the local authority's charge through deputyship.

BROKERING AND CONTRACTING

1–217   The statutory guidance discusses "brokering" services in paras 10.15 to 10.19. This is where the local authority supports the individual to make a choice about and enter into a contract with the care provider. The local authority would not need to "hold" the contract with the provider but would need to be satisfied that the provider and terms of the contract were appropriate to meet the person's needs. However, the individual themselves funds the provision of services.

The statutory guidance states that brokering would only be an effective way of meeting a person's needs in "exceptional circumstances", such as where a self-funder wishes to retain control of the contract with their provider but asks the local authority to meet their needs under s.18(3) and where the person is not using alternative care arrangements

---

[1] Bill 123–EN 2013–2014, Explanatory Notes to the Bill, para.123.
[2] *Hansard* (House of Commons: Public Bill Committee), 16 January 2014 (AM): Fifth Sitting, col.180 (Norman Lamb MP).
[3] *House of Commons Written Answers and Statements Daily Report*, Cap on Care Costs: Written Statement – HCWS145, 20 July 2015, pp.162 to 164 (Alastair Burt MP).
[4] *Hansard* (House of Lords), 16 January 2013, Vol.747, col.745 (Earl Howe) and *Hansard* (House of Commons: Public Bill Committee), 16 January 2014 (AM): Fifth Sitting, col.180 (Norman Lamb MP).
[5] Care Act 2014: Explanatory Notes para.140.

such as an individual service fund. It also suggests that when deciding whether or not to use brokerage, local authorities should:

". . . have regard to the likelihood of the person continuing to be willing and able to manage such arrangements in the future, including their ability to pay the charges due (e.g. to mitigate against a future loss of capacity or disposal of their assets, such that the local authority may be required to take over the contract with the provider). The local authority would continue to support the person in meeting any other needs, offer ongoing support and keep the arrangements under review to ensure that the needs were met. The person would have a care and support plan as usual."[1]

The statutory guidance also emphasises that people must be made aware that they have a right to request the local authority to meet their needs, and that they may be liable to pay an arrangement fee. Also, local authorities should offer support to people in meeting their own needs such as providing information on different options, and "may offer to arrange contracts with providers".[2] In addition, the guidance explains that where a local authority is arranging care and support for someone with resources above the financial limit, it may charge the person the full costs of their care and support. The person "remains responsible for the costs of their care and support, but the local authority takes on the responsibility for meeting those needs".[3]

Elsewhere the guidance states that:

"In supporting self-funders to arrange care, the local authority may choose to enter into a contract with the preferred provider, or may broker the contract on behalf of the person. Where the local authority is arranging and managing the contract with the provider, it should ensure that there are clear arrangements in place as to how the costs will be met, including any 'top-up' element.

Ultimately, the local authority should assure itself that robust contractual arrangements are in place in such circumstances that clearly set out where responsibilities for costs lie and ensure that the person understands those arrangements. Self-funders will have to pay for the costs of their care and support including, in cases where they choose a setting that is more expensive than the amount identified in their personal budget, the top-up element of the costs of that setting."[4]

IMPACT ON THE PROVIDER MARKET

Most self-funders do not pay local authority rates for care homes. To some degree this is **1–218** because local authorities take advantage of procurement at scale and secure a lower rate for those residents funded by the authority. Many people see this as a case where local authorities underpay and that if homes only existed under local authority rates many of them would not be viable. In effect, self-funders subsidise the people in care homes who are paid for by the local authority.

A number of concerns were raised (during the Government's consultation on the draft guidance and regulations) about the possible impact of section 18(3) on the provider market. In particular, consultees suggested that the cost-differential would be eroded, and that there would be additional demand for local authority services, particularly in areas with high levels of self-funders. In reply, the Government argued that there was little consensus on the size of the risk, how and where it may impact or the extent it could be mitigated by local practices and robust information and advice. It admitted that some data suggested different prices paid by local authorities and self-funders in certain cases, but "this is not sufficiently robust to determine whether or how such risks may manifest, or to quantify

---

[1] Department of Health, *Care and Support Statutory Guidance* (2014), para.10.17.
[2] Department of Health, *Care and Support Statutory Guidance* (2014), paras 8.56, 8.58 and 8.61.
[3] Department of Health, *Care and Support Statutory Guidance* (2014), para.8.62.
[4] Department of Health, *Care and Support Statutory Guidance* (2014), Annex A, paras 42 to 43.

accurately any impact on local authorities and providers". Moreover, it felt that any impact would be significantly less in 2015/16 than in 2016/17 when the capped costs system and independent personal budgets were originally due to be introduced. The Government therefore announced the delay in the implementation of s.18(3) for one year, until April 2016, insofar as it relates to people whose needs are to be met in care homes. The additional time was intended to allow for further analysis and a clearer understanding of the risks, and to develop "appropriate strategies for implementing this most effectively".[1] However, in July 2015 the Government announced that the full introduction of the duty on local authorities under s.18(3) would be further delayed until April 2020.[2] In the meantime, local authorities have discretion to arrange care-homes for self-funders.[3]

See also discussion at para.1–320 above on the potential impact of independent personal budgets on local authorities and care providers.

Subsection (4)

1–219   Condition 3 provides that if the local authority does charge, the duty to meet eligible needs is triggered if the adult lacks the mental capacity to arrange care and support, and there is no other in a position to arrange that care and support on their behalf. In these circumstances, the duty applies, regardless of other factors such as finances. The Government described this condition as an "additional safety net" which enacts a provision set out previously in guidance.[4]

The Joint Committee noted that a self-funder who lacks the requisite mental capacity would not have the right to require their local authority to meet their needs if they had (for example) a lasting power of attorney—even if the attorney is unwilling or unable to make the care arrangements. Even if there is no attorney or equivalent, the duty would not arise if the local authority decided that someone (for example a family carer) was "in a position" to provide support on the person's behalf. The Committee argued it was wrong in principle to place a person with impaired mental capacity in such a disadvantaged position.[5]

The explanatory notes state that condition three applies where there is no other person "willing or able" to arrange the care and support.[6] Subsection (4) must therefore be read with this intention in mind. However, it is submitted that the correct position is that there must be no other person "willing *and* able". The ability of any person to undertake this role is not enough to satisfy condition three. There must be a willingness to arrange the care and support. In other words, the mere existence of a family member or carer should not lead a local authority to conclude that they are in a position to arrange the care and support; the individual is not obliged to take on this task. This principle applies even where the person who lacks capacity has an attorney or deputy acting on their behalf. That person must be both willing and able to make the arrangements. In particular, the local authority would need to be sure that this person had been given the appropriate legal authority under the terms of the lasting power of attorney or by Court of Protection.

---

[1] Department of Health, *Response to the Consultation on draft Regulations and Guidance for Implementation of Part 1 of the Care Act 2014* (2014) Cm 8955, pp.7 to 8.

[2] *House of Commons Written Answers and Statements Daily Report*, Cap on Care Costs: Written Statement – HCWS145, 20 July 2015, pp.162 to 164 (Alastair Burt MP).

[3] Department of Health, *Response to the Consultation on draft Regulations and Guidance for Implementation of Part 1 of the Care Act 2014* (2014) Cm 8955, pp. 7 to 8 and Department of Health, *Care and Support Statutory Guidance* (2014), paras 8.55 to 8.56.

[4] *Hansard* (House of Lords), 16 July 2013, Vol.747, col.745 (Earl Howe). The guidance being referred to was: LAC(98)19: Community Care (Residential Accommodation) Act 1998 paras 10 to 12).

[5] House of Lords House of Commons Joint Committee on the Draft Care and Support Bill, *Draft Care and Support Bill Report, Session 2012–13*, para.201.

[6] Care Act 2014: Explanatory Notes para.140.

Subsection (5)

The local authority is under a duty to meet an adult's needs for care and support which **1–220**
meet the eligibility criteria where the adult's accrued costs exceed the cap on care costs (see
s.15) if the adult is ordinarily resident in the local authority area (or has no settled residence
in any area, but is living in the local authority area at that time). As noted earlier, the introduction of the capped costs system has been delayed until 2020.

Subsection (6)

This sets out the circumstances in which there may be no charge for particular types of **1–221**
care and support, for the purposes of subs.(1)(c). These are that:

- regulations prohibit the local authority from charging for the type of care and support
  being provided by the local authority; or
- the local authority decides not to charge for the care and support being provided.

Subsection (7)

The local authority is not under a duty to meet any of the adult's eligible needs which are **1–222**
being met at that time by a carer. The explanatory notes state:

"When conducting the needs assessment and the eligibility determination, the local
authority will assess the totality of the adult's needs, regardless of whether a carer is currently meeting any of them. This is sometimes referred to as the assessment being 'carer-
sighted'.

However, the local authority is not under a duty to meet any eligible needs which are
being met by a carer, because the carer is already doing so. If a carer were to cease providing care and to stop meeting any eligible needs, this would trigger a review of the
adult's care and support plan, and may mean that the local authority is required to
meet the needs. If the carer has needs for support, they should be entitled to an assessment in their own right, under [s.10], and may receive support to meet their eligible
needs."[1]

The approach set out in the notes is sometimes referred to as the assessment being "carer
blind"—see para.1–098 above. The Government's intention is to "create an incentive to
ensure that the local authority supports the carer to maintain their caring role".[2]
However, this is subject to s.10(5)(a) and (b) which requires the carer's assessment to
include an assessment of the carer's willingness and ability to continue to provide support.
See also discussion under s.15(3)(b)—see para.1–187 above—which confirms that the
cap on care costs will not apply to needs which are being met by a carer. Arguably, as a
result of these reforms carers will have an incentive to withdraw informal support or be
less than completely open about the support being provided, because the cared-for person
will reach the cap on care costs sooner than they would otherwise have done.

Power to meet needs for care and support

19.—(1) A local authority, having carried out a needs assessment and (if **1–223**
required to do so) a financial assessment, may meet an adult's needs for care
and support if—
  (a) the adult is ordinarily resident in the authority's area or is present in its area
      but of no settled residence, and
  (b) the authority is satisfied that it is not required to meet the adult's needs
      under section 18.

---

[1] Care Act 2014: Explanatory Notes paras 143 to 144.
[2] *Hansard* (House of Commons: Public Bill Committee), 16 January 2014 (AM): Fifth Sitting, col.182
(Norman Lamb MP).

(2) A local authority, having made a determination under section 13(1), may meet an adult's needs for care and support which meet the eligibility criteria if—

(a) the adult is ordinarily resident in the area of another local authority,

(b) there is no charge under section 14 for meeting the needs or, in so far as there is such a charge, condition 1, 2 or 3 in section 18 is met, and

(c) the authority has notified the other local authority of its intention to meet the needs.

(3) A local authority may meet an adult's needs for care and support which appear to it to be urgent (regardless of whether the adult is ordinarily resident in its area) without having yet—

(a) carried out a needs assessment or a financial assessment, or

(b) made a determination under section 13(1).

(4) A local authority may meet an adult's needs under subsection (3) where, for example, the adult is terminally ill (within the meaning given in section 82(4) of the Welfare Reform Act 2012).

(5) The reference in subsection (2) to there being no charge under section 14 for meeting an adult's needs is to be construed in accordance with section 18(6).

GENERAL NOTE

1–224   The Law Commission recommended that local authorities should continue to have a power to meet needs that fall below the eligibility criteria and to provide temporary urgent services before an assessment is carried out.[1] This has been implemented by s.19 which enables local authorities to meet the needs of adults whose needs they are not otherwise required to meet.

Subsection (1)

1–225   This subsection provides that where an adult is ordinary resident—or of no settled residence but present in the authority's area—and has needs which fall below the eligibility threshold, the authority may meet those needs. The local authority must have carried out a needs assessment (and a financial assessment if required to do so) before this power arises.

Subsection (2)

1–226   Where a local authority is satisfied on the basis of a needs assessment that the adult has eligible needs, but that person is ordinary resident in another local authority's area, it may still meet those needs if:

● it has decided not to charge or is not able to charge for a particular type of care and support; or

● in so far as there is such a charge, conditions one to three in s.18 are met.

The authority must notify the other local authority of its intention to meet the needs.

The first condition in s.18 is that the adult's financial resources are assessed as being at or below the financial limit set in regulations under s.17. The second condition is that the adult requests that the local authority meets their needs, even if they have to pay for their care and support in full because their resources are assessed as above the financial limit. The third condition is that the adult lacks the mental capacity to arrange care and support, and there is no other in a position to arrange that care and support on their behalf.

The power does not allow a local authority to meet the needs of a person who is ordinarily resident elsewhere and which do not satisfy the minimum eligibility threshold.

---

[1] Law Commission, *Adult Social Care*, paras 6.11 and 12.19 to 12.21

Subsection (3)

The local authority may meet an adult's urgent needs for care and support. This applies **1–227** regardless of whether the adult is ordinarily resident in its area. The authority is not required to have first carried out a needs assessment and a financial assessment or made an eligibility decision. In some cases the local authority may need to respond to urgent needs by the provision of services. But the statutory guidance also recognises that in other cases, an immediate referral may be necessary, for example by completing the NHS Continuing Health Care Fast Track Pathway Tool.[1]

This provision is based on the previous local authority power under s.47(3) of the National Health Service and Community Care Act 1990 to provide temporary community care services without having undertaken an assessment where in the opinion of the authority the person requires those services as a matter of urgency. In addition, s.47(6) had stated that if, by virtue of subs.(5), services have been provided temporarily, then "as soon as practicable thereafter" an assessment of the person's needs must be made in accordance with s.47(1). The Care Act does not contain an equivalent requirement to s.47(6). However, clearly it will be in a local authority's interest to ensure that as a matter of practice a full assessment is carried out or an eligibility decision is made as soon as possible. The explanatory notes state that when urgent care and support is provided, "the local authority must still carry out the assessments, but can do so in due course so as to not delay care and support being put in place".[2] The statutory guidance confirms that the person should be informed that a full assessment and other procedures will follow.[3]

Following the assessment or eligibility decision, services may be withdrawn, changed, or provided subject to a charge. Previous statutory guidance had advised that after the initial response individuals should be informed that such changes might occur.[4] It is likely that a similar approach would be expected in respect of service provision under subs.(3).

The meaning of the term "urgent" is not defined in the Act. The courts have however considered that under the previous power under s.47(3) of the National Health Service and Community Care Act 1990 the following cases could qualify:

- the provision of temporary residential accommodation to a destitute asylum seeker suffering from hepatitis B[5] ; and
- the provision of a temporary residential placement for a young man of 19 who was autistic and had learning difficulties, where a local authority's flawed decision-making process had ruled out a placement on the grounds of cost and had not identified suitable alternatives and where the urgency had resulted from the lateness of the decisions by the authority.[6]

The statutory guidance points to the example of where an individual's condition deteriorates rapidly or they have an accident.[7]

Subsection (4)

Originally the Care Bill did not refer to cases of terminal illness. The Joint Committee **1–228** had recommended that the legislation should require local authorities to fast-track assessments for terminally ill people, other than those for whom the NHS has continuing health care responsibilities.[8] In response, the Government argued that this was unnecessary given

---

[1] Department of Health, *Care and Support Statutory Guidance* (2014), para.6.26.
[2] Care Act 2014: Explanatory Notes para.146.
[3] Department of Health, *Care and Support Statutory Guidance* (2014), para.6.26.
[4] LAC(2002)13, *Fair Access to Care Services: Guidance on Eligibility Criteria for Adult Social Care*, para.69.
[5] *R. (AA) v Lambeth LBC* [2001] EWHC Admin 741; (2002) 5 CCLR 36.
[6] *R. (Alloway) v Bromley LBC* [2004] EWHC 2108 (Admin); (2005) 8 CCLR 61.
[7] Department of Health, *Care and Support Statutory Guidance* (2014), para.6.26.
[8] House of Lords House of Commons Joint Committee on the Draft Care and Support Bill, *Draft Care and Support Bill Report, Session 2012–13*, para.181.

that local authorities had powers to meet urgent needs for care and support without carrying out a full assessment under subs.(3).[1]

However, during the passage of the Care Bill in the House of Lords the Government faced further pressure on this issue led by Lord Warner, Lord Patel and Baroness Greengross.[2] The Government responded by introducing subs.(4) as an amendment at report stage. It provides that a local authority may regard the care and support needs of people at the end of life as urgent. But it does not require this. The Government Minster explained the intention in the following terms:

". . . I have tabled an amendment to make it explicit that the end of life is an example of when local authorities may treat cases as urgent. We do not believe that it would be right to require local authorities to treat all cases in this way—circumstances have to dictate the approach taken—but we agree that clarity around end-of-life cases as examples of urgent situations for the purposes of [s.19] may provide a useful indication to improve practice."[3]

The Government faced further pressure in the House of Commons to introduce a duty to meet all needs at the end of life urgently. However, the Government argued that it would not be appropriate for there to be such a duty "as there are many instances where it would be appropriate first to carry out financial assessment and eligibility in the normal way".[4]

The Government also rejected an amendment which would have specified that a local authority may meet a carer's needs under subs.(3) where the adult needing support is terminally ill. It argued that an express provision was unnecessary because:

"When a carer's needs for support are deemed urgent it is usually as a result of the adult's needs being urgent, and so usually that would be best remedied by providing care to the adult urgently, for which there is already provision in [s.19]. Where it is clear that local authorities need to put in place support for a carer quickly, they should obviously do so. We would expect provisions in the [Care Act] to be applied proportionately, so that there need not be a delay in providing the support carers need, especially in urgent circumstances."[5]

Subsection (4) cross-refers to the definition of a terminal illness provided in s.82(4) of the Welfare Reform Act 2012. This defines a person as being "terminally ill" if "the person suffers from a progressive disease and the person's death in consequence of that disease can reasonably be expected within 6 months". In the House of Lords Baroness Finlay outlines some of the problems with this definition:

". . . we cannot predict prognosis. That is always the catch with defining terminal illness. We are making our best guess, as it says in the Welfare Reform Act, as to whether someone can 'reasonably be expected' to die within six months, but it is no better than that. It is a guess. There are patients who outlive their prognosis."[6]

1–229 END OF LIFE CARE. In the House of Lords the Government also faced pressure to amend the Bill to provide that terminally ill patients should where practicable be able to choose their place of death and be exempt from social care charges.[7] On the first issue,

---

[1] Department of Health, *The Care Bill explained—including a response to consultation and pre-legislative scrutiny on the draft Care and Support Bill* (TSO, July 2012), Cm.8386, para.59.

[2] *Hansard* (House of Lords), 29 July 2013, Vol.747, cols 1593 to 1599.

[3] *Hansard* (House of Lords), 14 October 2013, Vol.478, col.289 (Earl Howe).

[4] *Hansard* (House of Commons: Public Bill Committee), 16 January 2014 (PM): Sixth Sitting, col.199 (Norman Lamb MP).

[5] *Hansard* (House of Commons: Public Bill Committee), 16 January 2014 (PM): Sixth Sitting, col.199 (Norman Lamb MP).

[6] *Hansard* (House of Lords), 14 October 2013, Vol.478, col.294.

[7] *Hansard* (House of Lords), 29 July 2013, Vol.747, cols 1593 to 1599 and 14 October 2013, Vol.478, col. 289 to 291.

Macmillan Can Support estimated that 36,400 cancer patients who die in hospital each year would have preferred to die at home where that was possible. The national bereavement survey found that around half of people die in hospital despite the fact that only 2 per cent actually stipulated that as their preference. The National Audit Office found that for 40 per cent of those who die in hospital, there was no clinical reason for them to be there.[1] The Government responded by saying it had made a commitment in *Liberating the NHS: Greater Choice and Control* to support people's preferences at the end of life and this is being taken forward in the *End of Life Care Strategy*.[2] It also pointed out that there is already a power in s.6E of the National Health Service Act 2006 to make regulations, or standing rules, to require NHS England and clinical commissioning groups to make arrangements for patient choice in respect of specified treatments or services. It confirmed that these were the powers that would be used to implement a choice offer in end-of-life care. The Government also stated:

"It would be in no one's interests if the upfront investment required to enhance community services came at the expense of existing services. That is why the Department of Health and NHS England will be working together, and with organisations from across the end-of-life and palliative care sector, on a review of the timescale for introducing this choice offer at a time that will be right for patients and for those in the NHS working in this vital area. We have to ensure that when a choice offer is introduced, it will be a real choice backed by a system that is able to deliver it."[3]

On the charging issue, the Government had stated that it is funding eight pilot sites on free social care at the end of life (due to report in 2015), and confirmed that primary legislation is not required to enable social care to be provided free at the end of life as this can be introduced through regulations under s.14(6) of the Care Act.[4] In the House of Commons the Government Minister stated that he was determined to achieve the objective of free social care at the end of life, but recognised he was not in a position to commit the Government.[5]

In March 2015 the Health Select Committee recommended that the Government provide free social care at the end of life and expressed disappointment at the lack of progress on developing a method for calculating the costs.[6]

Duty and power to meet a carer's needs for support

20.—(1) A local authority, having made a determination under section 13(1), **1–230** must meet a carer's needs for support which meet the eligibility criteria if—

(a)   the adult needing care is ordinarily resident in the local authority's area or is present in its area but of no settled residence,

(b)   in so far as meeting the carer's needs involves the provision of support to the carer, there is no charge under section 14 for meeting the needs or, in so far as there is, condition 1 or 2 is met, and

---

[1] Macmillan Cancer Research, *Time to Choose: Making Choice at the End of Life A Reality* (October 2013), Office for National Statistics, *National Bereavement Surry (VOICES) 2012* (2013), National Audit Office, *End of Life Care* (November 2008) HC 1043.

[2] *Hansard* (House of Lords), 29 July 2013, Vol.747, col.1600 (Earl Howe).

[3] *Hansard* (House of Lords), 14 October 2013, Vol.478, col.297 (Earl Howe).

[4] *Hansard* (House of Lords), 21 May 2013, Vol.745, col.827 (Earl Howe). See also, *Hansard* (House of Commons: Public Bill Committee), 16 January 2014 (PM): Sixth Sitting, cols 200 and 204 (Norman Lamb MP).

[5] *Hansard* (House of Commons: Public Bill Committee), 16 January 2014 (PM): Sixth Sitting, col.201 (Norman Lamb MP).

[6] House of Commons Health Committee: End of Life Care: Fifth Report of Session 2014-15 (2015) HC 805, paras 120 to 137.

(c) in so far as meeting the carer's needs involves the provision of care and support to the adult needing care—
  (i) there is no charge under section 14 for meeting the needs and the adult needing care agrees to the needs being met in that way, or
  (ii) in so far as there is such a charge, condition 3 or 4 is met.

(2) Condition 1 is met if the local authority is satisfied on the basis of the financial assessment it carried out that the carer's financial resources are at or below the financial limit.

(3) Condition 2 is met if—

(a) the local authority is satisfied on the basis of the financial assessment it carried out that the carer's financial resources are above the financial limit, but

(b) the carer nonetheless asks the authority to meet the needs in question.

(4) Condition 3 is met if—

(a) the local authority is satisfied on the basis of the financial assessment it carried out that the financial resources of the adult needing care are at or below the financial limit, and

(b) the adult needing care agrees to the authority meeting the needs in question by providing care and support to him or her.

(5) Condition 4 is met if—

(a) the local authority is satisfied on the basis of the financial assessment it carried out that the financial resources of the adult needing care are above the financial limit, but

(b) the adult needing care nonetheless asks the authority to meet the needs in question by providing care and support to him or her.

(6) A local authority may meet a carer's needs for support if it is satisfied that it is not required to meet the carer's needs under this section; but, in so far as meeting the carer's needs involves the provision of care and support to the adult needing care, it may do so only if the adult needing care agrees to the needs being met in that way.

(7) A local authority may meet some or all of a carer's needs for support in a way which involves the provision of care and support to the adult needing care, even if the authority would not be required to meet the adult's needs for care and support under section 18.

(8) Where a local authority is required by this section to meet some or all of a carer's needs for support but it does not prove feasible for it to do so by providing care and support to the adult needing care, it must, so far as it is feasible to do so, identify some other way in which to do so.

(9) The reference in subsection (1)(b) to there being no charge under section 14 for meeting a carer's needs for support is a reference to there being no such charge because—

(a) the authority is prohibited by regulations under section 14 from making such a charge, or

(b) the authority is entitled to make such a charge but decides not to do so.

(10) The reference in subsection (1)(c) to there being no charge under section 14 for meeting an adult's needs for care and support is to be construed in accordance with section 18(6).

GENERAL NOTE

Prior to the Care Act, local authorities had a power to provide services to carers but not **1–231** an express duty.[1] In exercising this power, authorities could, but were not required to, apply an eligibility framework and set a minimum threshold for service provision. Department of Health guidance had advised that local authorities should implement an eligibility framework based on the extent of the risk to the sustainability of the caring role, but this was non-statutory guidance.[2] This advice was cross-referenced in statutory guidance—and the eligibility framework for carers was reproduced—but it did not comment on whether the framework should be adopted by local authorities.[3]

In broad terms, the remit of the Law Commission's review of adult social care did not extend to the creation of new legal rights or entitlements to services. However, it considered that there was a strong case—in law reform terms—to provide for a new legal duty to meet carers' needs. In part this reflected an important principle that carers should have parity with the people they support in the new statute; as noted in para.1–113 above in respect of carer's assessments, the Commission concluded that there was no convincing reason why the threshold for carer's rights should differ from those of adults in need of care and support.

In addition, it considered the economic consequences of this approach. Research carried out by the Commission for the purposes of its consultation paper found that many local authorities were already using an eligibility framework to decide whether to provide services to carers. It was therefore argued that a duty to provide a carer service is accepted in practice even if it did not exist in law, and consequently the proposal would not have negligible resource implications. However, the eligibility framework used differed between local authorities, with practice ranging from applying the same eligibility framework that is used for service users, adding in further indicia to the service user eligibility framework, to using the eligibility framework for carers set out in practice guidance. In order to address this inconsistency the Commission proposed at consultation that there should be a mandatory national eligibility framework which local authorities must use to decide whether or not to provide services to individual carers, and a duty to meet the eligible needs of carers.[4]

However, a number of local authorities and other consultees—even those supporting the proposal—disagreed that the proposal would have negligible resource implications. In its final report, the Law Commission rejected these arguments. It pointed out that local authorities were already required to respond to certain needs of carers in some circumstances (for example, where a carer's needs gave rise to a critical risk to the sustainability of the caring role—see paras 1–120 and 1–333 above) and could not adopt a policy never to exercise the power to provide services, since this would amount to fettering its discretion. Moreover it was argued that in practice, local authorities did provide services to carers. The effect of the proposal would therefore be to provide greater clarity on how a local authority exercises this power and what level of needs it will provide services to meet. In effect, any cost implications would arise from where the eligibility threshold was set by the local authority or central government (depending on whether a national eligibility threshold would be introduced). The reform could be made within the same level of funding or the Government could decide to provide additional funding to meet carers' needs. For these reasons, the Commission recommended that there should be such a prescribed eligibility framework in the new statute and a duty to meet the eligible needs of carers.[5]

---

[1] Carers and Disabled Children Act 2000 s.2(1).

[2] Department of Health, *Carers and Disabled Children Act 2000: Carers and People with Parental Responsibility for Disabled Children: Practice Guidance* (2001), para.70.

[3] Department of Health, *Prioritising Need in the Context of Putting People First: A Whole System Approach to Eligibility for Social Care: Guidance on Eligibility Criteria for Adult Social Care, England 2010* (2010), paras 97 to 103.

[4] Law Commission, *Adult Social Care: A Consultation Paper*, Consultation Paper No.192 (2010), paras 6.48 to 6.65.

[5] Law Commission, *Adult Social Care*, paras 7.13 to 7.16.

In its response to the Law Commission, the Government accepted the principle of parity between carers and the people they support. It agreed that the statute should place a duty on local authorities to meet the eligible needs of carers.[1] This is provided for by s.20. See paras 1–150 to 1–163 above on the eligibility criteria for carers with support needs.

The statutory guidance does not discuss carers separately, although it does contain individual carer sections throughout. This is deliberate. The Department of Health has described its approach as "mainstreaming" the guidance relating to carers throughout the document "to ensure that consideration of carers is embedded throughout the reformed system".[2] However, the Association of Directors of Adult Social Services has produced a guide on implementing the carers' duties in the Care Act. The document also summarises the key elements of the statutory guidance that apply to carers.[3] This is not statutory guidance but it has been produced with the approval of the Department of Health (see 1–770 below).

Subsection (1)

1–232   This subsection sets out the criteria that trigger the local authority's duty to meet a carer's needs for support. The criteria are linked to the question of whether meeting the carer's needs involves the provision of support direct to the carer or whether it involves the provision of care and support direct to the adult needing care. An example of how the carer's needs for support might be met by providing care and support direct to the adult for whom they are caring could be the provision of replacement care to allow the carer to have a break from caring.

The criteria can be summarised as follows:

1. the adult needing care must be ordinarily resident in the local authority's area or has no settled residence, but is living in the local authority's area at that time (see discussion at paras 1–430 to 1–431 below on ordinary residence);

2. the carer has been assessed by the local authority and has been determined to have eligible needs for support – that is, the carer has needs that meet the national eligibility criteria (see s.13 and Care and Support (Eligibility Criteria) Regulations 2015 (SI 2015/313));

3. where the carer's eligible needs are to be met by support directly to them,

    (a) there is no charge (under s.14); or
    (b) one of the conditions in subss.(2) and (3) is met;

4. where the carer's eligible needs are being met by care and support to the adult needing care,

    (a) the adult agrees to its provision; or
    (b) one of the conditions in subss.(2) and (3) is met.

See paras 1–150 to 1–163 above on the eligibility criteria for carers with support needs.

Subsection (2)

1–233   The first condition that will trigger the duty to meet a carer's eligible needs is that— where meeting the carer's needs involves the provision of support to the carer—the carer's financial resources are at or below the financial limit.

---

[1] Department of Health, *Reforming the Law for Adult Care and Support: The Government's Response to Law Commission Report 326 on Adult Social Care* (TSO, July 2012), Cm.8379, paras 7.13 to 7.16.

[2] Department of Health, *Response to the Consultation on draft Regulations and Guidance for Implementation of Part 1 of the Care Act 2014* (2014) Cm 8955, p.9.

[3] Association of Directors of Adult Social Services, *A guide to interventions for implementing the Care Act 2014 as it applies to carers* (April 2015).

Subsection (3)

The second condition that will trigger the duty to meet a carer's eligible needs is that— **1–234**
where meeting the carer's needs involves the provision of support to the carer—the carer's
financial resources are above the financial limit (in effect they are a self-funder) but nevertheless they request that the local authority meet their needs.

In such cases s.14(1)(b) provides that a local authority can charge a fee for arranging the
provision of support to the carer.

Subsection (4)

The third condition that will trigger the duty to meet a carer's eligible needs is that— **1–235**
where meeting the carer's needs involves the provision of care and support to the adult
needing care—the adult needing care's financial resources are at or below the financial
limit, and that the adult concerned agrees to receive such support.

Subsection (5)

The fourth condition that will trigger the duty to meet a carer's eligible needs is that— **1–236**
where meeting the carer's needs involves the provision of care and support to the adult
needing care—the adult needing care's financial resources are above the financial limit
(in effect they are a self-funder) but nevertheless they request that the local authority
meet their needs by providing care and support to them.

In such cases s.14(1)(b) provides that a local authority can charge a fee for arranging the
provision of care and support to the adult.

Subsection (6)

Local authorities are given a broad power to meet the needs of carers who are not other- **1–237**
wise eligible, including the provision of care and support to the person needing care, as long
as that person agrees.

Subsection (7)

Where meeting the carer's needs involves the provision of care and support to the adult **1–238**
needing care, s.20 does not require that the adult themselves must have eligible needs. In
other words, it does not matter that there may be no duty to meet that adult's needs in their
own right.

Subsection (8)

Where a local authority considers the best way of meeting a carer's needs for support is **1–239**
by providing care and support to the adult needing care but it is not possible to do so (for
example, if that adult does not agree to such provision), the authority is required, as far as it
is feasible, to identify some other way of supporting the carer.

The term feasible confirms a focus on whether the identification of alternative support is
possible, rather than whether the provision of such support is considered to be the most
appropriate option.

Subsection (9)

This clarifies the reference in subs.(1)(b) to there being no charge for meeting a carer's **1–240**
need. This refers to s.14(3) which makes clear that where the needs are met by providing
care and support direct to the adult needing care, the charge may not be imposed on the
carer. Alternatively, it refers to where the authority exercises a discretion not to charge.

Exception for persons subject to immigration control

21.—(1) A local authority may not meet the needs for care and support of an **1–241**
adult to whom section 115 of the Immigration and Asylum Act 1999 ("the
1999 Act") (exclusion from benefits) applies and whose needs for care and support have arisen solely—

(a) because the adult is destitute, or

(b) because of the physical effects, or anticipated physical effects, of being destitute.

(2) For the purposes of subsection (1), section 95(2) to (7) of the 1999 Act applies but with the references in section 95(4) and (5) to the Secretary of State being read as references to the local authority in question.

(3) But, until the commencement of section 44(6) of the Nationality, Immigration and Asylum Act 2002, subsection (2) is to have effect as if it read as follows—

"(2) For the purposes of subsection (1), section 95(3) and (5) to (8) of, and paragraph 2 of Schedule 8 to, the 1999 Act apply but with references in section 95(5) and (7) and that paragraph to the Secretary of State being read as references to the local authority in question."

(4) The reference in subsection (1) to meeting an adult's needs for care and support includes a reference to providing care and support to the adult in order to meet a carer's needs for support.

(5) For the purposes of its application in relation to the duty in section 2(1) (preventing needs for care and support), this section is to be read as if—

(a) for subsection (1) there were substituted—

"(1) A local authority may not perform the duty under section 2(1) in relation to an adult to whom section 115 of the Immigration and Asylum Act 1999 ("the 1999 Act") (exclusion from benefits) applies and whose needs for care and support have arisen, or for whom such needs may in the future arise, solely—

(a) because the adult is destitute, or

(b) because of the physical effects, or anticipated physical effects, of being destitute.", and

(b) subsection (4) were omitted.

GENERAL NOTE

1–242   The interface between adult social care and immigration and asylum law has been mainly defined through, what has become known as, the "destitution-plus test". This was introduced into s.21 of the National Assistance Act 1948 (s.21(1A)) by the Immigration and Asylum Act 1999 in an attempt to set up a national asylum support scheme and remove from local authorities the "burden of looking after able bodied asylum seekers".[1]   The background to this provision is described by Baroness Hale in *R. (M) v Slough Borough Council*.[2]

The effect of the test has been that a local authority may not meet the care and support needs of such an adult which arise solely because the adult is destitute, or because of the physical effects or anticipated physical effects, of being destitute. The House of Lords confirmed that the word "solely" in this context means that the "able bodied destitute" are excluded from service provision, but the "infirm destitute", whose need for care and attention arises because "they are infirm as well as destitute", are not so excluded.[3]   In other words, the Home Office is responsible for asylum seekers whose need for care and attention arises solely because they are destitute or from the effects of destitution, while social

[1]   *R. (M) v Slough Borough Council* [2008] UKHL 52; [2008] 1 W.L.R. 1808 at [22] by Baroness Hale quoting from a 1998 Government White Paper, *Fairer, Faster and Firmer—A Modern Approach to Immigration and Asylum*, Cm.4018, para.8.23.

[2]   *R. (M) v Slough Borough Council* [2008] UKHL 52; [2008] 1 W.L.R. 1808 at [7] to [29].

[3]   *Westminster County Council v National Asylum Support Service* [2002] UKHL 38; [2002] 1 W.L.R. 2956 at [32].

services authorities are responsible for asylum seekers whose need arises out of matters additional to being destitute. The presence of a disability would not exclude the existence of purely destitution-related needs.[1]

The Law Commission's remit did not extend to considering the merits of Government policy in this area. Instead, it considered how the proposed adult social care statute could reflect the existing division of responsibilities for asylum seekers between social services authorities and the Home Office—while also expressly stating that this should not be taken as an endorsement of Government policy.[2] Prior to the Care Act, the destitution-plus test had been applied inconsistently to the provision of non-residential services. It had been applied to the provision of services to older people under s.45 of the Health Services and Public Health Act 1968 and services by social services authorities under the National Health Service Act 2006. However, the destitution-plus test did not apply to the provision of services under s.29 of the National Assistance Act 1948, s.2(1) of the Chronically Sick and Disabled Persons Act 1970 and s.2 of the Carer's and Disabled Children Act 2000. The test also did not apply to the provision of services (residential and non-residential) under s.117 of the Mental Health Act 1983. At consultation the Law Commission pointed out that the logic of a single statute for adult social care—which no longer provided that certain services are only available to certain service user groups—would mean that the destitution plus test would apply consistently to all forms of care and support. This would extend the test to all non-residential social care services and not just those provided under the Health Services and Public Health Act 1968 and National Health Service Act 2006. The Commission therefore asked what would be the likely consequences of retaining the destitution-plus test.[3]

A significant number of consultees provided evidence on the effect of the test and pointed to the negative impact on people's mental and physical health. Many argued that a review of political policy was required.[4] In its final report the Law Commission made no recommendation in relation to the prohibition on providing adult social care services to those subject to immigration control. Instead it stated:

"If the policy of the Government and the Welsh Assembly Government towards asylum seekers continues, the likely consequences identified by consultees are that vulnerable asylum seekers will continue to be excluded from access to support, with the result that their physical health and well-being may deteriorate, and existing mental health problems will be exacerbated. Retaining the prohibition would continue to place a heavy burden on surrounding families, including children, to care for the asylum seekers, and would also perpetuate the existing legal confusion about the assessment process for asylum seekers".[5]

The Government did not address this issue in its response to the Law Commission. However, s.21 of the Care Act provides that the destitution-plus has been extended to all forms of care and support.

Subsection (1)

This establishes that a local authority may not meet the care and support needs of an adult **1–243** who is subject to immigration control where those needs arise solely because the adult is destitute, or because of the physical effects or anticipated physical effects, of being destitute. It replaces the previous exclusions set out in, for example, ss.21(1A) and (1B) of the National Assistance Act 1948 and s.45(4A) Health Services and Public Health Act 1968.

---

[1] *R. (M) v Slough Borough Council* [2008] UKHL 52; [2008] 1 W.L.R. 1808 at [40].
[2] Law Commission, *Adult Social Care: A Consultation Paper*, Consultation Paper No.192 (2010), para.9.76.
[3] Law Commission, *Adult Social Care: A Consultation Paper*, Consultation Paper No.192 (2010), para.9.72 to 9.81.
[4] Law Commission, *Adult Social Care: Consultation Analysis* (2011), p.198.
[5] Law Commission, *Adult Social Care*, para.11.37.

An adult subject to immigration control means a person to whom s.115 of the Immigration and Asylum Act 1999 applies. Under s.115(9) of the 1999 Act, a person is subject to immigration control if he or she is not a national of a European Economic Area state and:

- requires leave to enter or remain in the UK but does not have it;
- has leave to enter or remain in the UK but subject to the condition that he does not have recourse to public funds;
- has leave to enter or remain in the UK which is given as a result of a maintenance undertaking; or
- has leave to enter or remain only because they are appealing against certain immigration decisions.

Section 95(3) of the 1999 Act provides that a person is destitute if:

- they do not have adequate accommodation or any means of obtaining it (whether or not their other essential living needs are met); or
- they have adequate accommodation or the means of obtaining it, but cannot meet their other essential living needs.

Section 95(4) ensures that if a person has dependants, subs.(3) is to be read as referring to that person and their dependants taken together.

Sections 95(5) and (6) provide that when determining whether a person's accommodation is adequate, regard may not be had to:

- the fact that the person concerned has no enforceable right to occupy the accommodation;
- the fact that the person shares the accommodation, or any part of the accommodation, with one or more other persons;
- the fact that the accommodation is temporary; or
- the location of the accommodation.

1–244   OTHER RESTRICTIONS ON THE PROVISION OF CARE AND SUPPORT.   The following groups are excluded from nearly all forms of care and support by virtue of the Nationality, Immigration and Asylum Act 2002 (s.55 and Sch.3(1)):

- individuals with refugee status in other European Economic Area countries;
- citizens of other European Economic Area countries;
- failed asylum seekers who have not co-operated with removal directions; and
- those unlawfully in the UK and who are not asylum seekers.

The main exception is services under s.117 of the Mental Health Act 1983.

The Care Act 2014 and Children and Families Act 2014 (Consequential Amendments) Order 2015 amended the 2002 Act to exclude Pt 1 of the Care Act.[1]

Subsections (2) and (3)

1–245   These provisions confirm that s.95 of the Immigration and Asylum Act 1999 applies for the purpose of subs.(1). However, whereas s.95 refers to the Secretary of State as the decision-maker, subs.(2) provides that the relevant references should be read as meaning the local authority in question.

---

[1] The Care Act 2014 and Children and Families Act 2014 (Consequential Amendments) Order 2015 (SI 2015/914).

Subsection (4)

This confirms that the prohibition in subs.(1) includes the provision of care and support **1–246** to the adult in order to meet a carer's needs for support.

Subsection (5)

This subsection provides that the restrictions imposed by this section also apply where a **1–247** local authority is doing anything in discharge of its duty under s.2 aimed at preventing, delaying or reducing needs.

Exception for provision of health services

22.—(1) A local authority may not meet needs under sections 18 to 20 by pro- **1–248** viding or arranging for the provision of a service or facility that is required to be provided under the National Health Service Act 2006 unless—

(a) doing so would be merely incidental or ancillary to doing something else to meet needs under those sections, and

(b) the service or facility in question would be of a nature that the local authority could be expected to provide.

(2) Regulations may specify—

(a) types of services or facilities which, despite subsection (1), may be provided or the provision of which may be arranged by a local authority, or circumstances in which such services or facilities may be so provided or the provision of which may be so arranged;

(b) types of services or facilities which may not be provided or the provision of which may not be arranged by a local authority, or circumstances in which such services or facilities may not be so provided or the provision of which may not be so arranged;

(c) services or facilities, or a method for determining services or facilities, the provision of which is, or is not, to be treated as meeting the conditions in subsection (1)(a) and (b).

(3) A local authority may not meet needs under sections 18 to 20 by providing or arranging for the provision of nursing care by a registered nurse.

(4) But a local authority may, despite the prohibitions in subsections (1) and (3), arrange for the provision of accommodation together with the provision of nursing care by a registered nurse if—

(a) the authority has obtained consent for it to arrange for the provision of the nursing care from whichever clinical commissioning group regulations require, or

(b) the case is urgent and the arrangements for accommodation are only temporary.

(5) In a case to which subsection (4)(b) applies, as soon as is feasible after the temporary arrangements are made, the local authority must seek to obtain the consent mentioned in subsection (4)(a).

(6) Regulations may require a local authority—

(a) to be involved in the specified manner in processes for assessing a person's needs for health care and for deciding how those needs should be met;

(b) to make arrangements for determining disputes between the authority and a clinical commissioning group or the National Health Service Commissioning Board about whether or not a service or facility is required to be provided under the National Health Service Act 2006.

(7) Nothing in this section affects what a local authority may do under the National Health Service Act 2006, including entering into arrangements under regulations under section 75 of that Act (arrangements with NHS bodies).

(8) A reference to the provision of nursing care by a registered nurse is a reference to the provision by a registered nurse of a service involving—

(a) the provision of care, or

(b) the planning, supervision or delegation of the provision of care, other than a service which, having regard to its nature and the circumstances in which it is provided, does not need to be provided by a registered nurse.

(9) Where, in a case within subsection (4), the National Health Service Commissioning Board has responsibility for arranging for the provision of the nursing care, the reference in paragraph (a) of that subsection to a clinical commissioning group is to be read as a reference to the Board.

(10) For the purposes of its application in relation to the duty in section 2(1) (preventing needs for care and support), this section is to be read as if references to meeting needs under sections 18 to 20 were references to performing the duty under section 2(1).

GENERAL NOTE

1–249 The division of health and social care provision dates back to the inception of the NHS, when the question of what is health and what is social care appeared relatively straightforward. The National Assistance Act 1948 was established to cater for those in need of "care and attention" through residential accommodation, and to provide otherwise for the welfare of older and disabled people. The National Health Service Act 1946 provided for specialist medical services which were the responsibility of the NHS. In the ensuing years, however, this division has become increasingly blurred as a result of fundamental changes to the way that health and social care is provided:

> "In practice the boundary between the two services has shifted over time, so that the long term care responsibilities of the NHS have reduced substantially, and people who in the past would have been cared for in NHS long stay wards are now often accommodated in nursing homes. This means that responsibility for funding long term care has to a major extent been shunted from the NHS to local authorities and individual patients and their families."[1]

This divide is significant for service users and their families because, in general terms, NHS services are provided free of charge, while social care services are subject to a means-tested charge. The difficulties that can arise in this respect are evident in the following example:

> "'Telehealth' allows the remote monitoring of conditions such as diabetes, congestive heart failure or chronic obstructive pulmonary disease (health care), while 'telecare' can establish whether someone has opened the fridge in the morning, or has had a fall (social care). When both can be provided in one piece of equipment, which part of this device and its associated services qualifies as free-at-the-point-of-use health care and which as means-tested social care?"[2]

The health and social care divide also has significant financial implications for public resources. As the Joint Committee stated:

---

[1] House of Commons Health Committee, *NHS Continuing Care: Sixth Report of the Session 2004–05, Volume 1* (2005), HC 399–1, para.41.

[2] King's Fund, *Securing Good Care for Older People: Taking a Long-Term View (2006)*, pp.12 to 13.

"Since the earliest days the boundary between health care, which is free at point of use, and social care, which is not, has been highly problematic. Clarity over the boundary is of fundamental importance . . . If the boundary is moved, it could result in either (a) a dilution of the NHS's responsibilities, and as a consequence more people having to pay for their care (since it would no longer be deemed NHS care); or (b) more people becoming entitled to free NHS care (since it would no longer be deemed a social services responsibility), which would have substantial financial implications for the taxpayer."[1]

The divide is also significant because almost all of the duties placed on the NHS are general target duties owed towards the general population rather than individuals.[2] In contrast adult social care law has in the past contained, and continues to contain, a number of specific public law duties which are amenable to enforcement by individuals.[3] Whether a service is provided by health or social services, therefore, may determine whether an individual can enforce their right to that service. The difference between general and specific duties is discussed at para.1–001 above. The disputed boundary between health and social care has been at its most acute over the provision of NHS continuing health care (see below).

THE QUANTITY AND QUALITY TEST

Prior to the Care Act, the boundary between health and social care services was deter- **1–250** mined largely by reference to the National Assistance Act 1948 and the National Health Service Act 2006 (a descendant of the 1946 Act). Section 21(8) of the 1948 Act stated that nothing in s.21 (provision of accommodation) authorised or required a local authority to make any provision "authorised or required to be provided under" the National Health Service Act 2006. This was considered by the Court of Appeal in *R. v North and East Devon Health Authority ex parte Coughlan*, which held that s.21(8) did not prevent a local authority from providing *any* health services, but instead:

"The subsection's prohibitive effect is limited to those health services which, in fact, have been authorised or required to be provided under the [National Health Service Act 2006]. Such health services would not therefore include services which the Secretary of State legitimately decided under section 3(1) of the [National Health Service Act 2006] it was not necessary for the NHS to provide."[4]

This did not mean, however, that local authorities were responsible for providing all health services that the Secretary of State had decided it is not necessary for the NHS to provide; the health services that could be provided by local authorities as part of a social care package were restricted to those services that could be provided lawfully under s.21.

In order to identify which health services it was lawful for a local authority to provide under s.21 of the 1948 Act, the courts developed the "quantity and quality test". This test provided that health care services could be provided by a local authority if those services were:

- merely incidental or ancillary to the provision of the accommodation which a local authority was under a duty to provide pursuant to s.21 of the 1948 Act (the *quantity* of the service provided); and

---

[1] House of Lords House of Commons Joint Committee on the Draft Care and Support Bill, *Draft Care and Support Bill Report, Session 2012–13*, para.53.

[2] *R. v Cambridgeshire Health Authority Ex p B* [1995] 1 W.L.R. 898.

[3] Previous individual duties include s.2(1) of the Chronically Sick and Disabled Persons Act 1970. Examples in the Care Act include ss.18(1) and 20(1).

[4] *R. v North and East Devon Health Authority Ex p Coughlan* [2001] Q.B. 213 at 232.

- of a nature which it could be expected that an authority whose primary responsibility was to provide social services could be expected to provide (the *quality* of the service provided).[1]

Section 22 of the Care Act imports the quantity and quality test into statute law (see discussion below under subs.(1)).

NHS CONTINUING HEALTH CARE

1–251   The effect of the quantity and quality test has been the legislative possibility of a gap between the provision of health care and the provision of social care services together with incidental or ancillary health care. Notwithstanding this possibility, it has been the longstanding policy of Government that such a gap should not arise.

To assist in deciding, in individual cases, which health services it is appropriate for the NHS to provide, and to distinguish between those and the services which local social services authorities must provide, the Government has developed the concept of a "primary health need". Where a person has been assessed to have a primary health need they are eligible for NHS continuing health care—which is defined as "a package of care arranged and funded solely by the health service for a person aged 18 or over to meet physical or mental health needs which have arisen as a result of disability, accident or illness".[2] In general terms, it is available to people who are not in hospital but have complex and on-going health care needs.

The *National Framework for NHS Continuing Health Care and NHS-funded Nursing Care* sets out four characteristics of need—namely "nature", "intensity", "complexity" and "unpredictability"—which help determine whether the quantity or quality of care required is beyond the limit of a local authority's responsibilities. Each of these characteristics may, alone or in combination, demonstrate a primary health need, because of the quality and/or quantity of care that is required to meet the individual's needs.[3]

In addition, a *Decision Support Tool* provides guidance on whether the nature, complexity, intensity or unpredictability of a person's needs are such that they have a primary health need. It divides needs into 12 care domains, or generic areas of need. These are sub-divided into statements of need, representing low, moderate, high, severe, or priority levels of need, depending on the domain. The care domains range from "behaviour" and "cognition" to "continence", "skin (including tissue viability)" and "breathing", and include a catchall of "other significant needs". Cases qualify for NHS continuing health care according to formulae which weigh the severity of the case across different domains.[4]

If a person does not qualify for NHS continuing health care, the NHS may still have a responsibility to contribute to that person's health needs. This could be provided as part of a joint package of care (including NHS funded nursing care[5] and other NHS services which are beyond the powers of the local authority to meet) under which the NHS is responsible for the provision of health care services and the local authority is responsible for the provision of social care services together with any health care services which are within their powers to provide.[6]

---

[1] *R. v North and East Devon Health Authority Ex p Coughlan* [2001] Q.B. 213 at 233.

[2] The National Health Service Commissioning Board and Clinical Commissioning Groups (Responsibilities and Standing Rules) Regulations 2012 (SI 2010/2996) reg.20(1).

[3] Department of Health, *The National Framework for NHS Continuing Healthcare and NHS-funded Nursing Care* (2012), paras 35 to 36.

[4] Department of Health, *Decision Support Tool for NHS Continuing Healthcare* (2012).

[5] If a person requires some nursing care, but nursing is not his or her primary need, the NHS will pay part of the care costs. This contribution is known as funded nursing care.

[6] Department of Health, *The National Framework for NHS Continuing Healthcare and NHS-funded Nursing Care* (2012), paras 113 to 117.

OTHER PROHIBITIONS

Prior to the Care Act, there were two further statutory prohibitions (in addition to s.21(8) **1–252** of the National Assistance Act 1948) on the provision of health services by local authorities. First, s.29(6) of the 1948 Act prohibited local authorities from providing any services under s.29 which were "required to be provided under" the National Health Service Act 2006. In general terms, s.29 enabled local authorities to provide a range of non-residential services for disabled people. The s.29(6) prohibition applied only where there was a duty on the NHS to provide a service and did not extend to services that the NHS had been authorised to provide by the Secretary of State as a matter of policy. It followed that a range of community care services could be provided for a person living in the community who was eligible for NHS continuing health care, notwithstanding Government policy that the NHS was responsible for service provision. Where disputes arose, the courts applied an adjusted version of the quantity and quality test.

Secondly, s.49(1) of the Health and Social Care Act 2001 prevented local authorities from providing nursing care by a registered nurse. This prohibition did not apply to any services which were in fact provided by a registered nurse but only those services that were required to be provided by a registered nurse. This provision has been retained by s.22(6) of the Care Act.

LAW COMMISSION RECOMMENDATIONS

The Law Commission's remit in this area was limited to examining how best to express **1–253** the existing divide and did not attempt to alter the responsibilities of health and social services. However, its final recommendations did contain some alterations which it felt were necessary in order for the prohibitions to operate effectively in the context of a single adult social care statute.

First, the Law Commission expressed concern about the incomprehensibility of the statutory prohibitions. It argued that the meaning of the prohibitions is not obvious from their wording—noting that the precise meaning has needed "detailed analysis" by the courts.[1] The Commission therefore recommended that the existing language of the prohibitions should be reviewed and where appropriate revised to clarify their meaning, and emphasised the importance of legislation in this area being as comprehensible as possible to the very many non-lawyer users.

Secondly, the Law Commission concluded that the quantity and quality test should be codified in statute law. It noted that the wording of the 1948 Act makes no explicit reference to the limits of a local authority's ability to provide health services, and the prohibitions can only be understood correctly when read in light of the quantity and quality test established in *Coughlan*. The Commission concluded that a clear provision on the face of the statute setting out the full meaning of the prohibition would help to ensure greater legal clarity.

Finally, while the Law Commission argued there would be advantages to closing the potential gap between health and social care, not least in terms of legal clarity, this was seen as a matter for political policy not law reform. However, it argued that the statute should allow for the development of Government policy on this issue. The Secretary of State should therefore be given a power to establish in regulations an eligibility framework for the provision of NHS continuing health care and to specify what combination of needs establish a primary health need. This would allow the Governments to decide, if it so wishes, to close the potential gap between health and social care in law.[2]

---

[1] *R. v North and East Devon Health Authority Ex p Coughlan* [2001] Q.B. 213 at 232, per Lord Woolf.
[2] Law Commission, *Adult Social Care*, paras 11.4 to 11.6.

The Government accepted all the Commission's recommendations in this area.[1] The statutory guidance discusses the boundary between care and support and the NHS in paras 19.29 to 15.36. It also discusses transition from children's to adults NHS continuing health care in paras 19.79 to 16.82, and NHS continuing care for prisoners in paras 17.66 to 17.67.

Subsection (1)

1–254   This subsection sets the boundary between what is NHS-provided and free at the point of delivery, and what is social care. It provides that a local authority in meeting an adult's needs for care and support may not provide health services which are required to be provided under the National Health Service Act 2006, unless:

- doing so would be incidental or ancillary to the provision of care and support; and
- the service is of a nature that the local authority could be expected to provide.

According to the explanatory notes, examples of services which the local authority would be prohibited from providing include primary medical, dental and ophthalmic services provided by clinical commissioning groups, the NHS Commissioning Board, or any other NHS body.[2] The courts have also said that the suctioning and changing of a tracheostomy tube does not constitute social care—albeit in the context of social care for children.[3]

The subsection imports the quantity and quality test into statute law. Therefore, a local authority may provide some health care services in certain circumstances, that is, where the service provided is "minor and accompanies some other care and support service which the local authority is permitted to provide and is of a nature that a local authority would be expected to provide".[4]

The Government has on several occasions stated that its intention is not to alter the divide between health and social care.[5] However, despite these reassurances, there are differences between the wording adopted in s.22 of the Care Act and that contained in the previous prohibitions in the National Assistance Act 1948. For example, s.21(8) of the 1948 Act set the prohibition at anything "authorised or required to be provided under" the National Health Service Act 2006, whereas the s.22(1) of the Care Act refers to "the provision of a service or facility that is required to be provided". In other words, s.22(1) keeps the words "required to be" but loses the word "authorised". Therefore, it only restricts social services provision to situations where there is a duty, rather than a power, under the National Health Service Act 2006. As noted above, this would make no difference for community-based services, but would constitute a material change for residential accommodation. Indeed the Joint Committee suggested that this change could have significant financial implications for local authorities (since residential accommodation is generally the most expensive social care service) and "would have the unintended effect of shifting the boundary so that fewer people would qualify for NHS continuing health care funding".[6]

1–255   In its response to the Joint Committee the Government stated that:

---

[1] Department of Health, *Reforming the Law for Adult Care and Support: The Government's Response to Law Commission Report 326 on Adult Social Care* (TSO, July 2012), Cm.8379, paras 11.4 to 11.10.

[2] Care Act 2014: Explanatory Notes para.159.

[3] *R. (T) v Haringey LBC* [2005] EWHC 2235 (Admin); (2006) 9 CCLR 58.

[4] Care Act 2014: Explanatory Notes para.160.

[5] For example, see, Department of Health, *Reforming the Law for Adult Care and Support: The Government's Response to Law Commission Report 326 on Adult Social Care* (TSO, July 2012), Cm.8379, para.11.4.

[6] House of Lords House of Commons Joint Committee on the Draft Care and Support Bill, *Draft Care and Support Bill Report, Session 2012–13*, para.55.

"The intention of this clause is not to change the boundary between local authorities and the NHS but to enable the current boundary to be replicated and to continue to work as before albeit with the new NHS landscape brought about as a result of the Health and Social Care Act 2012. We have made some clarifications to address this feedback, and we are satisfied that the clause enables the existing boundary between the care and support system and the NHS to be maintained."[1]

The Government's position was confirmed during the passage of the Care Bill in the House of Lords:

"The word 'authorised' in Section 21 of the 1948 Act has resulted in much confusion and case law. The intention behind [s.22] is therefore to simplify the language and to make the boundary clearer without moving it. Make no mistake: where nursing care is being funded by the health service, it will continue to be unlawful for a local authority to recover the cost of this from the individual. It is the relevant clinical commissioning group that would be responsible for this cost."[2]

In the House of Commons, at Committee stage, Paul Burstow MP—the chair of the Joint Committee—repeated the Committee's concerns:

"The Pandora's box is that clinical commissioning groups are still relatively immature bodies finding their feet and developing their policies and practices. They may well argue that the *Coughlan* judgment no longer applies, as the wording in s.21(8) of the National Assistance Act 1948, on which that judgment is based, no longer exists . . . Wherever budget pressures are great—we can debate how great they are now compared with the past and what they might be in the future—primary legislation where there are separate bodies with separate statutory duties comes into play."[3]

The Government responded by repeating its argument that the changes are not intended to alter the boundary set by the 1948 Act. It was also argued that the 1948 Act established a different prohibition depending on whether the health care provision was through accommodation or by other means. The Care Act removes this distinction and therefore the removal of "authorised" would make the boundary clearer, while also retaining the ability to fix the boundary where it currently lies, through regulations.[4]

Schedule 1, which deals with cross-border placements, provides that the divide established by subs.(1) also applies where a local authority is meeting needs by arranging for the provision of accommodation in Wales, Scotland or Northern Ireland.

Subsection (2)

This confers a power to make provision in regulations about the types of services which **1–256** (despite the prohibition in subs.(1)) may, or may not, be provided or arranged by local authorities, and in which circumstances.

The Joint Committee raised concerns that subs.(2)(a) would allow local authorities to provide, and by implication to charge for, types of services prescribed by regulations which would otherwise be provided under the National Health Service Act 2006, and hence free at point of use. In oral evidence to the Committee a Government official argued that:

"This kind of proposal is about things like NHS continuing health care, where the local authority may well arrange for the provision of that because it might well be provided by

---

[1] Department of Health, *The Care Bill explained—including a response to consultation and pre-legislative scrutiny on the draft Care and Support Bill* (TSO, July 2012), Cm.8386, para.79.

[2] *Hansard* (House of Lords), 9 July 2013, Vol.747, col.195.

[3] *Hansard* (House of Commons: Public Bill Committee), 16 January 2014 (PM): Sixth Sitting, col.206.

[4] *Hansard* (House of Commons: Public Bill Committee), 16 January 2014 (PM): Sixth Sitting, cols 206 to 207 (Norman Lamb MP).

a residential care provider. The local authority and the local Clinical Commissioning Group would need an arrangement to cross charge each other for it, but it would not be that you would be charging the actual individual for that continuing health care, because it would be free".[1]

The Committee recommended that the legislation must be amended to make clear that, where a local authority provides services on behalf of a Clinical Commissioning Group, the authority may not recover the cost from the individual whose needs are being met.[2]

The Government's response to the Joint Committee stated: "There is no intention to change the existing charging policy through which NHS services are provided free at the point of use". It also set out its intention that regulations will make clear the boundaries between health and social care.[3]

In the House of Commons, at Committee stage, Paul Burstow MP—the chair of the Joint Committee—argued that the ability to make regulations under subs.(2) would allow future Governments to decisively shift the boundary between health and social care, rather than through the additional scrutiny that primary legislation requires.[4] In response, the Government argued that regulations would allow matters to be clarified where there is uncertainty and allow it to "clarify and detail the types of service that may or may not be provided by local authorities and in which circumstances". In effect, the regulation-making power would provide "greater flexibility to control the boundary and prevent gaps or undesirable overlaps in provision".[5]

By virtue of s.125(4)(d) regulations made under subs.22(2)(b) are subject to the affirmative procedure in Parliament. The affirmative procedure is discussed at para.1–161 above under s.13(7).

Subsection (3)

1–257   This re-enacts the prohibition contained previously in s.49(1) of the Health and Social Care Act 2001 (see above). The background to s.49(1) is set out in detail in *R (Forge Care Homes Ltd.) v Cardiff and Vale University Health Board*.[6] Section 22(3) of the Care Act prevents local authorities from providing or arranging for the provision of nursing care (a term that is defined in subs.(8)—see below) by a registered nurse. This kind of nursing care may only be provided by the NHS. However, this must be read alongside subs.(4). The courts have confirmed that this prohibition is not subject to some general discretion by the NHS, although there is discretion as to how the NHS provides the relevant services.[7]

The Joint Committee felt there was a potential conflict between what may be done by regulations under subs.(2) and the qualified prohibition on provision by a local authority of nursing care by a registered nurse. It recommended that any regulations should not be able to override the prohibition.[8] In its response, the Government confirmed that its policy is to reflect the current position with regards to the limits of local authority provision of

---

[1] House of Lords House of Commons Joint Committee on the Draft Care and Support Bill, *Draft Care and Support Bill Report, Session 2012–13*, para.59.

[2] House of Lords House of Commons Joint Committee on the Draft Care and Support Bill, *Draft Care and Support Bill Report, Session 2012–13*, paras 58 to 59.

[3] Department of Health, *The Care Bill explained—including a response to consultation and pre-legislative scrutiny on the draft Care and Support Bill* (TSO, July 2012), Cm.8386, p.60.

[4] *Hansard* (House of Commons: Public Bill Committee), 16 January 2014 (PM): Sixth Sitting, cols 206 and 209.

[5] *Hansard* (House of Commons: Public Bill Committee), 16 January 2014 (PM): Sixth Sitting, col.207 (Norman Lamb MP).

[6] *R (Forge Care Homes Ltd.) v Cardiff and Vale University Health Board* [2015] EWHC 601 (Admin), at [25] to [42].

[7] *R (Forge Care Homes Ltd.) v Cardiff and Vale University Health Board* [2015] EWHC 601 (Admin), at [109].

[8] House of Lords House of Commons Joint Committee on the Draft Care and Support Bill, *Draft Care and Support Bill Report, Session 2012—13*, para.60.

registered nursing care. It also stated that it is not the intention to use the regulation making power in subs.(2) to override this subsection (and subs.(4)), and indeed it did not consider that it could do so.[1]

Subsections (4) and (5)

The local authority may arrange the provision of accommodation which includes the pro- **1–258** vision of nursing care by a registered nurse provided it has first obtained the agreement of whichever clinical commissioning group regulations require. The local authority may arrange the provision of such accommodation on a temporary basis as a matter of urgency, provided it obtains the agreement of the relevant clinical commissioning group as soon as possible afterwards.

Regulation 2 of the Care and Support (Provision of Health Services) Regulations 2014 (SI 2014/2821) imposes a requirement to obtain such consent from the clinical commissioning group which has the responsibility for arranging for the provision of nursing care by a registered nurse in respect of the person concerned. That responsibility is established by reference to certain provisions of the National Health Service Act 2006 and regulations made under the 2006 Act. See para.A1–161 below.

In most cases, the clinical commissioning group is responsible for arranging for the provision of nursing care. But, as subs.(9) acknowledges, it may in certain circumstances be the NHS Commissioning Board (known as NHS England). In those circumstances, the reference in subs.4(a) to a clinical commissioning group is to be read as a reference to the Board.

Subsection (6)

This sets out two other matters which may be provided for in regulations. The first is to **1–259** detail the steps which the local authority must take to contribute to an assessment as to whether an adult requires health care services. The second is to require the establishment of a process for dealing with disputes between local authorities and NHS bodies, should there be a disagreement over the responsibility for providing a particular service in an individual case. These matters have been implemented by regs 3 and 4, respectively, of the Care and Support (Provision of Health Services) Regulations 2014 (SI 2014/2821)—see paras A1–162 and A1–163 below.

Subsection (7)

Local authorities generally may not provide health care services (which are for the NHS **1–260** to provide under the National Health Service Act 2006). However, this subsection clarifies that local authorities are not prohibited from doing anything that they have the power to do under the 2006 Act (such as entering into partnership arrangements with NHS bodies under s.75 of the 2006 Act).[2]

Subsection (8)

This defines nursing care by a registered nurse as the provision of a service involving: **1–261**

- the provision of care; or
- the planning, supervision or delegation of the provision of care, other than a service which, having regard to its nature and the circumstances in which it is provided, does not need to be provided by a registered nurse.

Subsection (8) is based on s.49(2) of the Health and Social Care Act 2001 (see also discussion under subs.(3) above). For instance, like s.49(2) "nursing care by a registered nurse" is not defined simply in terms of tasks that only a registered nurse could undertake,

---

[1] Department of Health, *The Care Bill explained—including a response to consultation and pre-legislative scrutiny on the draft Care and Support Bill* (TSO, July 2012), Cm.8386, p.60.
[2] Care Act: Explanatory Notes para.166.

and is not defined simply in terms of the provision of care, but rather services "involving the provision of care".[1]

However, there is an important difference. Section s.49(2) of the 2001 Act had defined "nursing care by a registered nurse" as the provision of care, other than a service which, having regard to its nature and the circumstances in which it is provided, does not need to be provided by a registered nurse. In contrast, s.22(8) of the Care Act does not apply this exception to the provision of care (it now applies only to planning, supervision or delegation). In effect, the definition of nursing care by a registered nurse has been widened. Nevertheless, the effect may be minimal. The courts confirmed that under s.49(2) it had been unlawful for the NHS to adopt a task-based approach to the provision of nursing care by a registered nurse, in order to restrict the "services" to the tasks which only a registered nurse can perform because of the skills and experience required. The NHS must pay the costs of registered nurses working as such in a care home.[2]

Subsection (9)

1–262   See subs.(4) and (5) above.

Subsection (10)

1–263   This subsection provides that the restrictions imposed by this section also apply where a local authority is doing anything in discharge of its duty under s.2 aimed at preventing, delaying or reducing needs.

Exception for provision of housing etc.

1–264   **23.**—(1) A local authority may not meet needs under sections 18 to 20 by doing anything which it or another local authority is required to do under—

(a) the Housing Act 1996, or

(b) any other enactment specified in regulations.

(2) "Another local authority" includes a district council for an area in England for which there is also a county council.

(3) For the purposes of its application in relation to the duty in section 2(1) (preventing needs for care and support), this section is to be read as if, in subsection (1), for "meet needs under sections 18 to 20" there were substituted "perform the duty under section 2(1)".

GENERAL NOTE

1–265   Local housing authorities have statutory functions relating to homeless persons and people seeking social housing. However, local social services authorities also have long-standing responsibilities for the provision of residential accommodation. Case law has established that under s.21 of the National Assistance Act 1948 the range of accommodation that can be provided by social services is:

" 'wide and flexible' and embraces residential care, nursing homes, ordinary and sheltered housing, housing associations, other registered social landlords and 'private sector housing which may have to be purchased by the [local authority].'"[3]

Section 8(1)(a) of the Care Act also provides for a wide range of accommodation which can be provided by local social services departments (see para.1–089 above). There is, therefore, a potential overlap between accommodation that can be provided by a local

---

[1] See, *R (Forge Care Homes Ltd. and others) v Cardiff and Vale University Health Board and others* [2015] EWHC 601 (Admin), at [34] in respect of s.49(2) of the Health and Social Care Act 2001.

[2] *R (Forge Care Homes Ltd. and others) v Cardiff and Vale University Health Board and others* [2015] EWHC 601 (Admin) at [112].

[3] *R. (Banantu) v Islington LBC* (2001) 4 CCLR 445 at 451(G).

social services authority and that which can be provided by the housing department under the Housing Act 1996.

In addition, the general duties to promote integration in s.3 and the co-operation duty in s.6 require consideration of housing issues where relevant to care and support. Section 3(5) clarifies that housing is a health-related service which local authorities must aim to integrate.

Prior to the Care Act, the main statutory prohibition to the provision of s.21 accommodation was s.21(8) of the National Assistance Act 1948, which provided that:

> "Nothing in this section shall authorise or require a local authority to make any provision authorised or required to be made (whether by that or by any other authority) by or under any enactment not contained in this Part of the Act".

The Law Commission's review concluded that this position should be maintained in the new statute. However, it also felt that the statutory language should be reviewed and where appropriate revised to clarify its meaning.[1] The Government accepted the Commission's recommendation.[2]

Subsection (1)

This subsection sets the boundary between general housing and social care housing pro- **1–266** vision. It provides that a local authority in meeting an adult's needs for care and support may not provide housing or anything else which is required to be provided under the Housing Act 1996 (or under any other enactment added in regulations). During the passage of the Care Bill through the House of Commons, the Government explained its intention:

> "The point of [s.23] is to clarify the difference in law between a local authority's duties to provide adult care and support, which may include certain specialised housing services, and its duties to provide general housing under other legislation so as to avoid duplication. The [section] does not place a bar on local authorities providing accommodation where that is necessary to meet care and support needs. What it does is prohibit local authorities from using care and support law to provide general or social housing that is not related to a person's care and support needs. That is only right and proper to ensure clarity about roles and responsibilities."[3]

The explanatory notes state that s.23 does not prevent local authorities in their care and support role from providing more specific services (such as housing adaptations), or from working jointly with housing authorities.[4] However, in the House of Lords, the Government had also explained some of the limits of social services powers in this area:

> "Providing information and advice about general housing options and ensuring that there is sufficient suitable housing available is clearly the responsibility of the local housing authority, which is not always the local authority responsible for care and support in that area. It simply is not reasonable to ask local authorities, in their care and support functions, to carry out those other functions."[5]

Despite the Law Commission's recommendation that the previous boundary should be retained, s.23 does not maintain the exact position established in s.21(8) of the National Assistance Act 1948. The new prohibition refers to anything that a local authority "is required to do under" (rather than any provision "authorised or required to be made . . . by or under the Housing Act 1996". This means that the new prohibition applies only

---

[1] Law Commission, *Adult Social Care*, para.11.35.
[2] Department of Health, *Reforming the Law for Adult Care and Support: The Government's Response to Law Commission Report 326 on Adult Social Care* (TSO, July 2012), Cm.8379, para.11.12.
[3] *Hansard* (House of Commons: Public Bill Committee), 16 January 2014 (PM): Sixth Sitting, col.212 (Norman Lamb MP).
[4] Care Act 2014, Explanatory Notes para.170.
[5] *Hansard* (House of Lords), 9 October 2013, Vol.748, cols 106 to 107 (Earl Howe).

where the local authorities are subject to a duty to provide housing under the Housing Act 1996. There is no prohibition when a housing authority is authorised or empowered to provide housing. As a matter of law, this broadens the range of people who may be eligible potentially for social services accommodation. It also produces the potential for greater overlap between social services and housing authorities. Under the provisions of the Housing Act 1996 local housing authorities almost always have a residual power to offer accommodation should they wish, unless the person is expressly ineligible. Many such people may also now be eligible for the provision of residential accommodation by the social services authority.

In the past the courts have taken a narrow interpretation of the prohibition contained in s.21(8) of the National Assistance Act 1948, whereby the provision of residential accommodation by a social services authority is only prohibited where the housing authority has provided or will provide accommodation under the Housing Act 1996.[1] In other words, it was a factual test of whether housing is otherwise available than under s.21. For example, an individual that is intentionally homeless can be eligible for accommodation under s.21, even though the housing authority remains authorised to provide accommodation but chooses not to under the Housing Act 1996. It is possible that a similar approach may be adopted under the Care Act.

Subsection (3)

1–267   This applies the prohibition on housing provision to the duty to provide prevention services under s.2(1).

NEXT STEPS AFTER ASSESSMENTS

1–268   Once the local authority has determined that it will meet one or more of the person's needs, then care and support arrangements will need to be put in place. This process is often referred to as "care planning". The statutory guidance discusses care planning in Ch.10. Prior to the Care Act, the courts had confirmed on several occasions that resources can be a relevant consideration at the care planning stage. For example, the Supreme Court in *R(KM) a Cambridgeshire County Council* held that whilst a local authority is obliged to meet all eligible needs regardless of its resources, when determining *how* to meet those needs the authority is entitled to take into account its resources. Thus, if the person qualifies for a direct payment then the authority may ask what is the reasonable cost of securing provision of the necessary services to meet the person's eligible needs, and at this stage a Resource Allocation System can be used (see para.1–299 below).[2] In *McDonald v United Kingdom* the European Court of Human Rights held that a properly considered decision to remove night-time care from a dependent incontinent person falls within the state's margin of appreciation and would not violate art.8 of the European Convention on Human Rights. The court noted that states are afforded a wide margin of appreciation in issues of general policy and that margin is particularly wide when the issues involve an assessment of the priorities in the context of the allocation of limited state resources.[3]

This basic position is maintained under the Care Act. The statutory guidance confirms that in determining how to meet needs, the local authority may take into account "reasonable consideration of its own finances and budgetary position" and its related public law duties, such as ensuring that the funding available to the local authority is sufficient to meet the needs of the entire local population". It also states that:

"However, the local authority should not set arbitrary upper limits on the costs it is willing to pay to meet needs through certain routes – doing so would not deliver an approach that is person-centred or compatible with public law principles. The authority may take

---

[1] *R. (Mooney) v Southwark LBC* [2006] EWHC 1912 (Admin); (2006) 9 CCLR 670.
[2] *R(KM) v Cambridgeshire County Council* [2012] UKSC 23.
[3] *McDonald v United Kingdom* (20 May 2014) Application No.4241/12.

decisions on a case-by-case basis which weigh up the total costs of different potential options for meeting needs, and include the cost as a relevant factor in deciding between suitable alternative options for meeting needs. This does not mean choosing the cheapest option; but the one which delivers the outcomes desired for the best value."[1]

In addition to resources, the views, wishes and preferences of the person will be highly relevant at the care planning stage. In *Gunter v South Western Staffordshire Primary Care Trust,* a disabled person sought to challenge the decision that a residential package was the preferred package of care. Mr Justice Collins, giving judgement, considered that removing the person from their parent's home was an "obvious" interference with family life under art.8 of the European Convention of Human Rights and so must be justified as proportionate:

"Cost is a factor which can properly be taken into account. But the evidence of the improvement in [the claimant's] condition, the obvious quality of life within her family environment and her expressed views that she does not want to move are all important factors which suggest that to remove her from her home will require clear justification."[2]

The importance of a person's views, wishes and preferences in care planning has been recognised in a line of community care decisions. For example, it has been held that:

- where a person's preference forms part of their psychological needs, then this preference can be elevated to a need that must be met—as in the case of an entrenched wish for a particular care home, which is typical of and caused by Down's Syndrome[3] ; and
- where two care packages are both capable of meeting the assessed needs of a person, and if there were no resource implications, then the local authority might be forced to provide the care package that corresponds to the person's preference.[4]

Whilst these decisions pre-date the Care Act, it is likely that the basic principles, outlined above, will remain good law. Indeed, it might be argued that the Care Act places much greater emphasis (at least in statutory law) on the importance of the person's views, wishes, and preferences, than the previous legal framework. Most significantly, s.1(2)(d) requires decision-makers to promote control by the individual over day-to-day life (including over care and support, and support, provided to the individual and the way in which it is provided) and s.1(3)(a) requires decision-makers to start from the assumption that the individual is best placed to judge their own individual well-being. In addition, s.30 of the Care Act provides that in some cases a local authority will be obliged to arrange an adult's preferred accommodation. Also, ss.31 and 32 set out that direct payments can only be provided where a request has been made by the person, or, where the person lacks capacity to make a request, the request has been made on a best interests basis by someone authorised under the Mental Capacity Act 2005 or a "suitable person".

The statutory guidance states that if the adult has been assessed as having eligible needs, as a precursor to the care planning process the local authority must:

"Agree with the adult which of their needs they would like the local authority to meet. The person may not wish to have support in relation to all their needs—they may, for example, intend to arrange alternative services themselves to meet some needs. Others may not wish for the local authority to meet any of their needs, but approach the authority only for the purposes of determining eligible needs."[5]

---

[1] Department of Health, *Care and Support Statutory Guidance* (2014), para.10.27.
[2] *Gunter v South Western Staffordshire Primary Care Trust* [2005] EWHC 1894 (Admin); (2006) 9 CCLR 121 at [20].
[3] *R. v Avon CC Ex p M* (1999) 2 CCLR 185.
[4] *R. v Southwark LBC Ex p Khana* [2001] EWCA Civ 999; (2001) 4 CCLR 267 at [59] by Mance L.J.
[5] Department of Health, *Care and Support Statutory Guidance* (2014), para.6.140.

When discussing care and support planning, the statutory guidance emphasises that "above all, the local authority should refrain from any action that could be seen to restrict choice and impede flexibility". In particular it warns that:

"Lists of allowable purchases should be avoided as the range of possibilities should be very wide and will be beyond what the local authority is able to list at any point in time. While many authorities may choose to operate lists of quality accredited providers to help people choose (for example some authorities include trading standards-style 'buy with confidence' approaches) the use of such lists should not be mandated as the only choice offer to people. Limited lists of 'prescribed providers' that are only offered to the person on a 'take it or leave it' basis do not fit with the Government's vision of personalised care and should be avoided. "[1]

The statutory guidance discusses care planning for people who lack capacity in paras 10.59 to 10.72 (including where the person is subject to the Deprivation of Liberty Safeguards under the Mental Capacity Act 2005). Amongst other matters, it suggests that if a person lacks capacity, "the local authority must commence care planning in the person's best interests".[2]

CARE PLANNING, CHOICE AND CONSENT

1–269   Once a local authority has decided which care and support package it is willing to fund, the person still must decide whether to accept the offer. In the context of residential accommodation, the statutory guidance states that:

"A local authority must do everything it can to take into account a person's circumstances and preferences when arranging care. However, in all but a very small number of cases, such as where a person is being placed under Guardianship under s.7 of the Mental Health Act 1983, a person has a right to refuse to enter a setting whether that is on an interim or permanent basis. Where a person unreasonably refuses the arrangements, a local authority is entitled to consider that it has fulfilled its statutory duty to meet needs and may then inform the person in writing that as a result they need to make their own arrangements. This should be a step of last resort and local authorities should consider the risks posed by such an approach, for both the authority itself and the person concerned. Should the person contact the local authority again at a later date, the local authority should re-assess the needs as necessary and re-open the care and support planning process."[3]

The courts have set out that where a person has capacity to consent, the options available are to accept the offer, privately fund their preferred package elsewhere, or seek to negotiate with the authority.[4] The Court of Appeal in *R (Khana) v London Borough of Southwark* accepted the submission that if a person living at home refuses a residential package of care (reasonably or unreasonably) the local authority cannot treat themselves as discharged from any further duty to provide community services at home.[5] Although the point was not fully argued, it is possible that in some cases a local authority may need to reconsider its offer, particularly if a breach of art.8 would arise.

If a person lacks capacity to consent to the offer, a best interests decision would need to be made under the Mental Capacity Act 2005. This could therefore lead to a scenario where the care package is rejected on the basis that it is not in the person's best interests, but the public authority does not think that an alternative care package would be appropriate. In

---

[1] Department of Health, *Care and Support Statutory Guidance* (2014), para.10.48.

[2] Department of Health, *Care and Support Statutory Guidance* (2014), para.10.64.

[3] Department of Health, *Care and Support Statutory Guidance* (2014), Annex A, para.18.

[4] *Re S (Vulnerable Adult)* [2007] 2 FLR 1095 at [11] and *ACCG v MN* [2013] EWHC 3859 (COP) at [53] (approved in *Re MN* [2015] EWCA Civ 411 at [54]).

[5] *R (Khana) v London Borough of Southwark* [2001] EWCA Civ 999, (2001) 4 CCLR 267 at [51].

such cases the best interests decision-maker would need to consider whether an alternative care package (which they consider is in the person's best interests) could be privately funded elsewhere, or seek to negotiate with the authority. Ultimately, this issue may need to be decided by the courts. In such cases it is important to recognise the distinction between statutory duties in a private law context (namely deciding the best interests of a person lacking capacity under the Mental Capacity Act), with public law decisions under the Care Act. In the case of the former, the Court of Protection has no more power, just because it is acting on behalf of an adult who lacks capacity, to obtain resources or facilities from a third party, whether a private individual or a public authority, than the adult if they had capacity would be able to obtain themselves.[1] In contrast, the decision by a local authority to provide a service is a public law decision, and judicial review remains the proper vehicle through which to challenge unreasonable or irrational decisions.[2] The role of the Court of Protection in respect of care planning decisions, and the overlap with the Mental Capacity Act is discussed at para.1–703 below.

SUPPORTED DECISION-MAKING

Supported decision-making refers to the process of providing support to people whose **1–270** decision-making ability is impaired, to enable them to make their own decisions wherever possible. Supported decision-making therefore starts from the assumption that most people are capable of making decisions in all aspects of their life, if they are provided with appropriate support to do so. One of the main drivers for supported decision-making has been the UN Convention on the rights of Persons with Disabilities. The UN Disability Committee's general comment on art.12 of the UN Convention indicates that national laws should provide supports to the person to ensure that their will and preferences are respected, and must prohibit substituted decision-making based on a person's objective best interests[3].

A form of supported decision-making can be found in s.1(3) of the Mental Capacity Act 2005 which provides that a person is not to be treated as unable to make a decision unless all practical steps have been taken to help them to do so have been taken without success. The courts have required measures such as providing sex education, and presenting the person with "detailed options", rather than starting with a "blank canvas" to help a person attain the capacity to make a particular decision.[4]

Supported decision-making is not mentioned in the Care Act, but it is recognised in the statutory guidance (mainly in respect of care and support planning). Thus, the guidance states that:

- supported decision-making must be carried out if the person is unable to request an assessment or struggles to express their needs[5];
- the "modern care and support system should routinely enable supported decision-making"[6];
- the local authority must, when care planning for people who lack capacity, "support the person to understand and weigh up information, to offer choices and help people to exercise informed choice" and give the person "all practicable help to make the specific decision before being assessed as lacking capacity to make their own decisions"[7]; and
- in respect of continuity of care, where a person lacks capacity to make a decision about a move and their family wants them to move closer, the local authority

---

[1] *Re MN* [2015] EWCA Civ 411 at [80].

[2] *Re MN* [2013] EWHC 3859 (COP).

[3] Committee on the Rights of Person with Disabilities, *General Comment No 1* (2014) paras 20 to 21.

[4] *D Borough Council v AB* [2011] EWHC 101 (COP) and *CC v KK* [2012] EWHC 2136 (COP).

[5] Department of Health, *Care and Support Statutory Guidance* (2014), para.6.9.

[6] Department of Health, *Care and Support Statutory Guidance* (2014), para.10.4.

[7] Department of Health, *Care and Support Statutory Guidance* (2014), para.10.61.

must first carry out supported decision-making before proceeding to a mental capacity assessment and best interests decision under the Mental Capacity Act 2005[1].

NEEDS BEING MET BY A THIRD PARTY

1–271   Prior to the Care Act, case law confirmed that a need which is being met or could be met by a "third party" (such as a carer or a housing authority responsible for the making of disabled facilities grants) can nonetheless be an eligible need. Whether the local authority needs to provide services to meet the need, or whether that need could continue to be met by the third party or by other means, is properly a matter to be decided at the care planning stage and recorded in the care plan.[2] This position has been retained by the Care Act (see s.18(7) in respect of carers). See also discussion under para.1–282 below.

In the past, the Independent Living Fund provided services and direct payments to disabled people to help them lead independent lives in the community, and was an example of a "third party" meeting social care needs. In 2003 it was estimated that over 19,000 people were in receipt of assistance through the Fund which cost the Government over £350 million. Due to increasing costs, the Government closed the Fund completely from 30 June 2015. The Fund has been absorbed into local authority mainstream budgets in England.

The steps for the local authority to take

1–272   **24.**—(1) Where a local authority is required to meet needs under section 18 or 20(1), or decides to do so under section 19(1) or (2) or 20(6), it must—

(a) prepare a care and support plan or a support plan for the adult concerned,

(b) tell the adult which (if any) of the needs that it is going to meet may be met by direct payments, and

(c) help the adult with deciding how to have the needs met.

(2) Where a local authority has carried out a needs or carer's assessment but is not required to meet needs under section 18 or 20(1), and does not decide to do so under section 19(1) or (2) or 20(6), it must give the adult concerned—

(a) its written reasons for not meeting the needs, and

(b) (unless it has already done so under section 13(5)) advice and information about—

(i) what can be done to meet or reduce the needs;

(ii) what can be done to prevent or delay the development by the adult concerned of needs for care and support or of needs for support in the future.

(3) Where a local authority is not going to meet an adult's needs for care and support, it must nonetheless prepare an independent personal budget for the adult (see section 28) if—

(a) the needs meet the eligibility criteria,

(b) at least some of the needs are not being met by a carer, and

(c) the adult is ordinarily resident in the authority's area or is present in its area but of no settled residence.

GENERAL NOTE

1–273   This section sets out the steps local authorities must take after carrying out a needs assessment or carer's assessment. In particular it requires the provision of a care and

---

[1] Department of Health, *Care and Support Statutory Guidance* (2014), paras 20.17 to 20.18.

[2] See, for example, *R (Spink) v Wandsworth London Borough Council* [2005] EWCA Civ 302, [2005] 1 WLR 2884 *and R v Sefton Metropolitan Borough Council ex parte Help the Aged* (1997–98) 1 CCLR 57, 68(E).

support plan (for adults with care and support needs) and a support plan (for carers). In simple terms, such plans are produced following an assessment for the purpose of recording a person's assessed and eligible needs and detailing how a local authority plans to meet those needs. The content of care and support plans and support plans is dealt with by s.24.

The Law Commission recommended that the statute should place a duty on local authorities to produce a care plan for people who have been assessed as having eligible needs (including carers and self-funders). This, it was argued, would improve the clarity of law since at the time there was no statutory reference to care plans and the requirement to produce one, and what it should contain, had to be discerned through reference to a range of statutory and practice guidance.[1] Furthermore, it was argued care plans were of fundamental importance since, in particular, they specify what services an individual is entitled to receive and all other salient information connected with the delivery of those services. The Commission therefore concluded that a new duty would help to underline the centrality of a care plan to the adult social care process. The Commission also recommended that if a person falls below the eligibility criteria, the local authority should be required to put the reasons for that decision in writing and make a written record of the assessment available to the individual.[2]

The Government accepted the Law Commission's recommendations. In doing so it accepted that a statutory duty was "overdue", and further observed that:

"... the concept of a care and support plan has changed markedly over the years, moving from a simple summary record of the services that someone will receive from particular agencies, to one in which the user or carer is placed centre-stage and takes a more active part in its development and the outcomes associated with it."[3]

Section 24 therefore implements the Law Commission's recommendations, and also adds further detail about the information and support that must be provided at this stage.

TIMESCALES FOR CARE PLANS

In the House of Lords the Government stated that guidance will include indicative but **1–274** not definitive timescales for the completion of care and support plans.[4] During the passage of the Care Bill, at Committee stage in the House of Commons, the Government rejected an amendment which would have provided for a timescale to be set for the completion of a care and support plan.

"It is vitally important that local authorities retain the ability to be proportionate to the needs to be met. For some people the care planning process may be relatively simple, and therefore can occur relatively quickly. That may not be the case for people with multiple complex needs. That is not to say that it is right that there should be any delay. It may just take longer to do a proper and thorough assessment in some cases. There may also be a need for experts and independent advocates to be engaged in some cases, as we have previously debated. That should not be overlooked in order to meet a centralised target of timescale. Introducing a prescribed timescale for the completion of the care-planning process may also have the unintended consequence ... of some plans being rushed in order to meet the deadline."[5]

---

[1] For example, Department of Health, *Caring for People: Community Care in the Next Decade and Beyond: Policy Guidance* (1990), para.3.24

[2] Law Commission, *Adult Social Care*, paras 8.32 to 8.44.

[3] Department of Health, *Reforming the Law for Adult Care and Support: The Government's Response to Law Commission Report 326 on Adult Social Care* (TSO, July 2012), Cm.8379, paras 8.12 and 8.13.

[4] *Hansard* (House of Lords), 16 July 2013, Vol.747, col.746 (Earl Howe).

[5] *Hansard* (House of Commons: Public Bill Committee), 16 January 2014 (PM): Sixth Sitting, col.214 (Norman Lamb MP).

The statutory guidance stresses the need for a proportionate plan and that this does not equate to a light-touch approach, since "in many cases a proportionate plan will require a more detailed and thorough examination of needs".[1] It goes on to state that:

"While there is no defined timescale for the completion of the care and support planning process, the plan should be completed in a timely fashion, proportionate to the needs to be met. Local authorities must ensure that sufficient time is taken to ensure the plan is appropriate to meet the needs in question, and is agreed by the person the plan is intended for. The planning process should not unduly delay needs being met."[2]

Subsection (1)

1–275   This subsection applies when a local authority has:

- a duty under s.18 to meet an adult's needs for care and support;
- a duty under s.20(1) to meet a carer's needs for support;
- exercised its discretion under s.19(1) or (2) to meet an adult's needs for care and support following an assessment; or
- exercised its discretion under s.20(6) to meet a carer's needs for support.

It requires the local authority to do all of the following:

- prepare a care and support plan for an adult with needs for care and support, or a support plan for a carer;
- inform the adult which of their needs that the authority will meet may be met through direct payments; and
- help the adult in deciding how to have the needs met.

The need to inform the person about which of their needs can be met by direct payments is significant because under s.31(1)(b) the adult has a right to request direct payments and if certain conditions are met the local authority must comply with the request. The requirement in subs.(1)(b) is to "tell" the adult this information. This suggests that the information does not necessarily need to be given in writing. However, it is submitted that local authorities should as a matter of course, provide this information in writing in order to demonstrate they have met this requirement. The Equality Act 2010 may also be relevant and if necessary, the information should be provided in alternative formats and using different methods of communication. The statutory guidance advises that people should be offered the choice of direct payments "more than once in the process" and provided with examples of how others have used direct payments, including via direct peer support, for example from user-led organisations.[3] It goes on to state that the person must be provided with appropriate information and advice concerning the usage of direct payments, and lists certain matters that must be addressed in the advice provided.[4]

The guidance also advises that a named contact or lead professional should be considered both as part of care planning, and in the final plan, so that the person knows how to contact the local authority. In addition, where the assessment has been carried out by a person with specific expertise or training in a particular condition (for example, deafblindness), someone with similar knowledge (and preferably the same person) should also be involved in the production of the plan.[5]

---

[1] Department of Health, *Care and Support Statutory Guidance* (2014), para.10.43.
[2] Department of Health, *Care and Support Statutory Guidance* (2014), para.10.84.
[3] Department of Health, *Care and Support Statutory Guidance* (2014), para.10.3.
[4] Department of Health, *Care and Support Statutory Guidance* (2014), para.10.46.
[5] Department of Health, *Care and Support Statutory Guidance* (2014), paras 10.33 to 10.34.

Subsection (2)

This subsection applies when a local authority is not required to meet the person's needs **1–276** under ss.18 or 20(1), and decides not to exercise its discretion to meet any needs. For example, it may be that the adult has needs which meet the eligibility criteria but there is no duty to meet those needs because the adult is ordinarily resident elsewhere, or their needs are being met by a carer. The subsection also applies when the local authority decides not to exercise its discretion to meet the person's non-eligible needs.

It requires the local authority to provide the person with the following:

- a written explanation of the reasons why it is not going to meet the needs (subs.2(a)); and
- information and advice on how the adult can meet or reduce their needs, including information on how the adult can prevent or delay their needs (unless the adult or carer has received such advice and information already as required by s.13(5) in cases where none of their needs meet the eligibility criteria) (subs.2(b)).

The duty under subs.(2)(a) is to give written reasons for not meeting the needs. The Equality Act 2010 may be relevant to the performance of this duty and if necessary, the explanation should be provided in alternative formats and using different methods of communication, as well as being in writing. The statutory guidance also states that a copy should be given to the person's advocate, and "where the person cannot request this, then a copy should be given to the person's advocate or appropriate individual if this is in the best interests of the person".[1] The duty under subs.(2)(b) is to provide information and advice about how to prevent or delay needs. According to the explanatory notes this should be provided in writing.[2] However, the wording of the subsection contains no such requirement, and indeed does not specify any particular formalities about how the information and advice should be given to the person. The statutory guidance also does not expressly state that this should be in writing.[3] Nevertheless, it is submitted that local authorities should as a matter of course, provide this information in writing in order to demonstrate they have met this requirement. The Equality Act 2010 may also be relevant and if necessary, the information should be provided in alternative formats and using different methods of communication.

Subsection (2)(b) also says that the information and advice should be about what can be done to prevent or delay "the development by the adult concerned" of needs for care and support. The explanatory notes suggest that this means, how the adult can meet or reduce their needs "independently".[4] However, this should not be taken to mean that the adult should be left to fend for themselves. The adult should be signposted towards, and where necessary given assistance in accessing, relevant support services in the community. The statutory guidance emphasises that the information should be personal and not a generalised reference to prevention services or signpost to a general website.[5]

Local authorities retain discretion to provide additional information to those whose needs they are not required to meet, and where they have not exercised their power to provide services. They could also provide something similar to a formal care plan to such people.

Subsection (2)(a) and (b) does not specify or indicate how much detail should be provided when giving written reasons, and advice and information. The extent of the detail is likely to depend upon the specific circumstances of the individual case. For example, where the person is not seeking local authority assistance and agrees with the decision, it may be acceptable to provide relatively brief and straightforward reasons, and advice

---

[1] Department of Health, *Care and Support Statutory Guidance* (2014), para.10.29.
[2] Care Act 2014, Explanatory Notes para.173.
[3] See, Department of Health, *Care and Support Statutory Guidance* (2014), para.10.29.
[4] Care Act 2014, Explanatory Notes para.173.
[5] Department of Health, *Care and Support Statutory Guidance* (2014), para.10.29.

and information. But where for example the decision is disputed by the person and the family, more detail might be appropriate.

If a local authority meets some but not all of the person's needs it must provide a care plan under subs.(1) and information and advice on how to prevent or delay the needs it is not meeting as required under subs.(2).[1]

Subsection (3)

1–277   This subsection applies where the adult has eligible needs for care and support, but the local authority does not have a duty to meet these needs. In most cases this will be because the adult does not want to have their needs met by the local authority (see s.18). The subsection requires the local authority to prepare an independent personal budget for the adult (as required by s.28).

Care and support plan, support plan

1–278   **25.**—(1) A care and support plan or, in the case of a carer, a support plan is a document prepared by a local authority which—

(a)   specifies the needs identified by the needs assessment or carer's assessment,

(b)   specifies whether, and if so to what extent, the needs meet the eligibility criteria,

(c)   specifies the needs that the local authority is going to meet and how it is going to meet them,

(d)   specifies to which of the matters referred to in section 9(4) the provision of care and support could be relevant or to which of the matters referred to in section 10(5) and (6) the provision of support could be relevant,

(e)   includes the personal budget for the adult concerned (see section 26), and

(f)   includes advice and information about—

(i)   what can be done to meet or reduce the needs in question;

(ii)   what can be done to prevent or delay the development of needs for care and support or of needs for support in the future.

(2) Where some or all of the needs are to be met by making direct payments, the plan must also specify—

(a)   the needs which are to be so met, and

(b)   the amount and frequency of the direct payments.

(3) In preparing a care and support plan, the local authority must involve—

(a)   the adult for whom it is being prepared,

(b)   any carer that the adult has, and

(c)   any person whom the adult asks the authority to involve or, where the adult lacks capacity to ask the authority to do that, any person who appears to the authority to be interested in the adult's welfare.

(4) In preparing a support plan, the local authority must involve—

(a)   the carer for whom it is being prepared,

(b)   the adult needing care, if the carer asks the authority to do so, and

(c)   any other person whom the carer asks the authority to involve.

(5) In performing the duty under subsection (3)(a) or (4)(a), the local authority must take all reasonable steps to reach agreement with the adult or carer for whom the plan is being prepared about how the authority should meet the needs in question.

(6) In seeking to ensure that the plan is proportionate to the needs to be met, the local authority must have regard in particular—

---

[1]   Department of Health, *Care and Support Statutory Guidance* (2014), para.10.30.

(a) in the case of a care and support plan, to the matters referred to in section 9(4);

(b) in the case of a support plan, to the matters referred to in section 10(5) and (6).

(7) The local authority may authorise a person (including the person for whom the plan is to be prepared) to prepare the plan jointly with the authority.

(8) The local authority may do things to facilitate the preparation of the plan in a case within subsection (7); it may, for example, provide a person authorised under that subsection with—

(a) in the case of a care and support plan, information about the adult for whom the plan is being prepared;

(b) in the case of a support plan, information about the carer and the adult needing care;

(c) in either case, whatever resources, or access to whatever facilities, the authority thinks are required to prepare the plan.

(9) The local authority must give a copy of a care and support plan to—

(a) the adult for whom it has been prepared,

(b) any carer that the adult has, if the adult asks the authority to do so, and

(c) any other person to whom the adult asks the authority to give a copy.

(10) The local authority must give a copy of a support plan to—

(a) the carer for whom it has been prepared,

(b) the adult needing care, if the carer asks the authority to do so, and

(c) any other person to whom the carer asks the authority to give a copy.

(11) A local authority may combine a care and support plan or a support plan with a plan (whether or not prepared by it and whether or not under this Part) relating to another person only if the adult for whom the care and support plan or the support plan is being prepared agrees and—

(a) where the combination would include a plan prepared for another adult, that other adult agrees;

(b) where the combination would include a plan prepared for a child (including a young carer), the consent condition is met in relation to the child.

(12) The consent condition is met in relation to a child if—

(a) the child has capacity or is competent to agree to the plans being combined and does so agree, or

(b) the child lacks capacity or is not competent so to agree but the local authority is satisfied that the combining the plans would be in the child's best interests.

(13) Regulations may specify cases or circumstances in which such of paragraphs (a) to (f) of subsection (1) and paragraphs (a) and (b) of subsection (2) as are specified do not apply.

(14) The regulations may in particular specify that the paragraphs in question do not apply as regards specified needs or matters.

GENERAL NOTE

This section sets out the information that must be included in the care and support plan, **1–279** or the support plan. It also sets out requirements for how the plan must be prepared, who should be given copies of the plan and for combining different plans.

The Law Commission had recommended that—in order to ensure flexibility and future-proof the statute—the content of care and support plans should be set out in regulations.[1]

The Government agreed with the Commission that the inclusion of care and support plans more prominently in the new legislation is overdue. However the Government disagreed that regulations should specify the core content of the care and support plans and instead felt that primary legislation should set out "the few, high-level items which should be included in the plans provided both to people who use care, and to carers" such as details of the assessed needs, any assessed financial contributions, the care and support to be provided, and the amount of the personal budget. This would, it argued, "reflect existing practice, and obviate the need for further regulations".[2]

Timescales for the completion of plans are discussed above at para.1–274. The use of panels to sign-off care plans and personal budgets is discussed below at para.1-302.

CHALLENGING CARE PLANS

1–280   Prior to the Care Act, there was no statutory reference to care plans. Instead, the requirements concerning the production and content of such plans were contained in a range of statutory and non-statutory guidance. The courts had therefore tended to approach care plans as providing prima facie evidence of whether or not a local authority had breached its statutory community care responsibilities. For example, in *R. v Islington LBC Ex parte Rixon*, Mr Justice Sedley (as he then was) accepted that "a care plan is nothing more than a clerical record of what has been decided and what is planned" but went on to say:

"... far from marginalising the care plan, places it at the centre of any scrutiny of the local authority's duty to discharge its functions ... a care plan is the means by which the local authority assembles relevant information and applies it to the statutory ends, and hence affords good evidence to any inquirer of the due discharge of its statutory duties. It cannot, however, be quashed as it were a self-implementing document".[3]

The courts have also been at pains to emphasise the limits of their role in relation to care plans. In *R. (Lloyd) v Mayor and Burgesses of the London Borough of Barking and Dagenham*—which concerned a disabled woman who was being moved out of her long-term residential care home—the Court of Appeal accepted that it was at least arguable in this case that the care plan was deficient because it did not cater for her needs, but went on to say:

"... the Court is not the appropriate organ to be prescriptive as to the degree of detail which should go into a care plan ... In practice these are matters for the Council, and if necessary its complaints procedure. If the Council has failed to follow the Secretary of State's guidance and is arguably in breach of its statutory duties in relation to the way it carries out its assessment and what it puts into its care plans then aggrieved persons should in an appropriate case turn first to the Secretary of State. Where there is room for differences of judgment the Secretary of State and his advisers may have a useful input. The Court is here as a last resort where there is illegality."[4]

Nevertheless, the work of the courts will often involve sifting through care plans as the administrative record of what has been decided and what has been planned. The general approach of the courts is to adopt a cautious approach to passing adverse judgement upon the contents of care plans. In other words, the courts recognise and to extent defer

---

[1] Law Commission, *Adult Social Care*, para.8.44.
[2] Department of Health, *Reforming the Law for Adult Care and Support: The Government's Response to Law Commission Report 326 on Adult Social Care* (TSO, July 2012), Cm.8379, para.8.17.
[3] *R. v Islington LBC Ex p Rixon* (1997–1998) 1 CCLR 119.
[4] *R. (Lloyd) v Mayor and Burgesses of the London Borough of Barking and Dagenham* [2001] EWCA Civ 533 at [27].

to the expertise of social services departments on such matters. But this does not mean that the courts have been uncritical. In *Rixon*, for example, the court concluded that the care plan was inadequate to meet the needs of a 25-year old disabled man, and the authority had not complied with the relevant policy guidance in respect of the plan's content, the specification of objectives in the plan, agreement on implementation of the plan, the leeway for contingencies and the identification and feedback of unmet needs.[1] In *R. (B) v Cornwall CC* it was held that the approach taken by a local authority in devising a care plan was unlawful.[2] This case involved a disabled man who had originally been assessed as not being liable to be charged for services. The local authority then conducted a review of all such decisions and concluded that the financial assessments had been carried out incorrectly. After a paper review of the case it decided to charge him £68 per week. The court emphasised that the authority could not, on the one hand, make charging decisions on the basis of a care plan, whilst at the same time identifying defects in that plan and failing to consult the carers who might have provided the evidence lacking in the care plan itself.[3]

The introduction of statutory care and support plans and support plans in s.25 (and the **1–281** duty to provide such plans under s.24(1)(a)) should serve to reinforce and heighten their legal importance. It is submitted that by giving care plans a statutory footing, the ability to challenge the legal validity of such plans will expand. A failure by a local authority to produce a care plan or an adequate care plan could in itself amount to a breach of its statutory duty. In other words, care plans will no longer be just administrative records that evidence whether the local authority has discharged its statutory duties. Moreover a failure to produce the care plan in accordance with s.25—for example by not involving the relevant person—could also amount to a breach of statutory duty. As is currently the case, a failure to provide care and support in accordance with a care plan might also be unlawful. Furthermore, if the dispute over the care plan arises because the authority has failed in its general public requirements for example to act rationally and reasonably and have regard to all relevant considerations in its decision-making then, depending on the facts of the case, there may be grounds for judicial review.

It is instructive in this respect to consider the approach of the courts in other jurisdictions where care plans have been given a statutory footing. For example, in *R. (J) v Caerphilly County Borough Council*—which concerned the duty to provide pathway plans under the Children Act 1989, as amended by the Children (Leaving Care) Act 2000—Mr Justice Munby (as he was then) described the care plan produced by the local authority as "hopelessly inadequate" and "little more than worthless". Its deficiencies included the lack of detail about the nature and level of support to be provided, frequent vague statements of intent (such to arrange an appointment with someone else, or to "explore options", or to "develop" a programme) and no clear date by which actions will be completed (other than "ASAP" or "on going").[4] He went on to set out some minimum standards:

"Any judge who sits in the Family Division will be familiar with the depressing inadequacies and deficiencies in too many of the care plans presented to the court for its approval. A care plan is more than a statement of strategic objectives—though all too often even these are expressed in the most vacuous terms. A care plan is—or ought to be—a detailed operational plan. Just how detailed will depend upon the circumstances of the particular case. Sometimes a very high level of detail will be essential. But whatever the level of detail which the individual case may call for, any care plan worth its name ought to set out the operational objectives with sufficient detail—including detail

---

[1] *R. v Islington LBC Ex p Rixon* (1997–1998) 1 CCLR 119.

[2] *R. (B) v Cornwall CC* [2009] EWHC 491 (Admin); (2009) 12 CCLR 381.

[3] *R. (B) v Cornwall CC* [2009] EWHC 491 (Admin); (2009) 12 CCLR 381 at [67].

[4] *R. (J) v Caerphilly County Borough Council* [2005] EWHC 586 (Admin); [2005] 2 F.L.R. 860 at [42] to [43].

of the 'how, who, what and when'—to enable the care plan itself to be used as a means of checking whether or not those objectives are being met".[1]

Subsection (1)

1–282   This subsection defines a care and support plan, or a support plan, as a document containing certain information. Thus, it provides that the plan must specify the needs identified in the assessment and whether (and if so the extent to which) the needs meet the eligibility criteria. It also requires the plan to specify the needs the local authority will meet and to state how it will meet them. The statutory guidance sets out that if a person's needs are being met by alternative means—for example, by a carer or in an educational establishment—the local authority does not have to arrange or provide services (although they remain under a duty to meet the person's eligible needs). This applies irrespective of whether the services are self-funded. In such circumstances the authority should record those needs as eligible needs, and keep the arrangements under review. Where a person is entitled to other services which could meet their needs—but does not avail themselves of the services—the needs are unmet and the local authority remains under a duty to meet them.[2] See also discussion at para.1–271 above.

The care and support plan must specify to which of the following matters (covered in the assessment under s.9(4)) the provision of care and support could be relevant:

- the impact of the adult's needs for care and support on the matters specified in s.1(2);
- the outcomes that the adult wishes to achieve in day-to-day life; and
- whether, and if so to what extent, the provision of care and support could contribute to the achievement of those outcomes.

The support plan must specify to which of the following matters (covered in the assessment under s.10(5) and (6)) the provision support could be relevant:

- whether the carer is able, and is likely to continue to be able, to provide care;
- whether the carer is willing, and is likely to continue to be willing, to do so;
- the impact of the carer's needs for support on the matters specified in s.1(2);
- the outcomes that the carer wishes to achieve in day-to-day life;
- whether, and if so to what extent, the provision of support could contribute to the achievement of those outcomes;
- whether the carer works or wishes to do so; and
- whether the carer is participating in or wishes to participate in education, training or recreation.

The care and support plan, and the support plan, must also include the personal budget for the adult (s.26) and information and advice about how to prevent, delay or reduce the adult's needs for care and support or the carer's need for support.

During the passage of the Care Bill in the House of Lords, the Government emphasised that:

". . . it is vital that local authorities retain the ability to be proportionate to the needs to be met. For some people the care planning process may be relatively simple and therefore can occur relatively quickly, but that may not be the case for people with multiple complex needs. As we discussed earlier, there may be a need for experts to be engaged in some cases, and this should not be overlooked in order to meet a centralised target."[3]

---

[1] *R. (J) v Caerphilly County Borough Council* [2005] EWHC 586 (Admin); [2005] 2 F.L.R. 860 at [46].

[2] Department of Health, *Care and Support Statutory Guidance* (2014), paras 10.22 and 10.25.

[3] *Hansard* (House of Lords), 16 July 2013, Vol.747, col.745 (Earl Howe).

In response to whether health needs should be specified in the care plan, the Government went on to say:

"The Bill creates a clear legal framework to enable such integration to happen in practice. However, it is not for the local authority to specify in the care plan which needs the NHS should meet. [S.25] requires local authorities to involve the adult and carer, and take all reasonable steps to agree the plan with them, which would include whether to refer to any health needs."[1]

Subsection (2)

If the individual's needs are met by a direct payment, the plan must specify the needs that **1–283** will be met by the direct payment, and the amount and frequency of the direct payment. This confirms that direct payments must be spent on meeting need, and not on desires or wants. It is also in line with the decision in *R. (KM) v Cambridgeshire CC* that the amount of the direct payments must reflect a rational computation of the individual's assessed eligible needs (see para.1–300 below).[2]

Subsection (3)

In preparing a care and support plan, the local authority must involve the adult, any carer **1–284** they may have, and anyone else the adult may ask to be involved in the development of the plan. Where a person lacks capacity the local authority must also involve any person who appears to be interested in the individual's welfare.

The Government removed the qualification contained in the draft Care and Support Bill that engagement should only be undertaken "as far as feasible" in relation to developing the care and support plan (clause 24(3)). See discussion at paras 1–104 to 1–105 above in respect of the meaning of involve and when involvement might not be appropriate.

Involving a person may involve providing them with an advocate. The right to advocacy in s.67 of the Care Act expressly applies to this subsection (see s.67(3)(c)).

The statutory guidance emphasises throughout the need to involve the person fully. For example it states that:

"The person must be genuinely involved and influential throughout the planning process, and should be given every opportunity to take joint ownership of the development of the plan with the local authority if they wish, and the local authority agrees. There should be a default assumption that the person, with support if necessary, will play a strong pro-active role in planning if they choose to. Indeed, it should be made clear that the plan 'belongs' to the person it is intended for, with the local authority role to ensure the production and sign-off of the plan to ensure that it is appropriate to meet the identified needs."[3] However, there is recognition that the person may not wish to take control and may ask for more local authority support (for instance if they lack the skills or confidence to engage with the provider market), and the local authority should "respond accordingly".[4]

The guidance also states that "joint planning does not mean a 50:50 split" and "the person can take a bigger share of the planning where this is appropriate and the person wishes to do so". Moreover, the person "should not be required to go through lengthy processes which limit their ability to be actively involved, unless there are very strong reasons to add in elements of process and decision-making".[5]

---

[1] *Hansard* (House of Lords), 16 July 2013, Vol.747, col.746 (Earl Howe).
[2] *R. (KM) v Cambridgeshire CC* [2012] UKSC 23 at [38].
[3] Department of Health, *Care and Support Statutory Guidance* (2014), para.10.2.
[4] Department of Health, *Care and Support Statutory Guidance* (2014), para.10.21.
[5] Department of Health, *Care and Support Statutory Guidance* (2014), para.10.32.

The guidance emphasises that the carer must be involved in the planning process and the local authority should record the carer's willingness to provide care and the extent of this in the plan of the person and also the carer.[1]

Involving the person is also discussed at paras 10.49 to 10.54 of the statutory guidance. It advises that local authorities should include a prompt during the initial stages of the planning process to ask whether there is anyone else that the person wishes to be involved. Where the person lacks capacity, the local authority should make a best interests decision about who else should be involved.[2]

Subsection (4)

1–285   In preparing a support plan, the local authority must involve the carer, the adult receiving care, and anyone else the carer may ask to be involved in the development of the plan.

The Government removed the qualification contained in the draft Bill that engagement should be undertaken "as far as feasible" in relation to developing the support plan.[3] See discussion at paras 1–104 to 1–105 above in respect of the meaning of involve and when involvement might not be appropriate.

Involving a person may involve providing them with an advocate. The right to advocacy in s.67 of the Care Act expressly applies to this subsection (see s.67(3)(d)).

Subsection (5)

1–286   The local authority must take all "reasonable steps" to reach agreement with the person for whom the plan is being prepared about how the local authority is going to meet their needs. This largely repeats a previous requirement contained in the Community Care Assessment Directions 2004.[4] The explanatory notes recognise that in some cases the local authority will be required to make an advocate available under s.67.[5] In some cases it will not be possible to reach an agreement. In those cases, the Government has stated that "the local authority will have to act to ensure that the person's needs are met and that any risks to their safety are prevented".[6] The Supreme Court said in *R. (KM) v Cambridgeshire CC* that where it is not possible to reach agreement, the local authority should set out how in its opinion the service user might reasonably choose to deploy the offered sum and its assessment of the reasonable costs involved.[7]

The sign off and assurance of care plans is discussed in paras 10.81 to 10.87 of the statutory guidance. In the event that the plan cannot be agreed, the local authority should state the reasons and the steps which must be taken to ensure the plan is signed off. If the dispute remains the person should be directed to the complaints procedure.[8]

The use of approval panels to sign off care plans is discussed at para.1–302 below.

Subsection (6)

1–287   In seeking to ensure that the plan is proportionate to the needs to be met, the local authority is required to have regard in particular to various matters covered by the assessment (as specified in ss.9(4), 10(5) and 10(6)).

In the case of a care and support plan, these matters are:

- the impact of the adult's needs for care and support on the matters specified in s.1(2);
- the outcomes that the adult wishes to achieve in day-to-day life; and

---

[1] Department of Health, *Care and Support Statutory Guidance* (2014), para.10.40.
[2] Department of Health, *Care and Support Statutory Guidance* (2014), para.10.49.
[3] Department of Health, *Draft Care and Support Bill* (TSO July 2012), Cm.8386, cl.24(4).
[4] Community Care Assessment Directions 2004, dir 2(3).
[5] Care Act 2014, Explanatory Notes para.180.
[6] *Hansard* (House of Lords), 16 July 2013, Vol.747, col.749 (Earl Howe).
[7] *R. (KM) v Cambridgeshire CC* [2012] UKSC 23 at [38].
[8] Department of Health, *Care and Support Statutory Guidance* (2014), para.10.86.

- whether, and if so to what extent, the provision of care and support could contribute to the achievement of those outcomes.

In the case of a support plan, these matters are:

- whether the carer is able, and is likely to continue to be able, to provide care for the adult needing care;
- whether the carer is willing, and is likely to continue to be willing, to do so;
- the impact of the carer's needs for support on the matters specified in s.1(2);
- the outcomes that the carer wishes to achieve in day-to-day life;
- whether, and if so to what extent, the provision of support could contribute to the achievement of those outcomes;
- whether the carer works or wishes to do so; and
- whether the carer is participating in or wishes to participate in education, training or recreation.

Subsection (7)

The local authority can jointly prepare the plan with another person, including the adult **1–288** or carer who the plan is being prepared for. Authorising others (including the person) to prepare the plan jointly with the local authority is discussed in paras 10.55 to 10.58 of the statutory guidance. The sign off and assurance of care plans jointly prepared with the local authority is discussed in para.10.82.

Subsection (8)

The local authority must facilitate the development of the plan under subs.(7) by provid- **1–289** ing such a person with information, resources and access to facilities.

Subsection (9)

Local authorities are required to give a copy of a care and support plan to: **1–290**

- the adult;
- any carer (if the adult asks the authority to do so); and
- any other person that the adult may ask to be given a copy

The onus is on the adult to ask for their plan to be shared—as opposed to a presumption that information is shared by the local authority unless the adult disagrees. The statutory guidance notes that this should not restrict local authorities from making the draft plan available throughout the planning process and consideration should be given to sharing key points of the final plan with other professionals and supporters.[1]

Subsection (10)

Local authorities are required to give a copy of a support plan to: **1–291**

- the carer;
- the adult needing care (if the carer asks the authority to do so); and
- any other person that the carer may ask to be given a copy.

The onus is on the carer to ask for their plan to be shared—as opposed to a presumption that information is shared by the local authority unless the carer disagrees.

---

[1] Department of Health, *Care and Support Statutory Guidance* (2014), para.10.87.

Subsection (11)

1–292   Subsection (11) enables the local authority to combine a care and support plan or a support plan with any other plan, where those to whom the plans relate agree.

The Law Commission noted the clear message that service users and carers were concerned by the proliferation of multiple care plan regimes for different service users. It concluded that the law should not require professionals to produce multiple plans for the same person under different legal provisions (for example, the Care Act, the Care Programme Approach and the single assessment process). The Commission, therefore, recommended that the legislation should enable the production of a single plan across the different legal assessment regimes.[1] In Parliament, the Government stated to its expectation that where an adult has an Education, Health and Care Plan (as required up until the age of 25 by the Children and Families Act 2014) their care and support needs assessment and plan should be integrated with it.[2]

The statutory guidance discusses combining care plans in paras 10.73 to 10.80. It also discusses cooperation between professionals and organisations (including joint assessments) in the context of transition assessments in paras 16.40 to 16.49. See para.1–590 below.

Subsection (12)

1–293   Where one of the plans being combined under subs.(11) relates to a child who lacks capacity or is not competent to agree, the local authority must be satisfied that combining the plans is in the child's best interests.

This would allow for a combined care and support plan, for instance to reflect the needs of a family more holistically.

Subsection (13)

1–294   Regulations may specify circumstances where elements of subs.(1) and (2) do not apply.

Subsection (14)

1–295   This subsection was introduced as a Government amendment during Committee stage in the House of Commons. It clarifies that the regulation-making power in subs.(13) can:

> ". . . specify cases related to needs, or matters where aspects of the care plan, including the personal budget, are not required. This will allow regulations to exclude from the personal budget in the care plan the cost of meeting any specified prescribed care and support needs, which are otherwise incorporated in that plan. It was always the policy intention that there may be cases where aspects of care planning are not appropriate. An example is the inclusion of costs related to the provision of re-ablement. This is where the provision of care and support needs to be short-term, rapidly provided and may change often. Therefore it may not be appropriate for these types of care and support to follow the same processes as for long-term care and support. This also reflects current practice, and we intend to continue this arrangement through regulations under the Care Bill."[3]

Personal budget

1–296   **26.**—(1) A personal budget for an adult is a statement which specifies—

(a) the cost to the local authority of meeting those of the adult's needs which it is required or decides to meet as mentioned in section 24(1),

(b) the amount which, on the basis of the financial assessment, the adult must pay towards that cost, and

---

[1] Law Commission, *Adult Social Care*, para.8.52.

[2] *Hansard* (House of Lords), 16 July, 2013, Vol.747, cols 746 to 747 (Earl Howe).

[3] *Hansard* (House of Commons: Public Bill Committee), 16 January 2014 (PM): Sixth Sitting, col.215 (Norman Lamb MP).

(c) if on that basis the local authority must itself pay towards that cost, the amount which it must pay.

(2) In the case of an adult with needs for care and support which the local authority is required to meet under section 18, the personal budget must also specify—

(a) the cost to the local authority of meeting the adult's needs under that section, and

(b) where that cost includes daily living costs—

(i) the amount attributable to those daily living costs, and

(ii) the balance of the cost referred to in paragraph (a).

(3) A personal budget for an adult may also specify other amounts of public money that are available in the adult's case including, for example, amounts available for spending on matters relating to housing, health care or welfare.

(4) Regulations may make provision for excluding costs to a local authority from a personal budget if the costs are incurred in meeting needs for which the authority—

(a) does not make a charge, or

(b) is not permitted to make a charge.

GENERAL NOTE

A personal budget is a statement which sets out the cost to the local authority of meeting **1–297** an adult's care and support needs. It is normally developed in two stages. First, an indicative amount is allocated at the start of the care and support planning process. This is intended to provide a ballpark figure which provides individuals, at an early stage, with a rough idea of how much money will be available to meet their needs. Second, the final amount of the personal budget is confirmed. The individual can then choose to manage this money as a direct payment, or the local authority can manage the budget, or a third party or provider (known as an individual service fund) can manage the budget on the person's behalf, or there may be a combination of these approaches. The range of options is discussed in paras 11.29 to 11.41 of the statutory guidance. Personal budgets are seen as a key element of the Government's policy of personalisation and self-directed support. Supporters of personal budgets argue that if people know how much their care and support is costing, they are more likely to want to exercise greater choice and control over how their needs are met.

Prior to the Care Act, both the Labour and Coalition Governments had stated that local authorities must introduce personal budgets for everyone eligible for adult social care support—including carers.[1] The Law Commission raised concerns that despite this policy intention, no changes had been made to the legislative framework in order to accommodate personal budgets, and in some instances, they did not sit easily with the underlying legislation. It argued that the legal framework and the policy of personal budgets must be more closely aligned and that to leave this significant policy development without a statutory basis would leave local authorities uncertain of their legal obligations and individuals uncertain of their entitlements. The Commission therefore recommended that the statute should enable regulations to provide for a duty or power to provide a personal budget. The idea of setting this out in regulations was in part an attempt to accommodate the policy of the Welsh Government which had not embraced personal budgets (as noted at para.I1–008 above, the Law Commission had intended to establish identical statutes in both England and in Wales). The Social Services and Well-being (Wales) Act 2014 does provide for regulations which would enable personal budgets to be specified as part of the care and

---

[1] See, for example, HM Government and others, *Putting People First* (2007), p.3; Department of Health, *A Vision for Adult Social Care* (2010), para.4.9; and HM Government, *Recognised, Valued and Supported: Next Steps for the Carers Strategy* (2010), p.24.

support plan.[1] The Commission also felt that the use of regulations would also allow for changes in Government policy which in future may not be in favour of personal budgets.[2]

However, in its response to the Law Commission the Government argued that because personal budgets are a critical element of achieving its policy objectives, there should be a clear duty on the face of the statute to provide a personal budget. In effect, the provision of a personal budget would be the:

". . . default part of the care and support plan, to enable users or carers to decide how much control they wish to exercise in deciding how their needs for care and support will be met. This position would have only limited exceptions, for instance for certain one-off or short-term services where allocating costs upfront in a personal budget may be less relevant. We will specify such exceptions in regulations."[3]

1–298 Section 26 therefore defines a personal budget as a statement and sets out the financial information that must be included in the statement. It must be read alongside s.25(1)(e) of the Care Act which requires that a care and support plan, or support plan, must include the adult's personal budget. The duty to provide a personal budget applies to both those with care and support needs and carers.

During the passage of the Care Bill, Paul Burstow MP placed the significance of the personal budget into perspective:

"The personal budget is merely the means, and sometimes in some quarters the personal budget gets elevated to being more important than the goal, which is individualised, personalised care."[4]

However, the importance of personal budgets was further heightened by the confirmation that the Government intended to establish a cap on care costs and therefore the personal budget would act as a confirmation for the individual over what will count towards the cap on care costs (see para.1–181 above). Prior to the Care Act personal budgets had been an important aspect of achieving the Government's policy of personalisation, but as a result of the funding reforms they will also potentially have significant financial implications for many service users. The capped costs system is due to be implemented from April 2020.

RESOURCE ALLOCATION SYSTEMS

1–299 To calculate the personal budget many local authorities use a resource allocation system (RAS). There is a range of RASs in use. Some RASs use a points scored questionnaire which measures a person's levels of care and support needs in key areas (such as personal care, relationships and employment). Each point is given a value depending on the area of need and a calculation is made (often by a computation or by reference to a table) which converts the value into an overall sum of money. Other RASs estimate the sum of money directly from the number of hours of support that is needed. Most RASs generate an indicative sum which is then upgraded or deflated according to the individual circumstances of the service user.

The Court of Appeal in *R. (Savva) v Kensington and Chelsea Council* set out several important principles about how personal budgets should be calculated.[5] It was stated that the use of a RAS is not inherently unlawful. But the court placed some emphasis on the fact that in this case the computer's indicative budget was not used by the local authority

---

[1] Social Services and Well-being (Wales) Act 2014 s.54(5).

[2] Law Commission, *Adult Social Care*, paras 8.54 to 8.61.

[3] Department of Health, *Reforming the Law for Adult Care and Support: The Government's Response to Law Commission Report 326 on Adult Social Care* (TSO, July 2012), Cm.8379, para.8.19 to 8.22.

[4] *Hansard* (House of Commons: Public Bill Committee), 16 January 2014 (PM): Sixth Sitting, col.222.

[5] *R. (Savva) v Kensington and Chelsea Council* [2010] EWCA Civ 1209.

as anything other than a starting point and was subjected to a subsequent process. In broad terms a resource allocation panel had reviewed the budget generated by the RAS in the light of other information specifically from the formal assessment process to ensure that it could purchase sufficient services to meet the person's eligible needs. However, the court held that an individual is entitled to be told how the sum of money has been calculated in clear terms:

> "When a local authority converts an established right—the provision of services to meet an assessed eligible need—into a sum of money, the recipient is entitled to be told how the sum has been calculated. It is submitted on behalf of the Council that the imposition of such a duty is excessively onerous for a local authority. By way of illustration, there are some 5000 recipients within the area for which the Council is responsible. It is said that to require the Council to provide each of them with written reasons would be unduly costly. I accept that the burden would not be insignificant but it is what simple fairness requires. If a local authority were entitled to notify a bald figure without any explanation, the recipient would have no means of satisfying himself or herself that it was properly calculated. As the guidance from the Association of Directors of Social Services puts it, explanations of decisions 'make it possible for people and families to challenge these decisions'. Or, to put it the other way round, an absence of explanations may make it impossible to mount such a challenge, whether by way of complaint or by way of litigation."[1]

The court observed that the provision of adequate reasons could be achieved with reasonable brevity. In this case it was considered that the local authority explanation should include a list of the required services and assumed timings, together with the assumed hourly cost. However, service users with more complicated arrangements will need more expansive reasoning. The court, however, rejected the suggestion that every decision must include an explanation of the local authority's RAS. It was explained that:

> ". . . recipients and their advisers are entitled to know about the RAS but . . . this can be achieved by publishing the RAS on the Council's website in a user-friendly format".[2]

Lord Justice Kay also argued that the duty to provide reasons may be satisfied by notice **1–300** in the decision letter that reasons will be provided on request.[3]

In *R. (KM) v Cambridgeshire CC* the Supreme Court confirmed that a RAS is an unlawful tool for an authority to deploy even only "as a starting point".[4] What is crucial is that, once the indicative sum has been identified, the requisite services in the particular case should be costed in a reasonable degree of detail so that a judgement can be made whether the indicative sum is too high, too low or about right. The court also underlined the importance of providing an intelligible explanation of how the final sum has been calculated and described as "helpful guidance" the approach of the Court of Appeal in *Savva* to the giving of reasons. It was also stated that:

> "Even in a more complicated case, however, it may be enough for the authority, as here, to attribute a compendious cost to a group of requisite services of similar character, particularly if there are reasons for concluding that general assumptions have been made which, if reflective of error, would reflect error in the service-user's favour."[5]

In this case the local authority was criticised for failing to make a more detailed presentation of its own assessment of the reasonable cost of paying for carers.[6]

---

[1] *R. (Savva) v Kensington and Chelsea Council* [2010] EWCA Civ 1209 at [20].
[2] *R. (Savva) v Kensington and Chelsea Council* [2010] EWCA Civ 1209 at [21].
[3] *R. (Savva) v Kensington and Chelsea Council* [2010] EWCA Civ 1209 at [23].
[4] *R. (KM) v Cambridgeshire CC* [2012] UKSC 23.
[5] *R. (KM) v Cambridgeshire CC* [2012] UKSC 23 at [37].
[6] *R. (KM) v Cambridgeshire CC* [2012] UKSC 23 at [38].

Research by Series and Clements involving 20 local authorities concerning their use of RASs uncovered several key concerns.[1] First, the authors found a lack of transparency involving how RASs were being deployed. Some local authorities refused to disclose their algorithms which actually determine general the indicative amount. When the relevant information was supplied much of it was incomprehensible. Secondly, the research found that RASs differed in how they take into account informal support, with a small number of local authorities not taking this into account at all or doing so in a way that penalised individuals living with informal carers. Many questionnaires asked about the level of support that was actually provided rather than the level of support the carer was willing and able to provide (which is the legal requirement—see para.1–120 above). Thirdly, some local authorities felt that compliance with the Equality Act 2010 meant that a single RAS should apply to all service user groups while others took into account local variations in the unit costs of care for differing groups. The authors argued that the former view was based on a misunderstanding of the 2010 Act and of what equality of provision means (i.e. based on how much money is allocated rather than equality of outcomes). Moreover the research suggested that RASs do not predict accurately the value of personal budgets. They appeared to systematically over or underestimate the value of personal budgets in different local authority areas. The authors concluded:

> "The RAS appears to be a cog spinning inside a machine with which it does not engage. It neither reduces the labour of social care assessment, nor provides service users with enforceable 'entitlements'. However, the RAS is not merely a cog which serves no purpose at all, for in many cases it will serve as a decoy, a pseudo-explanation of how the value of a personal budget has been determined."[2]

The Joint Committee also questioned the secretive way in which RASs are developed and applied and expressed concern about their growing complexity. It made several recommendations. First, it recommended that RASs should be placed on a statutory footing, making it clear that they are subject to the well-being principle, and requiring local authorities to publicise their schemes and to include full details of how the amount included in the personal budget is calculated.[3] It also urged the Government to put beyond doubt that a RAS cannot include a blanket policy of reducing a person's personal budget or notional cost on the basis of the presence of a carer, without the carer's knowledge or consent.[4] The Joint Committee also recommended that the Government should review the efficacy of RASs and ensure that the code of practice or guidance makes clear that the development and application of any methodology for calculating the cost of meeting eligible needs is transparent, has regard for the well-being principle, and is subject to the duty to meet eligible needs.[5] Finally, the Joint Committee recommended that the Bill should require that the amount of a personal budget should be equivalent to the reasonable cost of securing the provision of the service concerned in the local area.[6]

1–301   The Government did not agree that RASs should be placed on a statutory footing. It argued that local authorities should be free to develop their own operational systems to suit their local populations. It stated that statutory guidance will expand on the processes which local authorities should use, and set expectations in relation to the transparency of

---

[1] L. Series and L. Clements, "Putting the Cart Before the Horse: Resource Allocation Systems and Community Care", (2013) 35 *Journal of Social Welfare and Family Law* 207 to 226.

[2] L. Series and L. Clements, "Putting the Cart Before the Horse: Resource Allocation Systems and Community Care", (2013) 35 *Journal of Social Welfare and Family Law* 207, 225.

[3] House of Lords House of Commons Joint Committee on the Draft Care and Support Bill, *Draft Care and Support Bill Report, Session 2012–13*, para.32.

[4] House of Lords House of Commons Joint Committee on the Draft Care and Support Bill, *Draft Care and Support Bill Report, Session 2012–13*, para.33.

[5] House of Lords House of Commons Joint Committee on the Draft Care and Support Bill, *Draft Care and Support Bill Report, Session 2012–13*, para.204.

[6] House of Lords House of Commons Joint Committee on the Draft Care and Support Bill, *Draft Care and Support Bill Report, Session 2012–13*, para.208.

any systems determined locally.[1] The Government argued that the following provision of the Care Act will ensure that a RAS cannot include a blanket policy of reducing a personal budget based on the presence of a carer, without their consent:

- the local authority must take all reasonable steps to agree with the person as to how their needs are to be met (s.25(5)) and places a duty on local authorities to consult with the adult, the carer and any other person the adult wishes (s.9(5)). Therefore, all parties "will be made aware of how the assessment of needs the local authority will meet and the personal budget have been derived";
- written records of assessments and eligibility determinations are to be provided (s.12(4) and 13(2)), so there will be "the ability to challenge any incorrect assumptions about carers' input"; and
- the personal budget must be based on the costs to the local authority of meeting the individual's needs (s.26(1)(a)).[2]

The Government did not accept the need to review the efficacy of RASs but agreed to work with the adult social care sector to ensure that RAS are transparent and reflect the requirements of the new legislation.[3] Finally, the Government accepted the Joint Committee's recommendation on reasonable costs and revised the legislation accordingly (see subs.(1)(a)).[4]

Calculating a person's budget is discussed in paras 11.22 to 11.28 of the statutory guidance. Amongst other matters, it warns against a "one size fits all" approach to resource allocation, and advises that alternative approaches should be considered for certain client groups (highlighting in particular the position of those with multiple complex and deafblind people).[5] The guidance also sets out a set of common principles on which all RASs should be based:

- transparency;
- timeliness; and
- sufficiency.[6]

FUNDING PANELS

Final decisions about the value of personal budgets and the approval of care plans are **1–302** often made by a panel of local authority officers based on information provided by the person with care and support needs, their social worker and the RAS indicative calculation. These are often referred to as "funding panels" or "approval panels". During the passage of the Care Bill through Parliament, Baroness Uddin raised concerns that these panels lack transparency in regard of their remit, obligations and decision-making. She also expressed concern that service users and their advocates were often forbidden from having adequate details about the panel making the decision and from being heard.[7] In reply the Government stated that s.25 sets out new duties on local authorities to involve the adult in care planning and to take all reasonable steps to reach agreement with the adult or carer on how their needs are to be met.[8]

---

[1] Department of Health, *The Care Bill explained—including a response to consultation and pre-legislative scrutiny on the draft Care and Support Bill* (TSO, July 2012), Cm.8386, p.57.
[2] Department of Health, *The Care Bill explained—including a response to consultation and pre-legislative scrutiny on the draft Care and Support Bill* (TSO, July 2012), Cm.8386, p.57.
[3] Department of Health, *The Care Bill explained—including a response to consultation and pre-legislative scrutiny on the draft Care and Support Bill* (TSO, July 2012), Cm.8386, p.71.
[4] Department of Health, *The Care Bill explained—including a response to consultation and pre-legislative scrutiny on the draft Care and Support Bill* (TSO, July 2012), Cm.8386, para.89.
[5] Department of Health, *Care and Support Statutory Guidance* (2014), para.11.23.
[6] Department of Health, *Care and Support Statutory Guidance* (2014), para.11.24.
[7] *Hansard* (House of Lords), 21 May 2013, Vol.745, col.815.
[8] *Hansard* (House of Lords), 21 May 2013, Vol.745, col.825 (Earl Howe).

The statutory guidance advises that:

"Due regard should be taken to the use of approval panels in both the timeliness and bureaucracy of the planning and sign-off process. In some cases, panels may be an appropriate governance mechanism to sign-off large or unique personal budget allocations and/or plans. Where used, panels should be appropriately skilled and trained, and local authorities should refrain from creating or using panels that seek to amend planning decisions, micro-manage the planning process or are in place purely for financial reasons. Local authorities should consider how to delegate responsibility to their staff to ensure sign-off takes place at the most appropriate level. In cases or circumstances where a panel is to be used, and where an expert assessor has been involved in the care and support journey, the same person or another person with similar expertise should be part of the panel to ensure decisions take into account complex or specialist issues."[1]

Practice guidance also points out that in some local authorities all care and support plans and personal budgets go through a panel financial control and formal sign off. It claims that this undermines person-centred planning. The guidance also suggests that local authorities should ask themselves whether going to a panel is the exception of the norm, and "the aim should be for exceptions, if used at all".[2] This is not statutory guidance but it has been produced with the approval of the Department of Health (see para.1–770 below).

PERSONAL HEALTH BUDGETS

1–303   Between 2009 and 2012 personal health budgets were piloted in over 60 sites across England. They work in a similar way to personal budgets for social care, and are intended to enable people to choose how their budget is spent (including by direct payment) to meet their individual needs, in line with a care plan which they agreed with the NHS. The pilot programme looked at the use of personal health budgets for people with conditions and services such as NHS continuing health care, diabetes, Chronic Obstructive Pulmonary Disease, mental health and other long-term conditions. There was an independent evaluation of the pilots, led by the University of Kent, which was generally positive about the use of personal health budgets.[3] The Government has since announced the national roll out of personal health budgets, initially aimed at NHS continuing health care. The National Health Service Commissioning Board and Clinical Commissioning Groups (Responsibilities and Standing Rules) Regulations 2012 requires the NHS to give due consideration to any request by or on behalf of a person eligible for a personal health budget (which can be managed as a direct payment) in respect of NHS continuing health care.[4] They also imposed obligations on the NHS to publicise and promote the availability of personal health budgets and provide information, advice and other support to eligible persons and their representatives.

The Government's view is that notional budgets (where the NHS makes the arrangements for the agreed care and support) and third party budgets (where someone independent of the individual and the NHS holds the budget and makes the arrangements for the agreed care and support) have always been available as a matter of law do not need changes to legislation or regulations. However, it was accepted that the use of direct payments did require changes to the law. Regulations therefore removed the previous pilot schemes limitation by repealing ss.12A(6) and 12C(1) to (4) of the National Health

[1] Department of Health, *Care and Support Statutory Guidance* (2014), para.10.85.
[2] Think Local Act Personal, *Delivering Care and Support Planning: Supporting Implementation of the Care Act 2014* (2015) p.31.
[3] J. Forder et al, *Evaluation of the Personal Health Budget Pilot Programme* (DH, November 2012).
[4] National Health Service Commissioning Board and Clinical Commissioning Groups (Responsibilities and Standing Rules) Regulations 2012 (SI 2012/2996), Pt 6A.

Service Act 2006.[1] The Government subsequently issued the National Health Service (Direct Payments) Regulations) 2013 which made provision for the making of direct payments for health care to secure the provision of certain health services under the National Health Service Act 2006.[2] This sets out a power to provide a direct payment to a person if they consent.

Subsection (1)

The personal budget is defined as a statement that must set out the total amount it costs **1–304** the local authority to meet the adult's needs, and certain other matters. It is not the cost to the individual of meeting their needs. A personal budget must be provided where a local authority is required to meet the needs of:

- an adult with care and support needs (under s.18); or
- a carer (under s.20(1)).

The personal budget must also be provided where the local authority exercises its discretion to provide care and support to an adult (under s.19(1)) or a carer (under s.20(1)). The statutory guidance confirms that local authorities can pool budgets, for instance between people in the same household or people in the community with similar needs.[3]

The personal budget must include the person's eligible needs which the local authority is required to meet and any other needs that the local authority has exercised its power to meet. The statement must also include the amount, if any, which the adult must pay towards the total cost and the amount, if any, which the local authority must pay. The amount the adult must pay is calculated on the basis of the financial assessment carried out under s.17. The elements of the personal budget are discussed in paras 11.10 to 11.21 of the statutory guidance.

Carers' personal budgets are discussed in paras 11.36 to 11.46 of the statutory guidance. Amongst other matters, it emphasises that decisions on which services are provided to meet a carer's needs and which are provided to meet the needs of the adult for whom they care, will impact on which personal budget includes the costs of meeting those needs. Under s.14(3) of the Care Act, if a service is provided directly to the adult needing care, even though it is to meet the carer's needs, the adult is liable to pay any charge. The guidance also suggests that joint personal budgets may be of benefit.[4] In some circumstances "replacement care" (or respite care) should be considered a service to the cared-for person and therefore the costs would appear in their personal budget (unless they do not have eligible needs and a personal budget) – see para 1–175 above.

THE COST TO THE LOCAL AUTHORITY OF MEETING NEEDS

As noted above, the equivalent provision in the draft Care and Support Bill was amended **1–305** in response to the Joint Committee's recommendation that the legislation should require that the amount of a personal budget should be equivalent to the reasonable cost of securing the provision of the service concerned in the local area. Clause 25(1)(a) of the draft Bill had stated that the personal budget must be "the amount which the local authority assesses as the cost of meeting" the adult's needs. Subsection (2)(a) now states that the amount must be the cost to the local authority of meeting the adult's needs. The revised drafting is intended

---

[1] National Health Service (Direct Payments) (Repeal of Pilot Schemes Limitation) Order 2013 (SI 2013/1563).
[2] National Health Service (Direct Payments Regulations) 2013 (SI 2013/1617).
[3] Department of Health, *Care and Support Statutory Guidance* (2014), para.11.34.
[4] Department of Health, *Care and Support Statutory Guidance* (2014), paras 11.36 to 11.37.

to make clear that "the personal budget *is* the cost to the local authority of meeting the needs it is required or has decided to meet".[1]

During the passage of the Care Bill, at Committee stage in the House of Commons, the Government rejected amendments which would have added that the personal budget should reflect the actual cost of care to the individual. Particular concerns were raised that service users in receipt of direct payments or an independent personal budget (see s.28) would face higher costs because a local authority can use their market power to get lower prices than an individual going into the market and buying services for themselves. This issue is also discussed at para.1–320 below. In reply the Government stated that:

"Everyone's personal budget must be based on the same principle: that it relates to the cost to the local authority. That ensures fairness and consistency. If a direct payment were the cost to the person, it might have the unintended consequence of incentivising people to source more expensive care and support to meet needs, and thus progress quicker to the cap on care costs. If a person is unable to use their direct payment to purchase care to meet their eligible needs, they can ask the local authority to review their care plan, and consider whether there are other ways to meet their needs, such as through the provision of care and support arranged by the local authority or a combination of such provision and direct payments."[2]

The Government went on to emphasise that the amount at which the personal budget is set must be "sufficient to meet the eligible needs of the person" and "there is no ability for the local authority to reduce the personal budget to an amount less than it would cost to meet the person's needs".[3] However, this statement does not appear to exclude the possibility of a local authority setting the personal budget at a level that it would cost the authority to meet the person's needs, which is less than it would cost an individual purchaser.

The statutory guidance discusses calculating a personal budget for direct payment recipients in paras 11.25 to 11.28. Amongst other matters it states that there may be concern that the "cost to the local authority" may result in the direct payment being insufficient to purchase care and support from the local market, this should be allayed by local authorities basing the personal budget on the cost of quality local provision. Generally the guidance sets out that when establishing the "cost to the local authority"—irrespective of whether or not direct payments will be used—consideration should be given to "local market intelligence and costs of local quality provision". Moreover, it states that these cost assumptions should be shared with the person.[4]

The statutory guidance also sets out that the personal budget "should not assume that people are forced to accept specific care options, such as moving into care homes, against their will because this is perceived to be the cheapest option".[5] It goes on to state:

"The personal budget is defined as the cost to the local authority of meeting the person's needs which the local authority chooses or is required to meet. However, the local authority should take into consideration cases or circumstances where this 'cost to the local authority' may need to be adjusted to ensure that needs are met. For example, a person may have specific dietary requirements that can only be met in specific settings. In all cases the local authority must have regard to the actual cost of good quality care in deciding the personal budget to ensure that the amount is one that reflects local market

---

[1] Department of Health, *The Care Bill explained—including a response to consultation and pre-legislative scrutiny on the draft Care and Support Bill* (TSO, July 2012), Cm.8386, para.89. Emphasis in the original.

[2] *Hansard* (House of Commons: Public Bill Committee), 16 January 2014 (PM): Sixth Sitting, col.221 (Norman Lamb MP).

[3] *Hansard* (House of Commons: Public Bill Committee), 16 January 2014 (PM): Sixth Sitting, col.222 (Norman Lamb MP).

[4] Department of Health, *Care and Support Statutory Guidance* (2014), para.11.25.

[5] Department of Health, *Care and Support Statutory Guidance* (2014), para.11.7.

conditions. This should also reflect other factors such as the person's circumstances and the availability of provision. In addition, the local authority should not set arbitrary amounts or ceilings for particular types of accommodation that do not reflect a fair cost of care."[1]

See also para.1–321 below on determining the cost to the local authority for the purpose of the independent personal budget.

Subsection (2)

In the case of an adult needing care and support, the personal budget must specify the **1–306** total cost to the local authority of meeting eligible needs which it is required to meet under s.18. The personal budget must also specify how much of that total cost is attributable to daily living costs. This is because daily living costs will not count towards the cap on care costs. Moreover, where a person has exceeded the cap, they will still be liable to pay for their daily living costs (see para.1–202 above). The capped costs system is due to be implemented in April 2020.

Subsection (3)

The personal budget may specify other amounts of public money that are available to the **1–307** person for spending on matters including those relating to housing, health care or welfare. The Government has stated that it:

". . . expects local areas to consider whether action could be taken to integrate personal budgets for care and support needs and personal health budgets to ensure a joint approach to assessment and care planning . . . Personal health budgets will not count towards the cap, so it will be important that integrated approaches remain clear about the specific costs of meeting care and support needs."[2]

Subsection (4)

This allows regulations to specify where certain costs do not have to form part of the per- **1–308** sonal budget (and thus will not count towards the cap on care costs). This subsection was added during the passage of the Care Bill by Government amendment at report stage in the House of Commons. The Government confirmed that:

"It has always been the intention that some provision, such as reablement, should be a universal, free service and therefore should not be incorporated in the personal budget. Such exemptions will not apply to general care and support that a local authority can charge for."[3]

The regulation-making power is therefore limited to services that the local authority cannot make a charge, or chooses not to. The relevant regulations made under this provision are the Care and Support and After-Care (Personal Budget: Exclusion of Costs) Regulations 2014 (SI 2014/2840). They are reproduced and discussed at para.A1–215 below. These regulations provide that where either intermediate care or reablement support is being provided to meet needs (i.e. under section 18, 19 or 20 of the Care Act) the cost of this must not be included in the personal budget. The statutory guidance discusses the regulations in paras 11.15 to 11.21.

The personal budget may include the above and other sources of funding that do not count towards the cap. For instance the personal budget may include the costs of meeting non-eligible needs or it may be pooled with that of another person or carer. Only the cost of meeting the person's eligible needs will count towards the cap and so this cost will need to

---

[1] Department of Health, *Care and Support Statutory Guidance* (2014), Annex A, para.11.
[2] Department of Health, *Caring for our future: Consultation on reforming what and how people pay for their care and support* (2013), para.70.
[3] *Hansard* (House of Commons), 10 March 2014, Vol.577, col.90 (Norman Lamb MP).

be distinguished clearly within the personal budget when the capped costs system is introduced.

Review of care and support plan or of support plan

1–309 27.—(1) A local authority must—

(a) keep under review generally care and support plans, and support plans, that it has prepared, and

(b) on a reasonable request by or on behalf of the adult to whom a care and support plan relates or the carer to whom a support plan relates, review the plan.

(2) A local authority may revise a care and support plan; and in deciding whether or how to do so, it—

(a) must have regard in particular to the matters referred to in section 9(4) (and specified in the plan under section 25(1)(d)), and

(b) must involve—

(i) the adult to whom the plan relates,

(ii) any carer that the adult has, and

(iii) any person whom the adult asks the authority to involve or, where the adult lacks capacity to ask the authority to do that, any person who appears to the authority to be interested in the adult's welfare.

(3) A local authority may revise a support plan; and in deciding whether or how to do so, it—

(a) must have regard in particular to the matters referred to in section 10(5) and (6) (and specified in the plan under section 25(1)(d)), and

(b) must involve—

(i) the carer to whom the plan relates,

(ii) the adult needing care, if the carer asks the authority to do so, and

(iii) any other person whom the carer asks the authority to involve.

(4) Where a local authority is satisfied that circumstances have changed in a way that affects a care and support plan or a support plan, the authority must—

(a) to the extent it thinks appropriate, carry out a needs or carer's assessment, carry out a financial assessment and make a determination under section 13(1), and

(b) revise the care and support plan or support plan accordingly.

(5) Where, in a case within subsection (4), the local authority is proposing to change how it meets the needs in question, it must, in performing the duty under subsection (2)(b)(i) or (3)(b)(i), take all reasonable steps to reach agreement with the adult concerned about how it should meet those needs.

GENERAL NOTE

1–310 This section provides for the review of the care and support plan, or the support plan, to ensure that it remains up to date and accurate. It also enables the revision of the plan and in certain circumstances requires fresh assessments and an eligibility decision. A review is therefore conceptually different to a re-assessment.

The statutory guidance discusses the review of care and support plans in Ch.13. It advises that local authorities should consider authorising others to conduct a review—including "the person themselves or carer, a third party (such as a provider) or another professional, with the local authority adopting an assurance and sign-off approach".[1] The range of review options include self-review, peer led review, reviews conducted remotely, or face-to-face reviews with a social worker or other relevant professional.[2] The review itself should be completed in a "timely manner" and in urgent cases, local authorities should consider interim packages while the plan is revised.[3]

Subsection (1)

A local authority is under a general duty to keep under review all plans that it has pre- **1–311** pared and a specific duty where a "reasonable request" is made by the adult to whom the plan relates or in the case of a care and support plan, someone on the person's behalf.

The Government has said that except where a reasonable request is made, reviews should be made at "an appropriate time, that will often be annually".[4] However, during the passage of the Care Bill through Parliament it rejected an attempt to amend this section to enable the Government to specify a review period that local authorities must adhere to. It explained that:

"A regular review would imply only that the frequency of a review was consistent over time; it would not necessarily mean that the frequency was right or that the review took place at the most appropriate time for an individual. Our proposal to keep the plan 'under review generally' would ensure that it was monitored constantly, and steps could be taken to change it as required."[5]

In the case of planned reviews, the statutory guidance states that the first review should be "an initial 'light-touch' review of the planning arrangements six to eight weeks after sign-off of the personal budget and plan".[6] The guidance also suggests that reviews may need to be more frequent than normal in cases where the person's condition is progressive and their health is deteriorating, and where the person is isolated socially.[7] Moreover, an immediate review should be conducted if "any information or evidence suggests that circumstances have changed in any way that may affect the efficacy, appropriateness or content of the plan".[8] The guidance goes on to explain that planned reviews should be conducted no later than every 12 months (except for the initial "light touch" review), and "light touch" reviews should be considered following a revision of the plan.

A REASONABLE REQUEST. The Government rejected attempts in the House of Lords to **1–312** amend this provision (and the similar provision in s.28(4)(b) in respect of independent personal budgets) to remove the determination of reasonableness and instead provide that any request will trigger the duty to review the plan. It argued that this amendment might:

". . . leave the process open to abuse and create frivolous reviews costs the local authority time and money. For example, it would not be reasonable to request a review when a review has recently been conducted and needs have not changed. If an adult request is considered unreasonable, then the adult should be informed of the grounds for the local authority decision."[9]

---

[1] Department of Health, *Care and Support Statutory Guidance* (2014), para.13.3.
[2] Department of Health, *Care and Support Statutory Guidance* (2014), para.13.16.
[3] Department of Health, *Care and Support Statutory Guidance* (2014), para.13.34.
[4] Department of Health, *Caring for our future: Consultation on reforming what and how people pay for their care and support* (2013), para.223.
[5] *Hansard* (House of Commons: Public Bill Committee), 16 January 2014 (PM): Sixth Sitting, col.226 (Norman Lamb MP).
[6] Department of Health, *Care and Support Statutory Guidance* (2014), para.13.15.
[7] Department of Health, *Care and Support Statutory Guidance* (2014), para.13.18.
[8] Department of Health, *Care and Support Statutory Guidance* (2014), para.13.19.
[9] *Hansard* (House of Lords), 16 July 2013, Vol.747, col.747 (Earl Howe).

The statutory guidance sets out that "local authorities should provide information and advice to people at the planning stage about how to make a request for a review". It also confirms that requests for a review do not have to be made directly by the person themselves, but can be made on the person's behalf by third parties such as a relative or neighbour.[1] The guidance states that following a request:

> "In most cases, it is the expectation that a review should be performed unless the authority is reasonably satisfied that the plan remains sufficient, or the request is frivolous, or is made on the basis of inaccurate information, or is a complaint; for example where a person lodges multiple requests for a review in a short period of time and there is no reason to believe that the person's needs have changed."[2]

If the request is not accepted, the local authority should set out its reasons "in a format accessible to the person, along with details of how to pursue the matter if the person remains unsatisfied". In most cases, this should set out that the authority will continue to monitor the plan, and that the decision does not affect the right to make a future request for review. The guidance also suggests that it may be prudent for the local authority to set out when the person can expect a formal review of the plan.[3]

Subsection (2)

1–313   The local authority may revise the care and support plan, and when making this decision or revising the plan, it must have regard to the following matters (as contained in s.9(4)):

- the impact of the adult's needs for care and support on the matters specified in s.1(2);
- the outcomes that the adult wishes to achieve in day-to-day life; and
- whether, and if so to what extent, the provision of care and support could contribute to the achievement of those outcomes.

These matters should be specified in the care and support plan (see s.25(1)(d)).

The authority must also involve the adult, any carer they may have, and anyone else the adult may ask to be involved. Where a person lacks capacity the local authority must also involve any person who appears to be interested in the individual's welfare.

See discussion at paras 1–104 to 1–105 above in respect of the meaning of involve and when involvement might not be appropriate.

Involving a person may entail providing them with an advocate. The right to advocacy in s.67 of the Care Act expressly applies to this subsection (see s.67(3)(e)).

In most cases, the care plan will only be revised following a full review. However, the statutory guidance states that:

> ". . . there are occasions when a change to a plan is required but there has been no change in the levels of need (for example, a carer may change the times when they are available to support). In addition, there can be small changes in need, at times temporary, which can be accommodated within the established personal budget . . . In these circumstances, it may not be appropriate for the person to go through a full review and revision of the plan. The local authority should respond to these 'light-touch' requests in a proportionate and reasonable way."[4]

The statutory guidance discusses revisions to care plans in paras 13.26 to 13.30. It sets out that any revisions should wherever possible "follow the process used in the assessment and care planning stages".[5] If the person's circumstances have changed in a way that affects the plan, then re-assessment may be necessary (see subs.(4)). A re-assessment

---

[1] Department of Health, *Care and Support Statutory Guidance* (2014), paras 13.20 and 13.22.
[2] Department of Health, *Care and Support Statutory Guidance* (2014), para.13.23.
[3] Department of Health, *Care and Support Statutory Guidance* (2014), para.13.25.
[4] Department of Health, *Care and Support Statutory Guidance* (2014), paras 13.6 to 13.7.
[5] Department of Health, *Care and Support Statutory Guidance* (2014), para.13.27.

cannot occur without the local authority first conducting a review and then deciding that a revision of a plan is necessary.

The guidance also reminds local authorities that:

"Periodic reviews and reviews in general must not be used to arbitrarily reduce a care and support package. Such behaviour would be unlawful under the Act as the personal budget must always be an amount appropriate to meet the person's needs. Any reduction to a personal budget should be the result of a change in need or circumstance."[1]

See also discussion under subs.(4) below on whether a re-assessment must take place before the plan is revised.

Subsection (3)

The local authority may revise the support plan, and when making this decision or revis- **1–314** ing the plan, it must have regard to the following matters (as contained in s.10(5) and (6)):

- whether the carer is able, and is likely to continue to be able, to provide care;
- whether the carer is willing, and is likely to continue to be willing, to do so;
- the impact of the carer's needs for support on the matters specified in s.1(2);
- the outcomes that the carer wishes to achieve in day-to-day life;
- whether, and if so to what extent, the provision of support could contribute to the achievement of those outcomes;
- whether the carer works or wishes to do so; and
- whether the carer is participating in or wishes to participate in education, training or recreation.

These matters should be specified in the care and support plan (see s.25(1)(d)).

The authority must also involve the carer, the adult needing care (if the carer asks the authority to do so) and anyone else the carer may ask to be involved. The main difference with the equivalent duty to involve under subs.(2) when revising a care and support plan, is the omission from subs.(3) of the requirement to include any person interested in their welfare where the carer lacks capacity.

See discussion at paras 1–104 to 1–105 above in respect of the meaning of involve and when involvement might not be appropriate.

Involving a person may involve providing them with an advocate. The right to advocacy in s.67 of the Care Act expressly applies to this subsection (see s.67(3)(f)).

The provisions of the statutory guidance on making revisions to a care plan and re-assessments—see discussion under subs.(3) above—also apply to a carer's support plan.

Subsection (4)

Where the local authority is satisfied that circumstances have changed in a way that **1–315** affects their plan (for example their needs or finances), the local authority must, "to the extent it thinks appropriate":

- carry out a new needs or carers assessment, or carry out a new financial assessment (or both); and
- consider whether the person's needs meet the eligibility criteria.

The local authority must then revise the care and support plan or support plan as appropriate. This is intended to ensure that the individual's care and support package, and the level to which the local authority contributes to it, are up-to-date and in line with the outcomes of the care and support plan review.

---

[1] Department of Health, *Care and Support Statutory Guidance* (2014), para.13.33.

It is submitted that a change in circumstances that affects the care plan would include any proposal to change for example the setting or manner in which the needs are met (including when retaining the same provider)—even if those needs have not changed. In effect, "circumstances" should be given a wider meaning than "needs". It is notable in this respect that the subsection does not require a change in the "adult's" circumstances to trigger the review, but instead that "circumstances have changed" in a way that affects the plan.

The duty to carry out a re-assessment applies if the local authority is satisfied that the person's circumstances have changed in a way that affects their care plan. However, the re-assessment can be to the extent that the local authority considers appropriate. The statutory guidance makes clear that the re-assessment should not start from the beginning but "pick up from what is already known about the person and should be proportionate". A re-assessment cannot occur without the local authority first conducting a review and then deciding that a revision of a plan is necessary.[1] The statutory guidance discusses revisions to care plans in paras 13.26 to 13.30.

Subsection (5)

1–316   As with the care and support plan in s.25, the local authority must involve the user of care services and carer and take all reasonable steps to reach agreement with the person for whom the plan is being prepared if there is to be a change in how the person's needs are met.

The Government removed the qualification contained in the draft Care and Support Bill that engagement should be undertaken "as far as feasible" in relation to conducting reviews (cl.26(2)(b) and 3(b)). For a discussion on how far people should be involved see paras 1–104 to 1–105 above.

1–317   CAN SERVICES BE CUT WITHOUT CONSULTATION?   The intention is clearly that the review of a care plan should be a collaborative process between the local authority and the person to whom the plan relates. For instance, subs.(2) provides that the adult must be involved in deciding whether to undertake a review or how to do so. Under subs.(5), the local authority must also take all reasonable steps to reach agreement if it is proposing to alter how it will meet the needs in question.

However, it is not clear how a local authority would proceed if it were considering cutting services and the service user refused to participate in the review process. This issue is not addressed directly in the statutory guidance.

Under subs.(4), if the relevant circumstances have changed, the local authority is placed under a duty to carry out the relevant assessment(s) and revise the care and support plan or support plan accordingly. However, the person would appear to have the right to refuse the assessment under s.11 (unless one of the exceptions apply).

The Government has stated that:

"If reconsideration of eligibility of a person's eligible needs determines they no longer have eligible needs or if they refuse a reasonable request from the local authority for a re-assessment, then their progress towards the cap will freeze at that point. The local authority will retain a record of all progress up to this point and should the person be determined to have eligible needs following a subsequent re-assessment, then progress will start from where they left off."[2]

This would appear to suggest that services could be cut, or even withdrawn entirely, in the face of a "unreasonable" refusal to engage in the review process. However, while there is an express provision in respect of an independent personal budget which would allow progress towards the cap on care costs to be frozen where the person refuses the assessment and the refusal is unreasonable—there is no equivalent provision in s.27 in respect of personal budgets.

---

[1] Department of Health, *Care and Support Statutory Guidance* (2014), para.13.27.

[2] Department of Health, *Caring for our future: Consultation on reforming what and how people pay for their care and support* (2013), para.225.

It is submitted that if the person exercises their right to refuse an assessment under s.11 (and the exceptions do not apply), the local authority may need to exercise its underlying power to assess (see para.1–127 above). If it did so, there may be a greater onus on the authority to ensure the involvement of the person's carer(s) and anyone the adult has asked to be involved, as well as other agencies involved in the person's care. There may also be a duty to appoint an advocate. The authority would need to document the service user's refusal to engage in the review process and the reasons for this, the reasons why it is proceeding with the assessment and the outcome of the assessment (if any) it has managed to conduct in such circumstances. If the authority remains satisfied that circumstances have changed in such a way to affect the care plan, it will need to document its reasons for this conclusion and how it will revise the plan. Any decision must be based on rational and cogent reasons, and the authority would need to have proper regard to the likely impact on the service user's well-being that will occur as a result of the revision and document this. The authority must in particular be satisfied that the person's needs will significantly worsen or increase in the foreseeable future due to the revision. It should also provide written explanations for the service user, carer(s) and other relevant person, and provide an opportunity for an appeal against the decision or a full assessment to take place.

Independent personal budget

28.—(1) An independent personal budget is a statement which specifies what **1–318** the cost would be to the local authority concerned (see section 24(3)) of meeting the adult's eligible needs for care and support.

(2) Where the amount referred to in subsection (1) includes daily living costs, the independent personal budget for the adult must specify—

(a) the amount attributable to those daily living costs, and

(b) the balance of the amount referred to in subsection (1).

(3) An adult's needs are "eligible needs" if, at the time they were met—

(a) they met the eligibility criteria,

(b) they were not being met by a carer, and

(c) the adult was ordinarily resident or present in the area of the local authority.

(4) A local authority must—

(a) keep under review generally independent personal budgets that it has prepared, and

(b) on a reasonable request by or on behalf of the adult to whom an independent personal budget relates, review the independent personal budget.

(5) A local authority may revise an independent personal budget; and in deciding whether or how to do so, it must, in so far as it is feasible to do so, involve—

(a) the adult to whom the independent personal budget relates,

(b) any carer that the adult has, and

(c) any other person whom the adult asks the authority to involve or, where the adult lacks capacity to ask the authority to do that, any person who appears to the authority to be interested in the adult's welfare.

(6) Where a local authority is satisfied that the circumstances of the adult to whom an independent personal budget applies have changed in a way that affects the independent personal budget, the authority must—

(a) to the extent it thinks appropriate, carry out a needs assessment and make a determination under section 13(1), and

(b) revise the independent personal budget accordingly.

(7) Where, in a case within subsection (6), an adult refuses a needs assessment and the local authority thinks that the adult's refusal is unreasonable, it need no longer keep an up-to-date care account in the adult's case.

(8) Having reviewed an independent personal budget, a local authority must—

(a) if it revises the independent personal budget, notify the adult to whom the independent personal budget relates of the revisions and provide an explanation of the effect of each revision, or

(b) if it does not revise the independent personal budget, notify the adult accordingly.

GENERAL NOTE

1–319   This section establishes the concept of independent personal budgets for adults who have eligible needs, but who do not have these needs met by their local authority (for example, if the person's resources are above the financial limit and they have not asked the local authority to meet their needs (s.18(3)—condition 2)). Such individuals will not have personal budgets under s.26 because the local authority is not under a duty to prepare a care and support plan for them, so a separate mechanism has been established to record their care costs for the purposes of measuring progress towards the costs cap.Whilst there is no duty to provide a care and support plan, the local authority can do so. This might be particularly helpful where setting the Independent Personal Budget rate at an average may not be appropriate, such as where people have needs for specialist care and support that is more expensive.[1]

The Department of Health has announced that the introduction of the cap on care costs system (including independent personal budgets) will be delayed until April 2020.[2]

SELF-FUNDERS AND RATES FOR CARE HOMES

1–320   Most self-funders do not pay local authority rates for care homes. To some degree this is because local authorities take advantage of procurement at scale and secure a lower rate for those residents funded by the authority. Many people see this as a case where local authorities underpay and that if homes only existed under local authority rates many of them would not be viable. In effect, self-funders subsidise the people in care homes who are paid for by the local authority.

A potential implication of the funding reforms (due to be implemented in 2010) is that self-funders will be able to see the cost to the local authority of meeting their eligible needs. This is because independent personal budgets will be set on the basis of this amount. Self-funders will be able to compare that with what they might pay on the open market and then will have the option to request the local authority to arrange their care for an administrative fee. Some members of the House of Lords warned that this greater transparency would lead inevitably to conflict between self-funders and people who are in receipt of support from their local authorities.

"There is a group of people who will be over the means-test threshold but will pay the full cost under the cap. They will suddenly be confronted with information in this new regime of transparency which will give them far more information about what other people are paying in the home, what the local authority is prepared to pay and what the local authority believes to be a reasonable fee for care. That could lead to conflict within individual care homes."[3]

It is also the case that all providers of health and social care registered with the Care Quality Commission must meet a registration requirement relating to fees. If a service

[1] Department of Health, *The Care Act 2014: Consultation on draft regulations and guidance to implement the cap on care costs and policy proposals for a new appeals system for care and support* (2015), para.11.24.
[2] *House of Commons Written Answers and Statements Daily Report*, Cap on Care Costs: Written Statement – HCWS145, 20 July 2015, pp 162 to 164 (Alastair Burt MP).
[3] *Hansard* (House of Lords), 16 July 2013, Vol.747, cols 707 to 708 (Lord Campbell-Savours).

user is responsible for paying the costs of their care or treatment, either in full or partially, the provider must produce a statement that sets out the terms and conditions of the services to be provided, including the amount—and method of payment—of any fees. That statement must be in writing and, as far as practicable, be provided before the commencement of services.[1]

See the discussion at para.1–218 above on the potential impact on the provider market of the ability for self-funders to seek local authority assistance in arranging their care. See subs.(1) below on determining the cost to the local authority for the purpose of the independent personal budget.

Subsection (1)

The independent personal budget is defined as a statement that shows the amount that it **1–321** would have cost the local authority to meet the adult's eligible needs. In other words, it is the equivalent to what it would cost the local authority to purchase the care for the individual, if it were doing so under s.18. Eligible needs are defined in subs.(3).

The Government set out its intention during the passage of the Care Bill through the House of Lords:

"The personal budget or independent personal budget must reflect the cost to the local authority of meeting the adult's needs, not the cost to the individual of doing so himself or herself. Otherwise, this would create an unfair advantage for those with more means who are able to pay more for their care and would therefore reach the cap quicker".[2]

The underlying policy aim is to establish a level playing field between people progressing towards the cap whether they are meeting the whole of their costs themselves or receiving local authority support.

In 2015 the Government consulted on how to calculate what the costs would be to the local authority of meeting a self-funder's eligible needs. In particular it noted that the costs to a local authority will depend on a number of factors such as the availability of beds on a particular day, or the status of any block contracts which may apply—and this presents challenges for calculating an independent personal budget. Three options were considered. First, a "dummy purchasing" process which would involve local authorities consulting a range of care providers to determine the cost of care on the particular date the independent personal budget is set. However this option was rejected because of the administrative burden and because it would lead to arbitrary variations in the personal budgets set for self-funders with similar needs based on which day their budgets had been set. Secondly, the Government considered requiring local authorities to set the independent personal budget at the upper end of the range of personal budgets the authority had given to people in that area with similar needs. But this option was rejected because it would create unfairness in the system, as self-funders would progress faster towards the cap than local authority-supported people with similar needs. Instead, the Government's preferred option at consultation was for local authorities to set independent personal budgets by taking the average of the personal budgets the authority had given to people in that area with similar needs. The draft guidance does not define the groupings for these averages; this is left to the authority to decide based on the circumstances in their area. However, the Government has stated that it does not want to re-introduce the concept of the "usual local authority rate". The draft guidance also requires local authorities to consider whether it is necessary to tailor the independent personal budget based on an average to a person's individual circumstances, for example where a person has needs which are low-level, complex or costly to meet.[3]

---

[1] Care Quality Commission, *Essential Standards of Quality and Safety* (March 2010), p.56.

[2] *Hansard* (House of Lords), 16 July 2013, Vol.747, col.747 (Earl Howe).

[3] See, Department of Health, *The Care Act 2014: Consultation on draft regulations and guidance to implement the cap on care costs and policy proposals for a new appeals system for care and support* (2015), paras 4.13 to 4.21, 11.15 to 11.17 and 11.22.

It is intended that the statutory guidance will specify that when self-funders approach local authorities to register for the cap, the local authority should ensure from the outset that the person is clear that the cost to the local authority of meeting needs may be different to the rate the person has been quoted or is paying.[1]

It should be noted that all the proposals, set out above, were published before the delay to the funding reforms was announced. It is possible that new proposals will be developed before 2020.

Subsection (2)

1–322 The independent personal budget must specify how much of the total represents daily living costs and the remaining amount of the independent personal budget that is for care costs which therefore contributes towards someone's progress towards the cap (see s.15(6)).

Subsection (3)

1–323 Eligible needs are those that meet the eligibility criteria and are not being met by a carer. The person must be ordinarily resident or present in the area of the local authority. The Government has proposed that the accrued costs of meeting eligible needs will be backdated to the date that the person requested the assessment. Where the assessment has been requested prior to the implementation of the capped costs system (due in April 2020), it is likely that the person's accrued costs will be backdated to this date.[2]

Subsection (4)

1–324 A local authority will be under a general duty to keep under review all independent personal budgets that it has prepared and a specific duty to review the budget where a "reasonable request" is made by the adult to whom the budget relates or someone on their behalf. The meaning of a reasonable request is discussed at para.1–312 above. It is expected that the statutory guidance will set out that unless a request is made, in most cases it would be appropriate to hold a review annually or more frequently if the person's needs are likely to change.[3]

It is also expected that the statutory guidance will confirm that—whilst local authorities must keep under review all budgets—the person is not under any obligation to meet their needs in any particular way in order to progress towards the cap. Therefore local authorities will not be able to require the person to provide evidence of having made arrangements to meet their needs in the same way as they might for direct payments. If a self-funder is choosing not to meet their needs at all or in part, the local authority must offer information and advice about how their needs can be met and how to prevent the development of further needs. The local authority will need to be alert to safeguarding issues—such as the use of coercion by a family member to force the person to buy cheaper services that do not meet their needs.[4]

---

[1] Department of Health, *The Care Act 2014: Consultation on draft regulations and guidance to implement the cap on care costs and policy proposals for a new appeals system for care and support* (2015), para.11.18.

[2] Department of Health, *The Care Act 2014: Consultation on draft regulations and guidance to implement the cap on care costs and policy proposals for a new appeals system for care and support* (2015), para.11.18.

[3] Department of Health, *The Care Act 2014: Consultation on draft regulations and guidance to implement the cap on care costs and policy proposals for a new appeals system for care and support* (2015), para.11.33.

[4] Department of Health, *The Care Act 2014: Consultation on draft regulations and guidance to implement the cap on care costs and policy proposals for a new appeals system for care and support* (2015), paras 11.26 to 11.29.

Subsection (5)

The local authority may revise the independent personal budget, and when making this **1–325** decision or revising the budget it must as far as "feasible" involve the adult, any carer and anyone else the adult may ask to be involved. Where a person lacks capacity the local authority must also involve any person who appears to be interested in the individual's welfare.

The term "feasible" suggests a focus on whether the involvement of others is possible, rather than whether it is appropriate. For a discussion of what "involve" means, and when a person should not be involved, see paras 1–104 to 1–105 above.

Subsection (6)

Where the local authority is satisfied that the person's circumstances have changed (for **1–326** example their needs or finances) in a way that affects their independent personal budget, it must to the extent it thinks appropriate, carry out a new needs assessment and determine if any of the person's needs meet the eligibility criteria (s.13(1)) and revise the budget accordingly.

If the determination concludes that the person no longer has eligible needs then their progress towards the cap will freeze at that point. The local authority will retain a record of all progress up to this point (see s.29) and should the person be determined to have eligible needs following a subsequent re-assessment, then progress will start from where they left off.

Subsection (7)

If the person refuses a reasonable request from the local authority for a re-assessment, **1–327** then their progress towards the cap will freeze at that point. The local authority will retain a record of all progress up to this point (see s.29) and should the person be determined to have eligible needs following a subsequent re-assessment, then progress will start from where they left off.

This subsection was amended by the Government in the House of Lords at committee stage to put beyond doubt that the provisions of s.11 (refusal of an assessment) should apply to any refusal of a needs assessment by an adult with an independent personal budget. As a result "where an adult lacks capacity or is at risk of abuse and neglect, the local authority must carry out the assessment if it believes it to be in the adult's best interests".[1]

Subsection (8)

Following a review, the local authority must notify the adult of the outcome and if the **1–328** independent personal budget has changed, must explain why.

Care account

29.—(1) Where an adult has needs for care and support which meet the eligi- **1–329** bility criteria, the local authority in whose area the adult is ordinarily resident or, if the adult is of no settled residence, in whose area the adult is present—

(a) must keep an up-to-date record of the adult's accrued costs (a "care account"), and

(b) once those costs exceed the cap on care costs, must inform the adult.

(2) Where a local authority which has been keeping a care account is no longer required to do so, it must nonetheless retain the account that it has kept so far until—

(a) the end of the period of 99 years beginning with the day on which it last updated the account, or

(b) where the adult dies, the local authority becomes aware of the death.

---

[1] *Hansard* (House of Lords), 16 July 2013, Vol.747, col.747 (Earl Howe).

(3) A care account must specify such amount as is attributable to the adult's daily living costs.

(4) A local authority which is keeping a care account must, at such times as regulations may specify, provide the adult concerned with a statement which—

(a) sets out the adult's accrued costs, and

(b) includes such other matters as regulations may specify.

(5) Regulations may specify circumstances in which the duty under subsection (4) does not apply.

GENERAL NOTE

1–330   This section requires local authorities to keep a care account for adults whose care costs are counted towards the costs cap. A care account is intended to be an up-to-date record of a person's total care costs accrued to that point in time. It is the record of a person's progress towards the cap on care costs, and therefore an important aspect of the new funding system. The Government has stated that it:

> ". . . wants to ensure everyone has a clear understanding of their responsibility for their care costs and be able to predict when they may reach the cap and therefore qualify for additional support towards the costs of meeting their eligible needs. We intend local authorities to provide individuals with an update of their care account at least annually or at the reasonable request of the individual. The annual care account statement should become an equivalent to a person's annual mortgage statement or pension statement."[1]

The care account will be adjusted annually by the same measure as the cap, so that everyone's rate of progress towards the cap remains the same (see s.16(2)).

The Department of Health has announced that the introduction of the cap on care costs system (including care accounts) will be delayed until April 2020.[2]

Subsection (1)

1–331   The care account is a statement of an adult's accrued care and support costs. The local authority must keep a record of the accrued costs of any adult who has or has had eligible needs at any time following the introduction of the cap on care costs in April 2020, and who is ordinary resident in its area or, if the adult is of no settled residence, in whose area the adult is present. Costs will begin accruing from the point the person contacted the local authority to request a needs assessment or the local authority identified that they might need one. If a person requested the assessment or was already receiving local authority support before the implementation of the capped costs system (due in April 2020), it is likely that their accrued costs will be backdated to this date.[3] Under subs.(1)(b) the local authority is also required to inform the adult if the level of accrued costs in their care account reaches the cap.

Accrued costs are the total costs of meeting a person's eligible needs which will count towards the cap on care costs. Accrued costs will not include:

- costs of meeting eligible care and support needs incurred before April 2020;
- costs of meeting non-eligible needs;
- daily living costs (for care home residents these are the costs at the level set in the regulations);

---

[1] Department of Health, *Caring for our future: Consultation on reforming what and how people pay for their care and support* (2013), para.228.

[2] *House of Commons Written Answers and Statements Daily Report*, Cap on Care Costs: Written Statement – HCWS145, 20 July 2015, pp.162 to 164 (Alastair Burt MP).

[3] Department of Health, *The Care Act 2014: Consultation on draft regulations and guidance to implement the cap on care costs and policy proposals for a new appeals system for care and support* (2015), para.12.4.

- "top-up payments" the person or a third party chooses to make, for example for a preferred choice of accommodation;
- costs of services not included in the personal budget such as prevention and reablement services;
- interest or fees charged under a deferred payment agreement;
- needs which are being met, and will continue to be met, by a carer;
- NHS-funded nursing care and continuing health care; and
- after-care under s.117 of the Mental Health Act.

If a person's care needs or circumstances change and their needs are no longer eligible, the record of their accrued costs will be retained by the local authority. If at a future point the person's needs again become eligible, then their new costs will be added to their previous care account.

Subsection (2)

It is expected that local authorities will retain and update the person's care account as **1–332** appropriate until it is requested by another authority. If the person chooses to move to another area in England the care account will be transferred to the new authority, they will retain the amount already credited to their care account and the new costs will be added. To avoid the risk of care accounts going missing when people move between local authorities, the originating local authority will be required to retain records of care accounts until the end of a person's life, or after 99 years.

It is expected that the statutory guidance will be amended to advise local authorities, in determining their local retention policy, to have regard to the need to allow sufficient time to resolve disputes (which may occur after a person's death) as well as their duties under the Data Protection Act 1998 and common law. The guidance is also likely to state that if a dispute arises relating to the account, that account should be retained until the dispute is resolved.[1]

Subsection (3)

This clarifies that the care account must set out such amount that relates to daily living **1–333** costs (see para.1–202 above). The explanatory notes state that "where the care account includes daily living costs, these must be specified separately".[2] The amount of daily living costs specified in the statement should be the same as that specified in the personal budget (which can be a weekly or monthly amount), but the local authority will not be required to keep a running total of the daily living costs a person has paid.[3]

Subsection (4)

This provides that regulations may specify how often local authorities must provide **1–334** adults with a statement of their care account, and any other matters which must be included in this statement. In February 2015, the Government published detailed proposals on these matters.[4] Under these proposals local authorities would be required to provide statements at least annually, as well as on the "reasonable request" of the person or their representative. The draft regulations would require that the annual statement includes:

---

[1] Department of Health, *The Care Act 2014: Consultation on draft regulations and guidance to implement the cap on care costs and policy proposals for a new appeals system for care and support* (2015), para.12.34.

[2] Care Act 2014, Explanatory Notes para.204.

[3] Department of Health, *The Care Act 2014: Consultation on draft regulations and guidance to implement the cap on care costs and policy proposals for a new appeals system for care and support* (2015), para.12.21.

[4] Department of Health, *The Care Act 2014: Consultation on draft regulations and guidance to implement the cap on care costs and policy proposals for a new appeals system for care and support* (2015).

- the current level of the cap;
- the current rate of progress towards the cap (the costs specified in the personal budget or independent personal budget that count towards the cap);
- progress towards the cap to date—ie the accrued costs; and
- any amount attributable to daily living costs excluded from the rate above.[1]

It was also proposed that the statement should make clear any adjustments which have been made to the accrued costs to date since the previous statement as a result of an adjustment to the level of the cap, and provide a clear explanation of why and how a person's accrued costs have been adjusted for other reasons (for instance if the person has had a long stay in hospital or has qualified for NHS continuing health care). Under the proposals, accrued costs should not be adjusted to reflect changes of less than six weeks in duration. The statutory guidance would also be amended to state that the statement should set out what responsibilities the person has to inform the local authority of any change in circumstances, and when the local authority expect to review a person's needs and /or finances.[2]

The Government consulted on whether care accounts should include projections of when the person would be expected to reach the cap.[3] It concluded that projections might not be appropriate in all cases, such as if the person has low-level or fluctuating needs. Therefore, it was proposed that the regulations should give local authorities discretion over when to provide a projection (for example, where the person is progressing towards the cap at a relatively fast rate). The only exception would be if the date the person is expected to reach the cap falls within 18 months of the statement being prepared.[4] This would be provided alongside other information that the local authority must provide at this stage—see paras 1–183 and 1–184 above.

The Government has stated:

"We recognise that providing projections of when people might reach the cap could open up local authorities to challenge and would also increase the complexity of implementation and operation of the care account. However, as long as the local authority acted fairly and properly in calculating the projection in accordance with the regulations, and made sure it set out that this is just for illustrative purposes, and retained the right to make future changes this risk should be small."[5]

The Government also consulted on whether care accounts should include projections of whether the person will qualify for financial support because their assets fall below the new financial limits.[6] However, this was not included in the draft regulations because it was concluded that such a projection would be misleading, as assumptions would need to be made about a person's spending and it was more important to provide "clear information

---

[1] Department of Health, *The Care Act 2014: Consultation on draft regulations and guidance to implement the cap on care costs and policy proposals for a new appeals system for care and support* (2015), para.5.40.

[2] Department of Health, *The Care Act 2014: Consultation on draft regulations and guidance to implement the cap on care costs and policy proposals for a new appeals system for care and support* (2015), paras.5.5 and 12.25 to 12.29.

[3] Department of Health, *Caring for our future: Consultation on reforming what and how people pay for their care and support* (2013), para.231.

[4] Department of Health, *The Care Act 2014: Consultation on draft regulations and guidance to implement the cap on care costs and policy proposals for a new appeals system for care and support* (2015), paras 5.7 to 5.9 and 12.23.

[5] Department of Health, *Caring for our future: Consultation on reforming what and how people pay for their care and support* (2013), para.232.

[6] Department of Health, *Caring for our future: Consultation on reforming what and how people pay for their care and support* (2013), para.231.

and advice about the changes in the person's circumstances that should prompt them to approach the local authority".[1]

The draft regulations did not specify the format of the statement. Instead, it was announced that the statutory guidance would be amended to specify that "as a minimum statements should be provided in hard copy by post" but they may be provided in other formats, including electronic formats, if the person consents. Local authorities would also be encouraged in the guidance to consider how they might provide people with secure online access, and combine care account statements with deferred payment statements.[2]

It should be noted that all the proposals, set out above, were published before the delay to the funding reforms was announced. It is possible that new proposals will be developed before 2020.

Subsection (5)

This provides that regulations may specify circumstances in which the duty to send a statement of the care account under subs.(4) does not apply. Under the proposals published in February 2015, local authorities would have discretion not to provide a care account statement where the cap has already been reached, the person has not received any care and support or accrued any costs in the year since the last statement, or the person does not have to pay towards the costs of meetings needs.[3]   **1–335**

Cases where adult expresses preference for particular accommodation

30.—(1) Regulations may provide that where—   **1–336**

   (a) a local authority is going to meet needs under sections 18 to 20 by providing or arranging for the provision of accommodation of a specified type,

   (b) the adult for whom the accommodation is going to be provided expresses a preference for particular accommodation of that type, and

   (c) specified conditions are met, the local authority must provide or arrange for the provision of the preferred accommodation.

(2) The regulations may provide for the adult or a person of a specified description to pay for some or all of the additional cost in specified cases or circumstances.

(3) "Additional cost" means the cost of providing or arranging for the provision of the preferred accommodation less that part of the amount specified in the personal budget for the purposes of section 26(1)(a) that relates to the provision of accommodation of that type.

GENERAL NOTE

Prior to the Care Act, directions issued in 1992 under s.7A of the Local Authority Social Services Act 1970 gave service users a right to choose the setting of their residential care.[4] The 1992 directions were intended to ensure that when a local authority had decided to place a person in a care home under s.21(1) of the National Assistance Act 1948, it must accommodate that person at the place of their choice within England and Wales. This duty applied provided that: **1–337**

---

[1] Department of Health, *The Care Act 2014: Consultation on draft regulations and guidance to implement the cap on care costs and policy proposals for a new appeals system for care and support* (2015), para.5.10.

[2] Department of Health, *The Care Act 2014: Consultation on draft regulations and guidance to implement the cap on care costs and policy proposals for a new appeals system for care and support* (2015), paras.5.3 and 12.9 to 12.11.

[3] Department of Health, *The Care Act 2014: Consultation on draft regulations and guidance to implement the cap on care costs and policy proposals for a new appeals system for care and support* (2015), paras 5.13 and 12.12 to 12.17.

[4] National Assistance Act 1948 (Choice of Accommodation) Directions 1992 and LAC(2004)20.

- the accommodation was suitable in relation to the person's assessed needs;
- to provide the accommodation would not cost the authority more than what it would usually expect to pay for accommodation for someone with the individual's assessed needs;
- the accommodation was available; and
- the person in charge of the accommodation was willing to provide accommodation, subject to the council's usual terms and conditions.

Where a person chose accommodation that was more expensive than the local authority would usually expect to pay, regulations allowed for him or her to be placed in the more expensive accommodation, provided that a third party, such as a relative or friend, is able and willing to top-up the difference.[1] The person themselves could also make top-ups themselves in certain cases—such as residents who were subject to the 12-week property disregard[2] or had entered into a deferred payment agreement.[3]

The Law Commission argued that the 1992 directions were one of the few examples of genuine choice that individuals had in relation to service provision and were an early example of self-directed support. However, at consultation there appeared to be widespread uncertainty over their existence and status, with some suggesting that the 1992 directions were being ignored by local authorities. In order to reflect their importance and give them additional prominence, the Commission recommended that the content of the 1992 directions should be placed in statute law. Significantly, this would also mean that the right to choose accommodation was placed on an equal footing with the right to choose non-residential services—which had been recognised in statute law through the direct payments legislation.[4] In order to address concerns raised at consultation that the new provisions must not become too inflexible, the Commission felt that the detail should be left to regulations. In effect the Secretary of State should be given a power to make regulations requiring or authorising local authorities to accommodate a person at the place of his or her choice, and the circumstances in which this applies, as well as the existing provisions on additional payments.[5]

The Law Commission's approach has been implemented by s.30 which provides regulation-making powers regarding preferred accommodation, and other matters. It sets out some further factors to be considered when it has been determined that an individual's needs would be best met through the provision of care and support in a care home or other type of accommodation.

During the House of Lords committee stage, the Government rejected amendments to this section which would have—amongst other matters—made it mandatory for the regulations to be made, and to establish a right to express a preference for the nature and location of accommodation. In doing so, the Government stated:

> "It is important that people should, as far as reasonably possible, be able to choose the accommodation they live in. People may wish to move into a care home in a new area—for example, to be close to relatives—and they should be able to do this even if this is in another local authority area. I can reassure the Committee that we intend to make regulations that enable people to exercise choice of accommodation both within and outside their current local authority. However, we do not believe that it would be appropriate to require local authorities to find and arrange care in another local authority area. While

---

[1] National Assistance (Residential Accommodation)(Additional Payments and Assessment of Resources) (Amendment)(England) Regulations 2001 (SI 2001/3441).

[2] The value of a resident's home was disregarded for the first 12 weeks of a permanent admission to a care home.

[3] An agreement whereby the value of the resident's property is disregarded when providing residential accommodation but the local authority recovers the fees from the sale of the property, normally after the resident's death. See ss.34 to 36.

[4] Health and Social Care Act 2001 s.57.

[5] Law Commission, Adult Social Care, paras 8.76 to 8.82.

some might choose to do so, others might lack the local knowledge effectively to undertake this task. The requirement may also potentially have significant costs and could reduce the funds available to support those with the greatest needs."[1]

The relevant regulations made under s.30 are the Care and Support and After-Care (Choice of Accommodation) Regulations 2014 (SI 2014/2670). They are reproduced and discussed at paras A1–101 to A1–110 below.. The statutory guidance discusses the regulations in paras 8.36 to 8.37 and Annex A. Whereas the previous 1992 directions had only applied to care homes, the regulations also enable people to exercise choice in respect of shared lives and supported living accommodation.

The regulations do not make any separate provisions for those who lack capacity to **1–338** choose between different types of accommodation. According to the statutory guidance, in such cases local authorities should:

". . . act on the choices expressed by the person's advocate, carer or legal guardian in the same way they would on the person's own wishes, unless in the local authority's opinion it would be against the best interests of the person."[2]

Service users who were receiving accommodation under s.117 of the Mental Health Act 1983 were not subject to the 1992 directions. However, the Care Act amends s.117 to provide that regulations can be made regarding choice of accommodation (see para.1–742 below in respect of s.75(6)).

Subsection (1)

Regulations may require a local authority to meet an individual's preference for specific **1–339** accommodation. The regulations may also provide conditions to be imposed on the provision of the preferred accommodation.

The Care and Support and After-Care (Choice of Accommodation) Regulations 2014 (SI 2014/2670) provide that the following conditions must be met for the provision of preferred accommodation:

- the local authority is meeting needs under ss.18 to 20 of the Act by providing or arranging care home, shared lives or supported living accommodation (reg.2(1)(a));
- the adult expresses a preference for particular accommodation of a specified type (reg.2(1)(b));
- the care and support plan specifies that the person's needs are going to be met by the provision of accommodation of a specified type (reg.3(1)(a));
- the preferred accommodation is of the same type as that specified in the care and support plan (reg.3(1)(b));
- the preferred accommodation is suitable to meet the person's needs (reg.3(1)(c));
- the preferred accommodation is available (reg.3(1)(d));
- the provider is willing to provide the accommodation to the person on the local authority's terms (reg.3(1)(e)); and
- where the cost of the preferred accommodation is greater than the amount specified in the personal budget for accommodation of the same type, a third party or (in certain cases) the person must be able and willing to pay the additional cost (regs 3(2) and 5).

The person has a right to choose between different settings or providers of a type of accommodation (provided that the other conditions are met). It does not enable the person to choose between different types of accommodation (for example a shared lives scheme rather than care home accommodation). The statutory guidance also specifies that the local authority must ensure that "the person has a genuine choice and must ensure that

---

[1] *Hansard* (House of Lords), 16 July 2013, Vol.747, cols 747 to 748 (Earl Howe).
[2] Department of Health, *Care and Support Statutory Guidance* (2014), Annex A, para.40.

at least one option is available and affordable within a person's personal budget and should ensure that there is more than one" accommodation option available.[1]

Subsections (2) and (3)

1–340   The regulations may allow the individual, or someone acting on their behalf, to make an additional payment to the local authority to cover the difference between the cost of their preferred accommodation, and the amount specified in the personal budget. This is known as a "top-up" payment.

Regulation 5 of the Care and Support and After-Care (Choice of Accommodation) Regulations 2014 (SI 2014/2670) provides that where the cost of an adult's preferred accommodation is more than the amount specified for the accommodation in the adult's personal budget (under s.26 of the Act), the local authority is not required to provide that accommodation unless the additional cost condition is met. In effect, the local authority must be satisfied that a third party or (in some cases) the person themselves is able and willing to pay the top-up payment. The amount of the top-up should therefore be the difference between the actual costs of the preferred provider and the amount the local authority would have set in the personal budget to meet the person's needs through the provision of accommodation of the same type (although the local authority can agree for the amount of the top-up to be less).

The statutory guidance makes clear that top-up payments enable a person to choose alternative and more expensive options, where a third party or in certain circumstances the resident is willing and able to pay the additional cost. However, "an additional payment must always be optional and never as a result of commissioning failures leading to a lack of choice".[2] The statutory guidance discusses in detail the use of top-up fees in Annex A.

FIRST PARTY TOP-UPS

1–341   The 1992 directions provided that a person with care and support needs could only make top-up payments if they were subject to the 12-week property disregard or had entered into a deferred payment agreement. This could be seen as impeding choice and discriminatory against single older adults without children, as top-ups have to be paid by third parties such as family members. During the passage of the Care Bill through Parliament the Government confirmed that it was considering allowing people to make their own top-up payments.[3] It had been announced that the restrictions on first party top-up arrangements would be lifted from April 2016.[4] However, the delay to the introduction of the funding reforms is likely to mean that first party top-ups will not be introduced until April 2020.

In the meantime, the Care and Support regulations and After-Care (Choice of Accommodation) Regulations 2014 (SI 2014/2670) consolidate the 1992 directions. People with care and support needs are still only able to make top-up payments if they are subject to the 12-week property disregard or a deferred payment agreement is in place. However, the regulations do enable adults who are receiving their accommodation under s.117 of the Mental Health Act 1983 to make top-up payments on the same basis as third parties.

---

[1] Department of Health, *Care and Support Statutory Guidance* (2014), para.8.37 and Annex A, para.9.

[2] Department of Health, *Care and Support Statutory Guidance* (2014), para.8.37.

[3] *Hansard* (House of Lords), 14 October 2013, Vol.748, col.287 (Earl Howe). See also *Hansard* (House of Commons: Public Bill Committee), 16 January 2014 (AM): Fifth Sitting, col.175 (Norman Lamb MP).

[4] See, Department of Health, *The Care Act 2014: Consultation on draft regulations and guidance to implement the cap on care costs and policy proposals for a new appeals system for care and support* (2015), pp. 41 to 42.

DIRECT PAYMENTS

As noted at para.I1–005 above, the introduction of direct payments was largely a **1–342** response to the rise of the disability rights and independent living movements in the 1990s that criticised the care management system as disabling and disempowering, and sought greater control. Direct payments are monetary payments made by local authorities directly to service users and carers so that they can purchase the care and support that the authority would otherwise provide. They have been described in statutory guidance as:

". . . fundamental to achieving the Government's aim of increasing people's independence, choice and control by providing personalised alternatives to the social care services offered by a council with social services responsibilities."[1]

Indeed the Joint Committee stated that:

". . . direct payments to persons in need, allowing them to have more control over the services they buy and the priorities they accord to them, are likely to become a much bigger feature of social care in the future."[2]

Direct payments were first introduced by the Community Care (Direct Payments) Act 1996 (which came into force on 1 April 2007). This Act gave local authorities a power to provide payments to certain categories of service users. Initially they were available only to people aged under 65 and eligible for services under s.29 of the National Assistance Act 1948 who were capable of managing a direct payment. The categories of those potentially eligible were later expanded to include older people, carers, people with parental responsibility for disabled children and disabled 16 and 17 year olds. The 1996 Act was replaced by s.57 of the Health and Social Care Act 2001 which provided that regulations may require or authorise local authorities to make direct payments to a person with eligible needs, with his or her consent (or if the person lacked capacity to consent, to a "suitable person") or to a carer.

In England, the regulations under the 2001 Act required local authorities to make a direct payment if:

- the person appeared to be capable of managing a direct payment alone or with assistance;
- the person is not subject to certain court orders;
- the direct payment is provided to secure the provision of a community care service within the meaning of s.46(3) of the National Health Service and Community Care Act 1990 or a carer's service under s.2 of the Carers and Disabled Children Act 2000; and
- the authority is satisfied that the person's need for the service can be met by securing the provision of it by means of direct payment.[3]

Under these regulations, the duty to make direct payments extended to most people who were subject to compulsory measures under the Mental Health Act 1983 and there was a power to make direct payments in respect of services which the person was under an obligation to accept as a result of the 1983 Act (such as Community Treatment Orders) or certain criminal justice legislation (such as during the supervision period of a suspended sentence under the Criminal Justice Act 2003).

---

[1] Department of Health, *Guidance on direct payments—For community care, services for carers and children's services: England 2009* (2009), p.1.

[2] House of Lords House of Commons Joint Committee on the Draft Care and Support Bill, *Draft Care and Support Bill Report, Session 2012–13*, para.209.

[3] The Community Care, Services for Carers and Children's Services (Direct Payments) (England) Regulations 2009 (SI 2009/1887).

There were several restrictions placed on the provision of direct payments. For example, direct payments could not be used to purchase:

- services from close family members or partners who live with the person, except if the local authority was satisfied that securing the service from such a person is necessary to meet satisfactorily the person's need for that service;
- long-term residential accommodation (although direct payments could be used to purchase short-term stays of not more than a period of four continuous weeks in any period of 12 months); and
- a service from a local authority.[1]

The Law Commission recommended that the new statute should retain the direct payment provisions and should not alter the balance between statute and regulations. In effect, statute law would set out the duty to provide direct payments, but most of the detail would be set out in regulations.[2] This recommendation has been implemented in ss.31 to 33 of the Care Act. The relevant regulations are the Care and Support (Direct Payment) Regulations 2014 (SI 2014/2871). They are reproduced in full and discussed further in paras A1–231 to A1–244 below..

Some local authorities have developed the use of pre-paid cards for recipients of direct payments. These are sometimes used to allow direct payments without the need for a separate bank account, or to ease the financial management of the payment. The statutory guidance suggests that pre-paid cards can be a "good option" for some people but they must not be used to constrain choice. Therefore pre-paid cards should not be the only option, should not be only available for use with restricted list of providers, and should be offered alongside the option of direct payments into a bank account.[3]

See para.1–304 above on calculating a personal budget for direct payment recipients.

PURPOSE OF DIRECT PAYMENTS

1–343   The Joint Committee recommended that the purposes for which direct payments can be used should be clarified, and the presumption should be that individuals can spend their direct payments as they like to achieve the agreed outcomes. This recommendation was in response to calls from witnesses for clarification on whether the person receiving a direct payment will be able to use it as the equivalent of a personal budget either for "whole family" purposes or to compensate another family member for loss of earnings, which is commonplace in some European countries.[4] The Government accepted that the general presumption should be that individuals can spend their direct payments as they like, to achieve the agreed outcomes. In response it removed a provision from the draft Care and Support Bill that required the care and support plan to state "how needs could be met by the direct payment". This had been criticised for inhibiting flexibility and implying that the person would need local authority permission for minor variations in how the direct payment is used.[5]

As noted above, since the introduction of direct payments there has been a requirement that they are spent on services provided in the independent sector. The Joint Committee questioned whether it is consistent with the well-being principle, particularly regarding the promotion of choice, and recommended that the Government should lift the ban on

[1] The Community Care, Services for Carers and Children's Services (Direct Payments) (England) Regulations 2009 (SI 2009/1887).
[2] Law Commission, *Adult Social Care*, paras 8.63 to 8.69.
[3] Department of Health, *Care and Support Statutory Guidance* (2014), paras 11.35 and 12.58.
[4] House of Lords House of Commons Joint Committee on the Draft Care and Support Bill, *Draft Care and Support Bill Report, Session 2012–13*, para.210.
[5] Department of Health, *The Care Bill explained—including a response to consultation and pre-legislative scrutiny on the draft Care and Support Bill*, p.71.

direct payments being used to pay for local authority direct services if the individual so chooses.[1] The Government rejected this, and argued that it would be more efficient and less bureaucratic for the local authority to provide this direct to the person as part of a managed service rather than as a direct payment.[2]

This policy has been continued in the statutory guidance, which states that:

> "As a general rule, direct payments should not be used to pay for local authority-provided services from the 'home' local authority. Where a person wishes to receive care and support from their local authority, it should be easier and less burdensome to provide the service direct to the person. This will also avoid possible conflicts of interest where the local authority is providing the direct payment, but also promoting their services for people to purchase."[3]

But the guidance also acknowledges that in some cases local authorities could exercise their discretion to provide care and support by receiving a direct payment amount. The example is given of "where a person who is using direct payments wants to make a one-off purchase from the local authority such as a place in day care"—and it would be less burdensome to accept the direct payment, rather than providing the service and then reducing the personal budget and direct payment accordingly. In these cases the local authority should "take into account" the wishes of the person when making a decision. The guidance also confirms that this does not preclude people from using their direct payment to purchase care and support from a different local authority, such as where "a person may live close to authority boundaries and another local authority could provide a particular service that their 'home' authority does not provide".[4]

DIRECT PAYMENTS AND RESIDENTIAL CARE

The Law Commission also recommended that direct payments should be extended to pay **1–344** for people to live in long-term care home placements. Prior to consultation this had been opposed by the Department of Health. It had argued that Government policy was to help people to remain living in their own homes and direct payments provided the key means of achieving this, whereas residential care was viewed as an option of last resort. Moreover, it argued that extending direct payments in this way was unnecessary given that the National Assistance Act 1948 (Choice of Accommodation) Directions 1992 already offered individuals entering care homes choice and control. Those responding to the Law Commission's consultation also expressed concern that direct payment recipients would be charged higher rates for their accommodation since the local authority would not be exercising its market power to negotiate a lower rate, and because there is a greater risk of default in the direct payment system. The Commission concluded that in principle service users should be given greater choice and control over the provision of accommodation and should no longer have to rely on their preference being acknowledged and implemented by local authority staff. It also rejected the practical concerns. First, it argued that the local authority would continue to exercise a high degree of market power in the local market for residential care through caps on direct payments rather than negotiating block contracts. Second it concluded that the danger of default is not a significant one and local authorities could take measures to minimise the risks—for example, through supervision of payments and reverting to direct service provision. Therefore, the Commission recommended that direct payments should be extended to residential care.[5]

---

[1] House of Lords House of Commons Joint Committee on the Draft Care and Support Bill, *Draft Care and Support Bill Report, Session 2012–13*, para.211.

[2] Department of Health, *The Care Bill explained—including a response to consultation and pre-legislative scrutiny on the draft Care and Support Bill*, para.88.

[3] Department of Health, *Care and Support Statutory Guidance* (2014), para.12.55.

[4] Department of Health, *Care and Support Statutory Guidance* (2014), paras 12.56 to 12.57.

[5] Law Commission, *Adult Social Care: A Consultation Paper*, Consultation Paper No.192 (2010), paras 10.10 to 10.18 and Law Commission, Adult Social Care, paras 8.62 to 8.75.

Regulation 6 of the Care and Support (Direct Payment) Regulations 2014 (SI 2014/2871) provides that direct payments can only be used to fund short-term care in a care home. See para.A1–237 below. But the statutory guidance points out that people in long-term placements may receive direct payments in relation to non-residential care services. It also confirms that the Government is testing the use of direct payments for long-term residential care at selected sites. The pilots started in the autumn of April 2013 and the original aim was to introduce direct payments to fund long-term residential care alongside the introduction of the cap on care costs in April 2016.[1] However, the Department of Health has announced that the introduction of the capped costs system will be delayed until April 2020.[2]

Whilst direct payments cannot be used for long-term care and support in a care home, the individual may request a direct payment to meet needs for other types of accommodation such as supported living and shared lives. The statutory guidance states that in such cases "the direct payment would be for the care but usually not the accommodation". Local authorities should therefore ensure that they have in place "effective, proportionate processes for recording how the individual chooses to meet their needs."[3]

CHARGING AND DIRECT PAYMENTS

1–345 Direct payments can be paid as a gross or net payment. A gross payment is where the local authority makes a direct payment that is equivalent to their estimate of the reasonable cost of the service, and can subsequently seek reimbursement of the assessed charge. A net payment involves the local authority deducting from their estimate the assessed charge before the payment is made. The statutory guidance makes clear that whether payments are made on a gross or net is a matter for local authorities to decide, following consultation with stakeholders. But it also emphasises that local authorities that make gross payments should consider the benefits of net payments such as reduced transaction and process costs.[4]

MONITORING DIRECT PAYMENTS

1–346 When a person chooses to receive direct payments, they take on responsibility for securing the necessary care and support to meet their eligible needs. However, the local authority remains accountable for the proper use of its public funds and will need to establish monitoring arrangements. Moreover the local authority is subject to a duty under s.33(3) to ensure that a direct payment must only be used for the purpose of meeting the needs specified in the care and support plan or support plan. Under s.33(4), the local authority must stop making direct payments if any of the conditions in ss.31 or 32 are no longer met. These duties reinforce the need to review the provision of direct payments.

The Secretary of State also has regulation-making powers to specify cases or circumstances in which a local authority making direct payments must review the making of those payments (s.33(2)(g)). Such provision is made in reg.7 of the Care and Support (Direct Payment) Regulations 2014 (SI 2014/2871). Reviewing direct payments is discussed at para.A1–238 below.

The statutory guidance makes clear that local authorities must be satisfied that the direct payment is being used to meet the needs set out in the care and support plan or support plan,

---

[1] Department of Health, *Care and Support Statutory Guidance* (2014), paras 12.46 to 12.47. See, also, Department of Health, *Caring for our future: Consultation on reforming what and how people pay for their care and support* (2013), paras 301 to 302.

[2] *House of Commons Written Answers and Statements Daily Report*, Cap on Care Costs: Written Statement – HCWS145, 20 July 2015, pp.162 to 164 (Alastair Burt MP).

[3] Department of Health, *Care and Support Statutory Guidance* (2014), para.19.35.

[4] Department of Health, *Care and Support Statutory Guidance* (2014), para.12.26.

and should therefore have systems in place to "proportionally monitor direct payment usage to ensure effective use of public money". It goes on to state that:

"Local authorities should not design systems that place a disproportionate reporting burden upon the individual. The reporting system should not clash with the policy intention of direct payments to encourage greater autonomy, flexibility and innovation. For example, people should not be requested to duplicate information or have onerous monitoring requirements placed upon them. Monitoring should be proportionate to the needs to be met and the care package. Thus local authorities should have regard to lowering monitoring requirements for people that have been managing direct payments without issues for a long period."[1]

In 2011, a serious case review into Buckinghamshire County Council's care of a 70-year old man with multiple health needs highlighted the tragic consequences of failing to keep a close check on direct payments. Mr C, a service user and recipient of direct payments, was murdered by his son. Although Mr C was being funded for four personal assistants there was no evidence they ever existed. Payments continued for months after his death, during which time the son continued to access the funds. It is not known what happened to this money. The review highlighted major shortcomings in the oversight of public funds by the local authority and concluded that:

"Direct Payments are a process and not an outcome. People do what is measured and rewarded. With little experience on which to draw, it appears that Adult Social Care operated under the assumption that what was agreed would occur. It appears too that Mr C was regarded as a client with a less complex care package and, as such, was subject to an unduly light-touch reviewing process captured via vague and arms-length recording . . . Although Direct Payments Recipients can be offered considerable flexibility in what they want to purchase, the local authority still has a duty to ensure that the money is spent for the purpose intended. Mr C's circumstances indicate that that duty was not enacted effectively in Buckinghamshire."[2]

A more robust approach was taken by the local authority in the case of *R. (G) v North Somerset Council*.[3] Direct payments were ceased immediately and without consulting those concerned once the local authority had become concerned about the misuse of the payments which had been revealed in its audit. The direct payments had been replaced by direct service provision. The court confirmed that the authority had been entitled to take those steps given the very serious concerns that had been raised.

General concerns have been raised that people using personal budgets, particularly direct payment users, may generally be at greater risk of abuse and neglect than people using conventionally commissioned care services, particularly if they hire unregulated care workers, or rely on relatives or others to manage their money. However, others argue that personal budgets and direct payments may enhance safety through increasing people's control over their own care. A 2014 study funded by the National Institute for Health Research School for Social Care Research found no strong evidence to suggest higher levels of safeguarding referrals among people with personal budgets compared with all social care users. In the three councils studied, although safeguarding referrals overall were equal to those for conventional services, there was a statistically significant higher proportion of referrals for financial abuse and abuse by home care workers in people using personal budgets.[4]

---

[1] Department of Health, *Care and Support Statutory Guidance* (2014), para.12.24.

[2] Margaret Flynn CPEA Ltd, *Executive Summary: The Murder of Mr C—A Serious Care Review (Commissioned by Buckinghamshire's Safeguarding Vulnerable Adults Board* (2011), p.15.

[3] *R. (G) v North Somerset Council* [2011] EWHC 2232 (Admin).

[4] M. Stevens and others, *Research Findings: Risk, Safeguarding and Persoanl Budgets: Exploring Relationships and Identifying Good Practice* (2014).

1–347   A local authority's general power of competence under s.1 of the Localism Act 2011 could be used to provide cash payments outside the direct payments scheme.

Section 12A of the National Health Service Act 2006 provides for direct payments for health services. These are discussed in more detail at para.1–303 above.

Regulation 10 of the Care and Support (Direct Payment) Regulations 2014 (SI 2014/2871) requires local authorities to take reasonable steps to co–ordinate its systems and processes in respect of the direct payment with those in place for the direct payment made under the s.12A of the 2006 Act (see para.A1–241 below).

Adults with capacity to request direct payments

1–348   **31.**—(1) This section applies where—

(a) a personal budget for an adult specifies an amount which the local authority must pay towards the cost of meeting the needs to which the personal budget relates, and

(b) the adult requests the local authority to meet some or all of those needs by making payments to the adult or a person nominated by the adult.

(2) If conditions 1 to 4 are met, the local authority must, subject to regulations under section 33, make the payments to which the request relates to the adult or nominated person.

(3) A payment under this section is referred to in this Part as a "direct payment".

(4) Condition 1 is that—

(a) the adult has capacity to make the request, and

(b) where there is a nominated person, that person agrees to receive the payments.

(5) Condition 2 is that—

(a) the local authority is not prohibited by regulations under section 33 from meeting the adult's needs by making direct payments to the adult or nominated person, and

(b) if regulations under that section give the local authority discretion to decide not to meet the adult's needs by making direct payments to the adult or nominated person, it does not exercise that discretion.

(6) Condition 3 is that the local authority is satisfied that the adult or nominated person is capable of managing direct payments—

(a) by himself or herself, or

(b) with whatever help the authority thinks the adult or nominated person will be able to access.

(7) Condition 4 is that the local authority is satisfied that making direct payments to the adult or nominated person is an appropriate way to meet the needs in question.

GENERAL NOTE

1–349   This section specifies the conditions that must be satisfied in order to trigger the local authority duty to provide a direct payment. It relates to adults who have the capacity to request a direct payment. Section 32 deals with those who lack capacity.

In broad terms, s.31 provides that direct payments must be provided if:

- an adult requests direct payments and has capacity to do so—and if they have nominated someone to manage the payments on their behalf, that person agrees to receive the payments;

- the local authority is required to contribute towards meeting the adult's needs;
- the local authority is satisfied that the adult or nominated person is capable of managing direct payments—by themselves or with help;
- the local authority is satisfied that making direct payments is an appropriate way to meet the needs in question; and
- the provision of direct payments is not prohibited by the regulations, and if the regulations give the authority discretion not to provide direct payments, it exercises that discretion. The relevant regulations are the Care and Support (Direct Payment) Regulations 2014 (SI 2014/2871).

Subsection (1)

A direct payment may not be made unless the local authority is required to contribute **1–350** towards the costs of meeting the adult's needs (and the amount must be specified in the person's personal budget) and the adult requests a direct payment to be made to the adult or to someone who is nominated by the adult to receive the direct payment.

REQUESTING A DIRECT PAYMENT. This right to request a direct payment should be read **1–351** alongside s.24(1)(b) which requires the local authority to tell an adult which (if any) of their needs can be met by making direct payments. There are no particular formalities about the format of the request. For example, it does not need to be in writing.

An individual can decide not to make a request and can instead choose to have services provided or arranged by the local authority. However, it is likely that under the Care Act a local authority would not be prevented from offering direct payments and suggesting that a request is made. In *P. (MP) v Hackney LBC* the court considered the previous legal requirement of consent to direct payments and held that this did not necessarily preclude the local authority from making an offer of direct payments. The local authority had further argued that refusal to consent cannot be for irrational reasons. Whilst the judge accepted that it was not necessary to decide this question, he opined that the expectation of the statute and regulations was that the recipient's reasons should be articulated and a dialogue takes place between them and the local authority with a view towards resolving any concerns. In deciding whether a local authority has exceeded a reasonable time to arrange services directly, the court may need to take into account whether the person's objections "have been reasonable or arbitrary and, if reasonable, whether they have met a reasonable response".[1]

The statutory guidance makes clear that:

"The route to a direct payment is for a person to request one, but the local authority should support the person's right to make this request by providing information and advice as detailed above. People must not be forced to take a direct payment against their will, but instead be informed of the choices available to them."[2]

It goes on to state:

". . . the gateway to receiving a direct payment must always be through the request from the person. Local authorities must not force people to take a direct payment against their will, or allow people to be placed in a situation where the direct payment is the only way to receive personalised care and support. However, local authorities are encouraged to prompt people to consider direct payments and how they could be used to meet needs."[3]

Subsection (2)

The local authority must make payments to the adult or nominated person, subject to any **1–352** regulations specified under s.33 and provided that the four conditions (set out in subs.(4) to

---

[1] *P. (MP) v Hackney LBC* [2007] EWHC 1365 (Admin) at [37] to [39].
[2] Department of Health, *Care and Support Statutory Guidance* (2014), para.12.5.
[3] Department of Health, *Care and Support Statutory Guidance* (2014), para.12.9.

(7)) are all met. If the request is refused, written reasons should be provided and the person should be made aware of how to appeal the decision.[1]

Subsections (4) to (7)

1–353   The four conditions that must be met for the purposes of the duty to provide direct payments under s.31 are:

- condition 1: the adult must have capacity to request direct payments, and any person nominated to receive a direct payment of their behalf must agree to doing so (subs.(4));
- condition 2: the local authority is not prohibited by regulations made under s.33 from making direct payments, and if the regulations give the authority discretion not to provide direct payments, it does not exercise that discretion (subs.(5));
- condition 3: the local authority must be satisfied that the adult (or anyone nominated on their behalf) is "capable of managing" a direct payment, either on their own or with help for instance from family members (subs.(6)); and
- condition 4: the local authority is satisfied that making direct payments (either to the adult or someone nominated) is an appropriate way of meeting the needs for care and support (subs.(7)).

The statutory guidance makes clear that all these conditions need to be met in their entirety and a failure in one would result in direct payments being declined.[2] The guidance also explains that where requests for direct payments are accepted, the decision should be recorded in the care and support plan, or support plan. Where refused, the person should be provided with written reasons that explain the decision, and be made aware of how to appeal the decision through the local complaints process.[3]

1–354   CAPACITY TO MAKE A REQUEST.   Condition 1 requires that the person must have sufficient capacity to request a direct payment. It is likely that understanding the purpose to which the direct payment will be put and the practical implications will be relevant to the capacity assessment.

The capacity to make a request is not the same as—and is a lower threshold for capacity than—the capacity to manage a direct payment. In other words, it would be possible for a person to have capacity to request a direct payment but lack capacity to manage the payment. However, the duty to provide a direct payment would not apply to such a person by virtue of condition 3 which requires that the person is capable of managing the direct payment. In such a case the person could nominate someone under subs.1(b) to receive the payment on their behalf or could be provided with assistance to manage the payment (condition 3).

The statutory guidance states that an assessment of whether the person has capacity to make a decision about direct payments should have taken place at the assessment of needs. It also lists a number of general considerations that will be relevant to this assessment.[4] The Care and Support (Direct Payments) Regulations 2014 (SI 2014/2871) allow for direct payments to continue to be made in cases of fluctuating capacity (regs 8 and 9).

1–355   NOMINATED PERSON.   Only the person with care and support needs can nominate someone else to manage the direct payment on their behalf. However, this would not preclude a local authority from suggesting that a certain person might be suitable to be nominated.

---

[1] Department of Health, *Care and Support Statutory Guidance* (2014), para.12.18.
[2] Department of Health, *Care and Support Statutory Guidance* (2014), para 12.14.
[3] Department of Health, *Care and Support Statutory Guidance* (2014), paras 12.18 and 12.22.
[4] Department of Health, *Care and Support Statutory Guidance* (2014), para.12.10.

In legal terms a "person" means anyone with a legal personality. Therefore s.31 enables the local authority to pay the direct payment to a person of a type specified by the adult, including user trusts set up as companies and organisations set up as companies.[1]

The regulations contain no further detail about the nominated person such as how they can be nominated and who can be nominated. However, condition 3 requires that the local authority must be satisfied that the nominated person is capable of managing the payment and condition 4 requires the authority to be satisfied that making direct payments to the nominated person is an appropriate way to meet the needs in question.

An enduring or lasting power of attorney can be used while the donor still has the requisite capacity, in order to manage their property and affairs. An attorney therefore could potentially be the person nominated to receive the direct payment on the donor's behalf. Indeed the donor could specify in the instrument that their attorney should manage their direct payment. However, the local authority would still need to be satisfied that the person is capable of managing the payment, and the donor will need to be clear that the care and support being purchased is within the scope of their authority.

The statutory guidance states that:

"Where a nominated person has been requested to receive the direct payment, the authority should involve the nominated person in any appropriate stages of the care planning journey, such as the development of the care plan, as long as the person with care needs agrees to this. Where the person does not specifically request this involvement, the local authority should consider whether to encourage the person to make that request. During this process, the nominated person should receive information regarding the local authorities direct payments processes, as well as information and advice on using and managing the direct payment, so that the nominated person understands their legal obligations as the direct payment recipient to act in the best interests of the person requiring care and support."[2]

CAPABLE OF MANAGING DIRECT PAYMENTS. The person making the request or their **1–356** nominated person must be capable of managing the direct payment. This form of words was also used in the previous regulations.[3] The 2009 statutory guidance on direct payments suggested that the following should be considered:

- the person's understanding of direct payments, including the actions required on their part;
- whether the person understands the implications of taking or not taking on direct payments;
- what help is available to the person;
- what kind of support the person might need to achieve their identified outcomes; and
- what arrangements the person would make to obtain this support.[4]

During the passage of the Care Bill through the House of Lords, an attempt was made by Lord Sharkey to amend the Bill to require a local authority to explain in writing and discuss with the applicant the criteria that it uses to satisfy itself that the adult is capable of managing a direct payment. His Lordship argued that people may underestimate the difficulties involved in administering payments, such as the contractual arrangements when employing a person directly, and there is no clarity about how local authorities would make the

---

[1] *Hansard* (House of Lords), 16 July 2013, Vol.747, col.742 (Earl Howe).
[2] Department of Health, *Care and Support Statutory Guidance* (2014), para.12.15.
[3] Community Care, Services for Carers and Children's Services (Direct Payments) (England) Regulations 2009 (SI 2009/1887) reg.2(a).
[4] Department of Health, *Guidance on direct payments—For community care, services for carers and children's services: England 2009* (DH, 2009), p.27.

decision about who was and was not a suitable recipient for payments. Lord Sharkey explained the effect of the amendment in the following terms:

"This would have the effect of bringing about a proper discussion of the implications for the applicant of managing direct payments and provide a proper and informed basis for the local authority to make a judgment. I hope that it would also ensure that the criteria for judgment were clear, understandable, user friendly and completely transparent. Making this simple change would greatly improve the chances of correctly matching direct payments with those who understand the implications and can effectively manage the system."[1]

In response, the Government argued that the amendment was unnecessary because the local authority would not be able to fulfil its duties under the legislation unless it "tells the adult what he or she needs to know in order to make a decision and reach agreement about whether or not to take a direct payment".[2]

The statutory guidance states that:

"A further condition is that the local authority must be satisfied that the person is able to manage the direct payment by him or herself, or whatever help or support the person will be able to access. Local authorities should therefore take all reasonable steps to provide this support to whoever may require it. To comply with this, many local authorities have contracts with voluntary or user-led organisations that provide support and advice to direct payment holders, or to people interested in receiving direct payments. This condition should not be used to deny a person from receiving a direct payment without consideration of support needs. Consideration should also be given to involving a specialist assessor in determination of support requirements, in particular if one was used earlier in the care and support process (such as assessment)."[3]

1–357 AN APPROPRIATE WAY TO MEET THE NEEDS. The local authority must be satisfied that making direct payments to the adult or nominated person is an appropriate way to meet the needs in question. The statutory guidance—while recognising that there may be some cases where a direct payment is not appropriate to meet needs—states that:

"Local authorities must not use this condition to arbitrarily decline a request for a direct payment. For example, there may be instances where a person is obliged to receive services as a condition of mental health legislation (including a community treatment order, guardianship or leave of absence from hospital under the Mental Health Act or provisions in other mental health legislation). In these cases, although the person is being obliged to receive services rather than choosing to present for services, it may still be appropriate to give the person the responsibility of meeting their needs via a direct payment, if this is what is requested. Particular consideration should be given to these cases when applying the conditions set out in the Act. In all cases, appropriateness is for local authorities to determine, although it is expected that in general, direct payments are an appropriate way to meet most care and support needs."[4]

Adults without capacity to request direct payments

1–358 **32.**—(1) This section applies where—

(a) a personal budget for an adult specifies an amount which the local authority must pay towards the cost of meeting the needs to which the personal budget relates, and

---

[1] *Hansard* (House of Lords), 16 July 2013, Vol.747, col.742.
[2] *Hansard* (House of Lords), 16 July 2013, Vol.747, col.748.
[3] Department of Health, *Care and Support Statutory Guidance* (2014), para.12.21.
[4] Department of Health, *Care and Support Statutory Guidance* (2014), paras 12.19 and 12.20.

(b) the adult lacks capacity to request the local authority to meet any of those needs by making payments to the adult, but

(c) an authorised person requests the local authority to meet some or all of those needs by making payments to the authorised person.

(2) If conditions 1 to 5 are met, the local authority must, subject to regulations under section 33, make the payments to which the request relates to the authorised person.

(3) A payment under this section is referred to in this Part as a "direct payment".

(4) A person is authorised for the purposes of this section if—

(a) the person is authorised under the Mental Capacity Act 2005 to make decisions about the adult's needs for care and support,

(b) where the person is not authorised as mentioned in paragraph (a), a person who is so authorised agrees with the local authority that the person is a suitable person to whom to make direct payments, or

(c) where the person is not authorised as mentioned in paragraph (a) and there is no person who is so authorised, the local authority considers that the person is a suitable person to whom to make direct payments.

(5) Condition 1 is that, where the authorised person is not authorised as mentioned in subsection (4)(a) but there is at least one person who is so authorised, a person who is so authorised supports the authorised person's request.

(6) Condition 2 is that—

(a) the local authority is not prohibited by regulations under section 33 from meeting the adult's needs by making direct payments to the authorised person, and

(b) if regulations under that section give the local authority discretion to decide not to meet the adult's needs by making direct payments to the authorised person, it does not exercise that discretion.

(7) Condition 3 is that the local authority is satisfied that the authorised person will act in the adult's best interests in arranging for the provision of the care and support for which the direct payments under this section would be used.

(8) Condition 4 is that the local authority is satisfied that the authorised person is capable of managing direct payments—

(a) by himself or herself, or

(b) with whatever help the authority thinks the authorised person will be able to access.

(9) Condition 5 is that the local authority is satisfied that making direct payments to the authorised person is an appropriate way to meet the needs in question.

GENERAL NOTE

This section specifies the conditions that must be satisfied in order to trigger the local **1–359** authority duty to provide a direct payment. It relates to adults who lack the capacity to request a direct payment. Section 31 deals with those who have capacity.

In broad terms, s.32 provides that direct payments must be provided if:

- a person authorised under the Mental Capacity Act or a suitable person requests direct payments to meet the adult's needs;
- the local authority is required to contribute towards meeting the adult's needs;
- the local authority is satisfied that the authorised person will act in the adult's best interests;

- the local authority is satisfied that the authorised person is capable of managing direct payments—by themselves or with help;
- the local authority is satisfied that making direct payments to the authorised person is an appropriate way to meet the needs in question; and
- the provision of direct payments is not prohibited by the regulations, and if the regulations give the authority discretion not to provide direct payments, it exercises that discretion. The relevant regulations are the Care and Support (Direct Payment) Regulations 2014 (SI 2014/2871).

Subsection (1)

1–360　　In order for the s.32 duty to apply, the adult must lack capacity to request direct payments. This is discussed above at para.1–354.

A direct payment may not be made unless the local authority is required to contribute towards the costs of meeting the adult's needs and an authorised person (defined in subs.(4)) requests the local authority to meet some or all of the adult's needs by making a direct payment to the authorised person.

Direct payments under s.32 must be discontinued if the person subsequently gains capacity. Regulation 9 of the Care and Support (Direct Payment) Regulations 2014 (SI 2014/2871) provides that if the gaining of capacity is temporary, the local authority can continue payments to the authorised person if during that period the adult will manage the payments themselves–see para.A1–240 below.

Subsection (2)

1–361　　The local authority must make payments to an authorised person (defined in subs.(4)), subject to any regulations specified under s.33 and provided that the five conditions (set out in subs.(5) to (9)) are all met.

Subsection (4)

1–362　　This sets out who is an "authorised person" for the purposes of the s.32 duty. An authorised person can be:

- someone who is authorised under the Mental Capacity Act 2005 to make decisions about the adult's needs for care and support; or
- a person who the local authority and a person who is so authorised agree is a "suitable person" to receive the direct payments; or
- if there is no person authorised under the Mental Capacity Act, a person who the local authority considers is a suitable person to whom to make the payment.

Section 80(3) of the Care Act provides that references to being authorised under the Mental Capacity Act 2005 mean being authorised (whether in general or specific terms) as:

- a donee of a lasting power of attorney; or
- a deputy appointed by the Court of Protection.

It is submitted that these people should also be consulted under the Care Act, as far as is reasonably practicable and appropriate.

1–363　　Suitable person.　　This term is not defined in the regulations or guidance. The determination as to whether someone is a suitable person must be made by the local authority and someone authorised under the Mental Capacity Act (if there is such a person). The determination itself must relate to whether they are a suitable person to whom to make direct payments. This suggests that any general concerns about the person's character or standing would only be relevant if they relate potentially to the management of direct payments. The term suitable person was also used in the Health and Social Care Act 2001.[1] The previous regulations provided that the local authority should, so far as is reasonably practicable and appropriate, consult and take into account the views of the following people before making the decision to make direct payments to a suitable person:

- anyone who has been named by an adult before they lost capacity as someone to be consulted on the subject of direct payments or related matters;
- anyone currently engaged in caring for the person or anyone with an interest in their personal welfare;
- the person who lacks capacity themselves (including any written statement of wishes and preferences made before they lost capacity); and
- any representative or surrogate of the person lacking capacity.[2]

Subsections (5) to (9)

The five conditions that must be met for the purposes of the duty to provide direct pay- **1–364** ments under s.32 are:

- condition 1: where the authorised person is not authorised under the Mental Capacity Act 2005 to make decisions, but there is someone who is so authorised under the 2005 Act, that person supports the request (subs.(5));
- condition 2: the local authority is not prohibited by regulations made under s.33 from making direct payments, and if the regulations give the authority discretion not to provide direct payments, it decides not to exercise that discretion (subs.6);
- condition 3: the local authority is satisfied that the authorised person will use the direct payment in the best interests of the adult (subs.7);
- condition 4: the local authority is satisfied that the authorised person is capable of managing the direct payment by themselves, or with assistance (subs.8); and
- condition 5: the local authority is satisfied that making a direct payment to the authorised person is an appropriate way of meeting the adult's needs (subs.(9)).

The statutory guidance makes clear that all these conditions need to be met in their entirety and a failure in one would result in direct payments being declined.[3] The guidance also explains that where requests for direct payments are accepted, the decision should be recorded in the care and support plan, or support plan. Where refused, the person should be provided with written reasons that explain the decision, and be made aware of how to appeal the decision through the local complaints process.[4]

The meaning of "capable of managing direct payments" is discussed at para.1–356 above.

Regulation 5 of the Care and Support (Direct Payments) Regulations 2014 (SI 2014/2871) sets out steps which a local authority must take in order to be satisfied that making direct payments to an authorised person is an appropriate way to meet the needs in question. These include consulting and taking into account the views of:

- anyone named by the adult as someone to be consulted on this matter;
- anyone caring for or interested in the adult's welfare; and

---

[1] Health and Social Care Act 2001 s.57(1C). This was inserted by s.146(2) of the Health and Social Care Act 2008.

[2] Community Care, Services for Carers and Children's Services (Direct Payments) (England) Regulations 2009 (SI 2009/1887) reg.8(3).

[3] Department of Health, *Care and Support Statutory Guidance* (2014), para. 12.17.

[4] Department of Health, *Care and Support Statutory Guidance* (2014), paras 12.18 and 12.22.

- any person who is authorised under the Mental Capacity Act 2005 to make decisions about the adult's needs for care and support.

They also include considering the adult's wishes and feelings, their beliefs and values and other relevant factors. In some cases an enhanced criminal record certificate will also be required. See para.A1–236 below.

The meaning of "an 'appropriate' way to meet the needs in question" is considered at para.1–357.

Direct payments: further provision

1–365   **33.**—(1) Regulations must make further provision about direct payments.

(2) The regulations may, in particular, specify—

(a) cases or circumstances in which a local authority must not, or cases or circumstances in which it has the discretion to decide not to, meet needs by making direct payments;

(b) conditions which a local authority may or must attach to the making of direct payments;

(c) matters to which a local authority may or must have regard when making a decision of a specified type in relation to direct payments;

(d) steps which a local authority may or must take before, or after, making a decision of a specified type in relation to direct payments;

(e) cases or circumstances in which an adult who lacks capacity to request the making of direct payments must or may nonetheless be regarded for the purposes of this Part or the regulations as having capacity to do so;

(f) cases or circumstances in which an adult who no longer lacks capacity to make such a request must or may nonetheless be regarded for any of those purposes as lacking capacity to do so;

(g) cases or circumstances in which a local authority making direct payments must review the making of those payments.

(3) A direct payment is made on condition that it be used only to pay for arrangements under which the needs specified under section 25(2)(a) in the care and support plan or (as the case may be) the support plan are met.

(4) In a case where one or more of conditions 1 to 4 in section 31 is no longer met or one or more of conditions 1 to 5 in section 32 is no longer met, the local authority must terminate the making of direct payments.

(5) In a case where a condition specified under subsection (2)(b) or the condition mentioned in subsection (3) is breached, the local authority—

(a) may terminate the making of direct payments, and

(b) may require repayment of the whole or part of a direct payment (with section 69 accordingly applying to sums which the local authority requires to be repaid).

GENERAL NOTE

1–366   This section makes further provisions about direct payments.

Subsections (1) and (2)

1–367   The Secretary of State is required to make regulations, which may specify a number of further matters in relation to direct payments. The relevant regulations are the Care and Support (Direct Payment) Regulations 2014 (SI 2014/2871). They are reproduced in full and discussed further in paras A1–231 to A1–244 below.

Subsection (2)(e) was added as a Government amendment at Committee stage in the House of Commons. It makes a mirror provision to subs.(2)(f) and allows regulations to be made so that adults for whom a direct payment is made under s.31 can be treated as continuing to have capacity notwithstanding some periods of incapacity. Subsection (2)(e) and (f) therefore allows regulations to make provision for cases where a person with a direct payment has a fluctuating capacity, so that the local authority can continue with the original direct payment arrangements. This is intended to "provide continuity and to prevent direct payments from having to be terminated unnecessarily".[1] This has been implemented by reg.9 of the Care and Support (Direct Payment) Regulations 2014 (SI 2014/2871).

As noted at para.1–346 above, subs.(2)(g) provides that the regulations may specify cases or circumstances in which a local authority making direct payments must review the making of those payments.

Subsection (3)

1–368 A direct payment must only be used for the purpose of meeting the needs specified in the care and support plan or support plan.

This provision reinforces the need to review the provision of direct payments (see para.1–346 above).

Subsection (4)

1–369 The local authority must stop making direct payments if any of the conditions in ss.31 or 32 are no longer met. This provision reinforces the need to review the provision of direct payments (see para.1–346 above).

One such condition is contained in s.31(4)(a) whereby a local authority must stop making direct payments if a person who has capacity to request direct payments subsequently loses capacity. However, reg.8 of the Care and Support (Direct Payment) Regulations 2014 provides that if the loss of capacity is temporary, the local authority can continue payments if there is someone who is suitable and willing to manage the payments on the person's behalf.

The statutory guidance discusses terminating direct payments at paras 12.67 to 12.84.

Subsection (5)

1–370 This subsection allows the local authority to stop making direct payments and to require repayment of direct payments it has already made if there is a breach of any condition imposed by the local authority as permitted by regulations made under subs.(2)(b) and (3) or if the direct payment is not used to pay for the needs specified in the care and support plan.

DEFERRED PAYMENT AGREEMENTS, ETC

1–371 The origins of deferred payments can be traced back to the 1999 Royal Commission on Long Term Care.[2] Its report—*With Respect to Old Age*—contained a note of dissent by Joel Joffee and David Lipsey which rejected the majority's recommendation that personal care should be provided free of charge paid from general taxation on the basis of a needs assessment. The note argued that:

". . . it would be wrong that people needing care could simply hang onto their homes and eventually bequeath them to their families without spending any of the capital that those homes represented to pay for their own care".[3]

---

[1] *Hansard* (House of Commons: Public Bill Committee), 16 January 2014 (PM): Sixth Sitting, col.227 (Norman Lamb MP).

[2] Royal Commission on Long Term Care, *With Respect to Old Age: Long Term Care—Rights and Responsibilities* (The Stationary Office, March 1999), Cm.4192–I.

[3] *Hansard* (House of Lords), 22 July 2013, Vol.747, col.1062, Lord Lipsey.

Whilst acknowledging the general public hostility to the means test, the note put forward several measures designed to "remove the sting of the current means-test and allow people who have accumulated modest assets to retain them". The first of these measures was deferred payments—which are local authority loans secured against the value of a person's home and repayable when the home is sold, often after the person has died. The note described deferred payments as "a virtual guarantee that no old person will have to sell their home against their will".[1]

This was implemented by the Government in 2001 when local authorities were given powers to arrange deferred payments by virtue of s.55 of the Health and Social Care Act 2001. They were intended to operate across England but in practice local authority provision was patchy and many people were unable to access a deferred payment. It is estimated that only 4,000 people each year took up a deferred payment.[2] Several factors contributed to this. First, local authorities did not have to offer deferred payments, although they were encouraged to do so. Secondly, local authorities were not able to charge interest on the loan and therefore running the scheme had a cost to them and there was a financial incentive not to make them. Interest could however be charged after the person had died. Moreover, some local authorities had preferred to use their general debt recovery powers under s.22 of the Health and Social Services and Social Security Adjudication Act 1983, which also involved a charge upon the property but did require the resident to consent. Lord Lipsey (as he is now known) has also argued that deferred payments were "sabotaged" by officials at local and national level who failed to appreciate the emotional reasons why people would want to hang on to their house when they were living in a care home, and they did not want to see "valuable homes left empty".[3]

In 2011, the Commission on Funding Care and Support recommended a universal deferred payment scheme. The key elements of this scheme were a consistent offer across the country and enabling local authorities to charge interest to recover their costs, to make the scheme cost neutral. The report stated that:

"At a minimum, the Commission recommends an extension to the current deferred payment scheme so that it is a full, universal offer across the country. Anyone who would be unable to afford care charges without selling their home should be able to take out a deferred payment."[4]

1–372   The Commission's recommendation was accepted by the Government. During the passage of the Care Bill through the House of Lords, the Government stated that:

"We agree with the Dilnot commission that deferred payments should become a full and universal offer across the country for people who have to sell their homes to pay for residential care. We intend the scheme to be cost neutral to local authorities, as the commission also recommended. We are proud to introduce this universal scheme from April 2015. It will provide much needed peace of mind to the 40,000 people who sell their homes each year to pay for care."[5]

Sections 34 to 36 of the Care Act provide for a deferred payments scheme, although the vast majority of the detail is contained in regulations. The relevant regulations are the Care and Support (Deferred Payment) Regulations 2014 (SI 2014/2671). They are reproduced in full and discussed further in paras A1–111 to A1–122 below. The regulations require for the first time all local authorities to offer deferred payments arrangements. The Government

---

[1]   Royal Commission on Long Term Care, *With Respect to Old Age: Long Term Care—Rights and Responsibilities, Note of Dissent*, para.57.

[2]   Department of Health, *Universal Deferred Payment Scheme: Impact Assessment* (DH 08/05/2013) IA No.7084, para.4.

[3]   *Hansard* (House of Lords), 22 July 2013, Vol.747, col.1062.

[4]   Commission on Funding of Care and Support, *Fairer Care Funding: the Report of the Commission on Funding of Care and Support: Volume I* (July 2011), p.41.

[5]   *Hansard* (House of Lords), 22 July 2013, Vol.747, col.1069 (Earl Howe).

has stated that £110 million will be made available in 2015–16 to fund the expansion of the scheme.[1]

During the passage of the Care Bill through Parliament, Paul Burstow MP summarised the main purpose of deferred payments:

"Deferred payment is fundamentally about having a mechanism that avoids the family facing the trauma of a fire sale of the property at the moment of crisis. Having a deferred payment gives that peace of mind of knowing that is not something they have to address at that point. It also ensures that the property is not sold at a point when everything else is going on, potentially at a lower price than it would achieve if properly marketed over time. It is an important protection of the asset, but a much more important protection of the emotional crisis that a family is in at the point at which this takes place. That is the best way to understand what deferred payment should be about."[2]

The Government rejected suggestions that deferred payments might provide a perverse incentive for people to go into care homes rather than receive care at home. It argued that the well-being principle in s.1 and the fact that local authorities will not be able to make a profit on deferred payments should address this concern.[3]

IMPLEMENTATION OF DEFERRED PAYMENTS

As noted above, the intention is to introduce the scheme from April 2015. During the **1–373** passage of the Care Bill, many questioned how viable this timetable would be. In response, the Government explained that its intention was to introduce a range of new measures for self-funders (including deferred payments) to encourage local authorities to engage with self-funders in preparation for the introduction of the capped costs system (now due in April 2020).[4] Questions were also asked about the cost of the scheme. A Local Government Association analysis of the ongoing costs of deferred payment suggested that the total value of loans would increase from £122 million in 2015–16 to £1.1 billion by 2024–25 which compares with £139 million to £230 million in the Government's impact assessment.[5]

In the House of Lords, Lord Lipsey questioned the 40,000 figure quoted (above) by the Government:

"I have spent a surprising—perhaps wasted—amount of my time trying to trace the figure that 40,000 people each year are forced to sell their home to pay for care. I have been doing it ever since I sat on the royal commission 15 years ago. When we were sitting on the royal commission, we eventually found a very dodgy piece of research, now more than 20 years old, which kind of concluded that the number might be about 40,000. Of course, what happened was not that the piece of research was examined and found to be accurate but that the figure got into the *Daily Mail* cuttings library, so that every time that paper campaigned against people having to sell their house to pay for care— I praise it for this—the figure was repeated, until it became accepted throughout the world as the number involved."[6]

He went on to question the notion that people have been forced to sell their home:

---

[1] *Hansard* (House of Commons: Public Bill Committee), 4 February 2014: Fifteenth Sitting, col.606 (Norman Lamb MP).

[2] *Hansard* (House of Commons: Public Bill Committee), 16 January 2014 (PM): Sixth Sitting, col.231 to 232.

[3] *Hansard* (House of Lords), 22 July 2013, Vol.747, col.1073 (Earl Howe).

[4] *Hansard* (House of Lords), 22 July 2013, Vol.747, col.1072 (Earl Howe).

[5] Local Government Association, *Funding Outlook for Councils From 2010/11 to 2019/20: Preliminary Modelling* (2012).

[6] *Hansard* (House of Lords), 14 October 2013, Vol.748, col.300.

"'Forced' is a funny word in this context. For most people who go into a home, selling their house is the sensible thing to do to fund the cost of care. You do not want to leave the house empty; that benefits nobody. It does not provide housing for anybody; the house starts to crumble and is worth less to you and your family, so you had best sell it and get something that is more suitable. However, the deferred payment scheme is so important because there are people for whom that is not true. For example, some people want their families to live in their house and therefore cannot get cash for it. That is why we have a deferred payment scheme. 'Forced' suggests that this is something dreadful in all cases, when in fact it is dreadful in some cases. It is absolutely right, as I said before, that we have such a scheme for some cases but not for all cases."[1]

In response the Government confirmed that the 40,000 figure—which should have been "up to 40,000"—was a Government figure which had been arrived at as its best estimate of people who could benefit from the deferred payment arrangements.[2]

A NATIONAL MODEL SCHEME

1–374   At Committee stage in the House of Lords there was an attempt to force the Government to design a model scheme in an attempt to avoid the new scheme becoming "a new kind of national lottery" and save local authorities costs in having to work out the details of their own scheme. As Lord Warner argued:

"The worst of all worlds would be not to take hold of this issue and leave it to the market-place of 152 without guidance or assistance with compatibility of IT and issues of that kind."[3]

In response, the Government stated that its intention was to provide for a "uniform approach to the essentials of the scheme", namely criteria for payments in national regulations over who qualifies and what fees they can defer, and a consistent policy on interest and charges.[4]

At report stage, Lord Hunt tabled a similar amendment to require the Secretary of State to make available to all local authorities a model deferred payment scheme, and all authorities must follow this model unless they can show due cause not to.[5] In response the Government said that a model scheme already existed for local authorities and it intended to build on and improve this scheme in partnership with local authorities. Moreover, this will be reinforced by statutory guidance on deferred payments which will have "a clear legal status".[6] The opposition lost the vote on this amendment by a majority of 63 votes.[7]

In the House of Commons during Committee stage the Government repeated its intention that the guidance will set out that local authorities should use the model scheme, unless there is good cause not to use it.[8] It also rejected an amendment to create a national body, underwritten by central government, to arrange deferred payments and loans. It was intended that this body would work in a way similar to the Student Loans Company and that local authorities would have a power to delegate their functions relating to s.34, to this body. The Government argued that such a body would create an "additional layer of bureaucracy", be stressful for the individual and their family to deal with, lead to delays and be costly to set up. It also pointed out that under s.79 local authorities already have

---

[1] *Hansard* (House of Lords), 14 October 2013, Vol.748, col.300.
[2] *Hansard* (House of Lords), 14 October 2013, Vol.748, col.305.
[3] *Hansard* (House of Lords), 22 July 2013, Vol.747, col.1065 (Lord Warner).
[4] *Hansard* (House of Lords), 22 July 2013, Vol.747, col.1074 (Earl Howe).
[5] *Hansard* (House of Lords), 14 October 2013, Vol.748, cols 302 to 303.
[6] *Hansard* (House of Lords), 14 October 2013, Vol.748, cols 306 to 307.
[7] *Hansard* (House of Lords), 14 October 2013, Vol.748, cols 308 to 312.
[8] *Hansard* (House of Commons: Public Bill Committee), 16 January 2014 (PM): Sixth Sitting, col.235 (Norman Lamb MP).

a power to delegate their functions, including deferred payment agreements, which would allow for a range of options in respect of the administration of deferred payments:

"[Section 79] does not force a national body that is remote from local conditions and lacking in local knowledge to make decisions that it is ill equipped to make. Instead, it allows local authorities to combine their collective resources and offer a regional solution that is tailored to local conditions and that allows the administrative burden to be shared."[1]

FINANCIAL ADVICE

The Joint Committee on the draft Care and Support Bill noted that a deferred payment is **1–375** potentially a complex agreement, especially for adults in a vulnerable position. It argued that adults should not enter into such an agreement without financial advice, and noted arguments that the local authority may face a conflict of interest in providing such advice about a financial product for which it is responsible while at the same time being responsible for the person's care and support needs. The Joint Committee stated that its other recommendation to ensure that the adult is informed of the importance of independent financial advice from an adviser regulated by the Financial Services Authority, and how to obtain it, was of particular importance in the case of deferred payment agreements.[2] The Government accepted the overall argument about the importance of ensuring access to financial information and advice, and revised s.4 to make this clear. It also stated that guidance "will emphasise the importance of access to an independent, regulated financial advice for anybody considering the deferred payment arrangements".[3]

The statutory guidance discusses providing information and advice on deferred payments at paras 9.19 to 9.31. Amongst other matters, the guidance sets out the minimum information that a local authority must provide to a person who may benefit from or is eligible for a deferred payment agreement. This includes suggesting that the person "may want to consider taking independent financial advice (including flagging the existence of regulated financial advice".[4]

The Government's approach to ensuring independent financial advice is set out in more detail at para.1–047 above.

Deferred payment agreements and loans

34.—(1) Regulations may, in such cases or circumstances and subject to such **1–376** conditions as may be specified, require or permit a local authority to enter into a deferred payment agreement with an adult.

(2) A "deferred payment agreement" is an agreement under which a local authority agrees not to require until the specified time either or both of the following—

(a) the payment of the specified part of the amounts due from an adult to the authority under such provision of this Part or of regulations under this Part as is specified in regulations;

(b) the repayment of the specified part of a loan made under the agreement by the authority to an adult for the purpose of assisting the adult to obtain the provision of care and support for the adult.

---

[1] *Hansard* (House of Commons: Public Bill Committee), 4 February 2014: Fifteenth Sitting, col.606 (Norman Lamb MP).

[2] House of Lords House of Commons Joint Committee on the Draft Care and Support Bill, *Draft Care and Support Bill Report—Session 2012–13*, paras 197 to 198.

[3] Department of Health, *The Care Bill explained—including a response to consultation and pre-legislative scrutiny on the draft Care and Support Bill* (2013), p.61.

[4] Department of Health, *Care and Support Statutory Guidance* (2014), para.9.26.

(3) The care and support mentioned in subsection (2)(b) includes care and support the provision of which—

(a) the authority does not consider to be necessary to meet the adult's needs;

(b) is in addition to care and support which is being provided, arranged for, or paid for (in whole or in part) by the authority.

(4) Regulations under subsection (1) may, in particular, prohibit a local authority from entering into, or permit it to refuse to enter into, a deferred payment agreement unless it obtains adequate security for the payment of the adult's deferred amount.

(5) Regulations may specify what constitutes adequate security for the purposes of subsection (4); they may, for example, specify—

(a) an obligation on the adult to give the authority a charge over the adult's legal or beneficial interest in the property which the adult occupies as his or her only or main residence (or in a property which the adult used to occupy as such) to secure payment of the adult's deferred amount;

(b) a guarantee from another person to pay the adult's deferred amount.

(6) A reference in this section or section 35 to an adult's deferred amount, in relation to a deferred payment agreement, is a reference to the amount of which the local authority agrees not to require payment or repayment until the specified time.

(7) "Specified", in relation to a time or a part of an amount or loan, means specified in or determined in accordance with regulations; and the specified part of an amount or loan may be 100%.

(8) This section applies in relation to an agreement under which a local authority agrees to make a loan to an adult for the purpose of assisting the adult to obtain the provision of care and support for the adult as it applies in relation to a deferred payment agreement; and for that purpose—

(a) the reference in subsection (3) to subsection (2)(b) is to be read as a reference to this subsection; and

(b) the references in subsections (4) and (5) to payment of the adult's deferred amount are to be read as references to repayment of the loan.

GENERAL NOTE

1–377   Section 34 enables the Secretary of State to make regulations concerning deferred payments and loans. As noted above, deferred payments are local authority loans secured against the value of a person's home and repayable when the home is sold, often after the person has died. The relevant regulations are the Care and Support (Deferred Payment) Regulations 2014 (SI 2014/2671). They are reproduced in full and discussed further in paras A1–111 to A–122 below.

How long can the deferred payment last?

1–378   Regulation 7 of the Care and Support (Deferred Payment) Regulations 2014 (SI 2014/2671) makes provision as to the time for repayment of the deferred amount—see para.A1–130 below. Deferred payments can be arranged for different periods of time depending on the person's circumstances. Many of the existing arrangements are short-term. Some people will arrange the deferred payment in order to make decisions and financial or practical arrangements following the move into residential care, especially if the move is sudden or the person lacks capacity. For example, as Lord Lipsey put it during the passage of the Care Bill through the House of Lords:

"It would also give the old person, who might initially have said, "Well, maybe I might return home one day", time to come to terms with the fact that that may not be so. That can take a bit of time—and some people, miraculously, can return home."[1]

This breathing space can also be achieved by treating the move as temporary (at least initially) and by the 12-week property disregard rule. The treatment of property is discussed at para.1–152 below.

A deferred payment may be made to enable a person to sell their home, in order to give them time to arrange the sale and to achieve a fair price, as well as to take care of property and possessions. For some, the deferred payment may be for a longer period of time to enable the person to retain ownership of their home during their lifetime.

RELATIONSHIP WITH THE CAP ON CARE COSTS

Taking out a deferred payment will not affect adversely a person's progress towards the **1–379** cap on care costs (due to be implemented in April 2020). People will progress towards the cap at the same rate, whether or not they have a deferred payment. Any amount that people defer will count as personal debt for the purposes of the financial assessment and all things being equal they will qualify for financial support at the same time as someone who pays directly for their care.

This was further explained by the Government during the passage of the Care Bill through the House of Commons:

"Deferred payment agreements do not have any relation to how much a person is expected to contribute towards the cost of their care and nor will they necessarily have any relation to the rate at which a person meters towards the cap. Instead deferred payment agreements are a mechanism that people can choose to use—if they wish to do so—to pay for their care costs. The method by which a person chooses to pay should not affect how much they are expected to pay before they reach the cap. I do not believe that people should meter towards the cap faster if they choose to pay through a deferred payment agreement than people who choose to pay, for example, through an immediate needs annuity, an insurance policy or, indeed, by selling their home."[2]

Subsection (1)

This provides that the Government may make regulations which specify when a local **1–380** authority may or must offer someone a deferred payment or loan. The Care and Support (Deferred Payment) Regulations 2014 (SI 2014/2671), in general terms, require a local authority to enter into a deferred payment agreement if:

- the adult's needs for care and support are being met by the provision of accommodation in a care home, or if the local authority had been asked to meet the person's needs, it would have provided care home accommodation;
- the person's home has not been disregarded for the purposes of the financial assessment because for instance it is occupied by a spouse of dependent relative;
- the adults assets are £23,250 or less, excluding the value of their home;
- the local authority has obtained adequate security for the payment of the deferred amount; and
- the adult agrees to the agreement.

In effect, people who qualify for state support during the 12 week disregard period will also be entitled to a deferred payment, available to start from the thirteenth week. Those who do not qualify will be those who could choose to remain in their own home and

---

[1] *Hansard* (House of Lords), 29 October 2013, Vol.748, col.1472.
[2] *Hansard* (House of Commons: Public Bill Committee), 16 January 2014 (PM): Sixth Sitting, cols 235 to 236 (Norman Lamb MP).

those with significant levels of non-housing assets, who according to the Government should have other financial options than a deferred payment.[1]

The regulations also provide that, in general terms, a local authority may enter into a deferred payment agreement if:

- the adult's needs for care and support are being met by the provision of accommodation in care home or supported living accommodation, or if the local authority had been asked to meet the person's needs, it would have provided such accommodation;
- the local authority has obtained adequate security for the payment of the deferred amount; and
- the adult agrees to the agreement.

If a person lacks capacity to request a deferred payment, the statutory guidance advises that a deputy appointed by the Court of Protection or attorney appointed by an enduring or lasting power of attorney may request it on the person's behalf. The local authority should where appropriate provide information about deputyship, legal powers of attorney and advocacy, and confirm what would happen if a person were to lose capacity and had not made their own arrangements.[2]

Local authorities will need to comply with relevant consumer protection legislation and guidance when offering deferred payments, such as the *Unfair terms in consumer contracts regulations*,[3] *Mortgage Sales Guidance for local authorities and registered social landlords*[4] and Consumer Credit Act 1974 in addition to the regulations and guidance which are published under the Care Act.

Lord Lipsey, during the passage of the Care Bill through the House of Lords, was critical of the £23,250 threshold arguing that "most people who have reasonably valuable houses, who are the people most likely to want to adopt this measure, will have far more than £23,250 worth of other assets". Such people will be forced to spend down until they have reached this threshold.[5] In support, Lord Warner confirmed that the Commission on Funding Care and Support had not supported this threshold, and had in fact concluded that it should be a full universal offer across the country.[6] The Government responded that it was consulting on the threshold, but pointed out that there would be a power for local authorities to offer deferred payments more widely.[7] Summing up the debate, Lord Lipsey noted that the consultation said that deferred payments would only be available to people who have "slightly more savings" than £23,250 and said that:

"This Bill does not provide a universal deferred payments scheme. It provides a deferred payments scheme only for people who have less than £23,250 in assets. There is no universal deferred payments scheme. Further, this has been done in a back-door manner which disgraces the Government. It was not in Dilnot. We have heard decisive testimony on that from my noble friend Lord Warner. It was not in the Government's announcement of their response to Dilnot. It was not in the Second Reading speeches. It came out between stages of the Bill in this consultation document."[8]

---

[1] Department of Health, *Caring for our future: Consultation on reforming what and how people pay for their care and support* (2013), paras 151 and 153.
[2] Department of Health, *Care and Support Statutory Guidance* (2014), paras 9.24 to 9.25.
[3] Office of Fair Trading, *Unfair Contract Terms Guidance: Guidance for the Unfair Terms in Consumer Contracts Regulations 1999* (September 2008), OFT 311.
[4] Office of the Deputy Prime Minister, Mortgage Sales Guidance for Local Authorities and Registered Social Landlords (November 2005).
[5] *Hansard* (House of Lords), 14 October 2013, Vol.748, col.301.
[6] *Hansard* (House of Lords), 14 October 2013, Vol.748, col.303.
[7] *Hansard* (House of Lords), 14 October 2013, Vol.748, col.305 (Earl Howe).
[8] *Hansard* (House of Lords), 14 October 2013, Vol.748, cols 307 to 308.

The House of Lords also debated this matter at Third Reading. Again Lord Lipsey contended that the threshold would exclude people on middle incomes—the very people that the scheme is intended for. It was also argued that the £23,250 threshold appears to have been determined by reference to the present upper limit for getting help under the means test, but under the new funding system this would be increased to £118,000. It was argued that this would be a more appropriate threshold. The Government agreed to review the threshold and consider increasing it to £118,000 as part of its consultation.[1]

In the House of Commons the opposition party also targeted the £23,250 threshold arguing that it will prevent almost half of those who would otherwise have been able to take advantage of the scheme from accessing it.[2] During Committee stage it was argued that the threshold would prevent the scheme from being universal.[3] The Government rejected this by arguing that deferred payments are intended to target those who need most support and should not be available for anyone, "even those with assets of great monetary value in addition to their main home".[4]

In its consultation on the funding reforms the Government confirmed its policy of retaining the £23,250 threshold, but to give local authorities discretion to give deferred payments if someone has slightly more savings and would qualify soon.[5] This has been implemented by regs.2 and 3 of the Care and Support (Deferred Payment) Regulations 2014 (SI 2014/2671)—see paras A1–113 to A1–114 below.

Subsection (2)

A deferred payment agreement is defined as an agreement where the sum or part of the **1–381** sum owed to the local authority does not have to be repaid until a specified time.

The Government's intention is that people will be able to defer the full costs of their residential care and accommodation, up to the equity in their home (plus other assets). The deferred payment will cover the cost of any registered care home the person might want to choose.[6]

In the House of Lords an amendment by Lord Lipsey attempted to make loans available not only for care home fees but to purchase care annuities which might cover hotel costs and the excess over what a local authority is prepared to pay for the person.[7] The Government argued this was unnecessary since the insurance market already offers such a mechanism through the use of equity release to purchase a care annuity.[8]

Subsection (3)

This subsection confirms that a deferred payment agreement may include services that **1–382** are not necessary to meet someone's needs. The explanatory notes state that examples include preventive or extra services which may be in addition to the care and support the authority is providing.[9]

Subsections (4) and (5)

These subsections allow regulations to be made as to whether a local authority must **1–383** have, and if so what will constitute, security for the deferred payment. Adequate security

---

[1] *Hansard* (House of Lords), 29 October 2013, Vol.748, cols 1470 to 1475.

[2] *Hansard* (House of Commons), 16 December 2013, Vol.572, col.502 (Andy Burham MP).

[3] *Hansard* (House of Commons: Public Bill Committee), 16 January 2014 (PM): Sixth Sitting, col.230 (Liz Kendall MP).

[4] *Hansard* (House of Commons: Public Bill Committee), 16 January 2014 (PM): Sixth Sitting, col.236 (Norman Lamb MP).

[5] Department of Health, *Caring for our future: Consultation on reforming what and how people pay for their care and support* (2013), paras 150 to 154.

[6] Department of Health, *Caring for our future: Consultation on reforming what and how people pay for their care and support* (2013), para.158.

[7] *Hansard* (House of Lords), 22 July 2013, Vol.747, col.1064.

[8] *Hansard* (House of Lords), 22 July 2013, Vol.747, cols 1070 to 1071 (Earl Howe).

[9] Care Act 2014: Explanatory Notes para.225.

may include a charge on the individual's property or a guarantee from a third party. Regulation 4 of the Care and Support (Deferred Payment) Regulations 2014 (SI 2014/ 2671) makes such provision.

In the House of Lords, Lord Lipsey attempted to amend section 34 to prevent the use of third-party guarantees on the loans as well as their being secured against the value of the home. His Lordship explained:

> "That is belt and braces and I do not see why families should be providing braces when there is a perfectly good belt in place. It would particularly apply when the deferred payment is secured on where somebody else—perhaps the old person's son or daughter— lives. At the moment, case law provides that a local authority cannot in those circumstances force the sale of a property in order to redeem a mortgage on that property when somebody else lives there. However, if a guarantee was sought from the co-owner, the guarantor could be in a position where they are expected to repay the individual's care costs based on an unrealisable value of half of the property they live in. This provision may put off people who would otherwise have taken advantage of the scheme and I ask the Minister to look at it again."[1]

In response, the Government's stated that its guiding principle was that as many people as possible should benefit from deferred payments. In order to make deferred payments available widely such a provision was needed in order to cater for situations in which a local authority cannot secure its debt through a legal charge on the property, for example:

> ". . . when a charge cannot be secured by registration with the Land Registry or where there is reasonable doubt about the person's ability to afford the care home of their choice over the longer term".[2]

It was argued that in such cases it is necessary to allow for constructive ways forward which might include "a different form of guarantee such as a solicitor's agreement or the involvement of a third party".[3]

1–384   REPAYMENT.   Debt recovery could be used after a deferred payment had ended and the resident or estate is not taking steps to repay the amount owed to the local authority. For those who do choose to repay from their estate, the Government has suggested that authorities should wait for up to three months after someone has died before actively seeking repayment, allowing everyone time to settle their affairs.[4]

The Care Act contains general powers to recover debts but these cannot be used where an authority could enter into a deferred payment agreement, unless the authority offers someone this option and they refuse (see s.69(2)). Annex D of the statutory guidance covers debt recovery.

Subsection (6)

1–385   A "deferred amount" is the amount which the adult does not have to repay until the time specified or determined in accordance with regulations.

Subsection (7)

1–386   This subsection was amended during the passage of the Care Bill to make clear that deferred payments, whether they are deferred charges or a deferred repayment of a loan, can either be paid back in whole or in part.[5]

---

[1] *Hansard* (House of Lords), 22 July 2013, Vol.747, col.1063 (Lord Lipsey).

[2] *Hansard* (House of Lords), 22 July 2013, Vol.747, col.1070 (Earl Howe).

[3] *Hansard* (House of Lords), 22 July 2013, Vol.747, col.1070 (Earl Howe).

[4] Department of Health, *Caring for our future: Consultation on reforming what and how people pay for their care and support* (2013), para.168.

[5] *Hansard* (House of Lords), 7 May 2014, Vol.753, col.1478 (Earl Howe).

Section 34 applies to a loan—other than a deferred payment agreement—which a local **1–387** authority agrees to make to an adult to assist them to obtain care and support in relation to a deferred payment. The explanatory notes state that the loan may be for "care and support other than that which the authority considers is necessary for the purposes of meeting needs, for example preventive or extra services".[1]

Deferred payment agreements and loans: further provision

35.—(1) Regulations may require or permit a local authority to charge—   **1–388**
(a) interest on an adult's deferred amount;
(b) such amount relating to the authority's administrative costs as is specified in or determined in accordance with the regulations;
(c) interest on an amount charged under paragraph (b).

(2) The regulations may specify costs which are, or which are not, to be regarded as administrative costs for the purposes of subsection (1)(b).

(3) The regulations may—
(a) require or permit adequate security to be obtained for the payment of any interest or other amount referred to in subsection (1);
(b) require or permit any such interest or other amount to be treated in the same way as the adult's deferred amount;
(c) specify what constitutes adequate security for the purposes of paragraph (a).

(4) The authority may not charge interest under regulations made under subsection (1) or under a deferred payment agreement at a rate that exceeds the rate specified in or determined in accordance with the regulations; the regulations may, for example, provide for a rate to be determined by reference to a specified interest rate or other specified criterion.

(5) The regulations must enable the adult to terminate a deferred payment agreement by—
(a) giving the authority notice, and
(b) paying the authority the full amount for which the adult is liable with respect to the adult's deferred amount and any interest or other amount charged under regulations made under subsection (1) or under the agreement.

(6) The regulations may make other provision about the duration of a deferred payment agreement and for its termination by either party.

(7) The regulations may make provision as to the rights and obligations of the authority and the adult where the adult disposes of any legal or beneficial interest in a property to which a deferred payment agreement relates and acquires a legal or beneficial interest in another property (whether or not it is in the area of that authority); they may, for example, make provision—
(a) for the authority not to require payment of the amounts referred to in subsection (5)(b) until the time specified in or determined in accordance with the regulations;
(b) for the adult to give the authority a charge over the adult's legal or beneficial interest in the other property.

(8) The regulations may—
(a) require or permit terms or conditions of a specified description, or in a specified form, to be included in a deferred payment agreement;

---

[1] Care Act 2014: Explanatory Notes para.228.

(b) permit such other terms or conditions as the authority considers appropriate to be included in such an agreement;

(c) require statements or other information relating to specified matters, or in a specified form, to be included in such an agreement.

(9) The regulations may make provision for the purpose of enabling local authorities to protect (for example, by registration) or enforce security obtained for the payment of the adult's deferred amount or the payment of any interest or other amount referred to in subsection (1); and, for that purpose, the regulations may amend, repeal, or revoke an enactment, or provide for an enactment to apply with specified modifications.

(10) This section applies in relation to an agreement of the kind mentioned in section 34(8) as it applies in relation to a deferred payment agreement; and for that purpose—

(a) the references in subsections (1), (3) and (5) to the adult's deferred amount are to be read as references to the loan; and

(b) the reference in subsection (9) to payment of the adult's deferred amount is to be read as a reference to repayment of the loan.

GENERAL NOTE

1–389 This section contains further provisions concerning conditions associated with deferred payments, including interest and administration charges, which may be imposed by regulations made under s.34(1). As noted previously in para.1–371 above, the inability to charge interest was perceived to be one of the reasons why the scheme had not been implemented fully across the country.

The relevant regulations are the Care and Support (Deferred Payment) Regulations 2014 (SI 2014/2671). They are reproduced in full and discussed further in paras A1–111 to A1–122 below.

Subsection (1)

1–390 Regulations may require or allow authorities to charge interest upon a deferred sum, an amount to cover their administrative costs and interest on those costs. Regulations 9 and 10 of the Care and Support (Deferred Payment) Regulations 2014 (SI 2014/2671) make such provision.

1–391 INTEREST. During the passage of the Care Bill, in the House of Commons, the opposition party was critical of the ability to charge interest. It claimed that a loan to cover the average length of stay in a care home—two and a half years—would generate extra costs of £3,500 in interest alone. It was also pointed out that interest would not be included in the cap on care costs but would be outside it.

1–392 ADMINISTRATION FEE. Regulation 10 of the of the Care and Support (Deferred Payment) Regulations 2014 (SI 2014/2671) enables local authorities to charge an administration fee to cover the costs of offering a deferred payment—see para.A1–121 below. This can cover, for example, the costs associated with placing a charge on a property to secure the debt. The fee could potentially be added to the deferred payment.

The Joint Committee felt that it was excessive that the adult should pay interest on administrative costs, some of which may have been incurred many years previously and recommended that this provision should be removed.[1] The Government, however, argued that individuals should have the option of paying an upfront administrative fee or deferring it so it is repaid later with the rest of the payment, and in the case of the latter, it is

---

[1] House of Lords House of Commons Joint Committee on the Draft Care and Support Bill, *Draft Care and Support Bill Report, Session 2012–13*, para.199.

"reasonable to charge interest on the deferred amount so the authority does not make a loss over time". Moreover, the Government argued that "it will make a very small difference to what someone pays while ensuring overall fairness".[1]

Concerns were raised in the House of Lords that some local authorities may want to raise charges for administrative costs while others might not, leading to a lack of national uniformity. In reply the Government stated its intention that there will be uniformity on such matters.[2]

Subsection (2)

The regulations can specify what costs are administration costs—for example the cost to **1–393** a local authority of registering a charge at the Land Registry.[3] See reg.10(3) and (4) of the Care and Support (Deferred Payment) Regulations 2014 (SI 2014/2671).

Subsection (3)

This enables regulations to be made to allow or require a local authority to add any **1–394** interest or administrative costs to the charges or loan and obtain and specify what will constitute adequate security for the same. See regs 4 and 10 of the Care and Support (Deferred Payment) Regulations 2014 (SI 2014/2671).

Subsection (4)

A local authority may not charge interest at a rate which is higher than any rate specified **1–395** in regulations. See reg.9 of the Care and Support (Deferred Payment) Regulations 2014 (SI 2014/2671).

Subsection (5)

Regulations must be made to permit an adult to terminate the agreement before the date **1–396** or occurrence of the event specified in the agreement by giving notice and repaying the sum in full to the authority. See reg.8 of the Care and Support (Deferred Payment) Regulations 2014 (SI 2014/2671).

Subsection (6)

Regulations may make other provision about the duration or termination of the agree- **1–397** ment. See for instance reg.7 of the Care and Support (Deferred Payment) Regulations 2014 (SI 2014/2671).

Subsection (7)

Regulations can be made to address what may happen in a situation where somebody **1–398** sells or otherwise disposes of property. The explanatory notes state that this might apply:

"For example in a case where the agreement provides that it must be repaid when an adult sells their home, regulations might allow the deferred payment agreement to continue rather than to be repaid in cases where a property is sold in order that a new property can be bought as a home for the adult or the adult's partner and that new home can be used as security for the agreement.[4]

Subsection (8)

Regulations may require local authorities to include terms and conditions of a specified **1–399** type in a deferred payment agreement. The explanatory notes state that this is intended:

---

[1] Department of Health, *The Care Bill explained—including a response to consultation and pre-legislative scrutiny on the draft Care and Support Bill*, para.91.
[2] *Hansard* (House of Lords), 22 July 2013, Vol.747, col.1070.
[3] Care Act 2014: Explanatory Notes para.231.
[4] Care Act 2014: Explanatory Notes para.237.

". . . to allow local authorities to include such terms and conditions and others which they think are appropriate and to require statements relating to specified matters or in a specified form to be included in the agreement. Regulations under this subsection may provide, for example, that the agreement must contain a term which entitles the adult to receive an annual statement showing the amount they owe under the agreement."[1]

See reg.11 of the Care and Support (Deferred Payment) Regulations 2014 (SI 2014/2671).

Subsection (9)

1–400   This allows regulations to be made to enable a local authority to protect or enforce the security it has obtained for the payment of the deferred amount or loan, and for this purpose to make necessary amendments to other legislation. Regulations under this subsection can include provision that amends or repeals a provision of an Act of Parliament, and such regulations are subject to the affirmative resolution procedure in Parliament by virtue of s.125(4)(e). The affirmative procedure is discussed at para.1–161 above.

Subsection (10)

1–401   This clarifies that s.35 also applies to loan agreements.

Alternative financial arrangements

1–402   **36.**—(1) Regulations may, in such cases or circumstances and subject to such conditions as may be specified, require or permit a local authority to enter into alternative financial arrangements of a specified description with an adult.

(2) "Alternative financial arrangements" means arrangements which in the Secretary of State's opinion—

(a) equate in substance to a deferred payment agreement or an agreement of the kind mentioned in section 34(8), but

(b) achieve a similar effect to an agreement of the kind in question without including provision for the payment of interest.

(3) The regulations may make provision in connection with alternative financial arrangements to which they apply, including, in particular, provision of the kind that may (or must) be made in regulations under section 34 or 35 (apart from provision for the payment of interest).

GENERAL NOTE

1–403   Section 36 was introduced as a Government amendment during the Committee stage in the House of Lords. It enables regulations to be made to allow local authorities to make alternative arrangements for people who would not wish to have a deferred payment because of their religious objection to paying interest. The Islamic Bank of Britain provided assistance with the amendment.[2]

However, the Government consultation on the draft regulations and guidance under the Care Act produced mixed responses to the question of whether to develop a "Sharia law-compliant" deferred payment scheme:

"A number of responses voiced concerns over fairness and equity, fearing that the Sharia scheme might be more generous than the core scheme. Others questioned the place of Sharia law in the British legal system, while others still pointed out that there might be other products available for those wishing to pay for care in a Sharia-compliant way. Those supportive of introducing a Sharia-compliant scheme in the future largely

---

[1] Care Act 2014: Explanatory Notes para.238.
[2] *Hansard* (House of Lords), 22 July 2013, Vol.747, col.1070 (Earl Howe).

highlighted the desirability of offering the same protection from having to sell one's home to pay for care to everyone."[1]

The Government has therefore announced that it intends to conduct further research with the Muslim community to assess whether there is a demand for such a scheme and take a decision subsequently.[2]

Subsection (1)

This provides the regulation making power for "alternative financial arrangements". **1–404**

Subsection (2)

According to the explanatory notes, this subsection defines an alternative financial **1–405** arrangement as "one which is in essence the same as a deferred payment (as set out in s.34) and that achieves a similar effect without charging interest".[3]

Subsection (3)

This enables regulations to be made for alternative financial arrangements. The intention **1–406** is to enable such regulations to be made in relation to any issue on which it is possible to make deferred payment regulations, except for the charging of interest.[4] Regulations under this subsection may include provision that amends or repeals a provision of an Act of Parliament. Any such regulations are subject to the affirmative resolution procedure in Parliament by virtue of s.125(4)(e). The affirmative procedure is discussed at para.1–161 above.

CONTINUITY OF CARE AND SUPPORT WHEN ADULT MOVES

Continuity of care and support (also known as portability) refers to the ability of disabled **1–407** people and carers to ensure that their needs continue to be met when they move between local authority areas. The difficulties that many disabled people faced in this respect were described by Baroness Campbell, an independent peer and disability rights campaigner, during the Parliamentary debates on the Health and Social Care Bill 2007–08[5] :

"Currently, if a disabled person moves out of their local authority area they must give up whatever payments or services they are receiving and start again from scratch to negotiate a new package with the new local authority. This necessitates a costly re-assessment even if the person's needs have not changed. Needless to say, this presents a huge bureaucratic cost to the local authority and, at the same time, causes frustration and stress to the service user."[6]

In effect, the law was seen to impede service users' freedom of movement by failing to guarantee the continuity of their care package. Baroness Campbell went on to describe the impact that this has:

"As well as putting lives and mental well-being at risk, the absence of a right to portable support has a negative impact on employment opportunities. There is little point applying for a job in another part of the country unless you know that you can relocate in the sure knowledge that your support will be ready and waiting. It is stressful enough applying for a new job without knowing whether you will be able to get out of bed to get there.

---

[1] Department of Health, *Response to the Consultation on draft Regulations and Guidance for Implementation of Part 1 of the Care Act 2014* (2014) Cm 8955, p.28.

[2] Department of Health, *Response to the Consultation on draft Regulations and Guidance for Implementation of Part 1 of the Care Act 2014* (2014) Cm 8955, p.28.

[3] Care Act 2014: Explanatory Notes para.242.

[4] Care Act 2014: Explanatory Notes para.243.

[5] Which became the Health and Social Care Act 2008.

[6] *Hansard* (House of Lords), 22 May 2008, Vol.701, col.GC641.

It also has an extremely negative impact on family life. Many disabled and older people provide support to other relatives, but are prevented from moving closer to them because of this fundamental flaw in the system. The same case can be made for moving to areas where housing may be more affordable in retirement. We are all told to move, but if your portable support is not with you, then you cannot."[1]

Baroness Campbell argued that this situation means that many disabled people become "a prisoner of one's local authority, unable to enjoy the same social and economic mobility and freedom of movement as our non-disabled counterparts".[2]

There have been a number of failed attempts in Parliament to introduce a right to continuity of care. For example, Lord Kilmarnock tabled an amendment to the National Health Service and Community Care Bill 1988–89[3] to provide that, once a service user has moved, their existing assessment should apply in the new authority until that authority carries out a new assessment.[4] This amendment was later revised to include a period of 28 days in default of the new assessment.[5] The Government rejected both amendments.

Baroness Campbell attempted to amend the Health and Social Care Bill 2007–08 to give service users who are moving areas a right, for a transitional period, to "equivalent" services or direct payments to cover their needs before they undergo an assessment in the new authority.[6] Under this amendment, the original authority would be under a duty to give notice to the new authority if it became aware that a service user intended to become ordinarily resident in the new authority's area, and the original authority would retain responsibility for funding the individual's care needs for a prescribed period. The Government rejected this amendment.

Baroness Campbell also sponsored two Private Members Bills, the Social Care Portability Bill 2010–12 and 2012–13, which both received a first reading in the House of Lords, but failed to progress any further. They attempted to provide that on receipt of a notice from the first local authority that a service user was moving into its area, the second authority would be required to put in place an "equivalent" care package to that which was already in place for a limited period. Until the new care package was in place, the first authority would be responsible for the funding of the care package (subject to reimbursement).

1–408 One of the most challenging issues in securing rights to continuity of care and support is the extent to which an existing package of care and support services should be guaranteed when a person moves. For instance, it would be possible—at least in theory—to require the same or an equivalent level of services to be provided indefinitely or for a limited period of time when the person moves. The Law Commission doubted that any system could obviate entirely the need for a re-assessment when a service user moves areas since the very fact of moving may alter a person's needs and indeed this may be the very reason for the move (for example, the individual may be moving in order to be closer to their family). Furthermore the same package of care and support cannot be guaranteed since, for example, certain services may be unavailable.[7]

The Law Commission's final report recommended several measures aimed at securing greater portability of assessments and services. These measures included an enhanced duty to co-operate that would apply to both the first and new local authority when the latter becomes aware that the person wishes to move areas. Also, if the new local authority decided to give a significantly different support package, the Commission recommended that it should be required to produce a clear and written explanation to the service user

[1] *Hansard* (House of Lords), 22 May 2008, Vol.701, cols GC641 to GC642.
[2] *Hansard* (House of Lords), 1 July 2008, Vol.703, col.153.
[3] Which became the National Health Service and Community Care Act 1990.
[4] *Hansard* (House of Lords), 18 June 1990, Vol.520, col.617.
[5] *Hansard* (House of Lords), 25 June 1990, Vol.520, cols 1377 to 1378.
[6] *Hansard* (House of Lords), 22 May 2008, Vol.701, col.GC640 and *Hansard* (House of Lords), 1 July 2008, Vol.703, col.152.
[7] Law Commission, *Adult Social Care: A Consultation Paper*, Consultation Paper No.192 (2010), paras 8.37 to 8.40.

and where appropriate their carer. Finally, it recommended that the Secretary of State should have powers to make regulations requiring that when service users move from one authority to another, the new authority must provide the person with equivalent services or direct payments to those provided by the original authority to cover their support needs until they have undergone an assessment in the new authority. The aim was to remove any incentive on the new authority to delay an assessment so as to delay the provision of services and direct payments. It would be left to Government to decide, as a matter of policy, whether or not to introduce this provision.[1]

The Government's response accepted the proposed duty to co-operate and the principle that "an individual should have the ability to choose where they want to live and move between places without fear of losing the care and support they need". It proposed that a "portability duty" would apply up until the point that the new authority has carried out an assessment and put in place care and support to meet eligible needs. It did not, however, want to require that the same or equivalent services must be provided after the person has moved, since the same type of service may not always be available locally.[2] The draft Care and Support Bill provided that if a "sending" local authority was satisfied that the adult genuinely intends to move, the "receiving" authority must carry out an assessment of the person's care and support needs and provide care and support accordingly. If the receiving authority did not carry out the assessment before the person arrives in the new area, it must provide care and support based on the care and support plan of the sending authority until it is able to carry out its own assessment. The aim was therefore to ensure that assessment takes place as a matter of course upon a person's decision to move rather than guarantee a portable package of care.[3]

The Joint Committee criticised the use of the terms "sending authority" and "receiving authority" in the draft Bill which it felt reinforced a paternalistic culture whereby local authorities "behave as if they have some sort of control over where people in need of support should live". It argued that "in principle, people have a right to live where they choose" and decisions about where to live are separate from decisions about which body funds a care package.[4] The Government accepted this and agreed to revise the language in the relevant clauses to refer to "first" and "second" authorities.[5]

The Joint Committee accepted that after a move there should be continuity of care until a re-assessment takes place, and rejected suggestions that the first authority should remain responsible for funding the service user as long as they are eligible for support. However the Committee suggested that the Government might wish to consider whether there should be guidance on the minimum period during which an original assessment should be protected.[6] The Government accepted the Joint Committee's point, and stated that guidance will cover "the timings when both local authorities have to comply with the requirements on continuity of care", including the time frame in which the second authority has to undertake its assessment.[7]

Sections 37 to 38 of the Care Act set out the duties that local authorities are under when a service user (and potentially their carer) moves from one local authority area to another. In broad terms the new scheme is very similar to that contained in the draft Care and Support Bill (set out above). The provisions seek to ensure that service users can move between

---

[1] Law Commission, *Adult Social Care*, paras 10.15 to 10.22.

[2] Department of Health, *Reforming the Law for Adult Care and Support: The Government's Response to Law Commission Report 326 on Adult Social Care* (TSO, July 2012), Cm.8379, paras 10.5 to 10.8.

[3] Department of Health, *Draft Care and Support Bill* (TSO, July 2012) Cm.8386, pp.48 to 49 (cl.31).

[4] House of Lords House of Commons Joint Committee on the Draft Care and Support Bill, *Draft Care and Support Bill Report, Session 2012–13*, para.214.

[5] Department of Health, *The Care Bill explained—including a response to consultation and pre-legislative scrutiny on the draft Care and Support Bill*, para.93.

[6] House of Lords House of Commons Joint Committee on the Draft Care and Support Bill, *Draft Care and Support Bill Report, Session 2012–13*, paras 219 to 225.

[7] Department of Health, *The Care Bill explained—including a response to consultation and pre-legislative scrutiny on the draft Care and Support Bill*, p.72.

local authority areas with minimum interruption to their care. These sections also need to be read alongside the new national eligibility criteria (see s.13), which provide that if a person moves to another local authority area in England, they do so knowing that the same upper eligibility threshold will apply in the new area. This will assist continuity of care by removing local variation and providing that individuals in any part of the country are eligible for services at the level of "substantial" needs.

The continuity of care provisions are discussed mainly in Ch.20 of the statutory guidance. But they are also mentioned at para.7.29 (responsibility for providing advocacy when a person is moving), paras 17.49 to 17.54 (in respect of prisoners), and para.20.18 (the amendment of sight registers when a person moves).

Notification, assessment, etc.

1–409   **37.**—(1) This section applies where—
    (a) an adult's needs for care and support are being met by a local authority ("the first authority") under section 18 or 19,
    (b) the adult notifies another local authority ("the second authority") (or that authority is notified on the adult's behalf) that the adult intends to move to the area of the second authority, and
    (c) the second authority is satisfied that the adult's intention is genuine.
    (2) This section also applies where—
    (a) an adult is not having needs for care and support met under either of those sections but a local authority ("the first authority") is nonetheless keeping a care account in the adult's case,
    (b) the adult notifies another local authority ("the second authority") (or that authority is notified on the adult's behalf) that the adult intends to move to the area of the second authority, and
    (c) the second authority is satisfied that the adult's intention is genuine.
    (3) This section also applies where—
    (a) an adult's needs for care and support are being met by a local authority ("the first authority") under section 18 or 19 by the first authority arranging for the provision of accommodation in the area of another local authority ("the second authority"),
    (b) the adult notifies the second authority (or that authority is notified on the adult's behalf) that the adult intends to move out of that accommodation but to remain, and be provided with care and support at home or in the community, in its area, and
    (c) the second authority is satisfied that the adult's intention is genuine.
    (4) The second authority must—
    (a) provide the adult and, if the adult has or is proposing to have a carer, the carer with such information as it considers appropriate (in so far as it would not do so under section 4), and
    (b) notify the first authority that it is satisfied as mentioned in subsection (1)(c), (2)(c) or (3)(c).
    (5) The first authority, having received the notification under subsection (4)(b), must provide the second authority with—
    (a) a copy of any care and support plan prepared for the adult,
    (b) a copy of any independent personal budget prepared for the adult,
    (c) in a case within subsection (2), a copy of the most recent needs assessment in the adult's case,

(d) if the first authority has been keeping a care account in the adult's case, a copy of that account,

(e) if the adult has a carer and that carer is to continue as the adult's carer after the move, a copy of any support plan prepared for the carer, and

(f) such other information relating to the adult and, if the adult has a carer (whether or not one with needs for support), such other information relating to the carer as the second authority may request.

(6) The second authority must—

(a) assess whether the adult has needs for care and support and, if the adult does, what those needs are, and

(b) where the adult has or is proposing to have a carer and it is appropriate to do so, assess whether the carer has or is likely to have needs for support and, if the carer does or is likely to, what those needs are or are likely to be.

(7) In carrying out an assessment under subsection (6)(a) or (b), the second authority must have regard to the care and support plan provided under subsection (5)(a) or (as the case may be) the support plan provided under subsection (5)(e).

(8) This Part—

(a) applies to an assessment under subsection (6)(a) as it applies to a needs assessment, and

(b) applies to an assessment under subsection (6)(b) as it applies to a carer's assessment.

(9) Pending the adult's move, the first authority must keep in contact with the second authority in order to ascertain the progress that the second authority is making in preparing to meet—

(a) any needs for care and support under section 18 or 19 in the adult's case, and

(b) where the adult is proposing to have a carer immediately after the move, any needs for support under section 20 in the carer's case.

(10) The first authority must keep the adult (and, where applicable, the carer) informed about its contact under subsection (9) with the second authority and must involve the adult (and, where applicable, the carer) in the contact.

(11) Where the needs identified by an assessment under subsection (6)(a) carried out by the second authority are different from those specified in the care and support plan provided under subsection (5)(a), the second authority must provide a written explanation of the difference to—

(a) the adult,

(b) any carer that the adult has, if the adult asks the authority to do so, and

(c) any other person to whom the adult asks the authority to provide the explanation.

(12) Where the cost to the second authority of meeting the adult's eligible needs is different from the cost to the first authority of doing so, the second authority must provide a written explanation of the difference to—

(a) the adult,

(b) any carer that the adult has, if the adult asks the authority to do so, and

(c) any other person to whom the adult asks the authority to provide the explanation.

(13) Where the needs identified by an assessment under subsection (6)(b) carried out by the second authority are different from those in the support plan provided under subsection (5)(e), the second authority must provide a written explanation of the difference to—

(a) the carer,

(b) the adult needing care, if the carer asks the authority to do so, and

(c) any other person to whom the carer asks the authority to provide an explanation.

(14) Regulations may specify steps which a local authority must take for the purpose of being satisfied as mentioned in subsection (1)(c), (2)(c) or (3)(c).

(15) In this section—

(a) an adult's needs are "eligible needs" if they meet the eligibility criteria and are not being met by a carer,

(b) a reference to moving to an area is a reference to moving to that area with a view to becoming ordinarily resident there, and

(c) a reference to remaining in an area is a reference to remaining ordinarily resident there.

GENERAL NOTE

1–410 This section sets out the framework for continuity of care which applies when an adult service user intends to move from one local authority (the first authority) area to another (the second authority). In broad terms, s.37 provides that once the second authority has received a notification from the adult of their intention to move, it is obliged to carry out an assessment before the adult moves and take into account the first authority's care and support plan when doing so. The second authority must provide a written explanation if it assesses the person as having different needs to those identified in the first authority's care and support plan.

The continuity of care provisions apply only in respect of an adult with care and support needs. It does not apply independently to carers who wish to move. But where a person with care and support needs is moving, and their carer is also intending to move with them, the continuity of care provisions will apply to the carer in the same way as they do to the person with care and support needs. Where the person with care and support needs is not moving, but the carer is moving to another local authority, these provisions will not apply. The carer is still providing care in the original authority and that authority will continue to be responsible for meeting their needs.

During the passage of the Care Bill through Parliament, Baroness Campbell recognised that the greater part of her Social Care Portability Bill 2012–13 had been subsumed by the Care Act, but there was one "crucial difference", namely the right to an equivalent care package. Under her Bill, the first local authority must continue to provide services equivalent to the existing care package until a new care package was in place. As she described it:

"My Bill ensures that disabled people can move to another area, confident that they will receive the support they need to enable them to continue to play an active role in society. The manner in which the council meets those needs may be different because of the different configuration of local community and care services but it should not reduce choice and control, and the ability to achieve the outcomes they need."[1]

At report stage, Baroness Campbell said:

"Moving house is one of the most stressful days of your life. Let us give disabled people the confidence to move and, hopefully, improve their circumstances. To do that, they require three things: first, knowing that support is there; secondly, the knowledge about the process to reassure them during a time of potential anxiety; and, thirdly, the certainty that they can live their lives in the same way with the same outcomes in their new environment."[2]

---

[1] *Hansard* (House of Lords), 21 May 2013, Vol.745, col.758.

[2] *Hansard* (House of Lords), 14 October 2013, Vol.748, col.313.

Baroness Campbell's main concerns during the passage of the Care Bill through the House of Lords were the need to reference outcomes in the continuity provisions and the risk of a gap in provision of care and support. As a result of her pressure, amendments were made to this section (see subss.(9) and (10)). The Baroness also managed to secure from the Government a commitment to review of the continuity of care provisions after three years with the aim of understanding if the process can be improved.[1]

The statutory guidance emphasises that local authorities should provide service users and their carers with information and advice to help them to decide whether or not to move. As well as publicly available information, it states that local authorities should provide any extra information requested by the adult or their carer. It also warns that in providing information and advice, local authorities should guard against influence over the final decision whether or not to move (which is a matter for the adult and their carer).[2]

Subsections (1) to (3)

The continuity of care duties apply in three specific cases: **1–411**

1. when an adult whose care and support needs are being met by the first authority notifies the second authority of their intention to move and the second authority is satisfied that their intention to move is genuine (subs.(1));
2. where the first authority is keeping a care account on behalf of an individual who is funding their own care and he or she notifies the second authority of their intention to move and the second authority is satisfied that their intention to move is genuine (subs.(2)). This will allow for the person's care account to be transferred to the second authority;
3. where a person has their care and support arranged by the first authority and is residing in a care home in the second authority's area, and if that person notifies the second authority of their intention to leave the care home but remain resident in the second authority's area and the second authority is satisfied that their intention to move is genuine (subs.(3)).

In all three cases the duties are triggered only if the person notifies the second authority, or the second authority is notified on the person's behalf. The adult making the request does not necessarily need to have someone whose needs must be met by the local authority; the duties will still be triggered if the first authority is exercising its discretion to provide services. As noted above, the duties do not apply when a carer with support needs is moving but the service user is not moving.

When someone moves between local authority areas they will take their care account and independent personal budget with them. They will be re-assessed by their new local authority, so their independent personal budget may change. However, their accrued costs in their care account will remain the same. To ensure that people can be sure there is a record of their care costs when they move, the first authority is required to retain a record of their care account (see s.29(2)).

Once the second local authority has been notified, it must assure itself that the person's intention is genuine. In order to do this, the statutory guidance points to the need to contact the person and their carer, speak to the first local authority and access contacts and information supplied by the person.[3]

Subsection (4)

The second authority must provide the adult and their carer with "such information as it **1–412** considers appropriate". The Act does not define what information must be provided at this point. But the statutory guidance sets out that the second local authority must provide "accessible information", which includes details about:

---

[1] *Hansard* (House of Lords), 14 October 2013, Vol.748, col.316 (Earl Howe).
[2] Department of Health, *Care and Support Statutory Guidance* (2014), paras 20.7 to 20.9.
[3] Department of Health, *Care and Support Statutory Guidance* (2014), para.20.12.

- the types of care and support available to people with similar needs, so the adult can know how they are likely to be affected by differences in the range of services available;
- support for carers;
- the local care market and organisations that could meet their needs; and
- the local authority's charging policy, including any charges which the person may be expected to meet for particular services in that area.[1]

Whilst subs.(4)(a) places the duty to provide information on the second local authority, the statutory guidance also explains that the first authority should advise recipients of direct payments that they will need to consider how to meet any contractual arrangements put in place for the provision of their care and support (for instance, any contracts a person may have with personal assistants who may not be moving with them). The guidance also emphasises more generally that a person can request assistance from the first and second authority in understanding the implications of their move on the provision of care and support, and the authority should ensure they have access to the relevant information and advice (including advocacy support).[2]

Where a person lacks capacity to make a decision about the move and the family wants them to move closer, the statutory guidance states that the local authority must first "carry out supported decision-making" before proceeding to a mental capacity assessment and best interests decision under the Mental Capacity Act 2005.[3] The meaning of supported decision-making is considered in para.1–270 above.

Subsection (4) also requires the second authority to notify the first authority that it is satisfied the request to move is genuine. At this stage, the statutory guidance sets out that both authorities should identify a named staff member to lead on the case and be the ongoing contact during the move. These contacts should have joint responsibility for facilitating the person's move.[4]

Subsection (5)

1–413   The first authority must provide certain information to the second authority such as the person's care and support plan, and the carer's support plan (if they will continue as the carer after the move). The first authority must also provide any relevant information requested by the second authority. See paras 20.21 to 20.22 of the statutory guidance.

Where a child has had a transition assessment but is moving area before the transition to adult care and support takes place, the statutory guidance states that the first authority should ensure that the second authority is provided with a copy of the assessment and any resulting transition plan. Similarly, where a child's carer is having needs met by adult services following a transition assessment, the first local authority should ensure that the second authority is provided with a copy of the assessment and the carer's support plan.[5]

Subsection (6)

1–414   In the cases specified in subss.(1) to (3), the second authority must carry out an assessment of the needs of that individual, and potentially their carer. The assessment and care planning process in such cases is described in paras 20.24 to 20.38 of the statutory guidance. In general terms, it emphasises that all assessments should be carried out in line with the mainstream process for assessment and eligibility. Where the person also has health needs, the statutory guidance sets out the need for joint working, assessments and care plans with the clinical commissioning group. It also sets out the approach to be

---

[1] Department of Health, *Care and Support Statutory Guidance* (2014), paras 20.13 to 20.14.
[2] Department of Health, *Care and Support Statutory Guidance* (2014), paras 20.15 to 20.16.
[3] Department of Health, *Care and Support Statutory Guidance* (2014), paras 20.17 to 20.18.
[4] Department of Health, Care and Support Statutory Guidance (2014), para. 20.19.
[5] Department of Health, *Care and Support Statutory Guidance* (2014), para. 20.23.

followed where a person is moving and has equipment and adaptations installed in their home.[1] The Government's intention is that the assessment should be carried out before the individual moves.[2] However, this may not always be possible, for example if the second authority receives the notification a day before the person moves. Section 38 deals with cases where the assessment has not been completed on the day of the move.

Subsection (7)

The second authority must "have regard" to the first authority's care and support plan **1–415** when carrying out its assessment.

In the House of Lords, Baroness Campbell attempted to amend this provision to require the second authority to have "due regard" to the existing plan arguing that this would require "appropriate and conscious consideration—a stronger duty than having regard".[3] The Government in response argued that these changes were not necessary given that the second authority is required to have regard to the plan, and s.25(5) which requires the local authority to take all reasonable steps to agree with the adult how their needs will be met.[4]

At report stage Baroness Campbell tabled an amendment to require the local authority to have regard to the care plan with a view to securing, as far as reasonably practicable, the outcomes identified in the assessment.[5] The Government argued that assessments must look at the outcomes that the person or carer want to achieve, and confirmed that this will be emphasised in the statutory guidance.[6]

Subsections (9) and (10)

These subsections were added through a Government amendment in the House of Lords **1–416** to reflect concerns raised by Baroness Campbell about the potential for gaps in services when a person moves areas. At committee stage, Baroness Campbell attempted to amend subs.(4) to provide that service users and carers are informed about how their case is progressing. In response, the Government argued that this is unnecessary because subs.(6) requires the second authority to carry out an assessment as soon as it has established the adult's intention to move, which will require interaction from an early stage and an opportunity to inform them of progress. The Government also stated its intention to clarify this matter in statutory guidance.[7] In the event, however, the Government instead came back at report stage with an amendment containing subs.(9) and (10). These require the first authority "to contact the second authority and maintain this relationship so that it is aware of where the second authority is with putting services in place". They are also intended to require the first authority to "keep the person involved with discussions about their services and informed of progress for putting these in place. In other words, the amendment will put the person at the centre of the process."[8] Baroness Campbell welcomed this amendment, while suggesting that it would be enhanced by requiring the first authority to remain in contact with the second authority until the new care package is in place.[9]

Subsection (11)

The second authority must give the individual a written explanation where it has assessed **1–417** the person as having different needs compared with the original care and support plan.

---

[1] Department of Health, *Care and Support Statutory Guidance* (2014), paras 20.33 to 20.38.
[2] Care Act 2014: Explanatory Notes para.249 and Department of Health, *Care and Support Statutory Guidance* (2014), para. 20.30.
[3] *Hansard* (House of Lords), 22 July 2013, Vol.747, col.1079.
[4] *Hansard* (House of Lords), 22 July 2013, Vol.747, col.1086 (Baroness Northover).
[5] *Hansard* (House of Lords), 14 October 2013, Vol.748, col.312.
[6] *Hansard* (House of Lords), 14 October 2013, Vol.748, col.315 (Earl Howe).
[7] *Hansard* (House of Lords), 22 July 2013, Vol.747, col.1086 (Baroness Northover).
[8] *Hansard* (House of Lords), 14 October 2013, Vol.748, col.316 (Earl Howe).
[9] *Hansard* (House of Lords), 14 October 2013, Vol.748, col.313.

There are no requirements for the format or content of the explanation, other than for it being in writing. However, the Equality Act 2010 may be relevant to the performance of this duty and if necessary, the explanation should be provided in alternative formats and using different methods of communication, as well as being in writing.

Subsection (11) does not specify or indicate how much detail should be provided in the written explanation. The extent of the detail is likely to depend upon the specific circumstances of the individual case. For example, it may be appropriate for the explanation to be relatively brief where the person does not dispute the outcome of the assessment, compared to that given to a person who as a result of the assessment stands to lose care and support services and disagrees with the decision.

Subsection (12)

1–418 The second authority must give a written explanation to the person with care and support needs where the cost of providing the care (ie the personal budget) is different. The explanation must be in writing.

There are no requirements for the format or content of the explanation, other than for it being in writing. However, the Equality Act 2010 may be relevant to the performance of this duty and if necessary, the explanation should be provided in alternative formats and using different methods of communication, as well as being in writing.

Subsection (11) does not specify or indicate how much detail should be provided in the written explanation. The extent of the detail is likely to depend upon the specific circumstances of the individual case.

Subsection (13)

1–419 This places a similar requirement to subs.(11) (to provide a written explanation) on the second authority where the carer's needs are assessed as different. However, it does not place a similar requirement to subs.(12) to explain the difference in the cost of meeting the carer's needs. The Government explained that this is because carers will not have a care account as they are not eligible for a cap on care costs and therefore there is no need to require the second authority to inform them of any change in the costs of meeting their eligible needs.[1] However, the statutory guidance states that the second authority must provide a written explanation "if the adult's or carer's personal budget is different to that provided by the first authority".[2]

Subsection (14)

1–420 This enables regulations to specify steps which a local authority must take for the purpose of being satisfied that the adult's intention to move is genuine. No such regulations have so far been made.

Case where assessments not complete on day of move

1–421 **38.**—(1) If, on the day of the intended move as mentioned in section 37(1)(b), (2)(b) or (3)(b), the second authority has yet to carry out the assessment or assessments under section 37(6), or has done so but has yet to take the other steps required under this Part in the adult's case, it must—

(a) meet the adult's needs for care and support, and the needs for support of any carer who is continuing as the adult's carer, which the first authority has been meeting, and

(b) where the first authority has been keeping a care account in the adult's case, itself keep that account on the same basis as the first authority has been keeping it.

---

[1] *Hansard* (House of Lords), 22 July 2013, Vol.747, cols 1086 to 1087 (Baroness Northover).

[2] Department of Health, *Care and Support Statutory Guidance* (2014), para.20.39.

(2) The second authority is subject to the duty under subsection (1) until it has—

(a) carried out the assessment or assessments under section 37(6), and

(b) taken the other steps required under this Part in the adult's case.

(3) In deciding how to meet the adult's needs for care and support under subsection (1), the second authority must involve—

(a) the adult,

(b) any carer who is continuing as the adult's carer, and

(c) any person whom the adult asks the authority to involve or, where the adult lacks capacity to ask the authority to do that, any person who appears to the authority to be interested in the adult's welfare.

(4) In deciding how to meet the needs for support of any carer who is continuing as the adult's carer, the second authority must involve—

(a) the carer,

(b) the adult needing care, if the carer asks the authority to do so, and

(c) any other person whom the carer asks the authority to involve.

(5) In performing the duty under subsection (3)(a) or (4)(a), the second authority must take all reasonable steps to reach agreement with the adult or carer about how it should meet the needs in question.

(6) The first authority is not required to meet the adult's needs for care and support or, if the adult has a carer, such needs for support as the carer has, for so long as the second authority is subject to the duty under subsection (1).

(7) Where, having complied with the duty under subsection (1), the second authority is not required to meet the adult's needs for care and support under section 18 because the adult is still ordinarily resident in the area of the first authority, the second authority may recover from the first authority the costs it incurs in complying with the duty under subsection (1).

(8) Regulations may specify matters to which the second authority must have regard in deciding how to perform the duty under subsection (1).

GENERAL NOTE

The Joint Committee on the draft Care and Support Bill was concerned to ensure that an **1–422** adequate safety net was in place to deal with failures by local authorities to comply with their legal obligations, such as the failure of a second authority to carry out an assessment. In particular, the Local Ombudsman had told the Joint Committee that failures may occur which could have a major impact on the provision of care and the person's experiences. The Joint Committee therefore recommended that the first authority should be absolved from meeting the person's needs only once the second authority had itself begun to meet their needs, as it is required to do. Moreover, in order to remove a perverse incentive that a new authority might benefit financially from its delay, the second authority should be reimbursed its costs when the first authority fails to comply with its obligation to support a person who has moved.[1] The Government, however, did not agree:

"It is important that both local authorities are fully aware of their responsibilities to ensure that the person does not have any disruption to their care. There is a danger that requiring the first authority to continue to meet the person's needs could see the second authority delaying putting its own arrangements in place. The second authority will know its own market and any delay in it taking over responsibility for meeting the person's needs could see the person not receiving the most appropriate care and

[1] House of Lords House of Commons Joint Committee on the *Draft Care and Support Bill, Draft Care and Support Bill Report, Session 2012–13*, paras 226 to 229.

support for their new surroundings. To ensure there is no confusion over which authority is responsible to meet the individual's needs we reject this recommendation."[1]

Instead, s.38 provides that from the day of arrival in the new area, it is the new authority's responsibility to meet the adult's needs, and the first authority's previous duties are discharged. This is also discussed in the statutory guidance at paras 20.40 to 20.42.

Subsection (1)

1–423   When the second authority has not carried out the assessment required under s.37 before the person moves into its area, or has done so, but has not taken the other steps required to meet the adult's needs, that authority must meet the needs for care and support which the first authority was meeting. The statutory guidance states that in such cases arrangements should be in place on the day of the move, but a temporary care and support package should not be in place for a "prolonged period".[2]

The second authority is also required to continue to update the person's care account by the amount set by the first authority. Where the first authority has not been meeting the adult's needs under s.18, but has provided an independent personal budget, the second authority must only continue the adult's care account on the same basis that the first authority had been keeping it.

During the passage of the Care Bill through Parliament, Baroness Campbell tabled an amendment to provide that in cases where the second authority delays putting in such temporary measures, the first authority would be required to continue to provide care until the new arrangements were in place.[3] The Government argued that the second authority should be the one responsible, but in light of the concerns raised it amended s.37 (subss.(9) and (10)) with the aim of improving co-ordination between the person moving and the two local authorities.[4]

Subsection (2)

1–424   This confirms that the second authority must continue to meet the person's, and potentially their carer's, needs until it has carried out its own assessment or arranged the appropriate care and support.

Subsection (3)

1–425   In deciding how to meet the adult's needs for care and support under subs.(1), the second authority must involve the adult, any carer and any other person that the adult asks to be involved (and in the case of a person who lacks capacity to ask the authority to do that, any person who appears to the authority to be interested in the adult's welfare).

See discussion at paras 1–104 to 1–105 above on the meaning of "involve".

Subsection (4)

1–426   In deciding how to meet the carer's needs for support, the second authority must involve the carer, the adult needing care (if the carer asks the authority to do so) and any other person whom the carer asks the authority to involve.

See discussion at paras 1–104 to 1–105 above on the meaning of "involve".

Subsection (5)

1–427   In deciding how to meet the person's needs the second authority must take all reasonable steps to reach agreement with the adult or carer about how it should meet the needs in question.

---

[1] Department of Health, *The Care Bill explained—including a response to consultation and pre- legislative scrutiny on the draft Care and Support Bill*, p.73.
[2] Department of Health, *Care and Support Statutory Guidance* (2014), paras 20.41 and 20.47.
[3] *Hansard* (House of Lords), 14 October 2013, Vol.748, col.312 to 313.
[4] *Hansard* (House of Lords), 14 October 2013, Vol.748, col.316 (Earl Howe).

Subsection (7)

The second authority may recover the costs of care from the first authority if the individ- **1–428**
ual moving remains ordinarily resident in the area of the first authority. This only applies if
the second authority has not assessed the person prior to the move but is planning to provide
care and support based on the existing care plan. The statutory guidance states:

> "In deciding whether to recover these costs the second authority may want to consider,
> for example, whether the first authority was aware that the person was not going to move
> and had not told the second authority or whether the first authority was not aware and
> was unable to advise the second authority not to make arrangements. The second auth-
> ority should consider whether it would be reasonable to recover their costs depending on
> the circumstances of the case."[1]

In cases where the move has been delayed, the statutory guidance explains that both
authorities may have incurred expense, and therefore "each of the authorities should consider agreeing to cutting their losses incurred in preparing continuity of care".[2]

Subsection (8)

This enables regulations to specify matters to which the second authority must have **1–429**
regard in deciding how to perform the duty under subs.(1) where cases are not assessed
before the date of the move. The relevant regulations are the Care and Support
(Continuity of Care) Regulations 2014 (SI 2014/2825), which are reproduced in full in
paras A1–184 to A1–186. Regulation 2 provides that the second local authority must
have regard to a number of matters, including the contents of any care and support plan
and support plan supplied to them by the first local authority, the outcomes that the person
wishes to achieve and the person's views and preferences. The matters local authorities
must have regard to when making arrangements are also discussed at paras 20.43 to
20.47 of the statutory guidance.

ESTABLISHING WHERE A PERSON LIVES, ETC.

As Lord Justice Elias explained in the case of *R. (Cornwall Council) v Secretary of State* **1–430**
for Health:

> "Local authorities have a wide range of duties, imposed under a variety of statutes, to
> secure the provision of care and other types of assistance for certain children and vulner-
> able adults. Criteria have to be identified to determine which authority has the obligation.
> In a general sense it will be the authority with which the individual has the closest con-
> nection. Some test has to be adopted to reflect that general notion, and typically this is to
> ask where the person is ordinarily resident, although sometimes the alternative formulae
> of normal or habitual residence are used. Usually the application of that test is straight-
> forward and provides a clear answer, but not always. Human beings have the
> inconvenient habit of conducting their lives without regard to legal categories, and the
> application of the relevant test is sometimes highly problematic."[3]

The concept of ordinary residence is referred to throughout Pt 1 of the Care Act. For
example, the duty on a local authority to meet the eligible needs of an adult or a carer is
triggered if the person with care and support needs is ordinarily resident in the authority's
area (ss.18(1)(a) and 20(1)(a)). Moreover, local authorities have powers to meet the needs
of those adults whose needs they are not otherwise required to meet if they are ordinarily
resident (s.19(1)).

---

[1] Department of Health, *Care and Support Statutory Guidance* (2014), para. 20.50.
[2] Department of Health, *Care and Support Statutory Guidance* (2014), para. 20.49.
[3] *R. (Cornwall Council) v Secretary of State for Health* [2014] EWCA Civ 12 at [1].

However, there is no statutory definition of ordinary residence and the concept has instead been developed by the courts. The leading case is *R. v Barnet LBC Ex parte Shah*, where Lord Scarman said:

"Unless, therefore, it can be shown that the statutory framework or the legal context in which the words are used requires a different meaning, I unhesitatingly subscribe to the view that 'ordinarily resident' refers to a man's abode in a particular place or country which he has adopted voluntarily and for settled purposes as part of the regular order of his life for the time being, whether of short or of long duration."[1]

He added that:

"There are two, but no more than two, respects in which the mind of the 'propositus' is important in determining ordinary residence. The residence must be voluntarily adopted. Enforced presence by reason of kidnapping or imprisonment, or a Robinson Crusoe existence on a desert island with no opportunity of escape, may be so overwhelming a factor as to negative the will to be where one is.

And there must be a degree of settled purpose. The purpose may be one; or there may be several. It may be specific or general. All that the law requires is that there is a settled purpose. This is not to say that the 'propositus' intends to stay where he is indefinitely; indeed his purpose, while settled, may be for a limited period. Education, business or profession, employment, health, family or merely love of the place spring to mind as common reasons for the choice of a regular abode. And there may well be many others. All that is necessary is that the purpose of living where one does has a sufficient degree of continuity to be properly described as settled."[2]

In this case, Lord Scarman applied the tax cases of *Levene v Inland Revenue Commissioners* and *Inland Revenue Commissioners v Lysaght*.[3] In the former, Viscount Cave said: "I think that it connotes residence in a place with some degree of continuity and apart from accidental or temporary absences."[4] Lord Warrington also explained that:

"Ordinary residence also seems to me to have no such technical or special meaning. In particular it is in my opinion impossible to restrict its connotation to its duration. A member of this House may well be said to be ordinarily resident in London during the Parliamentary session and in the country during the recess. If it has any definite meaning I should say it means according to the way in which a man's life is usually ordered."[5]

1–431   In *Lysaght*, Viscount Sumner said: "I should think the converse to ordinarily is extraordinarily and that part of the regular order of a man's life, adopted voluntarily and for settled purposes is not extraordinary."[6]

The principles set out in *Shah* are based upon the assumption that the person has capacity to decide where to live. But difficult questions can arise where the relevant person lacks capacity or where the place of residence has not been voluntarily adopted. For example, in the case of *R. v Waltham Forest LBC Ex p Vale* the court adapted the *Shah* test and established a two-part approach for determining the ordinary residence of a person unable to make decisions about where to live.[7] This case concerned an English woman called Judith with severe learning disabilities who had been in residential care in Ireland for over 20 years. When her parents returned to England, she became distressed and it was thought to be in her best interests to return to live near them. On return she lived with

---

[1] *R. v Barnet LBC Ex p Shah* [1983] 2 A.C. 309 at 343.

[2] *R. v Barnet LBC Ex p Shah* [1983] 2 A.C. 309 at 344.

[3] *Levene v Inland Revenue Commissioners* [1928] A.C. 217; *Inland Revenue Commissioners v Lysaght* [1928] A.C. 234.

[4] *Levene v Inland Revenue Commissioners* [1928] A.C. 217 at 225.

[5] *Levene v Inland Revenue Commissioners* [1928] A.C. 217 at 232.

[6] *Inland Revenue Commissioners v Lysaght* [1928] A.C. 234 at 243.

[7] *R. v Waltham Forest LBC Ex p Vale* (1985), *The Times*, 25 February 1985.

her parents temporarily for a month before being placed in a residential home in another English local authority. Mr Justice Taylor (as he was then) set out a two-part approach, but on either approach he considered that residence with her parents could be treated as sufficiently settled to satisfy the *Shah* test. Under the first approach he explained that:

"Where the propositus . . . is so mentally handicapped as to be totally dependent upon a parent or guardian, the concept of her having an independent ordinary residence of her own which she has adopted voluntarily and for which she has a settled purpose does not arise. She is in the same position as a small child. Her ordinary residence is that of her parents because that is her 'base', to use the word adopted by Lord Denning in the infant case cited."[1]

The alternative approach involved considering her as if she were a person of normal mental capacity. In this case, Mr Justice Taylor adopted the first approach.

The statutory guidance refers to these approaches as "Vale 1" and "Vale 2". It sets out that whereas *Shah* should be the starting point in the case of people who have capacity, an alternative approach should be adopted because *Shah* requires the voluntary adoption of residence. It states that:

"In the case of a person whose parents are deceased, people who have become ordinarily resident in an area and then lost capacity or have limited contact with their parents, the approach known as Vale 2 is appropriate to determine ordinary residence. This involves considering a person's ordinary residence as if they had capacity. All the facts of the person's case must be considered, including physical presence in a particular place and the nature and purpose of that presence but without requiring the person to have voluntarily adopted the place of residence."[2]

The guidance also refers in Annex H to the idea of a "child's base" which had been referred to in the *Vale* case (see para.1–430 above).

In *R(Cornwall) v Secretary of State for Health* the Supreme Court considered the approaches set out in *Vale* and held that:

"With hindsight, it was perhaps unhelpful to elide the *Shah* test with the idea of a "base", used by Lord Denning MR in a different context and for a different purpose. The [passage in *Vale* quoted in para.1–430 above] cannot be read as supporting any more general proposition than that Judith's ordinary residence was to be equated with that of her parents, without reference to the period of her own actual residence with them. Nor in my view should Taylor J's two approaches be treated as separate legal tests. Rather they were complementary, common-sense approaches to the application of the *Shah* test to a person unable to make decisions for herself; that is, to the single question whether her period of actual residence with her parents was sufficiently "settled" to amount to ordinary residence."[3]

Sections 18 and 20 of the Care Act provide that local authorities have a duty to meet the eligible needs of people if they are present in its area but of "no settled residence". The meaning of no settled residence was considered by Mr Justice Potts in *R. v Redbridge LBC*.[4] This case concerned adult twins with learning difficulties who attended a residential school in East Sussex but their parents, who had been ordinarily resident in Redbridge, left this country to live in Nigeria. Soon after the parents' departure the residential school attended by the twins closed. Applying the Vale 1 approach, it was held that the twins were no longer resident in Redbridge. Instead they had no ordinary residence but that the duty to provide for them fell on East Sussex, on the basis that they were in that county

---

[1] See above footnote. The judgment of Lord Denning to which reference is made was *Re P (GE) an infant* [1965] Ch.568.

[2] Department of Health, *Care and Support Statutory Guidance* (2014), para.19.21.

[3] *R. (Cornwall Council) v Secretary of State for Health* [2015] UKSC 46 at [47].

[4] *R. v Redbridge LBC Ex p East Sussex CC* [1993] COD 293.

and suffering from a mental disorder. The statutory guidance states that it will "only be in rare circumstances that local authorities conclude that someone is of no settled residence". It also provides examples of where a person would be of no settled residence—such as if a person has clearly and intentionally left their previous residence and moved to stay elsewhere on a temporary basis during which time their circumstances change, and if a person arrives from abroad.[1]

The statutory guidance discusses in Ch.19 how to determine ordinary residence, including in situations where a person is in receipt of s.117 after-care under the Mental Health Act 1983, takes temporary absence from the area, has more than one home, or funds and arranged their own care. Annexes H1 to H8 provide guidance on specific cases and scenarios. The ordinary residence principles that apply when young people move from children's to adult's services, and when they move away to university are discussed in paras 16.75 to 16.78, Ch.19 and Annex J. The ordinary residence of people leaving prison is discussed in paras 17.55 to 17.58.

In addition to the above, s.39 of the Care Act makes provision for determining the ordinary residence of people whose needs can only be met through the provision of certain types of accommodation, including when the accommodation is being provided or arranged in a different local authority area in England. Broadly this ensures that the person's ordinary residence remains with the local authority in which they were ordinarily resident immediately before moving into the accommodation. This is often referred to as the "deeming principle".

CARERS AND ORDINARY RESIDENCE

1–432   A local authority's duty to provide support to a carer does not require him or her to be ordinarily resident in its area. But the adult needing care is required to be ordinarily resident (or present but of no settled residence) in order to trigger the local authority's responsibilities towards the carer (see s.20(1)(a)). Put simply, the local authority in which the adult needing care lives is responsible in most cases for meeting the carer's eligible needs for support.

There are two main policy reasons for this. First, the local authority where the adult needing care lives benefits from the informal care being provided by the carer, since it would otherwise need to provide care and support to meet the needs that are being met by the carer. Second, carers' services are often delivered in the form of services to the cared-for person, for example in order to give the carer a break, the adult needing care may be given a place at a day-centre. Therefore, it makes sense from an organisational perspective to have the same authority making decisions about services for both the carer and the adult needing care.

Particular difficulties may be faced by carers who provide care for people who live a long way from them and/or who live across local authority boundaries (especially when they are caring for more than one person). The statutory guidance emphasises that where there is more than one local authority involved, those authorities should "consider how best to cooperate on and share the provision of support", for example through joint funding or by agreeing that one takes overall responsibility for certain aspects.[2] Previous guidance also set out the following principles, which are likely to remain relevant under the Care Act:

- where the carer cares long distance for only one cared-for person and that person is eligible for services, the cared-for person's authority is responsible for the carers assessment and provision of services, even if carers services (such as buying a washing machine) might need to be provided in a different local authority area;

---

[1] Department of Health, *Care and Support Statutory Guidance* (2014), paras 19.22 and 19.24. See also Annex H6.
[2] Department of Health, *Care and Support Statutory Guidance* (2014), para.19.8.

- where the carer cares for more than one person in more than one local authority area, but only one cared-for person is eligible for services, the home local authority of the eligible cared-for person has responsibility for the carers assessment and for leading any co-ordination that may be required between authorities; and
- where two cared-for people in two different authorities are eligible for services, the authorities should agree how a carer's assessment may best be conducted and negotiate how carers' services may need to be provided.[1]

NHS RULES

Concern has also been raised about the complex inter-relationship between local auth- **1–433** ority rules on ordinary residence and NHS rules on establishing who is responsible for providing NHS care. Section 3(1A) of the National Health Services Act provides that a clinical commissioning group has responsibility for all people who are:

- provided with primary medical services by GP practices who are members of the clinical commissioning group; or
- who are usually resident in the area covered by the clinical commissioning group and are not provided with primary medical services by a member of any clinical commissioning group.

Regulations make further provision for the responsibilities of clinical commissioning groups including the responsibility to commission urgent and emergency care services for everyone present in their geographic area.[2] In general, clinical commissioning groups are responsible for commissioning all health services, with the exception of:

- certain services commissioned directly by the NHS Commissioning Board (primary care, high secure psychiatric services, specialised services and the majority of health services for prisoners/those detained in "other prescribed accommodation" and members of the armed forces);
- health improvement services commissioned by local authorities; and
- health protection and promotion services provided by Public Health England.[3]

The complex inter-relationship between the local authority and NHS rules means that a person could be living in one area but be provided with health care services from clinical commissioning group and care and support from a local authority in another area.

The rules that apply to ordinary residence when a person goes into hospital or other NHS accommodation are contained in s.39(5) of the Care Act.

Where a person's ordinary residence is

39.—(1) Where an adult has needs for care and support which can be met only **1–434** if the adult is living in accommodation of a type specified in regulations, and the adult is living in accommodation in England of a type so specified, the adult is to be treated for the purposes of this Part as ordinarily resident—

(a) in the area in which the adult was ordinarily resident immediately before the adult began to live in accommodation of a type specified in the regulations, or

---

[1] Department of Health, *Carers and Disabled Children Act 2000: Carers and People with Parental Responsibility for Disabled Children: Practice Guidance* (2001), paras 24 to 27.

[2] The National Health Service Commissioning Board and Clinical Commissioning Groups (Responsibilities and Standing Rules) Regulations 2012 (SI 2012/2996).

[3] NHS England, *Who Pays? Determining Responsibility for Payments to Providers: Rules and Guidance for Clinical Commissioning Groups* (August 2013), pp.5 to 6.

(b) if the adult was of no settled residence immediately before the adult began to live in accommodation of a type so specified, in the area in which the adult was present at that time.

(2) Where, before beginning to live in his or her current accommodation, the adult was living in accommodation of a type so specified (whether or not of the same type as the current accommodation), the reference in subsection (1)(a) to when the adult began to live in accommodation of a type so specified is a reference to the beginning of the period during which the adult has been living in accommodation of one or more of the specified types for consecutive periods.

(3) The regulations may make provision for determining for the purposes of subsection (1) whether an adult has needs for care and support which can be met only if the adult is living in accommodation of a type specified in the regulations.

(4) An adult who is being provided with accommodation under section 117 of the Mental Health Act 1983 (after-care) is to be treated for the purposes of this Part as ordinarily resident in the area of the local authority in England or the local authority in Wales on which the duty to provide the adult with services under that section is imposed; and for that purpose—

(a) "local authority in England" means a local authority for the purposes of this Part, and

(b) "local authority in Wales" means a local authority for the purposes of the Social Services and Well-being (Wales) Act 2014.

(5) An adult who is being provided with NHS accommodation is to be treated for the purposes of this Part as ordinarily resident—

(a) in the area in which the adult was ordinarily resident immediately before the accommodation was provided, or

(b) if the adult was of no settled residence immediately before the accommodation was provided, in the area in which the adult was present at that time.

(6) "NHS accommodation" means accommodation under—

(a) the National Health Service Act 2006,

(b) the National Health Service (Wales) Act 2006,

(c) the National Health Service (Scotland) Act 1978, or

(d) Article 5(1) of the Health and Personal Social Services (Northern Ireland) Order 1972.

(7) The reference in subsection (1) to this Part does not include a reference to section 28 (independent personal budget).

(8) Schedule 1 (which makes provision about cross-border placements to and from Wales, Scotland or Northern Ireland) has effect.

GENERAL NOTE

1–435   Section 39 makes provision for determining the ordinary residence of people whose needs can only be met through the provision of certain types of accommodation, including when the accommodation is being provided or arranged in a different local authority area in England. This replaces s.25(5) and (6) of the National Assistance Act 1948. In general terms, s.39 ensures that the person's ordinary residence remains with the local authority in which they where ordinarily resident immediately before moving into the accommodation. So, for example, if a local authority determines that an adult needs accommodation of a specified type in a different local authority area, their ordinary residence remains with the first local authority. Therefore the first authority remains responsible for funding, reviewing and managing the person's care plan. This is often referred to as the "deeming principle" because it "deems a person to be ordinarily resident in a local authority area when [he or she] is in fact ordinarily resident elsewhere.[1] As the Court of Appeal set out in *R(Kent County Council) v Secretary of State for Health* the purpose of the deeming principle is to provide continuity of financial responsibility whilst a person is being provided with residential care:

"It is not uncommon for those who are eligible for such assistance, for practical reasons or reasons connected with securing their best interests, to be placed outside the area of the local authority with the statutory responsibility. The deeming provision avoids complications arising in connection with funding in those circumstances. It also avoids the possibility of a local authority placing someone outside its own area to ease its financial burdens".[2]

Whilst the Court was referring to the deeming principle under the 1948 Act, the underlying rationale also applies to s.39. However, the Care Act makes two significant changes to the deeming principle. First, it is not necessary for the local authority to have arranged the accommodation in order for the deeming principle to apply (see discussion under subs.(1) below). Secondly, whereas the deeming principle under the 1948 Act only applied to care home accommodation, s.39 enables regulations to specify a wider range of accommodation. The relevant regulations are the Care and Support (Ordinary Residence) (Specified Accommodation) Regulations 2014 (SI 2014/2828), which are reproduced in full in paras A1–195 to A1–200 below. They specify and define three types of accommodation for these purposes: care home accommodation, shared lives scheme accommodation and supported living accommodation.

The statutory guidance discusses the deeming principle at paras 19.25 to 19.38. Amongst other matters it clarifies that if a person is placed out of area into specified accommodation, or an individual has arranged this themselves via direct payments, the first local authority should inform the host local authority and:

". . . ensure that satisfactory arrangements are made before the accommodation begins for any necessary support services which are provided locally, such as day care, and that clear agreements are in place for funding all aspects of the person's care and support."[3]

It also acknowledges that in practice "the first local authority may enter into agreements to allow the authority where the accommodation is located to carry out functions on its behalf".[4]

The changes introduced by s.39 will only apply to arrangements made after 1 April 2015. For arrangements made before 1 April, the previous law on deeming ordinary residence, under s.24 of the 1948 Act, applies. For example, a person who moved before 1 April 2015 into supported living out of area will normally have had their ordinary residence moved to that of their new area, under the 1948 Act. Their status will not change with the implementation of the Care Act.[5]

Subsection (1)

An adult whose needs can only be met by the provision of accommodation (of a type **1–436** specified in regulations) is to be treated as ordinarily resident—

- in the area in which they were ordinarily resident immediately before living in the accommodation; or
- if they had no settled residence, in the area where they were present before living in the accommodation.

---

[1] *R(Kent County Council) v Secretary of State for Health* [2015] EWCA Civ 81 at [1].
[2] *R(Kent County Council) v Secretary of State for Health* [2015] EWCA Civ 81 at [13].
[3] Department of Health, *Care and Support Statutory Guidance* (2014), paras 19.36 to 19.37.
[4] Department of Health, *Care and Support Statutory Guidance* (2014), paras 19.36 to 19.37.
[5] Care Act 2014 (Transitional Provision) Order 2015 (SI 2015/995).

As noted above, the Care and Support (Ordinary Residence) (Specified Accommodation) Regulations 2014 (SI 2014/2828) specify and define three types of accommodation for these purposes: care home accommodation, shared lives scheme accommodation and supported living accommodation.

The deeming principle applies if it has been determined that an adult's needs can only be met through the specified type of accommodation. The statutory guidance emphasises that this determination should be evidenced in the care and support plan. Moreover, it confirms that the deeming principle applies where the person uses direct payments to purchase supported living or shared lives accommodation (and the care plan states that their needs can only be met through this type of accommodation) in a different local authority area. However, if the person moves to accommodation outside what was specified in the care plan or of a type of accommodation not specified in the regulations, then the deeming principle would not apply.[1]

The statutory guidance suggests that s.39 only applies where the accommodation is being "arranged" for the person by the local authority.[2] However, the Government has stated that it intends to amend the guidance to make clear that the deeming principle applies when the local authority considers that a person's needs can only be met in a specified type of accommodation in the area of another local authority, and it is not necessary for the local authority to be arranging the accommodation. It will also make clear that an absence of evidence that needs can only be met in a certain way is not the same as proof that there are other viable options.[3]

Privately arranged moves

The statutory guidance sets out that the local authority must have carried out an assessment in order to have determined that the person's needs can only be met by the provision of the specified accommodation—and the deeming principle therefore "does not apply to cases where a person arranges their own accommodation and the local authority does not meet their needs".[4] Self-funders who arrange their own care and choose to move to another area, are likely to become ordinarily resident in the local authority area that they have moved to. The guidance states that if such a person find that their funds have depleted, they can apply to the local authority area that they have moved to in order to have their needs assessed, and "if it is decided that they have eligible needs for care and support, the person's ordinary residence will be in the place where they moved to and not the first authority".[5] Where a local authority is arranging a self-funder's accommodation pursuant to s.18(3) of the Care Act (ie, where a self-funder who has eligible needs, has asked the local authority to meet their needs), the guidance suggests that the the deeming provision will apply and the person will keep the ordinary residence of the arranging local authority.[6]

Prior to the Care Act, many had pointed to an incentive for local authorities to encourage (but not to make the arrangements for) self-funders to move into a care home in another authority, because when the person's capital falls below the financial threshold they would become the responsibility of the new local authority. Under the Care Act the deeming principle does not apply on the basis that the local authority arranged the accommodation, and it is therefore less likely that disputes will arise on this basis. Instead, there is likely to be a signicant amount of focus on local authority decisions regarding whether the person's needs can only be met by the provision of the accommodation.

---

[1] Department of Health, *Care and Support Statutory Guidance* (2014), paras 19.31 and 19.34.
[2] Department of Health, *Care and Support Statutory Guidance* (2014), para.19.3.
[3] Department of Health, *Update on the Final Orders under the Care Act 2014* (2015) paras 22 to 23.
[4] Department of Health, *Update on the Final Orders under the Care Act 2014* (2015) para.19.31.
[5] Department of Health, *Update on the Final Orders under the Care Act 2014* (2015), para.19.52.
[6] Department of Health, *Update on the Final Orders under the Care Act 2014* (2015), Annex H4. p.473.

What happens if a care home de-registers?

In the past, problems were caused when care homes de-registered and, for example, started providing services to residents under supported living arrangements. This meant that the placing authority no longer retained financial responsibility for their clients' personal support costs, and instead those people became the responsibility of the local authority in which they had been placed. Lord Low had therefore pointed to a perverse financial incentive for placing authorities to encourage homes to de-register, and significant budgetary implications for those authorities well served by residential care facilities and which therefore received a lot of out-of-area placements.[1]

The Care Act alters this position. Care homes that de-register will be caught by s.39 if they fall within the definition of shared lives or supported living accommodation. The statutory guidance states that:

> "There may be occasions where a provider chooses to change the type of care which it provides, for instance to de-register a property as a care home and to redesign the service as a supported living scheme. Where the person remains living at the same property, and their needs continue to be met by the new service, then ordinary residence should not be affected, and the duty to meet needs will remain with the first authority. This will occur even if the person temporarily moves to another address whilst any changes to the property occur.[2] "

What happens when the person moves out of the accommodation?

In the past, it has been argued that the deeming principle provided a perverse incentive for placing authorities to encourage disabled people living in registered care homes to move into the local community. This would mean that responsibility for meeting the person's needs would be transferred to the local authority in which they had been placed.[3] Under the Care Act this incentive continues, unless the person is moving into supported living or shared lives accommodation and the placing local authority determines that the person's needs can only be met by the provision of the accommodation.

Subsection (2)

This subsection applies where before beginning to live in their current accommodation, **1–437** the adult was living in accommodation of a specified type. The reference in subs.(1)(a) to when the adult began to live in the accommodation refers to the beginning of the period during which the adult has been living in accommodation of one or more of the specified types for consecutive periods.

Subsection (3)

Regulations may specify how to determine if an adult has needs for care and support **1–438** which can be met only if the adult is living in accommodation for the purposes of subs.(1).

Subsection (4)

Where an adult is being provided with accommodation under s.117 of the Mental Health **1–439** Act 1983—rather than the Care Act—they are treated as ordinarily resident in the local authority in England or Wales on which the s.117 duty is imposed.

The references to Wales were added as a Government amendment in the House of Lords The intention (along with other amendments) was to apply consistent ordinary residence rules in England and Wales in respect of after-care under the Mental Health Act 1983, and reflect the Department of Health's agreement with Wales that Welsh Ministers or the Secretary of State will determine cross-border disputes according to agreed arrangements.[4]

---

[1] *Hansard* (House of Lords), 23 July 2007, Vol.694, col.609.
[2] Department of Health, Care and Support Statutory Guidance (2014), para.19.38.
[3] *Hansard* (House of Lords), 23 July 2007, Vol.694, col.609.
[4] *Hansard* (House of Lords), 14 October 2013, Vol.748, col.317 (Earl Howe).

The application of the ordinary residence rules to s.117 after-care is considered in para.1–736 below.

Subsections (5) and (6)

1–440   This provides that anyone who is admitted to NHS accommodation (including a hospital or a nursing home) will be ordinarily resident in the area immediately before the move. For example, if a person suffers a fall at home and is admitted to hospital and from there admitted to a care home, ordinary residence is determined by where the person was ordinarily resident before the hospital admission. The statutory guidance confirms that this applies regardless of the length of stay in hospital.[1] Alternatively, if the person has no settled residence they will be treated as ordinarily resident in the location of the accommodation they have been admitted to.

NHS accommodation is defined in subs.(6) as accommodation provided as part of the NHS under any relevant NHS legislation in the UK. According to the explanatory notes, this ensures that a stay in a hospital in England, Scotland, Wales or Northern Ireland will not affect a person's ordinary residence, and this means that their care and support "must continue to be provided by the local authority in whose area they were ordinarily resident before their hospital stay".[2]

Subsection (5) was amended (and subs.(6) was added) in the House of Lords to address a potential lacuna in respect of people who may live in England (and therefore be ordinarily resident in an English local authority) but who are treated entirely within the NHS of a devolved administration. The amendments ensure that they would remain ordinarily resident in England.[3]

These subsections are discussed in the statutory guidance at paras 19.39 to 19.41.

Subsection (7)

1–441   This was added as a result of a Government amendment in the House of Lords to clarify the position of a person who has an independent personal budget (s.28). The local authority where the person is ordinarily resident is responsible for preparing the person's independent personal budget and keeping the care account. The Government's intention was to clarify "that if such a person is in residential care and moves to the area of a different local authority, they will be able to become ordinarily resident in that new area".[4]

Disputes about ordinary residence or continuity of care

1–442   **40.**—(1) Any dispute about where an adult is ordinarily resident for the purposes of this Part, or any dispute between local authorities under section 37 about the application of that section, is to be determined by—

(a) the Secretary of State, or

(b) where the Secretary of State appoints a person for that purpose (the "appointed person"), that person.

(2) The Secretary of State or appointed person may review a determination under subsection (1), provided that the review begins within 3 months of the date of the determination.

(3) Having carried out a review under subsection (2), the Secretary of State or appointed person must—

(a) confirm the original determination, or

(b) substitute a different determination.

---

[1] Department of Health, *Care and Support Statutory Guidance* (2014), paras 19.40.

[2] Care Act 2014: Explanatory Notes para.258.

[3] *Hansard* (House of Lords), 14 October 2013, Vol.748, cols 316 to 317 (Earl Howe).

[4] *Hansard* (House of Lords), 22 July 2013, Vol.747, col.1088 (Baroness Northover).

(4) Regulations may make further provision about resolution of disputes of the type mentioned in subsection (1); the regulations may, for example, include—

(a) provision for ensuring that care and support is provided to the adult while the dispute is unresolved;

(b) provision requiring the local authorities in dispute to take specified steps before referring the dispute to the Secretary of State or (as the case may be) the appointed person;

(c) provision about the procedure for referring the dispute to the Secretary of State or appointed person;

(d) where a review of a determination has been carried out under subsection (2) and a different determination substituted, provision requiring a local authority to take specified steps (including paying specified amounts) in relation to the period before the determination was substituted.

GENERAL NOTE

Chapter 19 of the statutory guidance is intended to assist local authorities in making **1–443** decisions about ordinary residence. However, there are occasions when two or more authorities do not agree on where a person should be considered ordinarily resident. Lord Low, during the passage of the Care Bill through Parliament, described some of the difficulties that can arise:

". . . with ordinary residence disputes, the individual themselves becomes invisible in the midst of financial wrangling between authorities. If an individual is prevented or delayed from moving because of a dispute between local authorities over who pays, they have been denied the choice and control that are said to lie at the heart of this legislation. Funding rather than individual well-being has become the prime consideration."[1]

Subsection 40 provides that if such cases cannot be resolved locally, the local authorities involved may request a determination of ordinary residence to be made by the Secretary of State or a person appointed by the Secretary of State. Further detail on this process is contained in the Care and Support (Disputes Between Local Authorities) Regulations 2014 (SI 2014/2829). These are reproduced and discussed at paras A1–201 to A1–208 below. The statutory guidance sets out the process for resolving disputes and seeking determinations in paras 19.53 to 19.70. A similar dispute resolution process was in place prior to the Care Act provided for by directions made under the National Assistance Act 1948 and s.7A of the Local Authority Social Services Act 1970.[2]

The procedures for determining ordinary residence disputes have been criticised as costly and time consuming. For example, a 2007 report by the Voluntary Organisations Disability Group estimated that at least 500 people are caught up in ordinary residence disputes at any one time, costing an estimated £3 million a year in legal fees and administrative costs for local authorities.[3] Part of the reason for delay may be ongoing negotiations between local authorities to resolve the dispute informally. In addition, the Department of Health has been criticised for the length of time taken to make ordinary residence determinations. The Department has stated that it aims to have a determination sent to the parties within three months of receipt of a full set of papers and where cases take longer it is often because further documentation has been requested.[4]

---

[1] *Hansard* (House of Lords, 22 July 2013, Vol.747, col.1082.

[2] The Ordinary Residence Disputes (National Assistance Act 1948) Directions 2010.

[3] Voluntary Organisations Disability Group, *No Place Like Home* (July 2007), pp.35 to 36.

[4] M. Pedler, "Ordinary Residence under the National Assistance Act 1948: a Department of Health Perspective" (2008) 11 CCLR 207, 213.

Subsection (1)

1–444   This provides that ordinary residence disputes must be determined by the Secretary of State or someone appointed by the Secretary of State.

Subsection (2)

1–445   Local authorities may request a review within three months of the original determination being made. In the House of Lords, the Government stated that as a result of this subsection "there is no excuse for authorities deliberately to stall the process in order to postpone meeting their financial responsibility."[1]

Subsection (3)

1–446   The powers of the Secretary of State or the appointed person following a review are to confirm the original determination, or substitute a different determination.

Subsection (4)

1–447   This provides that regulations may make further provision about resolution of disputes. As noted above, the relevant regulations are the Care and Support (Disputes Between Local Authorities) Regulations 2014 (SI 2014/2829).

Financial adjustments between local authorities

1–448   **41.**—(1) This section applies where—

  (a) a local authority has been meeting an adult's needs for care and support, but
  (b) it transpires (whether following the determination of a dispute under section 40 or otherwise) that the adult was, for some or all of the time that the authority has been meeting the adult's needs, ordinarily resident in the area of another local authority.

  (2) This section also applies where—

  (a) a local authority has been meeting a carer's needs for support, but
  (b) it transpires (whether following the determination of a dispute under section 40 or otherwise) that the adult needing care was, for some or all of the time that the authority has been meeting the carer's needs, ordinarily resident in the area of another local authority.

  (3) The local authority concerned may recover from the other local authority the amount of any payments it made towards meeting the needs in question at a time when the other local authority was instead liable to meet them under section 18 or 20(1) (as the case may be).

  (4) Subsection (3) does not apply to payments which are the subject of a deferred payment agreement entered into by the local authority in question, unless it agrees with the other local authority to assign its rights and obligations under the deferred payment agreement to that other authority.

  (5) Any period during which a local authority was meeting the needs in question under section 19 or 20(6) is to be disregarded for the purposes of this section.

GENERAL NOTE

1–449   Following a dispute which is being considered under s.40, or by some other process, it may become apparent that a local authority has been funding a person's care and support when that person is not in fact ordinarily resident in their area. In such circumstances, s.41 allows for that local authority to reclaim the costs they have paid for that person's care and support from the local authority where they are or were ordinarily resident. This section does not apply where the local authority has chosen to meet the person's needs in the

---

[1] *Hansard* (House of Lords, 22 July 2013, Vol.747, col.1090 (Baroness Northover).

knowledge they are ordinarily resident elsewhere (s.19(2)). The statutory guidance discusses financial adjustments in paras 19.67 to 19.68.

Subsections (1) and (2)

This section applies where a local authority has been meeting the needs of an adult with **1–450** care and support needs, or a carer, but it transpires (whether following the determination of a dispute under s.39 or otherwise) that the adult or the carer was ordinarily resident elsewhere.

Subsection (3)

The costs that can be recovered are the amount of any payments the local authority made **1–451** towards meeting the needs in question when the other local authority was instead liable to meet them. This applies to the adult's or carer's needs that the local authority was required to meet under s.18 or s.20(1).

Subsection (4)

The costs that can be recovered under subs.(3) do not include any payments which are the **1–452** subject of a deferred payment agreement, unless it agrees with the other local authority to assign its rights and obligations under the deferred payment agreement to that other authority.

Subsection (5)

Any period during which the local authority was exercising a discretion to provide ser- **1–453** vices to the adult or the carer (under s.19 or 20(6)) is to be disregarded for the purposes of this section.

SAFEGUARDING ADULTS AT RISK OF ABUSE OR NEGLECT

GENERAL NOTE

The Law Commission's 2011 final report described the legal framework for adult safe- **1–454** guarding as "neither systematic nor co-ordinated, reflecting the sporadic development of safeguarding policy over the last 25 years".[1] Prior to the Care Act, there was no single or coherent statutory framework for adult safeguarding in England. Instead, the law had to be discerned through reference to a wide range of laws including general NHS and community care legislation and guidance, mental health and mental capacity legislation, the common law, public law responsibilities and the civil and criminal justice systems. The Law Commission identified this lack of coherence as a major deficiency in the law and recommended the creation of a new statutory framework which included a duty to investigate and statutory safeguarding boards.[2]

At consultation, some had argued that there should be a stand-alone adult safeguarding statute which placed joint duties on local authorities, health services and the police. The Law Commission did not agree. It concluded that the law must establish clear responsibilities for adult safeguarding and argued that the introduction of joint multi-agency duties could lead to blurred accountability for taking action in individual cases. It recommended that local social services authorities should have the lead co-ordinating responsibility for safeguarding, and therefore the best vehicle for this new framework was the adult social care statute rather a stand-alone safeguarding statute. Nevertheless the Commission accepted that the new statute should reflect the importance of a multi-agency approach to adult safeguarding. This was evident in its recommendations for new duties to co-operate and Adult Safeguarding Boards.[3]

---

[1] Law Commission, *Adult Social Care*, para.9.1.
[2] Law Commission, *Adult Social Care*, Pt 9.
[3] Law Commission, *Adult Social Care*, paras 9.13 to 9.14.

Sections 42 to 47 of, and Sch.2 to, the Care Act implement almost all of the Law Commission's recommendations in this area. These provisions establish the first ever statutory framework for adult safeguarding in England which requires local authorities to ensure enquiries are made into allegations of abuse or neglect and establish a safeguarding adults board in their area. The Government also accepted the Law Commission's recommendation that the law must establish clearly that the local authority has the lead co-ordinating responsibility for safeguarding. It explained that:

"This should frame the responsibility as being the lead co-ordinating agency, as other agencies also need to contribute to adult safeguarding in their day-to-day work within their existing statutory duties (for example, within health care for the delivery of NHS services and within law enforcement and crime prevention for the police)".[1]

The statutory guidance discusses safeguarding in Ch.14. In addition, organisations such as the Social Care Institute for Excellence have produced a range of documents on the new safeguarding framework.[2] These documents are not statutory guidance but they have been produced with the approval of the Department of Health (see 1–770 below).

The introduction of a statutory framework for adult safeguarding is compatible with the United Nations Convention on the Rights of Persons with Disabilities. Article 16 (Freedom from Exploitation, Violence and Abuse) requires that:

"States Parties shall take all appropriate legislative, administrative, social, educational and other measures to protect persons with disabilities, both within and outside the home, from all forms of exploitation, violence and abuse, including their gender-based aspects."

Article 16 also includes requirements for the State to put in place measures to:

- independently monitor services provided to people with disabilities in order to prevent exploitation, violence and abuse;
- support the recovery of people with disabilities who are victims of exploitation, violence and abuse; and
- provide effective legislation and policies for the effective identification, investigation and, where appropriate, prosecution of exploitation, violence and abuse.

THE INCIDENCE OF ABUSE AND NEGLECT IN ENGLAND

1–455 There is a growing body of research into the abuse and neglect of adults with care and support needs. In 2007, the first national survey into the abuse and neglect of older people found that 2.6 per cent of people aged 66 and over living in private households in the UK reported that they had experienced "mistreatment" involving a family member, friend or care worker during the past year. This equates to about 227,000 people aged 66 and over experiencing mistreatment, and around 1 in 40 of the older population. The overall prevalence increased to 4 per cent when the enquiry is broadened to include incidents involving neighbours and acquaintances. The survey also found that the proportion of mistreatment cases coming to the attention of adult protection services is likely to be small: approximately 3 per cent.[3]

A Department of Health survey conducted in 2004 based on adult protection referrals to local authorities found that most referrals concerned abuse against older people (4436 referrals), followed by abuse of those with learning disabilities (3047 referrals), mental

---

[1] Department of Health, *Reforming the Law for Adult Care and Support: The Government's Response to Law Commission Report 326 on Adult Social Care* (TSO, July 2012), Cm.8379, para.9.8.

[2] A comprehensive list of resources on safeguarding can be found on the Local Government Association's website

[3] M. O'Keefe et al, *UK Study of Abuse and Neglect of Older People: Prevalence Survey Report* (2007) and A. Mowlam et al, *UK Study of Abuse and Neglect of Older People: Qualitative Findings* (2007).

health problems (1100 referrals) and physical disability (1086 referrals). The most common form of abuse reported was physical abuse (in 65 per cent of authorities), followed by financial abuse.[1]

Figures from the Health & Social Care Information Centre show that the number of cases referred for investigation by councils in England rose from 108,000 in 2011–12 to 112,000 in 2012–13. While 45 per cent of these cases took place in a care home, 38 per cent of the alleged abuse took place in the older person's own home. Physical abuse and neglect were the most common types of abuse reported (38,000 referrals). There were 24,500 referrals for financial abuse, the third highest. In 6 per cent of cases the abuser was the older person's partner; in 16 per cent it was another family member; and in 37 per cent it was a social care worker. Three-fifths of the referrals were for vulnerable adults—those described in the report as people who may be in need of community care services because they are elderly or suffer mental illness, disability or another ailment and are aged 65 or older.[2]

The Confidential Inquiry into Premature Deaths of People with Learning Disabilities published its findings in March 2013. It looked at the deaths of 233 adults and 14 children with a learning disability in the south-west and found that for 20 per cent of the people safeguarding concerns had previously been raised. While some of these may have been due to financial abuse, it is more likely that they concerned other forms of abuse: in particular, neglect. The study showed that 37 per cent of deaths would have been potentially avoidable if good-quality health care had been provided.[3]

SAFEGUARDING AND ADULT PROTECTION

The Law Commission distinguished between safeguarding and adult protection. It **1–456** argued that while safeguarding relates to the general prevention of abuse and neglect and "has a broad focus that extends to all aspects of a person's general welfare", adult protection refers to "investigation and intervention" where an adult is experiencing or is at risk of abuse and neglect. Safeguarding, considered in this context, is therefore properly part of the general approach to be taken to assessment and the provision of care and support services. The Commission therefore recommended that the well-being principle should require decision-makers to always consider the need to safeguard adults from abuse and neglect when making any decision or undertaking any action under the new statute, including in non-adult protection cases.[4]

The Joint Committee on the draft Care and Support Bill recommended that the safeguarding provisions should be moved to the part of the legislation which sets out local authorities' general responsibilities (ss.1 to 7). This was in response to concerns that the first reference to safeguarding in the draft Care and Support Bill was in relation to an enquiry which does not recognise the need for local authorities to take steps to prevent abuse occurring in the first place. The Joint Committee also recommended that local authorities should be placed under a statutory duty to take steps to empower individuals to understand what abuse is, and how to protect themselves from it, whether by seeking help or otherwise.[5]

The Government did not accept that the safeguarding provisions should be moved. It argued that unlike the general responsibilities, these provisions have a threshold that must be met before they are triggered and also that having separate safeguarding provisions

---

[1] Department of Health, *Action on Elder Abuse: Report on the Project to Establish a Monitoring and Reporting Process for Adult Protection Referrals Made in Accordance With 'No Secrets'* (2005).
[2] Health and Social Care Information Centre, *Abuse of Vulnerable Adults in England—2013–13, Provisional Report, Experimental Statistics* (12 September 2013).
[3] P. Heslop et al, *Confidential Inquiry into Premature Deaths of People with Learning Disabilities: Final Report* (University of Bristol, 2013).
[4] Law Commission, *Adult Social Care*, para.9.12.
[5] House of Lords House of Commons Joint Committee on the Draft Care and Support Bill, *Draft Care and Support Bill Report, Session 2012–13*, paras 148 to 149.

"underlines the importance of these responsibilities for local authorities and others". The Government further argued that a new duty to empower individuals was unnecessary. It pointed specifically to s.4(2)(e) which places a duty on local authorities to provide information and advice on how to raise concerns about the safety and well-being of an adult who has needs for care and support, and the role of safeguarding adults boards in raising awareness on the issues of abuse and neglect. The Government also argued that the general focus of the new legislation "on assessment on empowerment, choice, control and management of risk" supported the approach suggested by the Joint Committee.[1]

LOCAL AUTHORITY SAFEGUARDING POWERS

1–457   Local authorities have a number of statutory powers and duties to safeguard adults in cases of abuse and neglect. Some of these powers and duties are contained in the Care Act and relate to the provision of care and support to adults and carers. Sections 9 and 10, for instance, establish the core duties to assess an adult with care and support needs and a carer. Where a local authority becomes aware of potential or actual abuse or neglect concerning or being perpetrated by a person who may have care and support needs, then in the vast majority of cases these duties will be triggered. Moreover, the local authority must carry out the needs assessment in a safeguarding case even if the adult refuses (s.11(2)(b)). If the person has eligible needs then the authority must ensure that care and support is provided to meet those needs (provided that the additional criteria in ss.18 and 20 are met). It is also likely that the duty to make inquiries would be triggered in safeguarding cases (s.42). See para.1–475 below for discussion on the inter-relationship between the assessment and enquiry duties.

Outside of the Care Act, local authorities have statutory powers to take more coercive action in safeguarding cases. These powers are set out below. The circumstances in which such powers may be used include where the person lacks the requisite level of capacity or when they have decision-making capacity, particularly where their conduct affects others.

The Mental Health Act 1983

1–458   The Mental Health Act 1983 enables the detention of mentally disordered people in hospital if this is necessary in the interests of the person's health and safety or with a view to the protection of others.[2] The local social services authority's role is central to the use of such powers, mainly through the Approved Mental Health Professional who acts on behalf of the authority and in most cases makes the application for detention in hospital.

The option of hospital admission might be appropriate in some safeguarding cases, for example if as a result of mental disorder the person is neglecting themselves or putting themselves in danger of being abused by others, or where a carer is at risk of harm. There is no requirement that, in order to be detained, the person must lack capacity to make decisions about their care and treatment; in practice, the prevalence of mental incapacity amongst detained patients is high but not invariable.[3] However, the powers of the 1983 Act focus on the risks that occur as a result of mental disorder, rather than abuse and neglect by others. Moreover, these powers are only available if the person needs to be detained in hospital in order to assess or treat their mental disorder, which may not be relevant in many safeguarding cases.

The 1983 Act also establishes regimes, which include coercive elements, under which care and treatment can be provided in the community, such as Guardianship and Supervised Community Treatment.[4] These regimes enable safeguarding measures to be

---

[1] Department of Health, *The Care Bill explained—including a response to consultation and pre-legislative scrutiny on the draft Care and Support Bill*, pp.66 to 67.

[2] Mental Health Act 1983 ss.2 to 4.

[3] G. Owen et al, "Mental Capacity to Make Decisions on Treatment in People Admitted to Psychiatric Hospitals: Cross Sectional Study" (2008) 337 *British Medical Journal 40.*

[4] Mental Health Act 1983 ss.7 and 17A.

put in place such as requiring a person to live in a specified place or requiring access to the person.

Section 115 of the 1983 Act provides a power for an Approved Mental Health Professional to enter and inspect any premises (other than a hospital) in which a person with a mental disorder is living, if there is reasonable cause to suspect that the person is not receiving proper care.

In addition, s.135(1) of the 1983 Act allows a person to be removed from their home to a place of safety where it is believed that they have been or are being "ill-treated, neglected or kept otherwise than under proper control". This power can be granted by a magistrates court, on application from an Approved Mental Health Professional. It is often assumed that this power can only be used as a precursor to an assessment under the 1983 Act, but it can also be used for the purposes of making alternative arrangements for care and support, for example informal hospital admission or follow up support from community mental health services. But the utility of s.135(1) will also be limited because removal to a place of safety is only permitted for up to 72 hours during which time it may be unlikely that adequate safeguarding arrangements can be put in place.

The Mental Capacity Act 2005

The Mental Capacity Act 2005 provides that any action or decision on behalf of a person **1–459** who lacks capacity must be done or made in the person's "best interests". Such action can include the use of restraint. In safeguarding cases, local authorities may need to make a best interests decision on behalf of a person who lacks capacity who is at risk of abuse or neglect. However, a person cannot be treated as lacking in capacity merely on the basis that they make an unwise decision. This could include decisions that put the person at risk of harm. Before making a best interests decision, the person must consider whether it is possible to decide or act in a way that would interfere less with the person's rights and freedom of action.[1]

Regulations under the 2005 Act give local authorities and NHS bodies the power to appoint an Independent Mental Capacity Advocate where it is alleged that a person who lacks capacity is or has been abused or neglected by another person, or the person is abusing or neglecting another person. In addition, protective measures must have been taken or proposed by the local authority or NHS body.[2]

Schedules 1A and A1 to the 2005 Act also provide a procedural framework (known as the Deprivation of Liberty Safeguards) to enable people who lack capacity to consent to their care or treatment, to be deprived of their liberty if it is considered necessary in their best interests. The safeguards apply only to deprivations of liberty in care homes and hospitals, and require that the local authority must authorise the detention. In some cases, the safeguards may be an appropriate response to safeguarding concerns, for example to ensure that a person with dementia does not wander out of the care home at night unaccompanied and put themselves at risk. In some cases the process may uncover unauthorised deprivations of liberty which in themselves may constitute abuse or neglect.

The Mental Capacity Act 2005 also established the Court of Protection, which has the full powers of the High Court to make decisions on financial or welfare matters affecting people who lack the relevant decision-making capacity. The Court has further powers to make declarations as to whether a person has capacity or not. Local authorities may need to apply to the Court in certain cases, particularly when significant decisions are being considered in respect of a person who lacks or may lack capacity. The Court might have a role to play if there were uncertainties about whether the alleged victim had capacity and where staff were being denied entry; for example by granting injunctions to enable a proper capacity assessment.[3] In some cases the Court has been prepared to

---

[1] Mental Capacity Act 2005 s.1(4) and (6).

[2] Mental Capacity Act 2005 (Independent Mental Capacity Advocates) (Expansion of Role) Regulations 2006 (SI 2006/2883).

[3] *Re F* [2010] 2 F.L.R. 28.

authorise the removal of a person who lacks capacity from family carers where the adult's needs are being neglected.[1] The Court also has powers to appoint deputies to act on behalf of an incapacitated person or remove deputies or donees of a lasting power of attorney and an enduring power of attorney. The Act also established the Public Guardian who amongst other matters is responsible for investigating (or making referrals to the appropriate agencies) where it is alleged that a donee of a lasting power of attorney or enduring power of attorney or a court-appointed deputy is abusing or exploiting the donor or person subject to deputyship.

In practice the Mental Capacity Act 2005 has limitations. For example, it can be difficult to assess the capacity of a person who is being abused and neglected (particularly where they are reluctant to engage with services), and unless the person can be shown to lack the requisite capacity then the Act cannot be utilised. The Act also provides limited options to address directly the acts or omissions of a third party who is abusing or neglecting a person lacking capacity. It has also been suggested that the ethos of safeguarding, based on risk aversion and paternalism, differs to that of the 2005 Act based on empowerment and autonomy.[2]

The statutory guidance discusses safeguarding and the Mental Capacity Act in paras 14.44 to 14.50. It also discusses how mental capacity should be taken into account when undertaking a safeguarding enquiry (paras 14.80 to 14.81) and considering what happens after an enquiry (paras 14.92 to 14.93).

Inherent jurisdiction of the High Court

1–460   The local authority can apply to the High Court to exercise its inherent jurisdiction in safeguarding cases. The court's powers when exercising the inherent jurisdiction are wide and can include declaratory relief and the use of injunctions. The inherent jurisdiction exists to remedy lacunae left by the common law or statute. Prior to the commencement of the Mental Capacity Act 2005, the courts developed this jurisdiction primarily in relation to those who lacked capacity to make decisions.[3] It can still be relevant for adults who lack capacity if the matter is not covered by the Mental Capacity Act, for instance when making a declaration of non-recognition of a marriage.[4] But the inherent jurisdiction has also been, and continues to be, used in cases of adults who have capacity but who are "vulnerable".

In *Re SA*, Mr Justice Munby (as he was then) described a "vulnerable adult" for the purposes of the inherent jurisdiction as a person who is not necessarily lacking mental capacity but is reasonably believed to be:

- under constraint;
- subject to coercion or undue influence; or
- for some other reason "deprived of the capacity to make the relevant decision, or disabled from making a free choice, or incapacitated or disabled from giving or expressing a real and genuine consent".[5]

He went on to say:

"In the context of the inherent jurisdiction I would treat as a vulnerable adult someone who, whether or not mentally incapacitated, and whether or not suffering from any mental illness, or mental disorder, is or may be unable to take care of him or herself, or unable to protect him or herself against significant harm or exploitation, or who is deaf, blind or

---

[1] For example, *A Local Authority v WMA* [2013] EWHC 2580 (COP).
[2] See, for example, Care Quality Commission, *Monitoring the Use of the Mental Capacity Act Deprivation of Liberty Safeguards in 2011/12* (2013), p.44 and House of Lords Select Committee on the Mental Capacity Act, *Mental Capacity Act 2005: Post Legislative Scrutiny* (2014), HL Paper 139, paras 15 and 104.
[3] See, for example, *Re F (Mental patient: Sterilisation)* [1990] 2 A.C. 1.
[4] *XCC v AA* [2012] EWHC 2183 (COP).
[5] *Re SA (Vulnerable Adult with Capacity: Marriage)* [2005] EWHC 2942; [2006] 1 F.L.R. 867 at [77].

dumb, or who is substantially handicapped by illness, illness or congenial deformity. This, I emphasise, is not and is not intended to be a definition. It is descriptive, not definitive; indicative rather than prescriptive."[1]

This particular case involved an 18-year-old woman suffering from a range of disabilities, for example she was deaf, unable to communicate orally, and visually impaired. The local authority assessment was that she functioned at the intellectual level of a 13 or 14 year old, with a reading age of about 7 or 8. The issue before the court was whether it had jurisdiction to protect her from an unsuitable arranged marriage. On the facts of the case, the court made an order requiring that she be properly informed, in a manner she could understand, about any specific marriage before entering into it, and made a number of injunctions to put this into effect.

Since then, the courts have confirmed that the risk of significant harm is not determinative to the use of the inherent jurisdiction; the court's concern is instead with the person's "safety and welfare" and it will intervene "only where there is a need to protect a vulnerable adult from abuse or the real possibility of abuse".[2] However, the inherent jurisdiction cannot be used to compel a capacitated but vulnerable person to do or not do something which they have, after due consideration, decided to do or not to do; the jurisdiction acts to "facilitate the process of unencumbered decision-making" by those who have capacity "free of external pressure or physical restraint in making those decisions".[3]

The Court of Appeal has confirmed that the High Court's inherent jurisdiction had not been displaced by the Mental Capacity Act 2005 and it continues to exist for vulnerable adults whose ability to make decisions for themselves has been compromised by matters other than those covered by the 2005 Act. This particular case concerned an elderly couple—both of whom had capacity to make decisions about their living arrangements—who lived with their son. The local authority had become concerned that the son was inflicting physical and mental abuse upon his parents, for example by restricting their access to friends and family, and trying to coercive his mother into residential care. The local authority sought an injunction to prevent him from continuing with this behaviour, which was granted. The Court of Appeal upheld the injunction. In doing so, it explained that the purpose of this jurisdiction is "in part aimed at enhancing or liberating the autonomy of the vulnerable adult" whose autonomy has been compromised for one of the reasons outlined in *Re SA*.[4] The Court went on to dismiss the suggestion that the inherent jurisdiction would be used by local authorities in order to pursue a "Big Brother agenda":

". . . there can be no power of public intervention simply because an adult proposes to make a decision, or to tolerate a state of affairs, which most would consider neither wise nor sensible. There has to be much more than simply that for any intervention to be justified: and any such intervention will indeed need to be justified as necessary and proportionate."[5]

However, the inherent jurisdiction can be expensive and slow. This may make local authorities reluctant to use this option when budgets are stretched.

Public health powers

Local authority public health powers may particularly be an option in safeguarding cases **1–461** involving self-neglect. The Public Health (Control of Disease) Act 1984 allows a local authority to apply to a magistrate for an order to remove a person from a house where an infectious disease has occurred, and to place or detain a person in hospital if they are

---

[1] *Re SA (Vulnerable Adult with Capacity: Marriage)* [2005] EWHC 2942; [2006] 1 F.L.R. 867 at [82].

[2] *Local Authority X v MM* [2007] EWHC 2003 (Fam); (2008) 11 CCLR 119 at [115] and [118].

[3] *LBL v RYJ* [2010] EWHC 2665 (COP) at [62].

[4] *DL v A Local Authority* [2012] EWCA Civ 253; [2012] 3 W.L.R. 1439 at [54].

[5] *DL v A Local Authority* [2012] EWCA Civ 253; [2012] 3 W.L.R. 1439 at [76].

suffering from a notifiable disease. There is further power for a magistrate to order the removal of people who are or may be infected or contaminated in such a way that presents a significant risk of harm to human health.

Under the Environmental Health Act 1990 a local authority has powers of entry in order to determine if a statutory nuisance exists or to take action or execute work. Statutory nuisances can include premises, an animal kept in a place or manner or any accumulation or deposit prejudicial to health or a nuisance.[1] The Public Health Act 1936 gives local authorities powers in respect of filthy, unwholesome, verminous premises, verminous persons or clothing (including the removal of the person), and cleaning or destroying filthy or verminous articles.[2] These powers include the ability to require vacation of premises during fumigation.[3] There is also a power of entry to premises, suing force if necessary. An order can be obtained from the magistrates' court for this purpose.[4]

However, environmental health departments often set high thresholds for intervention under this legislation and accordingly the powers are only used as a last resort. In any event, these powers are aimed at protecting *public* health, rather than being focused on the harm that may be caused to the person responsible for the insanitary conditions.

Other relevant legal provisions

1–462   The Anti-Social Behaviour, Crime and Policing Act 2014 introduced a civil injunction available in the County Court for adults and in the youth court for those under the age of 18. The injunction replaces previous anti-social provisions such as the anti-social behaviour order and anti-social behaviour injunction. Along with prohibitions, the injunction could include positive requirements to get the individual to deal with the underlying cause of the behaviour, for example the misuse of alcohol. Applications for the injunction can be made to the court by a local authority, housing provider or police officer.

AUTONOMY VERSUS PROTECTION

1–463   For both policy makers and practitioners, there is a difficult balance to be struck between maximising freedom of choice and autonomy and ensuring adequate protection for those who need it. Public intervention in the lives of children is often based on the assumption that they are incapable of providing for themselves, but with adults the contrary assumption applies. There are links between safeguarding adults and mental capacity, since the need for intervention may be heightened where an adult lacks the capacity to make a certain decision and is placed at risk as a result. This was summed up by Mr Justice Thorpe in *Re C (Adult: Refusal of Treatment)* when he opined that "the further the capacity is reduced, the lighter autonomy weighs".[5] However, safeguarding adults is not confined to those who lack capacity and can, depending on the form it takes, extend to those with decision-making capacity. Whether or not the person lacks capacity, determining whether intervention is justified and the types of intervention that are warranted is often difficult to gauge and will vary according to the circumstances of the case. Even the most clearly drafted law or guidance will not provide clear solutions for every scenario. However, the law does provide a framework to assist the practitioner to decide on the most appropriate response, and provides a range of possible interventions to implement that decision.

The principles of the Care Act are particularly relevant to decision-making in this context. Section 1(3)(a) emphasises the importance of beginning with the assumption that the person is best placed to judge their own well-being. Alongside this starting point, the decision-maker must have regard to the other principles, including the need to protect

---

[1]   Environmental Health Act 1990 s.79.
[2]   Public Health Act 1936 ss.83 to 85.
[3]   Public Health Act 1936 s.83(3).
[4]   Public Health Act 1936 s.287.
[5]   *Re C (Adult: Refusal of Treatment)* [1994] 1 W.L.R. 290 at 292.

people from abuse and neglect (s.1(3)(g)) and ensure that any restriction is kept to the minimum necessary (s.1(3)(h)).

The Human Rights Act 1998 has been described as "potentially one of the most powerful instruments for protecting people against neglect and abuse".[1] Section 6 of the Act provides that it is unlawful for a public body such as a local authority to act in a way that is incompatible with a right protected by the European Convention on Human Rights and listed in Sch.1. This is intended to ensure that human rights are part and parcel of the development and delivery of public services. Article 8 of the Convention, for example, provides that everyone has the right to respect for their private and family life, and this right can be restricted only in specified circumstances, such as to protect health and the rights and freedoms of others. Any interference must also be in accordance with the law, legitimate and necessary. Although art.8 is often interpreted by practitioners as preventing intervention by the state against the citizen, in legal terms this is not necessarily correct. It requires a balance between the rights of the individual and the need to, for example, protect the wider needs of the community. In some cases it may also lead to positive safeguarding obligations. The positive obligations under art.8 are discussed in more detail at para.1–153 above.

The framework of the Human Rights Act described above is based on the principle of proportionality. In deciding what action (if any) to take in safeguarding cases, practitioners are required to weigh up all of the relevant considerations in the light of the particular circumstances of the individual case. The Social Care Institute for Excellence guide on safeguarding powers sums up the position in the following terms:

"Any interference by the state (meaning public bodies, or sometimes private bodies carrying out functions of a public nature) must be lawful and proportionate. The stipulation of necessity encompasses a requirement of proportionality—that is, not 'taking a sledgehammer to crack a nut'. Where a power of entry is though necessary, it should be exercised proportionately, in relation to the risk and the apparent gravity of the situation."[2]

It is submitted that practitioners should consider their available safeguarding powers, starting with the least restrictive. Where any such powers could be used, a local authority might have to explain any failure to investigate the case or take further action, particularly where that failure has led to a situation where a person suffers harm. For example, the victims of abuse or neglect might claim damages against the local authority that failed to act (for negligence, breach of a specific duty or breach of the European Convention on Human Rights) or the local authority may be the subject of an investigation carried out by the Local Government Ombudsman, the Care Quality Commission, or incidentally through a Coroner's investigation into a death in which system failure is alleged.

Practitioners should be mindful of judicial concern that some local authorities are heavy-handed and too eager to intervene without proper legal authority, for example to remove service users arbitrarily from domestic settings.[3] Mr Justice Munby (as he was then) said that when public bodies are considering whether to intervene to protect an adult from harm:

"The emphasis must be on sensible risk appraisal, not striving to avoid all risk, whatever the price, but instead seeking a proper balance and being willing to tolerate manageable or acceptable risks as the price appropriately to be paid in order to achieve some other good—in particular to achieve the vital good of the elderly or vulnerable person's *happiness*. What good is it making someone safer if it merely makes them miserable?"[4]

---

[1] *Hansard* (House of Lords), 22 July 2013,Vol.747, col.1102.

[2] Social Care Institute for Excellence, *Gaining access to an adult suspected to be at risk of neglect or abuse: a guide for social workers and their managers in England* (Oct 2014), p.6.

[3] *A Local Authority v A* [2010] EWHC 978 (Fam); (2010) 13 CCLR 404 at [99], per Munby L.J.

[4] *Local Authority X v MM* [2007] EWHC 2003 (Fam); (2008) 11 CCLR 119 at [120] (emphasis in original).

The statutory guidance also recognises the need for a balanced and proportionate approach. For instance, it states that:

"Any intervention in family or personal relationships needs to be carefully considered. While abusive relationships never contribute to the wellbeing of an adult, interventions which remove all contact with family members may also be experienced as abusive interventions and risk breaching the adult's right to family life if not justified or proportionate. Safeguarding needs to recognise that the right to safety needs to be balanced with other rights, such as rights to liberty and autonomy, and rights to family life."[1]

THE COMMON LAW DUTY OF CARE

1–464   In tort law, a duty of care is an obligation placed on an individual requiring that they exercise a reasonable standard of care while doing something (or possibly omitting to do something) that could foreseeably harm others. For an action to succeed in negligence, the claimant must prove that the defendant owed them a duty of care. The likelihood of any proceedings being successful will only arise where a duty of care is breached through negligent acts or omissions and an individual suffers damage caused by the breach of the duty, which was not too remote.[2]

In *X v Hounslow LBC*, the Court of Appeal held that a local authority did not owe a common law duty of care to protect tenants living in one of its flats by moving them into alternative accommodation in response to "the unusual but dangerous situation which had developed".[3] The couple, who had learning difficulties, lived in local housing authority accommodation with their children, and local youths had taken to using the couple's flat for illicit activity, including taking drugs, underage sexual activity and storing stolen goods, and on several occasions the couple had been subjected to threatening and abusive behaviour. Social services had referred them to the housing department to be re-housed, but the local authority failed to do so before the youths imprisoned the couple in their home for the duration of a weekend and subjected them to serious and degrading sexual and physical assaults. The Court of Appeal held that in order to establish a duty of care to protect one party against the criminal acts of a third party, something more than reasonable foreseeability of harm was needed. Examples of the necessary further ingredients include where the defendant creates the source of danger to the claimant, the third party who causes damage is under the control or supervision of the defendant, and the defendant has assumed a responsibility to the victim.[4]

The claimants argued that the local authority had assumed a responsibility for the family because it provided social work support to them, and had taken on the task of securing suitable and safe housing. The claimants also argued that, given the vulnerability of the couple, they could only live in the community with the assistance of the authority and there was a heavy degree of reliance by the vulnerable adults on the authority. The Court of Appeal, however, was not persuaded that those considerations led to the assumption of responsibility or some other factor which might give rise to the imposition of a duty of care on the local authority. The Court found that the local authority was seeking to carry out its statutory functions and no more; a complaint that the authority was not exercising its statutory duties and powers properly is not sufficient to give rise to a parallel common law duty of care.[5]

---

[1] Department of Health, *Care and Support Statutory Guidance* (2014), para.6.82.
[2] The test for whether a duty of care is owed is contained in *Caparo Industries Plc v Dickman* [1990] 2 A.C. 605. The case concerned liability for economic loss, but the conditions have subsequently been treated as being of general application.
[3] *X v Hounslow LBC* [2009] EWCA Civ 286; (2009) 12 CCLR 254 at [33].
[4] *X v Hounslow LBC* [2009] EWCA Civ 286; (2009) 12 CCLR 254 at [55].
[5] *X v Hounslow LBC* [2009] EWCA Civ 286; (2009) 12 CCLR 254 at [65] and [90].

The point at which a local authority will be held to have assumed responsibility towards an individual to protect them from harm caused by a third party is not capable of being defined precisely but it is more than merely providing services and other support to individuals; some other *special factor* is required. While the common law has not yet recognised a duty of care, if a local authority assumes a responsibility over an individual or increases or causes the danger they face, such a duty may be found in the future. This is in direct contrast with the situation in relation to children, which in many respects is a direct result of the statutory child protection regime that establishes a clear obligation on local authorities to use their powers to safeguard children at risk of significant harm. Nonetheless, this has been held by the courts not to be directly enforceable at common law, either as an action for breach of statutory duty, or by creating a separate duty of care in negligence.[1]

OTHER SAFEGUARDING LAW

There are other legal provisions that may apply in adult safeguarding cases which do not **1–465** give powers directly to the local authority. However, local authorities will need to be aware of these provisions and where powers are given to other bodies, consider sharing information with or initiating a referral to the relevant body in safeguarding cases where appropriate. As the lead safeguarding agency, the local authority may need to have an ongoing role in co-ordinating the use of such powers.

Health and social care service providers are regulated by the Care Quality Commission. The Health and Social Care Act 2008 and associated regulations provide for the registration requirements and standards of quality and care that all providers have to meet when they register with the Care Quality Commission, and on an on-going basis after that. The standards include a specific safeguarding outcome that service users must not be subject to abuse and improper treatment (and take action to prevent or respond to abuse) and other relevant outcomes such as treating service users with dignity and respect.[2] The Government also amended the Care Act during its passage through Parliament to introduce an explicit duty of candour on health and social care providers (see below).[3] The Care Quality Commission has a number of enforcement powers if the standards are not being met, including warning notices, cancelling registration and prosecution. The Care Act introduces provisions, in relation to organisations convicted of supplying or publishing false or misleading information, for "remedial orders" (requiring the organisation to take steps to correct the situation) and "publicity orders" (requiring the organisation to publicise the conviction, whether a remedial order has been issued by the court, and, if so, what steps it is taking to comply with that order).[4] In the past, the Care Quality Commission's prosecuting powers were criticised as ineffective because it was required to serve a notice against the company before prosecuting and if the company complied with the notice it could take no further action. However, from 2014 the Care Quality Commission will have powers to bring prosecutions to issue a warning notice in cases where there have been serious failings in care. In other cases it will retain a pre-prosecution notice system.[5]

One of the most important but often neglected areas of adult protection is the role of the UK regulators of health and social care professionals, such as the General Medical Council,

---

[1] *X (Minors) v Bedfordshire CC* [1995] 2 A.C. 633.
[2] Health and Social Care Act 2008 (Regulated Activities) Regulations 2014 (SI 2014/2936), regs 10 and 13.
[3] Care Act 2014 s.81.
[4] Care Act 2014 s.93.
[5] Department of Health, *Introducing Fundamental Standards: Consultation on Proposals to Change CQC Registration Requirements* (January 2014), p.14.

Nursing and Midwifery Council and Health and Care Professions Council.[1] The primary purpose of professional regulation is to ensure public safety. This is achieved not only by a process of weeding out those whose fitness to practise is impaired but also by encouraging high standards of professional practice and conduct, and thereby reducing the need for disciplinary intervention. The regulators are required to issue, for example, standards of conduct, performance and ethics and to determine from time to time the standards of proficiency for safe and competent practice which professionals are expected to follow. Professionals wishing to use titles such as "registered medical practitioner", "social worker" or "pharmacist" must be registered with the relevant regulator. It is a criminal offence for any person to use a protected title without being registered. Professional regulation is one element of a much broader system of ensuring patient and service user care. In broad terms, its focus is on the regulation of individual professionals rather than, for example, organisations and systems.

There are also more limited forms of individual regulation based on negative registration or barring schemes. Rather than providing a list of those who are qualified and fit to practise, a barring scheme lists only those who are prohibited from practising. Examples include the Disclosure and Barring Service's lists of people who are barred from working with children and vulnerable adults.[2] In broad terms, barring takes place where the person has been convicted of certain serious offences or where there is or may be harm to a child or vulnerable adult. The statutory guidance discusses the role of the Disclosure and Barring Service in paras 14.61 to 14.62. The Health and Care Professions Council also maintains a barring scheme for social work students and is exploring the possibility for adult social care workers in England.[3]

The Employment Rights Act 1996 (as amended by the Public Disclosure Act 1998) gives workers who raise concerns about abuses and malpractice protection from dismissal and victimisation. Such "whistleblowers" are enabled to make a complaint to an employment tribunal. The NHS Constitution in England also includes an expectation that staff should raise concerns at an early stage and that NHS bodies should support staff that whistleblow by investigating the concerns and ensuring there is an independent person to speak to. The regulators of health and social care professionals (see above) issue codes and standards which cover raising concerns at work. For example, the Health and Care Professions Council's *Standards of Conduct, Performance and Ethics* requires registrants to "act immediately" if a situation comes to light where a service user may be put in danger, and inform the Council of any important information about their own, or other registrants' or health professionals' conduct or competence.[4] The Care Quality Commission also issues guidance to care providers to ensure robust whistleblowing policies.[5]

1–466   Adults with care and support needs are also protected by the same criminal law provisions as other people, such as the Offences Against the Person Act 1861 and common law offences such as assault or, in the case of financial abuse, theft or fraud. Local social services authorities may be involved in reporting possible criminal actions to the police or providing further evidence in criminal cases. There are also specific provisions aimed at, for example, disabled people and those with mental health problems, such as:

---

[1] For an overview of this are see Law Commission et al, *Regulation of Health Care Professionals, Regulation of Social Care Professionals in England* (2012), Consultation Paper No.202; Northern Ireland Law Commission Consultation Paper No.12; Scottish Law Commission Discussion Paper No.153. For a summary of the consultation paper see, T. Spencer-Lane, "Reforming the Professional regulatory Bodies: the Law Commission Review of Health and Social Care Professional Regulation", 14 *Journal of Adult Protection* 5, 237.

[2] Safeguarding Vulnerable Groups Act 2006.

[3] Health and Care Professions Council. *Proposal for Regulating Adult Social Care Workers in England* (2013).

[4] Health and Care Professions Council, *Standards of Conduct, Performance and Ethics* (2008), standards 1 and 4.

[5] Care Quality Commission, *Whistleblowing: Guidance for Providers who are Registered with the Care Quality Commission* (November 2013).

- The Criminal Justice Act 2003 provides that any offence can be "aggravated" by hostility to particular groups (including disabled people). Where an offence is aggravated in this sense, that fact must be taken into account in sentencing, and can result in an enhanced sentence.
- Section 127 of the Mental Health Act 1983 and s.44 of the Mental Capacity Act 2005 establish criminal offences of ill treatment or wilful neglect in relation to mental health patients and those who lack capacity respectively.
- The Sexual Offences Act 2003 establishes a range of criminal offences relating to people with mental disorders and sexual activity.
- Section 5 of the Domestic Violence, Crime and Victims Act 2004 makes it an offence to cause or allow the death or serious physical harm of a child or vulnerable adult.
- Section 4 of the Fraud Act 2006 makes it an offence for a person who occupies a position where he or she is required to safeguard, or not act against, the financial interests of another person, to dishonestly abuse that position, with the intent of self benefit or to benefit others.

The police have emergency powers which may be relevant in some safeguarding cases. The police have powers to enter and arrest a person for an indictable offence under s.17(1)(b) of the Police and Criminal Evidence Act 1984. An indictable offence would include ill-treatment and wilful neglect (see below). Under s.17(1)(e) of the 1984 Act the police may enter and search premises without a warrant for the purposes of "saving life or limb or preventing serious damage to property". The courts have confirmed that the threshold for the use of this power is high, reflecting the fact that it is a serious matter for a citizen to have their house entered against their will by police officers. Thus, s.17(1)(e) cannot be used where there is merely a concern for a person's welfare; something more serious is required.[1] Section 24 of the 1984 Act also provides for a power of arrest without a warrant where a police officer has reasonable grounds for suspecting that someone is about to, or is committing an offence. There also remains in common law a power of entry to stop or prevent a breach of the peace. The threat of a breach of the peace must be both real and imminent.[2]

The police have powers to issue Domestic Violence Protection Notices under s.24 of the Crime and Security Act 2010. The Notice can require a perpetrator to leave their home if they live with the victim. The police can also apply for a Domestic Violence Protection Order, which is a court order issued by a magistrates' court.

The statutory guidance discusses criminal offences and adult safeguarding (including vulnerable witnesses) in paras 14.70 to 14.76. See also commentary below under s.76(8) and (9) for further detail on the mechanisms that are in place in prisons to address cases of abuse and neglect.

A claim in tort may also be appropriate in safeguarding cases, relying on the torts of negligence, false imprisonment or trespass to the person. It may also be possible for the victim to apply for an injunction under s.3 of the Protection from Harassment Act 1997, or a non-molestation order or occupation order under the Family Law Act 1996. Other relevant law includes the offence of corporate manslaughter under the Corporate Manslaughter and Corporate Homicide Act 2007 and corporate neglect in s.37 of the Health and Safety at Work etc Act 1974.

New safeguarding powers

In 1995, the Law Commission recommended the introduction of a number of new compulsory intervention powers aimed specifically at adults at risk of abuse and neglect. These **1–467**

---

[1] *Baker v Crown Prosecution Service* [2009] EWHC 299 (Admin) and *Syed v Director of Public Prosecutions* [2010] EWHC 81 (Admin).
[2] *R. v Howell* [1981] 3 W.L.R. 501.

powers aimed to deal with two distinct problems. The first was the refusal by a service user of help and support when without them the person would no longer be able to live an independent life in the community. The second was where a carer or other person with whom the service user is living refuses access to that person or refuses the provision of services to them. This was, in part, a response to the case of Beverley Lewis, a disabled woman who died at home in 1989 after her mother, with whom she lived and who suffered from mental health problems, obstructed the attempts of the health and social services authorities to gain access to her daughter.[1] The main powers recommended in this respect were:

- a right for a local authority officer to enter premises and interview a vulnerable adult;
- a court order to allow a local authority officer to enter premises, by force if necessary, where a vulnerable adult may be at risk;
- a court order to allow the local authority to assess whether a person is at risk; and
- a compulsory power to remove and detain a person who is at risk.[2]

In response to the Law Commission Report, the Lord Chancellor's Department published a Green Paper *Who Decides* in December 1997. The Government accepted in principle these particular recommendations on compulsory powers but sought additional views on the practicalities of the proposals.[3] However, following the responses to the consultation the Government announced in a policy statement entitled *Making Decisions* in October 1999 that it would not be taking forward any new compulsory powers. However, it gave no reason for excluding these proposals from its plans for law reform.[4]

In 2003, the Joint Committee on the draft Mental Incapacity Bill recommended the introduction of new safeguarding powers.[5] In its response, the Government stated that it was already taking action to protect vulnerable adults against abuse. In particular, it pointed to:

- the *No Secrets* guidance on developing multi-agency procedures for the protection of vulnerable adults[6] ;
- the new Public Guardian which would have a role working with local authorities and other agencies; and
- the new criminal offence of ill-treatment or wilful neglect in the Bill which would be "another valuable tool in tackling potential abuse".[7]

During the passage of the Mental Capacity Bill through Parliament the Government rejected an amendment on new safeguarding powers, by pointing to the existing duty to investigate and compulsory powers under s.47 of the National Assistance Act 1947 which provided a compulsory power to remove people living in insanitary conditions and not receiving proper care and attention.[8]

---

[1] Law Commission, Mentally Incapacitated and Other Vulnerable Adults: Public Law Protection Consultation Paper No.130 (1993), p.6.

[2] Law Commission, *Mental Incapacity*, Law Com No.231 (1995), paras 9.19 to 9.34.

[3] Lord Chancellor's Department, Who Decides: *Making Decisions on Behalf of Mentally Incapacitated Adults* (TSO, December 1997), Cm.3803, paras 8.1 to 8.6 and 8.20 to 8.43.

[4] Lord Chancellor's Department, *Making decisions: The Government's Proposals for Making Decisions on behalf of Mentally Incapacitated Adults* (October 1999), Cm.4465, para.12.

[5] House of Lords House of Commons Joint Committee on the *Draft Mental Incapacity Bill, Draft Mental Incapacity Bill, Session 2002–03*, HL Paper 189-I, HC Paper 1083-I (TSO, November 2003), Vol.1, para.266.

[6] Department of Health and Home Office, *No Secrets: Guidance on Developing and Implementing Multi-agency Policies and Procedures to Protect Vulnerable Adults from Abuse* (2000).

[7] Department for Constitutional Affairs, *The Government Response to the Scrutiny Committees Report on the Draft Mental Incapacity Bill* (February 2004), Cm.6121, para.15.

[8] *Hansard* (House of Commons: Mental Capacity Bill in Standing Committee A) 2 November 2004, col.325 (Rosie Winterton MP).

Since then, the Adult Support and Protection (Scotland) Act 2007 has been implemented, which includes the following compulsory powers intended to protect adults who are unable to safeguard their own interests:

- the power for a council officer to visit premises to determine whether or not further action is needed to protect an adult at risk of harm, using warrants of entry if necessary;
- the power for a sheriff to issue an assessment order or an order to remove the adult at risk to a specified place; and
- the power to ban abusers from a specified place for up to six months.

In the summer of 2007, Ivan Lewis, the then Minister for Care Services, announced that *No Secrets* was to be reviewed. This announcement was made following the publication of the 2007 national survey into the abuse and neglect of older people (see para.1–455 above). The review which was launched a year later included consideration of the need for new safeguarding powers.[1] The responses to the consultation showed that:

- 60 per cent of respondents supported a new power to enter premises where it is suspected that a vulnerable adult is being abused (27 per cent did not support such a power);
- 22 per cent of respondents agreed that such a power should apply when an adult has capacity and may be self-neglecting or self harming (50 per cent did not want to see such a power);
- 13 per cent supported the introduction of a power to remove an adult who is thought to be subject to harm but who has capacity and who does not consent to being removed (57 per cent did not support such a power); and
- 12 per cent agreed that force should be used to remove a person who is self-neglecting or harming (60 per cent did not support this view).[2]

In summary, while there was quite high support for a power of entry, the level of support **1–468** significantly reduced in response to more invasive powers. There was also less support for compulsory powers in situations where the relevant person has decision-making capacity. In response the Government announced plans to introduce new legislation to place adult boards on a statutory footing and publish a guide to the law on safeguarding. But it made no mention of any new powers of intervention.[3]

The Law Commission's final report on adult social care did not recommend new safeguarding powers. It argued this was a matter for political policy rather than law reform. However, it did consider reforming the compulsory removal power under s.47 of the National Assistance Act 1948. While the Commission concluded that s.47 should be repealed mainly because it breached the European Convention on Human Rights, it also recommended that the Government should consider carrying out research and consulting on a new replacement power. The repeal of s.47 is considered in more detail at para.1–507 below. In addition, the Commission recommend that the following issues merited further consideration:

- amending the Mental Health Act 1983 to ensure that protection arrangements under Guardianship can apply to all people with learning disabilities and not just those

---

[1] Department of Health, Home Office, and the Ministry of Justice, *Safeguarding Adults: A Consultation on the Review of the "No Secrets" Guidance* (2008).

[2] Department of Health, Home Office, and the Ministry of Justice, *Safeguarding Adults: Report on the Consultation on the Review of "No Secrets"* (2009), pp.122 to 124.

[3] Department of Health, *Written Ministerial Statement: Government Response to the Consultation on Safeguarding Adults: The Review of the No Secrets Guidance* (2010).

whose disability is "associated with abnormally aggressive and seriously irresponsible conduct"; and

- implementing the power of local authorities to apply for occupation orders on the person's behalf under s.60 of the Family Law Act 1996 for use in safeguarding cases.[1]

In response the Government agreed that s.47 should be repealed but it also discounted any new powers in this area. Instead it announced that it would use the opportunity of pre-legislative scrutiny of the draft Care and Support Bill to consult on a more limited power to give local authorities access to a person who may be at risk of abuse. The Government also said that it was unpersuaded that amendments to Guardianship would offer any additional protection to such people over and above that provided by existing adult safeguarding powers, and that it had no plans to bring s.60 of the Family Law Act 1996 into force.[2]

In July 2012 the Government launched a consultation on a new safeguarding power which would apply where a local authority has reasonable cause for concern that a person with capacity is experiencing abuse or neglect, and someone else in the property is preventing the local authority from speaking with that person. In such circumstances the local authority would be able to apply for a warrant to enter the premises and speak with that person alone. In part the proposal was an attempt to mirror the existing remit of the inherent jurisdiction of the High Court (see para.1–460 above), and therefore avoid the need to resort to the courts in every case.[3] The Joint Committee recognised the "obvious dangers" of a new compulsory power but on balance felt that the safeguarding provisions should include a power of entry for local authority representatives in such cases.[4] However, the Government's consultation revealed no clear consensus. Of 212 respondents, 49 per cent backed a new power, with 40 per cent opposed and 11 per cent undecided. The majority of respondents in favour of a new power of access were health and social care professionals (90 per cent and 72 per cent, respectively) but among individuals, 77 per cent disapproved. The Government's response noted, in particular, the strength of feeling among the public and the risk of unintended consequences noted by some respondents. It concluded that the responses to the consultation did not provide a compelling case to legislate for a new power of entry.[5] However, the accuracy of the Government's analysis of consultation responses has been questioned.[6]

1–469 During the passage of the Care Bill, at report stage in the House of Lords, Baroness Greengross tabled an amendment to allow a social worker or another practitioner to conduct a private interview following an application to the court based on a reasonable suspicion of abuse or neglect.[7] In response the Government stated:

> "A fundamental truth at the heart of all this is that no amount of legislation will prevent abuse of adults vulnerable to abuse. Rather, it is through developing effective partnerships and ensuring the active engagement of the community that we can best protect individuals."[8]

---

[1] Law Commission, *Adult Social Care*, paras 9.96 and 9.138 to 9.146.

[2] Department of Health, *Reforming the Law for Adult Care and Support: The Government's Response to Law Commission Report 326 on Adult Social Care* (TSO, July 2012), Cm.8379, paras 9.17 to 9.19 and 9.27 to 9.29.

[3] Department of Health, *Consultation on New Safeguarding Power* (2012).

[4] House of Lords House of Commons Joint Committee on the Draft Care and Support Bill, *Draft Care and Support Bill Report, Session 2012–13*, para.159.

[5] Department of Health, *Government Response to the Safeguarding Power of Entry Consultation* (May 2013), paras 13 to 16 and 31 to 33.

[6] D. Hewitt, "You are not, any of you, my mother: what happened to the safeguarding power of entry?" (2014) 16 *Journal of Adult Protection* 1.

[7] *Hansard* (House of Lords), 14 October 2013, Vol.748, cols 331 to 332.

[8] *Hansard* (House of Lords), 14 October 2013, Vol.748, col.340 (Earl Howe).

In the division this amendment was defeated by 143 peers against 72, a majority of 71.[1] A similar amendment was tabled by Paul Burstow MP at Committee stage in the House of Commons. It would have required an application to have been made to a circuit judge authorised by the Court of Protection and included various notification requirements. In rejecting this amendment the Government argued that the Police and Criminal Evidence Act 1984 already allowed necessary action where appropriate.[2]

At report stage the issue was revisited. Paul Burstow MP quoted Action on Elder Abuse research which showed that 29 local authorities had reported at least one instance in the previous 12 months in which they had been unable to gain entry because a third party had denied them access. In 21 of those cases they had never gained access.[3] Once again the Government denied that there was a gap in powers that would prevent professionals from accessing those in urgent need of assistance. As well as quoting statements to confirm this position from the Association of Chief Police Officers, the Association of Directors of Adult Social Services and the chief social worker for adults, the Government pointed to the inherent jurisdiction of the High Court as providing a "crucial final safety net". It also confirmed that a clear statement on the use of existing safeguarding powers would be published in 2014.[4] This statement took the form of a guide produced by the Social Care Institute for Excellence on gaining access to adults suspected to be at risk of abuse or neglect, and was published in October 2014.[5]

As noted above, a provision on powers of entry already exists in the Adult Support and Protection (Scotland) Act 2007. Sections 37 to 41 set out the necessary procedures for applying to a sheriff or, in urgent cases, to a justice of the peace, for a warrant for entry. Section 127 of the Social Services and Well-being (Wales) Act 2014 also provides for adult protection and support orders to authorise entry to premises (if necessary by force) for the purpose of enabling an authorised officer of a local authority to assess whether an adult is at risk of abuse or neglect and, if so, what to do about it. Consequently there is no consistent UK-wide approach to adult safeguarding powers.

ILL-TREATMENT AND WILFUL NEGLECT

Both the Mental Health Act 1983 and the Mental Capacity Act 2005 establish criminal **1–470** offences of ill-treatment and wilful neglect in relation to mental health patients and those who lack capacity respectively.[6] An individual convicted of these offences faces a maximum sentence of five years imprisonment or an unlimited fine. In addition, the offence of child cruelty under s.1 of the Children and Young Persons Act 1933 applies in cases of wilful ill-treatment or neglect. Research indicates that in 2013–14, 349 charges were made and reached a first magistrates' court hearing in England and Wales in respect of the Mental Capacity Act offence. This was a rise from 168 in 2012–13. There were 47 prosecutions under the Mental Health Act offence in 2013–14, down from 57 in 2012–13.[7]

Ill-treatment and neglect are separate concepts and cases do not have to prove that both took place. The courts have confirmed that ill treatment does not necessarily need to cause physical harm, and can include the emotional and psychological damage that the actions have caused or have the potential to cause, both to the patient and to their family.[8] It

---

[1] *Hansard* (House of Lords), 14 October 2013, Vol.748, cols 343 to 344.
[2] *Hansard* (House of Commons: Public Bill Committee), 4 February 2014: Fifteenth Sitting, col.610 (Norman Lamb MP).
[3] *Hansard* (House of Commons), 10 March 2014, Vol.577, col.56.
[4] *Hansard* (House of Commons), 10 March 2014, Vol.577, col.85 (Norman Lamb MP).
[5] Social Care Institute for Excellence, *Gaining access to an adult suspected to be at risk of neglect or abuse: a guide for social workers and their managers in England* (Oct 2014).
[6] Mental Health Act 1983 s.127 and Mental Capacity Act 2005 s.44.
[7] Figures obtained by Dave Sheppard and reported by Community Care, see: A McNicholl, "Prosecutions Double for Abuse and Neglect of People who lack Capacity" (5/11/05).
[8] *R v Newington* (1990) 91 Cr App R 247, 254.

can include failing to protect the privacy and dignity of a vulnerable patient (even where the victim is not aware that they have been ill-treated) such as by taking a photograph of a semi-naked elderly patient in the bath.[1]

These offences apply to a "person", which can include an individual, corporate body or partnership. An organisation can only be found guilty of wilful neglect, if a "directing mind" of that organisation was also guilty of the offence, such as that the organisation as a whole was guilty of the offence. A person is a directing mind if they are sufficiently senior to be considered the embodiment of the company.[2] The difficulties in prosecuting companies for these types of offences led to the development of the corporate manslaughter offence.[3]

The meaning of "wilful" has also been developed through case law. According to *Archbold*:

> "The leading case is *R v Sheppard* [1981] A.C, HL, in which the majority held that a man 'wilfully' fails to provide adequate medical attention for a child if he *either* (a) deliberately does so, knowing that there is some risk that the child's health may suffer unless he receives such attention *or* (b) does so because he does not care whether the child may be in need of medical treatment or not."[4]

It does not include genuine error or accident, including where an experienced professional has failed to appreciate the full circumstances of an incident and did not seek appropriate medical attention.[5] The Court of Appeal has said that actions or omissions that reflected or were believed to reflect the protected autonomy of the individual needing care (for example where a patient was refusing help) did not constitute wilful neglect.[6] But it can include where a practitioner knows it is necessary to administer a clinical intervention but decides not to because they panicked. But the judge in this case did say that a failure to act as a result of stress could be taken into account when sentencing.[7]

The Law Commission's final report on adult social care recommended that the Government should consider extending the criminal offences of ill treatment or wilful neglect to include people with care and support needs who are not subject to the powers of the 1983 Act or mentally incapacitated. It noted that a situation could arise whereby three adults at risk had been placed in a care home where they suffered abuse and neglect—one has been placed there under the Mental Health Act 1983, one lacks capacity and has been admitted following a best interests decision under the Mental Capacity Act 2005 and the other person has capacity and has been placed there under adult social care legislation. A prosecution on their behalf for ill-treatment or wilful neglect could only be initiated in the case of the first two people. At consultation, the Commission had also been informed by police officers that prosecutions were being dropped in practice because doctors cannot confirm or have not documented that the person lacks capacity.[8] In response the Government argued that a new criminal offence was unnecessary and pointed to the

---

[1] *R v Dublas* (2009) Inner London County Court (unreported).

[2] *Tesco Supermarkets Ltd v Nattrass* [1971] UKHL 1.

[3] Home Office, *Corporate Manslaughter: The Government's Draft Bill for Reform* (March 2005), Cm.6497. The offence of corporate manslaughter/homicide established in the Corporate Manslaughter and Corporate Homicide Act 2007 does not require the identififcation of a single individual acting as the "directing mind" of the organisation, and then proving that this individual behaved wilfully, such that the organisation as a whole can be considered to be guilty of the offence. Instead, it focusses on the way an organisation managed or organised its activities, and on the duty of care that the organisation owed towards the victim.

[4] *Archbold: Criminal Pleading, Evidence and Practice 2014* (London: Sweet & Maxwell, 2014), para.11–47

[5] *R. v Morrell* [2002] EWCA Crim 2547.

[6] *R. (Ligaya) v Nursing and Midwifery Council* [2012] EWCA Crim 2521.

[7] *R. v Patel* [2013] EWCA Crim 965.

[8] Law Commission, *Adult Social Care*, paras 9.96 and 9.142 to 9.144.

inherent jurisdiction of the High Court which can protect adults with capacity who are subject to "coercion or undue influence".[1]

The Joint Committee also considered corporate accountability for abuse and neglect—mainly as a result of events at Winterbourne View. It recommended that:

". . . where abuse or neglect of an adult has resulted in the commission of an offence by an employee of a body corporate acting as such, and this is proved to have been committed with the consent of, or to have been attributable to any neglect on the part of, a director, manager or similar officer of the body corporate acting as such, he as well as the body corporate should be guilty of an offence."[2]

During the passage of the Care Bill in the House of Lords, amendments were tabled by **1–471** Lord Touhig to create a new offence of corporate manslaughter and by Baroness Greengross to create a new criminal offence of ill treatment or wilful neglect of an adult with care and support needs who is not covered by the Mental Health Act or Mental Capacity Act.[3] However, the Government rejected these amendments and pointed to alternative sources of redress such as the civil law in cases of neglect, the criminal law in cases of assault, and further specific offences under health and safety legislation.[4]

At second reading in the House of Commons, Nick Smith MP linked the need for a new criminal offence with the case of Operation Jasmine (see para.I1–012 above):

"I have previously told the House about the horrendous instances of historic neglect and abuse in care homes uncovered by Gwent police's Operation Jasmine. The £11.6 million investigation started in 2005 and gathered 10,500 exhibits and 12.5 tonnes of documents. It led our police to brand the negligence discovered as 'death by indifference'. There were 103 alleged victims of care home abuse and neglect, yet, like their relatives, I was dismayed that Operation Jasmine secured just three convictions for wilful neglect by carers. Worse, charges brought against a care home owner did not directly relate to poor care for residents in his homes, but instead to breaches of health and safety legislation and false accounting."[5]

However, the Government eventually reconsidered its position. This occurred mainly in the aftermath of events at the Mid Staffordshire NHS Foundation Trust (see para.I1–012 above). The Francis report on the standards of care provided by the Trust was published in February 2013, and part of the Government's response was to establish an independent review—chaired by Professor Don Berwick—on improving the safety of patients in England. The final report of this review recommended that there should be a new offence of wilful neglect or ill treatment of patients, which should apply to individuals and organisations whether or not they are registered with the Care Quality Commission.[6] The Government accepted this recommendation.[7] This was implemented by ss.20 to 25 of the Criminal Justice and Courts Act 2015. Section 20 makes it an offence for an individual who has the care of another individual by virtue of being a care worker to ill-treat or wilfully neglect that individual. The offence applies to most formal health and social care settings in England and Wales where there is a contractual or employment duty to provide services. On conviction on indictment, the penalty is imprisonment for a maximum of five

---

[1] Department of Health, *Reforming the Law for Adult Care and Support: The Government's Response to Law Commission Report 326 on Adult Social Care* (TSO, July 2012), Cm.8379, para.9.28.

[2] House of Lords House of Commons Joint Committee on the Draft Care and Support Bill, *Draft Care and Support Bill Report, Session 2012–13*, para.272.

[3] *Hansard* (House of Lords), 22 July 2013, Vol.747, col.1101 and *Hansard* (House of Lords), 14 October 2013, Vol.748, cols 331 to 332.

[4] *Hansard* (House of Lords), 14 October 2013, Vol.748, col.341 (Earl Howe).

[5] *Hansard* (House of Commons), 16 December 2013, Vol.572, col.530.

[6] National Advisory Group on the Safety of Patients in England, *A Promise to Learn—A Commitment to Act: Improving the Safety of Patients in England* (August 2013), p.34.

[7] Department of Health, *Hard Truths: The Journey to Putting Patients First: Vol.1* (November 2013) Cm.8777-1, para.55.

years, or a fine, or both. On summary conviction, the penalty is imprisonment for a maximum of 12 months, or a fine, or both. Section 21 applies the offence to care providers. The penalties include a fine, remedial order and publicity order.

Since these offences apply to organisations as well as individuals, there is some overlap with the role of the Care Quality Commission (see above). Its regulatory standard on safeguarding adults from abuse and improper treatment and abuse is defined as including ill-treatment and neglect.[1] The Commission is able, therefore, to pursue prosecutions against registered care providers where they judge the standard to have been breached. However, the criminal offences apply to cases of *wilful* neglect—where there is evidence of the perpetrator "acting or omitting to act either deliberately, even though they know there is some risk to the patient as a consequence, or because they do not care about that risk".[2] The Care Quality Commission standard does not refer to "wilful neglect", only neglect. There are also links between the criminal offences and the "fit and proper" test for directors (or equivalent) of service providers registered with the Care Quality Commission. Where a director is considered by the Commission to be unfit it could either refuse registration, in the case of a new provider, or require the removal of the director on inspection, or following notification of a new appointment by the imposition of a condition. Failure to remove the director without reasonable excuse would be an offence for breach of the condition.[3]

DUTY OF CANDOUR

1–472   The duty of candour refers to a requirement on health and social care services to be open and honest with patients and service users when things go wrong. For example, there is a contractual duty of candour on organisations that provide services under the NHS Standard Contract.[4] The regulators of health and social care professionals also normally include references to candour in their professional standards and guidance. Thus regulated professionals are expected to be candid with patients and service users when serious events occur and not to obstruct colleagues who seek to raise concerns. Any breach of these standards could lead to fitness to practise proceedings.[5]

The Francis report made a number of recommendations in this respect, including that health care providers must inform patients or other authorised person as soon as practicable when they believe that the treatment of care provided has caused death or serious injury to that patient, and provide such information and explanation as the patient may reasonably request. The report also recommended a duty of candour on individual professionals to inform their employer where they believe or suspect that treatment has caused death or serious injury, and a criminal offence to obstruct a person in the performance of these duties or provide misleading information. The Care Quality Commission would enforce these provisions.[6]

The Government accepted these recommendations. Section 81 of the Care Act (which amends the Health and Social Care Act 2008) therefore requires the Government to include a duty of candour as one of the registration requirements for providers registered with the Care Quality Commission. The relevant regulations provide that all providers are required to act in an open and transparent way with patients and service users about their care and

---

[1] Health and Social Care Act 2008 (Regulated Activities) Regulations 2014 (SI 2014/2936), reg.13.
[2] Department of Health, *New Offence of Ill-Treatment or Wilful Neglect: Consultation Document* (February 2014), paras 22 and 36.
[3] Health and Social Care Act 2008 (Regulated Activities) Regulations 2014 (SI 2014/2936), reg.5.
[4] NHS England, *NHS Standard Contrct 2015/16 Service Conditions* (2015) p.34.
[5] For example, Nursing and Midwifery Council, *The Code: Professional Standards of Practice and Behaviour for Nurses and Midwives* (2015), standard 14 and Health and Care Professions Council, *Standards of Conduct, Performance and Ethics* (2008), standard 1.
[6] R. Francis, *Report of the Mid Staffordshire NHS Foundation Trust Public Inquiry—Executive Summary*, HC 898 (2013).

treatment. There are also specific requirements to notify and provide information and support to the patient or service user (or person acting on their behalf) where an incident has resulted in (or appears to have resulted in) the death of a service user, or severe harm, moderate harm or prolonged psychological harm to the service user. The regulations also set out notification requirements (including an apology) and a criminal offence for breaches of the duty of candour.[1]

Some have raised concerns about a duty of candour, arguing that it hinders a learning environment because faced with the threat of prosecution, individuals are unlikely to be open and honest about serious incidents.[2]

Enquiry by local authority

42.—(1) This section applies where a local authority has reasonable cause to **1–473** suspect that an adult in its area (whether or not ordinarily resident there)—

  (a) has needs for care and support (whether or not the authority is meeting any of those needs),

  (b) is experiencing, or is at risk of, abuse or neglect, and

  (c) as a result of those needs is unable to protect himself or herself against the abuse or neglect or the risk of it.

(2) The local authority must make (or cause to be made) whatever enquiries it thinks necessary to enable it to decide whether any action should be taken in the adult's case (whether under this Part or otherwise) and, if so, what and by whom.

(3) "Abuse" includes financial abuse; and for that purpose "financial abuse" includes—

  (a) having money or other property stolen,

  (b) being defrauded,

  (c) being put under pressure in relation to money or other property, and

  (d) having money or other property misused.

GENERAL NOTE

In its 1995 report on mental incapacity, the Law Commission recommended that a statu- **1–474** tory duty should be placed on a local authority to make enquiries where it has reason to believe "that a vulnerable person in their area is suffering or likely to suffer significant harm or serious exploitation", and decide:

- whether the person is in fact suffering or likely to suffer such harm or exploitation; and
- if so, whether community care services should be provided or arranged or other action taken to protect the person from such harm or exploitation.[3]

This recommendation was not taken forward by the then Government. Instead, in 2000 it issued statutory guidance on safeguarding, *No Secrets*. Amongst other matters, this guidance set out the need for multi-agency action in response to the risk of abuse and neglect and tasked local social services authorities with playing a lead role in developing local policies and procedures for the protection of adults at risk. It did not, however, specify a requirement to make enquiries.[4]

---

[1] Health and Social Care Act 2008 (Regulated Activities) Regulations 2014 (SI 2014/2936), regs 20 and 22.

[2] See, for example, Care Quality Commission, A New Start: *Responses to Our Consultation on Changes to the Way CQC Regulates, Inspects and Monitors Care Services* (October 2013).

[3] *Mental Incapacity, Law Com No.231* (1995), para.9.16 and Draft Bill, cl.37(1).

[4] Department of Health and Home Office, No Secrets: *Guidance on Developing and Implementing Multi-agency Policies and Procedures to Protect Vulnerable Adults from Abuse* (2000).

The Law Commission's review of adult social care revisited this issue. It argued that existing law (which then included community care law, the *No Secrets* guidance, public law obligations, common law, the Mental Health Act 1983 and the Mental Capacity Act 2005—see paras 1–457 to 1–460 above) placed a duty on local authorities to investigate cases of abuse and neglect in certain circumstances. For example, where a local authority knows that a vulnerable adult may be deprived of their liberty by a private individual then its positive obligations under art.5 of the European Convention on Human Rights will be triggered, including a duty to investigate.[1] The Commission recommended that the new legal framework should clarify the overall legal position and establish a duty on local authorities to make enquiries in adult protection cases, or cause enquiries to be made by other agencies, in individual cases. The Commission also recommended that the statute should place a duty on the Secretary of State to make regulations prescribing the process for adult protection enquiries.[2]

In response the Government agreed with the establishment of a new statutory duty to make enquiries, but did not accept the need to take a power to make regulations about the duty to make enquiries:

"Our view is that regulations for adult safeguarding enquiries would be over-prescriptive, and would run the risk of governing the process by prescribed procedures, rather than emphasising the need for professional judgement and user and carer voice. Not all enquiries should or need to have the same breadth or depth, depending on the specific circumstances involved."[3]

Section 42 sets out the core duty to undertake an adult safeguarding enquiry. It is the first ever such duty in English law. By virtue of s.79(2) a local authority cannot delegate its s.42 duty. The statutory guidance discusses safeguarding in Ch.14. In addition, organisations such as the Social Care Institute for Excellence have produced a range of documents on the new safeguarding framework, incuding a guide on safeguarding powers and sharing information.[4] These documents are not statutory guidance but they have been produced with the approval of the Department of Health (see 1–770 below).

During the passage of the Care Bill through the House of Lords, the Government confirmed that it is of the upmost importance that the voice of the individual is heard in any safeguarding enquiry and that the individual is properly supported and that the principles in s.1 (which apply to safeguarding enquiries) should help to ensure this. It was also stated that where a person lacks capacity to take part in a safeguarding enquiry concerning them, the local authority should "involve any person appointed to act on their behalf, or, where there is no such a person, the local authority must itself act in the person's best interests".[5] This general approached is confirmed in paras 14.66 to 14.67 of the statutory guidance.

RELATIONSHIP WITH THE DUTY TO ASSESS

1–475   Sections 9 and 10 of the Care Act establish the core duties to assess an adult with care and support needs and a carer. Where a local authority becomes aware that a person with care and support needs is at risk of, or is experiencing, abuse or neglect, then the s.9 assessment duty would be triggered. In addition, the s.42 duty to make enquiries could arise. Section 19(3) establishes a power to provide temporary services in cases of urgency before a full

---

[1] *A Local Authority v A* [2010] EWHC 978 (Fam); (2010) 13 CCLR 404 at [95].

[2] Law Commission, Adult Social Care, paras 9.3 to 9.19.

[3] Department of Health, *Reforming the Law for Adult Care and Support: The Government's Response to Law Commission Report 326 on Adult Social Care* (TSO, July 2012), Cm.8379, paras 9.9 to 9.11.

[4] Social Care Institute for Excellence, *Gaining access to an adult suspected to be at risk of neglect or abuse: a guide for social workers and their managers in England* (Oct 2014) and Social Care Institute for Excellence, *Adult Safeguarding: Sharing Information* (February 2015). A comprehensive list of resources on safeguarding can be found on the Local Government Association's website.

[5] *Hansard* (House of Lords), 22 July 2013, Vol.747, col.1115 (Baroness Northover).

assessment takes place. This may also be relevant in safeguarding cases. The statutory guidance states that in relevant cases the needs assessment "should run parallel to the
safeguarding enquiry and the enquiry should not disrupt the assessment process or the
local authority meeting eligible needs".[1]

Much of what would be covered by the s.42 duty, could be covered by a general assessment. However, a general needs assessment is not designed to meet the specific demands of
some adult protection cases, and is often an unsatisfactory mechanism for dealing with
them. The Law Commission considered that:

"Enquiries into abuse and neglect often amount to a more formal process than a community care assessment, and may need to focus less on the need for services and more
on establishing the facts and validity of the allegations, especially if police inquiries
are also taking place. The most common outcome of a safeguarding investigation is
not the provision of care and support services but increased monitoring. Furthermore,
an adult protection investigation may need to consider compulsory forms of
intervention."[2]

Moreover, a safeguarding enquiry may involve interviewing the adult separately from
their family or even without the knowledge of the family. A number of formal mechanisms
may be triggered in an investigation, such as a strategy meeting or discussion, a case conference, an adult protection plan, protocols for sharing information, disciplinary procedures
and inter-agency working agreements.

The s.9 duty may however still be appropriate in safeguarding cases. For example, it
might help to establish the nature and degree of the abuse and neglect, and may prompt
referrals to other services and organisations, such as local safeguarding teams, mental
health services, the police and the Public Guardian. Once an assessment has been undertaken, the local authority must decide whether the person's needs call for the provision
of services. In many cases, the provision of such services is used to safeguard adults
from abuse and neglect. A person undergoing a general assessment could become the subject of adult protection enquiries if evidence came to light that they were at risk of abuse or
neglect. Conversely an adult protection investigation could easily revert to a general assessment if such allegations are discounted.

VULNERABLE ADULTS AND ADULTS AT RISK

The statutory guidance, *No Secrets*, referred to the definition of a "vulnerable adult" in **1–476**
order to identify the cohort of people who might need some form of safeguarding intervention. A vulnerable adult was defined as an adult who "is or may be in need of community
care services by reason of mental or other disability, age or illness" and "who is or may be
unable to take care of him or herself, or unable to protect him or herself against significant
harm or exploitation.[3] The use of legal categories, such as vulnerable adults, is an attempt
to move beyond mental incapacity and mental disorder in order to define those people who
are or may be unable to protect themselves from abuse or neglect. However, the Law
Commission pointed to concerns that the term vulnerable adult appears to locate the
cause of abuse with the victim, rather than placing responsibility with the actions or omissions of others, and suggested that vulnerability is an inherent characteristic of a person and
does not recognise that it might be the context, the setting or the place which makes a person vulnerable. It therefore recommended that the term vulnerable adults should be
replaced by "adults at risk of harm".[4]

The Government however pointed to concerns that the common understanding of the
term adult at risk would be very broad, "as anyone can be 'at risk' under certain

---

[1] Department of Health, *Care and Support Statutory Guidance* (2014), para 6.57.
[2] Law Commission, *Adult Social Care*, para.9.11.
[3] Department of Health and Home Office, *No Secrets* (2000), para.2.3.
[4] Law Commission, *Adult Social Care*, paras 9.20 to 9.21.

circumstances." It argued that "any particular descriptive term in the legislation will be problematic and unlikely to be future-proof or suitable for a modern care and support statute".[1] The Care Act therefore merely sets out the parameters of the duty to make enquiries without using any descriptive terminology of the people to whom the duty applies.

ENQUIRIES AND INVESTIGATIONS

1–477   The Law Commission doubted the significance of the difference between the terms "enquiry" and "investigation" and used them interchangeably in its final report.[2] Indeed, in its consultation paper the Commission said:

> "Many different bodies have a statutory investigative function. For example, the police have a duty to investigate crime and indeed, the word *investigation* has, for some, become synonymous with a criminal inquiry. However, there are different types of investigation, the precise nature of which will vary according to the powers and role of the relevant organisation. For example, where a service user is at risk of abuse or neglect, the social services authority will normally need to make enquiries in order to decide what action, if any, it *can* and *should* take. The nature of the investigation will, therefore, be circumscribed by the powers available to the authority and a social services investigation is not the same as a criminal investigation."[3]

In its response to the Law Commission report, the Government explained its use of the term enquiry rather than investigation:

> "We feel the term 'investigation' is too closely associated with police functions. We must remain very clear that the police's role is to investigate when an alleged or suspected criminal offence has been committed. It will often be appropriate to conduct an adult safeguarding enquiry when no criminal offence has been committed."[4]

The statutory guidance states clearly that "a criminal investigation by the police takes priority over all other enquiries", although a multi-disciplinary approach should be agreed to ensure that the interests and wishes of the person are considered throughout.[5]

CASE CONFERENCES

1–478   A case conference is often held following the completion of the safeguarding enquiry. The purpose of a case conference is to consider the evidence and decide what plan (if any) is necessary in order to protect the person from abuse or neglect. In doing so, the conference will need to make decisions about current and future risks, and how any plan should be reviewed or monitored.

In *Davis v West Sussex CC* the safeguarding procedures adopted by the local authority, and in particular the decisions made by the safeguarding vulnerable adults case conference, were held to be unlawful and heavily criticised by the court.[6] The claimants, Mr and Mrs Davis, were care home owners and sought judicial review of the decisions made following the alleged abuse of vulnerable adults residing in one of their care homes. It was held that the local authority's procedures were unfair and resulted in a breach of natural justice. For instance, the court stated that:

---

[1] Department of Health, *Reforming the Law for Adult Care and Support: The Government's Response to Law Commission Report 326 on Adult Social Care* (TSO, July 2012), Cm.8379, paras 9.12 to 9.13.
[2] Law Commission, *Adult Social Care*, para.9.18.
[3] Law Commission, *Adult Social Care: A Consultation Paper*, para.12.5 (emphasis in the original).
[4] Department of Health, *Reforming the Law for Adult Care and Support: The Government's Response to Law Commission Report 326 on Adult Social Care* (TSO, July 2012), Cm.8379, para.9.10.
[5] Department of Health, Care and Support Statutory Guidance (2014), para.14.75.
[6] *Davis v West Sussex CC* [2012] EWHC 2152.

"West Sussex was aware of Mrs Davis's limited role as owner not manager of Nyton House. The chair refused an adjournment, gave Mrs Davis no proper opportunity to prepare for the meeting, refused even to consider her solicitors' letter, continued for eight hours knowing that she was an elderly lady, where the meeting was ten on one side and one on the other and where even the informality of a brief lunch break was abused. Nevertheless conclusions were drawn about Mrs Davis's credibility and her fitness to own a care home. These were in part based on detailed matters relating to individual carers and patients . . . which West Sussex knew or should have known were outside Mrs Davis's knowledge given the impossibility of looking into all these allegations in such an absurdly short time and its decision (for reasons which were of themselves legitimate) to exclude from the meeting those who would have had the answers. West Sussex, as Mr McGuire put it, considered that Mrs Davis had 'made a long series of admissions'. I again remind myself that the prime object of the investigation was to protect vulnerable adults and to prevent abuse not to give particular consideration to Mrs Davis. But her treatment at and around the meeting was deplorable."[1]

This decision underlines that, even when exercising important safeguarding functions to protect vulnerable people, local authorities must not abuse their powers by acting unfairly.

Subsection (1)

The duty to make enquiries applies where a local authority has reasonable cause to suspect that an adult in its area: **1–479**

- has needs for care and support;
- is experiencing, or is at risk of, abuse or neglect; and
- as a result of their care and support needs, is unable to protect themselves.

The duty applies to adults. The statutory guidance states that where the person is over 18 and still receiving children's services (for example, residential education), the matter should be dealt with by adult safeguarding services—but in co-operation with children's safeguarding services where appropriate.[2]

The s.42 duty is not based on the consent of the adult. The statutory guidance states:

"Practitioners should wherever practicable seek the consent of the adult before taking action. However, there may be circumstances when consent cannot be obtained because the adult lacks the capacity to give it, but it is in their best interests to undertake an enquiry. Whether or not the adult has capacity to give consent, action may need to be taken if others are or will be put at risk if nothing is done or where it is in the public interest to take action because a criminal offence has occurred. It is the responsibility of all staff and members of the public to act on any suspicion or evidence of abuse or neglect and to pass on their concerns to a responsible person or agency."[3]

REASONABLE CAUSE TO SUSPECT.

Case law on the investigation duty under s.47 of the Children Act 1989 confirms that **1–480** having reasonable cause to suspect—as opposed to reasonable cause to believe—is a standard that is "quite low".[4] For example, it is lower than the "balance of probabilities".[5] But there still must be objectively reasonable grounds for believing that the criteria is

---

[1] *Davis v West Sussex CC* [2012] EWHC 2152 at [46] to [47].
[2] Department of Health, *Care and Support Statutory Guidance* (2014), para.14.5.
[3] Department of Health, *Care and Support Statutory Guidance* (2014), para.14.79.
[4] *R. (S) v Swindon Borough Council and Wiltshire CC* [2001] EWHC Admin 334 at [36].
[5] Re S (Sexual Abuse Allegations: Local Authority Response) [2001] EWHC Admin 334; [2001] 2 F.L.R. 776.

satisfied, not simply grounds which the decision-maker thinks reasonable.[1] That said, in *Gogay v Hertfordshire CC*, Lady Justice Hale (as she was then) held that what is reasonable has to be judged on the information available at the time the decision was made. It was also held that:

> "Courts should be slow indeed to hold that a local authority does not have reasonable grounds such as will justify it in making further inquiries".[2]

Based on the case law on the 1989 Act, it is submitted that examples of "reasonable cause to suspect" might include:

- past evidence, such as previous allegations of abuse or neglect and court proceedings[3] ;
- a report from a clinician[4] ; and
- accusations made by the victim to their social worker.[5]

During the passage of the Care Bill through Parliament, Baroness Greengross tabled an amendment to require agencies to notify the local authority if they believed that an adult is at risk of abuse or neglect.[6] The Government responded that:

> "Existing regulations and guidance are clear that partners and staff are required to report abuse and we will be issuing new guidance on safeguarding under the powers in the [Care Act]. Professional codes of practice, regulators' requirements and employers' policies should provide clarity in this respect. Furthermore, the changes we propose to its registration requirements would make it easier for the Care Quality Commission to take action against registered providers in cases of abuse."[7]

In contrast, s.128 of the Social Services and Well-being (Wales) Act 2014 places a duty on relevant partners to inform the relevant local authority if they have a reasonable cause to suspect that an adult is at risk of abuse or neglect.

1–481   AN ADULT IN ITS AREA. The local authority has a responsibility to make enquiries if the adult is currently physically present in its geographical area of responsibility whether or not the person is ordinarily resident there. Adults may be physically present in the area of a local authority if, for example, they live in the area, attend services in the area or are temporarily housed in the area.

In the House of Lords, the Government confirmed its intention that "adult safeguarding applies regardless of location" and that s.42:

> ". . . will require a local authority to make inquiries or cause them to be made where abuse and neglect are suspected in respect of an adult with care and support needs, regardless of the particular setting where the abuse or neglect is suspected to have occurred."[8]

---

[1] *Gogay v Hertfordshire CC* [2001] 1 F.L.R. 280.
[2] *Gogay v Hertfordshire CC* [2001] 1 F.L.R. 280.
[3] *R. (S) v Swindon Borough Council and Wiltshire CC* [2001] EWHC Admin 334 at [36].
[4] *A v Enfield LBC* [2008] EWHC 1886 (Admin).
[5] *Gogay v Hertfordshire CC* [2001] 1 F.L.R. 280.
[6] *Hansard* (House of Lords), 14 October 2013, Vol.748, cols 331 to 332.
[7] *Hansard* (House of Lords), 14 October 2013, Vol.748, col.340 (Earl Howe). The new registration requirements referred to here are set out in Department of Health, *Introducing Fundamental Standards: Consultation on Proposals to Change CQC Registration Requirements* (January 2014).
[8] *Hansard* (House of Lords), 22 July 2013, Vol.747, col.1115 (Baroness Northover).

There may be cases where the relevant local authority—even though it has formal responsibility—may not be best placed to undertake the enquiry. Examples might include care homes where large numbers of residents have been placed there by another local authority. In such cases the local authority may want to cause the enquiry to be made by the placing authority. This could be backed up by the specific power to request co-operation in s.7. If more than one local authority is involved it is submitted that the priority must be the safety of the person and arguments about which authority is responsible should not delay the investigation.

NEEDS FOR CARE AND SUPPORT. The duty to makes enquiries applies to all adults who **1–482** have any level of care and support needs, including relatively low level needs. The duty applies regardless of whether the person's needs meet the eligibility criteria or the person is currently receiving services from the local authority or anyone else. This is confirmed by the explanatory notes, which state that:

"Safeguarding enquiries should be made on the understanding of the risk of neglect or abuse, irrespective whether the individual would meet the criteria for the provision of services."[1]

The Law Commission considered the case for expanding the duty beyond those with care and support needs to include people with health-only needs.[2] Consultees had argued that joint working with the NHS would be enhanced by including those with health-only needs, and moreover confining the duty to social care needs would allow other agencies to abrogate their safeguarding responsibilities. On the other side it was argued that the law must establish clear responsibilities and partnership working does not require that each agency should have some formal responsibility for the area of operation of the other agencies. On balance, the Commission felt that the duty should include reference to people with only health needs, as well as those with social care needs. But it also argued this would make very little difference in practical terms:

"While very many of the people with whom safeguarding and adult protection are generally concerned as a matter of practice do, indeed, have health needs, the overwhelmingly large majority also have at least some social care needs."[3]

The Law Commission also argued that the duty to investigate should include carers who are at risk of harm as a result of their caring role.[4] For example, if a carer was being abused by the person they are supporting the duty to make enquiries might be triggered. However, this has not been taken forward in s.42 which is confined to the abuse or neglect of those with care and support needs.

If the carer was experiencing, or was at risk of, abuse and neglect, then this should trigger the carer's assessment duty under s.10. If the carer exercised their right to refuse the assessment under s.11(5), the local authority may need to consider their capacity to refuse the assessment or whether undue influence is being brought to bear upon them. If the carer lacked capacity to refuse the assessment, they could be treated as a person with care and support needs, in which case the s.42 safeguarding duty may be triggered or there could be a duty to carry out a needs assessment under s.9. In respect of the s.9 assessment duty, the individual would not be able to refuse the assessment under s.11(1) since they are experiencing or at risk of abuse or neglect.

---

[1] Care Act 2014: Explanatory Notes para.274.
[2] Law Commission, *Adult Social Care*, paras 9.34 to 9.36.
[3] Law Commission, *Adult Social Care*, para.9.36.
[4] Law Commission, *Adult Social Care*, para.9.39.

In the case of undue influence, an application for the exercise of the inherent jurisdiction of the High Court may need to be considered (see para.1–460 above). In the case of *DL v A Local Authority* the inherent jurisdiction was invoked in order to protect two elderly parents who lacked capacity as a result of undue influence brought to bear upon them by their son.[1] Other possible options may include the use of the criminal law or a civil injunction under the Anti-Social Behaviour, Crime and Policing Act 2014 (see paras 1–462 and 1–465 to 1–466 above).

It is also possible that the carer may have some level of care and support needs (even a relatively low level) which may trigger the s.42 duty (assuming the other criteria are met). The consequences could also be caught in the needs assessment of the cared-for person.

It is submitted that in a small number of cases of sufficient severity, the European Convention on Human Rights may require a response from a local authority in the case of the abuse or neglect of a carer. Under the European Convention, a local authority has a positive duty to take reasonable action to prevent a person for whom it is responsible from being subjected to inhuman or degrading treatment and to ensure respect for private home and family life under arts 3 and 8 respectively (see discussion at paras 1–134 and 1–153 above).

The statutory guidance discusses carers and safeguarding in paras 14.35 to 14.39.

1–483 ABUSE OR NEGLECT. Prior to the Care Act, the relevant threshold for the purposes of adult safeguarding was "significant harm".[2] The Law Commission consulted on retaining this threshold. However, this divided opinion. Some argued that a significant harm requirement would help to limit the numbers of investigations to manageable levels. Others felt it set the bar too high and would imply that some forms of abuse and neglect were acceptable and not worthy of being investigated. The Commission accepted the general tenor of the criticism, and argued that the trigger should be "somewhere above *minor* or *trivial* on the spectrum of harm, but not so high as *serious*." It recommended therefore that the duty should only require "harm", and it should be left to the other criteria to do the main work of refining the category of adult at risk.[3]

The Government was not minded to follow this approach. It preferred the concepts of "abuse" and "neglect" over the term "harm", arguing that the core work of adult safeguarding should be a response to the actions and omissions of others in a way that "harm" cannot capture alone.[4] This is reflected in s.42(1) where the local authorities' enquiry duty applies to adults who are either at risk of or experiencing abuse or neglect.

The Care Act does not define the terms abuse and neglect. The Law Commission had recommended the statute should provide a non-exhaustive definition of harm, which included ill-treatment, financial abuse, self-harm and neglect and exploitation. It stated that:

> "We agree that some degree of detail can assist clarity. However, a degree of caution is appropriate in this respect. Too much detail may lead to confusion and unnecessarily protracted discussions over whether some activity—which is clearly adversely affecting the service user—can be defined in legal terms as *harm*. In other words, we do not want the law to get in the way of adopting a common sense approach."[5]

However, the draft Care and Support Bill did not include any statutory definition of abuse and neglect. The Government argued that statutory definitions might suggest that the local authority enquiry duty was restricted to a prescribed list, and instead wanted to

[1] *DL v A Local Authority [2011] EWHC 1022* (Fam); *DL v A Local Authority* [2012] EWCA Civ 253.
[2] Department of Health and Home Office, *No Secrets: Guidance on Developing and Implementing Multi-agency Policies and Procedures to Protect Vulnerable Adults from Abuse* (2000), para.7.2.
[3] Law Commission, *Adult Social Care*, para.9.26 (emphasis in the original).
[4] Department of Health, *Reforming the Law for Adult Care and Support: The Government's Response to Law Commission Report 326 on Adult Social Care* (TSO, July 2012), Cm.8379, para.9.15.
[5] Law Commission, *Adult Social Care*, para.9.30 (emphasis in the original).

rely on the natural meaning of abuse and neglect. It also argued that this approach would "keep the scope of the duty to make inquiries as wide and flexible as possible".[1]

Despite criticism by some witnesses over the lack of a statutory definition, the Joint Committee concluded that "abuse is an ordinary English word, capable of being understood without being defined" and moreover, "to attempt an exhaustive definition always has the danger of omitting something which, as subsequent events make clear, should have been included."[2]

At report stage in the House of Lords, Lord Rix attempted to introduce a full statutory definition of "abuse".[3] In response the Government said:

"It seems to us inevitable that creating any list of types of abuse risks excluding something which a local authority or its partners may wish to inquire into. I think that is a real danger. We have made an exception regarding financial abuse to be absolutely clear on our intention for financial abuse to be included within the scope of the duty when it may not necessarily be considered as falling within the natural meaning of 'abuse'."[4]

This issue was raised again in the House of Commons. At second reading Tom Clarke MP—who had sponsored the Disabled Persons (Services, Consultation and Representation) Act 1986—said:

"I believe that reference only to financial abuse is unbalanced and critically makes other forms of abuse appear less relevant or important. Again, recalling the recent institutional abuse and neglect highlighted by Winterbourne View, Mid Staffs and the confidential inquiry into the premature deaths of people with a learning disability, it is crucial that other forms of abuse are set out in the Bill. They may be covered by guidance, but evidence has shown that this has not protected people with a learning disability who may well be subject to multiple abuses. I agree with the Government that an exhaustive list might be wrong and difficult to defend. However, the Bill should be amended to include reference to physical, sexual and psychological abuse, as well as neglect. It can make further reference to 'other as guidance may specify'."[5]

At Committee stage the Government confirmed its intention to rely on the "ordinary **1–484** meaning" of abuse and neglect and did not "restrict the scope of local authorities' enquiry duty to a prescribed list".[6] Subsection (3) does confirm that abuse includes financial abuse.

The statutory guidance sets out the following non-exhaustive list of the types of abuse and neglect:

- physical abuse;
- domestic violence;
- sexual abuse;
- psychological abuse;
- financial and material abuse;
- modern slavery;
- discriminatory abuse;
- organisational abuse;
- neglect and acts of omission; and
- self-neglect.[7]

---

[1] *Hansard* (House of Lords) 22 July 2013, Vol.747, col.1115 (Baroness Northover).
[2] House of Lords House of Commons Joint Committee on the Draft Care and Support Bill, *Draft Care and Support Bill Report, Session 2012–13*, para.155.
[3] *Hansard* (House of Lords), 14 October 2013, Vol.748, cols 333 to 334.
[4] *Hansard* (House of Lords), 14 October 2013, Vol.748, col.341 (Earl Howe).
[5] *Hansard* (House of Commons), 16 December 2013, Vol.572, col.573.
[6] *Hansard* (House of Commons: Public Bill Committee), 21 January 2014 (AM): Seventh Sitting, col.276 (Norman Lamb MP).
[7] Department of Health, *Care and Support Statutory Guidance* (2014), para.14.17.

Self-harm and self-neglect

The inclusion of self-neglect in the statutory guidance list (above) represents an important clarification. The equivalent list contained in the previous guidance *No Secrets* had not referred expressly to self-harm or self-neglect.[1] This had led to confusion and inconsistent practice. The Law Commission recommended that the statute should put beyond doubt that the definition of neglect includes self-harm or self-neglect.[2] However, the Government originally did not agree:

> "Adult safeguarding activity should be focused on cases where a person is at risk as a result of the act or omission of another person. Cases of self-harm or self-neglect may raise professional concerns, but we do not believe they should be specifically set out as examples of where a *safeguarding* response would always be necessary. This, of course, would not stop Safeguarding Adults Boards making local decisions to consider activity in this area, if that is thought to be a local priority."[3]

Whilst the statutory guidance now confirms the inclusion of self-neglect, it does not mention self-harm. It is submitted that the natural meaning of neglect would clearly include self-harm. Since self-harm is not ruled out expressly in the statute, s.42(1)(b) must be read as including self-harm. Further guidance on self-neglect can be found in the Social Care Institute for Excellence guide on safeguarding practice. Amongst other matters it suggests that:

> " . . . although self-neglect in some circumstances may be raised as a safeguarding concern, it is usually likely to be dealt with as an intervention under the parts of the Care Act dealing with assessment, planning, information and advice, and prevention".[4]

During the passage of the Care Bill through the House of Lords, the Government confirmed that a person should not be considered as suffering abuse or neglect if they have refused medical treatment.[5]

Historic Abuse and Neglect

In its written evidence to the Joint Committee, the Law Commission expressed concern that the duty to make enquiries may not extend to safeguarding cases where abuse or neglect has or may have occurred in the past. This was because the duty appears to require that the abuse is occurring at the present time or is likely to occur in the future. The Commission cited events at Winterbourne View where procedures had been put in place to address the past episode of abuse but the local authority still needed to investigate to ensure that the residents were not at risk. The Joint Committee recommended that the matter should be put beyond doubt and that the duty should be amended to ensure that it includes cases where abuse or neglect has occurred in the past but still needs to be investigated.[6] In response the Government stated that "it has always been our intention that local authorities (as part of the [Safeguarding Adults Board]) can hold reviews into past cases of abuse or neglect" and agreed to amend s.44 to state this power expressly. However, it disagreed that the duty to make enquiries needed to be amended to this effect, because the duty "relates to immediate action on present risk so changing it would not address the concern raised".[7]

---

[1] Department of Health and Home Office, *No Secrets: Guidance on Developing and Implementing Multi-agency Policies and Procedures to Protect Vulnerable Adults from Abuse* (2000), para.2.7.

[2] Law Commission, *Adult Social Care*, para.9.49.

[3] Department of Health, *Reforming the Law for Adult Care and Support: The Government's Response to Law Commission Report 326 on Adult Social Care* (TSO, July 2012), Cm.8379, para.9.16.

[4] Social Care Institute for Excellence, *Adult Safeguarding Practice Questions* (April 2015), p.12.

[5] *Hansard* (House of Lords), 22 July 2013, Vol.747, col.1115 (Baroness Northover).

[6] House of Lords House of Commons Joint Committee on the Draft Care and Support Bill, *Draft Care and Support Bill Report, Session 2012–13*, paras 151 to 153.

[7] Department of Health, *The Care Bill explained—including a response to consultation and pre-legislative scrutiny on the draft Care and Support Bill*, p.67.

Poor care and safeguarding

Abuse or neglect can arise as a result of deficient care or treatment. In some cases the s.42 duty will be triggered. However the Social Care Institute for Excellence guide on safeguarding practice emphasises that many instances of "poor practice or poor-quality care" are not rooted in "malicious harm" (such as falls, pressure sores, wrongly administered medication and poor nutritional care). It suggests that it is important to differentiate between the two in order to address problems in the right way and avoid:

". . . making safeguarding enquiries unnecessarily, so that police and adult safeguarding teams are able to focus on potentially criminal acts and malicious behaviour rather than on poor care practices".[1]

The guide also warns that "repeated instances of poor care may indicate serious underlying problems and point towards institutional abuse". Pressure sores are discussed as an example of the difficulties of determining whether an issue is caused by poor care or avoidable neglect, or whether it is the unavoidable result of a person's current condition.[2]

UNABLE TO PROTECT HIMSELF OR HERSELF. The Law Commission recommended the **1–485** inclusion of this criterion in order to recognise that many people can safeguard themselves from abuse and neglect, either by themselves or with the assistance of others. In determining whether a person may be unable to safeguard themselves, the Commission felt it would be necessary to consider the person's mental capacity to make the relevant decision (while also recognising that some people who lack capacity may still be able to safeguard themselves). But a person's ability to safeguard themselves should not be solely a matter of mental capacity. Some people with capacity may be unable to safeguard themselves, for example due to a physical disability.[3]

The inability to protect themselves must be a result of the person's care and support needs. The Law Commission saw this as an important condition which helped to ensure that the duty to make enquiries is kept within the broad ambit of social services authorities' core functions.[4]

Subsection (2)

If the criteria in subs.(1) is satisfied, the local authority is required to make (or cause to be **1–486** made) whatever enquiries it thinks necessary to enable it to decide whether any action should be taken in the adult's case (whether under this Part or otherwise) and, if so, what and by whom. The statutory guidance states that an enquiry could range from "a conversation with the adult" through to a formal multi-agency plan or course of action.[5] See also discussion above at para.1–475 on the relationship with the duty to assess. The guidance further suggests that a social worker would be the most appropriate lead where abuse or neglect is suspected within a family or informal relationship.[6] It also states clearly that "a criminal investigation by the police takes priority over all other enquiries", although a multi-disciplinary approach should be agreed to ensure that the interests and wishes of the person are considered throughout.[7]

Whilst subs.(2) establishes a duty to conduct an enquiry, it does not expressly rule out an enquiry in other cases. It is therefore submitted that there is an underlying power to conduct

---

[1] Social Care Institute for Excellence, *Adult Safeguarding Practice Questions* (April 2015) p.13.
[2] Social Care Institute for Excellence, *Adult Safeguarding Practice Questions* (April 2015) pp.13 to 14.
[3] Law Commission, *Adult Social Care*, para.9.45.
[4] Law Commission, *Adult Social Care*, para.9.46.
[5] Department of Health, *Care and Support Statutory Guidance* (2014), para.14.64. See also, Social Care Institute for Excellence, *Adult Safeguarding Practice Questions* (April 2015) pp.16 to 17.
[6] Department of Health, *Care and Support Statutory Guidance* (2014), para.14.68.
[7] Department of Health, *Care and Support Statutory Guidance* (2014), para.14.75. See also para.14.85.

a safeguarding enquiry in cases that fall outside subs(1). This interpretation appears to be supported by the Social Care Institute for Excellence guide on safeguarding practice which states that:

> "Non-statutory enquiries (known as 'other safeguarding enquiries') may also be carried out or instigated by local authorities in response to concerns about carers, or about adults who do not have care and support needs but who may still be at risk of abuse or neglect and to whom the local authority has a 'wellbeing' duty under Section 1 of the Care Act 2014."[1]

This is not statutory guidance but it has been produced with the approval of the Department of Health (see 1–770 below).

1–487 CAUSE TO BE MADE. As noted above, by virtue of s.79(2) a local authority cannot delegate its s.42 duty to make enquiries. Nevertheless, s.42(2) establishes that local authorities can cause enquiries to be made by others. In other words, it recognises that local authorities have the lead responsibility for adult safeguarding but also acknowledges the need for multi-agency work. The specific wording had been recommended by the Law Commission in order to:

> ". . . ensure that this duty can be discharged through a range of pathways or different routes through safeguarding. For example, the social services authority could undertake enquiries themselves, refer the matter to the appropriate agency or initiate a multi-agency investigation."[2]

But it went on to say:

> "However, by referring the matter to another agency, the local authority would not be entitled necessarily to treat its duty to enquire as discharged; the referral would be a means through which the duty is performed and it may be necessary, for example, for the local authority to continue to monitor the case to ensure that it is dealt with by the agency appropriately. The extent of a local authority's ongoing role and responsibilities would vary according to the individual circumstances of the particular case."[3]

However, the Joint Committee agreed with concerns that it was not clear from the legislation what "cause to be made" means in practice and recommended that guidance was needed on this point.[4] The Government response stated:

> "We will make the safeguarding responsibilities of local authorities clear, while ensuring we do not lose local flexibility or impose unjustified burdens on other organisations."[5]

It is submitted that if necessary the local authority could use its power to request the co-operation of a "relevant partner" in specific cases under s.7 as a way of ensuring that others undertake this task. A relevant partner would include the NHS or the police.

The statutory guidance advises that if the local authority decides that another organisation should make the enquiry, the authority "should be clear about timescales, the need to know the outcomes of the enquiry and what action will follow if this is not done".[6] It also states that "health professionals should undertake enquiries and treatment plans relating to medicines management or pressure sores".[7] The guidance discusses multi-

---

[1] Social Care Institute for Excellence, *Adult Safeguarding Practice Questions* (April 2015), p.17.

[2] Law Commission, *Adult Social Care*, para.9.16.

[3] Law Commission, *Adult Social Care*, para.9.38.

[4] House of Lords House of Commons Joint Committee on the Draft Care and Support Bill, *Draft Care and Support Bill Report, Session 2012–13*, para.154.

[5] Department of Health, *The Care Bill explained—including a response to consultation and pre-legislative scrutiny on the draft Care and Support Bill*, para.49.

[6] Department of Health, *Care and Support Statutory Guidance* (2014), para.14.65.

[7] Department of Health, *Care and Support Statutory Guidance* (2014), para.14.69.

agency safeguarding roles in paras 14.51 to 14.55 and who can carry out an enquiry in paras 14.84 to 14.87. Amongst other matters, it emphasises that the local authority retains the lead role and should assure itself that the enquiry satisfies its duty to decide what action is necessary. If necessary, it should challenge the body making the enquiry.[1]

The statutory guidance also confirms that while the local authority can cause the enquiry to be made by another organisation, the authority is still responsible for taking action:

"Once enquiries are completed, the outcome should be notified to the local authority which should then determine with the adult what, if any, further action is necessary and acceptable. It is for the local authority to determine the appropriateness of the outcome of the enquiry."[2]

DECIDE WHETHER ANY ACTION SHOULD BE TAKEN. Subsection (2) provides that the pur- **1–488** pose of the safeguarding enquiry is to decide whether any action should be taken. According to the guide on safeguarding powers produced by the Social Care Institute for Excellence, in almost every case it is likely to be necessary to "physically see and talk to the adult in order to make that decision".[3] The action that might be taken following an enquiry can include the provision of care and support under Pt 1 of the Care Act. It can also include the initiation of other powers available to local authorities (such as public health powers and an application to the High Court under its inherent jurisdiction—see para.1–460 above). Alternatively the enquiries could conclude that action is needed by others, such as the NHS, mental health services or the police. If so, the s.42 enquiries must determine what must be done and by whom.

The courts have been careful to emphasise that local authorities must act within their statutory functions.[4] The mere existence of a duty to make enquiries does not in itself give local authorities any new powers to force individuals to be assessed or give any power to enter property or remove people from their property. In other words, if the local authority finds evidence of abuse and neglect it must act within its existing statutory powers. On the other hand, the local authority must consider the powers of other agencies to act. For example, a referral to the police or a joint investigation with the police would be lawful and might be justified in such cases. Moreover, the local authority can apply to the courts in cases where it lacks powers to intervene.

The case of *Re Z* concerned a woman who was suffering from an incurable and irreversible condition and who wished to be assisted to commit suicide in Switzerland (where assisted suicide is legal). She had received extensive support from the local authority. Her husband, who had initially been opposed to his wife's wishes, had kept the authority informed of the situation, and in particular had informed them when he changed his mind and proposed to make all the necessary arrangements and accompany his wife to Switzerland for the assisted suicide. It was held that the local authority's duties in such cases were:

- to investigate the person's position and consider what was their true position and intention;
- to consider whether the person was legally competent to make and carry out her decision and intention;
- to consider whether any other (and, if so, what) influence could be operating on the person's position and intention and to ensure that they had all relevant information and knew all the available options;

---

[1] Department of Health, *Care and Support Statutory Guidance* (2014), para.14.84.
[2] Department of Health, *Care and Support Statutory Guidance* (2014), para.14.94.
[3] Social Care Institute for Excellence, Gaining access to an adult suspected to be at risk of neglect or abuse: a guide for social workers and their managers in England (October 2014), p.4.
[4] See, for example, *A Local Authority v A* [2010] EWHC 978 (Fam); (2010) 13 CCLR 404 at [99] by Munby L.J.

- to consider whether to invoke the inherent jurisdiction of the High Court so that the question of competence could be judicially investigated and determined;
- in the event of the adult not being competent, to provide all such assistance as might be reasonably required both to determine and give effect to their best interests;
- in the event of the adult being competent, to allow them in any lawful way to give effect to their decision although that should not preclude the giving of advice or assistance in accordance with what were perceived to be their best interests;
- where there were reasonable grounds to suspect that the commission of a criminal offence might be involved, to draw that to the attention of the police; and
- in very exceptional circumstances, to invoke the jurisdiction of the court under s.222 of the Local Government Act 1972.[1]

This case was decided prior to the Care Act but it is likely that it will remain good law under the new legislation.

The statutory guidance discusses the following matters which are relevant to safeguarding actions:

- reporting and responding to abuse and neglect (paras 14.31 to 14.34);
- adult safeguarding procedures (paras 14.40 to 14.43);
- responding to abuse and neglect in a regulated care setting (paras 14.56 to 14.62);
- procedures for responding in individual cases (paras 14.77 to 14.87);
- what should an enquiry take into account (paras 14.80 to 14.83); and
- what happens after an enquiry—including safeguarding plans, taking action and the person alleged to be responsible for abuse and neglect (paras 14.88 to 14.103).

See also discussion above at para.1–478 on case conferences.

Subsection (3)

1–489   Section 42(3) does not define "abuse", but states that it includes financial abuse which includes having money or property stolen or misused, being defrauded, and being put under pressure in relation to money or property.

The Joint Committee had concluded that "abuse is an ordinary English word, capable of being understood without being defined", but since it might not however normally be thought of as including financial abuse, it is right that the legislation should put this beyond doubt.[2] In its response, the Government explained that the reason for highlighting financial abuse is that "the term 'abuse' in other legislation does not usually include financial abuse." However, it agreed to redraft the relevant subsection in the draft Care and Support Bill "to make clear that financial abuse is only one type of abuse that people might experience."[3]

The statutory guidance discusses financial abuse in paras 14.22 to 14.26.

Safeguarding Adults Boards

1–490   **43.**—(1) Each local authority must establish a Safeguarding Adults Board (an "SAB") for its area.

(2) The objective of an SAB is to help and protect adults in its area in cases of the kind described in section 42(1).

(3) The way in which an SAB must seek to achieve its objective is by co-ordinating and ensuring the effectiveness of what each of its members does.

---

[1] *Re Z* [2004] EWHC 2817 (Fam); [2005] 1 W.L.R. 959.

[2] House of Lords House of Commons Joint Committee on the Draft Care and Support Bill, *Draft Care and Support Bill Report, Session 2012–13*, para.155.

[3] Department of Health, *The Care Bill explained—including a response to consultation and pre-legislative scrutiny on the draft Care and Support Bill*, para.105.

(4) An SAB may do anything which appears to it to be necessary or desirable for the purpose of achieving its objective.

(5) Schedule 2 (which includes provision about the membership, funding and other resources, strategy and annual report of an SAB) has effect.

(6) Where two or more local authorities exercise their respective duties under subsection (1) by establishing an SAB for their combined area—

(a) a reference in this section, section 44 or Schedule 2 to the authority establishing the SAB is to be read as a reference to the authorities establishing it, and

(b) a reference in this section, that section or that Schedule to the SAB's area is to be read as a reference to the combined area.

GENERAL NOTE

Safeguarding Adults Boards are multi-agency partnerships, made up of a wide range of **1–491** representatives from statutory and voluntary bodies, and other individuals. They are aimed at facilitating joint working in adult protection and their responsibilities include ensuring that multi-agency policies and procedures are in place, conducting serious case reviews, and providing training and information. Prior to the Care Act, these boards had not been provided for in statute law, although they were mentioned briefly in statutory guidance.[1]

The Law Commission argued the introduction of statutory safeguarding boards would enhance the status of boards and allow for greater leverage in encouraging other agencies to participate. Furthermore, it would help to strengthen local safeguarding leadership and address inconsistencies in the current operation of boards. The Commission therefore recommended that safeguarding boards should be placed on a statutory footing, and in order to achieve this, the statute should:

- give local social services authorities the lead role in establishing and maintaining the boards;
- specify the functions of a board as being to review the procedures and practices of public bodies, give information or advice to any public body and improve the skills and knowledge of professionals;
- require social services, the NHS and the police to nominate a board member who has the appropriate skills and knowledge; and
- provide that Adult Safeguarding Boards should commission serious case reviews and establish a duty to contribute to these reviews.[2]

The Government accepted the principle of this recommendation and the majority of the detail. Section 43 therefore establishes for the first time statutory Safeguarding Adults Boards in England.

Further details about Safeguarding Adults Boards are set out in Sch.2. The statutory guidance discusses Safeguarding Adults Boards in paras 14.104 to 14.149. It also discusses local roles and responsibilities in paras 14.167 to 14.206—including the requirement that each Safeguarding Adults Board member should have a Designated Adults Safeguarding Manager.[3]

Research carried out prior to the implementation of the Care Act indicated that the size and composition of boards varied considerably. For example the number of members varied between 10 and 47. In some cases the board restricted its membership but created an operational board or group with responsibility for implementing board strategy. In other cases the board was a wide and inclusive group but a small executive group sat above it. Most

---

[1] Department of Health and Home Office, *No Secrets: Guidance on Developing and Implementing Multi-agency Policies and Procedures to Protect Vulnerable Adults from Abuse* (2000), para.3.4.

[2] Law Commission, *Adult Social Care*, paras 9.103 to 9.126.

[3] Department of Health, *Care and Support Statutory Guidance* (2014), para.14.176.

boards had established sub-groups to take forward different strands of activity, such as promoting service user involvement and training and work force development.[1]

Subsection (1)

1–492   The local authority is required to establish a Safeguarding Adults Board. This reinforces the overall point that local authorities have the lead co-ordinating responsibility overall for safeguarding, including strategic responsibility and putting in place multi-agency arrangements.

Subsection (2)

1–493   As noted above, the Law Commission had recommended that the boards should be given three main overarching functions in respect of safeguarding: reviewing the procedures and practices of public bodies, giving information or advice to any public body, and improving the skills and knowledge of professionals. Subsection (2) however adopts a different approach and gives a Safeguarding Adults Board a single objective of helping and protecting adults in its area who have care and support needs and who are at risk of neglect and abuse and unable to protect themselves. It is notable that this is drafted as being "the objective", as opposed to the primary or main objective which is common in other statutes when describing objectives of a body. This means that there are no other objectives that a Safeguarding Adults Board must take into account. It is submitted that a board could have regard to other objectives as long as these were compatible with, or at least were interpreted in a way which did not undermine, its objective. This might include the need to run the board efficiently and cost-effectively. Moreover, this is a broad objective and could be used to justify various activities (see subs.(4)).

In addition to this objective, Safeguarding Adults Boards are given three specific duties: to publish a strategic plan (Sch.2 para.3); to publish an annual report (Sch.2 para.4); and conduct Safeguarding Adults Reviews (s.44).

Subsection (3)

1–494   This sets out that a Safeguarding Adults Board must achieve its objective through the co-ordination of members' activities in relation to safeguarding and ensuring the effectiveness of what those members do for safeguarding purposes. This underlines the multi-agency nature of safeguarding adults.

Subsection (4)

1–495   A Safeguarding Adults Board may undertake any lawful activity which is necessary and desirable to achieve its objective. The explanatory note states that "the functions which [a Safeguarding Adults Board] can exercise in pursuit of its objective are those of its members".[2]

The activities that might be undertaken include, for example, all of the functions recommended by the Law Commission (see above). Other activities that might fall within this objective could include carrying out research into abuse and neglect, the agreement of multi-agency protocols and, where necessary, arranging operational strategic meetings. The statutory guidance also emphasises the role of Safeguarding Adults Boards in prevention (paras14.105, 4.110 and 4.111), providing advice and assistance (para.14.106) and recruitment and training (paras 14.199 to 14.204).

Subsection (6)

1–496   This subsection confirms that two or more local authorities may establish a Safeguarding Adults Board for their combined geographical area of responsibility. In such cases, the duty in subs.(1) to establish a Board is placed on all the relevant local authorities.

---

[1] S. Braye et al, *The Governance of Adult Safeguarding: Findings From Research into Safeguarding Adults Boards* (University of Bedfordshire and University of Sussex, November 2010).
[2] Care Act 2014: Explanatory Notes para.278.

Some local areas have developed joint working arrangements between children safe-guarding boards and adult safeguarding boards, including joint serious case reviews and joint working groups. During the passage of the Care Bill through the House of Lords, how-ever, Baroness Wheeler on behalf of the opposition, said they were "cautious about bringing adult and children's safeguarding together under one structure as some councils have done" because "adult and children's safeguarding issues are not the same".[1] The Association of Directors of Adult Social Services and Local Government Association have also warned that a single board for adults and children would be a "retrograde step and should be discouraged" since "adult safeguarding leadership, improvement and effec-tiveness would be overshadowed by children's priorities".[2]

Safeguarding adults reviews

44.—(1) An SAB must arrange for there to be a review of a case involving an **1–497** adult in its area with needs for care and support (whether or not the local authority has been meeting any of those needs) if—

(a) there is reasonable cause for concern about how the SAB, members of it or other persons with relevant functions worked together to safeguard the adult, and

(b) condition 1 or 2 is met.

(2) Condition 1 is met if—

(a) the adult has died, and

(b) the SAB knows or suspects that the death resulted from abuse or neglect (whether or not it knew about or suspected the abuse or neglect before the adult died).

(3) Condition 2 is met if—

(a) the adult is still alive, and

(b) the SAB knows or suspects that the adult has experienced serious abuse or neglect.

(4) An SAB may arrange for there to be a review of any other case involving an adult in its area with needs for care and support (whether or not the local authority has been meeting any of those needs).

(5) Each member of the SAB must co-operate in and contribute to the carrying out of a review under this section with a view to—

(a) identifying the lessons to be learnt from the adult's case, and

(b) applying those lessons to future cases.

GENERAL NOTE

Serious case reviews are investigations or enquiries into serious failures in individual **1–498** safeguarding cases. In broad terms the aim of such reviews is not to reinvestigate the event or apportion blame but to learn lessons retrospectively and make improvements to local practices, procedures and services (see subs.(5)). For many years, investigations or enquiries into serious failures in the adult sector have been on a voluntary or non-statutory basis, and have been based on the long-established models of serious case reviews in chil-dren's services and mental health. This led to inconsistency over when they occurred and how they were conducted.

The Law Commission recommended that Safeguarding Adults Boards should be given statutory responsibility for commissioning serious case reviews and that there should be a

---

[1] *Hansard* (House of Lords), 22 July 2013, Vol.747, col.1111.

[2] Association of Directors of Adult Social Services and Local Government Association, *Response fron ADASS and LGA in Relation to Safeguarding: Joint Response on the Draft Care Act Guidance and Regulations* (2014), para.14.106.

duty to contribute to these reviews.[1] The Government accepted this recommendation.[2] Section 44 therefore requires Safeguarding Adults Boards to arrange for there to be a serious case review (known as a Safeguarding Adults Review) into certain cases in specific circumstances. The statutory guidance discusses Safeguarding Adults Reviews in paras 14.133 to 14.149. There are no statutory timescales for the completion of reviews. However, the guidance advises that a review should be completed within six months of its initiation unless there are good reasons for a longer period being required.[3] In addition, the Social Care Institute for Excellence has produced a guide on undertaking Safeguarding Adults Reviews.[4] This is not statutory guidance but it has been produced with the approval of the Department of Health (see 1–770 below).

Subsections (1) to (3)

1–499   The duty on the Safeguarding Adults Board is to arrange for there to be a review, and not necessarily to conduct it itself. Indeed, many reviews will be triggered due to concerns about the actions or omissions of the Board itself, or it members, in which case it would not be appropriate for the Board to conduct the review due to its conflict of interests.

All of the following criteria must be satisfied in order to trigger the duty.

1. the case must involve an adult in its area;
2. the adult has needs for care and support (whether or not the local authority has been meeting any of those needs); and
3. there is reasonable cause for concern about how the Safeguarding Adults Board, members of it, or other persons with relevant functions worked together to safeguard the adult.

In addition, one of the following conditions must apply:

1. the adult has died, and the Safeguarding Adults Board knows or suspects that the death resulted from abuse or neglect (whether or not it knew about or suspected the abuse or neglect before the adult died) (subs.(2)); or
2. the adult is still alive, and the Safeguarding Adults Board knows or suspects that the adult has experienced "serious abuse or neglect" (subs.(3)).

There is no definition provided of serious abuse or neglect. However, the statutory guidance advises that:

". . . something can be considered serious abuse or neglect where, for example the individual would have been likely to have died but for an intervention, or has suffered permanent harm or has reduced capacity or quality of life (whether because of physical or psychological effects) as a result of the abuse or neglect."[5]

Subsection (4)

1–500   Safeguarding Adults Boards may carry out a Safeguarding Adults Review in any other case involving an adult with care and support needs where they feel it would be appropriate.

Subsection (5)

1–501   Every member of the Safeguarding Adults Board must co-operate in and contribute to carrying out the review. The aim of such co-operation and contribution should be to identify the lessons to be learnt from the case, and apply those lessons to future cases. As the explanatory notes state:

---

[1] Law Commission, *Adult Social Care*, para.9.124.

[2] Department of Health, *Reforming the Law for Adult Care and Support: The Government's Response to Law Commission Report 326 on Adult Social Care* (TSO, July 2012), Cm.8379, para.9.24.

[3] Department of Health, *Care and Support Statutory Guidance* (2014), para.14.144.

[4] Social Care Institute for Excellence, *Safeguarding Adults Reviews Under the Care Act: Implementation Support* (March 2015).

[5] Department of Health, *Care and Support Statutory Guidance* (2014), para.14.134.

"The aim of a review is to ensure that lessons are learned from such cases, not to allocate blame but to improve future practice and partnership working, and to minimise the possibility of it happening again."[1]

Supply of information

45.—(1) If an SAB requests a person to supply information to it, or to some **1–502** other person specified in the request, the person to whom the request is made must comply with the request if—

(a) conditions 1 and 2 are met, and

(b) condition 3 or 4 is met.

(2) Condition 1 is that the request is made for the purpose of enabling or assisting the SAB to exercise its functions.

(3) Condition 2 is that the request is made to a person whose functions or activities the SAB considers to be such that the person is likely to have information relevant to the exercise of a function by the SAB.

(4) Condition 3 is that the information relates to—

(a) the person to whom the request is made,

(b) a function or activity of that person, or

(c) a person in respect of whom that person exercises a function or engages in an activity.

(5) Condition 4 is that the information—

(a) is information requested by the SAB from a person to whom information was supplied in compliance with another request under this section, and

(b) is the same as, or is derived from, information so supplied.

(6) Information may be used by the SAB, or other person to whom it is supplied under subsection (1), only for the purpose of enabling or assisting the SAB to exercise its functions.

GENERAL NOTE

The Law Commission's 2010 consultation paper had proposed that the statute should set **1–503** out requirements to share information with a Safeguarding Adults Board.[2] During consultation many pointed to failures to share information in safeguarding cases and several consultees supported an express duty to share information with Safeguarding Adults Boards.[3] However, in its final report the Commission did not recommend such a duty. It argued that there is already a vast amount of law regulating the sharing of information in adult protection, and introducing a new duty would add another layer to this and may obscure the existing legal responsibilities to share information. Examples of such law include the common law duty of confidentiality, Data Protection Act 1998 and Human Rights Act 1998. Moreover, a duty may have the unfortunate consequence of giving the impression that non-specified bodies cannot share information or non-specified information cannot be shared. Instead, the Commission recommended that information-sharing with Safeguarding Adults Boards should be addressed in the guidance.[4]

The Government originally accepted the Law Commission's analysis and the draft Care and Support Bill did not contain an express duty to share information with a Safeguarding Adults Board. However, the Joint Committee felt that Safeguarding Adults Reviews would not have the same statutory authority to obtain information as serious case reviews

[1] Care Act 2014: Explanatory Notes para.291.

[2] Law Commission, *Adult Social Care: A Consultation Paper, Consultation Paper No.192* (2010), para.12.79.

[3] Law Commission, *Adult Social Care: Consultation Analysis* (31 March 2011) paras 12.38 to 12.39 and 12.201 to 12.202.

[4] Law Commission, *Adult Social Care*, para.9.126.

involving children. The Children Act 2004 gives Children's Safeguarding Boards an express power to require a person or body to comply with a request for information from the Board where the information relates to the Board's duties.[1] The Committee argued that the absence of any express power in Safeguarding Adults Reviews "leaves a gap which could undermine the ability of such reviews to learn the lessons from serious cases of abuse and neglect".[2]

In response, the Government argued that the Data Protection Act 1998 should provide sufficient powers for information relevant to reviews to be obtained, but in the interests of clarity and transparency it agreed to include an express duty.[3] Section 45 therefore establishes a duty to supply information, which mirrors the duty in the Children Act 2004.

The duty is placed on a "person" to share information when requested by the Safeguarding Adults Board. As noted in para.1–470 above, a person can include an individual, corporate body, or partnership.

This is a reactive duty which only applies in response to a specific request from the Board, and it is not a proactive duty to raise safeguarding concerns. In contrast, s.128 of the Social Services and Well-being (Wales) Act 2014 places a duty on relevant partners to inform the relevant local authority if they have a reasonable cause to suspect that an adult is at risk of abuse or neglect.

The statutory guidance discusses information sharing and safeguarding in paras 14.150 to 14.166. For instance, it states that:

> "In the past, there have been instances where the withholding of information has prevented organisations being fully able to understand what 'went wrong' and so has hindered them identifying, to the best of their ability, the lessons to be applied to prevent or reduce the risks of such cases reoccurring. If someone knows that abuse or neglect is happening they must act upon that knowledge, not wait to be asked for information."[4]

The s.45 duty is summarised in para.14.156 of the guidance but is not considered further.

Section 45 exists alongside other legal provisions governing information sharing which are relevant to adult safeguarding. For instance s.115 of the Crime and Disorder Act 1998 states that any person who would not otherwise have the power to disclose information to a "relevant authority", does have such a power where disclosure is necessary or expedient for the purposes of the 1998 Act (namely, reduction and prevention of crime and disorder). A relevant authority includes the police, local authority, and NHS body. The Home Office guidance emphasises that this is a power and does not override other legal considerations, such as the common law duty of confidentiality, Data Protection Act 1998 and Human Rights Act 1998.[5]

The Social Care Institute for Excellence has produced a guide on safeguarding and sharing information.[6] This is not statutory guidance but it has been produced with the approval of the Department of Health (see 1–770 below).

Subsections (1) to (5)

1–504   All of the following criteria must be satisfied in order to trigger the duty:

1. the information must be requested for the purpose of enabling or assisting the Safeguarding Adults Board to perform its functions (subs.(2));

---

[1] Children Act 2004 s.14B.

[2] House of Lords House of Commons Joint Committee on the Draft Care and Support Bill, *Draft Care and Support Bill Report*, Session 2012–13, para.165.

[3] Department of Health, *The Care Bill explained—including a response to consultation and pre-legislative scrutiny on the draft Care and Support Bill*, para.107 and p.68.

[4] Department of Health, *Care and Support Statutory Guidance* (2014), para 14.155.

[5] Home Office, *National Support Framework: Delivering Safer and Confident Communities* (2010), para.2.4.1.1.

[6] Social Care Institute for Excellence, *Adult Safeguarding: Sharing Information* (February 2015).

2. the requested person must have functions or engage in activities such that the Board considers it likely to have information relevant to a function of the Board (subs.(3)). The explanatory notes provide the following explanation:

> "This would potentially encompass, for instance, a GP who provided medical advice or treatment to an adult in respect of whom a [Safeguarding Adults Board] was carrying out a serious case review, or to a family member or carer of that adult. It would also potentially encompass a person carrying out voluntary work that brought him or her into contact with such an adult or with a family member or carer, or a minister of a church attended by such an adult or by a family member or carer."[1]

In addition, one of the following conditions must apply:

1. the information relates to the requested person, a function or activity of that person, or a person in respect of whom that person exercises a function or engages in an activity (subs.(4)); or
2. the information was supplied to a person or body by a third party following a previous request (subs.(5)). The explanatory notes provide the following explanation:

> "Subsection (5) effectively enables the onward transmission to a [Safeguarding Adults Board] of information that it has previously requested, under the section, to be supplied to a third party, for instance to a NHS body, for collation and onward transmission to the [Safeguarding Adults Board]. But a [Safeguarding Adults Board] may request that information be supplied to a third party for collation and onward transmission only if the third party itself is within subsection (3))."[2]

It is notable that the s.45 duty is expressed without caveat. Normally duties of this nature provide for some degree of flexibility by setting out that the duty applies where "appropriate" or having regard to other data protection law. The statutory guidance, in the context of discussing confidentiality and safeguarding, does acknowledge that unless there is an overriding public interest it might not be appropriate to share information (although s.45 is not referred to directly).[3] In addition, the Social Care Institute for Excellence guide on sharing information suggests that if a s.45 request is made "then the reluctant party would only have grounds for refusal if it would be 'incompatible with their own duties or have an adverse effect on the exercise of their functions'".[4] This is not statutory guidance but it has been produced with the approval of the Department of Health (see 1–770 below). In making this statement, the Social Care Institute for Excellence guide appears to be applying by analogy s.7 of the Care Act. However, in the absence of such wording in s.45 it is doubtful that this approach is correct. It is submitted that instead s.45 should be interpreted as being subject to general public law principles to act reasonably and lawfully, and in particular regard must be had to the common law duty of confidentiality, Data Protection Act 1998 and Human Rights Act 1998.

Subsection (6)

A Safeguarding Adults Board may use information provided under this section only for **1–505** the purposes of its functions.

---

[1] Care Act 2014: Explanatory Notes para.266.
[2] Care Act 2014: Explanatory Notes para.297.
[3] Department of Health, *Care and Support Statutory Guidance* (2014), paras 14.157 to 14.161.
[4] Social Care Institute for Excellence, *Adult Safeguarding: Sharing Information* (February 2015), p.17.

Abolition of local authority's power to remove persons in need of care

1–506   **46.**—Section 47 of the National Assistance Act 1948 (which gives a local authority power to remove a person in need of care from home) ceases to apply to persons in England.

GENERAL NOTE

1–507   Section 47 of the National Assistance Act 1948 gave local authorities a power to apply to a magistrates' court for an order to remove certain people (those suffering from grave chronic illness, or being aged, infirm or physically incapacitated) to "suitable premises" (such as a hospital, care home or other place) if they were living in insanitary conditions and not receiving proper care and attention. In addition, a medical officer of health had to certify that removal was necessary in the interests of the person or for the prevention of injury to the health of, or serious nuisance to, other persons. The order could authorise the person's detention for up to three months, renewable for further periods of three months. In addition, the National Assistance (Amendment) Act 1951 provided an emergency procedure if a person needed to be removed without delay. The principles behind the s.47 power dated back to the old poor law and its wording was based on local legislation drafted in Bradford in 1925, designed to assist in slum clearance.[1]

The Law Commission's consultation paper argued that s.47 should be repealed for three main reasons:

- it breached art.5 of the European Convention on Human Rights (for example, because of the limited ability of the person to appeal against their detention);
- it has several operational difficulties (for example, the medical certificate was provided by public health specialists who were not necessarily medically qualified or had not conducted clinical examinations for some time); and
- it and has been rendered largely obsolete as a result of alternative and modern legal powers that can be used on a non-consensual and emergency basis (such as those under the Mental Health Act 1983 and Mental Capacity Act 2005).[2]

However, the views expressed at consultation—albeit from a minority of consultees—forced the Law Commission to reconsider this issue. In particular it was argued that the repeal of s.47 would leave a gap in the law whereby certain groups of vulnerable adults would be left unprotected. The Law Commission's analysis suggested that the s.47 power could be repealed in relation to people with grave chronic illness and people who lack capacity. The former were covered by public and environmental health powers (while the detention of those with non-infectious illness was prohibited under art.5(1) of the European Convention on Human Rights) and the latter were covered by the Mental Capacity Act 2005. Taking into account the relevant Strasbourg jurisprudence, the Commission concluded that if s.47 were repealed entirely, public bodies would lose powers to intervene only if the person:

- was of "unsound mind" but not of a nature or degree to warrant hospital admission under the Mental Health Act 1983;
- made a capacitous decision, which was free of external pressure or physical restraint (thereby ruling out the inherent jurisdiction of the High Court), to live in insanitary conditions (and those conditions are not such to necessitate intervention under public and environmental health powers); and

---

[1] E. Counsell, "Compulsory Removal and Medical Discretion" (1990) 140 *New Law Journal* 750 and J.A. Muir, "Section 47: Bradford 1925—United Kingdom 1988" (1990) 12 *Journal of Public Health Medicine* 28.

[2] Law Commission, *Adult Social Care: A Consultation Paper*, Consultation Paper No.192, (2010), paras 12.47 to 12.71.

- was unable to devote to themselves and are not otherwise receiving proper care and attention.

The Law Commission also noted the lack of any robust evidence—either from academic sources or from its consultation—on whether s.47 was still being used, and if so what is the level of activity. It argued that s.47 cannot become compliant with the European Convention on Human Rights and operationally workable without substantial reform which would radically transform its nature. The final report therefore concluded that s.47 should be repealed and that the Government should consider commissioning research into the use of s.47 and on the basis of that research decide if it would be appropriate to reform the power, following public consultation.[1]

The Department of Health accepted that s.47 should be repealed. However, it ruled out any replacement powers in this area.[2] As noted above, the Government instead consulted on (and as a result of that consultation rejected) the introduction of a more limited compulsory assessment power. Section 46 of the Care Act therefore repeals s.47 of the National Assistance Act 1948.

Protecting property of adults being cared for away from home

47.—(1) This section applies where—   **1–508**

(a) an adult is having needs for care and support met under section 18 or 19 in a way that involves the provision of accommodation, or is admitted to hospital (or both), and

(b) it appears to a local authority that there is a danger of loss or damage to movable property of the adult's in the authority's area because—

(i) the adult is unable (whether permanently or temporarily) to protect or deal with the property, and

(ii) no suitable arrangements have been or are being made.

(2) The local authority must take reasonable steps to prevent or mitigate the loss or damage.

(3) For the purpose of performing that duty, the local authority—

(a) may at all reasonable times and on reasonable notice enter any premises which the adult was living in immediately before being provided with accommodation or admitted to hospital, and

(b) may deal with any of the adult's movable property in any way which is reasonably necessary for preventing or mitigating loss or damage.

(4) A local authority may not exercise the power under subsection (3)(a) unless—

(a) it has obtained the consent of the adult concerned or, where the adult lacks capacity to give consent, the consent of a person authorised under the Mental Capacity Act 2005 to give it on the adult's behalf, or

(b) where the adult lacks capacity to give consent and there is no person so authorised, the local authority is satisfied that exercising the power would be in the adult's best interests.

(5) Where a local authority is proposing to exercise the power under subsection (3)(a), the officer it authorises to do so must, if required, produce valid documentation setting out the authorisation to do so.

---

[1] Law Commission, *Adult Social Care*, paras 9.60 to 9.96.
[2] Department of Health, *Reforming the Law for Adult Care and Support: The Government's Response to Law Commission Report 326 on Adult Social Care* (TSO, July 2012), Cm.8379, para.9.17.

(6) A person who, without reasonable excuse, obstructs the exercise of the power under subsection (3)(a)—

(a) commits an offence, and

(b) is liable on summary conviction to a fine not exceeding level 4 on the standard scale.

(7) A local authority may recover from an adult whatever reasonable expenses the authority incurs under this section in the adult's case.

GENERAL NOTE

1–509 This section restates the duty originally set out at s.48 of the National Assistance Act 1948, for local authorities to prevent or mitigate loss or damage to the property of adults who have been admitted to a hospital or to a residential care home, and are unable to protect it or deal with it themselves. This is based on a Law Commission recommendation.[1] But there are some amendments to the 1948 Act duty. Some of these amendments are minor and are intended to fit the duty into the new framework, while others provide additional clarity. The statutory guidance discusses the duty to protect property in paras 10.88 to 10.94.

Subsection (1)

1–510 The following criteria must be satisfied in order to trigger the duty:

1. the adult has care and support needs (eligible needs or otherwise) which are being met through the provision of accommodation and/or the adult is admitted to hospital;
2. there is a danger of loss or damage to the adult's movable property;
3. the property is in the local authority's area;
4. the loss or damage is because the adult is unable (whether permanently or temporarily) to protect or deal with the property, and no suitable arrangements have been or are being made.

The Law Commission concluded that the duty should not apply only as a last resort where no-one else is considered to be in a position to protect the property. However, it also felt that the duty should not impose onerous demands on local authorities and that, where appropriate, friends and family members should be expected to look after a person's property in such cases (supported by the local authority if necessary). This flexibility is reflected by subs.(1)(b)(ii) which requires action by the local authority only if no other suitable arrangements can be made.[2]

Subsection (2)

1–511 The duty is placed on the local authority to take reasonable steps to prevent or mitigate the loss or damage. In cases where the person is admitted to hospital it may be more appropriate for the NHS to perform this duty. The Law Commission noted that this function could be delegated or carried out in partnership with health services under s.75 of the National Health Service Act 2006.[3] It could also be delegated under s.79 of the Care Act.

Subsections (3) to (5)

1–512 The local authority may (at a reasonable time and after giving reasonable notice) enter any premises which the adult was living in immediately before being provided with accommodation or admitted to hospital. However, the consent of the adult is required. If the adult lacks capacity to give consent (and no one has been authorised under the Mental Capacity Act 2005 to make this decision under a lasting power of attorney) the local authority must make a best interests decision under s.4 of the 2005 Act. See also paras 10.90 to 10.91 of the statutory guidance on this point.

[1] Law Commission, *Adult Social Care*, paras 9.97 to 9.102.
[2] Law Commission, *Adult Social Care*, para.9.101.
[3] Law Commission, *Adult Social Care*, para.9.102.

Once it has gained access to the premises, the local authority may deal with any of the adult's property in any way which is reasonably necessary for preventing or mitigating loss or damage. This applies to any tangible, physical moveable property belonging to the adult in question. In law, there is a distinction between movable and immovable property. Movable property roughly corresponds to personal property, while immovable property corresponds to real estate or real property. A fixture would normally be considered real property, although those that can be detached may become personal property.

The definition of personal property includes pets. Therefore a local authority may need to consider putting in place arrangements to ensure that the person's pets are looked after while their owner is away, including where necessary arranging alternative accommodation.

The duty to protect movable property means that in practice a local authority will need at a minimum to secure the accommodation. Emergency protection for the property itself may be provided by the police in cases of criminal damage.

Subsection (6)

Any person who obstructs the local authority's exercise of this duty is liable on summary **1–513** conviction to pay a fine, and provides a defence of reasonable excuse. See paras 10.92 to 10.93 of the statutory guidance on this point.

Subsection (7)

Local authorities are able to recover from the adult any reasonable expenses incurred in **1–514** protecting that adult's property. It had been put to the Law Commission that this power should be extended to allow local authorities to recover *any* reasonable costs from family members. The Commission rejected this, arguing that it would amount to a reintroduction of the "outdated" principle of liable relatives, which had been abolished by the Health and Social Care Act 2008.[1]

PROVIDER FAILURE

Temporary duty on local authority

48.—(1) This section applies where a person registered under Ch.2 of Part 1 of the Health **1–515** and Social Care Act 2008 (a "registered care provider") in respect of the carrying on of a regulated activity (within the meaning of that Part) becomes unable to carry on that activity because of business failure.

(2) A local authority must for so long as it considers necessary (and in so far as it is not already required to do so) meet those of an adult's needs for care and support and those of a carer's needs for support which were, immediately before the registered care provider became unable to carry on the regulated activity, being met by the carrying on of that activity in the authority's area by the provider.

(3) A local authority is accordingly required to meet needs under subsection (2) regardless of—

(a) whether the relevant adult is ordinarily resident in its area;

(b) whether the authority has carried out a needs assessment, a carer's assessment or a financial assessment;

(c) whether any of the needs meet the eligibility criteria.

(4) Where a local authority is meeting needs under subsection (2), it is not required to carry out a needs assessment, a carer's assessment or a financial assessment or to determine whether any of the needs meet the eligibility criteria.

---

[1] Law Commission, *Adult Social Care*, para.9.101.

(5) A local authority may make a charge for meeting needs under subsection (2) (except in so far as doing so involves the provision of information or advice); and a charge under this subsection may cover only the cost that the local authority incurs in meeting the needs to which the charge applies.

(6) Subsection (5) does not apply if section 49 (cross-border cases) applies (see subsection (3) of that section).

(7) If the relevant adult is not ordinarily resident in the area of the local authority which is required to meet needs under subsection (2), that authority—

(a) must, in meeting needs under that subsection which were being met under arrangements made by another local authority, co-operate with that authority (in so far as it is not already required to do so by section 6);

(b) must, in meeting needs under that subsection which were being met under arrangements all or part of the cost of which was paid for by another local authority by means of direct payments, co-operate with that authority (in so far as it is not already required to do so by section 6);

(c) may recover from the other local authority mentioned in paragraph (a) or (b) (as the case may be) the cost it incurs in meeting those of the adult's or carer's needs referred to in the paragraph in question.

(8) Any dispute between local authorities about the application of this section is to be determined under section 40 as if it were a dispute of the type mentioned in subsection (1) of that section.

(9) "The relevant adult" means—

(a) in a case involving an adult's needs for care and support, that adult;

(b) in a case involving a carer's needs for support, the adult needing care.

GENERAL NOTE

1–516 Section 48 sets out local authorities' responsibilities for ensuring continuity of care where a provider sustains business failure and ceases to provide a service. It requires authorities to step in temporarily and meet the needs of people whose provider has failed in their geographic area. In some cases provider failure will cause minor changes for service users. For example, staff would be retained and in the case of residential care, and the person may be able to stay in the same home under new ownership. But also individuals could be forced to move into a new home or receive care from different staff. Moreover, financial problems are linked to poor quality of care through for example cuts in staff, refurbishment of the fabric of buildings, food and staff training.

Section 48 provides that local authorities will continue to have the lead role in this area. However, the need to manage provider failure should be balanced against the important principle that the company, its directors and investors are responsible for the operation of the company and must face the consequences of their decisions.

Section 48 should be read alongside ss.53 to 57 which give the Care Quality Commission responsibility for monitoring the financial position of providers that are difficult to replace for example due to their size, concentration or specialism. This central system is intended to provide local authorities with an early warning that a provider could fail and support local authorities to prepare and to manage continuity of care. Section 48 should also be read alongside the local authority market shaping duty under s.5, and especially the need to support the sustainability of care providers and publish a Market Position Statement.[1]

---

[1] See, Department of Health, *Care and Support Statutory Guidance* (2014), paras 4.36 and 4.55.

CONTINUITY OF NHS SERVICES

The Health and Social Care Act 2012 enables the Government to introduce through regu- **1–517** lations a Health Special Administration scheme which is aimed at securing access to certain essential services (known as Commissioner Requested Services) in the event of provider failure.[1] It also enables Monitor to establish mechanisms for providing financial assistance in cases where providers are subject to special administration.[2] However, the Government has announced that—following public consultation—it will not implement these provisions at the present time.[3]

Therefore, there is currently no specific legal framework to secure patients' access to services where an independent provider of NHS funded health care sustains financial failure. In such cases, the provider would be subject to administration proceedings under the Insolvency Act 1986. In addition, all providers require a licence from Monitor—which includes special continuity of service conditions—and Monitor has issued a Risk Assessment Framework to assess whether there are significant financial risks to the delivery of services. Using licence conditions it can intervene in order to safeguard those services.[4]

The Government has stated that:

"Should an independent provider of [Commissioner Requested Services] become insolvent, this will be dealt with on an individual case-by-case basis, taking into account the specific circumstances surrounding the failure. Safeguarding quality services for patients will always remain a priority, Monitor and where necessary, the Department of Health, will seek to work with the provider and relevant organisations as appropriate to determine the right solution and ensure that patients have access to the services that they need."[5]

Subsection (1)

This clarifies that the temporary duty on a local authority applies when there is a business **1–518** failure of a provider of care and support that is regulated by the Care Quality Commission.

The House of Lords Delegated Powers Committee expressed concern that the legislation does not define what is meant by "business failure" or "market failure". The Government therefore amended the Care Bill to provide that regulations under s.52(12) will define the circumstances in which a provider can be deemed to have failed:

"Those circumstances may include a situation in which a provider is struggling to service its debts as they fall due or has breached its financial covenants under loan agreements, or an administrator, liquidator or receiver has been appointed—which is a clear-cut case of failure. As I said, this will be defined in regulations because we want to capture these various different scenarios where a business can be deemed to have failed."[6]

The relevant regulations are the Care and Support (Business Failure) Regulations 2014 (SI 2015/301). See paras A1–254 to A1–256 below.

---

[1] Health and Social Care Act 2012 ss.129 to 132 and 304.
[2] Health and Social Care Act 2012 ss.134 to 135.
[3] Department of Health, *Protecting Patients' Interests—Ensuring Continuity of NHS Services: Proposals for a Health Special Administration Procedure for Companies: Government Response* (April 2014).
[4] Monitor, *Risk Assessment Framework* (August 2013).
[5] Department of Health, *Protecting Patients' Interests—Ensuring Continuity of NHS Services: Proposals for a Health Special Administration Procedure for Companies: Government Response* (April 2014), para.6.7.
[6] *Hansard* (House of Lords), 22 July 2013, Vol.747, col.1144 (Earl Howe).

Subsection (2)

1–519   The local authority in whose area the care provider was providing a service must meet needs which were being met by the failed service provider immediately before it became unable to do so. In the House of Lords, the Government explained that:

> "This means that the responsibility to ensure continuity of care falls on the local authority most able to meet needs, not necessarily the same local authority who made the arrangements with the failed provider to meet the needs of the adult."[1]

This subsection also provides that the duty does not apply in cases where the local authority is already under a duty to meet the needs. The explanatory notes state that:

> " . . . the duty to meet needs applies so far as the authority is not already required to do so such as where needs were being met by the provision of services paid for by an individual, or where another local authority was paying for services to meet the needs of an individual (or was making direct payments in respect of those needs). There is no need to apply the duty where the local authority is already required to meet needs because such a requirement does not change simply because there is a business failure of the provider who was meeting the needs."[2]

Subsection (3)

1–520   The duty to meet needs for temporary care and support under subs.(2) applies to any person whether or not they are ordinarily resident and irrespective of whether the local authority has carried out an assessment (a needs, carer's or financial assessment) and the adult has eligible needs.

Subsection (4)

1–521   When meeting need under subs.(2), the local authority is not required to carry out a needs, carer's or financial assessment, or to determine if the person has eligible needs. The explanatory notes state that:

> "The effect of this is to suspend the provisions of sections 9 to 13 and 17 for the temporary period during which the local authority is meeting needs under section 48. This ensures that the temporary duty to meet needs applies regardless of the results of the relevant assessments so that the provision of a substitute service is not delayed and individuals are not left without the care they need."[3]

Subsection (5)

1–522   This allows local authorities to charge for meeting needs under subs.(2), but they can only cover the costs involved in meeting those needs. The subsection confirms that charges cannot be made for providing information and advice under subs.(2).

Subsection (6)

1–523   Subsection (5) does not apply if s.49 applies (i.e. cross-border cases where the person's needs were being met by a local authority in Wales or Scotland or a Health and Social Care trust in Northern Ireland). This is because "in such a case there is already provision in section 49(3) for local authorities to recover costs".[4]

Subsection (7)

1–524   If the adult is ordinarily resident in another local authority, the local authority with the temporary duty must co-operate with the placing local authority (if any) in respect of

---

[1] *Hansard* (House of Lords), 22 July 2013, Vol.747, col.1089 (Baroness Northover).
[2] Care Act 2014: Explanatory Notes para.304.
[3] Care Act 2014, Explanatory Notes para.305.
[4] Care Act 2014, Explanatory Notes para.307.

meeting needs which were being met by the placing authority and to recover from that authority the costs incurred in meeting the needs during the temporary period.

Subsection (8)

The ordinary residence dispute resolution procedure in s.40 applies to any disputes **1–525**
between local authorities about the application of this section (for example "as to the duration of the temporary period for which there is a duty to meet needs").[1]

Section 48: cross-border cases

49.—(1) This section applies where, in a case within section 48, immediately **1–526**
before the registered care provider became unable to carry on the regulated
activity, some or all of the adult's needs for care and support or the carer's
needs for support were being met by the carrying on of that activity by the provider under arrangements made—
  (a) by a local authority in Wales discharging its duty under section 35 or 40, or
      exercising its power under section 36 or 45, of the Social Services and Well-
      being (Wales) Act 2014,
  (b) by a local authority in Scotland discharging its duty under section 12 or 13A
      of the Social Work (Scotland) Act 1968 or section 25 of the Mental Health
      (Care and Treatment) (Scotland) Act 2003, or
  (c) by a Health and Social Care trust under Article 15 of the Health and
      Personal Social Services (Northern Ireland) Order 1972 or section 2 of
      the Carers and Direct Payments Act (Northern Ireland) 2002.
  (2) This section also applies where, in a case within section 48—
  (a) immediately before the registered care provider became unable to carry on
      the regulated activity, some or all of the adult's needs for care and support or
      the carer's needs for support were being met by the carrying on of that
      activity by the provider, and
  (b) all or part of the cost of the accommodation or other services provided by
      the provider to meet those needs was paid for by means of direct payments
      made—

  (i) under section 50 or 52 of the Social Services and Well-being (Wales) Act
      2014,

  (ii) as a result of a choice made by the adult pursuant to section 5 of the Social
       Care (Self-directed Support) (Scotland) Act 2013, or

  (iii) by virtue of section 8 of the Carers and Direct Payments Act (Northern
        Ireland) 2002.

  (3) The local authority which is required to meet needs under section 48(2)—
  (a) must, in meeting needs under section 48(2) which were being met by the
      authority which made the arrangements referred to in subsection (1), co-
      operate with that authority;
  (b) must, in meeting needs under section 48(2) which were being met by the
      provision of accommodation or other services all or part of the cost of
      which was paid for by an authority by means of direct payments as referred
      to in subsection (2), co-operate with that authority;

---

[1] Care Act 2014, Explanatory Notes para.309.

(c) may recover from the authority referred to in paragraph (a) or (b) (as the case may be) the cost it incurs in meeting those of the adult's or carer's needs referred to in the paragraph in question;

(d) may recover from the adult or carer the cost it incurs in meeting those of the adult's or carer's needs other than those referred to in paragraph (a) or (b) (as the case may be).

(4) Any dispute between a local authority and a local authority in Wales, a local authority in Scotland or a Health and Social Care trust about the application of section 48 or of this section is to be resolved in accordance with paragraph 5 of Schedule 1.

(5) "Local authority in Wales" and "local authority in Scotland" each have the meaning given in paragraph 12 of Schedule 1.

(6) The references in paragraphs (a) and (b) of subsection (3) to an authority are references to a local authority in Wales, a local authority in Scotland or a Health and Social Care trust (as the case may be).

GENERAL NOTE

1–527   This section applies to cross-border cases where a person is in receipt of services in England and those services are being provided through arrangements made by a local authority in Wales or Scotland or a Health and Social Care trust in Northern Ireland. In most cases this will mean that they have been placed in a residential care home in England.

Subsections (1) and (2)

1–528   This applies the temporary duty in s.48(2) to cases where the failed service provider was meeting the person's needs under arrangements made by a local authority in Wales or Scotland or a Health and Social Care trust in Northern Ireland. This includes cases where a direct payment was being made (see subs.(2)).

Subsection (3)

1–529   This provides that the local authority in England must co-operate with the local authority in Wales or Scotland or the Health and Social Care trust in Northern Ireland. It also allows the local authority in England to recover costs it incurs in meeting the needs of the adult from the local authority or trust, or the adult themselves (except for needs being met by the local authority or trust).

Subsection (4)

1–530   In meeting the adult's needs, a local authority in Wales must co-operate with the authority or trust which made the arrangements or direct payments, and may recover costs it incurs from that authority and trust.

Subsection (5)

1–531   This provides that any dispute between a local authority in England and an authority in Wales or Scotland or a trust in Northern Ireland must be resolved in accordance with the dispute resolution procedure in para.5 of Sch.1.

Temporary duty on local authority in Wales

1–532   **50.**—(1) This section applies where a person registered under Part 2 of the Care Standards Act 2000 in respect of an establishment or agency—

(a) becomes unable to carry on or manage the establishment or agency because of business failure, and

(b) immediately before becoming unable to do so, was providing an adult with accommodation or other services in Wales under arrangements made—

(i) by a local authority meeting an adult's needs for care and support or a carer's needs for support under this Part,

(ii) by a local authority in Scotland discharging its duty under section 12 or 13A of the Social Work (Scotland) Act 1968 or section 25 of the Mental Health (Care and Treatment) (Scotland) Act 2003, or

(iii) by a Health and Social Care trust under Article 15 of the Health and Personal Social Services (Northern Ireland) Order 1972 or section 2 of the Carers and Direct Payments Act (Northern Ireland) 2002.

(2) This section also applies where a person registered under Part 2 of the Care Standards Act 2000 in respect of an establishment or agency—

(a) becomes unable to carry on or manage the establishment or agency because of business failure, and

(b) immediately before becoming unable to do so, was providing an adult with accommodation or other services in Wales all or part of the cost of which was paid for by means of direct payments made—

(i) under this Part of this Act,

(ii) as a result of a choice made by the adult pursuant to section 5 of the Social Care (Self-directed Support) (Scotland) Act 2013, or

(iii) by virtue of section 8 of the Carers and Direct Payments Act (Northern Ireland) 2002.

(3) The local authority in Wales in whose area the accommodation is situated or the services were provided must for so long as it considers necessary meet those of the adult's needs for care and support or the carer's needs for support which were being met by the registered person by the provision of the accommodation or other services.

(4) A local authority in Wales which is required to meet needs under subsection (3)—

(a) must, in meeting needs under that subsection which were being met by the authority which made the arrangements referred to in subsection (1)(b), co-operate with that authority;

(b) must, in meeting needs under subsection (3) which were being met by the provision of accommodation or other services all or part of the cost of which was paid for by an authority by means of direct payments as referred to in subsection (2)(b), co-operate with that authority;

(c) may recover from the authority referred to in paragraph (a) or (b) (as the case may be) the cost it incurs in meeting those of the adult's or carer's needs referred to in the paragraph in question.

(5) Any dispute about the application of this section is to be resolved in accordance with paragraph 5 of Schedule 1.

(6) "Local authority in Wales" and "local authority in Scotland" each have the meaning given in paragraph 12 of Schedule 1.

(7) The references in paragraphs (a) and (b) of subsection (4) to an authority are references to a local authority, a local authority in Scotland or a Health and Social Care trust (as the case may be).

GENERAL NOTE

1–533   This requires local authorities in Wales to step in temporarily and meet the needs of people whose provider has failed in their geographic area. It applies where a person is in receipt of services in Wales and those services are being provided through arrangements made by a local authority in England or Scotland or a Health and Social Care trust in Northern Ireland. In most cases this will mean that they have been placed in a residential care home in Wales.

Subsection (3)
1–534   The authority in Wales must meet the needs for so long as it considers necessary.

Subsection (4)
1–535   This provides that the local authority in Wales must co-operate with the local authority in England or Scotland or the Health and Social Care trust in Northern Ireland. It also allows the local authority in Wales to recover costs it incurs in meeting the needs of the adults from the local authority or trust, or the adult themselves (except for needs being met by the local authority or trust).

Subsection (5)
1–536   This provides that any dispute between a local authority in Wales and an authority in Wales or Scotland or a trust in Northern Ireland must be resolved in accordance with the dispute resolution procedure in para.5 of Sch.1.

Temporary duty on Health and Social Care trust in Northern Ireland
1–537   **51.**—(1) This section applies where a person registered under Part 3 of the Health and Social Services (Quality, Improvement and Regulation) (Northern Ireland) Order 2003 in respect of an establishment or agency—

   (a) becomes unable to carry on or manage the establishment or agency because of business failure, and

   (b) immediately before becoming unable to do so, was providing an adult with accommodation or other services in Northern Ireland under arrangements made—

   (i) by a local authority meeting an adult's needs for care and support or a carer's needs for support under this Part,

   (ii) by a local authority in Wales discharging its duty under section 35 or 40, or exercising its power under section 36 or 45, of the Social Services and Well-being (Wales) Act 2014, or

   (iii) by a local authority in Scotland discharging its duty under section 12 or 13A of the Social Work (Scotland) Act 1968 or section 25 of the Mental Health (Care and Treatment) (Scotland) Act 2003.

(2) This section also applies where a person registered under Part 3 of the Health and Personal Social Services (Quality, Improvement and Regulation) (Northern Ireland) Order 2003 in respect of an establishment or agency—

   (a) becomes unable to carry on or manage the establishment or agency because of business failure, and

   (b) immediately before becoming unable to do so, was providing an adult with accommodation or other services in Northern Ireland, all or part of the cost of which was paid for by means of direct payments made—

   (i) under this Part of this Act,

(ii) under section 50 or 52 of the Social Services and Well-being (Wales) Act 2014, or

(iii) as a result of a choice made by the adult pursuant to section 5 of the Social Care (Self-directed Support) (Scotland) Act 2013.

(3) The Health and Social Care trust in whose area the accommodation is situated or the services were provided must for so long as it considers necessary meet those of the adult's needs for care and support or the carer's needs for support which were being met by the registered person by the provision of the accommodation or other services.

(4) A Health and Social Care trust which is required to meet needs under subsection (3)—

(a) must, in meeting needs under that subsection which were being met by the authority which made the arrangements referred to in subsection (1)(b), co-operate with that authority;

(b) must, in meeting needs under subsection (3) which were being met by the provision of accommodation or other services all or part of the cost of which was paid for by an authority by means of direct payments as referred to in subsection (2)(b), co-operate with that authority;

(c) may recover from the authority referred to in paragraph (a) or (b) (as the case may be) the cost it incurs in meeting those of the adult's or carer's needs referred to in the paragraph in question.

(5) Any dispute about the application of this section is to be resolved in accordance with paragraph 5 of Schedule 1.

(6) "Local authority in Wales" and "local authority in Scotland" each have the meaning given in paragraph 12 of Schedule 1.

(7) The references in paragraphs (a) and (b) of subsection (4) to an authority are references to a local authority, a local authority in Wales or a local authority in Scotland (as the case may be).

GENERAL NOTE

This requires a Health and Social Care trust in Northern Ireland to step in temporarily **1–538** and meet the needs of people whose provider has failed in its geographic area. It applies where a person is in receipt of services in Northern Ireland and those services are being provided through arrangements made by a local authority in England, Scotland or Wales. In most cases this will mean that they have been placed in a residential care home in Northern Ireland.

Subsection (3)

The trust must meet the needs for so long as it considers necessary. **1–539**

Subsection (4)

This provides that the Health and Social Care trust in Northern Ireland must co-operate **1–540** with the local authority in England, Scotland or Wales. It also allows the trust to recover costs it incurs in meeting the needs of the adults from the local authority or the adult themselves (except for needs being met by the local authority or trust).

Subsection (5)

This provides that any dispute between a Health and Social Care trust in Northern Ireland **1–541** and an authority in England, Scotland or Wales must be resolved in accordance with the dispute resolution procedure in para.5 of Sch.1.

Sections 48 to 51: supplementary

1–542   **52.**—(1) An authority becomes subject to the duty under section 48(2), 50(3) or 51(3) as soon as it becomes aware of the business failure.

(2) Section 8 (how to meet needs) applies to meeting needs under section 48(2) as it applies to meeting needs under section 18.

(3) Section 34 of the Social Services and Well-being (Wales) Act 2014 (how to meet needs) applies to meeting needs under section 50(3) as it applies to meeting needs under section 35 of that Act.

(4) In deciding how to meet an adult's needs for care and support under section 48(2), 50(3) or 51(3), an authority must involve—

(a) the adult,

(b) any carer that the adult has, and

(c) any person whom the adult asks the authority to involve or, where the adult lacks capacity to ask the authority to do that, any person who appears to the authority to be interested in the adult's welfare.

(5) In deciding how to meet a carer's needs for support under section 48(2), 50(3) or 51(3), an authority must involve—

(a) the carer, and

(b) any person whom the carer asks the authority to involve.

(6) In carrying out the duty under subsection (4)(a) or (5)(a), an authority must take all reasonable steps to reach agreement with the adult or carer about how it should meet the needs in question.

(7) Sections 21 to 23 (exceptions to duty to meet needs) apply to meeting needs under section 48(2) as they apply to meeting needs under section 18.

(8) Sections 46 to 49 of the Social Services and Well-being (Wales) Act 2014 (exceptions to, and restrictions on, duty to meet needs) apply to meeting needs under section 50(3) as they apply to meeting needs under section 35 of that Act.

(9) Where an adult whose case comes within section 48 is being provided with NHS continuing healthcare under arrangements made by a clinical commissioning group no part of whose area is in the local authority's area, the group is to be treated as a relevant partner of the authority for the purposes of sections 6 and 7.

(10) "NHS continuing healthcare" is to be construed in accordance with standing rules under section 6E of the National Health Service Act 2006.

(11) Where a local authority considers it necessary to do so for the purpose of carrying out its duty under section 48(2), it may request the registered care provider, or such other person involved in the provider's business as it considers appropriate, to provide it with specified information.

(12) Regulations must make provision as to the interpretation for the purposes of sections 48, 50 and 51 and this section of references to business failure or to being unable to do something because of business failure; and the regulations may, in particular, specify circumstances in which a person is to be treated as unable to do something because of business failure.

(13) Pending the commencement of Part 4 of the Social Services and Well-being (Wales) Act 2014—

(a) a reference in section 49 or 51 to making arrangements to meet needs under section 35 or 36 of that Act is to be read as a reference to making arrangements or providing services under—

(i) Part 3 of the National Assistance Act 1948,

(ii) section 45 of the Health Services and Public Health Act 1968,

(iii) section 117 of the Mental Health Act 1983, or

(iv) Schedule 15 to the National Health Service (Wales) Act 2006;

(b) a reference in section 49 or 51 to making arrangements to meet needs under section 40 or 45 of that Act is to be read as a reference to providing services as referred to in section 2 of the Carers and Disabled Children Act 2000;

(c) a reference in section 49 or 51 to making direct payments under section 50 or 52 of that Act is to be read as a reference to making direct payments by virtue of section 57 of the Health and Social Care Act 2001;

(d) subsection (8) is to be read as if there were substituted for it—

"(8) Sections 21(1A) and (8) and 29(6) of the National Assistance Act 1948 apply to meeting needs under section 50(3) as they apply to the exercise of functions under sections 21 and 29 of that Act by a local authority in Wales (within the meaning given in paragraph 12 of Schedule 1)."

(14) Pending the commencement of section 5 of the Social Care (Self-directed Support) (Scotland) Act 2013—

(a) sections 49(2)(b)(ii) and 50(2)(b)(ii) are to be read as if there were substituted for each of them—

"(ii) under section 12B of the Social Work (Scotland) Act 1968,", and

(b) section 51(2)(b)(iii) is to be read as if there were substituted for it—

"(iii) under section 12B of the Social Work (Scotland) Act 1968.".

GENERAL NOTE

This section makes further provision and clarification in relation to the provider failure **1–543** duties contained in ss.48 to 52.

Subsection (1)

An authority in England and Wales or a trust in Northern Ireland becomes subject to the **1–544** provider failure duty as soon as it becomes aware of the business failure.

Subsection (2)

This clarifies that a local authority in England can meet needs through any of the forms of **1–545** care and support provided for under s.8. In other words it is not required to meet needs in the same way as they were being met by the service provider that has failed.

Subsection (3)

This clarifies that a local authority in Wales can meet needs through any of the forms of **1–546** care and support provided for under s.34 of the Social Services and Well-being (Wales) Act 2014. This is the equivalent provision to s.8 of the Care Act. In other words the authority in Wales is not required to meet needs in the same way as they were being met by the service provider.

The explanatory notes explain that there is no such provision for Northern Ireland because there is no provision equivalent to s.8 in Northern Irish legislation.[1]

Subsections (4) and (5)

In deciding how to meet needs the authority or trust is required to involve the adult, their **1–547** carer, and any person asked by the adult to act on their behalf, or, if the adult lacks capacity, any person whom the authority considers would be interested in the adult's welfare. Subsection (5) makes similar provision for carers.

The meaning of "involve" is discussed further at paras 1–104 to 1–105 above.

---

[1] Care Act 2014: Explanatory Notes para.326.

Subsections (6)

1–548   In deciding how to meet needs the authority or trust is required to take all reasonable steps to reach agreement with the adult or carer.

Subsections (7) and (8)

1–549   This confirms that that local authorities in England are not required to meet needs which are subject to the prohibitions contained in ss.21 to 23 of the Care Act. Subsection (8) applies similar exceptions in cases where a local authority in Wales is under a duty to meet needs.

Subsection (9)

1–550   This subsection applies where a failed provider in England is providing the adult with NHS continuing health care which is commissioned by a clinical commissioning group that is not in the area of the local authority in which the care is being provided. It amends the definition of "relevant partner" for the purposes of ss.6 and 7 to make clear that the duties to co-operate apply.

Subsection (11)

1–551   This makes clear that a local authority in England may request from the failed provider, or such other person involved in the business, information that it must have in order to comply with the provider failure duty.

Subsection (12)

1–552   This requires regulations to make provision to interpret references to business failure or to being able to do something because of a business failure. By virtue of s.125(4)(f) such regulations are subject to the affirmative procedure in Parliament. The affirmative procedure is discussed at para.1–161 above. See also 1–518 above for the background to subs.(12).

The relevant regulations issued are the Care and Support (Business Failure) Regulations 2014 (SI 2015/301), which are reproduced in full in paras A1–254 to A1–265 below. They set out that the meaning of business failure by reference to various types of insolvency, such as administration and winding up (see reg.2).

MARKET OVERSIGHT

GENERAL NOTE

1–553   Sections 53 to 57 represent the first time that a national regime on provider failure in the care sector has been introduced. Most care providers are relatively small and should they fail, local authorities are able to ensure that people's care needs are met with minimum disruption. However, corporate ownership has increased. An estimated 182,000 residential and nursing home beds were available in corporate owned care homes by the end of 2013/14 (39 per cent of the total of around 465,000 beds), compared with 172,000 (37 per cent) at the end of 2012/13.[1]

Prior to the Care Act, local authorities had oversight of their local care markets and had been responsible for managing provider failure. However, in 2011 the collapse of Southern Cross—then the largest independent provider of residential care services—illustrated the deficiencies with this system. At its peak, Southern Cross owned or operated over 750 care homes across the UK for 31,000 residents (predominately older people). It had 9 per cent of the market nationally and a much greater share of the market in certain areas such as the north and northeast of England. The company had expanded rapidly through the purchase of existing care businesses and selling freeholds of the care homes it acquired

---

[1] Care Quality Commission, *The State of Health Care and Adult Social Care in England 2013/14* (2014) HC 691, p.30.

to property management companies and leasing or renting the properties back. The company's business model worked during times of increasing property values and buoyant occupancy levels in care homes, but the contracts it entered into with its landlords proved to be unsustainable. Southern Cross was particularly reliant on local authority funding: only 20 per cent of its residents were self-funders compared with a national average of 40 per cent.[1]

The collapse of Southern Care proved particularly difficult to manage not just due to its size and the number of service users affected, but also because of the complexity of the business capital structures. Southern Cross had been brought by the American private equity firm Blackstone Capital Partners in 2004. The same year Blackstone purchased Nursing Home Properties whose business included leasing care homes to providers; Southern Cross was its biggest tenant. In 2006 Blackstone floated Southern Cross on the stock market and sold it for a profit of £500 million. It also sold Nursing Home Properties to an investment fund, Three Delta. The case of Southern Cross provides an example of the increasingly complex operating and financial business models emerging in the sector; for example, large corporate providers can be backed by a large investment group with a wide portfolio of interests. Some of these complexities were described in Parliament by Lord Warner during the passage of the Care Bill:

"People are assembling packages of money to buy groups of homes, and they put groups of homes together in what is often basically a hedge fund or private equity-type process, essentially consolidating providers in this sector. The days of mom and pop homes seem to be passing quite quickly, as the sector tries to secure greater financial capability to respond to the buffets of a market system."[2]

Following Southern Cross' failure, the National Audit Office argued that the market development of large providers operating across different local authority areas can create uncertainty over who has responsibility for managing failures. Moreover, it pointed out that there was no system to capture early warnings that a provider is facing difficulties and to take action to stop the situation deteriorating. The National Audit Office therefore recommended that the case of Southern Cross demonstrated that greater Government oversight was necessary at a national and local level to protect users from provider failure.[3]

The Care Act sets out a new legal framework for managing and monitoring the failure or potential failure of care providers. In the House of Lords, Earl Howe set out the policy reasons behind these provisions:

". . . it is unacceptable for care users to be left without the services that they need, particularly where the interruption of those services, or the worry that this might happen, could badly affect their well-being and place unacceptable stress on them and their families, friends and carers . . . [T]he collapse of Southern Cross in the autumn of 2012 highlighted the importance of this principle. Although no one was ultimately left without the services they needed, many people suffered from a considerable amount of stress and anxiety as a result of worries over whether the services that they, their friend or their relative relied on would stop being provided. At the time, there were no formal mechanisms for the Government to ensure that that was the case."[4]

This framework operates at two levels. First, s.48 sets out the responsibilities of local authorities in England for ensuring continuity of care where a provider sustains business failure and ceases to provide a service. In addition, ss.49 to 51 make provision for cross-border cases in the UK. Second, the Care Quality Commission is given responsibility

---

[1] See National Audit Office, *Oversight of User Choice and Provider Competition* (September 2011) and Institute of Public Care, *Care Quality Commission: The Stability of the Care Market and Market Oversight in England: Report* (February 2014).
[2] *Hansard* (House of Lords), 22 July 2013, Vol.747, cols 1338 to 1139.
[3] National Audit Office Oversight of User Choice and Provider Competition (September 2011), p.9.
[4] *Hansard* (House of Lords), 22 July 2013, Vol.747, col.1141.

under ss.53 to 57 for monitoring the financial position of providers in England who are difficult to replace for example due to their size, concentration or specialism. The objective of the market oversight regime is to:

". . . provide early warning to local authorities, to support them in ensuring that no one will suffer because the failure of a provider leaves a gap in the service on which they depend".[1]

Overall the market oversight regime is based on the premises that:

- the failure of any of the largest (or most significant) providers would be more likely to threaten the stability of the market than failure of a less significant provider;
- if a "difficult to replace" provider is at risk of failing, then putting in place contingency plans may avoid this outcome; and
- where an outcome of failure is not avoided, then through the involvement of the regulator, the continuity plan can help to avoid distress and disturbance to the service users.[2]

The aim is not to prevent failure but to ensure that, if it happens, arrangements are in place to secure continuity of care.

1–554   The Government's initial modelling suggests that the regime will cover 50 to 60 organisations in total at any given time.[3]

For issues relating to corporate neglect, see discussion on ill-treatment and wilful neglect at paras 1–470 to 1–471 above.

During the passage of the Care Bill in Parliament, Lord Patel argued that Monitor, as the financial regulator for health services, was better placed to assume this role. Moreover, it was suggested that the Care Quality Commission was undergoing significant structural change and lacked the capacity and expertise to take on this role.[4]   The Government described the decision to give responsibility to the Care Quality Commission as "a finely balanced one". But three key reasons were given:

- it ensures there will be a single regulator for social care providers, and the Care Quality Commission will therefore be able to assess both care quality and financial performance which is especially important given that financial performance can be an indicator of quality failures;
- the Care Quality Commission has existing working relations with providers; and
- the Care Quality Commission has established working relationships with local authority commissioners who will be responsible for managing the failure of a difficult to replace provider.

Moreover, it was argued that Monitor did not have the necessary experience in the care and support services market and essentially operates a failure regime whereby it may take control of the organisation—rather than ensuring that individuals continue to receive the services they depend upon during the failure.[5]

The Government also confirmed that where there is a danger of double regulation (such as providers that offer both social care and NHS-funded services) care providers will be exempt from Monitor's licensing regime. Regulations will create this exemption where

---

[1] *Hansard* (House of Commons: Public Bill Committee), 23 January 2014 (AM): Ninth Sitting, col.336 (Norman Lamb MP).

[2] Institute of Public Care, *Care Quality Commission: The Stability of the Care Market and Market Oversight in England: Report* (February 2014) p.13.

[3] Department of Health, *Oversight in Adult Social Care: The Consultation Response (May 2013)*, para.36.

[4] For example, see *Hansard* (House of Lords), 22 July 2013, Vol.747, cols 1136 to 1137 (Lord Patel).

[5] *Hansard* (House of Lords), 22 July 2013, Vol.747, cols 1142 to 1143 (Earl Howe).

the services provided are NHS continuing health care or NHS-funded nursing care. The exemption will expire in April 2015, at which point the Government will review whether it should be renewed.[1]

Similar concerns to those raised by Lord Patel were also raised at Committee stages in the House of Commons, that the Care Quality Commission had no expertise in insolvency or understanding complicated financial structures. During Committee stage, the Health Select Committee published a report on the Care Quality Commission which stated that the Government should reconsider its decision to allocate responsibility to the Commission and that it should ask Monitor to undertake this role.[2] The Minister confirmed that the Care Quality Commission will have sufficient funding and time to recruit the expertise it requires, and stated:

> "I think that aligning financial risk with quality makes the [Care Quality Commission] absolutely the right choice. It gives the right body the opportunity to focus on the import-ance of sustainability, because of its link to high-quality care. The [Care Quality Commission] will be able to give the intelligence to the local authorities, where homes might exist under a large and complex care provider, so that the local authority is pre-warned and can take action to prevent disaster from happening in its area."[3]

Specifying criteria for application of market oversight regime

53.—(1) Regulations must specify criteria for determining whether (subject to **1–555** regulations under subsection (4)) section 55 (financial sustainability assessment) applies to a registered care provider who is registered in respect of the carrying on of a regulated activity relating to the provision of social care for adults.

(2) In specifying the criteria, the Secretary of State must have regard to the fol-lowing in particular—

(a) the amount of social care provided by a registered care provider,

(b) the geographical concentration of a registered care provider's business,

(c) the extent to which a registered care provider specialises in the provision of particular types of care.

(3) The Secretary of State must—

(a) at such times as the Secretary of State considers appropriate, review the cri-teria for the time being specified in the regulations, and

(b) publish information about how the matters mentioned in subsection (2), and any other matters to which the Secretary of State has regard in specifying the criteria, are to be measured.

(4) Regulations may provide that section 55 does not apply, or applies only to the extent specified, to a specified registered care provider or to a registered care provider of a specified description, regardless of whether that provider or a pro-vider of that description would satisfy the criteria.

(5) Regulations may provide that section 55 applies, or applies to the extent specified, to a specified registered care provider or to a registered care provider of a specified description, regardless of whether that provider or a provider of that description would satisfy the criteria.

(6) The circumstances in which regulations may be made under subsection (4) include those in which the Secretary of State is satisfied that certain registered

---

[1] *Hansard* (House of Lords), 22 July 2013, Vol.747, col.1143 (Earl Howe).

[2] House of Commons Health Committee, *2013 Accountability Hearing with the Care Quality Commission: Sixth Report of Session 2013–14*, HC 761, (TSO, 22 January 2014), para.57.

[3] *Hansard* (House of Commons: Public Bill Committee), 21 January 2014 (PM): Eighth Sitting, col.326 (Norman Lamb MP).

care providers are already subject to a regulatory regime comparable to that provided for by sections 55 and 56; and regulations made in such circumstances may, for example, make provision requiring specified persons to co-operate or to share information of a specified description.

(7) "Social care" has the same meaning as in Part 1 of the Health and Social Care Act 2008.

GENERAL NOTE

1–556   This section enables the identification of care and support providers that are most difficult to replace and therefore will be subject to central oversight by the Care Quality Commission. The oversight system is provided for under ss.55 and 56.

Subsection (1)

1–557   This requires the Secretary of State to make regulations that specify the criteria for determining whether the care and support provider will be subject to the central oversight system. By virtue of s.125(4)(g) such regulations are subject to the affirmative procedure in Parliament. The affirmative procedure is discussed at para.1–161 above.

The relevant regulations issued under subs.(1) are the Care and Support (Market Oversight Criteria) Regulations 2015 (SI 2015/314). They are reproduced in full in paras A1–276 to A1–279 below. Regulation 2 sets out the criteria for entry applicable to providers of personal (non-residential) care. A provider becomes subject to the central oversight system if it is not a local authority and where it provides at least:

- 30,000 hours of care in a week anywhere in England; or
- 2,000 people with care in a week anywhere in England; or
- 800 people with care in a week anywhere in England and the number of hours of care provided in the same week divided by that number of people exceeds 30.

Regulation 3 sets out the criteria for entry applicable to providers of residential care. A provider becomes subject to the central oversight system if it is not a local authority and where it has a bed capacity of:

- at least 2,000 anywhere in England; or
- between 1,000 to 1,999 overall, with 1 bed or more in at least 16 local authorities in England; or
- between 1,000 to 1,999 anywhere in England and where their bed capacity in each of three or more local authorities in England exceeds 10 per cent of the total bed capacity in each of those local authorities.

Subsection (2)

1–558   In setting the criteria, the Secretary of State must have regard to the provider's size, its concentration in a particular area or areas, and its level of specialism.

Subsection (3)

1–559   The Secretary of State is required to review the criteria and publish information on how the matters mentioned in subs.(2) and any other factors considered in setting out the criteria are to be measured.

Subsection (4)

1–560   This enables the regulations to ensure that certain providers are exempt from the central oversight system, or parts of the system. By virtue of s.125(4)(h) such regulations are subject to the affirmative procedure in Parliament (this procedure is discussed at para.1–161 above). Subsection (6) clarifies that the regulations may be used to exempt providers who are already subject to a comparable regulatory system.

Subsection (5)
The regulations may specify that the central oversight system, or parts of the system, **1–561** applies only to the extent specified, to certain providers who would otherwise not fall within the regime.

Subsection (6)
Section 9(3) of the Health and Social Care Act 2008 defines "social care" as including **1–562** all forms of personal care and other practical assistance provided for individuals who by reason of age, illness, disability, pregnancy, childbirth, dependence on alcohol or drugs, or any other similar circumstances, are in need of such care or other assistance.

Determining whether criteria apply to care provider

54.—(1) The Care Quality Commission must determine, in the case of each **1–563** registered care provider, whether the provider satisfies one or more of the criteria specified in regulations under section 53.

(2) If the Commission determines that the provider satisfies one or more of the criteria, section 55 applies to that provider unless, or except in so far as, regulations under section 53(4) provide that it does not apply.

(3) Where section 55 applies to a registered care provider (whether as a result of subsection (2) or as a result of regulations under section 53(5)), the Commission must inform the provider accordingly.

GENERAL NOTE

Section 54 provides that the Care Quality Commission has responsibility for determining **1–564** whether care and support providers will be subject to the central oversight system. It must make this decision by reference to the criteria specified in the regulations made under s.53. The relevant regulations issued are the Care and Support (Market Oversight Criteria) Regulations 2015 (SI 2015/314). They are reproduced in full in paras A1–276 to A1–279 below. The Care Quality Commission is required to inform providers that satisfy the entry criteria that they are subject to the central oversight system.

Assessment of financial sustainability of care provider

55.—(1) Where this section applies to a registered care provider, the Care **1–565** Quality Commission must assess the financial sustainability of the provider's business of carrying on the regulated activity in respect of which it is registered.

(2) Where the Commission, in light of an assessment under subsection (1), considers that there is a significant risk to the financial sustainability of the provider's business, it may—
(a) require the provider to develop a plan for how to mitigate or eliminate the risk;
(b) arrange for, or require the provider to arrange for, a person with appropriate professional expertise to carry out an independent review of the business.

(3) Where the Commission imposes a requirement on a care provider under subsection (2)(a), it may also require the provider—
(a) to co-operate with it in developing the plan, and
(b) to obtain its approval of the finalised plan.

(4) Where the Commission arranges for a review under subsection (2)(b), it may recover from the provider such costs as the Commission incurs in connection with the arrangements (other than its administrative costs in making the arrangements).

(5) Regulations may make provision for enabling the Commission to obtain from such persons as it considers appropriate information which the Commission believes will assist it to assess the financial sustainability of a registered care provider to which this section applies.

(6) Regulations may make provision about the making of the assessment required by subsection (1).

(7) The Commission may consult such persons as it considers appropriate on the method for assessing the financial sustainability of a registered care provider's business; and, having done so, it must publish guidance on the method it expects to apply in making the assessment.

GENERAL NOTE

1–566   Section 55 sets out the core elements of the Care Quality Commission's central oversight system. It is based on an assessment of the provider's financial sustainability. In cases where there is a risk to the provider's business sustainability and ability to ensure continuity of care, the Care Quality Commission is given a number of powers to manage these risks.

Subsection (1)

1–567   When it has been determined that a provider satisfies the criteria set out in regulations under s.53, the Care Quality Commission is required to assess the provider's financial sustainability. During the passage of the Care bill the Government explained that:

> "In carrying out such assessments of financial sustainability, we would expect the [Care Quality Commission] to take into consideration a range of factors, including not only any risks to the business, but the reasons behind those risks. Those might include, as the amendment suggests, debts or charges owed to other individuals or organisations."[1]

Subsections (2)

1–568   Where the Care Quality Commission identifies a significant risk to the financial sustainability of the provider's business, it has powers to:

- require the provider to develop a sustainability plan to manage any risk of failure; and
- commission (or require the provider to arrange) an independent business review to help the provider to return to financial stability.

Subsection (3)

1–569   In cases where the provider is required to develop a sustainability plan, it can also be required to co-operate with the Care Quality Commission in developing the plan. The final plan may also be subject to the Care Quality Commission's approval.

Subsection (4)

1–570   Where an independent business review has been arranged, the Care Quality Commission can recover costs from the provider (other than its administrative costs).

Subsection (5)

1–571   This enables regulations to make provision for enabling the Care Quality Commission to obtain from any person it considers appropriate, information to assist it with the financial sustainability assessment. The explanatory notes set out that:

> "The type of information the [Care Quality Commission] may need is likely to be information which relates to the finances of the care provider or which relates to the financial

---

[1] *Hansard* (House of Commons: Public Bill Committee), 23 January 2014 (AM): Ninth Sitting, col.346 (Norman Lamb MP).

position of the particular entity—if the care provider is financially dependent on such entity. The type of person that may be described in such regulations may include companies within the same group as the provider, and companies that hold a significant ownership stake in the provider."[1]

The relevant regulations issued under ss.(5) are the Care and Support (Market Oversight Information) Regulations 2014 (SI 2014/2822). They are reproduced in full in paras A1–165 to A1–170 below. These regulations make provision for the Care Quality Commission to obtain information from persons other than the registered care provider to assist it in making this assessment. Regulation 2 provides that a registered care provider may be required to obtain from a group undertaking of the provider, a legally enforceable undertaking to provide information. Regulations 3 to 5 make further provision in relation to the information undertaking.

Subsection (6)

The Secretary of State may make provision about the making of financial sustainability **1–572** assessments.

Subsection (7)

The Care Quality Commission may consult such persons as it considers appropriate on **1–573** how to assess financial sustainability, and must then publish guidance on the methods it expects to apply in making its assessments.

Informing local authorities where failure of care provider likely

56.—(1) This section applies where the Care Quality Commission is satisfied **1–574** that a registered care provider to which section 55 applies is likely to become unable to carry on the regulated activity in respect of which it is registered because of business failure as mentioned in section 48.

(2) The Commission must inform the local authorities which it thinks will be required to carry out the duty under section 48(2) if the provider becomes unable to carry on the regulated activity in question.

(3) Where the Commission considers it necessary to do so for the purpose of assisting a local authority to carry out the duty under section 48(2), it may request the provider, or such other person involved in the provider's business as the Commission considers appropriate, to provide it with specified information.

(4) Where (as a result of subsection (3) or otherwise) the Commission has information about the provider's business that it considers may assist a local authority in carrying out the duty under section 48(2), the Commission must give the information to the local authority.

(5) Regulations may make provision as to the circumstances in which the Commission is entitled to be satisfied for the purposes of subsection (1) that a registered care provider is likely to become unable to carry on a regulated activity.

(6) The Commission may consult such persons as it considers appropriate on the methods to apply in assessing likelihood for the purposes of subsection (1); and, having carried out that consultation, it must publish guidance on the methods it expects to apply in making the assessment.

GENERAL NOTE

This section provides for when the Care Quality Commission must inform a local auth- **1–575** ority that a provider of care and support is likely to fail. This is intended to support local authorities in ensuring continuity of care by informing them when such a failure is likely

---

[1] Care Act 2014: Explanatory Notes para.346.

and providing information they need, such as details of individuals receiving services from the provider in their area. Under s.48(2) local authorities in England are required to step in temporarily and meet the needs of people whose provider has failed in their geographic area.

Subsection (1)

1–576   The duty to inform a local authority applies where the Care Quality Commission is satisfied that a provider is likely to become unable to continue carrying on the regulated activity in respect of which it is registered.

The relevant provider is one which has satisfied the criteria set out in regulations under s.53, and where the Care Quality Commission is required to assess the provider's financial sustainability.

Subsection (2)

1–577   The Care Quality Commission must inform the local authorities which it thinks will be required to carry out the duty under s.48(2)—the duty to meet temporary needs for care and support—if the provider becomes unable to carry on the regulated activity in question. The explanatory notes highlight that the duty only applies to local authorities in England and therefore the Care Quality Commission is not required to inform authorities in other countries.[1] However, in relevant cases the Care Quality Commission would have a power to inform such authorities or any other relevant bodies (including where appropriate Social Care and Social Work Improvement Scotland, Healthcare Improvement Scotland, the Health and Social Care Regulation and Quality Improvement Authority in Northern Ireland and the devolved UK Governments).

Subsections (3)

1–578   The Care Quality Commission may request from the provider (and any other person involved in the provider's business) any information that is necessary to assist a local authority in carrying out its duty under s.48(2).

Subsection (4)

1–579   The Care Quality Commission is required to share with a local authority any information that is necessary to assist the authority in carrying out its duty under s.48(2).

Subsection (5)

1–580   Regulations may make provision as to the circumstances in which the Care Quality Commission must inform local authorities about a provider under subs.(1).

Subsection (6)

1–581   The Care Quality Commission may consult such persons as it considers appropriate on how it will assess a provider's likelihood of becoming unable to continue carrying on the regulated activity, and must then publish guidance on how it will make this assessment.

Sections 54 to 56: supplementary

1–582   **57.**—(1) For the purposes of Part 1 of the Health and Social Care Act 2008, the duties imposed on the Care Quality Commission under sections 54(1) and 55(1) are to be treated as regulatory functions of the Commission.

(2) For the purposes of that Part of that Act, the doing by the Commission of anything for the purpose of assisting a local authority to carry out the duty under section 48(2) is to be treated as one of the Commission's regulatory functions.

---

[1] Care Act 2014: Explanatory Notes para.350.

(3) For the purposes of sections 17 and 18 of that Act (cancellation or suspension of registration under Part 1 of that Act), a requirement imposed on a registered care provider under or by virtue of any of sections 54 to 56 (or by virtue of subsection (1) or (2)) is to be treated as a requirement imposed by or under Chapter 6 of Part 1 of that Act.

(4) The Commission must, in exercising any of its functions under sections 54 to 56, have regard to the need to minimise the burdens it imposes on others.

GENERAL NOTE

This section clarifies the extent of the Care Quality Commission's powers under the central oversight system. **1–583**

Subsection (1)

This provides that the Care Quality Commission's duties to determine whether care and **1–584** support providers will be subject to the central oversight system and assess the financial sustainability of providers are to be treated as "regulatory functions" of the Care Quality Commission for the purposes of the Health and Social Care Act 2008. The explanatory notes explain:

"This establishes that the [Care Quality Commission] will be able to rely on its existing powers under the 2008 Act, such as requiring information and explanations from a provider (sections 64 and 65 of the 2008 Act). The [Care Quality Commission] will also be able to rely on its enforcement powers, for instance under sections 64(4) and 65(4) of the 2008 Act."[1]

Sections 64(4) and 65(4) provide that a person is guilty of an offence and liable on summary conviction to a fine.

Subsection (2)

This provides that anything which the Care Quality Commission may do to assist a local **1–585** authority in carrying out its duty under s.48(2) is to be treated as one of the Commission's "regulatory functions" for the purposes of the 2008 Act. See subs.(1), above, which sets out the significance of this.

Subsection (3)

The Care Quality Commission may, when imposing requirements on providers as part of **1–586** exercising the functions set out in ss.54 to 56, rely on ss.17 and 18 of the 2008 Act which provide for the cancellation or suspension of a care provider's registration.

Subsection (4)

The Care Quality Commission must have regard to the need to minimise the burdens it **1–587** may impose on a provider in exercising any of its functions under ss.54 to 56.

TRANSITION FOR CHILDREN TO ADULT CARE AND SUPPORT, ETC.

Prior to the Care Act, most community care legislation applied to those aged 18 and over. **1–588** However, the following legislation also applied to children:

- s.2(1) of the Chronically Sick and Disabled Persons Act 1970;
- s.4 of the Disabled Persons (Services, Consultation and Representation) Act 1986;
- s.117 of the Mental Health Act 1983;
- para.3 of Sch.20 to the National Health Service Act 2006;

---

[1] Care Act 2014: Explanatory Notes para.354.

- Carers (Recognition and Services) Act 1995; and
- Carers and Disabled Children Act 2000.

The Law Commission concluded that this overlap created confusion, and recommended that the adult social care statute should apply to those aged 18 and above. In general terms, this would mean that children's services would be provided primarily under Pt 3 of the Children Act 1989, and adults' services under the new adult statute. It also recommended that the Government should consider amending the 1989 Act to incorporate the same rights to services for disabled children that are contained in the legislation listed above (most notably the Chronically Sick and Disabled Persons Act 1970).[1]

These recommendations were aimed at establishing greater legal clarity, but the Law Commission also considered how the law should encourage a smooth transition for children who will need continuing services into adulthood. During the second reading of the Care Bill in the House of Commons, Stuart Andrew MP described some of the relevant issues:

"A successful transition needs to address both the transfer of responsibility for young people from children's to existing adults' social care, health and education services, and the development of new adult services that are tailored to young people's additional needs. The transition needs to be planned for years in advance, but, at present, planning is often disjointed and poor. The reduced services and support routinely offered by adult agencies, which are often focused on older people and end-of-life care, come as a distressing shock to many young people and their families. Parents have described the transition as like 'standing on the edge of a cliff, about to fall into a black hole'. Poor transitions lead to increased illness, adverse social and educational outcomes, and sometimes even premature death."[2]

In the House of Lords, Lord Patel also highlighted the particular difficulties faced by the children needing palliative care during the transition from children's to adult's services:

"There are about 45,000—repeat: 45,000—children or young people from newborns to the age of 19 who have long-term health conditions which will eventually end the lives of most of them and for which they may require palliative care. Medical advances mean that more young people with a range of different conditions are living into adulthood than ever before. The greatest increase is among those aged 16 to 19, who now account for 4,000, or one in 10, newborns to 19 year-olds needing palliative care. The majority of young people who may require palliative care have a range of severe disabilities and complex health needs. Cancer represents just under 14 per cent of diagnoses. Many young people have cognitive impairments, meaning that they lack capacity, and many are cared for over long periods by parent carers. Many young people with life-limiting or life-threatening conditions who are more cognitively able struggle to achieve independence or to enter education or employment because plans are not made for them. Those who are unlikely to be cured by treatment are offered palliative care. Transition for children after their 16th birthday is complex. Successful transition needs to address the transfer of responsibility for young people from children to existing adult social care, health and education services, and the development of new adult services tailored to young people's additional needs."[3]

1-589   The Law Commission's final report made recommendations to address the transition needs of three groups: children with care and support needs, child's carers (including parent carers) and young carers. These recommendations are described below in the general notes to ss.58 to 66 of the Care Act. But in broad terms, the Commission recommended that local authorities should be given powers to assess and provide services to 16 and 17 year olds

---

[1] Law Commission, *Adult Social Care*, paras 11.38 to 11.43.
[2] *Hansard* (House of Commons), 16 December 2013, Vol.572, col.533.
[3] *Hansard* (House of Lords), 22 July 2013, Vol.747, col.1147.

under the adult statute, supplemented by a right for the relevant child and parents to request an assessment.

The Government agreed with the Law Commission's analysis of the confusion at the boundary of children and adults, and accepted that the new statute should establish a clear general principle that adult care and support is for people aged 18 years and over. It also agreed that the law must support local authorities to "plan effectively and tailor transition around the needs of the individual, and not create a 'cliff edge' at the age of 18 years".[1] However, the detail of the Government's approach to transition (set out in ss.58 to 66 of the Care Act) differs in places to that recommended by the Law Commission. In particular, there are duties (rather than powers) to undertake transition assessments in certain circumstances, and no powers to provide services. The statutory guidance discusses the transition to adult care and support in Ch.16. In addition, the Social Care Institute for Excellence has produced a range of guides on the Care Act and the transition from childhood to adulthood.[2] These documents are not statutory guidance but have been produced with the approval of the Department of Health (see 1–770 below).

It is also important to note that other legislation also attempts to encourage a smooth transition for children into adult life. For example:

- the Children Act 1989, as amended by Children (Leaving Care) Act 2000, places duties on local authorities to support young people leaving care up until the age of 21 and in some cases beyond; and
- the Children and Families Act 2014 includes a right for those with special educational needs to an Education, Health and Care Plan up until the age of 25 (see also discussion at 1-071 above).

WHOLE FAMILY APPROACH

During the development and passage of the Care Bill, the Government fre- **1–590** quently emphasised its policy of encouraging a "whole family approach" to assessments.[3] Consequently, there are a number of provisions in the Care Act which enable children with care and support needs and young carers to be included in the adult assessment. For example, s.12(1)(a) provides a power to make regulations that require the local authority to have regard to the needs of the family of the person to whom an assessment relates. Section 12(5) also allows for the assessment of the adult to be linked to any other assessment. Under s.65 the local authority has powers to combine transition assessments jointly with another assessment (which could include an assessment of a family member). These provisions are intended to enable practitioners to consider the effect of an individual's support needs on the rest of the family, and provide appropriate services that address the needs of the whole family.

The whole family approach is discussed at paras 6.65 to 6.73 of the statutory guidance. In addition, the Association of Directors of Adult Social Services has produced a guide on

---

[1] Department of Health, *Reforming the Law for Adult Care and Support: The Government's Response to Law Commission Report 326 on Adult Social Care* (TSO, July 2012), Cm.8379, paras 11.15 to 11.16.

[2] For example, Social Care Institute for Excellence, *Transition From Children's to Adult Services: Early and Comprehensive Identification* (March 2015), Social Care Institute for Excellence, Adult Carer Transition in Practice under the Care Act 2014 (March 2015), and Social Care Institute for Excellence, *Young Carer Transition in Practice under the Care Act 2014* (March 2015).

[3] See, for example, Department of Health, *The Care Bill explained—including a response to consultation and pre-legislative scrutiny on the draft Care and Support Bill*, para.122.

whole family approaches.[1] This is not statutory guidance but have been produced with the approval of the Department of Health (see 1–770 below).

Assessment of a child's needs for care and support

1–591   **58.**—(1) Where it appears to a local authority that a child is likely to have needs for care and support after becoming 18, the authority must, if it is satisfied that it would be of significant benefit to the child to do so and if the consent condition is met, assess—

(a) whether the child has needs for care and support and, if so, what those needs are, and

(b) whether the child is likely to have needs for care and support after becoming 18 and, if so, what those needs are likely to be.

(2) An assessment under subsection (1) is referred to in this Part as a "child's needs assessment".

(3) The consent condition is met if—

(a) the child has capacity or is competent to consent to a child's needs assessment being carried out and the child does so consent, or

(b) the child lacks capacity or is not competent so to consent but the authority is satisfied that carrying out a child's needs assessment would be in the child's best interests.

(4) Where a child refuses a child's needs assessment and the consent condition is accordingly not met, the local authority must nonetheless carry out the assessment if the child is experiencing, or is at risk of, abuse or neglect.

(5) Where a local authority, having received a request to carry out a child's assessment from the child concerned or a parent or carer of the child, decides not to comply with the request, it must give the person who made the request—

(a) written reasons for its decision, and

(b) information and advice about what can be done to prevent or delay the development by the child of needs for care and support in the future.

(6) "Parent", in relation to a child, includes—

(a) a parent of the child who does not have parental responsibility for the child, and

(b) a person who is not a parent of the child but who has parental responsibility for the child.

(7) "Carer", in relation to a child, means a person, other than a parent, who is providing care for the child, whether or not under or by virtue of a contract or as voluntary work.

(8) The reference to providing care includes a reference to providing practical or emotional support.

GENERAL NOTE

1–592   The Law Commission recommended that local authorities should have a general power to assess and provide services to children aged 16 and 17 under the adult social care statute. In addition, such children (and their parents on their behalf) would be given a power to request that they be assessed under the adult statute rather than the Children Act 1989, and the local authority would then be required to give written reasons if it decided not to carry out the assessment. The request could be made by any child aged 16 or 17 years

---

[1] Association of Directors of Adult Social Services, *The Care Act and Whole Family Approaches* (January 2015).

old irrespective of their capacity, and a parent or carer could make a request on their behalf if:

- the child person has capacity and gives consent; or
- the child lacks capacity and an assessment under the adult legislation is in their "best interests" under the Mental Capacity Act 2005.

The Commission also recommended that the Government should have regulation-making powers to create a duty to assess certain children under the adult social care statute and to specify groups to whom this duty is owed.[1]

The Government agreed that, to support planning ahead of transition, local authorities should have a power to assess a child under 18 years old under the adult statute—along with a request mechanism for children, guardians, carers and parents. However it disagreed that there should be a general power to provide services (see discussion at para.1–653 below).[2]

Originally, the Care Bill—as introduced in the House of Lords—provided that the local authority power to undertake a child's needs assessment would only apply if:

- a request was made by the child, or their parent or carer, for an assessment;
- the child was likely to have needs for care and support after becoming 18;
- the assessment would be of "significant benefit" to the child; and
- the child had capacity or competence to make the request or consent to the request by a parent or carer, or the request was made by a parent or carer and an assessment is in the child's best interests.[3]

However, the Government faced pressure in the House of Lords to establish a duty to **1–593** undertake a transition assessment. For example, at committee stage Lord Patel tabled an amendment to require an assessment to take place when a child receiving services reaches 14 or a request is made.[4] Setting the age threshold at 14 was based on the statutory requirement for every young person aged 14 with a statement of special educational needs to have a transition plan.[5] In rejecting the amendment, the Government argued that any requirement for a transition assessment at a particular age would be too rigid and fail to take into account the individual's needs or circumstances. The Minister went on to argue that:

"Some young people will not have needs for care and support after the age of 18. It will not be appropriate, nor indeed will it be in a young person's interests, to assess in every case."[6]

However, by report stage the Government had been persuaded to alter its approach and tabled amendments to remove the need to request the assessment and introduce a duty to assess where this would be of significant benefit to the individual.[7] The Government however did not agree that there should be a duty to assess at the age of 14. The Minister explained that:

"The clauses are formulated in this way precisely so that assessments happen at the right time, whether that is before or after the age of 14, depending on the individual. The Bill

---

[1] Law Commission, *Adult Social Care*, paras 11.44 to 11.60.
[2] Department of Health, *Reforming the Law for Adult Care and Support: The Government's Response to Law Commission Report 326 on Adult Social Care* (TSO, July 2012), Cm.8379, paras 11.19 to 11.20.
[3] HL Bill 001 2013–2014 as introduced, cl.55.
[4] *Hansard* (House of Lords), 22 July 2013, Vol.747, cols 1147 to 1150.
[5] Education (Special Educational Needs) (England) (Consolidation) Regulations 2001 (SI 2001/3455).
[6] *Hansard* (House of Lords), 22 July 2013, Vol.747, col.1155 (Earl Howe).
[7] *Hansard* (House of Lords), 16 October 2013, Vol.748, cols 570 to 578.

approaches transition planning with a firm focus on assessing at the right time for the individual by the new duty to assess where it would be of significant benefit to the individual. I am not persuaded that the interests of young people are best served by prescribing when assessment should take place."[1]

The s.58 assessment duty does not extend to a child's carer and young carers, who are dealt with separately under ss.60 to 64. It also does not enable the provision of services to children. Indeed, there is no power under the Care Act to provide services to a child. Instead, s.66 provides a right to "continuity of care" for a child who is receiving services under s.17 of the Children Act 1989, an Education, Health and Care Plan (under s.37(2) of the Children and Families Act 2014) or s.2 of the Chronically Sick and Disabled Persons Act 1970. If a transition assessment has been requested, and the relevant assessment has not taken place or a conclusion has not been reached, then services must continue when the child reaches 18 until a conclusion has been reached.

Subsections (1) to (4)

1–594   The duty to undertake a child's needs assessment only applies if:

- the child is likely to have needs for care and support after becoming 18; and
- the assessment would be of significant benefit to the child.

In addition, one of the following must apply

- the child consents and has capacity or competence to do so (subs.(3)(a));
- the child lacks capacity or competence to consent, but carrying out the assessment is in their best interests (subs.(3)(b)); or
- the child refuses the assessment, but they are experiencing (or at risk of) abuse and neglect (subs.(4)).

A child does not have to be receiving any specific service under the Children Act 1989 or any other legislation, such as the Chronically Sick and Disabled Persons Act 1970, in order to qualify for an assessment. Similarly, there is no restriction on the age of child, or their proximity to their 18th birthday. These points are confirmed in the statutory guidance.[2] The guidance also discusses how to identify children who are not receiving services in paras 16.18 to 16.19.

The Joint Committee on the draft Care and Support Bill had recommended that the provision of an assessment should be extended to any child (or young carer) who may have needs for care and support at the time of the request for the assessment or on reaching 18.[3] The first of these criteria has not been implemented by the Care Act. The relevant test is that the child is likely to have needs after 18. The Joint Committee also recommended that there should be a presumption that the following groups should qualify for a transition assessment:

- any child in receipt of an Education, Health and Care Plan under the Children and Families Act 2014; and
- any child receiving care and support, or who has family members receiving care and support, under other legislation.[4]

---

[1] *Hansard* (House of Lords), 16 October 2013, Vol.748, col.571 (Earl Howe).

[2] Department of Health, *Care and Support Statutory Guidance* (2014), paras 16.7 to 16.8.

[3] House of Lords House of Commons Joint Committee on the Draft Care and Support Bill, *Draft Care and Support Bill Report, Session 2012–13*, para.238.

[4] House of Lords House of Commons Joint Committee on the Draft Care and Support Bill, *Draft Care and Support Bill Report, Session 2012–13*, para.238.

Section 58 contains no automatic duty to assess such groups. But the statutory guidance notes it is "highly likely" that those in receipt of children's services would be "likely to have needs" and therefore eligible for a transition assessment as they approach adulthood.[1]

SIGNIFICANT BENEFIT.   The statutory guidance explains that "significant benefit" is not **1–595** related to the level of needs, but rather to the timing of the transition assessment. It also states several factors that should be considered, including the stage they have reached at school and any upcoming exams, and any planned medical treatment. For those with special educational needs with an Education, Health and Care Plan the guidance states that preparation for adulthood must begin from year 9.[2]   Where the child is likely to have needs for care and support after turning 18, but it is not yet of significant benefit to carry out a transition assessment, the local authority "should consider indicating (when providing its written reasons for refusing the assessment) when it believes the assessment will be of significant benefit". The onus is then on the authority to contact the child to agree the timing of the transition assessment, rather than leaving the child to make repeated requests[3]

CAPACITY, COMPETENCE AND BEST INTERESTS.   The child's ability to consent to the **1–596** assessment depends on their capacity or competence to do so. The concepts of capacity and competence have similarities but are in legal terms distinct. The Mental Capacity Act 2005 will determine if a child has capacity to consent. This Act applies to anyone aged 16 or over, and on the basis that the lack of capacity results from an impairment of, or a disturbance in the functioning of, the mind or brain. The 2005 Act does not apply if the person aged 16 or 17 is unable to consent to the assessment for some other reason, for example because they are overwhelmed by the implications. The competence of the child to consent to the assessment will be determined by the principles set out in *Gillick v West Norfolk and Wisbech Area Health Authority*.[4]   This case provided that if a child is of sufficient age and understanding, they can give valid consent to contraceptive advice and treatment, without the consent of the parents. The principles elucidated in *Gillick* will apply where the child is aged under 16.

PURPOSE OF THE ASSESSMENT.   The purpose of the assessment is twofold: **1–597**

- whether the child has needs for care and support (and what those needs are); and
- whether the child is likely to have needs for care and support after becoming 18 (and what those needs are likely to be).

According to the explanatory notes:

"The purpose of this assessment would be to consider what needs for care and support the child may have at their 18th birthday, to support planning for transition to adult care and support. The local authority will therefore assess the child's needs by reference to the adult care and support arrangements, and this power is not intended to be used to assess needs for children's services."[5]

Further provision about the content and process of the assessment and the information which must be provided following an assessment is made in s.59.

---

[1] Department of Health, *Care and Support Statutory Guidance* (2014), para.16.9.
[2] Department of Health, *Care and Support Statutory Guidance* (2014), paras16.10 to 16.11.
[3] Department of Health, *Care and Support Statutory Guidance* (2014), para.16.15.
[4] *Gillick v West Norfolk and Wisbech Area Health Authority* [1986] A.C. 112.
[5] Care Act 2014: Explanatory Notes para.361.

Subsection (5)

1–598 A child, or a parent or carer acting on their behalf, can request an assessment and this may trigger an appearance of need for the purposes of this duty. This provision is discussed in paras 16.14 to 16.16 of the statutory guidance. There are no particular formalities about the format of the request. For example, it does not need to be in writing.

Any child, parent or carer can make a request, irrespective of their capacity or competence to make the request. However, the capacity or competence of the child to consent to the assessment will be relevant to the duty to assess (see subss.(3)(a) and (3)(b)). Where the local authority does not comply with the request it must explain why in writing and provide information and advice about what can be done to prevent or delay the development of needs.

The duty under subs.(5)(a) is to give written reasons for its decision not to comply with the request. The Equality Act 2010 may be relevant to the performance of this duty and if necessary, the explanation should be provided in alternative formats and using different methods of communication, as well as being in writing.

The duty under subs.(5)(b) is to provide information and advice about how to prevent or delay needs. It does not specify any particular formalities about how the information and advice should be given to the person. Nevertheless, it is submitted that local authorities should as a matter of course, provide this information in writing in order to demonstrate they have met this requirement. The Equality Act 2010 may also be relevant and if necessary, the information should be provided in alternative formats and using different methods of communication.

Under subs.(5)(a) and (b) the written reasons, and information and advice, must be given to the person who made the request. Where the child has not made the request, it is submitted that the local authority has discretion to provide the child with the written reasons, and information and advice.

Subsection (5)(a) and (b) does not specify or indicate how much detail should be provided when giving written reasons, and advice and information. The extent of the detail is likely to depend upon the specific circumstances of the individual case. For example, where the child is refusing the assessment (and there is no despite about their capacity or competence), it may be acceptable to provide relatively brief and straightforward reasons, and advice and information. But where for example the decision is disputed by the child and their family, more detail might be appropriate.

Subsections (6) and (7)

1–599 A child's parent or carer can make the request even though they do not have parental responsibility. "Parent" is defined in subs.(6) and "carer" is defined in subs.(7).

Child's needs assessment: requirements etc.

1–600 **59.**—(1) A child's needs assessment must include an assessment of—

(a) the impact on the matters specified in section 1(2) of what the child's needs for care and support are likely to be after the child becomes 18,

(b) the outcomes that the child wishes to achieve in day-to-day life, and

(c) whether, and if so to what extent, the provision of care and support could contribute to the achievement of those outcomes.

(2) A local authority, in carrying out a child's needs assessment, must involve—

(a) the child,

(b) the child's parents and any carer that the child has, and

(c) any person whom the child or a parent or carer of the child requests the local authority to involve.

(3) When carrying out a child's needs assessment, a local authority must also consider whether, and if so to what extent, matters other than the provision of

care and support could contribute to the achievement of the outcomes that the child wishes to achieve in day-to-day life.

(4) Having carried out a child's needs assessment, a local authority must give the child—

(a) an indication as to whether any of the needs for care and support which it thinks the child is likely to have after becoming 18 are likely to meet the eligibility criteria (and, if so, which ones are likely to do so), and

(b) advice and information about—

(i) what can be done to meet or reduce the needs which it thinks the child is likely to have after becoming 18;

(ii) what can be done to prevent or delay the development by the child of needs for care and support in the future.

(5) But in a case where the child is not competent or lacks capacity to understand the things which the local authority is required to give under subsection (4), that subsection is to have effect as if for "must give the child" there were substituted "must give the child's parents".

(6) Where a person to whom a child's needs assessment relates becomes 18, the local authority must decide whether to treat the assessment as a needs assessment; and if the authority decides to do so, this Part applies to the child's needs assessment as if it were a needs assessment that had been carried out after the person had become 18.

(7) In considering what to decide under subsection (6), a local authority must have regard to—

(a) when the child's needs assessment was carried out, and

(b) whether it appears to the authority that the circumstances of the person to whom the child's needs assessment relates have changed in a way that might affect the assessment.

(8) "Carer" has the same meaning as in section 58.

GENERAL NOTE

This section sets out what a child's needs assessment under s.58 must address. It also **1–601** contains certain procedural requirements governing who should be involved in the assessment and the information that should be provided following the completion of the assessment.

The local authority may combine a child's needs assessment with any other assessment it is carrying out of the child or another person, or carry out the assessment on behalf of or jointly with another body (see s.65(2) and (5)).

Subsection (1)

The assessment must address: **1–602**

- the impact of the child's needs on their well-being (as set out in s.1(2)) after they become 18;
- the outcomes the child wants to achieve; and
- whether the provision of care and support will contribute to meeting those outcomes.

Subsection (2)

The assessment must involve the child, the child's parents, the child's carers and any **1–603** other person who the child or the child's parent or carer wants to be involved.

The meaning of "involve" is discussed at paras 1–104 to 1–105 above.

Involving a person may involve providing them with an advocate. The right to advocacy in s.67 of the Care Act expressly applies to this subsection (see s.67(3)(g)).

Subsection (3)

1–604   When carrying out the assessment the local authority must also consider whether there are matters (other than the provision of care and support) that could help the child achieve the outcomes that they wish to achieve. Originally this provision was listed in subs.(1) as a matter which must be included in the assessment.[1] However, concerns were raised in the House of Lords that this blurred the distinction between assessing needs and how to meet needs.[2] This led to the introduction of Government amendments to ensure that such matters are considered separate to, but alongside, the needs assessment (see discussion on s.9(6) relating to the adult needs assessment at paras 1–108 to 1–110 above).

In the House of Lords, Baroness Pitkeathley raised concerns that in considering other matters that could help the child—which could include the child's own capabilities and support from others—there could be "undue reliance" on family and friends to provide support.[3] In response the Government explained its intention:

> ". . . consideration of 'other matters', a person's own capabilities and the other support that may be available does not exclude the provision of more conventional care and support services where needed. Indeed, when the child becomes 18, if the individual's needs are eligible, the local authority must meet them, in accordance with [s.18], if the adult wants the authority to do so, and those requirements are not diminished by these three paragraphs. The intention is to recognise that, in order to make the right connections to the local community and the variety of support available, the local authority should consider how these matters, along with more formal care and support provision, could be of benefit in achieving the adult's outcomes. The noble Baroness suggested that carers might be pressurised by these provisions into providing care. It is certainly not our intention that pressure is put on carers. The clauses make it very clear that a carer must be willing and able to provide support and that the impact upon carers' well-being must be considered."[4]

Subsection (4)

1–605   Following the assessment, the local authority must give the child who was the subject of the needs assessment:

- an indication of whether any of the needs identified (and if so, which ones) are likely to be eligible needs when the child reaches 18; and
- advice and information about what can be done to reduce the needs that are likely to become eligible needs, and what can be done to prevent or delay the development of needs for care and support in the future.

This requirement applies irrespective of whether or not the child consented to the assessment (subject to subs.(5)).

There are no particular formalities about how the indication, and advice and information should be given to the child. For example, it does not need to be in writing. However, it is submitted that local authorities should as a matter of course, provide the indication, and advice and information, in writing in order to demonstrate they have met the requirement in subs.(4). The Equality Act 2010 may be relevant to the performance of this duty and if necessary, the indication, and advice and information, should be provided in alternative formats and using different methods of communication.

---

[1] HL Bill 001 2013-2014 as introduced, cl.56(1)(c).
[2] *Hansard* (House of Lords), 22 July 2013, Vol.747, col.1151.
[3] *Hansard* (House of Lords), 22 July 2013, Vol.747, col.1151.
[4] *Hansard* (House of Lords), 22 July 2013, Vol.747, col.1156 to 1157 (Earl Howe).

Subsection (4) does not specify or indicate how much detail should be provided when giving the required indication, and advice and information. The extent of the detail is likely to depend upon the specific circumstances of the individual case. For example, where the child and their family do not dispute the decision and are not seeking local authority assistance, the indication, and information and advice, may be relatively brief and straightforward. But where the decision is disputed by the child and their family and where the child may lose services as a result, more detail might be appropriate.

The statutory guidance discusses providing information and advice following the completion of the transition assessment in paras16.50 to 16.57.

Subsection (5)

Where the child is not competent or lacks capacity to understand the things that the local **1–606** authority is required to give under subs.(4), the information must be given to the child's parents.

Subsections (6) and (7)

Once the young person becomes 18 the local authority must decide whether to treat this **1–607** assessment as their "needs assessment" under s.9. In doing so, the local authority must take into account when the assessment was carried out and whether the young person's circumstances have changed. The statutory guidance points out that few moves to adult's services will take place on someone's 18th birthday and in most cases will take place at the end of school term or another milestone—and may be staged over many months or years.[1]

Assessment of a child's carer's needs for support

60.—(1) Where it appears to a local authority that a carer of a child is likely to **1–608** have needs for support after the child becomes 18, the authority must, if it is satisfied that it would be of significant benefit to the carer to do so, assess—

(a) whether the carer has needs for support and, if so, what those needs are, and

(b) whether the carer is likely to have needs for support after the child becomes 18 and, if so, what those needs are likely to be.

(2) An assessment under subsection (1) is referred to in this Part as a "child's carer's assessment".

(3) Where a child's carer refuses a child's carer's assessment, the local authority is not required to carry out the assessment (and subsection (1) does not apply in the carer's case).

(4) Where, having refused a child's carer's assessment, a child's carer requests the assessment, subsection (1) applies in the carer's case (and subsection (3) does not).

(5) Where a child's carer has refused a child's carer's assessment and the local authority concerned thinks that the carer's needs or circumstances have changed, subsection (1) applies in the carer's case (but subject to further refusal as mentioned in subsection (3)).

(6) Where a local authority, having received a request to carry out a child's carer's assessment from the carer concerned, decides not to comply with the request, it must give the carer—

(a) written reasons for its decision, and

(b) information and advice about what can be done to prevent or delay the development by the carer of needs for support in the future.

---

[1] Department of Health, *Care and Support Statutory Guidance* (2014), para.16.61.

(7) "Carer", in relation to a child, means an adult (including one who is a parent of the child) who provides or intends to provide care for the child (but see subsection (8)).

(8) An adult is not a carer for the purposes of this section if the adult provides or intends to provide care—

(a) under or by virtue of a contract, or

(b) as voluntary work.

(9) But in a case where the local authority considers that the relationship between the child and the adult providing or intending to provide care is such that it would be appropriate for the adult to be regarded as a carer, the adult is to be regarded as such (and subsection (8) is therefore to be ignored in that case).

(10) The references to providing care include a reference to providing practical or emotional support.

GENERAL NOTE

1–609   A child's carer (which can include a parent carer) is an adult who has needs for support as a result of caring for a child. These needs may arise where, for example, the child is disabled. As Baroness Pitkeathley explained during the passage of the Care Bill through the House of Lords:

> ". . . we must understand that the responsibility we gladly take for our non-disabled children is very different from what we expect from the parents of a child with special needs. These parent carers can find themselves providing care for many years and often at the very heavy end of caring—for example, someone who has severe mental and physical disabilities may need lifting and continence care—and for 24 hours a day."[1]

Prior to the Care Act (and the Children and Families Act 2014), a child's carers had a right to a separate carer's assessment under s.1(2) of the Carers (Recognition and Services) Act 1995. In addition, a person with parental responsibility for a disabled child had a right to a separate carer's assessment under s.6 of the Carers and Disabled Children Act 2000. Under both pieces of legislation, the local authority was required to take the results of the assessment into account when deciding what services, if any, will be provided under the Children Act 1989. Child's carers also had a right to have their needs addressed as part of an assessment carried out under s.17 of the 1989 Act.

The Law Commission recommended that this legal framework should be consolidated and reformed (see para.1–610 below). It also proposed that parent carers should have a right to a transition assessment under the adult social care statute where the child (aged 16 or 17) is themselves receiving a transition assessment under the same statute.[2]   In response, the Government expressed support for the principle behind the Law Commission's recommendations "to ensure the whole family-focus by services working together around the needs of the family" and accepted that local authorities should be required to assess parent carers under the adult statute, on request.[3]

Originally, the Care Bill—as introduced in the House of Lords—provided that the local authority duty to undertake a transition assessment in respect of a child's carer only applied if:

- a request was made by the carer;
- the child was in receipt of services;
- the carer was likely to have needs for support after the child becomes 18; and

---

[1] *Hansard* (House of Lords), 22 July 2013, Vol.747, cols 1151 to 1152.

[2] Law Commission, *Adult Social Care*, paras 11.69 to 11.70.

[3] Department of Health, *Reforming the Law for Adult Care and Support: The Government's Response to Law Commission Report 326 on Adult Social Care* (TSO, July 2012), Cm.8379, paras 11.24 to 11.25.

- the assessment would be of "significant benefit" to the carer.

If the child was not in receipt of services, there was a power to assess.[1] However, this was amended during the passage of the Care Bill at report stage in the House of Lords (along with the provisions governing a child's needs assessment and a young carer's assessment) to remove the need to request the assessment (see paras 1–592 to 1–593 above). Instead, s.60 provides a duty to assess where the carer is likely to have needs for support after the child reaches 18 and the assessment would be of "significant benefit" to the carer—see para.1–595 above.

The power to provide transition support to a child's carer is contained in s.62.

PARENT CARERS AND THE CHILDREN ACT 1989

As noted above, the previous legal framework gave a child's carer's rights to a separate **1–610** carer's assessment by virtue of s.1(2) of the Carers (Recognition and Services) Act 1995 and s.6 of the Carers and Disabled Children Act 2000. However, the duty to assess only applied if (amongst other matters) the carer requested the assessment and was providing a substantial amount of support on a regular basis.

The Law Commission noted that if this legislation was retained, child's carers would face a higher threshold for an assessment in comparison to a carer's assessment under the adult social care statute (which would be based on the appearance of need—see para.1–113 above). Therefore it recommended that the duties to assess in the 1995 and 2000 Acts should be amended to make them consistent with the lower threshold for a carer's assessment under the adult statute. The Commission further recommended that the 1995 and 2000 Acts should be consolidated to create a single young carer's statute (which would include the rights of child's carers) or the Acts should be repealed and the provisions incorporated into an amended Children Act 1989.[2]

Initially, these recommendations were not taken forward by the Care Bill or the Children and Families Act Bill 2012–13 which was being considered by Parliament at the same time. Baroness Pitkeathley attempted to amend the Care Bill to provide that all child's carers are included in the duty to assess a carer's needs for support under s.10.[3] This was, in part, an attempt to ensure that the rights of child's carers to assessments and support were consistent with the rights of other carers. In response the Government stated:

> "In the Government's view, the main provision for assessing and supporting those caring for disabled children should be in children's legislation, so that the family's need for support can be looked at holistically. In most cases, the best way of supporting a parent carer of a disabled child and other members of the family is by the provision of support directly to the child concerned. It would not be appropriate for adult care and support to be undertaking an assessment of those needs, when adult support is not best placed to meet them. The view of the Minister for Children and Families is that there is already sufficient provision under Section 17 of the Children Act 1989 to provide for the assessment and support of children in need, including disabled children and their parents."[4]

However, the Joint Committee on Human Rights rejected the Government's position and recommended that child's carers should be given equivalent rights to a needs assessment and support—either in children's legislation or the Care Act.[5]

The Government was persuaded to change its view, and amended the Children and Families Bill 2013–14. Consequently, s.97 of the Children and Families Act 2014

---

[1] HL Bill 001 2013-2014 as introduced, cl.57.

[2] Law Commission, Adult Social Care, paras 11.65 and 11.69 to 11.70.

[3] *Hansard* (House of Lords), 9 October 2013, Vol.748, col.90.

[4] *Hansard* (House of Lords), 9 October 2013, Vol.748, col.97 (Earl Howe).

[5] House of Lords House of Commons Joint Committee on Human Rights, *Legislative Scrutiny: Care Bill: Eleventh Report of Session 2013–14*, HL Paper 121, HC 1027, (27 January 2014), para.114.

consolidates into Pt 3 of the Children Act 1989 the provisions relating to the assessment of parent carers, particularly those contained in the Carers and Disabled Children Act 2000. It removes the requirement for such carers to be providing "a substantial amount of care on a regular basis" in order to be assessed, and requires local authorities to assess on the appearance of need, as well as on request. Local authorities must have regard to the well-being of parent carers (as defined in the Care Act) in undertaking an assessment of their needs and must take reasonable steps to identify the extent to which there are parent carers within their area who have needs for support. The Secretary of State is also given a power to make regulations making provision about the carrying out of a parent carer's needs assessment. Those regulations may, in particular, specify matters to which a local authority is to have regard or is to determine in carrying out the assessment, the manner in which an assessment is to be carried out and the form that assessment is to take.

Subsections (1) to (3)

1–611   The duty to undertake a child's carer's assessment only applies if:

- the carer is likely to have needs for support after the child becomes 18 (subs.(1));
- the assessment would be of significant benefit to the carer (subs.(1)); and
- the carer does not refuse the assessment (subs.(3)).

The child needing care does not have to be receiving any specific service under the Children Act 1989 or any other legislation, such as the Chronically Sick and Disabled Persons Act 1970. Similarly, there is no restriction on the age of child, or their proximity to their 18th birthday.

The refusal of the assessment prevents an assessment from taking place even if the child's carer lacks capacity to consent to the assessment. In such cases it is likely that the carer would be eligible for a needs assessment under s.9 and would not be able to refuse the assessment (see s.11(2)(a))—see also discussion at para.1–133 above on carers and the refusal of an assessment.

The purpose of the assessment is twofold:

- whether the carer has needs for support (and what those needs are); and
- whether the carer is likely to have needs for support after the child becomes 18 (and what those needs are likely to be).

According to the explanatory notes:

"The purpose of the assessment would be to consider what needs for support the child's carer may have at the child's 18th birthday, to support planning for transition to adult care and support. The local authority will therefore assess the child's carer's needs by reference to the adult care and support arrangements, and this power is not intended to be used to assess needs for children's services."[1]

Further provision about the content and process of the assessment and the information that must be provided following an assessment is made in s.61.

Subsections (4) and (5)

1–612   The duty to assess a child's carer can be re-triggered following a refusal if the carer requests the assessment or if the local authority thinks the needs or circumstances have changed (unless the carer continues to refuse). This mirrors s.11 (6) and (7).

---

[1] Care Act 2014: Explanatory Notes para.373.

The child's carer can request an assessment and this may trigger an appearance of need **1–613** for the purposes of this duty. There are no particular formalities about the format of the request. For example, it does not need to be in writing. A child's carer can make a request, irrespective of their capacity or competence to make the request.

Where the local authority does not comply with the request it must explain why in writing. The Equality Act 2010 may be relevant to the performance of this duty and if necessary, the explanation should be provided in alternative formats and using different methods of communication, as well as being in writing.

In addition, where the local authority does not comply with the request it must provide information and advice about what can be done to prevent or delay the development of needs. This information and advice must be given to the carer. There are no particular formalities about how the information and advice should be given to the carer. For example, it does not need to be in writing. However, it is submitted that local authorities should as a matter of course, provide this information and advice in writing in order to demonstrate they have met this requirement. The Equality Act 2010 may also be relevant and if necessary, the information and advice should be provided in alternative formats and using different methods of communication.

Subsection (6) does not specify or indicate how much detail should be provided when giving written reasons, and advice and information. The extent of the detail is likely to depend upon the specific circumstances of the individual case. For example, where the assessment is refused for the simple reason that the carer is providing care by virtue of a contract, it may be acceptable to provide relatively brief and straightforward reasons, and advice and information. But where, for instance, the decision is disputed by the carer, more detail might be appropriate.

Subsection (7) to (10)
This defines a child's carer as an adult (including but not limited to the parent of the **1–614** child) who provides or intends to provide care for the child (including practical and emotional support).

The definition of a child's carer is subject to the proviso that those who care on a contractual or volunteering basis are not considered to be carers for the purposes of the Act. However, if the local authority thinks it is appropriate for such an individual (even if there is a contractual or volunteering element to the relationship) to be treated as a carer, then the adult is regarded as a carer and the duty to assess may apply. See also discussion under s.10(9) and (10).

Child's carer's assessment: requirements etc.

61.—(1) A child's carer's assessment must include an assessment of— **1–615**
  (a) whether the carer is able to provide care for the child and is likely to continue to be able to do so after the child becomes 18,
  (b) whether the carer is willing to do so and is likely to continue to be willing to do so after the child becomes 18,
  (c) the impact on the matters specified in section 1(2) of what the carer's needs for support are likely to be after the child becomes 18,
  (d) the outcomes that the carer wishes to achieve in day-to-day life, and
  (e) whether, and if so to what extent, the provision of support could contribute to the achievement of those outcomes.

  (2) A local authority, in carrying out a child's carer's assessment, must have regard to—
  (a) whether the carer works or wishes to do so, and
  (b) whether the carer is participating in or wishes to participate in education, training or recreation.

(3) A local authority, in carrying out a child's carer's assessment, must involve—

(a) the carer, and

(b) any person whom the carer asks the local authority to involve.

(4) When carrying out a child's carer's assessment, a local authority must also consider whether, and if so to what extent, matters other than the provision of support could contribute to the achievement of the outcomes that the carer wishes to achieve in day-to-day life.

(5) Having carried out a child's carer's assessment, a local authority must give the carer—

(a) an indication as to whether any of the needs for support which it thinks the carer is likely to have after the child becomes 18 are likely to meet the eligibility criteria (and, if so, which ones are likely to do so), and

(b) advice and information about—

(i) what can be done to meet or reduce the needs which it thinks the carer is likely to have after the child becomes 18;

(ii) what can be done to prevent or delay the development by the carer of needs for support in the future.

(6) Where, in the case of a carer to whom a child's carer's assessment relates, the child becomes 18, the local authority must decide whether to treat the assessment as a carer's assessment; and if the authority decides to do so, this Part applies to the child's carer's assessment as if it were a carer's assessment that had been carried out after the child had become 18.

(7) In considering what to decide under subsection (6), a local authority must have regard to—

(a) when the child's carer's assessment was carried out, and

(b) whether it appears to the authority that the circumstances of the carer to whom the child's carer's assessment relates have changed in a way that might affect the assessment.

(8) "Carer" has the same meaning as in section 60.

GENERAL NOTE

1–616   This section sets out what a child's carer's assessment under s.60 must address. It also contains certain procedural requirements governing who should be involved in the assessment and the information that should be provided following the completion of the assessment.

The local authority may combine a child's carer's assessment with any other assessment it is carrying out of the carer or another person, or carry out the assessment on behalf of or jointly with another body (see s.65(3) and (5)).

Subsection (1)

1–617   The assessment must address:

- the carer's ability and willingness to provide care (including after the child becomes 18);
- the impact of the carer's needs on their well-being (as set out in s.1(2)) after the child becomes 18;
- the outcomes the carer wants to achieve; and
- whether the provision of support will contribute to meeting those outcomes.

Subsection (2)

In carrying out the assessment, regard must be had to the carer's employment, education, **1–618** training and recreation needs.

This subsection replaces and largely consolidates the previous requirements in s.6(2A) of the Carers and Disabled Children Act 2000. This aspect of the assessment a crucial element of the carer's ability and willingness to carer under subs.(1) and the implication is that local authorities must not for example assume a willingness to give up work in order to care.

Subsection (3)

The assessment must involve the carer and any other person who the carer wants to be **1–619** involved.

The meaning of "involve" is discussed at paras 1–104 to 1–105 above.

Involving a person may involve providing them with an advocate. The right to advocacy in s.67 of the Care Act expressly applies to this subsection (see s.67(3)(h)).

Subsection (4)

When carrying out the assessment the local authority must also consider whether there **1–620** are matters (other than the provision of support) that could help the child's carer achieve the outcomes that they wish to achieve. Originally this was listed in subs.(1) as a matter which must be included in the assessment.[1] However, concerns were raised in the House of Lords that this blurred the distinction between assessing needs and how to meet needs.[2] This led to Government amendments to ensure that such matters are considered separate to, but alongside, the needs assessment (see discussion on s.9(6) relating to the adult needs assessment at paras 1–108 to 1–110 above).

Subsection (5)

Following the assessment, the local authority must give the child's carer: **1–621**

- an indication of whether the carer's needs identified after the child turns 18 are likely to be eligible;
- advice and information about what can be done to meet any of the carer's needs after the child becomes 18 and what can be done to prevent or delay the development of needs for support in the future.

There are no particular formalities about how the indication, and advice and information should be given to the child's carer. For example, it does not need to be in writing. However, it is submitted that local authorities should as a matter of course, provide this indication, and advice and information, in writing in order to demonstrate they have met the requirement in subs.(5). The Equality Act 2010 may also be relevant and if necessary, the indication, and advice and information, should be provided in alternative formats and using different methods of communication.

Subsection (5) does not specify or indicate how much detail should be provided when giving the required indication, and advice and information. The extent of the detail is likely to depend upon the specific circumstances of the individual case. For example, where the carer does not dispute the decision and is not seeking local authority assistance, the indication, and information and advice, may be relatively brief and straightforward. But where for instance the decision is disputed by the carer and where they may lose services as a result, more detail might be appropriate.

Subsections (6) and (7)

Where the child—who is being provided with support—becomes 18, the local authority **1–622** is required to decide whether to treat the child's carer assessment as a carer's assessment. In

---

[1] HL Bill 001 2013-2014 as introduced, cl.58(1)(f).

[2] *Hansard* (House of Lords), 22 July 2013, Vol.747, col.1151.

making this decision the authority must have regard to when the assessment was carried out and whether the circumstances of the carer have changed.

These subsections were introduced by Government amendments at Committee stage in the House of Commons. The Government explained that they:

". . . reflect a policy intention about which we have always been clear—that a transition assessment can be treated as a full assessment under the [Care Act] where that is appropriate and proportionate. That power already existed for children and young carers, but due to an oversight was not replicated for children's carers. The amendments correct that oversight . . .".[1]

Power to meet child's carer's needs for support

1–623 **62.**—(1) Where a local authority, having carried out a child's carer's assessment, is satisfied that the carer has needs for support, it may meet such of those needs as it considers appropriate.

(2) Regulations may make provision in connection with the exercise of the power under subsection (1); the regulations may, in particular, provide for provisions of this Part to apply with such modifications as may be specified.

(3) In deciding whether or how to exercise the power under subsection (1), a local authority must have regard to any services being provided to the carer under section 17 of the Children Act 1989.

(4) "Carer" has the same meaning as in section 60.

GENERAL NOTE

1–624 The Law Commission recommended that where a child's carer is receiving a transition assessment under the adult social care statute, they should able to establish the same rights to services that are given to carers under the same statute (as set out in s.20 of the Care Act). Otherwise, it recommended that the child's carer should continue to have the right to:

- have their needs addressed as part of an assessment carried out under s.17 of the Children Act 1989 Act; and
- have the results of their separate carer's assessment (under the Carers (Recognition and Services) Act 1995 or Carers and Disabled Children Act 2000) taken into account when deciding what services, if any, will be provided under the 1989 Act.[2]

In response, the Government agreed that child's carers should have the option of receiving adult support, as well as that provided to the family via children's services. It concluded that local authorities should have a power to meet the needs of parent carers "so that any services available only through adult care and support can be provided".[3] Section 62 therefore provides a power (but not a duty) for a local authority to meet a child's carer's needs for support.

This means that child's carers are not able to establish enforceable rights to services. As noted at para.1–610 above, Baroness Pitkeathley attempted to amend the Care Bill to ensure that the rights of child's carers to assessments and support were consistent with the rights of other carers. In response the Government made clear that in its view there is already sufficient provision under s.17 of the Children Act 1989 to provide for the

---

[1] *Hansard* (House of Commons: Public Bill Committee), 23 January 2014 (AM): Ninth Sitting, cols 346 to 347 (Norman Lamb MP).

[2] Law Commission, *Adult Social Care*, paras 11.69 to 11.70.

[3] Department of Health, *Reforming the Law for Adult Care and Support: The Government's Response to Law Commission Report 326 on Adult Social Care* (TSO, July 2012), Cm.8379, paras 11.24 to 11.25.

assessment and support of children in need and their families, including disabled children and their parents.

However, the Government did decide to amend the Children and Families Bill 2013–14 to clarify the existing power to provide parent carers with support under Pt 3 of the Children Act 1989. Consequently, s.97 of the Children and Families Act 2014 inserts a new s.17ZF into the 1989 Act which provides that once a local authority has carried out a "parent carer's needs assessment" it must decide whether the needs of the parent carer or disabled child could be satisfied by services under s.17 of the 1989 Act and if so, whether or not to provide any such services in relation to the parent carer or the disabled child.

Subsection (1)

This provides the local authority power to meet the needs of a child's carer following a **1–625** transition assessment. The statutory guidance confirms that a support plan and personal budget should be provided –and a financial assessment carried out where the carer is subject to charges for the support they receive. It also confirms that the local authority may not meet the adult's needs by providing services to the child.[1] See also para.1–590 above.

Subsection (2)

Regulations can be made in relation to the exercise of the power to meet needs under **1–626** subs.(1). By virtue of s.125(4)(i) such regulations are subject to the affirmative procedure in Parliament. The affirmative procedure is discussed at para.1–161 above. The relevant regulations issued under subs.(2) are the Care and Support (Children's Carers) Regulations 2014 (SI 2015/305). These regulations are reproduced in full in para.A1– 257 to A1–271 below. In broad terms, the regulations modify certain provisions of the Care Act to esure that the power under subs.(1) is implemented in the same way as the power under s.20(6) to meet the support needs of a carer.

Subsection (3)

In deciding whether or how to exercise the power under subs.(1), the local authority is **1–627** required to have regard to any services being provided to the carer under s.17 of the Children Act 1989. The Government's intention is that "a child's carer's needs will usually be met under s.17 of the Children Act 1989" however s.62 allows for "additional support to be provided, where appropriate, for instance, because a certain type of support is only available under adult care and support".[2] In the House of Lords the Government further explained:

> "Support should be available where it is needed. The question is the source and nature of that support. [Section 62] provides a power, rather than a duty, for local authorities to provide support because existing children's legislation already includes provision for support to a child's carer. Duplication of existing legislation may cause confusion and is unnecessary. This power is intended to enable support to be provided under adult legislation where a certain service is available only locally via that route."[3]

Assessment of a young carer's needs for support

63.—(1) Where it appears to a local authority that a young carer is likely to have **1–628** needs for support after becoming 18, the authority must, if it is satisfied that it would be of significant benefit to the young carer to do so and if the consent condition is met, assess—

(a) whether the young carer has needs for support and, if so, what those needs are, and

---

[1] Department of Health, *Care and Support Statutory Guidance* (2014), para.16.57.
[2] Care Act 2014: Explanatory Notes para.379.
[3] *Hansard* (House of Lords), 22 July 2013, Vol.747, col.1155 (Earl Howe).

(b) whether the young carer is likely to have needs for support after becoming 18 and, if so, what those needs are likely to be.

(2) An assessment under subsection (1) is referred to in this Part as a "young carer's assessment".

(3) The consent condition is met if—

(a) the young carer has capacity or is competent to consent to a young carer's assessment being carried out and the young carer does so consent, or

(b) the young carer lacks capacity or is not competent so to consent but the authority is satisfied that carrying out a young carer's assessment would be in the young carer's best interests.

(4) Where a young carer refuses a young carer's assessment and the consent condition is accordingly not met, the local authority must nonetheless carry out the assessment if the young carer is experiencing, or is at risk of, abuse or neglect.

(5) Where a local authority, having received a request to carry out a young carer's assessment from the young carer concerned or a parent of the young carer, decides not to comply with the request, it must give the person who made the request—

(a) written reasons for its decision, and

(b) advice and information about what can be done to prevent or delay the development by the young carer of needs for support in the future.

(6) "Young carer" means a person under 18 who provides or intends to provide care for an adult (but see subsection (7)).

(7) A person is not a young carer for the purposes of this section if the person provides or intends to provide care—

(a) under or by virtue of a contract, or

(b) as voluntary work.

(8) But in a case where the local authority considers that the relationship between the adult and the person under 18 providing or intending to provide care is such that it would be appropriate for the person under 18 to be regarded as a young carer, that person is to be regarded as such (and subsection (7) is therefore to be ignored in that case).

(9) The references to providing care include a reference to providing practical or emotional support.

GENERAL NOTE

1–629   A young carer is a person under 18 who provides or intends to provide care for an adult. In its evidence to the Joint Committee on the draft Care and Support Bill the Government discussed the issues raised when assessing the needs of a young carer:

> "Provisions are not the same, and never will be the same, because, when you are talking about young carers, you are talking about a child, so it is not just about identifying a young carer and saying, 'Okay, what does that person need to support them in their caring role?' Actually, there is a question of, 'Is that an appropriate caring role and is this in fact a child in need who needs support in different ways?'"[1]

Prior to the Care Act (and the Children and Families Act 2014), young carers had a right to a separate carer's assessment under s.1(1) of the Carers (Recognition and Services) Act 1995 and s.(1) of the Carers and Disabled Children Act 2000. In addition, young carers could have their needs assessed as a "child in need" under s.17 of the Children Act 1989.

---

[1] House of Lords House of Commons Joint Committee on the Draft Care and Support Bill, *Draft Care and Support Bill Report, Session 2012–13*, para.246.

The Law Commission recommended that this legal framework should be consolidated and reformed (see para.1–631 below). In order to support a smooth transition, the Commission recommended that local authorities should have a general power to assess and provide services to young carers aged 16 and 17 under the adult social care statute. Local authorities would be required to give written reasons if a young carer aged 16 and 17 (or their parents on their behalf) requested to be assessed under the adult statute, and the local authority decided not to comply with the request.[1] The Government agreed that local authorities should have a power to assess a young carer child under the adult statute—along with a request mechanism and a duty to explain the reasons for not assessing. However it disagreed that there should be a general power to provide services (see discussion under s.66 at para.1–653 below).[2]

Originally, the Care Bill—as introduced in the House of Lords—provided that the local authority power to undertake a young carer's assessment only applied if:

- a request was made by the young carer or their parent;
- the young carer was likely to have needs for support after becoming 18; and
- the assessment would be of "significant benefit" to the carer.[3]

However, this was amended at report stage (along with the provisions governing a child's **1–630** needs assessment and a child's carer's assessment) to remove the need to request the assessment (see paras 1–592 to 1–593 above). Instead, s.63 provides a duty to assess where the young carer is likely to have needs for support after becoming 18 and the assessment would be of "significant benefit" to them—see para.1–595 above.

Young carers may also be included in the adult assessment through a number of provisions in the Care Act that are aimed at encouraging a "whole family approach" (see para.1–590 above).

Section 63 does not enable the provision of transition services to young carers. Indeed, there is no power under the Care Act to provide services to a child. Instead, s.66 provides a right to "continuity of care" for a child (including a young carer) who is receiving services under s.17 of the Children Act 1989, an Education, Health and Care Plan (under s.37(2) of the Children and Families Act 2014) or s.2 of the Chronically Sick and Disabled Persons Act 1970. If a transition assessment has been requested, and the relevant assessment has not taken place or a conclusion has not been reached, then services must continue when the young carer reaches 18 until a conclusion has been reached.

The statutory guidance discusses adult carers and young carers in paras 16.20 to 16.23.

Young carers and the children act 1989

Prior to the Care Act, statutory guidance had made clear that young carers should be **1–631** "routinely assessed under the Children Act 1989" rather than under carers legislation.[4] This was because children should "not be expected to carry inappropriate levels of caring which have an adverse impact on their development and life chances" and in particular, "it should not be assumed that children should take on similar levels of caring responsibilities as adults".[5] Practice guidance had also advised that an exception might be where a carer

---

[1] Law Commission, *Adult Social Care*, paras 11.61 to 11.68.
[2] Department of Health, *Reforming the Law for Adult Care and Support: The Government's Response to Law Commission Report 326 on Adult Social Care* (TSO, July 2012), Cm.8379, para.11.23.
[3] HL Bill 001 2013-2014 as introduced, cl.60.
[4] Department of Health, *Carers and Disabled Children Act 2000 and Carers (Equal Opportunities) Act 2004: Combined Policy Guidance* (2005), para.10.
[5] See Department of Health, *Framework for the Assessment of Children in Need and their Families* (2004), para.3.62 and Department of Health, A Practitioner's Guide to Carers' Assessments under the Carers and Disabled Children Act 2000 (2001), para.12.

aged 17, expresses "a very strong wish" to be involved in providing care to a parent, but only if it is in the carer's "best interests to be allowed to continue" in this caring role.[1]

As noted above, the previous legislative framework gave young carers rights to a separate carer's assessment by virtue of s.1(1) of the Carers (Recognition and Services) Act 1995 and s.1(1) of the Carers and Disabled Children Act 2000. However, the duty to assess only applied if (amongst other matters) the carer requested the assessment and was providing a substantial amount of support on a regular basis.

The Law Commission noted that if this legislation was retained, young carers would face a higher threshold for an assessment in comparison to a carer's assessment under the adult social care statute (which would be based on the appearance of need—see para.1–113 above). Therefore it recommended that the duties to assess in the 1995 and 2000 Acts should be amended to make them consistent with the lower threshold for a carer's assessment under the adult statute. The Commission further recommended that the 1995 and 2000 Acts should be consolidated to create a single young carer's statute, or the Acts should be repealed and the provisions incorporated into an amended Children Act 1989.[2]

The Joint Committee also expressed concern that young carers would be left with lesser rights than adults, and argued that the most straightforward solution would be to bring updated legislation for young carers into the adult social care statute.[3] However, the Government did not agree that the adult statute was the right place to make provision for children. Instead it wanted to encourage a "whole family" approach to ensure that an individual is not looked at in isolation.[4]

But in Parliament the Government faced further pressure to address the situation of young carers, and was eventually persuaded to act by amending the Children and Families Act Bill 2012–13 which was being considered by Parliament at the same time as the Care Bill.[5] Consequently s.96 of the Children and Families Act 2014 consolidates young carer's rights—in particular from the Carers (Recognition and Services) Act 1995 and the Carers and Disabled Children Act 2000—and inserts new sections 17ZD and 17ZE into Pt 3 of the Children Act 1989. Local authorities are placed under a duty to undertake a "young carer's needs assessment" on request or on the appearance of need. Such assessments can be combined with an assessment of the person being cared for. Once a local authority has carried out a young carer's needs assessment it must decide whether the needs of the young carer could be satisfied by services under s.17 of the 1989 Act and if so, whether or not to provide any such services in relation to the young carer.

Local authorities are required to take reasonable steps to identify the extent to which there are young carers within their area who have needs for support. The Secretary of State is also given a power to make regulations making provision about the carrying out of a young carer's needs assessment. Those regulations may, in particular, specify matters to which a local authority is to have regard or is to determine in carrying out the assessment, the manner in which an assessment is to be carried out and the form that assessment is to take.

Subsections (1) to (4)

1–632   The duty to undertake a young carer's assessment only applies if:

- the young carer is likely to have needs for support after becoming 18; and

---

[1] Department of Health, *A Practitioner's Guide to Carers' Assessments under the Carers and Disabled Children Act 2000* (2001), pp.5 to 6.

[2] Law Commission, *Adult Social Care*, paras 11.61 and 11.65.

[3] House of Lords House of Commons Joint Committee on the Draft Care and Support Bill, *Draft Care and Support Bill Report*, Session 2012–13, paras 245 to 254.

[4] Department of Health, *The Care Bill explained—including a response to consultation and pre-legislative scrutiny on the draft Care and Support Bill*, p.74.

[5] *Hansard* (House of Lords), 2 July 2013, Vol.746, cols 1201 to 1202 (Lord Nash) and *Hansard* (House of Commons), 8 October 2013, Vol.568, cols 11WS to 12WS (Michael Gove MP).

- the assessment would be of significant benefit to the young carer.

In addition, one of the following must apply

- the young carer consents and has capacity or competence to do so (subs.(3)(a));
- the young carer lacks capacity or competence to consent, but carrying out the assessment is in their best interests (subs.(3)(b)); or
- the young carer refuses the assessment, but they are experiencing (or at risk of) abuse and neglect (subs.(4)).

It is noteworthy that a young carer does not have the same right to refuse a carer's assessment that is given to carers (under s.11(5)) and child's carers (under s.60(3)) which cannot be overridden.

A young carer does not have to be receiving any specific service under the Children Act 1989 or any other legislation in order to qualify for an assessment. Similarly, there is no restriction on the age of a young carer, or their proximity to their 18th birthday. These points are confirmed in the statutory guidance.[1] But the guidance further notes that it is "highly likely" that those in receipt of children's services would be "likely to have needs" and therefore eligible for a transition assessment as they approach adulthood.[2] The guidance also discusses how to identify young carers who are not receiving services in paras 16.18 to 16.19.

The meaning of "significant benefit" is discussed at para.1–595 above. For a discussion of capacity, competence and best interests see para.1–596 above.

The purpose of the assessment is twofold:

- whether the young carer has needs for support (and what those needs are); and
- whether the young carer is likely to have needs for support after becoming 18 (and what those needs are likely to be).

According to the explanatory notes:

"The purpose of this assessment would be to consider what needs for support the young carer may have after their 18th birthday to support planning for transition to adult care and support. The local authority will therefore assess the child's needs by reference to the adult care and support arrangements, and this power is not intended to be used to assess needs for children's services."[3]

Further provision about the content and process of the assessment and the information which must be provided following an assessment is made in s.64.

Subsection (5)

A young carer or their parent can request an assessment and this may trigger an appear- **1–633** ance of need for the purposes of this duty. There are no particular formalities about the format of the request. For example, it does not need to be in writing.

Any young carer or parent can make a request, irrespective of their capacity or competence to make the request. However, the capacity or competence of the child to consent to the assessment will be relevant to the duty to assess.

Where the local authority does not comply with the request it must explain why in writing. The Equality Act 2010 may be relevant to the performance of this duty and if necessary, the explanation should be provided in alternative formats and using different methods of communication, as well as being in writing. The explanation must be provided to the person who made the request.

---

[1] Department of Health, *Care and Support Statutory Guidance* (2014), paras 16.7 to 16.8.
[2] Department of Health, *Care and Support Statutory Guidance* (2014), para.16.9.
[3] Care Act 2014: Explanatory Notes para.386.

In addition, where the local authority does not comply with the request it must provide information and advice about what can be done to prevent or delay the development of needs. This information and advice must be given to the person who made the request. There are no particular formalities about how the information and advice should be given to the person. For example, it does not need to be in writing. However, it is submitted that local authorities should as a matter of course, provide this information and advice in writing in order to demonstrate they have met this requirement. The Equality Act 2010 may also be relevant and if necessary, the information and advice should be provided in alternative formats and using different methods of communication.

The explanation, and information and advice, must be given to the person who made the request. Where the young carer has not made the request it is sumitted that the local authority would have discretion to provide the young carer with the explanation, and information and advice. Similarly, if a young carer made the request, there would be a power to provide the parents with the explanation, and information and advice. Local authorities would need to have regard to their existing data protection responsibilities in such cases.

Subsection (5) does not specify or indicate how much detail should be provided when giving the written explanation, and information and advice. The extent of the detail is likely to depend upon the specific circumstances of the individual case. For example, where the assessment is refused for the simple reason that the young carer does not want to be assessed (and there is no dispute about their capacity or competence), it may be acceptable to provide relatively brief and straightforward reasons, and advice and information. But where for instance the decision is disputed by the carer and the family, more detail might be appropriate.

Subsection (6) to (9)

1–634   This defines a young carer as a person under 18 who provides or intends to provide care for an adult (including practical and emotional support).

The definition of a young carer is subject to the proviso that those who care on a contractual or volunteering basis are not considered to be carers for the purposes of the Act. However, if the local authority thinks it is appropriate for such an individual (even if there is a contractual or volunteering element to the relationship) to be treated as a carer, then the adult is regarded as a carer and the duty to assess may apply. See discussion under s.10(9) and (10).

Young carer's assessment: requirements etc.

1–635   **64.**—(1) A young carer's assessment must include an assessment of—

(a) whether the young carer is able to provide care for the person in question and is likely to continue to be able to do so after becoming 18,

(b) whether the young carer is willing to do so and is likely to continue to be willing to do so after becoming 18,

(c) the impact on the matters specified in section 1(2) of what the young carer's needs for support are likely to be after the young carer becomes 18,

(d) the outcomes that the young carer wishes to achieve in day-to-day life, and

(e) whether, and if so to what extent, the provision of support could contribute to the achievement of those outcomes.

(2) A local authority, in carrying out a young carer's assessment, must have regard to—

(a) the extent to which the young carer works or wishes to work (or is likely to wish to do so after becoming 18),

(b) the extent to which the young carer is participating in or wishes to participate in education, training or recreation (or is likely to wish to do so after becoming 18).

(3) A local authority, in carrying out a young carer's assessment, must involve—

(a) the young carer,

(b) the young carer's parents, and

(c) any person whom the young carer or a parent of the young carer requests the authority to involve.

(4) When carrying out a young carer's assessment, a local authority must also consider whether, and if so to what extent, matters other than the provision of support could contribute to the achievement of the outcomes that the young carer wishes to achieve in day-to-day life.

(5) Having carried out a young carer's assessment, a local authority must give the young carer—

(a) an indication as to whether any of the needs for support which it thinks the young carer is likely to have after becoming 18 are likely to meet the eligibility criteria (and, if so, which ones are likely to do so), and

(b) advice and information about—

(i) what can be done to meet or reduce the needs for support which it thinks the young carer is likely to have after becoming 18;

(ii) what can be done to prevent or delay the development by the young carer of needs for support in the future.

(6) But in a case where the young carer is not competent or lacks capacity to understand the things which the local authority is required to give under subs.(5), that subsection is to have effect as if for "must give the young carer" there were substituted "must give the young carer's parents".

(7) Where a person to whom a young carer's assessment relates becomes 18, the local authority must decide whether to treat the assessment as a carer's assessment; and if the authority decides to do so, this Part applies to the young carer's assessment as if it were a carer's assessment that had been carried out after the person had become 18.

(8) In considering what to decide under subs.(7), a local authority must have regard to—

(a) when the young carer's assessment was carried out, and

(b) whether it appears to the authority that the circumstances of the person to whom the young carer's assessment relates have changed in a way that might affect the assessment.

GENERAL NOTE

This section sets out what a young carer's assessment under s.63 must address. It also **1–636** contains certain procedural requirements governing who should be involved in the assessment and the information that should be provided following the completion of the assessment.

The local authority may combine a young carer's assessment with any other assessment it is carrying out of the carer or another person, or carry out the assessment on behalf of or jointly with another body (see s.65(2) and (5)).

Subsection (1)

The assessment must address: **1–637**

● the young carer's ability and willingness to provide care (including after the child becomes 18);

- the impact of the young carer's needs on their well-being (as set out in s.1(2)) after the child becomes 18;
- the outcomes the young carer wants to achieve; and
- whether the provision of support will contribute to meeting those outcomes.

Subsection (2)

1–638   In carrying out the assessment, regard must be had to the carer's employment, education, training and recreation needs.

This subsection replaces and largely consolidates the previous requirements in the Carers (Recognition and Services) Act 1995 and the Carers and Disabled Children Act 2000. This aspect of the assessment is a crucial element of the carer's ability and willingness to care under subs.(1) and the implication is that local authorities must not, for example, assume a willingness to give up work in order to care.

Subsection (3)

1–639   The assessment must involve the young carer, their parents and any other person who the young carer or a parent wants to be involved.

The meaning of "involve" is discussed at paras 1–104 to 1–105 above.

Involving a person may involve providing them with an advocate. The right to advocacy in s.67 of the Care Act expressly applies to this subsection (see s.67(3)(i)).

Subsection (4)

1–640   When carrying out the assessment the local authority must also consider whether there are matters (other than the provision of support) that could help the young carer achieve the outcomes that they wish to achieve. Originally this was listed in subs.(1) as a matter which must be included in the assessment.[1] However, concerns were raised in the House of Lords that this blurred the distinction between assessing needs and how to meet needs.[2] This led to Government amendments to ensure that such matters are considered separate to, but alongside, the needs assessment (see discussion on s.9(6) relating to the adult needs assessment at paras 1–108 to 1–110 above).

Subsection (5)

1–641   Following the assessment, the local authority must give the young carer:

- an indication of whether the needs identified after they turn 18 are likely to be eligible;
- advice and information about what can be done to meet any of the young carer's needs after they become 18 and what can be done to prevent or delay the development of needs for support in the future.

This requirement applies irrespective of whether or not the young carer consented to the assessment (subject to subs.(6)).

There are no particular formalities about how the indication, and advice and information should be given to the young carer. For example, it does not need to be in writing. However, it is submitted that local authorities should as a matter of course, provide the indication, and advice and information, in writing in order to demonstrate they have met the requirement in subs.(4). The Equality Act 2010 may be relevant to the performance of this duty and if necessary, the indication, and advice and information, should be provided in alternative formats and using different methods of communication.

Subsection (5) does not specify or indicate how much detail should be provided when giving the required indication, and advice and information. The extent of the detail is likely to depend upon the specific circumstances of the individual case. For example, where a

---

[1] HL Bill 001 2013–2014 as introduced, cl.56(1).
[2] *Hansard* (House of Lords), 22 July 2013, Vol.747, col.1151.

lack capacity or competence but the local authority thinks that a combined assessment would be in their best interests. For example, an assessment of likely needs after the age of 18 could be included in a young person's Education, Health and Care Plan, provided for in the Children and Families Act 2014.[1] See discussion at para.1-071 above on the relationship between the Care Act and Education, Health and Care Plans.

In addition, where the assessment is being combined with an assessment of another child, then that child must agree or if they lack capacity or competence then the combined assessment must be in their best interests. Where the assessment is being combined with an assessment of an adult, then the adult must agree.

For a discussion of capacity, competence and best interests see para.1–596 above.

Subsection (3)

A local authority may combine a child's carer's assessment with any other assessment **1–648** provided that the child's carer agrees. Where the assessment is being combined with an assessment of another adult, then that adult must also agree. Where the assessment is being combined with an assessment of a child, then that child must agree or if they lack capacity or competence then the combined assessment must be in their best interests.

For a discussion of capacity, competence and best interests see para.1–596 above.

Subsection (5)

A child's needs assessment, a child's carer's assessment or a young carer's assessment **1–649** may be carried out jointly with an external body or person when that body or person is carrying out an assessment of the child or carer. Alternatively the local authority could carry out the other assessment on behalf of the body or person. For example, if carrying out a child's needs assessment the local authority could carry out an NHS continuing health care assessment of his or her carer jointly with the relevant health body.[2] The statutory guidance discusses cooperation between professionals and organisations (including joint assessments) in the context of transition assessments in paras 16.40 to 16.49. Amongst other matters, it suggests that local authorities should consider designating a named person (often referred to as a key worker or care coordinator) to coordinate assessments and transition planning across agencies.[3]

Subsection (6)

The references to an assessment include a reference to part of an assessment. This means **1–650** that for example a part of an assessment can be combined with another assessment.

Continuity of services under other legislation

66.—(1) Before section 17A of the Children Act 1989 insert— **1–651**

"17ZH Section 17 services: transition for children to adult care and support

(1) Subsections (2) to (4) apply where a local authority in England providing services for a child in need in the exercise of functions conferred by section 17—

(a) are required by section 58(1) or 63(1) of the Care Act 2014 to carry out a child's needs assessment or young carer's assessment in relation to the child, or

(b) are required by section 60(1) of that Act to carry out a child's carer's assessment in relation to a carer of the child.

(2) If the local authority carry out the assessment before the child reaches the age of 18 and decide to treat it as a needs or carer's assessment in accordance with

---

[1] Care Act 2014: Explanatory Notes para.3.98.
[2] Care Act 2014: Explanatory Notes para.3.98.
[3] Department of Health, *Care and Support Statutory Guidance* (2014), paras 16.48 to 16.49.

section 59(6), 61(6) or 64(7) of the Care Act 2014 (with Part 1 of that Act applying to the assessment as a result), the authority must continue to comply with section 17 after the child reaches the age of 18 until they reach a conclusion in his case.

(3) If the local authority carry out the assessment before the child reaches the age of 18 but decide not to treat it as a needs or carer's assessment in accordance with section 59(6), 61(6) or 64(7) of the Care Act 2014—

(a) they must carry out a needs or carer's assessment (as the case may be) after the child reaches the age of 18, and

(b) they must continue to comply with section 17 after he reaches that age until they reach a conclusion in his case.

(4) If the local authority do not carry out the assessment before the child reaches the age of 18, they must continue to comply with section 17 after he reaches that age until—

(a) they decide that the duty under section 9 or 10 of the Care Act 2014 (needs or carer's assessment) does not apply, or

(b) having decided that the duty applies and having discharged it, they reach a conclusion in his case.

(5) Subsection (6) applies where a local authority in England providing services for a child in need in the exercise of functions conferred by section 17—

(a) receive a request for a child's needs assessment or young carer's assessment to be carried out in relation to the child or for a child's carer's assessment to be carried out in relation to a carer of the child, but

(b) have yet to be required by section 58(1), 60(1) or 63(1) of the Care Act 2014 to carry out the assessment.

(6) If the local authority do not decide, before the child reaches the age of 18, whether or not to comply with the request, they must continue to comply with section 17 after he reaches that age until—

(a) they decide that the duty under section 9 or 10 of the Care Act 2014 does not apply, or

(b) having decided that the duty applies and having discharged it, they reach a conclusion in his case.

(7) A local authority reach a conclusion in a person's case when—

(a) they conclude that he does not have needs for care and support or for support (as the case may be), or

(b) having concluded that he has such needs and that they are going to meet some or all of them, they begin to do so, or

(c) having concluded that he has such needs, they conclude that they are not going to meet any of those needs (whether because those needs do not meet the eligibility criteria or for some other reason).

(8) In this section, "child's needs assessment", "child's carer's assessment", "young carer's assessment", "needs assessment", "carer's assessment" and "eligibility criteria" each have the same meaning as in Part 1 of the Care Act 2014.

Section 17 services: provision after EHC plan no longer maintained

1–652   **17ZI.**—(1) This section applies where a local authority in England providing services for a person in the exercise, by virtue of section 17ZG, of functions conferred by section 17 are required to carry out a needs assessment in that person's case.

(2) If the EHC plan for the person ceases to be maintained before the local authority reach a conclusion in the person's case, they must continue to comply with section 17 until they do reach a conclusion in his case.

(3) The references to the local authority reaching a conclusion in a person's case are to be read with section 17ZH(7).

(4) In this section, "needs assessment" has the same meaning as in Part 1 of the Care Act 2014."

(2) In section 17ZG of that Act (continued provision of services under section 17 where EHC plan maintained), in subsection (2), after "after the EHC plan has ceased to be maintained" insert ", except in so far as the authority is required to do so under section 17ZH or 17ZI".

(3) After section 2 of the Chronically Sick and Disabled Persons Act 1970 insert—

"2A Welfare services: transition for children to adult care and support

(1) Subsections (2) to (4) apply where a local authority in England making arrangements for a disabled child under section 2 are required by section 58(1) of the Care Act 2014 to carry out a child's needs assessment in relation to the child.

(2) If the local authority carry out the assessment before the child reaches the age of 18 and decide to treat it as a needs assessment in accordance with section 59(6) of the Care Act 2014 (with Part 1 of that Act applying to the assessment as a result), the authority must continue to comply with section 2 after the child reaches the age of 18 until they reach a conclusion in his case.

(3) If the local authority carry out the assessment before the child reaches the age of 18 but decide not to treat it as a needs assessment in accordance with section 59(6) of that Act—

(a) they must carry out a needs assessment after the child reaches the age of 18, and

(b) they must continue to comply with section 2 after he reaches that age until they reach a conclusion in his case.

(4) If the local authority do not carry out the assessment before the child reaches the age of 18, they must continue to comply with section 2 after he reaches that age until—

(a) they decide that the duty under section 9 of the Care Act 2014 (needs assessment) does not apply, or

(b) having decided that the duty applies and having discharged it, they reach a conclusion in his case.

(5) Subsection (6) applies where a local authority in England making arrangements for a disabled child under section 2—

(a) receive a request for a child's needs assessment to be carried out in relation to the child, but

(b) have yet to be required by section 58(1) of the Care Act 2014 to carry out the assessment.

(6) If the local authority do not decide, before the child reaches the age of 18, whether or not to comply with the request, they must continue to comply with section 2 after he reaches that age until—

(a) they decide that the duty under section 9 of the Care Act 2014 does not apply, or

(b) having decided that the duty applies and having discharged it, they reach a conclusion in his case.

(7) A local authority reach a conclusion in a person's case when—

(a) they conclude that he does not have needs for care and support,

(b) having concluded that he has such needs and that they are going to meet some or all of them, they begin to do so, or

(c) having concluded that he has such needs, they conclude that they are not going to meet any of those needs (whether because those needs do not meet the eligibility criteria or for some other reason).

(8) In this section, "child's needs assessment", "needs assessment" and "eligibility criteria" each have the same meaning as in Part 1 of the Care Act 2014."

GENERAL NOTE

1–653 The Law Commission recommended that local authorities should have a general power to provide services to 16 and 17 year olds (including young carers) under the new adult social care statute. It felt that in some cases the young person would benefit from, for example, the greater availability of direct payments under adult legislation and being able to establish individually enforceable entitlements to services that are not available under the Children Act 1989.[1] However, the Government did not agree and instead argued that:

"There will be very few, if any, cases in which it is in the child's best interests to move to adult care and support sooner. We want the law to promote the involvement of adult care and support considerations in multi-agency planning, rather than to take over service provision unnecessarily."[2]

The Joint Committee on the draft Care and Support Bill agreed with the Law Commission's recommendation on the provision of services to 16 and 17 year olds. It further recommended that this should be done in a way that recognises that the aims of support to young carers will often be different from those for adult carers.[3] In its response, the Government stated:

"We . . . do not believe it would be appropriate for children to receive adult care and support before the age of 18. The adult care and support system is designed with adults in mind, and includes factors such as charging that do not apply to children's services. It is right to maintain a clear distinction between what can reasonably be expected for adults and what we would expect for children, and we wish to ensure children are supported as children. As such, we do not think it would be in a child's best interests for adult support to be provided before the point of transition."[4]

Consequently, the Care Act does not enable the provision of services to a child (including a young carer). Instead, s.66 provides a right to "continuity of care" for a child who is receiving services under s.17 of the Children Act 1989, an Education, Health and Care Plan (under s.37(2) of the Children and Families Act 2014) or s.2 of the Chronically Sick and Disabled Persons Act 1970. If the local authority is required to carry out a transition assessment (a child's needs assessment, child's carer's assessment or young carer's assessment) under the Care Act, and the necessary care and support was not in place when the child reached 18, then the local authority must continue to provide services until the relevant steps have been undertaken. The relevant steps are if the local authority concludes that the person:

---

[1] Law Commission, *Adult Social Care*, para.11.49.

[2] Department of Health, *Reforming the Law for Adult Care and Support: The Government's Response to Law Commission Report 326 on Adult Social Care* (TSO, July 2012), Cm.8379, para.11.20.

[3] House of Lords House of Commons Joint Committee on the Draft Care and Support Bill, *Draft Care and Support Bill Report, Session 2012–13*, para.256.

[4] Department of Health, *The Care Bill explained—including a response to consultation and pre-legislative scrutiny on the draft Care and Support Bill*, para.121.

- does not have needs for adult care and support; or
- does have needs for adult care and support and begins to meet some or all of them under the Care Act; or
- does have such needs but decides they are not going to meet any of those needs (for instance, because their needs do not meet the eligibility criteria under the Care Act).

This is intended to ensure "no gap in provision during the transition to adult care and support".[1]

The right to continuity of care also applies where a local authority receives a request for the transition assessment in accordance with s.58(1), 60(1) or 63(1) of the Care Act and has not decided whether or not to comply with the request. In the House of Lords, Baroness Tyler expressed some concerns about these provisions:

"However, the benefits outlined in [s.66] apply only if a request has been made for a child's needs assessment by the time that child turns 18. The concern remains that some young people will not be able to benefit from this protection because they or their parents or carers will not be aware that they need to request an assessment by the time they are 18."[2]

In response the Government said s.4 requires local authorities to establish and maintain an accessible system for information and advice including information and advice about how to access the care and support that is available.[3]

The statutory guidance discusses the s.66 provisions in paras 16.66 to 16.73. In particular it emphasises that in some cases the provision of children's services may be the best way to meet a person's needs even after they reach 18 (for example, people with complex special educational needs and care needs). The guidance also explains that where a person over 18 is receiving services under children's legislation through their Health, Education and Care Plan which then ceases, the transition process must be undertaken and where this has not happened at the point of transition, the requirement under the Care Act to continue to provide children's services applies.[4] If there are safeguarding concerns in relation to someone who is over 18 but still receiving children's services, the matter should be dealt with by the adult safeguarding team.[5]

INDEPENDENT ADVOCACY SUPPORT

GENERAL NOTE

Sections 67 and 68—which provide for rights to advocacy—were added to the Care Bill **1–654** by Government amendments introduced at report stage in the House of Lords. In welcoming the amendments, Baroness Barker, a Liberal Democrat peer, stated:

"My Lords, I think I am right in saying that in the Inuit language there are more than 300 words for snow. I suspect that if historians were to go back through the annals of the British Civil Service, they would come across thousands of ways in which officials have briefed Ministers to say "no" to requests for advocacy. During the 20 years that I have followed these sorts of issues, during which advocacy has became part of social care, Governments have had to find ways to say, 'It's a very good thing, but we're not going to fund it'. It was therefore a real joy to see the Government's Amendments 118 and 119 in this group."[6]

---

[1] Care Act 2014: Explanatory Notes para.401 and Department of Health, Care and Support Statutory Guidance (2014), para.16.67.

[2] *Hansard* (House of Lords), 22 July 2013, Vol.747, col.1152.

[3] *Hansard* (House of Lords), 22 July 2013, Vol.747, col.1156 (Earl Howe).

[4] Department of Health, *Care and Support Statutory Guidance* (2014), paras 16.70 and 16.72.

[5] Department of Health, *Care and Support Statutory Guidance* (2014), para.16.74.

[6] *Hansard* (House of Lords), 9 October 2013, Vol.748, col.117.

As Baroness Barker suggests, statutory rights to advocacy have frequently been achieved only as a result of concerted Parliamentary pressure and in the face of Government resistance. For example, the draft Mental Capacity Bill did not contain any provisions on advocacy, and the right to an Independent Mental Capacity Advocate was added only following criticism by the Joint Parliamentary Scrutiny Committee.[1] Similarly, the rights to an Independent Mental Health Advocate were added to the Mental Health Bill 2006–07 as a result of amendments introduced by the Government at a late stage in Parliament and following concerted pressure from the House of Lords in particular.[2] The right to advocacy contained in the Care Act is no exception to this tradition.

It is also relevant to note in this context that the Disabled Persons (Services, Consultation and Representation) Act 1986, which contained rights to advocacy for disabled people, originated as a Private Members Bill sponsored by Tom Clarke MP and had originally been opposed by Government. The 1986 Act gave the Government regulation-making powers to make provision for the appointment of "authorised representatives of disabled persons". It went on to require local authorities to permit representatives to, amongst other matters, make representations following a community care assessment and if services are not being provided.[3] These provisions, however, were never enacted.

The Law Commission did not consult on the issue of advocacy. However, it was persuaded to consider advocacy as a result of the arguments presented at consultation which made it clear that advocacy services play an essential role in assisting people to make and communicate decisions, safeguarding people from abuse and neglect and helping people to enforce their rights, secure access to justice and obtain an effective remedy.[4] The Commission noted the existing right to advocacy contained in the 1986 Act, and recommended that—in line with its stated aim of not removing existing rights—these provisions should be retained and modernised to bring them in line with modern understandings.[5]

1–655 The Government rejected this recommendation. It argued that the availability of advocacy services should be encouraged through a "broader focus" on information, advice and support and that specific advocacy provisions, such as those contained in the 1986 Act, "demonstrate a service-orientated approach to care and support which does not accord with our focus on needs and outcomes".[6] Instead the draft Care and Support Bill provided that "advocacy" was listed as an example of what a local authority may provide to meet an adult's or carer's needs (now s.8 of the Care Act), but it was not mentioned in the general duty to provide information and advice (now s.4 of the Care Act). The Joint Committee criticised this omission and recommended that the general duty to provide information and advice should be amended to make clear that independent advocacy is to be available before the assessment process has begun.[7] The Department of Health agreed that advocacy might be necessary in some circumstances, but considered that this was already covered by s.4. The Department concluded that—while a specific reference to advocacy in s.4 was not necessary—it would revise the duty to make clear that in meeting this duty local authorities

---

[1] House of Lords and House of Commons Joint Committee on the Mental Incapacity Bill, *Draft Mental Incapacity Bill, Report of the House of Lords and House of Commons Joint Committee*, HL 189-1, HC1083-1 (2002–03). The original Mental Capacity Bill provided for an "independent consultee service" which was amended by the Government during the passage of the Bill (as a result of pressure from backbenchers) and became the "independent mental capacity advocacy service". The relevant provisions are contained in the Mental Capacity Act 2005 ss.35 to 41.

[2] Mental Health Act 2007 s.30 (which inserted ss.130A to 130D into the Mental Health Act 1983).

[3] Disabled Person (Services, Consultation and Representation) Act 1986 ss.1 to 3.

[4] See Law Commission, Adult Social Care: Consultation Analysis (2011), paras 14.2 to 14.19.

[5] Law Commission, *Adult Social Care*, paras 12.2 to 12.9.

[6] Department of Health, *Reforming the Law for Adult Care and Support: The Government's Response to Law Commission Report 326 on Adult Social Care* (TSO, July 2012), Cm.8379, paras 11.39 to 11.41.

[7] House of Lords House of Commons Joint Committee on the Draft Care and Support Bill, *Draft Care and Support Bill Report, Session 2012–13*, paras 94 to 99.

must provide information that is accessible and proportionate to all, and that this would be judged on a case-by-case basis and could include in some cases advocacy.[1]

However, the Government faced further pressure from stakeholders and in the House of Lords during the passage of the Care Bill.[2] As a result, the Government finally relented and introduced ss.67 to 68 at report stage in the House of Lords. In doing so, the Minster explained the intention behind the new provisions:

"Following close work with the sector, we agree that the people who need this assistance most are those who have substantial difficulty in understanding, retaining, using or weighing the necessary information to allow this involvement, as well as those who have difficulty in communicating their wishes and feelings. For these people, our amendment states that local authorities would be under a duty to provide an independent advocate if there was no appropriate person to represent the individual who was not also involved in that person's care or treatment. This would usually be a friend or family member. The Government's amendments go further by proposing a similar duty to provide independent advocates to facilitate people's involvement in the safeguarding processes. We consider it vital that people are at the heart of these processes, rather than having these processes done to them."[3]

In the House of Commons, the Government's amendments were welcomed by Tom Clarke MP who argued that they built on the principles of the Disabled Persons (Services, Consultation and Representation) Act 1996 which he had sponsored.[4]

WHAT IS ADVOCACY?

Advocacy can be seen to have developed out of the disability rights and independent living movements over the last few decades. The role of the advocate is to assist disabled people to speak up for themselves, or if the disabled person is unable to do so, to communicate and represent the disabled person's needs and wishes. Advocacy is, therefore, seen as a vital component of achieving independent living and full citizenship for disabled people.[5] Some also highlight the importance of advocacy services in securing access to justice and obtaining an effective remedy. As one commentator argues: **1–656**

"For many people with disabilities, traditional legal methods for resolving disputes, such as litigation, are inappropriate as these often do not take account of the nature of disability and are also prohibitive in terms of cost and time. The additional effect of intellectual disability can result in a situation where people are unaware of their rights and do not understand how to obtain their entitlements. Therefore, an innovative measure, such as a state-operated advocacy service, should be made available to people with disabilities to enable more effective access to justice."[6]

There are many different types of advocacy, including:

- *self advocacy*—where the person is supported to advocate for themselves;
- *citizen advocacy*—where the advocacy role is taken on by a volunteer;
- *peer advocacy*—which involves the provision of advocacy by people who have the same or similar experiences as the person they are acting as an advocate for;

---

[1] Department of Health, *The Care Bill explained—including a response to consultation and pre-legislative scrutiny on the draft Care and Support Bill* (TSO, July 2012), Cm.8386, para.39.
[2] See, for example, *Hansard* (House of Lords), 21 May 2013, Vol.745, col.777 (Lord Patel).
[3] *Hansard* (House of Lords), 9 October 2013, Vol.748, col.121 (Earl Howe).
[4] *Hansard* (House of Commons), 16 December 2013, Vol.572, col.572.
[5] Prime Minister's Strategy Unit, *Improving the Life Chances of Disabled People: A Final Report* (2005), para 4.1.
[6] E. Flynn, *"Ireland's compliance with the Convention on the Rights of Persons with Disabilities: Towards a Rights-Based Approach for Legal Reform?"* 3 Dublin University Law Journal 357, 370.

Apart from the general functions given to Independent Mental Capacity Advocates, s.39D advocates are given a number of specific functions, such as helping the person and representative to:

- understand the authorisation, any conditions, the Deprivation of Liberty Safeguards assessments and the relevant rights; and
- take steps to exercise the right to apply to court and exercise the right of review (if the person or representative wishes to do so).[1]

Section 39D advocacy differs from the other Independent Mental Capacity Advocate provisions since it is available upon request to support the person, and to support a family member or carer if they are acting as the representative. Furthermore, the role of the s.39D advocacy is not primarily to gather information for decision-makers, but to help the person and representative to understand and exercise their rights. This is a much stronger and forceful role compared to the other Independent Mental Capacity Advocate provisions, and is intended to support the individual in challenging decisions.

Independent mental health advocates

1–660   The Mental Health Act 1983 requires local authorities to make arrangements for Independent Mental Health Advocates to be made available to help "qualifying patients". A qualifying patient includes all those liable to detention under the Act (except those subject to emergency short-term detention) or subject to guardianship, a community treatment order, and conditional discharge and those transferred from prison to hospital. In certain limited cases, informal patients will be qualifying patients (for example, in respect of treatment which requires consent and a second opinion).[2]

The role of the Independent Mental Health Advocates is to assist the patient in obtaining information about and understanding:

- the provisions of the Act that make them a qualifying patient;
- any conditions or restrictions to which they are subject;
- what medical treatment is being given or proposed, and why;
- the authority under which the treatment is to be given; and
- the requirements under the Act which apply in connection with the giving of treatment.[3]

In addition, the Independent Mental Health Advocate should assist the patient in obtaining information about and understanding their rights under the Act and the rights of the nearest relative, and provide help in exercising those rights. To assist in undertaking this role the Independent Mental Health Advocate has the right to visit a patient in private, to interview the medical staff and (with patient consent) to see the patient's medical and social services records.[4]

Other rights to advocacy

1–661   International law and treaties are supportive of rights to advocacy. For example, in certain exceptional circumstances, a right to advocacy can be derived from the State's positive procedural obligations under art.8 of the European Convention on Human Rights.[5] The United Nations Convention on the Rights of Persons with Disabilities reinforces the

---

[1] Mental Capacity Act 2005, s.39D(7) to (9) and Sch.A1, paras 49 and 95.

[2] Mental Health Act 1983, ss.130A and 130C.

[3] Mental Health Act 1983, ss.130B(1).

[4] Mental Health Act 1983, ss.130B(2) and (3).

[5] *CF v Secretary of State for the Home Department* [2004] EWHC 111 (Fam) at [166] and [167] and S v Local Authority X [2003] EWHC 551 (Fam) at [45] and [59]. See also Munby L.J., "Making Sure the Child is Heard: Part 2—Representation" (2004) 34 Family Law 427.

need to consider advocacy support. The preamble to the Convention sets out that disabled people "should have the opportunity to be actively involved in decision-making processes about policies and programmes including those directly affecting them".[1] Although art.29, which deals with involvement in detail, focuses on political rights and public affairs, arguably when read in light of the Convention as a whole there is implicit support for the right to advocacy.[2] The relevant provisions in this respect are:

- the right to an adequate standard of living and social protection (art.28);
- the right to accessible information (art.8);
- the right to access justice (art.13);
- the right to live independently (art.19); and
- to be included in the community and the right to participate in cultural life, recreation, leisure and sport (art.30).

The status of the United Nations Convention is discussed at para.1–704 below.

Advocacy is also provided for elsewhere in the Care Act. The general duty to provide information and advice (s.4) might involve in some individual cases access to advocacy services (see para.1–049 above). In s.8(1)(e) of the Act, "advocacy" is listed as an example of what a local authority may provide to meet an adult's or carer's needs following an assessment.

OVERLAPPING ADVOCACY ROLES

There is significant overlap between the various advocacy roles, particularly the Care **1–662** Act advocate and Independent Mental Capacity Advocates. Where a person who lacks capacity is receiving a needs assessment or a review of their care and support plan, they may be eligible for a Care Act advocate. If the local authority is considering long-term residential accommodation, then the person may also become eligible for an Independent Mental Capacity Advocate. Overlap also arises in safeguarding cases concerning people who lack capacity, where they might be entitled to a Care Act advocate and the local authority retains a power to appoint an Independent Mental Capacity Advocate. There is a danger that advocacy becomes atomised leading to a lack of continuity of support and also potentially overlapping and replication of activities. The statutory guidance advises that where people qualify for advocacy under the Care Act and the Mental Capacity Act, the same advocate can provide the support under each Act, and that commissioning arrangements should ensure that the advocate who is appointed is qualified to carry out both roles. But the advocate must meet the appropriate requirements for advocacy under whichever legislation they are acting.[3]

Nevertheless, it is likely that undertaking a dual role will prove challenging because the advocacy roles are different in key respects. The provision of an Independent Mental Capacity Advocacy is restricted to a relatively small number of defined decisions and its role is limited (with the notable exception of s.39D advocacy) to assisting decision-makers to reach best interests decisions—which may not necessarily be consistent with the person's wishes and feelings. In contrast, Care Act advocacy has a wider role which is focused on helping people to understand and exercise their rights and challenge decision-makers. This is discussed in more detail below.

Under the Mental Capacity Act, people who lack capacity and are alleged to be responsible for abuse may be entitled to the help of an Independent Mental Capacity Advocate to

---

[1] United Nations, *Convention on the Rights of Persons with Disabilities and Optional Protocol* (2006), Preamble (o).

[2] For a more detailed argument see, E. Flynn, "Ireland's Compliance with the Convention on the Rights of Persons with Disabilities: Towards a Rights-Based Approach for Legal Reform?" (2010) 3 *Dublin University Law Journal* 357, 370.

[3] Department of Health, *Care and Support Statutory Guidance* (2014), paras 7.9, 7.65 and 10.51.

support and represent them in the enquiries that are taking place. The statutory guidance confirms this is separate from the decision whether or not to provide the victim of abuse with an independent advocate under the Care Act.[1]

As noted above, certain mental health patients are entitled to support from an Independent Mental Health Advocate. In the context of discussing s.117 after-care and the Care Programme Approach, the statutory guidance states that those people who do not retain a right to an Independent Mental Health Advocate, whose care and support needs are being assessed, planned or reviewed should be considered for an advocate under the Care Act.[2]

Regulation 7 of the Care and Support (Independent Advocacy Support) (No.2) Regulations 2014 (SI 2014/2889) makes provision about circumstances in which, if an assessment is combined with another person's assessment, each person may be represented and supported by the same advocate or by different advocates.

OLDER PERSONS COMMISSIONERS

1–663   Recent years have seen the establishment of Older Persons Commissioners in the UK who are frequently described as advocates for the interests of older people. The Older People's Commissioner for Wales is a statutory office-holder—established by the Commissioner for Older People (Wales) Act 2006. The role of the Commissioner includes ensuring that the interests of older people in Wales, who are aged 60 or over, are safeguarded and promoted, promoting the elimination of discrimination and keeping under review the adequacy of the law affecting the interests of older people. The Commissioner is also able to examine individual cases and support individuals in taking court action in certain circumstances, undertake research, issue guidance on best practice and make reports to the National Assembly for Wales on the exercise of the Commissioner's functions.[3]

The Commissioner for Older People for Northern Ireland was established by the Commissioner for Older People Act (Northern Ireland) 2011. The Commissioner has a number of duties under this legislation including promoting awareness of the interests of older people in Northern Ireland and keeping under review the adequacy and effectiveness of the law as it affects the interests of older people. The Commissioner's office is set up as a non-departmental public body.

At report stage in the House of Lords Baroness Barker attempted to amend the Care Bill to introduce an Older Persons Commissioner for England.[4] A similar amendment was tabled by Paul Burstow MP at Report State in the House of Commons.[5] However, the Government argued that the interests of older people were already protected through a number of routes, such as:

- the role of The Care Quality Commission, in particular the new chief inspectors of hospitals, adult social care and general practice;
- the new Chief Social Worker for Adults post;
- Healthwatch England;
- the UK Advisory Forum on Aging; and
- the new provisions in the Care Act such as safeguarding and advocacy.[6]

---

[1] Department of Health, *Care and Support Statutory Guidance* (2014), para.14.98.
[2] Department of Health, *Care and Support Statutory Guidance* (2014), para.7.23.
[3] Commissioner for Older People (Wales) Act 2006 ss.2, 9, 10, 12 and 15.
[4] *Hansard* (House of Lords), 16 October 2013, Vol.748, cols 624 to 631.
[5] *Hansard* (House of Commons), 10 March 2014, Vol.577, col.60.
[6] *Hansard* (House of Lords), 16 October 2013, Vol.748, cols 634 to 635 (Earl Howe).

Involvement in assessments, plans etc.

67.—(1) This section applies where a local authority is required by a relevant **1–664** provision to involve an individual in its exercise of a function.

(2) The authority must, if the condition in subsection (4) is met, arrange for a person who is independent of the authority (an "independent advocate") to be available to represent and support the individual for the purpose of facilitating the individual's involvement; but see subsection (5).

(3) The relevant provisions are—

(a) section 9(5)(a) and (b) (carrying out needs assessment);

(b) section 10(7)(a) (carrying out carer's assessment);

(c) section 25(3)(a) and (b) (preparing care and support plan);

(d) section 25(4)(a) and (b) (preparing support plan);

(e) section 27(2)(b)(i) and (ii) (revising care and support plan);

(f) section 27(3)(b)(i) and (ii) (revising support plan);

(g) section 59(2)(a) and (b) (carrying out child's needs assessment);

(h) section 61(3)(a) (carrying out child's carer's assessment);

(i) section 64(3)(a) and (b) (carrying out young carer's assessment).

(4) The condition is that the local authority considers that, were an independent advocate not to be available, the individual would experience substantial difficulty in doing one or more of the following—

(a) understanding relevant information;

(b) retaining that information;

(c) using or weighing that information as part of the process of being involved;

(d) communicating the individual's views, wishes or feelings (whether by talking, using sign language or any other means).

(5) The duty under subsection (2) does not apply if the local authority is satisfied that there is a person—

(a) who would be an appropriate person to represent and support the individual for the purpose of facilitating the individual's involvement, and

(b) who is not engaged in providing care or treatment for the individual in a professional capacity or for remuneration.

(6) For the purposes of subsection (5), a person is not to be regarded as an appropriate person unless—

(a) where the individual has capacity or is competent to consent to being represented and supported by that person, the individual does so consent, or

(b) where the individual lacks capacity or is not competent so to consent, the local authority is satisfied that being represented and supported by that person would be in the individual's best interests.

(7) Regulations may make provision in connection with the making of arrangements under subsection (2); the regulations may in particular—

(a) specify requirements that must be met for a person to be independent for the purposes of subsection (2);

(b) specify matters to which a local authority must have regard in deciding whether an individual would experience substantial difficulty of the kind mentioned in subsection (4);

(c) specify circumstances in which the exception in subsection (5) does not apply;

(d) make provision as to the manner in which independent advocates are to perform their functions;

(e) specify circumstances in which, if an assessment under this Part is combined with an assessment under this Part that relates to another person, each person may or must be represented and supported by the same independent advocate or by different independent advocates;

(f) provide that an independent advocate may, in such circumstances or subject to such conditions as may be specified, examine and take copies of relevant records relating to the individual.

(8) This section does not restrict the provision that may be made under any other provision of this Act.

(9) "Relevant record" means—

(a) a health record (within the meaning given in section 68 of the Data Protection Act 1998 (as read with section 69 of that Act)),

(b) a record of, or held by, a local authority and compiled in connection with a function under this Part or a social services function (within the meaning given in section 1A of the Local Authority Social Services Act 1970),

(c) a record held by a person registered under Part 2 of the Care Standards Act 2000 or Chapter 2 of Part 1 of the Health and Social Care Act 2008, or

(d) a record of such other description as may be specified in the regulations.

GENERAL NOTE

1–665   Section 67 places a duty on local authorities to arrange an independent advocate to be available to facilitate the involvement of an adult or carer who is the subject of an assessment, or the care planning and review process. The duty applies only if the local authority considers that the adult would experience substantial difficulty in understanding the processes or information relevant to those procedures or communicating their views, wishes, or feelings. Most of the detail setting out the role and powers of an advocate is set out in the Care and Support (Independent Advocacy Support) (No.2) Regulations 2014 (SI 2014/2889). These have been made under powers conferred by ss.(4). They are reproduced and discussed at paras A1–245 to A1–253 below. The statutory guidance discusses advocacy in Ch.7.

In the House of Lords, the Government described two main ways of quality assuring the work of advocates:

"The first is through the commissioning process, whereby local authorities set out what they expect of the advocacy service in terms of quantity and quality and monitor it through performance indicators and regular meetings. Secondly, the department has also funded a sector-specific quality assurance framework, whereby organisations start by carrying out a self-assessment and then are visited by assessors, who examine and report on the quality of the work. This is called the quality performance mark, and many commissioners require it."[1]

Subsection (1)

1–666   The duty to arrange for an advocate only applies where a local authority is required by a provision in the Care Act to involve the individual. The relevant provisions in this respect are listed in subs.(3). Section 72 of the Care Act provides that regulations may be made to establish an appeals system against local authority decisions—this is due to be implemented in April 2020—and includes reference to the provision of advocacy support (see. s.72(6)). The statutory guidance confirms that "where appropriate arrangements for independent advocacy in respect of supporting a person's involvement in an appeal will look to mirror the arrangement set out here".[2]

---

[1] *Hansard* (House of Lords), 9 October 2013, Vol.748, col.122 (Earl Howe).

[2] Department of Health, *Care and Support Statutory Guidance* (2014), para.7.2.

The guidance also states that people should benefit from the provision of one advocate "for their whole experience of care or safeguarding work" and:

". . . it rarely makes sense to have one advocate for assessment and another for care and support planning; the two are interrelated, and people who have substantial difficulty in engaging should not be expected to have to tell their story repeatedly to different advocates."[1]

Subsection (2)

The duty is to arrange an "independent advocate". The distinction between independent **1–667** advocacy and other forms of advocacy is an attempt to recognise that many people advocate on an informal basis (such as family members, friends or carers) or as part of their professional role (for example nurses, social workers and care workers) but they cannot properly be described as independent because of the perceived or actual conflict of interests. For example, the needs of a family carer in respect of their quality of life may conflict with those of the person needing care they are advocating for, or a care worker may be employed by the body responsible for directly supplying or funding services to the person they are advocating for. Independent advocacy should also be separate (or at least as separate as possible) from statutory agencies and service providers. This is normally achieved through a combination of governance and funding arrangements. However, in practice public bodies (including the bodies whose decisions the advocate may be seeking to challenge) will fund and contract with independent advocacy services, thus leading some to question the independence of the advocacy provided.

The duty to involve

The purpose of independent advocacy is to facilitate the individual's involvement. In the House of Lords the Government explained its intention:

"My noble friend asked about the term 'involve'. The change in the duty to involve a person as opposed to consulting them in the assessment, care-planning and review processes was made as a result of public consultation. It represents a significant shift by changing the emphasis on the process from being one that is led by the local authority to one carried out jointly with the individual. In practice, this means that people will need to be actively involved throughout the process, meaning that local authorities take their views into account rather than being able to perform tick-box assessment exercises, which is sometimes the accusation now. This fits with our whole approach to reforming care and support, shifting from a paternalistic view and a system where the authorities know best to a system that is driven around people and their individual preferences."[2]

The statutory guidance also discusses the meaning of the duty to involve, emphasising that people should be "active partners" and the requirement applies "no matter how complex a person's needs" and in all settings (except for safeguarding enquiries and safeguarding adults reviews in prisons).[3]

Subsection (3)

This lists when the duty to provide advocacy applies for the purposes of s.67. The list **1–668** does not include adult safeguarding enquiries or safeguarding adults reviews which are provided for separately under s.68. The statutory guidance emphasises that the local authority should keep under review the need for an advocate throughout the assessment, care and support planning and review process. Where the local authority has outsourced or

---

[1] Department of Health, *Care and Support Statutory Guidance* (2014), para.7.60.
[2] *Hansard* (House of Lords), 9 October 2013, Vol.748, col.122 (Earl Howe).
[3] Department of Health, *Care and Support Statutory Guidance* (2014), paras 7.6 to 7.7.

commissioned this process, or any aspect of it, the authority will maintain "overall responsibility for this judgement".[1]

The guidance also provides that the requirement to consider the need for an advocate also applies to people whose needs are being jointly assessed by the NHS and the local authority or where a joint package of care is, planned, commissioned or funded by both a local authority and a clinical commissioning group. In addition, it states that local authorities (with clinical commissioning groups) will want to:

> "consider the benefits of providing access to independent advice or independent advocacy for those who do not have substantial difficulty and/or those who have an appropriate person to support their involvement".[2]

Subsection (4)

1–669 The duty to provide an advocate applies only if the local authority considers that, without an advocate, the individual would experience substantial difficulty in one or more of the following:

- understanding relevant information;
- retaining that information;
- using or weighing that information as part of the process of being involved; or
- communicating the individual's views, wishes or feelings (whether by talking, using sign language or any other means).

The meaning of each of these areas of difficulty is discussed (with examples) in paras 7.10 to 7.16 of the statutory guidance. In addition, reg.3 of the the Care and Support (Independent Advocacy Support) (No. 2) Regulations 2014 (SI 2014/2889) makes provision about matters to which a local authority must have regard when deciding whether a person would experience substantial difficulty in doing the things mentioned in ss.(4). These include any illness, learning disability or disability the individual has. See para.A1–248 below.

In addition, the Social Care Institute for Excellence has produced a guide to the meaning of substantial difficulty.[3] This is not statutory guidance but it has been produced with the approval of the Department of Health (see 1–770 below).

Subsections (5) and (6)

THE APPROPRIATE PERSON

1–670 The duty to provide an advocate does not apply if the local authority is satisfied there is an appropriate person to represent the adult, who is not engaged in providing care or treatment to the adult in a professional or paid capacity (ss.(5)). In addition, the adult must consent to being represented by that person, or where the adult lacks capacity to consent, the local authority must be satisfied that it would be in the adult's best interests to be represented by that person (ss.(6)).

During the passage of the Care Bill through the House of Commons, Tom Clarke MP sought reassurances that the appointment of an appropriate person will not become a default position for family members, and argued that some may be unable or unwilling to perform this role, and it would be "highly inappropriate" if such people felt pressured to do so.[4] The Government did not respond to this specific point, but it is submitted that the mere presence of a carer would not be sufficient to disapply the duty under subs.(2). The appropriate person must be willing and able to undertake this role.

---

[1] Department of Health, *Care and Support Statutory Guidance* (2014), para.7.18.
[2] Department of Health, *Care and Support Statutory Guidance* (2014), paras 7.21 to 7.22.
[3] Social Care Institute for Excellence, *Handout: Substantial Difficulty* (Oct 2014).
[4] *Hansard* (House of Commons), 16 December 2013, Vol.572, col.572.

Under the Mental Capacity Act, the duty to appoint an Independent Mental Capacity Advocate does not apply if the decision-maker considers that there is a person (who is not a professional or paid carer) who it would be appropriate to consult to determine the adult's best interests. However, the "appropriate consultee" is not given any specific powers, nor is it conceived to be a formal statutory role—it is merely a drafting device which serves to limit the availability of advocacy support. In respect of the Care Act, a straightforward reading of subs.(5) and (6) might suggest that that the "appropriate person" has a similar purpose. However, the statutory guidance sets out an expanded role for the appropriate person. It makes clear that the appropriate person is expected to undertake an active role and therefore would be unlikely to be able to fulfil this role if they live at distance or do not understand local authority processes. The statutory guidance sets out in no uncertain terms that "it is not sufficient to know the person well or to love them deeply; the role of the appropriate individual is to support the person's active *involvement with the local authority processes*". It also should not be someone who expresses their own opinions before asking the adult or is linked to safeguarding concerns.[1]

The draft guidance had originally contained a statement that "the person's wish not to be supported by that individual should be respected regardless of whether the person is assessed to have or lack capacity" and that "the person must agree to the appropriateness of the individual who is proposed to support them".[2] However this was removed from the final version. The statutory guidance now states that the person's wish not to be supported by that person should be respected. If a person has capacity and does not wish to be supported by an individual, their wishes must be followed. But if the adult lacks capacity, it must be in their best interests to be supported and represented by that individual.[3] This would appear to leave open the possibility that a person might have an appropriate person appointed against their wishes, which is likely to be problematic from the perspective of that person when supporting them to make decisions or advocating for them.

There is also guidance on the potential for conflicts of interest, and the circumstances in which an advocate may need to be appointed even if there appears to be an appropriate person.[4] Moreover, reg.4 of the Care and Support (Independent Advocacy Support) (No.2) Regulations 2014 (SI 2014/2889) provides that, in two specific sets of circumstances, a person must be provided with an advocate even though there is an appropriate person to support their involvement. The first is where the assessment or care planning function might result in a placement in NHS-funded provision in a hospital (for more than 28 days) or a care home (for more than eight weeks), and the local authority is satisfied it would be in the best interests of the person to arrange an advocate. The second is where there is a dispute between the appropriate person and the local authority, and the authority and the appropriate person considers it would be in the best interests of the individual to arrange an advocate. See para.A1–248 below.

Subsection (7)

The Government has powers to make regulations governing the provision of advocacy, **1–671** including:

- setting out the requirements for an independent advocate;
- specifying what a local authority must have regard to in determining whether an individual would experience substantial difficulties in their involvement in the assessment;
- specifying any circumstance in which the exception in subs.(5) does not apply; and

---

[1] Department of Health, *Care and Support Statutory Guidance* (2014), paras 7.35 to 7.36 (emphasis in original).

[2] Department of Health, *Care and Support Statutory Guidance: Issued under the Care Act 2014* (June 2014), para.7.25.

[3] Department of Health, *Care and Support Statutory Guidance* (2014), para.7.34.

[4] Department of Health, *Care and Support Statutory Guidance* (2014), paras 7.37 to 7.41.

- making provision as to the manner in which independent advocates are to perform their duties.

As noted above, the relevant regulations are the Care and Support (Independent Advocacy Support) (No. 2) Regulations 2014 (SI 2014/2889). In particular, regs 2 to 7 set out in detail the role and powers of an advocate. These are are discussed in detail at A1–247 to A1–252 below.

The role of advocacy under the Care Act can be usefully compared to that under the Mental Capacity Act. Independent Mental Capacity Advocacy is restricted to a relatively small number of defined decisions and its role limited to assisting decision-makers to reach best interests decisions (with the notable exception of section 39D advocacy). In contrast, Care Act advocacy has a wider role which is focused on helping people to understand and exercising their rights and challenge decision-makers. This goes much further than merely writing a report on the person's best interests (which may not necessarily be consistent with the person's wishes and feelings). For example, reg.4 requires that a Care Act advocate must:

- assist the individual in understanding the relevant function, communicating their views, wishes or feelings, understanding how their needs could be met by the local authority or otherwise, making decisions in respect of care and support arrangements, and challenging the local authority's decisions if the individual so wishes;
- so far as is practicable, ensure that the individual understands the local authority's duties and the individual's rights and obligations under the Care Act;
- make such representations as are necessary for the purpose of securing the individual's rights; and
- where the advocate has concerns about the assessment or planning function, prepare a report for the local authority outlining those concerns.

Moreover, where the individual lacks capacity, the advocate must communicate the person's views, wishes or feelings, to the extent the advocate can ascertain them, and challenge the decision if the advocate considers the decision to be inconsistent with the local authority's general duty under s.1 to promote the individual's well-being (reg.5). The local authority is required to "take into account any representations" made by the advocate and "take reasonable steps to assist the independent advocate to represent and support the individual". The local authority is also required to provide an independent advocate with a written response to any report made (reg.6).

See also discussion at paras 1-657 to 1-662 above.

Safeguarding enquiries and reviews

1–672   **68.**—(1) This section applies where there is to be—
   (a) an enquiry under section 42(2),
   (b) a review under section 44(1) of a case in which condition 2 in section 44(3) is met or a review under section 44(4).

(2) The relevant local authority must, if the condition in subsection (3) is met, arrange for a person who is independent of the authority (an "independent advocate") to be available to represent and support the adult to whose case the enquiry or review relates for the purpose of facilitating his or her involvement in the enquiry or review; but see subsections (4) and (6).

(3) The condition is that the local authority considers that, were an independent advocate not to be available, the individual would experience substantial difficulty in doing one or more of the following—
   (a) understanding relevant information;

(b) retaining that information;

(c) using or weighing that information as part of the process of being involved;

(d) communicating the individual's views, wishes or feelings (whether by talk-ing, using sign language or any other means).

(4) The duty under subsection (2) does not apply if the local authority is satis-fied that there is a person—

(a) who would be an appropriate person to represent and support the adult for the purpose of facilitating the adult's involvement, and

(b) who is not engaged in providing care or treatment for the adult in a pro-fessional capacity or for remuneration.

(5) For the purposes of subsection (4), a person is not to be regarded as an appropriate person unless—

(a) where the adult has capacity to consent to being represented and supported by that person, the adult does so consent, or

(b) where the adult lacks capacity so to consent, the local authority is satisfied that being represented and supported by that person would be in the adult's best interests.

(6) If the enquiry or review needs to begin as a matter of urgency, it may do so even if the authority has not yet been able to comply with the duty under subsec-tion (2) (and the authority continues to be subject to the duty).

(7) "Relevant local authority" means—

(a) in a case within subsection (1)(a), the authority making the enquiry or caus-ing it to be made;

(b) in a case within subsection (1)(b), the authority which established the SAB arranging the review.

GENERAL NOTE

Section 68 places a duty on local authorities to arrange an independent advocate to be **1–673** available to represent and support an adult who is the subject of an adult safeguarding enquiry or a safeguarding adults review, if that local authority considers that the adult would experience substantial difficulty in understanding the processes or information rel-evant to those processes or communicating their views, wishes, or feelings. It is a separate advocacy duty to that contained in s.67. This is because s.67 applies where a local authority is required by a relevant provision to involve an individual in its exercise of a function, which is not the case for adult safeguarding enquiries or safeguarding adults reviews. The separation of the duties is potentially significant because it means that the extensive regulation power provided for under s.67(7)—which has been used to specify detailed powers for the advocate (see para.1–671 above)—is not applicable to s.68 advocacy. The statutory guidance states that where an independent advocate has already been arranged under s.67 of the Care Act or under the Mental Capacity Act 2005 then, unless inappropriate, the same advocate should be used.[1]

The statutory guidance discusses advocacy in Ch.7. Most of this is generic and applies to ss.67 and 68 advocacy. However, it addresses s.68 advocacy specifically in paras 7.2 to 7.5, 7.24 to 7.28, and 7.49. The guidance also makes clear that people should benefit from the provision of one advocate "for their whole experience of care or safeguarding work".[2]

Under the Mental Capacity Act, people who lack capacity and are alleged to be respon-sible for abuse, may be entitled to the help of an Independent Mental Capacity Advocate, to support and represent them in the enquiries that are taking place. The statutory guidance

---

[1] Department of Health, *Care and Support Statutory Guidance* (2014), para.7.24.

[2] Department of Health, *Care and Support Statutory Guidance* (2014), para.7.60.

Subsection (3)

1–682   Sums are recoverable within six years (if they become due following commencement of this section), or within three years (if they became due before commencement). See para.23.25 and Annex D, para.11 of the statutory guidance.

Subsection (4)

1–683   When someone misrepresents or fails to disclose any material fact in connection with the provisions in this Part, the authority may recover as a debt, expenditure incurred as a result of the misrepresentation or failure and any sum it would have recovered but for the misrepresentation or failure.

During the passage of the Care Bill, at committee stage in the House of Lords, concerns were raised by Lord Lipsey that a failure to disclose any material fact—even inadvertently—would make an individual liable to recovery proceedings and therefore deter people from seeking care and support.[1] Baroness Barker also spoke about problems that occur when relatives take over the finances of someone and discover after they have died, financial accounts of which they were not aware (for example money set aside to pay for a funeral).[2]

The Government however rejected Lord Lipsey's amendment to prevent local authorities recovering debt in cases where people have inadvertently misled the local authority, arguing that this would require local authorities to prove intent which would result in complex and expensive legal proceedings. Moreover the Minister also stated:

"I think that the ability of a local authority to recover costs ought to act as a disincentive to people to be careless about what they are doing. They should make sure that what they declare is accurate and should be made aware that if they make a mistake, it might prove a little more costly to them than just rectifying the error. This is not about imposing recriminations on people. It is right for local authorities not to be out of pocket when other people out there could be benefiting from the public money that is available."[3]

At report stage Lord Lipsey tabled a further amendment to provide that a local authority can recover where a claim fraudulently or negligently misrepresents or fails to disclose any material fact that they might have reasonably been aware would have a bearing on expenditure incurred by the local authority.[4] The Government also rejected this amendment, arguing that it would provide an incentive for people to take advantage of the system and avoid charges. It also stated:

"We recognise that there may be a number of reasons why someone has not paid the full amount of the charges due to the local authority, including misrepresentations of their assets which were entirely unintentional. But even where the reason is an accident or a mistake, local authorities still suffer a loss and must be able to recover that loss if there is no other means of doing so. This is public money."[5]

The Minister went on to state:

"A local authority should not, as a matter of course, use these powers to recover debts without first having discussed other options with the individual concerned. In most cases, especially those where the failure to pay the correct charges was inadvertent, there would be other simpler routes to follow, such as agreeing a repayment plan which allows for recovery over time in a way that is manageable. The noble Lord suggests that local authorities may exercise these powers in a way that will drive people out of their own homes. Quite aside from the fact that we have no evidence that local

---

[1] *Hansard* (House of Lords), 16 July 2013, Vol.747, col.689.
[2] *Hansard* (House of Lords), 16 July 2013, Vol.747, col.691.
[3] *Hansard* (House of Lords), 16 July 2013, Vol.747, col.696 (Earl Howe).
[4] *Hansard* (House of Lords), 16 October 2013, Vol.748, cols 578 to 580.
[5] *Hansard* (House of Lords), 16 October 2013, Vol.748, cols 581 to 582 (Earl Howe).

   (b) retaining that information;

   (c) using or weighing that information as part of the process of being involved;

   (d) communicating the individual's views, wishes or feelings (whether by talking, using sign language or any other means).

   (4) The duty under subsection (2) does not apply if the local authority is satisfied that there is a person—

   (a) who would be an appropriate person to represent and support the adult for the purpose of facilitating the adult's involvement, and

   (b) who is not engaged in providing care or treatment for the adult in a professional capacity or for remuneration.

   (5) For the purposes of subsection (4), a person is not to be regarded as an appropriate person unless—

   (a) where the adult has capacity to consent to being represented and supported by that person, the adult does so consent, or

   (b) where the adult lacks capacity so to consent, the local authority is satisfied that being represented and supported by that person would be in the adult's best interests.

   (6) If the enquiry or review needs to begin as a matter of urgency, it may do so even if the authority has not yet been able to comply with the duty under subsection (2) (and the authority continues to be subject to the duty).

   (7) "Relevant local authority" means—

   (a) in a case within subsection (1)(a), the authority making the enquiry or causing it to be made;

   (b) in a case within subsection (1)(b), the authority which established the SAB arranging the review.

GENERAL NOTE

   Section 68 places a duty on local authorities to arrange an independent advocate to be **1–673** available to represent and support an adult who is the subject of an adult safeguarding enquiry or a safeguarding adults review, if that local authority considers that the adult would experience substantial difficulty in understanding the processes or information relevant to those processes or communicating their views, wishes, or feelings. It is a separate advocacy duty to that contained in s.67. This is because s.67 applies where a local authority is required by a relevant provision to involve an individual in its exercise of a function, which is not the case for adult safeguarding enquiries or safeguarding adults reviews. The separation of the duties is potentially significant because it means that the extensive regulation power provided for under s.67(7)—which has been used to specify detailed powers for the advocate (see para.1–671 above)—is not applicable to s.68 advocacy. The statutory guidance states that where an independent advocate has already been arranged under s.67 of the Care Act or under the Mental Capacity Act 2005 then, unless inappropriate, the same advocate should be used.[1]

   The statutory guidance discusses advocacy in Ch.7. Most of this is generic and applies to ss.67 and 68 advocacy. However, it addresses s.68 advocacy specifically in paras 7.2 to 7.5, 7.24 to 7.28, and 7.49. The guidance also makes clear that people should benefit from the provision of one advocate "for their whole experience of care or safeguarding work".[2]

   Under the Mental Capacity Act, people who lack capacity and are alleged to be responsible for abuse, may be entitled to the help of an Independent Mental Capacity Advocate, to support and represent them in the enquiries that are taking place. The statutory guidance

---

[1] Department of Health, *Care and Support Statutory Guidance* (2014), para.7.24.
[2] Department of Health, *Care and Support Statutory Guidance* (2014), para.7.60.

confirms this is separate from the decision whether or not to provide the victim of abuse with an independent advocate under the Care Act.[1]

Subsection (1)

1–674   The duty to arrange for an advocate applies where a local authority is required to make safeguarding enquiries under s.42(2), required to arrange a safeguarding adults review under s.44(1) (where the subject of the review is still alive) or exercises its power to arrange a safeguarding adults review under s.44(4). By virtue of subs.(7) the duty falls on the local authority making the enquiry or causing it to be made (in respect of a safeguarding adults enquiry), or the authority that established the Safeguarding Adults Board (in respect of a safeguarding adults review).

Subsection (2)

1–675   The duty is to arrange an "independent advocate". The role of the advocate is to represent and support the individual for the purpose of facilitating their involvement. The wording of subs.(2) is almost identical to that of s.67(2) and is discussed at para.1–667 above.

Subsection (3)

1–676   The duty to provide an advocate applies only if the local authority considers that, without an advocate, the individual would experience substantial difficulty in:

- understanding relevant information;
- retaining that information;
- using or weighing that information as part of the process of being involved; or
- communicating the individual's views, wishes or feelings (whether by talking, using sign language or any other means).

The wording of subs.(3) is almost identical to that of s.67(4)—see para.1–668 above.

Subsections (4) and (5)

1–677   The duty to provide an advocate does not apply if the local authority is satisfied there is an appropriate person to represent the adult, who is not engaged in providing care or treatment to the adult in a professional or paid capacity. In addition, the adult must consent to being represented by that person, or where the adult lacks capacity to consent, the local authority must be satisfied that it would be in the adult's best interests to be represented by that person.

See discussion at para.1–670 above (under s.67(5) and (6)) on the appropriate person.

Subsection (6)

1–678   This provides that urgent safeguarding enquiries or reviews can begin even if an advocacy has not been arranged under subs.(2). But the authority continues to be subject to the duty. The statutory guidance states that if an enquiry needs to start "urgently" then it can begin before an advocate is appointed but one must be appointed "as soon as possible".[2]

ENFORCEMENT OF DEBTS

Recovery of charges, interest etc.

1–679   **69.**—(1) Any sum due to a local authority under this Part is recoverable by the authority as a debt due to it.

---

[1] Department of Health, *Care and Support Statutory Guidance* (2014), para.14.98.
[2] Department of Health, *Care and Support Statutory Guidance* (2014), para.7.27.

(2) But subsection (1) does not apply in a case where a deferred payment agreement could, in accordance with regulations under section 34(1), be entered into, unless—

(a) the local authority has sought to enter into such an agreement with the adult from whom the sum is due, and

(b) the adult has refused.

(3) A sum is recoverable under this section—

(a) in a case in which the sum becomes due to the local authority on or after the commencement of this section, within six years of the date the sum becomes due;

(b) in any other case, within three years of the date on which it becomes due.

(4) Where a person misrepresents or fails to disclose (whether fraudulently or otherwise) to a local authority any material fact in connection with the provisions of this Part, the following sums are due to the authority from the person—

(a) any expenditure incurred by the authority as a result of the misrepresentation or failure, and

(b) any sum recoverable under this section which the authority has not recovered as a result of the misrepresentation or failure.

(5) The costs incurred by a local authority in recovering or seeking to recover a sum due to it under this Part are recoverable by the authority as a debt due to it.

(6) Regulations may—

(a) make provision for determining the date on which a sum becomes due to a local authority for the purposes of this section;

(b) specify cases or circumstances in which a sum due to a local authority under this Part is not recoverable by it under this section;

(c) specify cases or circumstances in which a local authority may charge interest on a sum due to it under this Part;

(d) where interest is chargeable, provide that it—

(i) must be charged at a rate specified in or determined in accordance with the regulations, or

(ii) may not be charged at a rate that exceeds the rate specified in or determined in accordance with the regulations.

GENERAL NOTE

1–680   This section allows local authorities to recover as a debt any sums owed, such as unpaid charges and interest. It replaces ss.22 and 24 of the Health and Social Services and Social Security Adjudications Act 1983 and s.45 of the National Assistance Act 1948. Ultimately the local authority may institute County Court proceedings to recover the debt. The statutory guidance states that in deciding how to proceed a local authority should consider the circumstances of the case and for instance, consider whether it was a deliberate avoidance of payment or due to circumstances beyond the person's control. Moreover, the option of court proceedings should only be used if other reasonable alternatives have been exhausted.[1] The statutory guidance discusses the recovery of debts in Annex D.

Subsection (2)

1–681   The power to recover a debt does not apply where an authority could (in accordance with regulations under s.34(1)) enter into a deferred payment agreement, unless the authority offers someone this option and they refuse.

---

[1] Department of Health, *Care and Support Statutory Guidance* (2014), paras 8.29 to 8.30.

Subsection (3)

1–682   Sums are recoverable within six years (if they become due following commencement of this section), or within three years (if they became due before commencement). See para.23.25 and Annex D, para.11 of the statutory guidance.

Subsection (4)

1–683   When someone misrepresents or fails to disclose any material fact in connection with the provisions in this Part, the authority may recover as a debt, expenditure incurred as a result of the misrepresentation or failure and any sum it would have recovered but for the misrepresentation or failure.

During the passage of the Care Bill, at committee stage in the House of Lords, concerns were raised by Lord Lipsey that a failure to disclose any material fact—even inadvertently—would make an individual liable to recovery proceedings and therefore deter people from seeking care and support.[1] Baroness Barker also spoke about problems that occur when relatives take over the finances of someone and discover after they have died, financial accounts of which they were not aware (for example money set aside to pay for a funeral).[2]

The Government however rejected Lord Lipsey's amendment to prevent local authorities recovering debt in cases where people have inadvertently misled the local authority, arguing that this would require local authorities to prove intent which would result in complex and expensive legal proceedings. Moreover the Minister also stated:

"I think that the ability of a local authority to recover costs ought to act as a disincentive to people to be careless about what they are doing. They should make sure that what they declare is accurate and should be made aware that if they make a mistake, it might prove a little more costly to them than just rectifying the error. This is not about imposing recriminations on people. It is right for local authorities not to be out of pocket when other people out there could be benefiting from the public money that is available."[3]

At report stage Lord Lipsey tabled a further amendment to provide that a local authority can recover where a claim fraudulently or negligently misrepresents or fails to disclose any material fact that they might have reasonably been aware would have a bearing on expenditure incurred by the local authority.[4] The Government also rejected this amendment, arguing that it would provide an incentive for people to take advantage of the system and avoid charges. It also stated:

"We recognise that there may be a number of reasons why someone has not paid the full amount of the charges due to the local authority, including misrepresentations of their assets which were entirely unintentional. But even where the reason is an accident or a mistake, local authorities still suffer a loss and must be able to recover that loss if there is no other means of doing so. This is public money."[5]

The Minister went on to state:

"A local authority should not, as a matter of course, use these powers to recover debts without first having discussed other options with the individual concerned. In most cases, especially those where the failure to pay the correct charges was inadvertent, there would be other simpler routes to follow, such as agreeing a repayment plan which allows for recovery over time in a way that is manageable. The noble Lord suggests that local authorities may exercise these powers in a way that will drive people out of their own homes. Quite aside from the fact that we have no evidence that local

---

[1] *Hansard* (House of Lords), 16 July 2013, Vol.747, col.689.
[2] *Hansard* (House of Lords), 16 July 2013, Vol.747, col.691.
[3] *Hansard* (House of Lords), 16 July 2013, Vol.747, col.696 (Earl Howe).
[4] *Hansard* (House of Lords), 16 October 2013, Vol.748, cols 578 to 580.
[5] *Hansard* (House of Lords), 16 October 2013, Vol.748, cols 581 to 582 (Earl Howe).

authorities behave in that way and have used their existing powers like that, I have to say that I find that assertion particularly unconvincing. Local authorities are bound by the public law principle of acting reasonably at all times and must act in accordance with human rights legislation, as well as the well-being principle, which we have already debated . . . whether or not the person could have been reasonably aware of something that needed to be included in the financial assessment is one of the factors that the local authority should consider when deciding whether it is appropriate to recover a debt."[1]

In the division, Lord Lipsey's amendment was defeated by 224 to 198 votes.[2]

Subsection (5)

A local authority can recover as a debt the legal and administrative costs it incurs in pursuing that debt. **1–684**

Subsection (6)

This subsection provides a power for regulations to determine the date when a debt **1–685** becomes due, to specify exceptions to when an authority can recover a debt and to specify when an authority may charge interest on the sum owed (at a rate in accordance with the regulations).

Transfer of assets to avoid charges

70.—(1) This section applies in a case where an adult's needs have been or are **1–686** being met by a local authority under sections 18 to 20 and where—

(a) the adult has transferred an asset to another person (a "transferee"),

(b) the transfer was undertaken with the intention of avoiding charges for having the adult's needs met, and

(c) either the consideration for the transfer was less than the value of the asset or there was no consideration for the transfer.

(2) The transferee is liable to pay to the local authority an amount equal to the difference between—

(a) the amount the authority would have charged the adult were it not for the transfer of the asset, and

(b) the amount it did in fact charge the adult.

(3) But the transferee is not liable to pay to the authority an amount which exceeds the benefit accruing to the transferee from the transfer.

(4) Where an asset has been transferred to more than one transferee, the liability of each transferee is in proportion to the benefit accruing to that transferee from the transfer.

(5) "Asset" means anything which may be taken into account for the purposes of a financial assessment.

(6) The value of an asset (other than cash) is the amount which would have been realised if it had been sold on the open market by a willing seller at the time of the transfer, with a deduction for—

(a) the amount of any incumbrance on the asset, and

(b) a reasonable amount in respect of the expenses of the sale.

(7) Regulations may specify cases or circumstances in which liability under subsection (2) does not arise.

---

[1] *Hansard* (House of Lords), 16 October 2013, Vol.748, cols 582 to 583 (Earl Howe).

[2] *Hansard* (House of Lords), 16 October 2013, Vol.748, cols 584 to 587.

GENERAL NOTE

1–687 Where a person's needs for care and support have been or are being met by a local authority, the local authority may impose a charge on the person to cover all or part of the cost of meeting the person's needs. If the person has transferred assets to another individual in order to avoid these charges, subss.(2) and (4) enable the local authority to recover the lost income from the individual, or individuals. Such cases may range from an older person gifting their life savings to the grandchildren before entering care, to more sinister planned transfers of property in an attempt to evade paying for care. It may even be necessary to pursue the estate of a deceased person in some cases. Case law has confirmed that the intention to avoid charges does not have to be the sole intention of the transfer; it is sufficient for this to be significant purpose.[1] Section 423 of the Insolvency Act 1986 can apply in such cases. The transfer of an asset which places it out of the reach of a local authority can make it a "victim" for the purposes of the Act. The statutory guidance discusses deprivation of assets in Annex E.

The Law Society has issued a practice note on making gifts of assets.[2]

Subsection (3)

1–688 This limits the amount the local authority may recover so that it cannot recover more than the individual gained from the transfer.

REVIEW OF FUNDING PROVISIONS

Five-yearly review by Secretary of State

1–689 **71.**—(1) The Secretary of State must review—

   (a) the level at which the cap on care costs is for the time being set under regulations under section 15(4),

   (b) the level at which the amount attributable to an adult's daily living costs is for the time being set under regulations under section 15(8), and

   (c) the level at which the financial limit is for the time being set under regulations under section 17(8).

  (2) In carrying out the review, the Secretary of State must have regard to—

   (a) the financial burden on the state of each of those matters being at the level in question,

   (b) the financial burden on local authorities of each of those matters being at the level in question,

   (c) the financial burden on adults who have needs for care and support of each of those matters being at the level in question,

   (d) the length of time for which people can reasonably be expected to live in good health,

   (e) changes in the ways or circumstances in which adults' needs for care and support are being or are likely to be met,

   (f) changes in the prevalence of conditions for which the provision of care and support is or is likely to be required, and

   (g) such other factors as the Secretary of State considers relevant.

  (3) The Secretary of State must prepare and publish a report on the outcome of the review.

  (4) The first report must be published before the end of the period of five years beginning with the day on which section 15 comes into force.

---

[1] *Yule v South Lanarkshire County Council* [1999] 1 CCLR 546.
[2] Law Society, *Making Gifts of Assets* (2011).

(5) Each subsequent report must be published before the end of the period of five years beginning with the day on which the previous report was published.

(6) The Secretary of State may arrange for some other person to carry out the whole or part of a review under this section on the Secretary of State's behalf.

(7) The Secretary of State must lay before Parliament a report prepared under this section.

GENERAL NOTE

Section 71 requires the Secretary of State every five years to review and report on the **1–690** level of the cap on care costs, of daily living costs to be disregarded for the purposes of the cap, and the threshold for the financial assessment. According to the explanatory notes, this review is intended to "inform decisions on whether to change the level of the cap, or other parameters, such as general living costs, in the system."[1] The capped costs system is due to be implemented in April 2020.

During the passage of the Care Bill, in the House of Lords, the Government agreed that the capped costs system requires oversight to ensure that it delivers the stated benefits, such as "peace of mind and protection against catastrophic costs". It therefore stated:

"To that end, we will be reviewing and assuring both implementation and funding, and have committed to reviewing the core elements of the capped-costs system within each five-year period."[2]

Lord Warner tabled an amendment to require the Government to publish a review of the working of the reforms ahead of the first five-yearly review.[3] The Government rejected this amendment. The Minister stated in response:

"Reviewing and evaluating those reforms is indeed essential . . . That is why we will conduct post-legislative scrutiny, as the Government have committed to do across the board for all new Acts. The agreement we have with the House Liaison Committee in another place is that that should be done between three and five years after Royal Assent. The joint programme and implementation board, which we have set up in collaboration with the Local Government Association and the Association of Directors of Adult Social Services, will also assure implementation, and we will work with local government on continuing assurance and improvement. I truly do not believe that it would be necessary or desirable to supplement those arrangements with further reviews, either by Government or by other bodies. Such additional oversight would cut across the scrutiny conducted by the Health Select Committee and cross-government planning on spending through the spending round. I am sure the noble Lords will agree that it is only right that decisions on care and support are taken at the same time as spending plans are set for all areas of government."[4]

Subsection (2)

This lists six factors which the Secretary of State must consider in the review. These **1–691** include the financial burden on the state and local authorities and health life expectancy. In addition, the Secretary of State can consider any other relevant factors.

Subsection (3)

A report of the review must be prepared and published. By virtue of sub.(7), this report **1–692** must also be laid in Parliament.

---

[1] Care Act 2014: Explanatory Notes para.416.
[2] *Hansard* (House of Lords), 14 October 2013, Vol.748, col.287 (Earl Howe).
[3] *Hansard* (House of Lords), 16 October 2013, Vol.748, cols 559 to 590.
[4] *Hansard* (House of Lords), 16 October 2013, Vol.748, col.592 (Earl Howe).

1–693　The first report must be published within five years of the commencement of this section. Subsequent reports must be published within five years of each previous report.

Subsection (6)
1–694　This confirms that the Secretary of State can commission other people to carry out the review.

APPEALS

Part 1 appeals
1–695　**72.**—(1) Regulations may make provision for appeals against decisions taken by a local authority in the exercise of functions under this Part in respect of an individual (including decisions taken before the coming into force of the first regulations made under this subsection).

(2) The regulations may in particular make provision about—

(a) who may (and may not) bring an appeal;

(b) grounds on which an appeal may be brought;

(c) pre-conditions for bringing an appeal;

(d) how an appeal is to be brought and dealt with (including time limits);

(e) who is to consider an appeal;

(f) matters to be taken into account (and disregarded) by the person or body considering an appeal;

(g) powers of the person or body deciding an appeal;

(h) what action is to be taken by a local authority as a result of an appeal decision;

(i) providing information about the right to bring an appeal, appeal procedures and other sources of information and advice;

(j) representation and support for an individual bringing or otherwise involved in an appeal;

(k) investigations into things done or not done by a person or body with power to consider an appeal.

(3) Provision about pre-conditions for bringing an appeal may require specified steps to have been taken before an appeal is brought.

(4) Provision about how an appeal is to be dealt with may include provision for—

(a) the appeal to be treated as, or as part of, an appeal brought or complaint made under another procedure;

(b) the appeal to be considered with any such appeal or complaint.

(5) Provision about who is to consider an appeal may include provision—

(a) establishing, or requiring or permitting the establishment of, a panel or other body to consider an appeal;

(b) requiring an appeal to be considered by, or by persons who include, persons with a specified description of expertise or experience.

(6) Provision about representation and support for an individual may include provision applying any provision of or made under section 67, with or without modifications.

(7) The regulations may make provision for—

(a) an appeal brought or complaint made under another procedure to be treated as, or as part of, an appeal brought under the regulations;

(b) an appeal brought or complaint made under another procedure to be considered with an appeal brought under the regulations;

(c) matters raised in an appeal brought under the regulations to be taken into account by the person or body considering an appeal brought or complaint made under another procedure.

(8) The regulations may include provision conferring functions on a person or body established by or under an Act (including an Act passed after the passing of this Act); for that purpose, the regulations may amend, repeal, or revoke an enactment, or provide for an enactment to apply with specified modifications.

(9) Regulations may make provision, in relation to a case where an appeal is brought under regulations under subsection (1)—

(a) for any provision of this Part to apply, for a specified period, as if a decision ("the interim decision") differing from the decision appealed against had been made;

(b) as to what the terms of the interim decision are, or as to how and by whom they are to be determined;

(c) for financial adjustments to be made following a decision on the appeal.

(10) The period specified under subsection (9)(a) may not begin earlier than the date on which the decision appealed against was made, or end later than the date on which the decision on the appeal takes effect.

GENERAL NOTE

In its scoping report, the Law Commission concluded that its review should consider the **1–696** efficacy of the legal structures in place for complaining about, and seeking redress for, failures in decision-making and service provision by local authorities (see also para.I1–006 above). This would have included consideration of whether there was a need to establish a tribunal to provide independent merits reviews of local authority community care decisions, analogous to that provided by the Special Education Needs and Disability Tribunal.[1] While the Department of Health approved the scoping report as providing the agenda for the law reform project, the one area it did not wish the Commission to cover was the system for service user redress.[2] Accordingly, the Law Commission's consultation paper did not examine the efficacy of the complaints and redress system, nor did it make any proposals on this issue. Notwithstanding this decision, a large number of consultees argued that the quality of local authorities' complaints procedures was such that proposals for reform should be made in this area. Within this theme, a number of consultees argued in favour of a tribunal to resolve complaints and disputes. In particular, it was argued that such a system would save money since local authority complaints procedures were shown to be more expensive than operating a tribunal.[3] Consequently, the Law Commission's final report recommended that, while this issue was formally outside of the project's remit, the Government should consider reviewing the complaints and redress system and whether a community care tribunal should be established.[4] The Government's response stated that it was planning to improve the complaints system and did not believe that any substantial law reform was needed in this area.[5]

The Joint Committee argued that the introduction of a capped costs system would result in "a large influx of people into the local authority assessment system for the first time"

---

[1] Law Commission, *Adult Social Care: Scoping Report* (26 November 2008) para.4.348.

[2] Law Commission, *Better law for disabled people, older people and carers—reforming adult social care legislation* (press release, 26 November 2008).

[3] See Law Commission, *Adult Social Care: Consultation Analysis* (2011), paras 14.20 to 14.31.

[4] Law Commission, *Adult Social Care*, paras 12.37 to 12.38.

[5] Department of Health, *Reforming the Law for Adult Care and Support: The Government's Response to Law Commission Report 326 on Adult Social Care* (TSO, July 2012), Cm.8379.

and that the arrangements for "determining a person's eligibility and then capping care costs by setting a notional cost to be accumulated in a care account will be highly contested".[1] It concluded that:

". . . the significant extension of local authority responsibility for assessment, and the introduction of the well-being principle into decision-making, warrant an urgent review of arrangements for providing redress and complaints resolution."[2]

The Committee therefore recommended that the Government should reconsider establishing a care and support tribunal to provide independent merit reviews of decisions made by local authorities, and consider giving this tribunal responsibility for resolving disputes over NHS continuing health care.[3]

However, the Government argued that a formal independent tribunal process "would slow down the process of resolving complaints, is likely to be expensive and would add a further burden to the existing system". Instead, it would look at existing complaints arrangements in the light of the findings of the *Review of NHS Complaints* led by Ann Clwyd and Professor Tricia Hart and its consultation on the capped costs scheme. This review had been set up by the Government in the light of the Francis Report into the failings at Mid Staffordshire NHS Foundation Trust (see para.I1–011 above).[4]

The Care Bill, as introduced into the House of Lords, therefore contained no provisions on appeals. At Committee stage in the House of Lords, Lord Dubs tabled an amendment to enable adults to make an appeal to the First-tier Tribunal if they disagreed with the local authority about its decisions relating to matters such as eligibility, financial assessments, care and support plans and other obligations under the legislation.[5] The Government responded that it was reviewing the current arrangements regarding complaints and as part of this review it will be considering redress and the advantages and disadvantages of the tribunal system.[6]

In the House of Commons at Committee stage, Paul Burstow MP tabled an amendment which would enable the Government to make regulations to introduce a mechanism for dispute resolution and redress.[7] In response the Government said that it already had the power to make such regulations under the Health and Social Care (Community Health and Standards) Act 2003 and those regulations already require local authorities to have in place systems for dealing with complaints. It was also confirmed that an announcement on the outcome of the review of the complaints system was expected soon.[8]

1–697   Indeed, this announcement came much sooner than expected. On the last day of the Committee stage, the Government tabled s.72 to be added to the Bill, which provides for a broad regulation-making power specific to appeals of decisions made under Pt 1 of the Care Act. In doing so, the Government stated that the Care Act:

---

[1] House of Lords House of Commons Joint Committee on the Draft Care and Support Bill, *Draft Care and Support Bill Report, Session 2012–13*, para.262.

[2] House of Lords House of Commons Joint Committee on the Draft Care and Support Bill, *Draft Care and Support Bill Report, Session 2012–13*, para.263.

[3] House of Lords House of Commons Joint Committee on the Draft Care and Support Bill, *Draft Care and Support Bill Report, Session 2012–13*, paras 263 to 264.

[4] Department of Health, *The Care Bill explained—including a response to consultation and pre-legislative scrutiny on the draft Care and Support Bill*, para.128; A. Clwyd and T. Hart, *A Review of the NHS Hospitals Complaints System: Putting Patients Back in the Picture: Final Report (October 2013)*.

[5] *Hansard* (House of Lords), 29 July 2013, Vol.747, cols 1561 to 1562.

[6] *Hansard* (House of Lords), 29 July 2013, Vol.747, col.1566 (Earl Howe).

[7] *Hansard* (House of Commons: Public Bill Committee), 9 January 2014: Second Sitting (PM), cols 67 to 69.

[8] *Hansard* (House of Commons: Public Bill Committee), 9 January 2014: Second Sitting (PM), cols 70 to 71 (Norman Lamb MP).

". . . establishes a new legal framework that puts the well-being of individuals at the heart of care and support and puts them in control of their own care. [The Care Act] will also put in place a new statutory framework for assessment and care planning, extending the duty to assess carers' needs and allowing people who pay for their own care to count the reasonable cost of meeting their eligible needs towards the cap. Given those changes, it is important that individuals have confidence in the system, and that they are able to challenge decisions without having to resort to judicial review."[1]

The Minister also referred to the "wide-ranging consultation"[2] which had been held in 2013 to seek opinions on the system of appeals which had persuaded the Government of the need for reform in this area. The Government further explained that s.72 will provide the "scope to develop detailed proposals for an appeals system, along with stakeholders" and it is possible that an existing statutory body will be involved in the appeals arrangements, "to bring particular expertise to the process", and so the power is wide enough to enable the Government to confer functions on such bodies.[3]

The Government's proposed appeal scheme was published in February 2015. It set out a three stage process:

- the early resolution stage—where the local authority undertakes dialogue with the person to resolve the issue locally (30 days);
- the independent review stage—where the local authority appoints an Independent Reviewer to review the original decision and make a recommendation (30 days); and
- the local authority decision—where the local authority makes a decision considering the Independent Reviewer's recommendation (five days).

The range of decisions proposed to be within scope of the appeals scheme were: assessment (s.9); eligibility (s.13); care planning (s.25); direct payments (s.31); personal budgets (s.26); independent personal budgets and care accounts (s.28); deferred payments agreements (s.34); transition (s.58); and advocacy (s.67). Under the proposals, the Independent Reviewer could not have been an employee of the local authority for the past three years prior to being appointed. The Independent Reviewer's role was to review whether the decision was reasonable with reference to the relevant regulations, guidance, facts and local policy, and where necessary could call upon relevant professional expertise (such as medical or social work expertise).[4] Originally the appeals scheme was due to be implemented on 1 April 2016. However, the Department of Health has announced that this reform will be delayed until April 2020.[5]

By virtue of s.125(4)(j) regulations made on the first exercise of the power in s.72 establishing the care and support appeals must be subject to the affirmative procedure in Parliament. Subsequent regulations that amend, repeal or modify the application of an Act of Parliament are also subject to the affirmative procedure (see s.125(4)(1)(k)). The affirmative procedure is discussed at para.1–161 above.

---

[1] *Hansard* (House of Commons: Public Bill Committee), 4 February 2014: Fifteenth Sitting, col.584 (Norman Lamb MP).

[2] Presumably this is a reference to A. Clyyd and Professor T. Hart, *A Review of the NHS Hospitals Complaints System*. See fn.4 above.

[3] *Hansard* (House of Commons: Public Bill Committee), 4 February 2014: Fifteenth Sitting, col.584 (Norman Lamb MP).

[4] See, Department of Health, The Care Act 2014: Consultation on draft regulations and guidance to implement the cap on care costs and policy proposals for a new appeals system for care and support (2015), Pt 2.

[5] *House of Commons Written Answers and Statements Daily Report*, Cap on Care Costs: Written Statement – HCWS145, 20 July 2015, pp.162 to 164 (Alastair Burt MP).

COMPLAINTS AND REDRESS

1–698   The following forms of complaints and redress remain available to individuals seeking to challenge the decision of a local authority.

Local authority complaints

1–699   Complaints about a local authority's discharge or failure to discharge a relevant function are handled according to regulations made under the Health and Social Care (Community Health and Standards) Act 2003.[1] The regulations establish a single complaints system for NHS and adult social care services.[2] Every "responsible body" (which includes the NHS, local authority and some independent providers) is required to set up arrangements for handing and considering complaints and designate a "responsible person" who must ensure compliance with the 2009 regulations, and a "complaints manager". But there is no prescribed process for dealing with complaints—this is left to the discretion of the NHS and local authority. The regulations provide that action must be taken, if necessary, in the light of the complaint.[3] This could include changes to practice and procedures to ensure a similar failure does not occur. The final report on the complaint must include details of any remedial action necessary and confirmation as to whether that action has been taken or will be taken.[4] The Local Government Act 2000 provides that the local authority can award financial compensation.

Local Government Ombudsman

1–700   A person who claims to have suffered an injustice as a result of maladministration in connection with any action taken by or on behalf of a local authority may complain to the Local Government Ombudsman.[5] It is not within its jurisdiction to determine the legality of administrative action or adjudicate on points of law—this remains the preserve of courts and tribunals. Before investigating a complaint, the ombudsman must be satisfied that the complaint has been drawn to the attention of the local authority in question and the authority has been afforded a reasonable opportunity to investigate and reply to the complaint.[6] In practice, the ombudsman will investigate a complaint before the statutory process has been exhausted where there has been a break down in trust between the complainant and authority, or where both parties agree.[7] Its jurisdiction includes self-funders who have arranged care from a registered provider without any local authority involvement and people whose care and support is being provided through a direct payment.[8]

In relation to remedies, the general objective of the ombudsman is to put the complainant in the position he or she would have been in but for the maladministration.[9] The ombudsman can recommend that the local authority take various actions, including providing an explanation, reconsidering a decision and providing compensation.[10] It can also recommend specific action, which in the sphere of social care may include the carrying out of a needs or carer's assessment, providing disabled facilities, reinstating services to

---

[1] Local Authority Social Services Complaints (England) Regulations 2009 (SI 2009/309).
[2] Complaints about social care services under the Children Act 1989 are subject to a separate statutory regime.
[3] Local Authority Social Services Complaints (England) Regulations 2009 (SI 2009/309) reg.4.
[4] Local Authority Social Services Complaints (England) Regulations 2009 (SI 2009/309) reg.14.
[5] Local Government Act 1974 s.25.
[6] Local Government Act 1974 s.26.
[7] J. White, "Community Care and the Local Government Ombudsman for England", (2006) 9 *Community Care Law Reports* 8.
[8] Local Government Act 1974 Pt 3A.
[9] Local Government Ombudsman, *Remedies: Guidance on Good Practice* 6 (2005), p.3.
[10] J. White, "Community Care and the Local Government Ombudsman for England" (2006) 9 *Community Care.*

implement a care plan, providing an independent advocate for an especially disadvantaged service user, and providing an apology for a service failure.[1]

Judicial review

A complainant may apply to the High Court for a review of the lawfulness of a decision, **1–701** action or failure to act in relation to the exercise of a public function, including by local authorities and NHS bodies.[2] The High Court can find that a decision is unlawful on the grounds that it is illegal, irrational or procedurally flawed. In such circumstances, the Court has the discretion to order the decision-maker to act, or abstain from acting, in a specified manner or can quash a decision and may remit or substitute its own decision. The court may also make a declaration or grant an injunction preventing or compelling action by a public body. The High Court may award damages in judicial review cases, but only in very limited circumstances.

It has been observed that judicial review has limitations as a remedy for many social care disputes of a factual nature. As noted in para.11–006 above, one of the proposals made to the Law Commission to review this area of law was based on concerns about the inadequacy of the system for challenging local authority decision-making. In particular, it was argued that courts undertaking judicial review were reluctant to interfere with local authority discretion over the outcome of decisions and confined their judgments to the process whereby decisions are made.[3] This has been confirmed in a line of community care cases which emphasise that the court should leave issues of fact:

"to the public authority to whom Parliament has entrusted the decision-making power, save in cases where it is obvious that the public body, consciously or unconsciously, are acting perversely".[4]

Mr Justice Collins acknowledged in *Gunter v South Western Staffordshire Primary Care Trust* that judicial review was an "unsatisfactory means" of dealing with cases where there are judgments to be made and factual issues in dispute:

"At best, it can identify failures to have regard to material considerations and a need for reconsideration. Very rarely if ever will it result in mandatory orders to the body which has the responsibility to reach the relevant decision".[5]

Human Rights Act 1998

The Human Rights Act 1998 gives further effect to rights and freedoms guaranteed under **1–702** the European Convention on Human Rights by bringing these rights into the sphere of domestic law. The "Convention rights" for the purpose of the 1988 Act are listed in Sch.1 to that Act.

The 1998 Act makes it unlawful for a public authority, such as a local authority, to act in a way that breaches a person's Convention rights.[6] Procedurally, an individual can bring an application for judicial review in the Administrative Court alleging that a public authority has breached s.6 of the 1998 Act. If the court finds the public authority has engaged in an

---

[1] J. White, "Community Care and the Local Government Ombudsman for England" (2006) 9 Community Care Law Reports 8, 11.

[2] Civil Procedure Rules r.54.1(2). A broad range of administrative decision-making is amenable to judicial review.

[3] Email from Michael and Henrietta Spink to the Law Commission (16 March 2007).

[4] *R (Ireneschild) v London Borough of Lambeth* [2007] EWCA Civ 234, at [44], referring to *Puhlhofer v Hillingdon London Borough Council* [1986] 84 LGR at [413] to [414].

[5] *Gunter v South Western Staffordshire Primary Care Trust* [2005] EWHC 1894 (Admin); 86 BMLR 60 at [19]. See also Mr Justice Collins, "Community Care and the Administrative Court" 9 *Community Care Law Reports* 5.

[6] Defined in s.1 of the Human Rights Act 1998. The Convention rights most relevant in the community care context are arts 2, 3, 5, 6, 8 and 14 of the ECHR.

unlawful act, it may grant such relief or remedy, or make such order within its powers as it considers just and appropriate.[1]

See also discussion at paras 1–715 to 1–720 below in respect of the remit of the Human Rights Act 1998, which has been extended by the Care Act.

THE MENTAL CAPACITY ACT AND PUBLIC LAW DECISIONS

1–703   In some cases, individuals who lack mental capacity (or someone on their behalf) have sought to challenge the local authority by arguing that a service or funding decision was not in their best interests under the Mental Capacity Act 2005. However, the courts have warned of the danger of a blurring of the distinction between statutory duties in a private law context (namely, to consider the best interests of an incapacitated adult), with public law challenges.[2] Fundamentally, the decision by a local authority to provide, or not to provide, a service is a public law decision, and judicial review remains the proper vehicle through which to challenge unreasonable or irrational decisions.[3] In contrast, decisions taken under the Mental Capacity Act are made when the assent of an individual is required. Section 1(5) requires that "an act done, or decision made . . . for or on behalf of the person who lacks capacity" must be in their best interests. The best interests decision-making criteria and procedures contained in s.4 are, therefore, "designed to be a substitute for the lack of independent capacity of the person to act or take decisions for him or herself" and "they come into play in circumstances where a person with capacity would take, or participate in the taking of, a decision".[4]

Therefore, where the decision to be reviewed is an incapacitated person's refusal to accept treatment or services which a public authority is willing to provide, this must be resolved by the best interests test. If the task is to review the decision of a public authority exercising its statutory responsibilities, this must be resolved through public law principles and the decision is susceptible to judicial review. The Supreme Court has confirmed that on an application under the Mental Capacity Act, "the court has no greater powers than the patient has if he were of full capacity".[5] In other words, the court may choose only between the available options; a best interest decision cannot be used as a way of putting pressure on a local authority to allocate its resources in a particular way.

Notwithstanding this distinction, there have been a number of cases where the Court of Protection has explored with public authorities the possibility of funding being made available for alternative packages of care, and sometimes has been assertive in doing so. For example, the Court has directed a local authority to make a decision whether it is prepared to fund an alternative package of support, and placed a condition on a local authority and care provider to ensure that "within available resources" reasonable steps are taken to increase the number of visits to the marital home for a woman deprived of her liberty in a care home.[6] But whilst "rigorous probing, searching questions and persuasion are permissible, pressure is not".[7] The court cannot create options where none exist,[8] and any negotiations:

"... are however a far cry from the court embarking on a 'best interests' trial with a view to determining whether or not an option which has been said by care provider (in the

---

[1] Human Rights Act 1998 s.8(3).
[2] *ACCG v MN* [2013] EWHC 3859 (COP) at [34].
[3] *Re MN* [2015] EWCA Civ 411.
[4] *R (Chatting) v Viridian Housing* [2012] EWHC 3595 (Admin) at [100] by Nicholas Paines QC.
[5] *Aintree University Hospitals NHS Foundation Trust v James* [2013] UKSC 67 at [11].
[6] *A Local Authority v PB* [2011] EWCOP 2675 at [21] to [22] and Bedford Borough Council v C [2015] EWCOP 25 at [182].
[7] *Re MN* [2015] EWCA Civ 411 at [36] and [81].
[8] *Holmes-Moorhouse v Richmond-upon-Thames London Borough Council* [2009] 1 WLR 413, by Baroness Hale at [30].

exercise of their statutory duties) not to be available, is nevertheless in the patient's best interest".[1]

The Court of Protection will however have a more direct role in cases where a public authority has assessed that a person who lacks capacity will be provided with services and has identified alternative packages of care that it is willing to fund. The Court can, in such cases, make a best interests decision in order to choose between the available options.[2] In effect, this would place the person in the same position as a person who had capacity who would normally participate in deciding which of the options should be provided.

In some cases the Court of Protection will be asked to approve the care plan put forward by the public authority. The only power of the court is to approve or refuse the care plan put forward, and it "cannot dictate to the public authority what the care plan should say".[3] However, in rare cases an impasse may occur where the Court does not approve the care plan, for example on the basis that it would breach the person's art.8 rights. The Court must then "select the lesser of two evils" endorsing the plan or dismissing the proceedings.[4]

UNITED NATIONS CONVENTION ON THE RIGHTS OF PERSONS WITH DISABILITIES

The United Nations Convention on the Rights of Persons with Disabilities does not pro- **1–704** vide a complaints and redress system for those seeking to challenge local authority decision-making. However, it does have an indirect influence on how those systems operate, particularly judicial review and the Human Rights Act 1998.

The United Nations General Assembly adopted the Convention in 2006. The Convention's stated purpose is to "promote, protect and ensure the full and equal enjoyment of all human rights and fundamental freedoms by all persons with disabilities, and to promote respect for their inherent dignity."[5] It has a wide field of application and encompasses civil and political rights as well as economic, social and cultural ones. These rights are extensive and cover matters such as the right to life, access to justice, independent living, education, work and cultural life. It also makes specific provision in respect of the rights of disabled women and disabled children.

The UK Government signed the Convention on 30 March 2007 and the optional protocol (which covers implementation and monitoring of the Convention) on 3 March 2009. The UK Parliament ratified the Convention on 8 June 2009. Consequently, the Convention is now legally binding on the Government in international law. However, the Convention has not been incorporated into UK law and is therefore not directly justiciable in UK courts. In other words, an individual cannot go to a UK court to complain about a breach of any of the rights in the Convention.

While the Convention does not form part of domestic law, it has an interpretative influence, particularly in human rights cases. The UK courts can—and do—refer to it when difficult questions need to be resolved or ambiguous provisions need to be interpreted.[6] Furthermore, the European Court of Human Rights has taken into account the Convention in assisting its interpretation of the European Convention on Human Rights.[7] The UK courts are required by the Human Rights Act 1998 to take account of this jurisprudence and the Government is bound by its judgments in cases against the

---

[1] *ACCG v MN* [2013] EWHC 3859 (COP) at [57]. Approved by Lord Justice Munby in *Re MN* [2015] EWCA Civ 411 at [81]
[2] *ACCG v MN* [2013] EWHC 3859 (COP).
[3] *Re MN* [2015] EWCA Civ 411 at [34].
[4] *Re MN* [2015] EWCA Civ 411 at [34]. Approved by Lord Justice Munby in *Re MN* [2015] EWCA Civ 411 at [81].
[5] UN Convention on the Rights of Persons with Disabilities art.1.
[6] *Burnip v Birmingham City Council* [2012] EWCA Civ 629 at [19] to [22].
[7] See, for example, *Stanev v Bulgaria* (17 January 2012) Application no.36760/06.

UK. Also, the EU ratified the Convention in 2010. This means that it must interpret EU law and regulation compatibly with the Convention. This gives the Convention some degree of direct influence on UK law.

The Convention requires the Government to report periodically to explain how the rights are being implemented. The Committee on the Rights of Persons with Disabilities will then examine the report and can make suggestions and general recommendations for appropriate changes to law and practice. The Optional Protocol to the Convention gives the Committee competence to examine individual complaints with regard to alleged violations of the Convention by States parties to the Protocol.

Article 19 of the Convention enshrines the right to independent living. This provision is considered in more detail at paras 1–019 to 1–020 above. The links between the Convention and rights to advocacy are discussed at para.1–661 above.

Subsection (1)

1–705   This gives the Secretary of State the power to make regulations providing for a process through which appeals may be made against decisions taken by a local authority in respect of individuals under Pt 1 of the Care Act. The subsection expressly provides that the decisions covered by the appeal system include those made prior to the coming into force of the first set of regulations under s.72. The explanatory notes state that:

> "It is the intention that regulations made under this section will come into force at the same time as the provisions relating to the funding cap, in April 2016. This means there will be a gap between the coming into force of the main provisions of Part 1 in April 2015 and the coming into force of regulations establishing a system under which decisions taken under Part 1 can be challenged. The regulations may therefore provide that such 'pre-commencement' decisions may be challenged under the system set up by the regulations, once it is established."[1]

As noted earlier, the reforms due to be implemented from 1 April 2016, including the cap on care costs system and the appeals system have been delayed until April 2020.

Subsection (2)

1–706   Amongst other things, the regulations may specify the type of decision that can be appealed and the details of the process that must be followed.

Subsection (2)(k) was introduced as a Government amendment at report stage in the House of Commons. It provides for investigations to be carried out into things done or not done by the person or body with power to consider the appeal (for example maladministration). This would enable overview of the appeals process itself and would, for example, enable the Secretary of State to provide for the involvement of the Local Government Ombudsman in the overall appeal process.[2]

Subsection (3)

1–707   This enables the regulations to include pre-conditions for bringing an appeal.

Subsection (4)

1–708   The regulations may provide for the appeal to be treated as, or as part of, an appeal brought or complaint made under another procedure, or for the appeal to be considered with any such appeal or complaint.

Subsection (5)

1–709   This provides for the establishment of a panel or other body to consider an appeal, and requiring an appeal to be considered by certain specified persons with relevant expertise or experience.

---

[1] Care Act: Explanatory Notes para.420.
[2] *Hansard* (House of Commons), 10 March 2014, Vol.577, col.90 (Norman Lamb MP).

Subsection (6)

Provision about representation and support for an individual may include provision relat- **1–710** ing to the provision of advocacy under s.67.

Subsection (7)

The regulations may make provision for an appeal or complaint to be made under **1–711** another procedure to be treated as, or as part of, an appeal brought under s.72, or considered with an appeal brought under s.72. Moreover, the regulations may make provision for matters raised in an appeal under s.72 to be taken into account by the person or body under the other procedure. This is intended to enable provision to be made concerning the interaction of the appeals system with other appeal and complaints systems.[1]

Subsection (8)

Regulations may include provision conferring functions on a statutory body. In order to **1–712** do so the regulations may need to amend or repeal primary legislation. Any such regulations are required to be made using the affirmative procedure in Parliament (see s.121(4)(k)). The affirmative procedure is discussed at para.1–161 above.

Subsection (9)

This allows for interim decisions to be made under the appeals process and for financial **1–713** adjustments to be made following a decision on the appeal.

MISCELLANEOUS

Human Rights Act 1998: provision of regulated care or support etc a public function

73.—(1) This section applies where— **1–714**

(a) in England, a registered care provider provides care and support to an adult or support to a carer, in the course of providing—

(i) personal care in a place where the adult receiving the personal care is living when the personal care is provided, or

(ii) residential accommodation together with nursing or personal care;

(b) in Wales, a person registered under Part 2 of the Care Standards Act 2000 provides care and support to an adult, or support to a carer, in the course of providing—

(i) personal care in a place where the adult receiving the personal care is living when the personal care is provided, or

(ii) residential accommodation together with nursing or personal care;

(c) in Scotland, a person provides advice, guidance or assistance to an adult or support to a carer, in the course of providing a care service which is registered under section 59 of the Public Services Reform (Scotland) Act 2010 and which consists of the provision of—

(i) personal care in a place where the adult receiving the personal care is living when the personal care is provided, or

(ii) residential accommodation together with nursing or personal care;

(d) in Northern Ireland, a person registered under Part 3 of the Health and Personal Social Services (Quality, Improvement and Regulation)

---

[1] Care Act: Explanatory Notes para.422.

(Northern Ireland) Order 2003 provides advice, guidance or assistance to an adult or services to a carer, in the course of providing—

(i) personal care in a place where the adult receiving the personal care is living when the personal care is provided, or

(ii) residential accommodation together with nursing or personal care.

In this section "the care or support" means the care and support, support, advice, guidance, assistance or services provided as mentioned above, and "the provider" means the person who provides the care or support.

(2) The provider is to be taken for the purposes of section 6(3)(b) of the Human Rights Act 1998 (acts of public authorities) to be exercising a function of a public nature in providing the care or support, if the requirements of subsection (3) are met.

(3) The requirements are that—

(a) the care or support is arranged by an authority listed in column 1 of the Table below, or paid for (directly or indirectly, and in whole or in part) by such an authority, and

(b) the authority arranges or pays for the care or support under a provision listed in the corresponding entry in column 2 of the Table.

TABLE

Authority	Provisions imposing duty or conferring power to meet needs
Local authority in England	Sections 2, 18, 19, 20, 38 and 49 of this Act.
Local authority in Wales	Part 4 and section 189 of the Social Services and Well-being (Wales) Act 2014. Section 51 of this Act.
Local authority in Scotland	Sections 12, 13A, 13B and 14 of the Social Work (Scotland) Act 1968. Section 3 of the Social Care (Self-directed Support) (Scotland) Act 2013.
Health and Social Care trust	Article 15 of the Health and Personal Social Services (Northern Ireland) Order 1972. Section 52 of this Act.
Authority (within the meaning of section 10 of the Carers and Direct Payments Act (Northern Ireland) 2002)	Section 2 of the Carers and Direct Payments Act (Northern Ireland) 2002.

(4) In this section—

"local authority in England" means a local authority for the purposes of this Part;

"local authority in Wales" means a local authority for the purposes of the Social Services and Well-being (Wales) Act 2014;

"local authority in Scotland" means a council constituted under section 2 of the Local Government etc. (Scotland) Act 1994;

"nursing care", for England, Wales and Northern Ireland, has the same meaning as in the Health and Social Care Act 2008 (Regulated Activities) Regulations 2010, as amended from time to time;

"personal care"—
(a) for England, Wales and Northern Ireland, has the same meaning as in the Health and Social Care Act 2008 (Regulated Activities) Regulations 2010, as amended from time to time;
(b) for Scotland, has the same meaning as in Part 5 of the Public Services Reform (Scotland) Act 2010, as amended from time to time.

GENERAL NOTE

The Human Rights Act 1998 applies to all public authorities and to other bodies when **1–715** they are performing functions of a public nature.[1] This means that individuals have a direct cause of action against such bodies and access to legal remedies envisaged in the 1998 Act in relation to any incompatibility with Convention rights. However, the case of *YL v Birmingham City Council* identified a loophole whereby care home services provided by private and third sector organisations under a contract with the local authority were not considered to fall within the definition of public function under the 1998 Act.[2] Therefore it was argued that many service users had no direct legal remedy to hold their providers to account under the Human Rights Act. The then Government attempted to close this loophole through s.145 of the Health and Social Care Act 2008 which clarified that residential care services provided or arranged by local authorities under the National Assistance Act 1948 are covered by the Human Rights Act.

JOINT COMMITTEE ON THE DRAFT CARE AND SUPPORT BILL

However, concerns were expressed to the Joint Committee on the draft Care and Support **1–716** Bill that s.145 continued to exclude home care services provided under contact to local authorities and care home residents not placed under the National Assistance Act 1948 (for example, those provided with residential care under s.117 of the Mental Health Act 1983). The Government's view, as stated in a note submitted to the Joint Committee, was that all providers of publicly arranged care and support services:

". . . including private and voluntary sector providers, should consider themselves to be bound by the duty imposed by section 6 of the Human Rights Act and not to act in a way that is incompatible with a Convention right".

However, the Joint Committee concluded that, as a result of the decision in the *YL* case, statutory provision is required to ensure this.[3] This was rejected by the Government.[4]

HOUSE OF LORDS AMENDMENT (CLAUSE 48)

The issue was raised in the House of Lords during the passage of the Care Bill. At **1–717** Committee stage, Lord Pannick—in support of an amendment to deem all service providers

---

[1] Human Rights Act 1998 s.6.
[2] *YL v Birmingham City Council* [2007] UKHL 27; [2008] 1 A.C. 95.
[3] House of Lords House of Commons Joint Committee on the Draft Care and Support Bill, *Draft Care and Support Bill Report, Session 2012–13*, paras 285 to 289.
[4] Department of Health, *The Care Bill explained—including a response to consultation and pre-legislative scrutiny on the draft Care and Support Bill*, pp.76 to 77.

regulated by the Care Quality Commission as exercising a public function for the purposes of the Human Rights Act 1998—said:

> "The vulnerability of the person receiving care, and the risk of abuse, mean that the law should now impose duties on the provider under the Human Rights Act in all these circumstances to encourage the maintenance of high standards and provide a direct remedy for the victim in appropriate cases."[1]

However, the Government rejected this amendment and set out that:

> "The Government's position has been that all providers of publicly arranged health and social care services, including those in the private and voluntary sectors, should consider themselves to be bound by the duty imposed by Section 6 of the Human Rights Act 1998 not to act in a way that is incompatible with the convention rights. The Care Quality Commission, as the regulator, is subject to the Human Rights Act, which may give rise to a positive obligation to ensure that individuals are protected from treatment that is contrary to their convention rights. As noble Lords will know, the Ministry of Justice is concerned that every time you add a provision, you may inadvertently have an effect on the umbrella application of the Act."[2]

The Government also confirmed that following the repeal of the National Assistance Act 1948, there would be a consequential amendment to s.145 of the Health and Social Care Act 2008 "so that there will be no regression in human rights legislation".[3]

The issue was raised again at report stage. Lord Low tabled a similar amendment to that tabled at Committee stage, arguing that the phrase "should consider themselves to be bound" is not the same as "covered by law".[4] The amendment was supported by Lord Hope, having recently returned from a period of disqualification following his retirement from the Supreme Court. He described s.6 as "rather difficult to apply in practice" and (quoting Lord Neuberger, in *YL*) agreed that any reasoned decision about the meaning of functions of a public nature, "risked falling foul of . . . circularity, preconception and arbitrariness".[5] He also criticised the Government position that all providers should consider themselves bound by s.6 of the Human Rights Act:

> "Comments of the kind that were made, that people should consider themselves bound by a Convention right, however well intentioned, do not have the force of law. They could not be relied upon, for example, in a court to guide a judge about the meaning of Section 6(3)(b) in the particular context. Therefore, they leave the law in a state of uncertainty because they do not have the force of law, and they have no relevance to a decision that the court would have to take."[6]

The Government had also been quoted as saying that the case law supports a broad application of s.6 and provides that individual factors should be considered in each case. Therefore, *YL* was "a case on the particular facts, and it does not necessarily follow that the reasoning in that case will be applied to other social care settings".[7] Lord Hope disagreed and suggested that that the implications of the *YL* go far wider than its own facts, due to the distinction between private, profit-making bodies on the one hand and state or Government-owned bodies with public functions on the other.[8] He went on to say:

> "A failure by Parliament to grasp this opportunity now and to make it clear will be noticed. There is a risk that, if that opportunity is not taken by Parliament now, courts

---

[1] *Hansard* (House of Lords), 22 July 2013, Vol.474, col.1107.
[2] *Hansard* (House of Lords), 22 July 2013,Vol.747, col.1118 (Baroness Northover).
[3] *Hansard* (House of Lords), 22 July 2013,Vol.747, col.1118 (Baroness Northover).
[4] *Hansard* (House of Lords), 16 October 2013, Vol.748, cols 544 to 546.
[5] *Hansard* (House of Lords), 16 October 2013, Vol.748, col.548.
[6] *Hansard* (House of Lords), 16 October 2013, Vol.748, col.549.
[7] *Hansard* (House of Lords), 16 October 2013, Vol.748, col.547 (Lord Willis).
[8] *Hansard* (House of Lords), 16 October 2013, Vol.748, col.550.

may take this as a sign that Parliament is content with the law as it stands and may be understood to be on the basis of *YL*."[1]

On the question of whether the amendment would have wider implications, he saw no real risk that, by dealing with the matter in a targeted way, it will be taken as a signal in the courts that there is some wider reach in s.6 from that which was being discussed in *YL*.[2]

The amendment was also supported by Lord Warner who pointed out that the Care Act will alter matters due to the introduction of the cap on care costs, in that any self-funder who reached the cap would have their care funded by the state and therefore fall within the remit of the Human Rights Act.[3]

The Government opposed the amendment on the basis that it would expand s.6 of the Human Rights Act into privately arranged contracts with no state involvement and include claims that cannot be brought before the European Court of Human Rights. It also argued that the reformed role of the Care Quality Commission would address poor care.[4] However, the Government lost the division and the amendment was agreed by 247 to 218 votes.[5] It became cl.48 of the Care Bill.[6]

HOUSE OF COMMONS: DELETION OF CLAUSE 48

This issue was revisited in the House of Commons. At Committee stage, the Government **1–718** tabled an amendment to delete cl.48. It argued that if this became law:

". . . it would be the first time the [Human Rights Act] extended into the purely private sphere, in this case the relationship between an individual and a private care provider. If that principle were established, other interest groups self-evidently could argue that they should also be able to challenge private providers on human rights grounds in other areas, taking us further and further from the purpose of the Act into duplication and overlap with other legislation."[7]

It also referred to the clause as "tokenism, not real protection"—arguing that the risk of prosecution by the Care Quality Commission was a greater protection than the risk of a claim under the Human Rights Act in a civil court.[8]

The Government also clarified that its argument that care providers should consider themselves covered by the Human Rights Act, related to providers of publicly funded non-residential care. It did not apply to care given by an entirely private provider to a person who pays for it themselves; instead such persons have rights in contract. The Government also explained that where the care is arranged by the local authority but funded privately, the individual may make a claim against the public body that arranged the service, namely the local authority—which is covered by the Human Rights Act.[9]

Finally the Government argued that self-funders are in a fundamentally different position to other service users:

". . . while an individual with private funding has the choice of state and private providers, the relationship is different for those who are funded publicly because they have less choice, perhaps only through publicly provided services? The only option being

---

[1] *Hansard* (House of Lords), 16 October 2013, Vol.748, col.550.
[2] *Hansard* (House of Lords), 16 October 2013, Vol.748, col.550.
[3] *Hansard* (House of Lords), 16 October 2013, Vol.748, col.555.
[4] *Hansard* (House of Lords), 16 October 2013, Vol.748, cols 558 to 559 (Earl Howe).
[5] *Hansard* (House of Lords), 16 October 2013, Vol.748, cols 562 to 565.
[6] Care Bill 123 2013–2–14.
[7] *Hansard* (House of Commons: Public Bill Committee), 21 January 2014 (PM): Eighth Sitting, col.298 (Norman Lamb MP).
[8] *Hansard* (House of Commons: Public Bill Committee), 21 January 2014 (PM): Eighth Sitting, col.300 (Norman Lamb MP).
[9] *Hansard* (House of Commons: Public Bill Committee), 21 January 2014 (PM): Eighth Sitting, col.305 (Norman Lamb MP).

The section establishes that care providers who are regulated by the Care Quality Commission in England or by equivalent bodies in the rest of the UK, when providing care and support arranged or funded in whole or in part by local authorities, are exercising a public function for the purposes of the Human Rights Act. This applies to the provision of residential and non-residential care and support. The Government stated:

> "It makes it clear that providers of publicly arranged or funded care and support, both residential and non-residential, provided on behalf of a local authority to an individual, are bound by the Human Rights Act."[1]

The Government described the Human Rights Act as "an entrenched enactment which the devolved legislatures cannot modify, but its application should be the same across the UK".[2] Section 73 therefore includes reference to Wales, Scotland and Northern Ireland.

However, the Government was concerned to make clear that this amendment did not establish any precedent. Earl Howe stated:

> "It is important to bear in mind that the scope of application of the Human Rights Act matters to lots of other people beyond the care sector. The Government believe that it is not appropriate to pick and choose which people or bodies are expressly made subject to the Human Rights Act. That is why I want to make it clear that this amendment would not set a precedent for any future occasions where there are perceived to be gaps in the coverage of the Human Rights Act."[3]

The amendment was supported by Lord Lester on behalf of the Joint Committee on Human Rights.[4] Lord Hope also added his view that it does not set a precedent:

> "So far as the judges are concerned, they would not regard it as such at all; the precedent is in the Act itself . . . It is a precisely targeted measure."[5]

In the House of Commons, Paul Burstow MP welcomed the amendment, stating that it marked "the end of a story of seven years of dealing with a gap in the law that was opened by a court judgment".[6]

Subsections (1) and (2)

1–721   These subsections make clear that registered care providers are bound by the Human Rights Act if they are providing personal care in the person's home or residential accommodation with nursing or personal care. Subsections (1) and (2) must be read alongside subs.(3) which also requires that such care must have been arranged or funded by a local authority.

Section 48(1) defines a registered care provider in England as a person registered under Ch.2 of Pt 1 of the Health and Social Care Act 2008.

In the House of Commons the Government was asked whether the provision of non-personal care was covered (such as assisting people with learning disabilities and mental health problems to participate in activities or to get to appointments). The Government stated that:

> ". . . like clause 48 of the Bill, as originally drafted, and s.145 of the Health and Social Act 2008, which was the preceding provision, Lords amendment 11B relates to providers of social care registered with the Care Quality Commission, covering personal care provided at home and in residential care settings. The amendment covers physical

---

[1] *Hansard* (House of Lords), 7 May 2014, Vol.753, col.1486 (Earl Howe).
[2] *Hansard* (House of Lords), 7 May 2014, Vol.753, col.1486 (Earl Howe).
[3] *Hansard* (House of Lords), 7 May 2014, Vol.753, col.1486 (Earl Howe).
[4] *Hansard* (House of Lords), 7 May 2014, Vol.753, col.1486 (Lord Lester).
[5] *Hansard* (House of Lords), 7 May 2014, Vol.753, col.1488 (Lord Hope).
[6] *Hansard* (House of Commons), 12 May 2014, Vol.580, col.445 (Paul Burstow MP).

assistance—for example, prompting someone to take their medication, dress, eat, drink and perform activities of daily living—but not non-personal care."[1]

The Government was also asked to clarify whether self-funders who exercise their right under s.18(3) to ask the authority to arrange their care, would enjoy the protection of the Human Rights Act. In response the Government confirmed that "when self-funders start to receive support from the local authority, they will indeed be covered by the Human Rights Act 1998."[2]

Subsection (3)

This provides that registered care providers are bound by the Human Rights Act only if **1–722** the care and support has been arranged or paid for (directly or indirectly) by the local authority. In England, this applies when care and support has been arranged or paid for under:

- s.2 (duty to prevent needs);
- s.18 (duty to meet needs for care and support);
- s.19 (power to meet needs for care and support);
- s.20 (duty and power to meet a carer's needs for support);
- s.38 (duty to meet needs in cases where an adult has moved local authority areas and an assessment has not been completed on the day of the move); and
- s.48 (duty to provide temporary services in cases of provider failure).

In the House of Lords, the Government confirmed that the wording of subs.(3)(a) ensures that the definition of a public function covers social care provided by regulated providers paid for by direct payments:

"The words used are: if the local authority pays 'directly or indirectly'. 'Indirectly' is to cover direct payments when the local authority provides the money to the individual who then goes to the regulated provider him or herself."[3]

The Government clarified its intention that the list in subs.(3) should cover all care and support arranged or paid for by all relevant authorities in the UK:

". . . all relevant regulated care and support across England and the Devolved Administrations is included in the list. It is our intention that the effect of this clause should be the same across the UK. We have worked very closely with the devolved Administrations to ensure that this is the case as far as possible. There is a potential source of confusion in the wording because in Scottish legislation social care is referred to in different terminology, but the net effect of what we are doing should mean that this applies in an even-handed way across the country."[4]

The Government also clarified that the wording of subs.(3)(a) ("paid for (directly or indirectly, and in whole or in part) by such an authority") also covers situations where a personal contribution is made towards the cost of care and support arranged by the local authority:"in other words, even if the local authority funds only part of the care, it will be covered".[5] In response to a question by Lord Hope, the Government confirmed that it also covers cases where the local authority itself is providing the regulated care or support (Lord Hope had raised a specific query regarding the position of people with mental health problems or learning disabilities who need assistance to enable them to participate in the activities being provided or get access to them).[6]

---

[1] *Hansard* (House of Commons), 12 May 2014, Vol.580, col.449 (Dr Daniel Poulter MP).
[2] *Hansard* (House of Commons), 12 May 2014, Vol.580, col.449 (Dr Daniel Poulter MP).
[3] *Hansard* (House of Lords), 7 May 2014, Vol.753, col.1490 (Earl Howe).
[4] *Hansard* (House of Lords), 7 May 2014, Vol.753, col.1490 (Earl Howe).
[5] *Hansard* (House of Lords), 7 May 2014, Vol.753, col.1490 (Earl Howe).
[6] *Hansard* (House of Lords), 7 May 2014, Vol.753, col.1490 (Earl Howe).

Discharge of hospital patients with care and support needs

1–723   **74.**—Schedule 3 (which includes provision about the discharge of hospital patients with care and support needs) has effect.

GENERAL NOTE

Section 74 introduces the provisions about delayed discharges, the details of which are set out in Sch.3 (see para.1–845 below).

After-care under the Mental Health Act 1983

1–724   **75.**—(1) In section 117 of the Mental Health Act 1983 (after-care), in subsection (2), after "to provide" insert "or arrange for the provision of".

(2) In subsection (2D) of that section, for the words from "as if" to the end substitute "as if the words "provide or" were omitted."

(3) In subsection (3) of that section, after "means the local social services authority" insert "—

(a) if, immediately before being detained, the person concerned was ordinarily resident in England, for the area in England in which he was ordinarily resident;

(b) if, immediately before being detained, the person concerned was ordinarily resident in Wales, for the area in Wales in which he was ordinarily resident; or

(c) in any other case".

(4) After that subsection insert—

"(4) Where there is a dispute about where a person was ordinarily resident for the purposes of subsection (3) above—

(a) if the dispute is between local social services authorities in England, section 40 of the Care Act 2014 applies to the dispute as it applies to a dispute about where a person was ordinarily resident for the purposes of Part 1 of that Act;

(b) if the dispute is between local social services authorities in Wales, section 195 of the Social Services and Well-being (Wales) Act 2014 applies to the dispute as it applies to a dispute about where a person was ordinarily resident for the purposes of that Act;

(c) if the dispute is between a local social services authority in England and a local social services authority in Wales, it is to be determined by the Secretary of State or the Welsh Ministers.

(5) The Secretary of State and the Welsh Ministers shall make and publish arrangements for determining which of them is to determine a dispute under subsection (4)(c); and the arrangements may, in particular, provide for the dispute to be determined by whichever of them they agree is to do so."

(5) After subsection (5) insert—

"(6) In this section, "after-care services", in relation to a person, means services which have both of the following purposes—

(a) meeting a need arising from or related to the person's mental disorder; and

(b) reducing the risk of a deterioration of the person's mental condition (and, accordingly, reducing the risk of the person requiring admission to a hospital again for treatment for mental disorder)."

(6) After section 117 of that Act insert—
"117A After-care: preference for particular accommodation
    (1) The Secretary of State may by regulations provide that where—

    (a) the local social services authority under section 117 is, in discharging its duty under subsection (2) of that section, providing or arranging for the provision of accommodation for the person concerned;
    (b) the person concerned expresses a preference for particular accommodation; and
    (c) any prescribed conditions are met, the local social services authority must provide or arrange for the provision of the person's preferred accommodation.

    (2) Regulations under this section may provide for the person concerned, or a person of a prescribed description, to pay for some or all of the additional cost in prescribed cases.

    (3) In subsection (2), "additional cost" means the cost of providing or arranging for the provision of the person's preferred accommodation less the amount that the local social services authority would expect to be the usual cost of providing or arranging for the provision of accommodation of that kind.

    (4) The power to make regulations under this section—

    (a) is exercisable only in relation to local social services authorities in England;
    (b) includes power to make different provision for different cases or areas."

(7) The ways in which a local authority may discharge its duty under section 117 of the Mental Health Act 1983 include by making direct payments; and for that purpose Part 1 of Schedule 4 (which includes modifications of the provisions of this Part relating to direct payments) has effect.

(8) In section 53 of the Social Services and Well-being (Wales) Act 2014 (direct payments: further provision), at the end insert—

    "(11) The ways in which a local authority may discharge its duty under section 117 of the Mental Health Act 1983 include by making direct payments; and for that purpose Schedule A1 (which includes modifications of sections 50 and 51 and this section) has effect."

(9) Before Schedule 1 to that Act insert the Schedule A1 contained in Part 2 of Schedule 4 to this Act.

(10) In section 163 of that Act (ordinary residence), after subsection (4) insert—

    "(4A) A person who is being provided with accommodation under section 117 of the Mental Health Act 1983 (after-care) is to be treated for the purposes of this Act as ordinarily resident in the area of the local authority, or the local authority in England, on which the duty to provide that person with services under that section is imposed."

(11) In consequence of subsections (7) to (9), in subsection (2C) of section 117 of the Mental Health Act 1983—

    (a) in paragraph (a), for "regulations under section 57 of the Health and Social Care Act 2001 or" substitute "—

> (i) sections 31 to 33 of the Care Act 2014 (as applied by Schedule 4 to that Act),
>
> (ii) sections 50, 51 and 53 of the Social Services and Well-being (Wales) Act 2014 (as applied by Schedule A1 to that Act), or
>
> (iii) regulations under",
>
> > (b) in paragraph (b), after "apart from" insert "those sections (as so applied) or".

(12) In the case of a person who, immediately before the commencement of subsections (3) and (4), is being provided with after-care services under section 117 of the Mental Health Act 1983, the amendments made by those subsections do not apply while those services are continuing to be provided to that person.

(13) In section 145 of the Mental Health Act 1983 (interpretation), for the definition of "local social services authority" substitute—

"local social services authority" means—

(a) an authority in England which is a local authority for the purposes of Part 1 of the Care Act 2014, or

(b) an authority in Wales which is a local authority for the purposes of the Social Services and Well-being (Wales) Act 2014."

GENERAL NOTE

1–725   Section 117 of the Mental Health Act 1983 requires the NHS and local social services authorities, in co-operation with voluntary agencies, to provide after-care to patients detained in hospital for treatment under ss.3, 37, 45A, 47 or 48 of the 1983 Act, who then cease to be detained and leave hospital. The s.117 duty applies to relevant patients who:

- have been discharged from hospital;
- are granted leave of absence under s.17 of the 1983 Act;
- have been placed on a Community Treatment Order or Guardianship;
- leave hospital, having remained in hospital voluntarily after ceasing to be detained; and
- have been released from prison having spent part of their sentence detained in hospital under a relevant section of the 1983 Act.

In the House of Lords, Lord Patel set out the reasons why these patients are singled out under s.117:

"The group of people to whom section 117 applies are the most vulnerable in the mental health system. They have been detained in hospital for psychiatric treatment following an established diagnosis. There are two groups, one of which is made up of those detained under section 3 of the Act, and the other of those detained by the criminal justice system for in-patient treatment. It is likely that those in both groups will have had extensive previous contact with psychiatric services and support, which have failed them and been unsuccessful, hence they require longer-term detention for treatment."[1]

In respect of the duty to provide after-care services, Maden and Spencer-Lane argue that:

"The term 'after-care' is a misnomer left over from the days when mental health care was mainly given in hospitals. In modern services, the vast majority of mental health treatment is delivered to patients in the community. Admission is the exception and

---

[1] *Hansard* (House of Lords), 29 July 2013, Vol.747, col.1569.

community care the norm. After-care has unfortunate resonance with the word 'after-thought'. Yet to focus on inpatient care to the detriment of management in the community is to allow the tail to wag the dog in a way that increases risks for patients and staff alike. Most criticism in homicide inquiries is directed at community care rather than inpatient management or discharge decisions; and the period following discharge is one of the times of highest risk for suicide."[1]

At an early stage of its review, the Law Commission concluded that s.117 should remain as a separate duty to provide after-care services in the 1983 Act and will not be consolidated into the adult social care statute. The main reasons were:

- s.117 applies to a specific group of former mental health patients whose needs are linked directly to the 1983 Act since services are required in order to reduce their chance of being readmitted to hospital; and
- s.117 cannot be described as a pure social care enactment, since it establishes a joint duty on social services and the NHS, and would not fit easily into the new scheme.[2]

Instead, the Commission considered how s.117 could be more fully integrated within the new adult social care legal framework. Its recommendations (discussed in more detail below) included defining after-care services and extending to s.117 service users the ordinary residence rules, choice of accommodation provisions, and top-up payments.[3] Section 75 of the Care Act implements most of the Law Commission's recommendations in this area.

It should be noted that the Care Act 2014 and Children and Families Act 2014 (Consequential Amendments) Order 2015 provides that the duty to assess under s.47 of the National Health Service and Community Care Act 1990 will continue to apply in England for the purposes of after-care services under s.117 of the Mental Health Act 1983.[4]

THE STRENGTH OF THE SECTION 117 DUTY

Section 117 originated as an opposition amendment to the Mental Health (Amendment) **1–726** Bill 1981. The then Government initially opposed the amendment, but later accepted it in the mistaken belief that it merely duplicated the general duties to provide services under the National Health Service Act 1977.[5] However, case law has confirmed that s.117 goes much further by placing an enforceable joint duty on both social services and the NHS to consider the after-care needs of each individual to whom it relates.[6] Once it has been decided that a patient needs specific services under s.117, there is a duty on the authorities to provide the service in question irrespective of resource considerations. This means that the NHS and social services cannot refuse to make suitable aftercare arrangements on the sole ground of lack of resources. However, in some cases the courts have accepted that there may be practical difficulties in carrying out this duty; for example, if there are no places available in the required residential care. In these types of cases, it is accepted that mental health services must use their best endeavours to arrange suitable aftercare services.[7]

---

[1] A. Maden and T. Spencer-Lane, *Essential Mental Health Law: A Guide to the Revised Mental Health Act and the Mental Capacity Act 2005* (London: Hammersmith press, 2010), p.113.

[2] Law Commission, *Adult Social Care: Scoping Report* (2008), para.4.192.

[3] Law Commission, *Adult Social Care*, paras 11.71 to 11.129.

[4] The Care Act 2014 and Children and Families Act 2014 (Consequential Amendments) Order 2015 (SI 2015/914).

[5] *Hansard* (House of Lords), 23 February 1982, Vol.427, cols 913 to 915 (Lord Elton).

[6] *R. v Ealing Health Authority Ex p Fox* [1993] 1 W.L.R. 373.

[7] *R. (IH) v Secretary of State* [2003] UKHL 59.

CHARGING FOR SECTION 117 SERVICES

1–727   In *R. (Stennett) v Manchester City Council*, the House of Lords considered whether s.117 itself required the provision of after-care services or whether it merely operates as a gateway section to trigger provisions under other statutory provisions. Counsel for the local authority had argued that s.117 services were provided under other provisions, such as community care legislation, and therefore local authorities may charge for such services. However, Lord Steyn concluded that s.117 was incapable of being read in this way, and held that s.117 imposes a free-standing duty to provide after-care services and is not a gateway duty. Since s.117 contains no charging provision, it follows that there is no right to charge for the after-care services.[1]

It should be stressed that the prohibition on charging only applies to s.117 after-care. Patients who are not under s.117—for example, those detained under s.2 of the 1983 Act or informal patients—can be charged for services. Some of those who responded to the Law Commission's consultation paper argued it was inequitable that such patients are not eligible for free s.117 services, while those detained under s.3 were eligible even though their needs are often not objectively different.[2] In *Stennett*, counsel for the local authority described this scenario as "the anomaly of the compliant and non-compliant patients in adjacent beds"; although the point was rejected by Lord Steyn as being "too simplistic" on the basis that there "may well be a reasonable view that generally patients admitted under ss.3 and 37 pose greater risks . . . than compliant patients" and moreover "Parliament necessarily legislates for the generality of cases".[3]

It is worth noting that the adjacent beds argument can be used to support the view that the right to free s.117 services should be abolished, and the view that the provision of free after-care services should be extended to all formal and informal patients under the 1983 Act.

RECIPROCITY

1–728   Establishing entitlement under s.117 is of key importance for service users. This is not just because of the inability to charge for services, but also because of the strong individually enforceable nature of the s.117 duty (see above). On the one hand, it has been argued that s.117 reflects the legal principle of reciprocity, that "when society imposes the exercise of compulsory powers on a person, there is a reciprocal right for that person to have services provided to help them get better".[4] This argument was evident during the passage of the Care Bill, at Committee stage in the House of Commons, when Grahame M. Morris MP stated that s.117 services must be free of charge in recognition of the fact that the individual has been detained by the state and therefore the state has a "duty of care to do everything possible to give them back their freedom and support outside hospital".[5] On the other side, s.117 can be described as a historical accident, the significance of which has arisen as a result of a misunderstanding by the Government at the time of its introduction (see above) and unclear drafting rather than any underlying legal principle. The decision in *Stennett*, for instance, was not reached primarily on the basis of reciprocity but on the technical question of whether the construction of s.117 established a gateway or free-standing duty. Indeed, no such principle of reciprocity has been found in other contexts involving the detention of vulnerable people; for instance, case law has confirmed that it is permissible to charge care home residents who are deprived of their liberty under the Mental Capacity Act

---

[1]   *R. (Stennett) v Manchester City Council* [2002] UKHL 34; [2002] 2 A.C. 1127 at [7] and [10].

[2]   See Law Commission, *Adult Social Care: Consultation Analysis* (2011), paras 11.267 to 11.269.

[3]   *R. (Stennett) v Manchester City Council* [2002] UKHL 34; [2002] 2 A.C. 1127 at [13].

[4]   *The Draft Mental Health Bill*, Report of the House of Lords and House of Commons Joint Committee, Volume 1 HL 79-1, HC 95-1 (2004–05), para.346.

[5]   *Hansard* (House of Commons: Public Bill Committee), 23 January 2014 (PM):Tenth Sitting, col.376.

2005.[1] Nevertheless, the observations of Lord Steyn in *Stennett* do suggest an element of reciprocity, at least in respect of non-voluntary after-care services, when he concluded:

> "If the argument of the authorities is accepted that there is a power to charge these patients such a view of the law would not be testimony to our society attaching a high value to the need to care after the exceptionally vulnerable."[2]

JOINT DUTY

Section 117 is a joint duty placed on the NHS and social services authorities. In *R.* **1–729** *(Watson) v Richmond upon Thames LBC,* Lord Justice Otton recognised that as a joint duty, s.117 may help to prevent people from falling between the gaps between services and encourage cross funding.[3]

The Law Commission felt that it was not clear whether the s.117 duty falls jointly and severally on health and social services authorities, in that both are responsible for the entire duty, or whether the duty falls primarily on health authorities to provide health care after-care and social services authorities to provide social care after-care. However, the Commission argued that it would be unlikely for a court to regard a health body as being accountable for the provision of social care after-care, or a social services authority as being accountable for health care after-care. But in its consultation paper the Commission accepted that the position is not clear in law and this could cause difficulties.[4]

By the time the Law Commission came to write its final report the Government had already introduced the Health and Social Care Bill 2010–11 into Parliament which, amongst other matters proposed to amend s.117 to provide that the NHS is responsible only for the health (rather than social care) services provided under s.117.[5] The Commission concluded that the case for dividing the s.117 duty had been strengthened as a result of the Government's Bill, and it would be confusing to retain s.117 as a joint duty as it relates to social care services, when health care after-care is the sole responsibility of the NHS.[6] However, as a result of opposition in Parliament, the Government was forced to abandon an attempt to amend s.117. The Government subsequently confirmed its intention to preserve the joint duty in s.117.[7]

GATEWAY DUTY

As noted above, case law has confirmed that s.117 imposes a free-standing duty to pro- **1–730** vide after-care services and is not a gateway provision that leads to services being provided under other statutory provisions.[8] In other words, services are provided under s.117 itself, and not under other legislation that normally governs the provision of health and social care services, for example the National Health Service Act 2006 and the Children Act 1989. The Law Commission was attracted to the possibility of recasting s.117 from a free-standing duty to a gateway provision. In effect, any adult social care after-care services would be in law regarded as services provided under the new adult social care statute. The main advantage would be that the rules that applied to a person's care package would be the same, irrespective of whether the service user was eligible for s.117 after-care or whether they were a non-s.117 service user, and that a number of uncertainties, complications and

---

[1] *DM v Doncaster Metropolitan Council* [2011] EWHC 3652 (Admin).

[2] *R. (Stennett) v Manchester City Council* [2002] UKHL 34; [2002] 2 A.C. 1127 at [15].

[3] *R. (Watson) v Richmond upon Thames LBC* (2000) 3 CCLR 276 at 285(A).

[4] Law Commission, *Adult Social Care: A Consultation Paper*, Consultation Paper No.192 (2010), paras 11.73 to 11.77.

[5] Bill 132 2010–11, cl.32(2).

[6] Law Commission, *Adult Social Care*, paras 11.93 to 11.99.

[7] Department of Health, Reforming the Law for Adult Care and Support: The Government's Response to Law Commission Report 326 on Adult Social Care (TSO, July 2012), Cm.8379, para.11.30.

[8] *R. (Stennett) v Manchester City Council* [2002] UKHL 34; [2002] 2 A.C. 1127 at [7] and [10].

anomalies would be removed. For example, the Commission was concerned that the choice of accommodation directions and additional payment regulations did not apply to s.117 services, and the relationship between s.117 and the eligibility criteria was uncertain. It therefore recommended that s.117 should become a gateway duty but only on the basis that s.117 services would remain free of charge.[1]

In the Health and Social Care Bill 2010–11—which was published before the Law Commission's final report—the Government proposed to introduce a form of gateway for the provision of s.117 health care after-care services. The Bill provided that the duty on the NHS must be regarded as being a duty under s.3 of the National Health Act 2006. As a result, references in legislation to services under s.3 of the 2006 Act (or the 2006 Act generally) would automatically include references to services commissioned by the NHS consortia under s.117.[2] But as a result of opposition in Parliament, it was forced to abandon this reform. The Government subsequently confirmed its intention not to change the status of s.117 as a free-standing duty.[3]

DURATION OF SECTION 117

1–731   Although the duty to provide aftercare begins when the patient leaves hospital, the *Mental Health Act Code of Practice* advises that planning should begin immediately after admission.[4] The Code also recognises that whilst the NHS and social services are under a duty to provide s.117 services, the patient is under no obligation to accept them, but any refusal should be fully informed and should not prevent a patient from receiving services at a later stage if there is a change of mind.[5]

There is no time limit on the s.117 obligation. Section 117(2) states that the duty to provide after-care services will cease if the NHS and social services authority are satisfied "that the person concerned is no longer in need of such services" and that they shall not be so satisfied in the case of patients subject to a Community Treatment Order. In effect, the duty to provide after-care continues for as long as the patient needs the service, including for the entire period of a Community Treatment Order in all cases, and after the cessation of a Community Treatment Order when necessary.

A joint health services and local authority circular provides that:

> "It is for the authority responsible for providing particular services to take the lead in deciding whether those services are no longer required. The patient, his/her carer and other agencies should always be consulted."[6]

The Mental Health Act Code of Practice advises that after-care services should not be withdrawn solely on the grounds that:

- the patient has been discharged from specialist mental health services;
- an arbitrary period has passed since the care was first provided;
- the patient is deprived of their liberty under the Mental Capacity Act 2005;
- the patient returns to hospital informally or under s.2; or
- the patient is no longer on a Community Treatment Order or s.17 leave.[7]

---

[1] Law Commission, *Adult Social Care*, paras 11.102 to 11.111.

[2] Bill 132 2010–11, cl.32(4).

[3] Department of Health, *Reforming the Law for Adult Care and Support: The Government's Response to Law Commission Report 326 on Adult Social Care* (TSO, July 2012), Cm.8379, para.11.31.

[4] Department of Health, *Code of Practice: Mental Health Act 1983* (2008), para.27.8.

[5] Department of Health, *Code of Practice: Mental Health Act 1983* (2008), para.27.22.

[6] HSC 2000/003 and LAC (2000)3, After-Care Under the Mental Health Act 1983, para.4.

[7] Department of Health, *Code of Practice: Mental Health Act 1983* (2008), para.27.20.

The Code also advises clinicians to fully involve the patient in the decision to end s.117 after-care.[1]

SECTION 117 AND NHS CONTINUING HEALTH CARE

The relevant guidance states that because there is no power to charge for s.117 services, it **1–732** is not necessary to assess for NHS continuing health care if all of the services that the person will receive are s.117 services; only needs that are not s.117 after-care needs should be considered for NHS continuing health care.[2]

Local authorities and the NHS are advised to have agreements in place detailing how they will carry out their s.117 responsibilities, and these agreements should clarify which services fall under s.117 and which authority should fund them.[3]

Different regions have different ways of working out how s.117 funding costs should be apportioned; however, where this results in the NHS fully funding a s.117 package this does not constitute NHS continuing health care. The Government has recommended that the NHS should have separate budgets for s.117 and NHS continuing health care, and where they are funded from the same budget they should still continue to be distinct and separate entitlements.[4]

CARE PROGRAMME APPROACH

The Care Programme Approach was established in 1991 through a joint health and social **1–733** services circular.[5] It is the system that is used to organise the care and treatment of many people with mental health problems in the community by secondary mental health services, such as community mental health teams and assertive outreach services. The relevant guidance is currently *Refocusing the Care Programme Approach*.[6] The guidance explains that the Care Programme Approach applies mainly to those with complex needs and who require multi-agency support.[7] The Care Programme Approach applies irrespective of s.117, but nevertheless will apply to many s.117 service users.

In broad terms, there are four distinct aspects to support provided under the Care Programme Approach:

- arrangements for assessing the health and social needs of people accepted by the specialist mental health services;
- the formation of a care plan which addresses the identified health and social care needs;
- the appointment of a care co-ordinator to keep in close touch with the person and monitor care; and
- regular review, and if need be, agreed changes to the care plan.

Subsection (1)

COMMISSIONING SECTION 117 SERVICES. This amends s.117 of the Mental Health Act **1–734** 1983 to clarify that local authorities may commission as well as provide after-care services. Until 2012, the s.117 duty was to "provide" after-care but apart from the reference to doing

---

[1] Department of Health, Code of Practice: Mental Health Act 1983 (2008), para.27.19.
[2] Department of Health, *The National Framework for NHS Continuing Healthcare and NHS-funded Nursing Care* (2012), para.121.
[3] HSC 2000/003 and LAC (2000)3, *After-Care Under the Mental Health Act 1983*.
[4] Department of Health, *The National Framework for NHS Continuing Healthcare and NHS-funded Nursing Care* (2012), paras 64.1 to 64.3.
[5] Joint Health and Social Services Circular, *The Care Programme Approach for people with a mental illness, referred to specialist psychiatric services*, HC(90)23/LASSL(90)11 (DH (1990)).
[6] Department of Health, *Refocusing the Care Programme Approach: Policy and Positive Practice Guidance* (2008).
[7] Department of Health, *Refocusing the Care Programme Approach: Policy and Positive Practice Guidance* (2008), pp.13 to 14.

so "in co-operation with relevant voluntary agencies", there was nothing stating that the NHS and social services authorities may commission services from other providers. The Law Commission argued that, in practice, the NHS and local authorities did commission s.117 services and felt that it was likely that a court would agree that "provide" must imply "commission". But it recommended that this matter should be put beyond doubt by the new statute.[1] This was accepted by the Government.[2]

The Health and Social Care Bill 2012 amended s.117 to make clear that the duty on commissioning consortia is to "commission", rather than "provide", healthcare after-care. But it did not amend the local authority side of the duty.[3] Subsection (1) therefore addresses this imbalance.

Subsection (2)

1–735   This amendment follows as a consequence of subs.(1). It preserves the effect of s.117(2D) that a clinical commissioning group is under a duty to commission rather than provide s.117 services.

Subsections (3) and (4)

1–736   ORDINARY RESIDENCE.   Prior to the Care Act, the concept of ordinary residence did not apply to s.117 services. Instead, the duty to provide after-care services fell upon those bodies responsible "for the area in which the person concerned is resident or to which he is sent on discharge by the hospital in which he was detained".[4] Case law confirmed that the relevant after-care bodies were those for the area in which the patient was resident before being detained in hospital, notwithstanding that the patient can be discharged to a different part of the country and is not likely to return. But where a patient had no place of residence, the relevant bodies would be those to which the patient was sent on discharge by the hospital.[5]

The Law Commission noted that anomalies could arise, particularly where one local authority was responsible for providing s.117 services whilst another commissions any other services a person may need. Some of the considerable practical problems had been demonstrated in the case of *R. (Hertfordshire CC) v Hammersmith and Fulham LBC*. The applicant, who had a history of Korsakoff's syndrome, had lived in local authority A for 15 years. Following a serious traffic accident, he was admitted to a general hospital and upon discharge was placed by local authority A in a hostel in local authority B. Under the ordinary residence rules borough A retained funding responsibility. However, after nine months the applicant's mental health deteriorated and he was detained under s.3 of the 1983 Act for 11 months before being discharged to a residential placement in local authority C. It was held that the ordinary residence rules no longer applied because the applicant was now subject to s.117 by virtue of his s.3 detention, and therefore local authority B became responsible for funding his after-care.[6]

The Law Commission therefore recommended that the concept of ordinary residence should be extended to include s.117 services.[7] This was accepted by the Government.[8] Subsections (3) and (4) therefore apply the ordinary residence rules and dispute procedures to s.117.

---

[1] Law Commission, *Adult Social Care*, paras 11.100 to 11.101.
[2] Department of Health, Reforming the Law for Adult Care and Support: The Government's Response to Law Commission Report 326 on Adult Social Care (TSO, July 2012), Cm.8379, para.11.32.
[3] Mental Health Act 1983 s.117(2D).
[4] Mental Health Act 1983 s.117(3).
[5] *R. v Mental Health Review Tribunal Ex p Hall* [1999] 2 CCLR 361, 371(J).
[6] *R. (Hertfordshire CC) v Hammersmith and Fulham LBC* [2011] EWCA Civ 77.
[7] Law Commission, *Adult Social Care*, paras 11.83 to 11.92.
[8] Department of Health, *Reforming the Law for Adult Care and Support: The Government's Response to Law Commission Report 326 on Adult Social Care* (TSO, July 2012), Cm.8379, para.11.29.

Section 117(3) of the 1983 Act (as amended by s.75(3) of the Care Act) makes provision for which local authority is to be responsible for providing such mental health after-care services in individual cases:

- if, immediately before being detained, the person was ordinarily resident in England, the responsible local authority will be the authority for the area in England in which the person was ordinarily resident;
- if, immediately before being detained, the person was ordinarily resident in Wales, the responsible local authority will be the authority for the area in Wales in which the person was ordinarily resident; and
- in any other case (for example, if the person has no settled residence) the responsible local authority will be the authority for the area in which the person concerned is resident or to which they are sent on discharge by the hospital to which they are detained.

The explanatory notes confirm that the intention behind these reforms is:

". . . to avoid anomalies which can currently arise where one local authority is responsible for commissioning section 117 services whilst another commissions any other services a person may need. They apply consistent after-care ordinary residence rules in England and Wales, in particular, in relation to which health body and local authority are responsible for commissioning after-care services."[1]

Therefore, the effect would be to alter the outcome of future cases where the facts are similar to those that arose in *R. (Hertfordshire CC) v Hammersmith and Fulham LBC*. If that case had been considered under the amendments introduced by s.75(3) of the Care Act provisions, local authority A would have retained funding responsibility. This is because the applicant had been placed by local authority A, and by virtue of the deeming principle in s.39 would be considered ordinarily resident there.

The statutory guidance explains that following discharge, any change in the person's ordinary residence will affect the local authority responsible for their social care services, it will not affect the local authority responsible for s.117 after-care. Thus, if a person is ordinarily resident in local authority A prior to detention, and moves on discharge to local authority B and moves again to local authority C, local authority A will remain responsible for s.117 after-care. However, if the person, having become ordinarily resident after discharge in local authority area B or C, is detained again, the local authority in whose area the person was ordinarily resident immediately before their subsequent admission (local authority B or C) will be responsible for their after-care when they are discharged from hospital.[2]

If the person's ordinary residence immediately before being detained cannot be established, the local authority in which they were resident immediately before the detention will be responsible for s.117 after-care. The statutory guidance explains:

"Only if that cannot be established, either, will the responsible local authority be the one for the area to which the patient is sent on discharge. However, local authorities should only determine that a person is not resident anywhere as a last resort."[3]

The Government intends to amend the statutory guidance to clarify that the local authority responsible for someone's after-care under s.117(3) will be identified based on where the person is resident immediately before being detained under the Mental Health Act if the person's ordinary residence immediately before being detained cannot be established.[4]

The Law Commission had recognised that a considerable benefit of this reform would be to ensure that s.117 service users could access the dispute resolution procedures that apply

---

[1] Care Act 2014: Explanatory Notes para.448.
[2] Department of Health, *Care and Support Statutory Guidance* (2014) para.19.44.
[3] Department of Health, *Care and Support Statutory Guidance* (2014) para.19.45.
[4] Department of Health, Update on the Final Orders under the Care Act 2014 (2015) para.24.

to ordinary residence.[1] Previously disputes over the residency of a s.117 service user had to be resolved ultimately by the courts. Section 117(4) of the 1983 Act (as amended by s.75(4) of the Care Act) makes the following provision for determining disputes about where the person is ordinarily resident for the purposes of s.117(3):

- if the dispute is between local authorities in England, s.40 of the Care Act applies to the dispute as it applies to a dispute about where a person was ordinarily resident for the purposes of Pt 1 of that Act (and therefore the dispute will be determined by the Secretary of State);
- if the dispute is between local authorities in Wales, s.194 of the Social Services and Well-being (Wales) Act 2014 applies to the dispute as it applies to a dispute about where a person was ordinarily resident for the purposes of that Act (and until s.194 is commenced in April 2016, transitional legislation will provide that the dispute will be determined by the Welsh Ministers); and
- if the dispute is between a local authority in England and a local authority in Wales, the dispute is to be determined by the Secretary of State or the Welsh Ministers.

Section 117(5) of the 1983 Act (also inserted by s.74(4) of the Care Act) requires the Secretary of State and Welsh Ministers to make and publish arrangements for determining cross-border disputes. These arrangements were published in March 2015.[2]

Subsection (12) provides that the changes to the commissioning responsibility made by subss.(3) and (4) will not apply where a person is already in receipt of s.117 services when these changes come into force. The explanatory notes state that: "The current authority will remain responsible for commissioning those services for as long as the person concerned continues to need them."[3]

1–737   NHS RESPONSIBILITY FOR AFTER-CARE.   The National Health Service Commissioning Board and Clinical Commissioning Groups (Responsibilities and Standing Rules) Regulations 2012 provide that the obligation on a Clinical Commissioning Group (CCG) may be imposed on another CCG or in some circumstances on the NHS Commissioning Board.[4]   The circumstances in which another CCG may be required to provide after-care include by virtue of s.3(1A) of the National Health Service Act 2006 which makes CCGs responsible for commissioning health services for individuals who are provided with primary medical services by a member of the CCG and individuals who are not provided with primary medical services by a member of any CCG but who usually reside in the group's area. It also applies in respect of certain categories of children. The explanatory memorandum sets out that the purpose of the regulations is to ensure that, wherever possible, the CCG responsible for commissioning after-care services is the same as that for meeting the patient's other needs for health services.[5]

Subsection (5)

1–738   THE DEFINITION OF AFTER-CARE SERVICES.   Prior to the Care Act there was no statutory definition of after-care services. However, case law established that such services are wide-ranging and would normally include:

---

[1] Law Commission, *Adult Social Care*, para.11.89.

[2] Department of Health and Welsh Government, *Mental Health Aftercare in England and Wales: Arrangements for Resolving Disputes Over Ordinary Residence Involving Local Authorities in England and Wales* (March 2015).

[3] Care Act 2014: Explanatory Notes para.454.

[4] The National Health Service Commissioning Board and Clinical Commissioning Groups (Responsibilities and Standing Rules) Regulations 2012 (SI 2012/2996).

[5] Explanatory Memorandum: National Health Service Commissioning Board and Clinical Commissioning Groups (Responsibilities and Standing Rules) Regulations 2012, para.4.7.

". . . social work, support in helping the ex-patient with problems of employment, accommodation or family relationships, the provision of domiciliary services and the use of day centre and residential facilities."[1]

Similarly, the Mental Health Act Code of Practice does not give any specific examples but lists a broad range of needs that the provision of after-care services could address.[2]

However, some of the relevant case law has also developed a restrictive approach to the purpose of such services, particularly residential accommodation. The authorities in this respect date back to the following comments by Lord Steyn in *R. (Stennett) v Manchester City Council*:

"Clearly, caring residential care (ensuring for example, that prescribed medication is taken) may be essential. It takes the place of the hospital environment. It can hardly be said that the mentally ill patient freely chooses such accommodation."[3]

It is likely that Lord Steyn was in fact contemplating a particular situation where on discharge pursuant to a direction by a mental health tribunal a patient still needs medical and other care. However, in some cases these words have been given wider significance. The notion that s.117 residential care was an extension of compulsory care in hospital was strongly supported by the observations of Mr Justice Langstaff in *DM v Doncaster Metropolitan Borough Council*.[4] In the case of *R. (Afework) v Camden LBC*, the High Court developed this argument even further. Mr Justice Mostyn opined that the term "after-care services" as a single compound noun with two components, and with the hyphenated linking of the word "after" with "care" within the first, indicates that the services in question must be consequential to the detention in hospital.[5] He went on to hold that s.117 is only engaged in respect of accommodation if:

- the need for accommodation is a direct result of the reason the ex-patient was detained in the first place ("the original condition");
- the requirement is for enhanced specialist accommodation to meet needs directly arising from the original condition; and
- the ex-patient is being placed in the accommodation on an involuntary (in the sense of being incapacitated) basis arising as a result of the original condition.[6]

The Law Commission did not consult expressly on the definition of after-care services, but some consultees argued that it needed to be clarified. In its final report (published before *Afework*) the Commission concluded that the establishment of a statutory definition would help to establish greater certainty, rather than leaving this matter entirely to case law, and help remove any notion that s.117 services must be compulsory. It recommended that after-care services should be defined in the 1983 Act as any service:

- necessary to meet a need arising from the former patient's mental disorder; and
- aimed at reducing that person's chance of being readmitted to hospital for treatment for that disorder.[7]

This was based on the definition set out by Professor Richard Jones in his influential pub- **1–739** lication the *Mental Health Act Manual*.[8] This formulation was also approved by Mr Justice Hickinbottom in *R. (Mwanza) v Greenwich LBC*.[9]

---

[1] *Clunis v Camden and Islington Health Authority* [1998] Q.B. 978 at 992, per Beldam LJ.
[2] Department of Health, Code of Practice: Mental Health Act 1983 (2008), para.27.13.
[3] *R. (Stennett) v Manchester City Council* [2002] UKHL 34; [2002] 2 A.C. 1127 at [15].
[4] *DM v Doncaster Metropolitan Borough Council* [2011] EWHC 3652 (Admin) at [63] to [64].
[5] *R. (Afework) v Camden LBC* [2013] EWHC 1637 (Admin) at [8].
[6] *R. (Afework) v Camden LBC* [2013] EWHC 1637 (Admin) at [19].
[7] Law Commission, *Adult Social Care*, para.11.122.
[8] R. Jones, *Mental Health Act Manual*, 13th edn (London: Sweet and Maxwell, 2010), para.1–1071.
[9] *R. (Mwanza) v Greenwich LBC* [2010] EWHC 1462 (Admin); (2010) 13 CCLR 454 at [67] and [79].

In the case of *Mwanza* the High Court held that the s.117 duty does not extend to providing normal accommodation simply on the basis that there is an increased risk to the person if accommodation is not provided, rather than a need arising from the person's mental disorder. If the person is in need of care and attention—which is not mental health related—then s.21 of the National Assistance Act 1948 (which was in place at the time of the judgment) was the more appropriate provision for seeking assistance. The court considered the contention that the need for basic or ordinary accommodation will never fall within the concept of after-care, since the need could not be said to have arisen from an individual's mental disorder. Mr Justice Hickinbottom rejected this but went on to say that the circumstances in which ordinary accommodation could fall within s.117 were difficult to envisage.[1] In *Afework* Mr Justice Mostyn went further and concluded there were no such circumstances.[2] The Law Commission accepted that it was correct legally that s.117 "does not include services that are not necessary to meet the needs arising from a person's mental disorder". But it recommended that the code of practice should provide guidance on distinguishing between accommodation which is and is not related to a mental disorder.[3]

The Government agreed with the Law Commission's recommended definition.[4] The wording used in the draft Care and Support Bill was therefore almost identical to that suggested by the Commission.[5] However, the definition has been the subject of some controversy. For example, in written evidence to the Joint Committee, Mind argued:

"In practice, it can be very difficult to establish which needs arise directly from an individual's mental health problem and which don't. We are concerned that narrowing the criteria for aftercare in this way will lead to disputes over what constitutes section 117 care, causing delays in the provision of services, distress for the people concerned and leaving them eligible to be charged for care that is essential to prevent their readmission to hospital. For example, under this new definition it seems likely that many local authorities will begin to charge for accommodation or residential care needed to prevent readmission to hospital, as it could be argued that the need for accommodation does not arise directly from a person's mental health problem. People would have to go through difficult financial assessments while being discharged from hospital, with some likely to refuse crucial elements of their care that they worry they will be charged for."[6]

However, the Joint Committee agreed with the Law Commission that the proposed definition was correct legally. But it also recommended that the Government should ensure that in the guidance that is given to local authorities "the risks are recognised and the well-being principle upheld".[7]

The wording used in the draft Care and Support Bill was revised by the Government to recognise some of the concerns noted above, and further amendments were introduced by the Government during the passage of the Care Bill through the House of Lords. These changes are discussed in detail below. Subsection (5) now provides that after-care services means services which have both of the following purposes:

---

[1] *R. (Mwanza) v Greenwich LBC* [2010] EWHC 1462 (Admin); (2010) 13 CCLR 454 at [67] and [75] to [76].

[2] *R. (Afework) v Camden LBC* [2013] EWHC 1637 (Admin) at [16].

[3] Law Commission, *Adult Social Care*, para.11.124.

[4] Department of Health, *Reforming the Law for Adult Care and Support: The Government's Response to Law Commission Report 326 on Adult Social Care* (TSO, July 2012), Cm.8379, para.11.32.

[5] Department of Health, *Draft Care and Support Bill* (TSO, July 2012) Cm.8386, p.60 (cl.48(5)).

[6] House of Lords House of Commons Joint Committee on the Draft Care and Support Bill, *Draft Care and Support Bill Report, Session 2012–13*, para.137.

[7] House of Lords House of Commons Joint Committee on the Draft Care and Support Bill, *Draft Care and Support Bill Report, Session 2012–13*, para.139.

- meeting a need arising from or related to the person's mental disorder; and
- reducing the risk of a deterioration of the person's mental condition (and, accordingly, reducing the risk of the person requiring admission to a hospital again for treatment for mental disorder)

The Government stated in the House of Lords during the passage of the Care Bill that nothing in subs.(5):

". . . will change the guidance in chapter 27 of the code of practice. [Section 117] covers housing, employment counselling, and cultural and spiritual needs. The professionals involved include mental health professionals, GPs, employment experts, independent advocates and others."[1]

It also stated that a definition was necessary as a result of the existing disputes that have arisen over the meaning of after-care services.[2] In the House of Commons the Government further argued that:

"One advantage of introducing a clear definition will be that the scope of after-care will no longer be entirely open to interpretation by the courts, whose views have varied and led to uncertainty over time."[3]

The Government went on to say that:

"[Section 117] has carefully drawn limits, because the Government do not consider it would be appropriate for the Mental Health Act to impose a duty on the responsible bodies to provide or commission services that are based on needs that neither arise from nor are related to a mental disorder. That is what the purpose of the provision is all about."[4]

A NEED ARISING FROM OR RELATED TO THE PERSONS MENTAL DISORDER

Section 117 services must be provided to meet needs "arising from or related to the per- **1–740** son's mental disorder". The words "related to" were not included in the equivalent cause in the draft Care and Support Bill, but were added by the Government in order to address concerns that "the wording in the Draft Bill could lead to after-care being interpreted only as services directly arising from a mental disorder".[5] During the passage of the Care Bill the Government confirmed that the inclusion of "related to" was "an important broadening of the definition so that a wide breadth of services is covered".[6]

In the House of Lords, Lord Patel tabled an amendment which would have removed the first limb of the definition altogether. Instead, after-care services would be defined as any services that reduce the risk of a deterioration of the person's mental condition. In particular he disagreed with the *Mwanza* judgment:

". . . because it suggests that the focus of Section 117 should be only on the mental disorder of the patient. As I have previously stated, Section 117 cannot just be tied to the needs around the mental disorder. It should be tied to the overall needs of the person

---

[1] *Hansard* (House of Lords), 29 July 2013, Vol.747, col.1576 (Baroness Northover).
[2] *Hansard* (House of Lords), 29 July 2013, Vol.747, cols 1575 to 1577 (Baroness Northover).
[3] *Hansard* (House of Commons: Public Bill Committee), 23 January 2014 (PM):Tenth Sitting, col.378 (Norman Lamb MP).
[4] *Hansard* (House of Commons: Public Bill Committee), 23 January 2014 (PM):Tenth Sitting, col.379 (Norman Lamb MP).
[5] Department of Health, *The Care Bill explained—including a response to consultation and pre-legislative scrutiny on the draft Care and Support Bill*, para.125.
[6] *Hansard* (House of Commons: Public Bill Committee), 23 January 2014 (PM):Tenth Sitting, col.378 (Norman Lamb MP).

for both healthcare and social care, to enable them to get out of hospital and back into the community as quickly as possible."[1]

The Government however rejected this amendment on the basis that it would confuse rather than clarify the circumstances in which after-care services should be provided.[2] Lord Patel's amendment was defeated by 198 to 178 votes.[3]

1–741 REDUCING THE RISK OF A DETERIORATION OF THE PERSON'S MENTAL CONDITION (AND, ACCORDINGLY, TO REDUCE THE RISK OF THE PERSON REQUIRING ADMISSION TO A HOSPITAL AGAIN FOR TREATMENT FOR THE DISORDER). At report stage in the House of Lords the Government amended this limb of the definition to reflect concerns raised by Lord Patel. In particular, the clause had referred to "the mental disorder" in the singular, which Lord Patel felt would be interpreted to refer only to the medical treatment of a single diagnosis, rather than looking at a person holistically. The Government explained its purpose:

> "We have added a positive objective to prevent deterioration as well as preventing read-mission to hospital, and have further changed the clause to remove the definite article when referring to 'the mental disorder', for which the noble Lord made the case in Committee. This is intended to remove any doubt about our intention that the scope of aftercare covers more than just one form of mental disorder, and is not necessarily limited to the specific disorder or disorders for which a person was previously detained under the Act and which gave rise to the right to after-care."[4]

This was an important clarification. As noted above, in *Afework* the court had said that s.117 services must "relate to the reason, and only to the reason, for the detention in hospital".[5] This suggests that after-care services must in some way be aimed at addressing the specific circumstances that led to the previous s.3 detention (or detention under one of the other relevant sections of the 1983 Act relevant to s.117). In contrast, the judgment in *Mwanza* stated that s.117 services must be aimed at "reducing that person's chance of being readmitted to hospital for treatment for that disorder". This suggests that s.117 could include services aimed generally at preventing any future re-admission to a psychiatric hospital-including an informal admission or an admission for a new condition not related to the previous illness. The Law Commission considered that in practice, it would be extremely difficult to distinguish between services aimed at preventing s.3 admissions and those aimed at preventing admission under other sections of the 1983 Act and therefore preferred the *Mwanza* interpretation. Whilst the Commission recognised that this may lead to lifelong funding responsibilities for some former mental health patients, it argued that this makes a strong case for robust review procedures in individual cases of the ongoing need for s.117 after-care and the discharge of people where it is no longer appropriate.[6]

Subsection (6)

1–742 PREFERRED ACCOMMODATION. Prior to the Care Act, the choice of accommodation directions and the additional payments regulations did not apply to residential accommodation provided under s.117.[7] The Law Commission concluded that in principle, all service

---

[1] *Hansard* (House of Lords), 29 July 2013, Vol.747, col.1572.

[2] *Hansard* (House of Lords), 29 July 2013, Vol.747, cols 1575 to 1577 (Baroness Northover).

[3] *Hansard* (House of Lords), 16 October 2013, Vol.748, cols 601 to 604.

[4] *Hansard* (House of Lords), 16 October 2013, Vol.748, cols 559 to 600 (Earl Howe).

[5] *R. (Afework) v Camden LBC* [2013] EWHC 1637 (Admin) at [8].

[6] Law Commission, *Adult Social Care*, para.11.123.

[7] National Assistance Act 1948 (Choice of Accommodation) Directions 1992 and National Assistance (Residential Accommodation) (Additional Payments and Assessment of Resources) (Amendment) (England) Regulations 2001 (SI 2001/3441).

users should be given the same right to choose the accommodation that is being provided by a local authority and make top-up payments, irrespective of whether or not s.117 applies.[1] The Government accepted both of these recommendations.[2]

Subsection (6) inserts a new s.117A into the 1983 Act. This empowers the Secretary of State to make regulations to place a duty on a local authority to enable a person who qualifies for accommodation under s.117 to live in accommodation of their choice. This may involve the person themselves or another person paying some or all of the additional cost. The relevant regulations are the Care and Support and After-Care (Choice of Accommodation) Regulations 2014 (SI 2014/2670). They are reproduced and discussed at paras A1–101 to A1–110 below. Regulation 4 requires a local authority, which in discharging its duty to provide or arrange for the provision of mental health after-care under s.117 of the Mental Health Act 1983, is providing or arranging for the provision of a specified type of accommodation to an adult to provide or for arrange the provision of the adult's preferred accommodation of that type, if specified conditions are met. The conditions are as follows:

- the local authority is providing or arranging care home, shared lives or supported living accommodation in England;
- the preferred accommodation is of the same type as that the local authority is providing;
- the preferred accommodation is suitable to meet the adult's needs;
- the preferred accommodation is available;
- the provider is willing to provide the accommodation to the person on the local authority's terms; and
- where the cost of the preferred accommodation is greater than the usual cost of accommodation of that kind, the person or a third party must be able and willing to pay the additional cost.

The statutory guidance discusses choice of accommodation and mental health after-care in Annex A, paras 44 to 50.

Subsection (7)

This subsection provides that a local authority may exercise its duty under s.117 by mak- **1–743** ing direct payments, subject to Sch.4. See reg.11 of the Care and Support (Direct Payments) Regulations 2014 (SI 2014/2871).

Subsections (8) and (9)

Subsection (8) inserts a new s.53(11) in the Social Services and Well-being (Wales) Act **1–744** 2014 to provide that a local authority in Wales may discharge its duty under s.117 by making direct payments, and subs.(9) inserts a new Sch.A1 into the same Act for that purpose.[3]

Subsection (10)

This was added to the Care Bill by a Government amendment during report stage in the **1–745** House of Lords and is intended to apply consistent ordinary residence rules in England and Wales in respect of after-care under s.117.[4] It inserts a new subsection in s.163 of the Social Services and Well-being (Wales) Act 2014 to provide that an adult will be treated as ordinarily resident in the area of the local authority in England or Wales in which that person is being provided with accommodation under s.117 of the Mental Health Act 1983.

---

[1] Law Commission, *Adult Social Care*, paras 11.74 to 11.82.
[2] Department of Health, Reforming the Law for Adult Care and Support: The Government's Response to Law Commission Report 326 on Adult Social Care (TSO, July 2012), Cm.8379, para.11.28.
[3] Care Act 2014: Explanatory Notes, para.453.
[4] *Hansard* (House of Lords), 14 October 2013, Vol.748, col.317 (Earl Howe).

1–746   This updates the references to legislation in s.117(2C) under which direct payments for mental health after-care services may be made.

Prisoners and persons in approved premises etc.

1–747   **76.**—(1) In its application to an adult who is detained in prison, this Part has effect as if references to being ordinarily resident in an area were references to being detained in prison in that area.

(2) In its application to an adult who is residing in approved premises, this Part has effect as if references to being ordinarily resident in an area were references to being resident in approved premises in that area.

(3) In its application to an adult who is residing in any other premises because a requirement to do so has been imposed on the adult as a condition of the grant of bail in criminal proceedings, this Part has effect as if references to being ordinarily resident in an area were references to being resident in premises in that area for that reason.

(4) The power under section 30 (preference for particular accommodation) may not be exercised in the case of an adult who is detained in prison or residing in approved premises except for the purpose of making provision with respect to accommodation for the adult—

(a) on his or her release from prison (including temporary release), or

(b) on ceasing to reside in approved premises.

(5) Sections 31 to 33 (direct payments) do not apply in the case of an adult who, having been convicted of an offence, is—

(a) detained in prison, or

(b) residing in approved premises.

(6) Sections 37 and 38 (continuity of care), in their application to an adult who is detained in prison or residing in approved premises, also apply where it is decided that the adult is to be detained in prison, or is to reside in approved premises, in the area of another local authority; and accordingly—

(a) references to the adult's intention to move are to be read as references to that decision, and

(b) references to carers are to be ignored.

(7) Sections 42 and 47 (safeguarding: enquiry by local authority and protection of property) do not apply in the case of an adult who is—

(a) detained in prison, or

(b) residing in approved premises.

(8) An SAB's objective under section 43(2) does not include helping and protecting adults who are detained in prison or residing in approved premises; but an SAB may nonetheless provide advice or assistance to any person for the purpose of helping and protecting such adults in its area in cases of the kind described in section 42(1) (adults with needs for care and support who are at risk of abuse or neglect).

(9) Section 44 (safeguarding adults reviews) does not apply to any case involving an adult in so far as the case relates to any period during which the adult was—

(a) detained in prison, or

(b) residing in approved premises.

(10) Regulations under paragraph 1(1)(d) of Schedule 2 (membership of Safeguarding Adults Boards) may not specify the governor, director or controller of a prison or a prison officer or prisoner custody officer.

(11) "Prison" has the same meaning as in the Prison Act 1952 (see section 53(1) of that Act); and—

(a) a reference to a prison includes a reference to a young offender institution, secure training centre or secure children's home,

(b) the reference in subsection (10) to the governor, director or controller of a prison includes a reference to the governor, director or controller of a young offender institution, to the governor, director or monitor of a secure training centre and to the manager of a secure children's home, and

(c) the reference in that subsection to a prison officer or prisoner custody officer includes a reference to a prison officer or prisoner custody officer at a young offender institution, to an officer or custody officer at a secure training centre and to a member of staff at a secure children's home.

(12) "Approved premises" has the meaning given in section 13 of the Offender Management Act 2007.

(13) "Bail in criminal proceedings" has the meaning given in section 1 of the Bail Act 1976.

(14) For the purposes of this section—

(a) a person who is temporarily absent from prison is to be treated as detained in prison for the period of absence;

(b) a person who is temporarily absent from approved premises is to be treated as residing in approved premises for the period of absence;

(c) a person who is temporarily absent from other premises in which the person is required to reside as a condition of the grant of bail in criminal proceedings is to be treated as residing in the premises for the period of absence.

GENERAL NOTE

Research carried out into the circumstances of prisoners, indicates a broad range of needs **1–748** among the prison population. For example, it has been shown that, relative to the general population, prisoners experience poorer physical and mental health,[1] and that between seven and 14 per cent of prisoners have learning disabilities, compared to two per cent of people in the community.[2] The incidence of health and social care needs will continue to rise due, not least, to the increasing number of prisoners and, more specifically, older prisoners.[3] On 30 June 2014, there were 11,080 prisoners aged 50 and over in England and Wales (including 3,720 aged 60 and over) which equates to 13 per cent of the total prison population. People aged 60 and over and those aged 50–59 are respectively the first and second fastest growing age groups in the prison population.[4] Research suggests that the psychological strains of prison life further accelerate the ageing process, and that older prisoners possess a physiological age approximately 10 years in excess of their chronological age.[5]

There are 58 local authorities in England which have prisons within their boundaries. However, prior to the Care Act there were few examples of local authorities providing

[1] Dyer, W and Biddle, P (2013), "Prison health discharge planning – evidence of an integrated care pathway or the end of the road?", *Social Policy and Society* 12, 4, 521-532 and Fazel, S and Baillargeon, J (2011), "The health of prisoners", *The Lancet*, 377, 9769, 956-965.

[2] Ministry of Justice, *Ensuring Equality*, PSI 32/2011, (14 April 2011), para.H1.

[3] S Ginn (2012) "Elderly Prisoners", *British Medical Journal* 345, 4.

[4] Prison Reform Trust, *Bromley Briefings Prison Factfile* (Autumn 2014).

[5] A Moll, *Losing Track of Time: Dementia and the ageing prison population: treatment challenges and examples of good practice* (Mental Health Foundation, 2013).

social care services to prisoners. For example, a review in 2004 by Her Majesty's Inspectorate of Prisons found that local social service authorities were in general "extremely reluctant" to carry out needs assessments for older prisoners and still less to offer support either during or after imprisonment. The reasons for this are varied but some organisations have pointed to the lack of legal clarity.[1] In 2013, an inquiry into older prisoners undertaken by the House of Commons Justice Committee concluded that social care provision in prisons was "sparse, variable and in some cases non-existent".[2]

The responsibilities of the Prison Service and of local authorities under the Children Act 1989 were considered in *R. (Howard League for Penal Reform) v The Secretary of State for the Home Department*.[3] It was held that the assessment duty under the Children Act 1989 for children in need does not cease to be owed by reason of the fact that the child is detained in custody—although the functions, duties and responsibilities owed by a local authority to a child in need were nevertheless affected by the fact that the child was in custody. The only limitation was the obligations placed on the prison governor under the Prison Act 1952 which themselves must be fully compatible with the Human Rights Act 1998.[4] In giving his judgment, Mr Justice Munby (as he was then) recognised that local authorities need to take into account the limitations upon their resources and that, therefore, an authority can lawfully take the view that, whilst a child is detained in custody "his or her needs for services would (at least ordinarily) be adequately met by the facilities provided by the Prison Service".[5]

The Law Commission's review of adult social care argued that there was no reason why the same principle would not apply to adult prisoners. It noted that there was nothing in community care law which excluded prisoners expressly from the class of persons to whom assessments and services can be provided. However, this situation had arisen not by design but by oversight. For example, the possibility of receiving direct payments was circumscribed by a number of exclusions which referred to people who were subject to certain criminal justice community orders, but none of these excluded prisoners. In practice there were significant barriers to the provision of care and support, such as the ordinary residence rules and eligibility criteria. The Commission therefore recommended that the new statute must clarify, one way or the other, the position of prisoners.[6] The Government accepted this recommendation.[7]

Section 76 sets out for the first time local authorities' responsibilities for the provision of care and support for adult prisoners and people residing in approved premises (this refers to premises approved under s.13 of the Offender Management Act 2007 which includes bail accommodation). These responsibilities include duties to assess care and support needs and meet eligible needs. According to the Government:

---

[1] Her Majesty's Inspectorate of Prisons, *'No Problems—Old and Quiet': Older Prisoners in England and Wales: A Thematic Review by HM Chief Inspector of Prisons* (2004), paras 4.42 to 4.47. Also, Prison Reform Trust, *Doing Time: the Experiences and Needs of Older People in Prison* (2008), p.5.

[2] House of Commons Justice Committee, Older Prisoners: Fifth Report of Session 2013-14 (TSO 2013), HC 89, para.71.

[3] *R. (Howard League for Penal Reform) v Secretary of State for the Home Department* [2002] EWHC 2497 (Admin); (2003) 6 CCLR 47.

[4] *R. (Howard League for Penal Reform) v Secretary of State for the Home Department* [2002] EWHC 2497 (Admin); (2003) 6 CCLR 47 at [142].

[5] *R. (Howard League for Penal Reform) v Secretary of State for the Home Department* [2002] EWHC 2497 (Admin); (2003) 6 CCLR 47 at [156].

[6] Law Commission, *Adult Social Care*, paras 11.133 to 11.134.

[7] Department of Health, *Reforming the Law for Adult Care and Support: The Government's Response to Law Commission Report 326 on Adult Social Care* (TSO, July 2012), Cm.8379, paras 11.36 to 11.37.

"This will provide consistency of approach between institutions and ensure prisoners and residents in approved premises receive services equivalent to people with similar needs in the community."[1]

The explanatory notes confirm that:

- the eligibility framework will apply to prisoners and residents in approved premises;
- youth offenders with care and support needs should receive the same transition procedures to adult care and support as young people in the community. A request for an assessment can be made on the youth offender's behalf by the professional responsible for their care in the Young Offenders' Institution, Secure Children's Home or Secure Training Centre; and
- charging arrangements for care and support services received by prisoners will be the same as for people in the community.[2]

The statutory guidance discusses prisons, approved premises and bail accommodation in Ch.17. Amongst other matters, it confirms Government policy that:

"All adults in custody, as well as offenders and defendants in the community, should expect the same level of care and support as the rest of the population. This principle of equivalence of care forms the basis of the policy intent for the Act and this guidance."[3]

PRISONERS WHO ARE CARERS

Many prisoners provide care for disabled and older prisoners, including assistance with getting dressed, cell cleaning and personal hygiene. A small number of carers are paid and receive support from the prison authorities, including the provision of training.[4] However, s.76 refers throughout to the application of Pt 1 to "adults" rather than carers. Whilst s.76 does not expressly rule out the provision of support to prisoners or residents in approved premises who take on the role of carer, the statutory guidance includes the following statement: **1–749**

"It is not the intention of the Care Act that any prisoner, resident of approved premises or staff in prisons or approved premises should take on the role of carer as defined by the Act and should therefore not in general be entitled to a carer's assessment. Separate guidance will be issued to prison and approved premises staff on the role of prisoners and residents of approved premises in providing assistance to others."[5]

This statement appears to leave open the possibility that a carer's assessment might be required in some cases. It is submitted therefore that as a matter of law Pt 1 can still apply to prisoners and residents of approved premises who are carers for other prisoners and residents, but the policy intention is that this should be avoided wherever possible.

---

[1] Department of Health, *The Care Bill explained—including a response to consultation and pre-legislative scrutiny on the draft Care and Support Bill*, para.126.

[2] Care Act 2014: Explanatory Notes paras 464 to 466.

[3] Department of Health, *Care and Support Statutory Guidance* (2014), para.17.9.

[4] Her Majesty's Inspectorate of Prisons, *'No Problems—Old and Quiet': Older Prisoners in England and Wales: A Thematic Review by HM Chief Inspector of Prisons* (2004), para.1.63; Care Services Improvement Partnership West Midlands Development Centre and University of Birmingham, *Adult Social Care in Prisons: A Strategic Framework* (2007); House of Commons Justice Committee, *Older Prisoners: Fifth Report of Session 2013-14* (TSO 2013), HC 89, paras 76 to 77.

[5] Department of Health, *Care and Support Statutory Guidance* (2014), para.17.36.

SERVICE PROVISION BY PRISON AND HEALTH AUTHORITIES

1–750   The Prison Service has responsibility for those in its care, including a common law duty of care.[1] Under s.6 of the Human Rights Act 1998 it is unlawful for a public authority to act incompatibly with the European Convention on Human Rights. The prison service is a public authority for these purposes, and private companies running prisons are likely to fall within this definition on the basis that they are exercising a function of a public nature. Protection against inhuman and degrading treatment or punishment is provided by art.3 of the European Convention on Human Rights, including a positive duty to prevent a violation of that right.[2] The lack of appropriate treatment can breach art.3, particularly where the person is in a "position of inferiority and powerlessness".[3] Treatment not amounting to inhuman or degrading treatment may breach the art.8 right to a family life if it has a sufficiently adverse effect on physical and moral integrity.[4]

In addition, the Equality Act 2010 makes it unlawful for public authorities, including prison authorities, to discriminate without justification against a disabled person when exercising its functions, and includes a requirement to make "reasonable adjustments" for disabled people. Section 149 places a duty on public authorities to promote equality of opportunity for disabled people. In *R. (Gill) v the Secretary of State for Justice*, it was held that the Secretary of State was guilty of disability discrimination for failing to provide access to an offending behaviour programme for a prisoner with a learning disability, where the completion of the course was necessary in order to be eligible for parole.[5]

Prison Service Instructions issued in 2011 outline Governors' responsibilities towards disabled prisoners, including the need to make reasonable adjustments. Examples given include the provisions of an auxiliary aid (such as special computer software) or a change to a particular policy or practice which puts a disabled person at a disadvantage.[6] The statutory guidance states that aids for individuals, as defined in the Care and Support (Preventing Needs for Care and Support) Regulations 2014 (SI 2014/2673) (which are reproduced at paras A1–153 to A1–158 below), are the responsibility of the local authority, whilst "more significant adaptations would the responsibility of the custodial establishment".[7]

Since 2003, the Secretary of State for Health has assumed responsibility from the Home Secretary for securing a range of health services to prisoners and as a result of the Health and Social Care Act 2012, responsibility for commissioning services has been delegated to NHS England. A longstanding principle of Government policy on offender health care is that standards of health care for those in custody should be the same as for those in the wider community.[8] Examples of prison-based health care include general medical services, nurse-led health care teams and mental health in-reach teams. Some of these services will involve an element of adult social care, for example, some mental health in-reach teams include social workers and some prison-based health care assistants undertake "by default" social care tasks such as assistance with bathing and dressing.[9] The statutory guidance states that in the context of commissioning services or delegating functions:

---

[1] *Racz v Home Office* [1994] 2 A.C. 45.

[2] *A v United Kingdom* [1998] 2 F.L.R. 959; (1999) 27 EHRR 611.

[3] *Herczegfalvy v Austria* (1993) 15 EHRR 437.

[4] *X v Netherlands* (1986) 3 EHRR 235.

[5] *R. (Gill) v Secretary of State for Justice [2010] EWHC 364 (Admin).*

[6] Ministry of Justice, *Ensuring Equality*, PSI 32/2011 (14 April 2011), paras 8.1 to 8.5 and Annexes G and H.

[7] Department of Health, *Care and Support Statutory Guidance* (2014), para.17.42.

[8] Joint Prison Service and National Health Service Executive Working Group, *The Future Organisation of Prison Health Care* (1999), p.iii.

[9] CSIP West Midlands Development Centre and University of Birmingham, *Adult Social Care in Prisons: A Strategic Framework* (2007), p.19.

"Local authorities should consider how this fits alongside the commissioning of health and substance misuse services in prison directly commissioned by NHS England and the commissioning of education services by the Skills Funding Agency. If such an arrangement is implemented, local authorities should consider retaining the functions relating to requirements for continuity of care between settings and must retain the functions in relation to charging and safeguarding."[1]

The guidance discusses partnerships and interdependencies, end of life care and NHS continuing health care in paras 17.59 to 17.67. See also commentary under subs.(7) and subss.(8) and (9) which sets out the mechanisms that are in place in prisons to address cases of abuse and neglect.

Subsections (1) and (2)

These subsections confirm that the provisions of Pt 1 of the Care Act apply to "adults" **1–751** who are prisoners and those residing in approved premises (subject to certain prohibitions). They also confirm that the local authority in whose area a prison or approved premises is located is responsible for providing assessments and meeting needs. Thus, an adult's previous ordinary residence will not be a consideration while they are in these settings, and responsibility will fall to the local authority area in whose area the prison or approved premises is located without reference to the general ordinary residence rules.[2]

The statutory guidance advises that prisons and prison health services should inform local authorities when someone they believe has care and support needs arrives at their establishment (and if necessary either party can utilise the power to require co-operation contained in s.7).[3] Assessments of need are discussed in paras 17.24 to 17.35 and next steps after assessments are discussed in paras 17.38 to 17.45. Clearly, the custodial regime will limit the range of care and support options available, and by virtue of subs.(5) direct payments are prohibited.

The guidance suggests that local authorities should consider "light touch" financial assessments where the person is unlikely to be required to contribute towards the cost of their care and support, and that individuals who want to purchase their own services should be referred to the National Offender Management Service.[4]

The guidance also discusses the transition to adult services, rights to advocacy, and the complaints and appeals (in the context of prisoners and young offenders) in paras 17.70 to 17.80.

Subsection (3)

The rule in subss.(1) and (2), regarding which local authority is responsible for an indi- **1–752** vidual's care and support needs, applies to people bailed to addresses other than approved premises.

Subsection (4)

Prisoners and those in approved premises will not be able to express a preference for par- **1–753** ticular accommodation under s.30 except where the individual is being released or resettled into the community. Release into an approved premises amounts to moving from one custodial setting to another.[5]

Subsection (5)

Sections 31 to 33 on the provision of direct payments do not apply to prisoners or resi- **1–754** dents in approved premises, except those who have not been convicted of an offence, for

---

[1] Department of Health, *Care and Support Statutory Guidance* (2014), para.17.43.
[2] Care Act 2014: Explanatory Notes para.457.
[3] Department of Health, *Care and Support Statutory Guidance* (2014), para.17.23.
[4] Department of Health, *Care and Support Statutory Guidance* (2014), para.17.37.
[5] Department of Health, *Care and Support Statutory Guidance* (2014), para.17.33.

example some people in bail accommodation. Prisoners and residents in approved premises who have been convicted of an offence will not be eligible to receive direct payments.[1] See also paras 17.46 to 17.47 of the statutory guidance.

Subsection (6)

1–755 This covers continuity of care for prisoners and those in approved premises whose needs for care and support are being met by a local authority. The continuity provisions in ss.37 and 38 will apply to such prisoners and residents in approved premises being moved between different custodial settings and on release to the community. Continuity of care and support when an adult in custody moves is discussed in paras 17.48 to 17.54 of the statutory guidance. The ordinary residence of people leaving prison is discussed in paras 17.55 to 17.58.

Subsection (7)

1–756 The duties on local authorities to make enquiries under s.42 and to protect people's property under s.47 do not apply to people in prison or approved premises. The statutory guidance makes clear that prisons must have clear safeguarding policies that are explained to all visiting staff.[2]

At report stage in the House of Lords, Lord Patel attempted to amend the Bill to ensure that people in prison and those residing in approved premises are not excluded from the duty to undertake safeguarding enquiries.[3] In response the Government outlined existing procedures in cases of abuse and neglect, namely:

- prison governors and directors, and the probation trust in the case of approved premises, are responsible for safeguarding and must have in place appropriate procedures and provide assurance on this to the National Offender Management Service; and
- Her Majesty's Chief Inspector of Prisons and the Prison and Probation Ombudsman require assurance that safeguarding procedures are in place and their implementation provides equivalent protection to that available in the community.[4]

It concluded that:

"The important thing is not to impose a duty on another body to conduct inquiries in prisons and approved premises, but to ensure that the procedures within the prisons and approved premises are informed by best practice and local expertise."[5]

The Government also clarified that when a person is in the community, for example, in a bail hostel, the responsible body for safeguarding is the probation trust.[6] However, at third reading in the House of Lords concerns were raised that probation trusts are due to be abolished in 2016. The Government replied that probation services will be contracted out in due course, so these will be approved premises provided by the probation service and by voluntary or private providers. It stated that the guidance will make it clear that "the provider running the accommodation has a duty of care and a safeguarding responsibility".[7]

At third reading in the House of Lords, the Government—in response to a specific query from Lord Patel—confirmed an "important distinction" that while subs.(7) says that the duty to conduct an enquiry does not apply, it does not say that local authorities should not conduct an enquiry.[8] In other words, there is still an underlying power to conduct a safeguarding enquiry in a prison.

---

[1] Care Act 2014: Explanatory Notes para.460.
[2] Department of Health, *Care and Support Statutory Guidance* (2014), para.17.68.
[3] *Hansard* (House of Lords), 16 October 2013, Vol.748, cols 621 to 623.
[4] *Hansard* (House of Lords), 16 October 2013, Vol.748, cols 623 to 624 (Earl Howe).
[5] *Hansard* (House of Lords), 16 October 2013, Vol.748, cols 624 (Earl Howe).
[6] *Hansard* (House of Lords), 16 October 2013, Vol.748, cols 625 (Earl Howe).
[7] *Hansard* (House of Lords), 16 October 2013, Vol.748, col.1480 (Earl Howe).
[8] *Hansard* (House of Lords), 29 October 2013, Vol.748, col.1481 (Earl Howe).

These subsections were added by amendments moved by Government during the **1–757** Committee stage in the House of Lords. Their aim is to further clarify the relationship between prisons, approved premises and local safeguarding adults boards. Subsection (8) provides that the objective of a Safeguarding Adults Boards under s.43(2) does not include helping and protecting prisoners or those in approved premises, but it may still provide advice or assistance for such persons. Subsection (9) provides that the duty or power to carry out a safeguarding adult review under s.44 does not apply in the case of prisoners or those in approved premises.

In explaining these amendments, the Government stated:

"Obviously prisons and approved premises retain a duty of care towards and responsibility for the safety of all their detainees. Mechanisms are already in place to hold them to account if there are concerns about the care or safety of prisoners . . . As such, local safeguarding boards will not conduct inquiries or serious case reviews in relation to incidents occurring while someone is in prison or approved premises with care and support needs. However, we want there to be open dialogue between prisons and approved premises and local safeguarding adults boards so that the prisons and approved premises receive the information and advice which the board can provide for the benefit of prisoners and residents . . . It is therefore our intention that safeguarding adults boards will be free to invite governors or other prison officers to sit on the board and, whether or not a member, governors, directors or controllers of prisons will be able to approach a safeguarding adults board to ask for advice and guidance in improving their safeguarding arrangements."[1]

The Government went on to explain the mechanisms that are in place in prison:

". . . prison governors and directors have in place procedures to follow in response to allegations of abuse or neglect. Governors and directors will provide assurance to the National Offender Management Service and Her Majesty's Chief Inspector of Prisons, through their inspection regimes, that those procedures and their implementation provide similar protection to that available in the community. The Prisons and Probation Ombudsman will investigate individual complaints and incidents . . . The governor or, in the case of contracted prisons, the director, has the primary duty of care for prisoners and is the appropriate first point for reporting concerns. There is an investigations procedure in place for cases in which prisoners suffer significant harm. Prisons are monitored by a range of inspectorates, including the [Care Quality Commission]."[2]

At third reading in the House of Lords, the Government also stressed the importance of joint working:

"The Ministry of Justice encourages prison and probation staff to be involved with local safeguarding adults boards. The guidance on how safeguarding should be carried out in conjunction with local authority partners can draw attention to the duty in [section] 6 that local authorities and their partners must co-operate in the exercise of their respective functions relating to adults with needs for care and support."[3]

It went on to say:

"For approved premises, the probation provider has a clear responsibility in relation to safeguarding but there is nothing to prevent it seeking advice from either the safeguarding adults board or the local authority safeguarding team. This already happens in many areas. Since a local authority's duties in relation to safeguarding would not extend to safeguarding adults who are at risk of abuse or neglect by reason of their detention or

---

[1] *Hansard* (House of Lords), 29 July 2013, Vol.747, col.1578 (Baroness Northover).
[2] *Hansard* (House of Lords), 29 July 2013, Vol.747, col.1584 to 1585 (Baroness Northover).
[3] *Hansard* (House of Lords), 29 October 2013, Vol.748, col.1479 (Earl Howe).

their offence, a joint approach would be much more effective where there is a particularly difficult safeguarding challenge in an approved premises."[1]

The statutory guidance confirms that local authorities should consider inviting prison and probation staff to be members of Safeguarding Adults Boards.[2] It also sets out the role of the Prisons and Probation Ombudsman, Her Majesty's Inspectorate of Prisons and Her Majesty's Inspectorate of Probation in paras.17.81 to 17.85.

Subsection (10)

1–758 Governors and officers of a prison cannot be required by regulations to become members of Safeguarding Adult Boards. By virtue of subs.(11))(b), this also extends to governors and officers of young offender's institutions, secure training centres and secure children's homes.[3]

In the House of Lords, the Government explained the reason for this provision:

"Prisons have their own safeguarding procedures, so we believe that it should be left to local discretion to determine whether it is appropriate for a governor or other prison staff to become members, rather than a statutory duty."[4]

Subsection (11)

1–759 "Prison" has the same meaning as the Prison Act 1952, s.53(1). A reference to a prison includes a reference to a young offender institution, secure training centre or secure children's home (subs.(11)(a)). A reference to a governor, director or controller of a prison includes a reference to the governor, director or controller of a young offender institution, to the governor, director or monitor of a secure training centre and to the manager of a secure children's home (subs.(11)(b)). A reference to a prison officer or prisoner custody officer includes a reference to a prison officer or prisoner custody officer as a young offender institution, to an officer or custody officer at a secure training centre and to a member of staff at a secure children's home (subs.(11)(c)).

Subsection (14)

1–760 This provides that a temporary absence from prison or approved premises will lead to someone continuing to be treated as detained in prison or residing in approved premises or other bail addresses for the purposes of this section. This means, for example, that if someone is receiving care or support from the local authority in which their prison is based and they are temporarily in hospital in the area of a different local authority, the responsibility for providing the support does not change local authorities.[5]

Registers of sight-impaired adults, disabled adults, etc.

1–761 **77.**—(1) A local authority must establish and maintain a register of sight-impaired and severely sight-impaired adults who are ordinarily resident in its area.

(2) Regulations may specify descriptions of persons who are, or are not, to be treated as being sight-impaired or severely sight-impaired for the purposes of this section.

(3) A local authority may establish and maintain one or more registers of adults to whom subsection (4) applies, and who are ordinarily resident in the local authority's area, for the purposes in particular of—

(a) planning the provision by the authority of services to meet needs for care and support, and

---

[1] *Hansard* (House of Lords), 29 October 2013, Vol.748, col.1480 (Earl Howe).
[2] Department of Health, Care and Support Statutory Guidance (2014), para.17.69.
[3] Care Act 2014: Explanatory Notes para.463.
[4] *Hansard* (House of Lords), 29 July 2013, Vol.747, col.1578 (Baroness Northover).
[5] Care Act 2014: Explanatory Notes para.467.

(b) monitoring changes over time in the number of adults in the authority's area with needs for care and support and the types of needs they have.

(4) This subsection applies to an adult who—

(a) has a disability,

(b) has a physical or mental impairment which is not a disability but which gives rise, or which the authority considers may in the future give rise, to needs for care and support, or

(c) comes within any other category of persons the authority considers appropriate to include in a register of persons who have, or the authority considers may in the future have, needs for care and support.

(5) "Disability" has the meaning given by section 6 of the Equality Act 2010.

GENERAL NOTE

Prior to the Care Act, local authorities were required to establish and maintain registers **1–762** of disabled people in their area.[1] Disabled people were defined by reference to s.29(1) of the National Assistance Act 1948 as adults who are "blind, deaf or dumb, or who suffer from mental disorder of any description" and "who are substantially and permanently handicapped by illness, injury, or congenital deformity". The purpose of the register was to assist local authorities to plan services and for "certain statutory purposes unconnected with s.29" such as establishing eligibility for certain welfare benefits.[2] In addition to the requirement to maintain a register, there were requirements to collect information about service users and carers. For example, statutory guidance obliged local authorities to collect and analyse data on which groups are referred for assessment and receive services, and to "identify, make contact with and keep a record of deafblind people in their catchment area".[3]

The Law Commission originally proposed that the disability register should be abolished. This was on the basis that the registers failed to provide an accurate record or source of information since few disabled people choose to register and the definition of disability was restrictive. Moreover, it felt that for the purposes of strategic planning the registers were largely irrelevant, and the majority of services, welfare benefits or concessions provided for disabled people do not rely on registration. The consultation paper did, however, recognise that the register was more accurate in relation to blind and partially sighted people and most of the benefits linked to registration were directed at this group.[4]

But a significant minority of consultees disagreed with the proposal. It was argued that in areas where there is a strong local commitment to make the registers work they can be an effective tool for planning and other purposes. Furthermore, groups representing blind and partially sighted people argued that the registers remained an important mechanism for gaining access to certain benefits. The Law Commission therefore recommended that local authorities should be required to establish and maintain a register of blind and partially sighted people. In all other cases, local authorities should be given a power to establish and maintain registers. Also, it recommended that the code of practice should retain the requirements on local authorities to analyse data on a number of issues including which groups are referred for assessment and receive services, and identify, make contact

---

[1] National Assistance Act 1948 s.29(4)(g) and LAC (93)10; Chronically Sick and Disabled Persons Act 1970, s.1.

[2] LAC (93)10 appendix 4 para.2 and DHSS Circular 12/70; *Chronically Sick and Disabled Persons Act 1970*, para.5.

[3] Department of Health, *Prioritising Need in the Context of Putting People First: A Whole System Approach to Eligibility for Social Care: Guidance on Eligibility Criteria for Adult Social Care, England 2010* (2010), paras 156 to 161 and LAC(DH)(2009)6, *Social Care for Deafblind Children and Adults*, para.14.

[4] Law Commission, *Adult Social Care: A Consultation Paper*, Consultation Paper No.192 (2010), paras 13.2 to 13.13.

with and keep a record of deafblind people in their catchment area.[1] The Government accepted these recommendations.[2]

Section 77 therefore places a requirement on local authorities to establish and maintain a register of people who are ordinarily resident in their area and are sight-impaired and severely sight-impaired. There is no legal definition of "sight impairment", but according to the explanatory notes:

". . . clinical guidelines make it clear that someone can be certified as sight impaired if they are 'substantially and permanently handicapped by defective vision caused by congenital defect or illness or injury'."[3]

The current system is based on the Certificate of Vision Impairment form. Certification happens when someone's vision has fallen below a certain threshold and their consultant ophthalmologist completes this form. When a form is completed, one copy is sent to the Certifications Office at Moorfields Eye Hospital for national monitoring purposes. Another copy of the form is sent to the person's local authority. The expectation is that the person should be offered a needs assessment within 10 days of receiving the form,[4] and is formally registered as severely sight-impaired (blind) or sight-impaired (partially sighted). This generates two sources of data, certification figures which form the basis of the Public Health Indicator and registration figures which are collected on a triennial basis and are managed by the Health and Social Care Information Centre.

Under Sch.2 to the Children Act 1989 every local authority is required to maintain a register of disabled children in its area. The changes in the Care Act do not affect this duty.

Sight registers and other registers are discussed in Ch.22 of the statutory guidance. It makes clear that:

"Registration is voluntary, however individuals should be encouraged to consent to inclusion on the register as it may assist them in accessing other concessions and benefits. The data which local authorities are provided on registration are also of benefit in service planning for health and care and support. However, individuals' access to care and support is not dependent upon registration, and those with eligible needs for care and support should continue to receive it regardless of whether they consent to inclusion on the register."[5]

Subsection (1)

1–763   This places a duty on each local authority to keep a register of sight-impaired and severely sight-impaired adults who are ordinarily resident in its area. Lord Low tabled an amendment during Committee stage in the House of Lords in order to ensure that local authorities have a duty to make contact with adults shortly after they have been issued a Certificate of Vision Impairment form. The Government however felt that this should be a matter on which there should be some flexibility—for example people who lose their sight suddenly may need more time to come to terms with their loss—and therefore should be a matter for guidance.[6]

The statutory guidance states that upon receipt of the Certificate of Vision Impairment, the local authority should make contact with the person (regardless of whether the person has decided to register or not) within two weeks to arrange their inclusion on the register

---

[1] Law Commission, *Adult Social Care*, paras 12.10 to 12.18.

[2] Department of Health, Reforming the Law for Adult Care and Support: The Government's Response to Law Commission Report 326 on Adult Social Care (TSO, July 2012), Cm.8379, para.11.44.

[3] Care Act 2014: Explanatory Notes para.469.

[4] Department of Health, *Certificate of Vision Impairment: Explanatory Notes for Consultant Ophthalmologists and Hospital Eye Clinic Staff* (2013), para.35 and Association of Directors of Social Services, *Progress in Sight: National Standards of Social Care for Visually Impaired People* (October 2002), para.8.5.

[5] Department of Health, *Care and Support Statutory Guidance* (2014), para.22.2.

[6] *Hansard* (House of Lords), 29 July 2013, Vol.747, col.1591 to 1592 (Baroness Northover).

(with the person's informed consent). If there is an appearance of need for care and support, local authorities must arrange an assessment "in a timely manner".[1] The policy guidance on care and support for deafblind children and adults states that local authorities are "required to identify, make contact with, and keep a record of deafblind people in their catchment area".[2]

Subsection (2)

This provides that regulations may describe persons who are to be treated as sight-impairment or severely sight-impairment for the purposes of compiling a local authority register. The relevant regulations are the Care and Support (Sight-impaired and Severely Sight-impaired Adults) Regulations 2014 (SI 2014/2854). They are reproduced at paras A1–228 to A1–230 below. Regulation 2 provides that persons certified as such by a consultant ophthalmologist are to be treated as sight-impaired or severely sight-impaired. **1–764**

Subsection (3)

Local authorities may establish and maintain registers of people living in their area who require care and support or who might in the future. According to the explanatory notes: **1–765**

"This . . . will allow those people whose needs may change over time to be accurately recorded-for instance, to take account of an individual with a progressive neurological condition who may need care and support at some point in the future."[3]

The statutory guidance confirms that inclusion on such registers is voluntary and with the individual's informed consent. But it also suggests that "local authorities should encourage individual's consent to inclusion on the register" because such registers may support "the establishment of an accurate and useful local record of people whose needs may change over time".[4]

Subsections (4) and (5)

This defines the categories of people who might be included in the voluntary general registers: **1–766**

- a disabled people within the meaning of s.6 of the Equality Act 2010;
- a person with a physical or mental impairment which is not a disability but which gives rise or may give rise to needs for care and support; or
- any other category of persons which is appropriate to include, who have or are likely to have needs for care and support.

It is submitted, however, that s.6 of the Equality Act 2010 does not provide an appropriate definition of a disabled person for the purpose of a local authority register. Section 6 provides that a person has a disability if he or she has a physical or mental impairment and the impairment has a substantial and long-term adverse effect on the person's ability to carry out normal day-to-day activities. It therefore requires explicit consideration of the effects of the impairment on the individual. This is largely because the definition was constructed to ensure that employers and service providers fulfil their duty to make reasonable adjustments so that protected persons are not put at "substantial disadvantage" in comparison with persons who are not disabled. The definition in section must be seen in this context. Moreover, the s.6 definition sets a high threshold which would exclude many people with care and support needs, including those with short-term conditions and drug and alcohol problems.

---

[1] Department of Health, *Care and Support Statutory Guidance* (2014), para.22.16.
[2] Department of Health, *Care and Support for Deafblind Children and Adults Policy Guidance* (December 2014) para.13.
[3] Care Act 2014: Explanatory Notes para.470.
[4] Department of Health, *Care and Support Statutory Guidance* (2014), para.22.25.

Guidance, etc.

1–767 **78.**—(1) A local authority must act under the general guidance of the Secretary of State in the exercise of functions given to it by this Part or by regulations under this Part.

(2) Before issuing any guidance for the purposes of subsection (1), the Secretary of State must consult such persons as the Secretary of State considers appropriate.

(3) The Secretary of State must have regard to the general duty of local authorities under section 1(1) (promotion of individual well-being)—

(a) in issuing guidance for the purposes of subsection (1);

(b) in making regulations under this Part.

GENERAL NOTE

1–768 The Law Commission criticised the proliferation, over many years, of central government guidance on adult social care. For example, at the time of the scoping report it was estimated that in order to undertake a comprehensive needs and a carer's assessment a professional would need to have regard to four sets of general assessment guidance, four sets of general guidance on carer's assessments, specific user group assessment guidance and various other policy documents.[1] The Commission argued that the sheer volume of guidance led to unnecessary duplication and overload. Moreover the legal status of much of this guidance was unclear. Case law has established that guidance issued under s.7 of the Local Authority Social Services Act 1970 (known as "statutory guidance") must be followed by local authorities unless there is good reason to deviate from it but without freedom to take a substantially different course (see paras 1–772 to 1–773 below).[2] However, most Government guidance is "practice guidance" which is inherently weaker in status than statutory guidance—although local authorities must still take account of it and give it due weight in accordance with general public law principles. The status of the guidance was sometimes—but not always—stated in the preface or the inside page of the document. Finally, the Commission also noted that the language used in statutory guidance was often "too vague to be instructive" and contained "policy-laden and generalised statements" rather than giving clear legal guidance for legal authorities on how to exercise their statutory functions.[3]

The Law Commission recommended that the Secretary of State should be required to issue a consolidated code of practice for the adult social care statute. This could be achieved through a single document or a consolidated series of documents. But if multiple documents were issued then the Commission considered they "should be published in a form which allows them to be presented as a coherent whole, and they should be available in a single accessible location, such as on one webpage".[4] The Commission also warned that:

> "The purpose of the consolidated guidance would be to guide social services authorities on the exercise of their functions under the statute, including the exercise of any discretion conferred by the Act. In our view this extends to guidance about the implementation and operation of the legislation, giving concrete examples where that helps to explain what is required and clarifying the correct legal interpretation of aspects of the law (for example, by summarising case law). The purpose of the guidance does not extend to policy exhortations or vague statements about the 'direction of travel' of social services functions. The consolidated guidance should set out the course of action that a social worker or other decision-maker should take, unless there is a good reason for not taking that course of action."[5]

---

[1] Law Commission, *Adult Social Care: Scoping Report* (26 November 2008), para.2.22.
[2] *R. v Islington LBC, Ex p Rixon* (1998) 1 CCLR 119.
[3] Law Commission, *Adult Social Care*, paras 3.24 and 3.26.
[4] Law Commission, *Adult Social Care*, para.3.25.
[5] Law Commission, *Adult Social Care*, para.3.26.

The Law Commission went on to recommend that the statute should specify the following matters:

- that local authorities must follow the code in exercising their functions and only deviate from it where there is good reason to do so, but without freedom to take a substantially different course;
- that the draft code, and any revisions to it, must be subject to public consultation; and
- that the draft code, or any revision to the code, must be laid in Parliament and subject to the negative resolution procedure.[1]

In respect of Parliamentary scrutiny, the Commission stated:

"The guidance plays a crucial role in our scheme as it will be the means by which the Secretary of State and Welsh Ministers can guide the exercise of local authority functions under the statute, and it will carry substantial legal force. Accordingly, it is important that any changes are given an appropriate degree of scrutiny. This is consistent with the approach adopted by the Mental Health Act 1983 and Mental Capacity Act 2005."[2]

The Department of Health accepted the Law Commission's analysis of the difficulties caused by a plethora of guidance whose status is unclear, but disagreed with the particular solution of a code of practice. It argued:

"A 'code of practice', as distinct from other forms of statutory guidance, is particularly inflexible. Codes of practice require a sizeable lead-in time for amendment (being subject to Parliamentary timetabling), and so can quickly become out of date. They are unable to respond to more urgent situations for the same reason".[3]

The Department felt that the goal could be achieved through a suite or bank of guidance **1–769** that would "look and feel the same" as a code of practice and pointed to this practice in children's services. However, the Department did accept that it would minimise the inclusion of policy statements in guidance and in the future and when such documents are published, their legal status will be made clear.[4]

The Joint Committee disagreed with the Department's approach to the guidance:

"The guidance plays a crucial role. It is the means by which the Secretary of State can guide the exercise of local authority functions under the Bill, and it will carry substantial legal force. In our view, it is important that any changes are given an appropriate degree of Parliamentary scrutiny. We think the approach of the Law Commission is preferable. It is not the title of the document which matters-s.42 of the Mental Capacity Act 2005 makes clear that the codes of practice issued by the Lord Chancellor are 'for the guidance' of those involved-but their statutory status, their Parliamentary control, and the fact that courts may specifically take them into account."[5]

In its response, the Government argued:

"Our view remains that a code of practice would be too inflexible for adult care and support guidance that may quickly become out of date. Our new bank of statutory guidance would have the same legal status and be subject to consultation in the same way as a code of practice. However, because it would not need to be laid before Parliament each time it

---

[1] Law Commission, *Adult Social Care*, paras 3.28 to 3.32.
[2] Law Commission, *Adult Social Care*, para.3.30.
[3] Department of Health, *Reforming the Law for Adult Care and Support: The Government's Response to Law Commission Report 326 on Adult Social Care* (TSO, July 2012), Cm.8379, para.2.15.
[4] Department of Health, *Reforming the Law for Adult Care and Support: The Government's Response to Law Commission Report 326 on Adult Social Care* (TSO, July 2012), Cm.8379, paras 2.15 to 2.17.
[5] House of Lords House of Commons Joint Committee on the Draft Care and Support Bill, *Draft Care and Support Bill Report, Session 2012–13*, para.63.

is amended for any future changes, it could be kept up to date to reflect emerging policy and practice, which would be particularly important in relation to implementing new funding reforms. Our approach is consistent with children's social services legislation, which also uses statutory guidance rather than a code of practice. Where codes of practice are used in other cases, this is usually where the function impacts on fundamental individual rights (for example, in relation to mental health and mental capacity legislation) and the case for Parliamentary oversight is stronger."[1]

Section 78 gives the Secretary of State a power to issue guidance to local authorities about how they exercise their functions under this Part of the Act. Such guidance is given the same status as statutory guidance issued under s.7 of the Local Authority Social Services Act 1970 (see paras 1–772 to 1–773 below). In addition, the Secretary of State continues to have direct powers under s.7 of the 1970 Act to issue guidance to local authorities on the exercise of their social services functions.

During the passage of the Care Bill through Parliament the Government confirmed its intention to develop a "single, consolidated bank of guidance" covering all functions within Pt 1 of the Care Act. It also confirmed that the guidance will be available in accessible formats.[2] Following a consultation process the statutory guidance was published on 23 October 2014. This has been reproduced in Appendix 2, p.641 below. There has been some attempt to address the Law Commission's criticism that the language used in guidance too often lacks clarity. The Department of Health has explained that:

"Where the guidance uses the word "must" it is a reference to a legal requirement in the Act or regulations. Where it uses the word "should", it is a reference to expected best practice. Where it uses the word "may" a local authority has legal or general discretion to act as it chooses (in line with public law obligations to act lawfully)."[3]

The statutory guidance also includes several case studies. The Department has stated that:

"Case studies do not form part of the guidance itself, but are intended as an illustration of the principles or examples of how organisations have gone about implementing them in real circumstances. It is not expected that case studies will be followed in the same way."[4]

The statutory guidance was due to be amended in 2016 to take into account the funding reforms. However, the Government has announced that the introduction of these reforms has been delayed until April 2020.

RANGE OF SECTION 78 GUIDANCE

1–770   As noted above, the Law Commission recommended a single consolidated code of practice for adult social care. However, s.78 does not require a single document. It is clear that the Department of Health intends to use s.78 to issue a range of documents (in addition to the statutory guidance). For example, it has already used s.78 to issue policy guidance on

[1] Department of Health, *The Care Bill explained—including a response to consultation and pre-legislative scrutiny on the draft Care and Support Bill*, para.130.

[2] *Hansard* (House of Commons: Public Bill Committee), 23 January 2014 (PM): Tenth Sitting, col.384 (Norman Lamb MP).

[3] Department of Health, *The Care Act 2014: Consultation on draft regulations and guidance to implement the cap on care costs and policy proposals for a new appeals system for care and support* (2015), para.1.4. See also Department of Health, *Response to the Consultation on draft Regulations and Guidance for Implementation of Part 1 of the Care Act 2014* (2014) Cm 8955, p.9.

[4] Department of Health, *Response to the Consultation on draft Regulations and Guidance for Implementation of Part 1 of the Care Act 2014* (2014) Cm 8955, pp.9 to 10.

care and support for deafblind children and adults.[1] In addition, local authority circulars will be issued under s.78.[2] The Department has also commissioned a range of guidance to support the implementation of the Care Act from a range of bodies, including the Social Care Institute for Excellence and Think Local Act Personal. These publications are not statutory guidance, and their status is likely to be similar to that of practice guidance (see para.1–168 above). It is likely that the proliferation of central government guidance will continue under the Care Act.

AUTISM ACT 2009

The Autism Act 2009 is England's only disability-specific legislation in that it applies **1–771** only to people with autism. It requires the Secretary of State to publish and keep under review "the autism strategy", setting out a strategy for meeting the needs of adults with autistic spectrum conditions by improving the provision of relevant services by local authorities and the NHS.[3] The first autism strategy was published in March 2010, and an update to the strategy was published in April 2014.[4]

Section 2(1) places a duty on the Secretary of State to issue guidance on implementation of the autism strategy to local authorities and the NHS. The guidance must be kept under review and can be revised.[5] Section 2(5) stipulates a range of matters that must be addressed in the guidance. These are:

- the provision or commissioning of diagnostic services for adults with autistic spectrum conditions;
- the identification of adults with autistic spectrum conditions;
- the assessment of the needs of adults with autistic spectrum conditions for relevant services;
- planning in relation to transition arrangements for children with autistic spectrum conditions as they move into adulthood;
- other planning in relation to the provision of relevant services;
- training of staff who provide relevant services to adults with autistic spectrum conditions;
- local leadership arrangements in relation to the provision of relevant services.

Section 3 requires local authorities and the NHS to act under the guidance as if it were guidance issued under s.7 of the Local Authority Social Services Act 1970. Local authorities are therefore under the same duty to act under that guidance as they would be in the case of any s.7 guidance. Moreover, NHS bodies (but not NHS foundation trusts) are also under the same duty to act under the guidance as local authorities.

In the House of Commons, during the passage of the Care Bill, a number of Members of Parliament sought reassurance that the statutory guidance issued under the Autism Act 2009 would remain in place. It was pointed out that guidance issued under s.78 of the Care Act does not place duties on the NHS. This is in contrast to s.4 of the Autism Act which places a duty on local authorities and NHS bodies to act under guidance issued

---

[1] Department of Health, *Care and Support for Deafblind Children and Adults Policy Guidance* (December 2014). This guidance was issued under s.78 of the Care Act and s.7 of the Local Authority Social Services Act 1970 (for children).

[2] See, for example, LAC(DH)(2015) 1: *Social Care – Charging for Care and Support*; LAC(DH)(2015) 3: *Social Care – Deferred payment agreements maximum chargeable interest rate for period 1 July - 31 December 2015*.

[3] Autism Act 2009 s.1.

[4] HM Government, *Fulfilling and Rewarding Lives: The Strategy for Adults with Autism in England* (DH 2010) and HM Government, *Think Autism: Fulfilling and Rewarding Lives, the Strategy for Adults with Autism in England: An Update* (DH 2014).

[5] Autism Act 2009 s.2(3). The current guidance is Department of Health, *Statutory Guidance for Local Authorities and NHS Organisations to Support Implementation of the Autism Strategy* (DH 2015).

under that Act.[1] The Government confirmed that the Autism Act and the duty to issue guidance under it are not affected by s.78 and remain in place.[2] This is confirmed by the statutory guidance to the Care Act which refers assessors to the autism strategy.[3]

The statutory guidance under the Autism Act also cross refers to the duty under the Care and Support (Assessment) Regulations 2014 (SI 2014/2827) to ensure that the person carrying out an assessment has the skills, knowledge and competence to carry out the assessment in question and is appropriately trained (see para.A1–192 below).[4]

Subsection (1)

1–772 This subsection requires local authorities to "act under the general guidance of the Secretary of State". According to the explanatory notes it has been drafted "with the intention that this guidance will have the same legal effect as guidance issued under s.7 of the Local Authority Social Services Act 1970".[5]

The legal effect of guidance issued under s.7 has been considered in a number of cases. In *R v Islington LBC Ex parte Rixon* (1998), Mr Justice Sedley (as he was then) described it in these terms:

> "Clearly guidance is less than direction, and the word 'general' emphasises the non-prescriptive nature of what is envisaged . . . In my judgment Parliament . . . did not intend local authorities to whom ministerial guidance was given to be free, having considered it, to take it or leave it. Such a construction would put this kind of statutory guidance on a par with the many forms of non-statutory guidance issued by departments of state. . . . in my view Parliament by section 7(1) has required local authorities to follow the path charted by the Secretary of State's guidance, with liberty to deviate from it where the local authority judges on admissible grounds that there is good reason to do so, but without freedom to take a substantially different course."[6]

In *R. (Munjaz) v Mersey Care NHS Trust* the House of Lords considered guidance on the seclusion of mental health patients contained in the Mental Health Act Code of Practice issued under s.118 of the Mental Health Act 1983. While this case was not concerned with s.7 of the 1970 Act, Mr Justice Males has argued that what was said "applies equally" to guidance issued under s.7.[7] In *Munjaz*, Lord Bingham stated:

> "It is in my view plain that the Code does not have the binding effect which a statutory provision or a statutory instrument would have. It is what it purports to be, guidance and not instruction. But the matters relied on by Mr Munjaz show that the guidance should be given great weight. It is not instruction, but it is much more than mere advice which an addressee is free to follow or not as it chooses. It is guidance which any hospital should consider with great care, and from which it should depart only if it has cogent reasons for doing so. Where, which is not this case, the guidance addresses a matter covered by s.118(2), any departure would call for even stronger reasons. In reviewing any challenge to a departure from the Code, the court should scrutinise the reasons given by the hospital for departure with the intensity which the importance and sensitivity of the subject matter requires."[8]

Lord Hope added:

---

[1] *Hansard* (House of Commons), 16 December 2013, Vol.572, col.547 (Robert Buckland MP).
[2] *Hansard* (House of Commons: Public Bill Committee), 23 January 2014 (PM): Tenth Sitting, col.385 (Norman Lamb MP).
[3] Department of Health, *Care and Support Statutory Guidance* (2014), paras 6.89 to 6.90.
[4] Department of Health, *Statutory Guidance for Local Authorities and NHS Organisations to Support Implementation of the Autism Strategy* (DH 2015).
[5] Care Act 2014: Explanatory Notes para.472.
[6] *R. v Islington LBC Ex p Rixon* (1998) 1 CCLR 119 at 123(H to I).
[7] *R. (X) v Tower Hamlets LBC* [2013] EWHC 480 (Admin); (2013) 16 CCLR 227 at [28].
[8] *R. (Munjaz) v Mersey Care NHS Trust* [2005] UKHL 58; [2006] 2 A.C. 148 at [21].

"The Court of Appeal said in para 76 of its judgment that the Code is something that those to whom it is addressed are expected to follow unless they have good reason for not doing so: see *R v Islington London Borough Council, ex p Rixon* (1996) 1 CCLR 119, per Sedley J at p.123. Like my noble and learned friend Lord Bingham of Cornhill I would go further. They must give cogent reasons if in any respect they decide not to follow it. These reasons must be spelled out clearly, logically and convincingly. I would emphatically reject any suggestion that they have a discretion to depart from the Code as they see fit. Parliament by enacting s.118(1) has made it clear that it expects that the persons to whom the Code is addressed will follow it, unless they can demonstrate that they have a cogent reason for not doing so. This expectation extends to the Code as a whole, from its statement of the guiding principles to all the detail that it gives with regard to admission and to treatment and care in hospital, except for those parts of it which specify forms of medical treatment requiring consent falling within s.118(2) where the treatment may not be given at all unless the conditions which it sets out are satisfied."[1]

In the case of *Munjaz*, the House of Lords held that sufficient reason had been demon- **1–773** strated for departing from the Code.

In *R. (Forest Care Home Ltd) v Pembroke CC* Mr Justice Hickinbottom doubted whether a local authority's power to depart from statutory guidance was limited to cases where the departure was not "substantial", although the point was not decisive in that case:

"The learned judge went on to insert a restriction on the authority's ability to deviate from the guidance, namely: '. . . but without the freedom to take a substantially different course'. I hesitate to do anything but agree with that too, because of the eminence of (now) Sedley LJ as an administrative lawyer and the fact that the point is not going to be determinative in this claim: but it seems to me, as a matter of principle, Parliament has given the relevant decision-making power to the local authority and, despite the terms of section 7 of the 1970 Act, it would be open to an authority to depart even substantially from guidance if it had sufficiently compelling grounds for so doing. However, certainly, the more the proposed deviation from guidance, the more compelling must be the grounds for departure from it."[2]

That approach has been followed in subsequent High Court cases.[3] The formulation put forward by Mrs Justice Black in *B v Lewisham LBC*—that local authorities have a duty "substantially to follow" the guidance unless there is good reason not to do so—would appear to amount to the same approach.[4]

The current position was thus summarised by Mr Justice Males in *R. (X) v Tower Hamlets LBC*:

"In summary, therefore, the guidance does not have the binding effect of secondary legislation and a local authority is free to depart from it, even 'substantially'. But a departure from the guidance will be unlawful unless there is a cogent reason for it, and the greater the departure, the more compelling must that reason be. Conversely a minor departure from the letter of the guidance while remaining true to its spirit may well be easy to justify or may not even be regarded as a departure at all. The court will scrutinise carefully the reason given by the authority for departing from the guidance. Freedom to depart is not necessarily limited to reasons resulting from 'local circumstances' (see [18]

---

[1] *R. (Munjaz) v Mersey Care NHS Trust* [2005] UKHL 58; [2006] 2 A.C. 148 at [69].

[2] *R. (Forest Care Home Ltd) v Pembroke CC* [2010] EWHC 3514 (Admin); (2011) 14 CCLR 103 at [29].

[3] *R. (Members of the Committee of Care North East Northumberland) v Northumberland CC* [2013] EWHC 234 (Admin) at [34] and *R. (X) v Tower Hamlets LBC* [2013] EWHC 480 (Admin); (2013) 16 CCLR 227 at [32].

[4] *B v Lewisham LBC* [2008] EWHC 738 (Admin); [2013] 2 F.L.R. 523 at [54]. Considered in *R. (X) v Tower Hamlets LBC* [2013] EWHC 480 (Admin); (2013) 16 CCLR 227 at [34] by Males J.

above), although if there are particular local circumstances which suggest that some aspect of the guidance ought not to apply, that may constitute a cogent reason for departure. However, except perhaps in the case of a minor departure, it is difficult to envisage circumstances in which mere disagreement with the guidance could amount to a cogent reason for departing from it." [1]

Subsection (2)

1–774   This subsection requires the Secretary of State to consult relevant persons including stakeholders before issuing guidance under this section.

Subsection (3)

1–775   When the Care Bill was introduced into the House of Lords, the well-being principle applied only to local authorities but not the Secretary of State. The Joint Committee had proposed that the duty should also apply to the Secretary of State when making regulations or guidance. [2] This was rejected by the Government on the basis that the well-being principle is intended to apply at an individual level when a local authority makes a decision and it would therefore not be appropriate for the Secretary of State to be subject to the same duty, as he or she does not make decisions at the individual level. [3] In addition, the Government argued that:

> "It is already the case that the Secretary of State must have regard to the general duty of local authorities to promote an individual's well-being when making guidance or issuing regulations. This is because, when making regulations or issuing guidance, the Secretary of State must consider how local authorities can fulfil their statutory obligations. He cannot ignore those obligations . . .". [4]

However, due to the strength of feeling in the House of Lords, the Government was persuaded to amend s.78 (even though it felt an amendment in this respect was not essential) to explicitly require the Secretary of State to have regard to the local authority well-being duty when issuing regulations and guidance. [5]

Delegation of local authority functions

1–776   **79.**—(1) A local authority may authorise a person to exercise on its behalf a function it has under—

(a) this Part or regulations under this Part (but see subsection (2)), or

(b) section 117 of the Mental Health Act 1983 (after-care services).

(2) The references in subsection (1)(a) to this Part do not include a reference to—

(a) section 3 (promoting integration with health services etc.),

(b) sections 6 and 7 (co-operating),

(c) section 14 (charges),

(d) sections 42 to 47 (safeguarding adults at risk of abuse or neglect), or

(e) this section.

(3) An authorisation under this section may authorise an employee of the authorised person to exercise the function to which the authorisation relates; and for that purpose, where the authorised person is a body corporate, "employee" includes a director or officer of the body.

---

[1] *R(X) v London Borough of Tower Hamlets* [2013] EWHC 480 (Admin), (2013) 16 CCLR 227 at [35]

[2] House of Lords House of Commons Joint Committee on the Draft Care and Support Bill, *Draft Care and Support Bill. Report—Session 2012–13*, para.83.

[3] *Hansard* (House of Lords), 21 May 2013, Vol.745, col.829 (Earl Howe).

[4] *Hansard* (House of Lords), 3 July 2013, Vol.746, col.1271 (Earl Howe).

[5] *Hansard* (House of Lords), 9 October 2013, Vol.748, col.85 (Earl Howe).

(4) An authorisation under this section may authorise the exercise of the function to which it relates—

(a) either wholly or to the extent specified in the authorisation;

(b) either generally or in cases, circumstances or areas so specified;

(c) either unconditionally or subject to conditions so specified.

(5) An authorisation under this section—

(a) is for the period specified in the authorisation;

(b) may be revoked by the local authority;

(c) does not prevent the local authority from exercising the function to which the authorisation relates.

(6) Anything done or omitted to be done by or in relation to a person authorised under this section in, or in connection with, the exercise or purported exercise of the function to which the authorisation relates is to be treated for all purposes as done or omitted to be done by or in relation to the local authority.

(7) But subsection (6) does not apply—

(a) for the purposes of the terms of any contract between the authorised person and the local authority which relate to the function, or

(b) for the purposes of any criminal proceedings brought in respect of anything done or omitted to be done by the authorised person.

(8) Schedule 15 to the Deregulation and Contracting Out Act 1994 (which permits disclosure of information between local authorities and contractors where that is necessary for the exercise of the functions concerned, even if that would otherwise be unlawful) applies to an authorisation under this section as it applies to an authorisation by virtue of an order under section 70(2) of that Act.

(9) The Secretary of State may by order—

(a) amend subsection (2) so as to add to or remove from the list a provision of this Part;

(b) amend subsection (1) so as to add to or remove from the list a provision relating to care and support for adults or support for carers;

(c) impose conditions or other restrictions on the exercise of the power under subsection (1), whether by amending this section or otherwise.

(10) The provision which may be made in an order under subsection (9) in reliance on section 125(8) (supplementary etc. provision in orders under this Act) includes, in particular, provision as to the rights and obligations of local authorities and persons authorised under this section in light of the provision made by the order.

(11) "Function" includes a power to do anything that is calculated to facilitate, or is conducive or incidental to, the exercise of a function.

GENERAL NOTE

This section provides an express power for local authorities to authorise a third party to **1–777** carry out certain care and support functions. An express power is necessary because generally in public law, a discretion conferred by statute is intended to be exercised by the authority on which the statute has conferred it and cannot be delegated, although this presumption "may be rebutted by any contrary indications found in the language, scope or object of the statute".[1] The delegation of local authority functions is discussed in Ch.18 of the statutory guidance.

---

[1] H. Woolf, J. Jowell and A. Le Suer, *De Smith's Judicial Review*, 6th edn (2007), para.5–139 citing J. Willis *"Delegatus non potest delegare"* (1943) 21 *Canadian Bar Review* 257, 259.

The use of delegation of statutory social work services has been increasing in recent years, particularly in respect of children and families services. Part 1 of the Children and Young Persons Act 2008 makes provision for local authorities to delegate functions relating to children looked after and care leavers to third parties. The Government has proposed to make regulations allowing a local authority to enter into arrangements with a body corporate for the discharge of a wider range of its social services functions relating to children.[1] Recent years has also seen the piloting of Independent Social Work Practices which are social worker-led organisations (including social enterprises) that have responsibility for undertaking delegated social work functions, managing day-to-day support, co-ordinating and monitoring service provision.[2] These were originally piloted in respect of children's services but were subsequently developed for adult care and support.[3] The White Paper, *Caring for Our Future*, set out the policy intention that many new providers (such as social enterprises and carers' centres) should be able to offer assessment services.[4]

Section 75 of the National Health Service Act 2006 permits delegation and sharing of functions between local authorities and NHS bodies.

Subsection (2)

1–778   This sets out the functions which are excluded, and which therefore may not be delegated to a third party. These excluded functions are:

- s.3 (promoting integration with health services);
- ss.6 and 7 (co-operating generally and in specific cases);
- s.14 (power of a local authority to charge);
- ss.42 to 47 (safeguarding adults at risk of abuse or neglect); or
- this section.

See para.18.16 of the statutory guidance which explains why these functions have been excluded. The guidance also confirms that local authorities may still commission or arrange for other parties to carry out certain related activities (for instance arranging for the NHS to undertake a safeguarding enquiry or commissioning an external agency to bill and collect fees for care and support).[5]

Originally, this subsection had included a prohibition on the delegation of direct payments. However, this prohibition was removed as a result of a Government amendment at report stage in the House of Commons after feedback from local authorities suggested it would "make sense for them to have flexibility to be able to delegate functions relating to direct payments if they so wish".[6]

Subsection (4)

1–779   The local authority may determine the extent to which it delegates the function in any particular case. The explanatory notes state that:

"For example, a local authority may delegate the carrying out of all needs assessments to a third party organisation, or it may choose to delegate assessments only for certain groups of people, but carry out other assessments itself. When delegating any function, the local authority may impose conditions on the way the third party may exercise the function."[7]

---

[1] Department for Education, *Powers to Delegate Children's Social Care Functions* (17 April 2014).
[2] Department for Education, *Social Work Practices: Report of the National Evaluation* (27 September 2012).
[3] See, Social Care Institute for Excellence, *Social Work Practice Pilots and Pioneers in Social Work for Adults* (May 2013) and Social Care Workforce Research Unit, *Evaluation of the Social Work Practices with Adults Pilots* (July 2014).
[4] HM Government, *Caring for Our Future: Reforming Care and Support* (July 2012), Cm.8378, p.33.
[5] Department of Health, *Care and Support Statutory Guidance* (2014), paras 18.16 to 18.21.
[6] *Hansard* (House of Commons), 10 March 2014, Vol.577, col.90 (Norman Lamb MP).
[7] Care Act 2014: Explanatory Notes para.477.

An example of such a condition might be that a qualified practitioner must carry out assessments, and that their training must be kept up-to-date. The statutory guidance confirms that delegated organisations can be authorised to take final decisions, or the local authority can retain responsibility for final decisions. The authority can continue to exercise the function it has delegated (for instance by offering a choice between the external organisation and itself).[1] The guidance also makes clear that conditions can be used to mitigate conflicts of interest (for example by delegating care and support planning but retaining control of signing off the personal budget), and that— in line with standard anti-fraud practice—where local authorities delegate their functions relating to assessment of needs or calculation of personal budgets to an external party, any direct payment should be made by the local authority.[2]

Subsection (5)

Any delegation under this section is only for the period specified in the authorisation. **1–780** The local authority may revoke the authorisation at any time during that period and delegating the function does not prevent the local authority from being able to carry out the function itself.

Subsections (6)

Anything done (or failed to be done) by the third party in carrying out any function dele- **1–781** gated to them is treated as done (or not done) by the local authority itself. According to the explanatory notes:

> "This means that the delegation of any function does not absolve the local authority from ultimate responsibility for ensuring the function is carried out properly and in accordance with all relevant statutory obligations."[3]

During the passage of the Care Bill, in the House of Lords, the Government confirmed that the Human Rights Act 1998 applies to the discharge of public functions so that when a local authority delegates its public functions to a third party, that function must still be carried out in a way that complies with the 1998 Act. It follows that "any failure to carry out the function in a way that is compliant with the Human Rights Act will be considered a failure by the local authority".[4] However, Lord Low pointed out that this is not the same as the third party being subject to the Human Rights Act; the third party would be failing its obligations to the local authority, but to no one else.[5]

At report stage in the House of Lords, Lord Low revisited this general issue and attempted to amend the Bill to make it clear that a person with delegated authority is subject to the same legal obligations as a local authority itself. This reflected a similar point made by the Joint Committee that there should be a clear chain of accountability by which the individual could hold the third party, not just the local authority, responsible if their rights were infringed.[6]

The Government argued that this amendment was unnecessary because when it delegates its functions, s.79(6) provides that the local authority remains responsible for the way that that function is discharged:

> "The person using care and support will therefore always have a route of redress against the local authority even if the local authority has delegated the discharge of the function to a third party . . . By making both the local authority and the contractor liable, [the

---

[1] Department of Health, *Care and Support Statutory Guidance* (2014), paras 18.14 to 18.15.

[2] Department of Health, *Care and Support Statutory Guidance* (2014), paras 18.22 to 18.25.

[3] Care Act 2014: Explanatory Notes para.479.

[4] *Hansard* (House of Lords), 29 July 2013, Vol.747, col.1586 (Baroness Northover).

[5] *Hansard* (House of Lords), 29 July 2013, Vol.747, col.1587 (Lord Low).

[6] *Hansard* (House of Lords), 16 October 2013, Vol.748, col.544 and House of Lords House of Commons Joint Committee on the Draft Care and Support Bill, *Draft Care and Support Bill Report, Session 2012–13*, para.284.

amendment] could create a lack of clarity about who is ultimately responsible for complying with the local authority's statutory obligations when a function is delegated".[1]

The statutory guidance confirms the position established under subs.(6):

"Since care and support functions are public functions, they must be carried out in a way that is compatible with all of the local authority's legal obligations. For example, the local authority would be liable for any breach by the delegated party, of its legal obligations under the Human Rights Act or the Data Protection Act. Local authorities should therefore draw up its contracts so as to ensure that third parties carry out functions in a way that is compatible with all of their legal obligations."[2]

It also confirms that delegated organisations will be responsible for any criminal proceedings brought against them.[3]

Subsection (7)

1–782   When a local authority arranges with the third party to carry out a public function, the local authority will have contractual recourse against that third party for any breach of contract. Moreover, a third party cannot avoid liability for any criminal actions. The explanatory notes state that:

"This means that the delegation of any function does not absolve the local authority from ultimate responsibility for ensuring the function is carried out properly and in accordance with all relevant statutory obligations."[4]

The statutory guidance also explains that:

"The delegated organisation will be liable to the local authority for any breach of the contract, and as such this is the mechanism through which local authorities are able to ensure that its functions are carried out properly, and through which they may hold the contractor to account."[5]

Subsection (8)

1–783   This permits the disclosure of information between the local authority and the third party where it is necessary for the exercise of the delegated function, even where the disclosure would otherwise be unlawful. It does this by applying the provisions of Sch.15 of the Deregulation and Contracting Out Act 1994 to any delegation made under this provision. The explanatory notes explain that the third party is then subject to the confidentiality requirements in respect of that information as was the local authority.[6]

Subsection (9)

1–784   The Secretary of State is given an order-making power to change the list of functions to which this power applies, and also to impose conditions and limitations on the exercising of the power. An order under this provision is subject to the affirmative procedure in Parliament (see s.125(4)(l)). The affirmative procedure is discussed at para.1–161 above.

Subsections (11)

1–785   This confirms that the term "function" has a wide meaning which includes anything that is calculated to facilitate, or is conducive or incidental to, the exercise of a function.

---

[1] *Hansard* (House of Lords), 16 October 2013, Vol.748, col.559 (Earl Howe).
[2] Department of Health, *Care and Support Statutory Guidance* (2014), para.18.12.
[3] Department of Health, *Care and Support Statutory Guidance* (2014), para.18.13.
[4] Care Act 2014: Explanatory Notes para.479.
[5] Department of Health, *Care and Support Statutory Guidance* (2014), para.18.9.
[6] Care Act 2014: Explanatory Notes para.480.

GENERAL

Part 1: Interpretation

80.—(1) For the purposes of this Part, an expression in the first column of the following table is defined or otherwise explained by the provision of this Act specified in the second column.

1–786

Expression	Provision
Abuse	Section 42(3)
Accrued costs	Section 15(5)
Adult	Section 2(8)
Adult needing care	Section 10(3)
Authority under the Mental Capacity Act 2005	Subsection (3) below
Best interests	Subsection (2) below
Cap on care costs	Section 15(4)
Capacity, having or lacking	Subsection (2) below
Care and support plan	Section 25
Care account	Section 29
Carer (other than in sections 58 to 62)	Section 10(3)
Carer's assessment	Sections 10(2) and 12(8) and (9)
Child's carer's assessment	Section 60(2)
Child's needs assessment	Section 58(2)
Daily living costs, amount attributable to	Section 15(8)
Deferred payment agreement	Section 34
Direct payment	Sections 31 and 32
Eligibility criteria	Section 13
Financial assessment	Section 17(5)
Financial limit	Section 17(10)
Financial year	Section 126
The health service	Section 126
Independent personal budget	Section 28
Local authority	Section 1(4)
Needs assessment	Sections 9(2) and 12(8) and (9)
Parent	Section 58(6)
Personal budget	Section 26
Registered care provider	Section 48
Support plan	Section 25
Well-being	Section 1(2)
Young carer	Section 63(6)
Young carer's assessment	Section 63(2)

(2) A reference in this Part to having or lacking capacity, or to a person's best interests, is to be interpreted in accordance with the Mental Capacity Act 2005.

(3) A reference in this Part to being authorised under the Mental Capacity Act 2005 is a reference to being authorised (whether in general or specific terms) as—

(a) a donee of a lasting power of attorney granted under that Act, or

(b) a deputy appointed by the Court of Protection under section 16(2)(b) of that Act.

GENERAL NOTE

1–787   Section 80 sets out an index of defined terms used in Pt 1 of the Care Act.

SCHEDULES

Section 39   SCHEDULE 1

GENERAL NOTE

A cross-border placement describes a situation where a person with care and support **1–788**
needs is being, or has been, placed by a public authority into residential accommodation
in a different UK country.

Schedule 1 applies to cross-border placements made by local authorities (in England,
Scotland, and Wales) and Health and Social Care Trusts (in Northern Ireland). Health
and social care are devolved under each settlement to Wales, Scotland and Northern
Ireland. Accordingly, the Scottish Parliament, National Assembly for Wales and
Northern Ireland Assembly have legislative competence for health and social care, and
the devolved governments in each country have executive powers and responsibilities.
The NHS and social services are therefore now administered differently in each of the
four countries of the UK. The provisions contained in Sch.1 and the relevant statutory guidance contained in Ch.21 have therefore been developed with the agreement of the four UK
governments.

The overarching principle of Sch.1 is that the placing authority retains responsibility for
the care of those individuals placed cross-border. This responsibility is not interrupted even
if the individual requires a period in hospital or other health care accommodation. This
means that, amongst other matters, the cap on care costs (if any) that has been set in the
jurisdiction of the placing authority will continue to apply to the individual. Paragraphs
9 and 10 of the schedule also enable regulations to apply the cross-border provisions to
accommodation that is being paid for by direct payments and to individuals placed in a setting other than a traditional care home, for example supported living arrangements.[1]

During the passage of the Care Bill through the House of Commons, it was queried why
cross-border provisions had not been introduced for community-based care packages.[2] In
response the Government stated that in such a situation the individuals would normally
become ordinarily resident in their new local authority, and that local authority would
therefore be the responsible authority should the individual need care and support.
However, it said it would work with the devolved administrations to "develop understandings in principle about cross-border continuity of care that achieve the same practical effect
as further legislation".[3]

Similarly the cross-border provisions do not apply if a person moves to a care home with- **1–789**
out being placed by their local authority or trust. Such individuals will usually become
ordinarily resident in the new area and the appropriate contribution they should make to
the costs of their care will be determined by the arrangements in the relevant country.

The four UK governments have agreed the following guiding principles which should be
applied to all cross-border placements:

- authorities should ensure a person-centred process and take into account the outcomes an adult wishes to achieve;
- authorities should work together and share information about their local care and
  support system and services;

---

[1] *Hansard* (House of Lords), 14 October 2013, Vol.748, col.317 (Earl Howe).
[2] *Hansard* (House of Commons), 16 December 2013, Vol.572, col.565 (Shelia Gilmore MP) and
   Hansard (House of Commons: Public Bill Committee), 21 January 2014 (AM): Seventh Sitting,
   cols 245 to 246 (Liz Kendall MP).
[3] *Hansard* (House of Commons: Public Bill Committee), 21 January 2014 (AM): Seventh Sitting,
   col.247 (Norman Lamb MP).

- the adult moving should be given relevant information, in an accessible format, about local care and support provision in the authority they are moving to;
- authorities should work together to support a move across national boundaries to ensure the adult's care and support is continued during the move; and
- authorities should share relevant information about the adult's care and support needs and any other information which it believes necessary in a timely manner and with the consent of the adult involved.[1]

WHAT IS MEANT BY A PLACEMENT?

1–790 In order for a cross-border placement to arise the authority must have arranged the residential care placement with the care provider by entering into a contract. It therefore follows that a cross-border placement will not normally arise in cases where a person moves of their volition into permanent residential accommodation in a new country having contracted privately with the provider, and is funding their own care. In this type of scenario the person will usually become the responsibility of the new authority into whose area they have moved. If they subsequently become in need of care and support (or their capital falls below the relevant threshold), they would usually need to approach the authority in which their residential accommodation is situated.

The meaning of residential accommodation is explained in para.1–824 below.

SELF-FUNDERS AND CROSS-BORDER PLACEMENTS

1–791 A cross-border placement can be made when the authority or the individual is paying, according to their means, some or all of the costs for the residential accomodation. The essential feature of a Sch.1 placement is that the accommodation has been arranged or provided by the authority. The mere fact that a person has capital in excess of the relevant threshold for financial support from the authority does not mean that a cross-border placement cannot or should not be made. In England, Wales and Northern Ireland, the authority will need to consider whether the person is able to manage their own affairs and whether the person has someone who can make the necessary arrangements on their behalf. If the answer to both of these questions is "no", it is likely that a cross-border placement will need to be arranged by the authority for the self-funder.

In determining whether there is anyone else in a position to act on the adult's behalf, the authority should consider if there is someone both willing and able to make suitable arrangements. There is no legal obligation to take on this role and it should not be assumed that just because a person is a family member or a carer, they should be expected to make the necessary arrangements. The ability to make arrangements includes having the appropriate legal authority (for instance under the relevant mental capacity legislation).

The approach is different in Scotland where the duty to provide accommodation does not depend on these questions. Rather, it arises simply on identification of need and the person in such need being physically present in the authority's area.

DID THE AUTHORITY MAKE THE ARRANGEMENTS?

1–792 A Sch.1 placement means that an authority has made the arrangements to provide the accommodation. The making of arrangements entails more than just facilitating a move. An authority can assist a person with care and support needs with their move by helping them to select the accommodation, and by transporting them to visit potential new care homes. The authority can even advise on the assessment and suitability of the accommodation and can go on to help the person move in and settle. However, unless the local authority makes the arrangements by entering into a contract with the provider, it is

---

[1] Department of Health, *Principles for Maintaining Continuity of Care When Moving Across Borders Within the United Kingdom* (26 March 2015).

unlikely that the person will be considered to have been placed by the authority under Sch.1.

This principle will also apply where the person lacks capacity to decide their living arrangements. If the relevant arrangements have been undertaken for or on behalf of the person—for instance by an appointed decision-maker (such as a guardian, attorney or deputy) or by a private individual (such as a friend, family member or carer) in accordance with the relevant law—this is likely to be a privately arranged move. In contrast, if the authority has made the arrangements to provide the accommodation by entering into a contract—even with the involvement of the appointed decision-makers and private individuals—this is likely to be a cross-border placement.

It should be noted that authorities cannot escape responsibility if they are legally obliged to make the necessary arrangements for the placements. In such a case the person would continue to be the responsibility of the area in which they resided immediately before the accommodation should have been provided.[1]

THE 12-WEEK PROPERTY DISREGARD

Where an authority arranges permanent residential care for a person, the value of the **1–793** resident's main or only home is normally disregarded for the purposes of the financial assessment for the first 12 weeks of local authority arranged care (see para.A1–152 below). During the 12-week disregard period, the person remains the responsibility of the authority in which they lived prior to moving into residential care. The authority in these circumstances will have entered into a contract with the provider. However, at the end of the 12-week period, the value of the person's home is taken into account (unless it remains the home of the person's spouse, civil partner, partner or certain other relatives). This may result in the person becoming a self-funder and entering into a private contract with the care home for the provision of their care on a permanent basis, rather than continuing to be provided with accommodation by their placing authority. In such a case, the placement would have ended and the person is likely to become ordinarily resident in the area of their care home. However, the ending of a placement will depend on a number of factors including the ability of the person to manage their affairs, and the ability and willingness of someone else to make the necessary arrangements on the person's behalf. In Scotland, different rules apply. If a person with capacity moved into a care home in Scotland under private arrangement and was self-funding, the 12-week disregard would not apply. The disregard would only be provided when the authority itself is required—because of need and/or eligibility for free personal and nursing care—to provide the accommodation and accordingly is required to assess the person's ability to pay for it.

DEFERRED PAYMENT AGREEMENTS

The responsibility for offering and funding a deferred payment is with the placing auth- **1–794** ority. Normally this option is made available during or at the end of the 12-week property disregard period (see above). If the person accepts the offer and enters into a deferred payment agreement, the placing authority remains responsible for funding their care and maintaining a contract with the care home on their behalf. These actions (ie, the making and maintenance of the contract) constitute "the making of arrangements" for the purposes of a cross-border placement.

If the person decides against having a deferred payment, they may revert to self-funding status at the end of the 12-week property disregard period. If this is the case, and they later require local authority funded care and support services (including the option to enter into a deferred payment agreement), they would need to approach the authority in which the care home is located.

---

[1] *R. (London Borough of Greenwich) v Secretary of State for Health* [2006] EWHC 2576 (Admin); (2007) 10 CCLR 60.

If the placing authority had failed to offer the person information about deferred payment agreements during the 12-week property disregard period, the placing authority would remain responsible for the provision of a deferred payment agreement should the person require one in the future.

TRANSITION AND CROSS-BORDER PLACEMENTS

1–795   When a young person with social care needs reaches the age of 18, the duty on local authorities to provide accommodation and services under children's legislation usually ends. If a child or young person has been placed in residential accommodation in a different UK country—and they subsequently turn 18—they are likely to remain the responsibility of the placing authority.

In *R.(Cornwall) v Secretary of State for Health* the Supreme Court held that a young person—who had been placed in foster care in South Gloucestershire which had been arranged by Wiltshire Council under the Children Act 1989—continued to be ordinarily resident in Wiltshire when he reached 18.[1] The Court set out that the underlying purpose of both children's and adult legislation is that "an authority should not be able to export its responsibility for providing the necessary accommodation by exporting the person who is in need of it" and it would be highly undesirable for there to be a hiatus in the legislation whereby a young person placed in a different area would become ordinarily resident in that area on their 18th birthday.[2]

1–796   In some cases the young person may have "looked after status". This broadly means that the child or young person is in a local authority's care by virtue of a care order or is provided with accommodation by a local authority in the exercise of their social services functions. A young person's "looked after status" ends when they reach 18. But sometimes the local authority which was formerly responsible for them retains some ongoing duties, for example to provide an advisor and support. These duties continue after the person has reached 18, and would normally be the responsibility of the placing authority. However, the residential accommodation will normally be provided under adult legislation.

WHAT IF THE PERSON LEAVES THE ACCOMMODATION?

1–797   If the person who has been placed subsequently leaves the accommodation of his or her own volition and for instance enters a tenancy agreement in rented accommodation in the area in which they had been placed, the person will normally become ordinarily resident in that area. The position is different in Scotland. A person in this case would only become ordinarily resident in a Scottish authority if he or she had capacity to make decisions about their living disparagements or the decision to reside there had been taken by someone authorised to do so on their behalf.

This will be the case even if the person's needs remain the same. However, there may be cases where the person leaves the accommodation provided by the local authority in circumstances which don't suggest a settled intention to reside elsewhere. For example, this may occur because of provider failure or a dispute with the authority about the quality of the accommodation or the services being provided. In such cases it is possible that the person would remain the responsibility of the first authority and practitioners would need to consider the relevant ordinary residence guidance in the light of the circumstances of the case.

WHAT IF THE CARE HOME DE-REGISTERS?

1–798   Sometimes a care home may de-register and become accommodation with support, with the individual signing his or her own tenancy agreement (if they have capacity to do so). In

---

[1]   *R. (Cornwall Council) v Secretary of State for Health* [2015] UKSC 46.
[2]   *R. (Cornwall Council) v Secretary of State for Health* [2015] UKSC 46 at [54].

some cases the individual will be agreeing to continue with the same arrangements, live in the same place and receive the same services. It is suggested in the statutory guidance that where the person remains living at the same property and their needs continue to be met by the new service, then their ordinary residence should not be affected and the duty to meet their needs will remain with the placing authority.[1] If a person lacks capacity to sign the tenancy agreement the relevant mental capacity legislation will need to be considered. For instance, in Scotland only the person with legal authority would be authorised to sign.

PROVIDER FAILURE

Regulations made under the Care Act 2010 set out what should happen in respect of **1–799** cross-border placements when the provider is unable to continue to provide care services. The relevant regulations are the Care and Support (Cross-border Placements)(Business Failure Duties of Scottish Local Authorities) Regulations 2014 (SI 2014/2839) and Care and Support (Cross-border Placements and Business Failure: Temporary Duty)(Dispute Resolution Regulations 2014 (SI 2014/2843)). In general terms these regulations provide that if a care provider fails and ceases to provide a service, the authority in whose area that individual is placed should ensure the person's needs are being met for as long as appropriate. The first authority will normally continue to have overall responsibility.

HAGUE CONVENTION

The Hague Convention on the International Protection of Adults 2000 may be relevant to **1–800** some cross-border placements.[2] It sets out rules on the recognition and enforcement of enforcement measures in all Contracting States. Therefore, if a person is being placed cross-border, and is subject to some form of protective measure (such as a court order) in the country of the placing authority, the Convention allows the measure to be recognised in the new country in certain circumstances. There is also provision for co-operation to support the workings of the Convention.

The position in relation to the Convention in the UK is not straightforward. Only Scotland has ratified it. But s.63 and Sch.3 to the Mental Capacity Act 2005 give effect to the Convention in England and Wales. In particular this provides for mutual recognition, enforcement and implementation of "protection measures" imposed by a foreign court regardless of whether the country has ratified the Convention. However, some parts of the Convention have not been included in the Mental Capacity Act.

Mr Justice Baker in *Health Service Executive of Ireland v PA* held that by including Sch.3 in the Mental Capacity Act, Parliament must be assumed to have permitted foreign orders to be recognised notwithstanding that they may be inconsistent with the law and procedures in England and Wales. As the definition of "adult" in Sch.3 "plainly extends to persons who may not be incapacitated", it follows that the court must recognise and enforce orders of a foreign court in terms that could not be included in an order made under the domestic jurisdiction under the Mental Capacity Act. It is only where the court concludes that recognition of the foreign measure would be manifestly contrary to public policy that the discretionary ground to refuse recognition will arise.[3]

Placements from England to Wales, Scotland or Northern Ireland
1.—(1) Where a local authority in England is meeting an adult's needs for care and support by **1–801** arranging for the provision of accommodation in Wales, the adult—
   (a) is to be treated for the purposes of this Part as ordinarily resident in the local authority's area, and

---

[1] Department of Health, *Care and Support Statutory Guidance* (2014), para.19.38.
[2] Hague Convention on the International Protection of Adults (13 January 2000).
[3] *Health Service Executive of Ireland v PA* [2015] EWCOP 38 at [93] and [98].

(b) is accordingly not to be treated for the purposes of the Social Services and Well-being (Wales) Act 2014 as ordinarily resident anywhere in Wales.

(2) Where a local authority in England, in reliance on section 22(4), is making arrangements which include the provision of accommodation in Wales, section 22(4) is to have effect as if for paragraph (a) there were substituted—

"(a) the authority has obtained consent for it to arrange for the provision of the nursing care from the Local Health Board for the area in which the accommodation is provided,".

(3) Where a local authority in England is meeting an adult's needs for care and support by arranging for the provision of accommodation in Scotland—

(a) the adult is to be treated for the purposes of this Part as ordinarily resident in the local authority's area, and

(b) no duty under Part 2 of the Social Work (Scotland) Act 1968 or sections 25 to 27 of the Mental Health (Care and Treatment) (Scotland) Act 2003 applies in the adult's case.

(4) Where a local authority in England is meeting an adult's needs for care and support by arranging for the provision of accommodation in Northern Ireland—

(a) the adult is to be treated for the purposes of this Part as ordinarily resident in the local authority's area, and

(b) no duty under the Health and Personal Social Services (Northern Ireland) Order 1972 or the Health and Social Care (Reform) Act (Northern Ireland) 2009 to provide or secure the provision of accommodation or other facilities applies in the adult's case.

(5) Section 22 (prohibition on provision of health services) is to have effect—

(a) in its application to a case within sub-paragraph (1)—

(i) as if the references in subsections (1) and (6) to the National Health Service Act 2006 included a reference to the National Health Service (Wales) Act 2006, and

(ii) as if the reference in subsection (6) to a clinical commissioning group or the National Health Service Commissioning Board included a reference to a Local Health Board;

(b) in its application to a case within sub-paragraph (3)—

(i) as if the references in subsections (1) and (6) to the National Health Service Act 2006 included a reference to the National Health Service (Scotland) Act 1978, and

(ii) as if the reference in subsection (6) to a clinical commissioning group or the National Health Service Commissioning Board included a reference to a Health Board or Special Health Board;

(c) in its application to a case within sub-paragraph (4)—

(i) as if the references in subsections (1) and (6) to a service or facility provided under the National Health Service Act 2006 included a reference to health care provided under the Health and Personal Social Services (Northern Ireland) Order 1972 or the Health and Social Care (Reform) Act (Northern Ireland) 2009, and

(ii) as if the reference in subsection (6) to a clinical commissioning group or the National Health Service Commissioning Board included a reference to a Health and Social Care trust.

(6) Regulations may make further provision in relation to arrangements of the kind referred to in this paragraph.

(7) The regulations may specify circumstances in which, in a case within subparagraph (3), specified duties under Part 2 of the Social Work (Scotland) Act 1968 are nonetheless to apply in the case of the adult concerned (and paragraph (b) of that sub-paragraph is to be read accordingly).

GENERAL NOTE

1–802   Paragraph 1 provides that if a local authority in England places someone in residential care in Wales, Scotland or Northern Ireland, that person will remain the responsibility of the English local authority. They do not acquire ordinary residence in their new location and for example the cap on care costs that is set in England will continue to apply to them.

Sub-paragraph (5)

1–803   This was added by at Government amendment during the passage of the Care Bill, at Committee stage of the House of Lords. The intention was to ensure that the prohibition on English local authorities providing NHS care in England in s.22 of the Care Act is mirrored when the English local authority places someone in residential accommodation across the border. The provision also mirrors the regulation-making power in s.22(6), to require the English local authority to be involved, as necessary, in processes for assessing a person's health needs, which would be led by the relevant NHS body.[1]

Sub-paragraph (7)
This enables the regulations to specify circumstances in which, in the case of a person **1–804** who has been placed in accommodation in Scotland, certain duties of Scottish local authorities under Pt 2 of the Social Work (Scotland) Act 1968 will nonetheless apply in the case of the adult concerned. The relevant regulations are the Care and Support (Cross-border Placements) (Business Failure Duties of Scottish Local Authorities) Regulations 2014 (SI 2014/2839). They are reproduced at paras A1–209 to A1–214 below. Regulation 3 sets out that the circumstances are that the care provider with whom the arrangements have been made is unable to continue to provide the care service in respect of which those arrangements have been made and this inability arises following any of the events set out in reg. 4. The duties are to continue to be discharged for so long as the local authority considers necessary. Regulation 5 sets out the duties under the 1968 Act which are to apply.

Placements from Wales to England, Scotland or Northern Ireland
2.—(1) Where a local authority in Wales is discharging its duty under section 35 of the Social **1–805** Services and Well-being (Wales) Act 2014 by arranging for the provision of accommodation in England, the adult concerned—
    (a) is to be treated for the purposes of that Act as ordinarily resident in the local authority's area, and
    (b) is accordingly not to be treated for the purposes of this Part of this Act as ordinarily resident anywhere in England.
(2) Where a local authority in Wales is arranging for the provision of accommodation in England in the exercise of its power under section 36 of the Social Services and Well-being (Wales) Act 2014—
    (a) the adult concerned is to be treated for the purposes of that Act—
        (i) in a case where the adult was within the local authority's area immediately before being provided by the local authority with accommodation in England, as remaining within that area;
        (ii) in a case where the adult was outside but ordinarily resident in the local authority's area immediately before being provided by the local authority with accommodation in England, as remaining outside but ordinarily resident in that area, and
    (b) the adult concerned is not to be treated for the purposes of this Part of this Act as ordinarily resident anywhere in England (unless the adult was so ordinarily resident immediately before being provided by the local authority with accommodation in England).
(3) Where a local authority in Wales is discharging its duty under section 35 of the Social Services and Well-being (Wales) Act 2014 by arranging for the provision of accommodation in Scotland—
    (a) the adult is to be treated for the purposes of that Act as ordinarily resident in the local authority's area, and
    (b) no duty under Part 2 of the Social Work (Scotland) Act 1968 or sections 25 to 27 of the Mental Health (Care and Treatment) (Scotland) Act 2003 applies in the adult's case.
(4) Where a local authority in Wales is arranging for the provision of accommodation in Scotland in the exercise of its power under section 36 of the Social Services and Well-being (Wales) Act 2014—
    (a) the adult concerned is to be treated for the purposes of that Act—
        (i) in a case where the adult was within the local authority's area immediately before being provided by the local authority with accommodation in Scotland, as remaining within that area;
        (ii) in a case where the adult was outside but ordinarily resident in the local authority's area immediately before being provided by the local authority with accommodation in Scotland, as remaining outside but ordinarily resident in that area, and
    (b) no duty under Part 2 of the Social Work (Scotland) Act 1968 or sections 25 to 27 of the Mental Health (Care and Treatment) (Scotland) Act 2003 applies in the adult's case.
(5) But paragraph (b) of sub-paragraph (4) does not prevent a duty mentioned in that paragraph from applying in the case of an adult who was ordinarily resident in Scotland immediately before being provided by the local authority with accommodation in Scotland.

---

[1] *Hansard* (House of Lords), 22 July 2013, Vol.747, cols 1088 to 1089 (Baroness Northover).

(6) Where a local authority in Wales is discharging its duty under section 35 of the Social Services and Well-being (Wales) Act 2014 by arranging for the provision of accommodation in Northern Ireland—

    (a) the adult is to be treated for the purposes of that Act as ordinarily resident in the local authority's area, and

    (b) no duty under the Health and Personal Social Services (Northern Ireland) Order 1972 or the Health and Social Care (Reform) Act (Northern Ireland) 2009 to provide or secure the provision of accommodation or other facilities applies in the adult's case.

(7) Where a local authority in Wales is arranging for the provision of accommodation in Northern Ireland in the exercise of its power under section 36 of the Social Services and Well-being (Wales) Act 2014—

    (a) the adult concerned is to be treated for the purposes of that Act—

        (i) in a case where the adult was within the local authority's area immediately before being provided by the local authority with accommodation in Northern Ireland, as remaining within that area;

        (ii) in a case where the adult was outside but ordinarily resident in the local authority's area immediately before being provided by the local authority with accommodation in Northern Ireland, as remaining outside but ordinarily resident in that area, and

    (b) no duty under the Health and Personal Social Services (Northern Ireland) Order 1972 or the Health and Social Care (Reform) Act (Northern Ireland) 2009 to provide or secure the provision of accommodation or other facilities applies in the adult's case.

(8) But paragraph (b) of sub-paragraph (7) does not prevent a duty mentioned in that paragraph from applying in the case of an adult who was ordinarily resident in Northern Ireland immediately before being provided by the local authority with accommodation in Northern Ireland.

(9) Regulations may make further provision in relation to arrangements of the kind referred to in this paragraph.

(10) The regulations may specify circumstances in which, in a case within subparagraph (3) or (4), specified duties under Part 2 of the Social Work (Scotland) Act 1968 are nonetheless to apply in the case of the adult concerned (and paragraph (b) of each of those sub-paragraphs is to be read accordingly).

GENERAL NOTE

1–806   Paragraph 2 provides that if a local authority in Wales places someone in residential care in England, Scotland or Northern Ireland, that person will remain the responsibility of the Welsh local authority. They do not acquire ordinary residence in their new location.

Placements from Scotland to England, Wales or Northern Ireland

1–807   **3.**—(1) Where a local authority in Scotland is discharging its duty under section 12 or 13A of the Social Work (Scotland) Act 1968 or section 25 of the Mental Health (Care and Treatment) (Scotland) Act 2003 by securing the provision of accommodation in England, the adult in question is not to be treated for the purposes of this Part of this Act as ordinarily resident anywhere in England.

(2) Where a local authority in Scotland is discharging its duty under a provision referred to in sub-paragraph (1) by securing the provision of accommodation in Wales, the adult in question is not to be treated for the purposes of the Social Services and Well-being (Wales) Act 2014 as ordinarily resident anywhere in Wales.

(3) Where a local authority in Scotland is discharging its duty under a provision referred to in sub-paragraph (1) by securing the provision of accommodation in Northern Ireland, no duty under the Health and Personal Social Services (Northern Ireland) Order 1972 or the Health and Social Care (Reform) Act (Northern Ireland) 2009 to provide or secure the provision of accommodation or other facilities applies in the case of the adult in question.

(4) In section 5 of the Community Care and Health (Scotland) Act 2002 (local authority arrangements for residential accommodation outside Scotland)—

    (a) in subsection (1), after "the 1968 Act" insert "or under section 25 of the Mental Health (Care and Treatment) (Scotland) Act 2003 (care and support)",

    (b) in subsection (2), for "such arrangements" substitute "persons for whom such arrangements are made", and

    (c) for subsections (5) and (6) substitute—

"(5) In subsections (1) and (3) above, "appropriate establishment" means an establishment of such description or conforming to such requirements as may be specified in regulations under subsection (1)."

(5) Regulations may make further provision in relation to arrangements of the kind referred to in this paragraph.

GENERAL NOTE

Paragraph 3 provides that if a local authority in Scotland places someone in residential **1–808** care in England, Wales or Northern Ireland, that person will remain the responsibility of the Scottish local authority. They do not acquire ordinary residence in their new location.

Placements from Northern Ireland to England, Wales or Scotland

4.—(1) Where there are arrangements under Article 15 of the Health and Personal Social Services **1–809** (Northern Ireland) Order 1972 for the provision of accommodation in England, the adult in question—
  (a) is to be treated for the purposes of that Order and the Health and Social Care (Reform) Act (Northern Ireland) 2009 as ordinarily resident in the area of the relevant Health and Social Care trust, and
  (b) is accordingly not to be treated for the purposes of this Part of this Act as ordinarily resident anywhere in England.

(2) Where there are arrangements under Article 15 of the Health and Personal Social Services (Northern Ireland) Order 1972 for the provision of accommodation in Wales, the adult in question—
  (a) is to be treated for the purposes of that Order and the Health and Social Care (Reform) Act (Northern Ireland) 2009 as ordinarily resident in the area of the relevant Health and Social Care trust, and
  (b) is accordingly not to be treated for the purposes of the Social Services and Well-being (Wales) Act 2014 as ordinarily resident anywhere in Wales.

(3) Where there are arrangements under Article 15 of the Health and Personal Social Services (Northern Ireland) Order 1972 for the provision of accommodation in Scotland—
  (a) the adult in question is to be treated for the purposes of that Order and the Health and Social Care (Reform) Act (Northern Ireland) 2009 as ordinarily resident in the area of the relevant Health and Social Care trust, and
  (b) no duty under Part 2 of the Social Work (Scotland) Act 1968 or sections 25 to 27 of the Mental Health (Care and Treatment) (Scotland) Act 2003 applies in the adult's case.

(4) The reference to the relevant Health and Social Care trust is a reference to the Health and Social Care trust in whose area the adult in question was ordinarily resident immediately before the making of arrangements of the kind referred to in this paragraph.

(5) Regulations may make further provision in relation to arrangements of the kind referred to in this paragraph.

(6) The regulations may specify circumstances in which, in a case within sub-paragraph (3), specified duties under Part 2 of the Social Work (Scotland) Act 1968 are nonetheless to apply in the case of the adult concerned (and paragraph (b) of that sub-paragraph is to be read accordingly).

GENERAL NOTE

Paragraph 3 provides that if a Health and Social Care trust in Northern Ireland places **1–810** someone in residential care in England, Scotland or Wales, that person will remain the responsibility of the Northern Irish trust. They do not acquire ordinary residence in their new location.

Dispute resolution

5.—(1) Any dispute about the application of any of paragraphs 1 to 4 to an adult's case is to be deter- **1–811** mined in accordance with this paragraph.

(2) If the dispute is between a local authority in England and a local authority in Wales, it is to be determined by the Secretary of State or the Welsh Ministers.

(3) If the dispute is between a local authority in England and a local authority in Scotland, it is to be determined by the Secretary of State or the Scottish Ministers.

(4) If the dispute is between a local authority in England and a Health and Social Care trust, it is to be determined by the Secretary of State or the Northern Ireland Department.

(5) If the dispute is between a local authority in Wales and a local authority in Scotland, it is to be determined by the Welsh Ministers or the Scottish Ministers.

(6) If the dispute is between a local authority in Wales and a Health and Social Care trust, it is to be determined by the Welsh Ministers or the Northern Ireland Department.

(7) If the dispute is between a local authority in Scotland and a Health and Social Care trust, it is to be determined by the Scottish Ministers or the Northern Ireland Department.

(8) In Article 36 of the Health and Personal Social Services (Northern Ireland) Order 1972, after paragraph (2) insert—

"(2A) Any question under this Order as to the ordinary residence of a person is to be determined by the Department."

(9) Regulations must make provision for determining which of the persons concerned is to determine the dispute; and the regulations may, in particular, provide for the dispute to be determined by whichever of them they agree is to do so.

(10) Regulations may make provision for the determination of disputes between more than two parties.

(11) Regulations may make further provision about determination of disputes under this paragraph or under regulations under sub-paragraph (10); the regulations may, for example, include—

   (a) provision requiring parties to a dispute to take specified steps before referring the dispute for determination under this paragraph;

   (b) provision about the procedure for referring the dispute under this paragraph.

GENERAL NOTE

1–812   If a local authority or trust which has made a cross-border placement falls into dispute with the authority or trust where that person is placed, and cannot resolve the question locally, the local authorities or trust involved may request a determination of ordinary residence to be made. Such determinations must be made by the Secretary of State (or a person appointed by the Secretary of State) in England or the relevant Minister or Department in Scotland, Wales or Northern Ireland, depending on the circumstances. Further detail on the dispute resolution process is set out in the Care and Support (Cross-border Placements and Business Failure: Temporary Duty) (Dispute Resolution) Regulations 2014 (SI 2014/2843). These are reproduced and discussed at paras A1–218 to A1–227 below. See also paras 21.58 to 21.68 of the statutory guidance.

Financial adjustments

1–813   **6.**—(1) This paragraph applies where—

   (a) an adult has been provided with accommodation in England, Wales, Scotland or Northern Ireland, and

   (b) it transpires (whether following the determination of a dispute under paragraph 5 or otherwise) that an authority in another of the territories was, for some or all of the time that the accommodation was being provided, liable to provide the adult with accommodation.

(2) The authority which made the arrangements may recover from the authority in the other territory the amount of any payments it made towards the making of the arrangements at a time when the other authority was liable to provide the adult with accommodation.

(3) A reference to an authority is a reference to a local authority in England, Wales or Scotland or a Health and Social Care trust in Northern Ireland.

1–814   **7.**—(1) In section 86 of the Social Work (Scotland) Act 1968 (adjustments between authorities providing accommodation), in subsections (1) and (10), after "a local authority in England or Wales" insert "and to a Health and Social Care trust in Northern Ireland".

(2) In subsection (2) of that section, after "the ordinary residence of a person shall" insert ", in a case where there is a dispute about the application of any of paragraphs 1 to 4 of Schedule 1 to the Care Act 2014 (cross-border placements), be determined in accordance with paragraph 5 of that Schedule; and in any other case, the question shall".

(3) After subsection (10) of that section insert—

"(10A) A person who, as a result of Schedule 1 to the Care Act 2014 (crossborder placements), is treated as ordinarily resident in an area in England, Wales or Northern Ireland (as the case may be) is to be treated as ordinarily resident in that area for the purposes of this section.

(10B) A person who, as a result of that Schedule, is not treated as ordinarily resident anywhere in England or Wales (as the case may be) is not to be treated as ordinarily resident there for the purposes of this section."

(4) In section 97 of that Act (extent)—

(a)   in subsection (1), for "sections 86 and 87" substitute "section 87", and

(b)   after that subsection insert—

"(1A) Section 86 of this Act shall extend to England and Wales and to Northern Ireland."

GENERAL NOTE

Paragraph 6 provides that local authorities or trusts can reclaim the costs they have paid **1–815** for a person's care and support from an authority or a trust in another territory. This applies following a dispute where it becomes apparent that a local authority or trust has been funding a person's care and support when that person is not in fact ordinarily resident in its area.

Paragraph 7 amends the Social Work (Scotland) Act 1968 so that a local authority in Scotland can recover from a health and social care trust in Northern Ireland any expenditure it incurs in the provision of accommodation or services under Pt II of that Act for a person ordinarily resident in the area of the trust, in the same way as is already the case if it incurs expenditure for the same reasons for a person who is ordinarily resident in England or Wales. It also amends the 1968 Act so that if there is any overlap between the dispute resolution mechanism in that Act and the procedure in Sch.1 to the Care Act, the provisions in the Care Act will prevail.[1]

Provision of NHS accommodation not to affect deemed ordinary residence etc.

8.—(1) In a case where, as a result of this Schedule, an adult is treated as ordinarily resident in an **1–816** area in England, Wales or Northern Ireland (as the case may be), the adult does not cease to be so treated merely because the adult is provided with NHS accommodation.

(2) In a case where, as a result of this Schedule, an adult is not treated as ordinarily resident anywhere in England or Wales (as the case may be), the adult continues not to be so treated even if the adult is provided with NHS accommodation.

(3) In a case where, as a result of this Schedule, no duty under a relevant enactment applies, the duty does not apply merely because the adult in question is provided with NHS accommodation; and for this purpose "relevant enactment" means—

(a)   Part 2 of the Social Work (Scotland) Act 1968,

(b)   sections 25 to 27 of the Mental Health (Care and Treatment) (Scotland) Act 2003,

(c)   the Health and Personal Social Services (Northern Ireland) Order 1972, or

(d)   the Health and Social Care (Reform) Act (Northern Ireland) 2009.

(4) In a case where, as a result of paragraph 2(2), (4) or (7), an adult is treated as remaining within, or as remaining outside but ordinarily resident in, an area in Wales, the adult does not cease to be so treated merely because the adult is provided with NHS accommodation.

GENERAL NOTE

This paragraph is intended to ensure that the general principles of non-transfer of **1–817** responsibility under paras.1 to 4 of Sch.1 remain unaffected when the adult in question is provided with NHS accommodation (as defined by s.39(6)).[2]

If NHS or health accommodation is needed during the placement, for any period of time, responsibility for the person's care and support needs will not alter. In other words, the first authority will continue to be responsible overall for the individual's residential care placement and social care needs. During the placement in NHS or health accommodation it is normal practice for a "retention fee" to be paid to the care provider to ensure the individual's place is secured. This is the responsibility of the first authority. In England, Scotland and Wales if a care home resident requires nursing care, but nursing is not his or her primary need, the relevant NHS body will pay part of the care costs. This contribution is known as NHS-funded nursing care. In Northern Ireland, the relevant Health and Social Care Trust is responsible for the provision of nursing care to people in care homes. The four UK

---

[1]   *Hansard* (House of Lords), 22 July 2013, Vol.747, cols 1088 to 1089 (Baroness Northover).

[2]   Care Act 2014: Explanatory Notes para.265.

governments have reached separate bilateral agreements as to which NHS body (or Trust in Northern Ireland) should be responsible for the cost of NHS funded nursing care required for individuals placed cross-border into a care home. In general terms:

- where the cross-border placement is between England and Scotland or between England and Northern Ireland (in either direction) the health service of the country of the first authority will be responsible for nursing costs;
- where the cross-border placement is between England and Wales (in either direction), the second authority's health service will be responsible for the costs of NHS nursing care; and
- where the cross-border placement is between Wales and Scotland, Wales and Northern Ireland, or between Scotland and Northern Ireland, the first authority's health service will retain responsibility for the costs of NHS funded nursing care.

Direct payments

1–818   **9.**—(1) Regulations may provide for this schedule to apply, with such modifications as may be specified, to a case where accommodation in England, Wales, Scotland or Northern Ireland is provided for an adult by means of direct payments made by an authority in another of the territories.

(2) The reference in sub-paragraph (1) to direct payments accordingly includes a reference to direct payments made—
- (a) under section 50 or 52 of the Social Services and Well-being (Wales) Act 2014,
- (b) as a result of a choice made by the adult pursuant to section 5 of the Social Care (Self-directed Support) (Scotland) Act 2013, or
- (c) by virtue of section 8 of the Carers and Direct Payments Act (Northern Ireland) 2002.

GENERAL NOTE

1–819   This provides that regulations may apply the cross-border provisions where accommodation is being paid for by direct payment. It is intended that in such cases the individual concerned would remain the responsibility of the original local authority or trust.[1]

Particular types of accommodation

1–820   **10.**—(1) Regulations may provide for this Schedule to apply, with such modifications as may be specified, to a case where—
- (a) an adult has needs for care and support which can be met only if the adult is living in accommodation of a type specified in the regulations,
- (b) the adult is living in accommodation in England, Wales, Scotland or Northern Ireland that is of a type so specified, and
- (c) the adult's needs for care and support are being met by an authority in another of the territories providing or arranging for the provision of services other than the accommodation.

(2) In section 5 of the Community Care and Health (Scotland) Act 2002 (the title to which becomes "Local authority arrangements for residential accommodation etc. outwith Scotland"), in subsection (1), at the end insert "or for the provision in England and Wales or in Northern Ireland of a service or facility of such other description as may be specified in the regulations".

GENERAL NOTE

1–821   This enables the regulations to apply the cross-border provisions to specified types of accommodation, for instance supported living placements. It is intended that in such cases the individual concerned would remain the responsibility of the original local authority or trust (whilst receiving other care and support services from an authority or trust in another country).[2]

Regulations

1–822   **11.**—Regulations under this Schedule—

---

[1] Care Act 2014: Explanatory Notes para.262.
[2] Care Act 2014: Explanatory Notes para.262.

(a) if they include provision relating to Wales, may not be made without the consent of the Welsh Ministers;

(b) if they include provision relating to Scotland, may not be made without the consent of the Scottish Ministers;

(c) if they include provision relating to Northern Ireland, may not be made without the consent of the Northern Ireland Department.

Interpretation

12.—(1) This paragraph applies for the purposes of this Schedule.   **1–823**

(2) "Accommodation in England" means accommodation in England of a type specified in regulations under section 39 but not of a type specified in regulations under this paragraph.

(3) "Accommodation in Wales" means accommodation in Wales of a type specified in regulations under section 194 of the Social Services and Wellbeing (Wales) Act 2014 but not of a type specified in regulations under this paragraph.

(4) "Accommodation in Scotland" means residential accommodation in Scotland of a type which may be provided under or by virtue of section 12 or 13A of the Social Work (Scotland) Act 1968, or section 25 of the Mental Health (Care and Treatment) (Scotland) Act 2003, but not of a type specified in regulations under this paragraph.

(5) "Accommodation in Northern Ireland" means residential or other accommodation in Northern Ireland of a type which may be provided under Article 15 of the Health and Personal Social Services (Northern Ireland) Order 1972.

(6) "Local authority in England" means a local authority for the purposes of this Part.

(7) "Local authority in Wales" means a local authority for the purposes of the Social Services and Well-being (Wales) Act 2014.

(8) "Local authority in Scotland" means a council constituted under section 2 of the Local Government etc. (Scotland) Act 1994.

(9) "The Northern Ireland Department" means the Department of Health, Social Services and Public Safety in Northern Ireland.

(10) "NHS accommodation" has the meaning given in section 39(6).

GENERAL NOTE

Paragraph 12 includes definitions of residential accommodation for the purposes of **1–824** cross-border placements. The meaning of residential accommodation differs according to the legislation in each country. So, for instance, residential accommodation in England is defined as meaning care home, shared lives and supported living accommodation.[1] Residential accommodation in Scotland means any accommodation which may be provided under s. 12 or 13A of the Social Work (Scotland) Act 1968, or s.25 of the Mental Health (Care and Treatment) (Scotland) Act 2003. In effect, this means that accommodation is defined as a residential care home. Residential accommodation in Northern Ireland means residential or other accommodation which may be provided under art.15 of the Health and Personal Social Services (Northern Ireland) Order 1972. Following the implementation of the Social Services and Well-being (Wales) Act 2014 residential accommodation in Wales will be defined as meaning care home accommodation.[2]

The relevant meaning of residential accommodation is that which applies in the country where the person has been placed. It is not the meaning that applies in the country of the placing authority. So, for example, if a person is moved from England into supported living accommodation in Wales, this could not constitute a cross-border placement (since the definition of residential accommodation in Wales does not include supported living). Whereas, if a person is moved from Wales into supported living accommodation in England, this could (in theory at least) constitute a cross-border.

In practice, however, it is likely that most UK cross-border placements will involve the provision of care home accommodation. Usually in supported living, shared lives and other

---

[1] Care Act 2014, Sch.1, para.12(2), and the Care and Support (Ordinary Residence) (Specified Accommodation) Regulations 2014 (SI 2014/2828).

[2] Care Act 2014, Sch.1, para.12(3) and draft Care and Support (Ordinary Residence) (Specified Accommodation) (Wales) Regulations 2015.

forms of non-care home accommodation, the tenancy will be private and it is unlikely that an authority will have placed the person.

Consequential provision

1–825   **13.**—In section 194 of the Social Services and Well-being (Wales) Act 2014 (ordinary residence), at the end insert—

"(8) For provision about cross-border placements to and from England, Scotland or Northern Ireland, see Schedule 1 to the Care Act 2014.

(8) Am ddarpariaeth ynghylch lleoliadau trawsffiniol i Loegr, yr Alban neu Ogledd Iwerddon neu o Loegr, yr Alban neu Ogledd Iwerddon, gweler Atodlen 1 i Ddeddf Gofal 2014."

Transitory provision

1–826   **14.**—(1) Pending the commencement of Part 4 of the Social Services and Well-being (Wales) Act 2014, this Schedule is to have effect with the modifications set out in this paragraph.

(2) A reference to that Act in paragraphs 1, 3 and 4 is to be read as a reference to Part 3 of the National Assistance Act 1948.

(3) In paragraph 2—

(a)   the references in sub-paragraphs (1), (3) and (6) to discharging a duty under section 35 of the Social Services and Well-being (Wales) Act 2014 by arranging for the provision of accommodation are to be read as references to providing residential accommodation under Part 3 of the National Assistance Act 1948;

(b)   the references in paragraph (a) of each of those sub-paragraphs to the Social Services and Well-being (Wales) Act 2014 are to be read as references to Part 3 of the National Assistance Act 1948;

(c)   sub-paragraphs (2), (4) and (7) are to be ignored; and

(d)   in sub-paragraph (10), the references to sub-paragraph (4) and paragraph (b) of sub-paragraph (4) are to be ignored.

(4) In paragraph 9, the reference to sections 50 and 52 of the Social Services and Well-being (Wales) Act 2014 is to be read as a reference to section 57 of the Health and Social Care Act 2001.

(5) In paragraph 12, sub-paragraph (3) is to be read as if the following were substituted for it—

"(3) "Accommodation in Wales" means residential accommodation in Wales of a type that may be provided under Part 3 of the National Assistance Act 1948 but not of a type specified in regulations under this paragraph."

(6) In that paragraph, sub-paragraph (7) is to be read as if the following were substituted for it—

"(7) "Local authority in Wales" means a local authority in Wales for the purposes of Part 3 of the National Assistance Act 1948."

(7) This paragraph does not affect the generality of section 124(2).

Section 43   SCHEDULE 2

SAFEGUARDING ADULTS BOARDS

GENERAL NOTE

1–827   The statutory guidance discusses Safeguarding Adults Boards at paras 14.104 to 14.122. In addition, the Social Care Institute for Excellence has produced a guide on Safeguarding Adults Boards.[1] This is not statutory guidance but it has been produced with the approval of the Department of Health (see 1–770 below).

Membership, etc.

1–828   **1.**—(1) The members of an SAB are—

---

[1]   Social Care Institute for Excellence, *Safeguarding Adults Boards Checklists and Resources* (2015).

(a) the local authority which established it,

(b) a clinical commissioning group the whole or part of whose area is in the local authority's area,

(c) the chief officer of police for a police area the whole or part of which is in the local authority's area, and

(d) such persons, or persons of such description, as may be specified in regulations.

(2) The membership of an SAB may also include such other persons as the local authority which established it, having consulted the other members listed in sub-paragraph (1), considers appropriate.

(3) A local authority, having consulted the other members of its SAB, must appoint as the chair a person whom the authority considers to have the required skills and experience.

(4) Each member of an SAB must appoint a person to represent it on the SAB; and the representative must be a person whom the member considers to have the required skills and experience.

(5) Where more than one clinical commissioning group or more than one chief officer of police comes within sub-paragraph (1), a person may represent more than one of the clinical commissioning groups or chief officers of police.

(6) The members of an SAB (other than the local authority which established it) must, in acting as such, have regard to such guidance as the Secretary of State may issue.

(7) Guidance for the local authority on acting as a member of the SAB is to be included in the guidance issued for the purposes of section 78(1).

(8) An SAB may regulate its own procedure.

GENERAL NOTE

The Law Commission recommended that the adult social care statute should require cer- **1–829** tain key agencies to nominate a representative to be a Safeguarding Adults Board member who has the appropriate skills and knowledge. These agencies were the local social services authority, the NHS, and the police.[1] The Commission also recommended that:

- the Secretary of State should be given a regulation-making power to add to the list of agencies required to nominate a representative;
- the Care Quality Commission should be given a power to nominate an appropriate representative to attend meetings; and
- the local authority should have a power to appoint as a Board member any other person with the necessary skills and knowledge and be given responsibility for appointing the chair.[2]

Many consultees had argued that General Practitioners should be required to attend Board meetings because of their vital role in safeguarding adults. However, the Law Commission felt this would be difficult to achieve in law because General Practitioners are contracted individually to the NHS. The Commission also did not agree that the statute should require local authorities in all cases to appoint an independent chair, but recommended that local authorities should retain this option subject to the person possessing the appropriate skills and knowledge.[3] The Government accepted all of the Law Commission's recommendations.[4]

The Joint Committee argued that the membership list should include the relevant Health and Well-being Board and appropriate housing representation. It also felt that the schedule should be amended to specify the circumstances in which a local authority should not take part in the proceedings of the Board. In particular it had in mind cases when a Board will be investigating alleged failures by the local authority.[5] The Department of Health rejected the need to add to the membership list arguing that local areas should have the freedom to decide the composition of their Boards in line with local circumstances. It also expected

---

[1] Law Commission, *Adult Social Care*, para.9.120.

[2] Law Commission, *Adult Social Care*, para.9.121.

[3] Law Commission, *Adult Social Care*, paras 9.122 to 9.123.

[4] Department of Health, *Reforming the Law for Adult Care and Support: The Government's Response to Law Commission Report 326 on Adult Social Care* (TSO, July 2012), Cm.8379, para.9.25.

[5] House of Lords House of Commons Joint Committee on the Draft Care and Support Bill, *Draft Care and Support Bill Report, Session 2012–13*, paras 160 to 164.

Boards "to develop protocols to deal with both the routine operation of their business as well as any exceptional circumstances, for example, a perceived conflict of interest".[1]

The statutory guidance discusses membership of Safeguarding Adults Boards in paras 14.116 to 14.122. It also discusses local roles and responsibilities in paras 14.167 to 14.206.[2]

Sub-paragraph (1)

1–830   The core members of the Safeguarding Adults Board are the local authority, each clinical commissioning group for the Board's area, and each chief officer of police for the Board's area. The Secretary of State may prescribe other core members of the Board through regulations.

Sub-paragraph (2)

1–831   The Safeguarding Adults Board may include other members that the local authority considers appropriate, after the local authority has consulted the other representatives mentioned in subparagraph (1).

Sub-paragraph (3)

1–832   The local authority must appoint a chair who has "the required skills and experience", after it has consulted all the other members of the Board. This could include—but does not require—the appointment of an independent chair. The statutory guidance advises that the local authority should consider appointing an independent chair.[3]   Research carried out prior to the implementation of the Care Act found that independent chairs were often believed to provide greater "transparency, challenge and scrutiny". On the other hand it was feared that independent chairs were difficult to reconcile with the local authority's accountability for the operation of the Board and were only effective where the Board was well-established and robust.[4]

Sub-paragraph (4)

1–833   Each Board member must appoint a representative to attend meetings who has "the required skills and experience".

Sub-paragraph (5)

1–834   The appointed representative for the clinical commissioning group or the police may represent more than one clinical commissioning group or chief officer of police where there is more than one within the Board's area.

Sub-paragraphs (6) and (7)

1–835   The local authority must act under the guidance issued by the Secretary of State in accordance with section 78(1) of the Care Act, whilst other Board members must have regard to such guidance.

Sub-paragraph (8)

1–836   Other than the matters specified in para.1 of Sch.2, there are no particular governance procedures that a Board must follow, and the Safeguarding Adults Board can regulate its own procedure.

---

[1] Department of Health, *The Care Bill explained—including a response to consultation and pre-legislative scrutiny on the draft Care and Support Bill*, para.14 and p.68.
[2] Department of Health, *Care and Support Statutory Guidance* (2014), para.14.176.
[3] Department of Health, *Care and Support Statutory Guidance* (2014), para.14.121.
[4] S. Braye et al, *The Governance of Adult Safeguarding: Findings From Research into Safeguarding Adults Boards* (University of Bedfordshire and University of Sussex, November 2010) pp.80 to 85.

Funding and other resources

2.—(1) A member of an SAB listed in paragraph 1(1) may make payments towards expenditure **1–837**
incurred by, or for purposes connected with, the SAB—
(a) by making the payments directly, or
(b) by contributing to a fund out of which the payments may be made.

(2) A member of an SAB listed in paragraph 1(1) may provide staff, goods, services, accommodation
or other resources for purposes connected with the SAB.

GENERAL NOTE

Safeguarding Adults Board members may contribute financially to the cost of running **1–838**
the Board by making payments directly or contributing to a single pooled fund.
Paragraph 2(2) confirms that Board members can provide non-pecuniary resources (such
as staff, goods, services or accommodation) in support of the activities of the Board.
The statutory guidance discusses funding in para.4.113.

Strategic plan

3.—(1) An SAB must publish for each financial year a plan (its "strategic plan") which sets out— **1–839**
(a) its strategy for achieving its objective (see section 43), and
(b) what each member is to do to implement that strategy.

(2) In preparing its strategic plan, the SAB must—
(a) consult the Local Healthwatch organisation for its area, and
(b) involve the community in its area.

(3) In this paragraph and paragraph 4, "financial year", in relation to an SAB, includes the period—
(a) beginning with the day on which the SAB is established, and
(b) ending with the following 31 March or, if the period ending with that date is 3 months or less,
ending with the 31 March following that date.

GENERAL NOTE

A Safeguarding Adults Board must publish for each financial year a strategic plan that **1–840**
sets how it will meet its main objective (in s.43(2)) and what each Board member will do to
achieve that objective (provided for under s.43(3) and (4)). This plan must be developed by
involving the local community, and the Board must consult the Local Healthwatch organisation in the development of the plan. The statutory guidance discusses strategic plans in
paras 14.123 to 14.125.

Annual report

4.—(1) As soon as is feasible after the end of each financial year, an SAB must publish a report on— **1–841**
(a) what it has done during that year to achieve its objective,
(b) what it has done during that year to implement its strategy,
(c) what each member has done during that year to implement the strategy,
(d) the findings of the reviews arranged by it under section 44 (safeguarding adults reviews) which
have concluded in that year (whether or not they began in that year),
(e) the reviews arranged by it under that section which are ongoing at the end of that year (whether
or not they began in that year),
(f) what it has done during that year to implement the findings of reviews arranged by it under that
section, and
(g) where it decides during that year not to implement a finding of a review arranged by it under
that section, the reasons for its decision.

(2) The SAB must send a copy of the report to—
(a) the chief executive and the leader of the local authority which established the SAB,
(b) the local policing body the whole or part of whose area is in the local authority's area,
(c) the Local Healthwatch organisation for the local authority's area, and
(d) the chair of the Health and Well-being Board for that area.

(3) "Local policing body" has the meaning given by section 101 of the Police Act 1996.

GENERAL NOTE

A Safeguarding Adults Board must publish for each financial year an annual report. The **1–842**
statutory guidance discusses the annual report in paras 14.126 to 14.132.

1–843   The report must be published as soon as feasible at the end of each financial year. The term feasible suggests a focus on the earliest date possible, rather than for example what the Board might consider to be a more appropriate date for publication.

The report must include:

- what the Board has done during the year to achieve its main objective and its strategy;
- how each Board member has helped to contribute to the strategy;
- the findings of Safeguarding Adults Reviews under s.44 which have concluded in that year;
- details of ongoing Safeguarding Adults Reviews under s.44; and
- what actions have been taken to implement the findings of Safeguarding Adults Reviews under s.44 (and the reasons for not implementing any finding).

The final point was introduced by a Government amendment during the passage of the Care Bill in the House of Lords. At Committee stage, an amendment had been tabled by Lord Rix and Lady Hollins at Committee stage to provide that annual reports should not only include findings of reviews but what actions had been taken to implement the recommendations of reviews. This aimed to ensure that lessons are learnt from reviews and practice changes.[1]   The Government on reflection agreed with the arguments that had been put forward by Lord Rix and Lady Hollins and tabled subpara.4(1)(f) and (g). It stated that this amendment "will increase the transparency and accountability of boards".[2]

Sub-paragraph (2)

1–844   As well as being published, copies of the report must be sent to the:

- Chief Executive and the leader of the local authority which established the Board;
- local policing body;
- local Healthwatch organisation; and
- Chair of the Health and Well-being Board for the area.

The Joint Committee recommended that the Care Quality Commission should be added to the list of those who should receive copies of the annual reports of all Safeguarding Adults Boards.[3]   The Government did not agree since the reports will be publically available.[4]

In the House of Lords, Lord Rix and Lady Hollins attempted to amend the Bill to require reports to be sent to the Secretary of State in order that the reports could be collated and trends could be monitored.[5]   In response the Government stated:

"With a duty on boards to publish their annual report, we can be assured that they will be publicly available. We would expect the local Healthwatch and health and well-being boards to monitor the safeguarding adult board's progress and report to the Secretary of State if there are particular matters of concern. To require the board formally to submit a report to the Secretary of State would, if nothing else, undermine the primacy of local accountability, which is at the heart of our approach to safeguarding."[6]

---

[1]   *Hansard* (House of Lords), 22 July 2013, Vol.747, col.1096.

[2]   *Hansard* (House of Lords), 14 October 2013, Vol.748, col.342.

[3]   House of Lords House of Commons Joint Committee on the Draft Care and Support Bill, *Draft Care and Support Bill Report, Session 2012–13*, para.162.

[4]   Department of Health, *The Care Bill explained—including a response to consultation and pre-legislative scrutiny on the draft Care and Support Bill*, p.67.

[5]   *Hansard* (House of Lords), 22 July 2013, Vol.747, col.1096 and *Hansard* (House of Lords), 14 October 2013, Vol.748, col.334.

[6]   *Hansard* (House of Lords), 14 October 2013, Vol.748, col.342 (Earl Howe).

Similar amendments—to require copies to be sent to the Secretary of State and Chief Inspector of Adult Social Care—were also tabled at Committee stage in the House of Commons. In response the Government repeated its argument that it expected the local Healthwatch and Health and Well-being Boards to monitor the Safeguarding Adults Boards and report to the Secretary of State if there were particular matters of concern about their operation. The Government also confirmed that it would expect them to report to the Chief Inspector of Adult Social Care if there were particular matters of concern about a Board's operation, or about a registered provider of adult social care.[1]

Section 74   SCHEDULE 3

DISCHARGE OF HOSPITAL PATIENTS WITH CARE AND SUPPORT NEEDS

GENERAL NOTE

To a large degree, Sch. 3 re-enacts the delayed discharges provisions contained in the **1–845** Community Care (Delayed Discharges etc) Act 2003 and associated regulations.[2] The 2003 Act had been a response to the problems associated with patients who are occupying a hospital bed that they do not strictly need (so-called "bed blocking") as a result of a failure by local authorities to assess the patient's needs or put together the necessary package of care and support to enable them to be discharged safely.[3] In broad terms, the 2003 Act established time limits for the completion of social care assessments and the provision of care and support services for NHS hospital patients, and fines or reimbursements if any delay in discharge had been caused by the local authority. It also set requirements for communication between the NHS and local authority in relation to patients who were ready to be discharged and for the involvement of patients and carers during the discharge process. This general framework has been maintained in Sch.3. The delayed discharge regime— which is based on the issuing of assessment, discharge and withdrawal notices, and time limits for assessments and communications—is essentially a bureaucratic and process-driven system, which arguably is out of kilter with the rest of the Care Act and its emphasis on local authority discretion and innovation.

Supporters of the delayed discharge regime argue that hospital beds are a scarce resource and prolonged stays can lead to poor recovery rates through loss of physical functioning, hospital infection or increased dependency. On the other side it is argued that the regime has led to people being placed in unsuitable residential accommodation in order to avoid paying the reimbursement charges. Thus while delayed discharges from hospital may have been reduced, critics point to a corresponding rise in emergency readmissions and lack of choice for service users.

The Law Commission considered that the existing delayed discharge provisions should be incorporated into the new statute.[4] This was mainly on the basis of its overall objective to consolidate and rationalise the law. The Government accepted this recommendation and undertook "to simplify the provisions to improve understanding". Some respondents to the Law Commission consultation proposed that the entirety of the delayed discharge provisions and procedure be repealed. The Government considered this proposal but concluded that the provisions still provided "a useful framework for local authorities and the NHS to manage their relationship around hospital discharge, and complete removal might disadvantage some areas to the detriment of patients".[5]

---

[1] *Hansard* (House of Commons: Public Bill Committee), 21 January 2014 (PM): Eighth Sitting, col.296 (Norman Lamb MP).
[2] Delayed Discharges (England) Regulations 2003 (SI 2003/2277).
[3] Secretary of State for Health, *Delivering the NHS Plan: Next Steps on Investment, Next Steps on Reform* (TSO, April 2002), Cm.5503.
[4] Law Commission, *Adult Social Care*, paras 11.130 to 11.132.
[5] Department of Health, *Reforming the Law for Adult Care and Support: The Government's Response to Law Commission Report 326 on Adult Social Care* (TSO, July 2012), Cm.8379, para.11.34.

Whilst Sch.3 re-enacts much of the 2003 Act and relevant regulations, there have been changes to reflect the new NHS structures introduced by the Health and Social Care Act 2008 and to achieve the Government's aim of simplifying the provisions. In addition, the recovery of any reimbursement has been placed on a discretionary rather than a mandatory footing (see para.1-862 below). The statutory guidance discusses the Sch.3 provisions in paras 15.37 to 15.47 and Annex G.

The adequacy of housing provision is often a vital component of a safe and timely discharge. The Joint Committee recommended that the legislation should be amended to require local authorities to ensure the integration of care and support provision with health provision on discharge from hospital, "with particular emphasis on the adequacy of housing provision on discharge".[1] In response the Government argued that this was unnecessary because s.3 already requires local authorities to ensure the integration of care and support provision with health provision, and health-related provision (including housing), and this applies to hospital discharges. It also pointed out that other provisions in the Act apply to hospital discharges including:

- the requirements on local authorities and their relevant partners to co-operate generally and in specific cases (ss.6 and 7);
- the requirement for local authorities to assess adults and carers who it appears to them may have needs for care and support (ss.9 and 10); and
- Sch.3 which deals with discharges from the acute secondary sector.[2]

DISPUTES

1-846 Schedule 3 makes no express provision for dispute resolution. However, the Care and Support (Disputes Between Local Authorities) Regulations 2014 (SI 2014/2829) set out the procedures to be followed when disputes arise between local authorities regarding a person's ordinary residence. These apply in delayed discharge cases. These are reproduced and discussed at paras A1–201 to A1–208 below. The statutory guidance confirms that if no agreement can be reached on ordinary residence, the local authority must seek a determination from the Secretary of State or an appointed representative. All other disputes in relation to delayed discharge should be resolved between the NHS body and local authority, and where this is not possible by way of an application for judicial review to the High Court.[3]

Previous guidance confirmed that a patient could challenge a discharge decision through the complaints procedure but in the meantime they did not have the right to stay in hospital. In such cases it advised that the local authority should consider providing suitable non-acute care.[4] This remains a useful starting point for such disputes under the Care Act. If the dispute relates to NHS continuing health care decisions then the person can apply to an NHS review panel.

Cases where hospital patient is likely to have care and support needs after discharge

1-847 1.—(1) Where the NHS body responsible for a hospital patient considers that it is not likely to be safe to discharge the patient unless arrangements for meeting the patient's needs for care and support are in place, the body must give notice to—
(a) the local authority in whose area the patient is ordinarily resident, or

---

[1] House of Lords House of Commons Joint Committee on the Draft Care and Support Bill, *Draft Care and Support Bill Report, Session 2012–13*, para.134.
[2] Department of Health, *The Care Bill explained—including a response to consultation and pre-legislative scrutiny on the draft Care and Support Bill*, p.65.
[3] Department of Health, *Care and Support Statutory Guidance* (2014), Annex G, paras 49 to 50.
[4] LAC (2003)21: *Community Care (Delayed Discharge) Act 2003: Guidance for Implementation*, para.96.

(b)   if it appears to the body that the patient is of no settled residence, the local authority in whose area the hospital is situated.

(2) A notice under sub-paragraph (1) is referred to in this Schedule as an "assessment notice"; and the local authority to which an assessment notice is given is referred to in this Schedule as "the relevant authority".

(3) An assessment notice—

(a)   must describe itself as such, and

(b)   may not be given more than seven days before the day on which the patient is expected to be admitted to hospital.

(4) Before giving an assessment notice, the NHS body responsible for the patient must consult—

(a)   the patient, and

(b)   where it is feasible to do so, any carer that the patient has.

(5) An assessment notice remains in force until—

(a)   the patient is discharged (whether by the NHS body responsible for the patient or by the patient himself or herself),

(b)   the patient dies, or

(c)   the NHS body responsible for the patient withdraws the notice by giving a notice (a "withdrawal notice") to the relevant authority.

(6) A reference in this paragraph to a hospital patient includes a reference to a person who it is reasonable to expect is about to become one.

GENERAL NOTE

Paragraph 1 sets out certain requirements for the relevant NHS body which is responsible **1–848** for a hospital patient who is likely to have care and support needs after being discharged.

Subparagraphs (1) and (2)

The NHS body must inform the relevant local authority when a hospital patient cannot be **1–849** discharged safely unless arrangements for care and support are put into place first. This is known as the "assessment notice". The relevant local authority is the one in which the patient is ordinarily resident, or if the patient has no settled residence, the local authority area in which the hospital is situated.

The statutory guidance warns that NHS organisations should not issue assessment notices in a precautionary and/or routine way.[1] It also states that:

"A locally agreed protocol between the NHS and local authorities which allows NHS staff to identify those likely to need care and support on discharge will provide help and advice as to when a patient should be considered to have possible care and support needs, in order to ensure the NHS issue assessment notices appropriately."[2]

Subparagraph (3)

The assessment notice given by the NHS body must describe itself as such. According to **1–850** the explanatory notes and the statutory guidance, this means that the assessment notice must state that it is given under para.1(1) of Sch.3 to the Care Act. This is to ensure that the local authority can recognise this notice as the formal start of the process provided for under this schedule "so that the local authority is aware of the legal consequences that could flow from the assessment notice, such as the liability to pay the relevant NHS body for the costs of delayed discharge".[3] Further provision about the content of the assessment notice is contained in the Care and Support (Discharge of Hospital Patients) Regulations 2014 (SI 2014/2823). Regulation 2 requires that the assessment notice must be in writing and contain the date upon which it is given, and reg.3 sets out the details that an assessment notice must contain (such as the patient's name and NHS number). The statutory guidance emphasises that the information contained in an assessment notice is intended to be minimal in order to "reflect patient confidentiality requirements and to

---

[1]   Department of Health, *Care and Support Statutory Guidance* (2014), Annex G, para.6.

[2]   Department of Health, *Care and Support Statutory Guidance* (2014), Annex G, para.7.

[3]   Care Act 2014: Explanatory Notes para.430.

minimise bureaucracy", and also sets out a model template that may be used.[1] The assessment notice cannot be issued more than seven days before the patient is expected to be admitted into hospital. This is intended to ensure that the notice is not given too far in advance of admission "to avoid the risk of wasting preliminary planning in the event the patient's condition changes".[2] The statutory guidance emphasises that, in other cases, local authorities should be given as much notice as possible, and that a balance may need to be struck between early notice and the risk that the patient's condition may change.[3] It goes to state that:

> "Accordingly, if the NHS is able either to issue an assessment notice up to seven days before the date of the patient's admission into hospital and/or have a good indication of the likely proposed discharge date which is unlikely to change, then the NHS should issue the assessment notice as soon as possible.[4]

Subparagraph (4)

1–851   Before issuing an assessment notice, the NHS must consult with the patient and any carer. This is to avoid unnecessary assessments where, for example, "the patient wishes to make private arrangements for care and support without the involvement of the local authority".[5]

The duty to consult the carer applies where it is "feasible" to do so. According to the explanatory notes, this means that consultation with the carer should take place where "appropriate".[6] However, it is submitted that the term feasible suggests a focus on whether such consultation is possible (for example, if the NHS can identify the carer), rather than whether it is appropriate. This interpretation is supported by the statutory guidance which does not use the term appropriate and instead merely states that the NHS must consult "where applicable" with the carer.[7] For a discussion on the difference (if any) between "consult" and "involve" see paras 1–104 to 1–105 above.

Subsection (5)

1–852   An assessment notice remains in force until the patient is discharged, the patient dies, or the NHS body withdraws the notice by giving a "withdrawal notice". Regulation 2 of the Care and Support (Discharge of Hospital Patients) Regulations 2014 (SI 2014/2823) requires that the withdrawal notice must be in writing and contain the date upon which it is given. Whilst the regulations do not further prescribe what a withdrawal notice must contain, the statutory guidance states that:

> ". . . local systems should be established to ensure that the withdrawal notice provides sufficient information for both the NHS and local authority to be clear as to which patient and assessment notice the withdrawal notice refers to, and the reason(s) as to why the assessment notice is being withdrawn. In the context of identifying the person, mirroring either in full or part what is required for the assessment notice itself should be considered."[8]

Regulation 4 sets out the circumstances under which an NHS body must withdraw an assessment notice, for example if the patient needs NHS continuing health care or the patient's ordinary residence has changed. Otherwise the NHS body has discretion to withdraw the assessment notice at any time. The statutory guidance confirms that once it has

---

[1] Department of Health, *Care and Support Statutory Guidance* (2014), Annex G, paras 12 and 16.
[2] Care Act 2014: Explanatory Notes para.430 and Department of Health, *Care and Support Statutory Guidance* (2014), Annex G, para.10.
[3] Department of Health, *Care and Support Statutory Guidance* (2014), Annex G, paras 9 to 10.
[4] Department of Health, *Care and Support Statutory Guidance* (2014), Annex G, para.11.
[5] Department of Health, *Care and Support Statutory Guidance* (2014), Annex G, para.8.
[6] Care Act 2014: Explanatory Notes para.430.
[7] Department of Health, *Care and Support Statutory Guidance* (2014), Annex G, para.8.
[8] Department of Health, *Care and Support Statutory Guidance* (2014), Annex G, para.24.

been withdrawn "no liability to the local authority can accrue after that date", and this applies even if a discharge notice has been subsequently issued "but any liability which may have accrued before the withdrawal of the assessment notice is unaffected."[1]

Assessment notice given by responsible NHS body to local authority

2.—(1) The NHS body responsible for a hospital patient, having given the relevant authority an assessment notice, must— **1–853**

    (a) consult the authority before deciding what it will do for the patient in order for discharge to be safe, and

    (b) give the authority notice of the day on which it proposes to discharge the patient.

(2) A notice under sub-paragraph (1)(b) is referred to in this Schedule as a "discharge notice".

(3) A discharge notice must specify—

    (a) whether the NHS body responsible for the patient will be providing or arranging for the provision of services under the National Health Service Act 2006 to the patient after discharge, and

    (b) if it will, what those services are.

(4) A discharge notice remains in force until—

    (a) the end of the relevant day, or

    (b) the NHS body responsible for the patient withdraws the notice by giving a withdrawal notice to the relevant authority.

(5) The "relevant day" is the later of—

    (a) the day specified in the discharge notice, and

    (b) the last day of such period as regulations may specify.

(6) A period specified under sub-paragraph (5)(b) must—

    (a) begin with the day after that on which the assessment notice is given, and

    (b) last for a period of at least two days.

3.—(1) The relevant authority, having received an assessment notice and having in light of it carried out a needs assessment and (where applicable) a carer's assessment, must inform the NHS body responsible for the patient— **1–854**

    (a) whether the patient has needs for care and support,

    (b) (where applicable) whether a carer has needs for support,

    (c) whether any of the needs referred to in paragraphs (a) and (b) meet the eligibility criteria, and

    (d) how the authority plans to meet such of those needs as meet the eligibility criteria.

(2) Where, having carried out a needs assessment or carer's assessment in a case within section 27(4), the relevant authority considers that the patient's needs for care and support or (as the case may be) the carer's needs for support have changed, it must inform the NHS body responsible for the patient of the change.

GENERAL NOTE

    Paragraphs 2 and 3 set out the process that the NHS body and local authority must follow once the assessment notice has been issued. **1–855**

Subparagraph 2(1) and (2)

    Following the issuing of an assessment notice, the NHS body must consult the local authority before deciding what it will do for the patient in order to secure a safe discharge. This is to ensure that "a complete package of care can be put in place smoothly and without duplication or omission of any particular service".[2] The NHS body is also required to give the local authority notice of when it intends to discharge the patient. This is known as a "discharge notice". The statutory guidance explains that a separate notification of the discharge date is needed because this date "may not have been previously known at the time of the issue of the assessment notice or may have subsequently changed since the assessment notice was issued". It also confirms that the NHS cannot seek to recover any reimbursement from the local authority in respect of a delayed discharge unless it has first issued both an assessment notice and a discharge notice.[3] **1–856**

---

[1] Department of Health, *Care and Support Statutory Guidance* (2014), Annex G, para.24.

[2] Community Care (Delayed Discharges etc) Act 2003: Explanatory Notes para.27. Schedule 3 para.2 to the Care Act largely replicates s.5 of the 2003 Act.

[3] Department of Health, *Care and Support Statutory Guidance* (2014), Annex G, paras 26 to 27.

Provision about the content of the discharge notice is contained in the Care and Support (Discharge of Hospital Patients) Regulations 2014 (SI 2014/2823). Regulation 2 requires that the discharge notice must be in writing and contain the date upon which it is given, and reg.6 sets out the details which a discharge notice must contain (such as the patient's name and NHS number).

Subparagraph 2(3)

1–857   This provides that the discharge notice must specify whether or not the patient will receive any health care services upon discharge, and if so, what those services will be.

Subparagraphs 2(4) to (5)

1–858   To avoid any risk of reimbursement liability, the local authority must carry out a needs assessment and (if applicable) a carer's assessment and put in place any arrangements before "the relevant day". The relevant day is therefore crucial because it establishes the start of the period during which the local authority is responsible for making payments in the event that discharge is delayed,. The relevant date is either the date upon which the NHS proposes to discharge the patient (as specified in the discharge notice) or the end of a period which regulations may set out—whichever is the later. Regulation 8 of the Care and Support (Discharge of Hospital Patients) Regulations 2014 (SI 2014/2823) provides that the minimum period for which a discharge notice may remain in force is two days after the date on which an assessment notice is given or treated as being given in accordance with reg.11. The statutory guidance provides examples of how these timescales should work.[1]

A discharge notice remains in place until the relevant day, unless it is withdrawn by the NHS body by giving a "withdrawal notice". Regulation 7 of the Care and Support (Discharge of Hospital Patients) Regulations 2014 (SI 2014/2823) sets out the circumstances under which an NHS body must withdraw a discharge notice. In general terms this is where the NHS body considers that it is no longer safe for the patient to be discharged on the proposed discharge date. However, this does not apply where the only reason that it is no longer safe is that the local authority has not carried out a needs or carer's assessment, or put in place the proposed care and support. Otherwise the NHS body has discretion to withdraw the discharge notice at any time. The statutory guidance confirms that once it has been withdrawn no further liability for the local authority to pay the NHS for any delayed transfer of care arises.[2]

Regulation 5 specifies that a discharge notice may not be given less than one day in advance of the proposed discharge date. The statutory guidance provides examples of the timing of discharge notices.[3]

Subparagraph 3(1)

1–859   This sets out the responsibilities of the local authority that has received an assessment notice. The local authority must carry out an assessment of the patient's need for care and support and, where applicable, the carer's need for support. It must inform the NHS body:

- whether the patient has needs for care and support;
- whether a carer has needs for support;
- whether any of these needs meet the eligibility criteria; and
- how the eligible needs will be met.

---

[1] Department of Health, *Care and Support Statutory Guidance* (2014), Annex G, para.21.
[2] Department of Health, *Care and Support Statutory Guidance* (2014), Annex G, para.38.
[3] Department of Health, *Care and Support Statutory Guidance* (2014), Annex G, para.30.

Following an assessment, if the local authority considers that the patient's or a carer's **1–860** needs have changed it must inform the NHS body. This is intended to allow the authority to change its decision about what services to provide to enable a safe discharge, so as to cover situations where the patient's condition changes. This means that for example if a patient recovers more quickly than expected, the local authority would not have to provide all the services they originally said they would, even though some of them were no longer needed. However, the authority will not be able to make such a change without first consulting the NHS body.

Cases where discharge of the patient is delayed
4.—(1) If the relevant authority, having received an assessment notice and a discharge notice, has not **1–861** carried out a needs or (where applicable) carer's assessment and the patient has not been discharged by the end of the relevant day, the NHS body responsible for the patient may require the relevant authority to pay the specified amount for each day of the specified period.
(2) If the relevant authority has not put in place arrangements for meeting some or all of those of the needs under sections 18 to 20 that it proposes to meet in the case of the patient or (where applicable) a carer, and the patient has for that reason alone not been discharged by the end of the relevant day, the NHS body responsible for the patient may require the relevant authority to pay the specified amount for each day of the specified period.
(3) If, in a case within sub-paragraph (1) or (2), the assessment notice ceases to be in force, any liability arising under that sub-paragraph before it ceased to be in force is unaffected.
(4) A payment under sub-paragraph (1) or (2) must be made to—
(a) the NHS body responsible for the patient, or
(b) in such a case as regulations may specify, the person specified.
(5) The "relevant day" has the meaning given by paragraph 2(5).
(6) A reference to a requirement to pay the specified amount is a reference to a requirement to pay the amount specified in regulations; and the reference to the specified period is a reference to the period specified in or determined in accordance with regulations.
(7) In specifying the amount of a payment, the Secretary of State must have regard in particular to either or both of—
(a) costs to NHS bodies of providing accommodation and personal care to patients ready to be discharged, and
(b) costs to local authorities of meeting needs under sections 18 to 20 in the case of persons who have been discharged.

GENERAL NOTE
This provides that in the event that the discharge of the patient is delayed because the **1–862** local authority has not carried out the relevant assessments or put the required package of care and support in place, the NHS body may require the local authority to make payments for each day that a patient is unable to be discharged. This is a change to the previous legal position. Under s.6 of the Community Care (Delayed Discharges etc) Act 2003 the social services authority was required to make payments to an NHS body in respect of delayed discharges. Under the Care Act, the NHS body has discretion over whether or not to require the authority to make payments. This change was introduced "in light of the drive to improve integration between health and social care provision" and to provide the "opportunity to seek collaborative solutions to address barriers locally in the first instance".[1]
Regulation 9 of the Care and Support (Discharge of Hospital Patients) Regulations 2014 (SI 2014/2823) sets out how the period for which the local authority may be liable to the NHS for reimbursement for the costs of the patient's care is to be determined, and reg.10 specifies the daily amount the local authority may be required to pay the NHS body in the event that the local authority has not assessed the patient and put in place arrangements to meet some or all of those needs that it proposes to meet. The charge has been set at £130 per day for most authorities and £155 for London authorities. This is a

---

[1] Department of Health, *Care and Support Statutory Guidance* (2014), paras 15.37 and 15.41.

rise from the previous charges under the 2003 Act (in line with the CPI measure of inflation) which were £100 per day for most authorities and £120 for certain "higher rate authorities".[1]

The statutory guidance emphasises that NHS bodies should "not use reimbursement as the first approach to address any local difficulties around delayed transfers of care".[2] Further guidance about delayed discharge liability can be found at paras 39 to 47 of the statutory guidance.

Delegation to management of independent hospital

1–863
5.—(1) An NHS body may make arrangements with any person connected with the management of an independent hospital for that person (or an employee of that person) to do, on behalf of the NHS body and in accordance with the arrangements, anything which is required or authorised to be done by the NHS body by or under this Schedule in relation to hospital patients accommodated in that hospital.

(2) Anything done or omitted to be done by or in relation to the authorised person (or an employee of that person) under such arrangements is to be treated as done or omitted to be done by or in relation to the NHS body.

(3) Nothing in this paragraph prevents anything being done by or in relation to the NHS body.

GENERAL NOTE

1–864
Paragraph 5 provides that an NHS body may make arrangements with an independent hospital to implement the delayed discharge regime. This allows an NHS body which has commissioned acute treatment at an independent hospital to make arrangements for the independent provider to issue assessment or discharge notifications on its behalf. The statutory guidance confirms that such arrangements can be made with an independent hospital in the UK.[3] It goes on to describe the intended effect of para.5:

"This means that independent providers can take decisions such as whether the patient is likely to need care and support services, when the patient is to be discharged, what follow-up health needs they may have, etc. However, the NHS body will retain ultimate responsibility for the functions, including any claim for reimbursement that might be appropriate."[4]

Adjustments between local authorities

1–865
6.—(1) Regulations may modify, or otherwise make provision about, the application of a provision of this Schedule in a case where it appears to the NHS body responsible for a hospital patient that the patient is ordinarily resident in the area of another local authority.

(2) The regulations may, in particular, authorise or require a local authority—
(a) to accept an assessment notice given to it even though it may wish to dispute that it was the correct authority to which to give the notice;
(b) to become the relevant authority in the patient's case;
(c) to recover expenditure incurred—
    (i) in the exercise of functions under this Schedule;
    (ii) in meeting needs under sections 18 to 20 in a case under this Schedule.

GENERAL NOTE

1–866
There may be cases where there are disputes about where a patient is ordinarily resident and therefore which local authority is responsible for assessing the patent's needs, or making any payments should discharge be delayed. Paragraph 6 allows for regulations to be made to modify the provisions relating to delayed hospital discharges where it appears to the NHS body that the patient is ordinarily resident in the area of another local authority. This has been implemented by reg.12 of the Care and Support (Discharge of Hospital

---

[1] Delayed Discharges (England) Regulations 2003 (SI 2003/2277) reg.7. The higher rate authorities were mainly based in London and the South East.
[2] Department of Health, *Care and Support Statutory Guidance* (2014), Annex G, para.39.
[3] Department of Health, *Care and Support Statutory Guidance* (2014), para.15.46.
[4] Department of Health, *Care and Support Statutory Guidance* (2014), para.15.47.

Patients) Regulations 2014 (SI 2014/2823) which requires a local authority to which an assessment notice is given to accept that notice and be required to undertake the duties in relation to that patient notwithstanding that it may dispute that patient's ordinary residence. It also allows a local authority which has wrongly been given an assessment notice to claim reimbursement for any delayed discharge payment it has paid in that case from the local authority in whose area the patient is later agreed or determined to be ordinarily resident. The intention is to ensure that one local authority is always responsible for the patient and that they receive any necessary care and support as soon as possible, even where there is uncertainty as to which authority should bear responsibility.[1] The statutory guidance confirms that if no agreement can be reached on ordinary residence, the local authority must seek a determination from the Secretary of State or an appointed representative.[2]

Meaning of "hospital patient", "NHS hospital, "NHS body", etc.

1–867

7.—(1) A hospital patient is a person ordinarily resident in England who—

    (a) is being accommodated at an NHS hospital, or at an independent hospital as a result of arrangements made by an NHS body, and

    (b) is receiving (or has received or can reasonably be expected to receive) acute care.

(2) "NHS hospital" means a health service hospital (as defined by the National Health Service Act 2006) in England.

(3) "Independent hospital" means a hospital (as defined by that Act) in the United Kingdom which is not—

    (a) an NHS hospital,

    (b) a health service hospital as defined by section 206 of the National Health Service (Wales) Act 2006,

    (c) a health service hospital as defined by section 108 of the National Health Service (Scotland) Act 1978, or

    (d) a hospital vested in the Department of Health, Social Services and Public Safety in Northern Ireland or managed by a Health and Social Care trust.

(4) "NHS body" means—

    (a) an NHS trust established under section 25 of the National Health Service Act 2006,

    (b) an NHS foundation trust,

    (c) the National Health Service Commissioning Board, or

    (d) a clinical commissioning group.

(5) A reference to the NHS body responsible for a hospital patient is—

    (a) if the hospital is an NHS hospital, a reference to the NHS body managing it, or

    (b) if the hospital is an independent hospital, a reference to the NHS body that arranged for the patient to be accommodated in it.

(6) "Acute care" means intensive medical treatment provided by or under the supervision of a consultant, that lasts for a limited period after which the person receiving the treatment no longer benefits from it.

(7) Care is not "acute care" if the patient has given an undertaking (or one has been given on the patient's behalf) to pay for it; nor is any of the following "acute care"—

    (a) care of an expectant or nursing mother;

    (b) mental health care;

    (c) palliative care;

    (d) a structured programme of care provided for a limited period to help a person maintain or regain the ability to live at home;

    (e) care provided for recuperation or rehabilitation.

(8) "Mental health care" means psychiatric services, or other services provided for the purpose of preventing, diagnosing or treating illness, the arrangements for which are the primary responsibility of a consultant psychiatrist.

---

[1] Community Care (Delayed Discharges etc) Act 2003: Explanatory Notes para.47. Schedule 3 para.6 to the Care Act largely replicates s.10 of the 2003 Act.

[2] Department of Health, *Care and Support Statutory Guidance* (2014), Annex G, paras 49 to 50.

PART 2

PROVISION TO BE INSERTED IN SOCIAL SERVICES AND WELL-BEING (WALES) ACT 2014

"Schedule A1 Direct payments: after-care under the mental health act 1983

General

1-872 **1.** Sections 50 (direct payments to meet an adult's needs), 51 (direct payments to meet a child's needs) and 53 (direct payments: further provision) apply in relation to section 117 of the Mental Health Act 1983 but as if the following modifications were made to those sections.

Modifications to section 50

1-873 **2.** For subsection (1) of section 50 substitute—

"(1) Regulations may require or allow a local authority to make payments to an adult to whom section 117 of the Mental Health Act 1983 (after-care) applies that are equivalent to the cost of providing or arranging for the provision of after-care services for the adult under that section."

3. In subsection (3) of that section—
  (a) in paragraph (a), for "who has needs for care and support ("A")" substitute "in respect of the provision to the adult ("A") of after-care services under section 117 of the Mental Health Act 1983", and
  (b) in paragraph (c)(i), for "of meeting A's needs" substitute "of discharging its duty towards A under section 117 of the Mental Health Act 1983".

4. In subsection (4) of that section—
  (a) in paragraph (a), for "who has needs for care and support ("A")" substitute "to whom section 117 of the Mental Health Act 1983 applies ("A")", and
  (b) in paragraph (d)(i), for "meeting A's needs" substitute "discharging its duty towards A under section 117 of the Mental Health Act 1983".

5. In subsection (5) of that section—
  (a) in paragraph (a), for "A's needs for care and support" substitute "the provision to A of after-care services under section 117 of the Mental Health Act 1983", and
  (b) in paragraph (b), for "towards the cost of meeting A's needs for care and support" substitute "equivalent to the cost of providing or arranging the provision to A of aftercare services under section 117 of the Mental Health Act 1983".

6. In subsection (6)(b) of that section, for "A's needs for care and support" substitute "the provision to A of after-care services under section 117 of the Mental Health Act 1983".

Modifications to section 51

1-874 **7.** For subsection (1) of section 51 substitute—

"(1) Regulations may require or allow a local authority to make payments to a person in respect of a child to whom section 117 of the Mental Health Act 1983 (after-care) applies that are equivalent to the cost of providing or arranging the provision of after-care services for the child under that section."

8. In subsection (3)(a) and (b) of that section, for "who has needs for care and support" (in each place it occurs) substitute "to whom section 117 of the Mental Health Act 1983 applies".

9. In subsection (5)(a) of that section, for "meeting the child's needs" substitute "discharging its duty towards the child under section 117 of the Mental Health Act 1983".

Modifications to section 53

1-875 **10.** In subsection (1) of section 53—
  (a) in the opening words, for "50, 51 or 52" substitute "50 or 51",
  (b) omit paragraphs (a), (b) and (c),
  (c) in paragraph (i), for "a local authority's duty or power to meet a person's needs for care and support or a carer's needs for support is displaced" substitute "a local authority's duty under section 117 of the Mental Health Act 1983 (after-care) is discharged", and
  (d) in paragraph (k), for "50 to 52" substitute "50 and 51".

11. Omit subsections (2) to (8) of that section.

12. After subsection (8) of that section insert—

"(8A) Regulations under sections 50 and 51 must specify that direct payments to meet the cost of providing or arranging for the provision of after-care services under section 117 of the Mental Health Act 1983 (after-care) must be made at a rate that the local authority estimates to be equivalent to the reasonable cost of securing the provision of those services to meet those needs."

13. In subsection (9) of that section—
(a) for ", 51 or 52" substitute "or 51", and
(b) for "care and support (or, in the case of a carer, support)" substitute "after-care services".

14. In subsection (10) of that section, for "care and support (or, in the case of a carer, support) to meet needs" substitute "after-care services".

GENERAL NOTE

Part 1 of Sch.4 modifies the application of certain direct payments provisions of the Care **1–876** Act (ss.31, 32 and 33) to ensure that they also apply to services provided under s.117 of the Mental Health Act 1983. Part 2 inserts Sch.A1 (direct payments: after-care under the Mental Health Act 1983) into the Social Services and Well-being (Wales) Act 2014, which modifies the application of certain direct payments provisions of that Act (ss.34, 35 and 37) to apply to services provided or commissioned under s.117 by local authorities in Wales.

APPENDIX 1

STATUTORY INSTRUMENTS

THE CARE AND SUPPORT AND AFTER-CARE (CHOICE OF ACCOMMODATION) REGULATIONS 2014 (SI 2014/2670)

The Secretary of State makes these Regulations in exercise of the powers conferred by **A1–101** section 117A(1), (2) and (4) of the Mental Health Act 1983[1] and sections 30(1) and (2) and 125(7) and (8) of the Care Act 2014[2] .

GENERAL NOTE

Section 30 of the Care Act establishes a regulation-making power to provide that where an adult's needs are to be met by the provision of specified types of accommodation, and the adult has expressed a preference for particular accommodation of that type, the local authority must meet the adult's preference, provided that specified conditions are met. In addition, s.117A of the Mental Health Act 1983 establishes a regulation-making power to introduce similar provisions for people who are being provided with accommodation under s.117 of the 1983 Act (see para.1–742 above). These regulations implement both of these powers.

In relation to accommodation under the Care Act, the regulations provide that the following conditions must be met for the provision of preferred accommodation:

- the local authority is meeting needs under sections 18 to 20 of the Act by providing or arranging care home, shared lives or supported living accommodation (reg. 2(1)(a));
- the adult expresses a preference for particular accommodation of a specified type (reg.2(1)(b));
- the care and support plan specifies that the person's needs are going to be met by the provision of accommodation of a specified type (reg.3(1)(a));
- the preferred accommodation is of the same type as that specified in the care and support plan (reg.3(1)(b));
- the preferred accommodation is suitable to meet the person's needs (reg.3(1)(c));
- the preferred accommodation is available (reg.3(1)(d));
- the provider is willing to provide the accommodation to the person on the local authority's terms (reg.3(1)(e)); and
- where the cost of the preferred accommodation is greater than the amount specified in the personal budget for accommodation of the same type, a third party or (in certain cases) the person must be able and willing to pay the additional cost (regs. 3(2) and 5).

Where accommodation is being provided under section 117 of the 1983 Act, the relevant conditions are very similar to those above (see reg. 4). The main difference is that a person receiving accommodation under section 117 has a greater ability to make top-up payments.

The statutory guidance discusses the regulations in paras 8.36 to 8.37 and Annex A.

---

[1] 1983 c.20. Section 117A is inserted by s.75(6) of the Care Act 2014.
[2] 2014 c.23; See s.125(1) for the powers to make regulations.

Citation, commencement and interpretation

A1–102   **1.**—(1) These Regulations may be cited as the Care and Support and After-care (Choice of Accommodation) Regulations 2014.

(2) These Regulations come into force as follows—

    (a) for the purposes of a case to which regulation 4(1)(a) applies, immediately after section 75(6) of the Care Act 2014 comes fully into force[1] ; and

    (b) for all other purposes, immediately after section 30 of the Care Act 2014 comes fully into force[2] .

(3) In these Regulations—

"the 1983 Act" means the Mental Health Act 1983;

"the Act" means the Care Act 2014;

"personal care" means—

    (a) physical assistance given to a person in connection with—
        (i) eating or drinking (including the administration of parenteral nutrition),
        (ii) toileting (including in relation to the process of menstruation),
        (iii) washing or bathing,
        (iv) dressing,
        (v) oral care,
        (vi) the care of skin, hair and nails (with the exception of nail care provided by a chiropodist or podiatrist); or
    (b) the prompting, together with supervision, of a person in relation to the performance of any of the activities listed in paragraph (a), where that person is unable to make a decision for themselves in relation to performing the activity without such prompting or supervision;

"preferred accommodation" means the accommodation for which the person for whom it is to be provided expresses a preference in accordance with—

    (a) in a case to which regulation 4 applies, regulation 4(1)(b);

    (b) in any other case, regulation 2(1)(b).

Choice of accommodation

A1–103   **2.**—(1) Where—

    (a) a local authority[3] is going to meet needs under sections 18 to 20 of the Act by providing or arranging for the provision of accommodation of a specified type in England;

    (b) the adult[4] for whom the accommodation is to be provided expresses a preference for particular accommodation (identifiable by reference to its address or provider) of a specified type; and

    (c) the conditions in regulation 3 are met, the local authority must provide or arrange for the provision of the preferred accommodation in accordance with these Regulations.

(2) The specified types of accommodation are—

    (a) care home accommodation (see regulation 6);

    (b) shared lives scheme accommodation (see regulation 7); or

    (c) supported living accommodation (see regulation 8).

---

[1] Section 75(6) was commenced for the purpose of making regulations by S.I. 2014/2473.
[2] Section 30 was commenced for the purpose of making regulations by S.I. 2014/2473.
[3] See s.1(4) of the Act for the meaning of "local authority"; the definition is limited to local authorities in England.
[4] See s.2(8) of the Act for the meaning of "adult".

GENERAL NOTE

Paragraph (1)(a)

The local authority must be meeting needs under sections 18 to 20 of the Care Act. Therefore it is not necessary for the person to have eligible needs and be owed a duty under section 18. A local authority could be providing accommodation through its power under section 19 and the regulations would still apply (provided that the relevant conditions are met). They also apply to accommodation being provided as a carer's service under section 20.

However, the regulations are limited to the provision of accommodation in England.

Paragraph (1)(b)

The adult has a right to choose between different providers of a type of accommodation (provided that the other conditions are met). The person's choice can be identified by reference to its address or provider. But this does not enable the person to choose between different types of accommodation (for example a shared lives scheme rather than care home accommodation). The statutory guidance explains that

"determining the appropriate type of accommodation should be made with the adult as part of the care and support planning process, therefore this choice only applies between providers of the same type".

The guidance also specifies that the local authority must ensure that "the person has a genuine choice and must ensure that at least one option is available and affordable within a person's personal budget and should ensure that there is more than one" accommodation option available.[1]

However, the choice is not limited to local authority accommodation or providers that the local authority contracts with. It is also not limited to accommodation within the authority's geographical area.[2]

The regulations do not make any separate provisions for those who lack capacity to choose between different types of accommodation. According to the statutory guidance, in such cases local authorities should:

". . . act on the choices expressed by the person's advocate, carer or legal guardian in the same way they would on the person's own wishes, unless in the local authority's opinion it would be against the best interests of the person."[3]

Some service users being provided with accommodation under the Care Act are not entirely free to choose their accommodation, such as those subject to Guardianship under the Mental Health Act 1983 or the Deprivation of Liberty Safeguards under the Mental Capacity Act 2005. However, the regulations may still be relevant even in these cases. Preferred accommodation can be provided even though a degree of coercion may be necessary. For example, Guardianship may be used where a person is moving into their preferred accommodation but there is concern that in the future their mental health may deteriorate causing them to try to leave their preferred accommodation.[4] Moreover, the use of the Deprivation of Liberty Safeguards will only be lawful if the care home regime is in the person's best interests under the Mental Capacity Act, which must include having regard to the person's wishes and feelings.[5]

---

[1] Department of Health, *Care and Support Statutory Guidance* (2014), para 8.37 and Annex A, paras 9 and 12.

[2] Department of Health, *Care and Support Statutory Guidance* (2014), para 8.37 and Annex A, paras 6 and 7.

[3] Department of Health, *Care and Support Statutory Guidance* (2014), para 8.37 and Annex A, para 40.

[4] Mental Health Act 1983 ss.7 and 8.

[5] Mental Capacity Act 2005 s.4, and Sch.1A para.16.

Paragraph (2)

Prior to the Care Act, the National Assistance Act 1948 (Choice of Accommodation) Directions 1992 had enabled service users to exercise choice if a person was being placed in a care home. However, para.2 provides that the choice of accommodation can be exercised in respect of care home, shared lives and supported living accommodation. These forms of accommodation are defined in regulations 6, 7 and 8 respectively.

Conditions for provision of preferred accommodation

A1–104   **3.**—(1) The following conditions must be met for the provision of preferred accommodation under regulation 2—

    (a) the care and support plan[1] for the adult specifies that the adult's needs are going to be met by the provision of accommodation of a specified type;

    (b) the preferred accommodation is of the same type as that specified in the adult's care and support plan;

    (c) the preferred accommodation is suitable to the adult's needs;

    (d) the preferred accommodation is available; and

    (e) where the preferred accommodation is not provided by the local authority, the provider of the accommodation agrees to provide the accommodation to the adult on the local authority's terms.

(2) If the cost to the local authority of providing or arranging for the provision of the preferred accommodation is greater than the amount specified in the adult's personal budget[2] that relates to the provision of accommodation of that type, the additional cost condition in regulation 5 must also be met[3].

GENERAL NOTE

Paragraph (1)(a)

The care and support plan must specify that the adult's needs will be met by the provision of one of the following types of accommodation: care home, shared lives or supported living.

Paragraph (1)(b)

The preferred accommodation must be of the same type as that specified in the care and support plan.

Paragraph (1)(c)

The local authority must ensure that the preferred accommodation is suitable to meet the person's assessed needs and outcomes that have been identified in the care and support plan. The statutory guidance links the issue of suitability to the care planning process. It states that:

"People are able to express a preference about the setting in which their needs are met through the care and support planning process. This process considers both the person's needs and preferences . . . Once this is agreed, the choice is between different settings, not different types. For example, a person cannot exercise the right to a choice of accommodation to choose a shared lives scheme when the care and support planning process, which involves the person, has assessed their needs as needing to be met in a care home."[4]

---

[1]   See s.25 of the Act for the meaning of "care and support plan".
[2]   See s.26 of the Act for the meaning of "personal budget".
[3]   See s.30(3) of the Act for the meaning of "additional cost".
[4]   Department of Health, *Care and Support Statutory Guidance* (2014), Annex A, para.9.

Paragraph (1)(d)

This requires that the preferred accommodation must be available.

When patients are being discharged from hospital practical difficulties may arise because their preferred accommodation has no vacancies. This may lead to delays in discharge or discharge to temporary accommodation while the preferred accommodation becomes available. The Law Commission recommended that the code of practice should provide concrete examples on how the new choice of accommodation regulations apply to hospital in-patients.[1]

The statutory guidance does not provide such specific examples. But it does advise, more generally, that where the preferred accommodation is not available and there may be a short wait, the local authority may need to put in place temporary arrangements. However, such arrangements "can be unsettling for the person and should be avoided wherever possible". Where interim arrangements are made and last for over 12 weeks, the person may be reassessed "to ensure that the interim and preferred option are still able to meet the person's needs and that remains their choice".[2]

The guidance also confirms that if the person's choice cannot be met (for instance if the provider does not have capacity to accommodate the person), the local authority must set out in writing why it has been unable to meet that choice and offer suitable alternatives. It should also provide detail of the local authority complaints procedure and when and if the decision is to be reviewed.[3] See also reg. 9 which provides that a local authority must give written reasons for a refusal to provide preferred accommodation.

Paragraph (1)(e)

As noted above, the choice of accommodation is not limited to providers that the local authority already contracts with. The statutory guidance states that contractual arrangements with providers who do not currently have an arrangement with the authority, should be broadly the same as those the authority would negotiate with any other providers (whilst taking into account individual circumstances). Moreover, "strict or unreasonable conditions should not be used as a means to avoid or deter the arrangement".[4]

Paragraph (2)

This provides that top-up payments may be made in cases where the costs of the preferred accommodation are greater than the amount specified in the personal budget. This is considered in more detail under reg. 5 below.

Application to after-care

A1–105

4.—(1) Where—
- (a) a local authority is, in discharging its duty under section 117(2) of the 1983 Act, providing or arranging for the provision of accommodation in England for a person;
- (b) the person expresses a preference for particular accommodation (identifiable by reference to its address or provider); and
- (c) the conditions in paragraph (2) are met, the local authority must provide or arrange for the provision of the preferred accommodation in accordance with these Regulations.

(2) The following conditions must be met for the provision of preferred accommodation under paragraph (1)—
- (a) the person must be aged 18 or over;

---

[1] Law Commission, *Adult Social Care*, para.11.79.
[2] Department of Health, *Care and Support Statutory Guidance* (2014), Annex A, paras 13 to 14.
[3] Department of Health, *Care and Support Statutory Guidance* (2014), Annex A, para.17.
[4] Department of Health, *Care and Support Statutory Guidance* (2014), Annex A, para.19.

(b) the accommodation which the local authority is providing or arranging must be of a specified type;

(c) the preferred accommodation must be of the same type that the local authority has decided to provide or arrange;

(d) the preferred accommodation must be suitable to meet the person's needs;

(e) the preferred accommodation must be available;

(f) where the preferred accommodation is not provided by the local authority, the provider of the accommodation must agree to provide the accommodation to the person on the local authority's terms; and

(g) where the cost to the local authority of providing or arranging for the provision of the preferred accommodation is greater than the amount that the local authority would expect to be the usual cost of providing or arranging for the provision of accommodation of that kind, the additional cost conditions in paragraph (3) must also be met.

(3) The additional cost conditions referred to in paragraph (2)(g) are that—

(a) the local authority is satisfied that the person for whom the accommodation is to be provided or another person ("the payer"), is willing and able to pay the additional cost of the preferred accommodation for the period during which the local authority expects to meet needs by providing or arranging for the provision of that accommodation; and

(b) the payer enters into a written agreement with the authority in which the payer agrees to pay the additional cost.

(4) In a case to which paragraph (3) applies, the local authority must comply with the requirements of regulation 5(2), (3)(a) and (c) to (f), and (4).

(5) For the purposes of this regulation the additional cost that is to be met by the payer may be less than the full amount of the additional cost referred to in section 117A(3) of the 1983 Act, if the local authority agrees that a lesser amount should be paid.

(6) The specified types of accommodation are those referred to in regulation 2(2) but for the purposes of this regulation any reference to "an adult" in regulations 7 and 8 should be read as a reference to "a person".

GENERAL NOTE

Regulation 4 is made under s.117A of the Mental Health Act 1983 (see para.1–742 above in respect of s.75(6)). It requires a local authority, which is providing or arranging the specified type of accommodation under s.117 of the Mental Health Act 1983, to provide or arrange the provision of the adult's preferred accommodation of that type, if certain conditions are met. The following conditions must be met:

• the local authority is providing or arranging care home, shared lives or supported living accommodation in England;

• the preferred accommodation is of the same type as that the local authority is providing;

• the preferred accommodation is suitable to meet the adult's needs;

• the preferred accommodation is available;

• the provider is willing to provide the accommodation to the person on the local authority's terms; and

• where the cost of the preferred accommodation is greater than the usual cost of accommodation of that kind, the person or a third party must be able and willing to pay the additional cost.

These conditions are very similar to the conditions under reg. 3 that apply to accommodation being provided under the Care Act. But there are differences. For instance, a person receiving accommodation under section 117 has a greater ability to make top-up payments (see reg. 5(5)). These differences are intended to reflect the fact that section 117 after-care must be provided free of charge and the care plan should be drawn up under the Care Programme Approach (see para 1-733 above).[1]

The statutory guidance sets out 2 options for the payment of top-up payments:
- they are made directly to the provider; and
- they are paid to the local authority.[2]

Some service users being provided with accommodation under section 117 are not entirely free to choose their accommodation, such as those subject to Guardianship, Supervised Community Treatment or Conditional Discharge under the Mental Health Act 1983. In many such cases the person will be excluded from these provisions because the local authority has assessed that his or her preferred type of accommodation is not suitable to meet their needs. Nevertheless, the person has a right to choose between different providers of a type of accommodation. Therefore the regulations may still be relevant if the person expresses a preference for particular accommodation of a specified type. Moreover, there may be cases where preferred accommodation can be provided even though a degree of coercion may be necessary. For example, Guardianship may be used where a person is moving into their preferred accommodation but there is concern that in the future their mental health may deteriorate causing them to try to leave their preferred accommodation.[3]

The additional cost condition

5.—(1) The additional cost condition is met if—   **A1–106**
  (a) the local authority is satisfied that—
      (i) a person other than the adult, or
      (ii) in a case to which paragraph (5) applies, the adult, ("the payer") is able and willing to pay the additional cost of the preferred accommodation for the period during which the local authority expects to meet the adult's needs by providing or arranging for the provision of that accommodation; and
  (b) the payer enters a written agreement with the local authority in which the payer agrees to pay the additional cost.

(2) The local authority must provide the payer with access to sufficient information and advice to enable the payer to understand the terms of the proposed written agreement before entering into it.

(3) The written agreement must include—
  (a) the additional cost;
  (b) the amount specified in the adult's personal budget in relation to the provision of accommodation;
  (c) the frequency of payments;
  (d) details of the person to whom the payments are to be made;
  (e) provision for review of the agreement;
  (f) provisions about the matters specified in paragraph (4).

(4) The specified matters are—
  (a) the consequences of ceasing to make payments;
  (b) the effect of increases in charges made by the provider of the preferred accommodation;
  (c) the effect of changes in the payer's financial circumstances.

---

[1] Department of Health, *Care and Support Statutory Guidance* (2014), Annex A, para.45.
[2] Department of Health, *Care and Support Statutory Guidance* (2014), Annex A, para.50.
[3] Mental Health Act 1983 ss.7 and 8.

(5) The local authority may not agree with the adult for whom the accommodation is to be provided for that adult to pay the additional cost unless—

(a) paragraph 2 of Schedule 2 to the Care and Support (Charging and Assessment of Resources) Regulations 2014[1] (the 12 week property disregard) applies to that adult; or

(b) the adult and the local authority agree to enter into a deferred payment agreement in accordance with the Care and Support (Deferred Payment) Regulations 2014[2] in respect of the additional cost.

(6) For the purposes of this regulation the additional cost that is to be met by the payer may be less than the full amount of the additional cost referred to in section 30(3) of the Act, if the local authority agrees that a lesser amount should be paid.

GENERAL NOTE

Where the cost of an adult's preferred accommodation is more than the amount specified for the accommodation in the adult's personal budget (under section 26 of the Act), the local authority is not required to provide that accommodation unless the additional cost condition is met. In effect, the local authority must be satisfied that a third party or (in some cases) the person themselves is able and willing to pay the additional cost of the preferred accommodation (known as the "top-up payment").

The additional cost provisions do not apply when someone is placed in more expensive accommodation solely because the local authority has been unable to make arrangements at the normal cost. In such cases the statutory guidance sets out that the personal budget should reflect this amount and the person would contribute towards the costs in accordance with the financial assessment.[3]

The guidance also notes that people should not have to pay top-ups "because of market inadequacies or commissioning failures and must ensure there is a genuine choice". The local authority therefore must ensure that at least one option is available that is affordable within a person's personal budget and should ensure that there is more than one. If no preference has been expressed and no suitable accommodation is available at the amount identified in a personal budget, the local authority "must arrange care in a more expensive setting and adjust the budget accordingly to ensure that needs are met". In such circumstances, the local authority must not ask for the payment of a top-up fee. Only when a person has chosen a more expensive accommodation can a top-up payment be sought.[4]

The Government intends to amend the statutory guidance to clarify that local authorities must ensure that at least one of the accommodation options provided by the local authority is within that person's personal budget and the authority should ensure that there is more than one accommodation option available.[5]

Paragraph (1)

The person paying the top-up must be willing and able to make the payment. Moreover, they must enter into a written agreement with the local authority.

In October 2014, the Local Government Ombudsman recommended that a local authority should reimburse a woman's estate the full amount of third party top-up payments. In this case the authority had reviewed the way it commissioned placements, and the home in which the woman lived was excluded from a new quality framework, despite meeting the set criteria. The woman was 80 and had dementia, and her son complained that she had to pay significant additional costs every week to remain in the home where she had lived in for the past three years. The guidance then in place (LAC(2004)20) had stated

---

[1] S.I. 2014/2672.

[2] S.I. 2014/2671.

[3] Department of Health, *Care and Support Statutory Guidance* (2014), Annex A, para.21.

[4] Department of Health, *Care and Support Statutory Guidance* (2014), Annex A, para.12.

[5] Department of Health, *Update on the Final Orders under the Care Act 2014* (2015) para.26.

that only when an individual expresses a wish for more expensive accommodation than that of the usual cost paid by the council, can a third party be asked to pay for a top-up fee. The woman in this case had not expressed such a wish. The guidance also stated that councils must contract to pay the full cost of accommodation including the top-up. It also stated that a resident cannot pay a top-up except in exceptional circumstances, which did not apply in this case, but a third party can pay on their behalf with everyone's agreement. In this case the man had paid the top-up from his mother's resources, of which the Council was aware, not because of a willingness to pay to pay but because he believed there was no option other than moving his mother from the care home where she was settled. There was also a failure to complete a financial assessment to establish the resident's ability and willingness to pay the extra charge, which should always be undertaken when there is a change to care fees which may impact on a resident.[1] This case remains relevant under the Care Act because the regulations and the statutory guidance contain almost identical provisions to those referred to under the previous guidance.

Paragraphs (3) and (4)

These list the minimum information and matters that must be addressed in the written agreement. The statutory guidance confirms that the list is not exhaustive.[2]

The agreement must specify the additional cost and the amount specified in the adult's personal budget in relation to the provision of accommodation. The amount of the top-up should be the difference between the actual costs of the preferred provider and the amount the local authority would have set in the personal budget to meet the person's needs through the provision of accommodation of the same type (although the local authority can agree for the amount to be less than the full amount – see para.6 below.).

The statutory guidance states that:

"The personal budget is defined as the cost to the local authority of meeting the person's needs which the local authority chooses or is required to meet. However, the local authority should take into consideration cases or circumstances where this 'cost to the local authority' may need to be adjusted to ensure that needs are met. For example, a person may have specific dietary requirements that can only be met in specific settings. In all cases the local authority must have regard to the actual cost of good quality care in deciding the personal budget to ensure that the amount is one that reflects local market conditions. This should also reflect other factors such as the person's circumstances and the availability of provision. In addition, the local authority should not set arbitrary amounts or ceilings for particular types of accommodation that do not reflect a fair cost of care."[3]

The statutory guidance states that when considering the costs of care in its area:

" . . . the local authority is likely to identify a range of costs which apply to different circumstances and settings. For the purposes of agreeing a "top-up" fee the local authority must consider what personal budget it would have set at the time care and support is needed. It should not default to the cheapest rate or to any other arbitrary figure."[4]

The agreement must specify the frequency of payments and details of the person to whom the payments are to be made. The statutory guidance sets out 3 options for the payment of top-up payments:

- they are treated as income and therefore recovered through the financial assessment;

---

[1] Local Government Ombudsman, Investigation into a compliant against Tamesside Metropolitan Borough Council (24 September 2014) Ref no. 12 019 862.
[2] Department of Health, *Care and Support Statutory Guidance* (2014), Annex A, para.23.
[3] Department of Health, *Care and Support Statutory Guidance* (2014), Annex A, para.11.
[4] Department of Health, *Care and Support Statutory Guidance* (2014), Annex A, para.26.

- they are made directly to the provider (although the guidance does not recommend this option); and
- they are paid to the local authority.[1]

The agreement must include provision for review of the agreement. This should include what should trigger the review and when a party can request a review, and there is an expectation that reviews should be held at least annually.[2]

The agreement must also include provisions for the consequences of ceasing to make payments, the effect of increases in charges made by the provider and the effect of changes in the payer's financial circumstances. The local authority remains responsible for the total cost of that placement. If the top-up fees were to cease for any reason, then the local authority would be liable for the fees. Local authorities should therefore "maintain an overview of all 'top-up' agreements" and hold reviews at least annually.[3]

Paragraph (5)

This provides for top-up payments to be made by the person with care and support needs. Such payment can only be made where they are subject to the 12-week property disregard, or a deferred payment agreement is in pace. In addition, under reg.4 the person can make top-up payments if they are receiving the accommodation under s.117 of the Mental Health Act 1983.

Paragraph (6)

The amount of the top-up should normally be the difference between the actual costs of the preferred provider and the amount the local authority would have set in the personal budget to meet the person's needs through the provision of accommodation of the same type. But this provision confirms the local authority can agree for the amount to be less than the full amount.

Care home accommodation

A1–107   **6.** For the purposes of these Regulations, "care home accommodation" means accommodation in a care home within the meaning given by section 3 of the Care Standards Act 2000[4] .

Shared lives scheme accommodation

A1–108   **7.** For the purposes of these Regulations, "shared lives scheme accommodation" means accommodation which is provided for an adult by a shared lives carer, and for this purpose—

"shared lives carer" means an individual who, under the terms of a shared lives agreement, provides, or intends to provide, personal care for adults together with, where necessary, accommodation in the individual's home;

"shared lives agreement" means an agreement entered into between a person carrying on a shared lives scheme and an individual for the provision, by that individual, of personal care to an adult together with, where necessary, accommodation in the individual's home; and

---

[1] Department of Health, *Care and Support Statutory Guidance* (2014), Annex A, para.29. See also para.25 regarding payments direct to the provider.

[2] Department of Health, *Care and Support Statutory Guidance* (2014), Annex A, paras 25 and 31 to 32.

[3] Department of Health, *Care and Support Statutory Guidance* (2014), Annex A, paras 25 and 31 to 32.

[4] 2000 c.14; s.3 was amended by the Health and Social Care Act 2008 (c.14), s.95 and para.4 of Sch.5.

"shared lives scheme" means a scheme carried on (whether or not for profit) by a local authority or other person for the purposes of—

(a) recruiting and training shared lives carers;

(b) making arrangements for the placing of adults with shared lives carers; and

(c) supporting and monitoring placements.

Supported living etc

8.—(1) For the purposes of these Regulations, "supported living accommodation" **A1–109** means—

(a) accommodation in premises which are specifically designed or adapted for occupation by adults with needs for care and support to enable them to live as independently as possible; and

(b) accommodation which is provided—

(i) in premises which are intended for occupation by adults with needs for care and support (whether or not the premises are specifically designed or adapted for that purpose), and

(ii) in circumstances in which personal care is available if required.

(2) The accommodation referred to in paragraph (1)(a) does not include adapted premises where the adult had occupied those premises as their home before the adaptations were made.

(3) For the purposes of paragraph (1)(b)(ii) personal care may be provided by a person other than the person who provides the accommodation.

Refusal to provide preferred accommodation

9. A local authority must give the adult its written reasons for a refusal to provide or **A1–110** arrange for the provision of preferred accommodation.

GENERAL NOTE

Regulation 9 provides that a local authority must give written reasons for a refusal to provide preferred accommodation.

THE CARE AND SUPPORT (DEFERRED PAYMENT) REGULATIONS 2014 (SI 2014/2671)

The Secretary of State makes the following Regulations in exercise of the powers con- **A1–111** ferred by sections 34(1), (2) and (4) to (8), 35 and 125(7) and (8) of the Care Act 2014[1] .

GENERAL NOTE

Section 34 enables the Secretary of State to make regulations concerning deferred payments and loans. Deferred payments are local authority loans secured against the value of a person's home and repayable when the home is sold, often after the person has died. These regulations make provision for local authorities to enter into a deferred payment agreement with an adult and specify the amount of the agreement and conditions which relate to the agreement.

Deferred payment agreements are covered in Pt 9 of the statutory guidance. Amongst other matters, it discusses providing information and advice on deferred payment agreements, and the minimum information that a local authority must provide to a person who may benefit from or be eligible for a deferred payment agreement. This includes suggesting that the person "may want to consider taking independent financial advice (including flagging the existence of regulated financial advice".[2]

---

[1] 2014 c.23.The powers to make regulations are exercisable by the Secretary of State; See s.125(1).

[2] Department of Health, *Care and Support Statutory Guidance* (2014), para.9.26.

In addition, Shills for Care has produced guidance on deferred payments.[1] These documents are not statutory guidance but have been produced with the approval of the Department of Health (see 1–770 above).

The statutory provisions for deferred payments, and the policy behind them, are discussed at paras 1–371 to 1–406 above.

Citation, commencement and interpretation

A1–112 **1.**—(1)These Regulations may be cited as the Care and Support (Deferred Payment) Regulations 2014 and come into force immediately after sections 34(1) and 35(1) of the Care Act 2014 are both fully in force[2] .

(2) In these Regulations—

"the Act" means the Care Act 2014 and a reference to a section is a reference to a section of the Act;

"care home" means a care home, within the meaning given in section 3 of the Care Standards Act 2000[3] , in respect of which a person is registered under the Health and Social Care Act 2008[4] for the regulated activity of the provision of accommodation together with nursing or personal care;

"long tenancy" is a tenancy granted for a term of years certain exceeding twenty one years, whether or not the tenancy is, or may become, terminable before the end of that term by notice given by or to the tenant or by re-entry, forfeiture or otherwise and includes a lease for a term fixed by law under a grant with a covenant or obligation for perpetual renewal unless it is a lease by sub-demise from one which is not a long tenancy;

"specified time" means the time specified in regulation 7;

"supported living accommodation" has the meaning in regulation 3(2);

"the 2011 Act" means the Budget Responsibility and National Audit Act 2011[5] .

Local authority required to enter into a deferred payment agreement

A1–113 **2.**—(1) A local authority[6] is required to enter into a deferred payment agreement with an adult if—

- (a) paragraph (2) applies to the adult;
- (b) the condition in regulation 4 is met; and
- (c) the adult agrees to all the terms and conditions included in the agreement in accordance with regulation 11.

(2) This paragraph applies to an adult if—

- (a) the adult's needs for care and support—
  - (i) are being met or are going to be met under section 18 or section 19(1) or (2) and the care and support plan[7] for the adult specifies that the local authority is going to meet the adult's needs by the provision of accommodation in a care home; or

---

1 Skills for Care, Making the DPA Handout (2014) and Skills for Care, *How much can be Deferred Handout* (2014).

2 Sections 34(1) and 35(1) have been commenced for the purpose of making regulations by S.I. 2014/2473.

3 2000 c.14.

4 2008 c.14.

5 2011 c.4.

6 See s.1(4) of the Act as to the meaning of "local authority"; the definition in s.1(4) is limited to local authorities in England.

7 See s.25 for the definition of "care and support plan".

(ii) are not being or going to be met by the local authority and the local authority considers that if it had been asked to meet the adult's needs it would have done so under section 18 or section 19(1) or (b) the local authority is satisfied that the adult has a legal or beneficial interest in a property which is the adult's main or only home, and
(i) where a financial assessment within the meaning of section 17(5) has been carried out in respect of the adult, that—

(aa) the value of that interest has not been disregarded for the purposes of calculating the amount of the adult's capital[1] ; and
(bb) the adult's capital less the value of that interest does not exceed £23,250; or
(ii) where such a financial assessment has not been carried out in respect of the adult that sub-paragraph (i) would be satisfied if such an assessment were carried out.

(3) But a local authority is only required to enter into a deferred payment agreement with an adult for amounts due from the adult to the authority under section 14, or for costs of care and support the provision of which the local authority considers to be necessary to meet the adult's needs.

GENERAL NOTE
This sets out when the duty arises to enter into a deferred payment agreement. In general terms, these provisions require a local authority to enter into a deferred payment agreement if:

- the adult's needs for care and support are being met by the provision of accommodation in a care home, or if the local authority had been asked to meet the person's needs, it would have provided care home accommodation (reg. 2(a));
- the person's home has not been disregarded for the purposes of the financial assessment because for instance it is occupied by a spouse of dependent relative (reg. 2(b)(i)(aa));
- the adults assets are £23,250 or less, excluding the value of their home (reg. 2(b)(i)(bb));
- the local authority has obtained adequate security for the payment of the deferred amount (reg.4); and
- the adult agrees to the agreement (regs. 2(c) and 11).

The statutory guidance lists a number of circumstances in which a local authority may refuse to defer any more charges including where a person's assets fall below the level of the means test and where they cease to have a need for accommodation in a care home.[2]

Local authority permitted to enter into a deferred payment agreement

3.—(1) A local authority is permitted to enter into a deferred payment agreement with an **A1–114** adult if—
(a) the adult's needs for care and support—
(i) are being met or are going to be met under section 18 or section 19(1) or (2) and the care and support plan for the adult specifies that the local authority is going to meet the adult's needs by the provision to the adult of accommodation in a care home or supported living accommodation; or
(ii) are not being or going to be met by the local authority and the local authority considers that if it had been asked to meet the adult's needs it would

---

[1] See s.17(11)(b) which provides that regulations under that section must make provision for calculating capital.
[2] Department of Health, *Care and Support Statutory Guidance* (2014), para.9.16.

have done so under section 18 or section 19(1) or (2) and it would have met the adult's needs by the provision to the adult of accommodation in a care home or supported living accommodation;

(b) the condition in regulation 4 is met; and

(c) the adult agrees to all the terms and conditions included in the agreement in accordance with regulation 11.

(2) For the purpose of paragraph (1), "supported living accommodation" means accommodation which is not a care home and is—

(a) in premises which are specifically designed or adapted for occupation by adults with needs for care and support to enable them to live as independently as possible; or

(b) provided—

(i) in premises which are intended for occupation by adults with needs for care and support (whether or not the premises are specifically designed or adapted for that purpose); and

(ii) in circumstances in which personal care is available if required.

(3) For the purposes of paragraph (2)(b)(ii), personal care may be provided by a person other than the person who provides the accommodation.

(4) The accommodation referred to in paragraph (2) does not include premises—

(a) in respect of which the adult is for the time being entitled to dispose of the fee simple, whether or not with the consent of other joint owners; or

(b) which the adult occupies other than under a licence or tenancy agreement.

(5) In paragraph (4) "tenancy" means a tenancy which is not a long tenancy.

GENERAL NOTE

This enables, but does not require, deferred payment arrangements to be put in place for those who do not meet the criteria in reg. 2. In general terms, a local authority may enter into a deferred payment agreement if:

- the adult's needs for care and support are being met by the provision of accommodation in care home or supported living accommodation, or if the local authority had been asked to meet the person's needs, it would have provided such accommodation (reg. 3(a));
- the local authority has obtained adequate security for the payment of the deferred amount (reg.4); and
- the adult agrees to the agreement (regs. 2(c) and 11).

The statutory guidance suggests that in exercising their discretion, local authorities may wish to take the following into account:

- whether meeting care costs would leave someone with very few accessible assets (this might include assets which cannot quickly/easily be liquidated or converted to cash);
- if someone would like to use wealth tied up in their home to fund more than just their core care costs and purchase affordable top-ups;
- whether someone has any other accessible means to help them meet the cost of their care and support; and/or
- if a person is narrowly not entitled to a deferred payment agreement given the criteria above, for example because they have slightly more than the £23,250 asset threshold. This should include people who are likely to meet the criteria in the near future.[1]

---

[1] Department of Health, *Care and Support Statutory Guidance* (2014), para.9.8.

In respect of supported living, the guidance states that a local authority should not exercise this discretion unless the person intends to retain their former home and pay the associated care and accommodation rental costs from their deferred payment, and deferred payment agreements cannot be entered into to finance mortgage payments on supported living accommodation.[1]

If a person lacks capacity to request a deferred payment, the statutory guidance advises that a deputy appointed by the Court of Protection or attorney appointed by an Enduring or Lasting Power of Attorney may request it on their behalf. The local authority should where appropriate provide information about deputyship, legal powers of attorney and advocacy, and confirm what would happen if a person were to lose capacity and had not made their own arrangements.[2]

Adequate security

A1–115

4.—(1) The local authority must obtain—

(a) adequate security for the payment of the adult's deferred amount[3] and any interest or administration costs which are treated in the same way as the adult's deferred amount; and

(b) the consent referred to in paragraph (4), if the authority considers it is necessary to do so.

(2) For the purposes of regulation 2, "adequate security" is a charge by way of legal mortgage for an amount which is at least equal to the deferred amount and any interest or administration costs which are to be treated in the same way as the adult's deferred amount and which is capable of being registered as a first legal charge in favour of the local authority in the land register[4].

(3) For the purposes of regulation 3, "adequate security" is—

(a) a charge by way of legal mortgage for an amount which is at least equal to the adult's deferred amount and any interest or administration costs which are to be treated in the same way as the adult's deferred amount and which is capable of being registered as described in paragraph (2); or

(b) any other security which the local authority considers is sufficient to secure payment of the deferred amount and any interest and administration costs which are to be treated in the same way as the adult's deferred amount.

(4) The consent required by paragraph (1) is consent which in the opinion of the local authority is genuine and informed consent given in writing to the matters specified in paragraph (5) by any person—

(a) who the authority considers has an interest in the land or other asset in respect of which a charge will be obtained; and

(b) whose interest the authority considers may prevent it from exercising a power of sale of the land or asset or recovering the deferred amount.

(5) The matters specified are—

(a) the creation of a charge; and

(b) the charge taking priority to and ranking before any interest the person has in the land or other asset which will be the subject of the charge.

---

[1] Department of Health, *Care and Support Statutory Guidance* (2014), para.9.9.
[2] Department of Health, *Care and Support Statutory Guidance* (2014), paras 9.24 to 9.25.
[3] See s.34(6) for the meaning of "deferred amount".
[4] See the Land Registration Act 2002 (c.9), s.132(1) for the meaning of "charge", "legal mortgage", "register".

(b) advance an instalment or part of an instalment under the loan agreement for the purpose of assisting the adult to obtain for that week the provision of care and support in a care home or supported living accommodation.

(2) But the amount which under this regulation the local authority may decide not to defer or advance in respect of that week may not exceed the amount by which the adult's income in that week exceeds £144.

(3) Where the local authority decides not to defer an amount or advance an instalment or part of an instalment under paragraph (1), it may include a term in the agreement to require the adult to pay or ensure payment of the amount due to the authority or the provider of the care and support in a care home or supported living accommodation.

(4) In paragraph (3) the amount due to the authority or provider of care and support is the amount which, in accordance with this regulation, the authority decides not to defer.

(5) The amount of the adult's weekly income must be calculated in accordance with regulations made under section 17.

[(6) But nothing in this regulation requires the local authority to—

(a) defer any amount which is due to it under section 14 or 30(2); or

(b) advance any or all of an instalment or part of an instalment under the loan agreement to the adult, if, under regulation 5(3) of these Regulations or in accordance with the terms of the agreement, the authority is required to, or is permitted to, cease to defer that amount or cease to advance any or all of the instalment or part of the instalment under the loan agreement.]

AMENDMENT
The amendment to this regulation was made by SI 2015/644 reg.2.

GENERAL NOTE
This provides that the local authority does not have to defer an amount where, after payment by the adult of the amounts due to the authority, or payment by the adult of the charges due to the provider of care and support in a care home or supported living accommodation, the adult would retain at least £144 of his or her weekly income. It also provides that the local authority may include a term in the agreement to require the adult to pay, or ensure payment of, the amounts which in accordance with the regulation the adult has decided not to defer.

Time for repayment of the deferred amount

A1–118 **7.** The specified time for repayment of the deferred amount and any interest and administration costs which have been treated in the same way as the deferred amount is the sooner of—

(a) the date of sale or disposal of the land or other asset in respect of which the authority has a charge; or

(b) 90 days after the date of the death of the adult with whom the agreement is made or such longer time as the authority may permit.

GENERAL NOTE
This makes provision as to the time for repayment of the deferred amount.

Termination

A1–119 **8.** The adult may terminate the deferred payment agreement at any time prior to the specified time by giving the authority reasonable notice in writing and paying to the local authority the deferred amount and any interest and administration costs which have been treated in the same way as the deferred amount.

GENERAL NOTE

This makes provision as to the adult's right to terminate the deferred payment agreement.

Interest

9.—(1) A local authority may charge interest on an adult's deferred amount and any **A1–120** amounts which are treated in the same way as the deferred amount provided that, before entering into the agreement, it informs the adult that it proposes to do so and of the rate at which interest will be charged.

(2) The interest may be treated in the same way as the adult's deferred amount, unless the adult requests to pay the interest separately.

(3) The interest rate is a rate that does not exceed the relevant rate for the relevant period plus 0.15%.

(4) The relevant rate is the weighted average interest rate on conventional gilts specified for the financial year in which the relevant period starts in the most recent report published before the start of the relevant period by the Office of Budget Responsibility[1] under section 4(3) of the 2011 Act[2].

(5) The relevant period is the period starting on—

    (a) 1st January and ending on 30th June in any year; or

    (b) 1st July and ending on 31st December in any year.

(6) "Financial year" has the meaning given in section 25(2) of the 2011 Act.

GENERAL NOTE

Regulation 9 makes provision as to the payment of interest. It is intended that the deferred payment scheme should run on a cost-neutral basis, with local authorities able to recoup the costs associated with deferring fees by charging interest. The Department of Health had originally proposed to have differential interest rates for deferred payment agreements formed under 'discretionary' and 'mandatory' powers. However, consultation responses argued this would produce complexity and confusion for local authorities and people with care and support needs. The Department accepted these points and reg.9 now makes clear that only one interest rate will apply to the entire scheme.[3] A local authority circular, issued under s.78 of the Care Act, has set out that the maximum interest rate chargeable will be 2.25 per cent for the period between July and December 2015.[4] The interest rate is discussed in the statutory guidance at paras 9.65 to 9.71.

Administration costs

10.—(1) The local authority may charge the adult its administration costs in accordance **A1–121** with paragraph (3) or (4) provided that it informs the adult that it proposes to do so, before entering into the agreement, and complies with sub–paragraphs (a) to (c) of paragraph (5).

(2) The administration costs may be treated in the same way as the adult's deferred amount, unless the adult requests to pay them separately.

(3) In this paragraph the administration costs are the total of any costs incurred by the authority in relation to the adult's deferred payment agreement including but not limited to—

    (a) the costs of postage, printing and photocopying;

    (b) the costs of time spent by persons in relation to the agreement;

---

[1] The Office of Budget Responsibility is established by s.3 of the 2011 Act.

[2] A copy of the report can be requested via careactconsultation@dh.gsi.gov.uk or the Department of Health, Richmond House, 79 Whitehall, London SW1A 2NS and is available at http://budgetresponsibility.org.uk/. [Accessed 27 July 2015]

[3] Department of Health, Response to the Consultation on draft Regulations and Guidance for Implementation of Part 1 of the Care Act 2014 (2014) Cm.8955, p.29.

[4] LAC(DH)(2015) 3: Social Care – Deferred payment agreements maximum chargeable interest rate for period 1 July - 31 December 2015.

(c) the costs of overheads, such as computer equipment and utility charges (to the extent that they are not already included in the costs of time spent by persons in relation to the agreement);

(d) the costs incurred for the purpose of ascertaining the value of the adequate security;

(e) the costs incurred in registering the charge on the land or land charges register;

(f) the costs incurred in perfecting the security obtained in respect of the deferred amount;

(g) the costs incurred in discharging or redeeming the security obtained in respect of the deferred amount; and

(h) the costs which are incurred by the authority for the purpose of ensuring compliance by the parties of the terms and conditions in the agreement.

(4) In this paragraph the administration costs are—

(a) the average cost to the local authority incurred in relation to deferred payment agreements generally, having regard to the costs and fees referred to in sub-paragraphs

(a) to (c) of paragraph (3), and for these purposes the local authority may provide for different average costs for different situations;

(b) the costs incurred for the purpose of ascertaining the value of the adequate security;

(c) the costs incurred in registering the charge on the land or land charges register;

(d) the costs incurred in perfecting the security obtained in respect of the deferred amount;

(e) the costs incurred in discharging or redeeming the security obtained in respect of the deferred amount; and

(f) the costs which are incurred by the authority for the purpose of ensuring compliance by the parties of its terms and conditions.

(5) But the local authority must—

(a) before entering into the agreement, give the adult an estimate of the amount of any charge it envisages levying in respect of making the agreement and registering any charge;

(b) before entering into the agreement give the adult an indication of its current charges for, and the matters in respect of which, it considers it may impose a charge under the agreement and information to enable the adult to ascertain the charges if they change during the period during which the agreement is in force;

(c) before requesting payment of any charge, or treating it in the same way as the deferred amount, provide the adult with a statement which sets out the amount of the charge—

(i) which, in a case where the administration costs are calculated in accordance with paragraph (3), is attributable to each of the items referred to in paragraph (3); or

(ii) which, in a case where the costs are calculated in accordance with paragraph 4, is attributable to the costs referred to in paragraph (4)(a) and each of the items referred to in sub-paragraphs (b) to (f) of that paragraph.

GENERAL NOTE

Local authorities can charge an adult for its administration costs. This is provided for in reg. 10. This will cover, for example, the costs associated with placing a charge on a property to secure the debt. The administration charge is discussed in the statutory guidance at paras 9.72 to 9.73.

Terms, conditions and information

11.—(1) The deferred payment agreement must include any terms, conditions and infor- **A1–122** mation, without which the adult is unable to ascertain his or her rights and obligations under the agreement including—

    (a) in the case of an agreement under which a local authority agrees to defer until the specified time the repayment of the part of the loan specified in regulation 5, a term to make clear that the local authority will make advances of that loan to the adult in instalments and when those instalments will be made;

    (b) a term to explain that the local authority must cease to defer amounts due to the authority under section 14 or 30(2) or advance instalments under the loan agreement if the adult is no longer receiving care and support in a care home or supported living accommodation or if the local authority no longer considers that the adult's needs should be met by the provision of such accommodation;

    (c) a term to explain any other circumstances in which the local authority will or may cease to defer amounts due to it under sections 14 or 30(2) or advance instalments under the loan agreement;

    (d) a term which requires the local authority to produce a written statement—

       (i) which is provided to the adult—

(aa) at the end of the period of six months beginning with the date on which the agreement is entered into;

(bb) every six months after that; and

(cc) within 28 days of a request made by the adult; and

       (ii) which shows—

(aa) the amount that the adult would have to pay to the local authority in order to terminate the agreement on the date on which the statement is sent by the authority to the adult or such later date as is requested by the adult; and

(bb) the amount of interest and administration charges which have accrued on the amounts deferred under section 14 or 30(2) or the loan instalments since the commencement of the loan;

    (e) a term which requires the local authority to give the adult 30 days written notice of the date on which the equity limit and, if different, the amount which the parties have agreed to defer is likely to be reached;

    (f) if the interest is to be treated in the same way as the adult's deferred amount, a term to explain how the interest will compound;

    (g) information as to administration costs which the authority may charge under the agreement;

    (h) in the case of a loan, a term to make clear that its purpose is to pay the costs of care and support in a care home or supported living accommodation, as the case may be, and that the adult must pay those costs as and when they fall due;

    (i) a term which explains that, subject to regulation 5(3), the maximum amount which may be deferred is the equity limit in regulation 5(5), and that this is likely to vary over the term of the agreement;

(j) a term which describes the adequate security accepted by the local authority;

(k) a term requiring the adult to obtain the consent of the local authority for any person to occupy the property; and

(l) a term to explain how the adult may exercise his or her right to terminate the agreement.

(2) The deferred payment agreement may include such other terms and conditions as the local authority considers appropriate.

GENERAL NOTE

Regulation 11 details the terms and conditions which must or may be in the agreement. The statutory guidance considers how agreements should be made at paras 9.74 to 9.84. It also considers the responsibilities of the local authority and the individual whilst the agreement is in place and termination of the agreement at paras 9.85 to 9.105. In respect of the former this includes the need to provide 6 monthly written updates and a statement on request within 28 days. It also confirms that local authorities may provide updates on a more frequent basis at their discretion.[1] This may be necessary where for instance when deferred payment agreements are relatively brief in length.

THE CARE AND SUPPORT (CHARGING AND ASSESSMENT OF RESOURCES) REGULATIONS 2014 (SI 2014/2672)

A1–123   The Secretary of State makes these Regulations in exercise of the powers in sections 14(5) to (8), 17(7) to (13) and 125(7) and (8) of the Care Act 2014[2] .

GENERAL NOTE

These regulations make provision under the Care Act 2014 for the limitations on the local authority powers to make a charge for meeting needs under s.14 of the Act (Pt 2) and in relation to financial assessments for the purposes of s.17 of the Act (Pts 3 to 5 and Schs 1 and 2). The duty to carry out a financial assessment under s.17 applies where the local authority thinks that if it were to meet an adult's needs for care and support, or a carer's needs for support, it would charge the adult or carer under s.14(1) of the Act. The statutory guidance covers charging and financial assessments in Pt 8 and in Annexes B and C.

In addition, the following non-statutory guidance has been produced on charging and financial assessments:

- Department of Health , Frequently asked questions on charging for care (June 2015);
- Skills for Care, Charging and Financial Assessment Workbook (2014); and
- Skills for Care, Deprivation of Assets Handout (2014).

The Skills for Care publications have been produced with the approval of the Department of Health (see 1–770 above).

Part 1

General

Citation and commencement

A1–124   1. These Regulations may be cited as the Care and Support (Charging and Assessment of Resources) Regulations 2014 and come into force immediately after sections 14(5) and 17(7) of the Act are both fully in force.

Interpretation

A1–125   2.—(1) In these Regulations—

"the Act" means the Care Act 2014;

---

[1] Department of Health, *Care and Support Statutory Guidance* (2014), para.9.85.

[2] 2014 c.23. The powers to make regulations are exercisable by the Secretary of State, See s.125(1). Sections 14(5) to (8) and 17(7) to (13) were commenced for the purposes of making regulations by S.I. 2014/2473. Section 17(8) was commenced in modified form.

"the 1992 Act" means the Social Security Contributions and Benefits Act 1992[1] ;

"the adult" in relation to a financial assessment carried out by a local authority for the purposes of section 17(1), (3) or (4) of the Act means the adult or, as the case may be, the carer in respect of whom the authority is carrying out the financial assessment;

"armed forces independence payment" means armed forces independence payment under the Armed Forces and Reserved Forces (Compensation Scheme) Order 2011[2] ;

"attendance allowance" has the same meaning as in the Income Support Regulations;

"care home" means a care home (within the meaning given in section 3 of the Care Standards Act 2000[3] in respect of which a person is registered under the Health and Social Care Act 2008[4] for the regulated activity of the provision of residential accommodation together with nursing or personal care;

"carer premium" means a carer premium under the Income Support Regulations;

"child benefit" means a child benefit under the 1992 Act;

"child tax credit" means a child tax credit under the Tax Credits Act 2002[5] ;

"council tax" is to be construed in accordance with section 1(1) of the Local Government Finance Act 1992[6] ;

"couple" has the same meaning as in the Income Support Regulations;

"disability living allowance" means a disability living allowance under the 1992 Act;

"disability premium" means a disability premium under the Income Support Regulations;

"employed earner" is to be construed in accordance with section 2(1)(a) of the 1992 Act[7] ;

"enhanced disability premium" means an enhanced disability premium under the Income Support Regulations;

"guardian's allowance" means a guardian's allowance under the 1992 Act;

"income support" means income support under the 1992 Act;

"Income Support Regulations" means the Income Support (General) Regulations 1987[8];

"lone parent" has the same meaning as in the Income Support Regulations;

"partner" has the same meaning as in the Income Support Regulations;

"Pension Credit Regulations" means the State Pension Credit Regulations 2002[9] ;

"pension credit age" means the qualifying age for state pension credit within the meaning of section 1(6) of the State Pension Credit Act 2002;

"permanent resident" means a resident who is not a temporary resident or a short-term resident;

---

[1] 1992 c.4.
[2] S.I. 2011/517.
[3] 2000 c.14.
[4] 2008 c.14.
[5] 2002 c.21.
[6] 1992 c.14.
[7] Section 2(1)(a) was amended by paras 169 and 171 of Sch.6 to the Income Tax (Earnings and Pensions) Act 2003 (c.1) and s.15(1) of the National Insurance Contributions Act 2014 (c.7).
[8] S.I. 1987/1967.
[9] S.I. 2002/1792.

"personal independence payment" means a personal independence payment under Part 4 of the Welfare Reform Act 2012[1] ;

"personal pension scheme" has the same meaning as in the Income Support Regulations;

"prospective resident" means a person for whom accommodation in a care home is proposed to be provided under the Act;

"resident" means a person who is provided with accommodation in a care home under the Act;

"savings credit" means a savings credit under the State Pension Credit Act 2002;

"self-employed earner" is to be construed in accordance with section 2(1)(b) of the 1992 Act;

"severe disablement occupational allowance" means a severe disablement occupational allowance paid under article 10 of the Naval, Military and Air Forces Etc. (Disablement and Death) Service Pensions Order 2006[2] or under article 16 of the Personal Injuries (Civilians) Scheme 1983[3] ;

"short-term resident" means a person who is provided with accommodation in a care home under the Act for a period not exceeding 8 weeks;

"temporary resident" means a resident whose stay is—

    (a) unlikely to exceed 52 weeks; or
    (b) in exceptional circumstances, unlikely to substantially exceed that period;

"working tax credit" means a working tax credit under the Tax Credits Act 2002.

(2) Where reference is made in these Regulations to the application of a provision in the Income Support Regulations, any reference to "claimant" in the provision of the Income Support Regulations is to be construed as a reference to the adult concerned.

(3) In these Regulations any reference to a resident's accommodation in a care home, or to accommodation provided for a resident in a care home, is to be construed in the case of a resident who is a prospective resident as a reference to accommodation to be provided for that resident under section 18, 19 or 20 of the Act.

PART 2

Power of the local authority to charge for care and support

Services to be provided free of charge

A1–126   **3.**—(1) A local authority[4] must not make a charge for meeting needs under section 14(1) of the Act where the care and support, or support which is provided to an adult, under section 18, 19 or 20 of the Act, is a service specified in paragraph (2)(a) or (b).

    (2) The following are specified—

        (a) a service which consists of the provision of community equipment (aids and minor adaptations);

---

[1] 2012 c.5.

[2] S.I. 2006/606. Article 10 was amended by S.I. 2008/679 and 2013/630.

[3] S.I. 1983/686. Article 16 was amended by S.I. 1984/1675 and 2001/420.

[4] See s.1(4) of the Act as to the meaning of "local authority"; the definition is limited to local authorities in England.

(b) intermediate care and reablement support services for the first 6 weeks of the specified period or, if the specified period is less than 6 weeks, for that period.

(3) In this regulation—

"community equipment (aids and minor adaptations)" means an aid, or a minor adaptation to property, for the purpose of assisting with nursing at home or aiding daily living and for the purposes of this paragraph, an adaptation is minor if the cost of making the adaptation is £1,000 or less;

"intermediate care and reablement support services" means care and support, or support provided to an adult by the local authority under section 18, 19 or 20 of the Act which—

(a) consists of a programme of care and support, or support;
(b) is for a specified period of time ("the specified period"); and
(c) has as its purpose the provision of assistance to an adult to enable the adult to maintain or regain the ability needed to live independently in their own home.

GENERAL NOTE

Section 14 of the Care Act provides that a local authority may make a charge for meeting needs under ss.18 to 20 of the Act. Regulation 3 specifies the services which are to be provided free of charge. These are community equipment (aids and minor adaptations) and, for the first six weeks only, intermediate care and reablement support services. The statutory guidance states that local authorities may wish to apply their discretion to offer this free of charge for longer than six weeks "where there are clear preventative benefits, such as when a person has recently become visually impaired".[1]

This provision must be read alongside the relevant case law which confirms that a local authority or the NHS cannot charge for after-care services under section 117 of the Mental Health Act 1983 (see para.1–727).

Adults to whom services are to be provided free of charge

4. A local authority must not make a charge for meeting needs under section 14(1) of the **A1–127** Act where the care and support is provided to an adult, under section 18, 19 or 20 of the Act, suffering from variant Creutzfeldt-Jakob disease.

GENERAL NOTE

Regulation 4 provides that adults suffering from variant Creutzfield-Jakob disease are to be provided with any services free of charge.

Costs of putting in place arrangements to meet needs

5. Where a local authority is meeting needs because Condition 2 in section 18, or **A1–128** Condition 2 or 4 in section 20, of the Act is met, the charge the authority may make under section 14(1)(b) of the Act may only cover the cost that the authority incurs in putting in place the arrangements for meeting those needs.

GENERAL NOTE

Regulation 5 provides that where a local authority is meeting needs because either Condition 2 in section 18 of the Care Act or Condition 2 or 4 in section 20 of the Care Act is met, a charge for putting in place the arrangements to meet needs must be no more than the cost incurred by a local authority.

---

[1] Department of Health, *Care and Support Statutory Guidance* (2014), para.8.14.

Appendix 1

Personal expenses allowance for residents or temporary residents provided with accommodation in a care home

A1–129   **6.** The amount specified for the purposes of section 14(7) of the Act[1] in relation to a resident or temporary resident provided with accommodation in a care home is [£24.90] each week.

AMENDMENT

The amendment to the amount of the personal expenses allowance was made by SI 2015/644 reg.3(a).

GENERAL NOTE

Section 14(7) of the Act provides that a local authority may not make a charge for services under s.14(1) of the Act if the adult or carer's income would, after deduction of the amount of the charge, fall below the amount specified in regulations. This is intended to enable a person with a specified amount to spend on personal items such as clothes and other items that are not part of their care. Regulation 6 specifies that the personal expenses allowance for residents or temporary residents provided with accommodation in a care home is £24.90 for each week. This is in addition to any income that the person receives from earnings.

The personal expenses allowance is normally adjusted annually and communicated by Local Authority Circular. The statutory guidance confirms that local authorities have discretion to apply a higher income allowance in individual cases, for example where the person needs to contribute towards the cost of maintaining their former home.[2] Further detail on the personal expenses allowance can be found at Annex E of the statutory guidance.

Payment of certain welfare benefits stop when a person in a care home begins to receive financial support from the local authority. These are Attendance Allowance, the care component of Disability Living Allowance or the daily living component of Personal Independence Payment.

When the new upper capital limit of £118,000 comes into effect, concerns have been raised that those with assets close to this limit will be worse off because they will only receive a small amount of local authority support which will be less than the benefits they were entitled to previously. The Government has therefore confirmed that the regulations will be amended to ensure that everyone in a care home who qualifies for local authority financial support will get a minimum level of financial support. This will be achieved by requiring a reduction in charges that is the equivalent to the maximum amount that a person would receive in any of the above benefits.[3]

Minimum income guaranteed amount for other adults and carers whose needs are being met otherwise than by the provision of accommodation in a care home

A1–130   **7.**—(1) Subject to paragraph (8), the amount specified for each week for the purposes of section 14(7) of the Act ("the minimum income guaranteed amount") in relation to the adult concerned specified in paragraph (2), (3), (4), (5), (6) or, as the case may be, (7) is the aggregate of—

   (a) the amount specified in relation to that adult in that paragraph[4] ;

---

[1] Under s.14(7) of the Act, the local authority may not make a charge under s.14(1) of the Act if the income of the adult concerned would, after deduction of the charge, fall below the amount specified in regulations.

[2] Department of Health, *Care and Support Statutory Guidance* (2014), para.8.35.

[3] Department of Health, *The Care Act 2014: Consultation on draft regulations and guidance to implement the cap on care costs and policy proposals for a new appeals system for care and support* (2015), paras 9.10 to 9.12.

[4] A buffer of 25 per cent has been added to each specified amount and the applicable premium.

(b) where the adult concerned is responsible for, and a member of the same household as, a child, the amount of [£83.65] in respect of each child; and

(c) any applicable premium under paragraphs (4) to (7).

(2) Where the adult concerned is a single person and—

(a) is aged 18 or older but less than 25, the amount of [£72.40];

(b) is aged 25 or older but less than pension credit age, the amount of [£91.40];

(c) has attained pension credit age, the amount of [£189.00].

(3) Where the adult concerned is a lone parent aged 18 or over, the amount of [£91.40].

(4) Where the adult concerned is a member of a couple and—

(a) one or both are aged 18 or over, the amount of [£71.80];

(b) one or both have attained pension credit age, the amount of [£144.30].

(5) Where the adult concerned is a single person who is in receipt of, or the local authority considers would, if in receipt of income support, be in receipt of—

(a) disability premium, the amount of the applicable premium is [£40.35];

(b) enhanced disability premium, the amount of the applicable premium is [£19.70].

(6) Where the adult concerned is a member of a couple and one member of that couple is in receipt of, or the local authority considers would, if in receipt of income support, be in receipt of—

(a) disability premium, the amount of the applicable premium is [£28.75];

(b) enhanced disability premium, the amount of the applicable premium is [£14.15].

(7) Where the adult concerned is in receipt of, or the local authority considers would, if in receipt of income support be in receipt of, carer premium, the amount of the applicable premium is [£43.25].

(8) Where a local authority provides non-care related support for the adult concerned the minimum income guaranteed amount in relation to that adult is the amount calculated in accordance with paragraph (1) less an amount equal to the cost the local authority incurs in providing that non-care related support for the adult concerned.

(9) In this regulation—

"the adult concerned" means—

(a) an adult who has needs for care and support under section 18, 19 or 20 of the Act other than the provision of accommodation in a care home;

(b) a carer who has needs for support under section 20 of the Act;

"non-care related support" includes support which consists of services or activities such as the provision of meals on wheels, shopping or transport services or recreational activities.

[(10) For the purposes of this regulation, the adult concerned is a single person if the adult neither has a partner nor is a lone parent.]

AMENDMENTS

The amendments to this regulation were made by SI 2015/644 reg.3(b) and (c).

GENERAL NOTE

Section 14(7) of the Act provides that a local authority may not make a charge for services under s.14(1) of the Act if the adult or carer's income would, after deduction of the amount of the charge, fall below the amount specified in regulations. Regulation 7 specifies the minimum income guaranteed amount for adults and carers whose needs are being met otherwise than through the provision of care home accommodation. The minimum income guaranteed amount is the aggregate of the amounts set out in regulation 7(1). The amounts reflect the applicable amounts for income support and an additional amount in respect of each child for whom the adult is responsible together with any applicable premiums, in each case together with a buffer of 25 per cent. Applicable premiums include carer premiums and disability premiums payable under the Income Support Regulations. The local authority can also include the listed premiums where it is satisfied that a person would be in receipt of the premium were they to be in receipt of income support. In addition, the financial assessment of their capital must exclude the value of the property which they occupy as their main or only home (Sch.2, para.6 of these regs).

The statutory guidance notes that local authorities have flexibility within this framework and may for instance choose to "disregard additional sources of income, set maximum charges or charge a person a percentage of their disposable income". But it warns that such discretion "should not lead to two people with similar needs, and receiving similar types of care and support, being charged differently".[1] In developing policies, local authorities should also consider how to protect a person's income:

> "The government considers that it is inconsistent with promoting independent living to assume, without further consideration, that all of a person's income above basic levels of Income Support or the Guarantee Credit element of Pension Credit plus 25% is available to be taken in charges."[2]

Local authorities are therefore advised to consider setting a maximum percentage of disposable income (over and above the guaranteed minimum income) which may be taken into account in charges and a maximum charge (for example as a maximum percentage of care home charges in a local area).[3]

Where the carer is being charged, local authorities must do so in accordance with the non-residential charging rules and will normally carry out a financial assessment.[4]

Power of the local authority to financially assess and charge a short-term resident as if the resident is receiving care and support or support other than the provision of accommodation in a care home

A1–131
8. A local authority may, if it thinks fit, financially assess and charge a short-term resident as if they are receiving care and support, or support under section 18, 19 or 20 of the Act other than the provision of accommodation in a care home.

GENERAL NOTE

Regulation 8 gives local authorities a power to charge and financially assess short-term residents – persons who are provided with accommodation in a care home for a period not exceeding eight weeks – as if they are in receipt of care and support in their own homes. The statutory guidance as an example suggests that in cases of respite care, for the first eight weeks a local authority may choose to charge based on its approach to charging those receiving care and support in other settings or in their own home.[5]

---

[1] Department of Health, *Care and Support Statutory Guidance* (2014), paras 8.43 to 8.44.
[2] Department of Health, *Care and Support Statutory Guidance* (2014), para.8.46.
[3] Department of Health, *Care and Support Statutory Guidance* (2014), paras 8.47 to 8.48.
[4] Department of Health, *Care and Support Statutory Guidance* (2014), para.8.53.
[5] Department of Health, *Care and Support Statutory Guidance* (2014), para.8.34.

PART 3

Assessment of financial resources

Financial assessment

9. A local authority must carry out a financial assessment of the adult under section **A1–132**
17(1), (3) or (4) of the Act in accordance with the provisions of Parts 3 to 5 of these
Regulations.

GENERAL NOTE

Part 3 makes provision in relation to the assessment of financial resources. Financial
assessments must be carried out in accordance with Pts 3 to 5 of these Regulations. The
statutory guidance notes that the local authority has no power to assess couples or civil partners according to their joint resources, and therefore each person must be treated
individually.[1] It goes on to confirm that people who lack capacity may still be assessed
as liable to contribute towards the cost of their care. However, local authorities must put
in place policies regarding how they communicate, carry out financial assessments and collect debts that "take into consideration the capacity of the person as well as any illness or
condition".[2] The guidance also confirms that where the person lacks capacity, the local
authority must find out "if the person has any of the following as the appropriate person
will need to be involved": their attorney, deputy or appointee. If such a person has not
been appointed with the appropriate authority, then the family (or if there is no family,
the local authority) may need to apply to the Court of Protection for the appointment of
a Property and Affairs Deputyship.[3] The charging rules also apply equally to people in
prison.[4]

10.—(1) A local authority is to be treated as having carried out a financial assessment in **A1–133**
an adult's case and being satisfied on that basis that the adult's financial resources exceed
the financial limit[5] where—

    (a) the adult has refused a financial assessment; or

    (b) the authority has been unable to carry out a full financial assessment because of
the adult's refusal to co-operate with the assessment and the local authority
nevertheless decides to meet some or all of the adult's needs for care and support, or for support.

(2) A local authority is to be treated as having carried out a financial assessment in an
adult's case and being satisfied on that basis that the adult's financial resources do not
exceed the financial limit where—

    (a) with the consent of the adult, the authority has not carried out a financial assess-
ment in accordance with these Regulations; and

    (b) the authority is satisfied from the evidence available to it that the adult's finan-
cial resources do not exceed the financial limit.

(3) A local authority is to be treated as having carried out a financial assessment in an
adult's case and being satisfied on that basis that the adult's financial resources exceed
the financial limit where—

    (a) with the consent of the adult, the authority has not carried out a financial assess-
ment in accordance with these Regulations; but

---

[1] Department of Health, *Care and Support Statutory Guidance* (2014), para.8.8.
[2] Department of Health, *Care and Support Statutory Guidance* (2014), para.8.9.
[3] Department of Health, *Care and Support Statutory Guidance* (2014), paras 8.18 to 8.19.
[4] Department of Health, *Care and Support Statutory Guidance* (2014), para.8.10.
[5] See s.17(10) of the Act as to the meaning of "the financial limit".

(b) the authority is satisfied from the evidence available to it that the adult's financial resources do exceed the financial limit.

GENERAL NOTE

In some circumstances an authority is to be treated as having carried out a financial assessment in an adult's case and being satisfied on that basis that their financial resources exceed, or as the case may be, do not exceed the financial limit. This includes where the authority, with the consent of the adult, has not carried out a financial assessment but is nevertheless satisfied from the evidence available to the authority that the adult's resources do not exceed the financial limit (for example, where the adult is in receipt of income support). This is known as a "light-touch" financial assessment and is discussed in the statutory guidance at paras 8.22 to 8.26. Amongst other matters the statutory guidance confirms that a local authority must inform the person when a light-touch financial assessment has taken place and make clear that the person has the right to request a full financial assessment should they wish to do so, and make sure they have access to "sufficient information and advice, including the option of independent financial information and advice" [1]

Rounding of fractions

A1–134   **11.** Where any financial assessment of the adult concerned, under section 17(1), (3) or (4) of the Act, results in a fraction of a penny, that fraction is, if it would be to that adult's advantage, to be treated as a penny, otherwise it is to be disregarded.

Financial limit - capital

A1–135   **12.**—(1) If the financial resources of an adult who is a permanent resident (in terms of capital) exceed £23,250, the local authority is not permitted to pay towards the cost of the provision of accommodation in a care home for that adult[2] .

(2) If the financial resources of an adult who has needs for care and support other than as a permanent resident (in terms of capital) exceed £23,250, the local authority may (but need not) pay towards the cost of that care and support.

(3) If the financial resources of a carer whose needs involve the provision of support (in terms of capital) exceed £23,250, the local authority may (but need not) pay towards the cost of the provision of that support for the carer[3] .

GENERAL NOTE

The financial limit establishes the point at which a person is entitled to access local authority support to meet their care and support needs. Regulation 12 sets the upper capital limit at £23,250. Below this a person can seek means-tested support from a local authority. The capital limits are discussed at paras 8.11 to 8.14 of the statutory guidance and the treatment of capital is considered in Annex B.

Only in care homes, where the financial assessment identifies that a person's resources exceed the capital limits, is a local authority precluded from paying towards the costs of care. The statutory guidance therefore states that local authorities should "develop and

---

[1] Department of Health, *Care and Support Statutory Guidance* (2014), para.8.17.

[2] See s.17(8) of the Act as to the requirement for regulations to make provision as to cases or circumstances in which, if the financial resources of an adult exceed a specified level, a local authority is not permitted to, or may (but need not) pay towards the cost of the provision of care and support for the adult. Section 17(8) has been commenced in modified form for the purposes of making regulations by S.I. 2014/2473. See also s.17(10) of the Act as to the meaning of "the financial limit".

[3] See s.17(9) of the Act as to the requirement for regulations to make provision as to cases circumstances in which, if the financial resources of a carer exceed a specified level, a local authority is not permitted to, or may (but need not), pay towards the cost of the provision of support for the carer. See also s.17(10) of the Act as to the meaning of "the financial limit".

maintain a policy setting out how they will charge people in settings other than care homes". [1]

The Government intends to amend the statutory guidance to clarify that local authorities have discretion to set their own capital limits in relation to adults receiving support in locations other than care homes, provided they are no lower that £23,250 for the higher limit and £14,250 for the lower limit.[2]

PART 4

Treatment and calculation of income

GENERAL NOTE

Part 4 and Schedule 1 make provision for the treatment and calculation of income. Schedule 1 sets out the income that must or may be disregarded by the local authority.

Calculation of income

13.—(1) The income of the adult is to be calculated on a weekly basis— **A1–136**
    (a) by determining, in accordance with this Part, the weekly amount of the adult's total income;
    (b) by adding to that amount the adult's weekly tariff income from capital calculated in accordance with regulation 25 (calculation of tariff income from capital).

(2) For the purposes of paragraph (1) income includes capital treated as income under regulation 16 and notional income under regulation 17.

Earnings to be disregarded

14.—(1) Earnings derived from employment as an employed earner or a self-employed **A1–137** earner are to be disregarded in the calculation of the adult's income for the purposes of the financial assessment.
    (2) For the purposes of this regulation—
        (a) earnings in relation to an employed earner has the same meaning—
            (i) as in regulation 35 of the Housing Benefit Regulations 2006[3] ;
            (ii) where the earner has attained the qualifying age for state pension credit, as in regulation 35 of the Housing Benefit (Persons who have attained the qualifying age for state pension credit) Regulations 2006 (earnings of employed earners)[4] ; and
        (b) earnings in relation to a self-employed earner has the same meaning as in regulation 37 of the Income Support Regulations (earnings of self-employed earners)[5] .

Other sums to be disregarded

15.—(1) There is to be disregarded in the calculation of the adult's total income for the **A1–138** purposes of the financial assessment any sum, where applicable, specified in Part 1 of Schedule 1, in accordance with Part 2 of that Schedule.
    (2) In a case where the adult has needs for care and support other than the provision of accommodation in a care home, or the carer has needs for support, a local authority may in carrying out the calculation of the adult or carer's income for the purposes of the financial

---

[1] Department of Health, *Care and Support Statutory Guidance* (2014), para.8.26.
[2] Department of Health, *Update on the Final Orders under the Care Act 2014* (2015), para.25.
[3] S.I. 2006/213. Regulation 35 was amended by S.I. 2007/2618, 2009/2655, 2012/757 and 2014/591.
[4] S.I. 2006/214. Regulation 35 was amended by S.I. 2009/2655, 2012/757 and 2014/591.
[5] Regulation 37 was amended by S.I. 1991/387, 1992/2155, 1994/2139 and 1999/2165.

assessment, disregard such other sums the adult or carer may receive as the authority considers appropriate.

Capital treated as income

A1–139   **16.**—(1) Any capital payable to the adult by instalments which are outstanding on the date on which the adult first becomes liable to pay for their care and support, or support, is to be treated as income if the aggregate of the instalments outstanding and the amount of the adult's capital calculated in accordance with Part 5 exceed the amount specified in regulation 41(1) of the Income Support Regulations (capital treated as income)[1] .

(2) Any payment received under an annuity is to be treated as income.

(3) Any earnings to the extent that they are not a payment of income are to be treated as income.

(4) Any payment of capital made or due to be made to a local authority by a third party pursuant to an agreement between the authority and the third party in connection with the liability of the adult to pay the local authority for accommodation provided under the Act is to be treated as part of the income of the adult, unless it is a voluntary payment made for the purposes of discharging any arrears of payments required by the local authority from the adult for their accommodation.

(5) Where an agreement or court order provides that payments are to be made to the adult in consequence of any personal injury to them and that such payments are to be made wholly or partly by way of periodical payments, any such periodical payments received by the adult, to the extent that they are not a payment of income, are to be treated as income.

Notional income

A1–140   **17.**—(1) The adult is to be treated as possessing income of which the adult has deprived themselves for the purpose of decreasing the amount they may be liable to pay towards the cost of meeting their needs for care and support, or their needs for support.

(2) The adult is to be treated as possessing any income which would be treated as income possessed by a claimant of income support under regulation 42(2) to (4A) of the Income Support Regulations (notional income)[2] .

(3) Subject to paragraph (4), the adult is to be treated as possessing any income paid or due to be paid to a local authority by a third party pursuant to an agreement between the local authority and the third party made in connection with the liability of the adult to pay towards the cost of accommodation provided for the adult under the Act.

(4) The adult is not to be treated as possessing any voluntary payment of income made by a third party to a local authority for the purpose of discharging any arrears of the payments required by the authority from the adult for accommodation provided under the Act.

GENERAL NOTE

Paragraph. (1)

Where a person has deliberately tried to avoid paying for care and support costs through depriving themselves of assets (capital or income), the local authority may charge the person as if they still owned the asset or (if the asset has been transferred to someone else) seek to recover the lost income from another person. The statutory guidance discusses the deprivation of assets at Annex E.

---

[1] Paragraph (1) was substituted by S.I. 1999/3178 and amended by S.I. 2005/2465.
[2] Relevant amending instruments are: S.I. 1991/1559, 1992/468, 1992/1198, 1993/315, 1994/527, 1995/2303, 1995/2792, 1996/206, 1998/563, 1998/663, 1998/1445, 1998/2117, 1999/2640, 1999/3156, 1999/3178, 1999/3324, 2001/859, 2001/1029, 2002/841, 2002/3019, 2003/455, 2005/574, 2005/2465, 2005/2687, 2005/2878, 2006/588, 2007/719, 2007/1749, 2008/698, 2008/2767, 2008/3157, 2009/2655, 2010/641, 2011/1707, 2011/2425 and 2013/276.

PART 5

Treatment and calculation of capital

GENERAL NOTE

Part 5 and Schedule 2 make provision for the treatment and calculation of capital.
Schedule 2 sets out the capital sums that must or may be disregarded by the local authority.

Calculation of capital

18.—(1) The capital of the adult to be taken into account in a financial assessment is, **A1–141**
subject to paragraph (2), to be the whole of the adult's capital calculated in accordance
with this Part and any income treated as capital under regulation 19.

(2) Any capital, where applicable, specified in Schedule 2 is to be disregarded in the calculation of the adult's capital under paragraph (1).

Income treated as capital

19.—(1) Any amount by way of refund of income tax deducted from profits or emolu- **A1–142**
ments chargeable to income tax under Schedule D or E is to be treated as capital.

(2) Any holiday pay which is not earnings is to be treated as capital.

(3) Except income derived from capital disregarded under paragraphs 1, 4, 9, 15, 22 and
24 of Schedule 2, any income of the adult which is derived from capital is to be treated as
capital but only on the date on which it is normally due to be paid to the adult.

(4) In the case of the adult's employment as an employed earner, any advance of earnings
or any loan made by the adult's employer is to be treated as capital.

(5) Any charitable or voluntary payment which is not made or due to be made at regular
intervals, other than one made under the Fund, the Eileen Trust, the Macfarlane Trust, the
Macfarlane (Special Payments) Trust, the Macfarlane (Special Payments) (No. 2) Trust or
the Independent Living Fund, is to be treated as capital.

(6) Any voluntary payment of income made by a third party to the adult for the purpose
of helping the adult to discharge any arrears of the payments required by the local authority
from the adult for accommodation provided under the Act is to be treated as the capital of
the adult.

(7) In this regulation, "the Fund", "the Eileen Trust", "the Macfarlane Trust", "the
Macfarlane (Special Payments) Trust", "the Macfarlane (Special Payments) (No. 2)
Trust" and "the Independent Living Fund" have the same meaning as in the Income
Support Regulations.

Calculation of capital in the United Kingdom

20. Capital which the adult possesses in the United Kingdom is to be calculated at its **A1–143**
current market or surrender value (whichever is the higher), less—

    (a) where there would be expenses attributable to sale, 10%; and

    (b) the amount of any encumbrance secured on it.

Calculation of capital outside the United Kingdom

21. Capital which the adult possesses outside of the United Kingdom shall be calculated **A1–144**
in accordance with the method set out in regulation 50 of the Income Support Regulations
(calculation of capital outside the United Kingdom).

Notional capital

22.—(1) The adult is to be treated as possessing capital of which the adult has deprived **A1–145**
themselves for the purpose of decreasing the amount that they may be liable to pay towards
the cost of meeting their needs for care and support, or their needs for support, except—

(a) where that capital is derived from a payment made in consequence of any personal injury and is placed on trust for the benefit of the adult;

(b) to the extent that the capital which the adult is treated as possessing is reduced in accordance with regulation 23; or

(c) any sum to which paragraph 44(1) or 45(a) of Schedule 10 to the Income Support

Regulations (disregard of compensation for personal injuries which is administered by the Court)[1] refers.

(2) Subject to paragraph (3), the adult may be treated as possessing any payment of capital which would be treated as capital possessed by a claimant of income support under regulation 51(2) or (3) of the Income Support Regulations (notional capital)[2] .

(3) For the purposes of paragraph (2), regulation 51(2)(c) of the Income Support Regulations applies as if for the reference to Schedule 10 to the Income Support Regulations there were substituted a reference to Schedule 2 to these Regulations.

(4) Where the adult is treated as possessing capital under paragraph (1) or (2), the provisions of this Part apply for the purposes of calculating its amount as if it were actual capital the adult does possess.

GENERAL NOTE

Paragraph (1)

Where a person has deliberately tried to avoid paying for care and support costs through depriving themselves of assets (capital or income), the local authority may charge the person as if they still owned the asset or (if the asset has been transferred to someone else) seek to recover the lost income from another person (see s.70 of the Care Act). The statutory guidance discusses the deprivation of assets at Annex E.

Diminishing notional capital rule

A1–146   **23.**—(1) Where the adult is treated as possessing capital under regulation 22 ("notional capital"), for each week or part of a week that the local authority has determined that the adult is liable to pay towards the cost of their care and support, or support, at a higher rate than that at which the adult would have been assessed as liable to pay if the adult had had no notional capital, the amount of the adult's notional capital is to be reduced by the method set out in paragraph (2).

(2) The local authority must reduce the amount of adult's notional capital by the difference between—

(a) the higher rate referred to in paragraph (1); and

(b) the rate at which the adult would have been assessed as liable to pay towards the cost of that care and support, or support for that week or part of a week if the adult had been assessed as possessing no notional capital.

Capital jointly held

A1–147   **24.**—(1) Where the adult and one or more other persons are beneficially entitled in possession to any capital asset except an interest in land—

(a) unless paragraph (2) applies, each person is to be treated as if each of them were entitled in possession to an equal share of the whole beneficial interest; and

(b) that asset is to be treated as if it were actual capital.

---

[1] Paragraphs 44 and 45 were inserted by S.I. 1994/2139. Paragraph 44 was substituted by S.I. 2006/2378. Paragraph 45 was amended by S.I. 1997/2197 and 2003/2279.

[2] Relevant amending instruments are: S.I. 1991/1559, 1993/315, 1995/2303, 1997/65, 1998/663, 1998/1445, 1998/2117, 1999/2640, 2001/3767, 2002/841, 2003/455, 2005/574, 2005/2465, 2005/2878, 2006/588, 2007/719, 2007/1749, 2008/3157 and 2010/641.

28. Any payment which would be disregarded under paragraph 31 or 31A of Schedule 9 to the Income Support Regulations (social fund payments and local welfare provision)[1] .

29. Any payment of income which under regulation 19 (income treated as capital) is to be treated as capital.

30. Any payment which would be disregarded under paragraph 33 of Schedule 9 to the Income Support Regulations (pensioner's Christmas bonus)[2] .

31. Any payment which would be disregarded under paragraph 39 of Schedule 9 to the Income Support Regulations (the Fund, the Macfarlane Trusts and other trusts and Funds and the Independent Living Fund)[3] .

32. Any amount which would be disregarded under paragraphs 40, 43 and 48 to 51 of Schedule 9 to the Income Support Regulations (housing benefit compensation, juror and witness payments, travelling expenses and health service supplies, welfare food payments, prison visiting scheme payments and disabled persons' employment payments)[4] .

33.—(1) Any child benefit, except in circumstances where the adult is accompanied by the child or qualifying young person in respect of whom the child benefit is payable, and accommodation is provided for that child or qualifying young person under the Act.

(2) In this paragraph, "child" and "qualifying young person" have the same meaning as in section 142 of the 1992 Act[5] .

34. Any payment which would be disregarded under paragraph 53 of Schedule 9 to the Income Support Regulations (increases in rates of benefits etc)[6] .

35. Any payment which would be disregarded under paragraphs 54 to 56 of Schedule 9 to the Income Support Regulations (supplementary pensions etc)[7] .

36. Any payment made by a local authority to or on behalf of the adult relating to the provision of a service, where—

    (a) that service is provided to develop or sustain the capacity of the adult to live independently in the community; and

    (b) any charge for that service would be a service charge of the kind specified in Schedule 1B to the Housing Benefit (General) Regulations 1987[8] as in force immediately before the 1st April 2003.

37. The amount of any payment made by the adult to the local authority in payment of a charge imposed on the adult by the authority under the Local Authorities (Charges for Specified Welfare Services) (England) Regulations 2003[9] .

38. Any guardian's allowance.

39. Any child tax credit.

40.—(1) Where the adult is in receipt of savings credit as a person who has no partner and has qualifying income not exceeding the standard minimum guarantee—

    (a) the amount of that savings credit where the amount received is £5.75 or less; or

---

[1] Paragraph 31 was substituted by S.I. 1992/468 and amended by S.I. 2008/3157. Paragraph 31A was inserted by S.I. 2013/443.

[2] Paragraph 33 was amended by S.I. 2008/3157.

[3] Paragraph 39 was inserted by S.I. 1988/663, substituted by S.I. 1991/1175 and amended by S.I. 1992/1101, 1993/963, 1993/1249, 2000/1981, 2004/2308, 2005/2877, 2005/3391, 2008/2767, 2010/641 and 2011/2425.

[4] Paragraph 40 was inserted by S.I. 1988/1445. Paragraph 43 was inserted by S.I. 1988/2022. Paragraphs 48 to 50 were inserted by S.I. 1990/1776. Paragraphs 48 and 49 were substituted by S.I. 2008/3157. Paragraph 50 was amended by S.I. 2007/2128 and 2008/3157. Paragraph 51 was inserted by S.I. 1992/468 and amended by S.I. 2004/565.

[5] Section 142 was substituted by s.1(2) of the Child Benefit Act 2005 (c.6).

[6] Paragraph 53 was inserted by S.I. 1994/527 and substituted by S.I. 2008/3157.

[7] Paragraphs 54 to 56 were inserted by S.I. 1994/2139. Paragraphs 55 and 56 were amended by S.I. 2005/2877 and para.56 amended by S.I. 2008/3157.

[8] S.I. 1987/1971. Schedule 1B was inserted by S.I. 1999/2734. The Regulations were revoked from 6 March 2006 by S.I. 2006/217.

[9] S.I. 2003/907.

(b) £5.75 of that savings credit where the amount received is greater than £5.75.

(2) Where the adult—
  (a) has no partner;
  (b) has attained the age of 65; and
  (c) has qualifying income in excess of the standard minimum guarantee, a sum of £5.75.

(3) Where the adult is in receipt of savings credit as a person who has a partner and has qualifying income not exceeding the standard minimum guarantee—
  (a) the amount of that savings credit where the amount received is £8.60 or less; or
  (b) £8.60 of that savings credit where the amount received is greater than £8.60.

(4) Subject to sub-paragraph (5), where the adult—
  (a) has a partner;
  (b) has—
  (i) attained the age of 65; or
  (ii) has attained pension credit age and the adult's partner has attained the age of 65; and
  (c) has qualifying income in excess of the standard minimum guarantee, a sum of £8.60.

(5) Where—
  (a) the sum referred to in sub-paragraph (4) has been disregarded in the assessment of the adult's partner's income under these Regulations; or
  (b) the adult's partner is in receipt of savings credit, sub-paragraph (4) does not apply to the adult.

(6) For the purposes of this paragraph—
  (a) the adult has a partner if the adult would be considered to have a partner for the purposes of the Pension Credit Regulations;
  (b) "qualifying income" is to be construed in accordance with regulation 9 of the Pension

Credit Regulations[1] and for the purposes of sub-paragraphs (3) and (4) the adult's qualifying income includes any qualifying income of the adult's partner;
  (c) "standard minimum guarantee" means, for the purposes of—
  (i) sub-paragraphs (1) and (2), the amount prescribed by regulation 6(1)(b) of the

Pension Credit Regulations[2] ; and
  (ii) sub-paragraphs (3) and (4), the amount prescribed by regulation 6(1)(a) of the Pension Credit Regulations.

41. Any payment made to a temporary resident in lieu of concessionary coal pursuant to section 19(1)(b) or (c) of the Coal Industry Act 1994[3] .

42. Any payment made to the adult under section 63(6)(b) of the Health Services and Public Health Act 1968[4] ("the 1968 Act") (travelling and other allowances to persons

---

[1] Regulation 9 was amended by S.I. 2008/1554 and 2013/630.
[2] The amounts in reg.6 were up-rated by S.I. 2014/516.
[3] 1994 c.21.
[4] 1968 c.46. Section 63(1)(a) was amended by para.95(2)(a) of Sch.1 to the Health Authorities Act 1995 (c.17), para.3(a) of Sch.4 to the Health Act 1999 (c.8), para.2 of Sch.5 to the National Health Service Reform and Health Care Professions Act 2002 (c.17), para.12(2) of Sch.5 to the Health and Social Care Act 2012 (c.7) and S.I. 2007/961.

availing themselves of instruction) for the purpose of meeting childcare costs where the instruction is provided pursuant to—

    (a) section 63(1)(a) of the 1968 Act; or

    (b) section 63(1)(b) of the 1968 Act and where the adult is employed, or has it in contemplation to be employed, in an activity involved in or connected with a service which must or may be provided or secured as part of the health service.

43. Any payment made in accordance with regulations made pursuant to section 14F of the Children Act 1989 (special guardian support services)[1] to an adult who is a prospective special guardian or a special guardian.

44.—(1) Where the adult is a student, any grant or other award, student loan, income used to make repayments on a student loan or other payment received by that student for the purposes of their course of study at an educational establishment.

(2) In this paragraph, "course of study", student and "student loan" have the same meaning as in the Income Support Regulations.

PART 2

Special provisions relating to charitable or voluntary payments and certain A1–151 pensions

45. Paragraph 15 does not apply to any payment which is made or due to be made—

    (a) by [a person] for the maintenance of any member of [the person's] family or of [the person's] former partner or of [the person's] children; or

    (b) by a third party pursuant to an agreement between the local authority and that third party in connection with the liability of [the resident] to pay the local authority for [the resident's] accommodation.

AMENDMENTS

The amendments to this regulation were made by SI 2015/644 reg.3(e).

46. The total income to be disregarded pursuant to paragraphs [15] and 17 must in no case exceed the amount per week specified in paragraph 36 of Schedule 9 to the Income Support Regulations (ceiling for aggregated disregards)[2] .

AMENDMENT

The amendment to this regulation was made by SI 2015/644 reg.3(f).

SCHEDULE 2   **Regulation 18(2)**

Capital to be disregarded   A1–152

GENERAL NOTE

Schedule 2 lists the types of capital assets that must be disregarded for the purposes of the financial assessment. The main examples of capital are property and savings. For instance, the main home owned by a person in residential care is "disregarded" from the financial assessment of their assets as long it was occupied in whole or in part by their partner, a relative who is aged 60 or over or who is incapacitated, or a child of the resident who is under 16. The person's home is also excluded from the financial assessment for the first 12 weeks of the move to a care home if that move is permanent, or is a temporary stay for up to one year.

---

[1] Section 14F was inserted by s.115(1) of the Adoption and Children Act 2002 (c.38).

[2] Paragraph 36 was amended by S.I. 1990/1657, 1996/462, 2000/1922 and 2006/2378.

In *R. (Walford) v Worcestershire CC* the Court of Appeal considered the equivalent property disregard provisions in the National Assistance (Assessment of Resources) Regulations 1992 (SI 1992/2977). In this case, the respondent's mother had moved into, and at the time her daughter (aged over 60) had a rented flat elsewhere but regarded her mother's property as her home. She had a bedroom and an office there, and kept many of her belongings there. She had paid for the maintenance of the property for over 20 years and had intended to live there when she retired. The Court of Appeal held that the disregard provisions applied only if the property was occupied at the date that the resident went into care, and could not be activated at a later date.[1] The 1992 regulations have now been repealed and replaced by the Care and Support (Charging and Assessment of Resources) Regulations 2014. The 2014 regulations deal more explicitly with the issue and specify that occupation must arise at the date when the resident goes into care (see para. 4 below).

In *R(ZYN) v Walsall MBC* the court considered whether capital derived from a personal injury settlement which is managed by a deputy appointed by the Court of Protection must be disregarded by a local authority when deciding whether the injured person can be required to contribute to the cost of services which he or she receives.[2] This case related to the previous National Assistance (Assessment of Resources) Regulations 1992 (SI 1992/ 2977) but the relevant provision has been retained by the Care and Support (Charging and Assessment of Resources) Regulations 2014 – see para.25 below. The court held that local authorities must disregard such capital managed by a deputy, and in doing so clarified that:

- The term "Court of Protection" in the Income Support Regulations refers to the current Court of Protection – and not the old Court of Protection under the Mental Health Act 1983, and
- Capital managed by a deputy appointed by the Court of Protection under the Mental Capacity Act 2005 is "administered on behalf of a person by the Court of Protection" within the meaning of the Income Support Regulations.[3]

Single premium investment bonds that contain an element of life insurance are currently disregarded in the financial assessment no matter how small the element of life insurance (see para.19 below). Consideration is being given to how these bonds should be treated in future.[4]

1.—(1) Where the adult is a temporary resident but not a prospective resident, the value of the adult's main or only home in circumstances where—

  (a) the adult is taking reasonable steps to dispose of the dwelling in order that they may acquire another dwelling which they intend to occupy as their main or only home; or

  (b) the adult intends to return to occupy that dwelling as their main or only home and the dwelling is still available to them.

(2) Where the adult is a temporary resident who is a prospective resident, the value of the adult's main or only home in circumstances where the adult intends, on being provided in fact with accommodation under the Act—

  (a) to take reasonable steps to dispose of the dwelling in order that they may acquire another dwelling which they intend to occupy as their main or only home; or

  (b) to return to occupy that dwelling as their main or only home and the dwelling to which the adult intends to return is available to them.

---

[1] *R. (Walford) v Worcestershire CC* [2015] EWCA Civ 22.
[2] *R(ZYN) v Walsall MBC* [2014] EWHC 1918 (Admin).
[3] *R(ZYN) v Walsall MBC* [2014] EWHC 1918 (Admin) at [67] and [76].
[4] Department of Health, Response to the Consultation on draft Regulations and Guidance for Implementation of Pt 1 of the Care Act 2014 (2014) Cm 8955, p.26.

2.—(1) Where the adult is a permanent resident the value of the adult's main or only home which the adult would otherwise normally occupy ("the adult's home") for a period of 12 weeks beginning with the day on which the adult first moves into accommodation in a care home ("the first period of residence").

(2) Where the adult—

(a) ceases to be a permanent resident; and

(b) subsequently becomes a permanent resident again at any time within the period of 52 weeks from the end of the first period of permanent residence, the value of the adult's home for such period (if any) which when added to the period disregarded under subparagraph

(1) in respect of their first period of permanent residence does not exceed 12 weeks in total.

(3) Where the adult—

(a) ceases to be a permanent resident and is not a person to whom sub-paragraph (2) has applied; and

(b) subsequently becomes a permanent resident again at any time after a period of more than

52 weeks from the end of the first period of residence, the value of the adult's home for a period of 12 weeks beginning with the day on which the second period of permanent residence begins.

(4) In this paragraph, "the second period of permanent residence" means the period of permanent residence beginning at any time after the period of 52 weeks referred to in sub-paragraph (3)(b).

3. Where the adult is a permanent resident and there is an unexpected change in their financial circumstances the local authority may disregard the value of the adult's main or only home which the adult would normally otherwise occupy for a period of 12 weeks.

4.—(1) The value of any premises—

(a) which would be disregarded under paragraph 2 or 4(b) of Schedule 10 to the Income Support Regulations (premises acquired for occupation, and premises occupied by a former partner)[1] but as if for the words "his home" in each provision there were substituted "his main or only home"; or

(b) which is occupied in whole or in part as their main or only home by a qualifying relative of the adult who has occupied the premises as their main or only home since before the date on which the adult was first provided with accommodation in a care home under the Act.

(2) A local authority may disregard the value of any premises which is occupied in whole or in part by a qualifying relative of the adult as their main or only home where the qualifying relative occupied the premises after the date on which the adult was first provided with accommodation in a care home under the Act.

(3) The value of any premises for a period of 12 weeks where the local authority has disregarded the value of the premises under sub-paragraph (1)(b) or (2) and that relative has died or is no longer occupying the premises because they have been provided with accommodation in a care home.

(4) The local authority may disregard the value of any premises for a period of 12 weeks where the premises were occupied in whole or in part by a qualifying relative of the adult as their main or only home and that relative is no longer occupying the premises because of an unexpected change in their circumstances.

(5) In this paragraph—

---

[1] Paragraph 2 was amended by S.I. 1988/1445. Paragraph 4(b) was amended by S.I. 1988/910 and 2005/2877.

"child" is to be construed in accordance with section 1 of the Family Law Reform Act 1987[1] ;

"qualifying relative" means the adult's—

(a) partner;

(b) other family member or relative who is aged 60 or over or who is incapacitated; or

(c) child who is under 18.

5. In the case of an adult who is a resident who has ceased to occupy what was formerly the dwelling occupied by them as their main or only home following their estrangement or divorce from their former partner, the value of the adult's interest in that dwelling where it is still occupied as the home by the former partner who is a lone parent.

6. In the case of an adult who is in receipt of care and support other than the provision of accommodation in a care home, the value of the adult's main or only home.

7. The value of the proceeds of sale of any premises which would be disregarded under paragraph 3 of Schedule 10 to the Income Support Regulations (proceeds of sale from premises formerly occupied).

8. Any future interest in property which would be disregarded under paragraph 5 of Schedule 10 to the Income Support Regulations (future interests in property other than in certain land or premises)[2] .

9. Any assets which would be disregarded under paragraph 6 of Schedule 10 to the Income Support Regulations (business assets)[3] , but as if in sub-paragraph (2) of that paragraph for the words from "the claim for income support" to the end of that sub-paragraph there were substituted—

(a) in the case of the adult who is a resident other than a prospective resident the words "the accommodation was initially provided";

(b) in the case of the adult who is a prospective resident, the words "the local authority began to assess the adult's ability to pay for their accommodation under these Regulations".

10. Any amount which would be disregarded under paragraph 7(1) of Schedule 10 to the Income Support Regulations (arrears of specified payments)[4] , but as if the words "Subject to subparagraph (2)" at the beginning of that sub-paragraph were omitted and as if the reference in paragraph (a) of that sub-paragraph to paragraphs 6, 8 or 9 of Schedule 9 to the Income Support Regulations (other income to be disregarded) were a reference to paragraphs 8 to 11 of Schedule 1 to these Regulations (other income to be disregarded).

11. Any arrears of, or any concessionary payment made to compensate for arrears due to the non-payment of—

(a) child tax credit;

(b) working tax credit;

(c) a payment which is made under any of—

(i) the Order in Council of 19th December 1881;

(ii) the Royal warrant of 27th October 1884;

(iii) the Order by his Majesty of 14th January 1922, to a widow, widower or surviving civil partner under any power of Her Majesty otherwise than under an enactment to make provision about pensions for or in respect of persons who have been disabled or have died in consequence of service as members of the armed forces of the Crown and whose service in such capacity terminated

---

[1] 1987 c.42. Section 1 was amended by para.51 of Schedule 3 to the Adoption and Children Act 2002, para.24 of Sch.6 to the Human Fertilisation and Embryology Act 2008 (c.22) and S.I. 2014/560.

[2] Paragraph 5 was substituted by S.I. 1995/2303.

[3] Paragraph 6 was amended by S.I. 1990/1776, 1998/1174 and 2000/2910.

[4] Paragraph 7(1) was amended by S.I. 1991/2742, 1996/1944, 2001/2333, 2002/2380, 2005/574, 2008/698, 2008/1554 and 2013/630.

before 31st March 1973, but only for a period of 52 weeks from the date of the receipt of the arrears or the concessionary payment.

12. Any amount which would be disregarded under paragraph 8 or 9 of Schedule 10 to the Income Support Regulations (property repairs and amounts deposited with a housing association).

13. Any personal possessions except those which had or have been acquired by the adult with the intention of reducing their capital in order to satisfy a local authority that they were unable to pay towards the cost of their care and support or support.

14. Any amount which would be disregarded under paragraph 11 of Schedule 10 to the Income Support Regulations (income under an annuity).

15. Any amount which would be disregarded under paragraph 12 of Schedule 10 to the Income Support Regulations (personal injury trusts)[1] .

16. Any amount which would be disregarded under paragraph 12A of Schedule 10 to the Income Support Regulations (personal injury payments)[2] with the exception of any payment or any part of any payment that has been specifically identified by a court to deal with the cost of providing care.

17. Any amount which would be disregarded under paragraph 13 of Schedule 10 to the Income Support Regulations (a life interest or a life rent).

18. The value of the right to receive any income which is disregarded under paragraph 21 of Schedule 1 (income to be disregarded).

19. Any amount which would be disregarded under paragraph 15, 16, 18, 18A or 19 of Schedule 10 to the Income Support Regulations (surrender value of life insurance policy, outstanding instalments, social fund payments, local welfare provision and tax refunds on certain loan interest)[3] .

20. Any capital which under regulation 16 (capital treated as income) is to be treated as income.

21. Any amount which would be disregarded under paragraphs 21 to 24 of Schedule 10 to the Income Support Regulations (charge or commission for converting capital into sterling, the Macfarlane Trusts, the Fund and the Independent Living Fund, value of the right to receive personal or occupational pension, value of funds under personal pension scheme and rent)[4] .

22. The value of any premises which would be disregarded under paragraph 27 or 28 of Schedule 10 to the Income Support Regulations (premises a claimant intends to occupy)[5] but as if for the words "his home" in each provision there were substituted "his main or only home".

23. Any amount which would be disregarded under paragraphs 29 to 31[6] , 34[7] and 36 to 43[8] of Schedule 10 to the Income Support Regulations (fund payments in kind, training

---

[1] Paragraph 12 was substituted by S.I. 1990/1776 and amended by S.I. 2006/2378.

[2] Paragraph 12A was inserted by S.I. 2006/2378.

[3] Paragraph 18 was substituted by S.I. 1992/468. Paragraphs 18 and 19 were amended by S.I. 2008/3157. Paragraph 18A was inserted by S.I. 2013/443.

[4] Paragraphs 22, 23 and 24 were inserted by S.I. 1988/663. Paragraph 22 was substituted by S.I. 1991/1175 and amended by S.I. 1992/1101, 1993/1249, 2000/1981, 2004/1141, 2005/2877, 2005/3391, 2008/2767, 2010/641 and 2011/2425. Paragraph 23 was amended by S.I. 1991/1559. Paragraph 23A was inserted by S.I. 1995/2303 and amended by S.I. 2007/1749. Paragraph 24 was amended by S.I. 1995/2303.

[5] Paragraphs 27 and 28 were inserted by S.I. 1988/910 and para 27 substituted by S.I. 1988/2202.

[6] Paragraphs 29 to 31 were inserted by S.I. 1988/1445. Paragraph 29 was amended by S.I. 1990/127, 1992/1101, 2007/2538, 2008/2767, 2010/641 and 2011/2425. Paragraph 30 was substituted by S.I. 2004/565.

[7] Paragraph 34 was inserted by S.I. 1988/2202.

[8] Paragraphs 36 and 37 were inserted by S.I. 1990/547 and para 36 amended by S.I. 1993/315, 2008/698 and 2013/443. Paragraphs 38 to 41 were inserted by S.I. 1990/1776 and paras 38 and 39 substituted by S.I. 2008/3157. Paragraph 39A was inserted by S.I. 2009/583. Paragraph 40 was amended by S.I. 2007/2128 and 2008/3157. Paragraph 41 was substituted by S.I. 2008/3157. Paragraphs 42 and 43 were inserted by S.I. 1992/468 and para.42 amended by S.I. 2004/565.

bonuses, housing benefit compensation, juror or witness payments, reduction of liability for personal community charge, housing grants, travelling expenses and health service supplies, welfare food payments, health in pregnancy grant, prison visiting scheme payments, special war widows payments, disabled persons' employment payments, and blind homeworkers' payments).

24. The value of any premises occupied in whole or in part by a third party where the local authority considers it would be reasonable to disregard the value of those premises.

25. Any amount which—

      (a) falls within paragraph 44(2)(a), and would be disregarded under paragraph 44(1)(a) or (b), of Schedule 10 to the Income Support Regulations[1] ; or

      (b) would be disregarded under paragraph 45(a) of that Schedule.

26. Any amount which would be disregarded under paragraph 61 of Schedule 10 to the Income Support Regulations (ex-gratia payment made by the Secretary of State in consequence of a person's imprisonment or internment by the Japanese during the Second World War)[2] .

27. Any payment which would be disregarded under paragraph 64 of Schedule 10 to the Income Support Regulations (payments under a trust established out of funds provided by the Secretary of State in respect of persons who suffered or are suffering from variant Creutzfeldt-Jakob disease)[3] .

28. Any payment made by a local authority to or on behalf of the adult relating to the provision of a service, where—

      (a) that service is provided to develop or sustain the capacity of the adult to live independently in the community; and

      (b) any charge for that service would be a service charge of the kind specified in Schedule 1B to the Housing Benefit (General) Regulations 1987 as in force immediately before 1st April 2003.

29. Any payment made by the adult to the local authority in payment of a charge imposed on the adult by the authority under the Local Authorities (Charges for Specified Welfare Services) (England) Regulations 2003.

30. Any payment made to the adult pursuant to regulations made under section 2(6)(b) or 3 of the Adoption and Children Act 2002.

31. Any payment made to the adult under section 2 or 3 of the Age-Related Payments Act 2004 (entitlement: basic or special cases)[4] .

32. Any payment made to the adult under Part 2 (payments to persons over the age of 65) or Part 3 (payments to persons in receipt of guarantee credit) of the Age-Related Payments Regulations 2005[5] .

33. Any payment made to the adult under section 63(6)(b) of the Health Services and Public Health Act 1968 ("the 1968 Act") (travelling and other allowances to persons availing themselves of instruction) for the purpose of meeting childcare costs where the instruction is provided pursuant to—

      (a) section 63(1)(a) of the 1968 Act; or

      (b) section 63(1)(b) of the 1968 Act and where the adult is employed, or has it in contemplation to be employed, in an activity involved in or connected with a service which must or may be provided or secured as part of the health service.

---

[1] Paragraphs 44 and 45 were inserted by S.I. 1994/2139. Paragraph 44 was substituted by S.I. 2006/2378. Paragraph 45 was amended by S.I. 1997/2197 and 2003/2279.

[2] Paragraph 61 was inserted by S.I. 2001/22 and amended by S.I. 2005/2877.

[3] Paragraph 64 was inserted by S.I. 2001/1118 and amended by S.I. 2005/2687 and 2006/718.

[4] 2004 c.10.

[5] S.I. 2005/1983.

34. Any payment made in accordance with regulations made pursuant to section 14F of the Children Act 1989 (special guardian support services) to an adult who is a prospective special guardian or a special guardian.

35. Any payment made to the adult under regulations made under section 7 of the Age-Related Payments Act 2004 (power to provide future payments)[1] .

THE CARE AND SUPPORT (PREVENTING NEEDS FOR CARE AND SUPPORT) REGULATIONS 2014 (SI 2014/2673)

The Secretary of State in exercise of the powers conferred by sections 2(3) and (4) and 125(7) of the Care Act 2014[2] makes the following Regulations.   **A1–153**

GENERAL NOTE

These regulations make provision for when a local authority can make a charge for the provision of prevention services under s.2 of the Care Act. Section 2(1) requires a local authority to provide or arrange for the provision of services, facilities or resources, or take other steps, which it considers will contribute towards preventing, delaying or reducing the needs for care and support of adults or for support in relation to carers. Section 2(3) provides the power to make regulations permitting a local authority to charge and prohibiting a local authority from making a charge. Section 2(5) provides that a charge may only cover the cost that the local authority incurs in providing or arranging for the provision of the service, facility or resource. Charging for preventative support is discussed in paras 2.54 to 2.62 of the statutory guidance. In particular it advises that a financial assessment is likely to be "disproportionate" in such cases, but that alternatives should be considered such as a light-touch assessment. In any event, a local authority should not charge more than it costs to provide or arrange for the service facility or resource.[3]

Citation and commencement

1. These Regulations may be cited as the Care and Support (Preventing Needs for Care   **A1–154** and Support) Regulations 2014 and come into force immediately after section 2(1) of the Care Act 2014 comes fully into force.

Interpretation

2. In these Regulations—   **A1–155**

"the Act" means the Care Act 2014;

"community equipment (aids and minor adaptations)" means an aid, or a minor adaptation to property, for the purpose of assisting with nursing at home or aiding daily living and, for the purposes of these Regulations, an adaptation is minor if the cost of making the adaptation is £1,000 or less;

"intermediate care and reablement support services" means facilities or resources provided to an adult by a local authority under section 2(1) of the Act which—

(a) consist of a programme of services, facilities or resources;

(b) are for a specified period of time ("the specified period"); and

(c) have as their purpose the provision of assistance to an adult to enable the adult to maintain or regain the ability needed to live independently in their own home.

---

[1] Section 7 was amended by S.I. 2013/1442.

[2] 2014 c.23. The powers to make regulations are exercisable by the Secretary of State, See s.125(1) of the Act ("the Act").

[3] Department of Health, *Care and Support Statutory Guidance* (2014), paras 2.57 to 2.58.

Making a charge

A1–156   **3.**—(1) Subject to these Regulations, a local authority[1] may make a charge for any provision made by it or arranged by it under section 2(1) of the Act.

(2) A charge must not reduce the income of the adult concerned below the amount specified in regulation 7 of the Care and Support (Charging and Assessment of Resources) Regulations 2014[2] (minimum income guaranteed amount).

(3) A carer must not be charged for any provision made under section 2(1) of the Act intended to prevent or delay the development by the carer of needs for support or to reduce the carer's needs for support which consists of provision made directly to the adult needing care.

GENERAL NOTE

Regulation 3 provides that a local authority can make a charge subject to these regulations. This is a power and not a duty on local authorities to make such charges.

Paragraph (2)

This provides that a charge must not reduce the adult's income to below the minimum income guarantee specified in the Care and Support (Charging and Assessment of Resources) Regulations 2014 (SI 2014/2672).

Paragraph (3)

This provides that a carer must not be charged for any provision intended to prevent or delay the development by the carer of needs for support or to reduce the carer's needs for support which consists of provision made directly to the adult needing care.

Services to be provided free of charge

A1–157   **4.** A local authority must not make a charge under regulation 3(1) where the provision made under section 2(1) of the Act is—

> (a) a service which consists of the provision of community equipment (aids and minor adaptations);
>
> (b) intermediate care and reablement support services for the first 6 weeks of the specified period or, if the specified period is less than 6 weeks, for that period.

GENERAL NOTE

Regulations 4 and 5 respectively specify the services which must always be provided free of any charge and the persons to whom services must always be provided free of any charge. Regulation 4 provides that the following services must be free of charge: community equipment (aids and minor adaptations) and, for the first six weeks only, intermediate care and reablement support services. The definitions of these terms are set out in reg.2.

Adults to whom services are to be provided free of charge

A1–158   **5.** A local authority must not make a charge under regulation 3(1) where the provision made under section 2(1) of the Act is to an adult suffering from variant Creutzfeldt-Jakob disease.

GENERAL NOTE

Regulations 4 and 5 respectively specify the services which must always be provided free of any charge and the persons to whom services must always be provided free of

---

[1] See s.1(4) of the Act as to the meaning of "local authority"; the definition is limited to local authorities in England.

[2] S.I. 2014/2672.

any charge. Regulation 5 provides that adults suffering from variant Creutzfield-Jakob disease are to be provided with any services free of charge.

THE CARE AND SUPPORT (PROVISION OF HEALTH SERVICES) REGULATIONS 2014
(SI 2014/2821)

The Secretary of State makes these Regulations in exercise of the powers conferred by **A1–159** sections 22(4)(a), 22(6) and 125(7) and (8) of the Care Act 2014[1] .

GENERAL NOTE

These regulations make provision for a number of issues which concern the relationship between local authorities and clinical commissioning groups (or, in certain cases, the National Health Service Commissioning Board). In broad terms they cover the provision of nursing care by a registered nurse, joint working between local authorities and clinical commissioning groups and disputes between local authorities and clinical commissioning groups.

Citation, commencement and interpretation

1.—(1) These Regulations may be cited as the Care and Support (Provision of Heath **A1–160** Services) Regulations 2014 and come into force immediately after section 22(1) of the Care Act 2014 comes fully into force.

(2) In these Regulations—

"the Act" means the Care Act 2014;

"the Board" means the National Health Service Commissioning Board[2] ;

"healthcare profession" means a profession which is concerned (wholly or partly) with the physical or mental health of individuals (whether or not a person engaged in that profession is regulated by, or by virtue of, any enactment);

"health service" means the health service continued under section 1(1) of the National Health Service Act 2006[3] ;

"local authority member" means a person appointed by the Board pursuant to regulation 23(1)(b)(ii) of the Standing Rules Regulations;

"multi-disciplinary team" means a team consisting of at least—

(a) two professionals who are from different healthcare professions, or
(b) one professional who is from a healthcare profession and one person who is responsible for assessing persons who may have needs for care and support under Part 1 of the Care Act 2014;

"National Framework" means the National Framework for NHS Continuing Healthcare and NHS-funded Nursing Care issued by the Secretary of State and dated 28th November 2012[4] ;

---

[1] 2014 c.23. The powers to make regulations are exercisable by the Secretary of State, See s.125(1).
[2] The National Health Service Commissioning Board is established by s.1H of the National Health Service Act 2006 (c.41) ("the 2006 Act"). Section 1H was inserted by s.9(1) of the Health and Social Care Act 2012 (c.7) ("the 2012 Act").
[3] Section 1 of the 2006 Act was substituted by s.1 of the 2012 Act.
[4] The National Framework for NHS Continuing Healthcare and NHS-funded Nursing Care can be found at https://www.gov.uk/government/publications/national-framework-for-nhs-continuing-healthcare-and-nhs-funded-nursing-care.[Accessed on 27 July 2015] A copy can be obtained from the following address: Department of Health, Quarry House, Leeds, LS2 7UE.

"NHS Continuing Healthcare" means a package of care arranged and funded solely by the health service in England for a person aged 18 or over to meet physical or mental health needs which have arisen as a result of disability, accident or illness;

"relevant body" means the Board or a clinical commissioning group[1] ;

"review panel" means the panel of members referred to in regulation 23(4) of the Standing Rules Regulations;

"Standing Rules Regulations" means the National Health Service Commissioning Board and Clinical Commissioning Groups (Responsibilities and Standing Rules) Regulations 2012[2] .

Arrangements for the provision of nursing care by a registered nurse: responsible clinical commissioning group

A1–161　　**2.**—(1) For the purposes of section 22(4) of the Act, the clinical commissioning group from which a local authority[3] must obtain consent for it to arrange for the provision of nursing care by a registered nurse in respect of any person is the responsible clinical commissioning group.

(2) The responsible clinical commissioning group in respect of any person is the clinical commissioning group which has responsibility for arranging for the provision of nursing care by a registered nurse in respect of that person, pursuant to the provisions of section 3(1), (1A) and (1E) of the National Health Service Act 2006 and any regulations made under section 3(1B) or (1D) of that Act[4] .

GENERAL NOTE

Local authorities are prohibited by s.22 of the Care Act 2014 from meeting needs by providing or arranging for the provision of services or facilities that it is the responsibility of the National Health Service to provide. However, s.22(4) of the Care Act provides that a local authority may arrange for the provision of accommodation which includes the provision of nursing care by a registered nurse, provided it has first obtained the agreement of whichever clinical commissioning group regulations require. A local authority can also arrange for the provision of such accommodation on a temporary basis as a matter of urgency, provided it obtains the agreement of the relevant clinical commissioning group as soon as possible afterwards. Regulation 2 imposes a requirement to obtain such consent from the clinical commissioning group that has the responsibility for arranging for the provision of nursing care by a registered nurse in respect of the person concerned. That responsibility is established by reference to certain provisions of the National Health Service Act 2006 and regulations made under the 2006 Act.

---

[1] A clinical commissioning group is a body established under s.14D of the 2006 Act. Section 14D was inserted by s.25(1) of the 2012 Act. See also s.1I of the 2006 Act, inserted by s.10 of the 2012 Act.
[2] S.I. 2012/2996. Regulation 21 and Sch.5 (which relates to reg.23) have been amended by the National Health Service Commissioning Board and Clinical Commissioning Groups (Responsibilities and Standing Rules) (Amendment) Regulations 2013 (S.I. 2013/2891, reg.2) and Sch.5 has been further amended by the National Health Service Commissioning Board and Clinical Commissioning Groups (Responsibilities and Standing Rules) (Amendment) (No. 3) Regulations 2014 (S.I. 2014/1611, reg.6).
[3] See s.1(4) of the Act as to the meaning of "local authority"; the definition is limited to local authorities in England.
[4] The National Health Service Commissioning Board and Clinical Commissioning Groups (Responsibilities and Standing Rules) Regulations 2012 (S.I. 2012/2996) have been made under, inter alia, the provisions in s.3(1B) of the 2006 Act. The National Health Service (Clinical Commissioning Groups – Disapplication of Responsibility) Regulations 2013 (S.I. 2013/350) have been made under the provisions of s.3(1D) of the 2006 Act.

In most cases, the clinical commissioning group is responsible for arranging for the provision of nursing care. But, as s.24(9) of the Care Act acknowledges, it may in certain circumstances be the NHS Commissioning Board (known as NHS England).

Requirements on local authorities: joint working with relevant bodies

3.—(1) A local authority must, as far as is reasonably practicable, provide advice and **A1–162** assistance to a relevant body which consults it pursuant to regulation 22(1)(a) of the Standing Rules Regulations (duty of relevant bodies: joint working with social services authorities).

(2) A local authority must, when requested to do so by a relevant body, co-operate with that body in arranging for a person or persons to participate in a multi-disciplinary team for the purposes of that body fulfilling its duty under regulation 21(5) of the Standing Rules Regulations (duty of relevant bodies: assessment and provision of NHS Continuing Healthcare).

(3) Nothing in this regulation affects a local authority's duty to carry out an assessment of a person's needs for care and support pursuant to section 9 of the Act (assessment of an adult's needs for care and support), and if it has carried out such an assessment, it must use the information obtained as a result of that assessment, so far as it is relevant, to comply with its duty under paragraph (1).

(4) In complying with its obligations under this regulation, a local authority must have due regard to the need to promote and secure the continuity of appropriate services for persons—

    (a) whose care and support needs are being met under Part 1 of the Act or who are being provided with aftercare under section 117 of the Mental Health Act 1983[1] on the date on which they are found to be eligible to receive NHS Continuing Healthcare;

    (b) who have been in receipt of NHS Continuing Healthcare but are determined to be no longer eligible for NHS Continuing Healthcare; or

    (c) who are otherwise determined to be ineligible for NHS Continuing Healthcare.

(5) Where, pursuant to regulation 24(1) of the Standing Rules Regulations (appointment and term of appointment), the Board requests that a local authority nominates a person to be appointed as a local authority member of a review panel, the local authority—

    (a) must nominate such a person as soon as is reasonably practicable; and

    (b) must ensure that local authority members are, so far as is reasonably practicable, available to participate in review panels.

GENERAL NOTE

    Section 22(6)(a) of the Care Act provides that regulations may detail the steps that a local authority must take to contribute to an assessment as to whether an adult requires health care services. This has been enacted by reg. 3 which makes provision about how local authorities must work with clinical commissioning groups in the processes for assessing a person's needs for health care and for deciding how those needs must be met. These provisions mirror similar requirements regarding joint working that are imposed on clinical commissioning groups by the National Health Service Commissioning Board and Clinical Commissioning Groups (Responsibilities and Standing Rules) Regulations 2012 (SI 2012/2996).

Paragraph (1)

    Regulation 22(1)(a) of the National Health Service Commissioning Board and Clinical Commissioning Groups (Responsibilities and Standing Rules) Regulations 2012 (SI 2012/2996) requires clinical commissioning groups, insofar as is reasonably practicable, to

---

[1] 1983 c.20. Section 117 is prospectively amended from a date to be appointed by s.75 of the Act.

consult with the relevant social services authority before making a decision about a person's eligibility for NHS continuing health care, including any decision that a person receiving NHS continuing health care is no longer eligible to do so.

When such consultation takes place, para.(1) requires the local authority to, as far as is reasonably practicable, provides advice and assistance. This must include relevant information obtained as a result of a needs assessment under s.9 of the Care Act (see para. (3)).

Paragraph (2)

Regulation 21(5) of the National Health Service Commissioning Board and Clinical Commissioning Groups (Responsibilities and Standing Rules) Regulations 2012 (SI 2012/2996) requires clinical commissioning groups, when carrying out an assessment of eligibility for NHS continuing health care, to ensure that a multi-disciplinary team undertakes an assessment of needs, which is then used to complete the Decision Support Tool for NHS continuing health care.

For the purposes of fulfilling this duty, para.(2) requires a local authority to co-operate with the clinical commissioning group when it is requested to do so.

Paragraph (5)

Regulation 24(1) of the National Health Service Commissioning Board and Clinical Commissioning Groups (Responsibilities and Standing Rules) Regulations 2012 (SI 2012/2996) provides for the nomination and appointment of Board members by the clinical commissioning group and the social services authority.

Under para. (5), social services authority appointments must be made as soon as reasonably practicable and local authorities must ensure that board members are available to participate in review panels (which are set up to consider appeals against NHS continuing health care decisions).

Requirements on local authorities: dispute resolution

A1–163   4. Where there is a dispute between a relevant body and a local authority about—

(a) a decision as to eligibility for NHS Continuing Healthcare; or

(b) the contribution of a relevant body or local authority to a joint package of care for a person who is not eligible for NHS Continuing Healthcare, the local authority must, having regard to the National Framework, agree a dispute resolution procedure with the relevant body, and resolve the dispute in accordance with that procedure.

GENERAL NOTE

Section 22(6)(b) of the Care Act provides that regulations may require the establishment of a process for dealing with disputes between local authorities and NHS bodies, should there be a disagreement over the responsibility for providing a particular service in an individual case. This has been enacted by reg.4 which requires local authorities to make arrangements for determining any disputes between themselves and clinical commissioning groups about eligibility for NHS continuing health care or contributions for a joint package of care. In making such arrangements the local authority must have regard to the *National Framework for NHS Continuing Healthcare and NHS-funded Nursing Care.*[1] These requirements mirror similar requirements imposed on NHS bodies by reg. 22(2) of the National Health Service Commissioning Board and Clinical Commissioning Groups (Responsibilities and Standing Rules) Regulations 2012 (SI 2012/2996).

---

[1] Department of Health, The National Framework for NHS Continuing Healthcare and NHS-funded Nursing Care (2012).

Transitional provisions

5.—(1) This paragraph applies in a case where, immediately before the coming into force **A1-164** of these Regulations, a local authority—

    (a) was, in accordance with any directions issued in exercise of the powers conferred by section 7A of the Local Authority Social Services Act 1970[1] —

        (i) providing advice and assistance to a relevant body which had consulted it pursuant to regulation 22(1)(a) of the Standing Rules Regulations (duty of relevant bodies: joint working with social services authorities); or

        (ii) cooperating with a relevant body in arranging for a person to participate in a multi-disciplinary team for the purposes of that body fulfilling its duty under regulation 21(5) of the Standing Rules Regulations (duty of relevant bodies: assessment and provision of NHS Continuing Healthcare);

    (b) was in receipt of a request from the Board, pursuant to regulation 24(1) of the Standing Rules Regulations (appointment and term of appointment), that it nominate a person to be appointed as a local authority member of a review panel but had not yet nominated such a person; or

    (c) was in dispute with a relevant body about—

        (i) a decision as to eligibility for NHS Continuing Healthcare; or

        (ii) the contribution of a relevant body or local authority to a joint package of care for a person who is not eligible for NHS Continuing Healthcare, and had either not yet agreed a dispute resolution procedure with the relevant body, in accordance with any directions issued in exercise of the powers conferred by section 7A of the Local Authority Social Services Act 1970, or had agreed such a dispute resolution procedure with the relevant body but had not yet resolved the dispute in accordance with that procedure.

(2) Where—

    (a) paragraph (1)(a) applies, the local authority is required to continue providing advice and assistance to the relevant body or cooperating with the relevant body as though such obligation had arisen under these Regulations;

    (b) paragraph (1)(b) applies, the local authority is required to nominate a person to be appointed as a local authority member of a review panel as though the obligation to nominate such a person had arisen under these Regulations;

    (c) paragraph (1)(c) applies, the local authority is required to—

        (i) if necessary, agree a dispute resolution procedure, and

        (ii) resolve the dispute in accordance with any procedure agreed with the relevant body, as though the obligation to agree such procedure and to resolve the dispute had arisen under these Regulations.

GENERAL NOTE

Regulation 5 makes transitional provisions to provide for continuity in those cases where (in accordance with directions issued under the provisions of section 7A of the Local Authority Social Services Act 1970) the local authority is already working jointly with NHS bodies in a particular case, or is already in receipt of a request to nominate a member to a review panel or is already working with an NHS body to settle a dispute.

---

[1] 1970 c.42. Section 7A was inserted by the National Health Service and Community Care Act 1990 (c.19) s.50. The NHS Continuing Healthcare (Responsibilities of Social Services Authorities) Directions 2013 were issued by the Secretary of State for Health under the powers conferred by s.7A of the Local Authority Social Services Act 1970 on 27 March 2013.

**THE CARE AND SUPPORT (MARKET OVERSIGHT INFORMATION) REGULATIONS
2014 (SI 2014/2822)**

A1–165   The Secretary of State makes these Regulations in exercise of the powers conferred by
sections 55(5), 125(7) and (8) of the Care Act 2014[1] .

GENERAL NOTE

Section 55(1) of the Care Act imposes a duty on the Care Quality Commission to assess
the financial sustainability of a registered care provider subject to the market oversight
regime. These regulations make provision for the Care Quality Commission to require providers to enter into information undertakings with their wider corporate group to ensure that
it has the information it needs in making this assessment. Regulation 2 provides that a registered care provider may be required to obtain from a group undertaking of the provider, a
legally enforceable undertaking to provide information. Regulations 3 to 5 make further
provision in relation to the information undertaking. The Government has explained that
if the information was not provided "the Care Quality Commission ultimately has the
enforcement powers available to it to close the business down. So, there is a clear interest
in the provider organisation's properly responding to the [Care Quality Commission's]
demands."[2]

Citation, commencement and interpretation
A1–166   **1.**—(1) These Regulations may be cited as the Care and Support (Market Oversight
Information) Regulations 2014 and come into force immediately after section 55(5) of
the Care Act 2014 comes fully into force[3] .

(2) In these Regulations—

"the Act" means the Care Act 2014;

"the Commission" means the Care Quality Commission[4] ;

"group undertaking" has the meaning given by section 1161(5) of the Companies Act
2006[5] and "undertaking" (except in the case of an information undertaking) has the
meaning given by section 1161(1) of that Act;

"information" means any information, documents, records or other material;

"information undertaking" is to be construed in accordance with regulation 2.

Undertaking to provide information
A1–167   **2.**—(1) This regulation applies where a registered care provider[6] to whom section 55 of
the Act applies is an undertaking.

(2) The Commission may require the registered care provider to obtain from a group
undertaking of the provider an "information undertaking" to provide the Commission
with such information as the Commission requests.

(3) An information undertaking must be in a form which is legally enforceable by the
registered care provider.

---

[1] 2014 c. 23 ("the Act"). The powers to make regulations are exercisable by the Secretary of State. See
s.125(1) of the Act.
[2] *Hansard* (House of Commons: Eighth Delegated Legislation Committee), 20 January 2015, col.13
(Norman Lamb MP).
[3] Section 55(5) was commenced for the purpose of making regulations by S.I. 2014/2473.
[4] Established by s.1(1) of the Health and Social Care Act 2008 (c. 14).
[5] 2006 c.46. See S.I. 2008/1911 as to the application of s.1161(5) with modifications to limited liability
partnerships.
[6] See s.48(1) of the Act for the meaning of "registered care provider".

Form of the information undertaking

3. The Commission may specify the form of an information undertaking and may pro- **A1–168**
vide in particular that—

(a) information must be provided at such times and such places as may be specified
by the Commission;

(b) an explanation of any information must be provided at such times and such
places as may be specified by the Commission;

(c) information and explanations must be provided in such manner or format as
may be specified by the Commission;

(d) the group undertaking must co-operate with the Commission in connection
with providing information and explanations; and

(e) information and explanations must be complete and accurate.

Time for provision of information undertaking, etc.

4.—(1) The registered care provider must obtain the information undertaking within **A1–169**
such period as the Commission specifies.

(2) The registered care provider must send to the Commission a copy of the information
undertaking within such period as the Commission specifies.

(3) The information undertaking must remain in force for as long as—

(a) the person required to provide information remains a group undertaking of the
registered care provider; and

(b) section 55 of the Act continues to apply to the registered care provider.

Breach, etc.

5.—(1) The registered care provider must inform the Commission immediately in writ- **A1–170**
ing if it becomes aware that—

(a) the information undertaking has ceased to be in force;

(b) the information undertaking has ceased to be legally enforceable; or

(c) any terms of the information undertaking have been breached.

(2) The registered care provider must comply with any request made by the Commission
to enforce the information undertaking.

THE CARE AND SUPPORT (DISCHARGE OF HOSPITAL PATIENTS) REGULATIONS 2014 (SI 2014/2823)

The Secretary of State makes these Regulations in exercise of the powers conferred by **A1–171**
paragraphs 2(5)(b), 4(6), 6 and 8 of Schedule 3 to, and section 125(7) of, the Care Act 2014[1].

GENERAL NOTE

These regulations make provision for the details of the scheme for the discharge of hospital patients with care and support needs. This scheme (often referred to as the "delayed
discharge" scheme) is introduced in s.74 of the Care Act, and the detail is set out in Sch.3.
In broad terms, the scheme enables the NHS to seek reimbursement from a local authority
where a patient's discharge has been delayed due to a failure of the local authority either to
arrange for relevant assessments or meet a patient's or (where applicable) that patient's
carer's needs which the local authority proposes to meet. It also set requirements for communication between the NHS and local authority in relation to patients who were ready to
be discharged and for the involvement of patients and carers during the discharge process.
The statutory guidance discusses the scheme at paras 15.37 to 15.47 and annex G.

---

[1] 2014 c.23 ("the Act"). The powers to make regulations are exercisable by the Secretary of State, See
s.125(1).

Citation, commencement and interpretation

A1–172   **1.**—(1) These Regulations may be cited as the Care and Support (Discharge of Hospital Patients) Regulations 2014 and come into force immediately after section 74 of the Care Act 2014 comes fully into force[1] .

(2) In these Regulations—

"the Act" means the Care Act 2014;

"delayed discharge period" means the period determined in accordance with regulation 9;

"NHS continuing health care" means a package of care arranged and funded solely by the health service for a person aged 18 or over to meet physical or mental health needs which have arisen as a result of disability, accident or illness.

(3) For the purposes of these Regulations, a reference to a section or a Schedule is a reference to that section of, or Schedule to, the Act, unless indicated otherwise.

Form of notices

A1–173   **2.**—(1) This regulation applies to the following—

    (a) an assessment notice[2] ;

    (b) a discharge notice[3] ; and

    (c) a withdrawal notice[4] given by an NHS body[5] to a local authority[6] under—

        (i) paragraph 1(5)(c) of Schedule 3; or

        (ii) paragraph 2(4)(b) of Schedule 3.

(2) The notice must—

    (a) be in writing; and

    (b) contain the date on which it is given.

GENERAL NOTE

Regulation 2 requires that all notices which the NHS body gives the local authority under Sch.3 to the Care Act must be in writing and contain the date upon which it is given. The statutory guidance emphasises that in order to be valid, notices must be legible.[7]

Assessment notice: contents

A1–174   **3.**—(1) An assessment notice must contain—

    (a) the name of the patient to whom the notice relates;

    (b) the patient's NHS number;

    (c) if given before the patient's admission, the expected date of admission and the name of the hospital to which the patient is expected to be admitted;

    (d) if given after the patient's admission, the name of the hospital in which the patient is being accommodated;

    (e) an indication of the likely date of the patient's discharge, if known;

    (f) a statement—

---

[1] Section 74 was commenced for the purpose of making regulations by S.I. 2014/2473.

[2] See para.1(2) of Sch.3 for the meaning of "assessment notice".

[3] See para.2(2) of Sch.3 for the meaning of "discharge notice".

[4] See para.1(5)(c) of Sch.3 for the meaning of "withdrawal notice".

[5] See para.7(4) of Sch.3 for the definition of "NHS body".

[6] See s.1(4) for the definition of "local authority"; the definition is limited to local authorities in England.

[7] Department of Health, *Care and Support Statutory Guidance* (2014), Annex 3, para.3.

(i) that the NHS body responsible for the patient has complied with its duty under paragraph 1(4) of Schedule 3 (duty to consult patient and any carer[1] that the patient has);

(ii) that the NHS body has considered whether or not to provide the patient with NHS continuing health care, and the result of that consideration; and

(iii) as to whether the patient or (where applicable) the patient's carer has objected to the giving of the assessment notice; and

(g) the contact details of the person at the hospital who will be responsible for liaising with the relevant authority[2] .

(2) In paragraph (1)(g), the reference to contact details in relation to that person means—

(a) their full name; and

(b) either or both of the following—

(i) their telephone number;

(ii) their electronic mail address.

GENERAL NOTE

Regulation 3 sets out the details that an assessment notice must contain.

Assessment notice: withdrawal

4. A notice withdrawing an assessment notice must be given where— **A1–175**

(a) the NHS body responsible for the patient considers that it is likely to be safe to discharge the patient without arrangements for meeting the patient's needs for care and support or (where applicable) the carer's needs for support being put in place;

(b) the NHS body considers that the patient needs NHS continuing health care;

(c) the NHS body, having received the information specified in paragraph 3(1)(d) of Schedule 3 (how local authority plans to meet needs), still considers that it is unlikely to be safe to discharge the patient from hospital unless further arrangements are put in place for meeting the patient's needs for care and support or (where applicable) the patient's carer's needs for support;

(d) the patient's proposed treatment is cancelled or postponed;

(e) the NHS body has been informed by the relevant authority that it is not required to carry out an assessment because the patient has refused a needs assessment[3] or (where applicable) the patient's carer has refused a carer's assessment[4] ; or

(f) the NHS body becomes aware that—

(i) the patient's ordinary residence has changed since the assessment notice was given; or

(ii) the notice was given to a local authority other than the one in whose area the patient is ordinarily resident.

GENERAL NOTE

Regulation 4 sets out the circumstances under which an NHS body must withdraw an assessment notice.

Discharge notice: minimum period of service

5. A discharge notice may not be given less than one day in advance of the proposed dis- **A1–176**
charge date.

---

[1] See s.10(3) for the meaning of "carer".

[2] See para.1(2) of Sch.3 for the meaning of "relevant authority".

[3] See s.9(2).

[4] See s.10(2).

Regulation 5 specifies that a discharge notice may not be given less than one day in advance of the proposed discharge date.

Discharge notice: contents

A1–177 **6.**—(1) A discharge notice must contain—
    (a) the name of the patient to whom the notice relates;
    (b) the patient's NHS number;
    (c) the name of the hospital in which the patient is being accommodated;
    (d) the contact details of the person at the hospital who will be responsible for liaising with the relevant authority;
    (e) the date on which it is proposed that the patient be discharged;
    (f) a statement confirming that the patient and, where applicable, the patient's carer has been informed of the date on which it is proposed that the patient be discharged; and
    (g) a statement that the discharge notice is given under paragraph 2(1)(b) of Schedule 3.

(2) In paragraph (1)(d), contact details in relation to that person means—
    (a) their full name; and
    (b) either or both of the following—
       (i) their telephone number;
      (ii) their electronic mail address.

GENERAL NOTE
Regulation 6 sets out the details which a discharge notice must contain.

Discharge notice: withdrawal

A1–178 **7.**—(1) Subject to paragraph (2), a notice withdrawing a discharge notice must be given where the NHS body responsible for the patient considers that it is no longer likely to be safe to discharge the patient on the proposed discharge date.

(2) Paragraph (1) does not apply where the only reason that the NHS body considers that it is no longer likely to be safe to discharge the patient on the proposed discharge date is that the relevant authority has—
    (a) not discharged its duty to carry out a needs assessment or (where applicable) a carer's assessment in relation to the patient; or
    (b) not put in place arrangements for meeting some or all of those needs that it proposes to meet under sections 18 to 20 in the case of the patient or (where applicable) the patient's carer.

GENERAL NOTE
Regulation 7 sets out the circumstances under which an NHS body must withdraw a discharge notice. In general terms this is where the NHS body considers that it is no longer safe for the patient to be discharged on the proposed discharge date. However, this does not apply where the only reason that it is no longer safe is that the local authority has not carried out a needs or carer's assessment, or put in place the proposed care and support.

Relevant day

A1–179 **8.** The period specified for the purposes of paragraph 2(5)(b) of Schedule 3 (relevant day in relation to discharge notice)[1] is the period—
    (a) beginning with the day after that on which the assessment notice is given or treated as given in accordance with regulation 11; and

---

[1] See also para.2(6) of Sch.3.

(b) ending two days after that date.

GENERAL NOTE
Regulation 8 specifies that the minimum period for which a discharge notice may remain in force (unless withdrawn by the local authority) is two days after the date on which an assessment notice is given or treated as being given in accordance with reg.11.

Delayed discharge period

9.—(1) The specified period for the purposes of paragraph 4(6) of Schedule 3 is to be **A1–180** determined in accordance with this regulation.

(2) The specified period begins on the day after the day which is the relevant day[1] in relation to that discharge notice.

(3) The specified period ends with the earliest of the days on which any of the following first occur—
>>> (a) the NHS body responsible for the patient withdraws the assessment notice or discharge notice relating to that patient;
>>> (b) the relevant authority gives notice to the NHS body responsible for the patient that it has—
>>>> (i) carried out a needs assessment and (where applicable) a carer's assessment in relation to the patient to whom the notice relates; and
>>>> (ii) put in place arrangements for meeting some or all of those needs that it proposes to meet under sections 18 to 20 in the case of the patient or (where applicable) the carer;
>>> (c) the relevant authority is no longer required to put in place arrangements to meet the needs of the patient and (where applicable) the carer under sections 18 to 20 because—
>>>> (i) the patient informs the relevant authority that they have arranged their own care or other care is arranged for the patient; and
>>>> (ii) where applicable the carer informs the relevant authority that they have arranged their own support or other support is arranged for the carer;
>>> (d) the patient discharges themself;
>>> (e) the NHS body responsible for the patient decides that the patient needs to remain in hospital for a further course of treatment; or
>>> (f) the patient dies.

(4) A day is not be to treated as a day of the specified period in the following circumstances—
>>> (a) the relevant authority has by 11am on that day put in place arrangements for meeting some or all of the needs that it proposes to meet under sections 18 to 20 in the case of the patient or (where applicable) the carer; or
>>> (b) the NHS body responsible for the patient considers that the patient is not able to be discharged due to a deterioration on that day.

GENERAL NOTE
Regulation 9 sets out how the period for which the local authority may be liable to the NHS for reimbursement for the costs of the patient's care is to be determined

Delayed discharge payment

10. For the purposes of paragraph 4(6) of Schedule 3 (amount to be paid for each day of **A1–181** delayed discharge period), the amount specified is—
>>> (a) £155 where the relevant authority is—
>>>> (i) a London borough council, or

---

[1] See para.2(5) of Sch.3 for the definition of "relevant day".

(ii) the Common Council of the City of London; and
(b) £130 in any other case.

GENERAL NOTE
Regulation 10 specifies the daily amount the local authority may be required to pay the NHS body in the event that the local authority has not assessed the patient and put in place arrangements to meet some or all of those needs that it proposes to meet.

Day on which assessment and discharge notice is to be regarded as given
A1–182   **11.** An assessment notice or a discharge notice which is given after 2pm on any day is to be treated as having been given on the following day.

GENERAL NOTE
Regulation 11 provides for the day on which an assessment and discharge notice is to be regarded as given.

Ordinary residence
A1–183   **12.**—(1) Subject to paragraph (2), a local authority to which an assessment notice has been given must accept that notice and carry out the duties of a relevant authority arising from it even though it may wish to dispute that it was the correct authority to which to give the notice.

(2) Where for a reason set out in paragraph (3), it is agreed or determined that the patient to whom the notice relates is ordinarily resident in the area of another local authority then that local authority is to become the relevant authority in the patient's case.

(3) The reasons referred to in paragraph (2) are that—
(a) the other local authority agrees that it is the correct authority; or
(b) a determination is made under section 40 to the effect that the patient is ordinarily resident in the area of the other local authority.

(4) Where paragraph (2) applies, the local authority to which the notice was given may recover from the local authority which is the correct authority in relation to that case any expenditure it has incurred in relation to making a payment under paragraph 4 of Schedule 3 (delayed discharge payment) in that case.

GENERAL NOTE
Regulation 12 requires a local authority to which an assessment notice is given to accept that notice and be required to undertake the duties in relation to that patient notwithstanding that it may dispute that patient's ordinary residence. It also allows a local authority which has wrongly been given an assessment notice to claim reimbursement for any delayed discharge payment it has paid in that case from the local authority in whose area the patient is later agreed or determined to be ordinarily resident. The intention is to ensure that one local authority is always responsible for the patient and that they receive any necessary care and support as soon as possible, even where there is uncertainty as to which authority should bear responsibility.

THE CARE AND SUPPORT (CONTINUITY OF CARE) REGULATIONS 2014 (SI 2014/2825)

A1–184   The Secretary of State makes these Regulations in exercise of the power conferred by section 38(8) of the Care Act 2014[1] .

---

[1] 2014 c.23; See s.125(1) for the powers to make regulations.

GENERAL NOTE

Sections 37 and 38 of the Care Act set out procedures to be followed when an individual who is receiving care and support from a local authority ("the first authority") wishes to move to the area of another local authority ("the second authority"). Under s.38(1), where a person has moved into the second authority's area but that authority has not yet carried out a full assessment of the person's needs, the second authority must meet the person's care and support needs from the date of the move; it must do this on the same basis as the first authority until it has carried out its own assessment. When carrying out this duty, the second authority must have regard to the matters set out in reg.2 below. These matters are also discussed at paras. 20.43 to 20.47 of the statutory guidance.

Citation, commencement and interpretation

1.—(1) These Regulations may be cited as the Care and Support (Continuity of Care) **A1–185** Regulations 2014 and come into force immediately after section 38(8) of the Care Act 2014 comes fully into force[1] .

(2) In these Regulations—

"the Act" means the Care Act 2014;

"relevant carer" means, in relation to an adult[2] , a person who is continuing as that adult's carer[3] as of the day of that adult's intended move; a reference to the day of an adult's intended move (howsoever expressed) is a reference to the day of that adult's intended move as mentioned in section 37(1)(b) or (3)(b) of the Act.

Matters to have regard to in deciding how to perform duty under section 38(1)

2.—(1) For the purposes of section 38(8) of the Act (cases where assessments are not **A1–186** complete on day of move), the second authority[4] must have regard to the following matters in deciding how to perform its duty under section 38(1) of the Act in respect of an adult ("the relevant adult")—

    (a) the contents of any care and support plan supplied to the authority under section 37(5)(a) of the Act (documents to be supplied by first authority where second authority is satisfied as to genuineness of intention to move) in relation to the relevant adult;

    (b) the contents of any support plan supplied to the authority under section 37(5)(e) of the Act in relation to any relevant carer of the relevant adult;

    (c) the outcomes that the relevant adult wishes to achieve in day-to-day life;

    (d) the outcomes that any relevant carer of that adult wishes to achieve in day-to-day life;

    (e) the views and preferences of the relevant adult as to how the authority should meet that adult's needs for care and support;

    (f) the views and preferences of any relevant carer of that adult as to how the authority should meet that carer's needs for support;

    (g) any relevant difference between the relevant adult's circumstances before and after the day of the adult's intended move, including in relation to—

        (i) access to a carer;

        (ii) suitability of living accommodation;

        (iii) location of living accommodation in terms of its proximity and accessibility to necessary facilities or services in the local community including—

---

[1] Section 38(8) was commenced for the purpose of making regulations by S.I. 2014/2473.
[2] See s.2(8) of the Act for the meaning of "adult".
[3] See s.10(3) of the Act for the meaning of "carer".
[4] See s.37(1) of the Act for the meaning of "second authority".

(aa) medical services,
(bb) public transport,
(cc) educational facilities, and
(dd) recreational facilities or services; and
    (iv) the availability of support from family members, friends, neighbours and the wider community.

(2) For the purposes of paragraph (1)(g), a difference is relevant if it is likely to have a significant effect on the well-being of the relevant adult during the period when that adult's needs for care and support are being met under section 38(1) of the Act.

THE CARE AND SUPPORT (ASSESSMENT) REGULATIONS 2014 (SI 2014/2827)

A1–187   The Secretary of State makes these Regulations in exercise of the powers conferred by s.12(1) and (2), 65(1) and 125(7) and (8) of the Care Act 2014[1] .

GENERAL NOTE

Sections 9 and 10 of the Care Act impose duties on a local authority to assess an adult's needs for care and support, and a carer's needs for support. These regulations make further provision about such assessments. They also apply to the following assessments carried out under the Care Act: a child's needs assessment (s.59), a child's carer's assessment (s.61) and a young carer's assessment (s.64).

- Regulation 2 makes provision for supported self-assessment, where the individual to whom the assessment relates and the local authority carry out the assessment jointly;
- Regulation 3 makes provision about the manner in which assessments are carried out (including appropriate and proportionate assessments, cases where the person has fluctuating needs and the provision of information);
- Regulation 4 imposes requirements on local authorities relating to the person's family and others involved in their care, including where it appears that any child is involved in providing care to any individual;
- Regulation 5 makes provision about the training and expertise of persons carrying out assessments;
- Regulation 6 makes specific provision about training and expertise in connection with the assessment of individuals who are deafblind; and
- Regulation 7 requires the local authority to make a referral to the health service where it appears that the individual whose needs are being assessed may have a need for NHS continuing health care.

The statutory guidance discusses the main features of a transition assessment in paras. 16.24 to 16.39. In addition, the guidance advises that in complex cases, social workers will often be the most appropriate lead professionals for transition assessments.[2]

Citation, commencement and interpretation

A1–188   **1.**—(1) These Regulations may be cited as the Care and Support (Assessment) Regulations 2014 and come into force immediately after section 12(1) of the Care Act 2014 comes fully into force[3] .

(2) In these Regulations—

"the Act" means the Care Act 2014;

---

[1] 2014 c.23 ("the Act"). The powers to make regulations is exercisable by the Secretary of State - See s.125(1).

[2] Department of Health, *Care and Support Statutory Guidance* (2014), para.16.16.

[3] Section 12(1) was commenced for the purpose of making regulations by S.I. 2014/2473.

"assessment" means—

    (a) a needs assessment[1] ;
    (b) a child's needs assessment[2] ;
    (c) a carer's assessment[3] ;
    (d) a child's carer's assessment[4] ;
    (e) a young carer's assessment[5] ;

"supported self-assessment" has the meaning given by regulation 2(1).

Supported self-assessment
2.—(1) A supported self-assessment is an assessment carried out jointly by the local **A1–189** authority[6] and the individual to whom it relates.

(2) A local authority proposing to carry out an assessment must ascertain whether the individual to whom the assessment is to relate wishes the assessment to be a supported self-assessment.

(3) A supported self-assessment must be carried out if the individual concerned is an adult and—

    (a) wishes the assessment to be a supported self-assessment; and
    (b) has the capacity[7] to take part in a supported self-assessment.

(4) A supported self-assessment may be carried out if the individual concerned is a child and—

    (a) wishes the assessment to be a supported self-assessment;
    (b) has the capacity, and is competent, to take part in a supported self-assessment; and
    (c) the local authority believes it appropriate for a self-supported assessment to be carried out having regard to all the circumstances.

(5) To facilitate the carrying out of the assessment a local authority must provide an individual taking part in a supported self-assessment with any relevant information it may have—

    (a) about that individual; and
    (b) providing the consent condition in paragraph (6) is met, in the case of—
        (i) a carer's assessment, about the adult needing care[8] ;
        (ii) a child's carer's assessment, about the child needing care;
        (iii) a young carer's assessment, about the adult needing care, if the local authority believes it is appropriate for the young carer to have that information having regard to all the circumstances.

(6) The consent condition referred to in paragraph (5)(b) is met if—

    (a) the adult or child needing care has capacity or is competent to agree to the information in paragraph (5)(b) being provided and does so agree, or
    (b) the adult or child needing care does not have capacity or is not competent so to agree but the local authority is satisfied that providing the information in paragraph (5)(b) would be in the best interests of the adult or child needing care.

---

[1] See s.9 of the Act.
[2] See s.58 of the Act.
[3] See s.10 of the Act.
[4] See s.60 of the Act.
[5] See s.63 of the Act.
[6] See s.1(4) of the Act for the meaning of "local authority"; the definition is limited to local authorities in England.
[7] A reference to having or lacking capacity is to be interpreted in accordance with the Mental Capacity Act 2005 (c.9), See s.80(2) of the Act.
[8] See s.10(3) of the Act for the meaning of "adult needing care".

(7) The information must be provided in a format which is accessible to the individual to whom it is given.

GENERAL NOTE

The statutory guidance defines a supported self-assessment in the following terms:

"A supported self-assessment is an assessment carried out jointly by the adult with care and support needs or carer and the local authority. It places the individual in control of the assessment process to a point where they themselves complete their assessment form. Whilst it is the person filling in the assessment form, the duty to assess the person's needs, and in doing so ensure that they are accurate and complete, remains with the local authority."[1]

The regulations provide that if a local authority is proposing to carry out an assessment, it must ascertain whether the person wishes to have a supported self-assessment. The duty to carry out a supported self-assessment applies if an adult wishes to have, and has the capacity to take part in, such an assessment. There is also a power to carry out a supported self-assessment where the local authority is carrying out a child's needs assessment or a young carer's assessment, and.
- the child wishes to have a supported self-assessment;
- the child has the capacity, and is competent, to take part in a supported self-assessment; and
- the local authority believes it appropriate for a self-supported assessment to be carried out having regard to all the circumstances.[2]

To facilitate the carrying out of a supported self-assessment, the local authority must provide an individual taking part in the assessment with any relevant information it may have about them. In addition, when a carer (including a child's care or young carer) is taking part in the supported self-assessment, the local authority is required to provide the carer with any relevant information about the person needing care. This requirement only applies if the person needing care agrees to this information being provided and has capacity or is competent to agree, or if the person lacks capacity or is not competent to agree but the local authority is satisfied that providing the information would be in their best interests. Moreover, in relation to a young carer, the local authority must believe it is appropriate for the young carer to have that information having regard to all the circumstances. The regulations also specify that information must be provided in a format which is accessible to the individual to whom it is given.[3] The statutory guidance explains that the requirements in the regulations to provide relevant information are intended to ensure that the person undertaking the assessment has "a full picture of their care and support history and is equipped with the same information an assessor would have when undertaking an assessment".[4]

More information on supported self-assessments is provided at paras 6.44 to 6.53 of the statutory guidance. Amongst other matters, the statutory guidance makes clear that:
- if the person does not wish to self-assess, then the local authority must undertake an assessment following one of the other processes (para.6.44);
- the supported self-assessment process is only complete once the local authority ensures that the information provided is accurate and complete (para.6.46);
- in the case of a person who requires a specialist assessment (for example if the person is deafblind), then the professional leading the assurance process must be seen as the assessor and so must have specific training and expertise relating to the individual's needs (para.6.46);

---

[1] Department of Health, *Care and Support Statutory Guidance* (2014), para.6.44.
[2] Care and Support (Assessment) Regulations 2014 (SI 2014/2827), reg.2(2) to (4).
[3] Care and Support (Assessment) Regulations 2014 (SI 2014/2827), reg.2(5) to (7).
[4] Department of Health, *Care and Support Statutory Guidance* (2014), para.6.45.

GENERAL NOTE

The regulations require local authorities to ensure that any person carrying out the assessment (other than in the case of a supported self-assessment) has the skills, knowledge and competence to carry out the assessment in question, and is appropriately trained. The regulations also require local authorities when carrying out an assessment to consult a person who has "expertise in relation to the condition or other circumstances of the individual whose needs are being assessed in any case where it considers that the needs of the individual concerned require it to do so". Such consultation may take place before, or during, the assessment. According to the statutory guidance:

> "A person with relevant expertise can be considered as somebody who, either through training or experience, has acquired knowledge or skill of the particular condition or circumstance. Such a person may be a doctor or health professional, or an expert from the voluntary sector, but there is no obligation for the local authority to source an expert from an outside body if the expertise is available in house."[1]

The statutory guidance discusses the training of assessors in paras 6.85 to 6.90. It underlines that staff must have the required skills, knowledge and competence no matter how the assessment is carried out, including first contact, and any assessment over the phone or online, or self-assessments where the person carrying out the assurance.[2] In relation to people with autism, the statutory guidance refers to *Think Autism 2014*, the April 2014 update to *Fulfilling and Rewarding Lives*, the strategy for adults with autism in England (2010)— see 1–771 above. It advises that Think Autism 2014 should be read with the statutory guidance, and that:

> "The Care Act strengthens [Think Autism 2014] in relation to assessors having specialised training to assess an adult with autism. The Act places a legal requirement on local authorities that all assessors must have the skills, knowledge and competence to carry out the assessment in question. Where an assessor does not have experience in a particular condition (such as autism, learning disabilities, mental health needs or other conditions), they must consult someone with relevant experience. This is so that the person being assessed is involved throughout the process and their needs, outcomes and the impact of needs on their well-being are all accurately identified."[3]

Local authorities must ensure that assessors undergo "regular, up-to-date training on an ongoing basis". They must also have the skills and knowledge to carry out assessments that relate to specific conditions or circumstances requiring expert insight, "for example when assessing an individual who has autism".

The guidance provides that the support of an expert may be sought "when assessing particularly complex or multiple needs". The need for such input should be considered "on a case-by-case basis, taking into account the nature of the needs of the individual, and the skills of those carrying out the assessment". In addition, a person with the relevant expertise "must" be consulted if the assessor does not have the necessary knowledge of a particular condition or circumstance.[4] It goes on to explain:

> "A person with relevant expertise can be considered as somebody who, either through training or experience, has acquired knowledge or skill of the particular condition or circumstance. Such a person may be a doctor or health professional, or an expert from the voluntary sector, but there is no obligation for the local authority to source an expert from an outside body if the expertise is available in house."[5]

---

[1] Department of Health, *Care and Support Statutory Guidance* (2014), para.6.88.
[2] Department of Health, *Care and Support Statutory Guidance* (2014), para.6.85.
[3] Department of Health, *Care and Support Statutory Guidance* (2014), para.6.90.
[4] Department of Health, *Care and Support Statutory Guidance* (2014), paras 6.87 to 6.88.
[5] Department of Health, *Care and Support Statutory Guidance* (2014), para.6.88.

Requirement for specialist expertise – deafblind individuals

A1–193   **6.**—(1) An assessment which relates to an individual who is deafblind must be carried out by a person who has specific training and expertise relating to individuals who are deafblind.

(2) A local authority must facilitate the carrying out of the assessment by providing any person carrying out such an assessment with any relevant information which it may have—

    (a) about the individual whose needs are being assessed; and

    (b) in the case of—

        (i) a carer's assessment, about the adult needing care;

        (ii) a child's carer's assessment, about the child needing care;

        (iii) a young carer's assessment, about the adult needing care.

(3) In this regulation, an individual is "deafblind" if the individual has combined sight and hearing impairment which causes difficulties with communication, access to information and mobility.

GENERAL NOTE

Any assessment which relates to a deafblind person must be carried out by a person who has specific training and expertise relating to individuals who are deafblind (defined as an individual who has "combined sight and hearing impairment which causes difficulties with communication, access to information and mobility"). The local authority must provide the person carrying out the assessment with any relevant information which it may have about the individual whose needs are being assessed, and (in the case of a carer's, child carer's or young carer's assessment) information about the adult or child needing carer.

The statutory guidance discusses the training and expertise of assessors at paras 6.85 to 6.97 (including those assessing deafblind people).

Amongst other matters it provides that:

- local authorities must ensure that an expert is involved in an assessment of adults, including where a deafblind person is carrying out a supported self-assessment (para 6.91);
- a person should be considered as deafblind "even if when taken separately each sensory impairment appears relatively mild" (para 6.92);
- the specialist assessment must be carried out by an assessor or team that has training of at least QCF or OCN level 3, or above where the person has higher or more complex needs (para 6.92);
- deafblindness is a dual sensory condition which requires a knowledge and understanding of the two respective conditions in unison, which cannot be replicated by taking an individual approach to both senses (para 6.94);
- the person ensuring that the self-assessment is complete and accurate must have specific training and expertise that will enable "maximum possible communication and an accurate and complete assessment" (para 6.95); and
- where necessary a qualified interpreter with training appropriate for the deafblind adult's communication should be used. A family member or carer should not normally be used, except for instance "where the adult's communication is idiosyncratic or personal to them and would only be understood by those close to them". This should only take place where the adult agrees or – if they lack capacity – where it is in their best interests (para 6.96).

In addition, the Social Care Institute for Excellence has produced a guide to assessments of deafblind people.[1] This is not statutory guidance but it has been produced with the approval of the Department of Health (see 1–770 above).

---

[1] Social Care Institute for Excellence, *Handout: People who are deafblind* (Oct 2014).

NHS Continuing Healthcare

7.—(1) Where it appears to a local authority carrying out a needs assessment that the **A1–194** individual to whom the assessment relates may be eligible for NHS continuing healthcare[1] , the local authority must refer the individual to the relevant body.

(2) Where it appears to a local authority carrying out a child's needs assessment that the child may, after becoming 18, be eligible for NHS continuing healthcare, the local authority must refer the individual to the relevant body.

(3) In performing its duties under this regulation, a local authority must have regard to the National Framework for NHS Continuing Healthcare and NHS-funded Nursing Care issued by the Secretary of State and dated 28 November 2012[2] .

(4) The "relevant body" means the National Health Service Commissioning Board[3] or a clinical commissioning group[4] as the case may be, which appears to the local authority to have responsibility for the individual by reason of regulation 20(2) of the National Health Service Commissioning Board and Clinical Commissioning Groups (Responsibilities and Standing Rules) Regulations 2012[5] .

GENERAL NOTE

Where a local authority is carrying out a needs assessment and it appears that a person may be eligible for NHS continuing health care, the authority must notify the relevant clinical commissioning group. In the case of a child's needs assessment, the same requirement applies where it appears that the child may, after becoming 18, be eligible for NHS continuing health care. In performing these duties, the local authority must have regard to the *National Framework for NHS Continuing Healthcare and NHS-funded Nursing Care.* NHS continuing health care is a package of care arranged and funded solely by health services where the individual has been found to have a 'primary health need'. It is discussed in more detail at para 1–251 above.

The duty to notify applies where it "appears" that the person "may be eligible" for NHS continuing health care. This is therefore a low threshold. The local authority does not have to be certain that the person is eligible and the person does not need to request the referral, formally or otherwise.

The statutory guidance states that:

"If, following an assessment for NHS CHC, a person is not found to be eligible for NHS CHC, the NHS may still have a responsibility to contribute to that person's health needs – either by directly commissioning services or by part-funding the package of support. Where a package of support is commissioned or funded by both an LA and a CCG, this is known as a 'joint package' of care. A joint package of care could include NHS-funded nursing care and other NHS services that are beyond the powers of a local authority to meet. The joint package could also involve the CCG and the local authority both contributing to the cost of the care package, or the CCG commissioning part of the package. Joint packages of care may be provided in a nursing or care home, or in a person's own home, and could be by way of joint personal budget."[6]

---

[1] See s.12(10) of the Act for the meaning of "NHS continuing healthcare".

[2] Copies available from the Department of Health, Richmond House, 79 Whitehall, London, SW1A 2NS and at http://www.gov.uk/government/uploads/system/uploads/attachment_data/file/213137/ National-Framework-for-NHS-CHC-NHSFNC-Nov-2012.pdf

[3] The National Health Service Commissioning Board is established by s.1H of the National Health Service Act 2006(c.41). Section 1H was inserted by s.9(1) of the Health and Social Care Act 2012 (c.7).

[4] A clinical commissioning group is a body established under s.14D of the National Health Service Act 2006. Section 14D was inserted by s.25(1) of the Health and Social Care Act 2012.

[5] S.I. 2012/2996.

[6] Department of Health, *Care and Support Statutory Guidance* (2014), para.6.82.

(2) In relation to a care provider who is an individual, the events specified for the purposes of regulation 3(2)(b) are—

    (a) the individual is adjudged bankrupt or sequestration of the individual's estate has been awarded under section 12 of the 1985 Act[1] ;

    (b) the nominee in relation to a proposal for a voluntary arrangement under Part 8 of the 1986 Act submits a report under section 256(1) or 256A(3) of that Act[2] which states that in the nominee's opinion a meeting of the creditors of the debtor (being the individual) should be summoned to consider the debtor's proposal;

    (c) a deed of arrangement made by or in respect of the affairs of the individual is registered in accordance with the Deeds of Arrangement Act 1914[3] ;

    (d) the individual executes a trust deed for the individual's creditors or enters into a composition contract.

(3) In relation to a care provider which is a partnership, the events specified for the purposes of regulation 3(2)(b) are—

    (a) an order for the winding up of the partnership is made by the court under any provision of the 1986 Act (as applied by an order under section 420 (insolvent partnerships) of that Act[4]);

    (b) sequestration is awarded on the estate of the partnership under section 12 of the 1985 Act or the partnership grants a trust deed for its creditors;

    (c) the nominee in relation to a proposal for a voluntary arrangement under Part 1 of the 1986 Act (as applied by an order under section 420 of that Act) submits a report to the court under section 2 (procedure where nominee is not the liquidator or administrator) of that Act which states that in the nominee's opinion meetings of the members of the partnership and the partnership's creditors should be summoned to consider the proposal;

    (d) the members of the partnership lodge with the court documents and statements in accordance with paragraph 7(1) of Schedule A1 (moratorium where directors propose voluntary arrangement) to the 1986 Act (as applied by an order under section 420 of that Act);

    (e) the partnership enters administration within the meaning of paragraph 1(2)(b) of Schedule B1 to the 1986 Act (as applied by an order under section 420 of that Act).

(4) In relation to any other care provider, the event specified for the purpose of regulation 3(2)(b) is an award of sequestration of the provider's estate made under section 12 of the 1985 Act or the Scottish Charitable Incorporated Organisations (Removal from Register and Dissolution) Regulations 2011[5] .

---

[1] Section 12 was amended by s.4(2) to (5) of the Bankruptcy (Scotland) Act 1995 (c.36), ss 14(8), 27(2) and (3) of, and para 10 of Sch.1 and para.1 of Sch.6 to, the Bankruptcy and Diligence etc. (Scotland) Act 2007 (asp 3) ("the 2007 Act") and s.9(3) of the Home Owner and Debtor Protection (Scotland) Act 2010 (asp 6) and is prospectively amended (from a date to be appointed) by s.11(4)(a) and 47 of, and para.9 of Sch.3 and para.1 of Sch.4 to, the Bankruptcy and Debt Advice (Scotland) Act 2014 (asp 11).

[2] Section 256 was amended by paras 1 and 6 of Sch.3 to the 2000 Act. There are other amendments to s.256 but none is relevant. Section 256A was inserted by paras 1 and 7 of Sch.3 to the 2000 Act. Subs.(3) was amended by paras 1 and 4 of Sch.19 to the Enterprise and Regulatory Reform Act 2013 (c.24) and by S.I. 2010/18.

[3] 1914 c.47.

[4] Section 420 was amended by paras 185 and 191 of Sch. 4 to the Constitutional Reform Act 2005 (c.4) and by S.I. 2002/1037. As to orders under s. 420, See S.I. 1994/2421 as amended by S.I. 1994/2421, 1996/1308, 2001/767, 2002/1308, 2005/1516 and 2006/622.

[5] S.S.I. 2011/237 as amended by S.S.I. 2013/362.

Specified duties

5.—(1) The duties specified for the purposes of regulation 3(1)(a) are the duties under **A1–214** sections 12 and 13A of the 1968 Act (social welfare services and residential accommodation with nursing)[1] in so far as the discharge of the duties would involve meeting the relevant adult's needs by taking the following steps—

(a) providing or securing the provision of accommodation; or

(b) providing, maintaining and making such arrangements as a local authority considers appropriate and adequate for the provision of suitable accommodation where nursing is provided for persons who are or appear to be in need of such accommodation by reason of infirmity, age, illness or mental disorder, dependency on drugs or alcohol or being substantially handicapped by any deformity or disability.

(2) In paragraph (1), "needs" means, in relation to an adult, the needs of the adult which were being met by the relevant care provider under relevant arrangements immediately before the provider became unable to continue to provide the care service in question as mentioned in regulation 3(2)(a).

THE CARE AND SUPPORT (PERSONAL BUDGET: EXCLUSION OF COSTS) REGULATIONS 2014 (SI 2014/2840)

The Secretary of State makes these Regulations in exercise of the powers conferred by **A1–215** sections 26(4) and 125(7) of the Care Act 2014[2] .

GENERAL NOTE

These regulations provide that the provision of intermediate care and reablement services, for which the local authority cannot or chooses not to make a charge, must be excluded from the personal budget. In other words, where either intermediate care or reablement is being provided to meet needs (i.e. under section 18, 19 or 20 of the Care Act) the cost of this must not be included in the personal budget. The statutory guidance discusses these provisions in paras. 11.15 to 11.21. Amongst other matters it explains that:

"Intermediate care/reablement should usually be provided as a free, universal service under section 2 of the Act, and therefore would not contribute to the personal budget amount. However, in some circumstances, a local authority may choose to combine either service with aspects of care and support to meet eligible or ongoing needs, which would require a personal budget to be developed. Removing the cost of provision of intermediate care/ reablement from the personal budget in these scenarios ensures that the allocation of both services is applied uniformly across all local authorities, and in future people progress towards the cap on care costs in a fair and consistent way." [3]

---

[1] 1968 c.49. Section 12 was amended by para.10(5) of Sch. 9 to the National Health Service and Community Care Act 1990 (c.19) ("the 1990 Act"), para.15(11) of Sch.4 to the Children (Scotland) Act 1995 (c.36), s.120(1) of the Immigration and Asylum Act 1999 (c.33) ("the 1999 Act") and s.3 of the Community Care and Health (Scotland) Act 2002 (asp 5) ("the CCHSA 2002"), and is prospectively amended (from a date to be appointed) by s.46(1) of the Nationality, Immigration and Asylum Act 2002 (c.41) ("the 2002 Act"). Section 13A was inserted by s.56 of the 1990 Act and amended by s.120(2) of the 1999 Act, s.72 of, and para.4(3) of Sch.3 to, the Regulation of Care (Scotland) Act 2001 (asp 8), para.1(4) of Sch. 2 to the CCHSA 2002 and by S.S.I. 2011/211, and is prospectively amended (from a date to be appointed) by s.46(2) of the 2002 Act.

[2] 2014 c.23. The powers to make regulations are exercisable by the Secretary of State; See s.125(1) of the Act ("the Act").

[3] Department of Health, *Care and Support Statutory Guidance* (2014), para.11.20.

as the dispute is between a local authority in England and a local authority in Wales, a local authority in Scotland or an HSC trust;

(b) section 50 (temporary duty on local authority in Wales) or 51 (temporary duty on Health and Social Care trust in Northern Ireland) of the Act to the case of an adult or a carer; or

(c) any of paragraphs 1 to 4 of Schedule 1 (cross-border placements) to the case of an adult;

"HSC trust" means Health and Social Care trust established under Article 10 of the Health and Personal Social Services (Northern Ireland) Order 1991 (Health and Social Care trusts)[1] ;

"lead authority" has the meaning given in regulation 3;

"needs" (except in regulation 5(3) and (5)) means—

(a) in respect of duties falling on local authorities in England, in relation to an adult, needs for care and support and in relation to a carer, needs for support;

(b) in respect of duties falling on local authorities in Scotland, needs which must be met under section 12 or 13A of the Social Work (Scotland) Act 1968 (social welfare services and residential accommodation with nursing)[2] or section 25 of the Mental Health (Care and Treatment) (Scotland) Act 2003 (care and support services etc.)[3] ;

(c) in respect of duties falling on local authorities in Wales, needs which must be met or are to be met under section 35, 36, 40 or 45 of the Social Services and Well-being (Wales) Act 2014 (meeting care and support needs of adults and support needs of a carer);

(d) in respect of duties falling on HSC trusts, needs which must be met under Article 15 of the Health and Personal Social Services (Northern Ireland) Order 1972 (general social welfare)[4] or which may be met under section 2 of the Carers and Direct Payments Act (Northern Ireland) 2002 (services for carers)[5] ;

"referred" in relation to a dispute, means referred for determination under paragraph 5 of Schedule 1 (dispute resolution), and "referral" is to be construed accordingly;

"Responsible Person" means the Secretary of State, the Welsh Ministers, the Scottish Ministers or the Northern Ireland Department;

"Schedule 1" means Schedule 1 to the Act.

---

[1] S.I. 1991/194 (N.I. 1). Article 10 has been amended by paras 1 and 13 of Sch. 6 to the Health and Social Care (Reform) Act (Northern Ireland) 2009 (c.1) ("the 2009 Act").

[2] 1968 c.49. Section 12 has been amended by para.10(5) of Schedule 9 to the National Health Service and Community Care Act 1990 (c.19) ("the 1990 Act"), para.15(11) of Schedule 4 to the Children (Scotland) Act 1995 (c.36), s.120(1) of the Immigration and Asylum Act 1999 (c.33) ("the 1999 Act") and s.3 of the Community Care and Health (Scotland) Act 2002 (asp 5) ("the CCHSA 2002"), and is prospectively amended (from a date to be appointed) by s.46(1) of the Nationality, Immigration and Asylum Act 2002 (c.41) ("the 2002 Act"). Section 13A was inserted by s.56 of the 1990 Act and amended by s.120(2) of the 1999 Act, s.72 of, and para.4(3) of Schedule 3 to, the Regulation of Care (Scotland) Act 2001 (asp 8) and para.1(4) of Schedule 2 to the CCHSA 2002, and by S.S.I. 2011/211, and is prospectively amended (from a date to be appointed) by s.46(2) of the 2002 Act.

[3] 2003 asp 13. Section 25 was amended by S.S.I. 2011/211.

[4] S.I. 1972/1265 (N.I. 14). Article 15 has been amended by s.121 of the 1999 Act, s.32 of, and paras 1 and 3 of Sch.6 to, the 2009 Act and by S.I. 1992/3204 (N.I. 20) and 1991/194 (N.I. 1); and is prospectively amended (from a date to be appointed) by s.46 of the 2002 Act.

[5] 2002 c.6. Section 2 has been amended by s.32 of, and para.1 of Sch.6 to, the 2009 Act.

(4) For the purposes of these Regulations, the following are Responsible Persons in relation to authorities—

    (a) in relation to a local authority in England, the Secretary of State;

    (b) in relation to a local authority in Wales, the Welsh Ministers;

    (c) in relation to a local authority in Scotland, the Scottish Ministers;

    (d) in relation to an HSC trust, the Northern Ireland Department.

(5) References in these Regulations to the date on which a dispute arises (however expressed) are references to the first date on which a written communication is sent by one of the authorities which are parties to the dispute to another of those authorities raising an issue about—

    (a) the application of any of sections 48 to 51 of the Act to the case of an adult or a carer; or

    (b) the application of any of paragraphs 1 to 4 of Schedule 1 to the case of an adult.

(6) In regulations 6 and 7 and for the purposes of the duty in regulation 8, a reference to the authorities which are parties to a dispute includes (where different) a reference to the lead authority in relation to that dispute, but this does not apply in relation to regulation 6(2)(a), (4)(a) or (5)(b) or to regulation 7(3)(h).

(7) In a case where a person is homeless, references in these Regulations (however expressed) to a person living in an area or a place are to be read as references to that person being physically present in that area or place.

Responsibility for determination of disputes

2.—(1) The Responsible Person which is to determine a dispute between authorities is to **A1–220** be determined as follows.

(2) Where the authorities which are parties to the dispute ("the authorities in dispute") include a local authority in England, and the adult or carer to whom the dispute relates ("the relevant person") is living in England as at the date the dispute is referred ("the relevant date"), the dispute is to be determined by the Secretary of State.

(3) Where the authorities in dispute include a local authority in Wales, and the relevant person is living in Wales as at the relevant date, the dispute is to be determined by the Welsh Ministers.

(4) Where the authorities in dispute include a local authority in Scotland, and the relevant person is living in Scotland as at the relevant date, the dispute is to be determined by the Scottish Ministers.

(5) Where the authorities in dispute include an HSC trust, and the relevant person is living in Northern Ireland as at the relevant date, the dispute is to be determined by the Northern Ireland Department.

(6) In any other case, the dispute is to be determined by whichever of the persons who are Responsible Persons in relation to the authorities in dispute, those persons agree is to do so.

GENERAL NOTE

Regulation 2 sets out who is to determine disputes. The effect of this is that where the adult or carer in question is living (or, in a case where the adult is homeless, is physically present) in the same territory as that in which an authority that is party to a dispute is situated, the dispute is to be determined by the "Responsible Person" in relation to that authority. In other cases, reg. 2(6) provides for the Responsible Persons in relation to the authorities in dispute, to agree between themselves as to who is to determine the dispute. The Responsible Person in relation to an authority is:

    • in relation to a local authority in England, the Secretary of State;

    • in relation to a local authority in Wales, the Welsh Ministers;

    • in relation to a local authority in Scotland, the Scottish Ministers; and

- in relation to a Health and Social Care trust in Northern Ireland, the Department of Health, Social Services and Public Safety in Northern Ireland.

Lead authority in relation to disputes

A1–221   **3.**—(1) For the purposes of these Regulations, the lead authority in relation to a dispute is the authority in whose area the adult or carer to whom the dispute relates is living as at the date on which the dispute arises.

(2) If that authority ("A") is not one of the authorities which are parties to the dispute—

- (a) those authorities must, without delay, bring to A's attention A's duties under these Regulations; and
- (b) A is not under those duties until the date on which A is aware of, or could reasonably be expected to have been aware of, those duties.

GENERAL NOTE

Regulation 3 sets out who is the "lead authority" for the purposes of duties imposed on such an authority under the regulations. The lead authority is the authority in whose area the relevant person is living (or physically present) as at the date on which the dispute arises.

Notification etc

A1–222   **4.**—(1) This regulation applies where a referral is—

- (a) made to a Responsible Person by authorities in accordance with regulation 8; or
- (b) sent to a Responsible Person by another Responsible Person pursuant to paragraph (4).

(2) In the following provisions of this regulation, the Responsible Person to whom the referral is made or sent is referred to as the "Relevant Responsible Person".

(3) If the dispute falls to be determined by the Relevant Responsible Person, that person must—

- (a) in determining the dispute, consult all persons who are Responsible Persons in relation to the authorities which are parties to the dispute ("the authorities in dispute"); and
- (b) prior to notifying those authorities of the outcome of the determination, notify those Responsible Persons of that outcome.

(4) If the dispute does not fall to be determined by the Relevant Responsible Person, that person must—

- (a) as soon as reasonably practicable after receiving the referral, send the referral to the Responsible Person by whom it appears to the Relevant Responsible Person the dispute falls to be determined or, in a case within regulation 2(6), to all persons who are Responsible Persons in relation to the authorities in dispute; and
- (b) notify the authorities in dispute of the action taken pursuant to sub-paragraph (a).

(5) For the purposes of this regulation, a reference to a dispute falling, or appearing to fall, to be determined by a Responsible Person (however expressed) is a reference to that dispute so falling, or appearing to fall, to be determined pursuant to regulation 2.

GENERAL NOTE

Regulation 4 imposes duties to be discharged by Responsible Persons upon receipt of a referral of a dispute. This includes a duty to consult other persons who are Responsible Persons in relation to the authorities in dispute when determining the dispute and to send on a referral to the appropriate Responsible Person where this has not been sent to the correct Responsible Person.

Responsibility for meeting needs pending determination of dispute etc

5.—(1) The authorities which are parties to a dispute must not allow the existence of the   **A1–223** dispute to prevent, delay, interrupt or otherwise adversely affect the meeting of the needs of the adult ("the adult") or carer to whom the dispute relates.

(2) This paragraph applies where a dispute concerns—

    (a) section 48(2), 50(3) or 51(3) of the Act (temporary duty to meet needs); or

    (b) any of paragraphs 1 to 4 of Schedule 1.

(3) Where paragraph (2) applies—

    (a) the authority which is meeting any needs for accommodation of the adult on the date on which the dispute arises must continue to meet those needs; and

    (b) if no authority is meeting those needs as at that date, the authority in whose area the adult is living as at that date must do so from that date.

(4) The duty under paragraph (3) must be discharged until the dispute in question is resolved.

(5) The meeting of an adult's needs by an authority pursuant to paragraph (3) does not affect the liability of that authority or any other authority for the meeting of those needs in respect of the period during which those needs are met.

GENERAL NOTE

Regulation 5 sets out duties on authorities in dispute in relation to the meeting of needs until a dispute is determined. This includes a requirement, in the case of certain disputes, for the authority in whose area the person is living (or physically present) to meet an adult's needs for accommodation in circumstances where no authority is meeting such needs as at the date on which the dispute arises. This does not affect the liability of that authority or any other authority for meeting those needs.

Steps to be taken prior to referral of a dispute including steps to try to resolve a dispute

6.—(1) The authorities which are parties to a dispute ("authorities in dispute") must,   **A1–224** prior to the referral of the dispute, take the steps specified in this regulation.

(2) As soon as reasonably practicable after the date on which the dispute arises—

    (a) the authority which is the lead authority in relation to the dispute must identify all the authorities which are parties to the dispute and co-ordinate discussions between those authorities in an attempt to resolve the dispute; and

    (b) each of the authorities in dispute must—

        (i) nominate an individual who will act as the point of contact within that authority in relation to the dispute; and

        (ii) provide the other authorities in dispute with the contact details of that individual.

(3) The lead authority must—

    (a) co-ordinate the discharge, by the authorities in dispute, of their duties under this regulation;

    (b) take steps to obtain, from the other authorities in dispute, information which may be relevant to the determination of the dispute;

    (c) disclose that information to the other authorities in dispute (if any); and

    (d) disclose to the other authorities in dispute any information the lead authority itself holds that may help to resolve the dispute.

(4) The authorities in dispute must—

    (a) take all reasonable steps to resolve the dispute between themselves; and

    (b) co-operate with each other in the discharge of their duties under this regulation.

(5) Each of the authorities in dispute must—

    (a) engage in a constructive dialogue with the other authorities in dispute, with a view to bringing about the speedy resolution of the dispute;

    (b) comply, without delay, with any reasonable request for relevant information made by the lead authority; and

    (c) keep the other authorities in dispute informed of information which appears to it to be relevant to the determination of the dispute.

(6) The lead authority in relation to the dispute must provide to the adult or carer to whom the dispute relates ("the relevant person"), or to the relevant person's representatives, such information as appears to it to be appropriate about progress in resolving the dispute.

GENERAL NOTE

Regulation 6 sets out steps that authorities in dispute have to take before referring a dispute for determination.

Contents of referral etc

A1–225   **7.**—(1) Where a referral is made in accordance with regulation 8, the authority which is the lead authority in relation to the dispute which is the subject of the referral, must send a copy of the referral to all persons who are Responsible Persons in relation to the authorities which are parties to the dispute.

(2) Subject to paragraphs (8) and (9), the referral must include the following documents—

    (a) a letter signed by the lead authority stating that the dispute is being referred and identifying the provision of the Act, the application of which the dispute is about;

    (b) a statement of facts signed by each of the authorities which are parties to the dispute ("the authorities in dispute") which includes the information specified in paragraph (3); and

    (c) copies of all correspondence between the authorities in dispute which relates to the dispute.

(3) The information referred to in paragraph (2)(b) is—

    (a) an explanation of the nature of the dispute;

    (b) a chronology of the events leading up to the referral of the dispute, including the date on which the dispute arose;

    (c) details of the needs of the adult ("the relevant adult") or carer ("the relevant carer") to whom the dispute relates since the beginning of the period to which the dispute relates;

    (d) a statement as to which authority has met those needs since then, how those needs have been met and the statutory provisions under which they have been met;

    (e) a statement as to any other steps taken by the authorities in dispute in relation to the relevant adult or the relevant carer and which may be relevant to the dispute;

    (f) details of the relevant adult's place of residence, and of any former places of residence which are relevant to the dispute;

    (g) in a case where the relevant adult's capacity to decide where to live is relevant to the dispute, either—

        (i) a statement that the authorities in dispute agree that the adult has, or lacks, such capacity; or

        (ii) information which appears to any of the authorities in dispute to be relevant to the question of whether the adult has, or lacks such capacity;

(h) details of the steps that the authorities in dispute have taken to resolve the dispute between themselves; and

(i) any other information which appears to any of the authorities in dispute to be relevant to the determination of the dispute.

(4) The authorities in dispute may submit legal arguments they are relying on in relation to the dispute provided that this is done within 14 days of the date on which the documents referred to in paragraph (2) are sent.

(5) If an authority submits legal arguments, it must—

(a) send a copy of those arguments to the other authorities in dispute; and

(b) provide evidence to the Responsible Person determining the dispute that it has done so.

(6) If the Responsible Person determining the dispute asks any of the authorities in dispute to provide further information, that authority must comply without delay.

(7) For the purposes of this regulation—

(a) a reference to lacking capacity (however expressed) is a reference to—

(i) lacking capacity within the meaning of section 2 of the Mental Capacity Act 2005[1] ;

(ii) being incapable within the meaning of section 1 of the Adults with Incapacity (Scotland) Act 2000[2] ; or

(iii) being incapable by reason of mental disorder within the meaning of Article 3(1) of the Mental Health (Northern Ireland) Order 1986[3] ;

(b) a reference to having capacity (however expressed) is a reference to not lacking capacity.

(8) Where the dispute is solely about the application of section 49(3)(c), 50(4)(c) or 51(4)(c) of the Act (recovery of costs), paragraph (3) is to be read as if sub-paragraphs (e), (f) and (g) were omitted and as if after sub-paragraph (i) there was inserted—

"(j) information as to the costs being sought to be recovered and a breakdown of those costs.".

(9) Where the dispute is solely about the application of section 49(3)(a) or (b), 50(4)(a) or (b) or 51(4)(a) or (b) of the Act (duty to co-operate), paragraph (3) is to be read as if sub-paragraphs (c) to (g) were omitted.

GENERAL NOTE

Regulation 7 requires the lead authority to send a copy of the referral of a dispute to relevant Responsible Persons and sets out what must or may be included with a referral. The documents to be included are a letter from the lead authority, a statement of facts and copies of relevant correspondence. The authorities may also submit supporting legal arguments. Where a dispute solely concerns the recovery of costs or a duty to co-operate, paras (8) and (9) omit the requirement to submit certain information and, in the case of a dispute solely concerning the recovery of costs, include a requirement to submit information concerning the costs being sought to be recovered.

Stage at which dispute must be referred

8. If the authorities which are parties to a dispute cannot resolve the dispute between **A1–226** themselves within four months of the date on which it arose, they must refer it for

---

[1] 2005 c.9.
[2] 2000 asp 4.
[3] S.I. 1986/595 (N.I. 4).

determination to the appropriate Responsible Person or, in a case within regulation 2(6), to all persons who are Responsible Persons in relation to the authorities in dispute.

GENERAL NOTE

Regulation 8 sets out a duty to refer disputes if they cannot be resolved within a specified time.

Transitory provision

A1–227   **9.** Pending the commencement of Part 4 of the Social Services and Well-being (Wales) Act 2014, in paragraph (c) of the definition of "needs" in regulation 1(3)—

    (a) the reference to section 35 or 36 of that Act is to be read as a reference to—

        (i) Part 3 of the National Assistance Act 1948[1] ,

        (ii) section 45 of the Health Services and Public Health Act 1968[2] ,

        (iii) section 117 of the Mental Health Act 1983[3] , or

        (iv) Schedule 15 to the National Health Service (Wales) Act 2006[4] ;

    (b) the reference to section 40 or 45 of that Act is to be read as a reference to section 2 of the Carers and Disabled Children Act 2000[5] .

GENERAL NOTE

Regulation 9 makes transitory provision in respect of the period before Part 4 of the Social Services and Well-being (Wales) Act 2014 is commenced

---

[1] 1948 c.29. Functions of a Minister of the Crown under the National Assistance Act 1948 were, so far as exercisable in relation to Wales, transferred to the National Assembly for Wales by Sch.1 to the National Assembly for Wales (Transfer of Functions) Order 1999 (S.I. 1999/672) ("the TOFO"). Functions of the National Assembly for Wales were transferred to the Welsh Ministers by s. 162 of, and para. 30 of Sch.11 to, the Government of Wales Act 2006 (c.32) ("the GOWA").

[2] 1968 c.46. Section 45 was amended by Sch.3 to the Local Authority Social Services Act 1970 (c.42), para.15 of Sch.23 to the Local Government Act 1972 (c.70), Pt 12 of Sch.1 to the Statute Law (Repeals) Act 1978 (c.45), Sch.2 to the Residential Homes Act 1980 (c.7), Pt 1 of Sch.10 to the Health and Social Services and Social Security Adjudications Act 1983 (c.41), s.42(7) of, and Sch.10 to, the 1990 Act, para 5(1) of Sch.10 to the Local Government (Wales) Act 1994 (c.19), s. 117(1) of the 1999 Act and paras 33 and 34 of Sch.1 to the National Health Service (Consequential Provisions) Act 2006 (c.43), and by S.I. 1968/1699, and is prospectively amended (from a date to be appointed) by s.45(6) of the Nationality, Immigration and Asylum Act 2002. S.45 has been repealed in relation to Scotland by s.14(4) of, and Pt 1 of Sch.9 to, the Social Work (Scotland) Act 1968 (c.49). The functions of the Secretary of State under s.45 were, so far as exercisable in relation to Wales, transferred to the National Assembly for Wales by Sch.1 to the TOFO. Functions of the National Assembly for Wales were transferred to the Welsh Ministers by s.162 of, and para.30 of Sch.11 to, the GOWA.

[3] 1983 c.20. Section 117 was amended by para.107 of Sch.1 to the Health Authorities Act 1995 (c.17), para.15 of Sch.1 to the Mental Health (Patients in the Community) Act 1995 (c.52), para. 12(17) of Sch. 4 to the Crime (Sentences) Act 1997 (c.43), paras 42 and 47 of Sch.2 to the National Health Service Reform and Health Care Professions Act 2002 (c.17), paras 1 and 24 of Sch.3 and Pt 5 of Sch.11 to the Mental Health Act 2007 (c.12), para. 3 of Sch.1 to the Health Act 2009 (c.21), s. 40 of the Health and Social Care Act 2012 (c.7) and by S.I. 2007/961. The functions of the Secretary of State under s.117 were, so far as exercisable in relation to Wales, transferred to the National Assembly for Wales by Sch.1 to the TOFO. Functions of the National Assembly for Wales were transferred to the Welsh Ministers by s.162 of, and para.30 of Sch.11 to, the GOWA.

[4] 2006 c.42.

[5] 2000 c.16.

THE CARE AND SUPPORT (SIGHT-IMPAIRED AND SEVERELY SIGHT-IMPAIRED ADULTS) REGULATIONS 2014 (SI 2014/2854)

The Secretary of State makes these Regulations in exercise of the power conferred by section 77(2) of the Care Act 2014[1] . **A1–228**

GENERAL NOTE

Section 77(1) of the Care Act sets out the requirement on local authorities to establish and maintain a register of adults who are ordinarily resident in their area and are sight-impaired or severely sight-impaired. Section 77(2) provides that regulations may describe persons who are to be treated as sight-impairment or severely sight-impairment for the purposes of compiling a local authority register. This provision has been given effect by the regulations below. Regulation 2 provides that persons certified as such by a consultant ophthalmologist are to be treated as sight-impaired or severely sight-impaired.

Citation, commencement and interpretation

1.—(1) These Regulations may be cited as the Care and Support (Sight-impaired and Severely **A1–229**
Sight-impaired Adults) Regulations 2014 and come into force immediately after section 77(1) of the Care Act 2014 comes fully into force.

(2) In these Regulations "consultant ophthalmologist" means a consultant or honorary consultant appointed in the medical speciality of ophthalmology, who is employed for the purposes of providing any service as part of the health service[2] .

Persons to be treated as sight-impaired or severely sight-impaired

2.—(1) For the purposes of section 77 of the Care Act 2014, a person is to be treated as **A1–230**
being sight-impaired if the person is certified as such by a consultant ophthalmologist.

(2) For the purposes of that section, a person is to be treated as being severely sight-impaired if the person is certified as such by a consultant ophthalmologist.

THE CARE AND SUPPORT (DIRECT PAYMENTS) REGULATIONS 2014 (SI 2014/2871)

The Secretary of State makes these Regulations in exercise of the powers conferred by **A1–231**
sections 33(1) and (2), 75(7), and 125(7) and (8) of the Care Act 2014[3] .

GENERAL NOTE

These regulations make provision for local authorities to meet a person's needs by the making of a direct payment in accordance with ss.31 to 33 of the Care Act. The regulations also make provision for making direct payments for the provision of after-care under s.117 of the Mental Health Act 1983.

In broad terms, s.31 provides that direct payments must be provided if:

- an adult requests direct payments and has capacity to do so – and if they have nominated someone to manage the payments on their behalf, that person agrees to receive the payments;
- the local authority is required to contribute towards meeting the adult's needs;
- the local authority is satisfied that the adult or nominated person is capable of managing direct payments – by themselves or with help;

---

[1] 2014 c. 23. The power to make regulations is exercisable by the Secretary of State - See s.125(1).
[2] This is defined in s.126 of the Care Act 2014.
[3] 2014 c.23. The powers to make regulations are exercisable by the Secretary of State, See s.125(1). Section 75(7) of the Act provides that a local authority may discharge its duty under s. 117 (after care) of the Mental Health Act 1983 (c.20) by making direct payments and that s.of, and para.1(10) of Sch.4 to, the Act modify s. 33(2) accordingly.

- the local authority is satisfied that making direct payments is an appropriate way to meet the needs in question; and
- the provision of direct payments is not prohibited by the regulations, and if the regulations give the authority discretion not to provide direct payments, it exercises that discretion.

Section 32 provides that direct payments must be provided if:
- an adult lacks capacity to request direct payments;
- a person authorised under the Mental Capacity Act or a suitable person requests direct payments to meet the adult's needs;
- the local authority is required to contribute towards meeting the adult's needs;
- the local authority is satisfied that the authorised person will act in the adult's best interests;
- the local authority is satisfied that the authorised person is capable of managing direct payments – by themselves or with help;
- the local authority is satisfied that making direct payments to the authorised person is an appropriate way to meet the needs in question; and
- the provision of direct payments is not prohibited by the regulations, and if the regulations give the authority discretion not to provide direct payments, it exercises that discretion.

Section 75(7) of the Care Act confirms that a local authority may discharge its duty under s.117 of the Mental Health Act by making direct payments.

The statutory guidance considers direct payments in Part 12.

Citation, commencement and interpretation

A1–232   **1.**—(1) These Regulations may be cited as the Care and Support (Direct Payments) Regulations 2014 and, subject to paragraph (2), come into force immediately after section 33(1) of the Care Act 2014 comes fully into force[1] .

(2) Regulation 11 comes into force immediately after section 33(1) of the Care Act 2014 comes fully into force unless section 75(7) of that Act comes fully into force later in which case it comes into force immediately after section 75(7) of that Act comes fully into force.

(3) In these Regulations—

"the Act" means the Care Act 2014;

"care home" has the meaning given by section 3 of the Care Standards Act 2000[2] .

Cases where a local authority must not meet needs by making a direct payment

A1–233   **2.** A local authority[3] must not meet needs by making a direct payment[4] if the adult[5] whose needs are to be met is a person to whom Schedule 1 applies.

GENERAL NOTE

Regulation 2 prohibits a local authority from meeting needs by making a direct payment in the case of a person to whom Sch.1 applies. In general terms, this sets out that direct payments cannot be made to people subject to a court order for a drug or alcohol treatment program or similar schemes.

---

[1] Section 33(1) was commenced for the purpose of making regulations by S.I. 2014/2473.

[2] 2000 c.14. Section 3 was amended by the Health and Social Care Act 2008 (c.14), Sch.5(1), para.4(2) and (3).

[3] See s.1(4) of the Act as to the meaning of "local authority"; the definition is limited to local authorities in England.

[4] Sections 31(3) and 32(3) interpret the expression "direct payment".

[5] See s.2(8) for the meaning of "adult".

Conditions which must apply to the making of direct payments

3.—(1) Direct payments must be made subject to the condition that they must not be used **A1–234** to pay any person mentioned in paragraph (3) to meet the needs of the adult in respect of whose needs the direct payment is made.

(2) Except that, if the local authority considers it is necessary to do so, direct payments may be used to pay a person mentioned in paragraph (3)—

    (a) to meet the care needs of the adult; or

    (b) to provide administrative and management support or services for the purpose of enabling a person to whom the direct payments are made to—

        (i) comply with legal obligations arising from the making of and use of the direct payment, or

        (ii) monitor the receipt and expenditure of the direct payment.

(3) The persons referred to in paragraph (1) are—

    (a) the spouse or civil partner of the adult;

    (b) a person who lives with the adult as if their spouse or civil partner;

    (c) a person living in the same household as the adult who is the adult's—

        (i) parent or parent-in-law,

        (ii) son or daughter,

        (iii) son-in-law or daughter-in-law,

        (iv) stepson or stepdaughter,

        (v) brother or sister,

        (vi) aunt or uncle, or

        (vii) grandparent;

    (d) the spouse or civil partner of any person specified in sub-paragraph (c) who lives in the same household as the adult; and

    (e) a person who lives with any person specified in sub-paragraph (c) as if that person's spouse or civil partner.

(4) A direct payment made under section 32 must be made subject to the condition that the authorised person[1] must—

    (a) notify the local authority if the authorised person reasonably believes that the adult no longer lacks the capacity to request the making of direct payments; and

    (b) if paragraph (5) applies, obtain—

        (i) an enhanced criminal record certificate issued under section 113B (enhanced criminal record certificate) of the Police Act 1997[2] , or

        (ii) verification that a satisfactory certificate of that type under that Act has been obtained, in respect of any person from whom a service in respect of which a direct payment is made is secured.

(5) This paragraph applies if the authorised person is—

    (a) a body corporate;

    (b) an unincorporated body of persons;

    (c) an individual who is not a person mentioned in paragraph (3); or

---

[1] See s.32(4) of the Act for the meaning of "authorised person".

[2] 1997 c.50; s.113B was inserted by s.163(2) of the Serious Organised Crime and Police Act 2005 (c.15) and was amended by the Safeguarding Vulnerable Groups Act 2006 (c.47), Sch.9, para.14(1) and (3); the Armed Forces Act 2006 (c.52), Sch.16, para.149; the Protection of Vulnerable Groups (Scotland) Act 2007 (asp 14), ss 79(1) and 80; the Policing and Crime Act 2009 (c.26), ss 97(2) and 112(2) and Sch. 8, Pt 8; the Criminal Justice and Licensing (Scotland) Act 2010 (asp 13), s.108(1) and (2); the Protection of Freedoms Act 2012 (c.9), ss 79(2)(b), 80(1), 82(1), 82(2) and (3) and Sch. 9, paras 35 and 37 and Sch. 10, Pts 5 and 6; the Crime and Courts Act 2013 (c.22), Sch. 8, Pt 2, paras 55 and 60; and by S.I. 2009/203, S.I. 2010/1146 and 2012/3006.

(d) an individual who is not a friend of the adult who is involved in the provision of care for the adult.

GENERAL NOTE

Regulation 3 sets out conditions which must be imposed in respect of direct payments. See also reg. 4 which gives local authorities discretion to impose certain conditions.

Paragraphs (1) to (3)

Direct payments cannot be used to pay for care from a close family member living in the same household. The exception is where the family member is providing administration/ management of the direct payment and the local authority determines this to be necessary. The policy intention behind this provision is to achieve the "right balance" between – on the one hand – making direct payments more attractive to people, providing people with greater flexibility and recognising the role that carers play in supporting people, and – on the other hand – concerns about safeguarding issues and the additional monitoring and accountability processes that would be required.[1] Paying family members is discussed in the statutory guidance at paras. 12.35 to 12.40.

Paragraphs (3) to (4)

In cases involving adults who lack capacity, the authorised person must notify the local authority if the adult no longer lacks capacity direct payments are being made. The termination of direct payments in such cases is covered in para 12.79 of the statutory guidance. In addition, the authorised person must apply for Disclosure and Barring Service checks for any person providing a service through the direct payment. This is discussed in para.12.50 of the statutory guidance.

Conditions which may apply to the making of direct payments

A1–235   4.—(1) A local authority may make a direct payment subject to other conditions.
(2) The conditions referred to in paragraph (1) may, in particular, require that—
    (a) the needs may not be met by a particular person;
    (b) the adult or authorised person (in the case of direct payments made under section 32 of the Act) must provide information to the authority.

(3) The conditions referred to in paragraph (1) may not require—
    (a) the needs of the adult to be met by any particular person; or
    (b) information to be provided to the authority—
        (i) more frequently and in more detail than is reasonably required by the authority for the purpose of enabling it to ascertain that—

(aa) making direct payments is an appropriate way to meet the needs in question, or
(bb) the conditions upon which it is made are complied with, or
        (ii) in a format which is not reasonably practicable for the adult or authorised person to provide.

GENERAL NOTE

This gives local authorities discretion to impose certain conditions. See also reg. 3 which sets out conditions which must be imposed.

Paragraph (1)

Local authorities may impose conditions in respect of direct payments.

---

[1] Department of Health, Response to the Consultation on draft Regulations and Guidance for Implementation of Part 1 of the Care Act 2014 (2014) Cm 8955, p 32.

Paragraph (2)

This provides two illustrative examples of conditions which may be imposed, namely that the payment cannot be used to secure services from a particular person or that information must be provided to the authority

Paragraph (3)

This sets some limitation to the setting of conditions. Such conditions cannot be used to require the person's needs to be met by a particular person. Also the provision of information cannot be required to be provided more frequently than is reasonably required or in a format that is not reasonably practical to provide.

The statutory guidance states that "there should be no blanket restrictions on cash withdrawals from pre-paid cards which could limit choice and control". Moreover, such cards should not be limited to an "online market that contains selected providers".[1]

The provision of information for the purpose of monitoring direct payments is considered in the statutory guidance at para.12.24 (see also para.1–346 above).

Steps which a local authority must take before making a direct payment under section 32 of the Act

5.—(1) A local authority must take the steps in paragraph (2) before it can be satisfied **A1–236** that condition 5 in section 32 of the Act is met (the local authority to be satisfied that making direct payments to the authorised person is an appropriate way to meet the needs in question).

(2) The steps referred to in paragraph (1) are that the authority must—

(a) so far as is reasonably practicable and appropriate, consult and take into account the views of—

(i) anyone named by the adult as someone to be consulted on the matter of whether direct payments should be made to the authorised person;

(ii) anyone engaged in caring for the adult or interested in the adult's welfare; and

(iii) any person who is authorised under the Mental Capacity Act 2005[2] to make decisions about the adult's needs for care and support; and

(b) so far as is reasonably ascertainable, consider—

(i) the adult's past and present wishes and feelings (and, in particular, any relevant written statement made by the adult when the adult had capacity[3] to request the local authority to meet his or her needs by making direct payments);

(ii) the beliefs and values that would be likely to influence the adult's decision if the adult had such capacity; and

(iii) other relevant factors that the adult would be likely to consider if he or she were able to do so; and

(c) obtain an enhanced criminal record certificate issued under section 113B of the Police Act 1997—

(i) in respect of the authorised person if he or she is an individual who is neither a person mentioned in regulation 3(3) nor a friend of the adult who is involved in the provision of care for the adult; and

(ii) (in a case where the authorised person is a body corporate or an unincorporated body of persons) in respect of the individual who will, on behalf of that body, have overall responsibility for the day to day management of the adult's direct payments.

---

[1] Department of Health, *Care and Support Statutory Guidance* (2014), para.12.56.

[2] 2005 c.9.

[3] Section 80(2) of the Act provides that a reference in Part 1 to having or lacking capacity is to be interpreted in accordance with the Mental Capacity Act 2005.

Regulation 5 sets out steps which a local authority must take in order to be satisfied that making direct payments under s.32 of the Care Act to an authorised person is an appropriate way to meet the needs in question.

Maximum periods of accommodation in a care home which may be secured by means of a direct payment

A1–237   **6.**—(1) A local authority may not make a direct payment for the provision of accommodation in a care home for an adult for a period of more than 4 consecutive weeks in any 12 month period, unless the local authority is one that is mentioned in Schedule 2.

(2) In calculating the period of 4 weeks mentioned in paragraph (1), a period of accommodation in a care home of less than 4 weeks shall be added to any succeeding period in such accommodation where the two periods are separated by a period of less than 4 weeks but not otherwise.

GENERAL NOTE
Direct payments cannot be used currently to pay for long-term care home placements. They can only be used to pay for short term care in a care home. Regulation 6 sets out the maximum periods of accommodation in a care home which may be secured by means of a direct payment. In general terms, it provides that direct payments can be made to fund a stay in a care home that does not exceed a period of four consecutive weeks in any 12 month period. Where the period between any two stays is less than four weeks, the two stays must be added together and the total should not exceed four weeks. The use of direct payments for short term stays in a care home is discussed at paras 12.41 to 12.45 of the statutory guidance.

Certain local authorities (listed in sch.2) are excluded from reg.6. These are local authorities that are involved in a Government pilot scheme to test the use of direct payments to pay for long-term care home placements. The Government's aim is to introduce this when the funding reforms are introduced (see para.1–344 above).

Review of direct payments

A1–238   **7.**—(1) A local authority must conduct a review for the purpose of ascertaining whether the making of direct payments is an appropriate way to meet the adult's needs—

> (a) at least once within the first 6 months of the direct payment being made and at intervals not exceeding 12 months thereafter;
>
> (b) if it considers that there has been a breach of a condition and that it may exercise its discretion under section 33(5) of the Act (power to terminate payments or require repayment) in respect of that breach;
>
> (c) in the case of a direct payment made to meet the needs of an adult under section 31 of the Act, whenever the local authority considers that—
>
>> (i) that adult no longer has the capacity to request it to meet any of those needs by the making of direct payments to the adult; or
>>
>> (ii) condition 3 (adult or nominated person is capable) or 4 (making direct payments to adult or nominated person is appropriate) of section 31 of the Act is no longer met;
>
> (d) in the case of a direct payment made to meet the needs of an adult under section 32 of the Act, whenever the local authority—
>
>> (i) considers that the adult no longer lacks the capacity to request the local authority to meet any of those needs by the making of direct payments to the adult; or
>>
>> (ii) is notified by any person of concerns that the direct payment may not have been used to meet the needs for which the payment was made; or
>>
>> (iii) considers, or is notified by any person of concerns, that condition 3, 4 or 5 of section 32 of the Act is no longer met.

(2) When complying with its duty in paragraph (1) the local authority must involve—
  (a) the adult;
  (b) any carer[1] that the adult has;
  (c) the authorised person to whom the direct payment is being made (in the case of direct payments made under section 32 of the Act);
  (d) any person who is providing administrative or management support or services in accordance with regulation 3(2)(b); and
  (e) either—
      (i) any person whom the adult asks the authority to involve, or
      (ii) if the adult lacks the capacity to do that—

(aa) the person who is authorised under the Mental Capacity Act 2005 to make decisions about the adult's needs for care and support (if different to the person in paragraph (c)), or

(bb) if there is no such person, any person who appears to the authority to be interested in the adult's welfare.

(3) The local authority must take all reasonable steps to reach agreement as to the outcome of the review with—
  (a) the adult concerned; or
  (b) if the adult lacks capacity to reach such agreement—
      (i) the person who is authorised under the Mental Capacity Act 2005 to make decisions about the adult's needs for care and support, or
      (ii) where there is no such person, any person who appears to the authority to be interested in the adult's welfare.

GENERAL NOTE

Regulation 7 makes provision for reviewing direct payments. The statutory guidance considers reviews at paras 12.61 to 12.66.

The monitoring of direct payments is discussed at para.1–346 above.

Paragraph (1)

The local authority is required to review the making of direct payments in certain circumstances. A review must be held within the first six months of making the first payment. The statutory guidance explains that this provision is intended for new direct payments made under the Care Act and not pre-existing ones.[2] Following this, reviews must take place no later than every 12 months. Reviews are also required to be held in other circumstances such as when a condition has been breached or if the person no longer has or lacks capacity to request direct payments.

Paragraph (2)

In broad terms, when reviewing direct payments the local authority must involve:
  • the adult;
  • any carer;
  • the authorised person (in the case of direct payments made under s.32 of the Care Act);
  • a family member providing administrative or management support or services (under reg. 3(2)(b); and
  • any person whom the adult asks the authority to involve, or if the adult lacks the capacity, a person authorised under the Mental Capacity Act 2005 or if there is no such person, any person interested in the adult's welfare.

The meaning of "involve" is considered at paras. 1–104 to 1–105 above.

---

[1] See s.10(3) of the Act as to the meaning of "carer".
[2] Department of Health, *Care and Support Statutory Guidance* (2014), para.12.61.

Paragraph (3)

The local authority must take reasonable steps to reach agreement as to the outcome of the review with the adult concerned, or if the adult lacks the capacity, a person authorised under the Mental Capacity Act 2005 or if there is no such person, any person interested in the adult's welfare.

Making of direct payments for an adult who no longer has capacity to request the making of direct payments

A1–239   **8.**—(1) For the purpose of ascertaining whether section 33(4) (termination of direct payments) of the Act applies, an adult who lacks capacity to request the making of direct payments may nonetheless be regarded by a local authority as having capacity to do so in the circumstances in paragraph (2).

(2) The circumstances are that—

(a) the authority is satisfied that the adult's lack of capacity to make the request is temporary; and

(b) another person who appears to the authority to be capable of managing a direct payment is prepared to accept and manage such payments on behalf of the adult during the period of the adult's incapacity.

GENERAL NOTE

Section 33(4) of the Care Act requires local authorities to stop making direct payments if any of the conditions in ss.31 or 32 are no longer met. This includes where a person who has capacity to request direct payments subsequently loses their capacity (s.31(4)(a)). Regulation 8 provides that if the loss of capacity is temporary, the local authority can continue payments if there is someone who is suitable and willing to manage the payments on the person's behalf. This provision is considered in paras 12.76 to 12.77 of the statutory guidance.

Regulation 9 covers cases where the local authority has reason to believe that someone who had lacked capacity to consent to direct payments subsequently gains capacity.

Making of direct payments for an adult who no longer lacks capacity to request the making of direct payments

A1–240   **9.**—(1) For the purpose of ascertaining whether section 32(1)(b) of the Act ceases to apply, an adult who no longer lacks capacity to request the making of direct payments may nonetheless be regarded by a local authority as lacking capacity to do so in the circumstances in paragraph (2).

(2) The circumstances are that—

(a) the authority is satisfied that the adult's capacity to request the authority to meet the needs to which the adult's personal budget[1] relates by making a direct payment is temporary; and

(b) the direct payments made during the period that the adult has the capacity to make such a request are made subject to an additional condition that the authorised person shall allow the adult to manage the direct payments themselves for any period in respect of which the authority is satisfied that the adult has the capacity to request the making of direct payments.

GENERAL NOTE

Section 32(1)(b) of the Care Act provides that in order for the s.32 duty to apply, the adult must lack capacity to request direct payments. Direct payments under s.32 must be discontinued if the person subsequently gains capacity. Regulation 9 provides that if the gaining of capacity is temporary, the local authority can continue payments to the authorised person if during that period the adult will mange the payments themselves. See also para.12.79 of the statutory guidance.

---

[1] See s.26 of the Act as to the meaning of "personal budget".

Regulation 8 covers cases where the local authority has reason to believe that someone who had capacity to consent to direct payments, subsequently loses capacity.

Harmonisation with payments made under other legislation

10. Where a direct payment is made for an adult for whom payments are made under section 12A (direct payments for health care) of the National Health Service Act 2006[1] ("the 2006 Act"), the local authority must take reasonable steps to co-ordinate the systems, processes and requirements which it applies or imposes in relation to the direct payment with those which apply in relation to the payments made under the 2006 Act with a view to minimising the administrative or other burdens which they place on the adult for whom, or the nominated or authorised person to whom, the local authority makes the direct payment. **A1–241**

GENERAL NOTE

Regulation 10 applies in cases where a direct payment is made to a person who is in receipt of direct payments under s.12A of the National Health Service Act 2006. It requires local authorities to take reasonable steps to co–ordinate its systems and processes in respect of the direct payment with those in place for the direct payment made under the 2006 Act. The statutory guidance states:

"The local authority must also have regard to where the direct payment can be integrated with other forms of public funding, such as personal health budget direct payments. Where this is apparent, the local authority should take steps to work with partners to combine the payments, as long as the person and all parties agree. For example, the local authority could agree with the NHS that the social care and health direct payments are combined and that the monitoring is performed solely by one organisation, reporting to the other as appropriate. This will avoid the person having multiple bank accounts, and having to supply similar information to public bodies to account for direct payment spend, while allowing both bodies to meet their statutory responsibilities."[2]

It goes on to state that:

"In circumstances where it is in the person's interest to combine the plan and budget with another form of state support (such as personal health budgets), and the person agrees that plans should be combined, the local authority should give consideration to whether the person is receiving direct payments from partner organisations, such as the NHS. If so, attempts should be made to harmonise the direct payments so that the person does not have multiple payments each with their own monitoring regime. For example, the local authority could work with the NHS partner to agree on a 'lead organisation' that oversees the overall budget and monitors the direct payments to ensure they are being to meet both health and care needs, while still allowing both bodies to satisfy themselves of their statutory responsibilities."[3]

Direct payments in respect of after-care under the Mental Health Act 1983

11.—(1) In respect of a direct payment to discharge the duty of a local authority under section 117 (after-care) of the 1983 Act[4] , these Regulations apply with the following modifications— **A1–242**

---

[1] 2006 c.41; s.12A was inserted by the Health Act 2009 (c.21), s.11 and amended by the Health and Social Care Act 2012 (c.7), Sch.4, para.10 and S.I. 2013/1563.

[2] Department of Health, *Care and Support Statutory Guidance* (2014), para.12.34.

[3] Department of Health, *Care and Support Statutory Guidance* (2014), para.12.60.

[4] 1983 c.20; s.117 was amended by the Health Authorities Act 1995 (c.17) Sch.1, paras 107(1) and (8)(b); the Mental Health (Patients in the Community) Act 1995 (c.52), Sch.1, para.15; the Crime (Sentences) Act 1997 (c.43), Sch.4, para.12(17); the National Health Service Reform and Health Care Professions Act 2002 (c.17), Sch. 2, paras 42 and 47; the Mental Health Act 2007 (c.12), Sch.3, paras 1 and 24 and Sch. 11, Part 5; the Health Act 2009 (c.21), Sch. 1, para. 3; the Health and Social Care Act 2012 (c.7), s. 40(1) to (4); and by S.I. 2007/961and is prosectively amended by s.75 of the Act.

  (a) in regulation 2 for "meet needs" substitute "discharge its duty under section 117 of the 1983 Act";

  (b) in regulation 3—

    (i) in paragraph (1), for "meet the needs of the adult in respect of whose needs the direct payment is made" substitute "provide after-care services to the adult to discharge the duty under section 117 of the 1983 Act", and

    (ii) in paragraph (2)(a), for "meet the care needs of the adult" substitute "provide after-care services to the adult to discharge the duty under section 117 of the 1983 Act";

  (c) in regulation 4—

    (i) in paragraph (2)(a), for "needs may not be met" substitute "after-care services may not be provided",

    (ii) in paragraph (3)(a), for "needs of the adult to be met" substitute "after-care services to be provided", and

    (iii) in paragraph (3)(b)(i)(aa), for "meet the needs in question" substitute "discharge its duty under section 117 of the 1983 Act";

  (d) in regulation 5, in paragraph (2)(b)(i), for "meet his or her needs by making direct payments" substitute "make payments to the adult or a person nominated by the adult that are equivalent to the cost of providing or arranging for the provision of after-care services for the adult under section 117 of the 1983 Act";

  (e) in regulation 7—

    (i) in paragraph (1), for "meet the adult's needs" substitute "discharge its duty under section 117 of the 1983 Act",

    (ii) in paragraph (1)(c), for "to meet the needs of an adult under section 31 of the Act" substitute "discharge its duty under section 117 of the 1983 Act",

    (iii) in paragraph (1)(c)(i), for "meet any of those needs" substitute "make payments to the adult or a person nominated by the adult that are equivalent to the cost of providing or arranging for the provision of after-care services for the adult under section 117 of the 1983 Act",

    (iv) in paragraph (1)(d), for "to meet the needs of an adult under section 32 of the Act" substitute "under section 32 of the Act to discharge its duty under section 117 of the 1983 Act",

    (v) in paragraph (1)(d)(i), for "meet any of those needs" substitute "make payments to the adult or a person nominated by the adult that are equivalent to the cost of providing or arranging for the provision of after-care services for the adult under section 117 of the 1983 Act",

    (vi) in paragraph (1)(d)(ii), for "to meet the needs" substitute "only to pay for arrangements under which after-care services for the adult are provided under section 117 of the 1983 Act",

    (vii) in paragraph (2)(e)(ii)(aa) and (3)(b)(i), for "the adult's needs for care and support" substitute "the provision of after-care services under section 117 of the 1983 Act"; and

  (f) in regulation 9, in paragraph (2), for "meet the needs to which the adult's personal budget relates" substitute "make payments to the adult or a person nominated by the adult that are equivalent to the cost of providing or arranging for the provision of after-care services for the adult under section 117 of the 1983 Act".

(2) In this regulation "the 1983 Act" means the Mental Health Act 1983.

GENERAL NOTE

Regulation 11 applies these regulations with modifications to cases where a direct payment is made under s.117 of the Mental Health Act 1983.

SCHEDULE 1   Regulation 2

Adults Whose Needs the Local Authority Must Not Meet By Making Direct Payments **A1–243**
This Schedule applies to a person if they are—

    (a) subject to a drug rehabilitation requirement, as defined by section 209 (drug rehabilitation requirement) of the Criminal Justice Act 2003 ("the 2003 Act")[1], specified in a community order (as defined by section 177 (community orders) of that Act[2], or a suspended sentence order (as defined by section 189[3] of that Act);

    (b) subject to an alcohol treatment requirement, as defined by section 212 of the Criminal Justice Act 2003[4], specified in a community order (as defined by section 177 of that Act), or a suspended sentence order (as defined by section 189 of that Act);

    (c) released from prison on licence—

        (i) under Chapter 6 of Part 12 (sentencing: release, licenses and recall) of the 2003 Act[5] or Chapter 2 of Part 2 (effect of custodial sentences: life sentences) of the Crime (Sentences) Act 1997 ("the 1997 Act")[6], subject to a non standard licence condition requiring the offender to undertake offending behaviour work to address drug or alcohol related behaviour; or

        (ii) subject to a drug testing requirement under section 64 (as amended by the Offender Rehabilitation Act 2014) (release on licence etc: drug testing)[7] or a drug appointment requirement under section 64A (release on licence etc: drug appointment) of the Criminal Justice and Courts Services Act 2000[8];

---

[1] 2003 c.44; s.209 was amended by the Criminal Justice and Immigration Act 2008 (c.4) ("the 2008 Act"), Sch.4 paras 71 and 88 and the Legal Aid, Sentencing and Punishment of Offenders Act 2012 (c.10) ("the 2012 Act"), s.74(1).

[2] Section 177 was amended by the 2008 Act, Sch.4, paras 71 and 82; the 2012 Act, ss 66(1) and (2), 70(1), 72(1) and (2) and 76(2) and (3); the Crime and Courts Act 2013 (c.22), Sch.16, paras 1 ,2, 11 and 12.

[3] Section 189 was amended by the 2012 Act, ss.68(1) to (5) and S.I. 2005/643.

[4] Section 212 was amended by the 2012 Act, s.75(1).

[5] Section 245 was repealed by the 2012 Act, Sch.10, para.22. Section 246 was amended by the Armed Forces Act 2006 (c.52) ("the 2006 Act"), Sch.16, para. 221; the 2008 Act, s.24; the 2012 Act, ss.110 to 112, Sch.10, para.23, Sch.20, para.5 and Sch.14, para.7; Section 246A was inserted by the 2012 Act, s.125. Section 247 was amended by the 2008 Act, Sch.28(2), para.1 and the 2012 Act, Sch.17, para.3. Section 248 was amended by the 2012 Act, s.116. Section 149 was amended by the 2012 Act, Sch.10, para.24, Sch.14, para.8 and Sch.17, para.4. Section 250 was amended by the 2012 Act, ss.111 and 117, Sch.10, para.25, Sch.14, para.9, Sch.20, para.6; the Offender Management Act 2007 (c.21), s.28; the Domestic Violence Crime and Victims Act 2004 (c.28) Sch.6, para.5. Section 252 was amended by the 2006 Act, Sch.16, para.224 of the 2012 Act, Sch.10, para.27. Section 253 was amended by the 2012 Act, s.114 and Sch. 10, para.28 and S.I. 2008/912.

[6] 1997 c.43. Section 31 was amended by the Crime and Disorder Act 1998 (c.37), Sch.8, para.131 and Sch.10, para.1; the Criminal Justice and Courts Services Act 2000 (c.43), Sch.7, para.4(1); the 2003 Act, Sch.18, para.1, s.32, para.83 and Sch.37, para.1; the Children Act 2004 (c.31), Sch.5; the 2008 Act, s.28; S.I. 2005/886; and 2008/91. Section 31A was inserted by the 2003 Act, Sch.18, para.2 and amended by the 2003 Act, s.18, para.2; the 2006 Act, Sch.16, para.141; the 2012 Act, s.117. Section 32 was amended by the 2003 Act, s.32, para.84 and the 2008 Act, s.31. Sections 32A and 32B were inserted by the 2012 Act, s.119.

[7] Section 64 is prospectively amended by the Offender Rehabilitation Act 2014 (c.11), s.11(2), Sch.3, para.13 and the prohibition on a person subject to a condition under that s.does not apply until the date that the amendment comes into force.

[8] 2000 c.43. Section 64A is prospectively inserted by s.12 of the Offender Rehabilitation Act 2014 which comes into force on a date to be appointed.

(d) required to comply with a drug testing or a drug appointment requirement specified in a notice given under section 256AA (supervision after end of sentence of prisoners serving less than 2 years) of the 2003 Act[1] ;

(e) required to submit to treatment for their drug or alcohol dependency by virtue of a community rehabilitation order within the meaning of section 41 of the Powers of Criminal Courts (Sentencing) Act 2000[2] or a community punishment and rehabilitation order within the meaning of section 51 of that Act;

(f) subject to a drug treatment and testing order imposed under section 52 of the Powers of Criminal Courts (Sentencing) Act 2000[3] ;

(g) required to submit to treatment for their drug or alcohol dependency by virtue of a requirement of a community payback or probation order within the meaning of sections 227 to 230 of the Criminal Procedure (Scotland) Act 1995[4] or subject to a drug treatment and testing order within the meaning of section 234B[5] of that Act; or

(h) released on licence under section 22 or section 26 of the Prisons (Scotland) Act 1989 (release on licence etc)[6] or under section 1 (release of short-term, long-term and life prisoners) or 1AA (release of certain sexual offenders) of the Prisoners and Criminal Proceedings (Scotland) Act 1993(**15**) and subject to a condition that they submit to treatment for their drug or alcohol dependency.

SCHEDULE 2　　　　　　　　　**Regulation 6(1)**

A1–244 List Of Local Authorities Who Are Not Prohibited From Making A Direct Payment For The Purpose Of Securing Long Term Care In A Care Home

> Bristol City Council
> Cornwall Council
> [. . .]
> Gateshead Council
> Hertfordshire County Council
> Hull City Council
> Lincolnshire County Council
> London Borough of Enfield
> [. . .]
> London Borough of Redbridge
> [. . .]
> Milton Keynes Council

---

[1] Section 256AA is prospectively inserted by s.2 of the Offender Rehabilitation Act 2014.

[2] 2000 c.6. Sections 41 and 51 were repealed, with savings, by Schedule 37 to the 2003 Act.

[3] 1995 c.46. Sections 227A to 227ZN (community payback orders) were inserted by s.14 of the Criminal Justice and Licensing (Scotland) Act 2010 (asp 13) ("the 2010 Act"). Sections 228 to 230 were repealed, with savings, by Sch.2(1), para.17 of the 2010 Act.

[4] Section 234B was inserted by s.89 of the Crime and Disorder Act 1998 (c.37).

[5] 1989 c.45. Section 22 was amended by the Prisoners and Criminal Proceedings (Scotland) Act 1993 (c. 9), s.47(3), Sch.7, Pt 1; the Criminal Justice and Public Order Act 1994 (c.33), s.134(5); the Criminal Justice (Scotland) Act 2003 (asp 7), ss.27(2) and 34(2). It was modified by the Crime (Sentences) Act 1997 (c.43), Schedule 5, para.11 and S.I. 1995/910. Section 26 was repealed, with savings, by s.47(3), Schedule 7, Part 1 to the Prisoners and Criminal Proceedings (Scotland) Act 1993.

[6] 1993 c.9. Section 1 was amended by para.98 of Sch.8 to the Crime and Disorder Act 1998, s.1(2) of the Convention Rights (Compliance) (Scotland) Act 2001 (asp 7) and s.15(2) of the Management of Offenders etc (Scotland) Act 2005 (asp 14) ("MOSA"). Section 1AA was inserted by s.15(3) of MOSA.

Norfolk County Council
North Lincolnshire Council
Nottinghamshire County Council
Staffordshire County Council
Stockport Council
Surrey County Council

AMENDMENTS
The amendments to this regulation (omitting Dorset County Council, London Borough of Havering and Manchester City Council) were made by SI 2015/644 reg.6.

THE CARE AND SUPPORT (INDEPENDENT ADVOCACY SUPPORT) (NO. 2) REGULATIONS 2014 (SI 2014/2889)

The Secretary of State makes these Regulations in exercise of the powers conferred by sections 67(7) and 125(7) and (8) of the Care Act 2014[1] .   **A1–245**

GENERAL NOTE
Section 67 of the Care Act 2014 requires local authorities to arrange for an independent advocate to represent and support certain individuals who would otherwise experience significant difficulty in doing certain things such as understanding information. These regulations make provision in connection with the making of such arrangements. The statutory guidance discusses advocacy in ch.7. In addition, the Social Care Institute for Excellence has produced guidance on the independent advocacy requirements of the Act.[2] These documents are not statutory guidance but have been produced with the approval of the Department of Health (see 1–770 above).

Citation, commencement and interpretation
1.—(1) These Regulations may be cited as the Care and Support (Independent Advocacy   **A1–246** Support) (No. 2) Regulations 2014 and come into force immediately after section 67(2) of the Care Act 2014 comes into force.

(2) In these Regulations—

"the Act" means the Care Act 2014;

"assessment or planning function" means a function, in the exercise of which a local authority[3] is required by a relevant provision to involve an individual;

"relevant provision" means a provision listed in section 67(3) of the Act.

Requirements for a person to be an independent advocate
2.—(1) A local authority must not make arrangements for a person to be an independent   **A1–247** advocate[4] under section 67(2) of the Act unless the authority is satisfied that the person—
  (a) has appropriate experience;
  (b) has undertaken appropriate training;
  (c) is competent to represent and support the individual for the purpose of facilitating that individual's involvement in any assessment and planning function;
  (d) has integrity and is of good character; and

---

[1] 2014 c.23 ("the Act"). The powers to make regulations is exercisable by the Secretary of State - See s.125(1).
[2] Social Care Institute for Excellence, *Independent Advocacy Workbook* (October 2014) and Social Care Institute for Excellence, *Care Act 2014: Commissioning Independent Advocacy* (March 2014).
[3] See s.1(4) of the Act for the meaning of "local authority"; the definition is limited to local authorities in England.
[4] See s.67(2) of the Act for the meaning of "independent advocate".

(e) has arrangements in place to receive appropriate supervision.

(2) A local authority must not make arrangements for a person to be an independent advocate under section 67(2) of the Act where that person is engaged in providing care or treatment in a professional capacity, or for remuneration—

    (a) for the individual to whom representation and support are to be made available; or

    (b) for—

        (i) that individual's carer, where the individual is an adult with care and support needs; or

        (ii) the adult in respect of whom that individual is providing care, where the individual is a carer.

(3) The requirements that must be met for a person to be independent for the purposes of section 67(2) of the Act are that—

    (a) the local authority is satisfied that the person demonstrates the ability to act independently of the local authority; and

    (b) the person is not employed by, or otherwise working for, the local authority.

(4) Before deciding whether a person has integrity and is of good character as mentioned in paragraph (1)(d), the local authority must obtain, in respect of that person, an enhanced criminal record certificate issued under section 113B of the Police Act 1997[1] which includes—

    (a) where the individual to whom representation and support are being made available is under 18 years of age, suitability information relating to children (within the meaning of section 113BA of that Act);

    (b) where the individual to whom representation and support are being made available is 18 years of age or older, suitability information relating to vulnerable adults (within the meaning of section 113BB of that Act).

(5) Where a local authority has made arrangements with any other person for that person to carry out the assessment or planning function on the local authority's behalf, the references in paragraph (3)(a) and (b) to a local authority include a reference to that other person.

GENERAL NOTE

Regulation 2 makes provision regarding the requirements that a person must meet in order to be an independent advocate, including having appropriate training and being of good character. These requirements are discussed in paras 7.43 to 7.45 of the statutory guidance. The guidance includes a reference to the Advocacy Quality Performance Mark which has been developed by the National Development Team for Inclusion. Essentially this is a quality assurance scheme that sets a number of standards (in conjunction with a code of practice) that advocacy organisations must achieve. Membership of the scheme is voluntary, but may be used by commissioners of advocacy services as a guarantee of the quality of services provided. It was launched in 2008 and over 80 organisations have been awarded the Advocacy Quality Performance Mark.

---

[1] 1997 c.50. Section 113B was inserted by the Serious Organised Crime and Police Act 2005 (c.15), s.163(2) and ss 113BA and 113BB were inserted by the Safeguarding Vulnerable Groups Act 2006 (c.47), s.63(1) and Sch.9, para.14(4).

Matters to which a local authority must have regard in deciding whether an individual would experience substantial difficulty of the kind mentioned in section 67(4) of the Act

3. In deciding whether an individual would experience substantial difficulty of the kind **A1–248** mentioned in section 67(4) of the Act (difficulty in understanding information etc.), a local authority must have regard to—

    (a) any health condition the individual has;

    (b) any learning difficulty the individual has;

    (c) any disability the individual has;

    (d) the degree of complexity of the individual's circumstances, whether in relation to the individual's needs for care and support or otherwise;

    (e) where the assessment or planning function is the carrying out of an assessment, whether the individual has previously refused an assessment[1] ; and

    (f) whether the individual is experiencing, or at risk of, abuse or neglect.

GENERAL NOTE

Regulation 3 makes provision about matters to which a local authority must have regard when deciding whether a person would experience substantial difficulty in doing certain things as mentioned in s.67(4) of the Act.

Circumstances in which the exception in section 67(5) of the Act does not apply

4.—(1) The exception in section 67(5) of the Act does not apply in the circumstances **A1–249** specified in paragraphs (2) and (3).

(2) The circumstances specified in this paragraph are that—

    (a) the exercise of the assessment or planning function in relation to the individual is likely to result in an NHS body making arrangements for the provision to that individual of accommodation in—

        (i) a hospital for a period of 28 days or more; or

        (ii) a care home for a period of 8 weeks or more; and

    (b) the local authority is satisfied that it would be in the best interests of the individual to make arrangements in relation to that individual under section 67(2) of the Act.

(3) The circumstances specified in this paragraph are that—

    (a) there is disagreement on a material issue between the local authority and the person referred to in section 67(5) of the Act in the case of the individual; and

    (b) the local authority and that person agree that making arrangements under section 67(2) of the Act in relation to the individual would be in the best interests of that individual.

(4) In this regulation—

"care home" means a care home (within the meaning given in section 3 of the Care Standards Act 2000[2]) in respect of a which a person is registered under the Health and Social Care Act 2008[3] for the regulated activity of the provision of residential accommodation together with nursing or personal care;

"hospital" means—

    (a) any institution for the reception and treatment of persons suffering from illness;

    (b) any maternity home; or

---

[1] See ss 11, 28(7), 58(4), 60(3) and 63(4) of the Act.
[2] 2000 c.14.
[3] 2008 c.14.

(c) any institution for the reception and treatment of persons during convalescence or persons requiring medical rehabilitation;

"the individual" refers to the individual in relation to whom the duty under section 67(2) of the Act would apply but for the exception in section 67(5) of the Act;

"NHS body" means—

(a) the National Health Service Commissioning Board[1] ;
(b) a clinical commissioning group[2] ; or
(c) a NHS trust or foundation trust.

GENERAL NOTE

Regulation 4 sets out circumstances in which the exception in subs.(5) of the Act does not apply. In other words, it provides for cases where a person will be eligible for an advocate even though there is an appropriate person to support their involvement. The first is where the assessment or care planning function might result in a placement in NHS-funded provision in a hospital (for more than 28 days) or a care home (for more than eight weeks), and the local authority is satisfied it would be in the best interests of the person to arrange an advocate. The second is where there is a dispute between the appropriate person and the local authority, and the authority and the appropriate person consider it would be in the best interests of the individual to arrange an advocate.

Manner in which independent advocates are to carry out their functions

A1–250   **5.**—(1) Independent advocates must perform their functions in the manner specified in this regulation.

(2) An independent advocate must determine in all the circumstances how best to represent and support the individual in question but at all times must act with a view to promoting the individual's well-being[3] .

(3) In particular, an independent advocate must, to the extent that it is practicable and appropriate to do so—

(a) meet the individual in private; and
(b) provided that the condition in paragraph (4) is met, with a view to promoting the individual's well-being, consult with—
    (i) persons who are, or have been, engaged in providing care or treatment for the individual in a professional capacity or for remuneration; and
    (ii) other persons who may be in a position to comment on the individual's wishes, beliefs or values, for example family members, carers or friends of the individual.

(4) The condition referred to in paragraph (3)(b) is that—

(a) the individual has capacity, or is competent, to consent to the independent advocate consulting with a person mentioned in that sub-paragraph, and does so consent; or
(b) the individual does not have capacity, or is not competent, so to consent but the independent advocate is satisfied that consulting with a person mentioned in that sub-paragraph would be in the individual's best interests.

(5) In particular, an independent advocate must—

---

[1] The National Health Service Commissioning Board is established by s.1H of the National Health Service Act 2006 (c.41). Section 1H was inserted by s.9(1) of the Health and Social Care Act 2012 (c.7).

[2] A clinical commissioning group is a body established under s.14D of the National Health Service Act 2006. Section 14D was inserted by s.25(1) of the Health and Social Care Act 2012.

[3] See s.1(2) of the Act for the meaning of "well-being".

(a) assist the individual in—
    (i) understanding the function in the exercise of which the individual is involved;
    (ii) communicating the individual's views, wishes or feelings;
    (iii) understanding how the individual's care and support, or support, needs could be met by the local authority or otherwise;
    (iv) making decisions in respect of care and support arrangements;
    (v) challenging the local authority's decisions if the individual so wishes;
(b) so far as is practicable, ensure that the individual understands the local authority's duties under Part 1 of the Act and the individual's rights and obligations under that Part and any other rights and obligations of the individual which may be relevant to those obligations;
(c) make such representations as are necessary for the purpose of securing the individual's rights in relation to the exercise of the function; and
(d) where the independent advocate has concerns about the manner in which the assessment or planning function has been exercised or the outcomes arising from it, prepare a report for the local authority outlining those concerns.

(6) In particular, an independent advocate may examine and take copies of any relevant records[1] relating to the individual in circumstances where—
(a) the individual has capacity, or is competent, to consent to the records being made available to the independent advocate and does so consent; or
(b) the individual does not have capacity, or is not competent, to consent to the records being made available to the independent advocate but the independent advocate considers it is in the best interests of the individual.

(7) Where the individual does not have capacity, or is not competent, to communicate his or her views, wishes or feelings, the independent advocate must do so to the extent the independent advocate can ascertain them.

(8) Where the individual does not have capacity, or is not competent, to challenge a decision made in the exercise of the assessment or planning function, the independent advocate must challenge the decision if the independent advocate considers the decision to be inconsistent with the authority's general duty under section 1 of the Act (duty to promote the individual's well-being).

GENERAL NOTE

Regulation 5 makes provision about the manner in which independent advocates must perform their functions. These matters are discussed in paras 7.47 to 7.52 of the statutory guidance. The role of advocacy under the Care Act can be usefully compared and contrasted to that under the Mental Capacity Act. Independent Mental Capacity Advocacy is restricted to a relatively small number of defined decisions and its role limited to assisting decision-makers to reach best interests decisions (with the notable exception of s.39D advocacy). In contrast, Care Act advocacy has a wider and proactive role which is focused on helping people to understand and exercising their rights and challenge decision-makers. This goes much further than merely writing a report on the person's best interests (which may not necessarily be consistent with the person's wishes and feelings). The statutory guidance therefore emphasises that this is a "responsible position", and sets out a clear expectation that the advocate must challenge decisions which do not promote the person's well-being (including where the person lacks capacity).[2] The different advocacy roles are also discussed at paras 1–657 to 1–662, and the appropriate person role is discussed at para.1–670 above.

---

[1] See s.67(9) of the Act for the meaning of "relevant record".

[2] Department of Health, *Care and Support Statutory Guidance* (2014), paras 7.50 to 7.52.

Paragraph (3)

This requires the advocate to meet the person in private and in certain cases consult carers and family members.

Paragraph (4)

Where a person has capacity, the advocate should ask their consent to talk to their carer, family, friends, care or support worker and others who can provide information about their needs and wishes, their beliefs and values. Where a person does not have capacity to consent, then the advocate should consult the family and others as appropriate, but only where the advocate considers this is in the person's best interests. See para.7.47 of the statutory guidance.

Paragraph (5)

This sets out detailed provisions concerning the role of an advocate. It provides that an independent advocate must:

- assist the individual in understanding the relevant function, communicating their views, wishes or feelings, understanding how their needs could be met by the local authority or otherwise, making decisions in respect of care and support arrangements, and challenging the local authority's decisions if the individual so wishes;
- so far as is practicable, ensure that the individual understands the local authority's duties and the individual's rights and obligations under the Care Act;
- make such representations as are necessary for the purpose of securing the individual's rights; and
- where the advocate has concerns about the assessment or planning function, prepare a report for the local authority outlining those concerns.

The statutory guidance states that in respect of assisting a person to understand the assessment, care and support planning and review and safeguarding processes:

"This requires advocates to understand local authority policies, and other agencies roles, and processes, the available assessment tools, the planning options, and the options available at the review of a care or support plan and required and good practice in safeguarding enquiries and SARs. It may involve advocates spending considerable time with the individual, considering their communications needs, their wishes and feelings and their life story, and using all this to assist the person to be involved and where possible to make decisions." [1]

The guidance also refers to the need to ensure individuals understand their rights to a care plan that is "personalised" and that promotes "a person's rights to liberty and to family life". It also confirms that where a person cannot challenge the decision even with assistance, then the advocate should challenge it on their behalf.[2]

Paragraph (6)

The advocate may examine and take copies of records relating to the individual (if the person consents – or where they lack capacity or competence, it is in their best interests). This mirrors the powers of an Independent Mental Capacity Advocate.

See para.7.47 of the statutory guidance.

Paragraphs (6) and (7)

Where the individual lacks capacity or competence to make the relevant decision, the advocate must communicate the person's views, wishes or feelings, to the extent the advocate can ascertain them, and challenge the decision if the advocate considers the decision to

---

[1] Department of Health, *Care and Support Statutory Guidance* (2014), para.7.48.
[2] Department of Health, *Care and Support Statutory Guidance* (2014), para.7.48.

be inconsistent with the authority's general duty under section 1 to promote the individual's well-being.

Local authority's dealings with the independent advocate

6.—(1) Where a local authority has arranged for an independent advocate under section **A1–251** 67(2) of the Act, it must, in exercising any assessment or planning function—

    (a) take into account any representations the independent advocate makes on behalf of the individual in question in relation to its exercise of that function or the impact of such exercise on the individual; and

    (b) take reasonable steps to assist the independent advocate to represent and support the individual.

(2) A local authority must provide an independent advocate with a written response to any report prepared for the authority by the advocate under regulation 5(5)(d).

(3) A local authority may make reasonable requests for information in connection with the performance of an independent advocate's functions and the independent advocate must comply with such requests.

GENERAL NOTE

Regulation 6 makes provision about how a local authority is to work with an independent advocate. For instance, it is required to "take into account any representations" made by the advocate and "take reasonable steps to assist the independent advocate to represent and support the individual". The local authority is also required to provide an independent advocate with a written response to any report made under reg.5(5)(d). A local authority may make reasonable requests for information in connection with the performance of an independent advocate's functions and the advocate must comply with such requests. These provisions are also discussed in paras 7.53 to 7.58 of the statutory guidance. For example, the guidance states that local authorities:

". . . should let other agencies know that an advocate is supporting a person, facilitating access to the person and to the records, they should propose a reasonable timetable for the assessment and the care and support plan (taking into consideration the needs of the person), and where the advocate wishes to consult family, friends or paid staff, the timetable should allow this. They should keep the advocate informed of any developments and of the outcome of the assessment and the care and support plan."[1]

Combined assessments

7.—(1) This regulation applies where— **A1–252**

    (a) a local authority combines an assessment of an individual under Part 1 of the Act with an assessment under that Part that relates to another individual; and

    (b) that authority is required to make arrangements under section 67(2) of the Act in respect of each of those individuals.

(2) Subject to paragraph (3), each of those individuals may be represented and supported by the same independent advocate in circumstances where the authority is satisfied that there would be no conflict of interest on a material issue—

    (a) between the individuals; or

    (b) between the independent advocate and either of the individuals.

(3) The local authority must ensure that each of those individuals is represented and supported by different independent advocates if so requested by—

    (a) either of those individuals; or

---

[1] Department of Health, *Care and Support Statutory Guidance* (2014), para.7.56.

"a members' voluntary winding up" means a winding up where a statutory declaration has been made under section 89 of the 1986 Act or article 75 of the 1989 Order[1] ;

"a provider" means—

(a) a registered care provider[2] ,

(b) a person registered under Part 2 of the Care Standards Act 2000[3] in respect of an establishment or agency, or

(c) a person registered under Part 3 of the Health and Social Services (Quality, Improvement and Regulation) (Northern Ireland) Order 2003[4] in respect of an establishment or agency;

"the relevant amount" means the amount specified in section 123(1)(a) of the 1986 Act (definition of inability to pay debts) or article 103(1)(a) of the 1989 Order (definition of inability to pay debts; the statutory demand) as the case may be.

Business failure

A1–256   **2.**—(1) For the purposes of sections 48 and 50 to 52 of the Act—

(a) business failure has the meaning given in paragraphs (2) to (5); and

(b) a provider is to be treated as unable to carry on a regulated activity[5] or to carry on or manage an establishment or agency because of business failure if the provider's inability to do so follows business failure.

(2) Where a provider is not an individual, business failure means that, in respect of that provider—

(a) the appointment of an administrator (within the meaning given by paragraph 1(1) of Schedule B1 to the 1986 Act[6] or paragraph 2(1) of Schedule B1 to the 1989 Order[7]) takes effect;

(b) a receiver is appointed;

(c) an administrative receiver as defined in section 251 of the 1986 Act[8] or article 5 of the 1989 Order is appointed;

(d) a resolution for a voluntary winding up is passed other than in a members' voluntary winding up;

(e) a winding up order is made;

(f) an order by virtue of article 11 of the Insolvent Partnerships Order 1994 (joint bankruptcy petition by individual members of insolvent partnership)[9] is made;

(g) an order by virtue of article 11 of the Insolvent Partnerships Order (Northern Ireland) 1995 (joint bankruptcy petition by individual members of insolvent partnership)[10] is made;

---

[1] See S.I. 2001/1090 and 2012/3013 as to the application of s.89 to Limited Liability Partnerships and Charitable Incorporated Organisations respectively. As to the application of s.89 to co-operative and community benefit societies, See s.123 of the Co-operative and Community Benefit Societies Act 2014 (c.14), and as to the application of art.75 of the 1989 Order to industrial and provident societies in Northern Ireland, See s.64 of the Industrial and Provident Societies Act (Northern Ireland) 1969 (c.24), as substituted by S.I. 2009/1941.

[2] See s.48(1) of the Act for the meaning of "registered care provider".

[3] 2000 c.14.

[4] S.I. 2003/431 (N.I. 9).

[5] See s.8 of the Health and Social Care Act 2008 (c.14) for the meaning of "regulated activity".

[6] Schedule B1 was inserted by s.248(2) of, and s.16 to, the Enterprise Act 2002 (c.40). As to the application of Pt 2 of the 1986 Act to co-operative and community benefit societies, See S.I. 2014/229 as amended by S.I. 2014/1822.

[7] Schedule B1 was inserted by S.I. 2005/1455 (N.I. 10).

[8] There are amendments to s.251 but none is relevant.

[9] S.I. 1994/2421.

[10] S.R. (N.I.) 1995 No. 225.

    (h) the charity trustees of the provider become unable to pay their debts as they fall due;

    (i) every member of the partnership (in a case where the provider is a partnership) is adjudged bankrupt; or

  (j) a voluntary arrangement proposed for the purposes of Part 1 of the 1986 Act[1] or Part 2 of the 1989 Order has been approved under that Part of that Act or Order.

(3) In relation to a provider who is an individual, business failure means that—

    (a) the individual is adjudged bankrupt; or

    (b) a voluntary arrangement pursuant to Part 8 of the 1986 Act or Part 8 of the 1989 Order is proposed by or entered into by the individual.

(4) For the purposes of paragraph (2)(h), a person is a charity trustee of a provider if—

    (a) the provider is a charity that is unincorporated; and

    (b) the person is a trustee of that charity.

(5) For the purposes of paragraph (2)(h), the charity trustees of a provider are to be treated as becoming unable to pay their debts as they fall due if—

    (a) a creditor to whom the trustees are indebted in a sum exceeding the relevant amount then due has served on the trustees a written demand requiring the trustees to pay the sum so due and the trustees have for 3 weeks thereafter neglected to pay the sum or to secure or compound for it to the reasonable satisfaction of the creditor;

    (b) in England and Wales, execution or other process issued on a judgment, decree or order of a court in favour of a creditor of the trustees is returned unsatisfied in whole or in part;

    (c) in Scotland, the induciae of a charge for payment on an extract decree, or an extract registered bond, or an extract registered protest, have expired without payment being made; or

    (d) in Northern Ireland, a certificate of unenforceability has been granted in respect of a judgment against the trustees.

THE CARE AND SUPPORT (CHILDRENS CARERS) REGULATIONS 2015 (SI 2015/305)

The Secretary of State makes these Regulations in exercise of the powers conferred by **A1–257** sections 62(2) and 125(7) and (8) of the Care Act 2014[2].

In accordance with section 125(4)(i) of the Care Act 2014, a draft of these Regulations was laid before Parliament and was approved by a resolution of each House of Parliament.

GENERAL NOTE

    Section 62(1) of the Care Act provides a power for a local authority to meet the support needs of the carer of a child in circumstances where the authority has carried out an assessment of the carer's needs under s.60 in advance of the child becoming 18. These regulations make provision in connection with the exercise of that power.

    Regulation 2 provides that certain provisions of the Act and regulations apply with modifications to the local authority's exercise of its power under s.62(1), as they would apply to the local authority's exercise of the power under s.20(6) to meet the support needs of a carer.

---

[1] As to the application of Part 1 of the 1986 Act to co-operative and community benefit societies, See S.I. 2014/229 as amended by S.I. 2014/1822.

[2] 2014 c.23. The powers to make regulations are exercisable by the Secretary of State, See s.125(1). Section 62 was brought into force on 1 October 2014 by S.I. 2014/2473 for the purposes of making regulations.

Regulation 3 prohibits a local authority, in exercising the power under s.62(1) of the Act, from meeting the needs of the child's carer by providing care and support to the child in question. As a result, s.4(3) does not apply to the exercise of the power under s.62(1).

Regulations 4 to 14 make modifications to certain provisions of the Act and regulations which are applied to the exercise of the power under s.62(1) by reg.2, to ensure they they have the intended effect. For instance, some of these modifications make straightforward substitutions of references to s.62(1) or to a "child's carer".

Citation, commencement and interpretation

A1–258   **1.**—(1) These Regulations may be cited as the Care and Support (Children's Carers) Regulations 2015 and come into force immediately after section 62(1) of the Care Act 2014 comes into force.

(2) In these Regulations, "the Act" means the Care Act 2014.

Application of Part 1 etc. in relation to the exercise of the power to meet a child's carer's needs for support

A1–259   **2.**—(1) The following apply, subject to any modifications specified in regulations 4 to 14, to the exercise of the power to meet a child's carer's[1] needs for support under section 62(1) of the Act insofar as they apply to the exercise of the power to meet a carer's[2] needs for support under section 20(6) of the Act—

(a) the provisions of Part 1 of the Act, insofar as they do not already apply to the exercise of the power under section 62(1) of the Act, except for the provisions listed in paragraph (2); and

(b) the Regulations specified in paragraph (3).

(2) The excepted provisions referred to in paragraph (1)(a) are—

(a) section 30 (cases where adult expresses preference for particular accommodation);

(b) section 41 (financial adjustments between local authorities); and

(c) section 74 and Schedule 3 (discharge of hospital patients with care and support needs).

(3) The Regulations referred to in paragraph (1)(b) are—

(a) the Care and Support (Independent Advocacy Support) (No. 2) Regulations 2014[3] ;

(b) the Care and Support (Charging and Assessment of Resources) Regulations 2014[4] ;

(c) the Care and Support (Personal Budget: Exclusion of Costs) Regulations 2014[5] ; and

(d) the Care and Support (Direct Payments) Regulations 2014[6] .

GENERAL NOTE

Regulation 2 provides that certain provisions of the Care Act and regulations apply with modifications to the local authority's exercise of its power under s.62(1), as they would apply to the local authority's exercise of the power under s.20(6) to meet the support needs of a carer. For example, certain provisions do not apply to the exercise of the s.20(6) power, and therefore do not apply under s.62(1). These include ss.15 (cap on

---

[1] See s.60(7) to (9) of the Act for the meaning of "carer" in relation to a child.
[2] See s.10(3) of the Act for the meaning of "carer".
[3] S.I. 2014/2889.
[4] S.I. 2014/2672.
[5] S.I. 2014/2840.
[6] S.I. 2014/2871.

care costs), 28 (independent personal budget), 29 (care account), 34 (deferred payments), 37 (continuity of care), 39 (ordinary residence deeming principle)—which do not apply because they relate to an adult with needs for care and support. Similarly, ss.13 (eligibility criteria), 42 to 46 (adult safeguarding) and 53 to 57 (market oversight) do not apply because they do not specifically apply to the exercise of the power under s.20(6). Certain provisions of the Care Act, such as ss.1 (individual well-being duty), 3 (integration duty) and 7 (cooperation in specific cases) already apply because they apply to the exercise of any function under Pt 1 of the Act. Regulation 2(2) excludes some provisions within Pt 1 which otherwise would apply to the exercise of the power under s.62(1).

Prohibition on providing support to a carer by providing care and support to a child
3. A local authority[1] may not meet a child's carer's needs for support under section 62(1) **A1–260** of the Act by providing care and support to the child.

Modification of section 8 (how to meet needs)
4. Section 8 of the Act applies as if, after "sections 18 to 20", wherever occurring, there **A1–261** were inserted "or section 62(1)".

Modification of section 14 (power of local authority to charge)
5. Section 14 of the Act applies as if, in subsection (1)(a), after "sections 18 to 20" there **A1–262** were inserted "or section 62(1)".

Modification of section 17 (assessment of financial resources)
6. Section 17 of the Act applies as if, after subsection (3), there were inserted—   **A1–263**

"(3A) Where a local authority thinks that, if it were to meet a child's carer's needs for support, it would charge the child's carer under section 14(1) for meeting at least some of the needs, it must assess—

   (a) the level of the child's carer's financial resources, and
   (b) the amount (if any) which the child's carer would be likely to be able to pay towards the cost of meeting the needs for support.".

Modification of section 22 (exception for provision of health services)
7. Section 22 of the Act applies as if, in subsections (1) and (3), after "sections 18 to 20", **A1–264** there were inserted "or section 62(1)".

Modification of section 23 (exception for provision of housing etc.)
8. Section 23 of the Act applies as if, in subsection (1), after "sections 18 to 20", there **A1–265** were inserted "or section 62(1)".

Modification of section 24 (the steps for the local authority to take)
9. Section 24 of the Act applies as if, in subsection (1), after "20(6)", there were inserted **A1–266** "or 62(1)".

Modification of section 25 (support plan)
10. Section 25 of the Act applies as if—   **A1–267**
   (a) in subsection (1), after "in the case of a carer", there were inserted "or child's carer";

---

[1] See s.1(4) of the Act for the meaning of "local authority"; the definition is limited to local authorities in England.

(b) in subsection (1)(a), after "carer's assessment", there were inserted "or child's carer's assessment";

(c) in subsection (1)(b), at the beginning, there were inserted "except in the case of a child's carer,";

(d) in subsection (1)(d), after "section 10(5) and (6)", there were inserted "or (in the case of a child's carer) section 61(1) and (2)";

(e) in subsection (4)(a), after "carer", there were inserted "or child's carer";

(f) in subsection (4)(b), at the beginning, there were inserted "in the case of a carer,";

(g) after subsection (4)(b), there were inserted—

"(ba) in the case of a child's carer, the child the child's carer cares for, if the child's carer asks the authority to do so, and";

(h) in subsection (4)(c), after "carer", there were inserted "or child's carer";

(i) in subsection (5), after "carer", there were inserted "or child's carer";

(j) in subsection (6)(b), after "section 10(5) and (6)", there were inserted "or (in the case of a child's carer) section 61(1) and (2)";

(k) in subsection (8)(b), after "carer", there were inserted "or child's carer" and after "adult needing care", there were inserted "or child the child's carer cares for";

(l) in subsection (10)(a), after "carer", there were inserted "or child's carer";

(m) in subsection (10)(b), at the beginning, there were inserted "in the case of a carer,";

(n) after subsection (10)(b), there were inserted—

"(ba) in the case of a child's carer, the child the child's carer cares for, if the child's carer asks the authority to do so, and"; and

(o) in subsection (10)(c), after "carer", there were inserted "or child's carer".

GENERAL NOTE

Regulation 10(c) modifies s.25 of the Act to ensure that there is no requirement for a support plan under s.24 to specify whether the child's carer's needs meet the local authority's eligibility criteria. This is because the exercise of the power under s.62(1) is not conditional upon needs meeting eligibility criteria.

Modification of section 27 (review of support plan)

A1–268　　**11.** Section 27 of the Act applies as if—

(a) in subsection (1)(b), after "carer", there were inserted "or child's carer";

(b) in subsection (3)(a), after "section 10(5) and (6)", there were inserted "or (in the case of a child's carer) section 61(1) and (2)";

(c) in subsection (3)(b)(i), after "carer", there were inserted "or child's carer";

(d) in subsection (3)(b)(ii), at the beginning, there were inserted "in the case of a carer,";

(e) after subsection (3)(b)(ii), there were inserted—

"(iia) in the case of a child's carer, the child the child's carer cares for, if the child's carer asks the authority to do so, and";

(f) in subsection (3)(b)(iii), after "carer", there were inserted "or child's carer";

(g) in subsection (4), after "or a support plan", there were inserted "in respect of a carer";

(h) after subsection (4), there were inserted—

"(4A) Where a local authority is satisfied that circumstances have changed in a way that affects a support plan in respect of a child's carer, the authority must—

(3) For the purpose of this regulation, where the registered care provider is an undertaking, the bed capacity of the provider includes the bed capacity of any group undertaking of the provider.

GENERAL NOTE

Regulation 3 sets out the criteria for entry applicable to providers of residential care, that is, providers who are registered in respect of the carrying on of the regulated activity set out in para.2 of Sch.1 to the   Health and Social Care Act 2008 (Regulated Activities) Regulations 2014 (SI 2014/2936). A provider becomes subject to the central oversight system if it is not a local authority and where it has a bed capacity of:

- at least 2,000 anywhere in England; or
- between 1,000 to 1,999 overall, with 1 bed or more in at least 16 local authorities in England; or
- between 1,000 to 1,999 anywhere in England and where their bed capacity in each of 3 or more local authorities in England exceeds 10 per cent of the total bed capacity in each of those local authorities.

Regulation 3 also provides that the bed capacity of a provider includes the bed capacity of any group undertaking.

THE CARE ACT 2014 AND CHILDREN AND FAMILIES ACT 2014 (CONSEQUENTIAL AMENDMENTS) ORDER 2015 (SI 2015/914)

The Secretary of State, in exercise of the powers conferred by sections 123(1) and (2) and **A1–280** 125(7) and (8) of the Care Act 2014[1] and sections 135(3) and 136(1) and (2) of the Children and Families Act 2014[2] makes the following Order.

In accordance with section 123(5) of the Care Act 2014, the Secretary of State has consulted the

Scottish Ministers and the Welsh Ministers before making this Order.

In accordance with section 125(4) of the Care Act 2014 and section 135(6) of the Children and

Families Act 2014, a draft of this Order was laid before Parliament and approved by a resolution of each House of Parliament.

GENERAL NOTE

This Order was made under the Care Act and the Children and Families Act 2014. It repealed (subject to certain savings for transitional purposes) the previous legislative framework governing community care in England. The Order also makes consequential and incidental amendments to other primary legislative provisions which refer, for various purposes, to the current social care legislation.

Citation, commencement and extent

1.—(1) This Order may be cited as the Care Act 2014 and Children and Families Act **A1–281** 2014 (Consequential Amendments) Order 2015.

(2) This Order comes into force on the day on which section 1 of the Care Act 2014 comes into force.

(3) Where this Order amends an enactment that is not yet in force, paragraph (2) does not affect how that enactment, as amended, comes into force.

(4) An amendment or repeal made by this Order has the same extent as the enactment amended or repealed.

---

[1] 2014 c. 23.
[2] 2014 c. 6.

Amendments

A1–282 **2.** The Schedule (amendments in consequence of provisions of the Care Act 2014 and the Children and Families Act 2014) has effect.

Savings and transitional provision

A1–283 **3.**—(1) Despite the amendments made by this Order, on or after the date on which this Order comes into force—

  (a) support or services may continue to be provided, and

    (b) payments towards the cost of support or services may continue to be made, in the case of a person to whom, or in relation to whom, support or services are being provided, or payments towards the cost of support or services are being made, immediately before this Order comes into force.

  (2) Paragraph (1) applies until—

    (a) Part 1 of the Care Act 2014 applies in relation to the provision of support or services, or the making of payments towards the cost of support or services, in that person's case by virtue of provision made for transitional purposes under a power conferred by that Act, or

    (b) if earlier, 31st March 2016.

  (3) Despite the amendments made by this Order—

    (a) any provision that operates in relation to, or by reference to, support or services provided, or payments towards the cost of support or services made, before or (in accordance with paragraph (1)) on or after the date on which this Order comes into force, and

    (b) anything done under such provision, continue to have effect for the purposes of that support or those services or payments, subject to paragraph (6).

  (4) The references in paragraph (3) to support or services provided, or payments made, before the date on which this Order comes into force include support or services that are not provided but are or may be required or permitted to be provided, or payments that are not made but are or may be required or permitted to be made, before that date.

  (5) The provision referred to in paragraph (3) includes in particular provision about—

    (a) costs and other amounts payable and their recovery;

    (b) civil legal services (within the meaning of Part 1 of the Legal Aid, Sentencing and Punishment of Offenders Act 2012[1]);

    (c) offences.

  (6) Paragraph (3) does not authorise a local authority to do any of the following on or after the date on which this Order comes into force—

    (a) create a charge under section 22(1) of the Health and Social Services and Social Security Adjudications Act 1983[2] ;

    (b) make an order under section 23(1) of that Act;

    (c) enter into a deferred payment agreement under section 55(1) of the Health and Social Care Act 2001[3]

  (7) Where under this Order an enactment ceases to have effect for a purpose for which a local authority holds land immediately before the Order comes into force, the land is to be treated as appropriated for whatever purposes of Part 1 of the Care Act 2014 the authority may designate.

---

[1] 2012 c. 10.

[2] 1983 c. 41.

[3] 2001 c. 15.

(8) Where under this Order an enactment ceases to have effect for a purpose for which a local authority has a right to use land immediately before the Order comes into force—

(a) the authority continues to have that right to use the land for whatever purposes of Part 1 of the Care Act 2014 the authority may designate, but

(b) that does not affect the circumstances (other than the enactment ceasing to have effect) in which the right ceases.

(9) This article is without prejudice to section 16 of the Interpretation Act 1978[1] (general savings).

(10) In this article "local authority" has the meaning given by section 1(4) of the Care Act 2014.

SCHEDULE   **ARTICLE 2**

AMENDMENTS IN CONSEQUENCE OF PROVISIONS OF THE CARE ACT 2014 AND THE CHILDREN AND FAMILIES ACT 2014

National Assistance Act 1948 (c. 29)   A1–284

1. The National Assistance Act 1948 is amended as follows.

2. In section 21 (duty of local authorities to provide accommodation) in subsection (4) after

"another local authority" insert ", including a local authority in England,".

3. In section 24 (authority liable for provision of accommodation) in subsection (4) after "another local authority" insert ", including a local authority in England,".

4.—(1) Section 32[2] (adjustments between authorities) is amended as follows.

(2) In subsection (1), after "a reference to a local authority in" insert "England or".

(3) After subsection (5) insert—

"(6) Subsections (3) to (5) do not apply to a question which involves a dispute to which paragraph 5 of Schedule 1 to the Care Act 2014 applies (corresponding provision about cross-border placements)."

5.—(1) Section 33(1)[3] (local authorities for purposes of Part 3 of that Act) is amended as follows.

(2) After ""local authority"" insert "(except in "local authority in England")".

(3) Omit "England or".

(4) At the end insert "and "local authority in England" means a council which is a local authority for the purposes of the Local Authority Social Services Act 1970 in England."

6.—(1) Section 47 (removal to suitable premises of persons in need of care and attention) is amended as follows.

(2) In subsection (1), after "for persons" insert "in Wales".

(3) In subsection (12), omit "the councils of districts and London Boroughs and the Common
Council of the City of London,".

(4) In subsection (12A)(a)[4] omit "England and".

7. In section 48(1) (duty of councils to provide temporary protection of property)—

---

[1] 1978 c. 30.

[2] Section 32(3) to (5) were substituted by the Health and Social Care Act 2008 (c. 14), s.48(2).

[3] Section 33(1) was amended by the Local Government Act 1972 (c. 70), Sch.23, para.2, the Local Government(Scotland) Act 1973 (c. 65), Sch.27, para.89, the Residential Homes Act 1980 (c. 7), s.11(5) and Sch.2, and the Local Government etc. (Scotland) Act 1994 (c. 39), Sch.13, para.31(2).

[4] Section 47(12A) was inserted by the Courts Act 2003 (c. 39), Sch.8, para.81.

(a) after "it appears to the council" insert ", in the case of any moveable property of that person that is for the time being situated in Wales,";
(b) for "any moveable property of his" substitute "the property".

8. In section 56(3)[1] (legal proceedings) after "1970" insert "in Wales".
9. In section 64 (interpretation), in subsection (1), in the definition of "local authority", for the words from "means", in the first place, to the end substitute "means the council of a county or county borough in Wales".
10. Section 66 of that Act (application to Isles of Scilly) ceases to have effect.

Disabled Persons (Employment) Act 1958 (c. 33)
A1–285   **11.** In section 3(2)[2] of the Disabled Persons (Employment) Act 1958 (provision of sheltered employment by local authorities) omit "paragraph 2 of Schedule 20 to the National Health Service Act 2006 or".

Health Services and Public Health Act 1968 (c. 46)
A1–286   **12.** Part 2 of the Health Services and Public Health Act 1968 (amendments connected with local authorities' services under the National Assistance Act 1948) is amended as follows.
13. In section 45(11) (local authorities' promotion of welfare of old people: meaning of local authority) for the words from "the council of a county" to "City of London" substitute "the council of a county or county borough in Wales".
14. Section 46 (application to Isles of Scilly) ceases to have effect.

Civil Evidence Act 1968 (c. 64)
A1–287   **15.** In section 12 of the Civil Evidence Act 1968 (findings of adultery and paternity as evidence in civil proceedings), in subsection (5), [3] in the definition of "relevant proceedings", omit paragraph (a).

Local Authority Social Services Act 1970 (c. 42)
A1–288   **16.** The Local Authority Social Services Act 1970 is amended as follows.
17. In section 7 (local authorities to act under general guidance of Secretary of State) after subsection (1) insert—

"(1A) Section 78 of the Care Act 2014 applies instead of this section in relation to functions given by Part 1 of that Act or by regulations under that Part."

18.—(1) Schedule 1[4] (social services functions) is amended as follows.
(2) In the entry for section 1 of the Chronically Sick and Disabled Persons Act 1970, after "welfare services" insert "; providing information about certain welfare services".

(3) After the entry for section 2 of that Act insert—

"Section 2A   Welfare services: transition for children to adult care and support in England."

(4) Omit the entry for the National Health Service Act 1977.

---

[1] Section 56(3) was substituted by the Local Government Act 1972 (c. 70), Sch.23, para.2.
[2] Section 3(2) was amended by the National Health Service (Consequential Provisions) Act 2006 (c. 43), Sch.1,para.19.
[3] In s.12(5), the definition of "relevant proceedings" was substituted by the Courts and Legal Services Act 1990 (c. 41), Sch.16, para.2.
[4] Schedule 1 was amended by the Health and Social Care Act 2001 (c.15), Sch.5, para.15.

(5) After the entry for section 117 of the Mental Health Act 1983 insert—

| "Section 117A | Functions under regulations about provision of preferred accommodation under section 117." |

(6) In column 1 of the entry for Part 4 of the Health and Social Care Act 2001 omit "England or".

(7) After the entries for the Mental Capacity Act 2005 insert—

"National Health Service (Wales) Act 2006

| Schedule 15 | Care of mothers and young children; prevention, care and aftercare; home help and laundry facilities." |

(8) At the end insert—

"Care Act 2014

Part 1, except section 78, so far as that Part and regulations under it give functions to local authorities in England	General responsibilities in relation to care and support services.
	Assessing and meeting needs for care and support, and carers' needs.
	Direct payments, deferred payment agreements and loans.
	Continuity of care and ordinary residence.
	Safeguarding adults.
	Provider failure.
	Children in transition to adult care and support.
	Independent advocacy support.
	Recovery of charges.
	Appeals against local authority decisions.
	Discharge of hospital patients.
	Registers.
	Delegation of functions."

Health and Social Services and Social Security Adjudications Act 1983 (c. 41)

A1–294   **30.** The Health and Social Services and Social Security Adjudications Act 1983 is amended as follows.

31.—(1) Section 17[1] (charges for local authority services in England and Wales) is amended as follows.

(2) Omit subsection (2)(a) to (d) and (f).

(3) In subsection (2)(e) omit the words from "other than" to the end.

(4) In subsection (3)(a), after "a service to which this section applies" insert "or a service within subsection (2A)".

(5) In subsection (5)—

> (a) for "This section has" substitute "Subsection (2A), and subsections (3) and (4) so far as they relate to it, have";
>
> (b) omit "15 or".

32.—(1) Section 22 (arrears of contributions charged on interest in land in England and Wales) is amended as follows.

(2) After subsection (2A) insert—

"(2B) A local authority in England may not create, or be required by directions under subsection (2A) to create, a charge under this section on or after the day on which section 1 of the Care Act 2014 came into force."

(3) Before subsection (4) insert—

"(3A) Subject to subsection (5) below, a charge under this section created by a local authority in England shall be in respect of any amount which is outstanding from time to time and is—

> (a) assessed as due to be paid by the person to the authority for the Part III accommodation, or
>
> (b) due by the person to the authority under Part 1 of the Care Act 2014 in respect of meeting needs for care and support by the provision of accommodation for the person, including anything provided in connection with that accommodation."

(4) In subsection (4), after "charge under this section" insert "created by a local authority in Wales or Scotland".

33.—(1) Section 23 (arrears of contributions secured over interest in land in Scotland) is amended as follows.

(2) After subsection (2A) insert—

"(2B) A local authority in England may not make, or be required by directions under subsection (2A) to make, a charging order on or after the day on which section 1 of the Care Act 2014 came into force."

(3) In subsection (3), for the words from "of securing" to the end substitute—

"mentioned in subsection (3A) or (as the case may be) (3B) below.

(3A) Where the charging order is made by a local authority in Scotland or Wales, the purpose referred to in subsection (3) above is the purpose of securing any debt due or to become due by the debtor to the local authority in respect of the provision of the Part III accommodation referred to in subsection (1) above, with interest on that amount as specified in section 24.

---

[1] Section 17 was amended by the National Health Service and Community Care Act 1990 (c. 19), Sch.9, para.25,the Carers and Disabled Children Act 2000 (c. 16), s.8, and the Community Care (Delayed Discharges etc.) Act 2003(c.5), s.17.

(3B) Where the charging order is made by a local authority in England, the purpose referred to in subsection (3) above is the purpose of securing any debt due or to become due by the debtor to the local authority—

(a) in respect of the provision of the Part III accommodation referred to in subsection (1) above, or

(b) under Part 1 of the Care Act 2014 in respect of meeting needs for care and support by the provision of accommodation for the person, including anything provided in connection with that accommodation, in either case, with interest on that amount as specified in section 24.

(3C) A local authority that records or registers a charging order as mentioned in subsection (1) above shall—

(a) intimate to the debtor in writing that they have made and recorded or registered the order, and (b) inform the debtor of the order's effect."

Public Health (Control of Disease) Act 1984 (c. 22)

34. In section 46 of the Public Health (Control of Disease) Act 1984 (burial and crem-   **A1–295** ation), in subs.(2)—

(a) after "immediately before his death" insert

"— (a) ", and

(b) after "section 29 of that Act" insert

", or (b) was being provided with accommodation under Part 1 of the Care Act 2014."

Transport Act 1985 (c. 67)

35. In section 104 of the Transport Act 1985 (travel concessions), in subsection (2)(b)   **A1–296** after "made with that Executive" insert

"—

(i) by any local authority within the meaning of the Care Act 2014 in the discharge of their functions under Part 1 of that Act (meeting needs for care and support), or (ii) ".

Disabled Persons (Services, Consultation and Representation) Act 1986 (c. 33)

36. The Disabled Persons (Services, Consultation and Representation) Act 1986 is   **A1–297** amended as follows.

37. In section 2 (rights of authorised representatives of disabled persons), in subsection (5)—

(a) in paragraph (b), after "Part III of the 1948 Act" insert "or Part 1 of the Care Act 2014", and

(b) in paragraph (c), after "section 26 of the 1948 Act" insert "or Part 1 of the Care Act 2014".

38.—(1) In section 3 (assessment by local authorities of needs of disabled persons), in subsection

(1) after "local authority" insert "in Wales or Scotland".

(2) In the heading of that section, after "local authorities" insert "in Wales or Scotland".

39.—(1) Section 4 (services under section 2 of the Chronically Sick and Disabled Persons Act 1970: duty to consider needs of disabled persons) is amended as follows.

(2) The existing words become subsection (1).

(3) In that subsection, after "2(1)" insert "or (4)".

(4) After that subsection insert—

"(2) In the case of a local authority in England this section applies only if the disabled person is aged under 18."

40.—(1) In section 8 (duty of local authority to take into account abilities of carer), in subsection

(1)(b) after "local authority" insert "in Wales or Scotland".

(2) In the heading of that section, after "local authority" insert "in Wales or Scotland".

41.—(1) Section 16[1] (interpretation) is amended as follows.

(2) In the definition of "disabled person", before paragraph (a) insert—

"(za) in relation to England, means—

> (i) in the case of a person aged 18 or over, a person who has a disability within the meaning of section 6 of the Equality Act 2010;
>
> (ii) in the case of a person aged under 18, a person who is disabled within the meaning of Part 3 of the Children Act 1989;".

(3) In paragraph (a) of that definition, omit "England and".

(4) In the definition of "the welfare enactments", before paragraph (a) insert—

"(za) in relation to England, Part 3 of the Children Act 1989 and Part 1 of the Care Act 2014,".

(5) In paragraph (a) of that definition, omit "England and" and "Schedule 20 to the 2006 Act and".

Local Government Finance Act 1988 (c. 41)

A1–298   **42.**—(1) In Schedule 5 to the Local Government Finance Act 1988 (non-domestic rating: exemption), paragraph 16 is amended as follows.

(2) After sub-paragraph (1) insert—

"(1A) For the purposes of this paragraph in its application to hereditaments in England, a person is disabled if he has a disability within the meaning given by section 6 of the Equality Act 2010."

(3) In sub-paragraph (2), at the beginning insert "For the purposes of this paragraph in its application to hereditaments in Wales,".

(4) In sub-paragraph (4) at the end insert "or, in the case of a local authority in England, had power to provide under that section immediately before it ceased to apply to local authorities in England."

Children Act 1989 (c. 41)

A1–299   **43.** The Children Act 1989 is amended as follows.

44. In section 17ZA[2] (young carers' needs assessments: England) in subsection (6)(b) after subparagraph

> (iii) add—

"(iv) Part 1 of the Care Act 2014."

45. In section 17ZD (parent carers' needs assessments: England) in subsection (8)(b) after subparagraph

> (iii) add—

"(iv) Part 1 of the Care Act 2014."

---

[1] Section 16 was amended by the Children (Scotland) Act 1995 (c. 36), Sch.4, para.39.
[2] Sections 17ZA to 17ZF were inserted by the Children and Families Act 2014 (c. 6), ss 96 and 97.

46.—(1) Section 17A[1] is amended as follows.

(2) For subsections (3) and (3A) substitute—

"(3) Regulations under this section may, in particular, make provision—

    (a) specifying circumstances in which the responsible authority are not required or authorised to make any payments under the regulations to a person, whether those circumstances relate to the person in question or to the particular service mentioned in subsection (2);

    (b) for any payments required or authorised by the regulations to be made to a person by the responsible authority ("direct payments") to be made to that person ("the payee") as gross payments or alternatively as net payments;

    (c) for the responsible authority to make for the purposes of subsection (3A) or (3B) such determination as to—

        (i) the payee's means, and

        (ii) the amount (if any) which it would be reasonably practicable for the payee to pay to the authority by way of reimbursement or contribution, as may be prescribed;

    (d) as to the conditions falling to be complied with by the payee which must or may be imposed by the responsible authority in relation to the direct payments (and any conditions which may not be so imposed);

    (e) specifying circumstances in which the responsible authority—

        (i) may or must terminate the making of direct payments,

        (ii) may require repayment (whether by the payee or otherwise) of the whole or part of the direct payments;

    (f) for any sum falling to be paid or repaid to the responsible authority by virtue of any condition or other requirement imposed in pursuance of the regulations to be recoverable as a debt due to the authority;

    (g) displacing functions or obligations of the responsible authority with respect to the provision of the service mentioned in subsection (2) only to such extent, and subject to such conditions, as may be prescribed;

    (h) authorising direct payments to be made to any prescribed person on behalf of the payee;

(j) as to matters to which the responsible authority must, or may, have regard when making a decision for the purposes of a provision of the regulations;

(k) as to steps which the responsible authority must, or may, take before, or after, the authority makes a decision for the purposes of a provision of the regulations;

(l) specifying circumstances in which a person who has fallen within subsection (3D) but no longer does so (whether because of fluctuating capacity, or regaining or gaining of capacity) is to be treated, or may be treated, as falling within subsection

(3D) for purposes of this section or for purposes of regulations under this section.

(3A) For the purposes of subsection (3)(b) "gross payments" means payments—

    (a) which are made at such a rate as the authority estimate to be equivalent to the reasonable cost of securing the provision of the service concerned; but

    (b) which may be made subject to the condition that the payee pays to the responsible authority, by way of reimbursement, an amount or amounts determined under the regulations.

(3B) For the purposes of subsection (3)(b) "net payments" means payments—

    (a) which are made on the basis that the payee will pay an amount or amounts determined under the regulations by way of contribution towards the cost of securing the provision of the service concerned; and

---

[1] Section 17A was substituted by the Health and Social Care Act 2001 (c. 15), s.58 and amended by the Health and Social Care Act 2008 (c. 14), Sch.14, para.1.

(b) which are accordingly made at such a rate below that mentioned in subsection

(3A)(a) as reflects any such contribution by the payee.

(3C) Regulations made for the purposes of subsection (3)(a) may provide that direct payments shall not be made in respect of the provision of residential accommodation for any person for a period in excess of a prescribed period.

(3D) A person falls within this subsection if the person lacks capacity, within the meaning of the Mental Capacity Act 2005, to consent to the making of direct payments."

(3) In subsection (4)—

(a) in paragraph (a), for the words from "(4)(a)" to the end substitute "(3A)(a)";
(b) in paragraph (b), for "(4)(b) of that section" substitute "(3A)(b)".

(4) In subsection (6)—

(a) omit the definition of "the 2001 Act";
(b) in the definition of "prescribed" omit the words from "(and has" to the end.

47.—(1) In section 17B[1] (vouchers for persons with parental responsibility for disabled children), in subsection (1) after "local authority" insert "in Wales".

(2) In the heading of that section, at the end insert ": Wales".

Opticians Act 1989 (c. 44)

A1–300   **48.** In section 27[2] of the Opticians Act 1989 (sale and supply of optical appliances), in subsection (3)(e)(i), after "so far as the seller knows," insert "registered as sight-impaired or severely sight-impaired in a register kept by a local authority under section 77(1) of the Care Act 2014 or".

National Health Service and Community Care Act 1990 (c. 19)

A1–301   **49.** The National Health Service and Community Care Act 1990 is amended as follows.

50. In section 46[3] (local authority plans for community care services), in paragraph (c) of the definition of "community care services" in subsection (3) omit "section 254 of, and Schedule 20 to, the National Health Service Act 2006, and".

51.—(1) Section 47 (assessment of needs for community care services) is amended as follows.

(2) In subsection (1) for "of community care services" substitute "of services under section 117 of the Mental Health Act 1983 (in the case of a local authority in England) or of community care services (in the case of a local authority in Wales)".

(3) In subsection (2) after "disabled person," insert "(and, in the case of a local authority in

England, that he is under 18)".

(4) In subsection (5) for "community care services" substitute "services mentioned in subsection

(1)".

(5) In subsection (6) omit "community care".

52.—(1) Section 48 (inspection of premises used for provision of community care services) is amended as follows.

(2) In subsection (1)—

(a) before "community care services" insert "services under section 117 of the Mental Health

---

[1] Section 17B was inserted by the Carers and Disabled Children Act 2000 (c. 16), s.7.
[2] Section 27 was amended by S.I. 2005/848.
[3] Section 46 was amended by the National Health Service (Consequential Provisions) Act 2006 (c. 43), Sch.1, para.129.

Act 1983, or services under Part 1 of the Care Act 2014 to meet adults' needs for care and support, are or are proposed to be provided by a local authority in England, or";
      (b) after "local authority" insert "in Wales".

(3) In subsection (2)(b), for "community care services" substitute "services mentioned in subsection (1)".

(4) In subsection (4)(a)(i), for "community care services" substitute "services mentioned in subsection (1) that are".

(5) In subsection (4)(a)(ii), for "the community care services" substitute "any of those services".

Water Industry Act 1991 (c. 56)

53. In paragraph 8(2) of Schedule 4A[1] to the Water Industry Act 1991 (premises that are not to be disconnected for non-payment of charges) in the definition of "care home" after paragraph (b) insert—   **A1–302**

"(c) a building or part of a building in which accommodation is provided under Part 1 of the Care Act 2014;".

Social Security Contributions and Benefits Act 1992 (c. 4)

54. In section 143 of the Social Security Contributions and Benefits Act 1992 (meaning of "person responsible for child or qualifying young person"), in subsection (3)(c)(i), omit "paragraph 2 of Schedule 20 to the National Health Service Act 2006 or".   **A1–303**

Local Government Finance Act 1992 (c. 14)

55. In paragraph 7(2) of Schedule 1[2] to the Local Government Finance Act 1992 (persons disregarded for purposes of council tax discount), in the definition of "care home" after paragraph (b) insert—   **A1–304**

", or (c) a building or part of a building in which accommodation is provided under Part 1 of the Care Act 2014;".

Carers (Recognition and Services) Act 1995 (c. 12)

56.—(1) Section 1[3] of the Carers (Recognition and Services) Act 1995 (assessment of ability of carers to provide care: England and Wales) is amended as follows.   **A1–305**

(2) In subsection (1)—
      (a) for "subsection (3)" substitute "subsections (3) and (3A)";
      (b) after "1990" insert "—
          (i) in the case of a local authority in England, of the needs of a child ("the relevant person") for after-care services under section 117 of the Mental Health Act 1983[4] , or
          (ii) in the case of a local authority in Wales,".

(3) In subsection (2) for "subsection (3)" substitute "subsections (3) and (3A)".
(4) After subsection (3) insert—

"(3A) In the case of a local authority in England, no request may be made under subsection (1) or (2) if, in relation to the relevant person or the disabled child, the carer is—

---

[1] Schedule 4A was inserted by the Water Industry Act 1999 (c. 9), s.17, and amended by the Care Standards Act 2000(c. 14), Sch. 4, para.18.

[2] Schedule 1 was amended by the Care Standards Act 2000 (c. 14), Sch.4, para.20.

[3] Section 1 was amended by the Carers (Equal Opportunities) Act 2004 (c.15), s.1.

[4] 1983 c. 20.

(a) a young carer, within the meaning given by section 17ZA of the Children Act 1989[1] , or

(b) a parent carer, within the meaning given by section 17ZD of that Act[2] ."

Housing Grants, Construction and Regeneration Act 1996 (c. 53)

A1–306 **57.**—(1) Section 100 of the Housing Grants, Construction and Regeneration Act 1996 (disabled persons for the purposes of Part 1) is amended as follows.

(2) In subsection (2), before paragraph (a) insert—

"(za) the person is registered in a register maintained under section 77(1) or (3) of the

Care Act 2014 (registers of sight-impaired adults, disabled adults, etc.),

(zb) in the opinion of the social services authority, the person falls within a category mentioned in section 77(4) of that Act (persons for whom register may be maintained),".

(3) In subsection (5)—

(a) after "regarded as" insert "having a disability for the purposes of section 77 of the Care Act 2014 or as";

(b) omit the words from "(which define" to the end.

Carers and Disabled Children Act 2000 (c. 16)

A1–307 **58.** The Carers and Disabled Children Act 2000 is amended as follows.

59.—(1) Section 1 (right of carers to assessment) is amended as follows.

(2) In subsection (1)(b) after "local authority" insert "in Wales".

(3) In subsection (4) for the words from the beginning to "Wales)" substitute "The Welsh

Ministers".

60.—(1) Section 6 (assessment: persons with parental responsibility for disabled children) is amended as follows.

(2) In subsection (1)(b) after "local authority" insert "in Wales".

(3) In subsection (3), for the words from the beginning to "Wales)" substitute "The Welsh

Ministers".

61.—(1) Section 11 (interpretation and regulations) is amended as follows.

(2) In subsection (1), in the definition of "regulations", for the words from "Secretary of State" to the end substitute "Welsh Ministers".

(3) In subsection (3) for "Secretary of State (or the National Assembly for Wales) thinks" substitute "Welsh Ministers think".

(4) Omit subsection (4).

Health and Social Care Act 2001 (c. 15)

A1–308 **62.** Part 4 of the Health and Social Care Act 2001 (social care) is amended as follows.

63. In section 50 (preserved rights: transfer to local authorities of responsibilities as to accommodation), in subsection (10), in the definition of "relevant premises" omit "England or".

64.—(1) Section 55 (power for local authorities to take charges on land instead of contributions) is amended as follows.

(2) After subsection (2) insert—

"(2A) A local authority in England may not enter into, or be required by directions under subsection (2) to enter into, a deferred payment agreement on or after the day on which section 1 of the Care Act 2014 came into force."

(3) For subsection (7) substitute—

---

[1] 1989 c. 41. Section 17ZA was inserted by the Children and Families Act 2014 (c. 6), s.96.
[2] Section 17ZD was inserted by the Children and Families Act 2014, s.97.

"(7) Any reference in this section to relevant contributions is—

(a) in relation to a local authority in Wales, a reference to so much of the payments which the resident is liable to pay to an authority for Part 3 accommodation (including any payments which are additional payments for the purpose of section

54) as may be specified in, or determined in accordance with, regulations made for the purposes of this subsection;

(b) in relation to a local authority in England, a reference to—

(i) so much of any payments such as are mentioned in paragraph (a) as may be so specified or determined, and

(ii) any sum due to an authority by the resident under Part 1 of the Care Act 2014 in respect of meeting needs for care and support by the provision of accommodation for the resident, including anything provided in connection with that accommodation."

65.—(1) Section 57 (direct payments) is amended as follows.
(2) In subsection (1)—

(a) after "subsection (2)" insert "or (2A)";

(b) for "paragraph (a) or (b) of that subsection" substitute "subsection (2) or (as the case may be) (2A)".

(3) In subsection (2), after "a local authority" insert "in Wales", and omit "("the responsible authority")".
(4) After subsection (2) insert—

"(2A) A person falls within this subsection if the person is under 18 and a local authority in England have decided under section 47 of the 1990 Act that the person's needs call for the provision by them of services under section 117 of the Mental Health Act 1983 (aftercare).

(2B) The local authority mentioned in subsection (2) or (2A) are referred to in this section as "the responsible authority"."

(5) In subsection (3)(a), for "paragraph (a) or (b) of subsection (2)" substitute "subsection (2) or (2A)".
(6) In subsection (3)(g), for "subsection (2)(a) or (b)" substitute "subsection (2) or (2A)".

66.—(1) Section 59(1) (interpretation of Part 4) is amended as follows.
(2) In the definition of "community care services", in paragraph (a) omit "England or".
(3) In the definition of "local authority"—

(a) before paragraph (a) insert—

"(za) does not, except in sections 55 and 57, include a local authority in England,";

(b) in paragraph (a) for "England or Wales," substitute "Wales or, in sections 55 and 57,

England or Wales,".

Nationality, Immigration and Asylum Act 2002 (c. 41)

67.—(1) Paragraph 1(1) of Schedule 3[1] to the Nationality, Immigration and Asylum Act **A1–309** 2002 (ineligibility for support) is amended as follows.

---

[1] Paragraph 1(1) of Sch.3 was amended by the National Health Service (Consequential Provisions) Act 2006 (c. 43), Sch.1, para.229.

(2) In paragraph (e) omit "section 254 of, and Schedule 20 to, the National Health Service Act

2006, or".

(3) Omit "or" at the end of paragraph (l);

(4) After paragraph (m) insert

", or

(n) Part 1 of the Care Act 2014 (care and support provided by local authority)."

Community Care (Delayed Discharges) Act 2003 (c. 5)

A1–310   **68.** The Community Care (Delayed Discharges) Act 2003 is amended as follows.

69. In section 1[1] (meaning of key terms), in the definition of "NHS body" omit paragraphs (ab),

(c) and (d) (but not "and" after (d)).

70.—(1) Section 4 (duties of responsible authority following notice under section 2) is amended as follows.

(2) In subsection (3)(a), after "2000 (c. 16)" insert "or Part 1 of the Care Act 2014".

(3) In subsection (4), after paragraph (b) insert—

"; or

(c) is entitled to an assessment under section 10(1) of the Care Act 2014."

(4) In each of subsections (9) and (10)—

    (a) before "(but without prejudice" insert "or, as the case may be, Part 1 of the Care Act 2014,";

    (b) after "that section" insert "or that Part".

71.—(1) Section 12 Section 12 was amended by the National Health Service (Consequential Provisions) Act 2006 (c. 43), Schedule 1, paragraph231, and by S.I. 2010/813, article 11.

(interpretation) is amended as follows.

(2) In the definition of "carer", after paragraph (b) insert—

"or a person who provides or intends to provide care for the patient and is entitled to an assessment under section 10(1) of the Care Act 2014;".

(3) After "community care service" insert

"—(a) in relation to England, means services under Part 1 of the Care Act 2014 or section

117 of the Mental Health Act 1983, and (b) in relation to Wales,".

(4) In the definition of "health service hospital" omit "the National Health Service Act 2006 or".

72.—(1) Section 14 (power to apply Part 1 to NHS patients in care homes) is amended as follows.

(2) In subsection (1) for "appropriate Minister" substitute "Welsh Ministers".

(3) In subsection (2)(a) for "appropriate Minister" substitute "Welsh Ministers".

73. Section 15 (free provision of services in England) ceases to have effect.

74. For section 16 substitute—

---

[1] Section 1 was amended by the Health and Social Care (Community Health and Standards) Act 2003 (c. 43), Sch.4, para.130, and by S.I. 2013/2341, art.3.

"16 Free provision of services in Wales

(1) The Welsh Ministers may by regulations require that the provision of any qualifying service of a description prescribed in the regulations is to be free of charge to the person to whom it is provided.

(2) The regulations may (without prejudice to the generality of subsection (1))—

    (a) prescribe circumstances in which a qualifying service is to be provided free of charge; and

    (b) limit the period for which a qualifying service is to be so provided.

(3) In this section "qualifying service" means—

    (a) the provision of accommodation under Part 3 of the National Assistance Act 1948 in pursuance of arrangements made by a local authority in Wales; or

    (b) any service which is provided to a person by, or in pursuance of arrangements made by, a local authority in Wales under an enactment mentioned in subsection (4).

(4) The enactments referred to in subsection (3)(b) are—

    (a) section 29 of the National Assistance Act 1948;

    (b) section 45(1) of the Health Services and Public Health Act 1968;

    (c) section 2 of the Carers and Disabled Children Act 2000.

(5) The regulations may not require any of the following services to be provided free of charge for a period of more than six weeks—

    (a) the provision of accommodation under Part 3 of the National Assistance Act 1948;

    (b) the provision of personal care to a person in any place where that person is living, other than accommodation provided under that Part of that Act;

    (c) a service provided to a carer under section 2 of the Carers and Disabled Children Act 2000 which consists of the provision of personal care delivered to the person cared for (in accordance with subsection (3) of that section).

(6) The regulations may—

    (a) make different provision for different descriptions of qualifying service; and

    (b) make supplementary, consequential, incidental, transitional or saving provision."

Carers (Equal Opportunities) Act 2004 (c. 15)

75. The Carers (Equal Opportunities) Act 2004 is amended as follows.   **A1–311**

76. In section 3(1)[1] (co-operation between authorities) after "local authority" insert "in Wales".

77. Section 6(5) and (6) (application of section 3 to Isles of Scilly) ceases to have effect.

Mental Capacity Act 2005 (c. 9)

78. The Mental Capacity Act 2005 is amended as follows.   **A1–312**

79.—(1) Section 39 (provision of accommodation by local authority) is amended as follows.

(2) After subsection (1) insert—

"(1A) But this section applies only if— in the case of a local authority in England, subsection (1B) applies; in the case of a local authority in Wales, subsection (2) applies."

(3) After subsection (1A) (inserted by paragraph (2)) insert—

"(1B) This subsection applies if the accommodation is to be provided in accordance with—

    (a) Part 1 of the Care Act 2014, or

---

[1] Section 3 was amended by the Health and Social Care Act 2012 (c. 7), Sch.5, para.125.

(b) section 117 of the Mental Health Act."

(4) In subsection (2), for "But this section applies only" substitute "This subsection applies".

80. In paragraph 183 of Schedule A1[1] (deprivation of liberty of hospital or care home residents: ordinary residence for purposes of identifying supervisory authority) after sub-paragraph (2) insert—

"(2A) Section 39(1), (2) and (4) to (6) of the Care Act 2014 and paragraphs 1(1), 2(1) and 8 of Schedule 1 to that Act apply to any determination of where a person is ordinarily resident for the purposes of paragraphs 180, 181 and 182 as they apply for the purposes of Part 1 of that Act."

National Health Service Act 2006 (c. 41)

A1–313   **81.** The National Health Service Act 2006 is amended as follows.

82.—(1) Section 254 (local social services authorities) is amended as follows.

(2) Omit subsection (1).

(3) In subsection (4) omit paragraph (b) and the "or" before it.

(4) In subsection (5) omit "and Schedule 20".

83. Omit Schedule 20.

National Health Service (Wales) Act 2006 (c. 42)

A1–314   **84.** In Schedule 15 to the National Health Service (Wales) Act 2006 (local social services authorities) after paragraph 2 insert—

"**2A.**—(1) Each local social services authority in Wales—

(a) must provide or arrange for the provision of home help, on a scale adequate for the needs of its area, for households where home help is required owing to the presence of a person to whom sub-paragraph (2) applies, and

(b) may provide or arrange for the provision of laundry facilities for households for which home help is being, or can be, provided under paragraph (a).

(2) This sub-paragraph applies to any person who—

(a) is suffering from illness,

(b) is pregnant or has recently given birth,

(c) is aged, or

(d) is handicapped as a result of having suffered from illness or by congenital deformity."

Safeguarding Vulnerable Groups Act 2006 (c. 47)

A1–315   **85.** The Safeguarding Vulnerable Groups Act 2006 is amended as follows.

86. In section 30 (provision of vetting information) (until it ceases to have effect by virtue of section 72(1) of the Protection of Freedoms Act 2012[2]), in subsection (8) after "section 57 of the Health and Social Care Act 2001 (c 15)" insert ", or in accordance with section 31 or 32 of the Care Act 2014,".

87. In paragraph 7 of Schedule 4[3] (regulated activity), after sub-paragraph (3E) insert—

"(3EA) Relevant assistance in the conduct of a person's own affairs is also representing or supporting the person in pursuance of arrangements made under section 67 or 68 of the

Care Act 2014 (independent advocacy support)."

---

[1] Schedule A1 was inserted by the Mental Health Act 2007 (c. 12), s.50, Sch.7.

[2] 2012 c. 9.

[3] Schedule 4 was amended by the Protection of Freedoms Act 2012, s.66.

Income Tax Act 2007 (c. 3)

88.—(1) Section 38 of the Income Tax Act 2007 (blind person's allowance) is amended **A1–316** as follows.

(2) In subsection (2), after "the individual is" insert

"—(a) registered as a severely sight-impaired adult in a register kept under section 77(1) of the Care Act 2014 (registers kept by local authorities in England), or

(b) ".

(3) In that subsection, omit "England and".

(4) In subsection (4)—

(a) in paragraph (a), after "section 29 of the National Assistance Act 1948" insert "or as a severely sight-impaired person in a register kept under section 77(1) of the Care Act 2014", and

(b) in paragraph (b), after "blindness" insert "or of severe sight-impairment".

Health and Social Care Act 2008 (c. 14)

89. The Health and Social Care Act 2008 is amended as follows.　　　　　**A1–317**

90. Section 145 ceases to have effect.

91. In section 156(2) (interpretation of provisions relating to financial assistance), in the definition of "social care services"—

(a) omit paragraphs (a) and (b);

(b) after paragraph (c) insert—

"(ca) Part 1 of the Care Act 2014,";

(c) omit paragraph (d).

92. In Schedule 14 (further amendments relating to Part 5), omit paragraph 1.

93.—(1) In paragraph 8 of Schedule 14 (further amendments relating to Part 5) the sub-sections inserted in section 6 of the Safeguarding Vulnerable Groups Act 2006[1] are amended as follows.

(2) In subsection (8A)—

(a) for " or section 57 of the Health and Social Care Act 2001" substitute ", section 57 of the Health and Social Care Act 2001 or sections 31 to 33 of the Care Act 2014";

(b) for "that section" substitute "any of those sections".

(3) After subsection (8B) insert—

"(8C) A person (S) who is authorised as mentioned in subsection (4)(a) of section 32 of the Care Act 2014 does not make arrangements for another to engage in a regulated activity by virtue of anything that S does under subsection (4)(b) of that section."

Welfare Reform Act 2009 (c. 24)

94. In section 50 of the Welfare Reform Act 2009 (interpretation of Part 2) in paragraph **A1–318** (a) of the definition of "community care services" for "(a) In relation to England and Wales," substitute—

"(a) in relation to England, services under Part 1 of the Care Act 2014 or section 117 of the Mental Health Act 1983; (aa) in relation to Wales,".

Personal Care at Home Act 2010 (c. 18)

95.—(1) Section 1 of the Personal Care at Home Act 2010 (which makes amendments to **A1–319** section 15 of the Community Care (Delayed Discharges) Act 2003[2] , with consequential amendments) is amended as follows.

---

[1] 2006 c. 47.
[2] 2003 c. 5.

(2) In subsection (1)—

(a) for "15" substitute "16";

(b) for "England" substitute "Wales".

(3) In subsections (7)(a) and (b) and (8), for "after "section 15" insert "or 16"" substitute "for

"section 15" substitute "section 16"".

Legal Aid, Sentencing and Punishment of Offenders Act 2012 (c. 10)

A1–320   **96.** In Part 1 of Schedule 1 to the Legal Aid, Sentencing and Punishment of Offenders Act 2012 (civil legal services), in paragraph 6(3), in the definition of "community care services"—

(a) omit paragraph (l);

(b) after paragraph (m) insert—

"(n) Part 1 of the Care Act 2014 (local authority's functions of meeting adult's needs for care and support);".

Children and Families Act 2014 (c. 6)

A1–321   **97.** In section 37 of the Children and Families Act 2014 (education, health and care plans), in subsection (2)(e), omit "(as it applies by virtue of section 28A of that Act)".

Social Services and Well-being (Wales) Act 2014 (anaw 4)

A1–322   **98.** In section 190 of the Social Services and Well-being (Wales) Act 2014 (provider failure: exception to temporary duty) in subsection (1)(d) after sub-paragraph (i) insert—

"(ia) by virtue of sections 31 to 33 of the Care Act 2014,".

the new provisions relating to care and support for adults, and support for carers.

APPENDIX 2

STATUTORY GUIDANCE

ISSUED UNDER THE CARE ACT 2014

DEPARTMENT OF HEALTH OCTOBER 2014

1. PROMOTING WELLBEING

This chapter provides guidance on section 1 of the Care Act 2014.

This chapter covers:
- Definition of wellbeing;
- Promoting wellbeing;
- Wellbeing throughout the Care Act.

1.1. The core purpose of adult care and support is to help people to achieve the outcomes that matter to them in their life. Throughout this guidance document, the different chapters set out how a local authority should go about performing its care and support responsibilities. Underpinning all of these individual "care and support functions" (that is, any process, activity or broader responsibility that the local authority performs) is the need to ensure that doing so focuses on the needs and goals of the person concerned.

1.2. Local authorities must promote wellbeing when carrying out any of their care and support functions in respect of a person. This may sometimes be referred to as "the wellbeing principle" because it is a guiding principle that puts wellbeing at the heart of care and support.

1.3. The wellbeing principle applies in all cases where a local authority is carrying out a care and support function, or making a decision, in relation to a person. For this reason it is referred to throughout this guidance. It applies equally to adults with care and support needs and their carers.

1.4. In some specific circumstances, it also applies to children, their carers and to young carers when they are subject to transition assessments (see chapter 16 on transition to adult care and support).

DEFINITION OF WELLBEING

1.5. "Wellbeing" is a broad concept, and it is described as relating to the following areas in particular:

- personal dignity (including treatment of the individual with respect);
- physical and mental health and emotional wellbeing;
- protection from abuse and neglect;
- control by the individual over day-to-day life (including over care and support provided and the way it is provided);
- participation in work, education, training or recreation;
- social and economic wellbeing;
- domestic, family and personal;
- suitability of living accommodation;
- the individual's contribution to society.

1.6. The individual aspects of wellbeing or outcomes above are those which are set out in the Care Act, and are most relevant to people with care and support needs and carers. There is no hierarchy, and all should be considered of equal importance when considering "wellbeing" in the round.

PROMOTING WELLBEING

1.7. Promoting wellbeing involves actively seeking improvements in the aspects of wellbeing set out above when carrying out a care and support function in relation to an individual at any stage of the process from the provision of information and advice to reviewing a care and support plan. Wellbeing covers an intentionally broad range of the aspects of a person's life and will encompass a wide variety of specific considerations depending on the individual.

1.8. A local authority can promote a person's wellbeing in many ways. How this happens will depend on the circumstances, including the person's needs, goals and wishes, and how these impact on their wellbeing. There is no set approach – a local authority should consider each case on its own merits, consider what the person wants to achieve, and how the action which the local authority is taking may affect the wellbeing of the individual.

1.9. The Act therefore signifies a shift from existing duties on local authorities to provide particular services, to the concept of 'meeting needs' (set out in sections 8 and 18-20 of the Act). This is the core legal entitlement for adults to care and support, establishing one clear and consistent set of duties and power for all people who need care and support.

1.10. The concept of 'meeting needs' recognises that everyone's needs are different and personal to them. Local authorities must consider how to meet each person's specific needs rather than simply considering what service they will fit into. The concept of meeting needs also recognises that modern care and support can be provided in any number of ways, with new models emerging all the time, rather than the previous legislation which focuses primarily on traditional models of residential and domiciliary care.

1.11. Whenever a local authority carries out any care and support functions relating to an individual, it must act to promote wellbeing – and it should consider all of the aspects above in looking at how to meet a person's needs and support them to achieve their desired outcomes. However, in individual cases, it is likely that some aspects of wellbeing will be more relevant to the person than others. For example, for some people the ability to engage in work or education will be a more important outcome than for others, and in these cases "promoting their wellbeing" effectively may mean taking particular consideration of this aspect. Local authorities should adopt a flexible approach that allows for a focus on which aspects of wellbeing matter most to the individual concerned.

1.12. The principle of promoting wellbeing should be embedded through the local authority care and support system, but how the local authority promotes wellbeing in practice will depend on the particular function being performed. During the assessment process, for instance, the local authority should explicitly consider the most relevant aspects of wellbeing to the individual concerned, and assess how their needs impact on them. Taking this approach will allow for the assessment to identify how care and support, or other services or resources in the local community, could help the person to achieve their outcomes.

During care and support planning, when agreeing how needs are to be met, promoting the person's wellbeing may mean making decisions about particular types or locations of care (for instance, to be closer to family).

1.13. The wellbeing principle applies equally to those who do not have eligible needs but come into contact with the system in some other way (for example, via an assessment that does not lead to ongoing care and support) as it does to those who go on to receive care and support, and have an ongoing relationship with the local authority. It should inform the delivery of universal services which are provided to all people in the local population, as well as being considered when meeting eligible needs. Although the wellbeing principle applies specifically when the local authority performs an activity or task, or makes a decision, in relation to a person, the principle should also be considered by the local authority when it undertakes broader, strategic functions, such as planning, which are not in relation to one individual. As such, "wellbeing" should be seen as the common theme around which care and support is built at local and national level.

1.14. In addition to the general principle of promoting wellbeing, there are a number of other key principles and standards which local authorities must have regard to when carrying out the same activities or functions:

(a) **the importance of beginning with the assumption that the individual is best-placed to judge the individual's wellbeing.** Building on the principles of the Mental Capacity Act, the local authority should assume that the person themselves knows best their own outcomes, goals and wellbeing. Local authorities should not make assumptions as to what matters most to the person;

(b) **the individual's views, wishes, feelings and beliefs.** Considering the person's views and wishes is critical to a person-centred system. Local authorities should not ignore or downplay the importance of a person's own opinions in relation to their life and their care. Where particular views, feelings or beliefs (including religious beliefs) impact on the choices that a person may wish to make about their care, these should be taken into account. This is especially important where a person has expressed views in the past, but no longer has capacity to make decisions themselves;

(c) **the importance of preventing or delaying the development of needs for care and support and the importance of reducing needs that already exist.** At every interaction with a person, a local authority should consider whether or how the person's needs could be reduced or other needs could be delayed from arising. Effective interventions at the right time can stop needs from escalating, and help people maintain their independence for longer (see chapter 2 on prevention);

(d) **the need to ensure that decisions are made having regard to all the individual's circumstances** (and are not based only on their age or appearance, any condition they have, or any aspect of their behaviour which might lead others to make unjustified assumptions about their wellbeing). Local authorities should not make judgments based on preconceptions about the person's circumstances, but should in every case work to understand their individual needs and goals;

(e) **the importance of the individual participating as fully as possible** in decisions about them and being provided with the information and support necessary to enable the individual to participate. Care and support should be personal, and local authorities should not make decisions from which the person is excluded;

(f) **the importance of achieving a balance between the individual's wellbeing and that of any friends or relatives who are involved in caring for the individual.** People should be considered in the context of their families and support networks, not just as isolated individuals with needs. Local authorities should take into account the impact of an individual's need on those who support them, and take steps to help others access information or support;

(g) **the need to protect people from abuse and neglect.** In any activity which a local authority undertakes, it should consider how to ensure that the person is and remains protected from abuse or neglect. This is not confined only to safeguarding issues, but should be a general principle applied in every case;

(h) **the need to ensure that any restriction on the individual's rights or freedom of action that is involved in the exercise of the function is kept to the minimum necessary** for achieving the purpose for which the function is being exercised. Where the local authority has to take actions which restrict rights or freedoms, they should ensure that the course followed is the least restrictive necessary.

1.15. All of the matters listed above must be considered in relation to every individual, when a local authority carries out a function as described in this guidance. Considering these matters should lead to an approach that looks at a person's life holistically, considering their needs in the context of their skills, ambitions, and priorities – as well as the other people in their life and how they can support the person in meeting the outcomes they want to achieve. The focus should be on supporting people to live as independently as possible for as long as possible.

1.16. As with promoting wellbeing, the factors above will vary in their relevance and application to individuals. For some people, spiritual or religious beliefs will be of great significance, and should be taken into particular account. For others, this will not be the case. Local authorities should consider how to apply these further principles on a case-by-case basis. This reflects the fact that every person is different and the matters of most importance to them will accordingly vary widely.

1.17. Neither these principles, nor the requirement to promote wellbeing, require the local authority to undertake any particular action. The steps a local authority should take will depend entirely on the circumstances. The principles as a whole are not intended to specify the activities which should take place. Instead, their purpose is to set common expectations for how local authorities should approach and engage with people.

"INDEPENDENT LIVING"

1.18. Although not mentioned specifically in the way that "wellbeing" is defined, the concept of "independent living" is a core part of the wellbeing principle. Section 1 of the Care Act includes matters such as individual's control of their day-to-day life, suitability of living accommodation, contribution to society – and crucially, requires local authorities to consider each person's views, wishes, feelings and beliefs.

1.19. The wellbeing principle is intended to cover the key components of independent living, as expressed in the UN Convention on the Rights of People with Disabilities[1] (in particular, Article 19 of the Convention). Supporting people to live as independently as possible, for as long as possible, is a guiding principle of the Care Act. The language used in the Act is intended to be clearer, and focus on the outcomes that truly matter to people, rather than using the relatively abstract term "independent living".

---

[1] http://www.un.org/disabilities/default.asp?id=279

WELLBEING THROUGHOUT THE CARE ACT

1.20. Wellbeing cannot be achieved simply through crisis management; it must include a focus on delaying and preventing care and support needs, and supporting people to live as independently as possible for as long as possible. (See chapter 2 for more detail on approaches to prevention).

1.21. Promoting wellbeing does not mean simply looking at a need that corresponds to a particular service. At the heart of the reformed system will be an assessment and planning process that is a genuine conversation about people's needs for care and support and how meeting these can help them achieve the outcomes most important to them. Where someone is unable to fully participate in these conversations and has no one to help them, local authorities will arrange for an independent advocate. Chapters 6 (Assessment and eligibility), 10 (Care and support planning), and 7 (Independent advocacy) discuss this in more detail.

1.22. In order to ensure these conversations look at people holistically, local authorities and their partners must focus on joining up around an individual, making the person the starting point for planning, rather than what services are provided by what particular agency. Chapter 15 (integration and cooperation) sets this out in more detail.

1.23. In particular, the Care Act is designed to work in partnership with the Children and Families Act 2014, which applies to 0-25 year old children and young people with SEN and Disabilities. In combination, the two Acts enable areas to prepare children and young people for adulthood from the earliest possible stage, including their transition to adult services. This is considered in more detail at chapter 16.

1.24. Promoting wellbeing is not always about local authorities meeting needs directly. It will be just as important for them to put in place a system where people have the information they need to take control of their care and support and choose the options that are right for them. People will have an opportunity to request their local authority support in the form of a direct payment that they can then use to buy their own care and support using this information. Chapters 3 (Information and advice) and 12 (Direct payments) explain this in more detail.

1.25. Control also means the ability to move from one area to another or from children's services to the adult system without fear of suddenly losing care and support. The Care Act ensures that people will be able to move to a different area without suddenly losing their care and support and provides clarity about who will be responsible for care and support in different situations. It also includes measures to help young people move to the adult care and support system, ensuring that no one finds themselves suddenly without care on turning 18. Chapters 20 (Continuity of care), 19 (Ordinary residence) and 16 (Transition to adult care and support set this out in more detail.

1.26. It is not possible to promote wellbeing without establishing a basic foundation where people are safe and their care and support is on a secure footing. The Care Act puts in place a new framework for adult safeguarding and includes measures to guard against provider failure to ensure this is managed without disruption to services. Chapters 14 (Safeguarding), and 5 (Managing provider failure) set this out in more detail.

2. PREVENTING, REDUCING OR DELAYING NEEDS

This chapter provides guidance on section 2 of the Care Act 2014.

This chapter covers:
- Defining "prevention";
- Primary prevention/promoting wellbeing;
- Secondary prevention/early intervention;
- Tertiary prevention/intermediate care and reablement;
- The focus of prevention;
- Developing local approaches to prevention;
- Working with others to focus on prevention;
- Identifying those who may benefit from prevention;
- Enabling access to preventative support;
- Charging for preventative services.

2.1. It is critical to the vision in the Care Act that the care and support system works to actively promote wellbeing and independence, and does not just wait to respond when people reach a crisis point. To meet the challenges of the future, it will be vital that the care and support system intervenes early to support individuals, helps people retain or regain their skills and confidence, and prevents need or delays deterioration wherever possible.

2.2. There are many ways in which a local authority can achieve the aims of promoting wellbeing and independence and reducing dependency. This guidance sets out how local authorities should go about fulfilling their responsibilities, both individually and in partnership with other local organisations, communities, and people themselves.

2.3. The local authority's responsibilities for prevention apply to all adults, including:

- people who do not have any current needs for care and support;

- adults with needs for care and support, whether their needs are eligible and/ or met by the local authority or not (see chapter 6);

- carers, including those who may be about to take on a caring role or who do not currently have any needs for support, and those with needs for support which may not be being met by the local authority or other organisation.

2.4. The term "prevention" or "preventative" measures can cover many different types of support, services, facilities or other resources. There is no one definition for what constitutes preventative activity and this can range from wide-scale whole-population measures aimed at promoting health, to more targeted, individual interventions aimed at improving skills or functioning for one person or a particular group or lessening the impact of caring on a carer's health and wellbeing. In considering how to give effect to their responsibilities, local authorities should consider the range of options available, and how those different approaches could support the needs of their local communities.

2.5. "Prevention" is often broken down into three general approaches – primary, secondary and tertiary prevention – which are described in more detail below. The use of such terms is aimed to illustrate what type of services, facilities and resources could be considered, arranged and provided as part of a prevention service, as well as to whom and when such services could be provided or arranged. However, services can cut across any or all of these three general approaches and as such the examples provided under each approach are not to be seen as limited to that particular approach. Prevention should be seen as an ongoing consideration and not a single activity or intervention.

PREVENT: PRIMARY PREVENTION/PROMOTING WELLBEING

2.6. These are aimed at individuals who have no current particular health or care and support needs. These are services, facilities or resources provided or arranged that may help an individual avoid developing needs for care and support, or help a carer avoid developing support needs by maintaining independence and good health and promoting wellbeing. They are generally universal (i.e. available to all) services, which may include, but are not limited to interventions and advice that:

- provide universal access to good quality information;

- support safer neighbourhoods;

- promote healthy and active lifestyles (e.g. exercise classes);

- reduce loneliness or isolation (e.g. befriending schemes or community activities such as the case study below); or,

- encourage early discussions in families or groups about potential changes in the future, e.g. conversations about potential care arrangements or suitable accommodation should a family member become ill or disabled.

Case Study:

The LinkAge programme aims to promote and enhance the lives of older people (55+ years old) through a range of activities, from walking groups to coffee mornings, through a number of older people-led "hubs" across the city. The main aim is to bring those people that feel socially isolated and lonely into their local communities.

In an evaluation of a new hub there was significant improvement on a friend-ship scale with scores moving from people feeling isolated or with a low level of social support at the beginning of the hub to very or highly socially con-nected at follow up. Eileen (85) said "I look forward to Fridays each week and enjoy the social aspect of the club too". Lyn said "if it wasn't for LinkAge I don't quite know what would have happened. It's made life bear-able, well more than bearable, it's made it life".

REDUCE: SECONDARY PREVENTION/EARLY INTERVENTION

2.7. These are more targeted interventions aimed at individuals who have an increased risk of developing needs, where the provision of services, resources or facilities may help slow down or reduce any further deterioration or prevent other needs from developing. Some early support can help stop a person's life tip-ping into crisis, for example helping someone with a learning disability with moderate needs manage their money, or a few hours support to help a family carer who is caring for their son or daughter with a learning disability and behav-iour that challenges at home.

2.8. Early intervention could also include a fall prevention clinic, adaptions to housing to improve accessibility or provide greater assistance, handyman services, short term provision of wheelchairs or telecare services. In order to identify those individuals most likely to benefit from such targeted services, local authorities may undertake screening or case- finding, for instance to identify individuals at risk of developing specific health conditions or experiencing certain events (such as strokes, or falls), or those that have needs for care and support which are not currently met by the local authority. Targeted interventions should also include approaches to identifying carers, including those who are taking on new caring responsibilities. Carers can also benefit from support to help them develop the knowledge and skills to care effectively and look after their own health and wellbeing.

DELAY: TERTIARY PREVENTION

2.9. These are interventions aimed at minimising the effect of disability or deterioration for people with established or complex health conditions, (including progressive conditions, such as dementia), supporting people to regain skills and manage or reduce need where possible. Tertiary prevention could include, for example the rehabilitation of people who are severely sight impaired (see also chapter 22 sight registers). Local authorities must provide or arrange services, resources or facilities that maximise independence for those already with such needs, for example, interventions such as rehabilitation/reablement services, e.g. community equipment services and adaptations and the use of joint case-management for people with complex needs.

2.10. Tertiary prevention services could also include helping improve the lives of carers by enabling them to continue to have a life of their own alongside caring, for example through respite care, peer support groups like dementia cafés, or emotional support or stress management classes which can provide essential opportunities to share learning and coping tips with others. This can help develop mechanisms to cope with stress associated with caring and help carers develop an awareness of their own physical and mental health needs.

2.11. Prevention is not a one off activity. For example, a change in the circumstances of an adult and/or carer may result in a change to the type of prevention activity that would be of benefit to them (see para 2.33). Prevention can sometimes be seen as something that happens primarily at the time of (or very soon after) a diagnosis or assessment or when there has been a subsequent change in the person's condition. Prevention services are, however, something that should always be considered. For example, at the end of life in relation to carers, prevention services could include the provision of pre-bereavement support.

INTERMEDIATE CARE AND REABLEMENT

2.12. There is a tendency for the terms "reablement", "rehabilitation" and "intermediate care" to be used interchangeably. The National Audit of Intermediate Care categorises four types of intermediate care:

- **crisis response** – services providing short-term care (up to 48 hours);

- **home-based intermediate care** – services provided to people in their own homes by a team with different specialities but mainly health professionals such as nurses and therapists;

- **bed-based intermediate care** – services delivered away from home, for example, in a community hospital; and,

- **reablement** – services to help people live independently which are provided in the person's own home by a team of mainly care and support professionals.

2.13. The term "rehabilitation" is sometimes used to describe a particular type of service designed to help a person regain or re-learn some capabilities where these capabilities have been lost due to illness or disease. Rehabilitation services can include provisions that help people attain independence and remain or return to their home and participate in their community, for example independent living skills and mobility training for people with visual impairment.

2.14. "Intermediate care" services are provided to people, usually older people, after they have left hospital or when they are at risk of being sent to hospital. Intermediate care is a programme of care provided for a limited period of time to assist a person to maintain or regain the ability to live independently – as such they provide a link between places such as hospitals and people's homes, and between different areas of the health and care and support system – community services, hospitals, GPs and care and support.

2.15. To prevent needs emerging across health and care, integrated services should draw on a mixture of qualified health, care and support staff, working collaboratively to deliver prevention. This could involve, for instance, reaching beyond traditional health or care interventions to help people develop or regain the skills of independent living and active involvement in their local community.

CARERS AND PREVENTION

2.16. Carers play a significant role in preventing the needs for care and support for the people they care for, which is why it is important that local authorities consider preventing carers from developing needs for care and support themselves. There may be specific interventions for carers that prevent, reduce or delay the need for carers' support. These interventions may differ from those for people without caring responsibilities. Examples of services, facilities or resources that could contribute to preventing, delaying or reducing the needs of carers may include but is not limited to those which help carers to:

- care effectively and safely – both for themselves and the person they are supporting, e.g. timely interventions or advice on moving and handling safely or avoiding falls in the home, or training for carers to feel confident performing basic care tasks;

- look after their own physical and mental health and wellbeing, including developing coping mechanisms;

- make use of adaptations, equipment IT and assistive technology;

- make choices about their own lives, for example managing care and paid employment;

- find support and services available in their area;

- access the advice, information and support they need including information and advice on welfare benefits and other financial information and about entitlement to carers' assessments (see chapter 6).

2.17. As with the people the care for, the duty to prevent carers from developing needs for support is distinct from the duty to meet their eligible needs (see chapter 6). While a person's eligible needs may be met through universal preventative services, this will be an individual response following a needs or carers assessment. Local authorities cannot fulfill their universal prevention duty in relation to carers simply by meeting eligible needs, and nor would universal preventative services always be an appropriate way of for meeting carers' eligible needs.

THE FOCUS OF PREVENTION
Promoting wellbeing

2.18. Local authorities must have regard to promoting wellbeing and the principles set out in chapter 1. Local authorities should look at an individual's life holistically. This will mean considering any care and support needs in the context of the person's skills, ambitions and priorities. This should include consideration of the role a person's family or friends can play in helping the person to meet their goals. This is not creating or adding to their caring role but including them in an approach supporting the person to live as independently as possible for as long as possible. In regard to carers, the local authority should consider how they can be supported to look after their own health and wellbeing and to have a life of their own alongside their caring responsibilities.

2.19. As highlighted in the case study, where people live alone a person may not always have the support from family or friends because they may not live close by. For this group of people prevention needs to be considered through other means, such as the provision of community services and activities that would help support people to maintain an independent life.

Case Study:

An older man lives alone with some support from his daughter who works full-time. He needs occasional personal care to remain living independently with dignity, and it is likely that these needs will increase. He has lost contact with family and friends following his wife's death and rarely goes out without support from his daughter who is restricted to taking him out at weekends because of work commitments.

An assessment would consider all of his needs, including those currently being met by his daughter, along with the outcomes he wishes to achieve. A separate carer's assessment offered to his daughter (or a combined assessment if both father and daughter agreed) would establish the daughter's willingness and ability to care and continue to care and how best to promote her own wellbeing, for example by having regard to the outcomes she wishes to achieve. This joint assessment would look at issues such as the possible impact on the daughter of supporting her father while in full-time employment as well as the father's isolation, ability to connect with others or be an active citizen.Community groups, voluntary organisations, and buddying services could support the father to reduce the social isolation that he may be feeling and maximise opportunitites to look after his own health and wellbeing and participate in local community activities. This, in turn could lessen the impact of caring on his daughter and enable her to continue to support her father effectively alongside paid employment. Such support can be identified/ suggested alongside other, perhaps more formal services to meet

---

personal care needs, and can be an effective way of promoting wellbeing. In this example, the aspects of wellbeing relating to social wellbeing and family relationships might be promoted.

DEVELOPING RESILIENCE AND PROMOTING INDIVIDUAL STRENGTH

2.20. In developing and delivering preventative approaches to care and support, local authorities should ensure that individuals are not seen as passive recipients of support services, but are able to design care and support based around achievement of their goals. Local authorities should actively promote participation in providing interventions that are co-produced with individuals, families, friends, carers and the community. "Co-production" is when an individual influences the support and services received, or when groups of people get together to influence the way that services are designed, commissioned and delivered. Such interventions can contribute to developing individual resilience and help promote self- reliance and independence, as well as ensuring that services reflect what the people who use them want.

Case Study:

Derby City Council used co-production to develop clear and easy to use customer information to support their new customer journey for self-directed support. New information that has been produced includes an assessment form, support planning tools for people using services, customer leaflets and a staff handbook.

A small project team held discussions and workshops to identify information that needed improving to be clearer and suggestions for improvement, e.g. a new assessment form. Staff working in adult social care assessment teams had training on how to make best use of the new suite of information.

The inclusive approach taken to re-designing the information took longer than an internally managed process, but has resulted in better information, informed people using services and bringing their own perspective and experience. The co-production approach led to the development of key principles which can be used in other areas of communication. The approach is being continued.

http://www.thinklocalactpersonal.org.uk/Browse/SDSandpersonalbudgets/
CaseStudies/ Resource/?cid=9598

2.21. Through the assessment process, an individual will have direct contact with a local authority. A good starting point for a discussion that helps develop resilience and promotes independence would be to ask "what does a good life look like for you and your family and how can we work together to achieve it?" Giving people choice and control over the support they may need and access to the right information enables people to stay as well as possible, maintain independence and caring roles for longer.

2.22. Social workers, Occupational Therapists, other professionals, service providers and commissioners who are effective at preventing, reducing, or delaying needs for care and support are likely to have a holistic picture of the individuals and families receiving support. This will include consideration of a person's strengths and their informal support networks as well as their needs and the risks they face. This approach recognises the value in the resources of voluntary and community groups and the other resources of the local area.

DEVELOPING A LOCAL APPROACH TO PREVENTATIVE SUPPORT

2.23. A local authority must provide or arrange for services, facilities or resources which would prevent, delay or reduce individuals' needs for care and support, or the needs for support of carers. Local authorities should develop a clear, local approach to prevention which sets out how they plan to fulfil this responsibility, taking into account the different types and focus of preventative support as described above. Developing a local approach to preventative support is a responsibility wider than adult care and support alone, and should include the involvement, by way of example, of those responsible for public health, leisure, transport, and housing services which are relevant to the provision of care and support.

2.24. Whilst local authorities may choose to provide some types of preventative support themselves, others may be more effectively provided in partnership with other local partners (e.g. rehabilitation or falls clinics provided jointly with the local NHS), and further types may be best provided by other organisations e.g. specialist housing providers or some carers' services. A local authority's commissioning strategy for prevention should consider the different commissioning routes available, and the benefits presented by each. This could include connecting to other key areas of local preventative activity outside care, including housing, planning and public health.

2.25. In developing a local approach to prevention, the local authority must take steps to identify and understand both the current and future demand for preventative support, and the supply in terms of services, facilities and other resources available.

2.26. Local authorities must consider the importance of identifying the services, facilities and resources that are already available in their area, which could support people to prevent, reduce or delay needs, and which could form part of the overall local approach to preventative activity. Understanding the breadth of available local resources will help the local authority to consider what gaps may remain, and what further steps it should itself take to promote the market or to put in place its own services.

2.27. Where the local authority does not provide such types of preventative support itself, it should have mechanisms in place for identifying existing and new services, maintaining contact with providers over time, and helping people to access them. Local approaches to prevention should be built on the resources of the local community, including local support networks and facilities provided by other partners and voluntary organisations (see paragraph 2.23).

2.28. Local authorities must promote diversity and quality in provision of care and support services, and ensure that a person has a variety of providers to choose from (see chapter 4). Considering the services, facilities and resources which contribute towards preventing or delaying the development of needs for care and support is a core element of fulfilling this responsibility. A local authority should engage local providers of care and support in all aspects of delivery and encourage providers to innovate and respond flexibly to develop interventions that contribute to preventing needs for care and support.

2.29. Local authorities should consider the number of people in its area with existing needs for care and support, as well as those at risk of developing needs in the future, and what can be done to prevent, delay or reduce those needs now and in the future. In doing so, a local authority should draw on existing analyses such as the Joint Strategic Needs Assessment, and work with other local partners such as the NHS to develop a broader, shared understanding of current and future needs, and support integrated approaches to prevention.

2.30. In particular, local authorities must consider how to identify "unmet need" – i.e. those people with needs which are not currently being met, whether by the local authority or anyone else. Understanding unmet need will be crucial to developing a longer-term approach to prevention that reflects the true needs of the local population. This assessment should also be shared with local partners, such as through the health and wellbeing board, to contribute to wider intelligence for local strategies. Preventative services, facilities or resources are often most effective when brought about through partnerships between different parts of the local authority and between other agencies and the community such as those people who are likely to use and benefit from these services.

2.31. Local authorities should consider how they can work with different partners to identify unmet needs for different groups and coordinate shared approaches to preventing or reducing such needs, for example working with the NHS to identify carers, and working with independent providers including housing providers and the voluntary sector, who can provide local insight into changing or emerging needs beyond eligibility for publically-funded care.

Case Study: Case Study: Midland Heart's re-ablement service

At 82, Beryl was diagnosed with stomach cancer and admitted to hospital. As a result of a major operation, she now has a permanent colostomy bag. After only a month Beryl was successfully discharged from hospital to her own home with a re-ablement package from Leicester City Council and support from the housing association, Midland Heart, to help her regain her independence

If Beryl had not received this support, she would have been discharged to a more costly care home. The re-ablement service ensured that Beryl's home was suitably adapted for her return, which allowed a speedy discharge and avoided the need for institutional care. The support service has assisted her attendance at medical appointments with her GP and monitored the impact of her medication.

WORKING WITH OTHER PARTNERS TO FOCUS ON PREVENTION

2.32. Developing and delivering local approaches to prevention, the local authority should consider how to align or integrate its approach with that of other local partners. Preventing needs will often be most effective when action is undertaken at a local level, with different organisations working together to understand how the actions of each may impact on the other.

2.33. Within the local authority, prevention of care and support needs is closely aligned to other local authority responsibilities in relation to public health, children's services, and housing, for example. Across the local landscape, the role of other bodies including the local NHS (e.g. GPs, dentists, pharmacists, opthamologists etc.), welfare and benefits advisers (e.g. at the Jobcentre Plus), the police, prisons in respect of those persons detained or released with care and support needs, service providers and others will also be important in developing a comprehensive approach.

2.34. Local authorities must ensure the integration of care and support provision, including prevention with health and health-related services, which include housing (see chapter 15). This responsibility includes in particular a focus on integrating with partners to prevent, reduce or delay needs for care and support.

2.35. A local authority must cooperate with each of its relevant partners and the partners must cooperate with the local authority (see chapter 15 on cooperation and details of specific relevant partners), for example, in relation to the provision of preventative services and the identification of carers, a local authority must cooperate with NHS bodies.

2.36. A local authority must also set up arrangements between its relevant partners and individual departments in relation to its care and support functions, which includes prevention. Relevant partners and individual departments include, but are not limited to, housing departments where, for example, housing services or officers may be well placed to identify people with dementia and their carers, and provide housing related support and or in partnership with others, home from hospital services or "step up step down" provision.

IDENTIFYING THOSE WHO MAY BENEFIT FROM PREVENTATIVE SUPPORT

2.37. Local authorities should put in place arrangements to identify and target those individuals who may benefit from particular types of preventative support. Helping people to access such types of support when they need it is likely to have a significant impact on their longer-term health and wellbeing, as well as potentially reducing or delaying the need for ongoing care and support from the local authority.

2.38. In developing such approaches, local authorities should consider the different opportunities for coming into contact with those people who may benefit from preventative support, including where the first contact may be with another professional outside the local authority, for example, GPs, pharmacists or welfare and benefit advisers. There are a number of interactions and access points that could bring a person into contact with the local authority or a partner organisation and act as a trigger point for the local authority to consider whether the provision of a preventative service, or some other step is appropriate. These might include, for instance:

- initial contact through a customer services centre, whether by the person concerned or someone acting on their behalf;
- contact with a GP, community nurses, housing officers or other professionals which leads to a referral to the local authority;
- an assessment of needs or a carer's assessment (see chapter 6 on assessment), which identifies that the person would benefit from a preventative service or other type of support available locally.

2.39. Prevention should be a consistent focus for local authorities in undertaking their care and support functions. However, there may be key points in a person's life or in the care and support process where a preventative intervention may be particularly appropriate or of benefit to the person. Approaches to identifying those people who may benefit from preventative support should consider how to locate people in such circumstances, for example:

- bereavement;

- hospital admission and /or discharge;

- people who have been recently admitted to or released from prison;

- application for benefits such as Attendance Allowance, or Carer's Allowance;

- contact with/use of local support groups;

- contact with/use of private care and support;

- changes in housing.

2.40. A local authority must establish and maintain a service for providing people with information and advice relating to care and support (see chapter 3). In addition to any more targeted approaches to communicating with individuals who may benefit from preventative support, this service should include information and advice about preventative services, facilities or resources, so that anyone can find out about the types of support available locally that may meet their individual needs and circumstances, and how to access them.

HELPING PEOPLE ACCESS PREVENTATIVE SUPPORT

2.41. Many different kinds of service, facility or resource can be preventative and can help individuals live well and maintain their independence or caring roles for longer.

2.42. Local authorities should be innovative and develop an approach to prevention that meets the needs of their local population. A preventative approach requires a broad range of interventions, as one size will not fit all.

2.43. Where a local authority has put in place mechanisms for identifying people who may benefit from a type of preventative support, it should take steps to ensure that the person concerned understands the need for the particular measure, and is provided with further information and advice as necessary.

2.44. Contact with a person who is identified as being able to benefit from preventative support may lead to the local authority becoming aware that the person appears to have needs for either or both care and support and support in a role as a carer. This appearance of need may trigger the requirement to carry out a needs assessment (in the case of an adult with needs for care and support), or a carer's assessment (see paragraphs 2.47-2.53 below). However, where a local authority is not required to carry out such an assessment under the Care Act, it should nonetheless take steps to establish whether the person identified will benefit from the type of preventative support proposed.

2.45. Where a person is provided with any type of service, or support to access any facility or resource as a preventative measure, the local authority should also provide the person with information in relation to the services offered or measure undertaken. The local authority is not required to provide a care and support plan or a support plan where it only take steps under section 2 of the Care Act; however, it should consider which aspects of a plan should be provided in these circumstances, and should provide such information as is necessary to enable the person to understand:

- what needs the person has or may develop, and why the intervention or other action is proposed in their regard;

- what the expected outcome for the action proposed is, and any relevant timescale in which those outcomes are expected; and

- what is proposed to take place at the end of the measure (for instance, whether an assessment of need or a carer's assessment will be carried out at that point).

2.46. The person concerned must agree to the provision of any service or other step proposed by the local authority. Where the person refuses, but continues to appear to have needs for care and support (or for support, in the case of a carer), then the local authority must proceed to offer the individual an assessment.

ASSESSMENT OF ADULTS' AND CARERS' NEEDS

2.47. In assessing whether an adult has any care and support needs or a carer has any needs for support, the local authority must consider whether the person concerned would benefit from the preventative services, facilities or resources provided by the local authority or which might otherwise be available in the community. This is regardless of whether, in fact, the adult or carer is assessed as having any care and support needs or support needs. This is to ensure that as part of the assessment process, the local authority considers the capacity of the person to manage their needs or achieve the outcomes which matter to them, and allows for access to preventative support before a decision is made on whether the person has eligible needs (see chapter 6 on assessment for more information).

2.48. As part of this process, the local authority should also take into account the person's own capabilities, and the potential for improving their skills, as well as the role of any support from family, friends or others that could help them to achieve what they wish for from day-to-day life. This should not assume that others are willing or able to take up caring roles, and where it appears to the local authority that a carer may have needs for support (whether currently or in the future) a carer's assessment must always be offered.

2.49. Children should not undertake inappropriate or excessive caring roles that may have an impact on their development. A young carer becomes vulnerable when their caring role risks impacting upon their emotional or physical wellbeing and their prospects in education and life. A local authority may become aware that a child is carrying out a caring role through an assessment or informed through family members or a school. A local authority should consider how supporting the adult with needs for care and support can prevent the young carer from under taking excessive or inappropriate care and support responsibilities. Where a young carer is identified, the local authority must undertake a young carer's assessment under part 3 of the Children Act 1989.

2.50. Considering the support from family, friends or others is important in taking a holistic approach to see the person in the context of their support networks and understanding how their needs may be prevented, reduced or delayed by others within the community, rather than by more formal services (also see chapter 6, paragraph 6.44 to 6.53 about the whole family approach to assessment).

2.51. If a person is provided with care and support or support as a carer by the local authority, the authority must provide them with information and advice about what can be done to prevent, delay, or reduce their needs as part of their care and support plan or support plan. This should also include consideration of the person's strengths and the support from other members of the family, friends or the community (see chapter 10 on care and support planning).

2.52. Regardless of whether or not a person is ultimately assessed as having either any needs at all or any needs which are to be met by the local authority, the authority must in any case provide information and advice in an accessible form, about what can be done to prevent, delay, or reduce development of their needs. This is to ensure that all people are provided with targeted, personalised information and advice that can support them to take steps to prevent or reduce their needs, connect more effectively with their local community, and delay the onset of greater needs to maximise their independence and quality of life. Where a person has some needs that are eligible, and also has some other needs that are not deemed to be eligible, the local authority must provide information and advice on services facilities or resources that would contribute to preventing, reducing or delaying the needs which are not eligible, and this should be aligned and be consistent with the care and support for care and support, or support as a carer plan or support plan.

2.53. It is important that people receive information in a timely manner about the services or interventions that can help or contribute to preventing an escalation in needs for care and support. Supporting people's access to the right information at the right time is a key element of a local authority's responsibilities for prevention.

CHARGING FOR PREVENTATIVE SUPPORT

2.54. Preventative services, like other forms of care and support, are not always provided free, and charging for some services is vital to ensure affordability. The Care and Support (Preventing Needs for Care and Support) Regulations 2014 continue to allow local authorities to make a charge for the provision of certain preventative services, facilities or resources. The regulations also provide that some other specified services must be provided free of charge.

2.55. Prevention services facilities or resources may not involve local authorities directly providing or commissioning a service. Some effective forms of prevention result from partnerships with other public services, voluntary and community organisations and other providers. In developing these partnerships local authorities should consider what obstacles there may be which might prevent people on low incomes from benefitting from the activities and take reasonable steps to avoid this.

2.56. Where a local authority chooses to charge for a particular service, it should consider how to balance the affordability and viability of the activity with the likely impact that charging may have on uptake. In some cases, charging may be necessary in order to make a preventative service viable or keep a service running.

2.57. When charging for any type of preventative support, local authorities should take reasonable steps to ensure that any charge is affordable for the person concerned. This does not need to follow the method of the financial assessment used for mainstream charging purposes; and the use of such a process is likely to be disproportionate.

2.58. However, local authorities should consider adopting more proportionate or "light- touch" approach which ensures that charges are only paid by those who can afford to do so. In any event, a local authority must not charge more than it costs to provide or arrange for the service, facility or resource.

2.59. The regulations require that intermediate care and reablement provided up to six weeks, and minor aids and adaptations up to the value of £1,000 must always be provided free of charge (see also 8.14).

2.60. Where local authorities provide intermediate care or reablement to those who require it, this must be provided free of charge for a period of up to six weeks. This is for all adults, irrespective of whether they have eligible needs for ongoing care and support. Although such types of support will usually be provided as a preventative measure under section 2 of the Act, they may also be provided as part of a package of care and support to meet eligible needs. In these cases, regulations also provide that intermediate care or reablement cannot be charged for in the first six weeks, to ensure consistency.

2.61. Whilst they are both time-limited interventions, neither intermediate care nor reablement should have a strict time limit, since the period of time for which the support is provided should depend on the needs and outcomes of the individual. In some cases, for instance a period of rehabilitation for a visually impaired person (a specific form of reablement)[1] may be expected to last longer than six weeks. Whilst the local authority does have the power to charge for this where it is provided beyond six weeks, local authorities should consider continuing to provide it free of charge beyond six weeks in view of the clear preventative benefits to the individual and, in many cases, the reduced risk of hospital admissions.

2.62. Local authorities should consider the potential impact and consequences of ending the provision of preventative services. Poorly considered exit strategies can negate the positive outcomes of preventative services, facilities or resources, and ongoing low-level care and support can have significant impact on preventing, reducing and delaying need.

Case Study:

Mr A is a 91 year old man who lives alone with his dog in his house. He is usually independent, is a passionate cook and enjoys socialising. He drives a car. Whilst out walking his dog he suffered a stroke, he fell, causing a fractured neck of femur. He was admitted to hospital and underwent surgery for a hip replacement which meant he had to follow hip precautions for 6 weeks. The stroke had left him with slight left-sided weakness and problems with concentration, sequencing and attention. He was transferred to a Community Hospital for rehabilitation where the Physiotherapists (PTs) and Occupational Therapists (OTs) worked on mobility, transfers, personal care following hip precautions, stair climbing and kitchen tasks. Cognitive screens were completed and the OTs targeted their input on helping improve concentration, sequencing and attention.

Mr A was discharged, independently mobile using a frame, independent transferring using equipment and stair climbing with supervision. He was discharged home with 4 calls per day from BEST plus (Bradford Enablement

---

[1] ADASS position statement on visual impairment rehabilitation in the context of personalisation (Dec 2013)

Support Team). Joint sessions between the PT and OT and BEST plus were completed to work on the following:

- Practising walking safely indoors using 2 walking sticks.
- Increase hip strength through exercises.
- To be safe and independent washing and dressing.
- To be safe and independent preparing hot drinks and simple snacks and transport safely using trolley.

The above goals were achieved and new goals were set in consultation with Mr A:

- To be safe and independent walking outdoors using 2 sticks.
- To be safe and independent bathing using bath lift.
- To be safe and independent preparing hot meals from scratch.
- To be safe and independent completing shopping using Access bus.
- To be safe and independent walking dog short distances using 4 wheeled walker. After 6 weeks of continued BEST plus input in Mr A's home, he was able to achieve all of his goals and all Social Services input was withdrawn. Aspects of Mr A's wellbeing have been promoted including physical wellbeing, social wellbeing, and control over day-to- day life.

3. INFORMATION AND ADVICE

This chapter provides guidance on section 4 of the Care Act 2014.

This chapter covers:
- The duty placed on local authorities to establish and maintain information and advice services relating to care and support for all people in its area;
- The broad audience for the information and advice service;
- The local authority role with respect to financial information and advice;
- The accessibility and proportionality of information and advice;
- The development of plans/strategies to meet local needs.

3.1. Information and advice is fundamental to enabling people, carers and families to take control of, and make well-informed choices about, their care and support and how they fund it. Not only does information and advice help to promote people's wellbeing by increasing their ability to exercise choice and control, it is also a vital component of preventing or delaying people's need for care and support.

3.2. Local authorities **must**: *"establish and maintain a service for providing people in its area with information and advice relating to care and support for adults and support for carers"*.

3.3. The local authority has an active and critical role in the provision of information and advice and **must** take an active role. To fulfil its duty under section 4 of the Act, a local authority is likely to need to go further than providing information and advice directly (though direct provision will be important) by working to ensure the coherence, sufficiency, availability and accessibility of information and advice relating to care and support across the local authority area. Importantly, this duty to establish and maintain an information and advice service relates to the whole population of the local authority area, not just those with care and support needs or in some other way already known to the system.

3.4. It is important to be clear that the duty to establish and maintain an information and advice service is distinct from the duty to meet eligible needs (see chapter 6): this is true for both people with care and support needs and their carers. While a person's eligible needs may be met by the provision of information and advice this will be an individual response following a needs or carers assessment. Local authorities cannot fulfil their universal information and advice duty simply by meeting eligible needs, and nor would information and advice always be an appropriate way of meeting eligible needs.

3.5. The local authority must ensure that information and advice services established cover more than just basic information about care and support and cover the wide range of care and support related areas set out in paragraph 3.22 below. The service should also address, prevention of care and support needs, finances, health, housing, employment, what to do in cases of abuse or neglect of an adult and other areas where required. In fulfilling this duty, local authorities should consider the people they are communicating with on a case by case basis, and seek to actively encourage them towards the types of information and/or advice that may be particularly relevant to them.

3.6. Local authorities **must** also have regard to identifying people that contact them who may benefit from financial information and advice independent of the local authority and actively facilitate those people to access to it (see paragraph 3.49). Separately to the duty to establish and maintain an information and advice service, local authorities must provide independent advocacy to facilitate the person's involvement in the care and support assessment, planning and review processes where an individual would experience substantial difficulty in understanding, retaining or using information given, or in communicating their views, wishes or feelings and where there is nobody else appropriate (see chapter 7).

3.7. The availability and provision of information and advice, whether more general information about the way the system operates in the local authority area or more personalised information on a person's specific needs, are essential building blocks to all of the reforms and many of the specific duties the Act introduces. This chapter of guidance should therefore be read in conjunction with guidance throughout this document, including:

- Promoting individual wellbeing (Chapter 1).

- Prevention of needs for care and support (Chapter 2).

- Integration of care and support with health and housing related services (Chapter 15).

- Promoting diverse and high quality services (Chapter 4).

- Assessment and eligibility (Chapter 6).

- Personal budgets, personal care and support planning and direct payments (Chapters 10-13).

- Deferred payment agreements (Chapter 9).

- Continuity of care (Chapter 20).

- Safeguarding (Chapter 14).

- Transition to adult care and support (Chapter 16).

- Independent advocacy (Chapter 7).

TERMINOLOGY

3.8. In this section of guidance, the term 'information' means the communication of knowledge and facts regarding care and support. 'Advice' means helping a person to identify choices and/or providing an opinion or recommendation regarding a course of action in relation to care and support.

3.9. This section of guidance also uses the term 'advocacy' to mean supporting a person to understand information, express their needs and wishes, secure their rights, represent their interests and obtain the care and support they need.

3.10. This guidance talks about 'financial information and advice' which includes a broad spectrum of services whose purpose is to help people plan, prepare and pay for their care costs. In places it talks of 'independent' financial information or advice which in this document means services independent of the local authority. This guidance also refers to 'regulated' financial advice which means advice from an organisation regulated by the Financial Conduct

Authority[1] (FCA) which can extend to individual recommendations about specific financial products. Local authorities should ensure that people are able to access all of these types of financial information and advice which help people plan and pay for their care.

THE DUTY TO ESTABLISH AND MAINTAIN A SERVICE

3.11. Local authorities **must** establish and maintain a service for providing people in their areas with information and advice relating to care and support for adults and support for carers. In doing so local authorities should take account of the services currently in place and actions already taken and plans with partner organisations resulting from Joint Strategic Needs Assessments and Joint Health and Wellbeing Strategies.[2] The information and advice service must cover the needs of all its population, not just those who are in receipt of local authority funded care or support. For example, people may often require information and advice before they need to access care or support services, to consider what actions they may take now to prevent or delay any need for care, or how they might plan to meet the cost of future care needs.

3.12. People need information and advice across many areas to support them to make informed choices about their care and support (see paragraph 3.23).

3.13. In establishing and maintaining an information and advice service, local authorities should ensure that they engage widely with people with care and support needs, carers, the wider public and local providers of information and advice and other types of care and support, to identify what is available and exactly what is needed locally, and how and where information and advice should best be provided.

3.14. It is important to recognise that while local authorities **must** establish and maintain a service, the duty does not require they *provide* all elements of this service. Rather, under this duty local authorities are expected to understand, co-ordinate and make effective use of other high quality statutory, voluntary and/ or private sector information and advice resources available to people within their areas. This may also include provision of a service or parts of a service in conjunction with one or more local authorities, health services, children's services,[3] or reuse of information from other local or national sources. When a local need for additional information and advice services is identified, local authorities should recognise the relevance of independent and impartial advice and should consider carefully whether services should be provided by the local authority directly or by another agency, including independent providers.

THE AUDIENCES FOR THE INFORMATION AND ADVICE SERVICE

3.15. Local authorities are responsible for ensuring that all adults including carers in their area with a need for information and advice about care and support are able to access it. This is a very broad group, extending much further than people who have an immediate need for care or support. It will only be achieved

---

[1] http://www.fca.org.uk/

[2] https://www.gov.uk/government/publications/joint-strategic-needs-assessment-and-joint-health-and-wellbeing-strategies-explained

[3] SEN Code of Practice (Department of Health, 2014). https://www.gov.uk/government/publications/send-code-of-practice-0-to-25

through working in partnership with wider public and local advice and information providers.

3.16. People (carers included) who are likely to need information and advice include, but are not restricted to:

- people wanting to plan for their future care and support needs;

- people who may develop care and support needs, or whose current care and support needs may become greater. Under the duty of prevention in Section 2 of the Act, local authorities are expected to take action to prevent, delay and/or reduce the care and support needs for these people (see chapter 2 on prevention);

- people who have not presented to local authorities for assessment but are likely to be in need of care and support. Local authorities are expected to take steps to identify such people and encourage them to come forward for an assessment of their needs (see chapter 2 on prevention);

- people who become known to the local authority (through referral, including self-referral), at first contact where an assessment of needs is being considered (see chapter 6 on assessments);

- people who are assessed by local authorities as currently being in need of care and support. Advice and information **must** be offered to these people irrespective of whether they have been assessed as having eligible needs which the local authority must meet (see chapter 6 on assessments);

- people whose eligible needs for care and support the local authority is currently meeting (whether the local authority is paying for some, all or none of the costs of meeting those needs) (see chapter 10 on care and support planning);

- people whose care and support or support plans are being reviewed (see chapter 13 on reviews of care and support plans);

- family members and carers of adults with care and support needs, (or those who are likely to develop care and support needs). Under Sections 2 of the Act, local authorities are expected to have regard to the importance of identifying carers and take action to reduce their needs for support (see chapter 6 on assessments);

- adults who are subject to adult safeguarding concerns (see chapter 14 on safeguarding);

- people who may benefit from financial information and advice on matters concerning care and support. Local authorities must have regard to the importance of identifying these people, to help them understand the financial costs of their care and support and access independent financial information and advice including from regulated financial advisers (see paragraph 3.49); and,

- care and support staff who have contact with and provide information and advice as part of their jobs.

3.17. In providing information and advice, local authorities must recognise and respond to the specific requirements that carers have for both general and personal information and advice. A carer's need for information and advice may be separate and distinct from information and advice for the person they are caring for. These distinct needs may be covered together, in a similar manner to the local authority combining an assessment of a person needing care and support with a carer's assessment (where both the individuals concerned agree) (see chapter 6 on assessments), but may be more appropriately addressed separately. This may include information and advice on:

- breaks from caring;
- the health and wellbeing of carers themselves;
- caring and advice on wider family relationships;
- carers' financial and legal issues;
- caring and employment;
- caring and education; and,
- a carer's need for advocacy.

ACCESS TO AND QUALITY OF INFORMATION AND ADVICE

3.18. The local authority must ensure that there is an accessible information and advice service that meets the needs of its population. Information and advice must be open to everyone who would benefit from it. People access information and advice from a wide variety of sources. The authority should take account of information standards[1] published by the Information Standards Board for Health and Social Care under the provisions of the Health and Social Care Act 2012.

3.19. Local authorities should ensure that information supplied is clear. Information and advice should only be judged as clear if it is understood and able to be acted upon by the individual receiving it. Local authorities will need to take steps to evaluate and ensure that information and advice is understood and able to be acted upon

3.20. Information and advice provided within the service should be accurate, up-to-date and consistent with other sources of information and advice. Staff providing information and advice within a local authority and other frontline staff should be aware of accessibility issues and be appropriately trained.

3.21. All reasonable efforts should be taken to ensure that information and advice provided meets the individual's requirements, is comprehensive and is given at an early stage. Local authorities must seek to ensure that all relevant information is available to people for them to make the best informed decision in their particular circumstances, and omission or the withholding of information would be at odds with the duty as set out in the Act.

3.22. There are some circumstances where it is particularly important for information and advice to be impartially provided. Local authorities should consider when this might most effectively be provided by an independent source rather than by the local authority itself. This is particularly likely to be the case when people need advice about how and whether to question or challenge the decisions of the local authority or other statutory body.

---

[1] More detail on the appeals system will be set out in the consultation on care and support funding reform, to be published in December 2014

WHAT SHOULD BE PROVIDED – INFORMATION AND ADVICE
CONTENT

3.23. In discharging this duty, local authorities must ensure that information and advice is provided on:

- *the care and support system locally* – about how the system works. An outline of what the 'process' may entail and the judgements that may need to be made. Including specific information on what the assessment process, eligibility, and review stage is, how to complain or make a formal appeal to the authority, what they involve and when independent advocacy should be provided and be widely available. This also includes wider information and advice to support individual wellbeing (see paragraph 3.25); the charging arrangements for care and support costs (utilising current and developing national resources (see paragraphs 3.66-3.67); how a person might plan for their future care and support needs and how to pay for them, including provision for the possibility that they may not have capacity to make decisions for themselves in the future;

- *how to access the care and support available locally* – where, how and with whom to make contact, including information on how and where to request an assessment of needs, a review or to complain or appeal against a decision;[1]

- *the choice of types of care and support, and the choice of care providers available in the local authority's area* – including prevention and reablement services and wider services that support wellbeing. Where possible this should include the likely costs to the person of the care and support services available to them. This should also include information on different types of service or support that allow people personal control over their care and support for example, details of Independent Service Funds, and direct payments (see chapter 4 on market shaping and commissioning);

- *how to access independent financial advice on matters relating to care and support* – about the extent of their personal responsibilities to pay for care and support, their rights to statutory financial and other support, locally and nationally, so that they understand what care and support they are entitled to from the local authority or other statutory providers. Including what information and advice people may wish to consider when making financial decisions about care so that they can make best use of their financial resources and are able to plan for their personal costs of care whether immediately or in the future. (See paragraphs 3.34-3.45.);

- *how to raise concerns about the safety or wellbeing of an adult with care and support needs (and* also *consider how to do the same for a carer with support needs)* (see paragraphs 3.49-3.50).

3.24. The breadth of the circumstances under which information and advice must be provided, and the overall duty to promote individual wellbeing, means that local authorities **must** ensure that the subject matters covered by their information and advice available to people in their areas go much further than a narrow

---

[1] As noted above, more detail on the appeals system will be set out in the consultation on care and support funding reform, to be published in December 2014

definition of care and support and cover all those subject matters listed in paragraph 3.22 above. Depending on local circumstances, the service should also include, but not be limited to, information and advice on:

- available housing and housing-related support options for those with care and support needs;
- effective treatment and support for health conditions, including Continuing Health Care arrangements;
- availability and quality of health services;
- availability of services that may help people remain independent for longer such as home improvement agencies, handyman or maintenance services;
- availability of befriending services and other services to prevent social isolation;
- availability of intermediate care entitlements such as aids and adaptations;
- eligibility and applying for disability benefits and other types of benefits;
- availability of employment support for disabled adults;
- children's social care services and transition;
- availability of carers' services and benefits;
- sources of independent information, advice and advocacy;
- the Court of Protection, power of attorney and becoming a Deputy;
- raise awareness of the need to plan for future care costs;
- practical help with planning to meet future or current care costs;
- accessible ways and support to help people understand the different types of abuse and its prevention.

WHEN INFORMATION SHOULD BE PROVIDED

3.25. Local authorities have a number of direct opportunities to provide – or signpost to – advice and information when people in need of care and support come into contact with them. These include:

- at first point of contact with the local authority;
- as part of a needs or carer's assessment, including joint Continuing Healthcare assessments;
- during a period of reablement;
- around and following financial assessment;
- when considering a financial commitment such as a deferred payment agreement or top-up agreement;
- during or following an adult safeguarding enquiry;
- when considering take up of a personal budget and/or Direct Payment;
- during the care and support planning process;
- during the review of a person's care and support plan;

- when a person may be considering a move to another local authority area;
- at points in transition, for example when people needing care or carers under 18 become adults and the systems for support may change.

3.26. Local authorities, working with their partners must use the wider opportunities to provide targeted information and advice at key points in people's contact with the care and support, health and other local services. These include, but are not limited to, known 'trigger points' during a person's life such as:

- contact with other local authority services;
- bereavement;
- hospital entry and/or discharge;
- diagnosis of health conditions – such as dementia, stroke or an acquired impairment for example;
- Consideration or review of Continuing Healthcare arrangements;
- take-up of power of attorney;
- applications to Court of Protection;
- application for, or review of, disability benefits such as Attendance Allowance and Personal Independence Payments, and for Carers Allowance;
- access to work interviews;
- contact with local support groups, charities, or user-led organisations including carers' groups and disabled person's organisations;
- contact with or use of private care and support services, including homes care;
- change or loss of housing;
- contact with the criminal justice system;
- admission to or release from prison;
- 'Guidance Guarantee' in the Pensions Act 2014;
- retirement.

ACCESSIBILITY OF INFORMATION AND ADVICE

3.27. The local authority should ensure that products and materials (in all formats) are as accessible as possible for all potential users. Websites should meet specific standards such as the Web Content Accessibility Guidelines[1] and guidance set out in the Government Digital Service's (GDS) service manual,[2] printed products should be produced to appropriate guidelines with important materials available in easy read, and telephone services should also be available to those with hearing impairments. Local authorities should particularly be aware

---

[1] http://www.w3.org/TR/WCAG20/
[2] https://www.gov.uk/service-manual/user-centred-design/accessibility.html

of the needs of individuals with complex but relatively rare conditions, such as deaf-blindness.[1]

3.28. As required under the Equality Act 2010,[2] reasonable adjustments should be made to ensure that disabled people have equal access to information and advice services. Reasonable adjustments could include the provision of information in accessible formats or with communication support.

3.29. Advice and information content should, where possible, be provided in the manner preferred by the person and will therefore often need to be available in a number of different formats. The duty in the Care Act will not be met through the use of digital channels alone, and information and advice channels are likely to include all of the following:

- face-to-face contact;
- use of peer-to-peer contacts;
- community settings;
- advice and advocacy services;
- telephone;
- mass communications, and targeted use of leaflets, posters etc. (e.g. in GP surgeries);
- use of 'free' media such as newspaper, local radio stations, social media;
- local authority's own and other appropriate internet websites, including support for the self-assessment of needs;
- third party internet content and applications;
- email.

3.30. Some groups in need of information and advice about care and support may have particular requirements. Local authorities must ensure that their information and advice service has due regard to the needs of these people. These include, but are not limited to:

- people with sensory impairments, such as visual impairment, deafblind and hearing impaired;
- people who do not have English as a first language;
- people who are socially isolated;
- people whose disabilities limit their physical mobility;
- people with learning disabilities;
- people with mental health problems.

3.31. Some people, including some people with dementia, may benefit from an independent person to help them to access or avail themselves of necessary

---

[1] Social care for deafblind adults and children LAC(DH)(2009)6 [under review] http://webarchive.nationalarchives.gov.uk/20130107105354/
http://www.dh.gov.uk/en/Publicationsandstatistics/Lettersandcirculars/LocalAuthorityCirculars/DH_101114
[2] https://www.gov.uk/equality-act-2010-guidance#public-sector-equality-duty

information and advice. Any such need for help to facilitate access to this universal information and advice needs to be considered in planning for delivery of the service, although the duty to make arrangements for an individual to have an independent advocate available to them in certain circumstances only applies in relation to an individual's involvement in the assessment, planning and review processes. From the point of first contact with or referral to the authority consideration of the duty to provide for independent advocacy to support involvement in assessment, planning and reviews should be undertaken (see chapter 7 on independent advocacy).

PROPORTIONALITY OF INFORMATION AND ADVICE

3.32. The type, extent and timing of information and advice provided should be appropriate to the needs of the person. More complex issues may require more intensive and more personalised information and advice, helping people to understand the choices available to them, while general enquiries may require a less intensive approach. It is also important that the right level of information and advice is provided at the right time, recognising that a person's need for information or advice may vary depending on the circumstance. For example, providing a person with too much information, more than they can take in, perhaps at a time of crisis, can be counter-productive.

3.33. There are clear messages from past public consultations and from research that people 'don't know what they need to know' in relation to their care and support. This can prevent them asking the right questions and can mask the articulation and identification of needs that they have, for which they could benefit from information and advice. All contact for information and advice should take account of this and be able to respond with an assessment of needs when appropriate (see chapter 6).[1]

3.34. Local authorities should help ensure that information and advice is proportionate to the needs of those for whom it is provided. This could include enabling access to the support of registered social work advice for those providing information and advice to people contacting the local authority. This can help ensure that the potential for complexity is recognised early on and the person receives help to access non-statutory services and/or initial statutory sector support proportionate to their needs.

3.35. In providing an information and advice service, local authorities must be providing more than just leaflets and web-based materials. The focus should be on enabling people to access what they need through a tailored range of services that assists people to navigate all points and aspects of their journey through care and support. In doing this, local authorities should think about how they are reaching out and joining up with other providers of information and advice to ensure the coherence of the overall "offer" (see chapter 14 on integration and cooperation).

FINANCIAL INFORMATION AND ADVICE

3.36. Financial information and advice is fundamental to enabling people to make well- informed choices about how they pay for their care. It is integral to a person's consideration of how best to meet care and support needs, immediately or in the future. People with good and impartial financial information and advice

---

[1] See Assessment chapter 6 on first contact

have a better understanding of how their available resources can be used more flexibly to fund a wider range of care options.

3.37. Financial information and advice is considered in a separate section due to the sometimes specialist and complex nature of what can be needed. This section should be read in the context of the overarching chapter and all requirements set out in this chapter, for example on accessibility and proportionality, must also be applied to financial information and advice. As set out at the start of the chapter, when this section refers to 'independent financial information and advice' it means services independent of the local authority. Where it refers to 'regulated' financial advice it means advice from an organisation regulated by the Financial Conduct Authority which can extend to individual recommendations about specific financial products.

3.38. The service that local authorities are required to establish and maintain must include financial information and advice on matters relevant to care and support. It should provide some of this information directly to people in its community. However, where it would not be appropriate for a local authority to provide it directly, the local authority must ensure that people are helped to understand how to access independent financial advice.

3.39. Care decisions are often made quickly and at a time of crisis, and they can often involve family and friends in the process. The local authority must have regard to the importance of identifying those who may benefit from financial advice or information as early as possible. This should be complemented by broader awareness raising about how care and support is funded. Local authorities may also include how care and support costs interact with retirement decisions. Actions taken by a local authority to do this should include:

- working with partners to get the right message to people in the authority's area: those who develop care and support needs, their carers, families and friends;

- working with partners to communicate messages about the benefits of financial information and advice for example with the voluntary sector, through hospitals, GPs, or solicitors who may be advising on wills or power of attorney; and

- considering a person's need for financial information and advice when they make first contact with the authority and throughout the assessment, care and support planning and review processes.

3.40. When making financial plans about how to pay for care and support, a person needs to have confidence in what to do in the present, a view ahead to the future and a plan for what to do if circumstances change. This long-term outlook means that people will want to access financial information and advice at different points in their journey to enable them to make sustainable plans to pay for their care. The local authority should provide a service that covers this breadth and that facilitates access to the full spectrum of financial information and advice – from basic budgeting tips to regulated advice – to ensure that people within its area who would benefit can access it. They should also be aware and provide for the fact that some people will be less able to protect themselves from theft, fraud and financial exploitations (see chapter 14).[1]

---

[1] See safeguarding chapter

3.41. The local authority service should include the following aspects of financial information and advice:

- understanding care charges;

- ways to pay;

- cap on care costs, when preparing for its introduction (April 2016), particularly early assessments;[1]

- money management;

- making informed financial decisions; and

- facilitating access to independent financial information and advice.

3.42. Before providing financial information or advice directly to a person the local authority should establish whether the person has a deputy of the Court of Protection or a person with Lasting Power of Attorney acting on their behalf.

UNDERSTANDING CARE CHARGES

3.43. The local authority must provide information to help people understand what they may have to pay, when and why and how it relates to people's individual circumstances. This must include the charging framework for care and support, how contributions are calculated (from both assets and income) and the means tested support available; top-ups (see chapter 8 on charging); and how care and support choices may affect costs. In the case of top-ups, local authority should ensure that someone is willing and able to pay for them – this information will be fundamental in helping with this. From April 2016, it will also need to include the capped costs system. The local authority should use the knowledge it has of the local care market – types of care and local providers of information and advice – to complement and develop the overarching narrative on how care funding works at the national level. This would include both domiciliary and residential care.

WAYS TO PAY

3.44. The local authority must provide people with information on the availability of different ways to pay for care including through income and assets (e.g. pension or housing wealth), a deferred payment agreement (see chapter 9 on deferred payment agreements), a financial product or a combination of these things. Local authorities should seek to give information that would be particularly pertinent to a person's individual circumstances and facilitate access to an independent source of information or advice where relevant. This will be of particular relevance where a person will be meeting the total cost of care and support themselves or may be considering taking out a deferred payment agreement (see chapter 9)[2] or purchasing a financial product.

MONEY MANAGEMENT

3.45. Different people will need different levels of support from the local authority and other providers of information and advice depending on their financial capability, their care needs and the amount they are expected to contribute. At the

---

[1] More detail will be set out in the consultation on funding reform, to be published in December 2014

[2] See deferred payment agreements chapter 9

lower end of the spectrum, people may just need some basic information and support to help them rebalance their finances in light of their changing circumstances. Topics may include welfare benefits, advice on good money management, help with basic budgeting and possibly on debt management. The local authority may be able to provide some of this information itself, for example of welfare benefits, but where it cannot, it should help people access it.

MAKING INFORMED FINANCIAL DECISIONS

3.46. The local authority must support people to make informed, affordable and sustainable financial decisions about their care throughout all stages of their life. In many situations the role of the local authority will be to understand the circumstances of the person, understand their preferences and help them to access the tailored information and advice that they need to make well-informed decisions. Where a person lacks capacity, the authority must establish whether a person has a deputy of the Court of Protection or a person with Lasting Power of Attorney acting on their behalf.

3.47. The local authority must offer to consider a person's specific circumstances and provide them with information about the methods of paying for their care and support that may be available to them. The local authority may consider the timing and context of any retirement decisions a person might be making and how this interacts with paying for their care and support. They should advise people of the ways to pay that others in similar circumstances would usually consider and the range of information and advice they should be considering to help make their decision.

3.48. To help people access the information and advice they need, the local authority should have a clear view of the information and advice services available locally and what they provide. The local authority should take a role in joining up information and advice organisations locally so they can work collaboratively. The local authority should help information and advice providers and people to understand the role of each information and advice provider so people can access the right provider at the right time and not be sent round in circles. Local authorities should provide and publicise links and information on access to wider sources of information and advice, including those available nationally.

3.49. Staff within a local authority and other frontline staff should have the knowledge to direct people to the financial information and advice they need explaining the differences and potential benefits from seeking regulated or non-regulated financial advice. Local authorities should ensure frontline staff are able to support people to access the information and advice they need to make good financial decisions.

FACILITATING ACCESS TO INDEPENDENT FINANCIAL INFORMATION AND ADVICE

3.50. A key role for local authorities, when it would be inappropriate to provide it itself, is to facilitate access to financial information and advice which is impartial and independent of a local authority. This should include both generic free and fee-based advice as well as services providing regulated forms of financial advice. 'Facilitating Access' may include making people aware of specific sources of information and advice that are available and giving information about how to use them. Local authorities should make people aware which independent services may charge for the information and advice they provide. Local authorities should be able to actively describe the general benefits of independent information and advice and be able to explain the reasons why it may be beneficial for a person to take independent financial advice based on what is known of their circumstances to an individual.

3.51. Where a person may be considering taking regulated financial advice local authorities are not required or encouraged to make a direct referral to one individual independent financial adviser, but they should actively help and direct a person to a choice of advisers regulated by the Financial Conduct Authority with the appropriate qualifications and accreditation. The local authority should ensure that they do this on a transparent basis.

INFORMATION AND ADVICE ON ADULT SAFEGUARDING

3.52. The Government expects local authorities and others to help people with care and support needs, who may be at risk of abuse or neglect as a result of those needs, keep safe. But this must not mean preventing them making their own choices and having control over their lives. Everyone in the community should understand the importance of safeguarding and help keep people safe (see chapter 14).[1]

3.53. The local authority must provide information and advice on how to raise concerns about the safety or wellbeing of an adult who has needs for care and support and should support public knowledge and awareness of different types of abuse and neglect, how to keep yourself physically, sexually, financially and emotionally safe, and how to support people to keep safe. The information and advice provided must also cover who to tell when there are concerns about abuse or neglect and what will happen when such concerns are raised, including information on how the local Safeguarding Board works.

COMPLAINTS

3.54. Current complaints provision in relation to local authority social services is set out in regulations.[2] The provisions of the regulations mean that anyone who is dissatisfied with a decision made by the local authority would be able to make a complaint about that decision and have that complaint handled by the local authority. The local authority must make its own arrangements for dealing with complaints in accordance with the 2009 regulations. As an essential part of how the whole system operates, under the 2009 Regulations the local authority's arrangements must ensure that those who make complaints receive, as far as reasonably practicable, assistance to enable them to understand the complaints procedure or advice on where to obtain such assistance.

REVIEWING AND DEVELOPING A PLAN OR STRATEGY

3.55. Local differences and different starting points will mean that each local authority will need to develop and implement a plan regarding their information and advice services that matches their circumstances and meets the needs of its population. The information and advice service should be aligned with wider local authority strategies such as market shaping and commissioning, and with

[1] See Safeguarding chapter 14
[2] Local Authority Social Services and NHS Complaints Regulations 2009, made under powers in Sections 113 to 115 of the Health and Social Care (Community Health and Standards) Act 2003.

joint area strategies with health. The development of such plans should have regard to some common principles, including:

- involving people who use services and carers, interested organisations and service providers in determining what is needed and how it is provided;

- being available at the right time for people who need it, in a range of accessible formats and through a range of channels;

- meeting the needs of all groups;

- being clear, comprehensive and impartial;

- be consistent, accurate and up-to-date;

- meeting quality standards, such as the Advice Quality Standard;[1]

- being based on a detailed analysis of the needs of the local population served by the local authority;

- being commissioned in tandem with other relevant support and independent advocacy services;

- avoiding unnecessary duplication;

- directing people to sources of further information;

- be used to inform future planning;

- ensuring appropriate quality assurance and review, including customer feedback to make sure that the service leans from experience and continuously improves.

3.56. The plan should build on local and national best practice and make best use of national resources. These national resources[2] include guidance on principles for local information and advice strategies, case studies and practice examples.

3.57. The local authority must exercise its functions under the Care Act, including the duty to provide an information and advice service, with a view to integrating care and support provision with health and health-related issues (including housing). It must also co-operate more generally with each of its relevant partners taking account of their respective functions (see chapter 15). The Local Government and Public Involvement in Health Act 2007 (as amended by the Health and Social Care Act 2012), provides that local authorities are under a duty to work with their local CCGs, and other partners through the Health and Wellbeing Board to undertake Joint Strategic Needs Assessments for their areas and to develop Joint Health and Wellbeing Strategies. Statutory Guidance[3] published in March 2013 makes clear that the Joint Strategic Needs Assessment and Joint Health and Wellbeing Strategies must be published, and have specific regard to "what health and social care information the community

---

[1] http://www.advicequalitystandard.org.uk/
[2] Available at: http://www.thinklocalactpersonal.org.uk/Browse/Informationandadvice/
[3] https://www.gov.uk/government/uploads/system/uploads/attachment_data/file/277012/Statutory-Guidance-on-Joint-Strategic-Needs-Assessments-and-Joint-Health-and-Wellbeing-Strategies-March-20131.pdf

needs, including how they access it and what support they may need to understand it".

3.58. The development and implementation of a wider plan or strategy on the provision of information and advice on care and support should be led by the local authority, acting as the coordinator and where appropriate the commissioners of information and advice services.

3.59. The development of information and advice plans and their implementation should be an ongoing and dynamic process, involving all relevant stakeholders, rather than a one off occurrence. The plan and the resulting service should adapt to changing needs and as a result of feedback and learning on what works best. The plan should be reviewed at agreed intervals. As a minimum, the process of developing a local plan should include:

- engagement with people, carers and family members, to understand what is working and not working for them, their preferences and how their information advice and advocacy needs can best be met;

- adopting a 'co-production' approach to their plan, involving user groups and people themselves, other appropriate statutory, commercial and voluntary sector service providers, and make public the plan once finalised;

- mapping to understand the range of information, advice and advocacy services, including independent financial advice and different providers available;

- coordination with other statutory bodies with an interest in care and support, including local Clinical Commissioning Groups, Health and Wellbeing Boards, local Healthwatch and neighbouring local authorities;

- building into the plan opportunities to record, measure and assess the impact of information and advice services rather than simply service outputs.

3.60. In deciding the types of information and advice services to be provided, each local authority will need to analyse and understand the specific needs of its population. Some of the factors and circumstances that local authorities should consider in doing this will often be identified in Joint Strategic Needs Assessments. These factors may include, but are not limited to:

- the ethnic composition of the local area, including languages used;

- the identity and nature of hard to reach groups;

- the split between those whose care and support is (or is likely to be) arranged or funded by the person and the state;

- demographic trends relating to health and care needs, age and disability;

- how people access information and advice at the moment and the quality of information and advice services;

- an appropriate balance between the needs of its local population for information and the needs people will have for access to advice;

- the current sufficiency of supply and the range of information and advice providers from different sectors (including their prospects for growth).

3.61. Local authorities should review and publish information about the effectiveness of the information and advice service locally, including customer satisfaction and may wish to build these into the local Joint Health and Wellbeing Strategies.

3.62. These actions will support local authorities to meet their duties for understanding and promoting the efficient and effective market of services for meeting care and support needs in its area (see chapter 4).

3.63. As part of their plans, local authorities should consider the persons and/or places most likely to come into contact with people in need of information and advice at these and other critical points in the person's care and support journey. This may be another statutory party, such as a GP or other NHS professional, other professionals, such as a solicitor or funeral director, care and support and housing providers, or a local group, user-led or charitable organisation, rather than the local authority itself. Local authorities should consider whether independent sources of information and advice may in some circumstances be more trusted – and therefore more effective – than the local authority itself (see chapter 15, paragraph 15.71).[1]

3.64. In addition or instead of direct provision, local authorities should consider whether it is in a person's best interests that they be signposted, directed or referred to independent sources of information and advice. In particular, people should be signposted to appropriate independent information and advice when they are entering into a legal agreement with a local authority or other third party, such as a deferred payment agreement or committing to a top-up, or they wish to question, challenge or appeal a decision of the local authority or other statutory body.

3.65. People often come into contact with care and support services and need to make important decisions at a time of crisis. A local authority plan should therefore allow for the urgent provision of information and advice when necessary. Local authorities should work with health organisations and other partners to provide targeted information and advice to people in these critical situations and where people have long-term health conditions such as dementia (see paragraph 3.25).

3.66. In their information and advice plan, local authorities will need to weigh up the likely demand and effectiveness of these different channels of communication, some of which will incur substantially higher costs than others. A plan that relies disproportionately on provision of information and advice through the authority's website, or third party websites, is unlikely to meet the authority's duty under the Act to establish and maintain a service to provide information and advice on care and support.

3.67. Local authorities will need to consider in their information and advice planning the appropriate interface and balance between local and national sources of information and advice. Where appropriate, local authorities should signpost or refer people to national sources of information and advice where these are recognised as the most useful source. Examples might include:

- the NHS Choices website, which contains online quality profiles of registered care providers in local areas. Local authorities are encouraged to add local sources of information and advice to the online profiles and

---

[1] See Integration chapter example in para 15.71 *et seq.*

make sure their local registered care providers add information on the services and support they offer. http://www.nhs.uk/CarersDirect/Pages/CarersDirectHome.aspx

- the NHS Choices website. Health A to Z, detailed information on specific health conditions and how/where to access health services http://www.nhs.uk/Pages/HomePage.aspx

- Carers Direct – national telephone helpline: Tel 0300 123 1053

- Money Advice Service https://www.moneyadviceservice.org.uk/

- the Care Quality Commission website http://www.cqc.org.uk/

- the Local Government Ombudsman www.lgo.org.uk

- consumer websites providing people with information and advice, including on managing their finances well, for example http://www.which.co.uk/elderly-care

- national charities and/or advice services supporting people with disabilities or older people and those with expert knowledge of specific conditions (e.g. deaf blind). For example, http://www.ageuk.org.uk/; http://www.independentage.org/; http://www.alzheimers.org.uk/ and http://www.sense.org.uk/, and their national telephone advice/ help lines

- national charities and advice services for carers, for example http://www.carersuk.org/ or http://www.ageuk.org.uk/

- national resources related to housing, accommodation and housing related support, for example http://www.firststopcareadvice.org.uk/ http://www.foundations.uk.com/home/

3.68. Some national providers, for example the Money Advice Service and NHS choices, may also offer free access to tools, resources and information content that can be integrated into local authority websites or delivered in paper formats. Local authorities are encouraged to explore how they can make the most of cost-effective partnership opportunities with national providers. Referral or signposting to national sources should only occur where this is deemed to be in the best interests of the person and their circumstances and should not take the place of local services necessary for local authorities to discharge their duty under the Act. Local authorities will need to find the appropriate balance between local and national provision to cost-effectively meet their local need.

3.69. Information and advice provided, whether directly by a local authority or by third parties as part of the information and advice service that the local authority establishes and maintains, should be of a good standard and, where appropriate, delivered by trained or suitably qualified individuals.

4. MARKET SHAPING AND COMMISSIONING OF ADULT CARE AND SUPPORT

This chapter provides guidance on section 5 of the Care Act 2014.

This chapter covers:
- The principles which should underpin market-shaping and commissioning activity:
- focusing on outcomes and wellbeing;
- promoting quality services, including through workforce development and remuneration and ensuring appropriately resourced care and support;
- supporting sustainability;
- ensuring choice;
- co-production with partners.
- The steps which local authorities should take to develop and implement local approaches to market-shaping and commissioning:
- designing strategies that meet local needs;
- engaging with providers and local communities;
- understanding the market;
- facilitating the development of the market;
- integrating their approach with local partners;
- securing supply in the market and assuring its quality through contracting.

4.1. High-quality, personalised care and support can only be achieved where there is a vibrant, responsive market of service providers. The role of the local authority is critical to achieving this, both through the actions it takes to directly commission services to meet needs, and the broader understanding and interactions it facilitates with the wider market, for the benefit of all local people and communities.

4.2. The Care Act places new duties on local authorities to facilitate and shape their market for adult care and support as a whole, so that it meets the needs of all people in their area who need care and support, whether arranged or funded by the state, by the individual themselves, or in other ways. The ambition is for local authorities to influence and drive the pace of change for their whole market, leading to a sustainable and diverse range of care and support providers, continuously improving quality and choice, and delivering better, innovative and cost-effective outcomes that promote the wellbeing of people who need care and support.

4.3. The market for care and support services is part of a wider system in which much of the need for care and support is met by people's own efforts, by their families, friends or other carers, and by community networks. Local authorities have a vital role in ensuring that universal services are available to the whole population and where necessary, tailored to meet the needs of those with additional support requirements (for example housing and leisure services). Market shaping and commissioning should aim to promote a market for care and support that should be seen as broadening, supplementing and supporting all these vital sources of care and support.

4.4. Local authorities should review the way they commission services, as this is a prime way to achieve effective market shaping and directly affects services for those whose needs are met by the local authority, including where funded wholly or partly by the state.

4.5. At a time of increasing pressure on public funds, changing patterns of needs, and increasing aspirations of citizens, together with momentum for integrated services, joint commissioning, and choice for individuals, it is suggested that fundamental changes to the way care and support services are arranged may be needed, driven through a transformation of the way services are led, considered and arranged.[1] Commissioning and market shaping are key levers for local authorities in designing and facilitating a healthy market of quality services.

DEFINITIONS

4.6. Market shaping means the local authority collaborating closely with other relevant partners, including people with care and support needs, carers and families, to facilitate the whole market in its area for care, support and related services. This includes services arranged and paid for by the state through the authority itself, those services paid by the state through direct payments, and those services arranged and paid for by individuals from whatever sources (sometimes called 'self-funders'), and services paid for by a combination of these sources. Market shaping activity should stimulate a diverse range of appropriate high quality services (both in terms of the types, volumes and quality of services and the types of provider organisation), and ensure the market as a whole remains vibrant and sustainable.

4.7. The core activities of market shaping are to engage with stakeholders to develop understanding of supply and demand and articulate likely trends that reflect people's evolving needs and aspirations, and based on evidence, to signal to the market the types of services needed now and in the future to meet them, encourage innovation, investment and continuous improvement. It also includes working to ensure that those who purchase their own services are empowered to be effective consumers, for example by helping people who want to take direct payments make informed decisions about employing personal assistants. A local authority's own commissioning practices are likely to have a significant influence on the market to achieve the desired outcomes, but other interventions may be needed, for example, incentivising innovation by user-led or third sector providers, possibly through grant funding.

4.8. Commissioning is the local authority's cyclical activity to assess the needs of its local population for care and support services, determining what element of this needs to be arranged by the authority, then designing, delivering, monitoring and evaluating those services to ensure appropriate outcomes. From the 1990s onwards care services have been increasingly procured from the independent sector (i.e. not directly commissioned from and provided by an authority itself) and covered all services that the authority arranged for people receiving state funding. Since 2007 when personalisation became a mainstream policy, commissioning has also covered activity to ensure that sufficient and appropriate services are available to meet the needs of growing numbers of people with personal budgets and direct payments. This has changed the commissioning role, as purchasing

---

[1] http://www.thinklocalactpersonal.org.uk/_library/Leadership_Framework_for_Empowered_and_Healthy_Communities_1.pdf

decisions have been increasingly devolved to individuals and families and direct procurement using block contracts has reduced. Commissioning has come to be shaped more by the outcomes commissioners and individuals identify, rather than volumes of activity expected and commissioners have sought to facilitate flexible arrangements with providers for other forms of service to support choice and control, such as Individual Service Funds (ISFs).

4.9. Procurement is the specific functions carried out by the local authority to buy or acquire the services which the local authority has duties to arrange to meet people's needs, to agreed quality standards so as to provide effective value for money to the public purse and deliver its commissioning strategy.

4.10. Contracting is the means by which that process is made legally binding. Contract management is the process that then ensures that the services continue to be delivered to the agreed quality standards. Commissioning encompasses procurement but includes the wider set of strategic activities.

4.11. This statutory guidance describes at a high level the themes and issues that local authorities should have regard to when carrying out duties to shape their local markets and commission services. Market shaping, commissioning, procurement and contracting are inter-related activities and the themes of this guidance will apply to each to a greater or lesser extent depending on the specific activity.

PRINCIPLES OF MARKET-SHAPING AND COMMISSIONING
Focusing on outcomes

4.12. Local authorities must ensure that the promotion of the wellbeing of individuals who need care and support, and the wellbeing of carers, and the outcomes they require, are central to all care and support functions in relation to individuals, emphasising the importance of enabling people to stay independent for as long as possible.

4.13. Local authorities will need to understand the outcomes which matter most to people in their area, and demonstrate that these outcomes are at the heart of their local strategies and approaches.

4.14. Local authorities should consider the Adult Social Care Outcomes Framework (ASCOF),[1] in addition to any locally-collected information on outcomes and experiences (for example, from local consumer research), when framing outcomes for their locality and groups of people with care and support needs. Local authorities should have regard to guidance from the Think Local Act Personal (TLAP) partnership[2] when framing outcomes for individuals, groups and their local population, in particular the Making It Real "I" statements, which set out what good personalised care and support should look like from the perspective of people with care and support needs, carers and family members. Outcomes should be considered both in terms of outcomes for individuals and outcomes for groups of people and populations. Local authorities should consider the emerging revised Care Quality Commission standards for quality and any emerging national frameworks for defining outcomes. Local authorities may find the Chartered Institute of Housing's Service Quality Tool for housing-related services useful. This builds on and updates the Quality Assessment Framework (QAF).

---

[1] https://www.gov.uk/government/publications/the-adult-social-care-outcomes-framework-2013-to-2014
[2] http://www.thinklocalactpersonal.org.uk/

4.15. Local authorities should consider analysing and presenting local needs for services in terms of outcomes required. Local authorities should ensure that achieving better outcomes is central to its commissioning strategy and practices, and should be able to demonstrate that they are moving to contracting in a way that has an outcome basis at its heart. Local authorities should consider emerging best practice on outcomes-based commissioning.

4.16. Outcomes-based services mean developing service arrangements that are defined on the basis of an agreed set of outcomes either for an individual or a group of people. Moving more to an outcomes-based approach therefore means changing the way services are bought: from units of provision to meet a specified need (for example, hours of care provided) to what is required to ensure specified measurable outcomes for people are met. The approach should emphasise prevention, enablement, ways of reducing loneliness and social isolation and promotion of independence as ways of achieving and exceeding desired outcomes, as well as choice in how people's needs are met. Moving to an outcomes-based approach will need to recognise that some outcomes are challenging to assess and local authorities may wish to consider involving service providers when considering how service evaluations can be interpreted. Outcomes should be used as a principal measure for quality assurance of services.

4.17. In encouraging outcomes-based services, consideration should be given to how services are paid for. Local authorities should consider incorporating elements of "payments- by-outcomes" mechanisms, where practical, to emphasise and embed this commissioning approach which is based on specifying the outcomes to be achieved, rather than the service outputs to be delivered. Whilst payments by outcomes may be theoretically the most appropriate approach for outcomes-based services, it is recognised that proxies for outcomes may be required to make the approach practical. For example, an outcome an authority may wish to measure might be someone's personal outcome 'I want to maintain a nutritious and balanced diet', but a proxy measure that is observable, attributable and capable of being described, may be the person receiving help with meal preparation at agreed and specified times. Care logs documenting punctual assistance in meal preparation, in conjunction with positive feedback from the person receiving care about support received might be used as part of the basis of payment. It is also recognised that whilst these mechanisms are more commonplace in other types of commissioning, they are in their infancy for adult social care.

4.18. The design of any mechanism should, however, be introduced in cooperation with stakeholders and partners to ensure it is sustainable and ensure that innovation, and individual choice and control are not undermined. Any move to payments by outcomes should be achieved such that smaller, specialist, voluntary sector and community-based providers are not excluded from markets or disadvantaged, because for example, they did not have appropriate IT systems.[1]

---

[1] Guidance on outcome based commissioning: http://www.thinklocalactpersonal.org.uk/_library/ Resources/ BetterCommissioning/BetterCommissioning_advice/Chap9AKerslake.pdf

4.19. Local authorities should keep under review emerging ideas and best practice about outcomes based commissioning and payments by outcomes.[1],[2],[3]

4.20. Section 2 of the Care Act outlines local authorities' role in preventing, reducing or delaying the need for care and support. This includes how the authority facilitates and commissions services and how it works with other local organisations to build community capital and make the most of the skills and resources already available in the area.[4] Local authorities should consider working not just with traditional public sector partners like health, but also with a range of other partners to engage with communities to understand how to prevent problems from arising.[5]

Promoting quality

4.21. Local authorities must facilitate markets that offer a diverse range of high-quality and appropriate services. In doing so, they must have regard to ensuring the continuous improvement of those services and encouraging a workforce which effectively underpins the market.[6],[7],[8] The quality of services provided and the workforce providing them can have a significant effect on the wellbeing of people receiving care and support, and that of carers, and it is important to establish agreed understandable and clear criteria for quality and to ensure they are met.

4.22. When considering the quality of services, local authorities should be mindful of the capacity, capability, timeliness, continuity, reliability and flexibility of services delivered to support well-being, where appropriate, using the definitions that underpin the CQC's fundamental standards of care as a minimum, and having regard to the ASCOF framework of population outcomes. High quality services should enable people who need care and support, and carers, to meet appropriate personal outcome measures, for example, a domiciliary care service which provides care two days a week so that a carer who normally provides care can go to work, is not a quality service if it is not available on the specified days, or the care workers do not arrive in time to allow the carer to get to work on time.

4.23. Local authorities should also consider other relevant national standards including those that are aspirational, for example, any developed by the National Institute of Health and Care Excellence (NICE).

---

[1] http://ipc.brookes.ac.uk/publications/pdf/
Wiltshire_Council_Help_to_Live_at_Home_IPC_Report_ April_2012.pdf
[2] http://www.birmingham.gov.uk/cs/Satellite?c=Page&childpagename=Housing%2FPage
Layout&cid=1223092722073&pagename=BCC%2FCommon%2FWrapper%2FWrapper
[3] http://b.3cdn.net/nefoundation/974bfd0fd635a9ffcd_j2m6b04bs.pdf
[4] For example, the Campaign to End Loneliness toolkit for health and wellbeing boards may be helpful: http://www.campaigntoendloneliness.org/for-local-government-and-healthcare/
[5] An example of preventative services effectively, taken from the Leeds Market Position Statement on Leeds Community Equipment Service, Telecare and Care Ring Services, can be found at: http://www.leeds.gov.uk/docs/LeedsAdultsMPS2012.pdf; there are also examples in the LGA final report on adult social care efficiency programme: http://www.local.gov.uk/documents/10180/11779/LGA+Adult+Social+Care+Efficiency+Programme+-+the+final+report/8e042c7f-7de4-4e42-8824-f7dc88ade15d Arthritis Research UK is developing a musculoskeletal (MSK) calculator to provide local estimates of the number of people with musculoskeletal conditions in England, for use in the planning of healthcare services and public health programmes for local populations.
[6] Standards (http://www.skillsforcare.org.uk/Standards/Standards.aspx)
[7] Skills (http://www.skillsforcare.org.uk/Skills/Skills.aspx)
[8] Qualifications and Apprenticeships (http://www.skillsforcare.org.uk/Qualifications-and-Apprenticeships/Qualifications-and-Apprenticeships.aspx)

4.24. Local authorities should encourage a wide range of service provision to ensure that people have a choice of appropriate services; appropriateness is a fundamental part of quality. For example, a working age person should be able to choose care and support tailored for their situation, and not be faced with only a choice of facilities designed for older people, as this is unlikely to be appropriate to their situation, regardless of how high quality the facilities may be in their own contexts. Appropriate services will meet people's needs and reasonable preferences.

4.25. When arranging services themselves, local authorities must ensure their commissioning practices and the services delivered on their behalf comply with the requirements of the Equality Act 2010, and do not discriminate against people with protected characteristics, this should include monitoring delivery against the requirements of that Act. When shaping markets for services, local authorities should work to ensure compliance with this Act for services provided in their area that are not arranged and/or paid for by them.[1],[2] Local authorities should consider care and support services for their appropriateness for people from different communities, cultures and beliefs.

4.26. Local authorities should encourage services that respond to the fluctuations and changes in people's care and support needs, for example someone with fluctuating mobility or visual impairment. Local authorities should support the transition of services throughout the stages of people with care and support needs' lives to ensure the services provided remain appropriate. This is particularly important, for example, for young people with care and support needs and young carers transitioning to adulthood.

For example: Ensuring provision of appropriate services

Young people move from children's to adult care and support or providing support for situations where young carers become adults

For instance, many young people with learning disabilities leave full-time education at around this age and require new forms of care and support to live independently thereafter. Ensuring that services are made available to meet those needs is better for the quality of life of the young person in question. This could include things such as employment support, training, developing friendships or advice on housing options. It is equally important to think about ways of supporting carers at this time: some parent carers need extra support to juggle caring and paid work after their child leaves full time education. Loss of paid employment can have a significant impact on the carer's wellbeing and self-esteem as well as a significant impact on the family's financial circumstances. Similar issues can affect young carers. Taking a whole family approach to care and support planning that sets out a "five-day offer" or appropriate supported living options for a young person, and support for a carer to manage an increased caring role (that allows them to stay in paid work if they wish to do so) can help families manage the transition and save money by avoiding unwanted out-of-county placements.

---

[1] https://www.gov.uk/equality-act-2010-guidance
[2] http://www.scie.org.uk/publications/ataglance/ataglance41.asp

4.27. Local authorities should commission services having regard to the cost-effectiveness and value for money that the services offer for public funds. The Local Government Association Adult Social Care Efficiency Programme has advice on these issues and may be helpful.[1]

4.28. People working in the care sector play a central role in providing high quality services. Local authorities must consider how to help foster, enhance and appropriately incentivise this vital workforce to underpin effective, high quality services.[2,3]

4.29. Local authorities should consider, in particular, how to encourage training and development for the care and support workforce, including for the management of care services, though, for example, national standards recommended by Skills for Care,[4,5,6,7,8] and have regard to funding available through grants to support the training of care workers in the independent sector.[9,10,11,12,13] Local authorities should consider encouraging the training and development of care worker staff to at least the standard of the emerging Care Certificate currently being developed by Health Education England, Skills for Care and Skills for Health.[14]

4.30. When commissioning services, local authorities should assure themselves and have evidence that service providers deliver services through staff remunerated so as to retain an effective workforce. Remuneration must be at least sufficient to comply with the national minimum wage legislation for hourly pay or equivalent salary. This will include appropriate remuneration for any time spent travelling between appointments. Guidance on these issues can be found at the HMRC website.[15]

4.31. When commissioning services, local authorities should assure themselves and have evidence that contract terms, conditions and fee levels for care and

---

[1] http://www.local.gov.uk/productivity/-/journal_content/56/10180/3371097/ARTICLE

[2] How to commission the adult social care workforce – North-West Joint Improvement Programme: http://ipc.brookes.ac.uk/publications/pdf/How_to_Commission_the_Adult_Social_Care_Workforce.pdf

[3] See Skill for Care resource on Workforce Redesign: http://www.skillsforcare.org.uk/NMDS-SC-intelligence-research-and-innovation/Workforce-redesign/Workforce-redesign.aspx

[4] See Skills for Care resources: Common Induction Standards: http://www.skillsforcare.org.uk/Home.aspx

[5] Common Induction Standards; http://www.skillsforcare.org.uk/Standards/Care-Quality-Commission- regulations/Care-Quality-Commission-regulations.aspx

[6] Care Certificate: http://www.skillsforcare.org.uk/Standards/Care-Certificate/Care-Certificate.aspx

[7] Manager Induction Standards: http://www.skillsforcare.org.uk/Standards/Manager-Induction-Standards/ Manager-Induction-Standards.aspx

[8] National Occupational Standards: http://www.skillsforcare.org.uk/Standards/NOS/National-Occupational-Standards.aspx

[9] An example of collaborative training by Surrey, East Sussex & Brighton & Hove can be found at: http://www.eastsussex.gov.uk/nr/rdonlyres/07194ab7-15a9-44b4-9f74-91c39fa479c5/0/

[10] Workforce Development Fund: http://www.skillsforcare.org.uk/Funding/Workforce-Development-Fund-2014/Workforce-Development-Fund.aspx

[11] Individual Employer Funding: http://www.skillsforcare.org.uk/Funding/Individual-employer-funding/Individual-employer-funding.aspx

[12] Workforce Development Innovation Fund: http://www.skillsforcare.org.uk/Funding/Workforce-development-innovation-fund/Workforce-development-innovation-fund-(WDIF).aspx

[13] Social Work—Assessed and Supported Year in Employment: http://www.skillsforcare.org.uk/Social-work/Assessed-and-Supported-Year-in-Employment/The-Assessed-and-Supported-Year-in-Employment-(ASYE).aspx

[14] http://hee.nhs.uk/work-programmes/the-care-certificate/

[15] http://www.hmrc.gov.uk/payerti/payroll/pay-and-deductions/nmw.htm

support services are appropriate to provide the delivery of the agreed care packages with agreed quality of care. This should support and promote the wellbeing of people who receive care and support, and allow for the service provider ability to meet statutory obligations to pay at least the national minimum wage and provide effective training and development of staff. It should also allow retention of staff commensurate with delivering services to the agreed quality, and encourage innovation and improvement. Local authorities should have regard to guidance on minimum fee levels necessary to provide this assurance, taking account of the local economic environment. The tools referenced may be helpful as examples of possible approaches.[1,2,3]

4.32. Local authorities should ensure that they themselves have functions to fulfil duties on market shaping and commissioning that are fit for purpose, with sufficient capacity and capability of trained and qualified staff to meet the requirements set out in the Care Act and this statutory guidance.[4,5] In particular, local authorities should encourage relevant staff to be trained or developed to meet the National Skills Academy standards and programmes of training for care and support commissioners 'Commissioning Now', or equivalent,[6] and appropriate standards for commissioning related services such as housing services where appropriate. Local authorities should consider the skills and capabilities needed to support new approaches to commissioning, for example, outcomes-based and integrated commissioning.

Supporting sustainability

4.33. Local authorities **must** work to develop markets for care and support that – whilst recognising that individual providers may exit the market from time to time – ensure the overall provision of services remains healthy in terms of the sufficiency of adequate provision of high quality care and support needed to meet expected needs. This will ensure that there are a range of appropriate and high quality providers and services for people to choose from.

4.34. Local authorities should understand the business environment of the providers offering services in their area and seek to work with providers facing challenges and understand their risks. Where needed, based on expected trends, local authorities should consider encouraging service providers to adjust the extent and types of service provision. This could include signalling to the market as a whole the likely need to extend or expand services, encourage new entrants to the market in their area, or if appropriate, signal likely decrease in needs – for example, drawing attention to a possible reduction in home care needs, and changes in demand resulting from increasing uptake of direct payments. The process of developing and articulating a Market Position Statement or equivalent should be central to this process.

---

[1] UKHCA Minimum Price for Homecare tool: http://www.ukhca.co.uk/pdfs/AMinimumPriceforHomecareVersion1020140202.pdf

[2] Laing and Buisson toolkit to understand fair price for residential care: https://www.laingbuisson.co.uk/ portals/1/media_packs/Fact_Sheets/Fair_Price_ThrdEd_2008.pdf

[3] ADASS paying for care calculator: http://www.adass.org.uk/Paying-for-care-calculator/

[4] Skills for Care resources: Care Act Capacity Planning: http://www.skillsforcare.org.uk/Standards/Care-Act/Care-Bill.aspx

[5] Workforce Capacity Planning: http://www.skillsforcare.org.uk/Standards/Care-Act/Workforce-capacity- planning/Workforce-capacity-planning.aspx

[6] https://www.nsasocialcare.co.uk/programmes/commissioning-now

4.35. Local authorities should consider the impact of their own activities on the market as a whole, in particular the potential impact of their commissioning and re-commissioning decisions, and how services are packaged or combined for tendering, and where they may also be a supplier of care and support. The local authority may be the most significant purchaser of care and support in an area, and therefore its approach to commissioning will have an impact beyond those services which it contracts. Local authorities **must not** undertake any actions which may threaten the sustainability of the market as a whole, that is, the pool of providers able to deliver services of an appropriate quality – for example, by setting fee levels below an amount which is not sustainable for providers in the long-term.

4.36. Local authorities should have effective communications and relationships with providers in their area that should minimise risks of unexpected closures and failures, and have effective interaction and communication with the Care Quality Commission (CQC) about the larger and most difficult to replace providers that CQC will provide financial oversight for. Local authorities should review the intelligence they have about the sustainability of care providers drawn from market shaping, commissioning and contract management activities. Where the authority believes there is a significant risk to a provider's financial viability, and where they consider it would be in the best interests of service users, the authority should consider what assistance may be provided or brokered to help the provider return to viability, and consider what actions might be needed were that provider to fail. For example, where a local authority has arranged services for people with a provider that appears to be at risk, undertaking early planning to identify potential replacement service capacity. Where it is apparent to a local authority that a provider is likely to imminently fail financially, either through its own intelligence or through information from the CQC, the authority should prepare to step in to ensure continuity of care and support for people who have their care and support provided by that provider (see chapter 5 on managing provider failure).

Ensuring choice

4.37. Local authorities **must** encourage a variety of different providers and different types of services. This is important in order to facilitate an effective open market, driving quality and cost-effectiveness so as to provide genuine choice to meet the range of needs and reasonable preferences of local people who need care and support services, including for people who choose to take direct payments, recognising, for example, the challenges presented in remote rural areas for low volume local services.

4.38. Local authorities **must** encourage a range of different types of service provider organisations to ensure people have a genuine choice of different types of service. This will include independent private providers, third sector, voluntary and community based organisations, including user-led organisations, mutual and small businesses. This should recognise that the different underpinning philosophies, cultural sensitivity and style of service of these organisations may be more suited to some people with care and support needs. Local authorities should consider encouraging and supporting providers or taking other steps to promote an appropriate balance of provision between types of provider, having regard to competition rules and the need for fairness and legal requirements for all potential providers who may wish to compete for contracts.[1] The TLAP guidance 'commissioning for provider diversity' may be helpful to commissioners.[2]

4.39. Where a local authority develops approved lists and frameworks that are used to limit the number of providers they work with, for example within a specific geographical area or for a particular service type to achieve strategic partnerships and value for money, the local authority must consider how to ensure that there is still a reasonable choice for people who need care and support.

4.40. Local authorities should encourage a genuine choice of service type, not only a selection of providers offering similar services, encouraging, for example, a variety of different living options such as shared lives, extra care housing, supported living, support provided at home, and live-in domiciliary care as alternatives to homes care, and low volume and specialist services for people with less common needs.

4.41. Choice for people who need care and support and carers should be interpreted widely. Local authorities should encourage choice over the way services are delivered, examples would include: developing arrangements so that care can be shared between an unpaid carer or relative and a paid care worker, a choice over when a service is delivered, choice over who is a person's key care worker, arranging for providers to collaborate to ensure the right provision is available, for example, a private provider and a voluntary organisation working together, choice over when a service is delivered.[3]

4.42. Local authorities must have regard to ensuring a sufficiency of provision – in terms of both capacity and capability – to meet anticipated needs for all people in their area needing care and support – regardless of how they are funded. This will include regularly reviewing trends in needs including multiple and complex needs, outcomes sought and achieved, and trends in supply, anticipating the effects and trends in prevention and community-based assets, and through understanding and encouraging changes in the supply of services and providers' business and investment decisions.[4]

4.43. When considering the sufficiency and diversity of service provision, local authorities should consider all types of service that are required to provide care and support for the local authority's whole population, including, for example:

- support services and universal and community services that promote prevention;
- domiciliary (home) care;
- homes and other types of accommodation care;
- nursing care;
- live-in care services;

[1] http://www.clinks.org/resources-reports/more-provider-role-voluntary-sector-commissioning-offender- services

[2] http://sharedlivesplus.invisionzone.com/index.php?/files/file/184-commissioning-for-provider-diversity/

[3] Shared Lives Plus/Community Catalyst guidance on commissioning for provider diversity. An example of a commissioning intervention to encourage diversity: http://sharedlivesplus.invisionzone.com/index.php?/ files/file/184-commissioning-for-provider-diversity/

[4] MENCAP guidance on commissioning for people with profound and multiple learning disabilities: http://www.mencap.org.uk/sites/default/files/documents/Raising-our-sights-Commissioning%20guide.pdf

- specialist care;
- support for carers;
- re-ablement services;
- sheltered accommodation and supported living;
- shared lives services;
- other housing options;
- community support;
- counselling;
- social work;
- information, brokerage, advocacy and advice services;
- direct payment support organisations.

4.44. This will include keeping up to date with innovations and developments in services, networking through for example, the Association of Directors of Adult Social Services (ADASS), TLAP, and the Local Government Association (LGA) etc.

4.45. Local authorities should facilitate the personalisation of care and support services, encouraging services (including small, local, specialised and personal assistant services that are highly tailored), to enable people to make meaningful choices and to take control of their support arrangements, regardless of service setting or how their personal budget is managed. Local authorities should have regard to the TLAP partnership agreement[1] that sets out how shaping markets to meet people's needs and aspirations, including housing options, can promote choice and control. Alongside the suitability of living accommodation in Section 1 of the Act, Local authorities should consider how they can encourage the development of accommodation options that can support choice and control and promote wellbeing. Personalised care and support services should be flexible so as to ensure people have choices over what they are supported with, when and how their support is provided and wherever possible, by whom. The mechanism of Individual Service Funds by service providers, which are applicable in many different service types, can help to secure these kinds of flexibilities for people and providers.[2]

4.46. Local authorities should help people who fund their own services or receive direct payments, to 'micro-commission' care and support services and/ or to pool their budgets, and should ensure a supporting infrastructure is available to help with these activities.[3] Many local authorities, for example, are utilising web-based systems such as e-Marketplaces for people who are funding their own care or are receiving direct payments to be able to search for, consider and buy care and support services on-line, consider joint purchases with others. This often involves offering information and advice about, for example, the

---

[1] http://www.thinklocalactpersonal.org.uk/Latest/Resource/?cid=10154
[2] http://www.thinklocalactpersonal.org.uk/Browse/commissioning/servicefunds/
[3] http://ipc.brookes.ac.uk/publications/pdf/Safeguarding_Vulnerable_Adults_through_better_commissioning. pdf

costs and quality of services and information to support safeguarding.[1] This activity should support people to become more effective consumers, helping to match people's wider needs with services.

4.47. Local authorities must facilitate information and advice to support people's choices for care and support.[2] This should include where appropriate through services to help people with care and support needs understand and access the systems and processes involved and to make effective choices. This is a key aspect of the new duty to establish and maintain a universal information and advice service locally as set out in Section 4 of the Care Act. Information and advice services should be reviewed for effectiveness using people's experiences and feedback; this feedback forms part of the overall information a local authority considers about people's needs and aspirations.

4.48. Local authorities should facilitate local markets to encourage a sufficiency of preventative, enablement and support services, including support for carers to make caring more sustainable, such as interpreters, signers and communicator guides, and other support services such as 'telecare', home maintenance and gardening that may assist people achieve more independence and supports the outcomes they want.

4.49. Local authorities should encourage flexible services to be developed and made available that support people who need care and support, and carers who need support, to take part in work, education or training.[3] Services should be encouraged that allow carers who live in one local authority area but care for someone in another local authority area to access services easily, bearing in mind guidance on ordinary residence.

Co-production with stakeholders

4.50. Local authorities should pursue the principle that market shaping and commissioning should be shared endeavours, with commissioners working alongside people with care and support needs, carers, family members, care providers, representatives of care workers, relevant voluntary, user and other support organisations and the public to find shared and agreed solutions. This should be in line with the Building Capacity and Partnership in Care Agreement.[4] The TLAP guidance on co-production may be helpful.[5]

Developing local strategies

4.51. Commissioning and market shaping should be fundamental means for local authorities to facilitate effective services in their area and it is important that authorities develop evidence- based local strategies for how they exercise these functions, and align these with wider corporate planning. Local authorities should have in place published strategies that include plans that show how their legislative duties, corporate plans, analysis of local needs and requirements (integrated with the Joint Strategic Needs Assessment and Joint Health and Wellbeing Strategy), thorough engagement with people, carers and families, market and supply analysis, market structuring and interventions, resource allocations and

---

[1] http://www.hertsdirect.org/services/emarketplace/
[2] http://www.pssru.ac.uk/pdf/dp2713.pdf
[3] See Carers Matter: http://www.skillsforcare.org.uk/Skills/Carers/Carers.aspx
[4] http://webarchive.nationalarchives.gov.uk/+/www.dh.gov.uk/en/Publicationsandstatistics/ Publications/ PublicationsPolicyAndGuidance/DH_4006241
[5] http://www.thinklocalactpersonal.org.uk/Browse/co-production/

procurement and contract management activities translate (now and in future) into appropriate high quality services that deliver identified outcomes for the people in their area and address any identified gaps.[1]

4.52. Since 2007 there has been a duty on local authorities and latterly clinical commissioning groups, through health and wellbeing boards, to undertake Joint Strategic Needs Assessments (JSNA). JSNA is a process that assesses and maps the needs and demand for health and care and support, supports the development of joint Health and Wellbeing Strategies to address needs, understands community assets and informs commissioning of local health and care and support services that together with community assets meet needs.

4.53. Market shaping and commissioning intentions should be cross-referenced to JSNA, and should be informed by an understanding of the needs and aspirations of the population and how services will adapt to meet them. Strategies should be informed and emphasise preventative services that encourage independence and wellbeing, delaying or preventing the need for acute interventions. Statutory guidance on JSNA and Joint Health and Wellbeing Strategies was published in March 2013.[2] The ambition is for market shaping and commissioning to be an integral part of understanding and delivering the whole health and care economy, and to reflect the range and diversity of communities and people with specific needs, in particular:

- people needing care and support themselves (through for example, consumer research);
- carers;
- carer support organisations;
- health professionals;
- care and support managers and social workers (and representative organisations for these groups);
- relevant voluntary, user and other support organisations;
- independent advocates;
- wider citizens;
- provider organisations (including where appropriate housing providers); and
- other tiers of local government.

4.54. A co-produced approach will stress the value of meaningful engagement with people at all stages, through design, delivery and evaluation, rather than simply as 'feedback'. Local authorities should publish and make available their local strategies for market shaping and commissioning, giving an indication of timescales, milestones and frequency of activities, to support local accountability and engagement with the provider market and the public.

---

[1] Examples of local authority strategies, development with stakeholders, links to JSNA, review processes, roles & responsibilities: http://www.hscic.gov.uk/jsna http://www.thinklocalactpersonal.org.uk/_library/ Resources/Personalisation/Personalisation_advice/298683_Uses_of_Resources.pdf

[2] https://www.gov.uk/government/uploads/system/uploads/attachment_data/file/223842/Statutory-Guidance-on-Joint-Strategic-Needs-Assessments-and-Joint-Health-and-Wellbeing-Strategies-March-2013.pdf

4.55. It is suggested that a local authority can best commence its duties under Sections 5 (market shaping and commissioning) and 48-52 (provider failure) of the Care Act by developing with providers and stakeholders a published Market Position Statement.[1] It may be helpful for Market Position Statements from neighbouring local authority areas to be coordinated to ensure a degree of consistency for people who will use the documents; this is particularly true for urban areas.

4.56. Local authorities should review strategies related to care and support together with stakeholders to ensure they remain fit for purpose, learn lessons, and adapt to incorporate emerging best practice, noting that peer review has a strong track record in driving improvement. It is suggested that reporting against strategies for care and support should form part of the local authority's Local Account.[2]

4.57. Many public sector bodies, including local authorities, have radically transformed services by reconsidering commissioning in a strategic context. The Government's Commissioning Academy[3] is working to promote such transformational approaches and local authorities should have regard to the emerging best practice it is producing.

4.58. Developing a diverse market in care and support services can boost employment and create opportunities for local economic growth, through for example, increasing employment opportunities for working-age people receiving care and carers, and developing the capacity of the care workforce. Local authorities should consider how their strategies related to care and support can be embedded in wider local growth strategies, for example, engaging care providers in local enterprise partnerships.[4]

4.59. Recognising that changes to adult care and support are taking place at a time of the need to deliver services from constrained resources, local authorities should have regard to best practice on efficiency and value for money, in particular the Local Government Association Adult Social Care Efficiency Programme.[5]

4.60. Local authority strategies should adhere to general standards, relevant laws and guidance, including the Committee of Standards in Public Life principles of accountability, regularity and ensuring value for money alongside quality,[6] and the HM Treasury guidance on Managing Public Money.[7]

4.61. Local authorities should develop standards on transparency and accountability to ensure citizens are able to contribute to and understand policy and review delivery. Standards should be in line with the codes of practice drawn up by the Department of Communities and Local Government.[8]

4.62. Local authorities should take the lead to engage with a wide range of stakeholders and citizens in order to develop effective approaches to care and

---

[1] http://ipc.brookes.ac.uk/dcmqc.html
[2] https://www.gov.uk/government/policies/making-local-councils-more-transparent-and-account-able-to- local-people
[3] https://www.gov.uk/the-commissioning-academy-information
[4] http://www.boroughofpoole.com/business/business-support-and-advice/locating-to-poole/dorset-local- enterprise-partnership/
[5] http://www.local.gov/productivity/journal_content/56/10180/3371097/ARTICLE
[6] https://www.gov.uk/government/uploads/system/uploads/attachment_data/file/228884/8519.pdf
https://www.gov.uk/government/publications/managing-public-money
[7] https://www.gov.uk/government/publications/managing-public-money
[8] https://www.gov.uk/government/policies/making-local-councils-more-transparent-and-account-able-to- local-people

support, including through developing the JSNA and a Market Position Statement. While the duties under section 5 of the Care Act fall upon local authorities, successful market shaping is a shared endeavour that requires a range of coordinated action by commissioners and providers, working together with the citizen at the centre. Local authorities should engage and cooperate with stakeholders to reflect the range and diversity of communities and people with specific needs, for example:

- people needing care and support themselves and their representative organisations;

- carers and their representative organisations;

- health professionals;

- social care managers and social workers;

- independent advocates;

- support organisations that help people who need care consider choices (including financial options);

- provider organisations (including where appropriate housing providers and registered social landlords);

- wider citizens and communities including individuals and groups who are less frequently heard (for example, LGBT communities where there may be a lack of data on care and support needs and preferences) or at risk from exclusion, including those who have communication issues and involving representatives of those who lack mental capacity.[1, 2]

4.63. Engagement with people needing care and support, people likely to need care and support, carers, independent advocates, families and friends, should emphasise understanding the needs of individuals and specific communities, what aspirations people have, what outcomes they would like to achieve, their views on existing services and how they would like services to be delivered in the future.[3] It should also seek to identify the types of support and resources or facilities available in the local community which may be relevant for meeting care and support needs, to help understand and build community capacity to reinforce the more formal, regulated provider market. In determining an approach to engagement, local authorities should consider methods that enable people to contribute meaningfully to:

- setting the strategic direction for market shaping and commissioning;

- engaging in planning – using methods that support people to identify problems and solutions, rather than relying on "downstream" consultation;

- identifying outcomes and set priorities for specific services;

---

[1] The recommendations of the All-Party Parliamentary Group on Dementia report, 'Building on the National Dementia Strategy: Change, progress and priorities' may be helpful http://www.alzheimers.org.uk/site/scripts/download_info.php?fileID=2249

[2] http://www.richmondcvs.org.uk/documents/Community%20Involvement/Enhancing%20Services%20 through%20Involvement.pdf

[3] Example of engagement with people using care and support: Warwickshire transformation assembly http://www.warwickshire.gov.uk/transformationassembly

- setting measures of success and monitor on-going service delivery, including through the experience of people who use services and carers;

- playing a leading role throughout tendering and procurement processes, from developing specifications to evaluating bids and selecting preferred providers;

- contributing to reviews of services and strategies that relate to decommissioning decisions and areas for new investment;

- managing any changes to service delivery, recognising that long-term relationships may have developed in the community and with individual people receiving care and support and carers.

4.64. Engagement with service providers should emphasise understanding the organisation's strategies, risks, plans, and encourage building trusting relationships and fostering improvement and innovation to better meet the needs of people in the area. Local authorities should consider engagement with significant suppliers of services to provider organisations, where this would help improve their understanding of markets, for example, engaging with employment and training services that might enable local authorities to gain access to frontline insights on care provision and the local workforce supply and training.

4.65. Local authorities should ensure that active engagement and consultation with local people is built into the development and review of their strategies for market shaping and commissioning, and is demonstrated to support local accountability (for example, via the Local Account).

4.66. Local authorities should engage positively with provider organisations to ensure fair play and necessary confidentiality. The Think Local Act Personal (TLAP) partnership has produced guidance that may assist in the process – Stronger Partnerships for Better Outcomes and Commissioning the future: start a new conversation.[1],[2]

4.67. Local authorities should make available to providers available routes to register concerns or complaints about engagement and commissioning activities. Local authorities should consider the adequacy and effectiveness of these routes and processes as part of their engagement and trust-building activities.

UNDERTAKING MARKET SHAPING AND COMMISSIONING
Understanding the market

4.68. Local authorities **must** understand local markets and develop knowledge of current and future needs for care and support services, and, insofar as they are willing to share and discuss, understand providers' business models and plans.[3] This is important so that authorities can articulate likely trends in needs and signal to the market the likely future demand for different types of services for their market as a whole, and understand the local business environment, to support effective commissioning. Activities to understand the market should appropriately reflect an authority's strategic plans for integrating health, social care and

---

[1] http://www.thinklocalactpersonal.org.uk/_library/NMDF/StrongerPartnerships_final.pdf
[2] http://www.thinklocalactpersonal.org.uk/Browse/marketdevelopment/
National_Market_Development_ Forum/Commissioning_the_future/?parent=9435&child=9324
[3] http://ipc.brookes.ac.uk/services/documents/DCMQC_MPS_example.pdf

related services and will require the cooperation of those other parties, as well as other authorities in the region, to ensure a complete picture.

4.69. Local authorities (through an engagement process, in concert with commissioners for other services where appropriate) should understand and articulate the characteristics of current and future needs for services. This should include reference to underpinning demographics, drivers and trends, the aspirations, priorities and preferences of those who will need care and support, their families and carers, and the changing care and support needs of people as they progress through their lives. This should include an understanding of:

- people with existing care needs drawn from assessment records;

- carers with existing care needs drawn from carers' assessment records;

- new care and support needs;

- those whose care and support needs will transition from young people's services to adult services;

- those transitioning from working-age adults to services for older people;

- people whose care and support needs may fluctuate;

- people moving to higher needs and specialised care and support; and

- those that will no longer need care and support.

4.70. It should include information and analysis of low incidence needs and multiple and complex conditions[1] as well as more common conditions such as sensory loss[2]. It should also include information about likely changes in requirements for specialist housing required by people with care and support needs. The online tool (shop@) developed by the Housing Learning and Improvement Network may be helpful.[3],[4]

4.71. Local authorities should have in place robust methods to collect, analyse and extrapolate this information about care and support needs, including as appropriate information about specific conditions (for example, neurological conditions such as Stroke, Parkinson's, Motor Neurone Disease), and multiple and complex needs. This should sit alongside information about providers' intentions to deliver support over an appropriate timescale – likely to be at least 5 years into the future, with alignment to other strategic timeframes. Data collection should include information on the quality of services provided in order to support local authority duties to foster continuous improvement. This could be achieved, for example, by collecting and acting on feedback from people who receive care, their families and carers alongside information on the specific nature of the services people receive (e.g. regularity and length of homecare visits). This will allow for an assessment of correlation between customer experience and service

---

[1] An analogy would be health care needs analysis based on risk stratification:

[2] RNIB has a tool to help local authorities scope the needs of people with sight impairment, Action on hearing loss intend to produce something similar for hearing loss shortly. http://www.rnib.org.uk/knowledge-and-research-hub-key-information-and-statistics/sight-loss-data-tool

[3] the online tool (shop@) developed by the Housing Learning and Improvement Network may be helpful http://www.housinglin.org.uk/Topics/browse/HousingExtraCare/ExtraCareStrategy/SHOP/SHOPAT/?

[4] Guidance around transition: www.preparingforadulthood.org.uk

provision. Data collection must be sufficient to allow local authorities to meet their duties under the Equality Act 2010.

4.72. Local authorities should include in their engagement and analysis, services and support provided by voluntary, community services, supported housing providers, and other groups that make up 'community assets' and plan strategically to encourage, make best use of and grow these essential activities to integrate them with formal care and support services.

4.73. Local authorities should also seek to understand trends and changes to the levels of support that are provided by carers, and seek to develop support to meet their needs, noting that amongst other sources, census data include information on carers and their economic activity. Local authorities should understand the trends and likely changes to the needs of carers in employment, so as to better plan future support.

4.74. In order to understand future trends in needs and demands, local authorities should include an understanding of people who are or are likely to be both wholly or partly state funded, and people who are or are likely to be self-funding. It should also include an analysis of those self-funding people who are likely to move to state funding in the future, including those who are likely to reach the cap on care costs, and people who are partly state-funded and likely to reach the cap on care costs.

4.75. The understanding of needs should also include an understanding of the likely demand for state-funded services that the local authority will need to commission directly, and state-funded services likely to be provided through direct payments and require individuals to 'micro-commission' services. Local authorities should also consider the extent to which people receiving services funded by the state may wish to 'top up' their provision to receive extra services or premium services – that is, the assessment of likely demand should be for services that people are likely to need and be prepared to pay for through top ups.

4.76. The assessment of needs should be integrated with the process of developing, refining and articulating a local authority's Joint Strategic Needs Assessment. Where appropriate, needs should be articulated on an outcomes basis.

4.77. In order to gather the necessary information to shape its market, local authorities should engage with providers (including the local authority itself if it directly provides services) to seek to understand and model current and future levels of service provision supply, the potential for change in supply, and opportunities for change in the types of services provided and innovation possible to deliver better quality services and greater value for money. Local authorities should understand the characteristics of providers' businesses, their business models, market concentration, investment plans etc. Information about both supply and expected demand for services should be made available publicly to help facilitate the market and empower communities and citizens when considering care and support.

4.78. Assessment of supply and potential demand should include an awareness and understanding of current and future service provision and potential demand from outside the local authority area where this is appropriate, for example in considering services to meet highly specialised and complex needs, care and support may not be available in the local authority area, but only from a small number of specialised providers in the country.

Facilitating the development of the market

4.79. Local authorities should collaborate with stakeholders and providers to bring together information about needs and demands for care and support with that about future supply, to understand for their whole market the implications for service delivery. This will include understanding and signalling to the market as a whole the need for the market to change to meet expected trends in needs, adapt to enhance diversity, choice, stability and sustainability, and consider geographic challenges for particular areas. To this picture, local authorities should add their own commissioning strategy and future likely resourcing for people receiving state-funding. Local authorities should consider co-ordinating these market shaping and related activities with other neighbouring authorities where this would provide better outcomes.

4.80. Local authorities should consider how to support and empower effective purchasing decisions by people who self-fund care or purchase services through direct payments, recognising that this can help deliver a more effective and responsive local market.

4.81. Local authorities should ensure that the market has sufficient signals, intelligence and understanding to react effectively and meet demand, a process often referred to as market structuring or signalling. Local authorities should publish, be transparent and engage with providers and stakeholders about the needs and supply analysis to assist this signalling. It is suggested that this is best achieved through the production and regular updating of a document like a Market Position Statement that clearly provides evidence and analysis and states the local authority's intent. A Market Position Statement is intended to encourage a continuing dialogue between a local authority, stakeholders and providers where that dialogue results in an enhanced understanding by all parties is an important element of signalling to the market.

4.82. A Market Position Statement should contain information on: the local authority's direction of travel and policy intent, key information and statistics on needs, demand and trends, (including for specialised services, personalisation, integration, housing, community services, information services and advocacy, and carers' services), information from consumer research and other sources about people's needs and wants, information to put the authority's needs in a national context, an indication of current and future authority resourcing and financial forecasts, a summary of supply and demand, the authority's ambitions for quality improvements and new types of services and innovations, and details or cross-references to the local authority's own commissioning intentions, strategies and practices.[1]

4.83. Developing and then making publicly available a Market Position Statement[2] is one way a local authority can meet its duties to make available information about the local market, and demonstrates activity to meet the other parts of Section 5 of the Act. Market Position Statements for care and support services should combine, cross-refer or otherwise complement other similar statements for

---

[1] See for example Warwickshire County Council's older people needs assessment projection a multi factor demographic, demand and finance model: http://apps.warwickshire.gov.uk/api/documents/ WCCC-568- 330 (N.B. published version includes only limited financial information)

[2] DCMQC web pages, including exemplar MPS and links to examples of good practice, http://ipc.-brookes.ac.uk/dcmqc.html

related services, particularly where there is an integrated approach or ambition, for example, housing.[1]

4.84. As part of developing and publishing a document like a Market Position Statement, local authorities should engage with stakeholders and partners to structure their markets. This could include:

- discussions with potential providers;
- actively promoting best practice and models of care and support;
- understanding the business planning cycles of providers;
- aligning interactions and supporting the provider's business planning;
- identifying and addressing barriers to market entry for new providers;
- facilitating entry to the market through advice and information;
- streamlining the authority's own procurement processes;
- promoting diversification of provider organisations;
- working with providers on an 'open-book accounting' approach[2] to cost current and future services and ensure provider sustainability;
- supporting providers through wider local authority activity – planning, business support and regeneration.

4.85. Local authorities may consider that market structuring activity – signalling to the market and providing assistance – is not achieving the strategic aims as quickly or as effectively as needed, and may wish to consider more direct interventions in the market. Market interventions may also be planned as part of the market shaping and commissioning strategies where there is an immediate need for intervention.

4.86. Market interventions could for example include: refocusing local authority business support initiatives onto the care and support sector, exploring how local care and support projects could attract capital investments and support and what guarantees may be needed, encouraging and supporting social enterprises, micro-enterprises, Community Interest Companies, and User-Led Organisations (for example, incentivising innovation by third sector providers, possibly through grant funding), exploring planning barriers and using planning law, offering access to training and development opportunities.

4.87. Local authorities should consider monitoring progress toward the ambitions set out in the Market Position Statement, and making that progress public along with information about its own commissioning decisions, as part of a commitment to transparency and accountability. This would demonstrate that the authority's commissioning activity is in line with the ambition and direction of travel articulated in its Market Position Statement, and might be achieved by including this information in regular updates to the Market Position Statement.

---

[1] The paper from the Housing Learning and Improvement Network on developing MPS for housing services may be helpful: http://www.housinglin.org.uk/_library/Resources/Housing/Support_materials/Practice_ briefings/HLIN_SHOPBriefing1_MPS_digitalversion03.pdf

[2] [typically sharing cost information between parties, sometimes with a third party acting as a broker – who surveys, anonymises, and analyses cost data from providers and arrives at a reasonable cost (based on weighted averages, and removing statistical outliers)]

Case Studies: Facilitating the market
Warwickshire Council's Market Position Statement for Older People identified a significant growth in the number of people living with dementia in the county, coupled with a declining trend in the number of people accessing traditional day services in the previous 4–5 years. Day services provide stimulation for the person living with dementia as well as a break for the person's carer.

Following this the Council undertook a full review of Dementia Community Support. This included evaluating the role of services funded by the NHS and the Council and also those provided directly by the voluntary and community sector.

The Council held an engagement event to establish what customers and carers want dementia Community Support services to look like and deliver. This identified the gaps between supply and demand in more detail and at a local level. The event also gathered information from providers and voluntary and community groups about the challenges of delivering services. Providers identified commissioning models which promote strong and stable service delivery whilst still allowing flexible responses to meet individual needs as particularly useful.

As a result of this activity, the Council are now in the process of procuring a new service model for Dementia Community Support. The model will include information and advice, community services, building-based respite and specialist support.

Promoting integration with local partners
4.88. The Health and Social Care Act 2012 sets out specific obligations for the health system and its relationship with care and support services. It gives a duty to NHS England, clinical commissioning groups, Monitor and Health and Wellbeing Boards to make it easier for health and social care services to work together to improve outcomes for people. Section 3 of the Care Act places a corresponding duty on local authorities to carry out their care and support functions with the aim of integrating services with those provided by the NHS or other health-related services, such as housing.

4.89. Local authorities should also consider working with appropriate partners to develop integration with services related to care and support such as housing, employment services, transport, benefits and leisure services. Local authorities should prioritise integration activity in areas where there is evidence that effective integration of services materially improves people's wellbeing, for example, end of life care, and should take account of the key national and local priorities and objectives of the Better Care Fund, for example, stopping people reaching crisis and reducing the emergency admissions to hospitals.

4.90. Integrated services built around an individual's needs are often best delivered through the home. The suitability of living accommodation is a core component of an individual's wellbeing and when developing integrated services, local authorities should consider the central role of housing within integration, with associated formal arrangements with housing and other partner organisations.

4.91. Local authorities should work towards providing integrated care and support, providing services that work together to provide better outcomes for individuals who need care and support and enhancing their wellbeing, noting that this will require the sharing of information about current and future needs and likely service provider's responses to underpin a holistic approach to developing integrated care and support pathways. Further information can be found in the chapters of this statutory guidance on integration (chapters 15 – 18). NHS guidance and LGA case studies on integration may be helpful,[1],[2] along with the toolkit for integration developed by North West London Whole System Integrated Care (particularly chapter 7 on budget pooling, governance arrangements and commissioning issues in general).[3]

4.92. Local authorities should consider with partners, the enabling activities, functions and processes that may facilitate effective integrated services.[4] These will include consideration of: joint commissioning strategies, joint funding, pooled budgets, lead commissioning, collaborative commissioning, working with potential service providers to consider innovative ways of arranging and delivering services, and making connections to public health improvement.

Securing supply in the market and assuring its quality and value for money through contracting

4.93. Local authorities should consider best practice on commissioning services, for example the NAO guidance[5] to ensure they deliver quality services with value for money. "Value for money" means optimal use of resources to achieve intended outcomes, and must reference the quality of service delivered and the outcomes achieved for people's wellbeing, and should not be solely based on achieving the lowest cost. Achieving value for money may mean arranging service provision collaboratively with other authorities, in order to secure viable, quality services that meet the demands identified, for example, low-volume services.

4.94. Commissioning and procurement practices must deliver services that meet the requirements of the Care Act and all related statutory guidance. Re-commissioning and replacing services represents a particular challenge and should be carried out so as to maintain quality and service delivery that supports the wellbeing of people who need care and support and carers, and guards against the risk of a discontinuity of care and support for those receiving services.[6],[7] For example, multiple contracts terminating around the same time may destabilise local markets if established providers lose significant business rapidly and staff do not transfer smoothly to new providers.

---

[1] http://www.england.nhs.uk/ourwork/part-rel/transformation-fund/bcf-plan/
[2] http://www.local.gov.uk/health/-/journal_content/56/10180/4060433/ARTICLE
[3] http://integration.healthiernorthwestlondon.nhs.uk/chapters
[4] Example of Bexley LA and CCG joint commissioning of preventative services: http://www.local.-gov.uk/web/guest/health/-/journal_content/56/10180/4060433/ARTICLE
http://www.bexley.gov.uk/CHttpHandler.ashx?id=12085&p=0
[5] http://www.nao.org.uk/successful-commissioning/
[6] http://www.nao.org.uk/decommissioning/
[7] http://ipc.brookes.ac.uk/publications/pdf/Decommissioning_and_reconfiguring_services.pdf

4.95. De-commissioning services where there is to be no replacement service should similarly be carried out so as to maintain the wellbeing of people who need care and support, and carers, and ensures that their eligible needs continue to be met.

4.96. Local authorities should consider the contract arrangements they make with providers to deliver services, including the range of block contracts, framework agreements, spot contracting or 'any qualified provider' approaches, to ensure that the approaches chosen do not have negative impacts on the sustainability, sufficiency, quality, diversity and value for money of the market as a whole – the pool of providers able to deliver services of appropriate quality.

4.97. A local authority's own commissioning should be delivered through a professional and effective procurement, tendering and contract management, monitoring, evaluation and decommissioning process that must be focussed on providing appropriate high quality services to individuals to support their wellbeing and supporting the strategies for market shaping and commissioning, including all the themes set out in this guidance.

4.98. Local authorities should ensure that they understand relevant procurement legislation, and that their procurement arrangements are consistent with such legislation and best practice. Local authorities should be aware that there is significant flexibility in procurement practices to support effective engagement with provider organisations and support innovation in service delivery, potentially reducing risks and leading to cost-savings. The Office of Fair Trading produced guidance[1] to help public purchasers understand the flexibilities so as to support service transformations through better commissioning. The TLAP National Market Development Forum has produced a briefing note summarising EU procurement rules and their impact on social care; Government has also produced guidance on when reserved contracts may be allowable for organisations employing a significant number of disabled people; these documents may be helpful to commissioners[2, 3].

4.99. Local authorities should ensure that their procurement and contract management and monitoring systems provide direct and effective links to care service managers and social workers to ensure the outcomes of service delivery matches individual's care and support needs and that where the local authority arranges services, people are given a reasonable choice of provider. Contract management should take account of feedback from people receiving care and support.

4.100. Local authorities should ensure that where they arrange services, the assessed needs of a person with eligible care and support needs is translated into effective, appropriate commissioned services that are adequately resourced and meet the wellbeing principle of the Act. For example, short home-care visits of 15 minutes or less are not appropriate for people who need support with intimate care needs, though such visits may be appropriate for checking someone has returned home safely from visiting a day centre, or whether medication has been taken (but not the administration of medicine) or where they are requested as a matter of personal choice.

---

[1] http://www.oft.gov.uk/OFTwork/competition-act-and-cartels/guidance-public-bodies/
[2] http://www.thinklocalactpersonal.org.uk/Latest/Resource/?cid=9003
[3] http://webarchive.nationalarchives.gov.uk/20100503135839/http:/www.ogc.gov.uk/documents/
Supported_Factories__Businesses.pdf

4.101. When commissioning services, local authorities should pay particular attention to ensuring that providers have clear arrangements in place to prevent abuse or neglect. This should include assuring themselves, through their contracting arrangements, that a provider is capable and competent in responding to allegations of abuse or neglect, including having robust processes in place to investigate the actions of members of staff. Local authorities should be clear what information they expect from providers (for example, where there are allegations of abuse, what action the provider is taking or has taken and what the outcome is) and where providers are expected to call upon local authorities to lead a section 42 enquiry (where the management of the provider is implicated for instance), or to involve the CCG (for health matters) or police (for example, in the case of potential crimes). There should be clear agreement about how local partners work together on investigations and what their respective roles and responsibilities are.

4.102. When commissioning services, local authorities should undertake due diligence about the financial sustainability and effectiveness of potential providers to deliver services to agreed criteria for quality, and should assure themselves that any recent breaches of regulatory standards or relevant legislation by a potential provider have been corrected before considering them during tendering processes. For example, where a provider has previously been in breach of national minimum wage legislation, a local authority should consider every legal means of excluding them from the tendering process unless they have evidence that the provider's policies and practice have changed to ensure permanent compliance.

4.103. Contracts should incentivise value for money, sustainability, innovation and continuous improvement in quality and actively reward improvement and added social value. Contracts and contract management should manage and eliminate poor performance and quality by providers and recognise and reward excellence.

4.104. Local authorities are under a duty to consider added social value when letting contracts through the Public Services (Social Value) Act 2012 and are required to consider how the services they procure, above relevant financial thresholds, might improve the economic, social and environmental well-being of the area.[1] Local authorities should consider using this duty to promote added value in care and support both when letting contracts to deliver care and support, and for wider goods and services. This should include considering whether integrated services, voluntary and community services and 'community capital' could be enhanced, recognising that these community assets provide the bedrock of care and support that commissioned and bought services supplement. Local authorities should consider the range of funding mechanisms that are available to support market interventions to support community based organisations such as seed funding and grants.

4.105. All services delivered should adhere to national quality standards, with procedures in place to assure quality, safeguarding, consider complaints and commendations, and continuing value for money, referencing the CQC standards for quality and CQC quality ratings.

---

[1] http://www.socialenterprise.org.uk/uploads/files/2012/03/public_services_act_2012_a_brief_guide_web_ version_final.pdf

4.106. Local authorities may consider delegating some forms of contracting to brokers and people who use care and support to support personal choice for people taking direct payments, with appropriate systems in place to underpin the delivery of safe, effective appropriate high quality services through such routes.[1] Where functions and activities are delegated, local authorities should ensure that appropriate elements of this statutory guidance are included in contractual conditions, for example, allowing engagement in developing Market Position Statements. Local authorities should also consider providing support to people who wish to use direct payments to help them make effective decisions through, for example, Direct Payment support organisations.

4.107. Local authority procurement and contract management activities should seek to minimise burdens on provider organisations and reduce duplications, where appropriate, using and sharing information, with for example the CQC.

4.108. Recognising that procurement is taking place against a backdrop of significant demand on commissioners to achieve improved value for money and make efficiencies, local authorities should consider emerging practice on achieving efficiencies without undermining the quality of care.[2]

Further information/best practice

4.109. The different approaches provided in footnotes in this guidance are meant as illustrative examples rather than recommendations or endorsements.

4.110. The Department of Health funded a programme in 2013/14 to support local authorities prepare for market shaping duties; further information is available at the website for the Developing Care Markets for Quality & Choice programme website.[3] The Department is also funding a project to develop commissioning standards for local authorities that will deliver guidance and standards by December 2014.

4.111. Both the Developing Care Markets programme and the commissioning standards and guidance will develop the themes presented in this statutory guidance and will themselves reference case studies of best practice and support tools that demonstrate how these themes have been introduced and delivered effectively.

---

[1] http://www.surreycc.gov.uk/__data/assets/pdf_file/0009/278640/Factsheet-7-Brokerage-v2Nov11.pdf

[2] http://www.local.gov.uk/productivity/-/journal_content/56/10180/3371097/ARTICLE

[3] http://ipc.brookes.ac.uk/dcmqc.html

5. MANAGING PROVIDER FAILURE AND OTHER SERVICE INTERRUPTIONS

This chapter provides guidance on:
- *Sections 19 and 48 to 57 of the Care Act 2014;*

- *The Care and Support (Business Failure) Regulations 2014.*

This chapter covers:
- service interruptions because of business failure. This chapter explains what local authorities must do if a provider is unable to carry on because of business failure;
- business failure involving a provider in the Care Quality Commission's (CQC) market oversight regime. This section explains CQC's role if business failure occurs and the link with the local authority's temporary duty;
- business failure involving a provider not in the CQC market oversight regime. This section explains what local authorities must do if the business failure involves a provider not in the CQC regime;
- administration and other insolvency procedures. This section explains the relationship between local authorities and persons such as an Administrator appointed in insolvency proceedings;
- service interruptions other than business failure. This section explains local authorities' powers where a service is interrupted for other reasons;
- the link with local authorities' duties in respect of market shaping. This section explains how local authorities' market shaping activities can play a part in effectively addressing service interruptions;
- the need for contingency planning. This section explains how local authorities should consider having contingency plans in advance to address the service interruptions that pose the greatest risk locally.

5.1. The possibility of interruptions to care and support services causes uncertainty and anxiety for people receiving services, their carers, family and friends. This guidance explains how the Care Act makes provision to ensure that, in such circumstances, the care and support needs of those receiving the service continue to be met. It describes local authorities' powers and duties when services are at risk of interruption in general and, in particular, when the interruption is because a provider's business has failed. It provides guidance to local authorities on the exercise of those powers and the discharge of those duties.

5.2. Interruptions can arise from a number of different causes. An example is when a provider of services faces commercial difficulties that put the continuation of their business under threat. In 2011, Southern Cross Healthcare, then the biggest provider of residential care services in the United Kingdom, ran into financial difficulties and it was possible the business would have to close down, putting services to residents at risk. While Southern Cross was a provider of services in all parts of the country, smaller local providers can also encounter commercial issues which cause uncertainty for people receiving care and support. Local authorities have an important role in situations where a provider is unable to continue to supply services because of business failure.

5.3. There are numerous other situations that can cause disruption to care and support services. Some may impact on the whole business – e.g. a provider decides to close the business down – while others impact on a particular service – e.g. a meningitis outbreak at a care home. Local authorities should use their powers to act in such cases, as set out below.

DEFINITIONS

5.4. "Business failure" is defined in The Care and Support (Business Failure) Regulations 2014. These Regulations define what is meant by "business failure" and explain the circumstances in which a person is to be treated as being unable to do something because of business failure. Business failure is defined by a list of different events such as the appointment of an administrator, the appointment of a receiver or an administrative receiver (the full list appears in the Regulations). Service interruption because of "business failure" relates to the whole of the regulated activity and not to parts of it.

5.5. "Temporary duty" or "duty" means the duty on local authorities to meet needs in the case of business failure. "Temporary" means the duty continues for as long as the local authority considers it necessary. The temporary duty applies regardless of whether a person is ordinarily resident in the authority's area. The duty applies from the moment the authority becomes aware of the business failure. The actions to be taken by authorities will depend on the circumstances, and may include the provision of information. The duty is to meet needs but authorities have discretion as to how they meet those needs.

SERVICE INTERRUPTIONS BECAUSE OF BUSINESS FAILURE

5.6. Business failure of a major provider is a rare and extreme event and does not automatically equate to closure of a service. It may have no impact on residents or the people who use the services. However, if a provider is unable to continue because of business failure, the duties on local authorities are as follows.

5.7. Local authorities are under a temporary duty to meet people's needs when a provider is unable to continue to carry on the relevant activity in question because of business failure. The duty applies when a service can no longer be provided and the reason for that is that the provider's business has failed. If the provider's business has failed but the service continues to be provided then the duty is not triggered. This often may happen in insolvency situations where an Administrator is appointed and continues to run the service.

5.8. The duty applies where a failed provider was meeting needs in the authority's area. It does not matter whether or not the authority has contracts with that provider, nor does it matter if all the people affected are self-funders (i.e. arranging and paying for their own care). The duty is in respect of people receiving care by that provider in that authority's area – it does not matter which local authority (if any) made the arrangements to provide services.

5.9. The needs that must be met are those that were being met by the provider immediately before the provider became unable to carry on the activity. Local authorities must ensure the needs are met but how that is done is for the local authority to decide, and there is significant flexibility in determining how to do so, as set out in section 8 of the Care Act. It is not necessary to meet those needs through exactly the same combination of services that were previously supplied. However, when deciding how needs will be met, local authorities must involve the person concerned, any carer that the person has, or anyone whom the person asks the authority to involve (see chapter 10 on care and support planning). Where the person lacks capacity to ask the authority to do that, the local authority must involve anyone who appears to the authority to be interested in the person's welfare. Where a carer's service is involved, local authorities must involve the carer and anyone the carer asks the authority to involve. The authority must take all reasonable steps to agree how needs should be met with the person concerned. It should seek to minimise disruption for people receiving care, in line with the wellbeing principle and, although authorities have discretion about how to meet needs, the aim should be to provide a service as similar as possible to the previous one.

5.10. An authority has the power, where it considers this necessary to discharge the temporary duty, to request that the provider, or anyone involved in the provider's business as it thinks appropriate, to supply it with information that it needs. This may involve, for example, up to date records of the people who are receiving services from that provider, to help the local authority to identify those who may require its support.

5.11. The authority should act promptly to meet people's needs. The lack of a needs or carer's assessment or a financial assessment for a person must not be a barrier to action. Neither is it necessary to complete those assessments before or whilst taking action. Similarly, authorities must meet needs irrespective of whether those needs would meet the eligibility criteria. All people receiving services in the local authority's area are to be treated the same. In particular, how someone pays for the costs of meeting their needs – for example, in full by the person themselves – must have no influence on whether the authority fulfils the duty However, an authority may charge the person for the costs of meeting their needs, and it may also charge another local authority which was previously meeting those needs, if it temporarily meets the needs of a person who is not ordinarily resident in its area. The charge must cover only the actual cost incurred by the authority in meeting the needs. No charge must be made for the provision of information and advice to the person.

5.12. The Care Act imposes certain restrictions on the provision of health services by local authorities and these apply to meeting needs in provider failure cases (section 52(7)). A local authority may not meet needs in provider failure cases by, for example, providing NHS Continuing Healthcare (NHS CHC). Where the failed provider's clientèle consists of persons in receipt of NHS CHC, unless their needs appear to have changed, it would be reasonable for the local authority to conclude that it was not necessary to do anything to meet those needs. This is because the duty to provide NHS CHC falls on the NHS and local authorities cannot provide it. The duties of the NHS in such situations are covered elsewhere and as such are beyond the scope of this guidance. Authorities should refer to the Standing Rules (the National Health Service Commissioning Board and Clinical Commissioning Groups (Responsibilities and Standing Rules) Regulations 2012 ,as amended); and to the National Framework for NHS Continuing Healthcare and NHS-funded Nursing Care and the NHS-Funded Nursing Care Best Practice Guidance for further guidance.

5.13. In fulfilling this function, authorities must follow the general duties to cooperate (see chapter 15). Where a person is not ordinarily resident in an authority's area, that authority must cooperate with the authority which was arranging for the needs to be met previously (i.e. before the provider became unable to carry on because of business failure). The duty of cooperation applies equally where the needs being met previously were paid for (in full or in part) by another authority through a direct payment to the person concerned.

5.14. Authorities that disagree on whether and/or how the law (i.e. section 48) applies in these circumstances may apply to the Secretary of State for a determination of a dispute under the procedure that applies to disputes over ordinary residence or continuity of care (see chapters 19 and 20).

5.15. All of the duties on local authorities described above apply equally if the needs the authority must meet were, at the time the provider became unable to carry on because of business failure, being met under arrangements made by local authorities in Wales, Scotland or Northern Ireland under the legislation that applies in those countries. English local authorities may recover from their counterparts in Wales, Scotland and Northern Ireland the costs incurred in meeting the person's needs. If applicable, English authorities can also recover costs from the person themselves (other than the costs of needs being met or funded by the authorities mentioned above).

5.16. Disputes between authorities in England, Wales, Scotland or Northern Ireland about whether or how the temporary duty applies in cross-border situations are to be resolved under the legislation governing disputes about cross-border placements in Schedule 1 and the relevant Regulations (see chapter 22).

BUSINESS FAILURE INVOLVING A PROVIDER IN THE CQC OVERSIGHT REGIME

5.17. From April 2015, the financial "health" of certain care and support providers will become subject to monitoring by the Care Quality Commission (CQC). The Care and Support (Market Oversight Criteria) Regulations 2014 set out the entry criteria for a provider to fall within the regime. These are intended to be providers which, because of their size, geographic concentration or other factors, would be difficult for one or more local authorities to replace, and therefore where national oversight is required. CQC will determine which providers satisfy the criteria using data available to it. It will notify the providers which meet the entry criteria.

5.18. CQC must then assess the financial sustainability of the provider's business. If it assesses there is a significant risk to the financial sustainability of the provider's business, there are certain actions CQC may take with that provider (none of which involve local authorities).

5.19. Where CQC is satisfied that a provider in the regime is likely to become unable to continue with their activity because of business failure, it is required to tell the local authorities which it thinks will be required to carry out the temporary duty, so that they can prepare for the local consequences of the business failure. CQC will inform local authorities once it is satisfied the provider is unlikely to be able to carry on because of business failure. CQC's trigger to contact authorities is that it believes the whole of the regulated activity in respect of which the provider is registered is likely to fail, not parts of it. It is not required to make contact with authorities if, say, a single home owned by the provider in the regime is likely to fail because it is unprofitable and the CQC is not satisfied that this will lead to the whole of the provider's relevant regulated activity becoming unable to continue. In these circumstances, it is the provider's responsibility to wind down and close the service in line with its contractual obligations and it is expected that providers would do so in a planned way that does not interrupt people's care.

5.20. Where CQC considers it necessary to do so to help a local authority to carry out the temporary duty, it may request the provider to provide it with information and CQC must then give the information, and any further relevant information it holds, to the local authorities affected.

5.21. If the CQC is of the view that a provider is likely to become unable to continue with its activity because of business failure, the CQC should work closely together with the affected local authorities to help them fulfil their temporary duty. Local authorities should consider the guidance which it is anticipated CQC will publish early in 2015 on its operation of the market oversight function and how it will work with authorities in such situations.

5.22. In exercising its market oversight functions, CQC must have regard to the need to minimise the burdens it imposes on others.

BUSINESS FAILURE INVOLVING A PROVIDER NOT IN THE CQC OVERSIGHT REGIME

5.23. Regulations set out the entry criteria into the CQC regime. It will be for CQC to apply those regulations and decide which providers are included. There are many thousands of providers in England and only a relatively small number of providers will fall in the regime. The providers outside the regime will in the main be those with small and medium size businesses.

5.24. The temporary duty on local authorities to meet needs in the case of business failure applies regardless of whether the provider is in the market oversight regime. Despite the CQC having a market oversight responsibility, local authorities have responsibility to ensure continuity of care in respect of business failure of all registered providers.

ADMINISTRATION AND OTHER INSOLVENCY PROCEDURES

5.25. Business failure (as defined) will usually involve an official being appointed e.g. an Administrator to oversee the insolvency proceedings. An Administrator represents the interests of the creditors of the provider that has failed and will try to rescue the company as a going concern. In these circumstances, the service will usually continue to be provided, and the exercise of local authorities' temporary duties may not be called for. It is not for local authorities to become involved in the commercial aspects of the insolvency, but they should cooperate with the Administrator if requested. Local authorities should, insofar as it does not adversely affect people's safety and wellbeing, support efforts to maintain service provision by, for example, not prematurely withdrawing people from the service that is affected, or ceasing to commission that service.

SERVICE INTERRUPTIONS OTHER THAN BUSINESS FAILURE

5.26. Sections 18 and 20 of the Care Act set out when a local authority must meet a person's eligible needs. They place duties on the local authority. If the circumstances described in the sections apply and the needs are eligible, the local authority must meet the needs in question. These duties apply whether or not business failure is at issue.

5.27. Section 19 of the Care Act covers the circumstances where care and support needs may be met i.e. circumstances where no duties arise under section 18 but the local authority may nevertheless meet an adult's needs. In particular, section 19(3) permits a local authority to meet needs which appear to it to be urgent. In this context, "urgent" takes its everyday meaning, subject to interpretation by the courts, and may be related to, for example, time, severity etc. This is likely to be the case in many situations where services are interrupted but business failure is not the cause. The power in section 19(3) can be exercised in order to meet urgent needs without having first conducted a needs assessment, financial assessment or eligibility criteria determination. The local authority may meet urgent needs regardless of whether the adult is ordinary resident in its area. This means the local authority can act quickly if circumstances warrant. The power to meet urgent needs is not limited by reference to services delivered by particular providers and is thus available where urgent needs arise as a result of service failure of an unregistered provider (i.e. a provider of an unregulated social care activity). The power may also be used in the context of quality failings of providers if that is causing people to have urgent needs.

5.28. This section gives local authorities a power to act to meet needs, but it does not require that authorities must act. Whether or not to act is a decision for the authority itself but authorities should consider the examples which follow.

5.29. In relation to service interruption, circumstances that might lead to the exercise of the power include where the continued provision of care and support to those receiving services is in imminent jeopardy and there is no likelihood of returning to a "business as usual" situation in the immediate future, leading to urgent needs. Not all situations where a service has been interrupted or closed will merit local authority involvement because not all cases will result in adults having urgent needs. For example, if a care home closes and residents have agreed to the provider's plans to move the residents to a nearby care home that the provider also owns, local authorities will not necessarily have to become actively involved as urgent needs might not arise. On the other hand, the local authority might wish to be satisfied that the alternative home can adequately meet the urgent needs. Whether to act under this power is a judgement for the local authority to make in the first instance.

5.30. If a provider has not failed, it is primarily the provider's responsibility to meet the needs of individuals receiving care in accordance with its contractual liabilities. The local authority may wish to be involved to help with this. The power provides an ultimate backstop for use where the provider cannot or will not meet its responsibilities, and where the authority judges that the needs of individuals are urgent (and where the local authority is not already under a duty to meet the adult's needs, e.g. under section 18).

5.31. A service closure may be temporary (e.g. unforeseen absence of qualified staff) or permanent (e.g. the home is to be sold on for use as a hotel). Similarly, an emergency closure or planned closure may be involved. What matters in deciding whether to meet needs is whether the needs of the people affected appear to be urgent. For example, the sale of a provider's business may be a positive development for residents, service users and commissioners alike and may not lead to urgent needs. These powers are not intended to inhibit the effective operation of a market in improving choice, quality and investment.

5.32. Where the local authority does get involved in ensuring needs continue to be met, that involvement might be short-lived (e.g. the giving of advice) or enduring over some months (e.g. overseeing the movement of residents following the closure of several homes owned by the same provider). Acts of God (e.g. flooding) or complications with suppliers (e.g. a nursing agency refuses to continue to provide qualified staff) should not in themselves automatically be considered to trigger the use of the power. In all cases, the test is whether the local authority considers there is an urgent need to be met.

5.33. When considering action in relation to service interruption or closure, there is a balance to be struck. On the one hand, if local authorities know there is a serious risk to the continued provision of a service, they may consider not using that service temporarily or reassigning people using that service to an alternative service. On the other hand, it may be possible and justifiable for the local authority to act in a way that maximises the provider's chances of continuing to provide the service and avoiding a business failure. Local authorities should weigh the consequences of their actions before deciding how to respond, in particular, how their actions might impact on the likelihood of the service continuing. Certain actions may increase the risk of precipitating the business failure.

5.34. In summary, each service interruption should be considered on its facts and assessed by the local authority through a process of risk assessment. It is for the local authority to decide if it will act to meet a person's needs for care and support which appear to it to be urgent. In exercising this judgement the local authority must act lawfully, including taking decisions that are reasonable.

THE LINK WITH LOCAL AUTHORITIES' DUTIES IN RESPECT OF MARKET SHAPING

5.35. Section 5 and the associated guidance sets out authorities' duties to promote the efficient and effective operation of the local market in care and support services (see chapter 4). Central to this function is the need to ensure that the authority has, and makes available, information about the providers of care and support services in its area and the types of services they provide. This gathering of market intelligence is equally relevant to authorities' responses to business failure and other service interruptions. Where alternative services are to be put in place, an effective response requires a thorough knowledge of the market, which providers provide which services, the quality of each provider's services and where there is spare capacity in service provision. In anticipating potential service interruptions, there is also a need to know the vulnerabilities in the operation of the market. For example, is there only one local provider of a particular service and no alternatives exist locally, or does one provider cater for a substantial part of the local market and alternative capacity could not be found easily? Service interruptions involving such providers are likely to be more difficult to address. Local authorities should have knowledge of market vulnerabilities, market capacity and capabilities such as this in order to respond effectively to service interruptions.

5.36. Local authorities should understand how providers in their area are coping with the current trading conditions through discussions with the providers themselves. Authorities can achieve this without the collection of detailed financial metrics, accounts and business plans that CQC might utilise in respect of the major corporate providers in the regime. The business failure of providers outside the CQC regime will be on a smaller scale, usually with lesser impact, and local authorities should take a proportionate approach to anticipating or getting early warning of business failure.

THE NEED FOR CONTINGENCY PLANNING

5.37. Most service interruptions are on a small scale and are easily managed but service interruptions on a large scale pose far greater problems. If a provider which operates nationwide fails, few local authorities are likely to be able to respond effectively on their own. Local authorities should consider how they would respond to different service interruptions and, where the involvement of neighbouring authorities would be essential in order to maintain services, ensure effective liaison and information sharing arrangements are set up in advance. Close cooperation between authorities may be particularly required where an authority has a substantial number of people placed within its area by other authorities.

5.38. As part of contingency planning, authorities should discuss with local providers which services they would be willing and able to provide if the need arose because another local provider had failed. This should help to facilitate a prompt response that would help to maintain continuity of care for the people affected. Through its market shaping activities, authorities should encourage trust between the parties so that effective relationships exist where urgent needs are to be met.

5.39. Service interruptions are often the cause of much anxiety and media attention. Local authorities should have the capacity to react quickly to any media reporting of service interruptions, whether large scale or small, if uncertainty and anxiety are to be minimised.

5.40. Local authorities should consider how to undertake contingency planning most effectively at a local level, to ensure preparedness for possible service interruptions in the future. Service interruptions are often unforeseen and require rapid response. Local authorities should review which service interruptions pose the greatest risk in their locality and consider developing contingency plans in advance, in conjunction with local partners. This may include regional activity with other local authorities in the same area, where risks are better shared between a number of neighbouring authorities.

5.41. Local authorities already plan and manage challenging situations as a matter of course, for example, school closures from public health outbreaks or the impact of extreme weather. The aim should be that contingency planning for social care sits alongside authorities' other emergency planning activities.

6. ASSESSMENT AND ELIGIBILITY

This chapter provides guidance on:
- *Sections 9 to 13 of the Care Act 2014;*
- *The Care and Support (Assessment) Regulations 2014;*
- *The Care and Support (Eligibility Criteria) Regulations 2014.*

This chapter covers:
- The purpose of needs and carers' assessments; refusal of assessment; first contact and relevant safeguarding, advocacy and capacity duties; supporting the person's involvement in the assessment; taking a preventative approach and looking at a person's strengths;
- The importance of appropriate and proportionate assessment, including supporting the person through the process, enabling supported self-assessment, combining assessments and referring to NHS Continuing Healthcare where appropriate;
- Taking into account the wider picture by considering fluctuating needs and the impact on the whole family;
- The importance of having assessors appropriately trained and with the experience and knowledge necessary to carry out the assessment, including specialist assessments for those who are deafblind;
- Carrying out integrated assessment where a person has other needs, for example where the person also has health as well as care and support needs; keeping records and delegating assessments;
- The eligibility framework to ensure that there is clarity and consistency around local authority determinations on eligibility.

ASSESSMENT

6.1. The assessment and eligibility process is one of the most important elements of the care and support system. The assessment is one of the key interactions between a local authority and an individual, whether an adult needing care or a carer. The process must be person- centred throughout, involving the person and supporting them to have choice and control.

6.2. The assessment process starts from when local authorities begin to collect information about the person, and will be an integral part of the person's journey through the care and support system as their needs change. It should not just be seen as a gateway to care and support, but should be a critical intervention in its own right, which can help people to understand their situation and the needs they have, to reduce or delay the onset of greater needs, and to access support when they require it. It can also help people to understand their strengths and capabilities, and the support available to them in the community and through other networks and services.

6.3. An 'assessment' must always be appropriate and proportionate. It may come in different formats and can be carried out in various ways, including but not limited to:

- A face-to-face assessment between the person and an assessor, whose professional role and qualifications may vary depending on the circumstances, but who must always be appropriately trained and have the right skills and knowledge.

- A supported self-assessment, which should use the same assessment materials as a face-to-face assessment, but where the person completes the assessment themselves and the local authority assures itself that it is an accurate reflection of the person's needs (for example, by consulting with other relevant professionals and people who know the person with their consent).

- An online or phone assessment, which can be a proportionate way of carrying out assessments (for example where the person's needs are less complex or where the person is already known to the local authority and it is carrying out an assessment following a change in their needs or circumstances).

- A joint assessment, where relevant agencies work together to avoid the person undergoing multiple assessments (including assessments in a prison, where local authorities may need to put particular emphasis on cross-agency cooperation and sharing of expertise).

- A combined assessment, where an adult's assessment is combined with a carer's assessment and/or an assessment relating to a child so that interrelated needs are properly captured and the process is as efficient as possible.

6.4. People may approach a local authority for an assessment, or be referred by a third party, for a number of reasons. The "assessment" which they receive must follow the core statutory obligations, but the process is flexible and can be adapted to best fit with the person's needs, wishes and goals. The nature of the assessment will not always be the same for all people, and depending on the circumstances, it could range from an initial contact or "triage" process which helps a person with lower needs to access support in their local community, to a more intensive, ongoing process which requires the input of a number of professionals over a longer period of time.

6.5. The aim of the assessment is to identify what needs the person may have and what outcomes they are looking to achieve to maintain or improve their well-being. The outcome of the assessment is to provide a full picture of the individual's needs so that a local authority can provide an appropriate response at the right time to meet the level of the person's needs. This might range from offering guidance and information to arranging for services to meet those needs. The assessment may be the only contact the local authority has with the individual at that point in time, so it is critical that the most is made of this opportunity.

6.6. The assessment and eligibility process provides a framework to identify any level of need for care and support so that local authorities can consider how to provide a proportionate response at the right time, based on the individual's needs. Prevention and early intervention are placed at the heart of the care and support system, and even if a person has needs that are not eligible at that time, the local authority must consider providing information and advice or other preventative services. Local authorities must also consider the person's own strengths or if any other support might be available in the community to meet those needs. The assessment and eligibility framework provides for ongoing engagement with the person so where they have eligible needs they are involved in the arrangements put in place to deliver the outcomes they want to achieve.

6.7. To provide a comprehensive assessment, the assessor must be appropriately trained. Registered social workers and occupational therapists can provide important support and may be involved in complex assessments which indicate a wide range of needs, risks and strengths that may require a coordinated response from a variety of statutory and community services.

6.8. Some of the duties and powers detailed in this chapter apply to children and young carers in transition as well as to adults. For more information on transition, see chapter 16 of this guidance, *Transition to adult care and support.*

THE PURPOSE OF AN ASSESSMENT

6.9. The purpose of an assessment is to identify the person's needs and how these impact on their wellbeing, and the outcomes that the person wishes to achieve in their day-to-day life. The assessment will support the determination of whether needs are eligible for care and support from the local authority, and understanding how the provision of care and support may assist the adult in achieving their desired outcomes. An assessment must be person- centred, involving the individual and any carer that the adult has, or any other person they might want involved. An adult with care needs could for example ask for their GP or a district nurse to be contacted to provide information relevant to their needs.

6.10. An assessment must seek to establish the total extent of needs before the local authority considers the person's eligibility for care and support and what types of care and support can help to meet those needs. This must include looking at the impact of the adult's needs on their wellbeing and whether meeting these needs will help the adult achieve their desired outcomes. The assessment process also provides the opportunity for local authorities to take a holistic view of the person's needs in the context of their wider support network. Local authorities must consider how the adult, their support network and the wider community can contribute towards meeting the outcomes the person wants to achieve.

6.11. An individual may be unable to request an assessment or may struggle to express their needs. The local authority must in these situations carry out supported decision making, helping the person to be as involved as possible in the assessment, and must carry out a capacity assessment. The requirements of the Mental Capacity Act and access to an Independent Mental Capacity Advocate apply for all those who may lack capacity.[1]

6.12. Eligibility determinations must be made on the basis of an assessment, and cannot be made without having first carried out an assessment. Once an eligibility determination has been made, and the local authority has determined whether it will meet the person's needs (whether eligible or not), it must then carry out a financial assessment if it wishes to charge the adult and confirm that the adult is ordinarily resident in the authority. The eligibility determination cannot take place until an assessment has been completed, except in cases where the local authority is meeting urgent needs. The financial assessment may in practice run parallel to the needs assessment, but it must never influence an assessment of needs. Local authorities must inform individuals that a financial assessment will determine whether or not they pay towards their care and support, but this must have no bearing on the assessment process itself.

---

[1] Mental Capacity Act, 2005. Online at http://www.legislation.gov.uk/ukpga/2005/9/contents

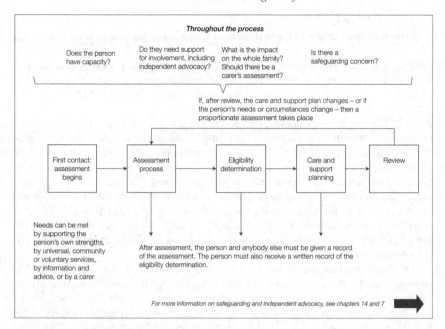

Throughout the process

Does the person have capacity?

Do they need support for involvement, including independent advocacy?

What is the impact on the whole family? Should there be a carer's assessment?

Is there a safeguardng concern?

If, after review, the care and support plan changes – or if the person's needs or circumstances change – then a proportionate assessment takes place

First contact: assessment begins → Assessment process → Eligibility determination → Care and support planning → Review

Needs can be met by supporting the person's own strengths, by universal, community or voluntary services, by information and advice, or by a carer

After assessment, the person and anybody else must be given a record of the assessment. The person must also receive a written record of the eligibility determination.

For more information on safeguarding and independent advocacy, see chapters 14 and 7

NEEDS ASSESSMENT

6.13. Local authorities must undertake an assessment for any adult with an appearance of need for care and support, regardless of whether or not the local authority thinks the individual has eligible needs or of their financial situation.

6.14. Wherever an individual expresses a need, or any challenges and difficulties they face because of their condition(s), the local authority should ensure that it has established the impact of that on the individual's day-to-day life. The local authority must also consider whether the individual's needs impact upon their wellbeing beyond the ways identified by the individual. For example where an adult expresses a need regarding their physical condition and mobility, the local authority must establish the impact of this on the adult's desired outcomes; and must also consider whether their need(s) have further consequences on their wider wellbeing such as on their personal health or the suitability of their living accommodation.

6.15. During the assessment, local authorities must consider all of the adult's care and support needs, regardless of any support being provided by a carer. Where the adult has a carer, information on the care that they are providing can be captured during assessment, but it must not influence the eligibility determination. After the eligibility determination has been reached, if the needs are eligible or the local authority otherwise intends to meet them, the care which a carer is providing can be taken into account during the care and support planning stage. The local authority is not required to meet any needs which are being met by a carer who is willing and able to do so, but it should record where that is the case. This ensures that the entirety of the adult's needs are identified and the local authority can respond appropriately if the carer feels unable or unwilling to carry out some or all of the caring they were previously providing.

CARER'S ASSESSMENT

6.16. Where an individual provides or intends to provide care for another adult and it appears that the carer may have any level of needs for support, local authorities must carry out a carer's assessment. Where an adult provides care under contract (e.g. for employment) or as part of voluntary work, they should not normally be regarded as a carer, and so the local authority would not be required to carry out the assessment.

6.17. There may be circumstances where the adult providing care, either under contract or through voluntary work, is also providing care for the same adult outside of those arrangements. In such a circumstance, the local authority must consider whether to carry out a carer's assessment for that part of the care they are not providing on a contractual or voluntary basis. There may also be cases where the person providing care does so as voluntary work or under contract, but the nature of their relationship with the person cared for is such that they ought to be considered as a "carer" within the scope of the Act. The local authority has the power to carry out an assessment in such cases, if it judges that there is reason to do so.

6.18. Carers' assessments must seek to establish not only the carer's needs for support, but also the sustainability of the caring role itself, which includes both the practical and emotional support the carer provides to the adult. Therefore, where the local authority is carrying out a carer's assessment, it must include in its assessment a consideration of the carer's potential future needs for support. Factored into this must be a consideration of whether the carer is, and will continue to be, able and willing to care for the adult needing care. Some carers may need support in recognising issues around sustainability, and in recognising their own needs. This will allow local authorities to make a realistic evaluation of the carer's present and future needs for support and whether the caring relationship is sustainable. Where appropriate these views should be sought in a separate conversation independent from the adult's needs assessment.

6.19. The carer's assessment must also consider the outcomes that the carer wants to achieve in their daily life, their activities beyond their caring responsibilities, and the impact of caring upon those activities. This includes considering the impact of caring responsibilities on a carer's desire and ability to work and to partake in education, training or recreational activities, such as having time to themselves. This impact should be considered in both a short-term immediate sense but also the impact of caring responsibilities over a longer term, cumulative sense.

REFUSAL OF ASSESSMENT

6.20. An adult with possible care and support needs or a carer may choose to refuse to have an assessment. The person may choose not to have an assessment because they do not feel that they need care or they may not want local authority support. In such circumstances local authorities are not required to carry out an assessment. However, where the local authority identifies that an adult lacks mental capacity and that carrying out a needs assessment would be in the adult's best interests, the local authority is required to do so. The same applies where the local authorities identifies that an adult is experiencing, or is at risk of experiencing, abuse or neglect.

6.21. In instances where an individual has refused a needs or carer's assessment but at a later time requests that an assessment is carried out, the local authority must do so. Additionally, where an individual previously refused an assessment and the local authority establishes that the adult or carer's needs or circumstances have changed, the local authority must consider whether it is required to offer an assessment, unless the person continues to refuse.

FIRST CONTACT WITH THE AUTHORITY

6.22. The assessment process starts from when local authorities start to collect information about the person. From their very first contact with the local authority, the person must be given as much information as possible about the assessment process, as early as possible, to ensure a personalised approach to the assessment. This should include detail of what can be expected during the assessment process (such as the format and timescale of assessment, complaints processes and possible access to independent advocacy) and allow them to be as involved in the process as possible. Local authorities must ensure that this information is in an accessible format for those to whom it is provided. For example, Braille may be an appropriate format for many with partial-sightedness or who are blind. Some formats are less accessible for certain groups, such as online platforms for those with particular sensory impairments.

6.23. From this early stage local authorities should consider whether the individual would have substantial difficulty in being involved in the assessment process and if so consider the need for independent advocacy (see chapter 7). Local authorities should also consider whether the person may have difficulty communicating (for example those with Autistic Spectrum Disorder or Profound and Multiple Learning Disabilities), and whether a specialist or interpreter may be needed to support communication.[1]

6.24. Getting the initial response right can save time and costs on assessment later. Some local authorities have found that putting in place a single access point for all new requests and people currently receiving care can speed up and simplify the process for people approaching the authority; and can also free up time for professional staff to focus on more complex cases.

6.25. Local authorities should not, however, remove people from the process too early. Early or targeted interventions such as universal services, a period of reablement and providing equipment or minor household adaptions can delay an adult's needs from progressing. The first contact with the authority, which triggers the requirement to assess, may lead to a pause in the assessment process to allow such interventions to take place and for any benefit to the adult to be determined. Local authorities must ensure that their staff are sufficiently trained and equipped to make the appropriate judgements needed to steer individuals seeking support towards information and advice, preventative services or a more detailed care and support assessment, or all of these. They must also be able to identify a person who may lack mental capacity and to act accordingly.

6.26. The Care Act provides local authorities with the powers to meet urgent needs where they have not completed an assessment. Authorities may meet urgent need for care and support regardless of the person's ordinary residence.[2] Where an individual with urgent needs approaches or is referred to the local authority, the local authority should provide an immediate response and meet the individual's

---

[1] For information on reasonable adjustments, see the Equality Act 2010. Online at http://www.legisla-tion.gov.uk/ukpga/2010/15/contents

[2] Care Act 2014, Section 19

care and support needs. For example, where an individual's condition deteriorates rapidly or they have an accident, they will need a swift response to ensure their needs are met. In some cases, the appropriate response may be that the local authority will meet the adult's needs. In other cases, an immediate referral may be the best way to meet a person's urgent needs, for example by completing the NHS Continuing Health Care Fast Track Pathway Tool. Following this initial response, the individual should be informed that a more detailed needs assessment, and any subsequent processes, will follow. Once the local authority has ensured these urgent needs are met, it can then consider details such as the person's ordinary residence and finances.

6.27. Staff who are involved in this first contact must have the appropriate training and should have the benefit of access to professional support from social workers, occupational therapists and other relevant experts as appropriate, to support the identification of any underlying conditions or to ensure that complex needs are identified early and that people are signposted appropriately.

6.28. Local authorities must ensure that any adult with an appearance of care and support needs, and any carer with an appearance of need for support, receives a proportionate assessment which identifies their level of needs. Where appropriate, an assessment may be carried out over the phone or online. In adopting such approaches, local authorities should consider whether the proposed means of carrying out the assessment poses any challenges or risks for certain groups, particularly when assuring itself that it has fulfilled its duties around safeguarding, independent advocacy, and assessing mental capacity. Where there is concern about a person's capacity to make a decision, for example as a result of a mental impairment such as those with dementia, acquired brain injury, learning disabilities or mental health needs, a face-to-face assessment should be arranged. Local authorities have a duty of care to carry out an assessment in a way that enables them to recognise the needs of those who may not be able to put these into words. Local authorities must ensure that assessors have the skills, knowledge and competence to carry out the assessment in question, and this applies to all assessments regardless of the format they take.

6.29. An assessment should be carried out over an appropriate and reasonable timescale taking into account the urgency of needs and a consideration of any fluctuation in those needs. Local authorities should inform the individual of an indicative timescale over which their assessment will be conducted and keep the person informed throughout the assessment process.

SUPPORTING THE PERSON'S INVOLVEMENT IN THE ASSESSMENT

6.30. Putting the person at the heart of the assessment process is crucial to understanding the person's needs, outcomes and wellbeing, and delivering better care and support. The local authority must involve the person being assessed in the process as they are best placed to judge their own wellbeing. In the case of an adult with care and support needs, the local authority must also involve any carer the person has (which may be more than one carer), and in all cases, the authority must also involve any other person requested. The local authority should have processes in place, and suitably trained staff, to ensure the involvement of these parties, so that their perspective and experience supports a better understanding of the needs, outcomes and wellbeing.

6.31. Where local authorities identify that an adult is unable to effectively engage in the assessment process independently, it should seek to involve somebody who can assist the adult in engaging with the process and helping them to articulate their preferred outcomes and needs as early as possible. This will include some people with mental impairments who will nevertheless have capacity to engage in the assessment alongside the local authority. They may require assistance whereby the local authority provides an assessment, tailored to their circumstances, their needs and their ability to engage. They should be supported in understanding the assessment process and assisted to make decisions wherever possible.

6.32. Where there is concern about a person's capacity to make a specific decision, for example as a result of a mental impairment such as dementia, acquired brain injury or learning disabilities, then an assessment of capacity should be carried out under the Mental Capacity Act (MCA). Those who may lack capacity will need extra support to identify and communicate their needs and make subsequent decisions, and may need an Independent Mental Capacity Advocate. The more serious the needs, the more support people may need to identify their impact and the consequences. Professional qualified staff, such as social workers, can advise and support assessors when they are carrying out an assessment with a person who may lack capacity.

INDEPENDENT ADVOCATES[1]

6.33. At the point of first contact, request or referral (including self-referral), local authorities must seek to ascertain whether an individual is able to be involved in their assessment and local authorities must therefore consider whether the individual has substantial difficulty in doing so. Local authorities must consider whether the adult would experience substantial difficulty in any of these four areas: understanding the information provided; retaining the information; using or weighing up the information as part of the process of being involved; and communicating the person's views, wishes or feelings. Where a person has substantial difficulty in any of these four areas, then they need assistance.

6.34. If a person does have substantial difficulty, the local authority must find someone appropriate and independent to support and represent the person, for the purpose of facilitating their involvement. This should be done as early as possible in the assessment process so that the individual's involvement can be supported throughout all stages of the process. Individuals may require help to understand information provided, assistance in weighing up the information, and support in communicating their wishes and preferences. Where there is a family member or friend who is willing and able to facilitate the person's involvement effectively, and who is acceptable to the individual and judged appropriate by the local authority, they may be asked to support the individual in the assessment process. Where there is no one thought to be appropriate for this role – either because there is no family member or friend willing and available, or if the individual does not want them to be a part of the assessment – the local authority must appoint an independent advocate.

APPROPRIATE AND PROPORTIONATE ASSESSMENTS

6.35. The assessment must be person-centred throughout. Local authorities must find out the extent to which the person being assessed wishes to be involved in the assessment and should meet those wishes as far as is practicable do so, as the

---

[1] See chapter 7

person is best placed to understand the impact of their condition(s) on their outcomes and wellbeing.

6.36. An assessment should be a collaborative process and it is therefore essential that the process is transparent and understandable so that the individual is able to:

- develop an understanding of the assessment process;

- develop an understanding of the implications of the assessment process on their condition(s) and situation;

- understand their own needs, the outcomes they want to achieve and the impact of their needs on their own wellbeing to allow them to engage effectively with the assessment process;

- start to identify the options that are available to them to meet those outcomes and to support their independence and wellbeing;

- understand the basis on which decisions are reached.

6.37. To support the person's involvement, the local authority should establish the individual's communication needs and seek to adapt the assessment process accordingly. In doing so local authorities must provide information about the assessment process in an accessible format.

6.38. To help the adult with needs for care and support, or the carer, prepare for the assessment the local authority should provide in advance, and in an accessible format, the list of questions to be covered in the assessment. This will help the individual or carer prepare for their assessment and think through what their needs are and the outcomes they want to achieve.

6.39. Some people being assessed may have severe communication needs, such as people with Profound and Multiple Learning Disabilities, Autistic Spectrum Disorder, or those who are deaf or blind. Such individuals may require the support of a specialist interpreter to help them to communicate and engage in the assessment.

6.40. Local authorities should also consider the impact of the assessment process itself on the individual's condition(s). People may feel uncertain and worried about what an assessment involves and may find the process itself to be strenuous. Local authorities should therefore give consideration to the preferences of the individual with regards to the timing, location and medium of the assessment.

6.41. The assessment should be designed to reflect the wishes of the person being assessed, taking into account their presenting need and their circumstances. An assessment process which benefits an individual in one instance may not necessarily be as effective for another. Local authorities should recognise this and in order to maintain a person-centred approach, local authorities must ensure that assessments are flexible to each individual case.

6.42. In carrying out a proportionate assessment local authorities must have regard to:

- the person's wishes and preferences and desired outcomes. For example, an individual who pays for their own care may wish to receive local authority support with accessing a particular service, but may not want the same interaction with the authority as someone who wants greater support;

- the severity and overall extent of the person's needs. For example, an individual with more complex needs will require a more detailed assessment, potentially involving a number of professionals. A person with lower needs may require a less intensive response;

- the potential fluctuation of a person's needs, both adults and carers. For example, where the local authority is aware that an adult's needs fluctuate over time, the assessment carried out at a particular moment may take into account the adult's history to get a complete picture of the person's needs.

6.43. Each local authority may decide to use an assessment tool to help collect information about the adult or carer and details of their wishes and feeling and their desired outcomes and needs. Where a local authority has decided that a person does not need a more detailed assessment, it should consider which elements of the assessment tool it should use and which are not necessary. When carrying out a proportionate assessment the assessor should continue to look for the appearance of further needs which may be the result of an underlying condition. Where the assessor believes that the person's presenting needs may be as a result of or a part of wider needs then the local authority should undertake a more detailed assessment and refer the person to other services such as housing or the NHS if necessary.

SUPPORTED SELF-ASSESSMENT

6.44. A supported self-assessment is an assessment carried out jointly by the adult with care and support needs or carer and the local authority. It places the individual in control of the assessment process to a point where they themselves complete their assessment form. Whilst it is the person filling in the assessment form, the duty to assess the person's needs, and in doing so ensure that they are accurate and complete, remains with the local authority. Local authorities can offer individuals a supported self-assessment, and must do so if the adult or carer is able, willing and has capacity to undertake it. If the person does not wish to self-assess, then the local authority must undertake an assessment following one of the other processes outlined above.

6.45. In order to support the person in carrying out a supported self-assessment, the local authority must give them any relevant information it has either about the person themselves or, for a carer's self-assessment, about the individual they care for. This is so that the person undertaking the assessment has a full picture of their care and support history and is equipped with the same information an assessor would have when undertaking an assessment. Before sharing any information, the local authority must ensure that the person consents to that information being shared. If the person lacks capacity, information must only be shared where the local authority is satisfied that doing so is in the person's best interests. In the case of a young carer, the local authority must also consider whether it is appropriate to share the information about the person the young carer cares for (see chapter 16).

6.46. Once the person has completed the assessment, the local authority must ensure that it is an accurate and complete reflection of the person's needs, outcomes, and the impact of needs on their wellbeing. The process of a supported self-assessment begins with first contact and is only complete when this assurance has been secured. Until the process of assurance is complete and the local authority has ensured that it is accurate, it will not have discharged its duties under section 9 of the Care Act. Where the person carrying out a supported self-assessment jointly with the local authority requires a specialist, for example people who are deafblind, then the professional leading this assurance process must be seen as the 'assessor' and so must have specific training and expertise relating to the individual's needs. When assuring itself that a self-assessment is comprehensive a local authority should not look to repeat the full assessment process again.

6.47. In assuring self-assessments local authorities may consider it useful to seek the views of those who are in regular contact with the person self-assessing, such as their carer(s) or other appropriate people from their support network, and any professional involved in providing care such as a housing support officer, a GP, a treating clinician, a district nurse, a rehabilitation officer or relevant prison staff. In doing this, the local authority should first seek the person's consent. This may be helpful in allowing local authorities to build an understanding of the individual's desires, outcomes, needs, and the impact on their wellbeing.

6.48. The person should be asked to complete the same assessment questionnaire that the authority uses in their needs or carers' assessments, which must assess the person's needs, their outcomes, and the impact of their needs on their wellbeing. Local authorities must also ensure they fulfill other relevant duties under the Act when supporting and assuring a person's self-assessment, such as those around independent advocacy. If at any point the local authority suspects that a person is experiencing, or is at risk of, abuse and neglect, it must begin a safeguarding enquiry (see chapter 14).

6.49. Before offering a supported self-assessment local authorities must ensure that the individual has capacity to fully assess and reflect their own needs. Local authorities must establish the individual's mental capacity in accordance with the Mental Capacity Act.[1]

6.50. If a local authority considers a person may lack capacity to understand and carry out a self-assessment, they must carry out a capacity assessment. If this shows that the person lacks the capacity to carry out a self-assessment, then the self-assessment should not be offered.

6.51. Where local authorities have established that the adult has capacity to undertake a self-assessment but experiences substantial difficulty in understanding, retaining and using the relevant information in relation to their self-assessment, they may wish to involve their carer or any other member of their family or support network in their self-assessment. Where the adult does not have the support required from a carer or family member who is willing and able to facilitate the person's involvement effectively and who is acceptable to the individual and judged appropriate by the local authority, the local authority must provide an independent advocate to assist them in their self-assessment. When a person who would otherwise receive a specialist assessment (for example, someone who is deafblind) chooses to undertake a self-assessment, the local authority must involve a person who has specific training and expertise when assuring that the person's assessment taken as a whole reflects the overall needs of the individual concerned.

6.52. Local authorities should ensure that self-assessments are completed in suitable time periods. If there is a delay in the person returning the self-assessment form the authority should assure itself that this is not because the person's condition(s) have deteriorated and is unable to complete the self-assessment.

---

[1] Mental Capacity Act, 2005. Online at http://www.legislation.gov.uk/ukpga/2005/9/contents

6.53. The local authority, once it has assured itself that the self-assessment has accurately captured the person's needs, must make an eligibility determination. Where appropriate this may include taking into account the person's own view. Although the local authority and the individual are working jointly to ascertain needs and eligibility, the final decision regarding eligibility will rest with the local authority. In all cases, the authority must inform the person of their eligibility judgement and why the local authority has reached the eligibility determination that it has. It must also discuss what needs are eligible and discuss how these might be met. Where the authority determines that the person has needs that are not eligible it must provide advice and information on what services are available in the community that can support the person in meeting those needs.

SAFEGUARDING

6.54. Where a person is at risk of harm or abuse, it is important that local authorities act swiftly and put in place an effective response. When carrying out an assessment local authorities must consider the impact of the adult's needs on their wellbeing. If it appears to local authorities that the person is experiencing, or at risk of, abuse or neglect, they must carry out a safeguarding enquiry and decide with the adult in question what action, if any, is necessary and by whom (see chapter 14).

6.55. The decision to carry out a safeguarding enquiry does not depend on the person's eligibility, but should be taken wherever there is reasonable cause to think that the person is experiencing, or is at risk of, abuse or neglect. Where this is the case, a local authority must carry out (or request others to carry out) whatever enquiries it thinks are necessary in order to decide whether any further action is necessary.

6.56. Where the actions required to protect the adult can be met by local authorities, they should take appropriate action. In some cases, safeguarding enquiries may result in the provision of care and support (under either section 18 or 19 of the Care Act), or the provision of preventative services (under section 2) or information and advice (under section 4). In the majority of cases the response will involve other agencies, for example, a safeguarding enquiry may result in referrals to the police, a change of accommodation, or action by CQC.

6.57. Where the adult has care and support needs, local authorities must continue to carry out a needs assessment and determine whether they have eligible needs, and if so, how these will be met. The assessment for care and support should run parallel to the safeguarding enquiry and the enquiry should not disrupt the assessment process or the local authority meeting eligible needs.

FLUCTUATING NEEDS

6.58. As the condition(s) of the individual at the time of the assessment may not be entirely indicative of their needs more generally, local authorities must consider whether the individual's current level of need is likely to fluctuate and what their on-going needs for care and support are likely to be. This is the case both for short-term fluctuations, which may be over the course of the day, and longer term changes in the level of the person's needs. In establishing the on-going level of need local authorities must consider the person's care and support history over a suitable period of time, both the frequency and degree of fluctuation. The local authority may also take into account at this point what fluctuations in need can be reasonably expected based on experience of others with a similar condition. It is important to recognise the benefit of adopting this comprehensive approach to assessment as the consideration of an individual's wider wellbeing may allow local authorities to provide types of care and support, or information and advice which delay or prevent the development of further needs in the future.

6.59. The assessment should also include a consideration of the individual's wider care and support needs. This may include types of care and support the individual has received in the past and their general medical history, which may be indicative of their current care and support needs.

FOCUSING ON PREVENTING NEEDS

6.60. The assessment and eligibility framework should be a key element of any prevention strategies authorities put in place. It is during the assessment where local authorities can identify needs that could be reduced, or where escalation could be delayed, and help people improve their wellbeing by providing specific preventive services, or information and advice on other universal services available locally. Early interventions can prevent or delay a person's needs from progressing.

6.61. In parallel with assessing a person's needs, local authorities must consider the benefits of approaches which delay or prevent the development of needs in individuals. This applies to both people with current needs that may be reduced or met through available universal services in the community, and those without needs who may otherwise require care and support in the future. This could include directing people to services such as community support groups which ensure that people feel supported, including an ability to participate in their local community. It may also include helping the person to access services which the local authority provides universally, such as preventative services. Local authorities can also support the person in understanding other types of support available to them, such as within their own support networks, for example to seek to promote access to appropriate employment, education or training, which can be an effective way of maintaining independence. Such interventions at an early stage will help to sustain the independence and wellbeing of people. More detail is available in chapter 2 on prevention and chapter 3 on information and advice.

6.62. Where the local authority judges that the person may benefit from such types of support, it should take steps to support the person to access those services. The local authority may 'pause' the assessment process to allow time for the benefits of such activities to be realised, so that the final assessment of need (and determination of eligibility) is based on the remaining needs which have not been met through such interventions. For example, if the local authority believes that a person may benefit from a short-term reablement service which is available locally, it may put that in place and complete the assessment following the provision of that service.

CONSIDERING THE PERSON'S STRENGTHS AND CAPABILITIES

6.63. At the same time as carrying out the assessment, the local authority must consider what else other than the provision of care and support might assist the person in meeting the outcomes they want to achieve. In considering what else might help, authorities should consider the person's own strengths and capabilities, and what support might be available from their wider support network or within the community to help. Strengths-based approaches might include co-production of services with people who are receiving care and support to foster mutual support networks. Encouraging people to use their gifts and strengths in a community setting could involve developing residents' groups and appropriate training to support people in developing their skills.

6.64. Local authorities might also consider the ways a person's cultural and spiritual networks can support them in meeting needs and building strengths, and explore this with the person. Any suggestion that support could be available from family and friends should be considered in light of their appropriateness, willingness and ability to provide any additional support and the impact on them of doing so. It must also be based on the agreement of the adult or carer in question.

CONSIDERING THE PERSON'S STRENGTHS: A CASE STUDY

Sally is 40 and has a physical disability. She receives a home care package to support her with her personal care needs, but spends a lot of time alone and has never worked. The home care worker refers her for a needs assessment because she fears Sally is in danger of isolation and depression.

The assessor asks Sally what outcomes she is looking for in day-to-day life and Sally says she would like to work but has never had the confidence to do so. The assessor refers Sally to a support-to-work service run by a local voluntary organisation.

After some training and support Sally finds a part-time job. She is now getting out of the house, socialising with colleagues and feels a valued part of a team. She is no longer in danger of isolation and depression.

WHOLE FAMILY APPROACH

6.65. The intention of the whole family approach is for local authorities to take a holistic view of the person's needs and to identify how the adult's needs for care and support impact on family members or others in their support network.

6.66. During the assessment the local authority must consider the impact of the person's needs for care and support on family members or other people the authority may feel appropriate. This will require the authority to identify anyone who may be part of the person's wider network of care and support.

6.67. In considering the impact of the person's needs on those around them, the local authority must consider whether or not the provision of any information and advice would be beneficial to those people they have identified. For example, this may include signposting to any support services in the local community.

6.68. The local authority must also identify any children who are involved in providing care. The authority may become aware that the child is carrying out a caring role through the assessment of the person needing care or their carer, or informed through family members or a school. Identification of a young carer in the family should result in an offer of a needs assessment for the adult requiring care and support and, where appropriate, the local authority must consider whether the child or young carer should be referred for a young carer's assessment or a needs assessment under the Children Act 1989,[1] or a young carer's assessment under section 63 of the Care Act. Local authorities should

---

[1] Children Act, 1989. Online at http://www.legislation.gov.uk/ukpga/1989/41/contents

ensure that adults' and children's care and support services work together to ensure the assessment is effective – for example by sharing expertise and linking processes.

6.69. When carrying out an adult's or carer's assessment, if it appears that a child is involved in providing care the local authority must consider:

- the impact of the person's needs on the young carer's wellbeing, welfare, education and development;

- whether any of the caring responsibilities the young carer is undertaking are inappropriate.

6.70. An assessment should take into account the parenting responsibilities of the person as well as the impact of the adult's needs for care and support on the young carer.

6.71. Local authorities must also consider whether any of the caring tasks the child is undertaking are inappropriate. They should consider how supporting the adult with needs for care and support can prevent the young carer from undertaking excessive or inappropriate care and support responsibilities. A young carer becomes vulnerable when their caring role risks impacting upon their emotional or physical wellbeing or their prospects in education and life. This might include:

- preventing the young carer from accessing education, for example because the adult's needs for care and support result in the young carer's regular absence from school or impacts upon their learning;

- preventing the young carer from building relationships and friendships;

- impacting upon any other aspect of the young carer's wellbeing.

6.72. Inappropriate caring responsibilities should be considered as anything which is likely to have an impact on the child's health, wellbeing or education, or which can be considered unsuitable in light of the child's circumstances and may include:

- personal care such as bathing and toileting;

- carrying out strenuous physical tasks such as lifting;

- administering medication;

- maintaining the family budget;

- emotional support to the adult.

6.73. When a local authority is determining whether the tasks a child carries out are inappropriate, it should also take into account the child's own view wherever appropriate.

COMBINING ASSESSMENTS

6.74. Local authorities may combine an assessment of an adult needing care and support or of a carer with any other assessment it is carrying out either of that person or another where both the individual and carer agree, and the consent condition is met in relation to a child. This will also avoid the authority carrying out two separate assessments when the two assessments are intrinsically linked. If either of the individuals concerned does not agree to a combined assessment, then the assessments must be carried out separately.

INTEGRATED ASSESSMENTS

6.75. People may have needs that are met by various bodies. Therefore, a holistic approach to assessment which aims to bring together all of the person's needs may need the input of different professionals such as adult care and support, children's services, housing, experts in the voluntary sector, relevant professionals in the criminal justice system, health or mental health professionals.

6.76. A local authority may carry out a needs or carer's assessment jointly with another body carrying out any other assessment in relation to the person concerned, provided that person agrees. In doing so, the authority may integrate or align assessment processes in order to better fit around the needs of the individual. An integrated approach may involve working together with relevant professionals on a single assessment. It may also include putting processes in place to ensure that the person is referred for other assessments such as an assessment for after-care needs under the Mental Health Act 1983.[1] In some settings, for example in prisons, local authorities should engage relevant professionals early to ensure assessors are prepared for carrying out an assessment in that environment.

6.77. Where more than one agency is assessing a person, they should all work closely together to prevent that person having to undergo a number of assessments at different times, which can be distressing and confusing.

6.78. Where a person has both health and care and support needs, local authorities and the NHS should work together effectively to deliver a high quality, coordinated assessment. To achieve this, local authorities should:

- Shape the process around the person, involving the person and considering their experience when coordinating an integrated assessment;

- Work with other professionals to ensure the person's health and care services are aligned. This will require flexibility of systems where possible, for example when sharing information. It will also be strengthened by a culture of common values and objectives at frontline level – joint visits can be helpful here.

- Link together various care and support plans to set out a single, shared care pathway, for example when following the Care Programme Approach for people with a severe mental disorder who need multi-agency support or intensive intervention, under the direction of a named care coordinator.[2] A multi-agency approach is particularly important where people are enrolled on the Proactive Care Programme, which was introduced through the Avoiding Unplanned Emergency Admissions Enhanced Service in the 2014/15 GP Contract.[3]

6.79. The local authority may carry out the care and support assessment jointly with any other assessment, and can also undertake the other assessment on behalf of the other body, where this is agreed. Where an assessment involves a body from outside of the local authority, the local authority should provide any resources or

---

[1] Mental Health Act, 1983. Available online at http://www.legislation.gov.uk/ukpga/1983/20/contents

[2] See chapter 34 of the revised "Code of Practice Mental Health Act 1983" (Department of Health, 2014)

[3] NHS Employers Publications: Avoiding Unplanned Admissions Guidance, 2014-15 (April 2014). Available online at http://www.nhsemployers.org/~/media/Employers/Publications/Avoiding%20 unplanned%20admissions%20guidance%202014-15.pdf (25/09/2014)

facilities which may be required to carry out the assessment. Sharing resources may include the provision of facilities or relative information relating to the person being assessed.[1]

NHS CONTINUING HEALTHCARE

6.80. Where it appears that a person may be eligible for NHS Continuing Healthcare (NHS CHC), local authorities must notify the relevant Clinical Commissioning Group (CCG). NHS CHC is a package of on-going care that is arranged and funded solely by the NHS where the individual has been found to have a 'primary health need' as set out in The National Framework for NHS Continuing Healthcare and NHS-funded Nursing Care (November 2012) (Revised).[2] Such care is provided to individuals aged 18 or over, to meet needs that have arisen as a result of disability, accident or illness. Eligibility for NHS CHC places no limits on the settings in which the package of support can be offered or on the type of service delivery.

6.81. Whilst local authorities have a duty to carry out an assessment where a person has an appearance of needs and a duty to meet eligible needs, local authorities cannot arrange services that are the responsibility of the NHS (e.g. care provided by registered nurses and services that the NHS has to provide because the individual is eligible for NHS CHC). However, the local authority may provide or arrange healthcare services where they are incidental or ancillary to doing something else to meet needs for care and support and the service or facility in question is of a nature that a local authority could be expected to provide. Ultimate responsibility for arranging and monitoring the services required to meet the needs of those who qualify for NHS CHC rests with the NHS.

6.82. Individuals may require care and support provided by their local authority and/or services arranged by CCGs. Local authorities and CCGs therefore have a responsibility to ensure that the assessment of eligibility for care and support and CHC respectively take place in a timely and consistent manner. If, following an assessment for NHS CHC, a person is not found to be eligible for NHS CHC, the NHS may still have a responsibility to contribute to that person's health needs – either by directly commissioning services or by part-funding the package of support. Where a package of support is commissioned or funded by both an LA and a CCG, this is known as a 'joint package' of care. A joint package of care could include NHS-funded nursing care and other NHS services that are beyond the powers of a local authority to meet. The joint package could also involve the CCG and the local authority both contributing to the cost of the care package, or the CCG commissioning part of the package. Joint packages of care may be provided in a nursing or care home, or in a person's own home, and could be by way of joint personal budget.

6.83. Local authorities and CCGs in each local area must agree a local disputes resolution process to resolve cases where there is a dispute between them about eligibility for NHS CHC, about the apportionment of funding in joint funded care and support packages, or about the operation of refunds guidance. Disputes should not delay the provision of the care package, and the protocol

---

[1] See chapters 15–18 of this guidance on Integration and Partnership Working
[2] NHS CHC National Framework, 2012. Available online at https://www.gov.uk/government/uploads/system/uploads/attachment_data/file/213137/National-Framework-for-NHS-CHC-NHS-FNC-Nov-2012.pdf (26/09/2014)

should make clear how funding will be provided pending resolution of the dispute. Where disputes relate to local authorities and CCGs in different geographical areas, the disputes resolution process of the responsible CCG should normally be used in order to ensure resolution in a robust and timely manner. This should include agreement on how funding will be provided during the dispute, and arrangements for reimbursement to the agencies involved once the dispute is resolved.

ROLES AND RESPONSIBILITIES

6.84. Assessments can be carried out by a range of professionals including registered social workers, occupational therapists and rehabilitation officers. Registered social workers and occupational therapists are considered to be two of the key professions in adult care and support. Local authorities should consider how adults who need care, carers, and assessors have access to registered social care practitioners, such as social workers or occupational therapists.

TRAINING

6.85. It is essential that the assessment is carried out to the highest quality. The assessment must: identify the person's needs, outcomes and how these impact on their wellbeing; consider the person's strengths and capabilities; and consider what universal services might help the person improve their wellbeing. Local authorities must ensure that their staff have the required skills, knowledge and competence to undertake assessments and that this is maintained. This applies no matter how the assessment is carried out, including first contact, any assessment over the phone or online, or self-assessments where the person carrying out the assurance will need to have the appropriate training.

6.86. Local authorities must ensure that assessors are appropriately trained and competent whenever they carry out an assessment. This means ensuring that assessors undergo regular, up-to-date training on an ongoing basis. The training must be appropriate to the assessment, both the format of assessment and the condition(s) and circumstances of the person being assessed. They must also have the skills and knowledge to carry out an assessment of needs that relate to a specific condition or circumstances requiring expert insight, for example when assessing an individual who has autism, learning disabilities, mental health needs or dementia. This training must be maintained throughout their career. As part of maintaining their registration, social workers and occupational therapists are required to evidence their Continuing Professional Development.

6.87. When assessing particularly complex or multiple needs, an assessor may require the support of an expert to carry out the assessment, to ensure that the person's needs are fully captured. Local authorities should consider whether additional relevant expertise is required on a case-by-case basis, taking into account the nature of the needs of the individual, and the skills of those carrying out the assessment. The local authority must ensure that the person is able to be involved as far as possible, for example by providing an interpreter where a person has a particular condition affecting communication – such as autism, blindness, or deafness.[1]

---

[1] See also the Equality Act for necessary provisions around reasonable adjustments. Online at http://www.legislation.gov.uk/ukpga/2010/15/contents

6.88. Where the assessor does not have the necessary knowledge of a particular condition or circumstance, they must consult someone who has relevant expertise. This is to ensure that the assessor can ask the right questions relating to the condition and interpret these appropriately to identify underlying needs. A person with relevant expertise can be considered as somebody who, either through training or experience, has acquired knowledge or skill of the particular condition or circumstance. Such a person may be a doctor or health professional, or an expert from the voluntary sector, but there is no obligation for the local authority to source an expert from an outside body if the expertise is available in house.

6.89. The Department has published guidance for certain groups of adults that refer to their assessment for care and support. Two specific areas are for people who are deafblind and people with autism and these pieces of guidance should be read with this guidance. *Think Autism 2014*, the April 2014 update to *Fulfilling and Rewarding Lives*, the strategy for adults with autism in England (2010), sets out that local authorities should:

- make basic autism training available for all staff working in health and social care;

- develop or provide specialist training for those in roles that have a direct impact on access to services for adults with autism; and

- include quality autism awareness training within general equality and diversity training programmes across public services.

6.90. The Care Act strengthens this guidance in relation to assessors having specialised training to assess an adult with autism. The Act places a legal requirement on local authorities that all assessors must have the skills, knowledge and competence to carry out the assessment in question. Where an assessor does not have experience in a particular condition (such as autism, learning disabilities, mental health needs or other conditions), they must consult someone with relevant experience. This is so that the person being assessed is involved throughout the process and their needs, outcomes and the impact of needs on their wellbeing are all accurately identified.

ASSESSMENT FOR PEOPLE WHO ARE DEAFBLIND

6.91. Local authorities must ensure that an expert is involved in the assessment of adults who are deafblind, including where a deafblind person is carrying out a supported self- assessment jointly with the authority. People are regarded as deafblind "if their combined sight and hearing impairment causes difficulties with communication, access to information and mobility. This includes people with a progressive sight and hearing loss" (Think Dual Sensory, Department of Health, 1995).

6.92. During an assessment if there is the appearance of both sensory impairments, even if when taken separately each sensory impairment appears relatively mild, the assessor must consider whether the person is deafblind as defined above. If a person is deafblind, this must trigger a specialist assessment. This specialist assessment must be carried out by an assessor or team that has training of at least QCF or OCN level 3, or above where the person has higher or more complex needs.

6.93. Training and expertise should in particular include; communication, one-to-one human contact, social interaction and emotional wellbeing, support with mobility, assistive technology and rehabilitation. The type and degree of specialism required should be judged on a case by case basis, according to the extent of the person's condition and their communication needs. Local authorities should also recognise that deafblindness is a dual sensory condition which requires a knowledge and understanding of the two respective conditions in unison, which cannot be replicated by taking an individual approach to both senses.

6.94. The combined loss of sight and hearing can have a significant impact upon the individual even where they are not profoundly deaf and totally blind, as it is the impact of one impairment upon the other which causes difficulties. Deafblindness can have significant impact on the adult's independence and their ability to achieve their desired outcomes. In particular deafblindness may have impact upon the adults:

- autonomy and ability to maintain choice and control;
- health and safety and daily routine; and
- involvement in education, work, family and social life.

6.95. Local authorities should recognise that adults may not define themselves as deafblind. Instead they may describe their vision and hearing loss in terms which indicate that they have significant difficulty in their day-to-day lives. The assessment must therefore take the initiative to establish maximum possible communication with the adult to ensure that individuals are as fully engaged as possible and have the opportunity to express their wishes and desired outcomes. This is particularly important where the person is carrying out a supported self-assessment jointly with the local authority. The person ensuring that the self-assessment is a complete and accurate reflection of needs must have specific training and expertise that will enable maximum possible communication and an accurate and complete assessment.

6.96. Whilst the person carrying out the assessment must have the suitable training and expertise, it may not be possible for them to carry out the assessment without an interpreter, for instance where the adult uses sign language. Therefore, where necessary a qualified interpreter with training appropriate for the deafblind adult's communication should be used. It is not normally appropriate to use a family member or carer as an interpreter, though sometimes this is appropriate, for instance where the adult's communication is idiosyncratic or personal to them and would only be understood by those close to them. This should only take place where the adult agrees or – if they lack capacity – where it is in their best interests.

6.97. The assessment should take into account both the current and future needs of the person being assessed, particularly where the adult's deafblindness is at risk of deteriorating. In such cases the adult may benefit from learning alternative forms of communication before their condition has deteriorated to a point where their current or preferred form of communication is no longer suitable.

RECORD KEEPING

6.98. Following their assessment, individuals must be given a record of their needs or carer's assessment. A copy must also be shared with anybody else that the individual requests the local authority to share a copy with. Where an independent advocate, an Independent Mental Capacity Advocate or an Independent Mental Health Advocate is involved in supporting the individual, the local authority should keep the advocate informed so that they can support the person to understand the outcome of the assessment and its implications.

DELEGATING ASSESSMENTS

6.99. Local authorities can delegate the majority of their care and support functions, including assessment (see chapter 18). In doing so they must ensure that the body carrying out an assessment complies with all the requirements and fulfils all relevant duties under the Act and regulations (such as providing an independent advocate – see chapter 7). Anything done by the body carrying out an assessment is treated as if done by the local authority. In respect of duties surrounding non-delegated functions, such as safeguarding (see chapter 14), local authorities must have appropriate processes in place to ensure they fulfill these functions, for example agreeing with the body that the local authority is notified if a safeguarding issue is spotted.

ELIGIBILITY

6.100. The national eligibility criteria set a minimum threshold for adult care and support needs and carer support needs which local authorities must meet. All local authorities must comply with this national threshold. Authorities can also decide to meet needs that are not deemed to be eligible if they chose to do so.

6.101. The introduction of a national eligibility threshold provides more transparency on what level of need is eligible. More clarity will support authorities in deciding whether the earlier provision of information and advice or preventative services would delay a person from developing needs which meet the eligibility criteria or whether longer-term care and support might be needed. It should also help the person needing care or their carer to think more broadly about what support might be available in the local community or through their support network to meet their needs and support the outcomes they want to achieve.

WHAT IS THE NATIONAL ELIGIBILITY THRESHOLD FOR ADULTS NEEDING CARE?

6.102. The eligibility threshold for adults with care and support needs is set out in the Care and Support (Eligibility Criteria) Regulations 2014 (the 'Eligibility Regulations'). The threshold is based on identifying how a person's needs affect their ability to achieve relevant outcomes, and how this impacts on their wellbeing.

6.103. In considering whether an adult with care and support needs has eligible needs, local authorities must consider whether:

- The adult's needs arise from or are related to a physical or mental impairment or illness.

- As a result of the adult's needs the adult is unable to achieve two or more of the specified outcomes (which are described in the guidance below).

- As a consequence of being unable to achieve these outcomes there is, or there is likely to be, a significant impact on the adult's wellbeing.

6.104. An adult's needs are only eligible where they meet all three of these conditions.

INTERPRETING THE ELIGIBILITY CRITERIA

The adult's needs arise from or are related to a physical or mental impairment or illness

6.105. The first condition that local authorities must be satisfied about is that the adult's needs for care and support are due to a physical or mental impairment or illness and that they are not caused by other circumstantial factors. Local authorities must consider at this stage if the adult has a condition as a result of either physical, mental, sensory, learning or cognitive disabilities or illnesses, substance misuse or brain injury. The authority should base their judgment on the assessment of the adult and a formal diagnosis of the condition should not be required.

As a result of the adult's needs, the adult is unable to achieve two or more of the outcomes set out in the regulations

6.106. The second condition that authorities must consider is whether the adult is "unable" to achieve two or more of the outcomes set out in the regulations. Authorities must also be aware that the regulations provide that "being unable" to achieve an outcome includes any of the following circumstances, where the adult:

- is unable to achieve the outcome without assistance. This would include where an adult would be unable to do so even when assistance is provided. It also includes where the adult may need prompting for example, some adults may be physically able to wash but need reminding of the importance of personal hygiene;

- is able to achieve the outcome without assistance but doing so causes the adult significant pain, distress or anxiety. For example, an older person with severe arthritis may be able to prepare a meal, but doing so will leave them in severe pain and unable to eat the meal;

- is able to achieve the outcome without assistance, but doing so endangers or is likely to endanger the health or safety of the adult, or of others – for example, if the health or safety of another member of the family, including any child, could be endangered when an adult attempts to complete a task or an activity without relevant support;

- is able to achieve the outcome without assistance but takes significantly longer than would normally be expected. For example, an adult with a physical disability is able to dress themselves in the morning, but it takes them a long time to do this, leaves them exhausted and prevents them from achieving other outcomes.

6.107. The Eligibility Regulations set out a range of outcomes. Local authorities must consider whether the adult is unable to achieve two or more of these outcomes when making the eligibility determination. The following section of the guidance provides examples of how local authorities should consider each outcome set out in the Eligibility Regulations (which do not constitute an exhaustive list) when determining the adult's eligibility for care and support:

(a) managing and maintaining nutrition Local authorities should consider whether the adult has access to food and drink to maintain nutrition, and that the adult is able to prepare and consume the food and drink.

(b) maintaining personal hygiene Local authorities should, for example, consider the adult's ability to wash themselves and launder their clothes.

(c) managing toilet needs Local authorities should consider the adult's ability to access and use a toilet and manage their toilet needs.

(d) being appropriately clothed Local authorities should consider the adult's ability to dress themselves and to be appropriately dressed, for instance in relation to the weather to maintain their health.

(e) being able to make use of the home safely Local authorities should consider the adult's ability to move around the home safely, which could for example include getting up steps, using kitchen facilities or accessing the bathroom. This should also include the immediate environment around the home such as access to the property, for example steps leading up to the home.

(f) maintaining a habitable home environment Local authorities should consider whether the condition of the adult's home is sufficiently clean and maintained to be safe. A habitable home is safe and has essential amenities. An adult may require support to sustain their occupancy of the home and to maintain amenities, such as water, electricity and gas.

(g) developing and maintaining family or other personal relationships Local authorities should consider whether the adult is lonely or isolated, either because their needs prevent them from maintaining the personal relationships they have or because their needs prevent them from developing new relationships.

(h) accessing and engaging in work, training, education or volunteering Local authorities should consider whether the adult has an opportunity to apply themselves and contribute to society through work, training, education or volunteering, subject to their own wishes in this regard. This includes the physical access to any facility and support with the participation in the relevant activity.

(i) making use of necessary facilities or services in the local community including public transport and recreational facilities or services Local authorities should consider the adult's ability to get around in the community safely and consider their ability to use such facilities as public transport, shops or recreational facilities when considering the impact on their wellbeing. Local authorities do not have responsibility for the provision of NHS services such as patient transport, however they should consider needs for support when the adult is attending healthcare appointments.

(j) carrying out any caring responsibilities the adult has for a child Local authorities should consider any parenting or other caring responsibilities the person has. The adult may for example be a step-parent with caring responsibilities for their spouse's children.

As a consequence there is, or there is likely to be, a significant impact on the adult's wellbeing

6.108. The third condition that must be met is that local authorities must consider whether the adult's needs and their inability to achieve the outcomes above cause or risk causing a significant impact on their wellbeing. The meaning of "wellbeing" is set out in Section 1 of the Care Act and more detail is described in chapter 1of this guidance.

6.109. Local authorities must determine how the adult's inability to achieve the outcomes above impacts on their wellbeing. Where the adult is unable to achieve more than one of the outcomes, the local authority does not need to consider the impact of each individually, but should consider whether the cumulative effect of being unable to achieve those outcomes is one of a "significant impact on wellbeing". In doing so, local authorities should also consider whether:

- the adult's inability to achieve the outcomes above impacts on at least one of the areas of wellbeing (as described in Section 1 of the Act and chapter 1 of this guidance) in a significant way; or,

- the effect of the impact on a number of the areas of wellbeing mean that there is a significant impact on the adult's overall wellbeing.

6.110. The term "significant" is not defined by the regulations, and must therefore be understood to have its everyday meaning. Local authorities will have to consider whether the adult's needs and their consequent inability to achieve the relevant outcomes will have an important, consequential effect on their daily lives, their independence and their wellbeing.

6.111. In making this judgment, local authorities should look to understand the adult's needs in the context of what is important to him or her. Needs may affect different people differently, because what is important to the individual's wellbeing may not be the same in all cases. Circumstances which create a significant impact on the wellbeing of one individual may not have the same effect on another.

6.112. The table below illustrates the interplay of the three conditions above, the outcomes listed in the eligibility regulations and the wellbeing principle, which is broken down into areas of wellbeing in (see chapter 1).

Eligibility decision process		
1. Needs	**2. Outcomes**	**3. Wellbeing**
The adult's needs arise from or are related to a physical or mental impairment or illness.	*As a result of the needs, the adult is unable to achieve two or more of the following:* a) managing and maintaining nutrition; b) maintaining personal hygiene; c) managing toilet needs; d) being appropriately clothed; e) maintaining a habitable home environment; f) being able to make use of the home safely; g) developing and maintaining family or other personal relationships; h) accessing and engaging in work, training, education or volunteering; i) making use of necessary facilities or services in the local community including public transport and recreational facilities or services; j) carrying out any caring responsibilities the adult has for a child.	*As a consequence, there is or is likely to be a significant impact on the adult's wellbeing, including the following:* a) personal dignity (including treatment of the individual with respect); b) physical and mental health and emotional wellbeing; c) protection from abuse and neglect; d) control by the individual over day-to-day life (including over care and support provided and the way it is provided); e) participation in work, education, training or recreation; f) social and economic wellbeing; g) domestic, family and personal relationships; h) suitability of living accommodation; i) the individual's contribution to society.

6.114. The case studies which follow demonstrate examples of how eligibility determinations may be made. The purpose of these case studies is to illustrate eligibility on the basis of significant impact on wellbeing where the person has needs caused by a physical or mental impairment or illness which mean they are unable to achieve two or more outcomes specified in the Eligibility Regulations. Significant impact on wellbeing is personal, so although two people are in similar circumstances, the impact on their wellbeing is different.

Case Study 1: John Taylor (Eligible)

John is 32 and has been referred by his mother for an assessment, who is concerned for John and his future. John is unemployed and lives with his mother and she is getting to an age where she realises that she might not be able to provide the same level of care and support for her son as she has done so far.

John is able to manage his own personal care, but his mother does all the housework for both of them. John feels increasingly isolated and will not leave the house without his mother. It is important to John that he is intellectually stimulated and there is a chess club nearby which he would like to join, but John does not feel confident about this due to his anxiety in social situations.

Needs	Outcomes	Impact on wellbeing	Decision: Eligible
Adult on the autistic spectrum.	John has severe difficulties socialising and co-operating with other people. He only has transactional exchanges and cannot maintain eye contact. John knows that others feel uneasy around him, and spends a lot of his time alone. As a result, John is unable to achieve the following outcomes: Developing and maintaining family or other personal relationships and making use of necessary facilities and services in the community.	John is too anxious to initiate developing friendships on his own although he would like to and he feels lonely and depressed most of the time. His nervousness also affects his ability to take advantage of facilities in the community, which could help him feel less lonely. Feeling anxious and lonely has a significant impact on his wellbeing.	**Next Actions:** John's local authority thinks John's needs are eligible. Both John and the local authority agree that the most effective way of meeting John's needs is to develop his confidence to join the chess club. John uses his personal budget to pay for a support worker to accompany him to an autism social skills group, and to the chess club and to travel with him on the bus to get there. John's local authority notes that John's mother could need support too and offers her a carer's assessment.

	Case study 2: Dave Brown (Not Eligible)

Dave is 32 and has been referred by his mother for an assessment, who is concerned for Dave and his future. Dave lives with his mother and she is getting to an age where she realises that she might not be able to provide the same level of care and support for her son as she has done so far.

Dave is able to manage his own personal care, but his mother does all the housework for both of them. Dave also works, but would like to get a job that is a better match for his intellectual abilities as his current job does not make the most of his numerical skills. Dave's social contact is mainly online because he feels more comfortable communicating this way and he spends a lot of time in his room on his computer.

Category	Needs	Impact on wellbeing	Decision: Not Eligible
Adult on the autistic spectrum.	Dave struggles severely in social situations leading to difficulties accessing work and cooperating with other people. He only has transactional exchanges with others and cannot maintain eye contact. Dave knows that others feel uneasy around him and spends a lot of his time alone.	Dave is not in ideal employment, but has access to and is engaged in work. This has some impact on his wellbeing but not to a significant extent. Dave prefers to socialise with people online. It emerges from conversations with Dave that he has access to those personal relationships that he considers essential. Dave is contributing to society, has contact with others, is in employment and is able to look after himself.	Dave has difficulties doing some of the things that many other people would think should be a natural part of daily living and he is unable to participate in recreational activities in a conventional sense. Those aspects of his wellbeing that are affected by the needs caused by his autism are not so significantly affected that Dave's overall wellbeing is at risk. The local authority decides that Dave's needs are not eligible, because they do not have a significant effect on his wellbeing despite his mother's concerns. **Next Actions:** The local authority records Dave's assessment and sends him a copy. They include information about a local autism support group. Dave's local authority notes that Dave's mother could well need support and offers her a carer's assessment.

FLUCTUATING NEEDS

6.117. Individuals with fluctuating needs may have needs which are not apparent at the time of the assessment, but may have arisen in the past and are likely to arise again in the future. Therefore local authorities must consider an individual's need over an appropriate period of time to ensure that all of their needs have been accounted for when eligibility is being determined. Where fluctuating needs are apparent, this should also be factored into the care plan, detailing the steps local authorities will take to meet needs in circumstances where these fluctuate. For example, an adult with a mental illness, which has been managed in the past eight months but which could deteriorate, if circumstances in the adult's life change. In such situations, local authorities must consider the nature of the adult's needs have been over the past year to get a complete picture of the adult's level of need.

6.118. When considering the type of needs an adult may have, local authorities should note that there is no hierarchy of needs or of the areas of wellbeing as described in chapter 1 of this guidance.

CONSIDERING NEEDS MET BY CARERS IN ELIGIBILITY DETERMINATIONS

6.119. The eligibility determination must be made based on the adult's needs and how these impact on their wellbeing. Authorities must only take consideration of whether the adult has a carer, or what needs may be met by a carer after the eligibility determination when a care and support plan is prepared. The determination must be based solely on the adult's needs and if an adult does have a carer, the care they are providing will be taken into account when considering whether the needs must be met. Local authorities are not required to meet any eligible needs which are being met by a carer, but those needs should be recognised and recorded as eligible during the assessment process. This is to ensure that should there be a breakdown in the caring relationship, the needs are already identified as eligible, and therefore local authorities must take steps to meet them without further assessment.

WHAT IS THE NATIONAL ELIGIBILITY THRESHOLD FOR CARERS?

6.120. Carers can be eligible for support in their own right. The national eligibility threshold for carers is also set out in the Care and Support (Eligibility Criteria) Regulations 2014. The threshold is based on the impact a carer's needs for support has on their wellbeing.

6.121. In considering whether a carer has eligible needs, local authorities must consider whether:

- the needs arise as a consequence of providing necessary care for an adult;

- the effect of the carer's needs is that any of the circumstances specified in the Eligibility Regulations apply to the carer; and

- as a consequence of that fact there is, or there is likely to be, a significant impact on the carer's wellbeing.

6.122. A carer's needs are only eligible where they meet all three of these conditions.

INTERPRETING THE CARERS' ELIGIBILITY CRITERIA
The needs arise as a consequence of providing necessary care for an adult

6.123. Local authorities must consider whether the carer's need for support arises because they are providing care to an adult. Carers can be eligible for support whether or not the adult for whom they care has eligible needs. The eligibility determination must be made based on the carer's needs and how these impact on their wellbeing. The determination should be made without consideration of whether or not the adult the carer cares for, has eligible needs.

6.124. The carer must also be providing "necessary" care. If the carer is providing care and support for needs which the adult is capable of meeting themselves, the carer may not be providing necessary support. In such cases, local authorities should provide information and advice to the adult and carer about how the adult can use their own strengths or services available in the community to meet their needs.

The effect of the carer's needs is that any of the circumstances specified in the Eligibility Regulations apply to the carer

6.125. The second condition that authorities must consider is whether the carer's physical or mental health is either deteriorating or is at risk of doing so, or whether the carer is unable to achieve any of a list of other outcomes which may apply.

6.126. Authorities must be aware that the regulations provide that 'being unable' to achieve outcomes, includes circumstances where the carer:

- Is unable to achieve the outcome without assistance. This includes where the carer would be unable to achieve an outcome even if assistance were provided. A carer might, for example, be unable to fulfill their parental responsibilities unless they receive support in their caring role.

- Is able to achieve the outcome without assistance, but doing so causes or is likely to cause significant pain, distress or anxiety or endangers. A carer might for example be able to care for the adult and undertake fulltime employment, but if doing both, this causes the carer significant distress, the carer should not be considered able to engage in employment.

- Is able to achieve the outcome without assistance but doing so is likely to endanger the health or safety of the carer or any adults or children for whom the carer provides care. A carer might for example be able to provide care for their family and deliver necessary care for the adult, but, where this endangers the adult with care and support needs, for example, because the adult receiving care would have to be left alone while other responsibilities are met, the carer should not be considered able to meet the outcome of caring for their family.

6.127. The eligibility Regulations set out a range of outcomes. Local authorities must consider whether the carer is able to achieve these outcomes or if due to nature of their needs they are unable to achieve any of the outcomes. The carer will have eligible needs met if they are unable to achieve any of these outcomes and as a result there is, or there is likely to be, a significant impact on their wellbeing.

6.128. The following section of the guidance provides examples of how local authorities should consider the outcomes set out in the Eligibility Regulations when they determine whether a carer meets the eligibility criteria. To be eligible, a carer must be unable to achieve any of the following outcomes:

(i) carrying out any caring responsibilities the carer has for a child Local authorities should consider any parenting or other caring responsibilities the carer has for a child in addition to their caring role for the adult. For example, the carer might be a grandparent with caring responsibilities for their grandchildren while the grandchildren's parents are at work.

(ii) providing care to other persons for whom the carer provides care Local authorities should consider any additional caring responsibilities the carer may have for other adults. For example, a carer may also have caring responsibilities for a parent in addition to caring for the adult with care and support needs.

(iii) maintaining a habitable home environment Local authorities should consider whether the condition of the carer's home is safe and an appropriate environment to live in and whether it presents a significant risk to the carer's wellbeing. A habitable home should be safe and have essential amenities such as water, electricity and gas.

(iv) managing and maintaining nutrition Local authorities should consider whether the carer has the time to do essential shopping and to prepare meals for themselves and their family.

(v) developing and maintaining family or other significant personal relationships Local authorities should consider whether the carer is in a position where their caring role prevents them from maintaining key relationships with family and friends or from developing new relationships where the carer does not already have other personal relationships.

(vi) engaging in work, training, education or volunteering Local authorities should consider whether the carer can continue in their job, and contribute to society, apply themselves in education, volunteer to support civil society or have the opportunity to get a job, if they are not in employment.

(vii) making use of necessary facilities or services in the local community Local authorities should consider whether the carer has an opportunity to make use of the local community's services and facilities and for example consider whether the carer has time to use recreational facilities such as gyms or swimming pools.

(viii) engaging in recreational activities Local authorities should consider whether the carer has leisure time, which might for example be some free time to read or engage in a hobby.

As a consequence of that fact there is, or there is likely to be, a significant impact on the carer's wellbeing

6.129. The third condition that must be met is that local authorities must consider whether the carer's needs and their inability to achieve the outcomes above present a significant impact on the carer's wellbeing. "Wellbeing" is defined by referring to examples of specific areas in Section 1 of the Care Act (see chapter 1). In doing so, local authorities should consider whether:

- The carer's needs and inability to achieve the outcomes impact on an area of the carer's wellbeing in a significant way; or

- The impact on a number of the areas of wellbeing is such that they have a significant impact on an adult's overall wellbeing.

6.130. The term 'significant' is not defined by the Regulations, and must therefore be understood to have its everyday meaning. Local authorities will have to consider whether the carer's needs and their inability to achieve the outcomes will have an important, consequential effect on their daily lives, their independence and their own wellbeing.

6.131. In making this judgment, local authorities should look to understand the carer's needs in the context of what is important to them. The impact of needs may affect different carers differently, because what is important to the individual's wellbeing may not be the same in all cases. Circumstances which create a significant impact on the wellbeing of one individual may not have the same effect on another.

6.132. When considering the type of needs a carer may have, local authorities should note that there is no hierarchy of needs or of the areas of wellbeing as described in chapter 1 of the guidance.

6.133. The table below illustrates the interplay of the outcomes listed in the eligibility regulations and the wellbeing principle, which is broken down into areas of wellbeing in chapter 1 of this guidance.

Carers' eligibility decision process		
1. Needs	**2. Outcomes**	**3. Wellbeing**
The needs arise as a consequence of providing necessary care to an adult, and the carer is 'unable' to achieve the following:	*As a result of the carer's needs, either:* a) the carer's physical; or mental health is, or is at risk of, deteriorating, or b) the carer is unable to achieve any of the following outcomes: i. carrying out any caring responsibilities the carer has for a child; ii. providing care to other persons for whom the carer provides care; iii. maintaining a habitable home environment; iv. managing and maintaining nutrition; v. developing and maintaining family or other significant personal relationships; vi. accessing and engaging in work, training, education or volunteering;	*As a consequence, there is or is likely to be a significant impact on the carer's wellbeing, including:* a) personal dignity (including treatment of the individual with respect); b) physical and mental health and emotional wellbeing; c) protection from abuse and neglect; d) personal dignity (including treatment of the individual with respect); e) physical and mental health and emotional wellbeing; f) protection from abuse and neglect; g) control by the individual over day-to-day life (including over care and support provided and the way it is provided);

	vii. accessing and engaging in work, training, education or volunteering;	h) participation in work, education, training or recreation;
	viii. making use of necessary facilities or services in the local community including recreational facilities or services;	i) social and economic wellbeing;
		j) domestic, family and personal relationships;
		k) suitability of living accommodation;
	x. engaging in recreational activities.	l) the individual's contribution to society.

6.134. The case studies which follow demonstrate examples of how eligibility determinations may be made. The purpose of these case studies is to illustrate eligibility on the basis of significant impact on wellbeing where the carer has needs caused by providing necessary care. Significant impact on wellbeing is personal, so although two people are in similar circumstances, the impact on their wellbeing is different.

Case Study 1: Deirdre (Not Eligible)
Deirdre is 58 and has been caring for her neighbour for the past six years.
Deirdre has been coping with her caring responsibilities, which include checking in on her neighbour, doing her shopping and cleaning and helping her with
the cooking every other day. Deirdre works 20 hours a week at the local school,
and she is also helping her daughter by picking up her grandchild after school.
Deirdre's son is concerned that she is taking on too much and notices that she is
tired. Deirdre's son persuades her to ask the local authority for a carer's
assessment.

Caring responsibilities	Outcomes	Impact on wellbeing	Decision: Not Eligible
Neighbour with COPD.	Deirdre enjoys the variety that her working life and caring role provide. She would like to be able to spend more time with her grandchild in the afternoons, but recognises that there is a balance between doing this and caring for her neigh-bour. Deirdre's needs impact on the following outcomes: • Carrying out caring responsi-bilities the carer has for a child. • Engaging in rec-reational activities.	Deirdre's needs are impacting on a few out-comes. Deirdre enjoys her caring responsi-bility for her grandchild and would like more free time. On the other hand, her caring roles are fulfill-ing so although Deirdre is tired at the end of the day, her local authority does not think her wellbeing is significantly affected.	The local authority deci-des that Deirdre is not eligible because her wellbeing is not signifi-cantly affected. **Next actions:** The local authority rec-ognises that Deirdre could do with some advice to help her man-age her day so that she can find some time for herself and so she does not get tired. They advise on how she may reduce some of her tasks such as sitting down with her neighbour to order their food shopping online rather than carrying them home. They make contact with a local carers' organisation and the local authority makes sure Deirdre is able to access it. The organisation is able to provide additional advice.

Case study 2: Sam (Eligible)

Sam is 38 and cares for his mother who has early-stage dementia. Sam's mother has telecare, but he still checks in on her daily, and does her shopping, cooking and laundry. Sam is a divorced father of two children, who live with him every other week. Sam works fulltime in an IT company and has come forward for an assessment as he is starting to feel unable to cope with his various responsibilities in the weeks when he looks after his children. Sam has made an arrangement with his employer that he can work longer hours on the weeks when the children are with their mother and fewer when he has the children.

Caring responsibilities	Outcomes	Impact on wellbeing	Decision: Eligible
Mother with early stage dementia.	Sam wants to spend more time with his children and for instance be able to free up an hour in the afternoon to help them with their homework, so it doesn't have to be done in the evening when the children are tired. Sam's needs impact on the following Outcomes: • Carrying out caring responsibilities the carer has for a child. • Engaging in recreational activities.	Sam's responsibilities impact on a few important outcomes. Sam is starting to feel like he is failing as a parent and it affects the relationship he has with his children, his ex-wife, and his mother. He also worries that his ability to stay in work would be in jeopardy unless he receives support. Sam seems quite stressed and anxious.	The local authority decides that Sam's fluctuating needs are eligible for support, because it perceives that they have a significant impact on his wellbeing. If the local authority supports Sam to maintain his current role, everyone is better off, because Sam can stay in employment, sustain his family relationships and provide security for his mother. **Next actions:** The local authority gives Sam a direct payment which he uses to pay for a care worker to come in for three days every other week to check on his mother and make her a meal. This gives Sam more time to spend with his children, doing homework with them and spending some more relaxed time with them. The local authority directs Sam to a carers' organisation which provides Sam with information about his rights at work and how to speak to his employers.

FLUCTUATING NEEDS

6.136. Carers with fluctuating needs may have needs which are not apparent at the time of the assessment, but may have arisen in the past and are likely to arise again in the future. Therefore local authorities must consider an individual's need over an appropriate period of time to ensure that all of their needs have been accounted for when the eligibility is being determined. Where fluctuating needs are apparent, this should also be factored into the care plan, detailing the steps local authorities will take to meet needs in circumstances where these fluctuate. For example, a carer could be caring for an adult with a mental illness, which has been managed in the past 8 months, but which could deteriorate, if circumstances in the adult's life change. In such situations, local authorities must consider what the nature of the carer's needs has been over the past year to get a complete picture of the carer's level of need.

6.137. The level of a carer's need can also fluctuate irrespective of whether the needs of the adult for whom thy care, fluctuate. For example, if the carer is a parent of school children, they may not have the same level of need for support during term time as during school holidays.

WHAT LOCAL AUTHORITIES MUST DO AFTER THE ELIGIBILITY DETERMINATION?

6.138. When the eligibility determination has been made, local authorities must provide the person to whom the determination relates (whether that is an adult with care and support needs, or a carer with support needs) with a copy of their decision.

6.139. Where the person is found to have no eligible needs, local authorities must provide information and advice on what can be done to meet or reduce the needs (for example what support might be available in the community to help the adult or carer) and what can be done to prevent or delay the development of needs in the future. Local authorities should consider how this package of information can be tailored to the needs which the person does have, with the aim of delaying deterioration and preventing future needs, and reflect the availability of local support (see also chapter 2 on preventative services and chapter 3 on information and advice).

6.140. If the adult has some eligible needs, the local authority must:

- Agree with the adult which of their needs they would like the local authority to meet. The person may not wish to have support in relation to all their needs – they may, for example, intend to arrange alternative services themselves to meet some needs. Others may not wish for the local authority to meet any of their needs, but approach the authority only for the purposes of determining eligible needs.

- Consider how the local authority may meet those needs. This does not replace or pre-empt the care and support planning process (see chapters 10 –13), but is an early consideration of the potential support options, in order to determine whether some of those may be services for which the local authority makes a charge. Where that is the case, the local authority must carry out a financial assessment (see chapter 8).

- Establish whether the person meets the ordinary residence requirement. This applies differently for adults with care and support needs and for carers. In the case of the adult, they must be ordinarily resident in the authority's area. In the case of the carer, the person for whom they care must be ordinarily resident in the authority's area. This is because carers' needs are met by local authorities where the adult with the needs for care and support lives, not the authority where the carer lives. Determining ordinary residence at this stage should not lead to a delay in meeting eligible needs – more guidance on ordinary residence can be found in chapter 19.

7. INDEPENDENT ADVOCACY

This chapter provides guidance on:
- *Sections 67 and 68 of the Care Act 2014;*

- *The Care and Support (Independent Advocacy) Regulations 2014.*

This chapter covers:
- Local authorities' responsibilities to provide independent advocacy;
- Matters which a local authority must consider in deciding whether an individual would experience substantial difficulty in being involved with care and support 'process' or safeguarding;
- Circumstances in which an advocate must be provided;
- The role of the advocate and how independent advocates are to carry out their functions.

7.1. The purpose of this section of guidance is to ensure that local authorities fully understand their duties in relation to the provision of independent advocacy and to assist them in carrying out these duties effectively.

7.2. There are duties to arrange an independent advocate for all adults, as part of their own assessment and care planning and care reviews and to those in their role as carers. It also applies to children who are approaching the transition to adult care and support, when a child's needs assessment is carried out, and when a young carer's assessment is undertaken. Section 72 of the Act provides that Regulations may be made for appeals against local authority decisions made under Part 1 of the Act and includes reference to the provision of independent advocacy. This, subject to development, consultation and Parliamentary process is expected to come into force from April 2016. Where appropriate arrangements for independent advocacy in respect of supporting a person's involvement in an appeal will look to mirror the arrangement set out here.

7.3. There is also a separate duty to arrange an independent advocate for adults who are subject to a safeguarding enquiry or Safeguarding Adults Review (SAR).

7.4. Local authorities must arrange an independent advocate to facilitate the involvement of a person in their assessment, in the preparation of their care and support plan and in the review of their care plan, as well as in safeguarding enquiries and SARs if two conditions are met. That if an independent advocate were not provided then the person would have substantial difficulty in being fully involved in these processes and second, there is no appropriate individual available to support and represent the person's wishes who is not paid or professionally engaged in providing care or treatment to the person or their carer. The role of the independent advocate is to support and represent the person and to facilitate their involvement in the key processes and interactions with the local authority and other organisations as required for the safeguarding enquiry or SAR.

7.5. Everyone should have access to information and advice on care and support and keeping safe from abuse or neglect (see chapter 3). Prior to making contact with the local authority, there may be some people who require independent advocacy to access that information and advice. Local authorities will need to consider such needs in ensuring that the information and advice service is accessible. Subsequently, once a person has contacted the local authority, or come to the local authority's attention as a result of a safeguarding concern, they must be actively involved in identifying their needs through assessment, in developing their care and support plan, and in leading their care reviews, where relevant, and being involved in any safeguarding enquiry or SAR. The aim of the duty to provide advocacy is to enable people who have substantial difficulty in being involved in these processes to be supported in that involvement as fully as possible, and where necessary to be represented by an advocate who speaks on their behalf. The Equality Act 2010, requires that reasonable adjustments should be made to ensure that disabled people have equal access to information and advice services. Provision of such adjustments, information in different formats for example, may reduce or remove a substantial difficulty a person may have in being involved. The ultimate aim is for people's wishes, feelings and needs to be at the heart of the assessment, care planning and review processes. This needs to be just as true for those who are the subject of a safeguarding enquiry or safeguarding adult review (SAR).

ADVOCACY AND THE DUTY TO INVOLVE

7.6. Local authorities must involve people in decisions made about them and their care and support or where there is to be a safeguarding enquiry or SAR. Involvement requires the local authority helping people to understand how they can be involved, how they can contribute and take part and sometimes lead or direct the process. People should be active partners in the key care and support processes of assessment, care and support and support planning, review and any enquiries in relation to abuse or neglect. No matter how complex a person's needs, local authorities are required to involve people, to help them express their wishes and feelings, to support them to weigh up options, and to make their own decisions.

7.7. The duty to involve applies in all settings, including for those people living in the community, in care homes or, apart from safeguarding enquiry and SAR, in prisons,[1] for example.

7.8. Local authorities must form a judgment about whether a person has substantial difficulty in being involved with these processes. If it is thought that they do, and that there is no appropriate individual to support and represent them for the purpose of facilitating their involvement, then the local authority must arrange for an independent advocate to support and represent the person.

7.9. Many of the people who qualify for advocacy under the Care Act will also qualify for advocacy under the Mental Capacity Act 2005. The same advocate can provide support as an advocate under the Care Act and under the Mental Capacity Act. This is to enable the person to receive seamless advocacy and not to have to repeat their story to different advocates. Under whichever legislation the advocate providing support is acting, they should meet the appropriate requirements for an advocate under that legislation.

Judging 'substantial difficulty' in being involved

7.10. Local authorities must consider for each person, whether they would have substantial difficulty in engaging with the local authority care and support

---

[1] Note: The advocacy duty under s.68 in relation to a safeguarding enquiry and SAR would not apply to prisoners: see s.76(7) and (9).

processes. The Care Act defines four areas in any one of which a substantial difficulty might be found, which are set out below.

Understanding relevant information

7.11. The first area to consider is *'understanding relevant information'*. Many people can be supported to understand relevant information, if it is presented appropriately and if time is taken to explain it. Some people, however, will not be able to understand relevant information, for example if they have mid-stage or advanced dementia.

Retaining information

7.12. The second area to consider is *'retaining information'*. If a person is unable to retain information long enough to be able to weigh up options and make decisions, then they are likely to have substantial difficulty in engaging and being involved in the process.

Using or weighing the information as part of engaging

7.13. The third area is *'using or weighing the information as part of the process of being involved.'* A person must be able to weigh up information, in order to participate fully and express preferences for or choose between options. For example, they need to be able to weigh up the advantages and disadvantages of moving into a care home or terminating an undermining relationship. If they are unable to do this, they will have substantial difficulty in engaging and being involved in the process.

Communicating their views, wishes and feelings

7.14. The fourth area involves *'communicating their views, wishes and feelings'*. A person must be able to communicate their views, wishes and feelings whether by talking, writing, signing or any other means, to aid the decision process and to make priorities clear. If they are unable to do this, they will have substantial difficulty in engaging and being involved in the process.

7.15. For example, a person with mid-stage or advanced dementia, significant learning disabilities, a brain injury or mental ill health may be considered to have substantial difficulty in communicating their views, wishes and feelings. But equally a person with Asperger's may be considered, as may a frail older person who does not have any diagnosis but is confused as a result of an infection, or a person who is near the end of their life and appears disengaged from involvement and decision-making. Within this context, it is the person's ability to communicate their views, wishes and feelings which is fundamental to their involvement rather than the diagnosis or specific condition.

7.16. Both the Care Act and the Mental Capacity Act recognise the same areas of difficulty, and both require a person with these difficulties to be supported and represented, either by family or friends, or by an advocate in order to communicate their views, wishes and feelings.

Case Study:

Stephen sustained a brain injury in a fall; he has completed six months in a specialist residential rehabilitation setting and the next step is an assessment of need for his continuing support.

Prior to this, the social worker telephones Stephen's treating clinician who confirms that because of his brain injury, Stephen lacks insight into the effects this has had on him and he also has difficulty processing lots of information quickly – this is a common symptom of brain injury.

Therefore the social worker decides on an initial short meeting to determine Stephen's needs and knows her first step will be to evaluate if Stephen has difficulty understanding and therefore being involved in the assessment process. If so, support could come from a carer, family member or friend or Mental Capacity Advocate, as she is aware lack of insight does not necessarily determine lack of capacity.

The social worker notes that Stephen is able to retain information about who she is and why she is meeting with him. He is articulate and can converse well about his plans for the future which includes detailed plans to meet up with friends and return to work again. However, a pre-assessment conversation with his mother, confirms that his friendship group has significantly diminished as his friends find it difficult to understand the differences in his behaviour since his fall and doubts whether he will be able to return to full-time employment. The social worker judges that because Stephen lacks insight into his personal relationships and future plans, he may well also have trouble estimating his true care and support needs. At this point the social worker decides that Stephen would have substantial difficulty in being fully involved in the rest of the assessment process and would therefore benefit from assistance.

Stephen is adamant that he wants to act and make decisions independently of his mother, though he is happy for her to inform the assessment process. The social worker decides that Stephen's mother would not be an appropriate person under the Care Act to support his involvement in the needs assessment. The social worker talks to Stephen about how an independent advocate could help him make sure his views, beliefs, wishes and aspirations are taken into account in the assessment, and with his agreement, arranges for an independent advocate with specialist brain injury training to support him. The independent advocate meets Stephen but also talks to his mother to get a true picture of Stephen's current needs and wishes and to ascertain the differences between how Stephen is now and prior to acquiring his brain injury. The social worker carries out the needs assessment with Stephen who is supported by his independent advocate, and with Stephen's approval, input from his mother.

WHEN THE DUTY TO PROVIDE INDEPENDENT ADVOCACY APPLIES
Assessment of needs

7.17. From the point of first contact, request or referral (including self-referral) for an assessment, the local authority must involve the person (see chapter 6).[1] They must initially consider the best way of involving the person in the assessment processes, which is appropriate and proportionate to the person's needs and circumstances. In some cases this may be relatively brief, in others it may consist of a series of interviews, in the person's own home or other care settings, over a period of time.

7.18. At the start of the assessment process, if it appears to the local authority that a person has care and support or support needs, and throughout any subsequent part of the process, the local authority must judge whether a person has *substantial difficulty in involvement* with the assessment, the care and support planning or review processes. The identification of a potential need for advocacy may arise through the process, from the person themselves, carers or family. Where an authority has outsourced or commissioned all or some of this process, the authority will maintain overall responsibility for this judgement.

7.19. Where the local authority considers that a person has substantial difficulty in engaging with the assessment process, then they must consider whether *there is anyone appropriate who can support the person be fully involved*. This might for example be a carer (who is not professionally engaged or remunerated), a family member or friend. If there is no one appropriate, then the local authority must arrange for an independent advocate. The advocate must support and represent the person in the assessment, in the care and support planning, and the review. This applies to the following:

- a needs assessment under section 9 of the Care Act;

- a carer's assessment under section 10;

- the preparation of a care and support plan or support plan under section 25;

- a review of care and support plan or support plan under section 27;

- a child's needs assessment under section 58;

- a child's carer's assessment under section 60 (therefore some people below 16 years of age);

- a young carer's assessment under section 63;

- safeguarding under section 68.

7.20. As part of the assessment and the care and support plan, the local authority must have regard to the need to help protect people from abuse and neglect. They should assist the person to identify any risks and ways to manage them. They should also assist the person to decide how much risk they can manage. The local authority must also have regard to ensuring that any restriction on the person's rights or freedom is kept to the minimum necessary. Restrictions should be carefully considered and frequently reviewed. Any potential deprivation of liberty must be authorised, either by a Deprivation of Liberty Authorisation by the local authority or the Court of Protection under the Deprivation of Liberty Safeguards in the Mental Capacity Act.

---

[1] See Assessment Ch.6.

7.21. Where it appears that a person may be eligible for NHS Continuing Healthcare (NHS CHC), local authorities must notify the relevant NHS body. NHS CHC is a package of on- going care that is arrange and funded solely by the NHS where the individual has complex ongoing healthcare needs of a type or quantity such that they are found to have a 'primary health need' as set out in The National Framework for NHS Continuing Healthcare and NHS- funded Nursing Care November 2012) (Revised).[1] Where an individual is not eligible for NHS CHC, local authorities still have a duty to carry out an assessment of needs where a person has an appearance of needs and a duty to meet those eligible needs (see chapter 6)[2] and therefore have a consequential duty to consider the need for an independent advocate to support the person's involvement in that assessment. This guidance applies equally to those people whose needs are being jointly accessed by the NHS and the local authority or where a package of support is, planned, commissioned or funded by both a local authority and a Clinical Commissioning Group (CCG), known as a 'joint package' of care.

7.22. These processes and arrangements have historically been difficult for individuals, their carers, family or friends, to understand and be involved in. Local authorities (with CCGs) will therefore want to consider the benefits of providing access to independent advice or independent advocacy for those who do not have substantial difficulty and/or those who have an appropriate person to support their involvement. Effective joint commissioning arrangements would involve:

- dealing with the person holistically, providing a seamless service and avoiding duplication;

- reducing communication break-down;

- involvement of the person, family and carers;

- effective partnership working for health and social care addressing needs together; and

- improved communication and continued care to achieve joint outcomes.

7.23. Under the Mental Health Act 1983 (MHA) certain people, known as 'qualifying patients', are entitled to the help and support from an Independent Mental Health Advocate (IMHA). Section 117 of the MHA places a duty on the NHS and local authorities to provide aftercare and this will usually involve a joint assessment (often under the Care Programme Approach) including an assessment of the person's care and support needs, a care and support or support plan and subsequent review (which may reach a decision that a person is no longer in need of aftercare). Those people who do not retain a right to an IMHA, whose care and support needs are being assessed, planned or reviewed should be considered for an advocate under the Care Act, if they have substantial difficulty in being involved and if there is no appropriate person to support their involvement (see paragraph 7.32).

---

[1] https://www.gov.uk/government/publications/national-framework-for-nhs-continuing-healthcare-and-nhs-funded-nursing-care
[2] See assessment Ch.6.

SAFEGUARDING ENQUIRIES AND SAFEGUARDING ADULT REVIEWS (SARS)

7.24. The local authority must arrange, where necessary, for an independent advocate to support and represent an adult who is the subject of a safeguarding enquiry or a safeguarding adult review. Where an independent advocate has already been arranged under s67 Care Act or under MCA 2005 then, unless inappropriate, the same advocate should be used.

7.25. Effective safeguarding is about seeking to promote an adult's rights as well as about protecting their physical safety[1] and taking action to prevent the occurrence or reoccurrence of abuse or neglect. It enables the adult to understand both the risk of abuse and actions that she or he can take, or ask others to take, to mitigate that risk.

7.26. There is increasing case law on adult safeguarding from the Court of Protection of which advocates and practitioners should be aware.[2]

7.27. If a safeguarding enquiry needs to start urgently then it can begin before an advocate is appointed but one must be appointed as soon as possible. All agencies need to know how the services of an advocacy can be accessed and what their role is.

7.28. It is critical in this particularly sensitive area (whether an enquiry or a SAR) that the adult is supported in what may feel a daunting process which may lead to some very difficult decisions. An individual who is thought to have been abused or neglected may be so demoralised, frightened, embarrassed or upset that independent advocacy provided under section 68 to help them to be involved will be crucial.

Case Study: Lynette

Lynette, who has learning disabilities, lives in a care home. A support worker contacted the local authority because another resident, Fred, has come into Lynette's room late at night shouting on several occasions and most recently was seen pushing her. A safeguarding enquiry is started and the local authority appoint an independent advocate to support Lynette as they are concerned that she cannot express herself easily.

When interviewed by the social worker Lynette cannot describe what happened. The social worker and advocate agree that the advocate will help Lynette to communicate how she feels.

The advocate spends time with Lynette. She explains what is happening and communicates with Lynette about different people that she lives with, including using photos, finding out more about her feelings. Lynette appears to be generally happy around the house and when going out, but is very distressed when she sees Fred in person, or even when she sees a picture of him. The advocate makes clear to the Local Authority what Lynette has communicated.

The local authority finds that whilst there is no doubt that Fred did what was reported, he may have done so as a result of his own confusion and distress. They agree a proposal from the registered manager of the care home that

---

alarms will be put on Fred's door and staffing numbers increased to prevent a recurrence.

The local authority agrees to review the situation after some weeks during which time the advocate stays in contact with Lynette in order to understand the impact of this decision on Lynette. The advocate finds that Lynette remains distressed by Fred's presence. She is concerned that the measures in place are not sufficient and writes this in a report to the local authority detailing what Lynette has communicated about where she lives and about Fred. The local authority agrees to look at what further action may be needed which might include considering whether Lynette and Fred should continue to share accommodation.

The main aspect of wellbeing promoted is protection from abuse and neglect, but also personal dignity and emotional wellbeing. The local authority has also demonstrated its regard for Lynette's views, wishes, feelings and beliefs.

CONTINUITY OF CARE AND ORDINARY RESIDENCE

7.29. The local authority which is carrying out the assessment, planning or review of the plan is responsible for considering whether an advocate is required. In the case of a person who is receiving care and support from one local authority and decides to move and live in another authority, the responsibility will move with the care and support assessment (see chapter 20). For a person whose care and support is being provided out of area (in a type of accommodation set out in the section on ordinary residence (see chapter 19) it will be the authority in which the person is ordinarily resident. Understanding of local communities may be an important consideration, so the advocacy/advocate should wherever possible be from the area where the person is resident at the time of the assessment, planning or review.

Consequences for local authorities
The local authority should have local policies to clarify the appointing of advocates:
- from advocacy services out of their area that they may not have a direct commissioning relationship with (as it currently is with Independent Mental Capacity Advocate (IMCA));
- for people placed out of area temporarily;
- for people who move from one area to another following an assessment and care and support planning in which an advocate is involved (the same advocate should be involved wherever practicable).

CARE AND SUPPORT REVIEWS

7.30. The local authority must involve the person, their carer and any other individual that the person wants to be involved in any review of their care and support plan, and take all reasonable steps to agree any changes (see chapter 13).

7.31. Local authorities must consider whether an advocate is required to facilitate the person's involvement in the review of a care and support plan and, if appropriate, appoint an advocate. This applies regardless of whether an advocate was involved at an earlier stage. Examples of when an advocate may be appointed at this stage despite not previously being involved include:

- The person's ability to be involved in the process without an advocate has changed.

- The circumstances have changed (e.g. the person's involvement was previously facilitated by a relative who is no longer able to perform that role).

- An advocate should have been involved at the care and support planning stage and was not.

- The requirement to involve an advocate at the care and support planning stage did not exist at that time.

JUDGEMENTS MADE BY THE LOCAL AUTHORITY
An appropriate individual to facilitate the person's involvement

7.32. Local authorities must consider whether there is an appropriate individual (or individuals) who can facilitate a person's involvement in the assessment, planning or review processes, and this includes three specific considerations.

7.33. First, it cannot be someone who is already providing the person with care or treatment in a professional capacity or on a paid basis (regardless of who employs or pays for them). That means it cannot be, for example, the person's GP, nurse, key worker or care and support worker.

Case Study: Janice

Janice is 43 and cares for her mother Sheena who is 72 who has advanced Parkinson's and increasing cognitive and communication difficulties. Janice cares for her mother in excess of 40 hours per week. Janice gave up work to care for her mother five years ago, and using her direct payment Sheena pays her daughter for 8 hours per week for care and support, including helping her with personal care, cooking meals and grocery shopping. Sheena preferred this to paying someone else – she prefers not to have strangers in the house and finds that others often do not understand her needs. As Janice is caring for her mother for many more hours than this, Janice has received a carers assessment and receives her own carers personal budget which she uses for breaks such as her weekly aerobics class which she finds helps her keep in touch with her friends, stay healthy, and deal with stress.

There is no-one else available to act as an appropriate individual to support Sheena in decision making. Both Sheena and Janice would be happy for Janice to take on this role. However, as Janice received a payment, she would not be regarded as an appropriate individual, though the guidance states that good practice should ensure Janice's views are sought as Sheena has made clear that she wishes this to happen.

7.34. Second the person's wish not to be supported by that individual should be respected. Where a person does not wish to be supported by a relative, for example, perhaps because they wish to be moving towards independence from their family, then the local authority cannot consider the relative appropriate. The person's wish not to be supported by that individual should be respected and if the person has capacity, or is competent to consent, the person's wishes must be followed. If the person has been judged to lack the capacity to make a decision, then the local authority must be satisfied that it is in a person's best interests to be supported and represented by the individual.

Case Study:

If the person already has an advocate, whose role so far has been to support the person on matters not under the Care Act, who is able and willing to facilitate their involvement in the assessment, planning and review processes then they may be an appropriate individual to support the person's involvement and represent them. They would not be acting as an appropriate person rather than an independent advocate under the Care Act. If, however, that advocate fulfils the requirements for an independent advocate under the Care Act then they can be appointed as such.

Additionally, if an advocate is required under the Mental Capacity Act, and the local authority is going to appoint the same person to be that advocate, then the instruction, appointment and qualification of the advocate must also meet the requirements of the Mental Capacity Act.

7.35. Third, the appropriate individual is expected to support and represent the person and to facilitate their involvement in the processes. It is unlikely that some people will be able to fulfil this role easily, for instance a family member who lives at a distance and who only has occasional contact with the person, a spouse who also finds it difficult to understand the local authority processes, a friend who expresses strong opinions of her own prior to finding out those of the individual concerned, or a housebound parent. It is not sufficient to know the person well or to love them deeply; the role of the appropriate individual is to support the person's active *involvement with the local authority processes* (see chapter 6).[1]

Case Study:

Jacinta is 26 and lives with her mother and father. She has two siblings aged 28 and 23 who have left the family home. Jacinta would also like to move to living more independently. Jacinta has moderate learning disabilities and finds it hard to retain information. Jacinta's parents are very worried that she won't be able to cope living in her own home and are against her doing so. In these circumstances Jacinta's parents would not be 'an appropriate person' who could effectively represent and support her involvement.

Case Study:

Brian is 84 and has advancing dementia. He lives alone in the house he owns. Brian has very limited mobility, has frequent falls and has difficulty in remembering to take medication and to eat. He has periods when he is confused and weighing up the longer term advantages and disadvantages of this care and support options, but has been judged to retain 'capacity'

---

[1] See Assessment chapter 6.9

> Brian says he feels very lonely. Social services are already providing some domiciliary care for which Brian is charged. The local authority is reviewing Brian's care plan. Brian's daughter and son in law who have had little contact with Brian over the past few years and will inherit the house are adamant that he can cope at home and does not need to go into a care home. In these circumstances, in addition to a lack of recent contact, there could be a conflict of interests and Brian's relatives would not be 'an appropriate person'.

7.36. It will clearly not be suitable for a person to be regarded as an appropriate individual where they are implicated in any enquiry of abuse or neglect or have been judged by a SAR to have failed to prevent an abuse or neglect.

7.37. Sometimes the local authority will not know at the point of first contact or at an early stage of the assessment whether there is someone appropriate to assist the person in engaging. They may need to appoint an advocate, and find later that there is an appropriate person in the person's own network. The advocate can at that stage 'hand over' to the appropriate person. Alternatively, the local authority may agree with the individual, the appropriate person and the advocate that it would be beneficial for the advocate to continue their role, though this is not a specific requirement under the legislation. Equally, it is possible that the local authority will consider someone appropriate who may then turn out to have difficulties in supporting the person to engage and be involved in the process. The local authority must at that point arrange for an advocate.

7.38. There may also be some cases where the local authority considers that a person needs the support of both a family member and an advocate; perhaps because the family member can provide a lot of information but not enough support, or because while there is a close relationship, there may be a conflict of interest with the relative, for example in relation to inheritance of the home.

7.39. If the local authority decides that they are required to appoint an independent advocate as the person does not have friends or family who can facilitate their involvement, the local authority must still consult with those friends or family members when the person asks them to (see chapter 6).[1]

7.40. It is the local authority's decision as to whether a family member or friend can act as an appropriate person to facilitate the individual's involvement. It is the local authority's responsibility to communicate this decision to the individual's friends and family where this may have been in question and whenever appropriate. The overall aim should be for people who need advocacy to be identified and when relevant, receive consistent support as early as possible and throughout the assessment, the care and support planning and the review processes.

7.41. The local authority may be carrying out assessments of two people in the same household. If both people agree to have the same advocate, and if the local authority consider there is no conflict of interest between the individuals or either of the individuals and the advocate, then the same advocate may support and represent the two people. For example, if they both wish to be supported to live together in their own home, then it may make sense for one advocate to support both. But where for example one wishes for the other to be moved away, there may

---

[1] See Assessment Chapter 6

be a conflict of interest and two advocates will be needed. If any of the people involved – the people being assessed or taking part in care and support or support planning or the advocate – consider that it would be better to have different advocates, then separate advocates should be provided.

THE EXCEPTIONS: PROVISION OF AN ADVOCATE EVEN WHERE THEY HAVE FAMILY OR OTHERS WHO CAN FACILITATE THE PERSON'S INVOLVEMENT

7.42. In general, a person who has substantial difficulty in being involved in their assessment, plan and review, will only become eligible for an advocate where there is no one appropriate to support their involvement. The exceptions are:

- where the exercising of the assessment or planning function might result in placement in NHS-funded provision in either a hospital for a period exceeding four weeks or in a care home for a period of eight weeks or more and the local authority believes that it would be in the best interests of the individual to arrange an advocate;

- where there is a disagreement, relating to the individual, between the local authority and the appropriate person whose role it would be to facilitate the individual's involvement, and the local authority and the appropriate person agree that the involvement of an independent advocate would be beneficial to the individual.

WHO CAN ACT AS AN ADVOCATE?
7.43. Advocates must have:

- a *suitable level of appropriate experience*: this may, for example, be in non-instructed advocacy or in working with those groups of people who may have substantial difficulty in engaging with assessments and care and support planning;

- *appropriate training*: this may, for example, initially be training in advocacy (non-instructed and instructed) or dementia, or working with people with learning disabilities. Once appointed, all independent advocates should be expected to work towards the National Qualification in Independent Advocacy (level 3) within a year of being appointed, and to achieve it in a reasonable amount of time;

- *competency in the task*: this will require the advocacy organisation assuring itself that the advocates who work for it are all competent and have regular training and assessments;

- *integrity and good character*: this might be assessed through: interview and selection processes; seeking and scrutinising references prior to employment and on-going DBS checks;[1]

- *the ability to work independently of the local authority or body carrying out assessments, planning or reviews on the local authority's behalf*: this would include the ability to make a judgement about what a person is

---

[1] Subject to necessary amendments being made to definition of "regulated activity related to vulnerable adults" in Schedule 4 of Safeguarding Vulnerable Groups Act 2006.

communicating and what is in a person's best interests, as opposed to in a local authority's best interests, and to act accordingly to represent this;

- *arrangements for regular supervision*: this will require that the person meets regularly and sufficiently frequently with a person with a good understanding of independent advocacy who is able to guide their practice and develop their competence.

7.44. The third updated version on the Advocacy Quality Performance Mark (QPM)[1] was published on 3 April 2014 by the National Development Team for Inclusion (NDTi). The QPM is a tool for providers of independent advocacy to show their commitment and ability to provide high quality advocacy services – essential for people to have their voices heard, to exercise choice and control and to live independently.

7.45. The independent advocate must not be working for the local authority, or for an organisation that is commissioned to carry out assessments, care and support plans or reviews for the local authority. In certain circumstances, in addition to their role under the Care Act, an advocate may assist an individual to develop their own care or support plan if requested to by the individual, but they cannot be the person to authorise the support plan or to approve care and support plans or reviews on behalf of the authority. Nor can an advocate be appointed if they are providing care or treatment to the individual in a professional or a paid capacity.

THE ROLE OF THE INDEPENDENT ADVOCATE

7.46. It is intended that advocates will decide the best way of supporting and representing the person they are advocating for, always with regard to the well-being and interest (including their views, beliefs and wishes) of the person concerned. This may involve creative approaches, for example, supporting someone to show film to help explain their needs, wishes or preferences.

Case Study:

Kate has profound and multiple learning disabilities. She doesn't use formal communication like words or signs. She communicates using body language and facial expressions. In her assessment, Kate's independent advocate supports her to show some film of her visiting a local market, enjoying the colours and sounds around her. In this way Kate is able to show the assessor some of the things that are important.

7.47. In addition, where practicable, they are expected to meet the person in private. Where a person has capacity, the advocate should ask their consent to look at their records and to talk to their carer, family, friends, care or support worker and others who can provide information about their needs and wishes, their beliefs and values. Where a person does not have capacity to decide whether an advocate should look at their relevant records or talk to their family and friends, then the advocate should consult the records and the family and others as appropriate, but consulting the family and others only where the advocate considers this is in the person's best interests. The Care Act allows advocates to examine and

---

[1] Available at www.qualityadvocacy.org.uk

take copies of relevant records in certain circumstances. This mirrors the powers of an Independent Mental Capacity Advocate.

7.48. Acting as an advocate for a person who has substantial difficulty in engaging with care and support or safeguarding processes is a responsible position. It includes:

- Assisting a person to understand the assessment, care and support planning and review and safeguarding processes. This requires advocates to understand local authority policies, and other agencies roles, and processes, the available assessment tools, the planning options, and the options available at the review of a care or support plan and required and good practice in safeguarding enquiries and SARs. It may involve advocates spending considerable time with the individual, considering their communications needs, their wishes and feelings and their life story, and using all this to assist the person to be involved and where possible to make decisions.

- Assisting a person to communicate their views, wishes and feelings to the staff who are carrying out an assessment or developing a care or support plan or reviewing an existing plan or to communicate their views, wishes and feelings to the staff who are carrying out safeguarding enquiries or reviews.

- Assisting a person to understand how their needs can be met by the local authority or otherwise – understanding for example how a care and support and support plan can be personalised, how it can be tailored to meet specific needs, how it can be creative, inclusive, and how it can be used to promote a person's rights to liberty and to family life.

- Assisting the person to make decisions about their care and support arrangements – assisting them to weigh up various care and support options and to choose the ones that best meet the person's needs and wishes.

- Assisting the person to understand their rights under the Care Act – for an assessment which considers their wishes and feelings and which considers the views of other people; their right to have their eligible needs met, and to have a care or support plan that reflects their needs and their preferences, and in relation to safeguarding, understanding their right to have their concerns. Also assisting the person to understand their wider rights, including their rights to liberty and family life. A person's rights are complemented by the local authority's duties, for example to involve the person, to meet needs in a way that is least restrictive of a person's rights.

- Assisting a person to challenge a decision or process made by the local authority; and where a person cannot challenge the decision even with assistance, then to challenge it on their behalf.

7.49. In terms of safeguarding there are some particular important issues for advocates to address. These include assisting a person to:

- decide what outcomes/changes they want;

- understand the behaviour of others that are abusive/neglectful;

- understand which actions of their own may expose them to avoidable abuse or neglect;

- understand what actions that they can take to safeguard themselves;

- understand what advice and help they can expect from others, including the criminal justice system;

- understand what parts of the process are completely or partially within their control;

- explain what help they want to avoid reoccurrence and also recover from the experience.

REPRESENTING

7.50. There will be times when an advocate will have concerns about how the local authority has acted or what decision has been made or what outcome is proposed. The advocate must write a report outlining their concerns for the local authority. The local authority should convene a meeting with the advocate to consider the concerns and provide a written response to the advocate following the meeting.

7.51. Where the individual does not have capacity, or is not otherwise able, to challenge a decision, the advocate must challenge any decision where they believe the decision is inconsistent with the local authority's duty to promote the individual's wellbeing.

7.52. Where a person has been assisted and supported and nevertheless remains unable to make their own representations or their own decisions, the independent advocate must use what information they have collected and found, and make the representations on behalf of the person. They must 'advocate' on their behalf, to put their case, to scrutinise the options, to question the plans if they do not appear to meet all eligible needs or do not meet them in a way that fits with the person's wishes and feelings, or are not the least restrictive of the person's life, and to challenge local authority decisions where necessary. The ultimate goal of this representation is to secure a person's rights, promote the individual's wellbeing and ensure that their wishes are taken fully into account.

THE LOCAL AUTHORITY ROLE IN SUPPORTING THE ADVOCATE

7.53. The local authority is expected to recognise that an advocate's duty is to support and represent a person who has substantial difficulty in engaging with the local authority processes. The local authority must take into account any representations made by an advocate. The local authority must provide a written response to a report from an advocate which outlines concerns about how the local authority has acted or what decision has been made or what outcome is proposed. The local authority should understand that the advocate's role incorporates 'challenge' on behalf of the individual.

7.54. The local authority is responsible for ensuring that the relevant people who work for the authority are aware of the advocacy service and the authority's duty to provide such services (see chapter 3).[1] It may engage with the advocates to support this awareness raising.

7.55. The local authority should consider including the identification and referral of those people likely to benefit from independent advocacy (during assessment, care and support planning, review and safeguarding) through the

---

[1] See Information and advice chapter 3

care and support services they may commission. In doing so, the local authority should engage with domiciliary and residential care and support workers and agencies.

7.56. The local authority should take reasonable steps to assist the advocate in carrying out their role. For example, they should let other agencies know that an advocate is supporting a person, facilitating access to the person and to the records, they should propose a reasonable timetable for the assessment and the care and support plan (taking into consideration the needs of the person), and where the advocate wishes to consult family, friends or paid staff, the timetable should allow this. They should keep the advocate informed of any developments and of the outcome of the assessment and the care and support plan.

7.57. The local authority may make reasonable requests of the advocate for information or for meetings both in relation to particular individuals and in relation to the advocate's work more generally, and the independent advocate should comply with these.

7.58. The local authority must meet its duties in relation to working with an Independent Mental Capacity Advocate (IMCA) provided under the Mental Capacity Act as well as those in relation to an advocate under the Care Act when the advocate is acting in both roles. These duties have been closely aligned so as to facilitate this.

AVAILABILITY OF ADVOCACY SERVICES TO PEOPLE IN THE AREA

7.59. All local authorities must ensure that there is sufficient provision of independent advocacy to meet their obligations under the Care Act. There should be sufficient independent advocates available for all people who qualify, and it will be unlawful not to provide someone who qualifies with an advocate (see also chapter 4).

7.60. Advocacy should be seamless for people who qualify, so that they can benefit from the support of one advocate for their whole experience of care or safeguarding work. It rarely makes sense to have one advocate for assessment and another for care and support planning; the two are interrelated, and people who have substantial difficulty in engaging should not be expected to have to tell their story repeatedly to different advocates.

7.61. The Local Government and Public Involvement in Health Act 2007 (as amended by the Health and Social Care Act 2012), provides that local authorities are under a duty to work with their local CCGs, and other partners through the Health and Wellbeing Board to undertake Joint Strategic Needs Assessments for their areas and to develop Joint Health and wellbeing Strategies. Statutory Guidance[1] published in March 2013 makes clear that the Joint Strategic Needs Assessment and Joint Health and Wellbeing Strategies must be published, and have specific regard to "what health and social care information the community needs, including how they access it and what support they may need to understand it".

7.62. Local authorities should be aware of and build on the current availability of independent advocacy services in its local area.

7.63. Independent advocacy under the duty flowing from the Care Act is similar in many ways to independent advocacy under the Mental Capacity Act (MCA).

---

[1] https://www.gov.uk/government/publications/joint-strategic-needs-assessment-and-joint-health-and-wellbeing-strategies-explained

Regulations have been designed to enable independent advocates to be able to carry out both roles. For both:

- the independent advocate's role is to support and represent people;
- the independent advocate's role is primarily to work with people who do not have anyone appropriate to support and represent them;
- the independent advocates require a similar skill set;
- regulations about the appointment and training of advocates are similar;
- local authorities are under a duty to consider representations made by both independent advocates;
- independent advocates will need to be well known and accessible;
- independent advocates may challenge local authority decisions;
- people who qualify for an Independent Mental Capacity Advocate (an IMCA) in relation to the care planning and care review – as that planning may result in an eligible change of accommodation decision – will (in nearly all cases) also qualify for independent advocacy under the Care Act. The provisions of the Care Act are however wider and apply to care planning irrespective of whether it may result in a change of accommodation decision. People for whom there is a power to instruct an IMCA in relation to care review will (in nearly all cases) also qualify for independent advocacy under the Care Act. The Care Act however creates a duty rather than a power in relation to advocacy and care reviews.

7.64. However, the duty to provide independent advocacy under the Care Act is broader and provides support to:

- people who have capacity but who have substantial difficulty in being involved in the care and support 'processes';
- people in relation to their assessment and/or care and support planning regardless of whether a change of accommodation is being considered for the person;
- people in relation to the review of a care and/or support plan;
- people in relation to safeguarding processes (though IMCAs may be involved if the authority has exercised its discretionary power under the MCA and appointed an IMCA if protective measures are being proposed for a person who lacks capacity, at the time to make the relevant decisions or understand their consequences);
- carers who have substantial difficulty in engaging – whether or not they have capacity;
- people for whom there is someone who is appropriate to consult for the purpose of best interests decisions under the Mental Capacity Act, but who is not able and/or willing to facilitate the person's involvement in the local authority process;
- adults who are subject to a safeguarding enquiry or SAR.

7.65. Frequently a person will be entitled to an advocate under the Care Act and then, as the process continues it will be identified that there is a duty to provide an advocate (IMCA) under the Mental Capacity Act.[1] This will occur for example when during the process of assessment or care and support planning it is identified that a decision needs to be taken about the person's long-term accommodation. It would be unhelpful to the individual and to the local authority for a new advocate to be appointed at that stage. It would be better that the advocate who is appointed in the first instance is qualified to act under the Mental Capacity Act (as IMCAs) and the Care Act and that the commissioning arrangements enable this to occur.

7.66. Local authorities do not have to commission one organisation to provide both types of advocacy. But there may be advantages of one organisation providing both:

- it is better for the person receiving the support;

- it is easier for those carrying out assessment and care planning to work with one advocate per individual rather than two; and

- it is easier for the local authority to manage and monitor one contract rather than two.

---

[1] See chapter 10 of the Mental Capacity Act 2005: Code of Practice on the functions of IMCAs.

8. CHARGING AND FINANCIAL ASSESSMENT

This chapter provides guidance on:
- *Sections 14, 17 and 69-70 of the Care Act 2014;*
- *the Care and Support (Charging and Assessment of Resources) Regulations 2014; and,*
- *the Care and Support and Aftercare (Choice of Accommodation) Regulations 2014.*

This chapter covers:
- Common issues for charging;
- Charging for care and support in a care home;
- Choice of accommodation when arranging care in a residential setting;
- Making additional payments for preferred accommodation;
- Charging for home care and support in a person's own home;
- Charging for support to carers;
- Requesting local authority support to meet eligible needs;

This chapter must be read in conjunction with Annexes A to F, which provide further technical and detailed information.

8.1. The Care Act provides a single legal framework for charging for care and support under sections 14 and 17. It enables a local authority to decide whether or not to charge a person when it is arranging to meet a person's care and support needs or a carer's support needs.

8.2. Where a local authority arranges care and support to meet a person's needs, it may charge the adult, except where the local authority is required to arrange care and support free of charge. The new framework is intended to make charging fairer and more clearly understood by everyone. The overarching principle is that people should only be required to pay what they can afford. People will be entitled to financial support based on a means-test and some will be entitled to free care. The framework is therefore based on the following principles that local authorities should take into account when making decisions on charging. The principles are that the approach to charging for care and support needs should:

- ensure that people are not charged more than it is reasonably practicable for them to pay;

- be comprehensive, to reduce variation in the way people are assessed and charged;

- be clear and transparent, so people know what they will be charged;

- promote wellbeing, social inclusion, and support the vision of personalisation, independence, choice and control;

- support carers to look after their own health and wellbeing and to care effectively and safely;

- be person-focused, reflecting the variety of care and caring journeys and the variety of options available to meet their needs;

- apply the charging rules equally so those with similar needs or services are treated the same and minimise anomalies between different care settings;

- encourage and enable those who wish to stay in or take up employment, education or training or plan for the future costs of meeting their needs to do so; and

- be sustainable for local authorities in the long-term.

8.3. Alongside this, local authorities should ensure there is sufficient information and advice available in a suitable format for the person's needs, in line with the Equality Act 2010 (in particular for those with a sensory impairment, with learning disabilities or for whom English is not their first language), to ensure that they or their representative are able to understand any contributions they are asked to make. Local authorities should also make the person or their representative aware of the availability of independent financial information and advice.

COMMON ISSUES FOR CHARGING

8.4. Local authorities have a duty to arrange care and support for those with eligible needs, and a power to meet both eligible and non-eligible needs. In all cases, a local authority has the discretion to choose whether or not to charge under section 14 of the Care Act following a person's needs assessment. Where it decides to charge, it must follow the Care and Support (Charging and Assessment of Resources) regulations and have regard to the guidance. The detail of how to charge is different depending on whether someone is receiving care in a care home, or their own home, or another setting. However, they share some common elements, which are set out in the following section.

8.5. The different approaches exist to reflect that the delivery model for care homes is relatively uniform across the country and it is therefore sensible to provide a single model for charging purposes. However, other models of care generally see a greater variety of approaches and innovation that we wish to continue.

8.6. Where a local authority chooses to charge, regulations determine the maximum amount a local authority can charge a person.

8.7. Only in care homes, where the financial assessment identifies that a person's resources exceed the capital limits, is a local authority precluded from paying towards the costs of care. Therefore, local authorities should develop and maintain a policy setting out how they will charge people in settings other than care homes. In deciding what it is reasonable to charge, local authorities must ensure that they do not charge more than is permitted under these regulations and as set out in this guidance.

8.8. The subsequent guidance and the supporting annexes assume that the appropriate assessment of needs has been carried out and the local authority has chosen to charge. It therefore provides detail on how to conduct the financial assessment for that person. The local authority has no power to assess couples or civil partners according to their joint resources. Each person must therefore be treated individually. For further guidance on assessment of needs see Chapter 6.

8.9. Where a person lacks capacity, they may still be assessed as being able to contribute towards the cost of their care. However, a local authority must put in place policies regarding how they communicate, how they carry out financial assessments and how they collect any debts that take into consideration the capacity of the person as well as any illness or condition. Local authorities are expected to use their social work skills both to communicate with people and also to design a system that works with, and for, very vulnerable people. Sometimes it is useful to consult with and engage with family members; however, family members may not have the legal right to access the person's bank accounts. Where possible, local authorities should work with someone who has the legal authority to make financial decisions on behalf of a person who lacks capacity. If there is no such person, then an approach to the Court of Protection is required.

8.10. The charging rules also apply equally to people in prison. Whilst prisoners have restricted access to paid employment and benefits (and earnings in prison are to be disregarded for the purposes of the financial assessments), any capital assets, savings and pensions will need specific consideration as set out in this chapter and relevant annexes. For more information on prisons and approved premises see Chapter 17.

CAPITAL LIMITS

8.11. The financial limit, known as the "upper capital limit", exists for the purposes of the financial assessment. This sets out at what point a person is entitled to access local authority support to meet their eligible needs. Full detail is set out in Annex B, and the local authority must read that guidance before undertaking a financial assessment.

8.12. The upper capital limit is currently set at £23,250. Below this level, a person can seek means-tested support from the local authority. This means that the local authority will undertake a financial assessment of the person's assets and will make a charge based on what the person can afford to pay. In the financial assessment capital below the lower capital limit – currently set at £14,250 – is disregarded in the assessment of what a person can pay. Where a person's resources are below the lower capital limit of £14,250 they will not need to contribute to the cost of their care and support from their capital.

8.13. A person with more in capital than the upper capital limit can ask their local authority to arrange their care and support for them. Where the person's needs are to be met by care in a care home, the local authority may choose to meet those needs and arrange the care, but is not required to do so. In other cases, the authority must meet the eligible needs if requested. However, these people are not entitled to receive any financial assistance from their local authority and in any case, may pay the full cost of their care and support until their capital falls below the upper capital limit.

8.14. The local authority must not charge for certain types of care and support which must be arranged free. These are:

- Intermediate care, including reablement, which must be provided free of charge for up to six weeks. However, local authorities must have regard to the guidance on preventative support set out in Chapter 2. This sets out that neither should have a strict time limit but should reflect the needs of the person. Local authorities therefore may wish to apply their discretion to offer this free of charge for longer than six weeks where there are clear preventative benefits, such as when a person has recently become visually impaired.

- Community equipment (aids and minor adaptations). Aids must be provided free of charge whether provided to meet or prevent/delay needs. A minor adaptation is one costing £1,000 or less.

- Care and support provided to people with Creutzfeldt-Jacob Disease.

- After-care services/support provided under section 117 of the Mental Health Act 1983.

- Any service or part of service which the NHS is under a duty to provide. This includes Continuing Healthcare and the NHS contribution to Registered Nursing Care.

- More broadly, any services which a local authority is under a duty to provide through other legislation may not be charged for under the Care Act 2014.

- Assessment of needs and care planning may also not be charged for, since these processes do not constitute "meeting needs".

CARRYING OUT A FINANCIAL ASSESSMENT

8.15. The legal framework for charging is set out in Sections 14 and 17 of the Care Act. When choosing to charge, a local authority must not charge more than the cost that it incurs in meeting the assessed needs of the person. It also cannot recover any administration fee relating to arranging that care and support. The only exception is in the case of a person with eligible needs and assets above the upper capital limit who has asked the local authority to arrange their care and support on their behalf. In such cases, the local authority may apply an administration fee to cover its costs. However, (see paragraphs 8.53 to 8.58 below) this must not be higher than the cost the local authority has incurred in arranging that care and support. This approach must also apply if the local authority has involved other organisations to deliver its duties in any way.

8.16. Where a local authority has decided to charge, except where a light touch assessment is permissible (see paragraph 8.22 below), it must carry out a financial assessment of what the person can afford to pay and, once complete, it must give a written record of that assessment to the person. This could be provided alongside a person's care and support plan or separately, including via online means. It should explain how the assessment has been carried out, what the charge will be and how often it will be made, and if there is any fluctuation in charges, the reason. The local authority should ensure that this is provided in a manner that the person can easily understand, in line with its duties on providing information and advice.

8.17. In carrying out the assessment, the local authority must have regard to the detailed guidance set out in Annexes B and C that set out how both capital and income should be treated. A local authority must regularly reassess a person's ability to meet the cost of any charges to take account of any changes to their resources. This is likely to be on an annual basis, but may vary according to individual circumstances. However, this should take place if there is a change in circumstance or at the request of the person.

8.18. At the time of the assessment of care and support needs, the local authority must establish whether the person has the capacity to take part in the assessment. If the person lacks capacity, the local authority must find out if the person has any of the following as the appropriate person will need to be involved:

- Enduring Power of Attorney (EPA);

- Lasting Power of Attorney (LPA) for Property and Affairs;

- Lasting Power of Attorney (LPA) for Health and Welfare;

- Property and Affairs Deputyship under the Court of Protection; or

- Any other person dealing with that person's affairs (e.g. someone who has been given appointee-ship by the Department for Work and Pensions (DWP) for the purpose of benefits payments).

8.19. People who lack capacity to give consent to a financial assessment and who do not have any of the above people with authority to be involved in their affairs, may require the appointment of a Property and Affairs Deputyship. Family members can apply for this to the Court of Protection or the local authority can apply if there is no family involved in the care of the person. While this takes some weeks, it then enables the person appointed to access information about bank accounts and financial affairs. A person with dementia for example should not be 'forced' to undertake a financial assessment, to sign documents they can no longer understand and should not be punished for any incomplete information that is elicited from them. The local authority should be working with an EPA, a LPA or a Deputy instead.

8.20. In the financial assessment, the person's capital is taken into account unless it is subject to one of the disregards set out in Schedule 2 to the regulations and described in Annex B. The main examples of capital are property and savings. Where the person receiving care and support has capital at or below the upper capital limit (currently £23,250), but more than the lower capital limit (currently £14,250), they may be charged £1 per week for every £250 in capital between the two amounts. This is called "tariff income". For example, if a person has £4,000 above the lower capital limit, they are charged a tariff income of £16 per week.

8.21. In assessing what a person can afford to pay, a local authority must take into account their income. However, to help encourage people to remain in or take up employment, with the benefits this has for a person's well-being, earnings from current employment must be disregarded when working out how much they can pay. There are different approaches to how income is treated depending on whether a person is in a care home or receiving care and support in their own home. Full details are set out in Annex C on the treatment of income in care homes and other settings.

"LIGHT-TOUCH" FINANCIAL ASSESSMENTS

8.22. In some circumstances, a local authority may choose to treat a person as if a financial assessment had been carried out. In order to do so, the local authority must be satisfied on the basis of evidence provided by the person that they can afford, and will continue to be able to afford, any charges due. This is known as a "light-touch" financial assessment.

8.23. The main circumstances in which a local authority may consider carrying out a light- touch financial assessment are:

(a) Where a person has significant financial resources, and does not wish to undergo a full financial assessment for personal reasons, but wishes none-theless to access local authority support in meeting their needs. In these situations the local authority may accept other evidence in lieu of carrying out the financial assessment and consider the person to have financial resources above the upper limit.

(b) Where the local authority charges a small or nominal amount for a particular service (e.g. for subsidised services) which a person is clearly able to meet and would clearly have the relevant minimum income left, and carrying out a financial assessment would be disproportionate.

(c) When an individual is in receipt of benefits which demonstrate that they would not be able to contribute towards their care and support costs. This might include income from Jobseeker's Allowance.

8.24. Ways a local authority may be satisfied that a person is able to afford any charges due might include evidence that a person has:

(a) property clearly worth more than the upper capital limit, where they are the sole owner or it is clear what their share is;

(b) savings clearly worth more than the upper capital limit; or,

(c) sufficient income left following the charge due.

8.25. Where the local authority is going to meet the person's needs, and it proposes to undertake a light-touch financial assessment, it should take steps to assure itself that the person concerned is willing, and will continue to be willing, to pay all charges due. It must also remember that it is responsible for ensuring that people are not charged more than it is reasonable for them to pay. Where a person does not agree to the charges that they have been assessed as being able to afford to pay under this route, a full financial assessment may be needed.

8.26. When deciding whether or not to undertake a light-touch financial assessment, a local authority should consider both the level of the charge it proposes to make, as well as the evidence or other certification the person is able to provide. They must also inform the person when a light-touch assessment has taken place and make clear that the person has the right to request a full financial assessment should they so wish, as well as making sure they have access to sufficient information and advice, including the option of independent financial information and advice.

DEPRIVATION OF ASSETS AND DEBTS

8.27. People with care and support needs are free to spend their income and assets as they see fit, including making gifts to friends and family. This is important for promoting their wellbeing and enabling them to live fulfilling and independent lives. However, it is also important that people pay their fair contribution towards their care and support costs.

8.28. There are some cases where a person may have tried to deliberately avoid paying for care and support costs through depriving themselves of assets – either capital or income. Where a local authority believes they have evidence to support this, it must read Annex E concerning the deprivation of assets. In such cases, the local authority may either charge the person as if they still possessed the asset or, if the asset has been transferred to someone else, seek to recover the lost income from charges from that person. However, the local authority cannot recover more than the person gained from the transfer.

8.29. Where a person has accrued a debt, the local authority may use its powers under the Care Act to recover that debt. In deciding how to proceed, the local authority should consider the circumstances of the case before deciding a course of action. For example, a local authority should consider whether this was a deliberate avoidance of payment or due to circumstances beyond the person's control.

8.30. Ultimately, the local authority may institute County Court proceedings to recover the debt. However, they should only use this power after other reasonable alternatives for recovering the debt have been exhausted. Further details on how to pursue debts are set out in Annex D.

CHARGING FOR CARE AND SUPPORT IN A CARE HOME

8.31. This section must be read in conjunction with Annex B on the treatment of capital and Annex C on the treatment of income in care homes.

8.32. Where a local authority has decided to charge and undertaken the financial assessment, it should support the person to identify options of how best to pay any charge. This may include offering the person a deferred payment agreement. In such cases, chapter 9 of the guidance must be considered.

8.33. Where a local authority is meeting needs by arranging a care home, it is responsible for contracting with the provider. It is also responsible for paying the full amount, including where a 'top-up' fee is being paid. However, where all parties are agreed it may choose to allow the person to pay the provider directly for the 'top-up' where this is permitted. In doing so it should remember that multiple contracts risk confusion and that the local authority may be unable to assure itself that it is meeting its responsibilities under the additional cost provisions in the Care Act. Local authorities must ensure they read the guidance at Annex A on the use of 'top-up' fees.

8.34. Where a person is a temporary or short-term resident in a care home, a local authority may choose to charge based on its charging policies outside of a care home. For example, where a person is resident in order to receive respite care, for the first eight weeks a local authority may choose to charge based on its approach to charging for those receiving care and support in other settings or in their own home.

8.35. People in a care home will contribute most of their income, excluding their earnings, towards the cost of their care and support. However, a local authority must leave the person with a specified amount of their own income so that the person has money to spend on personal items such as clothes and other items that are not part of their care. This is known as the personal expenses allowance (PEA). This is in addition to any income the person receives from earnings. Ministers have the power to adjust the PEA and have done so annually to ensure it maintains its value. These changes are communicated by Local Authority Circular and are binding. Local authorities have discretion to apply a higher income allowance in individual cases, for example where the person needs to contribute towards the cost of maintaining their former home. Further detail is set out in Annex C.

CHOICE OF ACCOMMODATION

8.36. Where the care planning process has determined that a person's needs are best met in a care home, the local authority must provide for the person's preferred choice of accommodation, subject to certain conditions. This also extends to shared lives, supported living and extra care housing settings. Determining the appropriate type of accommodation should be made with the adult as part of the care and support planning process, therefore this choice only applies between providers of the same type.

8.37. The local authority must ensure that the person has a genuine choice and must ensure that at least one option is available and affordable within a person's personal budget and should ensure that there is more than one. However, a person must also be able to choose alternative options, including a more expensive setting, where *a third party or in certain circumstances the resident is willing and able to pay the additional cost ('top- up')*. However, an additional payment must always be optional and never as a result of commissioning failures leading to a lack of choice. Detailed guidance is set out in Annex A which a local authority must have regard to.

CHARGING FOR CARE AND SUPPORT IN OTHER CARE SETTINGS INCLUDING A PERSON'S OWN HOME

8.38. This section should be read in conjunction with the regulations and Annex B on the treatment of capital and Annex C on the treatment of income in non-residential care.

8.39. These charging arrangements cover any setting for meeting care and support needs outside of a care home. For example, care and support received in a person's own home, and in other accommodation settings such as in extra care housing, supported living accommodation or shared lives arrangements.

8.40. The intent of the regulations and guidance is to support local authorities to assess what a person can afford to contribute towards their care costs. Local authorities should also consider how to use their discretion to support the principles of care and support charging.

8.41. This guidance does not make any presumption that local authorities will charge for care and support provided outside care homes, but enables them to continue to allow discretion.

8.42. Because a person who receives care and support outside a care home will need to pay their daily living costs such as rent, food and utilities, the charging rules must ensure they have enough money to meet these costs. After charging, a person must be left with the minimum income guarantee (MIG), equivalent to Income Support plus a buffer of 25%. In addition, where a person receives benefits to meet their disability needs that do not meet the eligibility criteria for local authority care and support, the charging arrangements should ensure that they keep enough money to cover the cost of meeting these disability- related costs.

8.43. Additionally, the financial assessment of their capital must exclude the value of the property which they occupy as their main or only home. Beyond this, the rules on what capital must be disregarded are the same for all types of care and support. However, local authorities have flexibility within this framework; for example, they may choose to disregard additional sources of income, set maximum charges, or charge a person a percentage of their disposable income. This will help support local authorities to take account of local circumstances and promote integration and innovation.

8.44. Although local authorities have this discretion, this should not lead to two people with similar needs, and receiving similar types of care and support, being charged differently.

8.45. Local authorities should develop and maintain a policy on how they wish to apply this discretion locally. In designing this policy local authorities should consider the objectives of care and support charging and how it can;

- ensure that people are not charged more than it is reasonably practicable for them to pay;

- be comprehensive, to reduce variation in the way people are assessed and charged;

- be clear and transparent, so people know what they will be charged;

- promote wellbeing, social inclusion, and support the vision of personalisation, independence, choice and control;

- support carers to look after their own health and wellbeing and to care effectively and safely;

- be person-focused, reflecting the variety of care and caring journeys and the variety of options available to meet their needs;

- apply the charging rules equally so those with similar needs or services are treated the same and minimise anomalies between different care settings;

- encourage and enable those who wish to stay in or take up employment, education or training or plan for the future costs of meeting their needs to do so;

- be sustainable for local authorities in the long-term; and

- administer a charging policy for people who lack capacity or are losing capacity in a way that considers what capacity remains and their rights.

8.46. Local authorities should consult people with care and support needs when deciding how to exercise this discretion. In doing this, local authorities should consider how to protect a person's income. The government considers that it is inconsistent with promoting independent living to assume, without further consideration, that all of a person's income above basic levels of Income Support or the Guarantee Credit element of Pension Credit plus 25% is available to be taken in charges.

8.47. Local authorities should therefore consider whether it is appropriate to set a maximum percentage of disposable income (over and above the guaranteed minimum income) which may be taken into account in charges.

8.48. Local authorities should also consider whether it is appropriate to set a maximum charge, for example these might be set as a maximum percentage of care home charges in a local area. This could help ensure that people are encouraged to remain in in their own homes, promoting individual wellbeing and independence.

CHARGING FOR SUPPORT TO CARERS

8.49. Where a carer has eligible support needs of their own, the local authority has a duty, or in some cases a power, to arrange support to meet their needs. Where a local authority is meeting the needs of a carer by providing a service directly to a carer, for example a relaxation class or driving lessons, it has the power to charge the carer. However, a local authority must not charge a carer for care and support provided directly to the person they care for under any circumstances.

8.50. Local authorities are not required to charge a carer for support and indeed in many cases it would be a false economy to do so. When deciding whether to charge, and in determining what an appropriate charge is, a local authority should consider how it wishes to express the way it values carers within its local community as partners in care, and recognise the significant contribution carers make. Carers help to maintain the health and wellbeing of the person they care for, support this person's independence and enable them to stay in their own homes for longer. In many cases of course, carers voluntarily meet eligible needs that the local authority would otherwise be required to meet. Local authorities should consider carefully the likely impact of any charges on carers, particularly in terms of their willingness and ability to continue their caring responsibilities. It may be that there are circumstances where a nominal charge may be appropriate, for example to provide for a service which is subsidised but for which the carer may still pay a small charge, such as a gym class. Ultimately, a local authority should ensure that any charges do not negatively impact on a carer's ability to look after their own health and wellbeing and to care effectively and safely.

8.51. While charging carers may be appropriate in some circumstances, it is very unlikely to be efficient to systematically charge carers for meeting their eligible needs. This is because excessive charges are likely to lead to carers refusing support, which in turn will lead to carer breakdown and local authorities having to meet more eligible needs of people currently cared for voluntarily. As an example, work carried out by Surrey County Council found that if even 10% of people with care and support needs in families supported by carers presented to the council with eligible needs as a result of carer breakdown, the resulting cost would be three times the current total budget for carer support.

8.52. Local authorities may also wish to consider whether charging is proportionate when light touch carers assessments are undertaken for small scale help. There is a risk that financial assessments might become the most costly part of the process and something that is administratively burdensome.

8.53. Where a local authority takes the decision to charge a carer, it must do so in accordance with the non-residential charging rules. In doing so, it should usually carry out a financial assessment to ensure that any charges are affordable. However, it may be more likely, in the case of a carer, that the carer and the local authority will agree that a full financial assessment would be disproportionate as carers often face significantly lower charges.

8.54. In such cases, a local authority may choose to treat a carer as if a financial assessment has been carried out. When deciding whether or not to undertake a light-touch financial assessment, a local authority should consider both the level of the charge it proposes to make as well as the evidence the person is able to provide that they will be able to afford the charge. They must also inform the person when a light-touch assessment has taken place and make clear from the outset that the person has the right to request a full financial assessment should they so wish.

REQUESTING LOCAL AUTHORITY SUPPORT TO MEET ELIGIBLE NEEDS

8.55. People with eligible needs and financial assets above the upper capital limit may ask the local authority to meet their needs. This could be for a variety of reasons such as the person finding the system too difficult to navigate, or wishing to take advantage of the local authority's knowledge of the local market of care and support services. Where the person asks the local authority to meet their eligible needs, and it is anticipated that their needs will be met by a care home placement, then the local authority may choose to meet their needs, but is not required to do so. In other cases, where the needs are to be met by care and support of some other type, the local authority must meet those eligible needs.

8.56. Local authorities should therefore take steps to make people aware that they have the right to request the local authority to meet their needs, in certain circumstances even when they have resources above the financial limits and would not be entitled to financial support with any charges. They should also be clear that this right does not extend to needs met by a care home placement, although local authorities may choose to apply the same approach locally. Local authorities should also offer support to people in meeting their own needs, including providing information and advice on different options, and may offer to arrange contracts with providers.

8.57. Where the person's resources are above the financial limit, the person's entitlement to local authority support in meeting their needs may be dependent and their needs are to be met through one or more types of care and support other than a care home, on the request having been made. Therefore it is important that the person, and any carer, advocate or other person they wish to involve, are aware of this ability and the consequences for their care and support. The local authority must make clear to the person that they may be liable to pay an arrangement fee in addition to the costs of meeting their needs to cover the costs of putting in place the care and support required.

8.58. Arrangement fees charged by local authorities must cover only the costs that the local authorities actually incur in arranging care. Arrangement fees should take account of the cost of negotiating and/or managing the contract with a provider and cover any administration costs incurred. Where a local authority chooses to meet the needs of a person with resources above the financial limit who requires a care home placement, it must not charge an arrangement fee. This is because it would support that person under its power (rather than its duty) to meet needs, and the ability to charge the arrangement fee applies only to circumstances when the authority is required to meet needs.

8.59. Local authorities must not charge people for a financial assessment, a needs assessment or the preparation of a care and support plan.

8.60. It may be appropriate for local authorities to charge a flat rate fee for arranging care. This can help ensure people have clarity about the costs they will face if they ask the local authority to arrange their care. However, such flat rate costs must be set at a level where they do not exceed the costs the local authority actually incurs.

8.61. The information provided to the person following a financial assessment should include information on the right to request the local authority to meet their needs – and how they would be charged – and the advice and support that is available to help people make arrangements to meet their own needs whatever type of support they require.

8.62. A local authority will be under a duty to meet a person's eligible needs when requested to do so and their needs are to be met by care and support other than in a care home. However, where the person has resources above the financial limits the local authority may charge the person for the full cost of their care and support. In such circumstances, the person remains responsible for paying for the cost of their care and support, but the local authority takes on the responsibility for meeting those needs. This means that the local authority may for example provide or arrange care and support, or make a direct payment which may be a paper based exercise, or some combination of these. Further information on how, to "meet needs" and the options available is provided in chapter 10.

8.63. The local authority must assure itself that whilst the person remains responsible for paying for their own care, they have sufficient assets for the arrangements that it puts in place to remain both affordable and sustainable. The local authority should also take steps to avoid disputes and additional liabilities by securing a person's agreement in writing to pay the costs that they are responsible for in meeting their needs, including payments to providers. Local authorities should make similar arrangements with any third parties that agree to contribute towards these costs.

PENSION REFORMS

8.64. Local authorities will also wish to be aware of reforms to defined contribution pensions that come into effect from April 2015. The aim of the reforms is to provide people with much greater flexibility in how they fund later life. The Government expects there to be a range of new products that people will use to manage and access money from their pensions as and when they need it, and where possible, these will be treated similarly to existing drawdown products for charging purposes.

8.65. Alongside the reforms is the introduction of a 'Guidance Guarantee' that will help people to make informed choices at the point of retirement. This will include information and advice on later life, including the risk that they will need, and have to pay for, care and support in the future.

8.66. For the purposes of charging, a local authority must follow the guidance set out on the treatment of income and capital in Annexes B and C and treat a person's assets accordingly. Where a person has chosen to withdraw funds from their pension pot and manage it directly, for example combining it with other assets rather than through a pensions product, this may be treated as capital under the rules laid out in Annex B.

COMPLAINTS

8.67. A person may wish to make a complaint about any aspect of the financial assessment or how a local authority has chosen to charge. A local authority must make clear what its complaints procedure is and provide information and advice on how to lodge a complaint.

8.68. Complaints about the level of charge levied by a local authority are subject to the usual Care and Support complaints procedure as set out in The Local Authority Social Services and NHS Complaints (England) Regulations 2009.

8.69. Where a local authority has established a special Panel or Fast track review processes to deal with financial assessment/charging issues, they should remind the person that they still have access to the statutory complaints procedure.

9. DEFERRED PAYMENT AGREEMENTS

This chapter provides guidance on:
- *sections 34-36 of the Care Act 2014; and*

- *the Care and Support (Deferred Payment Agreements) Regulations 2014.*

This chapter covers:
- Who to offer a deferred payment to;
- Provision of information and advice before making a deferred payment agreement;
- How much can be deferred, and security for the agreement;
- Interest rate for the deferral and administrative charges;
- Making the agreement, responsibilities while the agreement is in place and termination of the agreement.

DEFINITIONS

9.1. 'Care costs' – all costs charged to a person by a care provider, including any top-ups and core care costs. This includes where appropriate the costs associated with the provision of extra care.

9.2. 'Top ups' – this term has the usual meaning accorded to it within the care and support sector, but for the avoidance of doubt, top-ups are costs due to a local authority under Section 30 of the Care Act or costs for the provision of the type of care referred to in Section 34(3)(a) of the Care Act.

INTRODUCTION

9.3. The establishment of the universal deferred payment scheme will mean that people should not be forced to sell their home in their lifetime to pay for their care. By entering into a deferred payment agreement, a person can 'defer' or delay paying the costs of their care and support until a later date. Deferring payment can help people to delay the need to sell their home, and provides peace of mind during a time that can be challenging (or even a crisis point) for them and their loved ones as they make the transition into care.

9.4. A deferred payment agreement can provide additional flexibility for when and how someone pays for their care and support. It should be stressed from the outset that the payment for care and support is deferred and not 'written off' – the costs of provision of care and support will have to be repaid by the individual (or a third party on their behalf) at a later date.

9.5. The scheme will be universally available throughout England, and local authorities will be required to offer deferred payment agreements to people who meet certain criteria governing eligibility for the scheme. Local authorities will need to ensure that adequate security is in place for the amount being deferred, so that they can be confident that the amount deferred will be repaid in the future. Local authorities are also encouraged to offer the scheme more widely to anyone they feel would benefit who does not fully meet the criteria.

9.6. A deferral can last until death, however many people choose to use a deferred payment agreement as a 'bridging loan' to give them time and flexibility to sell their home when they choose to do so. This is entirely up to the individual to decide. Further details on deferred payment agreements are set out in the sections below.

WHO TO OFFER DEFERRED PAYMENTS TO
Criteria governing eligibility for deferred payment agreements
9.7. Deferred payment agreements are designed to prevent people from being forced to sell their home in their lifetime to meet the cost of their care. Local authorities must offer them to people who meet the criteria below and who are able to provide adequate security (see section entitled 'Obtaining Security' below). They must offer them to people who have local authority-arranged care and support, and also people who arrange and pay for their own care, subject to these criteria. The regulations specify that someone is eligible for and so must be offered a deferred payment agreement if they meet all three of the following criteria at the point of applying for a deferred payment agreement:
(a) anyone whose needs are to be met by the provision of care in a care home. This is determined when someone is assessed as having eligible needs[1] which the local authority decides should be met through a care home placement. This should comply with choice of accommodation regulations and care and support planning guidance and so take reasonable account of a person's preferences;
(b) anyone who has less than (or equal to) £23,250 in assets excluding the value of their home (i.e. in savings and other non-housing assets); and
(c) anyone whose home is not disregarded[2], for example it is not occupied by a spouse or dependent relative as defined in regulations on charging for care and support (i.e. someone whose home is taken into account in the local authority financial assessment and so might need to be sold).
9.8. As well as providing protection for people facing the prospect of having to sell their home to pay for care, deferred payment agreements can offer valuable flexibility, giving people greater choice over how they pay their care costs. Local authorities are, at their discretion, permitted to be more generous than these criteria and offer deferred payment agreements to people who do not meet the above criteria. In deciding whether someone who does not meet all of the criteria above should still be offered a deferred payment, some considerations a local authority may wish to take into account include (but are not limited to):
(a) whether meeting care costs would leave someone with very few accessible assets (this might include assets which cannot quickly/easily be liquidated or converted to cash);
(b) if someone would like to use wealth tied up in their home to fund more than just their core care costs and purchase affordable top-ups (see further guidance on 'How much can be deferred' below);
(c) whether someone has any other accessible means to help them meet the cost of their care and support; and/or
(d) if a person is narrowly not entitled to a deferred payment agreement given the criteria above, for example because they have slightly more than the £23,250 asset threshold. This should include people who are likely to meet the criteria in the near future.
9.9. Local authorities may also at their discretion enter into deferred payment agreements with people whose care and support is provided in supported living

---

[1] When someone is arranging their own care and support and the authority has not performed an assessment, this condition is satisfied when someone would be assessed as having eligible needs were the authority to have carried out such an assessment.
[2] Disregarded for the purposes of the financial assessment carried out under section 17 of the Act.

accommodation. The local authority should not exercise this discretion unless the person intends to retain their former home and pay the associated care and accommodation rental costs from their deferred payment. Further details on precisely what qualifies as supported living accommodation are set out in regulations. Deferred payment agreements cannot be entered into to finance mortgage payments on supported living accommodation.

Permission to refuse a deferred payment agreement

9.10. A local authority must offer a deferred payment to someone meeting the criteria governing eligibility for deferred payment agreements (DPAs) and who is able to provide adequate security for the debt (obtaining a land registry charge on their property, see 'Obtaining security' below); and may offer a deferred payment agreement to others who do not meet the criteria, at their discretion.

9.11. However there are certain circumstances in which a local authority may refuse a request for a deferred payment agreement ('permission to refuse'), even if a person meets the eligibility criteria and the local authority would otherwise be required to offer the person an agreement. This permission (or discretion) to refuse is intended to provide local authorities with a reasonable safeguard against default or non-repayment of debt.

9.12. A local authority may refuse a deferred payment agreement despite someone meeting the eligibility criteria:

(a) where a local authority is unable to secure a first charge on the person's property;
(b) where someone is seeking a top up[1] ; and/or
(c) where a person does not agree to the terms and conditions of the agreement, for example a requirement to insure and maintain the property.

9.13. In any of the above circumstances, a local authority should consider whether to exercise its discretion to offer a deferred payment anyway (for example, if a person's property is uninsurable but has a high land value, the local authority may choose to accept charges against this land as security instead).

Circumstances in which local authorities may stop deferring care costs

9.14. There are also circumstances where a local authority may refuse to defer any more charges for a person who has an active deferred payment agreement. Local authorities cannot demand repayment in these circumstances, and repayment is still subject to the usual terms of termination, as set out in the section entitled 'termination of the agreement' below.

9.15. The local authority should provide a minimum of 30 days, advance notice that further deferrals will cease; and should provide the person with an indication of how their care costs will need to be met in future. Depending on their circumstances, the person may either receive local authority support in meeting the costs of their care, or may be required to meet their costs from their income and assets. Local authorities exercising these powers to cease deferring additional amounts should consider their decision to do so whilst considering the person's circumstances and their overarching duties under the well-being principle.

---

[1] In these situations, a local authority should still seek to offer a deferred payment agreement but should be guided by principles in the section below (entitled 'how much to defer') to determine a maximum amount that is sustainable (or reflects their core care costs without any top-ups) and agree a deferral. The person can then choose whether they wish to agree.

9.16. Circumstances in which a local authority may refuse to defer any more charges include:[1]

 (a) when a person's total assets fall below the level of the means-test (see chapter 8), and the person becomes eligible for local authority support in paying for their care;

 (b) where a person no longer has need for care in a care home (or where appropriate supported living accommodation);

 (c) if a person breaches certain predefined terms of their contract (which must be clearly set out in the contract) and the local authority's attempts to resolve the breach are unsuccessful and the contract has specified that the authority will stop making further payments in such a case; or

 (d) if, under the charging regulations (see also chapter 8), the property becomes disregarded for any reason and the person consequently qualifies for local authority support in paying for their care, including but not limited to:

 • where a spouse or dependent relative (as defined in charging regulations) has moved into the property after the agreement has been made, where this means the person is eligible for local authority support in paying for care and no longer requires a deferred payment agreement; and

 • where a relative who was living in the property at the time of the agreement subsequently becomes a dependent relative (as defined in charging regulations). The local authority may cease further deferrals at this point.

9.17. Local authorities should not exercise these discretionary powers if a person would, as a result, be unable to pay any tariff income due to the local authority from their non-housing assets.

9.18. Local authorities must also cease deferring further amounts when a person has reached the 'equity limit' that they are allowed to defer (see 'how much can be deferred' below); or when a person is no longer receiving care and support in either a care home setting or in supported living accommodation. This also applies when the value of the security has dropped and so the equity limit has been reached earlier than expected[2].

Case study 1

Lucille develops a need for a home placement. She lives alone and is the sole owner of her home. Her home is valued at £165,000, and she has £15,000 in savings. Lucille meets the criteria governing eligibility for a deferred payment.

INFORMATION AND ADVICE

9.19. Under the Care Act, local authorities have responsibilities to provide information and advice about people's care and support. These extend to deferred payment schemes as well. This chapter should be read in combination with chapter 3 ('Information and Advice').

---

[1] In any of these cases, if the local authority chooses to charge it, interest would continue to accrue on the amount deferred until the agreement was terminated (either by sale of the property, the person's death or by the LA being repaid separately; as set out in the 'Termination of the Agreement' section below).

[2] The equity limit has been formulated such that, by this point in time, the person should qualify for full local authority support in paying for their care.

9.20. In order to be able to make well-informed choices, it is essential that people access appropriate information and advice before taking out a deferred payment agreement (DPA). It is also important that people are kept informed about their DPA throughout the course of the agreement, and that they (and the executor of their estate where appropriate) receive the necessary information upon termination of the agreement.

9.21. Information and advice requirements prior to taking out a DPA are discussed in this section; requirements on local authorities while the DPA is in place are discussed in a separate section below (see 'the local authority's responsibilities whilst the agreement is in place'); and the section entitled 'termination of the agreement' addresses the responsibilities on the local authority when the agreement is concluded. The requirements on local authorities to offer and facilitate access to financial information and advice on other options for paying for care are discussed in chapter 3.

9.22. Deferred payment agreements are often made during a time that is demanding for a person and their loved ones – a period when they are making a transition into a care home. People may need additional support during this period, and the local authority has a role in providing this support and facilitating their transition, particularly if their transition to care is made rapidly and/or at an unexpected point. The local authority must provide information in a way which is clear and easy to understand, and it should be designed to ease the process of transition for people, their carers and their families.

9.23. Carers and families often assist people in making decisions about their care and how they pay for it. Local authorities should as appropriate invite carers and/or families to participate in discussions, and should also provide them with all the information that would otherwise be given to the person they care for, subject (where required)[1] to the consent of the person with care and support needs (if they have capacity) or someone else with appropriate authorisation. In doing this, they must ensure compliance with mental capacity and data protection legislation, and the other duties pertaining to information and advice set out in chapter 3 of this guidance.

9.24. As a deferred payment agreement can take some time to set up and agree, it is important that both the local authority and the individual consider any potential issues around mental capacity. Where a person may lack capacity to request a deferred payment, a Deputy or Attorney (a person with a relevant Enduring Power of Attorney or Lasting Power of Attorney) may request a deferred payment on their behalf. If a family member requests a deferred payment and they do not have the legal power to act on behalf of the person, then the person and the family member should receive information and advice on how to obtain this, through Lasting Power of Attorney and Deputyships. Where the local authority is the Deputy for a person, then the local authority Deputy may apply for deferred payments where this is in the best interests of the person. Local authorities must not enter into deferred payment agreements with a person lacking the requisite mental capacity unless the proper arrangements are in place.

9.25. Local authorities and the person applying for a deferred payment (who has capacity) may also want to consider any potential issues around loss of capacity. The local authority should where appropriate provide the person with

---

[1] Not all information about a person's care will necessarily be confidential – so local authorities will need to apply data protection legislation to consider where seeking consent is and is not required.

information and advice on options for deputyship, legal power of attorney and advocacy. If a local authority and the person do discuss the issue, the local authority should confirm what would happen were the person to lose capacity and not have made their own arrangements. Further advice on capacity and financial arrangements is contained in the guidance on debt recovery in Annex D (a deferred payment being effectively a consensually-accruing debt to the local authority).

9.26. If a local authority identifies someone who may benefit from or be eligible for a DPA or a person approaches them for information, the local authority must tell them about the DPA scheme and how it works. This explanation should, at a minimum:

- set out clearly that the fees are being deferred or delayed and must still be paid back at a later date, for example through the sale of the home (potentially after the individual's death);

- explain the types of security that a local authority is prepared to accept (as set out by each local authority in a publicly – available policy; see the section entitled 'Obtaining Security' below for further details);

- explain that if a home is used as security, the home may need to be sold at a later date to repay the amount due;

- explain that the total amount they can defer will be governed by an equity limit (discussed in the section entitled 'How much can be deferred' below) which may change if the value of their security changes;

- explain the circumstances where the LA may cease to defer further amounts (such as when the person qualifies for LA support in paying for their care), and the circumstances where the LA has to stop deferring further amounts (such as when the person reaches their equity limit);

- explain how interest will be charged on any amount deferred;

- explain that they may be liable to pay administrative charges;

- explain what happens on termination of the agreement, how the loan becomes due and their options for repayment;

- explain what happens if they do not repay the amount due;

- set out the criteria governing eligibility for a DPA;

- detail the requirements that must be adhered to during the course of the DPA;

- explain the implications that a deferred payment agreement may have on their income, their benefit entitlements, and charging;

- provide an overview of some potential advantages and disadvantages of taking out a DPA, and explain that there are other options for paying for their care that they may wish to consider;

- note the existence of the 12-week disregard, which will afford those who qualify for it some additional time to consider their options in paying for care; and

779

- suggest that people may want to consider taking independent financial advice (including flagging the existence of regulated financial advice), in line with the guidance set out in chapter three.

9.27. Local authorities should provide easy to read information about how the scheme works. This may be in the form of a standardised information sheet.

9.28. Local authorities must provide this information and advice in formats that ensure compliance with the requirements of the Equality Act 2010 (in particular, they must ensure where appropriate that the information is accessible to the sensory impaired, people with learning disabilities, and people for whom English is not their first language). Further clarifications on information and advice requirements are detailed in chapter 3.

9.29. Where relevant, local authorities should provide information and advice on DPAs at the earliest appropriate opportunity during the period of the 12-week disregard.[1] Local authorities should aim to ensure that people are able to make a smooth transition from the 12- week disregard to the DPA if they opt to enter into an agreement. This means ensuring as far as possible that a DPA is available by the first day of week 13.

9.30. Local authorities should advise people (where appropriate) that they will need to consider how they plan to use, maintain and insure their property if they take out a DPA; that is whether they wish to rent, to prepare for sale, or to leave it vacant for a period. The local authority should advise if it intends to place conditions on how the property is maintained whilst the DPA is in place (authorities will usually include requirements for people to maintain and insure their homes in the terms and conditions of a deferred payment agreement; see the section entitled 'Making the Agreement' for further details).

9.31. Local authorities should develop basic information and advice for home-owners on how they may choose to use their property when they enter care, for example information on how they may go about renting their property, and the potential impact on other people living in the property if a sale is required after their death. They should signpost people to more specialist organisations who can provide further advice on this issue, including information about their legal responsibilities as landlords and their obligations to any potential tenants.

Case study 2

Lucille's son Buster has been providing informal care and support to her, and has heard of the deferred payments scheme. When Lucille decides she may benefit from a home placement, her son suggests they approach her local authority together for information and advice about deferred payment agreements.

Her local authority provides them both with a printed information sheet setting out further details on the authority's deferred payment scheme, and also provides them with contact details of some national and local services who provide financial information and advice

Lucille is interested in renting her property whilst residing in a care home. The local authority has an existing housing advice service, so signposts

---

[1] This refers to the first twelve weeks after entering local authority supported residential care in a care home during which local authorities must disregard the value of a person's home.

Lucille to them for further advice on lettings. The local authority's standard information sheet also includes information on how her rental income may be used to pay for her care and support.

HOW MUCH CAN BE DEFERRED?

9.32. In principle, a person should be able to defer the entirety of their care costs; subject to any contribution the local authority is allowed to require from the person's income. The local authority will need to consider whether a person can provide adequate security for the deferred payment agreement (see next section entitled 'Obtaining Security' – usually this requirement for 'adequate security' will be fulfilled by securing their deferred payment agreement against their property).

9.33. If the person is considering a top-up, the local authority should also consider whether the amount or size of the deferral requested is sustainable given the equity available from their chosen form of security. A discussion of sustainability may be helpful in all cases to ensure the person is aware of how much care their chosen form of security would afford them.

9.34. Three elements will dictate how much a person will defer, each of which is discussed below:

(a) The amount of *equity* a person has available in their chosen form of security (usually their property);

(b) The amount a person is *contributing to their care costs from other sources*, including income and (where they choose to) any contribution from savings, a financial product or a third-party; and

(c) The total *care costs* a person will face, including any top-ups the person might be seeking.

9.35. Local authorities should also satisfy themselves that any top-up they agree to is sufficiently sustainable. Some guidance for local authorities in assessing whether a top-up is sustainable is provided below.

Equity Limit

9.36. When considering the *equity available*, local authorities must be guided by an 'equity limit' for the total amount that can be deferred and ensure that the amount deferred does not rise above this limit. The equity limit will leave some equity remaining in the security used for the DPA – this will both act as a buffer to cover any subsequent interest which continues to accrue, and will provide a small 'cushion' in case of small variations in value of the security. In the majority of cases a property will be used as security, so the equity limit will provide a cushion against changes in house prices. When calculating progress towards the equity limit, the local authority must also include any interest or fees to be deferred.

9.37. If the person intends to secure their deferred payment agreement with a property, local authorities must obtain a valuation of the property. Reasonable property valuation costs are included in the list of administration charges that local authorities can pass on to people, should they wish to do so. People may request an independent assessment of the property's value (in addition to the local authority's valuation). If an independent assessment finds a substantially differing value to the local authority's valuation, the local authority and person should discuss and agree an appropriate valuation prior to proceeding with the agreement.

9.38. Where a property is used as security to offer a deferred payment agreement, the equity limit must be set at the value of the property minus ten percent, minus £14,250 (for financial year 2015/16, this is in line with the lower capital limit) and the amount of encumbrance secured on it. This limit provides some protection to local authorities against changes in the value of the security (such as possible house price fluctuations) and the risk that they may not be able to recoup the full amount owed, but also should mean that people qualify for local authority support if they deplete the equity available in their property (and are consequently not at risk of having to sell their home to pay for care)[1].

9.39. Local authorities should, when someone is approaching or reaches the point at which they have deferred 70% of the value of their chosen security, review the cost of their care with the person, discuss when the person might be eligible for any means tested support, discuss the implications for any top-up they might currently have, and consider jointly whether a deferred payment agreement continues to be the best way for someone to meet these costs.

9.40. The following example illustrates the equity limit principle.

Case study 3: The equity limit
Lucille decides to secure her deferred payment agreement with her house, which is worth £165,000.

The amount of equity available will be the value of the property minus ten percent, minus a further £14,250 (the lower capital limit).
£165,000 – £16,500 - £14,250 = £134,250

Therefore, her 'equity limit' for the total amount she could defer would consequently be £134,250, which would leave £30,750 in equity in her home.

9.41. Local authorities must not allow additional amounts to be deferred beyond the equity limit, and must refuse to defer care costs beyond this (see section above entitled 'permission to refuse'). However, interest can still accrue beyond this point, and administrative charges can still be deferred.

Contributing to care costs from other sources
9.42. A person may meet the costs of their care and support from a combination of any of four primary sources:

- income[2], including pension income;

- savings or other assets they might have access to, this might include any contributions from a third party;

- a financial product designed to pay for long-term care; or

- a deferred payment agreement which enables them to pay for their care at a later date out of assets (usually their home).

---

[1] Annex B of the Charging Guidance (chapter 8), paragraph 14 sub-paragraph A confirms that when assessing the value of a property, this should be less ten percent of the total value (to afford for sale costs), and should take into account only remaining equity in the property.
[2] See chapter eight for definition of income.

9.43. The share of care costs that someone defers will depend on the amount they will be paying from the other sources listed above.

9.44. Local authorities may require a contribution towards care costs from a person's income, but the person has a right to retain a proportion of their income (the 'disposable income allowance'). The disposable income allowance is a fixed amount (up to £144 per week) of a person's income which the local authority must allow the person to retain (if the person wants to retain it). The local authority can require the person to contribute the rest of their income, but must allow the person to retain as much of their disposable income allowance as they want to.

9.45. A person may choose to keep less of their income than the disposable income allowance. This might be advantageous to the person as they would be contributing more to the costs of their care from their income, and consequently reducing the amount they are deferring (and accruing less debt to their local authority overall). However this must be entirely at the individual's decision and the local authority must not compel someone to retain less than the disposable income allowance if the person wants to retain the full amount.

9.46. If a person decides to rent out their property during the course of their DPA, a local authority should permit that person to retain a percentage of any rental income they possess. Local authorities may want to consider whether to offer other incentives to individuals to encourage rental of properties, though the decision as to whether or not to rent a property must be the person's and theirs alone.

9.47. A person may also contribute to their care costs from payments by a third party (including any contributions available from a financial product) or from their savings. Contributing to care costs from another source would be beneficial for a person as it would reduce the amount they are deferring (and hence reduce their overall debt to the local authority). A local authority must not compel a person to contribute to their deferral from these sources.

Case study 4

Lucille identifies a care home placement that meets her care and support needs, costing £540 per week. She has an income provided by her pension of £230 per week. Lucille decides not to rent her home as she intends to sell it within the year.

Based on this provisional estimate of her care costs, Lucille would contribute £86 (230 – 144) per week from her income, and her weekly deferral would be £454.

Care costs

9.48. Before considering in detail how much they will be deferring, a person and usually the local authority should have a rough idea of their *likely care costs* as a result of the care planning process. Someone may wish to vary their care package (or any top-ups they may be considering) following consideration of what they could afford with a deferred payment agreement, but should approach the process with an approximate idea of what their care costs are likely to be.

9.49. In principle, people should be able to defer their full care costs including any top-ups[1] . At a minimum, when local authorities are required to offer a deferred payment agreement they must allow someone to defer their 'core' care costs. To ensure sustainability of the deferral, local authorities have discretion over the amount people are permitted to top- up[2] . Local authorities should consider any request for top-ups, but retain discretion over whether or not to agree to a given top-up. Local authorities should accept any top-up deemed to be reasonable given considerations of affordability, sustainability and available equity. Local authorities should be mindful of the duties set out in relation to top-ups and additional costs in the Care and Support and Aftercare (Choice of Accommodation) regulations 2014.

Sustainability

9.50. When deciding on the amount to be deferred in a discretionary deferred payment agreement (particularly when considering top-ups), both parties should consider a range of factors to satisfy themselves that the arrangement is *sustainable*:

- the likely period the person would want a DPA for (if they intend to use it as a 'bridging loan');

- the equity available;

- the sustainability of a person's contributions from their savings (if they are making one);

- the flexibility to meet future care needs; and

- the period of time a person would be able to defer their care costs for.

9.51. Deferred payment agreements should prevent people from having to sell their home in their lifetime to pay for their care. Local authorities should discuss with the person the projected limit of what their equity could cover, given their projected care costs, and how their care costs might change over time. This may include a discussion of when they are likely to reach any of the income thresholds and may begin to qualify for local authority support in paying for their care. If the person is requesting a top-up, it is important that the local authority discusses what might happen to any top-up requested if the person reaches the equity limit and moves on to local authority support in paying for their care, and ensures that a written agreement is in place (see Annex A: Choice of accommodation and additional payments). In particular, the local authority should make the person aware that once they have reached the equity limit, the local authority may not be willing to fund their top-up, and the person may need to find other ways to pay for it or be prepared for a change in their care package.

9.52. Local authorities and individuals should also consider the length of time that a person's intended contribution to care costs from savings would last, if they intend to contribute to their care costs from their savings. This should include

---

[1] Subject to any contribution from a person's income, as discussed above.

[2] As deferred payment agreements with top-up elements would fall under local authorities' discretionary powers, local authorities also retain broader overarching discretion as to whether to enter into any agreement involving a top-up.

consideration of the impact on their care if a person's savings are depleted (normally this would involve increasing the amount the person is deferring).

9.53. An important factor in the sustainability of a deferred payment agreement will be any *future care and support needs* someone might face, and local authorities and people should consider allowing flexibility for changes in circumstance, including possible escalations of needs, when deciding how much someone should defer. Local authorities and people should factor any potential changes in circumstances into their considerations of sustainability.

9.54. The Department will develop a tool to aid local authorities in assessing sustainability. Local authorities may use this tool to aid discussions and decisions about the amount to be deferred, but local authorities retain final responsibility for (and have discretion over) decisions taken about the agreements they enter into.

9.55. When agreement has been reached between a person and the local authority as to how much they want to defer, the local authority must ensure this is clearly and unambiguously set out in the deferred payment agreement. Further details on what happens once an amount has been agreed are set out in the section entitled 'making the agreement' below, and a model deferred payment agreement co-produced by the Department of Health and the sector is also available.

9.56. The amount being deferred should be reviewed on a regular basis to ensure the deferred amount does not exceed the equity limit as discussed above[1] . Local authorities should have particular regard to the amount deferred as it approaches the equity limit.

9.57. Further details of local authorities' responsibilities during the course of the DPA are set out in the relevant section below.

Case study 5

Lucille discusses her care home fees with the local authority. Based on the equity available in her home (£134,250, as set out in Case study 3 above), Lucille could afford her weekly deferral of £454 for around five years. Given an average length of stay in a care home care of 19.7 months (source: BUPA 2010, cited in Laing and Buisson 2012/13), the local authority deems her projected care costs to be sustainable.

Lucille enquires as to the cost of a room with a garden view. This would increase her weekly deferral to £525 which she could afford for around four and a half years. The local authority deems this to be sustainable, so agrees to Lucille's requested top-up.

OBTAINING SECURITY

9.58. A local authority must have adequate security in place when entering into a deferred payment agreement. The regulations set out one form of security that local authorities must accept, and also provide wider discretion for local authorities to accept other forms of security as they see fit. Local authorities should consider whether another type of security could be provided if a person cannot secure their deferred payment agreement with a charge on a property.

9.59. One form of 'adequate security' would be the local authority securing a first legal mortgage charge against a property on the Land Register. Local

---

[1] Annually may suffice, or more frequently if needs change or the value of the person's security changes substantially.

authorities must accept a first legal mortgage charge as adequate security and local authorities must offer a deferred payment to someone who meets the eligibility criteria for the scheme where the local authority is able to secure a first legal mortgage charge on the property.

9.60. In cases where an agreement is to be secured with a jointly-owned property, local authorities must seek both owners' consent (and agreement) to a charge being placed on the property. Both owners will need to be signatories to the charge agreement, and the co-owner will need to agree not to object to the sale of the property for the purpose of repaying the debt due to the local authority (following the same procedure as in the case where an individual is the sole owner of a property).

9.61. The local authority must obtain similar consent to a charge being created against the property from any other person who has a beneficial interest in the property.

9.62. Under the discretionary scheme, local authorities have discretion to decide what else may constitute 'adequate security' for a deferred payment agreement, in cases where a first charge cannot be secured. A local authority's decision should be based on an explicit and publicly-accessible policy of what other types of security they are willing to consider in addition to a first charge, but local authorities may consider the merits of each case individually. Other forms of security a local authority may choose to consider include (but are not limited to):

- a third-party guarantor – subject to the guarantor having / offering an appropriate form of security;

- a solicitor's undertaking letter;

- a valuable object such as a painting or other piece of art; or

- an agreement to repay the amount deferred from the proceeds of a life assurance policy.

9.63. A local authority has full discretion in individual cases to refuse a deferred payment agreement if it is not satisfied that adequate security is in place[1].

9.64. The security should also be revalued when the amount deferred equals or exceeds 50% of the value of the security to assess any potential change in the value (and consequently the person's 'equity limit' should be reassessed in turn). After this revaluation, local authorities should revalue the security periodically to monitor any potential further changes in value. If in either case there has been any substantial change the local authority should review the amount being deferred as well, as set out in the section "how much can be deferred" above.

INTEREST RATE AND ADMINISTRATION CHARGE

9.65. The deferred payment agreement scheme is intended to be run on a cost-neutral basis, with local authorities able to recoup the costs associated with deferring fees by charging interest. Local authorities can also recoup the administrative costs associated with DPAs, including legal and ongoing running costs, via administration charges which can be passed on to the individual. Administration charges and interest can be added on to the total amount deferred as they are accrued, although a person may request to pay these separately if they

---

[1] With the exception of an agreement that a local authority is required to enter into where a person meets the eligibility criteria and the authority can secure a first legal mortgage charge.

choose. The agreement must make clear that all fees deferred, alongside any interest and administrative charges incurred, must be repaid by the person in full. The local authority must also notify the individual in writing whenever they are liable for an administration charge.

9.66. Local authorities will have the ability to charge interest on any amount deferred, including any administration charge deferred. This is to cover the cost of lending and the risks to local authorities associated with lending, for example the risk of default. Where local authorities charge interest this must not exceed the maximum amount specified in regulations. A local authority may (but is not required to) charge the nationally-set maximum interest rate. The same interest rate must be charged on all deferred payments within a local authority[1] .

9.67. The national maximum interest rate will change every six months on 1st January and 1st June to track the market gilts rate specified in the most recently published report by the Office of Budget Responsibility. This is currently published in the Economic and Fiscal Outlook, which is usually published twice-yearly alongside the Budget and Autumn Statement. Local authorities must ensure that any changes to the national maximum rate are reflected within their authority and are applied to any agreements they have entered into (unless they are already charging less than the national maximum). Individual agreements must also contain adequate terms and conditions to ensure that the interest rate within any given agreement does not exceed the nationally-set maximum.

9.68. In extremely rare circumstances (such as a severe economic shock), Government may need to make new regulations to change the maximum interest rate which local authorities are permitted to charge before the next 1 January/1 June change date. These powers would only be exercised as a last resort.

9.69. Local authorities must inform people before they make the agreement if interest will be charged, what interest rates are currently set at, and when interest rates are likely to change. This is to enable people to make well-informed decisions about whether a deferred payment agreement is the best way for them to meet the costs of their care.

9.70. The interest charged and added to the deferred amount will be compounded, and local authorities should ensure when making the agreement that individuals understand that interest will accrue on a compound basis.

9.71. Interest can accrue on the amount deferred even once someone has reached the 'equity limit' (see 'how much can be deferred' above). It can also accrue after someone has died up until the point at which the deferred amount is repaid to the local authority. If the local authority cannot recover the debt and seeks to pursue this through the County Court system (as discussed in Annex D on debt recovery), the local authority may charge the higher County Court rate of interest.

9.72. Local authorities must set their administration charge at a reasonable level, and this level must not be more than the actual costs incurred by the local authority in provision of the Universal Deferred Payment Scheme, as set out in regulations. Relevant costs may include (but are not limited to) the costs incurred by a local authority whilst:

---

[1] When a local authority is reclaiming an outstanding amount due to it via debt recovery powers and the County Court system, the local authority may charge the higher County Court rate of interest.

- registering a legal charge with the Land Registry against the title of the property, including Land Registry search charges and any identity checks required;

- undertaking relevant postage, printing and telecommunications;

- costs of time spent by those providing the service;

- cost of valuation and re-valuation of the property;

- costs for removal of charges against property;

- overheads, including where appropriate (shares of) payroll, audit, management costs, legal service.

9.73. Local authorities should maintain a publicly-available list of administration charges that a person may be liable to pay. It is good practice to separate charges into a fixed set-up fee for deferred payment agreements, reflective of the costs incurred by the local authority in setting up and securing a typical deferred payment agreement, and other reasonable one-time fees during the course of the agreement (reflecting actual charges incurred in the course of the agreement).

MAKING THE AGREEMENT
9.74. Where someone chooses to enter into a deferred payment agreement, local authorities should aim to have the agreement finalised and in place by the end of the 12-week disregard period (where applicable) (see Annex B: Treatment of capital), or within 12 weeks of the person approaching the local authority regarding DPAs in other circumstances.

9.75. Decisions on a person's care and support package, the amount they intend to defer, the security they intend to use and the terms of the agreement should only be taken following discussion between the local authority and the individual. Once agreement in principle has been reached between the local authority and the person, it is the local authority's responsibility to transpose the details agreed into a deferred payment agreement, taking the legal form of a contract between the local authority and the person.

9.76. The local authority should provide a hardcopy of the deferred payment agreement to the person, and they should be provided with reasonable time to read and consider the agreement, including time for the individual to query any clauses and discuss the agreement further with the local authority.

9.77. The agreement must clearly set out all terms, conditions and information necessary to enable the person to ascertain his or her rights and obligations under the agreement. These include:
  (a) terms to explain how the interest will be calculated and that it will be compounded if it is to be added to the deferred amount;
  (b) information as to administrative costs the individual might be liable for;
  (c) terms to explain how the adult may exercise his or her right to terminate the agreement, which should explain the process for and consequences of terminating the agreement and specify what notice should be given (see the section entitled 'terminating the agreement' below);
  (d) terms to explain the circumstances in which the local authority might refuse to defer further fees (either when it is required to stop deferring, for example if the person has already deferred up to their 'equity limit', or when it has

powers to stop deferring, such as when a person qualifies for local authority support in paying for their care; as set out in the 'how much can be deferred' and 'permission to refuse' sections above);

(e) that the local authority will secure their debt either by placing a legal (Land Registry) charge against the property, or by some other means specified;

(f) a term requiring the local authority to provide the person with a written statement every six months and within 28 days of request by the person, setting out how much the person owes to the authority and the cost to them of repaying the debt;

(g) a term which explains that the maximum amount which may be deferred is the equity limit and that this is likely to vary over time;

(h) a term which requires the local authority to give the adult 30 days written notice of the date on which they are likely to reach the equity limit;

(i) a term which requires the adult to obtain the consent of the local authority for any person to occupy the property; and

(j) an explanation that the local authority will stop deferring its charges and making advances under a loan agreement if the person no longer receives care and support in a care home or supported living accommodation or if the local authority no longer considers that the adult's needs should be met in such accommodation.

9.78. If the agreement is not for the deferral of charges due to the authority (a 'loan'-style agreement), the agreement must also contain:

(a) a term to make clear that the authority will make advances of the loan to the adult in instalments;

(b) a term to make clear that the purpose of the loan is to pay for costs of care and support in a care home or supported living accommodation. This should explain –

- the consequences of any failure by the adult to pay those costs of care and support; and

- that the adult must inform the local authority if he or she no longer receives or intends to receive care in such accommodation.

9.79. The agreement should also stipulate:

(a) the value of any accrued or possible administrative charges, and where possible a breakdown of their calculation;

(b) the means of redress if either party feels the other has broken the terms of the agreement;

(c) the person's responsibilities regarding maintenance and insurance of their home;

(d) the person's responsibility to notify the local authority of any change to their income, home or care and support;

(e) the person's responsibility to notify the local authority if they intend to rent or sell their property and if someone has gained or may gain a beneficial interest in their property;

(f) the local authority's responsibility to give the person 30 days written notice if it intends to cease to defer charges (or make loan instalments) under the agreement

(g) a clear explanation of the consequences of taking out a DPA for the person and their property, including anybody who may reside in the property;

(h) the equity limit of their security (as discussed above in the section entitled 'how much can be deferred') and the scope for this to change upon revaluation of the security used for the DPA;

(i) the process for varying any part of the agreement; and

(j) the process by which the local authority can require a re-valuation of a person's chosen form of security.

9.80. Local authorities should ensure at a minimum that people sign or clearly and verifiably affirm they have received adequate information on options for paying for their care, that they understand how the DPA works and understand the agreement they are entering into; and that they have had the opportunity to ask questions about the contract. A term reflecting this should be included in the agreement itself.

9.81. Local authorities will need to consider whether the deferred payment agreements they enter into are regulated credit agreements to which the Consumer Credit Act 1974 (CCA) and Financial Services and Markets Act 2000 (FSMA) apply.

9.82. The scope of 'regulated credit agreements' is set out in article 60B of the Financial Services and Markets Act 2000 (Regulated Activities) Order 2001 ('the RAO'). A credit agreement is regulated unless exempt, and there are a number of exemptions in articles 60C to 60H of the RAO. It is likely that most DPAs will fall within such an exemption. If the agreement is regulated, it will need to comply with all applicable requirements of the CCA. In addition, the local authority will need a relevant permission from the Financial Conduct Authority (FCA), and to comply with the FCA's rules and principles, unless the exclusion in article 72G of the RAO applies (if the credit agreement is within the scope of the Consumer Credit Directive FCA authorisation is required).

9.83. All deferred payment agreements will be subject to the Unfair Terms in Consumer Contracts Regulations 1999, so the terms will have to be written in plain, intelligible English and will not be binding if they are unfair to the borrowers. Local authorities will also have to ensure that they do not contravene the Consumer Protection from Unfair Trading Regulations 2008.

9.84. Under Section 79 of the Care Act, local authorities may delegate responsibility for deferred payment agreements to another body. This could potentially allow a number of local authorities to combine their collective resources and offer a regional solution tailored to the local conditions and the administrative burden they face. If a local authority chooses to exercise their powers for delegation, the local authority must satisfy itself that the body taking on responsibility for DPAs is complying with all appropriate regulations and guidance (including but not limited to those governing deferred payments). Any and all duties in this guidance document, in the regulations and in the relevant sections of the Care Act apply equally to any delegated authority as they do to local authorities. The local authority should also seek feedback from people entering into DPAs to satisfy themselves that the service being provided meets the standards expected of the local authority. In the case of delegation of responsibility, the local authority remains ultimately responsible for (and liable for) the DPA.

THE LOCAL AUTHORITY'S RESPONSIBILITIES WHILST THE AGREEMENT IS IN PLACE

9.85. Local authorities must at a minimum provide people with six-monthly written updates of the amount of fees deferred, of interest and administrative charges accrued to date, and of the total amount due and the equity remaining in the home (the 'equity limit' discussed in the section entitled at 'how much can be deferred' above). Local authorities should also provide the person with a statement on request within 28 days. Local authorities may provide updates on a more frequent basis at their discretion. The update should set out the amount deferred during the previous period, alongside the total amount deferred to date, and should also include a projection of how quickly someone would deplete all equity remaining in their chosen form of security up to their equity limit.

9.86. Local authorities should reassess the value of the chosen form of security once the amount deferred exceeds 50% of the security (and periodically thereafter), and adjust the equity limit and review the amount deferred if the value has changed.

9.87. Local authorities may offer people a way to check their statement at any point in the year via an online facility.

9.88. Local authorities may choose to develop advice and guidance around maintaining a home, renting, and income. Local authorities may also offer services/ products to help the person meet the requirements for maintenance and insurance, but cannot compel a person to take on their product. Local authorities must accept reasonable alternative maintenance and insurance services.

Case study 6:

For illustrative purposes we have used an interest rate of 3.5%.

After six months, Lucille receives her first statement. It confirms she has deferred a total of £13,900, including £110 in interest and £100 in administration fees.

At this point, the local authority revalues her property, and finds its value has increased to £170,000. Based on the amount deferred and her care costs, her equity would afford her just over four and a half more years' care at this price.

CONTRACTUAL RESPONSIBILITIES ON THE INDIVIDUAL WHILST THE AGREEMENT IS IN PLACE

9.89. The deferred payment agreement sets out various contractual requirements on the individual as well as on the local authority. These are set out briefly in sections above, but the person's consequent responsibilities are recapped in more detail in the paragraphs below.

9.90. If the local authority is exercising its right to require the adult to make a contribution from income, it should include in the legal agreement provisions requiring the person to notify the local authority of any changes in their income.

9.91. The agreement should also contain provisions requiring the adult to notify the authority of changes in their need for care and support, if those changes are ones which will mean that the authority must or is entitled to stop making further instalments under the agreement or to alter the amount of the instalments.

9.92. Similarly if the agreement has been entered into on the basis that the adult's property has not been disregarded for the purposes of the financial assessment in section 17 and it is a term of the agreement that the local authority will cease making or reduce the amount of instalments it makes, the agreement should require the person to inform the authority of changes which mean that the property may be disregarded.

9.93. The local authority should include in a contract provisions requiring someone to ensure that appropriate arrangements are in place to maintain their home whilst they are in care. In particular, the contract should require that their home is maintained adequately, and require someone to have in place an arrangement for regular maintenance to take place. Local authorities should also require the person to have adequate insurance for their property. If their home is to be left empty for an extended period of time, the person will need to ensure their insurance covers this adequately and that any terms required by the insurer are met.

9.94. The local authority must include in a contract provisions which require the person to obtain the authority's consent before allowing someone to move into the property after the agreement has been made. In these circumstances, the local authority may (if it is reasonable to do so) require written consent from the person which places the debt owed to the local authority above any beneficial interest they may accrue in the property.

TERMINATION OF AGREEMENT

9.95. A deferred payment agreement can be terminated in three ways:

(a) at any time by the individual, or someone acting on their behalf, by repaying the full amount due (this can happen during a person's lifetime or when the agreement is terminated through the DPA holder's death);

(b) when the property (or form of security) is sold and the authority is repaid;[1] or

(c) when the person dies and the amount is repaid to the LA from their estate.

9.96. All three scenarios for the termination of the agreement are discussed below, alongside the various options for repayment. On termination, the full amount due (including care costs, any interest accrued and any administrative or legal fees charged) must be paid to the local authority.

9.97. If a *person decides sell their home*, they should notify the local authority during the sale process. They will be required to pay the amount due to the local authority from the proceeds of the sale, and the local authority will be required to relinquish the charge on their property.

9.98. A person may decide *to repay the amount due to the local authority from another source, or a third party may elect to repay the amount due on behalf of the individual*. In either case, the local authority should be notified of the person's/the third party's intention in writing, and the local authority must relinquish the charge on the property on receipt of the full amount due.

9.99. If the deferred payment is *terminated due to the person's death*, the amount due to the local authority must be either paid out of the estate or paid by a third party. A person's family or a third party may wish to settle the debt to the local authority by other means of repayment (as may be the case if the family wanted to avoid having to sell the property or means of security), and the local authority must accept an alternative means of payment in this case, provided this payment covers the full amount due to the local authority.

---

[1] In the case that a DPA is agreed on the basis of a form of security other than property, local authorities will need to make provision in the agreement for conclusion of the DPA in the event that the given security is disposed of/comes to fruition.

9. Deferred payment agreements

9.100. The executor of the will or Administrator of the Estate can decide how the amount due is to be paid; either from the person's estate (usually via the sale of the house or potentially via a life assurance policy) or from a third party source.

9.101. A local authority should wait at least two weeks following the person's death before approaching the executor with a full breakdown of the total amount deferred (but a family member or the executor can approach the local authority to resolve the outstanding amount due prior to this point).

9.102. Responsibility for arranging for repayment of the amount due (in the case of payment from the estate) falls to the executor of the will.

9.103. Interest will continue to accrue on the amount owed to the local authority after the individual's death and until the amount due to the local authority is repaid in full.

9.104. If terminated through a person's death, the amount owed to a local authority under a deferred payment agreement falls due 90 days after the person has died. After this 90 day period, if a local authority concludes active steps to repay the debt are not being taken, for example if the sale is not progressing and a local authority has actively sought to resolve the situation (or the local authority concludes the executor is wilfully obstructing sale of the property), the local authority may enter into legal proceedings to reclaim the amount due to it. Further information on debt recovery is included at Annex D of this guidance.

9.105. In whichever circumstance an agreement is terminated, the full amount due to the local authority must be repaid to cover all costs accrued under the agreement, and the person (and/or the third party where appropriate) must be provided with a full breakdown of how the amount due has been calculated. Once the amount has been paid, the local authority should provide the individual with confirmation that the agreement has been concluded, and confirm (where appropriate) that the charge against the property has been removed.

10. CARE AND SUPPORT PLANNING

This chapter provides guidance on sections 24 and 25 of the Care Act 2014.

This chapter covers:
- When to undertake care and support planning;
- What it means to "meet needs", and considerations in deciding how to meet needs;
- How to undertake care and support planning, and support planning;
- Production of the plan;
- Involving the person;
- Authorising others (including the person) to prepare the plan;
- Care planning for people who lack capacity;
- Minimising and authorising a deprivation of liberty (DOL) for people who lack capacity;
- Combining plans;
- Sign-off and assurance;
- Protecting property of adults being cared for away from home.

10.1. Care and support should put people in control of their care, with the support that they need to enhance their wellbeing and improve their connections to family, friends and community. A vital part of this process for people with ongoing needs which the local authority is going to meet is the care and support plan or support plan in the case of carers (henceforth referred to as 'the plan').

10.2. The person must be genuinely involved and influential throughout the planning process, and should be given every opportunity to take joint ownership of the development of the plan with the local authority if they wish, and the local authority agrees. There should be a default assumption that the person, with support if necessary, will play a strong pro-active role in planning if they choose to. Indeed, it should be made clear that the plan 'belongs' to the person it is intended for, with the local authority role to ensure the production and sign-off of the plan to ensure that it is appropriate to meet the identified needs.

10.3. The personal budget in the plan will give everyone clear information regarding the costs of their care and support and the amount that the local authority will make available, in order to help people to make better informed decisions as to how needs will be met. The ability to meet needs by taking a direct payment must be clearly explained to the person in a way that works best for them, so that they can make an informed decision about the level of choice and control they wish to take over their care and support. This should mean offering the choice more than once in the process and enabling that choice by providing examples of how others have used direct payments, including via direct peer support, for example from user-led organisations.

10.4. Some people will need assistance to make plans and decisions, and to be involved in the planning process. The modern care and support system should routinely enable supported decision making, where options and choices are presented simply and clearly. Independent advocates (if used) must be instructed early in the assessment and planning process for those who have substantial difficulty in engaging with the care system, and have no other means of accessing appropriate support through friends or relatives to facilitate their involvement. If the person's substantial difficulty only becomes apparent during the assessment, an advocate must be instructed as soon as this becomes known.[1]

10.5. Ultimately, the guiding principle in the development of the plan is that this process should be person-centred and person-led, in order to meet the needs and outcomes of the person intended in ways that work best for them as an individual or as part of a family. Both the process and the outcome should be built holistically around people's wishes and feelings, their needs, values and aspirations, irrespective of the extent to which they choose or are able to actively direct the process.

DEFINITIONS

10.6. This chapter applies to people in need of care and support and carers equally, unless specifically stated. It should be read in conjunction with the other chapters in this section (personal budgets, direct payments and review of care plans).

10.7. This chapter (and subsequent chapters in the section of 'Person Centred Care and Support Planning') applies to everyone whose needs are being met by the local authority, regardless of the setting in which the needs are met. For example, people in care homes must also receive a care and support plan and personal budget.

10.8. For the purposes of this chapter 'the plan' means either the care and support plan (in the case of adults with care and support needs) or the support plan (in the case of carers).

WHEN TO UNDERTAKE CARE AND SUPPORT PLANNING, AND SUPPORT PLANNING

10.9. Following the needs and carer's assessment and determination of eligibility (see chapter 6), a plan must be provided where a local authority is required to meet needs under section 18 or 20(1) of the Care Act, or decides to meet needs under section 19(1) or (2) and 20(6) of the Act. Where a local authority is required to meet needs under section 117 of the Mental Health Act 1983 this chapter should be read in conjunction with chapter 34 of the "Mental Health Act 1983 Code of Practice"[2] (on the Care Programme Approach) and "Refocusing the Care Programme Approach".[3]

WHAT DOES IT MEAN TO "MEET NEEDS"?

10.10. 'Meeting needs' is an important concept under the Act and moves away from the previous terminology of 'providing services'. This provides a greater variety of approach in how needs can be met, developed through care and support planning as described in this chapter. The concept of "meeting needs" is intended to be broader than a duty to provide or arrange a particular service. Because a person's needs are specific to them, there are many ways in which their needs can be met. The intention behind the legislation is to encourage this diversity, rather than point to a service or solution that may be neither what is best nor what the person wants. The purpose of the care and support planning process is to agree how a person's needs should be met, and therefore how the local authority will discharge its duty, or its power, to do so.

---

[1] See Ch.7
[2] "Mental Health Act 1983 Code of Practice" (Department of Health, 2014).
[3] "Refocusing the Care Programme Approach" (Department of Health, 2008).

10.11. There are a number of broad options for how needs could be met, and the use of one or more of these will depend on the circumstances. Section 8(2) of the Act gives some examples of ways of meeting needs, and would cover:

- the local authority directly providing some type of support, for example by providing a reablement or short-term respite service;

- the local authority arranging for a care and support provider to provide some type of support, for example by commissioning or contracting with a provider;

- making a direct payment, which allows the person to purchase their own care and support; or

- some combination of the above, for example the local authority arranging a homecare service whilst also providing a direct payment to meet other needs.

10.12. Where the local authority provides or arranges for care and support, the type of support may itself take many forms. These may include more traditional "service" options, such as care homes or home care, but may also include other types of support such as assistive technology in the home or equipment/adaptations, and approaches to meeting needs should be inclusive of less intensive or service-focused options.

10.13. Needs may be met through types of care and support which are available universally, including those which are not directly provided by the local authority. For example, in some cases needs could be met by a service which is also made available as part of a local authority's plans for preventing or reducing needs for care and support (under Section 2 of the Act). Needs could also be met, for example, by putting a person in contact with a local community group or voluntary sector organisation.

10.14. The examples of how needs can be met listed in the Act are not exhaustive, but cover the most common means of meeting needs. In addition, there are other methods which may be suitable for meeting a person's needs, for example by arranging an individual service fund (see chapter 11 on personal budgets which also includes detail on individual service funds). This is a budget held by a provider, rather than by the local authority or the individual. The local authority makes a payment to the provider, which then holds a budget over which the individual has control.

10.15. The local authority may also consider whether it can effectively meet a person's needs by "brokering" a service on behalf of an individual in certain cases. "Brokering" services are commonly offered by organisations which are independent of the local authority, and may be accessed by any person wishing to find care. However, the local authority may also provide such support where it meets a person's needs. "Brokering" would involve the local authority supporting an individual to make a choice about the provider of their care, and to enter into a contract with that provider. The local authority would not need to hold the contract with the provider, but would be required to assure itself that the chosen provider and terms of the contract were appropriate to meet the person's needs.

10.16. The local authority would remain under the duty to meet a person's eligible needs, and so would need to be satisfied both that this was an effective way of meeting those needs, and that the person was in agreement to this approach being used. It is likely that "brokering" would only be an effective way of meeting a person's needs in exceptional circumstances, for example where a person is fully funding their own care and wishes to retain control of the contract with their provider, but wants the local authority to meet their needs (under Section 18(3) of the Act). If there is a risk that a person's needs would not be met effectively by means of "brokering", the local authority should discount it as an option and proceed with other ways of meeting that person's needs, such as direct commissioning of services from a provider.

10.17. In considering such an option, the local authority should also have regard to the likelihood of the person continuing to be willing and able to manage such arrangements in the future, including their ability to pay the charges due (e.g. to mitigate against a future loss of capacity or disposal of their assets, such that the local authority may be required to take over the contract with the provider). The local authority would continue to support the person in meeting any other needs, offer ongoing support and keep the arrangements under review to ensure that the needs were met. The person would have a care and support plan as usual.

10.18. The individual's position in this approach would be in some respects akin to a person who had taken a direct payment to commission their own services, in that they would hold their own contract with a provider whilst the local authority is under a duty to meet their needs.

10.19. The difference would be that in the case of a direct payment, the money for commissioning the service comes from the local authority, whereas in the case of "brokering" it comes from the individual directly. This option, therefore, would only likely be of use for meeting the needs of people who are fully funding their own care but ask the local authority to meet their eligible needs, and who are not using alternative arrangements such as an individual service fund.

CONSIDERATIONS IN MEETING NEEDS

10.20. However the local authority is meeting needs, the principles in this chapter should be followed, such as ensuring the process is person-centred, and involving and taking all reasonable steps to agree the plan with the person.

10.21. The local authority must take into consideration the individual's preferences. The authority should consider the person's goals in approaching the authority for support, and the level or nature of support desired. Where the person wishes to take more control over their own care and support, this should be reflected in the route taken. Similarly, where the person asks for more local authority support (e.g. because they lack the skills or confidence to engage with the provider market), the authority should respond accordingly in the decision taken about how needs will be met.

Relationship with other services

10.22. Local authorities should also have regard to how needs may be met beyond the provision, or arrangement, of services by the authority. A person may already be in receipt of care and support which meets their needs (whether self-funded and arranged or not). For example, needs may be met by a carer, in an educational establishment or by another institution other than the local authority. In these circumstances the local authority, whilst remaining under a duty to meet the person's eligible needs, may not in practical terms have to arrange or provide any services to comply with that duty as long as the alternative means of meeting the needs is in place and the authority is satisfied that this alternative means is, in fact, meeting the person's eligible needs. However, the local authority should nonetheless record those needs through the assessment process, determine whether the needs meet the eligibility criteria and keep under review whether the authority needs to do anything in order to comply with its duty to meet the person's eligible needs (for example, if the alternative services being provided to meet the needs cease or the authority is no longer satisfied that the alternative services adequately meet the person's needs).

10.23. Sections 21 to 23 of the Act set out the limitations on the circumstances in which local authorities may meet care and support needs. In particular, they make clear that local authorities must not meet needs by providing or arranging any health service or facility which is required to be provided by the NHS, or doing anything under the Housing Act 1996. The aim of these provisions is to avoid duplication in the provision of services and facilities, and provide clarity about the limits of care and support, and the circumstances in which care and support should be provided as opposed to health services or housing services (or vice versa).

10.24. There may be other services to which a person is entitled under other legislation (but which could also be provided as part of the provision of care and support), which a local authority is not specifically prohibited from providing under the Act. Where there is a risk of overlapping entitlements (i.e. where two different organisations may be under a duty to provide a service in relation to the same needs), local authorities should take steps to support the individual to access the support to which they are entitled under other legislation. This may include, for example, helping the person to access some disability-related benefits and allowances. It may also include working with the housing authority to ensure that there is a clear process in place for access to disabled facilities grants to avoid the risk of duplication of work in meeting the same needs.

10.25. The duty to meet eligible needs is not discharged just because a person has another entitlement to a different service which could meet those needs, but which they are not availing themselves of. The needs remain 'unmet' (and so the local authority under a duty to meet them) until those needs are actually met by the relevant service bring provided or arranged. Local authorities should therefore consider how to inform and advise people on accessing any such entitlements at the earliest stage possible, as well as working collaboratively with other local services to share information.

Needs met by a carer

10.26. Local authorities are not under a duty to meet any needs that are being met by a carer. The local authority must identify, during the assessment process, those needs which are being met by a carer at that time, and determine whether those needs would be eligible. But any eligible needs met by a carer are not required to be met by the local authority, for so long as the carer continues to do so. The local authority should record in the care and support plan which needs are being met by a carer, and should consider putting in place plans to respond to any breakdown in the caring relationship.

Other considerations

10.27. In determining how to meet needs, the local authority may also take into reasonable consideration its own finances and budgetary position, and must comply with its related public law duties. This includes the importance of ensuring that the funding available to the local authority is sufficient to meet the needs of the entire local population. The local authority may reasonably consider how to balance that requirement with the duty to meet the eligible needs of an individual in determining *how* an individual's needs should be met (but not *whether* those needs are met). However, the local authority should not set arbitrary upper limits on the costs it is willing to pay to meet needs through certain routes – doing so would not deliver an approach that is person-centred or compatible with public law principles. The authority may take decisions on a case-by-case basis which weigh up the total costs of different potential options for meeting needs, and include the cost as a relevant factor in deciding between suitable alternative options for meeting needs. This does not mean choosing the cheapest option; but the one which delivers the outcomes desired for the best value.

NON-ELIGIBLE NEEDS

10.28. Where the local authority is not required to meet needs, it nonetheless may use its powers to meet any other needs. This may include, for example, meeting needs which are not "eligible" (i.e. those which do not meet the eligibility criteria), or meeting eligible needs in circumstances where the duty does not apply (for example, where the person is ordinarily resident in another area). Where the local authority exercises such a power to meet other needs, the same duties would apply regarding the next steps, and therefore a plan must be provided.

10.29. If the local authority decides not to use its powers to meet other needs, it must give the person written explanation for taking this decision, and should give a copy to their advocate if the person requests. If the person cannot request this, then a copy should be given to the person's advocate or appropriate individual if this in the best interests of the person. This explanation must also include information and advice on how the person can reduce or delay their needs in future. This should be personal and specific advice based on the person's needs assessment and not a generalised reference to prevention services or signpost to a general web-site. For example, this should involve consideration of alternative ways in which a person could reduce or delay their care and support needs, including signposting to support within the local community. Authorities may choose to provide this information after the eligibility determination, in which case this need not be repeated again. At whatever stage this is done, in all cases the person must be given a written explanation of why their needs are not being met. The explanation provided to the person must be personal to and should be accessible for the person.

10.30. Where a local authority is meeting some needs, but not others, a combination of the two approaches above must be followed. The person must receive a care and support plan for the needs the local authority is required, or decides to meet that accords to the Act and this guidance, and which also includes a tailored package of information and advice on how to delay and/or prevent the needs the local authority is not meeting. This information should be given to the person in a format accessible to them so they are clear what needs are being met by the local authority.

HOW TO UNDERTAKE CARE AND SUPPORT PLANNING, AND SUPPORT PLANNING

10.31. The plan must detail the needs to be met and how the needs will be met, and will link back to the outcomes that the adult wishes to achieve in day-to-day life as identified in the assessment process and to the wellbeing principle in the Act. This should reflect the individual's wishes, their needs and aspirations, and what is important to and for them, where this is reasonable.[1] This process is central to the provision of person-centred care and support that provides people with choice and control over how to meet their needs. The local authority should encourage creativity in planning how to meet needs, and refrain from judging unusual decisions as long as these are determined to meet needs in a reasonable way.

10.32. The guiding principle therefore is that the person be actively involved and is given every opportunity to influence the planning and subsequent content of the plan in conjunction with the local authority, with support if needed. Joint planning does not mean a 50:50 split; the person can take a bigger share of the planning where this is appropriate and the person wishes to do so. A further principle is that planning should be proportionate. The person should not be required to go through lengthy processes which limit their ability to be actively involved, unless there are very strong reasons to add in elements of process and decision-making. Wherever possible the person should be able to be fully involved in the development of their plan, and any revision if circumstances change, with minimum process.

PRODUCTION OF THE PLAN

10.33. The plan should be person-centred, with an emphasis on the individual having every reasonable opportunity to be involved in the planning to the extent that they choose and are able. This requires the local authority to ensure that information is available in a way that is meaningful to the person, and that they have support and time to consider their options. A named contact or lead professional should be considered both as part of care planning, and in the final plan, so that the person knows how to contact the local authority. The planning choices offered should range from support for the person, to jointly develop their plan with the local authority alone or with their family, friends or whoever they may wish to involve (this might include web-based resources, written information and peer support), through to one-to-one support from a paid professional, such as a social worker which may be the same person who undertook the assessment.

10.34. Where the person has substantial difficulty in being actively involved with the planning process, and they have no family and friends who are able to facilitate the person's involvement in the plan, the local authority must provide an independent advocate to represent and support the person to facilitate their involvement (see chapter 7). Likewise, where a person with specific expertise or training in a particular condition (for example, deafblindness) has carried out the assessment, someone with similar knowledge (and preferably the same person to ensure continuity) should also be involved in production of the plan.

---

[1] Reasonableness is to be agreed during care planning, and should take into account what is possible using the indicative personal budget as a guide (see chapter 11). However, this does not prevent the plan from detailing wider aspirations and wishes that may not form the person's eligible needs which the local authority is required to meet, but nonetheless are still important to the person.

10.35. In ensuring that the process is person-centred, the local authority should ensure that any staff responsible for developing the plan with the person are trained in the Mental Capacity Act if appropriate, familiar with best practice, and that there is sufficient local availability of independent advocacy and peer support, including access to social work advice.

10.36. When developing the plan, there are certain elements that must always be incorporated in the final plan, [unless excluded by the Care and Support (Personal Budget Exclusion of Costs) Regulations 2014]. These are:

- the needs identified by the assessment;

- whether, and to what extent, the needs meet the eligibility criteria;

- the needs that the authority is going to meet, and how it intends to do so;

- for a person needing care, for which of the desired outcomes care and support could be relevant;

- for a carer, the outcomes the carer wishes to achieve, and their wishes around providing care, work, education and recreation where support could be relevant;

- the personal budget (see chapter 11);

- information and advice on what can be done to reduce the needs in question, and to prevent or delay the development of needs in the future;

- where needs are being met via a direct payment (see chapter 12), the needs to be met via the direct payment and the amount and frequency of the payments.

10.37. These requirements should not encourage lengthy process where this is not necessary, or fixed decisions that cannot be changed easily. The maximum flexibility should be incorporated to allow adjustment and creativity, for example by allowing people to include personal elements into their plan which are important to them (but which the local authority is not under a duty to meet), or by developing the plan in a format that works for the person rather than a standard template.

10.38. Consideration of the needs to be met should take a holistic approach that covers aspects such as the person's wishes and aspirations in their daily and community life, rather than a narrow view purely designed to meet personal care needs.

10.39. Consideration of needs should also include the extent to which the needs or a person's other circumstances may mean that they are at risk of abuse or neglect. The planning process may bring to light new information that suggests a safeguarding issue, and therefore lead to a requirement to carry out a safeguarding enquiry (see chapter 14). Where such an enquiry leads to further specific interventions being put in place to address a safeguarding issue, this may be included in the care and support plan.

10.40. In considering the person's needs and how they may be met, the local authority must take into consideration any needs that are being met by a carer. The person may have assessed eligible needs which are being met by a carer at the time of the plan – in these cases the carer must be involved in the planning process. Provided the carer remains willing and able to continue caring, the local authority is not required to meet those needs. However, the local authority should record the carer's willingness to provide care and the extent of this in the plan of the person and also the carer, so that the authority is able to respond to any changes in circumstances (for instance, a breakdown in the caring relationship) more effectively. Where the carer also has eligible needs, the local authority should consider combining the plans of the adult requiring care and the carer, if all parties agree, and establish if the carer requires an independent advocate.

10.41. Local authorities should have regard to how universal services and community- based and/or unpaid support could contribute to the factors in the plan, including support that promotes mental and emotional wellbeing and builds social connections and capital. This may require additional learning and development skills and competencies for social workers and care workers which local authorities should provide.

10.42. Authorities are free, and are indeed encouraged, to include additional elements in the plan where this is proportionate to the needs to be met and agreed with the person the plan is intended for. For example, some people may value having an anticipated review date built into their plan in order for them to be aware of when the review will take place. As detailed in the review chapter, it is the expectation that the plan is reviewed no later than every 12 months, although a light-touch review should be considered 6-8 weeks after the plan and personal budget have been signed off.

10.43. The plan should be proportionate to the needs to be met, and should reflect the person's wishes, preferences and aspirations. However, local authorities should be aware that a "proportionate" plan does not equate to a light-touch approach, as in many cases a proportionate plan will require a more detailed and thorough examination of needs, how these will be met and how this connects with the outcomes that the adult wishes to achieve in day- to-day life.

10.44. For example, the person may have fluctuating needs, in which case the plan should make comprehensive provisions to accommodate for this, as well as indicate what contingencies are in place in the event of a sudden change or emergency. This should be an integral part of the care and support planning process, and not something decided when someone reaches a crisis point. Furthermore, specific consideration should be given to how planning is conducted in end of life care.

10.45. In all cases, additional content to the plan must be agreed with the adult and any other person that the adult requests, and should be guided by the person the plan is intended for. There should also be no restriction or limit on the type of information that the plan contains, as long as this is relevant to the person's needs and/or outcomes. It should also be possible for the person to develop their plan in a format that makes sense to them, rather than this being dictated by the recording requirements of the local authority.

Example – Fluctuating Needs

Miss S has Multiple Sclerosis and requires a frame or wheelchair for mobility. Miss S suffers badly with fatigue, but for the majority of the time she feels able to cope with daily life with a small amount of care and support. However, during relapses she has been unable to sit up, walk or transfer, has lost the use of an arm or lost hervision completely. This can last for a

---

few weeks, and happens two or three times a year; requiring 24 hour support for all daily activities.

In the past, Miss S was hospitalised during relapses as she was unable to cope at home. However, for the past three years, she has received a care and support package that include direct payments which allows her to save up one month's worth of 24 hour care for when she needs it, and this is detailed in the care and support plan.

Miss S can now instantly access the extra support she needs without reassessment and has reassurance that she will be able to put plans in place to cope with any fluctuating needs. She has not been hospitalised since.

10.46. In developing the plan, the local authority must inform the person which, if any, of their needs may be met by a direct payment (see chapter 12). In addition to this, the local authority should provide the person (and/or their independent advocate or any other individual supporting the person, if relevant and if the person wishes this) with appropriate information and advice concerning the usage of direct payments, how they differ from traditional services, and how the local authority will administer the payment (for example an explanation of the direct payment agreement or contract, and how it will be monitored). This advice should also include detail such as:

- the ability for someone else (such as a carer) to receive and manage the direct payment on behalf of the person;

- the ability to request to pay a close family member to provide care and/or administration and management of the direct payment if the local authority determines this to be necessary;

- the difference between purchasing regulated and unregulated services (for example regarding personal assistants);

- explanation of responsibilities that come with being an employer, managing the payment, and monitoring arrangements and how these can be managed locally without being a burden;

- signposting to direct payment support and support organisations available; in the area (e.g. employment, payroll, admin support, personal assistants, peer support);

- that there is no curtailment of choice on how to use the direct payment (within reason), with the aim to encourage innovation;

- local examples and links to people successfully using direct payment in similar circumstances to the person (providing these groups agree);

- the option to have needs met by a mixed package of direct payments and other forms of support or arrangements.

10.47. This information provided upfront should assist the person to decide whether they wish to request a direct payment to meet some or all of their needs and should also be available at various points in the process to ensure people have the best opportunities possible to consider how direct payments may be of benefit to them. However the person chooses to have their needs met, whether by direct payment, by the provision of local authority-arranged or directly provided care and support, or third-party provision, or a mix of these, there should be no constraint on how the needs are met as long as this is reasonable. The local authority has to satisfy itself that the decision is an appropriate and legal way to meet needs, and should take steps to avoid the decision being made on the assumption that the views of the professional are more valid than those of the person. Above all, the local authority should refrain from any action that could be seen to restrict choice and impede flexibility.

10.48. It is important that people are allowed to be very flexible to choose innovative forms of care and support, from a diverse range of sources, including quality providers but also "non-service" options such as Information and Communication Technologies (ICT) equipment, club membership, and massage. Lists of allowable purchases should be avoided as the range of possibilities should be very wide and will be beyond what the local authority is able to list at any point in time. While many authorities may choose to operate lists of quality accredited providers to help people choose (for example some authorities include trading standards- style "buy with confidence" approaches) the use of such lists should not be mandated as the only choice offer to people. Limited lists of 'prescribed providers' that are only offered to the person on a 'take it or leave it' basis do not fit with the Government's vision of personalised care and should be avoided.

INVOLVING THE PERSON

10.49. In addition to taking all reasonable steps to agree how needs are to be met, the local authority must also involve the person the plan is intended for, the carer (if there is one), any other person the adult requests to be involved. Where the person lacks capacity to ask the authority to do that, the local authority must involve any person who appears to the authority to be interested in the welfare of the person and should involve any person who would be able to contribute useful information. An independent advocate must be provided if section 67 of the Act applies (see chapter 7). The person, and their carers, will have the best understanding of how the needs identified fit into the person's life as a whole and connect to their overall wellbeing (see chapter 1). They are well placed to consider and identify which care and support options would best fit into their lifestyle and help them to achieve the day to day outcomes they identified during the assessment process. In practice, local authorities should give consideration to include a prompt to the person during the initial stages of the planning process to ask whether there is anyone else that the person wishes to be involved. Where the person lacks capacity, the local authority should make a best interests decision about who else should be involved.

10.50. The level of involvement should be agreed with the individual and any other party they wish to involve and should reflect their needs and preferences. This may entail local authorities involving the person through regular planning meetings, or there may be instances where remote involvement is just as effective, such as over the telephone, through video conferencing, or other means. In other circumstances, local authorities will need to seek the support of speech and language therapists or other specialists such as interpreters. Some people will need little help to be involved, others will need much more. Social workers or other relevant professionals should have a discussion with the person to get a sense of their confidence to take a lead in the process and what support they feel they need to be meaningfully involved.

10.51. The person should be supported to understand what is being discussed and what options are available for them. The local authority should make sure that a person's lack of confidence to take a lead in the process should not limit the extent to which they can play an active role, if they wish to do so. In all cases, people should be allowed to gain support from individuals who they choose to assist their involvement in the planning process. Where they have substantial difficulty in being actively involved in the process, then they should be assisted by a family member or friend. If the person already has an advocate, whose role has been to support the person on matters not under the Care Act, then it may be appropriate for them to support the individual's involvement and represent them. However, if an advocate is required under the MCA as well as the Care Act, then the instruction, appointment and qualification of the advocate must meet the requirements of the MCA.

10.52. The local authority must instruct an independent advocate if there is no one to represent and support the person's involvement (see chapter 7). This duty arises if the person would, without the representation and support of an independent advocate, experience substantial difficulty in any of the following:

- Understanding relevant information.

- Retaining that information.

- Using or weighing that information as part of the process of being involved.

- Communicating their views, wishes or feelings (whether by talking, using sign language, or any other means).

10.53. For example, there may be cases where a person who has substantial difficulty in the above, has no family or friend who can help, and therefore requires an independent advocate to understand the relevant information provided by the local authority, and to be able to use it to effectively plan for their care and support.

10.54. Genuine involvement will aid the development of the plan, increase the likelihood that the options selected will effectively support the adult in achieving the outcomes that matter to them, and may limit disputes as people involved will be fully aware and have agreed to decisions made. Local authorities should ensure that staff have appropriate learning and development opportunities in order to be able to facilitate involvement in the development of the plan.

AUTHORISING OTHERS (INCLUDING THE PERSON) TO PREPARE THE PLAN JOINTLY WITH THE LOCAL AUTHORITY

10.55. As stated earlier in this guidance, it is important that local authorities give people every opportunity to prepare their own plan in conjunction with the local authority if they wish.

10.56. Where a plan is being jointly prepared by the local authority and the person whose plan it is, or the local authority and a third party, the local authority should ensure that relevant information is shared securely, promptly and in accordance to the Data Protection Act to allow the plan to be prepared in a timely fashion.

10.57. A partnership approach should be taken, where each partner knows their role and the parties supported to identify options and choose between them. For example, the person may need help to weigh up different service options; to understand what each involves and to be able to choose the most appropriate and least restrictive option possible.

10.58. The local authority should also consider cases or circumstances where it may not be appropriate to jointly prepare the plan. For example, a person may not wish their family to be involved, or the authority may be aware that family members may have conflicting interests, or the person may have asked the local authority to prepare the plan with someone who lives far away from the person and even with the assistance of email, phone and other methods of communication is unable to prepare the plan in a timely fashion. The test for allowing the person and others to prepare the plan jointly with the local authority should start with the presumption that the person at the heart of the care plan should give consent for others to do so; and should also have safeguarding principles embedded to ensure that there is no conflict of interest between the person and the third party they wish to involve to prepare the plan jointly with. Where a person lacks capacity and cannot consent to third parties jointly preparing the plan, the local authority must always act in the best interests of the person requiring care and support.

PLANNING FOR PEOPLE WHO LACK CAPACITY[1]

10.59. Good, person-centred care planning is particularly important for people with the most complex needs. Many people receiving care and support have mental impairments, such as dementia or learning disabilities, mental health needs or brain injuries. The principles of the Care Act apply equally to them, in addition to the principles and requirements of the Mental Capacity Act 2005 (MCA) if the person lacks capacity.

10.60. The MCA requires local authorities to assume that people have capacity and can make decisions for themselves, unless otherwise established. Every adult has the right to make his or her own decisions in respect of his or her care plan, and must be assumed to have capacity to do so unless it is proved otherwise. This means that local authorities cannot assume that someone cannot make a decision for themselves just because they have a particular medical condition or disability.

10.61. The local authority must support the person to understand and weigh up information, to offer choices and help people to exercise informed choice. A person must be given all practicable help to make the specific decision before being assessed as lacking capacity to make their own decisions.

10.62. Local authorities must understand that people have the right to make what others might regard as an unwise or unusual decision. Everyone has their own values, beliefs and preferences which may not be the same as those of other people. People cannot be treated as lacking capacity for that reason. Sometimes the care and support plan may have unusual aspects; the question to explore is whether it will meet the assessed needs and lead to the desired outcomes.

10.63. If a local authority thinks a person may lack capacity to make a decision or a plan, even after they have offered them all practicable support, a social worker or other suitably qualified professional should carry out a capacity assessment in relation to the specific decision to be made. For example, the local

---

[1] See Chapter 7

authority may assess whether the person has the capacity to decide whether family members should be involved in their care planning or whether the person has the capacity to decide on whether a particular support option will meet their needs.

10.64. Where an individual has been assessed as lacking capacity to make a particular decision, then the local authority must commence care planning in the person's best interests under the meaning of the MCA. Furthermore a person making a decision concerning a plan on behalf of a person who lacks capacity must consider whether it is possible to make a decision or a plan in a way that would be less restrictive of the person's rights and freedoms of action. Any restriction must be in the person's best interests and necessary to prevent harm to the person, and a proportionate response to the likelihood of the person suffering harm and the seriousness of that harm.

10.65. The duty to involve the person remains throughout the process. If lack of capacity is established, it is still important that the person is involved as far as possible in making decisions. Planning should always be done with the person and not for them; should always start by the identification of their wishes, feelings, values and aspirations, not just their needs, and should always consider their wellbeing in the wider context of their rights to security, to liberty, and to family life.

10.66. Where a person has substantial difficulty in being fully involved in their care planning or lacks capacity to agree and consent to the care plan, they may be supported by family members or friends. If a person has no family or friend who is able to facilitate the person's involvement available and willing to do so, then an independent advocate must be appointed. A friend or family member is not appropriate to facilitate the person's involvement if the person has capacity to decide who they wish to support them and chooses not to be supported by that individual. If the person lacks such capacity, then the local authority must decide on the suitability of the friend or family member to act in the person's best interests. The role of the independent advocate is to:

- support and represent the person to facilitate their involvement in decision-making in the care planning process;

- assist the person in communicating their wishes, feelings, value and aspirations where possible; and

- to challenge the local authority's decisions if necessary to represent the person's wishes or to promote the person's wellbeing and rights to security, liberty and family life.

MINIMISING AND AUTHORISING DEPRIVATION OF LIBERTY (DOL) FOR PEOPLE WHO LACK CAPACITY

10.67. In line with the least restrictive principle in the MCA, local authorities and others drawing up plans must minimise planned restrictions and restraints on the person as much as possible. The MCA provides legal protection for acts of restraint only if the act is necessary to prevent harm to the person, a proportionate response to the likelihood of the person suffering harm and the seriousness of that harm, and in the person's best interests.[1] Planned restrictions and restraints must be documented and reported to a social worker to agree. Disagreements should be

---

[1] Mental Capacity Act 2005, sections 5 and 6.

resolved through formal Best Interests meetings, involving a wide range of people, including family members and/or an advocate to support and represent the person.

10.68. However, if the degree and intensity of restrictions and restraints are so significant that they amount to a deprivation of liberty, this must be authorised under the Deprivation of Liberty Safeguards (DOLS) under the MCA.

10.69. Developing effective person-centered processes for planning in line with the guidance and the Act in general may in most cases avoid circumstances where a deprivation of liberty will arise.

10.70. The difference between a deprivation of liberty and restraint is one of degree, intensity and duration, not necessarily nature or substance. The Supreme Court has clarified that there is a deprivation of liberty for the purposes of Article 5 of the European Convention on Human Rights in the following circumstances: the person is under continuous supervision and control and is not free to leave, and the person lacks capacity to consent to those arrangements.[1] The precise scope of the term "deprivation of liberty" is not fixed. It develops over time in accordance with case law.

10.71. In DOLS cases, MCA/DOLS staff and the independent advocate must go through the following steps when conducting the care planning process:

- Familiarise themselves with the provisions of the MCA, particularly the five principles and specifically the "least restrictive" principle.

- When designing and implementing new care and support plans for people lacking capacity, be alert to any restrictions and restraint which may be a degree or intensity that means a person is being, or is likely to be, deprived of their liberty (following the revised test supplied by the Supreme Court).

- Where a potential deprivation of liberty is identified at the planning or commissioning care stage, a full exploration of the alternative ways of providing the care and/or treatment should be undertaken, in order to identify any less restrictive ways of providing that care which will avoid a deprivation of liberty;

- Where the plan for an individual lacking capacity will unavoidably result in a deprivation of liberty judged to be in the person's best interests, this must be authorised before being implemented.

10.72. If the person will be accommodated in a hospital or care home, the local authority can issue a deprivation of liberty authorisation under Schedule 1A to the MCA (DOL authorisation). If the person will be accommodated in other settings, a Court of Protection Order under the MCA to authorise the deprivation of liberty is needed. If the independent advocate is concerned that there is a risk of deprivation of liberty which has not been authorised, the advocate should raise this with the local authority. The advocate may make an application to the Court of Protection (with the Court's permission) if they are dissatisfied with the local authority's response.

---

[1] P v Cheshire West and Chester Council and another; P and Q v Surrey County Council [2014] UKSC 19

COMBINING PLANS

10.73. Local authorities should not develop plans in isolation from other plans (such as plans of carers or family members, or Education, Health and Care plans) and should have regard to all of the person's needs and outcomes when developing a plan, rather than just their care and support needs.

10.74. The local authority should attempt to establish where other plans are present, or are being conducted and seek to combine plans, if appropriate. This should be considered early on in the planning process (at the same time as considering the person's needs and how they can be met in a holistic way) to ensure that the package of care and support is developed in a way that fits with what support is already being received or developed. For example, this may be where the plan can be combined with a plan being developed to meet other needs, or where a plan might usefully be combined with that of a carer, or family member. In all circumstances, the plan should only be combined if all parties to whom it is relevant agree and understand the implications of sharing data and information. It is the responsibility of the local authority to obtain consent from all parties involved, and the combination of plans should aim to maximize outcomes for all involved.

10.75. Where one of the plans to be combined is for a child (below 18 years old), the child must have capacity to agree to the combination, or if lacking capacity, the local authority must be satisfied that the combination of plans would be in the child's best interests. Often it will be; but where there is a conflict of interest (for example a parent does not wish to support their 17 year old daughter's wish for greater independence) it may not be (see chapter 16 on transition to adult care and support).

10.76. The local authority may be undertaking care and or support planning for two people in the same household who require independent advocacy to facilitate their involvement. If both people have the capacity to consent to having the same advocate, and the advocate and the local authority both consider there is no conflict of interest, then the same advocate may support and represent the two people. If either person lacks the capacity to consent to having the same advocate, the advocate and local authority must both consider that using the same advocate would not raise a conflict of interest and would be in the best interests of both persons (see chapter 7).

10.77. Consideration should also be given to how plans could be combined where budgets are pooled, either with people in the same household, or between members of a community with similar care needs where this is appropriate and all parties agree (see chapter 11 on personal budgets). Pooling arrangements should not be restricted to individuals using the same provider. Networks of pooling arrangements should be encouraged to bring groups of people together in a more effective manner.

10.78. Where it has been agreed to combine the plan with plans relating to other people, it is important that the individual aspects of each person's plan are not lost in the process of combining plans. The combined plan should reflect the individual needs and circumstance for each person involved, as well as any areas where a joint approach has been agreed to meet needs in a more effective way.

10.79. One key area where plans can be combined cases where the person is receiving both local authority care and support and NHS health care is an example would be a person with mental disorder who meets the criteria for care and support under the multi-agency Care Programme Approach.[1] The introduction of personal health budgets in health, similar to personal budgets in social care, provides a powerful tool to enable integrated health and care provision which focuses on what matters most to the person. Local authorities should provide information to the person of the benefits of combining health and social care support, and seek to work with health colleagues to combine health and care plans wherever possible.

10.80. In combining plans, whether among people or organisations (such as health, education or housing), it is vital to avoid duplicating process or introducing multiple monitoring regimes. Information sharing should be rapid and seek to minimise bureaucracy. Local authorities should work alongside health and other professionals (such as housing) where plans are combined to establish a 'lead' organisation who undertakes monitoring and assurance of the combined plan (this may also involve appointing a lead professional and detailing this in the plan so the person knows who to contact when plans are combined). Particular consideration should be given to ensuring that processes are aligned, coherent and streamlined, to avoid confusing the person with different systems (see chapter 14 on integration and cooperation).

SIGN-OFF AND ASSURANCE

10.81. The local authority must take all reasonable steps to agree with the person the manner in which the plan details how needs will be met, before the authority signs off the plan. Therefore, it should not introduce measures that place any undue burden on the person, especially where the person or third party is preparing the plan in conjunction with the local authority. The local authority should therefore avoid developing processes that undermine the joint preparation of plans, such as excessive quality control. For example, a local authority may have arrangements or contract with outside organisations/individuals to provide peer support for planning. If so, an important part of this contract should be around having agreement as to non-restrictive approaches that enhance the quality of plans and the local authority's trust in the detail as well as removing issues that can cause delay and problems.

10.82. The local authority's role where the person or third-party are undertaking the preparation of the plan jointly with the local authority includes overseeing and providing guidance for the completion of the plan; and ensuring that the plan sufficiently meets needs, is appropriate and represent the best balance between value for money and maximisation of outcomes for the person. For example, this may involve providing materials and approaches to support people jointly preparing the plan with the local authority. Where the local authority is preparing the plan on behalf of the person, or delegating this to a third-party to do so, the best interests of the person must be reflected throughout.

10.83. The local authority must take all reasonable steps to reach agreement with the person for whom the plan is being prepared. Wherever possible, local authority sign-off should occur when the person, any third party involved in the preparation of the plan and the local authority have agreed on the factors within the plan, including the final personal budget amount (which may have been subject to change during the planning process), and how the needs in question will be met. This is a key part of the planning process and the agreement should be

---

[1] See "Refocusing the Care Programme Approach" – Policy and Positive Practice Guidance" Department of Health, March 2008 http://www.nmhdu.org.uk/silo/files/dh-2008-refocusing-the-care-programme-approach-policy-and-positive-practice-guidance.pdf

recorded and a copy placed within the plan. Where an independent advocate has been involved, they should not be asked to sign off the plan – this is the responsibility of the local authority.

10.84. While there is no defined timescale for the completion of the care and support planning process, the plan should be completed in a timely fashion, proportionate to the needs to be met. Local authorities must ensure that sufficient time is taken to ensure the plan is appropriate to meet the needs in question, and is agreed by the person the plan is intended for. The planning process should not unduly delay needs being met.

10.85. Due regard should be taken to the use of approval panels in both the timeliness and bureaucracy of the planning and sign-off process. In some cases, panels may be an appropriate governance mechanism to sign-off large or unique personal budget allocations and/or plans. Where used, panels should be appropriately skilled and trained, and local authorities should refrain from creating or using panels that seek to amend planning decisions, micro-manage the planning process or are in place purely for financial reasons. Local authorities should consider how to delegate responsibility to their staff to ensure sign-off takes place at the most appropriate level. In cases or circumstances where a panel is to be used, and where an expert assessor has been involved in the care and support journey, the same person or another person with similar expertise should be part of the panel to ensure decisions take into account complex or specialist issues.

10.86. In the event that the plan cannot be agreed with the person, or any other person involved, the local authority should state the reasons for this and the steps which must be taken to ensure that the plan is signed-off. This may require going back to earlier elements of the planning process. People must not be left without support while a dispute is resolved. If a dispute still remains, and the local authority feels that it has taken all reasonable steps to address the situation, it should direct the person to the local complaints procedure. However, by conducting person-centred planning and ensuring genuine involvement throughout, this situation should be avoided.

10.87. Upon completion of the plan, the local authority must give a copy of the final plan which should be in a format that is accessible to the person for whom the plan is intended, any other person they request to receive a copy, and their independent advocate if they have one and the person agrees. This should not restrict local authorities from making the draft plan available throughout the planning process; indeed in cases where a person is preparing the plan in conjunction with the local authority, the plan should be in their possession. Consideration should also be given to sharing key points of the final plan with other professionals and supporters, with the person's consent (for example, as part of the person's health record), or sharing the plan in the best interests of a person who lacks capacity to decide on this matter.

PROTECTING PROPERTY OF ADULTS BEING CARE FOR AWAY FROM HOME

10.88. Local authorities must take all reasonable steps to protect the moveable property of an adult with care and support needs who is being cared for away from home in a hospital or in accommodation such as a care home, and who cannot arrange to protect their property themselves; this could include their pets as well as their personal property (e.g. private possessions and furniture). Local authorities must act where it believes that if it does not take action there is a risk of moveable property being lost or damaged.

10.89. For example, protecting property may include arranging for pets to be looked after when securing premises for someone who is having their care and support needs provided away from home in a care home or hospital, and who has not been able to make other arrangements for the care of their home or pets.

10.90. In order to protect moveable property in these circumstances the local authority may enter the property, at reasonable times, with the adult's consent; but reasonable prior notice to enter should be given. If the adult lacks the capacity to give consent to the local authority entering the property, consent should be sought from a person authorised under the Mental Capacity Act 2005 to give consent on the adult's behalf. This might be:

- an Attorney (also known as a donee with lasting power of attorney) that is someone appointed under the Mental Capacity Act 2005 who has the legal right to make decisions (e.g. decisions about their care and support) within the scope of their authority on behalf of the person (the donor) who made the power of attorney;

- a Deputy (also known as a Court-Appointed Deputy) that is a person appointed by the Court of Protection under the Mental Capacity Act 2005 to take specified decisions on behalf of someone who lacks capacity to take those decisions themselves; or

- the Court of Protection.

10.91. If the adult in question lacks capacity and no other person has been authorised to act on their behalf, then the local authority must act in the best interests of the adult in accordance with section 4 of the Mental Capacity Act 2005.

10.92. If a third party tries to stop an authorised entry into the home then they will be committing an offence, unless they can give a good reason for why they are obstructing the local authority in protecting the adult's property. Committing such an offence could, on conviction by a Magistrates' Court, lead to the person being fined up to a maximum fine not exceeding level 4 on the standard scale. If a local authority intends to enter a home then it must give written authorisation to an officer of the council and that person must be able to produce it if asked for.

10.93. The local authority has no power to apply for a warrant to carry out their duties to protect property. The enforcement power is prosecution for unreasonable obstruction. However, if the Court decides the obstruction is reasonable then the local authority would have no further power to force entry.

10.94. This duty on the local authority lasts until the adult in question returns home or makes their own arrangements for the protection of property or until there is no other danger of loss or damage to property; whichever happens first. Often a one off event is required such as the re-homing of pets or ensuring that the property is secured. However, if costs are incurred or if there are ongoing costs the local authority can recover any reasonable expenses they incur in protecting property under this duty from the adult whose property they are protecting.

LINKS TO EXTERNAL RESOURCES

Care and Support Planning Guide, National Voices, March 2014: http://www.nationalvoices.org.uk/read-our-guide

7 essential criteria of support planning, In Control 2005: http://bit.ly/1etdihV

Good practice in support planning and brokerage, PPF, 2008: http://bit.ly/1b4tfdS

Peer support and personalisation, NCIL, 2008: http://bit.ly/1fWs7Yz

Planning together – peer support and self-directed support, PPF, 2009: http://bit.ly/1fxsMOi

Support planning and brokerage with older people and people with mental health difficulties, PPF, 2010: http://bit.ly/LB7Igt

Personalisation through person-centre planning, DH, 2010: http://bit.ly/1iv3SBG

Rethinking support planning – ideas for an alternative approach, TLAP, 2011: http://bit.ly/1b4tYff

Empower and enable – a people led approach to support planning, Groundswell, 2012: http://bit.ly/1kYs93T

Using Individual Service Funds to deliver personalised care and support: http://www.groundswellpartnership.co.uk/choice-and-control-for-all

Implementing effective care planning, PHB Toolkit, NHSE, 2012: http://bit.ly/1cYCNWJ

PA toolkit, http://www.skillsforcare.org.uk/Employing-your-own-care-and-support/Support-for-individual-employers/Employing-personal-assistants-toolkit.aspx

Employing Staff, http://www.skillsforcare.org.uk/Employing-your-own-care-and-support/Employing-your-own-care-support-staff.aspx

The Common Core Principles to Self Care, http://www.skillsforcare.org.uk/Skills/Self-care/ Self-care.aspx

Personal budgets and mental health, http://www.ndti.org.uk/who-were-concerned-with/mental-health/paths-to-personalisation/

Carers' rights, http://www.skillsforcare.org.uk/Skills/Carers/Carers.aspx

Involve Me: involving people with profound and multiple learning disabilities in decision making www.mencap.org.uk/involveme

At a glance 42: Personalisation briefing: Implications for lesbian, gay, bisexual and transgendered (LGBT) people" (http://www.scie.org.uk/publications/ataglance/ataglance42.pdf)

11. PERSONAL BUDGETS

This chapter provides guidance on:
- Section 26 of the Care Act 2014;

- The Care and Support (Personal Budget Exclusion of Costs) Regulations 2014.

This chapter covers:
- The personal budget;
- Elements of the personal budget;
- Elements of care and support that are excluded from the personal budget;
- Calculating the personal budget;
- Agreeing the final budget;
- Use of the personal budget;
- Use of a carer's personal budget;
- Carers' personal budgets where the adult being cared for does not have eligible needs;
- Appeals/disputes.

11.1. Personal budgets are a key part of the Government's aspirations for a person-centred care and support system. Independent research shows that where implemented well, personal budgets can improve outcomes and deliver better value for money.[1,2,3,4]

11.2. The Act places personal budgets into law for the first time, making them the norm for people with care and support needs.

11.3. The personal budget is the mechanism that, in conjunction with the care and support plan, or support plan, enables the person, and their advocate if they have one, to exercise greater choice and take control over how their care and support needs are met. It means:

- knowing, before care and support planning begins, an estimate of how much money will be available to meet a person's assessed needs and, with the final personal budget, having clear information about the total amount of the budget, including proportion the local authority will pay, and what amount (if any) the person will pay;

- being able to choose from a range of options for how the money is managed, including direct payments, the local authority managing the budget and a provider or third party managing the budget on the individual's behalf (an individual service fund), or a combination of these approaches;

- having a choice over who is involved in developing the care and support plan for how the personal budget will be spent, including from family or friends;

---

[1] Glendinning, C. *et al.*, *Evaluation of the Individual Budgets Pilot Programme*, IBSEN, York, 2008.
[2] Audit Commission, Improving Value For Money in Adult Social Care, 2011. Thirty-six per cent of councils cited personalisation as a driver of better value for money in 2009/10. This rises to 45 per cent for 2010/11. Better value came mostly from improved outcomes, not savings.
[3] Audit Commission, Financial Management of Personal Budgets, 2010.
[4] Ipsos Mori, Users of Social Care Budgets, July 2011.

- having greater choice and control over the way the personal budget is used to purchase care and support, and from whom.

11.4. It is vital that the process used to establish the personal budget is transparent so that people are clear how their budget was calculated, and the method used is robust so that people have confidence that the personal budget allocation is correct and therefore sufficient to meet their care and support needs. The allocation of a clear upfront indicative (or 'ball- park') allocation at the start of the planning process will help people to develop the plan and make appropriate choices over how their needs are met.

11.5. The process of allocating the personal budget should be completed in a timely manner, proportionate to the needs to be met. At all times the person should be informed where they are in the care planning process, what will happen next and the likely timeframes.

11.6. This chapter applies to people in need of care and support and carers equally, unless specifically stated.

THE PERSONAL BUDGET

11.7. Everyone whose needs are met by the local authority, whether those needs are eligible, or if the authority has chosen to meet other needs, must receive a personal budget as part of the care and support plan, or support plan. The personal budget is an important tool that gives the person clear information regarding the money that has been allocated to meet the needs identified in the assessment and recorded in the plan. An indicative amount should be shared with the person, and anybody else involved, at the start of care and support planning, with the final amount of the personal budget confirmed through this process. The detail of how the personal budget will be used is set out in the care and support plan, or support plan. At all times, the wishes of the person must be considered and respected. For example, the personal budget should not assume that people are forced to accept specific care options, such as moving into care homes, against their will because this is perceived to be the cheapest option.

11.8. This allows the person, and anybody else the person wishes, to make informed decisions about how to meet their care and support needs. The person can choose for the personal budget allocation to remain with the local authority to arrange care and support on the person's behalf, and in line with their wishes. Alternatively, if available locally, it can be placed with a third-party provider on the same basis, often called an individual service fund (ISF). Where an ISF type arrangement is not available locally, the local authority should explore arrangements to develop this offer, and should be receptive to requests from personal budget recipients to create these arrangements with specified providers.

11.9. There may also be cases where a person prefers to use a mixed package of care and support. For example, this may be a direct payment to the person for some of their needs, with the remainder of the personal budget used to meet needs via local authority or third- party provision, or any combination of the above. The method of allocating the personal budget should be decided and agreed during the care and support planning process (see chapter 10). It is important that these arrangements can be subsequently adjusted if the person wishes this, with the minimum of procedure. The process for allocating and agreeing the personal budget via the planning process should be as straightforward and as timely as possible so that the person can access the budget without significant delay.

ELEMENTS OF THE PERSONAL BUDGET

11.10. The personal budget must always be an amount sufficient to meet the person's care and support needs, and must include the cost to the local authority of meeting the person's needs which the local authority is under a duty to meet, or has exercised its power to do so. This overall cost must then be broken down into the amount the person must pay, following the financial assessment, and the remainder of the budget that the authority will pay.

11.11. The personal budget may also set out other amounts of public money that the person is receiving, such as money provided through a personal health budget. Local authorities should consider requests from individuals to present their personal budget in this way. Integrated health and care, and integration of other aspects of public support are the long- term vision of the Government. This will provide the individual with a seamless experience, and can help to remove unnecessary bureaucracy and duplication that may exist where a person's needs are met through money from multiple funding streams.

11.12. Local authorities must carry out their care and support responsibilities with a view to promoting integration with health and other related services (such as housing), and therefore should take a lead in driving the integration of support services for their population. For example, this may involve agreeing with partner organisations how to integrate budgets and to what extent, and the establishment of a lead organisation that agrees to oversee monitoring and assurance of all budgets the person is receiving.

11.13. Where a local authority is meeting the eligible needs of a person whose financial resources are above the financial limit, but who has requested the local authority meet their needs, the local authority may make a charge for putting in place the necessary arrangements to meet needs (see chapter 8 on charging and financial assessment). Where this occurs, the local authority should consider how best to set this information out to the person, in a format accessible to them. This fee is not part of the personal budget, since it does not relate directly to meeting needs, but it may be presented alongside the budget to help the person understand the total charges to be paid. For example, a local authority may wish to specify this in both the plan and the personal budget for the person so all parties are clear on how costs are allocated.

11.14. Similarly, there will be cases where a person or a third party on their behalf is making an additional payment (or a "top-up") in order to be able to secure the care and support of their choice, where this costs more than the local authority would pay for such a type of care. In these cases, the additional payment does not form part of the personal budget, since the budget must reflect the costs to the local authority of meeting the needs. However, the local authority should consider how best to present this information to the individual, so that the total amount of charges paid is clear, and the link to the personal budget amount is understood.

ELEMENTS OF CARE AND SUPPORT THAT ARE EXCLUDED FROM THE PERSONAL BUDGET

11.15. Regulations set out the cases or circumstances where the costs of meeting the needs of care and support do not have to be incorporated into the personal budget. Because both the care and support plan and personal budget are mechanisms to enable people to have greater choice and control over their care and support, there are not many instances where this exclusion will apply.

11.16. The Care and Support (Personal Budget Exclusion of Costs) Regulations 2014 set out that the provision of intermediate care and reablement services, for which the local authority cannot or chooses not to make a charge,[1] must be excluded from the personal budget. This will mean that where either intermediate care or reablement is being provided to meet needs (i.e. under section 18, 19 or 20 of the Act) the cost of this must not be included in the personal budget.

11.17. Intermediate care services are usually provided to patients, often older people, after leaving hospital or when they are at risk of being sent to hospital. The services are a link between places such as hospitals and people's homes, and between different areas of the health and social care system – community services, hospitals, GPs and social care. "Reablement" is a particular type of intermediate care, which has a stronger focus on helping the person to regain skills and capabilities to reduce their needs, in particular through the use of therapy or minor adaptations. There is a tendency for the terms "reablement", "rehabilitation" and "intermediate care" to be used interchangeably. The National Audit of Intermediate Care categorises four types of intermediate care: crisis response – services providing short-term care (up to 48 hours); home-based intermediate care – services provided to people in their own homes by a team with different specialities but mainly health professionals such as nurses and therapists; bed-based intermediate care – services delivered away from home, for example, in a community hospital; and reablement – services to help people live independently provided in the person's own home by a team of mainly social care professionals.[2]

11.18. Three of the four types of intermediate care have historically been clinician-led and provided by health staff, with reablement being provided by local authorities. However, these are not concrete, mutually-exclusive categories – and, furthermore, with greater integration and co-operation between health and local authorities, there should be greater use of qualified staff from health and social care working together to provide intermediate care.

11.19. Local authorities should not include additional elements that would not normally be classified as intermediate care or reablement into this exclusion. Indeed, the Act restricts the regulations into specifying only care and support which the local authority cannot charge for, or chooses not to charge for. This ensures that long-term care and support will always be part of the personal budget, and in future, count towards the cap on care costs. Also, broader rehabilitation services could be included to an individual to meet identified health needs as part of a joint personal budget across health and social care.

11.20. Intermediate care/reablement should usually be provided as a free, universal service under section 2 of the Act, and therefore would not contribute to the personal budget amount. However, in some circumstances, a local authority may choose to combine either service with aspects of care and support to meet eligible or ongoing needs, which would require a personal budget to be developed. Removing the cost of provision of intermediate care/reablement from the personal

---

[1] The Care and Support (Charging and Assessment of Resources) Regulations 2014 state that intermediate care (including reablement) cannot be charged for, for the first six weeks. However, the charging guidance clearly sets out that, in line with the guidance on prevention, that neither should have a strict time limit but should reflect the needs of the person. Local authorities may therefore wish to apply their discretion to offer this free of charge for longer than six weeks where there are clear preventative benefits such as when a person has recently become visually impaired.

[2] See Chapter 2

budget in these scenarios ensures that the allocation of both services is applied uniformly across all local authorities, and in future people progress towards the cap on care costs in a fair and consistent way.

11.21. In cases where intermediate care/ reablement is provided to meet needs under section 18 or 20(1) or under section 19(1) or 20(6), either in isolation or combined with longer- term care and support, the plan should describe what the package consists of and how long it will last. This will help the person understand what is being provided to meet their needs. However, the person should not receive a personal budget, unless there are other forms of care and support being provided under these sections. In these cases, the personal budget amount must not include the cost of intermediate care/reablement which are provided free of charge.

CALCULATING THE PERSONAL BUDGET

11.22. It is important to have a consistent method for calculating personal budgets that provides an early indication of the appropriate amount to meet the identified needs to be used at the beginning of the planning process. Local authorities should ensure that the method used for calculating the personal budget produces equitable outcomes to ensure fairness in care and support packages regardless of the environment in which care and support takes place, for example, in a care home or someone's own home. Local authorities should not have arbitrary ceilings to personal budgets that result in people being forced to accept to move into care homes against their will.

11.23. There are many variations of systems used to arrive at personal budget amounts, ranging from complex algorithmic-based resource allocation systems (RAS), to more 'ready- reckoner' approaches. Complex RAS models of allocation may not work for all client groups, especially where people have multiple complex needs, or where needs are comparatively costly to meet, such as deafblind people. It is important that these factors are taken into account, and that a 'one size fits all' approach to resource allocation is not taken. If a RAS model is being used, local authorities should consider alternative approaches where the process may be more suitable to particular client groups to ensure that the personal budget is an appropriate amount to meet needs.

11.24. Regardless of the process used, the most important principles in setting the personal budget are transparency, timeliness and sufficiency. This will ensure that the person, their carer, and their independent advocate if they have one, is fully aware of how their budget was calculated, that they know the amount at a stage which enables them to effectively engage in care and support planning, and that they can have confidence that the amount includes all relevant costs that will be sufficient to meet their identified needs in the way set out in the plan. The local authority should also explain that the initial indicative allowance can be increased or decreased depending on the decisions made during the development of the plan. This should prevent disputes from arising, but it must also be possible for the person, carer or independent advocate (on the person's behalf) to challenge the local authority on the sufficiency of the final amount. These principles apply to both the indicative upfront budget and the final signed off personal budget that forms part of the care and support plan.

- Transparency: Authorities should make their allocation processes publicly available as part of their general information offer, or ideally provide this on a bespoke basis for each person the authority is supporting in a format accessible to them. This will ensure that people fully understand how the personal budget has been calculated, both in the indicative amount and the final personal budget allocation. Where a complex RAS process is used, local authorities should pay particular consideration to how they will meet this transparency principle, to ensure people are clear how the personal budget was derived.

- Timeliness: It is crucial when calculating the personal budget to arrive at an upfront allocation which can be used to inform the start of the care and support planning process. This 'indicative budget' will enable the person to plan how the needs are met. After refinement during the planning process, this indicative amount is then adjusted to be the amount that is sufficient to meet the needs which the local authority is required to meet under section 18 or 20(1), or decides to meet under section 19(1) or (2) or 20(6). This adjusted amount then forms the personal budget recorded in the care plan.

- Sufficiency: The amount that the local authority calculates as the personal budget must be sufficient to meet the person's needs which the local authority is required to meet under section 18 or 20(1), or decides to meet under section 19(1) or (2) or 20(6) and must also take into account the reasonable preferences to meet needs as detailed in the care and support plan, or support plan.

11.25. The Act states the personal budget must be an amount that is the cost to the local authority of meeting the person's needs. In establishing the 'cost to the local authority', consideration should therefore be given to local market intelligence and costs of local quality provision to ensure that the personal budget reflects local market conditions and that appropriate care that meets needs can be obtained for the amount specified in the budget. To further aid the transparency principle, these cost assumptions should be shared with the person so they are aware of how their personal budget was established. Consideration should also be given as to whether the personal budget is sufficient where needs will be met via direct payments, especially around any other costs that may be required to meet needs or ensure people are complying with legal requirements associated with becoming an employer (see chapter 12). There may be concern that the 'cost to the local authority' results in the direct payment being a lesser amount than is required to purchase care and support from the local market due to local authority bulk purchasing and block contract arrangements. However, by basing the personal budget on the cost of quality local provision, this concern should be allayed.

11.26. However, a request for needs to be met via a direct payment does not mean that there is no limit on the amount attributed to the personal budget. There may be cases where it is more appropriate to meet needs via directly-provided care and support, rather than by making a direct payment. For example, this may be where there is no local market for a particular kind of care and support that the person wishes to use the direct payment for, except for services provided by the local authority. It may also be the case where the costs of an alternate provider arranged via a direct payment would be more than the local authority would be able to arrange the same support for, whilst achieving the same outcomes for the individual.

11.27. In all circumstances, consideration should be given to the expected outcomes of each potential delivery route. It may be that by raising the personal budget to allow a direct payment from a particular provider, it is expected to deliver much better outcomes than local authority delivered care and support, or there may be other dynamics such as the preferred option reducing the need for travel costs, or out of hours care. In addition, efficiencies to the local authority (for example through an individual making their own arrangements) should also be considered. Decisions should therefore be based on outcomes and value for money, rather than purely financially motivated.

11.28. In cases where making a direct payment is a more expensive option to meet needs, the care plan should be reviewed to ensure that it is accurate and that the personal budget allocation is correct. The authority should work with the person, their carer and independent advocate (if there is one) to agree on how best to meet their care and support needs. It may be that the person can take a mixture of direct payment and local authority-arranged care and support, or the local authority can work with the person to discuss alternate uses for the personal budget. Essentially, these discussions will take place during the planning process and local authorities should ensure that their staff are appropriately trained to support personalised care and support, and to facilitate decision-making.

Example – Costs of direct payments

Andrew has chosen to meet his needs by receiving care and support from a PA. The local authority has a block contract with an agency which has been providing support to Andrew twice per week. Andrew would now like more flexibility in the times at which he receives support in order to better meet his needs by allowing him to undertake other activities and consider employment. He therefore requests a direct payment so that he can make his own arrangements with another agency, which is happy to arrange a much more flexible and personalised service, providing Andrew with the same carer on each occasion, and at a time that works best for him. The cost to the local authority of the block contracted services is £12.50 per hour. However, the more flexible support costs £17 per hour (inclusive of other employment costs). The local authority therefore increases Andrew's direct payment from £62.50 to £85 per week to allow him to continue to receive the care he requires. The solution through a direct payment delivers better outcomes for Andrew and therefore the additional cost is reasonable and seen as value for money as it may delay future needs developing. The local authority also agrees it is more efficient for them to allow Andrew to arrange and commission the hours he wants to receive support and handle the invoicing himself.

Example – Costs of direct payments (2)

Following George's assessment of needs, the local authority work out an indicative personal budget of £125 per week, based on their block contract rate of £12.50 per hour as an indication of the potential costs to meet his needs.

During care planning, George states that he has a neighbour that has recently trained to become a personal assistant, and George indicates a preference to use a direct payment to employ the neighbour instead of an arranged service. The local authority is satisfied that George will be able to manage the direct payment, and that he understands his responsibilities as an employer. George wants to pay the PA above the living wage and has provisionally agreed a hourly rate of £8 per hour.

The local authority agrees to this as George agrees that it will meet his needs and outcomes. The final personal budget is adjusted to £100 per week which factors in the new hourly rate, plus an additional allowance for employment responsibilities (PAYE, NI, insurance etc.)

USE OF THE PERSONAL BUDGET

11.29. The person should have the maximum possible range of options for managing the personal budget, including how it is spent and how it is utilised. Directing spend is as important for those choosing the council-managed option or individual service fund as for direct payments. Evidence suggests that people using council-managed personal budgets are currently not achieving the same level of outcomes as those using direct payments, and in too many cases do not even know they have been allocated a personal budget.

11.30. There are three main ways in which a personal budget can be deployed:

- As a managed account held by the local authority with support provided in line with the persons wishes;

- As a managed account held by a third party (often called an individual service fund or ISF) with support provided in line with the persons wishes;

- As a direct payment.

11.31. In addition, a person may choose a 'mixed package' that includes elements of some or all three of the approaches above. Local authorities must ensure that whatever way the personal budget is used, the decision is recorded in the plan and the person is given as much flexibility and choice as is reasonably practicable in how their needs are met. The mixed package approach can be a useful option for people who are moving to direct payments for the first time. This allows a phased introduction of the direct payment, giving the person time to adapt to the direct payment arrangements.

11.32. Where ISF approaches to personal budget management are available locally, the local authority should provide people with information and advice on how the ISF arrangement works and any contractual requirements, how the provider(s) will manage the budget on behalf of the person, and advice on what to do if a dispute arises. Consideration should be given to using real local examples that illustrate how other people have benefitted from ISF arrangements.

11.33. Where there are no ISF arrangements available locally, the local authority should consider establishing this as an offer for people. Additionally, the local authority should reasonably consider any request from a person for an ISF arrangement with a specified provider.

Case Studies: Using ISFs
Sally really enjoys dancing and night clubs and she needs support for this. Sally's ISF arrangement with her provider has given her the flexibility to employ staff that also like to do this, and they are paid time and a half after 11:00pm. The ISF arrangement also allows Sally to convert 'standard hours' into 'enhanced hours', for example, six standard hours equals four enhanced hours. Sally can plan late nights out knowing what it 'costs' from her allocation of twenty-four standard hours support, which is calculated from her personal budget.

Brian's ISF arrangement with his provider allows him to save up and then convert the hours of his support into money to purchase personal trainer time at a local gym.

In addition to promoting wellbeing in the areas of emotional and social wellbeing and personal relationships, these arrangements also demonstrate the local authority's regard for the importance of beginning with the assumption that an individual is best-placed to judge their own wellbeing.

11.34. Local authorities should also give consideration to how choice could be increased by people pooling their budgets together. For example, this may include pooling budgets of people living in the same household such as an adult and carer, or pooling budgets of people within a community with similar care and support needs, or aspirations. Pooling budgets in circumstances such as this may deliver increased choice, especially where managed budgets are concerned. Developing networks of 'budget poolers' could help create dynamic groups of people working together to meet needs.

11.35. Evidence suggests that in most cases people need to know the amount of their budget, be able to choose how it is managed, and have maximum flexibility in how it is used to achieve the best outcomes. Therefore the process and practice for personal budgets should follow the key principles of self-directed support.[1] Local authorities should aim to develop a range of means to enable anyone to make good use of direct payments and where people choose other options, should ensure local practice that maximises choice and control (for example use of Individual Service Funds). Local authorities should also take care not to inadvertently limit options and choices. For example "pre-paid cards" can be a good option for some people using direct payments, but must not be used to constrain choice or be only available for use with a restricted list of providers.

USE OF A CARER'S PERSONAL BUDGET
11.36. Specific consideration should be given to how a personal budget will be used by carers. The Act specifies that a carer's need for support can be met by providing care to the person they care for. However, decisions on for whom a particular service is to be provided may affect issues such as whether the service is chargeable, and who is liable to pay any charges. It is therefore important that it is clear to all individuals involved whose needs are intended to be met by a particular type of support, to whom the support will be provided directly, and

---

[1] http://www.in-control.org.uk/related-pages/seven-principles-of-self-directed-support.aspx

therefore who may pay any charges due. Where a service is provided directly to the adult needing care, even though it is to meet the carer's needs, then that adult would be liable to pay any charge, and must agree to doing so. Section 14 of the Act makes clear that where the needs are met by providing care and support direct to the adult needing care, the charge may not be imposed on the carer.

11.37. Decisions on which services are provided to meet carers' needs, and which are provided to meet the needs of the adult for whom they care, will therefore impact on which individual's personal budget includes the costs of meeting those needs. Local authorities should make this decision as part of the care planning process, in discussion with the individuals concerned, and should consider whether joint plans (and therefore joint personal budgets) for the two individuals may be of benefit.

11.38. Local authorities should consider how to align personal budgets where they are meeting the needs of both the carer and the adult needing care concurrently. Where an adult has eligible needs for care and support, and has a personal budget and care and support plan in their own right, and the carer's needs can be met, in part or in full, by the provision of care and support to that person needing care, then this kind of provision should be incorporated into the plan and personal budget of the person with care needs, as well as being detailed in a care and support plan for the carer.

Example – Flexible use of a carer's personal budget

Connor has been caring for his wife, who is in a wheelchair with ME and arthritis, for the last nine years. He does all the cooking, driving and general household duties for her. Connor received a personal budget which he requested in the form of a direct payment from his local authority for a laptop to enable him to be in more regular contact through Skype with family in the US. This now enables Connor to stay connected with family he cannot afford to fly and see. This family support helps Connor with his ongoing caring role.

Divya has four young children and provides care for her father who is nearing the end of his life. Her father receives a direct payment, which he used to pay a family member for a period of time to give his daughter a break from her caring role. Divya received a carers' direct payment, which she uses for her children to attend summer play schemes so that she get some free time to meet with friends and socialise when the family member providers care to her father. This gives Divya regular breaks from caring which are important to the family unit.

11.39. "Replacement care" may be needed to enable a carer to look after their own health and wellbeing alongside caring responsibilities, and to take a break from caring. For example, this may enable them to attend their own health appointments, or go shopping and pursue other recreational activities. It might be that regular replacement care overnight is needed so that the carer can catch up on their own sleep. In other circumstances, longer periods of replacement care may be needed, for example to enable carers to have a longer break from caring responsibilities or to balance caring with education or paid employment. In these circumstances, where the form of the replacement care is essentially a homecare service provided to the adult needing care that enables the carer to take a break, it should be considered a service provided to the cared-for person, and thus must be charged to them, not the carer.

11.40. The carer's personal budget must be an amount that enables the carer to meet their needs to continue to fulfil their caring role, and takes into account the outcomes that the carer wishes to achieve in their day to day life. This includes their wishes and/or aspirations concerning paid employment, education, training or recreation if the provision of support can contribute to the achievement of those outcomes. The manner in which the personal budget will be used to meet the carer's needs should be agreed as part of the planning process.

11.41. Local authorities must have regard to the wellbeing principle of the Act as it may be the case that the carer needs a break from caring responsibilities to look after their own physical/mental health and emotional wellbeing, social and economic wellbeing and to spend time with other members of the family and personal relationships. Whether or not there is a need for replacement care, carers may need support to help them to look after their own wellbeing. This may be, for example, a course of relaxation classes, training on stress management, gym or leisure centre membership, adult learning, development of new work skills or refreshing existing skills (so they might be able to stay in paid employment alongside caring or take up return to paid work), pursuit of hobbies such as the purchase of a garden shed, or purchase of laptop so they can stay in touch with family and friends.

CARERS' PERSONAL BUDGETS WHERE THE ADULT BEING CARED FOR DOES NOT HAVE ELIGIBLE NEEDS

11.42. The Act makes clear that the local authority is able to meet the carer's needs by providing a service directly to the adult needing care. However, there may be instances where the adult being cared for does not have eligible needs, so does not have their own personal budget or care plan. In these cases, the carer must still receive a support plan which covers their needs, and how they will be met. This would specify how the carer's needs are going to be met (for example, via replacement care to the adult needing care), and the personal budget would be for the costs of meeting the carer's needs.

11.43. The adult needing care would not receive a personal budget or care plan, because no matter what the service is in practice, it is designed to meet the carer's needs. However, it is essential that the person requiring care is involved in the decision-making process and agrees with the intended course of action.

11.44. In situations such as these, the carer could request a direct payment, and use that to commission their own replacement care from an agency, rather than using an arranged service from the local authority or a third party. The local authority should take steps to ensure that the wishes of the adult requiring care are taken into account during these decisions. For example, the adult requiring care may not want to receive replacement care in this manner.

11.45. If such a type of replacement care is charged for (and it may not be), then it would be the adult needing care that would pay, not the carer, because they are the direct recipient of the service. This is in part why it is so important that the adult needing care agrees to receiving that type of care. The decisions taken by the carer and adult requiring care and charging implications should be agreed and recorded in the support plan. If a dispute arises and the person refused to pay the charge, the local authority must, as far as it is feasible, identify some other way of supporting the carer.

11.46. For the purposes of charging, the personal budget which the carer receives must specify the costs to the local authority and the costs to the adult, based on the charging guidance (see chapter 8). In this case, "the adult" refers to the carer, because they are the adult whose needs are being met. However, in instances where replacement care is being provided, the carer should not be charged; if charges are due to be paid then these have to be met by the adult needing care. Any such charges would not be recorded in the personal budget, but should be set out clearly and agreed by those concerned.

APPEALS/DISPUTES

11.47. The local authority should take all reasonable steps to limit appeals or disputes regarding the personal budget allocation. This will include through effective care and support planning, and transparency in the personal budget allocation process. Additionally, many disputes may be avoided by informing people of the timescales that are likely to be involved in different stages of the process. Keeping people informed how their case is progressing may help limit the number of disputes.

11.48. Current complaints provision for care and support is set out in regulations.[1] The provisions of the regulations mean that anyone who is dissatisfied with a decision made by the local authority can make a complaint about that decision and have that complaint handled by the local authority. The local authority must make its own arrangements for dealing with complaints in accordance with the 2009 regulations.

LINKS TO EXTERNAL RESOURCES

The seven steps to being in control of my support, In Control, 2005: http://bit.ly/1c7cgSX

Managing the money – resource deployment options for personal budgets, PPF, 2008: http://bit.ly/1azdgUx

Financial management of personal budgets, Audit Commission, 2010: http://bit.ly/1dsWWzE

Enabling risk, ensuring safety – self-directed support and personal budgets, SCIE, 2010: http://bit.ly/1btZcqK

Self-directed support process – what good looks like, ADASS SW, 2010: http://bit.ly/1cYOXPi

Making resource allocation work in a financial environment, PPF/ADASS, 2010: http://bit.ly/1cYQpBh

Adult social care minimum process framework, TLAP, 2011: http://bit.ly/LBJym0

---

[1] Choice and control for all – the role of individual service funds in delivering personalised care and support, Groundswell, 2012: http://bit.ly/1dsYA4f. Local Authority Social Services and NHS Complaints Regulations 2009, made under powers in Sections 113 to 115 of the Health and Social Care (Community Health and Standards Act) 2003.

Keeping personal budgets personal – learning from the experiences of older people, people with mental health problems and their carers, SCIE, 2011: http://bit.ly/1iwYsFO

Personal budgets – taking stock, moving forward, TLAP, 2011: http://bit.ly/LTFDC3

Integrating personal budgets – early learning, PHB Toolkit, NHSE, 2012: http://bit.ly/Mv2F1Z

Integrating personal budgets – myths and misconceptions, PHB Toolkit, NHSE, 2012: http://bit.ly/1eXXz5j

Progressing personalisation – a review of personal budgets and direct payments for carers, Carers Trust, 2012: http://bit.ly/N8VzBj

Making it real – making progress towards personalised, community based support, TLAP, 2012: http://bit.ly/1nX2V8J

Groundswell, 2012: http://bit.ly/1dsYA4f

Personal health budgets – ways in which money can be held and managed, NHSE, 2012:http://bit.ly/1iv2Gyn

Improving personal budgets for older people, TLAP, 2013: http://bit.ly/1iuTGJq

Self-directed support: reducing process, increasing choice and control, TLAP, 2013: http://bit.ly/LBIqig

RAS Challenge information, In Control, 2013: http://bit.ly/1ndyaJe

Paths to personalisation in mental health, TLAP/NDTi, 2013: http://bit.ly/1b5mRmB

National personal budgets survey, TLAP, 2013: http://bit.ly/1crP3KG

Making it real for carers, TLAP, 2013: http://bit.ly/1ndEmkK

12. DIRECT PAYMENTS

This chapter covers:
- This chapter covers:
- Making direct payments available;
- Considerations for adults with and without capacity;
- Administering, monitoring and reviewing direct payments;
- Using the direct payment;
- Paying family members;
- Short-term and long-term care in a care home;
- Becoming an employer;
- Direct payments and hospital stays;
- Direct payments for local authority services;
- Direct payments in the form of pre-payment cards;
- Harmonisation of direct payments;
- Terminating direct payments.

12.1. Direct payments are monetary payments made to individuals who request to receive one to meet some or all of their eligible care and support needs. The legislative context for direct payments is set out in the Care Act, Section 117(2C) of the Mental Health Act 1983 (the 1983 Act) and the Care and Support (Direct Payments) Regulations 2014.

12.2. Direct payments have been in use in adult care and support since the mid-1990s and they remain the Government's preferred mechanism for personalised care and support. They provide independence, choice and control by enabling people to commission their own care and support in order to meet their eligible needs.[1]

12.3. Direct payments, along with personal budgets and personalised care planning, mandated for the first time in the Care Act, provide the platform with which to deliver a modern care and support system. People should be encouraged to take ownership of their care planning, and be free to choose how their needs are met, whether through local authority or third-party provision, by direct payments, or a combination of the three approaches.

12.4. For direct payments to have the maximum impact, the processes involved in administering and monitoring the payment should incorporate the minimal elements to allow the local authority to fulfil its statutory responsibilities. These processes must not restrict choice or stifle innovation by requiring that the adult's needs are met by a particular provider, and must not place undue burdens on people to provide information to the local authority. An effective monitoring process should also go beyond financial monitoring, and include aspects such as identifying wider risks and issues, for example non- payment of tax, and provision of employers' liability insurance where this is appropriate.

12.5. The local authority also has a key role in ensuring that people are given relevant and timely information about direct payments, so that they can make a

---

[1] In this guidance, references to care and support to meet an adult's eligible needs include care and support provided or commissioned by a local authority to discharge its duty under section 117 of the 1983 Act. References in this guidance to sections 31 and 32 of the Act also apply in respect of after-care services (as those sections are modified by Part 1 of Schedule 4 to the Act).

decision whether to request a payment, and, if doing so, are supported to use and manage the payment appropriately. The route to a direct payment is for a person to request one, but the local authority should support the person's right to make this request by providing information and advice as detailed above. People must not be forced to take a direct payment against their will, but instead be informed of the choices available to them.

12.6. This chapter should be read in conjunction with the sections on care and support planning and personal budgets (see chapters 10 and 11), and applies to people in need of care and support and carers equally, unless specifically stated.

MAKING DIRECT PAYMENTS AVAILABLE

12.7. The availability of direct payments should be included in the universal information service that all local authorities are required to provide. This should set out:

- what direct payments are;

- how to request one including the use of nominated and authorised persons95 to manage the payment;

- explanation of the direct payment agreement and how the local authority will monitor the use of the direct payment;

- the responsibilities involved in managing a direct payment and being an employer;

- making arrangements with social care providers;

- signposting to local organisations (such as user-led organisations and micro- enterprises) and the local authority's own internal support, who offer support to direct payment holders, and information on local providers;

- case studies and evidence on how direct payments can be used locally to innovatively meet needs.[1]

12.8. This will allow people to be fully aware what direct payments are and whether they are something that are of interest. In addition to this general information, authorities must also explain to people what needs could be met by direct payments during the care and support planning process.

12.9. Local authorities have a crucial role to play in promoting the use of direct payments, and enabling people to make requests to receive direct payments in an efficient way. However, the gateway to receiving a direct payment must always be through the request from the person. Local authorities must not force people to take a direct payment against their will, or allow people to be placed in a situation where the direct payment is the only way to receive personalised care and support. However, local authorities are encouraged to prompt people to consider direct payments and how they could be used to meet needs.

---

[1] A nominated person is anyone who agrees to manage a direct payment on behalf of the person with care needs. An authorised person is someone who agrees to manage a direct payment for a person who lacks capacity according to the Mental Capacity Act 2005.

STEPS FOLLOWING A REQUEST TO RECEIVE DIRECT PAYMENTS

12.10. It is expected that most requests to receive direct payments will occur during the care planning stage as this is when authorities must inform the person of the needs that could be met via direct payments. However, local authorities must consider requests for direct payments made at any time, and have clear and swift processes in place to respond to the requests. For example, a person may request a direct payment before a scheduled or anticipated review. In these cases, the local authority must assess the request on the same basis as a request made during care planning. In practice, it may be convenient to consider the request at the same time as a review of the care plan. In these cases, the review should be brought forward so as not to delay the consideration of the direct payment request (see chapter 13 on reviews). The steps to follow after receiving a request for a direct payment will depend on whether the person has been assessed as having capacity to make a decision about direct payments or not, which should have taken place at the assessment of needs (see chapter 6).

Assessing capacity

The following considerations should be made when assessing capacity:

- Does the person have a general understanding of what decisions they need to make and how they need to make them?
- Does the person have a general understanding of the consequences of making, or not making the decision?
- Is the person able to understand, retain, use and weigh up all relevant information to support the decision?
- Can the person communicate the decision? (This may involve the use of a specialist or independent advocate)
- Is there need to bring in additional expertise to aid the assessment?

12.11. Mental capacity is the ability to make a decision. Under the 2005 Mental Capacity Act, a person lacks capacity in relation to a matter if, at the material time, they are unable to make a decision in relation to the matter because of an impairment of, or a disturbance in the functioning of, the mind or brain.

12.12. Assessments of capacity must always be made on a case-by-case basis, in relation to the specific decision to be made. Assumptions should not be made due to the existence of a particular condition, nor on whole groups of people.

12.13. Consideration should also be given to whether capacity is constant or likely to fluctuate. Where it is clear that fluctuating capacity is a known issue, or likely to be, this should be covered in the care plan which details the steps to take where capacity fluctuates. The Care and Support (Direct Payments) Regulations 2014 allow for direct payments to continue to be made in cases of fluctuating capacity (see paragraphs 12.65-12.66 on terminating direct payments below).

ADULTS WITH CAPACITY

12.14. Where the local authority is satisfied that the person has capacity to make a request for direct payments to cover some or all of their care needs, it must consider each of the four conditions in section 31 of the Care Act. These conditions need to be met in their entirety; a failure in one would result in the request to receive a direct payment being declined. The conditions are:

- the adult has capacity to make the request, and where there is a nominated person, that person agrees to receive the payments;

- the local authority is not prohibited by regulations under section 33 from meeting the adult's needs by making direct payments to the adult or nominated person;

- the local authority is satisfied that the adult or nominated person is capable of managing direct payments either by himself or herself, or with whatever help the authority thinks the adult or nominated person will be able to access;

- the local authority is satisfied that making direct payments to the adult or nominated person is an appropriate way to meet the needs in question.

12.15. The authority must clarify at the earliest stage possible where the request originates from. The Care Act provides a power to enable direct payments to be made to the person in need of care and support, or a nominated person acting on their behalf if the adult so requests. Where a nominated person has been requested to receive the direct payment, the authority should involve the nominated person in any appropriate stages of the care planning journey, such as the development of the care plan, as long as the person with care needs agrees to this. Where the person does not specifically request this involvement, the local authority should consider whether to encourage the person to make that request. During this process, the nominated person should receive information regarding the local authorities direct payments processes, as well as information and advice on using and managing the direct payment, so that the nominated person understands their legal obligations as the direct payment recipient to act in the best interests of the person requiring care and support (see also becoming an employer below). The local authority must also satisfy itself that the nominated person meets the conditions in Section 31 of the Act.

ADULTS LACKING CAPACITY

12.16. In cases where the person in need of care and support has been assessed as lacking capacity to request the direct payment, an authorised person can request the direct payment on the person's behalf. In these cases, the local authority must satisfy itself that the person meets the five conditions as set out in section 32 of the Care Act.

12.17. As with direct payments for people with capacity, each of these conditions must be met in their entirety. Failure to meet any of the conditions would result in the request being declined. The conditions are:

- where the person is not authorised under the Mental Capacity Act 2005 but there is at least one person who is so authorised, that person who is authorised supports the person's request;

- the local authority is not prohibited by regulations under section 33 from meeting the adult's needs by making direct payments to the authorised person, and if regulations under that section give the local authority discretion to decide not to meet the adult's needs by making direct payments to the authorised person, it does not exercise that discretion;

- the local authority is satisfied that the authorised person will act in the adult's best interests in arranging for the provision of the care and support for which the direct payments under this section would be used;

- the local authority is satisfied that the authorised person is capable of managing direct payment by himself or herself, or with whatever help the authority thinks the authorised person will be able to access;

- the local authority is satisfied that making direct payments to the authorised person is an appropriate way to meet the needs in question.

CONSIDERATION OF THE REQUEST

12.18. After considering the suitability of the person requesting the direct payment against the appropriate conditions in the Care Act, the local authority must make a determination whether to provide a direct payment. Where accepted, the decision should be recorded in the care plan, or support plan. Where refused, the person or person making the request should be provided with written reasons that explain the decision, and be made aware of how to appeal the decision through the local complaints process.

12.19. The Care Act defines one of the conditions to be met is that the direct payment is an appropriate way to meet the needs in question (or, in respect of after-care services, an appropriate way to discharge its duty under section 117 of the 1983 Act).[1] Local authorities must not use this condition to arbitrarily decline a request for a direct payment. For example, there may be instances where a person is obliged to receive services as a condition of mental health legislation (including a community treatment order, guardianship or leave of absence from hospital under the Mental Health Act or provisions in other mental health legislation). In these cases, although the person is being obliged to receive services rather than choosing to present for services, it may still be appropriate to give the person the responsibility of meeting their needs via a direct payment, if this is what is requested. Particular consideration should be given to these cases when applying the conditions set out in the Act. In all cases, appropriateness is for local authorities to determine, although it is expected that in general, direct payments are an appropriate way to meet most care and support needs.

12.20. However, there may be cases where a direct payment is not appropriate to meet needs. The Regulations sets out that direct payments cannot be made to people subject to a court order for a drug or alcohol treatment program or similar schemes (schedule 1 of the Regulations).

12.21. A further condition is that the local authority must be satisfied that the person is able to manage the direct payment by him or herself, or whatever help or support the person will be able to access. Local authorities should therefore take all reasonable steps to provide this support to whoever may require it. To comply with this, many local authorities have contracts with voluntary or user-led organisations that provide support and advice to direct payment holders, or to people interested in receiving direct payments. This condition should not be used to deny a person from receiving a direct payment without consideration of support needs. Consideration should also be given to involving a specialist assessor in

---

[1] See sections 31(7) and 32(9) of the Act as modified respectively by paragraph (4) and (9) of Part 1 of Schedule 4 to the Act.

determination of support requirements, in particular if one was used earlier in the care and support process (such as assessment).

12.22. In all cases, the consideration of the request should be concluded in as timely a manner as possible. Where the request for a direct payment has been declined, the person in need of care and support, and any other person involved in the request (i.e. nominated or authorised person) should (subject to Data Protection Act requirements) receive the reasons in a format that is accessible to them. This should set out which of the conditions in the Care Act have not been met, the reasons as to why they have not been met, and what the person may need to do in the future to obtain a positive decision. The consideration stage should be performed as quickly as is reasonably practicable, and the local authority must provide interim arrangements to meet care and support needs to cover the period in question.

Case Study: Making direct payments support accessible

Abdul is a deafblind man; to communicate he prefers to use Braille, Deafblind Manual and email. He directly employs several staff through direct payments. He receives payroll support from his local direct payments support service. Abdul suggested ways to make direct payments management accessible to him. He communicates with the support service mainly via email but they also use Typetalk.

At the end of the month, Abdul emails the support service with details of the hours that his staff have worked. The support service work out any deductions from pay (such as National Insurance and Income Tax) and email him to tell him how much he should pay the staff via cheque. They then send him pay slips to be given to staff. The envelope that the payslips are sent in has two staples in the corner so that he knows who the letter is from. The payslips themselves are labelled in Braille so that he knows which staff to give them to.

Each quarter, the support service tells him how much he needs to pay on behalf of his employees in National Insurance and Income Tax. The service also fills in quarterly Inland Revenue paperwork. At the end of the year, the support service sends relevant information to the council, so that they are aware of how the direct payments are being spent.

Abdul has taken on only some of the responsibilities of employing people; he has delegated some tasks to the support service. Control still remains with Abdul and confidentiality is maintained by using accessible labelling. In terms of the wellbeing principle, the local authority has promoted Abdul's control over his day-to-day life.

12.23. Where the request has been declined, the local authority should continue the care planning process so that it can seek to agree with the person how best to meet the needs, without the use of direct payments (see chapter 10 on care and support planning).

ADMINISTERING DIRECT PAYMENTS

12.24. The local authority must be satisfied that the direct payment is being used to meet the care and support needs set out in the plan, and should therefore have systems in place to proportionally monitor direct payment usage to ensure effective use of public money. The Care and Support (Direct Payments) Regulations 2014 set out that the local authority must review the making of direct payments initially within six months, and thereafter every 12 months, and must not require information to be provided more often and in more detail than is reasonably required for the purpose of enabling the authority to know that making direct payment is still an appropriate way of meeting the needs, and that conditions upon which it is made are met. Local authorities should not design systems that place a disproportionate reporting burden upon the individual. The reporting system should not clash with the policy intention of direct payments to encourage greater autonomy, flexibility and innovation. For example, people should not be requested to duplicate information or have onerous monitoring requirements placed upon them. Monitoring should be proportionate to the needs to be met and the care package. Thus local authorities should have regard to lowering monitoring requirements for people that have been managing direct payments without issues for a long period.

12.25. The amount of the direct payment is derived from the personal budget as set out in the care and support plan, or support plan, and thus must be an amount which is sufficient to meet the needs the local authority has a duty or power to meet. The direct payment amount will reflect whether the person is required to make any financial contributions, or is requesting a direct payment for only a part of their care and support requirements. Local authorities cannot require financial contributions for a direct payment for after care services under the MHA; these must be provided without charge.

Example of reduced monitoring

Gina has a stable condition and has been successfully managing her direct payment for over two years. The local authority therefore decides to reduce monitoring to the lowest level due to the low perceived risk (while still complying with the required review in the Act and Regulations). Gina is now considered to have the skills and experience to manage on her own unless the local authority request otherwise or information suggested otherwise comes to the attention of the local authority.

12.26. It is ultimately for authorities to decide whether payments are made on a gross or net basis in consultation with appropriate stakeholders. However, local authorities who operate systems of providing gross direct payments should consider the benefits of moving to net payments as these reduce transaction and process costs for both the authority and the person receiving the direct payment.[1]

12.27. The local authority should have regard to whether there will be costs such as recruitment costs, Employers' National Insurance Contributions, and any other costs by reason of the way in which the adult's needs will be met with the direct payment.[2] If these costs will be incurred their amount must be

---

[1] Gross payments are for the full direct payment amount, and the local authority then recovers any applicable charges from the person. A net direct payment is allocated after any appropriate charges have been subtracted, and is generally seen as the easiest and most efficient way to administer direct payments.

[2] Employers (including direct payment holders) will be required to comply with the duty to automatically enrol eligible workers into a qualifying workplace pension scheme and to meet the minimum contributions required by law. More information for is available from The Pension Regulator at www.thepensionsregulator.gov.uk

included in the personal budget (and thus direct payment) if it is appropriate for the adult to meet the needs in a way which incurs the costs. Some local authorities include one-off payments within the direct payment to cover these factors. In addition, other authorities have commissioned support services such as brokerage, payroll and employment advice as part of their general direct payment offer.

12.28. Where a direct payment recipient is using their payment to employ a personal assistant (PA) or other staff, the local authority should ensure that there are clear plans in place of how needs will be met in the event of the PA being absent, for example due to sickness, maternity or holiday. Local authorities still have a duty to ensure needs are being met, even if the person makes their own arrangements via the direct payment, so contingencies may be needed. Where appropriate, these should be detailed in the care and support plan, or support plan.

12.29. Specific information should also be given to people about the requirements to have plans in place for redundancy payments due to circumstances such as moving home, a change in care and support needs, or the result of the death of the direct payment holder, or care recipient. If the person meets needs by directly employing someone, they will be responsible for all costs of employment including redundancy payments and this should be made clear to people as part of the information and advice process before a decision is made whether to request direct payments. The local authority must ensure that the direct payment is sufficient to meet these costs if it is appropriate for the adult to meet their needs by employing someone.

12.30. Normally, if someone dies any employment liabilities will be met by the person's estate, but with direct payments local authorities and adults have freedom to develop their own arrangements for dealing with this issue. This could include using any unspent direct payment to contribute to any redundancy costs, having insurance in place that covers redundancy, or the local authority agreeing to cover redundancy payments through the direct payment amount.

12.31. Whatever arrangements are made it is important that the local authority and direct payment holder are both clear as to their responsibilities in this regard to avoid any disputes at a sensitive time for family and carers. Decisions made should be recorded in care plans.

12.32. Local authorities should also consider how to recover unspent direct payments if the recipient dies. For example, if someone wishes to pay an agency in advance for its services, the local authority should bear in mind that it may be difficult to recover money paid for services that were not in fact delivered. Local authorities should also consider, if the direct payment recipient does leave unspent funds to be recovered, that before their death the direct payment recipient may have incurred liabilities that should legitimately be paid for using the direct payments (for example, they received services for which payment had not been made at the time of death). Local authorities may need to consider any redundancy costs payable to personal assistants and be prepared to provide advice on how these might be met. As with other costs the personal budget must be a sufficient amount to meet the person's needs, including the provision of any redundancy costs, if appropriate to meet needs, and subject to other arrangements that may have been made.

12.33. Local authorities should ensure all direct payment recipients are supported and given information in regards to having the correct insurance cover in place. Direct payments recipients should be given support to understand the benefits that insurance cover can provide, and the direct payment should therefore include an amount to cover the cost of employers' liability insurance and any other insurance that is required in order that the person can meet their needs in the way specified in the care plan.

12.34. The local authority must also have regard to where the direct payment can be integrated with other forms of public funding, such as personal health budget direct payments. Where this is apparent, the local authority should take steps to work with partners to combine the payments, as long as the person and all parties agree. For example, the local authority could agree with the NHS that the social care and health direct payments are combined and that the monitoring is performed solely by one organisation, reporting to the other as appropriate. This will avoid the person having multiple bank accounts, and having to supply similar information to public bodies to account for direct payment spend, while allowing both bodies to meet their statutory responsibilities.

USING THE DIRECT PAYMENT PAYING FAMILY MEMBERS

12.35. The direct payment is designed to be used flexibly and innovatively and there should be no unreasonable restriction placed on the use of the payment, as long as it is being used to meet eligible care and support needs.

Example – Direct Payment to pay a family member for administration support

David has been using direct payments to meet his needs for some time, and has used private agencies to provide payroll and administration support, funded by a one-off annual payment as part of his personal budget allocation.

David's wife, Gill provides care for him and is increasingly becoming more hands-on in arranging multiple PAs to visit and other administrative tasks as David's care needs have begun to fluctuate.

They jointly approach the local authority to request that Gill undertake the administration support instead of the agency as they want to take complete control of the payment and care arrangements so that they can best meet David's fluctuating needs and ensure that appropriate care is organized.

The local authority considers that Gill would be able to manage this aspect of the payment, and jointly revises the care plan to detail the aspects of the payment, and what services Gill will undertake to the agreement of all concerned. The personal budget is also revised accordingly.

The family now have complete control of the payment, Gill is reimbursed for her time in supporting David with his direct payment, and the local authority are able to make a saving in the one-off support allocation as there are no provider overheads to pay. In promoting David's wellbeing, the local authority has demonstrated regard for the balance between promoting an individual's wellbeing and that of people who are involved in caring for them. They have given Gill increased control in a way that David is comfortable with and supports.

12.36. The 2009 Direct Payment Regulations excluded the payment from being used to pay for care from a close family member living in the same household, except where the local authority determined this to be necessary.[1] While the Care and Support (Direct Payments) Regulations 2014 maintain this provision regarding paying a family member living in the same household for care, it provides a distinction between 'care' and 'administration/management' of the direct payment. This allows people to pay a close family member living in the same household to provide management and/or administrative support to the direct payment holder in cases where the local authority determines this to be necessary. This is intended to reflect the fact that in some cases, especially where there are multiple complex needs, the direct payment amount may be substantial.

---

[1] This does not include family members that live elsewhere to the direct payment recipient (i.e. it is allowed to pay a family member to provide care, as long as that member does not live in the same household).

Example – Direct payment paid to a family member where necessary
James has severe learning difficulties as well as various physical disabilities.
He has serious trust issues and a unique way of communicating that only his
family, through years of care as a child, can understand. The local authority
agrees that using a direct payment to pay for care from his parents is necessary
as it is the best way to meet James's needs and outcomes.

12.37. The management and administration of a large payment, along with
organising care and support can be a complex and time consuming task. This
allows family members performing this task to be paid a proportion of the direct
payment, similar to what many direct payment holders pay to third-party support
organisations, as long as the local authority allows this.

12.38. This is not intended to be income replacement, and people interested in
requesting this option should be informed of tax and employment implications,
any impacts upon other benefits and given (or signposted to) information and
advice to help them decide. The local authority should be satisfied that it is necessary to make the payment to the family member to provide this service and that the
direct payment will only be used for administration and management of the payment. The circumstances and payment amount should be decided and agreed with
the person requiring care and support, the family member, local authority and any
other person (i.e. advocate), with the local authority taking steps to ensure all parties agree.

12.39. These decisions should be recorded in the care plan and include the
amount of the payments, their frequency and the activities that are covered.
This arrangement must also be taken into account during allocation of the personal budget so that the amount remains sufficient to meet the person's needs.

12.40. Local authorities will need to have in place agreement between all parties about what steps to take in case of a dispute regarding the management of the
payment by a household family member. This will be especially relevant where
the person providing administrative and management is also the nominated or
authorised direct payment recipient. It would not be appropriate to allow this
where there is a risk that the direct payment may be abused, or there are other sen-
sitivities such as potential safeguarding issues.

SHORT-TERM CARE IN A CARE HOME

12.41. Direct payments cannot currently be used to pay for people to live in
long-term care home placements. They can be made to enable people to purchase
for themselves a short stay in care homes, provided that the stay does not exceed a
period of four consecutive weeks in any 12-month period. This could be used to
provide a respite break for a carer, for example.

12.42. The Regulations specify that where the interim period between two stays
in care homes is less than four weeks, then the two stays should be added together
to make a cumulative total, which should also not exceed four weeks if it is to be
paid for with direct payments. On the other hand, if two stays in care homes are
more than four weeks apart then they are not added together.

12.43. Once a direct payment recipient has had four consecutive weeks in care
homes, or two or more periods separated by less than four weeks which added
together total four weeks, then they cannot use their direct payments to pay for

any more home services care until 12 months have passed from the start of the four-week period. On the other hand, as long as each stay is less than four weeks and there is an interim period of at least four weeks between two or more stays which added together exceed four weeks, then the service recipient may use their direct payments to pay for residential breaks throughout the year.

Example – Direct Payments for short-term residential care
Mrs. H has one week in a care home every six weeks. Because each week in a care home is more than four weeks a part, they are not added together. The cumulative total is only one week and the four-week limit is never reached. Peter has three weeks in a care home, two weeks at home and then another week in a care home. The two episodes of time in a care home are less than four weeks apart and so they are added together making four weeks in total. Peter cannot use his direct payments to purchase any more care home services within a 12-month period.

12.44. People can receive additional weeks in a care home once they have reached the four-week maximum. They cannot purchase the stay using their direct payments, but if the local authority and the person agrees that a longer stay is needed, it can still arrange and fund stays for the person. There is no restriction on the length of time for which the local authority may arrange such accommodation for someone (see chapter 8 for guidance on choice of accommodation).

12.45. The time limit is imposed to promote people's independence and to encourage them to remain at home rather than moving into long-term home placement. Where a person is constantly using the direct payment to pay for a short-term care home stays, the local authority should consider whether to conduct a review to ensure that the care plan is still meeting needs.

LONG-TERM CARE IN A CARE HOME
12.46. People who are living in care homes may receive direct payments in relation to non- residential care services. For example, they may have temporary access to direct payments to try out independent living arrangements before making a commitment to moving out of their care home. Direct payments can also be used by people living in care homes to take part in day-time activities. This can be particularly empowering for young people in transition (see chapter 15).

12.47. Direct payments cannot currently be used to secure long-term stays in a care home. However, the Government is currently testing the use of direct payments in care homes, with the aim of introducing this in 2016. The learning from the trailblazer programme will be used to develop additional statutory guidance for local authorities.

BECOMING AN EMPLOYER
12.48. Local authorities should give people clear advice as to their responsibilities when managing direct payments, and whether the person in receipt of direct payments needs to register with HM Revenue & Customs (HMRC) as an employer. Becoming an employer carries with it certain responsibilities and

obligations, in particular to HMRC and people need to be aware of these before agreeing to take up a direct payment.[1]

12.49. The local authority should consider using the proportionality principle, whether to carry out checks to make sure any PAYE income tax and National Insurance contributions deducted from an employee's pay is in turn paid over to HMRC, and that employment payments do not breach the national minimum wage and conform to pension requirements if eligible. Some people may not need this check to be performed, but it may be more appropriate in other cases and conform to pension requirements if eligible.[2] Where it becomes clear that payments, or returns detailing employee information deductions, have not been made, or that the individual is failing to meet their obligations as an employer generally, the direct payment scheme should be reviewed and consideration given to whether alternative arrangements that result in the direct payment recipient no longer acting as the employer need to be made. Not doing so may result in the individual building up arrears of tax and National Insurance due to HMRC, which may then lead to enforcement action to recover any debt. This situation should be able to be avoided by effective monitoring where appropriate, and by providing clear, accessible upfront information about the responsibilities of becoming an employer. Many local authorities have commissioned voluntary and charity organisations to provide support to direct payment holders on these matters.

12.50. Many people are interested in using the direct payment to become an employer, for example, directly employing a personal assistant (PA). In these instances, the local authority should ensure that the person is given appropriate information and advice that explains the difference between a regulated and unregulated provider to help the person make a fully informed decision on how best to meet their needs. Where a direct payment is made under section 32 of the Act and to comply with the regulations, the local authority must also ensure that the authorised person is aware of how to access Disclosure and Barring Service Checks (DBS – previously CRB checks) on individuals they wish to employ, for example by ensuring that a check has been made by the agency providing the service, the local authority, or by another body. Individuals cannot apply for DBS checks on other individuals, and the local authority should make people aware of this, and the importance of thorough checks and employment references in the recruitment process.

12.51. Where a person wishes to directly employ their own PA, the local authority should also have regard to the guidance published by Skills for Care detailing minimum levels of support for individual employers and PAs. This guidance recommends local authorities should provide on-going support through access to training activities in a variety of ways and promote the Workforce Development Fund. It also proposes that local authorities promote apprenticeships for PAs.[3]

---

[1] Further information on being an employer, aimed at people using direct payments is available at www.disabilitytaxguide.org.uk

[2] Employers (including direct payment holders) will be required to comply with the duty to automatically enrol eligible workers into a qualifying workplace pension scheme and to meet the minimum contributions required by law. More information for is available from The Pension Regulator at www.thepensionsregulator.gov.uk

[3] Details of the advice note are available at: http://www.skillsforcare.org.uk/Document-library/ Employing- your-own-care-and-support/ADASS- and-Skills-for-Care-advice-note-2013.pdf

DIRECT PAYMENTS AND HOSPITAL STAYS

12.52. There may often be occasions when direct payment holders require a stay in hospital. However, this should not mean that the direct payment must be suspended while the individual is in hospital. Where the direct payment recipient is also the person requiring care and support, consideration should be given to how the direct payment may be used in hospital to meet non-health needs or to ensure employment arrangements are maintained. Suspending or even terminating the payment could result in the person having to break the employment contract with a trusted personal assistant, causing distress and a lack of continuity of care when discharged from hospital.

12.53. In these cases, the local authority should explore with the person, their carer and the NHS the options to ensure that both the health and care and support needs of the person are being fully met in the best way possible. For example, the person may prefer the personal assistant to visit hospital to help with personal care matters. This may be especially so where there has been a long relationship between the direct payment holder and the personal assistant. This should not interfere with the medical duties of hospital personnel, but be tailored to work alongside health provision.

12.54. In some cases, the nominated or authorised person managing the direct payment may require a hospital stay. In these cases, the authority must conduct an urgent review to ensure that the person continues to receive care and support to meet their needs. This may be through a temporary nominated/ authorised person, or through short-term authority arranged care and support.

Example of using a direct payment whilst in hospital

Peter is deafblind and is required to stay in hospital for an operation. Whilst the hospital pays for an interpreter for the medical interventions, Peter needs additional support to be able to move around the ward, and to communicate informally with staff and his family. The local authority and the NHS Trust agree that Peter's communicator guide continues to support him in hospital, and is paid for via the direct payment, as it was when Peter was at home. Personal and medical care is provided by NHS staff but Peter's communicator guide is on hand to provide specialist communication and guiding support to make his hospital stay is as comfortable as possible.

DIRECT PAYMENTS FOR LOCAL AUTHORITY SERVICES

12.55. As a general rule, direct payments should not be used to pay for local authority- provided services from the 'home' local authority. Where a person wishes to receive care and support from their local authority, it should be easier and less burdensome to provide the service direct to the person. This will also avoid possible conflicts of interest where the local authority is providing the direct payment, but also promoting their services for people to purchase.

12.56. There may be cases where the local authority exercises discretion to provide care and support by receiving a direct payment amount, for example this could be where a person who is using direct payments wants to make a one-off purchase from the local authority such as a place in day care. In these cases, the local authority should take into account the wishes of the person requiring care and support when making a decision. In one off cases such as these, it may be less burdensome to accept the direct payment amount, rather than providing the service and then reducing the personal budget and direct payment accordingly.

Example of local authority provided service
Graham has a direct payment for the full amount of his personal budget allowance. He decides to use a local authority run day service on an infrequent basis and requests to pay for it with his direct payment so that he retains flexibility about when he attends The local authority service is able to agree to this request and has systems already in place to take payments as self-funders often use the service. The authority advise Graham that if he wishes to use the day service on a frequent basis (i.e. once a week) it would be better to provide the service to him direct, and to reduce the direct payment amount accordingly.

12.57. This does not preclude people from using their direct payment to purchase care and support from a different local authority. For example, a person may live close to authority boundaries and another local authority could provide a particular service that their 'home' authority does not provide.

DIRECT PAYMENTS IN THE FORM OF PRE-PAID OR PRE-PAYMENT CARDS
12.58. Many local authorities have been developing the use of pre-paid cards as a mechanism to allow direct payments without the need for a separate bank account, or to ease the financial management of the payment. Whilst the use of such cards can be a useful step from managed services to direct payments, they should not be provided as the only option to take a direct payment The offer of a 'traditional' direct payment paid into a bank account should always be available if this is what the person requests and this is appropriate to meet needs. Consideration should be given to the benefit gained from this arrangement as opposed to receiving the payment via a pre-paid card.
12.59. It is also important that where a pre-paid card system is used, the person is still free to exercise choice and control. For example, there should not be blanket restrictions on cash withdrawals from pre-paid cards which could limit choice and control. The card must not be linked solely to an online market-place that only contains selected providers in which to choose from. Local authorities should therefore give consideration to how they develop card systems that encourage flexibility and innovation, and consider consulting care and support user groups on any proposed changes to direct payment processes.

HARMONISATION OF DIRECT PAYMENTS
12.60. In circumstances where it is in the person's interest to combine the plan and budget with another form of state support (such as personal health budgets), and the person agrees that plans should be combined, the local authority should give consideration to whether the person is receiving direct payments from partner organisations, such as the NHS. If so, attempts should be made to harmonise the direct payments so that the person does not have multiple payments each with their own monitoring regime. For example, the local authority could work with the NHS partner to agree on a 'lead organisation' that oversees the overall budget and monitors the direct payments to ensure they are being to meet both health and

care needs, while still allowing both bodies to satisfy themselves of their statutory responsibilities.

REVIEWING DIRECT PAYMENTS

12.61. In addition to monitoring direct payments generally to ensure they are being used to meet care and support needs, the Regulations set out that local authorities must also review the making of the direct payment within the first six months of making the first payment. This provision is intended to be used for direct payments made under the powers in the Care Act, rather than pre-existing ones.

12.62. This review is intended to be light-touch to ensure that the person is comfortable with using the direct payment, and experiencing no initial issues. It should ideally be incorporated within the initial review of the care and support plan 6-8 weeks after sign- off and include elements such as managing and using the direct payment and a discussion to consider any long-term support arrangements that may be appropriate such as payroll, insurance cover and third party support. Local authorities should ensure that reviewing officers are appropriately trained to review direct payments (for example are familiar with financial procedures and employment laws) This review is not intended to be a full review of the person's care and support plan. However, if this review raises concerns or requires actions that affect the detail recorded in the care plan, then a full review of the plan would need to be carried out.

12.63. If the direct payment recipient is employing people, the local authority should as part of the review, consider checking, if appropriate, to ensure the individual is fulfilling their responsibilities as the employer, in particular that they are submitting PAYE returns to HMRC as well as paying tax and National Insurance deductions made to HMRC.

12.64. The Regulations also set out that following the six-month review, the local authority must then review the making of the direct payment no later than every 12 months. In practice, after the initial six-month review period, local authorities may wish to consider aligning the annual review of the direct payment with the general review of the care plan. This will reduce bureaucracy and allow the local authority to review both at the same time.

12.65. Where a direct payment is being allocated to a nominated/authorised person, or where there may be a family carer being paid for administrative support, the review should incorporate all of these parties as well as the person in need of care and support. This will ensure that the local authority receives views from everyone involved in the direct payment, so that it can satisfy itself that there are no initial issues that require resolving.

12.66. The outcome of the review should be written down, and a copy given to all parties. Where there are issues that require resolving, the resolution method should be agreed with all parties involved, as far as is reasonably practicable. Where appropriate, local authorities should advise people of their rights to access the local authority complaints procedure.

TERMINATING DIRECT PAYMENTS

12.67. Direct payments should only be terminated as a last resort, or where there is clear and serious contradiction of the Regulations or where the conditions in sections 31 or 32 of the Act are no longer met (except in cases of fluctuating capacity – see below). Local authorities should take all reasonable steps to address any situations without the termination of the payment. Effective, but proportionate monitoring processes will help local authorities to spot any potential issues before a termination is necessary.

12.68. If terminating a direct payment, the local authority must ensure there is no gap in the provision of care support. Where a decision has been made to terminate a direct payment, the local authority should conduct a revision of the care and support plan, or support plan, to ensure that the plan is appropriate to meet the needs in question (see chapter 13 on reviews).

REASONS FOR DISCONTINUING DIRECT PAYMENTS

12.69. A person to whom direct payments are made, whether to purchase support for themselves or on behalf of someone else, may decide at any time that they no longer wish to continue receiving direct payments. In these cases, the local authority should ensure there are no outstanding contractual liabilities, and conduct a review of the care plan to consider alternate arrangements to meet needs.

12.70. The Care Act also sets out that a local authority shall cease making direct payments if the person no longer appears to be capable of managing the direct payments or of managing them with whatever support is necessary.

12.71. Direct payments should be discontinued when a person no longer needs the support for which the direct payments are made. This might happen in situations where the direct payments are for short-term packages when leaving care home or hospital. Direct payments for after-care services under section 117 of the Mental Health Act would also cease once the clinical commissioning group and local authority are satisfied that the person concerned is no longer in need of such services.

12.72. There may be circumstances in which the local authority discontinues direct payments temporarily. An example might be when an individual does not require assistance for a short period because their condition improves and they do not require the care and support that the direct payments are intended to secure. The local authority will need to discuss with the person, their carer, and any other person how best to manage this. The person should be allowed to resume responsibility for their own care after the interruption, if that remains their wish, unless there has been a change of circumstances which means that the conditions in the Act and/or Regulations are no longer met. If there is a change of circumstances that affects the care plan/support plan the local authority must revise the plan to ensure that it is still meeting needs (see chapter 13).

12.73. The local authority might also discontinue payments if the person fails to comply with a condition imposed under regulations to which the direct payments are subject or if for some reason the local authority no longer believes it is appropriate to make the direct payments. For example, the local authority might discontinue the direct payment if it is apparent that they have not been used to achieve the outcomes of the care plan.

12.74. The 2009 Direct Payment regulations set out that direct payments must not be provided under certain conditions, such as where the recipient is placed by the courts under a condition or requirement relating to a drug and/or alcohol dependency. The Care and Support (Direct Payments) Regulations 2014 retain this universal restriction. The groups and conditions remain substantially the same as the 2009 regulations and are set out in the schedule to the 2014 regulations.

12.75. Where direct payments are discontinued as a result of criminal justice legislative provisions, the local authority should make timely arrangements for services to be provided in lieu of the direct payments, to ensure continuity of support.

DISCONTINUING DIRECT PAYMENTS IN THE CASE OF PERSONS WITH CAPACITY TO CONSENT

12.76. Where someone with capacity was receiving direct payments but then loses capacity to consent, the local authority should discontinue direct payments to that person and consider making payments to an authorised person instead. In the interim, the local authority should make alternative arrangements to ensure continuity of support for the person concerned.

12.77. If the local authority believes the loss of capacity to consent to be temporary, it may continue to make payments if there is someone else who is willing to manage payments on the person's behalf. This situation should be treated as strictly temporary and closely monitored to ensure that, once the person has regained capacity, they are able to exercise overall control over the direct payments as before. If the person's loss of capacity to consent becomes prolonged, then the local authority should consider making more formal arrangements for an authorised person to take over receipt of the direct payments on that person's behalf. The local authority should make clear that the arrangement is designed to be temporary, so that the person managing the direct payment does not enter into any long- term contractual arrangements.

DISCONTINUING DIRECT PAYMENTS IN THE CASE OF PERSONS LACKING CAPACITY TO CONSENT

12.78. Direct payments must be discontinued if the local authority is no longer satisfied for whatever reason that the authorised person is acting in the best interests of the beneficiary, within the meaning of the 2005 Act. The local authority might also wish to discontinue the direct payments if it has sufficient reason to believe that the conditions imposed under regulations on the authorised person are not being met. The authority may wish to consider if someone else can act as an authorised person for the person lacking capacity, or whether it will have to arrange services for them in place of the direct payments.

12.79. Direct payments under section 32 of the Act must be discontinued where the local authority has reason to believe that someone who had lacked capacity to consent to direct payments has now regained that capacity on a long-term or permanent basis. The authority should not terminate direct payments to the authorised person before beginning to make direct payments to the service recipient themselves or to arrange services for them, according to their wishes. If the local authority is satisfied that the regaining of capacity will only be temporary, then it can continue to make direct payments to the authorised person if during the period that the adult has the capacity to make the request and is capable of managing the direct payment, the adult will manage the payments for him or herself.

HOW TO DISCONTINUE DIRECT PAYMENTS

12.80. In all cases, as soon as possible the local authority should discuss with individuals, their carers and any person managing the direct payments if it is considering discontinuing direct payments to them, in order to explore all available options before making the final decision to terminate the direct payments. For example, if ability to manage is an issue, the individual should be given an opportunity to demonstrate that they can continue to manage direct payments, albeit with greater support if appropriate. The local authority should not automatically assume when problems arise that the only solution is to discontinue or end direct payments.

12.81. If the local authority does decide to withdraw direct payments, it will need to conduct a review of the plan and agree alternative care and support provision with the person, their carer and independent advocate if they have one, unless the withdrawal was following a review after which the local authority concluded that the services were no longer needed. A minimum period of notice should be established that will normally be given before direct payments are discontinued. This should be included in the information to be provided to people who are considering receiving direct payments.

12.82. It will be extremely unlikely that a local authority will discontinue direct payments without giving notice, although in serious cases this may be warranted (for example, the authorised person is not acting in the best interests of the person). Local authorities should explain to people, before they begin to receive direct payments, the exceptional circumstances in which this might occur and discuss with them the implications this has for the arrangements that individuals might make.

12.83. If direct payments are discontinued, some people may find themselves with ongoing contractual responsibilities or having to terminate contracts for services (including possibly making employees redundant). Local authorities should take reasonable steps to make people aware of the potential consequences if direct payments end, and any obligations they may have.

12.84. There may be circumstances where the person has lost the capacity to manage the direct payment and there is no-one else to manage the payment on their behalf, or where a person needs additional support to terminate arrangements. In these cases the local authority should have regard as to whether it needs to step in or provide support to ensure that any contractual arrangements are appropriately terminated to ensure that additional costs are not incurred.

LINKS TO EXTERNAL RESOURCES

Status – check to see if the person engaged is employee or self-employed. http://www.hmrc.gov.uk/payerti/employee-starting/status.htm

Does the direct payment recipient need to register as an employer? http://www.hmrc.gov.uk/payerti/getting-started/register.htm

Becoming a new employer http://www.hmrc.gov.uk/payerti/getting-started/new-employer.htm

Information on taking on a new employee http://www.hmrc.gov.uk/payerti/employee-starting/new-employee.htm

Practical guide to taking on a personal assistant – www.disabilitytaxguide.org.uk

Best practice in direct payments support, TLAP, 2012: http://bit.ly/1fWbEDE

Direct payments in healthcare – a practical guide, HFMA, 2012: http://bit.ly/LBJym0

Appendix 2

Increasing the uptake of direct payments, TLAP, 2013: http://bit.ly/LBIqig

PA toolkit, http://www.skillsforcare.org.uk/Employing-your-own-care-and-support/Support-for-individual-employers/Employing-personal-assistants-toolkit.aspx

13. REVIEW OF CARE AND SUPPORT PLANS

This chapter provides guidance on section 27 of the Care Act 2014.

This chapter covers:
- Review of the care and support plan, support plan;
- Keeping plans under review generally;
- Planned and unplanned review;
- Considering a request for a review of a care plan, support plan;
- Considering a review;
- Revision of the care and support plan, support plan;
- Timeliness and regularity of reviews.

13.1. Ensuring all people with a care and support plan, or support plan have the opportunity to reflect on what is working, what is not working and what might need to change is a an important part of the planning process. It ensures that plans are kept up to date and relevant to the person's needs and aspirations, will provide confidence in the system, and mitigate the risk of people entering a crisis situation.

13.2. The review process should be person-centred and outcomes focused, as well as accessible and proportionate to the needs to be met. The process must involve the person needing care and also the carer where feasible, and consideration must be given whether to involve an independent advocate who local authorities are required to supply in the circumstances specified in the Act.

13.3. Reviewing intended outcomes detailed in the plan is the means by which the local authority complies with its ongoing responsibility towards people with care and support needs. The duty on the local authority therefore is to ensure that a review occurs, and if needed, a revision follows this. Consideration should also be given to authorising others to conduct a review – this could include the person themselves or carer, a third party (such as a provider) or another professional, with the local authority adopting an assurance and sign-off approach.

13.4. The review will help to identify if the person's needs have changed and can in such circumstances lead to a reassessment. It should also identify other circumstances which may have changed, and follow safeguarding principles in ensuring that the person is not at risk of abuse or neglect. The review must not be used as a mechanism to arbitrarily reduce the level of a person's personal budget.

13.5. In many cases, the review and revision of the plan should be intrinsically linked; it should not be possible to decide whether to revise a plan without a thorough review to ascertain if a revision is necessary, and in the best interests of the person. In addition, where a review is being undertaken where a person has a carer, the local authority should consider whether the carer's support plan requires reviewing, too.

13.6. However, there are occasions when a change to a plan is required but there has been no change in the levels of need (for example, a carer may change the times when they are available to support). In addition, there can be small changes in need, at times temporary, which can be accommodated within the established personal budget.

13.7. In these circumstances, it may not be appropriate for the person to go through a full review and revision of the plan. The local authority should respond to these 'light-touch' requests in a proportionate and reasonable way.

13.8. Where the local authority is satisfied that a revision is necessary, it must work through the assessment and care planning processes as detailed in sections 9-12 and 25 of the Act to the extent that it thinks appropriate (see chapter 6).

13.9. This chapter applies to people in need of care and support and carers equally, unless specifically stated. As many of the same principles apply to both care and support planning and reviews this chapter should be read in conjunction with the chapter on care and support planning. Where a plan is for a person with mental health problems, this chapter should be read in conjunction with chapter 34 of the "Mental Health Act 1983 Code of Practice" (on the Care Programme Approach)[1] and "Refocusing the Care Programme Approach".[2]

REVIEW OF THE CARE AND SUPPORT PLAN, SUPPORT PLAN
Keeping plans under review generally

13.10. Keeping plans under review is an essential element of the planning process. Without a system of regular reviews, plans could become quickly out of date meaning that people are not obtaining the care and support required to meet their needs. Plans may also identify outcomes that the person wants to achieve which are progressive or time limited, so a periodic review is vital to ensure that the plan remains relevant to their goals and aspirations.

13.11. The Act specifies that plans must be kept under review generally. Therefore, local authorities should establish systems that allow the proportionate monitoring of both care and support plans and support plans to ensure that needs are continuing to be met. This system should also include seeking cooperation with other health and care professionals who may be able to inform the authority of any concerns about the ability of the plan to meet needs (see chapter 14 on integration and cooperation).

13.12. The review should be a positive opportunity to take stock and consider if the plan is enabling the person to meet their needs and achieve their aspirations. The process should not be overly-complex or bureaucratic, and should cover these broad elements, which should be communicated to the person before the review process begins:

- Have the person's circumstances and/or care and support or support needs changed?

- What is working in the plan, what is not working, and what might need to change?

- Have the outcomes identified in the plan been achieved or not?

- Does the person have new outcomes they want to meet?

- Could improvements be made to achieve better outcomes?

- Is the person's personal budget enabling them to meet their needs and the outcomes identified in their plan, and

---

[1] "Code of Practice Mental Health Act 1983" (Department of Health, 2014).
[2] "Refocusing the Care Programme Approach" (Department of Health 2008).

- Is the current method of managing it still the best one for what they want to achieve, e.g. should direct payments be considered?[1]

- Is the personal budget still meeting the sufficiency test?

- Are there any changes in the person's informal and community support networks which might impact negatively or positively on the plan?

- Has there been any changes to the person's needs or circumstances which might mean they are at risk of abuse or neglect?

- Is the person, carer, independent advocate satisfied with the plan?

13.13. There are several different routes to reviewing a care and support or support plan including:

- a planned review (the date for which was set with the individual during care and support or support planning, or through general monitoring);

- an unplanned review (which results from a change in needs or circumstance that the local authority becomes aware of, e.g. a fall or hospital admission); and

- a requested review (where the person with the care and support or support plan, or their carer, family member, advocate or other interested party makes a request that a review is conducted. This may also be as the result of a change in needs or circumstances).

PLANNED REVIEWS

13.14. During the planning process, the person and their social worker, or relevant professional may have discussed when it might be useful to review the plan and therefore agree to record this date in the plan. This may be valuable to people in the care system so that they can anticipate when the review will take place, rather than the review being an unexpected experience. It also fits with the Government's view of personalised care and support, as the person may have a view as to a suitable time-frame for the review to occur. Additionally, setting out anticipated review dates may help authorities with future workload planning.

13.15. Even in cases with anticipated review dates, this should not reduce the requirement of the local authority to keep the plan under review generally. The first planned review should be an initial 'light-touch' review of the planning arrangements 6-8 weeks after sign-off of the personal budget and plan. Where relevant, this should also be combined with an initial review of direct payment arrangements. This will provide reassurance to all parties that the plan is working as intended, and will help to identify any teething problems. In addition, where plans are combined with other plans (for example the plan of a carer, or education, housing, and health and care plans which may be reviewed annually) the local authority should be aware of the review arrangements with these other plans and seek to align reviews together.

13.16. Local authorities should have regard to ensuring the planned review is proportionate to the circumstances, the value of the personal budget and any risks identified. In a similar way to care and support or support planning, there should be a range of review options available, which may include self-review,

---

[1] See Ch.11 on personal budgets.

peer led review, reviews conducted remotely, or face- to-face reviews with a social worker or other relevant professional. For example, where the person has a stable, longstanding support package with fixed or long term outcomes, they may wish to complete a self-review at the planned time which is then submitted to the local authority to sign-off, rather than have a face to face review with their social worker. This does not preclude their requesting a review at another time or a face to face review being needed if there is an unplanned change in needs or circumstances.

13.17. In all instances, the method of review should wherever reasonably possible be agreed with the person and must involve the adult to whom the plan relates, any carer the adult has and any person the adult asks the authority to involve. The local authority should take all appropriate measures to ensure their involvement and the involvement of other people if appropriate, such as an independent advocate where this is required by the circumstances specified in the Act.

13.18. Furthermore, if a person is recorded as having a mental impairment and lacking capacity to make some decisions, then the local authority should consider carefully when it will be appropriate for the next review to take place. In these instances, making appropriate use of a social worker as the lead professional should be encouraged. Where conditions are progressive, and the person's health is deteriorating, reviews may need to be much more frequent. Similarly where a person has few or no family members or friends involved in supporting them, the risks are higher, and again reviews or monitoring may need to be more frequent. It may beneficial to put a 'duty to request a review' into commissioned services so that employees are required to inform the local authority if they think that there is a need for a review. Where this occurs, the person should still be involved in the review process to ensure their views are taken account of.

UNPLANNED REVIEWS

13.19. If there is any information or evidence that suggests that circumstances have changed in a way that may affect the efficacy, appropriateness or content of the plan, then the local authority should immediately conduct a review to ascertain whether the plan requires revision. For example this could be where a carer is no longer able to provide the same level of care, there is evidence of a deterioration of the person's physical or mental wellbeing or the local authority receives a safeguarding alert. During the review process, the person the plan is intended for, or the person acting on their behalf should be kept fully involved and informed of what is occurring, the timescales involved and any likely consequences. This will help to alleviate anxiety at a time where things in the person's life may have changed substantially.

CONSIDERING A REQUEST FOR A REVIEW OF A PLAN

13.20. In addition to the duty on local authorities to keep plans under review generally, the Act provides a duty on the local authority to conduct a review if a request for one is made by the adult or a person acting on the adult's behalf.[1] Local authorities should provide information and advice to people at the planning stage about how to make a request for a review. This process should be accessible

---

[1] A similar provision exists in the Children & Families Act, where those with education, health and care (EHC) plans have a right to request a review of their EHC plan (as can others on their behalf). This will include any adult care components set out in the plan.

and include multiple routes to make a request – phone, email, text for example. The information given to people should also set out what happens after a request is made, and the timescales involved in the process.

13.21. The request process should be accessible and streamlined, with local authorities acting promptly after a request has been received. Consideration should also be given to the accessibility needs of the local population. This may, for example, include multiple language versions, and non-internet routes to request for people who may not have access to the internet, or in areas of digital exclusion. Local authorities should also consider the role that local community and voluntary organisations can play to help people log requests.

13.22. The right to request a review applies not just to the person receiving the care, but to others supporting them or interested in their wellbeing. For example a person with advanced dementia may not be able to request a review, but a relative or a neighbor may want to draw a deterioration in the person's condition to the attention of the local authority. The local authority should consider the request even if it is not made by the adult or their carer.

CONSIDERING A REVIEW

13.23. Upon receipt of a request to conduct a review, the local authority must consider this and judge the merits of conducting a review. In most cases, it is the expectation that a review should be performed unless the authority is reasonably satisfied that the plan remains sufficient, or the request is frivolous, or is made on the basis of inaccurate information, or is a complaint; for example where a person lodges multiple requests for a review in a short period of time and there is no reason to believe that the person's needs have changed. Local authorities should set out clearly the process that will be used to consider requests.

13.24. In considering whether to undertake a review the authority must involve the person, carer and anyone else the person requests to be involved where feasible. The local authority will need to identify those who may have significant difficulty in being fully involved in the decision to review and when there is no appropriate person who can represent or support their involvement and consider the duty to provide independent advocacy. More detail can be found in chapter 7 on advocacy.

Example 1

The local authority receives an email from a relative of an older person receiving care and support at home. The email provides details that the older person's condition is deteriorating and supplies evidence of recent visits to the GP. The local authority therefore decides to review their care and support plan to ensure that it continues to meet their needs.

Example 2

The local authority receives a phone call from Mr X who is angry as he feels that he has needs that have not been identified in his plan, during which he requests a review of his care plan. The authority has on a separate recent occasion reviewed his plan, and came to the conclusion that no revision was necessary, and informed Mr X of the decision and reasons for taking this. Therefore, in this case the local authority declines the request and

> provides a written explanation to Mr X, with an anticipated date of when the authority will be formally reviewing the plan as well as information on the local authority's complaints procedure.

13.25. Where a decision is made not to conduct a review following a request, the local authority should set out the reasons for not accepting the request in a format accessible to the person, along with details of how to pursue the matter if the person remains unsatisfied. In most cases, it would be helpful for this to set out that the authority will continue to monitor the plan to ensure that it remains fit for purpose, and that the decision does not affect the right to make a future request for review. Although not mandatory, it may also be prudent for the local authority to set out when the person can expect a formal review of the plan.

REVISION OF THE CARE AND SUPPORT PLAN, SUPPORT PLAN

13.26. Where a decision has been made following a review that a revision is necessary, the authority should inform the person, or a person acting on their behalf of the decision and what this will involve. Where the person has substantial difficulty in being actively involved with the review, and where there are no family or friends to help them being engaged, an independent advocate must be involved. More detail can be found in chapter 7 on advocacy.

13.27. When revising the plan the local authority must involve the person, their carer and any other persons the adult may want involved, and their advocate where the person qualifies for one. The local authority must take all reasonable steps to agree the revision. The revision should wherever possible follow the process used in the assessment and care planning stages. Indeed, the local authority must if satisfied that the circumstances have changed in a way that affects a care and support or support plan, carry out a needs or carer's assessment and financial assessment, and then revise the plan and personal budget accordingly. The assessment process following a review should not start from the beginning of the process but pick up from what is already known about the person and should be proportionate.[1]

13.28. In some cases a complete change of the plan may be required, whereas in others minor adjustments may be needed. In either case, the following aspects of care planning should be followed:

- the person's wishes and feelings should be identified as far as possible and they should be supported to be involved;

- the revision should be proportionate to the needs to be met;

- where the plan was produced in combination with other plans, this should be considered at the revision stage;

- the person, carer or person acting on their behalf should be allowed to self-plan in conjunction with the local authority where appropriate;

---

[1] This process may be referred to as a 're-assessment'. As noted above, this should not be a new assessment from the beginning of the care and support process, but should be a proportionate assessment that takes into consideration what is already known of the person and incorporates revised elements as appropriate. A 're-assessment' cannot occur without the local authority first conducting a review and then deciding that a revision of a plan is necessary.

- the development of the revised plan must be made with the involvement of the adult/carer, and any person the adult asks the authority to involve;

- any additional elements that were incorporated into the original plan should be replicated in the revised plan where appropriate and agreed by all parties; and

- there needs to be clarity on the sign-off process, especially where the revised plan is prepared by the person and the local authority.

13.29. Particular attention should be taken if the revisions to the plan proposes increased restraints or restrictions on a person who has not got the capacity to agree them. This may become a deprivation of liberty, which requires appropriate safeguards to be in place. The local authority should have policies to address how these are recognised and responded to, and the social worker, occupational therapist or other relevant social care qualified professional or Mental Capacity lead should be involved, as well as an advocate.

13.30. The local authority must consider in all cases whether an independent advocate may be required to facilitate the person's involvement in the revision of the plan. Where the plan was produced with the assistance of an independent advocate, then consideration should be given to whether an independent advocate is also required for the revision of the plan. In these scenarios, the advocate would ideally be the same person to ensure consistency and continuity with the case details. Likewise, where a specialist assessor has been used previously in the care and support journey, the local authority should have regard whether they need to employ the expertise of the assessor in the review.

TIMELINESS AND REGULARITY OF REVIEWS

13.31. In the absence of any request of a review, or any indication that circumstances may have changed, the local authority should conduct a periodic review of plan. As stated earlier, this could be indicated at the planning stage by including an anticipated review date to allow for future planning. In addition, local authorities may wish to align the periodic review of the plan, with the compulsory review of the direct payment arrangements, where this is appropriate.

13.32. It is the expectation that authorities should conduct a review of the plan no later than every 12 months, although a light- touch review should be considered 6– 8 weeks after agreement and sign-off of the plan and personal budget, to ensure that the arrangements are accurate and there are no initial issues to be aware of. This light-touch review should also be considered after revision of an existing plan to ensure that the new plan is working as intended, and in cases where a person chooses a direct payment, should be aligned with the review of the making of the direct payment (see chapter 12 on direct payments).

13.33. The periodic review should be proportionate to the needs to be met, and the process should not contain any surprises for the person concerned. Periodic reviews and reviews in general must not be used to arbitrarily reduce a care and support package. Such behaviour would be unlawful under the Act as the personal budget must always be an amount appropriate to meet the person's needs. Any reduction to a personal budget should be the result of a change in need or circumstance.

13.34. The review should be performed as quickly as is reasonably practicable. As with care and support planning, it is expected that in most cases the revision of the plan should be completed in a timely manner proportionate to the needs to be met. Where there is an urgent need to intervene, local authorities should consider implementing interim packages to urgently meet needs while the plan is revised. However, local authorities should work with the person to avoid such circumstances wherever possible by ensuring that any potential emergency needs are identified as part of the care and support planning stage and planned for accordingly.

LINKS TO EXTERNAL RESOURCES
Outcome focused reviews – a practical guide, PPF, 2009: http://bit.ly/1gP91Hr

Guidance notes for outcomes focused reviews, PPF, 2009: http://bit.ly/1fyJs8h

The headings used in a person-centred review, HSA, 2009: http://bit.ly/1fLbWxS

From a person-centred review to a person-centred plan, HSA, 2009: http://bit.ly/1nX5XtE

14. SAFEGUARDING

This chapter provides guidance on sections 42–46 of the Care Act 2014.

This chapter covers:
- Adult safeguarding – what it is and why it matters;
- Abuse and neglect:
  - Understanding what they are and spotting the signs;
  - Reporting and responding to abuse and neglect;
- Carers and adult safeguarding;
- Adult safeguarding procedures;
- Local authority's role and multi-agency working;
- Criminal offences and adult safeguarding;
- Safeguarding enquiries;
- Safeguarding Adults Boards;
- Safeguarding Adults Reviews;
- Information sharing, confidentiality and record keeping;
- Roles, responsibilities and training in local authorities, the NHS and other agencies.

14.1. This chapter replaces the 'No secrets' guidance.[1]

14.2. The safeguarding duties apply to an adult who:

- has needs for care and support (whether or not the local authority is meeting any of those needs) and;

- is experiencing, or at risk of, abuse or neglect; and

- as a result of those care and support needs is unable to protect themselves from either the risk of, or the experience of abuse or neglect.

14.3. The adult experiencing, or at risk of abuse or neglect will hereafter be referred to as the *adult* throughout this chapter.

14.4. The safeguarding duties have a legal effect in relation to organisations other than the local authority on for example the NHS and the Police.

14.5. Where someone is 18 or over but is still receiving children's services and a safeguarding issue is raised, the matter should be dealt with through adult safeguarding arrangements. For example, this could occur when a young person with substantial and complex needs continues to be supported in a residential educational setting until the age of 25 (see also chapter 16). Where appropriate, adult safeguarding services should involve the local authority's children's safeguarding colleagues as well as any relevant partners (e.g. the Police or NHS) or other persons relevant to the case. However, the level of needs is not relevant, and the young adult does not need to have eligible needs for care and support under the Care Act, or be receiving any particular service from the local authority, in order for the safeguarding duties to apply – so long as the conditions set out in paragraph 14.2 are met.

---

[1] https://www.gov.uk/government/publications/no-secrets-guidance-on-protecting-vulnerable-adults-in-care

14.6. Local authority statutory adult safeguarding duties apply equally to those adults with care and support needs regardless of whether those needs are being met, regardless of whether the adult lacks mental capacity or not, and regardless of setting, other than prisons and approved premises where prison governors and National Offender Management Service (NOMS) respectively have responsibility. However, senior representatives of those services may sit on the Safeguarding Adults Board and play an important role in the strategic development of adult safeguarding locally. Additionally, they may ask for advice from the local authority when faced with a safeguarding issue that they are finding particularly challenging.

ADULT SAFEGUARDING – WHAT IT IS AND WHY IT MATTERS

14.7. Safeguarding means protecting an adult's right to live in safety, free from abuse and neglect. It is about people and organisations working together to prevent and stop both the risks and experience of abuse or neglect, while at the same time making sure that the adult's wellbeing is promoted including, where appropriate, having regard to their views, wishes, feelings and beliefs in deciding on any action. This must recognise that adults sometimes have complex interpersonal relationships and may be ambivalent, unclear or unrealistic about their personal circumstances.

14.8. Organisations should always promote the adult's wellbeing in their safeguarding arrangements. People have complex lives and being safe is only one of the things they want for themselves. Professionals should work with the adult to establish what being safe means to them and how that can be best achieved. Professionals and other staff should not be advocating "safety" measures that do not take account of individual well-being, as defined in Section 1 of the Care Act.

14.9. Safeguarding is not a substitute for:

- providers' responsibilities to provide safe and high quality care and support;

- commissioners regularly assuring themselves of the safety and effectiveness of commissioned services;

- the Care Quality Commission (CQC) ensuring that regulated providers comply with the fundamental standards of care or by taking enforcement action; and

- the core duties of the police to prevent and detect crime and protect life and property.

14.10. The Care Act requires that each local authority **must:**

- make enquiries, or cause others to do so, if it believes an adult is experiencing, or is at risk of, abuse or neglect (see paragraph 14.16 onwards). An enquiry should establish whether any action needs to be taken to prevent or stop abuse or neglect, and if so, by whom;

- set up a Safeguarding Adults Board (SAB) (see paragraph 14.105 onwards);

- arrange, where appropriate, for an independent advocate to represent and support an adult who is the subject of a safeguarding enquiry or Safeguarding Adult Review (SAR) where the adult has 'substantial difficulty' in being involved in the process and where there is no other suitable person to represent and support them (see chapter 7 on advocacy);

- co-operate with each of its relevant partners (as set out in Section 6 of the Care Act) in order to protect the adult. In their turn each relevant partner must also co-operate with the local authority.

14.11. The aims of adult safeguarding are to:

- stop abuse or neglect wherever possible;

- prevent harm and reduce the risk of abuse or neglect to adults with care and support needs;

- safeguard adults in a way that supports them in making choices and having control about how they want to live;

- promote an approach that concentrates on improving life for the adults concerned;

- raise public awareness so that communities as a whole, alongside professionals, play their part in preventing, identifying and responding to abuse and neglect;

- provide information and support in accessible ways to help people understand the different types of abuse, how to stay safe and what to do to raise a concern about the safety or well-being of an adult; and

- address what has caused the abuse or neglect.

14.12. In order to achieve these aims, it is necessary to:

- ensure that everyone, both individuals and organisations, are clear about their roles and responsibilities;

- create strong multi-agency partnerships that provide timely and effective prevention of and responses to abuse or neglect;

- support the development of a positive learning environment across these partnerships and at all levels within them to help break down cultures that are risk-averse and seek to scapegoat or blame practitioners;

- enable access to mainstream community resources such as accessible leisure facilities, safe town centres and community groups that can reduce the social and physical isolation which in itself may increase the risk of abuse or neglect; and

- clarify how responses to safeguarding concerns deriving from the poor quality and inadequacy of service provision, including patient safety in the health sector, should be responded to.

14.13. The following six principles apply to all sectors and settings including care and support services, further education colleges, commissioning, regulation and provision of health and care services, social work, healthcare, welfare benefits, housing, wider local authority functions and the criminal justice system. The principles should inform the ways in which professionals and other staff work with adults. The principles can also help SABs, and organisations more widely, by using them to examine and improve their local arrangements.

Six key principles underpin all adult safeguarding work
- Empowerment – People being supported and encouraged to make their own decisions and informed consent.

"I am asked what I want as the outcomes from the safeguarding process and these directly inform what happens."

- Prevention – It is better to take action before harm occurs.

"I receive clear and simple information about what abuse is, how to recognise the signs and what I can do to seek help."

- Proportionality – The least intrusive response appropriate to the risk presented.

"I am sure that the professionals will work in my interest, as I see them and they will only get involved as much as needed."

- Protection – Support and representation for those in greatest need.

"I get help and support to report abuse and neglect. I get help so that I am able to take part in the safeguarding process to the extent to which I want."

- Partnership – Local solutions through services working with their communities. Communities have a part to play in preventing, detecting and reporting neglect and abuse.

"I know that staff treat any personal and sensitive information in confidence, only sharing what is helpful and necessary. I am confident that professionals will work together and with me to get the best result for me."

- Accountability – Accountability and transparency in delivering safeguarding.

"I understand the role of everyone involved in my life and so do they."

MAKING SAFEGUARDING PERSONAL

14.14. In addition to these principles, it is also important that all safeguarding partners take a broad community approach to establishing safeguarding arrangements. It is vital that all organisations recognise that adult safeguarding arrangements are there to protect individuals. We all have different preferences, histories, circumstances and life-styles, so it is unhelpful to prescribe a process that must be followed whenever a concern is raised; and the case study below helps illustrate this.

Two brothers with mild learning disabilities lived in their family home, where they had remained following the death of their parents some time previously. Large amounts of rubbish had accumulated both in the garden and inside the house, with cleanliness and self-neglect also an issue. They had been targeted by fraudsters, resulting in criminal investigation and conviction of those responsible, but the brothers had refused subsequent services from adult social care and their case had been closed.

They had, however, had a good relationship with their social worker, and as concerns about their health and wellbeing continued it was decided that the social worker would maintain contact, calling in every couple of weeks to see how they were, and offer any help needed, on their terms. After almost a year, through the gradual building of trust and understanding, the brothers asked to be considered for supported housing; with the social worker's help they improved the state of their house enough to sell it, and moved to a living environment in which practical support could be provided.

14.15. Making safeguarding personal means it should be person-led and out-come-focused. It engages the person in a conversation about how best to respond to their safeguarding situation in a way that enhances involvement, choice and control as well as improving quality of life, wellbeing and safety. Nevertheless, there are key issues that local authorities and their partners should consider [See decision tree at annex J] if they suspect or are made aware of abuse or neglect. See paragraph 14.204 for more detail about what such guidelines should cover.

WHAT ARE ABUSE AND NEGLECT?

14.16. This section considers the different types and patterns of abuse and neglect and the different circumstances in which they may take place. This is not intended to be an exhaustive list but an illustrative guide as to the sort of behaviour which could give rise to a safeguarding concern. This chapter also contains a number of illustrative case studies showing the action that was taken to help the adult stay or become safe.

14.17. Local authorities should not limit their view of what constitutes abuse or neglect, as they can take many forms and the circumstances of the individual case should always be considered; although the criteria at paragraph 14.2 will need to be met before the issue is considered as a safeguarding concern. Exploitation, in particular, is a common theme in the following list of the types of abuse and neglect.

- **Physical abuse** – including assault, hitting, slapping, pushing, misuse of medication, restraint or inappropriate physical sanctions.

- **Domestic violence** – including psychological, physical, sexual, financial, emotional abuse; so called 'honour' based violence.

- **Sexual abuse** – including rape, indecent exposure, sexual harassment, inappropriate looking or touching, sexual teasing or innuendo, sexual photography, subjection to pornography or witnessing sexual acts, indecent exposure and sexual assault or sexual acts to which the adult has not consented or was pressured into consenting.

- **Psychological abuse** – including emotional abuse, threats of harm or abandonment, deprivation of contact, humiliation, blaming, controlling, intimidation, coercion, harassment, verbal abuse, cyber bullying, isolation or unreasonable and unjustified withdrawal of services or supportive networks.

- **Financial or material abuse** – including theft, fraud, internet scamming, coercion in relation to an adult's financial affairs or arrangements, including in connection with wills, property, inheritance or financial transactions, or the misuse or misappropriation of property, possessions or benefits.

- **Modern slavery**[1] – encompasses slavery, human trafficking, forced labour and domestic servitude. Traffickers and slave masters use whatever means they have at their disposal to coerce, deceive and force individuals into a life of abuse, servitude and inhumane treatment.

- **Discriminatory abuse** – including forms of harassment, slurs or similar treatment; because of race, gender and gender identity, age, disability, sexual orientation or religion.[2]

- **Organisational abuse** – including neglect and poor care practice within an institution or specific care setting such as a hospital or care home, for example, or in relation to care provided in one's own home. This may range from one off incidents to on-going ill-treatment. It can be through neglect or poor professional practice as a result of the structure, policies, processes and practices within an organisation.

- **Neglect and acts of omission** – including ignoring medical, emotional or physical care needs, failure to provide access to appropriate health, care and support or educational services, the withholding of the necessities of life, such as medication, adequate nutrition and heating

- **Self-neglect** – this covers a wide range of behaviour neglecting to care for one's personal hygiene, health or surroundings and includes behaviour such as hoarding.

14.18. Incidents of abuse may be one-off or multiple, and affect one person or more. Professionals and others should look beyond single incidents or individuals to identify patterns of harm, just as the Care Quality Commission, as the regulator of service quality, does when it looks at the quality of care in health and care services. Repeated instances of poor care may be an indication of more serious problems and of what we now describe as organisational abuse. In order to see these patterns it is important that information is recorded and appropriately shared.

14.19. Patterns of abuse vary and include:

- serial abusing in which the perpetrator seeks out and 'grooms' individuals. Sexual abuse sometimes falls into this pattern as do some forms of financial abuse;

- long-term abuse in the context of an ongoing family relationship such as domestic violence between spouses or generations or persistent psychological abuse; or

- opportunistic abuse such as theft occurring because money or jewellery has been left lying around.

---

[1] https://www.gov.uk/government/uploads/system/uploads/attachment_data/file/328096/
Modern_slavery_ booklet_v12_WEB__2_.pdf
[2] Equalities Act 2010: https://www.gov.uk/discrimination-your-rights/types-of-discrimination

DOMESTIC ABUSE

14.20. In 2013, the Home Office announced changes to the definition of domestic abuse:

- Incident or pattern of incidents of controlling, coercive or threatening behaviour, violence or abuse. . . by someone who is or has been an intimate partner or family member regardless of gender or sexuality

- Includes: psychological, physical, sexual, financial, emotional abuse; so called 'honour' based violence; Female Genital Mutilation; forced marriage.

- Age range extended down to 16.

14.21. Many people think that domestic abuse is about intimate partners, but it is clear that other family members are included and that much safeguarding work (that meets the criteria set out in paragraph 14.2) that occurs at home is, in fact is concerned with domestic abuse. This confirms that domestic abuse approaches and legislation can be considered safeguarding responses in appropriate cases.[1]

FINANCIAL ABUSE

14.22. Financial abuse is the main form of abuse by the Office of the Public Guardian both amongst adults and children at risk. Financial recorded abuse can occur in isolation, but as research has shown, where there are other forms of abuse, there is likely to be financial abuse occurring. Although this is not always the case, everyone should also be aware of this possibility.

14.23. Potential indicators of financial abuse include:[2]

- change in living conditions;

- lack of heating, clothing or food;

- inability to pay bills/unexplained shortage of money;

- unexplained withdrawals from an account;

- unexplained loss/misplacement of financial documents;

- the recent addition of authorised signers on a client or donor's signature card; or

- sudden or unexpected changes in a will or other financial documents. This is not an exhaustive list, nor do these examples prove that there is actual abuse occurring. However, they do indicate that a closer look and possible investigation may be needed.

---

[1] This guide is being updated to include new legislation and Domestic Violence Protection Orders and is expected to be published by end 2014.
[2] http://www.cpa.org.uk/information/reviews/financialabuse240408[1].pdf

Mrs B is an 88 year old woman with dementia who was admitted to a care home from hospital following a fall. Mrs B appointed her only daughter G, to act for her under a Lasting Power of Attorney in relation to her property and financial affairs.

Mrs B's former home was sold and she became liable to pay the full fees of her care home. Mrs B's daughter failed to pay the fees and arrears built up, until the home made a referral to the local authority, who in turn alerted the Office of the Public Guardian (OPG).

OPG carried out an investigation and discovered that G was not providing her mother with any money for clothing or toiletries, which were being provided by the home from their own stocks. A visit and discussion with Mrs B revealed that she was unable to participate in any activities or outings arranged by the home, which she dearly wished to do. Her room was bare of any personal effects, and she had limited stocks of underwear and nightwear.

The Police were alerted and interviewed G, who admitted using the proceeds of the mother's house for her own benefit. The OPG applied to the Court of Protection for suspension of the power of attorney and the appointment of a deputy, who was able to seek recovery of funds and ensure Mrs B's needs were met.

14.24. The above case study highlights the need for local authorities not to underestimate the potential impact of financial abuse. It could significantly threaten an adult's health and wellbeing. Most financial abuse is also capable of amounting to theft or fraud and so would be a matter for the police to investigate. It may also require attention and collaboration from a wider group of organisations, including shops and financial institutions such as banks.

14.25. Where the abuse is by someone who has the authority to manage an adult's money, the relevant body should be informed, for example, the Office of the Public Guardian for deputies (see 14.48) and Department for Work and Pensions (DWP) in relation to appointees.

14.26. If anyone has concerns that a DWP appointee is acting incorrectly they should contact the DWP immediately. In addition to a name and address the DWP can get things done more quickly if it also has a National Insurance number. However, people should not delay acting because they do not know the adult's National Insurance number. The important thing is to alert DWP to their concerns. If DWP know that the person is also known to the local authority then they should also inform them.

WHO ABUSES AND NEGLECTS ADULTS?

14.27. Anyone can carry out abuse or neglect, including:

- spouses/partners;
- other family members;
- neighbours;
- friends;

- acquaintances;

- local residents;

- people who deliberately exploit adults they perceive as vulnerable to abuse;

- paid staff or professionals; and

- volunteers and strangers.

While a lot of attention is paid, for example, to targeted fraud or internet scams perpetrated by complete strangers, it is far more likely that the person responsible for abuse is known to the adult and is in a position of trust and power.[1]

14.28. Abuse can happen anywhere: for example, in someone's own home, in a public place, in hospital, in a care home or in college. It can take place when an adult lives alone or with others.

SPOTTING SIGNS OF ABUSE AND NEGLECT

14.29. Workers across a wide range of organisations need to be vigilant about adult safeguarding concerns in all walks of life including, amongst others in health and social care, welfare, policing, banking, fire and rescue services and trading standards; leisure services, faith groups, and housing. GPs, in particular, are often well-placed to notice changes in an adult that may indicate they are being abused or neglected. Findings from Serious Case Reviews have sometimes stated that if professionals or other staff had acted upon their concerns or sought more information, then death or serious harm might have been prevented. The following example illustrates that someone who might not typically be thought of, in this case the neighbour, does in fact have an important role to play in identifying when an adult is at risk.

Mr A is in his 40s, and lives in a housing association flat with little family contact. His mental health is relatively stable, after a previous period of hospitalisation, and he has visits from a mental health support worker.

He rarely goes out, but he lets people into his accommodation because of his loneliness. The police were alerted by Mr A's neighbours to several domestic disturbances. His accommodation had been targeted by a number of local people and he had become subjected to verbal, financial and sometime physical abuse. Although Mr A initially insisted they were his friends, he did indicate he was frightened; he attended a case conference with representatives from adult social care, mental health services and the police, from which emerged a plan to strengthen his own self-protective ability as well as to deal with the present abuse. Mr A has made different arrangements for managing his money so that he does not accumulate large sums at home. A community-based visiting service has been engaged to keep him company through visits to his home, and with time his support worker aims to help get involved in social activities that will bring more positive contacts to allay the loneliness that Mr A sees as his main challenge.

---

[1] http://www.hscic.gov.uk/catalogue/PUB13499/ abus-vuln-adul-eng-12-13-fin-rep.pdf

14.30. Anyone can witness or become aware of information suggesting that abuse and neglect is occuring. The matter may, for example, be raised by a worried neighbour (see above case study), a concerned bank cashier, a GP, a welfare benefits officer, a housing support worker or a nurse on a ward. Primary care staff may be particularly well-placed to spot abuse and neglect, as in many cases they may be the only professionals with whom the adult has contact. The adult may say or do things that hint that all is not well. It may come in the form of a complaint, a call for a police response, an expression of concern, or come to light during a needs assessment. Regardless of how the safeguarding concern is identified, everyone should understand what to do, and where to go locally to get help and advice. It is vital that professionals, other staff and members of the public are vigilant on behalf of those unable to protect themselves. This will include:

- knowing about different types of abuse and neglect and their signs;

- supporting adults to keep safe;

- knowing who to tell about suspected abuse or neglect; and

- supporting adults to think and weigh up the risks and benefits of different options when exercising choice and control.

Awareness campaigns for the general public and multi-agency training for all staff will contribute to achieving these objectives.

REPORTING AND RESPONDING TO ABUSE AND NEGLECT

14.31. It is important to understand the circumstances of abuse, including the wider context such as whether others may be at risk of abuse, whether there is any emerging pattern of abuse, whether others have witnessed abuse and the role of family members and paid staff or professionals.

14.32. The circumstances surrounding any actual or suspected case of abuse or neglect will inform the response. For example, it is important to recognise that abuse or neglect may be unintentional and may arise because a carer is struggling to care for another person. This makes the need to take action no less important, but in such circumstances, an appropriate response could be a support package for the carer and monitoring. However, the primary focus must still be how to safeguard the adult. In other circumstances where the safeguarding concerns arise from abuse or neglect deliberately intended to cause harm, then it would not only be necessary to immediately consider what steps are needed to protect the adult but also whether to refer the matter to the police to consider whether a criminal investigation would be required or appropriate.

14.33. The nature and timing of the intervention and who is best placed to lead will be, in part, determined by the circumstances. For example, where there is poor, neglectful care or practice, resulting in pressure sores for example, then an employer-led disciplinary response may be more appropriate; but this situation will need additional responses such as clinical intervention to improve the care given immediately and a clinical audit of practice. Commissioning or regulatory enforcement action may also be appropriate.

14.34. Early sharing of information is the key to providing an effective response where there are emerging concerns (see information sharing (14.150) and confidentiality (14.157) section). To ensure effective safeguarding arrangements:

- all organisations must have arrangements in place which set out clearly the processes and the principles for sharing information between each other, with other professionals and the SAB; this could be via an Information Sharing Agreement to formalise the arrangements; and,

- no professional should assume that someone else will pass on information which they think may be critical to the safety and wellbeing of the adult. If a professional has concerns about the adult's welfare and believes they are suffering or likely to suffer abuse or neglect, then they should share the information with the local authority and, or, the police if they believe or suspect that a crime has been committed.

CARERS AND SAFEGUARDING

14.35. Circumstances in which a carer (for example, a family member or friend) could be involved in a situation that may require a safeguarding response include:

- a carer may witness or speak up about abuse or neglect;

- a carer may experience intentional or unintentional harm from the adult they are trying to support or from professionals and organisations they are in contact with; or,

- a carer may unintentionally or intentionally harm or neglect the adult they support on their own or with others.

14.36. Assessment of both the carer and the adult they care for must include consideration of both their wellbeing. Section 1 of the Care Act includes protection from abuse and neglect as part of the definition of wellbeing. As such, a needs or carer's assessment is an important opportunity to explore the individuals' circumstances and consider whether it would be possible to provide information, or support that prevents abuse or neglect from occurring, for example, by providing training to the carer about the condition that the adult they care for has or to support them to care more safely. Where that is necessary the local authority should make arrangements for providing it.

14.37. If a carer speaks up about abuse or neglect, it is essential that they are listened to and that where appropriate a safeguarding enquiry is undertaken and other agencies are involved as appropriate.

14.38. If a carer experiences intentional or unintentional harm from the adult they are supporting, or if a carer unintentionally or intentionally harms or neglects the adult they support, consideration should be given to:

- whether, as part of the assessment and support planning process for the carer and, or, the adult they care for, support can be provided that removes or mitigates the risk of abuse. For example, the provision of training or information or other support that minimises the stress experienced by the carer. In some circumstances the carer may need to have independent representation or advocacy; in others, a carer may benefit from having such support if they are under great stress or similar; and

- whether other agencies should be involved; in some circumstances where a criminal offence is suspected this will include alerting the police, or in others the primary healthcare services may need to be involved in monitoring.

14.39. Other key considerations in relation to carers should include:

- involving carers in safeguarding enquiries relating to the adult they care for, as appropriate;

- whether or not joint assessment is appropriate in each individual circumstance;

- the risk factors that may increase the likelihood of abuse or neglect occurring; and

- whether a change in circumstance changes the risk of abuse or neglect occurring. A change in circumstance should also trigger the review of the care and support plan and, or, support plan.

Further information about these considerations can be found in an ADASS paper on carers and safeguarding.[1]

Mrs D lives with her husband, B. B has a long term brain injury which affects his mood, behaviour and his ability to manage close family relationships. This has often led to him shouting and hitting out at his wife, who is also his main informal carer. Mrs D told a professional who was involved in supporting her that she was becoming increasingly frightened by B's physical and verbal outbursts and at times feared for her personal safety.

Other family members were unaware of the extent of the harm and Mrs D was exhausted and considering leaving the situation. The local authority became involved. The situation presented significant personal risk to Mrs D but there was also a risk of fragmenting relationships if the local authority staff were not sensitive to the needs of the whole family. The practitioner, under supervision from her social work manager invested time in meeting with Mrs D to explore her preferences around managing her safety and how information about the situation would be communicated with the wider family and with B. This presented dilemmas around balancing the local authority's duty of care towards Mrs D with her wishes to remain in the situation with B. Placing emphasis on the latter inevitably meant that Mrs D would not be entirely free from the risk of harm but allowed the practitioner to explore help and support options which would enable Mrs D to manage and sustain her safety at a level which was acceptable to her.

The practitioner received regular supervision to allow time to reflect on the support being offered and to ensure that it was 'person centred'. The outcome for Mrs D was that she was able to continue to care for B by working in partnership with the local authority. The practitioner offered advice about how to safely access help in an emergency and helped her to develop strategies to manage her own safety – this included staff building rapport with B, building on his strengths and desire to participate in social activities outside the family home. The effect of this was that some of the trigger points of him being at home with his wife for sustained periods during the day were reduced because he was there less. Mrs D also had a number of pre-existing support avenues, including counselling and a good relationship with her son and her friends.

---

[1] http://static.carers.org/files/carers-and-safeguarding-document-june-2011-5730.pdf

> The situation will be reviewed regularly with Mrs D but for the time being she feels much more able to manage.

ADULT SAFEGUARDING PROCEDURES

14.40. In order to respond appropriately where abuse or neglect may be taking place, anyone in contact with the adult, whether in a volunteer or paid role, must understand their own role and responsibility and have access to practical and legal guidance, advice and support. This will include understanding local inter-agency policies and procedures.

14.41. In any organisation, there should be adult safeguarding policies and procedures. These should reflect this statutory guidance and the decision making tree diagram 1B and are for use locally to support the reduction or removal of safeguarding risks as well as to secure any support to protect the adult and, where necessary, to help the adult recover and develop resilience. Such policies and procedures should assist those working with adults how to develop swift and personalised safeguarding responses and how to involve adults in this decision making. This, in turn, should encourage proportionate responses and improve outcomes for the people concerned. Procedures may include:

- a statement of purpose relating to promoting wellbeing, preventing harm and responding effectively if concerns are raised;

- a statement of roles and responsibility, authority and accountability sufficiently specific to ensure that all staff and volunteers understand their role and limitations;

- a statement of the procedures for dealing with allegations of abuse, including those for dealing with emergencies by ensuring immediate safety, the processes for initially assessing abuse and neglect and deciding when intervention is appropriate, and the arrangements for reporting to the police, urgently when necessary;

- a full list of points of referral indicating how to access support and advice at all times, whether in normal working hours or outside them, with a comprehensive list of contact addresses and telephone numbers, including relevant national and local voluntary bodies;

- an indication of how to record allegations of abuse and neglect, any enquiry and all subsequent action;

- a list of sources of expert advice;

- a full description of channels of inter-agency communication and procedures for information sharing and for decision making;

- a list of all services which might offer access to support or redress; and,

- how professional disagreements are resolved especially with regard to whether decisions should be made, enquiries undertaken for example.

14.42. The SAB should keep policies and procedures under review and report on these in the annual report as necessary. Procedures should be updated to incorporate learning from published research, peer reviews, case law and lessons from recent cases and Safeguarding Adults Reviews. The procedures should also include the provisions of the law – criminal, civil and statutory – relevant to adult safeguarding. This should include local or agency specific information about obtaining legal advice and access to appropriate remedies.

14.43. The Care Act requires that each local authority must arrange for an independent advocate to represent and support an adult who is the subject of a safeguarding enquiry or Safeguarding Adult Review where the adult has 'substantial difficulty' in being involved in the process and where there is no other suitable person to represent and support them (see chapter 7).

THE MENTAL CAPACITY ACT 2005

14.44. People must be assumed to have capacity to make their own decisions and be given all practicable help before anyone treats them as not being able to make their own decisions. Where an adult is found to lack capacity to make a decision then any action taken, or any decision made for, or on their behalf, must be made in their best interests.

14.45. Professionals and other staff need to understand and always work in line with the Mental Capacity Act 2005 (MCA). They should use their professional judgement and balance many competing views. They will need considerable guidance and support from their employers if they are to help adults manage risk in ways and put them in control of decision- making if possible.

14.46. Regular face-to-face supervision from skilled managers is essential to enable staff to work confidently and competently in difficult and sensitive situations.

14.47. Mental capacity is frequently raised in relation to adult safeguarding. The requirement to apply the MCA in adult safeguarding enquiries challenges many professionals and requires utmost care, particularly where it appears an adult has capacity for making specific decisions that nevertheless places them at risk of being abused or neglected.[1]

14.48. The MCA created the criminal offences of ill-treatment and wilful neglect in respect of people who lack the ability to make decisions. The offences can be committed by anyone responsible for that adult's care and support – paid staff but also family carers as well as people who have the legal authority to act on that adult's behalf (i.e. persons with power of attorney or Court-appointed deputies).

14.59. These offences are punishable by fines or imprisonment. Ill-treatment covers both deliberate acts of ill-treatment and also those acts which are reckless which results in ill- treatment. Wilful neglect requires a serious departure from the required standards of treatment and usually means that a person has deliberately failed to carry out an act that they knew they were under a duty to perform.

14.50. Abuse by an attorney or deputy: If someone has concerns about the actions of an attorney acting under a registered Enduring Power of Attorney (EPA) or Lasting Power of Attorney (LPA), or a Deputy appointed by the Court of Protection, they should contact the Office of the Public Guardian (OPG). The OPG can investigate the actions of a Deputy or Attorney and can also refer concerns to other relevant agencies. When it makes a referral, the OPG will make sure that the relevant agency keeps it informed of the action it takes. The OPG can also make an application to the Court of Protection if it needs to take

---

[1] http://www.direct.gov.uk/prod_consum_dg/groups/dg_digitalassets/@dg/@en/@disabled/documents/ digitalasset/dg_186484.pdf

possible action against the attorney or deputy. Whilst the OPG primarily investigates financial abuse, it is important to note that that it also has a duty to investigate concerns about the actions of an attorney acting under a health and welfare Lasting Power of Attorney or a personal welfare deputy. The OPG can investigate concerns about an attorney acting under a registered Enduring or Lasting Power of Attorney, regardless of the adult's capacity to make decisions. Further information about the role and powers of the OPG and its policy in relation to adult safeguarding can be found here.[1]

MULTI-AGENCY SAFEGUARDING ROLE
Preventing abuse and neglect
14.51. Local authorities must cooperate with each of their relevant partners, as described in section 6(7) of the Care Act, and those partners must also cooperate with the local authority, in the exercise of their functions relevant to care and support including those to protect adults (see also chapter 15 which sets out general responsibilities in relation to co-operation).

14.52. Relevant partners of a local authority include any other local authority with whom they agree it would be appropriate to co-operate (e.g. neighbouring authorities with whom they provide joint shared services) and the following agencies or bodies who operate within the local authority's area including:

- NHS England;
- Clinical Commissioning Groups (CCGs);
- NHS trusts and NHS Foundation Trusts;
- Department for Work and Pensions;
- the Police;
- Prisons; and
- Probation services;

14.53. Local authorities must also co-operate with such other agencies or bodies as it considers appropriate in the exercise of its adult safeguarding functions, including (but not limited to) those listed in section 6(3):

- General Practitioners;
- dentists;
- pharmacists;
- NHS hospitals; and
- housing, health and care providers.

14.54. Agencies should stress the need for preventing abuse and neglect wherever possible. Observant professionals and other staff making early, positive interventions with individuals and families can make a huge difference to their lives, preventing the deterioration of a situation or breakdown of a support network. It is often when people become increasingly isolated and cut off from families and friends that they become extremely vulnerable to abuse and neglect.

---

[1] http://www.justice.gov.uk/downloads/protecting-the-vulnerable/mca/safeguarding-policy.pdf

Agencies should implement robust risk management processes in order to prevent concerns escalating to a crisis point and requiring intervention under safeguarding adult procedures.

14.55. Partners should ensure that they have the mechanisms in place that enable early identification and assessment of risk through timely information sharing and targeted multi- agency intervention. Multi-agency safeguarding hubs may be one model to support this but are not the only one. Policies and strategies for safeguarding adults should include measures to minimise the circumstances, including isolation, which make adults vulnerable to abuse.

Miss P's mental health social worker became concerned when she had received reports that two of Marissa's associates were visiting more regularly and sometimes staying over at her flat. Miss P was being coerced into prostitution and reportedly being physically assaulted by one of the men visiting her flat. There was also concern that she was being financially exploited. Miss P's vulnerability was exacerbated by her mental health needs and consequent inability to set safe boundaries with the people she was associating with.

The social worker recognised that the most appropriate way to enable Miss P to manage the risk of harm was to involve Miss P's family, to which she agreed to, and other professionals to develop and coordinate a plan which would enable her to continue living independently but provide a safety net for when the risk of harm became heightened. Guided initially by Miss P's wish for the two men to stay away from her, the social worker initiated a planning meeting between supportive family members and other professionals such as the police, domestic violence workers, support workers and housing officers. Although Miss P herself felt unable to attend the planning meeting, her social worker ensured that her views were included and helped guide the plan. The meeting allowed family and professionals to work in partnership, to openly share information about the risks and to plan what support Miss P needed to safely maintain her independence.

asks were divided between the police, family members and specialist support workers. The social worker had a role in ensuring that the plan was coordinated properly and that Miss P was fully aware of everyone's role. Miss P's family were crucial to the success of the plan as they had always supported her and were able to advocate for her needs. They also had a trusting relationship with her and were able to notify the police and other professionals if they thought that the risk to Miss P was increasing. The police played an active role in monitoring and preventing criminal activity towards Miss P and ensured that they kept all of the other professionals and family up to date with what was happening.

Miss P is working with a domestic violence specialist to help her develop personal strategies to keep safer and her support worker is helping her to build resilience through community support and activities.

RESPONDING TO ABUSE AND NEGLECT IN A REGULATED CARE SETTING

14.56. It is important that all partners are clear where responsibility lies where abuse or neglect is carried out by employees or in a regulated setting, such as a care home, hospital, or college. The first responsibility to act must be with the employing organisation as provider of the service. However, social workers or counsellors may need to be involved in order to support the adult to recover.

14.57. When an employer is aware of abuse or neglect in their organisation, then they are under a duty to correct this and protect the adult from harm as soon as possible and inform the local authority, CQC and CCG where the latter is the commissioner. Where a local authority has reasonable cause to suspect that an adult may be experiencing or at risk of abuse or neglect, then it is still under a duty to make (or cause to be made) whatever enquiries it thinks necessary to decide what if any action needs to be taken and by whom. The local authority may well be reassured by the employer's response so that no further action is required. However, a local authority would have to satisfy itself that an employer's response has been sufficient to deal with the safeguarding issue and, if not, to undertake any enquiry of its own and any appropriate follow up action (e.g. referral to CQC, professional regulators).

14.58. The employer should investigate any concern (and provide any additional support that the adult may need) unless there is compelling reason why it is inappropriate or unsafe to do this. For example, this could be a serious conflict of interest on the part of the employer, concerns having been raised about non-effective past enquiries or serious, multiple concerns, or a matter that requires investigation by the police.

14.59. An example of a conflict of interest where it is better for an external person to be appointed to investigate may be the case of a family-run business where institutional abuse is alleged, or where the manager or owner of the service is implicated. The circumstances where an external person would be required should be set out in the local multi-agency procedures. All those carrying out such enquiries should have received appropriate training.

14.60. There should be a clear understanding between partners at a local level when other agencies such as the local authority, CQC or CCG need to be notified or involved and what role they have. ADASS, CQC, LGA, ACPO and NHS England have jointly produced a high level guide on these roles and responsibilities.[1] The focus should be on promoting the wellbeing of those adults at risk. It may be that additional training or supervision will be the appropriate response, but the impact of this needs to be assessed. Commissioners of care or other professionals should only use safeguarding procedures in a way that reflects the principles above not as a means of intimidating providers or families. Transparency, open- mindedness and timeliness are important features of fair and effective safeguarding enquiries. CQC and commissioners have alternative means of raising standards of service, including support for staff training, contract compliance and, in the case of CQC, enforcement powers.

14.61. Commissioners should encourage an open culture around safeguarding, working in partnership with providers to ensure the best outcome for the adult. A disciplinary investigation, and potentially a hearing, may result in the employer taking informal or formal measures which may include dismissal and possibly referral to the Disclosure and Barring Service.

14.62. If someone is removed by being either dismissed or redeployed to a non-regulated activity, from their role providing regulated activity following a

---

[1] http://www.cqc.org.uk/sites/default/files/20140416_safeguarding_adults_-_roles_and_responsibilities-_revised_draf....pdf

safeguarding incident, or a person leaves their role (resignation, retirement) to avoid a disciplinary hearing following a safeguarding incident and the employer/volunteer organisation feels they would have dismissed the person based on the information they hold, the regulated activity provider has a legal duty to refer to the Disclosure and Barring Service.[1] If an agency or personnel supplier has provided the person, then the legal duty sits with that agency.[2] In circumstances where these actions are not undertaken then the local authority can make such a referral.

LOCAL AUTHORITY'S ROLE IN CARRYING OUT ENQUIRIES

14.63. Local authorities **must** make enquiries, or cause others to do so, if they reasonably suspect an adult who meets the criteria at paragraph 14.2 is, or is at risk of, being abused or neglected.

14.64. An enquiry is the action taken or instigated by the local authority in response to a concern that abuse or neglect may be taking place. An enquiry could range from a conversation with the adult, or if they lack capacity, or have substantial difficulty in understanding the enquiry their representative or advocate, prior to initiating a formal enquiry under section 42, right through to a much more formal multi-agency plan or course of action. Whatever the course of subsequent action, the professional concerned should record the concern, the adult's views and wishes, any immediate action has taken and the reasons for those actions.

14.65. The purpose of the enquiry is to decide whether or not the local authority or another organisation, or person, should do something to help and protect the adult. If the local authority decides that another organisation should make the enquiry, for example a care provider, then the local authority should be clear about timescales, the need to know the outcomes of the enquiry and what action will follow if this is not done.

14.66. What happens as a result of an enquiry should reflect the adult's wishes wherever possible, as stated by them or by their representative or advocate. If they lack capacity it should be in their best interests if they are not able to make the decision, and be proportionate to the level of concern.

14.67. The adult should always be involved from the beginning of the enquiry unless there are exceptional circumstances that would increase the risk of abuse. If the adult has substantial difficulty in being involved, and where there is no one appropriate to support them, then the local authority must arrange for an independent advocate to represent them for the purpose of facilitating their involvement.

14.68. Professionals and other staff need to handle enquiries in a sensitive and skilled way to ensure distress to the adult is minimised. It is likely that many enquiries will require the input and supervision of a social worker, particularly the more complex situations and to support the adult to realise the outcomes they want and to reach a resolution or recovery. For example, where abuse or neglect is suspected within a family or informal relationship it is likely that a social worker will be the most appropriate lead. Personal and family relationships within community settings can prove both difficult and complex to assess and intervene in. The dynamics of personal relationships can be extremely difficult

---

[1] https://www.gov.uk/government/publications/dbs-referrals-factsheets
[2] https://www.gov.uk/disclosure-and-barring-service-criminal-record-checks-referrals-and-complaints

to judge and rebalance. For example, an adult may make a choice to be in a relationship that causes them emotional distress which outweighs, for them, the unhappiness of not maintaining the relationship.

14.69. Whilst work with the adult may frequently require the input of a social worker, other aspects of enquiries may be best undertaken by others with more appropriate skills and knowledge. For example, health professionals should undertake enquiries and treatment plans relating to medicines management or pressure sores.

CRIMINAL OFFENCES AND ADULT SAFEGUARDING

14.70. Everyone is entitled to the protection of the law and access to justice. Behaviour which amounts to abuse and neglect, for example physical or sexual assault or rape, psychological abuse or hate crime, wilful neglect, unlawful imprisonment, theft and fraud and certain forms of discrimination also often constitute specific criminal offences under various pieces of legislation. Although the local authority has the lead role in making enquiries, where criminal activity is suspected, then the early involvement of the police is likely to have benefits in many cases.

> Miss Y is a young woman with a learning disability with limited support from her family and was not engaged with health and social care services. Miss Y was befriended by an individual who took her to parties where she was given drugs and alcohol and forced to have sex with different men. Sometimes she would be given money or gifts in return for having sex with the men. Miss Y disclosed this to a social worker and it was discovered that there were a number of young people and vulnerable adults who were being sexually exploited by multiple perpetrators. Miss Y lacked mental capacity in order to be able to consent to having sex, as well as in relation to her accommodation, finances or personal safety. The perpetrators sought out Miss Y and others because of their vulnerability – whether that was because of their age, disability, mental illness, or their previous history as a victim of abuse. The process to safeguard Miss Y involved a coordinated response between the police, social care, health and voluntary and community sector organisations. This included the police investigating the perpetrators for rape, sexual assault, trafficking and drug offences. The Court of Protection and Deprivation of Liberty Safeguards were also used initially to safeguard Miss Y.

14.71. For the purpose of court proceedings, a witness is competent if they can understand the questions and respond in a way that the court can understand. Police have a duty under legislation to assist those witnesses who are vulnerable and intimidated. A range of special measures are available to facilitate the gathering and giving of evidence by vulnerable and intimidated witnesses. Consideration of specials measures should occur from the onset of a police investigation.[1] In particular:

- immediate referral or consultation with the police will enable the police to establish whether a criminal act has been committed and this will give an

---

[1] http://www.justice.gov.uk/downloads/victims-and-witnesses/vulnerable-witnesses/vulnerable-intimidated- witnesses.pdf

opportunity of determining if, and at what stage, the police need to become involved further and undertake a criminal investigation;

- the police have powers to initiate specific protective actions which may apply, such as Domestic Violence Protection Orders (DVPO);

- a higher standard of proof is required in criminal proceedings ("beyond reasonable doubt") than in disciplinary or regulatory proceedings (where the test is the balance of probabilities) and so early contact with police may assist in obtaining and securing evidence and witness statements;

- early involvement of the police will help ensure that forensic evidence is not lost or contaminated;

- police officers need to have considerable skill in investigating and interviewing adults with a range of disabilities and communication needs if early involvement is to prevent the adult being interviewed unnecessarily on subsequent occasions. Research[1] has found that sometimes evidence from victims and witnesses with learning disabilities is discounted. This may also be true of others such as people with dementia. It is crucial that reasonable adjustments are made and appropriate support given, so people can get equal access to justice;

- police investigations should be coordinated with health and social care enquiries but they may take priority;

- guidance should include reference to support relating to criminal justice matters which is available locally from such organisations as Victim Support and court preparation schemes;

- some witnesses will need protection; and

- the police may be able to get victim support in place.

14.72. Special Measures were introduced through legislation in the Youth Justice and Criminal Evidence Act 1999 (YJCEA) and include a range of measures to support witnesses to give their best evidence and to help reduce some of the anxiety when attending court. Measures in place include the use of screens around the witness box, the use of live-link or recorded evidence-in-chief and the use of an intermediary to help witnesses understand the questions they are being asked and to give their answers accurately.

14.73. **Vulnerable adult Witnesses** (S.16 YJCEA) have a

- mental disorder

- learning disability, or

- physical disability

These witnesses are only eligible for special measures if the quality of evidence that is given by them is likely to be diminished by reason of the disorder or disability.

14.74. **Intimidated Witnesses** (S17 YJCEA 99): Intimidated witnesses are defined by Section 17 of the Act as those whose quality of evidence is likely to

---

[1] http://www.cps.gov.uk/publications/docs/mhld_cps_research.pdf

be diminished by reason of fear or distress. In determining whether a witness falls into this category the court takes account of:

- the nature and alleged circumstances of the offence;
- the age of the witness;
- the social and cultural background and ethnic origins of the witness;
- the domestic and employment circumstances of the witness;
- any religious beliefs or political opinions of the witness;
- any behaviour towards the witness by the accused or third party. Also falling into this category are:
- complainants in cases of sexual assault;
- witnesses to specified gun and knife offences;
- victims of and witnesses to domestic violence, racially motivated crime, crime motivated by reasons relating to religion, homophobic crime, gang related violence and repeat victimisation;
- those who are older and frail; and,
- the families of homicide victims.

Registered Intermediaries (RIs) have been facilitating communication with vulnerable witnesses in the criminal justice system in England and Wales since 2004.

14.75. A criminal investigation by the police takes priority over all other enquiries, although a multi-agency approach should be agreed to ensure that the interests and personal wishes of the adult will be considered throughout, even if they do not wish to provide any evidence or support a prosecution. The welfare of the adult and others, including children, is paramount and requires continued risk assessment to ensure the outcome is in their interests and enhances their wellbeing.

14.76. If the adult has the mental capacity to make informed decisions about their safety and they do not want any action to be taken, this does not preclude the sharing of information with relevant professional colleagues. This is to enable professionals to assess the risk of harm and to be confident that the adult is not being unduly influenced, coerced or intimidated and is aware of all the options. This will also enable professionals to check the safety and validity of decisions made. It is good practice to inform the adult that this action is being taken unless doing so would increase the risk of harm.

Mr P has mild learning disabilities. The safeguarding concern was financial and other abuse and neglect by his brother, with whom he lived. His support worker had noticed that Mr P had begun to appear agitated and anxious, that he looked increasingly unkempt and that he was often without money; then he suddenly stopped attending his day centre. When the support worker and the safeguarding officer followed up, Mr P told them that at times he was not allowed out at all by his brother and was confined to his bedroom. He was only allowed to use the bathroom when his brother said he could, and often

---

didn't get enough to eat. He was also very worried because his bank card no longer worked, and he had no money, so couldn't buy food for himself.

Mr P consented to move to temporary accommodation, and a case conference was held, which he attended with an advocate. At his request a move to a supported living flat was arranged and his belongings were retrieved from his brother's property. His bank account had been emptied by his brother, so he has made new arrangements for his money.

The police are investigating both the financial abuse and the harm Mr P suffered at his brother's hands. He has begun to talk about his experiences and is gradually regaining his confidence.

14. Safeguarding

Diagram 1A

Information gathering

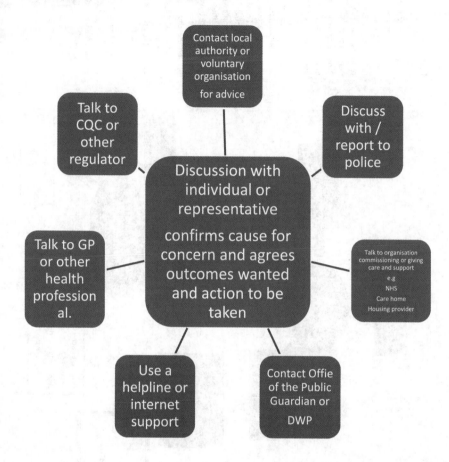

If the issue cannot be resolved through these means or the adult remains at risk of abuse or neglect (real or suspected)then the local authority's enquiry duty under section 42 continues until it decides what action is necessary to protect the adult and by whom and ensures itself that this action has been taken.

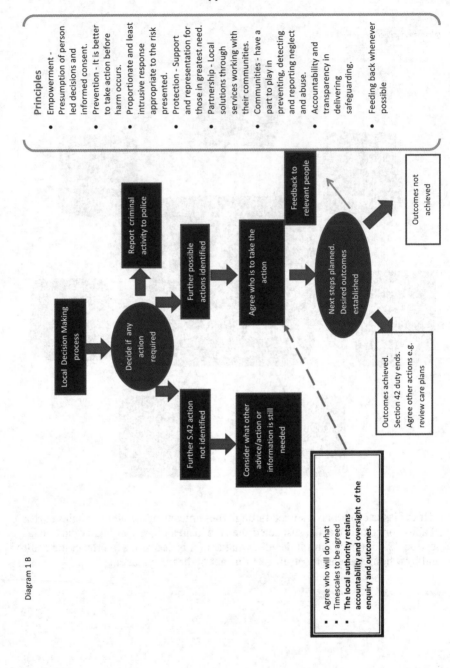

Appendix 2

Diagram 1 B

Principles

- Empowerment - Presumption of person led decisions and informed consent.
- Prevention - It is better to take action before harm occurs.
- Proportionate and least intrusive response appropriate to the risk presented.
- Protection - Support and representation for those in greatest need.
- Partnership - Local solutions through services working with their communities.
- Communities - have a part to play in preventing, detecting and reporting neglect and abuse.
- Accountability and transparency in delivering safeguarding.
- Feeding back whenever possible

Local Decision Making process

Decide if any action required

Report criminal activity to police

Further possible actions identified

Further S.42 action not identified

Consider what other advice/action or information is still needed

Agree who is to take the action

Feedback to relevant people

Next steps planned. Desired outcomes established

Outcomes not achieved

Outcomes achieved. Section 42 duty ends. Agree other actions e.g. review care plans

- Agree who will do what
- Timescales to be agreed
- **The local authority retains accountability and oversight of the enquiry and outcomes.**

Diagram 1 B

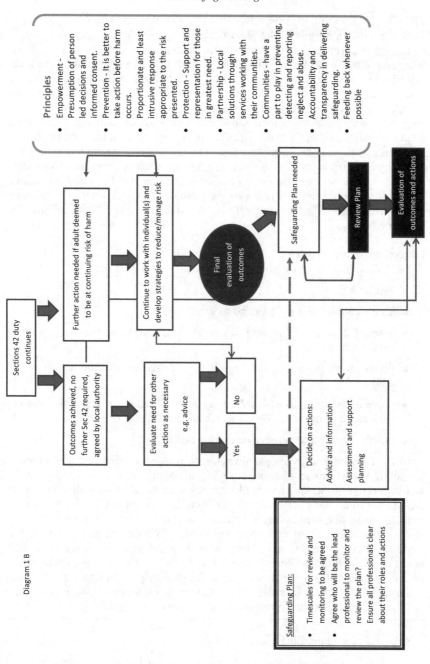

Principles

- Empowerment - Presumption of person led decisions and informed consent.
- Prevention - It is better to take action before harm occurs.
- Proportionate and least intrusive response appropriate to the risk presented.
- Protection - Support and representation for those in greatest need.
- Partnership - Local solutions through services working with their communities.
- Communities - have a part to play in preventing, detecting and reporting neglect and abuse.
- Accountability and transparency in delivering safeguarding.
- Feeding back whenever possible

Sections 42 duty continues

Further action needed if adult deemed to be at continuing risk of harm

Continue to work with individual(s) and develop strategies to reduce/manage risk

Outcomes achieved, no further Sec 42 required, agreed by local authority

Evaluate need for other actions as necessary

e.g. advice

No

Yes

Final evaluation of outcomes

Decide on actions:

Advice and information

Assessment and support planning

Safeguarding Plan needed

Review Plan

Evaluation of outcomes and actions

Safeguarding Plan:

- Timescales for review and monitoring to be agreed
- Agree who will be the lead professional to monitor and review the plan?

Ensure all professionals clear about their roles and actions

PROCEDURES FOR RESPONDING IN INDIVIDUAL CASES
When should an enquiry take place?

14.77. Local authorities must make enquiries, or cause another agency to do so, whenever abuse or neglect are suspected in relation to an adult and the local authority thinks it necessary to enable it to decide what (if any) action is needed to help and protect the adult. The scope of that enquiry, who leads it and its nature, and how long it takes, will depend on the particular circumstances. It will usually start with asking the adult their view and wishes which will often determine what next steps to take. Everyone involved in an enquiry must focus on improving the adult's well-being and work together to that shared aim. At this stage, the local authority also has a duty to consider whether the adult requires an independent advocate to represent and support the adult in the enquiry. The decision making tree at (see annex) highlights appropriate pauses for reflection, consideration and professional judgment and reflects the different routes and actions that might be taken.

Objectives of an enquiry

14.78. The objectives of an enquiry into abuse or neglect are to:

- establish facts;

- ascertain the adult's views and wishes;

- assess the needs of the adult for protection, support and redress and how they might be met;

- protect from the abuse and neglect, in accordance with the wishes of the adult;

- make decisions as to what follow-up action should be taken with regard to the person or organisation responsible for the abuse or neglect; and

- enable the adult to achieve resolution and recovery.

14.79. The first priority should always be to ensure the safety and well-being of the adult. The adult should experience the safeguarding process as empowering and supportive. Practitioners should wherever practicable seek the consent of the adult before taking action. However, there may be circumstances when consent cannot be obtained because the adult lacks the capacity to give it, but it is in their best interests to undertake an enquiry. Whether or not the adult has capacity to give consent, action may need to be taken if others are or will be put at risk if nothing is done or where it is in the public interest to take action because a criminal offence has occurred. It is the responsibility of all staff and members of the public to act on any suspicion or evidence of abuse or neglect and to pass on their concerns to a responsible person or agency.

BMA Adult safeguarding toolkit:

". . .where a competent adult explicitly refuses any supporting intervention, this should normally be respected. Exceptions to this may be where a criminal offence may have taken place or where there may be a significant risk of harm to a third party. If, for example, there may be an abusive adult in a position of authority in relation to other vulnerable adults [sic], it may be appropriate to breach confidentiality and disclose information to an appropriate authority. Where a criminal offence is suspected it may also be necessary to take legal advice. Ongoing support should also be offered. Because an adult initially refuses the offer of assistance he or she should not therefore be lost to or abandoned by relevant services. The situation should be monitored and the individual informed that she or he can take up the offer of assistance at any time."

What should an enquiry take into account?

14.80. The wishes of the adult are very important, particularly where they have capacity to make decisions about their safeguarding. The wishes of those that lack capacity are of equal importance. Wishes need to be balanced alongside wider considerations such as the level of risk or risk to others including any children affected. All adults at risk, regardless of whether they have capacity or not may want highly intrusive help, such as the barring of a person from their home, or a person to be brought to justice or they may wish to be helped in less intrusive ways, such as through the provision of advice as to the various options available to them and the risks and advantages of these various options.

14.81. Where an adult lacks capacity to make decisions about their safeguarding plans, then a range of options should be identified, which help the adult stay as much in control of their life as possible. Wherever possible, the adult should be supported to recognise risks and to manage them. Safeguarding plans should empower the adult as far as possible to make choices and to develop their own capability to respond to them.

14.82. Any intervention in family or personal relationships needs to be carefully considered. While abusive relationships never contribute to the wellbeing of an adult, interventions which remove all contact with family members may also be experienced as abusive interventions and risk breaching the adult's right to family life if not justified or proportionate. Safeguarding needs to recognise that the right to safety needs to be balanced with other rights, such as rights to liberty and autonomy, and rights to family life. Action might be primarily supportive or therapeutic, or it might involve the application of civil orders, sanctions, suspension, regulatory activity or criminal prosecution, disciplinary action or deregistration from a professional body.

14.83. It is important, when considering the management of any intervention or enquiry, to approach reports of incidents or allegations with an open mind. In considering how to respond the following factors need to be considered:

- the adult's needs for care and support;

- the adult's risk of abuse or neglect;

- the adult's ability to protect themselves or the ability of their networks to increase the support they offer;

- the impact on the adult, their wishes;

- the possible impact on important relationships;

- potential of action and increasing risk to the adult;

- the risk of repeated or increasingly serious acts involving children, or another adult at risk of abuse or neglect;

- the responsibility of the person or organisation that has caused the abuse or neglect; and

- research evidence to support any intervention.

Who can carry out an enquiry?

14.84. Although the local authority is the lead agency for making enquiries, it may require others to undertake them. The specific circumstances will often determine who is the right person to begin an enquiry. In many cases a professional who already knows the adult will be the best person. They may be a social worker, a housing support worker, a GP or other health worker such as a community nurse. The local authority retains the responsibility for ensuring that the enquiry is referred to the right place and is acted upon. The local authority, in its lead and coordinating role, should assure itself that the enquiry satisfies its duty under section 42 to decide what action (if any) is necessary to help and protect the adult and by whom and to ensure that such action is taken when necessary. In this role if the local authority has asked someone else to make enquiries, it is able to challenge the body making the enquiry if it considers that the process and/or outcome is unsatisfactory.

14.85. Where a crime is suspected and referred to the police, then the police must lead the criminal investigations, with the local authority's support where appropriate, for example by providing information and assistance. The local authority has an ongoing duty to promote the wellbeing of the adult in these circumstances.

Mr A is 24 and has autism and a mild learning disability. He is a very friendly and sociable young man who is prone to waving and talking to most people he comes across, seeing everyone as a potential friend. However, due to his disabilities, he struggles to read the intentions of others and is easily led astray and manipulated. He lives next door to a pub, where he knows the staff and the regulars. He also lives close to his GP, and is able to access his most frequently visited places. He does, however, like to walk into town to talk to people he meets out and about. On such occasions he has been repeatedly tricked into stealing items from a newsagent by a group of teenagers and given large amounts of money away to strangers he strikes up conversations with.

Due to his previous experiences, Mr A was identified during a needs assessment as being at risk of abuse and neglect. A safeguarding enquiry was triggered. The council found that, although Mr A was not currently experiencing abuse or neglect, he remained highly vulnerable to abuse due to his disabilities. To assure his safety in the future, a safeguarding plan was agreed between Mr A and a social worker. This focused on developing his social skills and understanding of relationships and boundaries and the social worker worked with Mr A to consider various support options such as having a buddy or circle of support. The social worker put Mr A in touch with an autism social group which provided sessions on skills for staying safe. As the group was based in town, Mr A's plan also included a support worker to accompany him. After the first 5 sessions Mr A was able to attend himself

---

882

but continued to meet with his support worker on a monthly basis as part of the risk management strategy set out in his safeguarding plan.

14.86. Employers must ensure that staff, including volunteers, are trained in recognising the symptoms of abuse or neglect, how to respond and where to go for advice and assistance. These are best written down in shared policy documents that can be easily understood and used by all the key organisations.

14.87. Employers must also ensure all staff keep accurate records, stating what the facts are and what are the known opinions of professionals and others and differentiating between fact and opinion. It is vital that the views of the adult are sought and recorded. These should include the outcomes that the adult wants, such as feeling safe at home, access to community facilities, restricted or no contact with certain individuals or pursuing the matter through the criminal justice system.

WHAT HAPPENS AFTER AN ENQUIRY?

14.88. Once the wishes of the adult have been ascertained and an initial enquiry undertaken, discussions should be undertaken with them as to whether further enquiry is needed and what further action could be taken.

14.89. That action could take a number of courses: it could include disciplinary, complaints or criminal investigations or work by contracts managers and CQC to improve care standards. Those discussions should enable the adult to understand what their options might be and how their wishes might best be realised. Social workers must be able to set out both the civil and criminal justice approaches that are open and other approaches that might help to promote their wellbeing, such as therapeutic or family work, mediation and conflict resolution, peer or circles of support. In complex domestic circumstances, it may take the adult some time to gain the confidence and self-esteem to protect themselves and take action and their wishes may change. The police, health service and others may need to be involved to help ensure these wishes are realised.

Safeguarding plans

14.90. Once the facts have been established, a further discussion of the needs and wishes of the adult is likely to take place. This could be focused safeguarding planning to enable the adult to achieve resolution or recovery, or fuller assessments by health and social care agencies (e.g. a needs assessment under the Care Act).This will entail joint discussion, decision taking and planning with the adult for their future safety and well-being. This applies if it is concluded that the allegation is true or otherwise, as many enquiries may be inconclusive.

14.91. The local authority must determine what further action is necessary. Where the local authority determines that it should itself take further action (e.g. a protection plan), then the authority would be under a duty to do so.

14.92. The MCA is clear that local authorities must presume that an adult has the capacity to make a decision until there is a reason to suspect that capacity is in some way compromised; the adult is best placed to make choices about their wellbeing which may involve taking certain risks. Of course, where the adult may lack capacity to make decisions about arrangements for enquiries or managing any abusive situation, then their capacity must always be assessed and any decision made in their best interests. If the adult has the capacity to make decisions in this area of their life and declines assistance, this can limit the intervention that organisations can make. The focus should therefore be, on harm reduction. It should not however limit the action that may be required to protect others who are at risk of harm. The potential for 'undue influence' will need to be considered if relevant. If the adult is thought to be refusing intervention on the grounds of duress then action must be taken.

14.93. In order to make sound decisions, the adult's emotional, physical, intellectual and mental capacity in relation to self-determination and consent and any intimidation, misuse of authority or undue influence will have to be assessed.[1]

Taking action

14.94. Once enquiries are completed, the outcome should be notified to the local authority which should then determine with the adult what, if any, further action is necessary and acceptable. It is for the local authority to determine the appropriateness of the outcome of the enquiry. One outcome of the enquiry may be the formulation of agreed action for the adult which should be recorded on their care plan. This will be the responsibility of the relevant agencies to implement.

14.95. In relation to the adult this should set out:

- what steps are to be taken to assure their safety in future;

- the provision of any support, treatment or therapy including on-going advocacy;

- any modifications needed in the way services are provided (e.g. same gender care or placement; appointment of an OPG deputy);

- how best to support the adult through any action they take to seek justice or redress;

- any on-going risk management strategy as appropriate; and,

- any action to be taken in relation to the person or organisation that has caused the concern.

Person alleged to be responsible for abuse or neglect

14.96. When a complaint or allegation has been made against a member of staff, including people employed by the adult, they should be made aware of their rights under employment legislation and any internal disciplinary procedures.

14.97. Where the person who is alleged to have carried out the abuse themselves has care and support needs and is unable to understand the significance of questions put to them or their replies, they should be assured of their right to the support of an 'appropriate' adult if they are questioned in relation to a suspected crime by the police under the Police and Criminal Evidence Act 1984 (PACE). Victims of crime and witnesses may also require the support of an 'appropriate' adult.[2]

---

[1] https://www.justice.gov.uk/protecting-the-vulnerable/mental-capacity-act
[2] https://www.justice.gov.uk/victims-and-witnesses/vulnerable-intimidated-witnesses-guidance

14.98. Under the MCA, people who lack capacity and are alleged to be responsible for abuse, are entitled to the help of an Independent Mental Capacity Advocate, to support and represent them in the enquiries that are taking place. This is separate from the decision whether or not to provide the victim of abuse with an independent advocate under the Care Act.

14.99. The Police and Crown Prosecution Service (CPS) should agree procedures with the local authority, care providers, housing providers, and the NHS/CCG to cover the following situations:

- action pending the outcome of the police and the employer's investigations;

- action following a decision to prosecute an individual;

- action following a decision not to prosecute;

- action pending trial; and

- responses to both acquittal and conviction.

14.100. Employers who are also providers or commissioners of care and support not only have a duty to the adult, but also a responsibility to take action in relation to the employee when allegations of abuse are made against them. Employers should ensure that their disciplinary procedures are compatible with the responsibility to protect adults at risk of abuse or neglect.

14.101. With regard to abuse, neglect and misconduct within a professional relationship, codes of professional conduct and/or employment contracts should be followed and should determine the action that can be taken. Robust employment practices, with checkable references and recent DBS checks are important. Reports of abuse, neglect and misconduct should be investigated and evidence collected.

14.102. Where appropriate, employers should report workers to the statutory and other bodies responsible for professional regulation such as the General Medical Council and the Nursing and Midwifery Council. If someone is removed from their role providing regulated activity following a safeguarding incident the regulated activity provider (or if the person has been provided by an agency or personnel supplier, the legal duty sits with them) has a legal duty to refer to the Disclosure and Barring Service. The legal duty to refer to the Disclosure and Barring Service also applies where a person leaves their role to avoid a disciplinary hearing following a safeguarding incident and the employer/volunteer organisation feels they would have dismissed the person based on the information they hold.

14.103. The standard of proof for prosecution is 'beyond reasonable doubt'. The standard of proof for internal disciplinary procedures and for discretionary barring consideration by the Disclosure and Barring Service (DBS) and the Vetting and Barring Board is usually the civil standard of 'on the balance of probabilities'. This means that when criminal procedures are concluded without action being taken this does not automatically mean that regulatory or disciplinary procedures should cease or not be considered. In any event there is a legal duty to make a safeguarding referral to DBS if a person is dismissed or removed from their role due to harm to a child or a vulnerable adult.

SAFEGUARDING ADULTS BOARDS

14.104. Each local authority must set up a Safeguarding Adults Board (SAB). The main objective of a SAB is to assure itself that local safeguarding arrangements and partners act to help and protect adults in its area who meet the criteria set out at paragraph 14.2.

14.105. The SAB has a strategic role that is greater than the sum of the operational duties of the core partners. It oversees and leads adult safeguarding across the locality and will be interested in a range of matters that contribute to the prevention of abuse and neglect. These will include the safety of patients in its local health services, quality of local care and support services, effectiveness of prisons and approved premises in safeguarding offenders and awareness and responsiveness of further education services. It is important that SAB partners feel able to challenge each other and other organisations where it believes that their actions or inactions are increasing the risk of abuse or neglect. This will include commissioners, as well as providers of services.

14.106. The SAB can be an important source of advice and assistance, for example in helping others improve their safeguarding mechanisms. It is important that the SAB has effective links with other key partnerships in the locality and share relevant information and work plans. They should consciously cooperate to reduce any duplication and maximise any efficiency, particularly as objectives and membership is likely to overlap.

14.107. A SAB has three core duties:

- It **must** publish a strategic plan for each financial year that sets how it will meet its main objective and what the members will do to achieve this. The plan must be developed with local community involvement, and the SAB must consult the local Healthwatch organisation. The plan should be evidence based and make use of all available evidence and intelligence from partners to form and develop its plan.

- It **must** publish an annual report detailing what the SAB has done during the year to achieve its main objective and implement its strategic plan, and what each member has done to implement the strategy as well as detailing the findings of any Safeguarding Adults Reviews and subsequent action.

- It **must** conduct any Safeguarding Adults Review in accordance with Section 44 of the Act.

14.108. Safeguarding requires collaboration between partners in order to create a framework of inter-agency arrangements. Local authorities and their relevant partners must collaborate and work together as set out in the co-operation duties in the Care Act and, in doing so, must, where appropriate, also consider the wishes and feelings of the adult on whose behalf they are working.

14.109. Local authorities may cooperate with any other body they consider appropriate where it is relevant to their care and support functions. The lead agency with responsibility for coordinating adult safeguarding arrangements is the local authority, but all the members of the SAB should designate a lead officer. Other agencies should also consider the benefits of having a lead for adult safeguarding.

14.110. Each Safeguarding Adults Board should:

- identify the role, responsibility, authority and accountability with regard to the action each agency and professional group should take to ensure the protection of adults;

- establish ways of analysing and interrogating data on safeguarding notifications that increase the SAB's understanding of prevalence of abuse and neglect locally that builds up a picture over time;

- establish how it will hold partners to account and gain assurance of the effectiveness of its arrangements;

- determine its arrangements for peer review and self-audit;

- establish mechanisms for developing policies and strategies for protecting adults which should be formulated, not only in collaboration and consultation with all relevant agencies but also take account of the views of adults who have needs for care and support, their families, advocates and carer representatives;

- develop preventative strategies that aim to reduce instances of abuse and neglect in its area;

- identify types of circumstances giving grounds for concern and when they should be considered as a referral to the local authority as an enquiry;

- formulate guidance about the arrangements for managing adult safeguarding, and dealing with complaints, grievances and professional and administrative malpractice in relation to safeguarding adults;

- develop strategies to deal with the impact of issues of race, ethnicity, religion, gender and gender orientation, sexual orientation, age, disadvantage and disability on abuse and neglect;

- balance the requirements of confidentiality with the consideration that, to protect adults, it may be necessary to share information on a 'need-to-know basis';

- identify mechanisms for monitoring and reviewing the implementation and impact of policy and training;

- carry out safeguarding adult reviews;

- produce a Strategic Plan and an Annual Report;

- evidence how SAB members have challenged one another and held other boards to account; and,

- promote multi-agency training and consider any specialist training that may be required. Consider any scope to jointly commission some training with other partnerships, such as the Community Safety Partnership.

14.111. Strategies for the prevention of abuse and neglect is a core responsibility of a SAB and it should have an overview of how this is taking place in the area and how this work ties in with the Health and Wellbeing Board's, Quality Surveillance Group's (QSG), Community Safety Partnership's and CQC's stated approach and practice. This could be about commissioners and the regulator, together with providers, acting to address poor quality care and the intelligence that indicates there is risk that care may be deteriorating and becoming abusive or neglectful. It could also be about addressing hate crime or anti-social behaviour in a particular neighbourhood. The SAB will need to have effective links and communication across a number of networks in order to make this work effectively.

14.112. Within the context of the duties set out at paragraph 14.2, safeguarding partnerships can be a positive means of addressing issues of self-neglect. The SAB is a multi-agency group that is the appropriate forum where strategic discussions can take place on dealing with what are often complex and challenging situations for practitioners and managers as well as communities more broadly.

Recent research has identified ways of working that can have positive outcomes for those who self-neglect.[1]

Mr M, in his 70s, lives in an upper-floor council flat, and had hoarded over many years: his own possessions, items inherited from his family home, and materials he had collected from skips and building sites in case they came in useful. The material was piled from floor to ceiling in every room, and Mr M lived in a burrow tunnelled through the middle, with no lighting or heating, apart from a gas stove. Finally, after years of hiding in privacy, Mr M had realised that work being carried out on the building would lead to his living conditions being discovered. Mr M himself recounted how hard it had been for him to invite access to his home, how ashamed and scared he was, and how important his hoard was to him, having learnt as a child of the war never to waste anything.

Through working closely together, Mr M, his support worker and experienced contractors have been able gradually to remove from his flat a very large volume of hoarded material and bring improvements to his home environment. It has taken time and patience, courage and faith, and a strong relationship based on trust. The worker has not judged Mr M, and has worked at his pace, positively affirming his progress. Both Mr M and his support worker acknowledge his low self-esteem, and have connected with his doctor and mental health services. The worker has recognised the need to replace what Mr M is giving up, and has encouraged activities that reflect his interests. Mr M has valued the worker's honesty, kindness and sensitivity, his ability to listen, and the respect and reciprocity within their relationship.

14.113. Members of a SAB are expected to consider what assistance they can provide in supporting the Board in its work. This might be through payment to the local authority or to a joint fund established by the local authority to provide, for example, secretariat functions for the Board. Members might also support the work of the SAB by providing administrative help, premises for meetings or holding training sessions. It is in all core partners' interests to have an effective SAB that is resourced adequately to carry out its functions.

14.114. Local SABs decide how they operate but they must ensure that their arrangements will be able to deliver the duties and functions under Schedule 2 of the Care Act.

---

[1] Braye, S., Orr, D. and Preston-Shoot, M. *Self-neglect Policy and Practice: Building an Evidence Base for Adult Social Care*. London: Social Care Institute for Excellence. http://www.scie.org.uk/publications/reports/report69.asp

14.115. The arrangements that the SAB needs to create include for example, how often it meets, the appointment of the Chair, any sub-groups to it and other practical arrangements. It also needs to be clear about how it will seek feedback from the local community, particularly those adults who have been involved in a safeguarding enquiry.

Membership of Safeguarding Adults Boards

14.116. The information about how the SAB works should be easily accessible to partner organisations and to the general public. The following organisations must be represented on the Board:

- the local authority which set it up;
- the CCGs in the local authority's area; and
- the chief officer of police in the local authority's area.

14.117. SABs may also include such other organisations and individuals as the establishing local authority considers appropriate having consulted its SAB partners from the CCG and police. The SAB may wish to invite additional partners to some meetings depending on the specific focus or to participate in its work more generally. Examples include:

- ambulance and fire services;
- representatives of providers of health and social care services, including independent providers;
- Department for Work and Pensions;
- representatives of housing providers, housing support providers, probation and prison services;
- General Practitioners;
- representatives of further education colleges;
- members of user, advocacy and carer groups;
- local Healthwatch;
- Care Quality Commission;
- representatives of children's safeguarding boards; and
- Trading Standards.

14.118. This is not a definitive list, but SABs should assure themselves that the Board has the involvement of all partners necessary to effectively carry out its duties. Additionally, there may also be effective links that can be made with related partnerships to maximise impact and minimise duplication and which would reflect the reality and interconnectivities of local partnerships. There are strong synergies between the work of many of these bodies, particularly when looking at a broader family agenda as well as opportunities for efficiencies in taking forward work. The following example illustrates a safeguarding children's board and the domestic abuse board work collaboratively to commission and deliver training.

A SAB has worked with the domestic abuse Board to develop a Multi-Agency Risk Assessment Conference (MARAC) e-learning package and to commission training in line with the domestic abuse training standards, such as: domestic abuse basic awareness; domestic abuse enhanced awareness; Domestic Abuse, Stalking and Harassment (DASH) and; MARAC awareness.

14.119. Partnerships may include:

- Community Safety Partnerships;
- Local Children Safeguarding Boards;
- Health and Wellbeing Boards;
- Quality Surveillance Groups;
- Clinical Commissioning Group Boards; and
- Health Overview and Scrutiny Committees (OSCs).

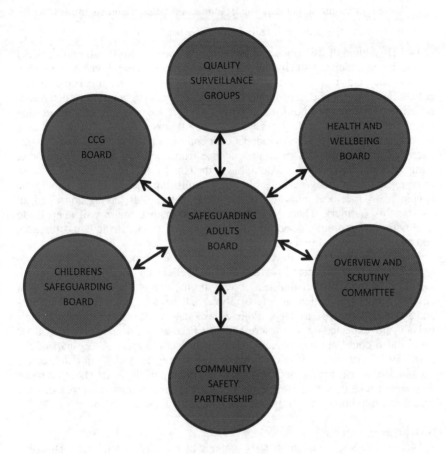

14.120. The local authority which establishes the SAB must ensure that between them, all members of the SAB have the requisite skills and experience necessary for the SAB to act effectively and efficiently to safeguard adults in its area. For example, a social worker's ability to understand the individual within complex social networks and other systems makes social work input a vital component in SAB arrangements; but the SAB will also require access to medical, nursing and legal expertise. Members who attend in a professional and managerial capacity should be:

- able to present issues clearly in writing and in person;
- experienced in the work of their organisation;
- knowledgeable about the local area and population;
- able to explain their organisation's priorities;
- able to promote the aims of the SAB;
- able to commit their organisation to agreed actions;

- have a thorough understanding of abuse and neglect and its impact; and

- understand the pressures facing front line practitioners.

14.121. Although it is not a requirement, the local authority should consider appointing an independent chair to the SAB who is not an employee or a member of an agency that is a member of the SAB. The Chair has a critical role to lead collaboratively, give advice, support and encouragement but also to offer constructive challenge and hold main partner agencies to account and ensure that interfaces with other strategic functions are effective whilst also acting as a spokesperson for the SAB. An independent chair can provide additional reassurance that the Board has some independence from the local authority and other partners. The Chair will be accountable to the Chief Executive of the local authority as the lead body responsible for establishing the SAB but should be appointed by the local authority in the name of the SAB having consulted all its statutory partners. There is a clear expectation that chairs will keep up to date with, and promote, good practice, developments in case law and research and any other relevant material.

14.122. The SAB must develop clear policies and processes that have been agreed with other interested parties, and that reflect the local service arrangements, roles and responsibilities. It will promote multi-agency training that ensures a common understanding of abuse and neglect, appropriate responses and agree how to work together. Policies will state what organisations and individuals are expected to do where they suspect abuse or neglect. The SAB should also consider any specialist training that is required. A key part of the SAB's role will be to develop preventative strategies and aiming to reduce instances of abuse and neglect in its area. Members of the SAB should also be clear about how they will contribute the financial and human resources of their organisation to both preventing and responding to abuse and neglect.

SAB strategic plans

14.123. The SAB must publish its strategic plan each financial year. This plan should address both short and longer-term actions and it must set out how it will help adults in its area and what actions each member of the SAB will take to deliver the strategic plan and protect better. This plan could cover 3-5 years in order to enable the Board to plan ahead as long as it is reviewed and updated annually.

14.124. When it is preparing the plan, the SAB must consult the local Healthwatch and involve the local community. The local community has a role to play in the recognition and prevention of abuse and neglect but active and on-going work with the community is needed to tap into this source of support.

14.125. SABs must understand the many and potentially different concerns of the various groups that make up its local community. These might include such things as scams targeted at older householders, bullying and harassment of disabled people, hate crime directed at those with mental health problems, cyber bullying and the sexual exploitation of people who may lack the capacity to understand that they have the right to say no. In order to make the plan understood as widely as possible, it should be free from jargon and written in plain English with an easy read version available.

SAB annual reports

14.126. After the end of each financial year, the SAB must publish an annual report that **must** clearly state what both the SAB and its members have done to carry out and deliver the objectives and other content of its strategic plan.

14.127. Specifically, the annual report must provide information about any Safeguarding Adults Reviews (SARs) that the SAB has arranged which are ongoing or have reported in the year (regardless whether they commenced in that year). The report must state what the SAB has done to act on the findings of completed SARs or, where it has decided not to act on a finding, why not.

14.128. The annual report must set out how the SAB is monitoring progress against its policies and intentions to deliver its strategic plan. The SAB should consider the following in coming to its conclusions:

- evidence of community awareness of adult abuse and neglect and how to respond;

- analysis of safeguarding data to better understand the reasons that lie behind local data returns and use the information to improve the strategic plan and operational arrangements;

- what adults who have experienced the process say and the extent to which the outcomes they wanted (their wishes) have been realised;

- what front line practitioners say about outcomes for adults and about their ability to work in a personalised way with those adults;

- better reporting of abuse and neglect;

- evidence of success of strategies to prevent abuse or neglect;

- feedback from local Healthwatch, adults who use care and support services and carers, community groups, advocates, service providers and other partners;

- how successful adult safeguarding is at linking with other parts of the system, for example children's safeguarding, domestic violence, community safety;

- the impact of training carried out in this area and analysis of future need; and

- how well agencies are co-operating and collaborating.

14.129. Safeguarding forms one of the domains in the Adult Social Care Outcomes Framework (ASCOF). The 2014/15 publication announced the development of a national measure on safeguarding outcomes – one of the first to focus on those who have been through an adult safeguarding enquiry and their views on how the enquiry was dealt with. A set of questions has been developed and cognitively tested in preparation for a pilot survey undertaken by volunteer local authorities in summer 2014. This testing has successfully created a number of questions which can be used in a face to face interview, with confidence by local authorities, to seek the views of adults, or relatives/friends/carers or IMCAs where appropriate. Findings from this work highlighted how pleased adults were to be asked about their experiences. The questionnaires and all survey documentation can be found on the HSCIC's website.[1]

14.130. Using these questions would enable local authorities to better understand the experience of those going through the safeguarding process in their locality but would also facilitate the comparison to other local authorities.

14.131. The report is meant to be a document that can be read and understood by anyone. Most SABs are likely to publish these reports on their websites. SABs should consider making the report available in a variety of media. SABs will need to establish ways of publicising the report and actively seeking feedback from communities.

14.132. Every SAB must send a copy of its report to:

- the Chief Executive and leader of the local authority;

- the Police and Crime Commissioner and the Chief Constable;

- the local Healthwatch; and

- the Chair of the Health and Wellbeing Board.

It is expected that those organisations will fully consider the contents of the report and how they can improve their contributions to both safeguarding throughout their own organisation and to the joint work of the Board.

SAFEGUARDING ADULTS REVIEWS (SARS)

14.133. SABs must arrange a SAR when an adult in its area dies as a result of abuse or neglect, whether known or suspected, and there is concern that partner agencies could have worked more effectively to protect the adult.

14.134. SABs must also arrange a SAR if an adult in its area has not died, but the SAB knows or suspects that the adult has experienced serious abuse or neglect. In the context of SARs, something can be considered serious abuse or neglect where, for example the individual would have been likely to have died but for an intervention, or has suffered permanent harm or has reduced capacity or quality of life (whether because of physical or psychological effects) as a result of the abuse or neglect. SABs are free to arrange for a SAR in any other situations involving an adult in its area with needs for care and support.

14.135. The SAB should be primarily concerned with weighing up what type of 'review' process will promote effective learning and improvement action to prevent future deaths or serious harm occurring again. This may be where a case can provide useful insights into the way organisations are working together to prevent and reduce abuse and neglect of adults. SARs may also be used to explore examples of good practice where this is likely to identify lessons that can be applied to future cases.

At the age of 72 years old, although registered disabled, Ms W was an active member in her community often seen helping at community events and visiting the local shops and swimming pool. Ms W had a fall in her home which left her lacking in confidence and fearful that she would fall again. As the winter approached, Ms W spent more time alone at home only venturing to the corner shop to buy groceries. As time passed her house came in disrepair

---

[1] http://www.hscic.gov.uk/article/4769/Safeguarding-Outcomes-Measure-Pilot-Study

and unhygienic as local youths began throw rubbish, including dog faeces into her front garden.

Within a five month period Ms W made seven complaints to the police about anti-social behaviour in her local area, and on two occasions was the victim of criminal damage to the front of her house, where her wheelchair accessibility ramp has been painted by graffiti. The police made a referral to social services. As a result, Ms W was placed on a waiting list for a support service.

Four weeks after she was last seen Ms W committed suicide. A Serious Case Review (SCR) was convened according to the local policy that stated 'the purpose of an SCR is not to reinvestigate or to apportion blame, but to establish whether there are lessons to be learnt from the circumstances of the case about the way in which local professionals and agencies work together to safeguard vulnerable adults. The published report and recommendations which followed demonstrated the lessons from this case. The resultant action plan included:

- Strengthened relationships and information sharing between police officers, health and the local authority.
- Clear lines of reporting and joint working arrangements with the Community Safety Partnerships.
- A robust multi-agency training plan.
- A targeted community programme to address anti-social behaviour.
- The development of a 'People's Panel' as a sub group to the Safeguarding Adults Board which includes people who access services, carers and voluntary groups.
- The development of a 'stay safe' programme involving local shops where adults at risk of abuse may report their concerns to a trusted member if their community.

14.136. Early discussions need to take place with the adult, family and friends to agree how they wish to be involved. The adult who is the subject of any SAR need not have been in receipt of care and support services for the SAB to arrange a review in relation to them.

14.137. SARs should reflect the six safeguarding principles. SABs should agree Terms of Reference for any SAR they arrange and these should be published and openly available. When undertaking SARs the records should either be anonymised through redaction or consent should be sought.

14.138. The following principles should be applied by SABs and their partner organisations to all reviews:

- there should be a culture of continuous learning and improvement across the organisations that work together to safeguard and promote the wellbeing and empowerment of adults, identifying opportunities to draw on what works and promote good practice;
- the approach taken to reviews should be proportionate according to the scale and level of complexity of the issues being examined;
- reviews of serious cases should be led by individuals who are independent of the case under review and of the organisations whose actions are being reviewed;

- professionals should be involved fully in reviews and invited to contribute their perspectives without fear of being blamed for actions they took in good faith; and

- families should be invited to contribute to reviews. They should understand how they are going to be involved and their expectations should be managed appropriately and sensitively.

14.139. SARs should seek to determine what the relevant agencies and individuals involved in the case might have done differently that could have prevented harm or death. This is so that lessons can be learned from the case and those lessons applied to future cases to prevent similar harm occurring again. Its purpose is not to hold any individual or organisation to account. Other processes exist for that, including criminal proceedings, disciplinary procedures, employment law and systems of service and professional regulation, such as CQC and the Nursing and Midwifery Council, the Health and Care Professions Council, and the General Medical Council.

14.140. It is vital, if individuals and organisations are to be able to learn lessons from the past, that reviews are trusted and safe experiences that encourage honesty, transparency and sharing of information to obtain maximum benefit from them. If individuals and their organisations are fearful of SARs their response will be defensive and their participation guarded and partial.

14.141. The process for undertaking SARs should be determined locally according to the specific circumstances of individual circumstances. No one model will be applicable for all cases. The focus must be on what needs to happen to achieve understanding, remedial action and, very often, answers for families and friends of adults who have died or been seriously abused or neglected. The recommendations and action plans from a SAR need to be followed through by the SAB.

14.142. The SAB should ensure that there is appropriate involvement in the review process of professionals and organisations who were involved with the adult. The SAR should also communicate with the adult and, or, their family. In some cases it may be helpful to communicate with the person who caused the abuse or neglect.

14.143. It is expected that those undertaking a SAR will have appropriate skills and experience which should include:

- strong leadership and ability to motivate others;

- expert facilitation skills and ability to handle multiple perspectives and potentially sensitive and complex group dynamics;

- collaborative problem solving experience and knowledge of participative approaches;

- good analytic skills and ability to manage qualitative data;

- safeguarding knowledge;

- inclined to promote an open, reflective learning culture.

14.144. The SAB should aim for completion of a SAR within a reasonable period of time and in any event within six months of initiating it, unless there are good reasons for a longer period being required; for example, because of potential prejudice to related court proceedings. Every effort should be made while the SAR is in progress to capture points from the case about improvements needed; and to take corrective action.

Links with other reviews

14.145. When victims of domestic homicide are aged between 16 and 18, there are separate requirements in statutory guidance for both a child Serious Case Review (SCR) and a Domestic Homicide Review (DHR). Where such reviews may be relevant to SAR (e.g. because they concern the same perpetrator), consideration should be given to how SARs, DHRs and SCRs can be managed in parallel in the most effective manner possible so that organisations and professionals can learn from the case. For example, considering whether some aspects of the reviews can be commissioned jointly so as to reduce duplication of work for the organisations involved.

14.146. In setting up a SAR the SAB should also consider how the process can dovetail with any other relevant investigations that are running parallel, such as a child SCR or DHR, a criminal investigation or an inquest.

14.147. It may be helpful when running a SAR and DHR or child SCR in parallel to establish at the outset all the relevant areas that need to be addressed, to reduce potential for duplication for families and staff. Any SAR will need to take account of a coroner's inquiry, and, or, any criminal investigation related to the case, including disclosure issues, to ensure that relevant information can be shared without incurring significant delay in the review process. It will be the responsibility of the manager of the SAR to ensure contact is made with the Chair of any parallel process in order to minimise avoidable duplication.

Findings from SARs

14.148. The SAB should include the findings from any SAR in its Annual Report and what actions it has taken, or intends to take in relation to those findings. Where the SAB decides not to implement an action then it must state the reason for that decision in the Annual Report. All documentation the SAB receives from registered providers which is relevant to CQC's regulatory functions will be given to the CQC on CQC's request.

14.149. SAR reports should:

- provide a sound analysis of what happened, why and what action needs to be taken to prevent a reoccurrence, if possible;

- be written in plain English; and

- contain findings of practical value to organisations and professionals.

INFORMATION SHARING
Record-keeping

14.150. Good record keeping is a vital component of professional practice. Whenever a complaint or allegation of abuse is made, all agencies should keep clear and accurate records and each agency should identify procedures for incorporating, on receipt of a complaint or allegation, all relevant records into a file to record all action taken. When abuse or neglect is raised managers need to look for past incidents, concerns, risks and patterns. We know that in many situations, abuse and neglect arise from a range of incidents over a period of time. In the case of providers registered with CQC, records of these should be available to service commissioners and the CQC so they can take the necessary action.

14.151. Staff should be given clear direction as to what information should be recorded and in what format. The following questions are a guide:

- What information do staff need to know in order to provide a high quality response to the adult concerned?

- What information do staff need to know in order to keep adults safe under the service's duty to protect people from harm?

- What information is not necessary?

- What is the basis for any decision to share (or not) information with a third party?

14.152. Records should be kept in such a way that the information can easily be collated for local use and national data collections.

14.153. All agencies should identify arrangements, consistent with principles and rules of fairness, confidentiality and data protection for making records available to those adults affected by, and subject to, an enquiry. If the alleged abuser is using care and support themselves, then information about their involvement in an adult safeguarding enquiry, including the outcome, should be included in their case record. If it is assessed that the individual continues to pose a threat to other people then this should be included in any information that is passed on to service providers or other people who need to know.

14.154. In order to carry out its functions, SABs will need access to information that a wide number of people or other organisations may hold. Some of these may be SAB members, such as the NHS and the police. Others will not be, such as private health and care providers or housing providers/housing support providers or education providers.

14.155. In the past, there have been instances where the withholding of information has prevented organisations being fully able to understand what "went wrong" and so has hindered them identifying, to the best of their ability, the lessons to be applied to prevent or reduce the risks of such cases reoccurring. If someone knows that abuse or neglect is happening they must act upon that knowledge, not wait to be asked for information.

14.156. An SAB may request a person to supply information to it or to another person. The person who receives the request must provide the information provided to the SAB if:

- the request is made in order to enable or assist the SAB to do its job;

- the request is made of a person who is likely to have relevant information and then either:
  i. the information requested relates to the person to whom the request is made and their functions or activities or;
  ii. the information requested has already been supplied to another person subject to an SAB request for information.

Confidentiality
14.157. Agencies should draw up a common agreement relating to confidentiality and setting out the principles governing the sharing of information,

based on the welfare of the adult or of other potentially affected adults. Any agreement should be consistent with the principles set out in the Caldicott Review published 2013[1] ensuring that:

- information will only be shared on a 'need to know' basis when it is in the interests of the adult;

- confidentiality must not be confused with secrecy;

- informed consent should be obtained but, if this is not possible and other adults are at risk of abuse or neglect, it may be necessary to override the requirement; and

- it is inappropriate for agencies to give assurances of absolute confidentiality in cases where there are concerns about abuse, particularly in those situations when other adults may be at risk.

14.158. Where an adult has refused to consent to information being disclosed for these purposes, then practitioners must consider whether there is an overriding public interest that would justify information sharing (e.g. because there is a risk that others are at risk of serious harm) and wherever possible, the appropriate Caldicott Guardian should be involved.[2]

14.159. Decisions about who needs to know and what needs to be known should be taken on a case by case basis, within agency policies and the constraints of the legal framework.

14.160. Principles of confidentiality designed to safeguard and promote the interests of an adult should not be confused with those designed to protect the management interests of an organisation. These have a legitimate role but must never be allowed to conflict with the welfare of an adult. If it appears to an employee or person in a similar role that such confidentiality rules may be operating against the interests of the adult then a duty arises to make full disclosure in the public interest.

14.161. In certain circumstances, it will be necessary to exchange or disclose personal information which will need to be in accordance with the law on confidentiality and the Data Protection Act 1998 where this applies. The Home Office and the Office of the Information Commissioner have issued general guidance on the preparation and use of information sharing protocols.

Information for staff, people who use care and support, carers and the general public

14.162. Information in a range of media should be produced in different, user-friendly formats for people with care and support needs and their carers. These should explain clearly what abuse is and also how to express concern and make a complaint. Adults with care and support needs and carers should be informed that their concern or complaint will be taken seriously, be dealt with independently and that they will be kept involved in the process to the degree that they wish to be. They should be reassured that they will receive help and support in

---

[1] https://www.gov.uk/government/uploads/system/uploads/attachment_data/file/192572/2900774_ InfoGovernance_accv2.pdf

[2] Guidance on public interest disclosure can be found here: https://www.gov.uk/government/uploads/ system/uploads/attachment_data/file/200147/Confidentiality_NHS_Code_of_Practice_ Supplementary_ Guidance_on_Public_Interest_Disclosures.pdf

taking action on their own behalf. They should also be advised that they can nominate an advocate or representative to speak and act on their behalf if they wish.

14.163. If an adult has no appropriate person to support them and has substantial difficulty in being involved in the local authority processes, they must be informed of their right to an independent advocate. Where appropriate local authorities should provide information on access to appropriate services such as how to obtain independent legal advice or counselling services for example. The involvement of adults at risk in developing such communication is sensible.

14.164. A number of local SABs or multi-agency safeguarding hubs (MASHs) have developed helpful and accessible information aimed at adults in order that they can protect themselves from abuse, such as the London Borough of Barnet's "Say NO to Abuse" booklet. Barnet has also produced a booklet "What happens after you report abuse".

14.165. All commissioners or providers of services in the public, voluntary or private sectors should disseminate information about the multi-agency policy and procedures. Staff should be made aware through internal guidelines of what to do when they suspect or encounter abuse of adults in vulnerable situations. This should be incorporated in staff manuals or handbooks detailing terms and conditions of appointment and other employment procedures so that individual staff members will be aware of their responsibilities in relation to safeguarding adults.

Camden has developed a leaflet for carers about the harm they may experience when caring for a relative or friend and the harm they may cause. This was developed in partnership with carers' organisations and carers themselves, and remains a partnership owned publication.

14.166. This information should emphasise that all those who express concern will be treated seriously and will receive a positive response from managers.

LOCAL ROLES AND RESPONSIBILITIES

14.167. Roles and responsibilities[1] should be clear and collaboration should take place at all the following levels:

- operational;
- supervisory line management;
- Designated Adult Safeguarding Managers (DASMs);
- senior management staff;
- corporate/cross authority;
- Chief officers/chief executives;
- local authority members and local police and crime commissioners;
- commissioners;
- providers of services;

---

[1] http://www.tcsw.org.uk/uploadedFiles/TheCollege/_CollegeLibrary/Policy/
RolesFunctionsAdviceNote.pdf

- voluntary organisations, and;
- regulated professionals.

Front line

14.168. Operational front line staff are responsible for identifying and responding to allegations of abuse and substandard practice. Staff at operational level need to share a common view of what types of behaviour may be abuse or neglect and what to do as an initial response to a suspicion or allegation that it is or has occurred. This includes GPs. It is employers' and commissioners' duty to set these out clearly and reinforce regularly.

14.169. It is not for front line staff to second-guess the outcome of an enquiry in deciding whether or not to share their concerns. There should be effective and well-publicised ways of escalating concerns where immediate line managers do not take action in response to a concern being raised.

14.170. Concerns about abuse or neglect must be reported whatever the source of harm is. It is imperative that poor or neglectful care is brought to the immediate attention of managers and responded to swiftly, including ensuring immediate safety and well-being of the adult. Where the source of abuse or neglect is a member of staff it is for the employer to take immediate action and record what they have done and why (similarly for volunteers and or students).

14.171. There should be clear arrangements in place about what each agency should contribute at this level. These will cover approaches to enquiries and subsequent courses of action. The local authority is responsible for ensuring effective co-ordination at this level.

A resident at a local care home told the district nurse that staff members spoke disrespectfully to her and that there were episodes of her waiting a long time for the call bell to be answered when wanting to use the commode. The resident wished to leave the home as she was very unhappy with the treatment she was receiving, and was regularly distressed and tearful.

The resident was reluctant for a formal safeguarding enquiry to take place, but did agree that the issues could be discussed with the manager. The district nurse negotiated some actions with the manager to promote good practice and address the issues that had been raised. When the district nurse reviewed the situation; the manager at the care home had dealt with the issues appropriately and devised an action plan. The resident stated that she was now happy at the care home – staff 'couldn't be more helpful' and she no longer wanted to move.

Line managers' supervision

14.172. Skilled and knowledgeable supervision focused on outcomes for adults is critical in safeguarding work. Managers have a central role in ensuring high standards of practice and that practitioners are properly equipped and supported. It is important to recognise that dealing with situations involving abuse and neglect can be stressful and distressing for staff and workplace support should be available.

14.173. Managers need to develop good working relationships with their counterparts in other agencies to improve cooperation locally and swiftly address any differences or difficulties that arise between front line staff or managers.

14.174. They should have access to legal advice on when proposed interventions, such as the proposed stopping of contact between family members, require applications to the Court of Protection.

Designated Adult Safeguarding Manager

14.175. Each SAB should establish and agree a framework and process for any organisation under the umbrella of the SAB to respond to allegations and issues of concern that are raised about a person who may have harmed or who may pose a risk to adults. The framework should have clear recording and information-sharing guidance and explicit timescales for action and be mindful of the need to preserve evidence. This will be whether the allegation or concern is current or historical.

14.176. Each member of the SAB should have a Designated Adult Safeguarding Manager (DASM) responsible for the management and oversight of individual complex cases and coordination where allegations are made or concerns raised about a person, whether an employee, volunteer or student, paid or unpaid. DASMs should keep in regular contact with their counterparts in partner organisations. They should also have a role in highlighting the extent to which their own organisation prevents abuse and neglect taking place.

14.177. The DASM should provide advice and guidance within their organisation, liaising with other agencies as necessary. The DASM should monitor the progress of cases to ensure that they are dealt with as quickly as possible, consistent with a thorough and fair process.

14.178. The DASMs will work with care and support providers and other service providers e.g. housing and NHS trusts to ensure that referral of individual employees to the DBS and, or, Regulatory Bodies (e.g. CQC, HCPC, GMC, NMC) are made promptly and appropriately and that any supporting evidence required is made available.

14.179. The DASMs will ensure that systems are in place to provide the employee with support and regular updates in respect of the adult safeguarding investigation. Particular care must be taken to not breach the right to a fair trial in Article Six of the European Convention on Human Rights as incorporated by the Human Rights Act 1998.

14.180. DASMs should ensure that appropriate recording systems are in place that provide clear audit trails about decision-making and recommendations in all processes relating to the management of adult safeguarding allegations against the person alleged to have caused the harm or risk of harm and ensure the control of information in respect of individual cases is in accordance with accepted Data Protection and Confidentiality requirements.

14.181. The local authority DASM will need to work closely with the children's services Local Authority Designated Officer (LADO) and other DASMs and LADOs for both adults and children in the region or nationally to ensure sharing of information and development of best practice.

14.182. There may be times when a person is working with adults and their behaviour towards a child or children may impact on their suitability to work with or continue to work with adults at risk. This may be referred to the DASM from a LADO, if it is not, then information should be shared with the LADO. Each situation will be risk assessed individually.

14.183. There may also be times when a person's conduct towards an adult may impact on their suitability to work with or continue to work with children. All these situations must be referred to the LADO.

14.184. Unless it puts the adult at risk or child in danger, the individual should be informed that the information regarding the allegation against them will be shared. Responsibility lies with the person receiving the information to obtain the consent of the individual to share information. The person with the allegation against them should be offered a right to reply, wherever possible seek their consent to share, and be informed what information will be shared, how and who with. Each case must be assessed individually as there may be rare cases where informing the person about details of the allegations may increase the risks to the adult or child.

14.185. Decisions on sharing information must be justifiable and proportionate, based on the potential or actual harm to adults or children at risk and the rationale for decision-making should always be recorded.

14.186. When sharing information about adults, children and young people at risk between agencies it should only be shared:

- where relevant and necessary, not simply all the information held;
- with the relevant people who need all or some of the information; and
- when there is a specific need for the information to be shared at that time.

Senior managers

14.187. Each agency should identify a senior manager to take a lead role in the organisational and in inter-agency arrangements, including the SAB. In order for the Board to be an effective decision-making body providing leadership and accountability, members need to be sufficiently senior and have the authority to commit resources and make strategic decisions. To achieve effective working relationships, based on trust and transparency, the members will need to understand the contexts and restraints within which their counterparts work.

Corporate/cross authority roles

14.188. To ensure effective partnership working, each organisation must recognise and accept its role and functions in relation to adult safeguarding. These should be set out in the SAB's strategic plan as well as its own communication channels. They should also have protocols for mediation and family group conferences and for various forms of dispute resolution.

Chief Officers and Chief Executives

14.189. As chief officer for the leading adult safeguarding agency, the Director of Adult Social Services (DASS) has a particularly important leadership and challenge role to play in adult safeguarding.

14.190. Responsible for promoting prevention, early intervention and partnership working is a key part of a DASS's role and also critical in the development of effective safeguarding. Taking a personalised approach to adult safeguarding requires a DASS promoting a culture that is person-centred, supports choice and control and aims to tackle inequalities.

personalisation, boards should seek assurances that directly employed staff (e.g. Personal Assistants) have access to training and advice on safeguarding.

14.201. Training is a continuing responsibility and should be provided as a rolling programme.[1] Whilst training may be undertaken on a joint basis and the SAB has an overview of standards and content, it is the responsibility of each organisation to train its own staff.

14.202. Regular face-to-face supervision from skilled managers and reflective practice is essential to enable staff to work confidently and competently with difficult and sensitive situations.

Rigorous recruitment practices relevant to safeguarding

14.203. There are three levels of a Disclosure and Barring Service (DBS) check. Each contains different information and the eligibility for each check is set out in law. They are:

- Standard check: This allows employers to access the criminal record history of people working, or seeking to work, in certain positions, especially those that involve working with children or adults in specific situations. A standard check discloses details of an individual's convictions, cautions, reprimands and warnings recorded on police systems and includes both 'spent' and 'unspent' convictions.

- Enhanced checks: This discloses the same information provided on a Standard certificate, together with any local police information that the police believe is relevant and ought to be disclosed.

- Enhanced with barred list checks: This check includes the same level of disclosure as the enhanced check, plus a check of the appropriate barred lists. An individual may only be checked against the children's and adults' barred lists if their job falls within the definition of 'regulated activity' with children and/or adults under the Safeguarding Vulnerable Groups Act 2006, as amended by the Protection of Freedoms Act 2012. It should be noted that in 'signing off' or agreeing a personal budget or personal health budget a local authority may add conditions such as a DBS check as part of its risk assessment of safeguarding in specific cases. The local authority may also require personal budget holders using Direct Payments to specify whom they are employing to the local authority.

14.204. Skills for Care has produced a recruitment and retention toolkit for the adult care and support sector. 'Finders Keepers'[2] is designed to help care providers, particularly smaller organisations, to improve the ways they recruit staff and retain them.

Internal guidelines for all staff

14.205. Provider agencies should produce for their staff a set of internal guidelines which relate clearly to the multiagency policy and which set out the responsibilities of all staff to operate within it. These should include guidance on:

- identifying adults who are particularly at risk;

---

[1] https://safe.bournemouth.ac.uk/
[2] http://www.skillsforcare.org.uk/Document-library/Finding-and-keeping-workers/Practical-toolkits/

- recognising risk from different sources and in different situations and recognising abusive or neglectful behaviour from other service users, colleagues, and family members;

- routes for making a referral and channels of communication within and beyond the agency;

- organisational and individual responsibilities for whistleblowing;

- assurances of protection for whistle blowers;

- working within best practice as specified in contracts;

- working within and co-operating with regulatory mechanisms; and,

- working within agreed operational guidelines to maintain best practice in relation to:

- challenging or distressing behaviour;

- personal and intimate care;

- control and restraint;

- gender identity and sexual orientation;

- medication;

- handling of people's money; and

- risk assessment and management.[1]

14.206. Internal guidelines should also explain the rights of staff and how employers will respond where abuse is alleged against them within either a criminal or disciplinary context.

---

[1] https://www.gov.uk/government/publications/nothing-ventured-nothing-gained-risk-guidance-for-people- with-dementia

15. INTEGRATION, COOPERATION AND PARTNERSHIPS

This chapter provides guidance on:
- *Sections 3, 6, 7, 22, 23, 74 and Schedule 3 of the Care Act 2014;*
- *The Care and Support (Provision of Health Services) Regulations 2014;*
- *The Care and Support (Discharge of Hospital Patients) Regulations 2014.*

This chapter covers:
- Integrating care and support with other local services;
- Strategic planning;
- Integrating service provision and combining and aligning processes;
- Cooperation of partner organisations;
- General duty to cooperate;
- Who must cooperate;
- Cooperation within local authorities;
- Cooperating in specific cases;
- Working with the NHS;
- The boundary between the NHS and care and support;
- Delayed transfers of care from hospitals;
- Working with housing authorities and providers;
- Working with welfare and employment support.

15.1. For people to receive high quality health and care and support, local organisations need to work in a more joined-up way, to eliminate the disjointed care that is a source of frustration to people and staff, and which often results in poor care, with a negative impact on health and wellbeing. The vision is for integrated care and support that is person-centred, tailored to the needs and preferences of those needing care and support, carers and families.

15.2. Sections 3, 6 and 7 of the Act require that:

- local authorities must carry out their care and support responsibilities with the aim of promoting greater integration with NHS and other health-related services;

- local authorities and their relevant partners must cooperate generally in performing their functions related to care and support; and, supplementary to this,

- in specific individual cases, local authorities and their partners must cooperate in performing their respective functions relating to care and support and carers wherever they can.

INTEGRATING CARE AND SUPPORT WITH OTHER LOCAL SERVICES

15.3. Local authorities must carry out their care and support responsibilities with the aim of joining-up the services provided or other actions taken with those provided by the NHS and other health-related services (for example, housing or leisure services). This general requirement applies to all the local authority's care and support functions for adults with needs for care and support and for carers, including in relation to preventing needs (see chapter 2), providing information and advice (see chapter 3) shaping and facilitating the market of service providers (see chapter 4), safeguarding (see chapter 14), cross-border placements (see chapter 21), and transition to adult care and support (see chapter 16).

15.4. This duty applies where the local authority considers that the integration of services will:

- promote the wellbeing of adults with care and support needs or of carers in its area;

- contribute to the prevention or delay of the development of needs of people;

- improve the quality of care and support in the local authority's area, including the outcomes that are achieved for local people.

15.5. The local authority is not solely responsible for promoting integration with the NHS, and this responsibility reflects similar duties placed on NHS England and clinical commissioning groups (CCGs) to promote integration with care and support.[1] Under the NHS Act, NHS England must encourage partnership arrangements between CCGs and local authorities where it considers this would ensure the integrated provision of health services and that this would improve the quality of services or reduce inequalities. Similarly, every CCG has a duty to exercise its functions with a view to securing that health services are provided in an integrated way, where this would improve the quality of health and/or reduce inequalities in access or outcomes. The Care Act adds further coherence by placing an equivalent duty on local authorities to integrate care and support provision with health services and health related services, for example housing (see paragraphs 15.7-15.8 below about the integration of health and health related services).

15.6. There are a number of ways in which local authorities can fulfil this duty at the strategic level; at the level of individual service; and in combining and aligning processes. Some examples are discussed below.

Case study:
Promoting the integration of housing, health and social care across Leicestershire

District Councils in Leicestershire have taken a strategic approach to working with county wide providers on priority issues, including housing, health and wellbeing. A District Chief Executive leads across the 7 District Councils working with a network of senior managers in each individual council.

This has built the influence and credibility of District Councils with health and social care leaders who now have an increasing understanding of the vital role housing and housing based services play in the delivery of better outcomes for vulnerable people.

The Housing Offer to Health in Leicestershire is built into the County's Better Care Fund priorities and work is underway across health, social care and housing in the following key areas:

---

[1] See sections 13N and 14Z1 of the National Health Service Act 2006 as inserted by the Health and Social Care Act 2012.

- Housing's Hospital to Home discharge pathway – looking to place housing options expertise within the day-day discharge assessment and planning work of both acute and mental health providers so that the planning and decisions around an individual's hospital discharge includes early consideration, and actioning of appropriate and supportive housing options.
- Establishing an integrated service to provide practical support to people in their own homes across all tenures so that aids, equipment, adaptations, handy person services and energy efficiency interventions are available and delivered quickly. Through this we hope to reduce the time taken to provide practical help to individual people with care and support needs, reduce process costs for services paid for through the public purse and support vulnerable people to access the low level practical support that helps them remain independently at home.
- Establishing a locality based approach to prevention and housing based support which includes Local Area Co-ordination, Timebanking and delivery of low level support services to vulnerable older people through a mixture of community volunteers and multi-skilled workers.

The district councils are therefore promoting wellbeing in the area of suitability of accommodation at population level, providing a basis for promoting individual wellbeing via transfers of care and universal preventative services.

STRATEGIC PLANNING
Integration with health and health-related services
15.7. A local authority must promote integration between care and support provision, health and health related services, with the aim of joining up services. To ensure greater integration of services, a local authority should consider the different mechanisms through which it can promote integration, for example;
 (a) Planning – using adult care and support and public health data to understand the profile of the population and the needs of that population. For example, using information from the local Joint Strategic Needs Assessments to consider the wider need of that population in relation to housing (see chapter 2 for further guidance in relation to prevention). The needs of older and vulnerable residents should be reflected within local authorities' development plans with reference to local requirements for inclusive mainstream housing and specialist accommodation and/or housing services. As part of this, local authorities can share population level data with partners to enable greater integration.
 (b) Commissioning – building on joint strategic needs assessments, joint commissioning can ensure better outcomes for populations in an area. A local authority may wish to have housing represented at the Health and Wellbeing Board/Clinical Commissioning Groups (CCGs) making a visible and effective link between preventative spend (including housing related) and preventing acute/crisis interventions. Ways to achieve this include jointly-commissioned advice services covering healthcare and housing, and services like housing-related support that can provide a range of preventative interventions alongside care.

(c) Assessment and information and advice – this may include integrating an assessment with information and advice about housing options on where to live, and adaptations to the home, care and related finance to help develop a care plan (if necessary), and understand housing choices reflecting the person's strengths and capabilities to help achieve their desired outcomes. There may be occasions where non-social care professional (e.g. a housing staff) knows the person best, and with their agreement may be able to contribute to the assessment process or provide information. As part of care and support planning (se chapter 10) a local area could introduce a single care plan for an individual spanning health, care and housing that is owned and directed by that person.

(d) Delivery or provision of care and support – that is integrated with an assessment of the home, including general upkeep or scope for aids and adaptations, community equipment of other modifications could reduce the risk to health, help maintain independence or support reablement or recovery. For example, some specialist housing associations and home improvement agencies may offer a support service which could form part of a jointly agreed support plan. A housing assessment should form part of any assessment process, in terms of suitability, access, safety, repair, heating and lighting (e.g. efficiency).

Joint strategic needs assessment

15.8. Local authorities and clinical commissioning groups already have an equal and joint duty to prepare Joint Strategic Needs Assessments (JSNAs) and Joint Health and Wellbeing Strategies (JHWS) through health and wellbeing boards.[1] JSNAs are local assessments of current and future health and care needs that could be met by the local authority, CCGs or the NHS Commissioning Board, or other partners. JHWSs are shared strategies for meeting those needs, which set out the actions that each partner will take individually and collectively.

15.9. Joint Strategic Needs Assessments and Joint Health and Wellbeing Strategies are therefore key means by which local authorities work with CCGs to identify and plan to meet the care and support needs of the local population, including carers. JHWSs can help health and care and support services to be joined up with each other and with health- related services. Local Authorities and CCGs can include in their JHWSs a statement of how arrangements for the provision of health, social care and health-related services might be better integrated.

15.10. Under the Act, local authorities must exercise its care and support functions with a view to ensuring integration with health and health-related services if doing so would achieve any or all of the objectives set in paragraph 15.4 above (promoting wellbeing; preventing or delaying needs; improving the quality of care). The JHWSs should also set the local context and frame the discussion with partners on how different organisations can work together to align and integrate services. However, local authorities should bear in mind that carrying out the JSNA and JWHS on their own will not be sufficient to fulfil the requirement to

---

[1] See sections 116 and 116A of the Local Government and Public Involvement Act 2007 (as amended by the Health and Social Care Act 2012) from which the requirement to produce SNAs and JHWSs is derived.

promote integration; it will be the agreed actions which follow the strategies and plans that will have the greatest impact on integration and on the experience and outcomes of people.

Integrating service provision and combining and aligning processes

15.11. There are many ways in which local authorities can integrate care and support provision with that of health and related provision locally. Different areas are likely to find success in different models. Whilst some areas may pursue for integrated organisational structures, or shared funding arrangements, others may join up teams of frontline professionals to promote multi-disciplinary working. There is no required format or mechanism for integrating provision, and local authorities should consider and develop their strategy jointly with partners.

15.12. At the strategic level, there are many examples of how local authorities can integrate services including:

- the use of "pooled budgets", which bring together funding from different organisations to invest jointly in delivering agreed, shared outcomes.[1] For example, the Better Care Fund, which provides local authorities and CCGs with a shared fund to invest in agreed local priorities which support health and care and support, will be a key opportunity to promote integration in provision to ensure access to, and availability of, a range of preventative care and support services in the community.[2]

- the development of joint commissioning arrangements to achieve health and wellbeing outcomes across traditional service boundaries of housing, health, care and support.

- Integrated management or provision of services.[3] This could, for example, include jointly funding home adaptations to ensure people with changing care needs are able to maximize their independence and live well at home for longer.

15.13. In terms of working practices to encourage greater integration at an individual level, this could include recruiting and training individual care coordinators who are responsible for planning how to meet an adult's needs through a number of service providers. Another example could be in relation to working with people who are being discharged from hospital, where staff from more than one body may be involved with providing or arranging care and support to allow the person to return home and live independently.[4] As with other examples of integration, this would not necessarily require structural integration – i.e. organisations merging – but a seamless service, from the point of view of the person, could be delivered by staff working together more effectively, for example, integrating an assessment with information and advice about housing

---

[1] http://www.england.nhs.uk/wp-content/uploads/2012/10/lga-nhscb-concordat.pdf

[2] Link to BCF guidance: http://www.england.nhs.uk/ourwork/part-rel/transformation-fund/bcf-plan/

[3] There are a number of powers within the 2006 NHS Act that enable local authorities and partners to operate in a more integrated way: Section 75 relates to pooled funding, lead commissioning arrangements, and integrated management or provision of services; Sections 76 and 256 allow service revenue or capital contributions to support specific additional services from health bodies to local authorities (and vice versa) where these offer a more efficient use of resources and can be used to create joint budgets for integrated services.

[4] Hospital 2 Home guide http://www.housinglin.org.uk/hospital2home_pack/

options, or co-locating housing support workers in health and care settings like GPs surgeries or hospitals. (see paragraphs 15.54-15.75 on housing and integration).

Case study:
Promoting the integration and social care with regards to carers support in Torbay and Southern Devon Health and Care NHS Trust

Torbay, a 'Care Trust' or organisation responsible for health and social takes a 'whole system' approach to the identification and support of carers. They worked with clinicians in primary care and the acute trust to develop an evidence base to show the positive impact early support and access to services has on carers' health and wellbeing. This led to recognition that carer support is the joint responsibility of primary and acute health services and social care as well as an understanding that carers can be a 'reluctant audience' and may not identify themselves until in crisis.

Torbay has used joint CQUINs (commissioning for quality and innovation payments) to drive change. They developed a model founded on having Carers Support Workers at key points in the carer's journey in all GP practices, in the Acute Hospital Discharge team and in specialist community teams such as Mental Health and Substance Misuse. These workers provide easy access to support, advice to other practitioners, and signpost carers through the system. They also target key staff groups for development; for example the 2013/14 focus has been on training and encouraging district and community nurses to identify and signpost carers to support. This has significantly increased referrals as well as raised awareness.

A pathway exercise was undertaken with staff and carers to map the carer's journey through the whole system and the points at which engagement did, or could, happen. This has led to changes such as Carer Contact Cards, which includes key information on where carers can get support, in all discharge folders and a new Carers Policy for Torbay Hospital.

Providing simple, easy to access services for all carers such as Signpost's information service, a Torbay carers' register and carer education programmes, that are not subject to eligibility criteria and has brought carers into support much earlier therefore reducing crises.

15.14. Local authorities, together with their partners, should consider combining or aligning key processes in the care and support journey, where there may be benefit to the individual concerned from linking more effectively. Combined assessments should only take place in suitable circumstances and where assessors are trained to do so. For example, combining assessments may allow for a clearer picture of the person's needs holistically, and for a single point of contact with the person to promote consistency of experience, so that provision of different types of support can be aligned. A number of assessments could be carried out on the same person, for example a care and support needs assessment, health assessment and continuing healthcare assessments. Where it is not practicable for assessments to be conducted by the same professional, it may nonetheless be possible to align processes to support a better experience, for example, the 2nd or 3rd assessor could be obliged to read the 1st assessment (provided there is a lawful basis for sharing the information) and not ask any information that has already been collected, or the different bodies could work together to develop a single, compatible assessment tool. Local authorities have powers to carry out assessments jointly with other parties, or to de-delegate the function in its entirety.

CO-OPERATION OF PARTNER ORGANISATIONS

15.15. All public organisations should work together and co-operate where needed, in order to ensure a focus on the care and support (including carers' support) and health and health- related needs of their local population. Whilst there are some local services where the local authority must actively promote integration, in other cases it must nonetheless co-operate with relevant local and national partners.

15.16. Co-operation between partners should be a general principle for all those concerned, and all should understand the reasons why co-operation is important for those people involved. The Act sets out five aims of co-operation between partners which are relevant to care and support, although it should be noted that the purposes of co-operation are not limited to these matters:

- promoting the wellbeing of adults needing care and support and of carers;

- improving the quality of care and support for adults and support for carers (including the outcomes from such provision);

- smoothing the transition from children's to adults' services;

- protecting adults with care and support needs who are currently experiencing or at risk of abuse or neglect;

- identifying lessons to be learned from cases where adults with needs for care and support have experienced serious abuse or neglect.

15.17. The processes and systems behind the areas noted above, as well as how working with partners is integral to achieving the best outcomes, are set out in more detail in other chapters of this guidance.

15.18. Local Authorities and relevant partners must co-operate when exercising any respective functions which are relevant to care and support. This requirement relates to organisations existing functions only, and the Act does not confer new functions.

15.19. "Co-operation", like integration, can be achieved through a number of means, and is intended to require the adoption of a common principle, rather than to prescribe any specific tasks. There are a number of powers which local authorities may use to promote joint working. For example, local authorities may share information with other partners, or provide staff, services or other resources to partners to improve co-operation. Some of the actions may be the same as those undertaken to promote integration, for example under section 75 of the NHS Act 2006, a local authority may contribute to a "pooled budget" with an NHS body – a shared fund out of which payments can be made to meet agreed priorities.

15.20. Other actions may be specific to particular circumstances or the needs of a specific group, for example the local authority co-operating with prisons in its area to develop a joint strategy for meeting the care and support needs of prisoners.

Who must co-operate?

15.21. The local authority must co-operate with each of its relevant partners, and the partners must also co-operate with the local authority, in relation to relevant functions. The Act specifies the "relevant partners" who have a reciprocal responsibility to co-operate. These are:

- other local authorities within the area (i.e. in multi-tier authority areas, this will be a district council);

- any other local authority which would be appropriate to co-operate with in a particular set of circumstances (for example, another authority which is arranging care for a person in the home area);

- NHS bodies in the authority's area (including the primary care, CCGs, any hospital trusts and NHS England, where it commissions health care locally) [see paragraphs 15.29-15.53 about care and support and the NHS];

- local offices of the Department for Work and Pensions (such as Job Centre Plus) [see paragraphs 14.81-14.87 about care and support, welfare and employment];

- police services in the local authority areas and prisons and probation services in the local area [see chapter 17 on care and support in Prisons].

15.22. In addition, there may be other persons or bodies with whom a local authority should co-operate if it considers this appropriate when exercising care and support functions, in particular independent or private sector organisations. Examples include, but are not limited to, care and support providers, NHS primary health providers, independent hospitals and private registered providers of social housing, the Care Quality Commission and regulators of health and social care professionals. In these cases, the local authority should consider what degree of co-operation is required, and what mechanisms it may have in place to ensure mutual co-operation (for example, via contractual means).

ENSURING CO-OPERATION WITHIN LOCAL AUTHORITIES

15.23. Local authorities fulfil a range of different functions that have an impact on the health and wellbeing of individuals, in addition to their care and support responsibilities (e.g. children's services, housing, public health). It is therefore important that, in addition to ensuring co-operation between the local authority and its external partners, there is internal co- operation between the different local authority officers and professionals who provide these services. Local authorities must make arrangements to ensure co-operation between its officers responsible for adult care and support, housing, public health and children's services, and should also consider how such arrangements may also be applied to other relevant local authority responsibilities, such as education, planning and transport. Arrangements that local authorities could make to ensure co-operation between officers include offering training and establishing systems for information sharing or multi-disciplinary teams.

15.24. For example, it is important that local authority officers responsible for housing work in co-operation with adult care and support, given that housing and suitability of living accommodation play a significant role in supporting a person to meet their needs and can help to delay that person's deterioration. Similarly, the transition from children's social care to adult care and support will require local authority officers in the respective departments to co- operate to share information, prepare for transition, and ensure the young person's needs are met on reaching the age of eighteen. Cooperation is also needed where there are children at risk of taking on inappropriate caring roles. In these cases local authorities should be referring children for a young carer's assessment under the Children Act and under the Care Act where the conditions in section 63 apply. Joint working with the Director of Public Health will be important when, for example, developing joint health and wellbeing strategies, and designing and commissioning preventative services.

Co-operating with partners in specific cases

15.25. Co-operation in relation to care and support functions should form part of a local authority and partners' general strategic thinking, which should, in turn, inform how they exercise these functions day-to-day. However, there will be individual cases where more specific co-operation will be required, and a local authority or partner will need to explicitly ask one another for co-operation, for example, by requesting specific action in an individual case. The Care Act provides an express duty for the local authority and partner to ask each other for co-operation in individual cases.

15.26. Where a local authority or partner requests co-operation from each other in relation to a particular individual case, the local authority or relevant partner must co-operate as requested, unless doing so would be incompatible with their own duties or have an adverse effect on the exercise of their functions.

15.27. This mechanism is intended to support partners with a means of identifying specific cases in which more targeted co-operation is required. In practice, it may be the case that general working protocols and relationships between organisations mean that this further process is not required. However, there will be situations that arise which that necessitate a more tailored response to fit around the person concerned. This might include, for example:

- when a person is planning to move from one area to another, and the authorities involved require co-operation to support that move;

- when an assessment of care and support needs identified other needs that should be assessed (for instance, health needs that may indicate eligibility for NHS Continuing Healthcare); and,

- when a local authority is carrying out a safeguarding enquiry or review, and requires the support of another organisation.

15.28. Where the local authority or relevant partner decide to use this mechanism, they should notify the other in writing, making clear the relevant Care Act provisions. If the local authority or the relevant partner decide not to co-operate with a request, then they must write to the other, setting out reasons for not doing so. Local authorities and their relevant partners must respond to requests to cooperate under their general public law duties to act reasonably, and failure to respond within a reasonable time frame could be subject to judicial review.

WORKING WITH THE NHS
The boundary between care and support and the NHS

15.29. Local authorities must carry out an assessment where someone appears to have needs for care and support. It has a duty to meet those needs for care and support that meet the eligibility criteria. Similarly, in the case of carers, the local authority must carry out an assessment if a carer appears to have, or is likely to have, needs for support and it has a duty to meet those needs for support that meet the eligibility criteria. However, local authorities cannot lawfully meet needs in either case by providing or arranging services that are legally the responsibility of the NHS.

15.30. In order to support joint working, it is important that all partners involved are clear about their own responsibilities, and how they fit together. Section 22 of the Care Act sets out the limits on what a local authority may provide by way of healthcare and so, in effect, sets the boundary between the responsibilities of local authorities for the provision of care and support, and those of the NHS for the provision of health care.

15.31. Where the NHS has a clear legal responsibility to provide a particular service, then the local authority may not do so. This general rule is intended to provide clarity and avoid overlaps, and to maintain the existing legal boundary. However, there is an exception to this general rule, in that the local authority may provide some limited healthcare services as part of a package of care and support, but only where the services provided are "incidental or ancillary" (that is, relatively minor, and part of a broader package), and where the services are the type of support that an authority whose primary responsibility if to provide social services could be expected to provide.

15.32. The two most obvious relevant examples of healthcare that are clearly the responsibility of the NHS (and thus not something a local authority may provide) are nursing care provided by registered nurses, and services that the NHS has to provide because the individual is eligible for NHS Continuing Healthcare.

15.33. NHS Continuing Healthcare is a package of ongoing care that is arranged and funded solely by the health service for individuals outside a hospital setting who have complex ongoing healthcare needs, of a type or quantity such that they are found to have a 'primary health need'. Such care is provided to people aged 18 or over, to meet needs that have arisen as a result of disability, accident or illness. NHS Continuing Healthcare is not dependent on a person's condition or diagnosis, but is based on their specific physical or mental health needs.

15.34. Where the person has a 'primary health need' as set out in regulations[1] and as determined following an assessment of need under national guidance (the National Framework for NHS Continuing Healthcare and NHS-funded Nursing Care[2] ('the National Framework'), it is the responsibility of the health service to meet all assessed health and associated care and support needs, including suitable accommodation, if that is part of the overall need.

15.35. The National Framework sets out a process for the NHS, working together with its local authority partners wherever practicable, to assess health needs, decide on eligibility for NHS Continuing Healthcare, and provide that assessed care. 'NHS-funded Nursing Care', is the funding provided by the NHS

---

[1] See regulations under the National Health Service Act 2006 and the Health and Social Care Act 2012 (see Part 6 of The National Health Service Commissioning Board and Clinical Commissioning Groups (Responsibilities and Standing Rules) Regulations 2012, as amended by The National Health Service Commissioning Board and Clinical Commissioning Groups (Responsibilities and Standing Rules) (Amendment) Regulations 2013) ('the Standing Rules').

[2] https://www.gov.uk/government/uploads/system/uploads/attachment_data/file/213137/National-Framework-for-NHS-CHC-NHS-FNC-Nov-2012. pdf

to care homes providing nursing, to support the provision of nursing care by a registered nurse. If an individual does not qualify for NHS Continuing Healthcare, the need for care from a registered nurse must be determined. If the person has such a need and it is determined that their overall needs would be most appropriately met in a care home providing nursing care, then this would lead to eligibility for NHS-funded Nursing Care. Once the need for such care is agreed, a CCG (or in some case NHS England) must pay a flat-rate contribution to the care home towards registered nursings care costs.

15.36. The regulations and guidance referred to above, set out how the 'primary health need' test takes account of the limits of local authority responsibility. Although the regulations and guidance pre-date the coming into force of the Care Act 2014, the limits of local authority responsibility have not been changed by the Care Act 2014.

Supporting discharge of hospital patients with care and support

15.37. The provisions on the discharge of hospital patients with care and support needs are contained in Schedule 3 to the Care Act 2014 and the Care and Support (Discharge of Hospital Patients) Regulations 2014 ("the Regulations"). These provisions enable the NHS to seek reimbursement from local authorities where they consider it necessary in order to assist the NHS and local authorities in working together effectively and efficiently to plan the safe and timely discharge of NHS hospital patients from NHS acute medical care facilities to local authority care and support. The purpose of these provisions is to maintain the existing scope of the reimbursement regime but to update existing provisions to reflect the current NHS and care and support landscape. Also, in light of the drive to improve integration between health and social care provision the recovery of any reimbursement has now been placed on a discretionary rather than mandatory footing.

15.38. Schedule 3 to the Care Act covers:

- the scope of the hospital discharge regime and the definition of the patients to whom it applies;

- the notifications which an NHS body must give a local authority where the NHS considers that it is not likely to be safe to discharge the patient unless arrangements for meeting the patient's needs for care and support are put in place;

- the period for which an NHS body can consider seeking reimbursement from a local authority, where that local authority has not fulfilled its requirements to assess or put in place care and support to meet needs, or (where applicable) to meet carers' needs for support, within the time periods set such that the patient's discharge from hospital is delayed.

15.39. The Regulations and this guidance both set out further details of the form and content of what the various types of NHS notification notices must and should contain to ensure the local authority has relevant information to comply with its requirements to undertake assessments, and to put in place any arrangements necessary for meeting any of the patient's care and support needs, or where applicable, the carer's needs for support. They set out the circumstances when assessment notices and discharge notices must be withdrawn, and determine the period and amount of any reimbursement liability which a local authority may be required to pay the NHS for any delay in the transfer of care.

15.40. This guidance seeks to support the effective implementation of the requirements of these regulations. However, it does not address the wider practice issues associated with planning safe and effective discharge which apply to all cases of hospital discharge regardless of they whether they fall within the scope of these provisions or not. In relation to all cases, both NHS and local authorities should, using the best evidence available, develop and apply local protocols that ensure that all patients receive appropriate and safe discharge procedures.

Reimbursement as part of the wider duties to cooperate and promote integration

15.41. The NHS may seek reimbursement from local authorities for a delayed transfer of care in the circumstances set out in Schedule 3 to the Care Act and its Regulations. The potential for reimbursement liability is intended to act as an incentive to improve joint working between the NHS and local government, but should not be seen in isolation. It is a part of a wider picture in which joint and integrated working is embedded in the Act. The opportunity to seek collaborative solutions to address barriers locally in the first instance is reflected in the use of these reimbursements being made discretionary: see paragraphs 4(1) and (2) of Schedule 3 to the Act.

15.42. NHS and local authorities should develop and adopt collaborative approaches to working together in order to reduce the number of delayed days where a patient is ready to be transferred from NHS acute medical care to other settings regardless of whether the patient falls within the scope of the reimbursement regime. Both the NHS and local authorities owe a common law duty of care to the people within their care. The duties to cooperate in the Care Act 2014 also apply to all transfers of care.

15.43. The majority of delayed discharge days are attributable to the NHS and because the issues behind them are within their gift to address, it is important that NHS organisations consider what actions they need to take to support reductions in delayed discharges for which the cause is wholly within the health sector. NHS organisations should report the days for as long as the delay occurs. This reporting is required irrespective of whether the patient concerned has potential social care needs and whether the patient comes within the scope of the potential reimbursement arrangements or not.

TO WHOM DO THE DISCHARGE OF HOSPITAL PATIENTS PROVISIONS APPLY

15.44. The discharge of hospital patients provisions only apply to NHS hospital patients in England who are receiving acute care, and who the NHS considers are likely to have care and support needs after discharge from hospital and who have not otherwise been expressly excluded. However, even where a patient falls outside the scope of these provisions, this does not means that the NHS and local authorities should not be working together to deliver the safe and timely discharge of all hospital patients with care and support needs.) More detail on the key criteria is set out below:

- NHS Hospital Patient in England: A hospital patient is a person who is ordinarily resident in England who is accommodated in an NHS hospital in

reduce the needs for care and support and contribute to preventing or delaying the development of such needs. Housing services should be used to help promote an individual's wellbeing, in which people in need of care and support and carers can build a full and active life. Suitability of living accommodation is one of the matters local authorities must take into account as part of their duty to promote an individual's wellbeing.

15.54. Consideration of housing issues in relation to a local authority's reasonability is an integral part of the health and care system and a local authority's responsibility for care and support. This could be in relation to a local authority's duty on prevention (see chapter 2) or through the duty to assess an adult or carer's needs for care and support (see chapter 6), or in providing advice and information (see chapter 3).

15.55. Enabling individuals to recognise their own skills, ambitions and priorities and developing personal and community connections in relation to housing needs can help promote an individual's wellbeing. Supporting people through the provision of good quality information and advice can help people make early choices about their housing options and related services in advance of a potential crisis. This avoids making such decisions when a person is in crisis or when such decisions have to be taken by relatives or carers. People can be helped to stay independent longer through adaptations and modifications to their homes or extra care or support being offered in their home.

15.56. Health, care and support and housing services should centre on the individual and family, by helping them to articulate the outcomes they want to achieve a local authority can consider what support it can provide in or through the home.

Considering accommodation within the wellbeing principle

15.57. Local authorities have a general duty to promote an individual's wellbeing when carrying out their care and support functions. The Act is clear that one specific component of wellbeing is the suitability of living accommodation. A local authority should consider suitable living accommodation in looking at a person's needs and desired outcomes.

15.58. Housing has a vital role to play in other areas relating to a person's wellbeing. For example access to a safe settled home underpins personal dignity. A safe suitable home can contribute to physical and mental wellbeing and can provide control over day to day life and protection from abuse and neglect. A home or suitable living accommodation can enable participation in work or education, social interactions and family relationships.

15.59. In relation to housing, a local authority can make an important contribution to an individual's wellbeing, for example by providing and signposting information that allows people to address care and support needs through specific housing related support services, or through joint planning and commissioning that enables local authorities to provide (or arrange for the provision of) housing and care services or housing adaptations to meet the needs of the local population.

HOUSING TO SUPPORT PREVENTION OF NEEDS

15.60. In many cases, the best way to promote someone's wellbeing will be through preventative measures that allow people to live as independently as possible for as long as possible.

15.61. A local authority must provide or arrange for the provision of services that contribute towards preventing, reducing or delaying the needs for care and support (see chapter 2). Housing and housing related support can be a way to prevent needs for care and support, or to delay deterioration over time. Getting housing right and helping people to choose the right housing options for them can help to prevent falls, prevent hospital admissions and readmissions, reduce the need for care and support, improve wellbeing, and help maintain independence at home.

15.62. Housing and housing services can play a significant part in prevention, for example, from a design/physical perspective, accessibility, having adequate heating and lighting, identifying and removing hazards or by identifying a person who needs to be on the housing register. In addition, housing related support, i.e. services that help people develop their capacity to live in the community, live independently in accommodation, or sustain their capacity to do so, such as help with welfare benefits, developing budgeting skills, help with developing social networks or taking up education, training and employment opportunities can prevent, reduce or delay the needs for care and support. Community equipment, along with telecare, aids and adaptations can support reablement, promote independence contributing to preventing the needs for care and support.

15.63. A local authority may wish to draw on the assistance of the housing authority and local housing services. Housing-related support staff and scheme managers can contribute to prevention, for example by being alert to early signs of ill health, e.g. dementia, and signposting or supporting individuals to access community resources which may prevent, reduce or delay the need for care and support or a move into residential care.

15.64. The links between living in cold and damp homes and poor health and wellbeing are well-evidenced.[1] Local authorities may wish to consider the opportunities to prevent the escalation of health and care and support needs through the delivery or facilitation of affordable warmth measures to help achieve health and wellbeing outcomes.[2,3]

Integrating information and advice on housing

15.65. A local authority must establish and maintain a service for providing information and advice relating to care and support, and this must include advice on relevant housing and housing services which meet care and support needs. The authority is not required to provide all elements of this service, rather, they are expected under this duty to understand, co-ordinate and make effective use of other statutory, voluntary and or private sector information and advice resources within their area in order to deliver more integrated information and advice.

15.66. A person-centred approach to information and advice will consider the person's strengths and capabilities and the information or advice that will help them to achieve their ambitions. Information and advice should include services in the home that bring health, care and housing services together. This means that information and advice on housing, on adaptations to the current home, or alternative housing options or housing related services should be included. This will

---

[1] (http://www.instituteofhealthequity.org/projects/the-health-impacts-of-cold-homes-and-fuel-poverty, www.gov.uk/government/collections/housing-health-and-safety-rating-system-hhsrs-guidance).
[2] The Energy Companies Obligation: https://www.gov.uk/government/policies/helping-households-to-cut-their-energy-bills/supporting-pages/energy-companies-obligation-eco
[3] Energy Saving Advice Service: http://www.energysavingtrust.org.uk/Organisations/Government-and-local-programmes/Programmes-we-deliver/Energy-Saving-Advice-Service

enable a person to choose how best they can meet or prevent their needs for care and support. (See chapter 3 on information and advice).

15.67. A person using care and support or carer should be supported to make fully informed decisions about how to prevent or meet their needs for care and support. A local authority should make use of information and advice that is already available at local and national levels. Examples of some national resources are; www.firststopcareadvice.org.uk

www.moneyadviceservice.org.uk

www.nhs.uk/CarersDirect/Pages/CarersDirectHome.aspx

www.foundations.uk.com

15.68. People's care and support needs, their housing circumstances and financial resources are closely interconnected. It is only with full knowledge of the care and support ptions open to them, including possible housing options and the related financial implications that people will be able to exercise informed choice. For example, some people with their families have made early decisions about moving into residential care possibly sooner than is necessary. Information and advice about the full range of accommodation/housing options and how these might be funded can contribute to more informed decision making for individuals and can extend independent living. Carers in their local population when drawing up Joint Strategic Needs Assessments, including their need to participate in paid employment alongside caring responsibilities.

Case study:
Putting health back into housing

The Gloucestershire Affordable Housing Landlords' Forum (GAHLF), comprising of the seven leading local housing providers in the county, have set out an 'offer' to the Health and Wellbeing Board that demonstrates how each is working to improve the quality of life of their residents, the neighbourhoods and wider communities, by investing in new homes, supporting independent living, developing the community and supporting older and vulnerable people.

£12 million is being invested, by Stroud District Council, over five years, to improve the quality of housing stock and reduce fuel poverty for tenants. Stroud has been upgrading the heating supply in properties not currently served by mains gas. Many properties have electric storage heating which does not give the same level of control and is more expensive than gas or renewable energy. Dryleaze Court is a Supported Housing unit where 5 properties have had mains gas installed this year. At the same time, the team has also installed uPVC privacy panels, replaced porches with insulated cavity brick walls and fitted new double-glazed windows. The works have improved tenants' quality of life, helping them to live more comfortably and reduce their fuel bills. All in all, over the three years ending March 2013, GAHLF has improved over 14,900 homes, with an estimated savings to the NHS of around £1.4 million per annum. http://www.housinglin.org.uk/_library/Resources/Housing/Regions/South_West/GAHLF_Health_and_Wellbeing_V.II1.pdf

---

Link to further Case Study – Commissioning Advice Services in Portsmouth

http://www.adviceuk.org.uk/wp-content/uploads/2013/06/Breaking-the-Mould- Portsmouth.pdf

---

WORKING WITH EMPLOYMENT AND WELFARE SERVICES

15.69. The Disability and Health Employment Strategy[1] identified that many disabled people and people with health conditions, particularly those with more complex needs, receive a range of different services at local level, for example, care and support, primary and secondary health services, as well as support offered by Jobcentre Plus and contracted providers. It highlighted feedback from stakeholders that the support on offer at a local level to disabled people and people with health conditions can be confusing and inconsistent and often results in them having to give the same information to different services.

15.70. Local authorities must establish and maintain an information and advice service, but they are not required to provide all elements of this service. Rather, local authorities are expected to understand, co-ordinate and make effective use of other statutory, voluntary and/or private sector information and advice resources available to people within their areas. The information and advice available to the local population should include information and advice on eligibility and applying for disability benefits and other types of benefits and, on the availability of employment support for disabled adults.

15.71. Different people will need different levels of support from the local authority and other providers of financial information and advice depending on their capability, their care needs and their financial circumstances. People may just need some basic information and support to help them rebalance their finances in light of their changing circumstances. Topics may include welfare benefits, advice on good money management, help with basic budgeting and possibly on debt management. The local authority may be able to provide some of this information itself, for example of welfare benefits, but where it cannot, it should work with partner organisations to help people access it.

15.72. Local authorities, working with their partners, must also use the wider opportunities to provide targeted information and advice at key points in people's contact with the care and support, health and other local services. This should include application for disability benefits such as Attendance Allowance and Personal Independence Payments, and for Carers Allowance and access to work interviews.

CONSIDERING INDIVIDUAL EMPLOYMENT, TRAINING AND EDUCATION NEEDS

15.73. In addition to considering how to join up care and support at a local level, local authorities must consider education, training and employment when working with individuals. In particular:

- local authorities must promote wellbeing when carrying out care and support functions, or making a decision in relation to a person. This applies

---

[1] https://www.gov.uk/government/uploads/system/uploads/attachment_data/file/266373/disability-and- health-employment-strategy.pdf

equally to people with care and support needs and their carers. In some specific circumstances, it also applies to children, their carers and to young carers (when they are subject to the transition assessments discussed in chapter 16). The definition of wellbeing includes participation in work education and training. As such local authorities must consider whether participation in work, education or training is a relevant consideration when they are promoting wellbeing.

- local authorities, when carrying out a needs assessment, carer's assessment or child's carer's assessment must have regard to whether the carer works or wishes to do so, and whether the carer is participating in or wishes to participate in education, training or recreation and this should be reflected, as appropriate in the way their needs are met. Local authorities and the Department for Work and Pensions should cooperate to ensure people are given appropriate employment support and opportunities – in particular where this is a person's preferred outcome. This should include consideration of how direct payments may be used for employment support.[1]

- sections 37 and 38 of the Act support people to move, including to pursue employment opportunities or move closer to family members. Local authorities must ensure continuity of care and support when people move between areas so that they can move without the fear that they will be left without the care and support they need (see chapter 20).

SOURCES OF INFORMATION

15.74. The integration clauses mirrors similar duties placed on Clinical Commissioning Groups and NHS England. There are a number of relevant documents that local authorities may find of interest:

- The Functions of Clinical Commissioning Groups, NHS England March 2013   http://www.england.nhs.uk/wp-content/uploads/2013/03/a-functions-ccgs.pdf

- Statutory Guidance on Joint Strategic Needs Assessments and Joint Health and Wellbeing Strategies, Department of Health, April 2012.
  See part 4: Promoting integration between services. http://www.wakefield.-gov.uk/NR/rdonlyres/37D0E9D1-C438-4388-B270-A527139D9F37/0/StatutoryGuidanceonJSNAsandJHWSs_DH2013.pdf

- National Voices, a national coalition of health and social care charities,have produced a narrative for person-centred co-ordinated care and support, showing what this would look like from the perspective of people with care and support needs: http://www.england.nhs.uk/wp-content/uploads/2013/05/nv-narrative-cc.pdf

15.75. The following links provide further sources of information in relation to housing service and practical examples which support integration with care and support on a local level:

- http://www.housinglin.org.uk/Topics/browse/Housing/hwb/?parent=3691 &child=8169

---

[1] An example of personal budgets being used as a way to support and enterprise and employment can be found at: http://www.serendipity-chic.co.uk/

- http://www.cih.org/publication-free/display/vpathDCR/templatedata/cih/
publication-free/data/Developing_your_local_housing_offer_for_health_
and_care

- https://www.gov.uk/government/collections/housing-health-and-safety-
rating-system-hhsrs-guidance

- http://www.housinglin.org.uk/hospital2home_pack/

16. TRANSITION TO ADULT CARE AND SUPPORT

This chapter provides guidance on:
- *Sections 58 to 66 of the Care Act;*
- *The Care and Support (Children's Carers) Regulations 2014.*

This chapter covers:
- When a transition assessment must be carried out;
- Identifying young people who are not already receiving children's services;
- Adult carers and young carers;
- Features of a transition assessment;
- Cooperation between professionals and organisation;
- Providing information and advice once a transition assessment is completed;
- Provision of age appropriate local services and resources;
- After the young person in question turns 18;
- Combining EHC plans with care and support plans after the age of 18;
- Continuity of care after the age of 18;
- Safeguarding after the age of 18;
- Ordinary residence and transition to higher education;
- Transition from children's to adult NHS Continuing Healthcare.

16.1. Effective person-centred transition planning is essential to help young people and their families prepare for adulthood. Transition to adult care and support comes at a time when a lot of change can take place in a young person's life. It can also mean changes to the care and support they receive from education, health and care services, or involvement with new agencies such as those who provide support for housing, employment or further education and training.

16.2. The years in which a young person is approaching adulthood should be full of opportunity. Some of the life outcomes that matter for young people approaching adulthood and their families, may include (but are not limited to):

- Paid employment;
- Good health;
- Completing exams or moving to further education;
- Independent living (choice and control over one's life and good housing options);
- Social inclusion (friends, relationships and community).

16.3. The wellbeing of each young person or carer must be taken into account so that assessment and planning is based around the individual needs, wishes, and outcomes which matter to that person (see chapter 1 on the wellbeing principle). Historically, there has sometimes been a lack of effective planning for people using children's services who are approaching adulthood. Looked-after children, young people with disabilities, and carers are often among the groups of people with the lowest life chances. Early conversations provide an opportunity for young people and their families to reflect on their strengths, needs and desired outcomes, and to plan ahead for how they will achieve their goals.

16.4. Professionals from different agencies, families, friends and the wider community should work together in a coordinated manner around each young person or carer to help raise their aspirations and achieve the outcomes that matter to them. The purpose of carrying out transition assessments is to provide young people and their families with information so that they know what to expect in the future and can prepare for adulthood.

16.5. Transition assessments can in themselves be of benefit in providing solutions that do not necessarily involve the provision of services, and which may aid planning that helps to prevent, reduce or delay the development of needs for care or support. The local authorities' own commissioning and procurement practices should take account of wider market shaping duties and therefore transition assessments should focus outcomes and well–being (see section 2.15 on Market shaping and commissioning). Transition assessments will also allow local authorities to better understand the needs of people in their population, and to plan resources and commission services for young people and carers accordingly.

DEFINITIONS

16.6. The Care Act contains provisions to help preparation for adulthood for three particular groups of people – children, young carers and child's carers.

Persons described	Definition
Child	In the context of this chapter, a child is most probably a young person in their teenage years preparing for their adult life. This chapter therefore uses the term 'young person' for people under 18 with care and support needs who are approaching transition, rather than the legal term "child" contained in the Care Act itself.
Young person	See above
Adult carer	An adult carer of a young person preparing for adulthood, this is equivalent to the term "child's carer" in the Care Act itself.
Young Carer	A young carer under 18 themselves preparing for adulthood.
Young person or carer	This is the general term in the chapter for all three groups – young people, adult carers and young carers. Where something does not apply to all three groups, the specific groups to whom it does apply are specified using the terms above.
Transition assessment	Each group has their own specific transition assessment respectively; a child's needs assessment, a young carer's assessment, and a child's carer's assessment. The term used in this chapter for all three is 'transition assessment'.
Likely need	The duty to conduct a transition assessment applies when someone is likely to have needs for care and support (or support as a carer) under the Care Act when they or the person they care for transitions to the adult system.

Persons described	Definition
Significant benefit	A transition assessment must be conducted for all those who have likely needs (see above), however the timing of this assessment will depend on when it is of *significant benefit* to the young person or carer. This will generally be at the point when their needs for care and support as an adult can be predicted reasonably confidently, but will also depend on a range of other factors discussed in the section below "When a transition assessment must be carried out".

WHEN A TRANSITION ASSESSMENT MUST BE CARRIED OUT

16.7. Transition assessments should take place at the right time for the young person or carer and at a point when the local authority can be reasonably confident about what the young person's or carer's needs for care or support will look like after the young person in question turns 18. There is no set age when young people reach this point; every young person and their family are different, and as such, transition assessments should take place when it is most appropriate for them.

16.8. Local authorities must carry out a transition assessment of anyone in the three groups when there is significant benefit to the young person or carer in doing so, and if they are likely to have needs for care or support after turning 18. The provisions in the Care Act relating to transition to adult care and support are not only for those who are already receiving children's services, but for anyone who is likely to have needs for adult care and support after turning 18.

16.9. That a young person or carer is 'likely to have needs' means they have any likely appearance of any need for care and support as an adult – not just those needs that will be deemed eligible under the adult statute. It is highly likely that young people and carers who are in receipt of children's services would be 'likely to have needs' in this context, and local authorities should therefore carry out a transition assessment for those who are receiving children's services as they approach adulthood, so that they have information about what to expect when they become an adult.

16.10. When considering if it is of 'significant benefit' to assess, the local authority should consider the circumstances of the young person or carer, and whether it is an appropriate time for the young person or carer to undertake an assessment which helps them to prepare for adulthood. The consideration of 'significant benefit' is not related to the level of a young person or carer's needs, but rather to the timing of the transition assessment. When considering whether it is of significant benefit to assess, a local authority should consider factors which may contribute to establishing the right time to assess (including but not limited to the following):

- The stage they have reached at school and any upcoming exams;
- Whether the young person or carer wishes to enter further/higher education or training;
- Whether the young person or carer wishes to get a job when they become a young adult;
- Whether the young person is planning to move out of their parental home into their own accommodation;

- Whether the young person will have care leaver status when they become 18;

- Whether the carer of a young person wishes to remain in or return to employment when the young person leaves full time education;

- The time it may take to carry out an assessment;

- The time it may take to plan and put in place the adult care and support;

- Any relevant family circumstances;

- Any planned medical treatment.

16.11. For young people with special educational needs (SEN) who have an Education, Health and Care (EHC) plan under the Children and Families Act, preparation for adulthood must begin from year 9.[1] The transition assessment should be undertaken as part of one of the annual statutory reviews of the EHC plan, and should inform a plan for the transition from children's to adult care and support.

16.12. Equally for those without EHC plans, early conversations with local authorities about preparation for adulthood are beneficial – when these conversations begin to take place will depend on individual circumstances. For care leavers, local authorities should consider using the statutory Pathway Planning process as the opportunity to carry out a transition assessment where appropriate.

16.13. Local authorities should not carry out the transition assessment at inappropriate times in a young person's life, such as when they are sitting their exams and it would cause disruption. The Special Educational Needs (SEN) Code of Practice similarly states that local authorities must minimise disruption to the child and their family – for example by combining multiple appointments where possible. Local authorities should seek to agree the best time for assessments and planning with the young person or carer, and where appropriate, their family and any other relevant partners.

16.14. A young person or carer, or someone acting on their behalf, has the right to request a transition assessment. The local authority must consider such requests and whether the likely need and significant benefit conditions apply – and if so it must undertake a transition assessment. If the local authority thinks these conditions do not apply and refuses an assessment on that basis, it must provide its reasons for this in writing in a timely manner, and it must provide information and advice on what can be done to prevent or delay the development of needs for support.

16.15. Where it is judged by the local authority that the young person or carer is likely to have needs for care and support after turning 18, but that it is not yet of significant benefit to carry out a transition assessment, the local authority should consider indicating (when providing its written reasons for refusing the assessment) when it believes the assessment will be of significant benefit. In these circumstances, the onus is on the local authority to contact the young person or carer to agree the timing of the transition assessment, rather than leaving the young person or carer in uncertainty or having to make repeated requests for an assessment.

---

[1] See SEN Code of Practice "Preparing for Adulthood" (Department of Health, 2014). https://www.gov.uk/government/publications/send-code-of-practice-0-to-25

Case study – when a transition assessment is of "significant benefit" – Isabelle's story

Isabelle is 15 years old with complex needs. She attends a residential school on a 38- week basis funded by education and social services. Care and support is currently required on the weekends and in holidays.

Isabelle's parents have approached the local authority requesting a transition assessment around the time of her 16th birthday. Initially the local authority's reaction is that this is too soon to be of significant benefit. Since the support from school can continue until she is 19, they feel transition will be straight-forward as adult services simply need to begin funding the package which is already in place.

However, when they talk in more detail to the school and the parents they realise that when Isabelle leaves school at 19 it will not be appropriate for her to live with her parents and she will require substantial supported living support and a college placement. Due to the nature of Isabelle's needs, she will need a lengthy transition in order to get used to new staff, a new environment and a new educational setting. The college has also indicated that that they will need up to a year to plan for her start.

It is therefore of significant benefit for the transition assessment to take place around the age of 16, looking at both the funding for support from age 18 – 19 and the longer-term options. Once the assessment has identified the support Isabelle will be entitled to on leaving school, the planning process can begin and suitable support can be put in place by the time she leaves school. If a transition assessment were to take place later, the local authority would be at risk of not promoting wellbeing in the areas of family relationships (because Isabelle could temporarily need to live with her parents while solutions are found at the last minute, which would not be appropriate) and control over day-to-day life (because Isabelle would very likely not have the same range of choices if planning and preparation were to be truncated).

16.16. Where someone is refused (or they themselves refuse) a transition assessment, but at a later time makes a request for an assessment, the local authority must again consider whether the likely need and significant benefit conditions apply, and carry out an assessment if so. In more complex cases, it can take some time not only to carry out the assessment itself but to plan and put in place care and support. Social workers will often be the most appropriate lead professionals for complex cases. Transition assessments should be carried out early enough to ensure that the right care and support is in place when the young person moves to adult care and support.

16.17. When transition assessments take place too late and care and support is arranged in a hurry, it can result in care and support which does not best meet the young person or carer's needs – and sometimes at greater financial cost to the local authority than if it had been planned properly in advance.

IDENTIFYING YOUNG PEOPLE AND YOUNG CARERS WHO ARE NOT
ALREADY RECEIVING CHILDREN'S SERVICES

16.18. Most young people who receive transition assessments will be children
in need under the Children Act 1989 and will already be known to local authorities. However, local authorities should consider how they can identify young
people who are not receiving children's services who are likely to have care
and support needs as an adult. Key examples include:

- young people with degenerative conditions;

- young people (for example with autism) whose needs have been largely met
  by their educational institution, but who once they leave, will require their
  needs to be met in some other way;

- young people detained in the youth justice system who will move to the
  adult custodial estate;

- young carers whose parents have needs below the local authority's eligibility threshold but may nevertheless require advice or support to fulfil
  their potential, for example a child with deaf parents who is undertaking
  communication support;

- young people and young carers receiving Children and Adolescent Mental
  Health Services (CAMHS) may also require care and support as adults even
  if they did not receive children's services from the local authority.[1]

Even if they are not eligible for services, a transition assessment with good information and advice about support in the community can be particularly helpful
for these groups as they are less likely to be aware of support available in the
community.

16.19. Often when young people who have not been in contact with children's
services present to the local authority as a young adult, they do so with a high level
of need for care and support. Local authorities should consider how to establish
mechanisms in partnership with local educational institutions, health services
and other agencies to identify these groups as early as possible in order to plan
and prevent the development of care and support needs. (see chapter 15 on cooperation and integration and SEN Code Of Practice chapter 4 on joint
commissioning, making effective relationships.[2]

ADULT CARERS AND YOUNG CARERS

16.20. Preparation for adulthood will involve not only assessing how the needs
of young people change as they approach adulthood but also how carers', young
carers' and other family members' needs might change. Local authorities must
assess the needs of an adult carer where there is a likely need for support after
the child turns 18 and it is of significant benefit to the carer to do so. For instance,
some carers of disabled children are able to remain in employment with minimal

---

[1] The new NHS service specification for transition from CAMHS to Adult Mental Health Services
(AMHS) includes all mental health care services having an organisation-wide transition policy
and a named professional responsible for it. It also emphasises the need to work with local authorities
where someone receiving CAMHS also has likely needs for care and support as an adult, to ensure
that a transition assessment takes place.

[2] See SEN Code of Practice (Department of Health, 2014). https://www.gov.uk/government/publica-
tions/send-code-of-practice-0-to-25

support while the child has been in school. However, once the young person leaves education, it may be the case that the carer's needs for support increase, and additional support and planning is required from the local authority to allow the carer to stay in employment.

16.21. The SEN code of practice sets out the importance of full-time programmes for young people aged 16 and over. For instance, some sixth forms or colleges offer five-day placements which allow parents to remain in employment full time. However, for young people who do not have this opportunity, for example if their college offers only three- day placements, transition assessments should consider if there is other provision and support for the young person such as volunteering, community participation or training which not only allows the carer to remain in full time employment, but also fulfils the young person's wishes or equips them to live more independently as an adult. (see SEN Code of Practice chapter 8[1] on preparation for adulthood, and chapter 4 of this guidance on market shaping).

16.22. Local authorities must also assess the needs of young carers as they approach adulthood. For instance, many young carers feel that they cannot go to university or enter employment because of their caring responsibilities. Transition assessments and planning must consider how to support young carers to prepare for adulthood and how to raise and fulfil their aspirations.

16.23. Local authorities must consider the impact on other members of the family (or other people the authority may feel appropriate) of the person receiving care and support. This will require the authority to identify anyone who may be part of the person's wider network of care and support. For example, caring responsibilities could have an impact on siblings' school work, or their aspirations to go to university. Young carers' assessments should include an indication of how any care and support plan for the person(s) they care for would change as a result of the young carer's change in circumstances. For example, if a young carer has an opportunity to go to university away from home, the local authority should indicate how it would meet the eligible needs of any family members that were previously being met by the young carer.

FEATURES OF A TRANSITION ASSESSMENT

16.24. The transition assessment should support the young person and their family to plan for the future, by providing them with information about what they can expect. All transition assessments must include an assessment of:

- current needs for care and support and how these impact on wellbeing;

- whether the child or carer is likely to have needs for care and support after the child in question becomes 18;

- if so, what those needs are likely to be, and which are likely to be eligible needs;

- the outcomes the young person or carer wishes to achieve in day-to-day life and how care and support (and other matters) can contribute to achieving them.

---

[1] Insert chapter number when COP published.

16.25. Transition assessments for young carers or adult carers must also specifically consider whether the carer:

- is able to care now and after the child in question turns 18;
- is willing to care now and will continue to after 18;
- works or wishes to do so;
- is or wishes to participate in education, training or recreation.

16.26. The same requirements and principles apply for carrying out transition assessments as for other needs assessments under the adult statute (chapter 6 sets out the requirements and principles for carrying out needs assessments under the adult statute).

16.27. For example, assessments must include an assessment of the outcomes, views and wishes that matter to the child or carer in question, and an assessment of their strengths and capabilities. The power to join up assessments also applies, so for example if an adult is caring for a 17 year-old in transition and a 12 year-old, the local authority could combine:

- the child's needs assessment of the 17 year old under the Care Act;
- any assessment of the 17 year old's needs under section 17 of the Children Act;
- any assessment of the 12 year old's needs under section 17 of the Children Act;
- the child's carer's assessment of the adult under the Care Act; and
- the parent carer assessment of the adult under the Children and Families Act.

16.28. The young person or carer in question must be involved in the assessment for it to be person centred and reflect their views and wishes. The assessment must also involve anyone else who the young person or carer wants to involve in the assessment. For example, many young people will want their parents involved in their process.

16.29. Transition assessments will often represent a very different context to that which the person is accustomed, so ensuring that people have general information and advice about adult care and support will sometimes be a prerequisite for giving more detailed information and advice. For example, the right to self-assessment applies as with other assessments under the Care Act (see chapter 6 again), however there is the important caveat that for children, the local authority must ensure that a self-assessment is appropriate. This means for example ensuring that a young carer conducting a self-assessment is clear about the support available both to them and the person(s) they care for, avoiding a situation where the young carer assumes the default of continuing in the same caring role through ignorance of other options.

16.30. When sharing information with a young carer about the person they care for a supported self-assessment during transition, local authorities must satisfy themselves that it is appropriate for the young carer to have the information. They must have regard to all circumstances in taking this decision, especially the age of the young carer, however each case will be different and there is no one age at which a young carer is necessarily old enough to receive information.

Local authorities must ensure that the adult consents to have their information shared in this way.

16.31. Transition assessments should be carried out in a reasonable timescale. Local authorities should inform the young person or carer of an indicative time-scale over which the assessment will be conducted and keep them informed.

16.32. While like all assessments transition assessments must identify all a person's needs for care and support, they should be proportionate to that person's needs. For someone with a low level of need, an assessment might be light-touch, but it many cases a more thorough examination will be required to fully establish a person's needs.

16.33. Transition assessments should consider the immediate short-term outcomes that a child or carer wants to achieve as well as the medium and longer-term aspirations for their life. Progress towards achieving outcomes should be monitored.

16.34. EHC plans must be person-centred, and must focus on preparation for adulthood from Year 9. Therefore, for young people with EHC plans, transition assessments should build on the plans which will already contain information about the person, their aspirations and progress towards achieving their desired outcomes.

16.35. Similarly, for young people and carers who do not have an EHC plan, but who already have other plans under children's legislation, the transition assessment should build on existing information.

16.36. In all cases, the young person or carer in question must agree to the assessment where they have mental capacity and are competent to agree. Where a young person or carer lacks mental capacity or is not competent to agree, the local authority must be satisfied that an assessment is in their best interests. Everyone has the right to refuse a transition assessment, however the local authority must undertake an assessment regardless if it suspects that a child is experiencing or at risk of abuse or neglect.

16.37. The right of young people to make decisions is subject to their capacity to do so as set out in the Mental Capacity Act 2005. The underlying principle of the Act is to ensure that those who lack capacity are supported to make as many decisions for themselves as possible, and that any decision made or action taken on their behalf, is done so in their best interests. This is a necessity if the transition assessment is to be person-centred.

16.38. For young people below the age of 16, local authorities will need to establish a young person's competence using the test of 'Gillick competence' (whether they are able to understand a proposed treatment or procedure). Where the young person is not competent, a person with parental responsibility will need to be involved in their transition assessment, – or an independent advocate provided if there is no one appropriate to act on their behalf (either with or without parental responsibility).

16.39. The Care Act places a duty on local authorities to provide an independent advocate to facilitate the involvement in the transition assessment where the person in question would experience substantial difficulty in understanding the necessary information or in communicating their views, wishes and feelings – and if there is nobody else appropriate to act on their behalf (see chapter 7 for more detail on the provision independent advocacy). This duty applies for all young people or carers who meet the criteria, regardless of whether they lack mental capacity as defined under the Mental Capacity Act.

CO-OPERATION BETWEEN PROFESSIONALS AND ORGANISATIONS

16.40. People with complex needs for care and support may have several professionals involved in their lives, and numerous assessments from multiple organisations. For children with special educational needs, the Children and Families Act 2014 brings these assessments together into a coordinated Education, Health and Care (EHC) Plan (see SEN Code of Practice Chapter 9).[1]

16.41. Local authorities must cooperate with relevant partners, and this duty is reciprocal (see chapter 15 on cooperation). This includes an explicit requirement which states that children and adult services must cooperate for the purposes of transition to adult care and support. Often, staff working in children's services will have built relationships and knowledge about the young person or carer in question over a number of years. As young people and carers prepare for adulthood, children's services and adults' services should work together to pass on this knowledge and build new relationships in advance of transition.

16.42. Local authorities should have a clear understanding of their responsibilities, including funding arrangements, for young people and carers who are moving from children's to adult services. Disputes between different departments within a local authority about who is responsible can be time consuming and can sometimes result in disruption to the young person or carer.

16.43. Local authorities must also cooperate with relevant external agencies including local GP practices, housing providers and educational institutions. Again, this duty is reciprocal. This cooperation is crucial to help ensure that assessments and planning are person-centred. Furthermore, local health services or schools are vital to identifying young people and carers who may not already be in contact with local authorities.

16.44. It can be frustrating for children and families who have to attend multiple appointments for assessments, and who have to give out the same information repeatedly. The SEN Code of Practice highlights the importance of the 'tell us once' approach to gathering information for assessments and this will be important in other contexts as well. Local authorities should consult with the young person and their family to discuss what arrangements they would prefer for assessments and reviews.

16.45. The local authority should ensure that all relevant partners are involved in transition planning where they are involved in the person's care and support. Equally, the local authority should be involved in transition planning led by another organisation, for example a child and adolescent mental health service, where there are also likely to be needs for adult care and support.

16.46. Agencies should agree how to organise processes so that all the relevant professionals are able to contribute. For example, this might involve arranging a multi- disciplinary team meeting with the young person or carer. However, it may not always be possible for all the professionals from different agencies to be present at appointments, but where this is the case, they should still be able to contribute. Transition assessments must be person- centred, which means that contributions by different agencies should reflect the views of the person to whom the assessment relates.

16.47. The local authority may also combine a transition assessment with any other assessment it is carrying out (see examples in paragraph 16.27), or it may

---

[1] See SEN Code of Practice (Department of Health, 2014). https://www.gov.uk/government/publications/send-code-of-practice-0-to-25

carry out assessments jointly with, or on behalf of, another body. All such cases must meet the consent condition around mental capacity or the competence condition set out above (paragraph

16.3. to be carried out jointly. For example, transition assessments should be combined with existing EHC assessments unless there are specific circumstances to prevent it.

16.48. Many people value having one designated person who coordinates assessments and transition planning across different agencies, and helps them to navigate through numerous systems and processes that can sometimes be complicated. Often there is a natural lead professional involved in a young person's care who fulfils this role and local authorities should consider formalising this by designating a named person to coordinate transition assessment and planning across different agencies. Local authorities may also wish to consider specialist posts in their workforce to carry out this coordination function for people who are preparing for adulthood and interacting with multiple agencies.

16.49. This coordinating role – sometimes referred to as a 'key working' or 'care coordination' can not only help to deliver person-centred, integrated care, but can also help to reduce bureaucracy and duplication for local authorities, the NHS and other agencies. Care coordinators are also often able to build close relationships with young people and families and can act as a valuable provider of information and advice both to the families and to local authorities. Care leavers will have Personal Advisers to provide support, for example by providing advice or signposting the young person to services. The Personal Adviser will be a natural lead in many cases to coordinate a transition from children's to adult care and support where relevant.

Case study: Matthew's story: person-centred transition planning, involving multiple agencies

To ensure that Matthew was fully involved in the transition process, four planning sessions were held with his Transition Officer and facilitated by an outside agency that had expertise in person-centred planning. Matthew's aspirations were to live independently in his own home and to have paid employment in an office.

It was vital to Matthew's preparation for adulthood that he was given information about what support he would be eligible for after 18 in order to plan for sustainable employment and to ensure the appropriate support would be available to enable Matthew to live independently. This involved considering:

- whether he would still have a Personal Budget;
- support with travel training;
- job coaching; and
- support to live independently, developing appropriate housing options locally. Matthew and his family worked with the local authority and the housing association to identify a suitable home for him. The housing association then bought the house for Matthew and another young man to live in, with a carer. This whole process took over three years. Early, person-centred planning has been crucial to Matthew achieving his goals. Without adequate transition planning, the local authority would not have been able to promote Matthew's wellbeing in terms of participation in work, suitability of accommodation, or control over day-to-day life.

Here is a link to an update video on what Matthew is doing today: http://www.media19.co.uk/production/matthews-story/

ON COMPLETION OF THE TRANSITION ASSESSMENT – PROVIDING INFORMATION AND ADVICE

16.50. Having carried out a transition assessment, the local authority must give an indication of which needs are likely to be eligible needs (and which are not likely to be eligible) once the young person in question turns 18, to ensure that the young person or carer understands the care and support they are likely to receive and can plan accordingly.

16.51. There is a particularly important role for local authorities in ensuring that young people and carers understand their likely situation when they reach adulthood. The different systems for children's and adult care and support mean that there will be circumstances in which needs that were being met by children's services may not be eligible needs under the adult system. Adult care and support is also subject to means-testing and charging. However, from April 2016, people who turn 18 with eligible care and support needs, will have those needs met for free by their local authority for the rest of their lifetime. Forthcoming guidance on funding reform (to be published for consultation later this year) will set out the detail of how this will work.

16.52. It is critical that families are able to understand what support they are likely to receive when the young person or carer is in the adult system, and that the transition period is planned and managed as far in advance as is practical and useful to the individual to ensure that there is not a sudden gap in meeting the young person's or carer's needs. Where the transition assessment identifies needs that are likely to be eligible, local authorities should consider providing an indicative personal budget, so that young people, carers and their families are able to plan their care and support before entering the adult system (see SEN code of practice for further information about right to a personal budget for people with EHC plans, and chapter 11 for personal budgets under the Care Act).

16.53. For any needs that are not eligible under the adult statute, local authorities must provide information and advice on how those needs can be met, and how they can be prevented from getting worse. Information and advice must be accessible and proportionate to whoever needs it and must consider individual circumstances. For example when providing information and advice to young people and young carers, it is often more effective if information is given face-to-face from a trusted source, such as the young person's care coordinator.

16.54. The Children and Families Act 2014 requires local authorities to publish a local offer, which includes provision of information and advice for children's social care in their local area, including specific requirements for young people who are preparing for adulthood (see chapter 4 SEN Code of Practice).[1] The Care Act places a similar duty on local authorities to provide information and advice about adult care and support (see chapter 3 for guidance on the provision of information and advice).

16.55. Given the similar requirements on both children and adult services to provide information and advice that is easily accessible, local authorities should consider jointly commissioning and delivering their information and advice services for both children's and adult care and support as part of their requirement to work together to smooth the transition between children and adult services.

16.56. The local authority and relevant partners should consider building on a transition assessment to create a person-centred transition plan that sets out the information in the assessment, along with a plan for the transition to adult care and support, including key milestones for achieving the young person or carer's desired outcomes. An advantage of a transition plan is that it is easier to update and refine without undertaking a new assessment – transition assessments and plans should be reviewed regularly to take account of changes both in circumstances and desired outcomes. The priorities of young people and young carers will often change a lot during their adolescent years, and plans should be updated frequently enough to reflect this. Local authorities should also accept reasonable requests from young people and their families to review transition plans (see chapter 13 for further on reviews of care plans).

---

[1] See SEN Code of Practice (Department of Health, 2014). https://www.gov.uk/government/publications/send-code-of-practice-0-to-25

Links to example templates of transition plans:

http://www.preparingforadulthood.org.uk/media/208807/william_s_draft_
transition_plan.pdf

http://www.hertsdirect.org/docs/pdf/p/PfAtransplan

16.57. In the case of an adult carer, if the local authority has identified needs through a transition assessment which could be met by adult services, it may meet these needs under the Care Act in advance of the child being cared for turning 18. In deciding whether to do this the local authority must have regard to what support the adult carer is receiving under children's legislation.[1] If the local authority decides to meet the adult carer's needs through adult services, as for anyone else under the adult legislation, the adult carer must receive a support plan and a personal budget – as well as a financial assessment if they are subject to charges for the support they will receive. A local authority may not meet an adult carer's needs for support under section the Care Act by providing care and support to the child cared for – this will always happen under children's legislation.

PROVISION OF AGE-APPROPRIATE LOCAL SERVICES AND
RESOURCES

16.58. The Care Act requires local authorities to arrange preventative services, and to ensure a diverse range of quality providers of care and support in their local area. There are similar requirements in relation to the Local Offer in the Children and Families Act (see chapter 4 on market shaping).

16.59. Promoting a local market that offers a choice of high quality services will include having regard to the needs of young people and young carers transferring from children's services after turning 18. In order to prepare to live independently as adults, many young people leaving full-time education will require different types of care and support to that which is typically provided to children or older people. For young adults with care and support needs or young adult carers, this might include things such as advice on housing options, support to help them live in their own home or job training.

16.60. Given the clear similarities in the statutory requirements under both Acts, local authorities should consider jointly planning and commissioning these services where there is potential to make better use of resources. It can cause significant disruption to young people and their families if they would prefer to stay local but are forced to travel out of area due to lack of adequate local provision. This will also often result in high transport costs and high costs of out-of- area placements.

AFTER THE YOUNG PERSON OR CARER TURNS 18

16.61. There is no obligation on local authorities to implement the move from children's social care to adult care and support as soon as someone turns 18. Very few moves will take place on the day of someone's 18th birthday. For the most part, the move to adult services begins at the end of a school term or another

---

[1] Specifically, to section 17 of the Children Act 1989 or section 2 of the Sick and Disabled Persons Act 1970 or section 2 of the Carers and Disabled Children Act 2000.

similar milestone, and in many cases should be a staged process over several months or years.

16.62. In advance of the move taking place, the local authority must decide whether to treat the transition assessment as a needs or carers assessment under the Care Act (i.e. an assessment for the adult care and support system as set out in chapter 6). In making this decision the local authority must have regard to when the transition assessment was carried out and whether the person's circumstances have changed.

16.63. If the local authority will meet the young person's or carer's needs under the Care Act after they have turned 18 (based either on the existing transition assessment or a new needs assessment if necessary), the local authority must undertake the care planning process as for other adults – including creating a care and support plan and producing a personal budget as set out in chapters 10 and 11. Local authorities should ensure that this happens early enough that a package of care and support is in place at the time of transition.

COMBINING EHC PLANS AND CARE AND SUPPORT PLANS AFTER THE AGE OF 18

16.64. Where young people aged 18 or over continue to have EHC plans under the Children and Families Act 2014, and they make the move to adult care and support, the care and support aspects of the EHC plan will be provided under the Care Act. The statutory care and support plan must form the basis of the 'care' element of the EHC plan (chapter 10 sets out the requirements and guidance for care and support plans).

16.65. Under the Children and Families Act, EHC plans must clearly set out the care and support which is reasonably required by the learning difficulties and disabilities that result in the young person having SEN. For people over 18 with a care and support plan, this will be those elements of their care and support which are directly related to their SEN. EHC plans may also include other care and support that is in the care and support plan, but the elements that are directly related to SEN should always be clearly marked out separately as they will be of particular relevance to the rest of the EHC plan.

CONTINUITY OF CARE AFTER THE AGE OF 18

16.66. Young people and their carers have sometimes faced a gap in provision of care and support when they turn 18, and this can be distressing and disruptive to their lives. Local authorities must not allow a gap in care and support when young people and carers move from children's to adult services.

16.67. If transition assessment and planning is carried out as it should be, there should not be any gap in provision of care and support. However, if adult care and support is not in place on a young person's 18th birthday, and they or their carer have been receiving services under children's legislation,[1] the local authority must continue providing services until the relevant steps have been taken, so that there is no gap in provision. The 'relevant steps' are if the local authority:

- concludes that the person does not have needs for adult care and support; or

---

[1] Specifically, under section 17 of the Children Act 1989 or section 2 of the Sick and Disabled Persons Act 1970 or section 2 of the Carers and Disabled Children Act 2000.

- concludes that the person does have such needs and begins to meet some or all of them (the local authority will not always meet all of a person's needs – certain needs are sometimes met by carers or other organisations); or

- concludes that the person does have such needs but decides they are not going to meet any of those needs (for instance, because their needs do not meet the eligibility criteria under the Care Act 2014).

16.68. In order to reach such a conclusion, the local authority must have conducted a transition assessment (that they will use as a needs or carers assessment under the adult statute). Where a transition assessment was not conducted and should have been (or where the young person's circumstances have changed), the local authority must carry out an adult needs or carer's assessment as described in chapter 6.

16.69. In the case of care leavers, the Staying Put Guidance[1] states that local authorities may choose to extend foster placements beyond the age of 18. All local authorities must have a Staying Put policy to ensure transition from care to independence and adulthood that is similar for care leavers to that which most young people experience, and is based on need and not on age alone.

16.70. For some people with complex SEN and care needs, local authorities and their partners may decide that children's services are the best way to meet a person's needs – even after they have turned 18. Both the Care Act 2014 and the Children and Families Act 2014 allow for this.[2]

16.71. The Children and Families Act enables local authorities to continue children's services beyond age 18 and up to 25 for young people with EHC plans if they need longer to complete or consolidate their education and training and achieve the outcomes set out in their plan. Under the Care Act 2014, if, having carried out a transition assessment, it is agreed that the best decision for the young person is to continue to receive children's services, the local authority may choose to do so. Children and adults' services must work together, and any decision to continue children's services after the child turns 18 will require agreement between children and adult services.

16.72. Where a person over 18 is still receiving services under children's legislation through their EHC plan and the EHC plan ceases, the transition assessment and planning process must be undertaken as set out elsewhere in this chapter. Where this has not happened at the point of transition, the requirement under the Care Act to continue children's services (as set out above) applies.

16.73. Both the Children and Families Act 2014 and the Care Act 2014 also require young people and their parents to be fully involved making decisions about their care and support. This includes decisions about the most appropriate time to make the transition to adult services. The EHC plan or any transition plan should set out how this will happen, who is involved and what support will be provided to make sure the transition is as seamless as possible.

---

[1] https://www.gov.uk/government/publications/staying-put-arrangements-for-care-leavers-aged-18-years- and-above

[2] Both Acts make insertions to the Children Act 1989 and "children's services" in the rest of this section means services provided under section 17 of that Act.

SAFEGUARDING AFTER THE AGE 18

16.74. Where someone is over 18 but still receiving children's services and a safeguarding issue is raised, the matter should be dealt with as a matter of course by the adult safeguarding team. Where appropriate, they should involve the local authority's children's safeguarding colleagues as well as any relevant partners (e.g. police or NHS) or other persons relevant to the case. The same approach should apply for complaints or appeals, as well as where someone is moving to a different local authority area after receiving a transition assessment but before moving to adult care and support.

ORDINARY RESIDENCE AND TRANSITION TO HIGHER EDUCATION

16.75. Where a young person is intending to move to a higher or further education institution which is out of the area where they were receiving children's services, they will usually remain ordinarily resident in the area where their parents live (or the local authority area which had responsibility for them as a child). However, this is not always the case and Chapter 20 and Annex J contain more detailed guidance about ordinary residence principles when young people move from children's to adult services, and when they move away to university. This includes example case studies to help local authorities in making decisions about which area is responsible – it will be an important aspect of transition planning to confirm as early as possible where someone will be ordinarily resident as an adult.

16.76. Where a young person or carer wishes to attend a higher or further education institution, local authorities should help them identify a suitable institution as part of transition planning (if they have not done so already). Once an offer has been accepted, local authorities should ensure the relevant institution is made aware as soon as possible of the young person's or carer's needs and desired outcomes and discuss a plan for meeting them. As set out in the SEN code of practice, an EHC plan will cease if someone progresses to further or higher education, but a care and support plan is likely to be required thereafter.

16.77. Wherever possible, this should be a conversation involving the young person or carer, anyone else they wish to involve, the local authority, and the institution – as well as the local authority where the institution is located where appropriate. All higher and further education institutions have clear duties and responsibilities under the Equality Act 2010 with regard to ensuring that disabled students do not face discrimination or less favourable treatment whilst applying to, and studying in these institutions. They are likely to have a learning support team or similar that can lead transition discussions on their behalf. These conversations should also ensure young people and carers are aware of their rights to the Disabled Students Allowance[1] and student loans.

16.78. The objective should be to ensure that there will be an appropriate package of care and support in place from the day the young person or carer starts at the institution. In many cases a young person or carer studying at university will have a dual location, for example coming home to stay with the parents during weekends or holidays. Where this is the case, local authorities must ensure their needs are met all year round.

---

[1] https://www.gov.uk/disabled-students-allowances-dsas/overview

TRANSITION FROM CHILDREN'S TO ADULT NHS CONTINUING HEALTH CARE

16.79. Clinical Commissioning Groups (CCGs) should use the National Framework for NHS Continuing Healthcare[1] and supporting guidance and tools (especially the Decision Support Tool) to determine what on-going care services people aged 18 years or over should receive. The framework sets out that CCGs should ensure that adult NHS continuing healthcare is appropriately represented at all transition planning meetings to do with individual young people whose needs suggest that there may be potential eligibility. CCGs and LAs should have systems in place to ensure that appropriate referrals are made whenever either organisation is supporting a young person who, on reaching adulthood, may have a need for services from the other agency.

16.80. The framework sets out best practice for the timing of transition steps as follows:

- Children's services should identify young people with likely needs for NHS CHC and notify the relevant CCGs when such a young person turns 14;

- There should be a formal referral for adult NHS CHC screening at 16;

- There should be a decision in principle at 17 so that a package of care can be in place once the person turns 18 (or later if agreed more appropriate).

16.81. Where a young person has been receiving children's continuing health care from a relevant CCG, it is likely that they will continue to be eligible for a package of adult NHS CHC when they reach the age of 18. Where their needs have changed such that they are assessed as no longer requiring such a package, they should be advised of their non-eligibility and of their right to request an independent review and mediation (see 16.83 below). The CCG should continue to participate in the transition process, in order to ensure an appropriate transfer of responsibilities, including consideration of whether they should be commissioning, funding or providing services towards a joint package of care.

16.82. As set out above, where it will benefit a young person with an EHC plan, local authorities have the power to continue to provide children's services past a young person's 18th birthday for as long as is deemed necessary. Where there is a change in CHC provision, this needs to be recorded in the young person's EHC plan, where they have one, and advised of their rights to ask the local authority for mediation (this is in the SEND Code of Practice and applicable up to age 25).

LINKS TO EXTERNAL RESOURCES
Code of Practice for Children with Special Educations Needs
https://www.gov.uk/government/publications/send-code-of-practice-0-to-25

Preparing for Adulthood website
http://www.preparingforadulthood.org.uk/

Together for Short Lives website
http://www.togetherforshortlives.org.uk/

---

[1] https://www.gov.uk/government/publications/national-framework-for-nhs-continuing-healthcare-and-nhs- funded-nursing-care

Transition Information Network website
http://www.transitioninfonetwork.org.uk/

Carers Trust *Transition*

Children's Society (2013) *Hidden From View: the experiences of young carers in England*

Cerebra (2013) *Transition to Adulthood A guide for practitioners working with disabled young people and their families*

Contact a family (2014) *Preparing for adult life and transition: Information for families*

17. PRISONS, APPROVED PREMISES AND BAIL ACCOMMODATION

This chapter provides guidance on section 76 of the Care Act 2014. It also pro-
vides guidance on other sections of the Act where they relate to care and support
for adults in prison, approved premises and bail accommodation and those
released from custody.

This chapter covers:
- Information sharing;
- Assessments of need;
- Assessments of a carer's needs;
- Charging and assessing financial resources;
- Next steps after assessments;
- Direct payments and deferred payment agreements;
- Continuity of care and support when an adult moves or is released;
- Partnerships and interdependencies;
- End of life care;
- Safeguarding adults at risk of abuse or neglect;
- Transition from children's to adult care and support;
- Independent advocacy support;
- Complaints;
- Standards and assessments.

17.1. People in custody or custodial settings who have needs for care and support should be able to access the care they need, just like anyone else. In the past, the responsibilities for meeting the needs of prisoners have been unclear, and this has led to confusion between local authorities, prisons and other organisations. This has created difficulties in ensuring people's eligible needs are met.

17.2. Prisoners can often have complex health and care needs and experience poorer health and mental health outcomes than the general population. Evidence demonstrates higher prevalence among the adult prison population of mental illness, substance misuse and learning disabilities than in the general population. Access to good integrated health and care support will be particularly important for these groups. Section 76 of the Care Act sets out to clarify local responsibilities, and to describe how the partners involved should work together.

17.3. Throughout this chapter, references to *custody* or *custodial settings* relate to prisons, approved premises and other bail accommodation. It can also apply to people aged over 18 years in young offender institutions, secure children's homes and secure training centres. Please see the *Definitions* section below. People bailed to a particular address in criminal proceedings are, like those in prison or approved premises, treated for the purposes of the Care Act as ordinarily resident in the local authority where they are required to reside and the provisions in the Care Act apply accordingly.

17.4. The guidance in this chapter relates only to custodial settings in England.

17.5. The Act and this chapter apply to adults who are detained or residing in a custodial setting. For the purposes of the Act, adults detained or residing in a custodial setting are treated as if they were ordinarily resident in the area where the custodial setting is located.

17.6. Where prisoners have previously been detained under sections 47 and 48 of the Mental Health Act 1983 and transferred back to prison, their entitlement to section 117 aftercare should be dealt with in the same way as it would be in the community, apart from any provisions which are disapplied in custodial settings, such as direct payments and choice of accommodation, which are set out in more detail below. Section 117(3), as amended by the Care Act 2014, will apply in determining which local authority is responsible for commissioning or providing the section 117 after-care.

17.7. If the person was ordinarily resident in the area of a local authority immediately before being detained in hospital, that local authority will be responsible for the after-care while the person is in prison and upon their release from prison (see Chapter 19 for further detail on determination). However, if the person was not ordinarily resident in any area immediately before detention, the local authority responsible will be where the person is resident or where they have been discharged (i.e. the local authority responsible for the prison to which the person has been discharged). The local authority will be jointly responsible for after-care with NHS England while the person is in prison.

17.8. This chapter of the guidance does not apply to individuals aged under 18 years. Details of where to find information on provision for children can be found at the end of this chapter. Please refer to paragraphs 17.62-17.63 of this chapter for information about transition from children's to adult care and support in custodial settings. For more detail please see chapter 16 in this guidance on transition from children's to adult care and support.

17.9. All adults in custody, as well as offenders and defendants in the community, should expect the same level of care and support as the rest of the population. This principle of equivalence of care forms the basis of the policy intent for the Act and this guidance. This is crucial in ensuring that those in need of care and support achieve the outcomes that matter to them, and that will support them to live as independently as possible at the end of their detention. In addition to ensuring that individual needs are met, this will contribute to the effectiveness of rehabilitation and improve community safety.

17.10. Local authorities are responsible for the assessment of all adults who are in custody in their area and who appear to be in need of care and support, regardless of which area the individual came from or where they will be released to. If an individual is transferred to another custodial establishment in a different local authority area this responsibility will transfer to the new area. The prison or approved premises to which an individual is allocated is a matter for the Ministry of Justice.

17.11. Local authorities should also be aware that prisoners, especially those serving long sentences, may develop eligible needs over time whilst in prison. Local authorities should consider how best to provide information and advice to both individuals and establishments on what can be done to prevent or delay the development of care and support needs. In doing so it is important to consider the level of access to electronic media and the most appropriate format, such as easy-read leaflets, of information and advice in custodial settings, and the custodial environment in which the care and support is to be provided.

17.12. Not all local authority areas contain prisons or approved premises. Those that do will assume responsibility for the eligible needs of the people residing in these sites. However, all local authorities will be responsible for continuity of care for offenders with a package of care coming into their area on release from prison.

Provision of care and support, where an adult has eligible needs, should be provided in line with chapter 6 of this guidance once these individuals move into the community. Early engagement in the resettlement plan of the local authority in the area to which the person is returning will reduce delays, particularly when resettlement is in a new area due to the nature of the original offence. Similarly local authorities must support continuity of care for any of their residents moving into custody. Either party may use the mechanism to require co-operation to support working in an individual case, set out in chapter 15.

17.13. Local authorities, provider organisations and their staff working in custodial settings should abide by all rules and practices for that establishment, including (but not restricted to) security policies such as restricted items and searches on entry, equality and safeguarding procedures.

DEFINITIONS
17.14. Prison: This has the same meaning as the Prison Act 1952, section 53(1). A reference to a prison includes a reference to a young offender institution, secure training centre or secure children's home (see Care Act section 76(11)(a)). A reference to a governor, director or controller of a prison includes a reference to the governor, director or controller of a young offender institution, to the governor, director or monitor of a secure training centre and to the manager of a secure children's home (see Care Act section 76(11)(b)). A reference to a prison officer or prisoner custody officer includes a reference to a prison officer or prisoner custody officer as a young offender institution, to an officer or custody officer at a secure training centre and to a member of staff at a secure children's home (see Care Act section 76(11)(c)).

17.15. Approved premises: Premises approved as accommodation under section 13 of the Offender Management Act 2007 for the supervision and rehabilitation of offenders, and for people on bail. They are usually supervised hostel-type accommodation.

17.16. National Offender Management Service (NOMS): An executive agency of the Ministry of Justice, its role is to commission and provide offender services in the community and in custody in England and Wales, ensuring best value for money from public resources. NOMS works to protect the public and reduce reoffending by delivering the punishment and orders of the courts and supporting rehabilitation by helping offenders to change their lives.

17.17. National Probation Service (NPS) and Community Rehabilitation Companies (CRCs): The Transforming Rehabilitation reforms are putting in place a new system of offender management and rehabilitation across England and Wales. The NPS is responsible for conducting all initial offender assessments for risk of harm, and allocating offenders to either the NPS or CRCs. It will manage all offenders who pose a high risk of serious harm to the public (including those whose risk level escalates during their period of supervision), offenders who have committed the most serious sexual and violent offences (including those managed under Multi Agency Public Protection Arrangements), foreign nationals who meet the criteria for deportation, and a small number of exceptional public interest cases. The 21 CRCs are responsible for managing the majority of offenders in the community (most low to medium risk offenders), The NPS sits within the National Offender Management Service, while the 21

- what can be done to prevent or delay the development of needs for care and support in the future.

17.30. The threshold for the provision of care and support does not change in custodial settings and will be the same as described in chapter 6. When an individual is in a custodial setting, this should not in any way affect the assessment and recording of eligible needs. Whilst the setting in which the care and support will be provided is likely to be different from community or other settings, and this should be taken into account when considering how to meet the need for care and support as part of the care planning process, the extent and nature of need should be identified before taking into account the environment in which the individual lives. This is particularly important when individuals move between prisons and/ or from prison into the community. Services which support the best outcomes which can be achieved should be provided where the built environment necessarily limits the type or quality of care and support which can be provided. If a safeguarding issue is identified then the prison or approved premises management needs to be notified in accordance with NOMS policy on adult safeguarding.

17.31. For any needs that are not eligible under the Act, local authorities must provide information and advice to the individual on how those needs can be met, and how they can be prevented from getting worse (as per Section 13 (5) of the Care Act). It is good practice to copy this information to managers of custodial settings, with the person's consent as this may be relevant to how the individual is managed in the custodial setting.

17.32. Prisoners, especially those serving long sentences, may develop eligible needs over time. Local authorities should consider how best to provide information and advice to both individuals and establishments on what can be done to prevent or delay the development of care and support needs. In doing so it is important to consider the prison regime and the environment, as well as the individual's capacity to understand the information that is being provided. Individuals in custodial settings, like people in the community, may benefit from low level preventative support and information and advice that will help them maintain their own health and wellbeing.

17.33. The right to a choice of accommodation does not apply to those in a custodial setting except when an individual is preparing for release or resettlement in the community. Release into an approved premises amounts to moving from one custodial setting to another.

17.34. It is important that, where appropriate, individuals in custodial settings, maintain links with their families, subject to consideration of the best interests of the individual and to public protection requirements which may limit family contact. While it may not always be possible or appropriate to involve family members directly in assessment or care planning, individuals should be asked whether they would like to involve others in their assessment or care planning.

17.35. If it is not possible to involve families directly, the local authority should ask the individual concerned whether they would like others to be informed that an assessment is taking place, the outcome of that assessment and whether they should see the care and support plan.

ASSESSMENTS OF A CARER'S NEEDS

17.36. It is not the intention of the Care Act that any prisoner, resident of approved premises or staff in prisons or approved premises should take on the role of carer as defined by the Act and should therefore not in general be entitled to a carer's assessment. Separate guidance will be issued to prison and approved premises staff on the role of prisoners and residents of approved premises in providing assistance to others.

CHARGING AND ASSESSING FINANCIAL RESOURCES

17.37. Those in custodial settings will be subject to a financial assessment to determine how much they may pay towards the cost of their care and support, as they would be in the community (see chapter 8). Consideration should be given to the best way of handling financial assessments, taking into account the resources required. In particular local authorities should consider how "light touch" assessments could be carried out where a person is unlikely to be required to contribute towards the cost of their care and support. As indicated previously, a high proportion of the prison population have a mental health problem or learning disability and they may have a poor understanding of their personal finances. Therefore forms and questions must be accessible and support provided to enable the individual to complete the financial assessment. Should the person not meet the eligibility threshold for local authority support, but they wish to purchase care services, this request should be referred for decision to NOMS.

NEXT STEPS AFTER ASSESSMENT

17.38. The local authority should ensure that all relevant partners are involved in care and support planning and take part in joint planning with health partners.

17.39. Where a local authority is required to meet needs it must prepare a care and support plan for the person concerned and involve the individual to decide how to have their needs met. The local authority should also speak to others concerned with the person's health and wellbeing, including prison staff, probation Offender Managers, staff of approved premises and health care staff, to ensure integration of care, and fit with the custodial regime as appropriate, including enabling access to regime services such as libraries and education. Any safeguarding issues are to be addressed in the care and support plan.

17.40. Whilst every effort should be made to put people in control of their care and for them to be actively involved and influential throughout the planning process (see chapter 10 on care and support planning) local authorities should make it clear to individuals that the custodial regime may limit the range of care options available, and some, such as direct payments, do not apply in a custodial setting. Where an individual's ability to exercise choice and control is limited by the custodial regime, this should be discussed with the individual and recorded as part of the care planning process. However, the plan must contain the elements defined in the Act, including the allocated personal budget. This will ensure that the person is clear about the needs to be met, the cost attributed to meeting those needs and how, if applicable, the custodial regime limited the individual's choice and control.

17.41. Local authorities should aim to ensure that consent is given so that individual care plans are shared with other providers of custodial and resettlement services including custodial services, probation service providers including Community Rehabilitation Companies, prison healthcare providers and managers of approved premises. For residents of approved premises, the local authority should always liaise with the responsible Offender Manager in probation services.

17.42. For those assessed as being in need of equipment or adaptations to their living accommodation to meet their needs, local authorities should discuss with their partners in prisons, approved premises and health care services where responsibility lies. Where this relates to fixtures and fittings (for instance a grab rail or a ramp), it will usually be for the prison to deliver this. But for specialised and moveable items such as beds and hoists, then it may be the local authority that is responsible. Aids for individuals, as defined in the Care and Support (Preventing Needs for Care and Support) Regulations 2014, are the responsibility of the local authority, whilst more significant adaptations would the responsibility of the custodial establishment. Further guidance on responsibility of custodial services for equipment aids and adaptations will be issued by NOMS. Custody services, healthcare providers and local authorities should agree local responsibilities.

17.43. Local authorities may commission or arrange for others to provide care and support services, or delegate the function to another party (see chapter 18 on delegation). Local authorities should consider how this fits alongside the commissioning of health and substance misuse services in prison directly commissioned by NHS England and the commissioning of education services by the Skills Funding Agency. If such an arrangement is implemented, local authorities should consider retaining the functions relating to requirements for continuity of care between settings and must retain the functions in relation to charging and safeguarding. Local authorities should make sure that any other party commissioned to provide care and support is aware of the policies and procedures to be followed when working in a custodial environment.

17.44. Care and support plans for those in custodial settings will be subject to the same review processes as all other plans (see chapter 13). Local authorities should also review an individual's care and support plan each time they enter custody from the community, or are released from custody.

17.45. People in custody may experience episodes of hospital care, for example following an incident such as a stroke. Local authorities should co-operate with hospital staff and prison health service providers and commissioners to prevent delays in discharge from hospital and support a timely return to custody.

DIRECT PAYMENTS

17.46. Any references to direct payments in the Act or this guidance will not apply in prisons and approved premises. Direct payments may not be made to people in custodial settings.

17.47. Individuals in bail accommodation and approved premises who have not yet been convicted are entitled to direct payments, as they would have been whilst in their own homes. For more information see the main guidance at chapter 12.

CONTINUITY OF CARE AND SUPPORT WHEN AN ADULT MOVES

17.48. Individuals in custody with care and support needs must have continuity of care where they are moved to another custodial setting or where they are being released from prison and are moving back in to the community. To ensure that the individual continues to receive care during the move, local authorities should follow a similar process to that set out in chapter 20 on continuity of care.

17.49. Individuals in custody cannot be said to be ordinarily resident there because the concept of ordinary residence relies on the person voluntarily living there and those in custody have not chosen to live there. As such, they might remain ordinarily resident where they previously resided. It is the local authority where the custodial setting is situated which is responsible for assessments, services etc. under Part 1 of the Care Act in relation to an individual in custody. Where the adult is being released from prison, their ordinary residence will generally be in the authority where they intend to live on a permanent basis, but see paragraphs 17.55-17.58 below.

17.50. There will be circumstances where the process to ensure continuity of care will need to differ, for example when a prisoner is moved between establishments or when they are released in another area because of the nature of their offence. The prison or approved premises to which an individual is allocated is a matter for the Ministry of Justice, and individuals may be moved between different custodial settings. In such cases, the Governor of the prison or a representative, should inform the local authority in which the prison is located (the first authority) that the adult is to be moved or is being released to a new area as soon as practicable. If this is a move to a custodial setting or release into the community in the same authority, then the first authority will remain responsible for meeting the individual's care and support needs. Where the new custodial setting or the community, if being released, is in a different local authority area (second authority), the first authority must inform the second authority of the move once it has been told by the prison.

17.51. The prison, both local authorities and where practicable, the individual, should work together to ensure that the adult's care is continued during the move. It is good practice for the first and second local authority (and the transferring and receiving prisons where appropriate) to have a named member of staff to lead on arrangements for individuals during the transfer. Both local authorities must share the relevant information as set out in chapter 20 on continuity of care, including their care and support plan.

17.52. The second authority should assess the individual before they are moved, but this may not always be possible as the authority could be informed of the transfer at short notice. In such circumstances the second authority must continue to meet the care and support needs that the first authority was meeting. It must continue to meet these needs until it has carried out its own assessment.

17.53. The requirements outlined in this guidance only apply to custodial settings in England. (Guidance to cover prisoners who are moved to Scotland, Wales or Northern Ireland is still to be developed.)

17.54. Under the Transforming Rehabilitation Programme, all prisons in England and Wales will be designated as either resettlement or non-resettlement prisons. Due to the nature of resettlement prisons, it is likely that they will experience a high turnover of prisoners and it is particularly important that the care needs of those serving short term sentences are identified and responded to.

PEOPLE LEAVING PRISON – ORDINARY RESIDENCE

17.55. The deeming provisions in section 39 of the Care Act, which provide that in most circumstances a person's ordinary residence is retained where they have their needs met in certain types of accommodation in another local authority area, do not apply to people who are leaving prison. However, local authorities can reasonably follow the approach set out in section 39 for people who are due for

and expertise to assist prison and probation staff in ensuring that all people in custodial settings are safeguarded.

TRANSITION FROM CHILDREN'S TO ADULT CARE AND SUPPORT

17.70. Local authorities should be aware of children and young people in Young Offender Institutions, Secure Children's Homes, Secure Training Centres or other places of detention as well as children and young people in the youth justice system, who are likely to have eligible needs for care and support as adults, and are approaching their eighteenth birthday. Local authorities should ensure that appropriate arrangements are in place to identify these young people and ensure they receive a transition assessment when appropriate. See chapter 16.

17.71. This also applies where an offender moves from the youth custodial estate to the adult custodial estate, which may include a change in the responsible local authority. A request for an assessment can be made on the young person's behalf by the professional responsible for their care in the Young Offenders' Institution, Secure Children's Home or Secure Training Centre. Good communication between professionals, institutions and local authorities is essential to prepare for transfer and ensure a smooth transition.

CARE LEAVERS

17.72. If a young person is entitled to support and services as a care leaver, this status remains unchanged while in custody and the local authority that looked after the young person retains responsibility for providing leaving care services during his/her time in custody and on release.

17.73. Responsibilities for planning continuing support applies to all care leavers until they reach the age of 21 or, if they are being helped with education or training, to the end of the agreed programme of education or training (which can take them beyond their 25th birthday).

17.74. Good communication is essential between the local authority responsible for leaving care services and the local authority responsible for providing care and support in custody.

INDEPENDENT ADVOCACY SUPPORT

17.75. Adults in custody are entitled to the support of an independent advocate during needs assessments and care and support planning and reviews of plans if they would have significant difficulty in being involved in the process. It is the local authority's duty to arrange an independent advocate, as they would for an individual in the community. See chapter 7 of this guidance for further details.

17.76. Local authorities should agree with managers of custodial establishments how the advocacy scheme will work in their establishments. Local arrangements for peers or prison officers to provide advocacy support or signpost people in custody have a role, however this does not fulfil the requirement under the Act for independent advocacy support.

COMPLAINTS AND APPEALS

17.77. Local authorities should provide information to those in custodial settings on how to make complaints, and seek redress about provision of care and support services.

17.78. Managers of custodial settings should inform local authorities where an offender wishes to make a complaint as soon as they are made aware. A prisoner may choose to complain or appeal by alternative methods, such as by letter or telephone to the care and support provider. This correspondence should be processed in the same way as all other appeals and complaints once received by local authorities.

17.79. Current complaints provision for care and support is set out in regulations.[1] The provisions of the regulations mean that anyone who is dissatisfied with a decision made by the local authority would be able to make a complaint about that decision and have that complaint handled by the local authority. The local authority must make its own arrangements for dealing with complaints in accordance with the 2009 regulations.

17.80. The Department of Health intends to develop detailed proposals for a system of reviewing local authority decisions which will be set out in regulations. The detail will specify the scope of decisions which will be covered by the new proposals, including whether decisions made by local authorities on care planning and personal budgets will be eligible for appeal. It is envisaged that the Department will consult on more detailed proposals late in 2014 and that the appeals system would come into force in April 2016, in line with funding reform.

STANDARDS AND ASSESSMENTS

17.81. The Prisons and Probation Ombudsman (PPO) conducts investigations in prisons following complaints about prison services, as well as deaths in custody or other significant events. The PPO will commission a relevant body to assist their investigations where it is felt that an aspect of care and support provision has contributed to the event. Local authorities should co- operate with any investigations as required.

17.82. The party commissioned by the PPO will investigate any relevant aspect of care and support provision and report back to the PPO for inclusion in the final report.

17.83. Both prisons and probation services are inspected by Her Majesty's Inspectorate of Prisons and Her Majesty's Inspectorate of Probation. Local authorities should make any relevant assessments and other documents available to inspecting bodies as part of the investigation.

17.84. Local authorities will receive copies of all investigation reports that are relevant to them. It is good practice for local authorities to contribute to the responses and action plans in conjunction with NOMS managers, prison managers and health care providers and commissioners. This could include work to prevent and reduce reoffending, and to prevent harm to others or to the offender.

17.85. Local authorities should co-operate with and attend any inquests that are held following a death in custody, where they are requested to do so or they have relevant information.

LINKS TO OTHER SOURCES OF INFORMATION/PRODUCTS WHICH SUPPORT IMPLEMENTATION

For information on the provision of social care for children visit https://www.gov.uk/childrens- services/childrens-social-care

---

[1] Local Authority Social Services and NHS Complaints Regulations 2009, made under powers in Sections 113 to of the Health and Social Care (Community Health and Standards) Act 2003

Appendix 2

For more information on the National Offender Management Service and contact details, visit https://www.justice.gov.uk/about/noms

18. DELEGATION OF LOCAL AUTHORITY FUNCTIONS

This chapter provides guidance on section 79 of the Care Act 2014.

This chapter covers:
- Overview of the policy;
- Local authorities retain ultimate responsibility for how its functions are carried out;
- Importance of contracts;
- Which functions may not be delegated;
- The difference between outsourcing a legal function and activities relating to the function;
- Conflicts of interest.

18.1. Part 1 of the Care Act sets out local authorities' functions and responsibilities for care and support. Sometimes external organisations might be better placed than the local authority itself to carry out some of its care and support functions. For instance, an outside organisation might specialise in carrying out assessments or care and support planning for certain disability groups, where the local authority does not have the in-house expertise. External organisations might also be able to provide additional capacity to carry out care and support functions.

18.2. The Care Act allows local authorities to delegate some, but not all, of their care and support functions to other parties. This power to delegate is intended to allow flexibility for local approaches to be developed in delivering care and support, and to allow local authorities to work more efficiently and innovatively, and provide better quality care and support to local populations.

18.3. As with all care and support, individual wellbeing should be central to any decision to delegate a function. Local authorities should not delegate its functions simply to gain efficiency where this is to the detriment of the wellbeing of people using care and support.

18.4. Local Authorities retain ultimate responsibility for how its functions are carried out. Delegation does not absolve the local authority of its legal responsibilities. When a local authority delegates any of its functions, it retains ultimate responsibility for how the function is carried out. The Care Act is clear that anything done (or not done) by the third party in carrying out the function, is to be treated as if it has been done (or not done) by the local authority itself. This is a core principle of allowing delegation of care and support functions.

18.5. People using care and support will always have a means of redress against the local authority for how any of its functions under Part 1 of the Act are carried out. For example, a local authority might delegate needs assessments to another organisation, which has its own procedures for handling complaints. If the adult to whom the assessment relates has a complaint about the way in which it was carried out, the adult might choose to take it up with the organisation in question. However, if this does not satisfy the adult, or if the adult simply chooses to complain directly to the local authority, the local authority will remain responsible for addressing the complaint.

18.6. In delegating care and support functions, local authorities should have regard to the local authority version of the NHS information governance toolkit,[1] in particular ensuring that all formal contractual arrangements include compliance with information governance requirements (requirement 12-146).

IMPORTANCE OF CONTRACTS

18.7. The success of a policy by a local authority to delegate its functions to a third party will be determined to a large extent, by the strength and quality of the contracts that the local authorities make with the delegated third party. Local authorities should therefore ensure that contracts are drafted by staff with the necessary skills and competencies to do so. Local authorities should consider the findings of the Social Work Practice pilot scheme,[2] which tested approaches to delegation, when considering how to construct contracts.

18.8. Through the terms of their contracts with authorised third parties, local authorities have the power to impose conditions on how the function is carried out. For example, when delegating assessments the local authority could choose to require that assessments must be carried out by people with a particular training or expertise, and that the training must be kept up to date.

18.9. The delegated organisation will be liable to the local authority for any breach of the contract, and as such this is the mechanism through which local authorities are able to ensure that its functions are carried out properly, and through which they may hold the contractor to account.

18.10. Where a local authority uses its power under the Act to authorise another party to carry out its care and support functions, it should specify how long the authorisation lasts, and it should make clear that it may revoke the authorisation at any time during that period.

18.11. Local authorities should put in place monitoring arrangements so that they can assure themselves that functions that have been delegated, are being carried out in an appropriate manner. This should involve building good working relationships which allow local authorities to guide third parties about how they are exercising the functions, but equally for the local authority to learn about innovations and knowledge that third parties may be able to provide.

18.12. Since care and support functions are public functions, they must be carried out in a way that is compatible with all of the local authority's legal obligations. For example, the local authority would be liable for any breach by the delegated party, of its legal obligations under the Human Rights Act or the Data Protection Act. Local authorities should therefore draw up its contracts so as to ensure that third parties carry out functions in a way that is compatible with all of their legal obligations.

18.13. Although local authorities retain overall responsibility for how its functions are carried out, delegated organisations will be responsible for any criminal proceedings brought against them.

18.14. Local authorities are able to choose the extent to which they delegate their functions. For example, they could authorise an external party to carry out all the elements of the function, including for example taking final decisions, or it can limit the steps the authorised organisation may take, leaving any final

---

[1] https://www.igt.hscic.gov.uk/RequirementsList.aspx?tk=418956179371111&lnv=2&cb=4fe9d316-e2ba-4a44-b92e-ec2b666fefcd&sViewOrgType=28&sDesc=Local Authority

[2] Insert link to final King's College evaluation when published.

decisions to the local authority. Local authorities should make clear in its contracts with authorised parties, the extent to which the function is being delegated.

18.15. The fact that a local authority delegates its functions does not mean that it cannot also continue to exercise that function itself. So, for instance the local authority could ask a specialist mental health organisation to carry out care and support planning for people with specific mental health conditions, but it may choose to do care and support planning for people with other mental health conditions itself. Or it may choose to offer people a choice between itself and the external organisation.

WHICH CARE AND SUPPORT FUNCTIONS MAY NOT BE DELEGATED?

18.16. The Care Act does not allow certain functions to be delegated. These are:

- **Integration and cooperation** – local authorities must cooperate and integrate with local partners. Delegating these functions would not be compatible with meeting their duties to work together with other agencies. However, local authorities should take steps to ensure that authorised parties co-operate with other partners, work in a way which supports integration, and is consistent with their own responsibilities.

- **Adult Safeguarding** – the Care Act puts in place a legal framework for adult safeguarding, including the establishment of Safeguarding Adults Boards (SABs), carrying out safeguarding adult reviews and making safeguarding enquiries. Since the local authority must be one of the members of SABs, and it must take the lead role in adult safeguarding, it may not delegate these statutory functions to another party. However, it may commission or arrange for other parties to carry out certain related activities (see paragraph 22.18 below).

- **Power to charge** – the Care Act gives local authorities the power to charge people for care and support in certain circumstances. Local policies relating to what can and cannot be charged for must rightly remain a decision of the local authority, and therefore the Act does not permit local authorities to delegate this decision to outside parties. However, it may commission or arrange for other parties to carry out related activities.

WHAT IS THE DIFFERENCE BETWEEN DELEGATING A STATUTORY CARE AND SUPPORT FUNCTION AND COMMISSIONING OTHER RELATED ACTIVITIES?

18.17. For those functions which may not be delegated (outlined in paragraph 18.15 above), as well as other functions which may be delegated, local authorities may wish to use outside expertise to assist in carrying out practical activities to support it in discharging those functions, rather than fully or formally delegating the function itself to be carried out by another party.

18.18. There can be some uncertainty about the difference between delegation of a statutory care and support function and commissioning, arranging or outsourcing other procedural activities relating to a function. Local authorities should seek legal advice about whether the activity it is seeking to commission another party to undertake is a legal function under Part 1 of the Act or not.

18.19. For example, as set out above local authorities may not delegate its functions relating to establishing Safeguarding Adult Boards, making safeguarding enquiries or arranging safeguarding reviews. However, the enquiry duty is for local authorities to make enquiries or cause them to be made, so a local authority can still have arrangements whereby NHS or others are asked to undertake the enquiries where necessary. So while a local authority can ask others to carry out an actual enquiry, it cannot delegate its responsibility for ensuring that this happens and ensuring that, where necessary, any appropriate action is taken.

18.20. Similarly, it may decide to authorise an external agency to run a contact centre for people to report safeguarding incidents, and manage referrals to the local authority. It may be that the contact centre is not carrying out the local authority's statutory functions (although its activities are related to the functions), and as such the local authority would not require any legal authority to outsource these activities, so may choose to do so.

18.21. Another example is the local authorities' function which allows them discretion over charging people for care and support. The Act does not allow delegation of this decision to other organisations. As such the local authority itself must decide its charging policies. However, local authorities may commission an external agency to carry out the administration, billing and collection of fees for care and support on its behalf. These activities may not be classed as care and support functions under the Care Act, even though they are related to the charging function. It should be noted that the care and support function relating to financial assessments (section 17 of the Act) may be delegated.

CONFLICTS OF INTEREST

18.22. There might be instances where there is the potential for a conflict of interest when delegating functions. For example, when the same external organisation carries out care and support planning, but also provides the resulting care and support that is set out in the plan. Local authorities should consider whether the delegation of its functions could give rise to any potential conflict and should avoid delegating their functions where they deem that there would be an inappropriate conflict.

18.23. Local authorities should consider imposing conditions in their contracts with delegated parties to mitigate against the risk of any potential conflicts. For example, the local authority may choose to delegate care and support planning, but retain the final decision- making, including signing off the amount of the personal budget (see chapter 10 on care and support planning and chapter 11 on personal budgets). Local authorities should also consider including conditions that allow the contract to be revoked at any time, if having authorised an external party to exercise its functions, a conflict becomes apparent.

CONFLICT OF INTEREST RELATING TO MAKING DIRECT PAYMENTS

18.24. The Act places various functions on local authorities relating to the provision of direct payments. These functions include determining whether someone is capable of managing a direct payment, being satisfied that the direct payment is being used in a way that is meeting the person's needs, and monitoring this periodically. Local authorities may choose to delegate these functions. For example, where an authorised external party is carrying out care and support planning, the local authority may decide that the direct payment functions could also usefully be delegated to that party (see chapter 12) for more detail on direct payments.

18.25. The Act also gives local authority the function of making direct payments to people, that is, paying them money to meet their care and support needs. This function may also be delegated to an external party. However, where local authorities delegate their functions relating to assessment of needs or calculation of personal budgets to an external party, they should not allow that same party to make direct payments. In these cases, the actual payment of money should be made directly from the local authority to the adult or carer. This is because it is not appropriate for an external party to determine both how public funds are to be spent, as well as handling and those funds. This is in line with standard anti-fraud practice.[1]

Case Study: delegation of local authority care and support functions

A local Authority has agreed a contract with a local user-led organisation (ULO), to carry out specialist needs assessments and care and support planning for people with learning disabilities. The expertise provided by the ULO allows for better interaction with the people undergoing assessments and a better understanding of their needs, resulting in more accurate and person-centred needs assessments.

The ULO's specialist knowledge of local facilities, befriending groups and employment schemes allows them to broker more personalised care and support planning which allows the person's needs to be met in a number of imaginative ways which support local people with learning disabilities to live independently, improves their wellbeing – and often with less costly care packages.

As part of the delegation, the local authority builds a good working relationship with the ULO, as it needs to monitor how the needs of the adults to whom they have a responsibility are being met. The local authority realises that the ULO has had some difficulty in advising its clients on employment laws for people who are employing personal assistants with their direct payments. The local authority has much experience of providing this type of advice to people with disabilities, and provides support to the ULO to help with this aspect of function.

Through the delegation, the local authority has been able to build its knowledge of specialist resources in its area that it did not previously know about, and has been able to learn about new practices in carrying out assessments and planning care and support packages more imaginatively and efficiently – learning which it is able to apply to other groups of people with care and support needs.

The more personalised assessment and care planning has resulted in fewer reviews of care plans. More people with learning disabilities in the area are supported to live independently for longer which results in better outcomes for them while simultaneously reducing costs to the local authority. The local authority has thus been able to use effective delegation as a way of promoting the wellbeing of its local population.

---

[1] http://webarchive.nationalarchives.gov.uk/20130129110402/
http://www.hm-treasury.gov.uk/psr_managing_risk_of_fraud.htm

19. ORDINARY RESIDENCE

This chapter provides guidance on:
- *Sections 39-41 of the Care Act 2014;*

- *The Care and Support (Ordinary Residence) (Specified Accommodation) Regulations 2014;*
  The Care and Support (Disputes Between Local Authorities.) Regulations 2014

This chapter covers:
- How ordinary residence affects the legal framework in the Care Act;
- How to determine ordinary residence;
- Determining ordinary residence when a person moves into certain types of accommodation out of area;
- Disputes between authorities, and the process for seeking a determination by the Secretary of State for Health or appointed person;
- Further information around ordinary residence and relevant scenarios (see Annexes H1-H8).

19.1. It is critical to the effective operation of the care and support system that local authorities understand for which people they are responsible; and that people themselves know who to contact when they need care and support. Many of the local authority's care and support responsibilities relate to the entire local population (for instance, in relation to information and advice or preventive services). However, when it comes to determining which individuals have needs which a local authority is required to meet, the local authority is only required to meet needs in respect of an adult who is "ordinarily resident" in their area (or is present there but has no settled residence (see paragraph 19.22 below).

19.2. "Ordinary residence" is crucial in deciding which local authority is required to meet the needs in respect of adults with care and support needs and carers. Whether the person is "ordinarily resident" in the area of the local authority is a key test in determining where responsibilities lie between local authorities for the funding and provision of care and support.

19.3. Ordinary residence is not a new concept – it has been used in care and support for many years. However, there have been in the past and will continue to be cases in which it is difficult to establish precisely where a person is ordinarily resident, and this guidance is intended to help resolve such situations. The Care Act also extends the principle of "deeming" certain people to be ordinarily resident in a particular local authority's area when some types of accommodation are arranged for them in another area, and the guidance also describes how these provisions should be put into practice. Local authorities cannot escape the effect of the deeming provision where they are under a duty to provide or to arrange for the provision of services, see paragraph 55 of R(Greenwich) v Secretary of State and Bexley (2006) EWHC 2576.

19.4. This chapter of the guidance should also be read with Annexes H1-H8, which provides further detailed guidance on specific situations and circumstances which may arise, and where the question of ordinary residence may be unclear.

HOW DOES ORDINARY RESIDENCE AFFECT THE PROVISION OF CARE AND SUPPORT?

19.5. Ordinary residence is one of the key tests which must be met to establish whether a local authority is required to meet a person's eligible needs. It is therefore crucial that local authorities establish at the appropriate time whether a person is ordinarily resident in their area, and whether such duties arise.

19.6. The test for ordinary residence, which determines which local authority would be responsible for meeting needs, applies differently in relation to adults with needs for care and support and carers. For adults with care and support needs, the local authority in which the adult is ordinarily resident will be responsible for meeting their eligible needs. For carers, however, the responsible local authority will be the one where the adult for whom they care is ordinarily resident.

19.7. Establishing responsibility for the provision of care and support for carers, therefore, requires the local authority to consider the ordinary residence of the adult needing care. However, there may be some cases where the carer provides care for more than one person in different local authority areas.

19.8. Where there is more than one local authority involved, those authorities should consider how best to cooperate on and share the provision of support. For example, where there are services or interventions that directly relate to the caring responsibilities towards one of the individuals (e.g. equipment installed in the carer's home to accommodate one of the people), then it would be a straightforward matter of the relevant authority being responsible. Where that same piece of equipment serves for both people cared-for, then the local authorities concerned should agree how to arrange the package. There might be an agreement to jointly fund the support for the carer, or the authorities concerned may agree that one takes overall responsibility for certain aspects. For example, one might lead on reviews because it is geographically closer to the carer's home.

19.9. The Act contains all the necessary powers for joint assessments and support planning, plus the duties to co-operate to provide a mechanism for one of the authorities in a case like this, to require the cooperation of the other, if needed.

19.10. Local authorities must determine whether an individual is ordinarily resident in their area following the needs or carer's assessment, and after determining whether the person has eligible needs (see chapter 6). Determining ordinary residence is a key additional requirement in establishing whether the duty to meet needs under section 18 or 20 of the Act is triggered, so this must be taken into consideration when deciding if the local authority is to meet the person's needs.

19.11. The determination of ordinary residence must not delay the process of meeting needs. In cases where ordinary residence is not certain, the local authority should meet the individual's needs first, and then resolve the question of residence subsequently. This is particularly the case where there may be a dispute between two or more local authorities.

HOW TO DETERMINE ORDINARY RESIDENCE

19.12. The local authority's responsibility for meeting a person's eligible needs under the Care Act is based on the concept of "ordinary residence". However, there is no definition of "ordinary residence" in the Act. Therefore, the term should be given its ordinary and natural meaning.

19.13. In most cases, establishing the person's ordinary residence is a straightforward matter. However, this is not always the case. There will be circumstances in which ordinary residence is not as clear cut, for example when people spend their time in more than one area, or move between areas. Where uncertainties arise, local authorities should always consider each case on its own merits.

19.14. The concept of ordinary residence involves questions of both fact and degree. Factors such as time, intention and continuity (each of which may be given different weight according to the context) have to be taken into account. The courts have considered the meaning of "ordinary residence" and the leading case is that of Shah v London Borough of Barnet (1983). In this case, Lord Scarman stated that:

> *'unless . . . it can be shown that the statutory framework or the legal context in which the words are used requires a different meaning I unhesitatingly subscribe to the view that "ordinarily resident" refers to a man's abode in a particular place or country which he has adopted voluntarily and for settled purposes as part of the regular order of his life for the time being, whether of short or long duration.'*

19.15. Local authorities must always have regard to this case when determining the ordinary residence of people who have capacity to make their own decisions about where they wish to live. For people who lack capacity to make decisions about their accommodation, an alternative approach is appropriate because a person's lack of mental capacity may mean that they are not able to voluntarily adopt a particular place.[1]

19.16. Local authorities should in particular apply the principle that ordinary residence is the place the person has voluntarily adopted for a settled purpose, whether for a short or long duration. Ordinary residence can be acquired as soon as the person moves to an area, if their move is voluntary and for settled purposes, irrespective of whether they own, or have an interest in a property in another local authority area. There is no minimum period in which a person has to be living in a particular place for them to be considered ordinarily resident there, because it depends on the nature and quality of the connection with the new place.

CASES WHERE A PERSON LACKS CAPACITY

19.17. All issues relating to mental capacity should be decided with reference to the Mental Capacity Act 2005 ("the 2005 Act").[2] Under this Act, it must be assumed that adults have capacity to make their own decisions, including decisions relating to their accommodation and care, unless it is established to the contrary.

19.18. The test for capacity is specific to each decision at the time it needs to be made, and a person may be capable of making some decisions but not others. It is not necessary for a person to understand local authority funding arrangements to be able to decide where they want to live.

19.19. If it can be shown that a person lacks capacity to make a particular decision, the 2005 Act makes clear who can take decisions on behalf of others,

---

[1] 144

[2] The Mental Capacity Act 2005 Code of Practice
The use of the approach – known as Vale 1, is currently the subject of litigation and the guidance will be amended in due course is available at the following address: http://www.dca.gov.uk/menincap/legis. htm#codeofpractice

in which situations and how they should go about doing this. For example, if a person lacks capacity to decide where to live, a best interests decision about their accommodation should be made under the 2005 Act. Under section 1(5) of the 2005 Act, any act done, or decision made (which would include a decision relating to where a person without capacity should live), must be done in the best interests of the person who lacks capacity. Section 4 of the 2005 Act sets out how to work out the best interests of a person who lacks capacity and provides a check-list of factors for this purpose.

19.20. Where a person lacks the capacity to decide where to live and uncertain-ties arise about their place of ordinary residence, the test in Shah will not assist since it requires the voluntary adoption of a place.

19.21. In the case of a person whose parents are deceased, people who have become ordinarily resident in an area and then lost capacity or have limited con-tact with their parents, the approach known as Vale 2 is appropriate to determine ordinary residence. This involves considering a person's ordinary residence as if they had capacity. All the facts of the person's case must be considered, including physical presence in a particular place and the nature and purpose of that presence but without requiring the person have voluntarily adopted the place of residence.

PEOPLE WITH NO SETTLED RESIDENCE

19.22. Where doubts arise in respect of a person's ordinary residence, it is usually possible for local authorities to decide that the person has resided in one place long enough, or has sufficiently firm intentions in relation to that place, to have acquired an ordinary residence there. Therefore, it should only be in rare circumstances that local authorities conclude that someone is of no set-tled residence. For example, if a person has clearly and intentionally left their previous residence and moved to stay elsewhere on a temporary basis during which time their circumstances change, a local authority may conclude the person to be of no settled residence.

19.23. Sections 18 and 20 of the Care Act make clear that local authorities have a duty to meet the eligible needs of people if they are present in its area but of no settled residence. In this regard, people who have no settled residence, but are physically present in the local authority's area, should be treated the same as those who are ordinarily resident.

19.24. A local authority may conclude that a person arriving from abroad is of no settled residence, including those people who are returning to England after a period of residing abroad and who have given up their previous home in this country. For more details on people returning to England after a period of living abroad, see Annex H6 (British citizens resuming permanent residence in England after a period abroad).

Scenario: persons of no settled residence

David is 20 years old and has a physical disability together with mild learning disabilities. Until four months ago, he lived with his family in local authority A. However, his family relationship broke down and his parents asked him to leave their home for good. They have since changed the locks on their house.

He sought help from local authority A and was placed in a care home for young people with disabilities located in local authority A. This placement was made on a short-term basis until a more permanent solution for David

---

could be found in a supported living type accommodation with his own tenancy. However, David chose to leave the care home after a few weeks and stayed with friends in local authority B for a short period. However, he has recently presented at local authority B seeking accommodation on the basis that he is a destitute adult who is in need of care and attention. Local authority B provides David with care home accommodation but falls into dispute with local authority A over his place of ordinary residence.

Local authority B contends that David remains ordinarily resident in local authority A, given his previous residence there and his recent discharge from their care. Local authority A argues that David has acquired a new ordinary residence in local authority B.

As David is being provided with a type of accommodation by local authority B, as specified by the regulations, S39(1)(a) applies. Therefore, he is deemed to continue to be ordinarily resident in the area in which he was ordinarily resident immediatelybeforethecare home accommodation was provided for him. The day before David presented at local authority B he was staying with friends in that local authority area. His friends made it clear that this was a short-term temporary arrangement, to prevent him becoming homeless upon leaving the care home in local authority A. He had not built up any community ties within the area of local authority B; nor had he chosen to reside in local authority B voluntarily and for settled purposes. Therefore, under the [Shah] test, David has not acquired an ordinary residence in local authority B.

However, nor does it appear that David has retained his ordinary residence in local authority A where he lived with his parents. He left the care home in local authority A intentionally and has no settled residence to which he can return. As David appears not to have been ordinarily resident in either local authority A or local authority B immediately before he presented at local authority B and was provided with accommodation, it is decided that he is a person of no settled residence. Section 18 of the Care Act 2014 makes clear that local authorities have a duty to meet the needs of someone, if they are present in its area but of no settled residence. Local authority B is therefore the authority responsible for David's eligible care and support needs and can therefore treat David as if he were ordinarily resident in their area and provide him with accommodation.

ORDINARY RESIDENCE WHEN ARRANGING ACCOMMODATION IN ANOTHER AREA

19.25. There may be some cases where the local authority considers it appropriate for the person's care and support needs to be met by the provision of accommodation in the area of another authority, in premises which could be a care home or premises that are designated (whether or not specifically designed or adapted for the purpose) for occupation by adults with needs for care and support, to help enable them to adjust to independent living or to live independently.

19.26. In addition to their involvement in the planning process, the person will also have a right to make a choice about their preferred accommodation (see chapter 8 and Annex A about choice of accommodation). This right allows the person to make a choice about a particular individual provider, including where that provider is located. Provided that certain conditions are met, the local authority must arrange for the preferred accommodation. Many people will either require or benefit from the support of an advocate, either under the Care Act or under the Mental Capacity Act. The role of the advocate is to support and represent the person. This may include helping them to make, or to express, a choice. It may include representing their interests when they are unable to engage with the care planning process.

19.27. This will mean that local authorities will in some circumstances arrange accommodation that is located in a different area. In any such case, it should be clear which local authority is responsible for meeting the person's needs in the future.

19.28. Section 39 of the Care Act, and the regulations made under it[1] set out what should happen in these cases, and specify which local authority is responsible for the person's care and support when the person is placed in another authority's area. Together, these create the principle that the person placed 'out of area' is deemed to continue to be ordinarily resident in the area of the first or 'placing' authority, and does not acquire an ordinary residence in the 'host' or second authority. The local authority which arranges the accommodation, therefore, retains responsibility for meeting the person's needs.

19.29. The regulations specify the types of accommodation to which this provision applies. The regulations explicitly set out three types of accommodation:

- nursing homes/care homes – accommodation which includes either nursing care or personal care;

- supported living/extra care housing; this is either;

  - specialist or adapted accommodation: this means accommodation which includes features that have been built in or changed to in order to meet the needs of adults with care and support needs. This may include safety systems and features which enable accessibility and navigation around the accommodation and minimise the risk of harm, as appropriate to the individual; or

  - accommodation which is intended for occupation by adults with care and support needs, in which personal care is also available, usually from a different provider.

  - shared lives schemes: accommodation which is provided together with care and support for an adult by a shared lives carer, approved by the scheme, in the shared lives carer's home under the terms of an agreement between the adult, the scheme the shared lives carer and any local authority responsible for making the arrangement. The shared lives carer will normally be providing personal care but they will not need to provide it in every case.

19.30. Where an adult has needs which can only be met by the provision of one of the specified types of accommodation and the accommodation arranged is in another area, then the principle of "deeming" ordinary residence applies. This means that the adult is treated as remaining ordinarily resident in the area where they were resident before the placement began. The consequence of this

---

[1] The Care and Support (Ordinary Residence) (Specified Accommodation) Regulations.

is that the local authority which arranges the accommodation will remain responsible for meeting the person's eligible needs, and responsibility does not transfer to the authority in whose area the accommodation is physically located. However, in circumstances where the person moves to accommodation of their own volition, without the local authority making the arrangements, their ordinary residence would be where the new accommodation is situated.

19.31. Need should be judged to "only be able to be met" through a specified type of accommodation where the local authority has made this decision following an assessment and a care and support planning process involving the person. Decisions on how needs are to be met, made in the latter process and recorded in the care and support plan, should evidence that needs can only be met in that manner. The local authority must have assessed those needs in order to make such a decision – the "deeming" principle therefore does not apply to cases where a person arranges their own accommodation and the local authority does not meet their needs.

19.32. The first, or placing, local authority's responsibility will continue in this way for as long as the person's eligible needs are met by a specified type of accommodation. This will include situations where the person moves between different specified types of accommodation in another (or more than one other) area.

19.33. As an example, if the first authority places someone in one type of accommodation in the area of the second authority (for example in a shared lives scheme or a care home) and the person's needs change, leading to them moving into another type of accommodation still in the second authority (for example a supported living scheme), the person would continue to be ordinarily resident in the first authority, and that authority would remain responsible for the care and support. However, should the person's needs no longer require a specified type of accommodation, and should the person choose to settle in their own accommodation in the second authority (or another area), then it is likely that their ordinary residence will change, and the first local authority will no longer retain responsibility.

19.34. The ordinary residence "deeming" principle applies most commonly where the local authority provides or arranges the accommodation directly. However, the principle also applies where a person takes a direct payment and arranges their own care (since the local authority is still meeting their needs). In such cases, the individual has the choice over how their needs are met, and arranges their own care and support. If the care plan stipulates that person's needs can be met only if the adult is living in one of the specified types of accommodation and the person chooses to arrange that accommodation[1] in the area of a local authority which is not the one making the direct payments then the same principle would apply; the local authority which is meeting the person's care and support needs by making direct payments would retain responsibility. However, if the person chose accommodation that is outside what was specified in the care plan or of a type of accommodation not specified in the regulations, then the 'deeming' principle would not apply.

19.35. At present, direct payments may not be made to meet needs by the provision of long-term care and support in a care home. However, the individual may request a direct payment to meet needs for other types of accommodation

---

[1] Care and Support (Ordinary Residence) (Specified Accommodation)) Regulations 2014.

specified in the regulations. Where someone chooses a type of supported living accommodation, the direct payment would be for the care but usually not the accommodation. Local authorities should therefore ensure that they have in place effective, proportionate processes for recording how the individual chooses to meet their needs. More information on direct payments can be found in chapter 12.

19.36. If a local authority arranges a type of accommodation as specified in the regulations in another area, or becomes aware that an individual with a direct payment has done so themselves, the authority should inform the host authority, to ensure the host authority is aware of the person in their area. The first authority should ensure that satisfactory arrangements are made before the accommodation begins for any necessary support services which are provided locally, such as day care, and that clear agreements are in place for funding all aspects of the person's care and support.

19.37. In practice, the first local authority may enter into agreements to allow the authority where the accommodation is located to carry out functions on its behalf. This may particularly be the case where the accommodation is located some distance away, and some functions can be performed more effectively locally. For example a carer may live in a different authority from the person he or she is caring for. Local authorities may make arrangements to reimburse to each other, any costs occurred through such agreements. However, local authorities should take account of their on-going obligations towards the individual when arranging for such types of accommodation

19.38. There may be occasions where a provider chooses to change the type of care which it provides, for instance to de-register a property as a care home and to redesign the service as a supported living scheme. Where the person remains living at the same property, and their needs continue to be met by the new service, then ordinary residence should not be affected, and the duty to meet needs will remain with the first authority. This will occur even if the person temporarily moves to another address whilst any changes to the property occur.

NHS ACCOMMODATION

19.39. Where a person goes into hospital, or other NHS accommodation, there may be questions over where they are ordinarily resident, especially if they are subsequently discharged into a different local authority area. For this reason, the Care Act makes clear what should happen in these circumstances.

19.40. A person for whom NHS accommodation is provided is to be treated as being ordinarily resident in the local authority where they were ordinarily resident before the NHS accommodation was provided. This means that where a person, for example, goes into hospital, they are treated as ordinarily resident in the area where they were living before they went into hospital. This applies regardless of the length of stay in the hospital, and means that responsibility for the person's care and support does not transfer to the area of the hospital, if this is different from the area in which the person lived previously.

19.41. This requirement also applies to NHS accommodation in Northern Ireland, Scotland and Wales. If a person who is ordinarily resident in England goes into hospital in Scotland, Wales or Northern Ireland, their ordinary residence will remain in England (in the local authority in which they resided before going into hospital) for the purposes of responsibility for the adult's care and support.

MENTAL HEALTH AFTER-CARE

19.42. Under section 117 of the Mental Health Act 1983, local authorities together with Clinical Commissioning Groups (CCGs)[1] have a joint duty to arrange the provision of mental health after-care services for people who have been detained in hospital for treatment under certain sections of the 1983 Act.[2] After-care services must have both the purposes of "meeting a need arising from or related to the person's mental disorder" and "reducing the risk of a deterioration of the person's mental condition and, accordingly, reducing the risk of the person requiring admission to a hospital again for treatment for mental disorder." The range of services which can be provided is broad.[3]

19.43. The duty on local authorities to commission or provide mental health after-care rests with the local authority for the area in which the person concerned was ordinarily resident immediately before they were detained under the 1983 Act, even if the person becomes ordinarily resident in another area after leaving hospital.

19.44. Although any change in the patient's ordinary residence after discharge will affect the local authority responsible for their social care services, it will not affect the local authority responsible for commissioning the patient's section 117 after-care. As amended by the Care Act 2014, section 117 provides that, if a person is ordinarily resident in local authority area (A) immediately before detention under the 1983 Act, and moves on discharge to local authority area (B) and moves again to local authority area (C), local authority (A) will remain responsible for providing or commissioning their after-care. However, if the patient, having become ordinarily resident after discharge in local authority area (B) or (C), is subsequently detained in hospital for treatment again, the local authority in whose area the person was ordinarily resident immediately before their subsequent admission (local authority (B) or (C)) will be responsible for their after-care when they are discharged from hospital.

19.45. If, however, the patient's ordinary residence immediately before being detained cannot be established, the local authority responsible for commissioning the patient's after- care will be the one for the area in which the patient was resident immediately before being detained under the 1983 Act. Only if that cannot be established,either, will the responsible local authority be the one for the area to which the patient is sent on discharge. However, local authorities should only determine that a person is not resident anywhere as a last resort.

19.46. If there is a dispute between local authorities in England about where the person was ordinarily resident immediately before being detained, this will be determined by the process set out in section 40 of the Care Act 2014. Disputes between a local authority in England and a local authority in Wales will be determined by the Secretary of State for Health or the Welsh Ministers. The Secretary

---

[1] Regulations made under section 117 may impose the duty of a CCG on another CCG or on NHS England instead. At the time of publication, see regulations 14 and 15 of the National Health Service Commissioning Board and Clinical Commissioning Groups (Responsibilities and Standing Rules) Regulations 2012/2996.

[2] These are patients who leave hospital after being detained on the basis of an application under section 3, a hospital order under section 37, or a hospital direction under section 45A, or a transfer direction under section 47 or 48.

[3] For detailed information on mental health after-care see the "Code of Practice Mental Health Act 1983".

of State and the Welsh Ministers shall publish arrangements for determining which of them will determine such disputes.

OTHER COMMON SITUATIONS
Temporary absences

19.47. Having established ordinary residence in a particular place, this should not be affected by the individual taking a temporary absence from the area.151 The courts have held that temporary or accidental absences, including for example holidays or hospital visits in another area,152 should not break the continuity of ordinary residence, and local authorities should take this into account.

19.48. The fact that the person may be temporarily away from the local authority in which they are ordinarily resident, does not preclude them from receiving any type of care and support from another local authority if they become in urgent need (see Annex H1 for further guidance regarding persons in "urgent need"). Local authorities have powers in the Care Act to meet the needs of people who are known to be ordinarily resident in another area, at their discretion and subject to their informing the authority where the person is ordinarily resident.

People with more than one home

19.49. Although in general terms it may be possible for a person to have more than one ordinary residence (for example, a person who divides their time equally between two homes), this is not possible for the purposes of the Care Act 2014. The purpose of the ordinary residence test in the Act is to determine which single local authority has responsibility for meeting a person's eligible needs, and this purpose would be defeated if a person could have more than one ordinary residence.

19.50. If a person appears genuinely to divide their time equally between two homes, it would be necessary to establish (from all of the circumstances) to which of the two homes the person has the stronger link. Where this is the case, it would be the responsibility of the local authority in whose area the person is ordinarily resident, to provide or arrange care and support to meet the needs during the time the person is temporarily away at their second home.

19.51. Further scenarios which may occur are set out in Annex H, and may be used by local authorities to support cases where there may be uncertainty as to an individual's ordinary residence.

People who arrange and fund their own care

19.52. People who self-fund and arrange their own care and choose to move to another area, and then find that their funds have depleted, can apply to the local authority area that they have moved to in order to have their needs assessed. If it is decided that they have eligible needs for care and support, the person's ordinary residence will be in the place where they moved to and not the first authority. Further information regarding self-funders is at annex H4.

RESOLVING ORDINARY RESIDENCE AND CONTINUITY OF CARE DISPUTES

19.53. In the majority of cases, determining ordinary residence should be straightforward. However, there will be occasions where a person's residency status is more complicated to establish.

19.54. A question as to a person's ordinary residence can only arise where two or more local authorities are in dispute about the place of ordinary residence of a person. In such a case, the authorities may apply for a determination to the Secretary of State or appointed person. Where the local authorities concerned are in agreement about a person's ordinary residence, but the person is unhappy with the decision, the person would have to pursue this with the authorities concerned and could not apply to the Secretary of State or an appointed person for a determination.

19.55. The Care and Support (Disputes Between Local Authorities) Regulations 2014 (the regulations), set out the procedures local authorities must follow when disputes arise between local authorities regarding a person's ordinary residence. When a dispute between two or more local authorities occurs, local authorities must take all reasonable steps to resolve the dispute between themselves. It is critical that the person does not go without the care they need, should local authorities be in dispute. The local authority that is meeting the needs of the adult or the carer on the date that the dispute arises, must continue to do so until the dispute is resolved. If no local authority is currently meeting the person's needs, then the local authority where the person is living or is physically present must accept responsibility until the dispute is resolved. The local authority which has accepted provisional responsibility is referred to as the "the lead authority".

19.56. The lead authority must identify all the authorities involved in the dispute and co- ordinate an ongoing dialogue between all parties involved. The parties involved must provide the lead authority with contact details of a named person in relation to the dispute. The lead authority must be responsible for the co-ordination of any information that may be relevant to the dispute and keep all parties informed of any developments that may be relevant to the dispute. The lead authority must also keep the person, or their carer if appropriate, fully informed of dispute in question and of progress regarding any resolution.

19.57. If, having taken appropriate legal advice and considered the position, and followed the procedure set out in the disputes regulations, the authorities are still unable to resolve a particular dispute, they must apply for a determination to the Secretary of State or appointed person. Applications for determinations must be submitted by the lead authority before or by the end of a period of four months from the date when the dispute arose. The provisional acceptance of responsibility by the lead authority will not influence any determination made by the Secretary of State.

PROCESS FOR SEEKING A DETERMINATION

19.58. The regulations place a duty on the parties involved in the dispute to provide specified information to the Secretary of State or appointed person. The lead local authority **must** make a request in writing to the Secretary of State or appointed person , together with a statement of facts and other documentation. The statement of facts must include certain specified information as set out in the regulations. Local authorities should endeavour to produce a statement of facts that is jointly agreed. If the parties cannot agree on particular information, they should make clear what information the parties say is agreed, what information the parties say is in dispute and, as regards the latter, what the parties' respective versions of the facts are. Local authorities should ensure that all documents sent to the Secretary of State or appointed person are in an indexed paginated bundle. Copies of any further document required will need to be added to the index for insertion into the bundle.

19.59. The Secretary of State or appointed person will not allow ordinary residence disputes to run on indefinitely once they have been referred for a determination. The Secretary of State – or appointed person – once satisfied that the parties have had adequate opportunities to make representations, will proceed to make a determination. Any local authority failing to have due regard to a determination by the Secretary of State or appointed person, would put itself at risk of a legal challenge by the resident or their representative or the other local authorities to the dispute.

19.60. Local authorities may wish to seek legal advice before making an application for a determination, although they are not required to do so. If legal advice is sought, local authorities may, in addition to the required documentation, provide a separate legal submission. Where legal submissions are included, these should be exchanged between the local authorities in dispute and evidence of this should be supplied to the Secretary of State. All applications for Secretary of State determinations should be sent to the Department of Health at the address below:

Department of Health Quality and Safety Team
Social Care Policy Division
Area 313B, Richmond House, 79 Whitehall
London SW1A 2NS

19.61. If during a determination of the ordinary residence dispute by the Secretary of State or appointed person, a local authority in dispute is asked to provide further information to the Secretary of State or appointed person, that local authority must provide that information without delay.

19.62. If the local authorities involved in the dispute reach an agreement whilst the Secretary of State is considering the determination, they should notify the Department of Health at the above address. Both parties must confirm that the dispute has been resolved after which the determination will be closed down.

19.63. If a determination by the Secretary of State or an appointed person subsequently finds another local authority to be the authority of ordinary residence, the lead local authority can recover costs from the authority which should have been providing the relevant care and support.

19.64. The Department of Health makes available anonymised copied of determinations it has made.[1] Although these do not set a precedent, as each case must be considered in light of its own particular facts, they may provide local authorities with useful guidance when faced with similar circumstances.

19.65. Disputes about a person's ordinary residence in connection with section 117 arising between a local authority in England and a local authority in Wales, can be referred to the Secretary of State, or Welsh Ministers for determination. The Secretary of State and the Welsh Ministers shall publish arrangements for determining which of them will determine such disputes.

19.66. As set out in Chapter 23 – Transition to the New Framework, provision will be made to deal with transitional issues related to ordinary residence disputes. Thus, for example, any dispute regarding ordinary residence that occurs and is submitted before April 2015 is likely to be considered under the old regulations.

---

[1] https://www.gov.uk/government/collections/ordinary-residence-pages

We will set out more detail around this in transitional provisions to be published early next year.

FINANCIAL ADJUSTMENTS BETWEEN LOCAL AUTHORITIES

19.67. Sometimes a local authority has been paying for a person's care and support, but it later becomes apparent (for example as a result of an ordinary residence determination) that the person is in fact ordinarily resident elsewhere. In these circumstances the local authority which has been paying for that person's care can reclaim the costs from the local authority where the person was ordinarily resident.

19.68. This can occur in cases where it is not clear initially where the person is ordinarily resident. In order to ensure that the individual does not experience any delay to their care due to uncertainty over their ordinary residence, local authorities should be able to recover any losses due to initial errors or delays in deciding where a person is ordinarily resident. This also extends to costs spent supporting the carer of the person whose ordinary residence was in dispute.

RECONSIDERING DISPUTES

19.69. If further facts come to light after a determination has been made, it may be appropriate for the Secretary of State or appointed person to reconsider the original determination. As a consequence of this, a different determination may be substituted. This may mean that payments made from one authority to another as a consequence of the first determination will need to be repaid.

19.70. Any review of the determination must begin within three months of the date of the original determination. This is needed to ensure clarity and fairness in the process and minimise the amount of time taken for determinations to be made.

20. CONTINUITY OF CARE

This section provides guidance on:
- *Sections 37-38 of the Care Act 2014;*
- *The Care and Support (Continuity of Care) Regulations 2014.*

This chapter covers:
- Making an informed decision to move to a different local authority; confirming intention to move; supporting people to be fully involved in the process;
- What local authorities take into account when they are planning the move with people;
- How to ensure continuity of the person's care if the second local authority has not carried out an assessment ahead of the day of the move;
- What happens if a person does not move.

20.1. People with care and support needs may decide to move home just like anyone else, such as to be closer to family or to pursue education or employment opportunities, or because they want to live in another area. Where they do decide to move to a new area and as a result their ordinary residence status changes (see chapter 19 on ordinary residence), it is important to ensure that care and support is in place during the move, so the person's wellbeing is maintained.

20.2. In circumstances where a person is receiving local authority support and moves within their current local authority (for example, moving between homes in the same area), they would remain ordinarily resident within that authority and it must continue to meet their needs. Where the person chooses to live in a different local authority area, the local authority that is currently arranging care and support and the authority to which they are moving must work together to ensure that there is no interruption to the person's care and support.

20.3. The continuity of care chapter sets out the process local authorities must follow to ensure that the person's care and support continue, without disruption, during and after the move. These procedures also apply where the person's carer is receiving support and will continue to care for adult after they have moved. In addition to meeting their responsibilities in these sections, authorities are reminded that the other requirements of Part 1 of the Act apply during this process, and authorities should refer to the guidance on wellbeing, prevention, information and advice, integration, assessment and eligibility, and care and support planning.

20.4. The aim of this process is to ensure that the person with care and support needs will be able to move with the confidence that arrangements to meet their needs will be in place on the day of the move. Local authorities are expected to achieve continuity of care by ensuring that the second authority has completed a needs assessment and care and support plan of the individual prior to the day of the move. It is possible that the second local authority might be unable to complete a needs assessment prior to the day of the move due to the logistics of assessing a person a long distance away or because they want to assess the adult in their new home. If the second authority has not carried out the assessment prior to the move, it must continue to meet the needs and take into account outcomes identified in the adult's current care and support plan until it has carried out its own assessment.

20.5. The key to ensuring that the adult's care is continued is through both local authorities working together and that the adult and their carer, if they are continuing to care for the adult, are at the centre of the process.

DEFINITIONS

20.6. For the purpose of this chapter the following meaning applies:

- 'Adult' means the person who needs care and support, and is or is intending to move to another authority.

- 'Carer(s)' refers to any carer(s) that the person may have who has decided to continue to care for the adult after they have moved to the new area.

- 'New carer' refers to any new person who will take over the caring role when the adult moves to the new area.

- 'Person' or 'individual' refer to both the adult needing care and support and the carer.

- 'First authority' means the local authority where the person lives and is ordinarily resident prior to moving.

- 'Second authority' means the local authority the person is wishing to move to.

- 'Assessment' refers to both a needs assessment and a carer's assessment.

MAKING AN INFORMED DECISION TO MOVE TO A DIFFERENT LOCAL AUTHORITY

20.7. When contemplating the possibility of moving, an adult may want to find out information about the care and support available in one or more authorities. Local authorities may already make much of this information publicly available in accordance with its general duties under the Care Act (see chapter 3), and they should provide any extra information requested by the adult and where relevant, their carer.

20.8. Local authorities can provide the adult and their carer with relevant information or advice to help inform their decision. When providing relevant information and advice, local authorities should guard against influence over the final decision. The authorities can, for example, provide advice on the implications for the individual's care and support (and their carer's support), but the final decision on whether or not to move is for the adult and, if relevant, the carer to make.

20.9. The prompt provision of this information will help the adult make an informed decision and assist the process if the adult decides that they want to move.

CONFIRMING THE INTENTION TO MOVE

20.10. The continuity of care process starts when the second authority is notified of the adult's intention to move. Local authorities may find out about the person's intention to move from the individual directly or through someone acting on their behalf, who may contact either the first authority or the second authority to tell them of their intentions. If the person has approached the first authority and informed them of their intention to move, the first authority should make contact with the second authority to tell them that the person is planning on moving to their area.

20.11. When the person has confirmed their intention to move with the second authority, the authority must assure itself that the person's intention is genuine. This is because the duties in the Act flow from this point.

20.12. To assure itself that the intention is genuine, the second authority should:

- establish and maintain contact with the person and their carer to keep abreast of their intentions to move;

- continue to speak with the first authority to get their view on the person's intentions;

- ask if the person has any information or contacts that can help to establish their intention.

20.13. When the second authority is satisfied that the person's intentions to move are genuine, it must provide the adult and the carer if also intending to move, with accessible information about the care and support available in its area. This should include but is not limited to, details about:

20.14. the types of care and support available to people with similar needs, so the adult can know how they are likely to be affected by differences in the range of services available:

- support for carers;

- the local care market and organisations that could meet their needs;

- the local authority's charging policy, including any charges which the person may be expected to meet for particular services in that area.

20.15. Where the person moving currently receives a direct payment to meet some or all of their needs, the first authority should advise the person that they will need to consider how to meet any contractual arrangements put in place for the provision of their care and support. For instance, any contracts a person may have with personal assistants who may not be moving with them.

SUPPORTING PEOPLE TO BE FULLY INVOLVED

20.16. The person may request assistance from either the first or second authority in helping them understand the implications of their move on their care and support, and the authority should ensure that they have access to all relevant information and advice. This should include consideration of the need for an independent advocate in helping the person to weigh up their options (see chapter 7 on advocacy).

20.17. There will be situations where the adult may lack capacity to make a decision about a move, but the family wish to move the adult closer to where they live.

20.18. The local authority must in these situations first carry out supported decision making, supporting the adult to be as involved as possible and must carry out a capacity assessment and where necessary then take "best interests" decisions. The requirements of the Mental Capacity Act 2005 apply to all those who may lack capacity.

PREPARING FOR THE MOVE

20.19. Once the second authority has assured itself that the adult's and where relevant the carer's intentions to move are genuine, it must inform the first authority. At this stage, both authorities should identify a named staff member to lead on the case and be the ongoing contact during the move. These contacts should make themselves known to the person and lead on the sharing of information and maintaining contact on progress towards arranging the care and support for the adult and support for the carer. These contacts should be jointly responsible for facilitating continuity of care within an acceptable timeframe, taking into consideration the circumstances behind the adult's intention to move, such as a job opportunity.

20.20. The second authority must provide the adult and carer with any relevant information that it did not supply when the person was considering whether to move.

20.21. When the first authority has been notified by the second authority that it is satisfied that the person's intention to move is genuine, the first authority must provide it with:

- a copy of the person's most recent care and support plan;

- a copy of the most recent support plan where the person's carer is moving with them; and

- any other information relating to the person or the carer (whether or not the carer has needs for support), that the second authority may request.

20.22. The information the second authority may request may include the most recent needs assessment if the person's needs are not likely to change as a result of the move, the adult's financial assessment, any safeguarding plan that have been completed for the individual, and, where a Deprivation of Liberty has been authorised for a person who is moving to a new local authority area, then a new referral for a Deprivation of Liberty must be made to the new local authority.[1]

PEOPLE RECEIVING SERVICES UNDER CHILDREN'S LEGISLATION

20.23. The continuity of care provisions will not apply for people receiving services under children's legislation. Where such a person has had a transition assessment (see chapter 16) but is moving area before the actual transition to adult care and support takes place, the first local authority should ensure that the second is provided with a copy of the assessment and any resulting transition plan. Similarly, where a child's carer is having needs met by adult care and support in advance of the child turning 18 (following a transition assessment), the first local authority should ensure that the second is provided with a copy of the assessment and the carer's support plan.

---

[1] More detail can be found in Deprivation Of Liberty Safeguards, Mental Capacity Act 2005 Code of Practice.

ASSESSMENT AND CARE AND SUPPORT PLANNING

20.24. If the person has substantial difficulty and requires help to be fully involved in the assessment or care planning process and there is no other suitable person who can support them, the Act requires that they must be provided with an independent advocate. In this case the advocate should be provided by the second authority because it takes over the responsibility for carrying out the assessment and care planning with the individual (see chapter 7).

20.25. The second authority must contact the adult and the carer to carry out an assessment and to discuss how arrangements might be made. The second authority should also consider whether the person might be moving to be closer to a new carer and whether that new carer would benefit from an assessment.

20.26. Throughout the assessment process, the first authority must keep in contact with the second authority about progress being made towards arranging necessary care and support for the day of the move. The first authority must also keep the adult and the carer informed and involved of progress so that they have confidence in the process. This should include involving them in any relevant meetings about the move. Meetings may not always be face-to-face where there are long distances between the local authorities involved. Having this three-way contact will keep the individuals at the centre of the process, and help ensure that arrangements are in place on the day of the move.

20.27. All assessments, for adults with care and support needs and carers, must be carried out in line with the processes described in chapter 6 of this guidance. The adult and the carer, and anyone else requested, must be involved in the respective assessments. The assessments must identify the person's needs and the outcomes they want to achieve. These could be the same as the outcomes the first authority was meeting or they could have changed with the person's circumstances.

20.28. The assessment must consider whether any preventative services or advice and information would help either person meet those outcomes. The assessments should also consider the individuals' own strengths and capabilities and whether support might be available from family, friends or within the new community to achieve their outcomes. In carrying out the assessments, the second authority must take into account the previous care and support plan (or support plan) which has been provided by the first authority.

20.29. Following the assessment and after determining whether the adult or carer has eligible needs, the second authority must involve the adult, the carer and any other individual the person requests, in the development of their care and support plan, or the carer's support plan as relevant, and take all reasonable steps to agree the plan. The development of the care and support plan or carer's support plan should include consideration of whether the person would like to receive a direct payment. Further guidance on care and support planning is provided in chapter 10.

20.30. The second authority should agree the adult's care and support plan and carer's support plan, including any personal budget, in advance of the move to ensure that arrangements are in place when the person moves into the new area. This should be shared with the individuals before the move so that they are clear how their needs will be met, and this must also set out any differences between the person's original plan and their new care and support or support plan. Such differences could arise where the range of services in one local authority differs from the range of services in another. The second authority must also explain to the adult or carer where there are any differences in their needs.

20.31. The care and support plan should include arrangements for the entire day of the move. This should be agreed by the adult, the carers (existing and new as relevant) and both authorities. The first authority should remain responsible for meeting the care and support needs the person has in their original home and when moving. The second authority is responsible for providing care and support when the person and their carer move in to the new area. The person moving is responsible for organising and paying for moving their belongings and furniture to their new home.

20.32. In considering the person's personal budget, the second authority should take into consideration any differences between the costs of making arrangements in the second authority compared with the first authority and provide explanation for such a difference where relevant. Where there is a difference in the amount of the personal budget, this should be explained to the person. It should also look to ensure that the person's direct payment is in place in a timely manner, for example, the person moving may have a personal assistant that is also moving and will requiring paying.

INTEGRATION

20.33. The adult and their carer may have health needs as well as care and support needs. Both local authorities should work with their local Clinical Commissioning Groups (CCGs) to ensure that all of the adult's and carer's health and care needs are being dealt with in a joined up way. Guidance to CCGs is set out in *Who Pays*.[1]

20.34. If the person also has health needs, the second authority should carry out the assessment jointly with their local CCG. Alternatively, if the CCG agrees, the second authority can carry out the assessment on its behalf. Having a joint assessment ensures that all of the person's needs are being assessed and the second authority can work together with the CCG to prepare a joint plan to meet the adult's care and support and health needs. Where relevant, the local authority may use the cooperation procedures set out in the Care Act to require cooperation from the CCG, or other relevant partners, in supporting with the move. More detail on these procedures is set out in chapter 15.

20.35. Providing joint care and support and health plans will avoid duplication of processes and the need for multiple monitoring regimes. Information should be shared as quickly as possible with the minimum of bureaucracy. Local authorities should work alongside health and other professionals where plans are developed jointly to establish a 'lead' organisation which undertakes monitoring and assurance of the combined plan. Consideration should be given to whether a person should receive a personal budget and a personal health budget to upport integration of services. More information about personal health budgets can be found in chapter 11.

EQUIPMENT AND ADAPTATIONS

20.36. Many people with care and support needs will also have equipment installed and adaptations made to their home. Where the first authority has provided equipment, it should move with the person to the second authority where

---

[1] NHS England (2013) *Who Pays? Determining Responsibility for Payments to Providers.*

this is the person's preference and it is still required and doing so is the most cost-effective solution. This should apply whatever the original cost of the item. In deciding whether the equipment should move with the person, the local authorities should discuss this with the individual and consider whether they still want it and whether it is suitable for their new home. Consideration will also have to be given to the contract for maintenance of the equipment and whether the equipment is due to be replaced.

20.37. As adaptations are fitted based on the person's accommodation, it may be more practicable for the second authority to organise the installation of any adaptations. For example, walls need to be checked for the correct fixing of rails.

20.38. Where the person has a piece of equipment on long-term loan from the NHS, the second local authority should discuss with the relevant NHS body. The parties are jointly responsible for ensuring that the person has adequate equipment when they move (see chapter 15 on cooperation and integration).

COPY OF DOCUMENTATION

20.39. The second authority must provide the adult and the carer and anyone else requested with a copy of their assessments. This must include a written explanation where it has assessed the needs as being different to those in the care and support plan or the carer's support plan provided by the first authority. The second authority must also provide a written explanation if the adult's or carer's personal budget is different to that provided by the first authority.

WHAT HAPPENS IF THE SECOND AUTHORITY HAS NOT CARRIED OUT AN ASSESSMENT BEFORE THE DAY OF THE MOVE?

20.40. The second local authority is generally expected to have carried out their needs assessment of the persons moving prior to the day of the move. However, there may be occasions where the authority has not carried out the assessments or has completed the assessments but has not made arrangements to have support in place. This might happen where the second authority wants to assess the person in their new home and consider if their needs have changed, for example because they have started a new job or are now in education, or they have moved to be closer to family. The second authority must still have made contact with the adult and their carer in advance of the move.

20.41. Where the full assessment has not taken place prior to the move, the second authority must put in place arrangements that meet the adult's or carer's needs for care and support as identified by the first authority. These arrangements must be in place on the day of the move and continue until the second authority has carried out its own assessment and put in place a care and support plan which has been developed with the person (see chapter 6-10).

20.42. The second authority must involve the adult and carer, and any relevant independent advocate, as well as any other individual that either person may request, when deciding how to meet the care and support needs in the interim period. The authority must take all reasonable steps to agree these temporary arrangements with the relevant person.

MATTERS LOCAL AUTHORITIES MUST HAVE REGARD TO WHEN MAKING ARRANGEMENTS

20.43. The Care and Support (Continuity of Care) Regulations 2014 require the second authority to have regard to the following matters when meeting the person's needs in advance of carrying out their own assessment:

- **Care and support plan:** The adult's care and support plan, and the carer's support plan if the carer is also moving, which were provided by the first authority. The second authority should discuss with the adult and the carer how to meet their eligible needs and any other needs that the first authority was meeting that are not deemed as eligible but were included in either plan.

- **Outcomes:** Whether the outcomes that the adult and the carer were achieving in day-to- day life in their first authority are the outcomes they want to achieve in the new authority, or whether their aims have changed because of the move.

- **Preferences and views:** The preferences and views of the adult and the carer on how their needs are met during the interim period.

20.44. The second authority must also consider any significant difference to the person's circumstances where that change may impact on the individual's well-being, including:

- Support from a carer: Whether the adult is currently receiving support from a carer and whether that carer is also moving with them. Where the carer is not moving the second authority must consider how to meet any needs previously met by the carer, even if the first authority was not providing any service in relation to those needs.

- Suitability of accommodation: Where the new accommodation is significantly different from the original accommodation and this changes the response needed to meet the needs. For example, the adult may move from a ground floor flat to a first floor flat and now need assistance to manage stairs.

- Where the person has received equipment or had adaptations installed in their original home by the first authority, the procedures as set out in paragraphs 20.36-20.39 should be followed.

- Access to services and facilities: Where the services and facilities in the new area are different, and in particular fewer than those in the originating area; for example access to food deliveries or other food outlets, access to public transport, or access to leisure or recreational facilities, the person's workplace. A move from an urban to a rural environment could bring this about.

- Access to other types of support: Where the person was receiving support from friends, neighbours or the wider community and this may not readily be available in their new area.

- Where the person makes use of universal services such as local authority day services, drop in support, or befriending schemes, and these are not available in the new area.

20.45. If the person has substantial difficulty in being fully involved in the assessment, care planning or review process the second authority should consider whether the person needs an independent advocate or whether their original advocate is moving with them (see chapter 7 on advocacy).

20.46. The second authority should ascertain this information from relevant documentation sent to them or by talking to the individuals involved, and the first authority.

20.47. The adult or carer should not be on an interim care and support (or support) package for a prolonged period of time as a tailored care and support (or support) plan must be put in place. The second authority should carry out the assessment in a timely manner.

WHEN THE ADULT DOES NOT MOVE OR THE MOVE IS DELAYED

20.48. There are a range of reasons why a person might not move on the designated day. This may be, for example, because they have become unwell, there has been a delay in exchanging contracts. Where there has been a delay because of unforeseen circumstances, both authorities should maintain contact with the person to ensure that arrangements are in place for the new date of the move.

20.49. If the person's move is delayed and they remain resident in the area of the first authority, they will normally continue to be ordinarily resident in that area and so the first authority will remain responsible for meeting the person's and the carer's needs. Both local authorities may have incurred some expense in putting arrangements in place before the move was delayed. In such circumstances each of the authorities should consider agreeing to cutting their losses incurred in preparing continuity of care.

20.50. In circumstances where the second authority has not assessed the person prior to the move and is planning to meet needs based on their original care and support plan, but it transpires that the individual does not move to the second authority (and so the first authority remains responsible for providing care and support), the Care Act does provide for the second authority to be able to recover any costs it incurred from the first authority. In deciding whether to recover these costs the second authority may want to consider, for example, whether the first authority was aware that the person was not going to move and had not told the second authority or whether the first authority was not aware and was unable to advise the second authority not to make arrangements. The second authority should consider whether it would be reasonable to recover their costs depending on the circumstances of the case.

DISPUTES ABOUT ORDINARY RESIDENCE AND CONTINUITY OF CARE

20.51. Where local authorities are in dispute over application of the continuity of care provisions, the authorities who are parties to the dispute must not allow their dispute to prevent, delay or adversely affect the meeting of the person's needs. Where the authorities cannot resolve their differences, the steps described in chapter 19 on ordinary residence disputes must be taken to ensure that the person is unaffected by the dispute and will continue to receive care for the needs that were identified by the first local authority.

MAKING COMPLAINTS

20.52. It is important that individuals have confidence in the assessment process and the wider care and support system. Therefore any individual should be able to make a complaint and challenge decisions where they believe a wrong decision has been made in their case. Current complaints provision for care and support is set out in regulations Local Authority Social Services and NHS Complaints Regulations 2009, made under powers in Sections 113 to 115 of the Health and Social Care (Community Health and Standards Act) 2003. The provisions of the regulations mean that anyone who is dissatisfied with a decision made by the local authority would be able to make a complaint about that decision and have that complaint handled by the local authority. The local authority must make its own arrangements for dealing with complaints in accordance with the Local Authority Social Services and National Health Service (England) Complaints Regulations 2009 No. 309.

21. CROSS-BORDER PLACEMENTS

This chapter provides guidance on:
- *Section 39 of and Schedule 1 to the Care Act 2014;*
- *The Care and Support (Cross-border Placements and Business Failure: Temporary Duty) (Dispute Resolution) Regulations 2014.*

This chapter covers:
- Local authorities' (in Northern Ireland, Health and Social Care (HSC) Trusts') responsibilities with respect to placing individuals into care home accommodation in different territories of the UK;
- Those matters local authorities (or HSC Trusts) should have regard to when considering, planning and carrying out a cross-border placement;
- Process for resolving disputes that may arise in relation to a cross-border placement.

DEFINITIONS

21.1. First authority – the local authority (or Health and Social Care (HSC) Trust in Northern Ireland) which places the individual in a cross-border residential placement.

21.2. Second authority – that local authority (or HSC Trust) into whose area the individual is placed or to be placed.

PRINCIPLES AND PURPOSE OF CROSS-BORDER PLACEMENTS

Purpose

21.3. People's health and wellbeing are likely to be improved if they are close to a support network of friends and family. In a small number of cases an individual's friends and family may be located in a different country of the UK from that in which they reside.

21.4. In the production of a care and support plan,[1] the authority[2] and the individual concerned may reach the conclusion that the individual's wellbeing is best achieved by a placement into care home in a different country of the UK. Schedule 1 to the Care Act sets out certain principles governing cross-border residential care placements.

21.5. As a general rule, responsibility for individuals who are placed in cross-border residential care remains with the first authority. This guidance sets out how the first and second authorities should work together in the interests of individuals receiving care and support through a cross-border residential placement.

Principles

21.6. The four administrations of the UK (England, Scotland, Wales and Northern Ireland) have worked together to agree Schedule 1 and this

---

[1] In Wales, the requirement to prepare a care and support plan will be commenced under the Social Services and Well-being (Wales) Act in April 2016. Until then, references in this document to "care and support plans" should be understood to refer to existing care management arrangements.

[2] Authority = Local Authority in England, Wales and Scotland. HSC Trust in Northern Ireland

ask the authority to involve others, any person who appears to the authority to be interested in the individual's welfare. In involving the individual, the authority should (and in England must) take all reasonable steps to reach agreement with the individual about how the authority should meet the needs in question.

21.21. The individual should be kept informed and involved throughout the process. Their views on suitable providers should be sought and their agreement checked before a final decision is made. The benefits of advocacy in supporting the individual to express their wishes should be considered throughout and relevant duties met (see earlier chapter on advocacy).

21.22. The individual should also be informed of the likelihood of the first authority giving notification of the placement to the second authority, seeking that authority's assistance with management of the placement or with discharge of other functions, for example reviews, and of what this would involve. Where, for example, this would involve the sharing of information or the gathering of information by the second authority on behalf of the first, (see next section) the individual should be informed of this at the outset and their consent sought.

21.23. Authorities should strive to offer people a choice of placements.[1]

Step two: initial liaison between "first" and "second" authority

21.24. Once the placement has been agreed in principle (with the individual concerned and/or their representative) and the authority has identified a potential provider they should immediately contact the authority in whose area the placement will be made.

21.25. The first authority should:

- notify the second authority of their intention to make a cross-border residential care placement;

- provide a provisional date on which they intend for the individual concerned to commence their placement;

- provide the second authority with details of the proposed care provider;

- seek that authority's views on the suitability of the residential accommodation.

21.26. The initial contact can be made by telephone, but should be confirmed in writing.

21.27. The second authority has no power to "block" a residential care placement into its area as the first authority contracts directly with the provider. In the event of the second authority objecting to the proposed placement, all reasonable steps should be taken by the first authority to resolve the issues concerned before making the placement.

21.28. Following the initial contact and any subsequent discussions (and provided no obstacles to the placement taking place have been identified) the first authority should write to the second authority confirming the conclusions of the discussions and setting out a timetable of key milestones up to the placement commencing.

---

[1] See section 9(5) of the Act as to the duties on English local authorities to involve persons in carrying out needs assessments the adult wishes to achieve.

21.29. The first authority should inform the provider that the placement is proposed – in the same way as with any care home placement. The first authority should ensure that the provider is aware that this will be a cross-border placement.

21.30. The first authority should contact the individual concerned and/or their representative to confirm that the placement can go ahead and to seek their final agreement. The first authority should also notify any family/friends that the individual has given permission and/ or requested to be kept informed.

21.31. The first authority should make all those arrangements that it would normally make in organising a residential care placement in its own area.

Step three: arrangements for ongoing management of placement

21.32. A key necessity is for the first authority to consider with the second authority, arrangements for the on-going management of the placement and assistance with the performance of relevant care and support functions.

21.33. The first authority will retain responsibility for the individual and the management and review of their placement. In this regard, the authority's responsibilities to the individual are no different than they would be if the individual was placed with a provider in the authority's own area.

21.34. However, it is recognised that the practicalities of day-to-day management of a placement potentially hundreds of miles distant from the authority may prove difficult.

21.35. As such, the first authority may wish to make arrangements for the second authority to assist with the day-to-day placement management functions for example where urgent in-person liaison is required with the provider and/or individual concerned, or with regular care reviews which are for the first authority to perform (in accordance with its statutory obligations),[1] but with which the second authority may be able to assist (e.g. by gathering information necessary for the review and passing this to the first authority to make a decision).

21.36. It should be made clear that ultimate responsibility for exercising the functions remains with the first authority (they are obtaining assistance with the performance of these functions or, where applicable, authorising the exercise of functions on their behalf).

21.37. Any such arrangement should be detailed in writing – being clear as to what role the second authority is to play and for how long. Clarity should also be provided on the regularity of any reporting to the first authority and any payment involved for services provided by the second authority.

Step four: confirmation of placement

21.38. When the placement has been confirmed, the first authority should notify the second authority and detail in writing all the arrangements made with the second authority for assistance with on-going placement management and other matters. The first authority should also confirm the date at which the placement will begin.

21.39. The second authority should acknowledge receipt of these documents/ information and give its agreement to the arrangements in writing.

---

[1] See section 27 of the Act as to the review of care and support plans by English local authorities. See section 79 as to delegation of functions by such authorities and the chapter in this guidance on delegation.

21.40. The first authority should provide the individual concerned and/or their representative with contact details (including whom to contact during an emergency) for both the first and second authority. If required, it is expected that the first authority will be responsible for organising suitable transport, and for the costs of it, to take the individual and their belongings to their new placement.

21.41. As would be the case normally, the first authority will normally be responsible for closing off previous placements or making other necessary arrangements regarding the individual's prior residence.

OTHER ISSUES TO BE CONSIDERED DURING THE ORGANISATION OF A PLACEMENT

Timeliness of organising and making a placement

21.42. Steps one to four should be conducted in a timely manner; the time taken should be proportionate to the circumstances.

Self-arranged placements

21.43. This guidance does not apply in relation to individuals who arrange their own care. Individuals who arrange and pay for their own care will normally become ordinarily resident in and/or the responsibility of the area to which they move. This guidance does apply to individuals who pay for their own care where that care is arranged by an authority.

ISSUES THAT MAY ARISE ONCE A PLACEMENT HAS COMMENCED

Where the individual requires a stay in NHS accommodation

21.44. Should the individual placed cross-border need to go into NHS accommodation[1] for any period of time then this stay will not interrupt the position regarding ordinary residence or responsibility deemed under Schedule 1.

21.45. If, while the individual is in NHS accommodation, a "retention" fee is payable to the care provider to ensure the individual's place is secured, this will be the responsibility of the first authority.

Where the individual requires NHS-funded nursing care

21.46. Should the individual being placed require NHS-funded nursing care, the arrangements for delivering this should be discussed between the first authority, the NHS body delivering the care, the NHS body funding the care and the care provider prior to the placement commencing. Early (indeed advance) engagement with the NHS in such circumstances is important in ensuring smooth and integrated provision of services in cross-border placements.

21.47. Where the need for nursing care becomes evident after the placement has commenced, the relevant authorities should work together to ensure this is provided without delay.

21.48. The four administrations of the UK have reached separate bilateral agreements as to which administration shall bear the cost of NHS funded nursing care required for individuals placed cross-border into a care home.

21.49. In the event of cross-border placements between England and Scotland or between England and Northern Ireland (in either direction) the health service of the country of the first authority will be responsible for nursing costs. (In England therefore, the individual's responsible Clinical Commissioning Group will pay

---

[1] See section 39(6) of the Care Act as to the meaning of "NHS accommodation".

the costs.) The NHS standing rules will be amended to facilitate this. The first authority should inform the CCG of the arrangements being made and their formal consent sought. It is not expected that the CCG would withhold consent – any change in costs associated with the care would be likely to be negligible.

21.50. In the event of a cross-border placement between England and Wales (in either direction), the second authority's health service will be responsible for the costs of NHS nursing care. However, in the event of a cross-border placement between Wales and Scotland, Wales and Northern Ireland, or between Scotland and Northern Ireland, the first authority's health service will retain responsibility for the costs of NHS funded nursing care.

Where the individual's care needs change during the placement

21.51. In the event that an individual's care and support needs change during the course of the placement, these should be picked up in the course of a review and the care and support plan amended as needed.

21.52. The first authority retains responsibility for review and amendment of the individual's care and support plan, although it may have agreed with the second authority that the latter will assist it in certain ways. In this case, clarity and communication will be important as to each authority's roles (see chapter 13 for more information on reviews of care and support plans and chapter 18 for more information on delegation).

HANDLING COMPLAINTS

21.53. If the complaint relates to the care provider, it should normally be made to the provider in the first instance and dealt with according to the complaints process of the provider as governed by the applicable legislation, which will normally be the legislation of the administration into which the individual has been placed.

21.54. If the complaint relates to NHS care, it should be dealt with according to the legislation governing such complaints in the relevant territory of the UK.

21.55. Complaints regarding the first authority should be dealt with by the first authority in accordance with the relevant legislation of that territory of the UK. As should complaints regarding the care and support plan. Complaints regarding the second authority should be dealt with by the second authority.

21.56. If referral to the health ombudsmen is necessary this should be made to the ombudsmen whose investigation the provider or authority in question is subject to, in accordance with the governing legislation. See subsequent section for how to deal with a dispute that might arise between two or more authorities.

REPORTING ARRANGEMENTS

21.57. There is no legal requirement for authorities to notify national authorities that a cross-border placement has taken place. However, as UK-wide cross-border placements will generally be a new occurrence, it will be sensible to record the number of placements occurring to best inform future application of the policy. Therefore, authorities should record the number of placements made into their area from other territories of the UK and vice versa.

DISPUTES BETWEEN AUTHORITIES

21.58. If authorities have regard to and apply the suggested process and procedures outlined above and, more importantly, if the first and second authority work together in a spirit of reciprocity and cooperation and promptly communicate in order to ensure matters go smoothly, then there should be no need for dispute resolution. A dispute is most likely to occur because of lack of communication or following a communication breakdown/ misunderstanding between first and second authority during the process of arranging the placement.

21.59. The four administrations of the UK have worked together on the contents of specific regulations governing the process of resolving a dispute. These regulations cover all disputes that arise about the application of paragraphs 1 to 4 of Schedule 1 to the Act (general non- transfer of responsibility in the case of placements).

21.60. The regulations under Schedule 1 state:

- A dispute must not be allowed to prevent, interrupt, delay or otherwise adversely affect the meeting of an individual's care and support needs.[1]

- The authority in whose area the individual is living at the date the dispute arises is the lead authority for the purposes of duties relating to coordination and management of the dispute.

21.61. In the event of a dispute between two authorities where the individual is living in the area of one of those authorities when the dispute is referred, the Ministers/Northern Ireland Department (NID) in whose jurisdiction that area lies would determine the dispute. In the event of other disputes between authorities, the Ministers/NID in whose jurisdiction those authorities sit would decide between themselves as to who would determine the dispute.

21.62. Before a dispute is referred to the relevant Ministers/NID, the authorities concerned must take a number of steps. These include the following. The lead authority must:

- Co-ordinate the discharge of duties by the authorities in dispute.

- Take steps to obtain relevant information from those authorities.

- Disclose relevant information to those authorities.

21.63. Authorities in dispute must:

- Take all reasonable steps to resolve the dispute between themselves.

- Co-operate with each other in the discharge of their duties.

21.64. Each authority in dispute must:

- Engage in constructive dialogue with other authorities to bring about a speedy resolution.

- Comply with any reasonable request made by the lead authority to supply information.

21.65. The regulations specify the requisite contents of a dispute referral as follows. When a dispute is referred, the following must be provided:

- A letter signed by the lead authority stating that the dispute is being referred and identifying the provision of the Act which the dispute is about.

- A statement of the facts.

---

[1] See further the meaning of "needs" in relation to the four territories under the regulations.

- Copies of related correspondence.

21.66. The statement of facts must include:

- Details of the needs of the individual to whom the dispute relates.

- Which authority, if any, has met those needs, how they have been met and the relevant statutory provision.

- Any relevant steps taken in relation to the individual.

- An explanation of the nature of the dispute.

- Details of the individual's place of residence and any former relevant residence.

- Chronology of events leading up to the referral.

- Details of steps authorities have taken to resolve dispute.

- Where the individual's mental capacity is relevant, relevant supporting information.

21.67. The authorities in dispute may make legal submissions and if they do, they must send a copy to the other authorities in dispute, and provide evidence that they have done so.

21.68. The Responsible Person (i.e. Minister or Northern Ireland Department) to whom the dispute has been referred must:

- Consult other responsible persons (i.e. Ministers or NI Department) in determining the dispute.

- Notify those responsible persons of their determination.

PROVIDER FAILURE

21.69. In the event that a provider with which cross-border arrangements for an individual have been made or funded fails and is unable to carry on the care activity as a result, the authority in whose area that individual's care and support needs were being met has duties to ensure those needs continue to be met for so long as that authority considers it necessary, in the case of residential placements, as the first authority will normally continue to have overall responsibility.

21.70. Close communication and cooperation between the first and second authority throughout will be important. The temporary duty to meet needs in the event of provider failure will apply to authorities in England and Northern Ireland but is not expected to apply to local authorities in Wales until April 2016.

21.71. In the event of provider failure in Scotland, local authorities are required to perform duties provided for under Part 2 of the Social Work (Scotland) Act 1968 as specified in regulations made by the Secretary of State under paragraphs 1(6) and (7), 2(9) and (10) and 4(5) and (6) of Schedule 1 to the Care Act 2014.

21.72. The Act enables the authority under the duty mentioned in paragraph 21.69 to recover costs from the authority which made or funded the arrangements. This power will be commenced in relation to local authorities in Wales at the same time as the temporary duty is commenced in relation to them.

21.73. If a dispute later emerges, for example regarding costs incurred as a result of the provider failure situation, then the Schedule 1 dispute regulations described above will apply (where this concerns duties on authorities in England, Wales or Northern Ireland).

POTENTIAL FUTURE CROSS-BORDER ARRANGEMENTS

21.74. Schedule 1 makes provision for regulation-making powers with respect to applying cross-border principles to direct payments and/ or other types of accommodation which are not arranged by a local authority.

21.75. The UK Government and the Devolved Administrations will be keeping under review the possibility of exercising these regulation-making powers, in light of the implementation of residential cross-border placements and policy developments across all UK administrations.

Case Study: Frances

Frances is a 78 year old lady with severe arthritis who lives alone in south London. Frances slips whilst walking down her stairs and breaks a wrist and leg. Frances is admitted to a local general hospital. At the hospital, Francis is visited by a local authority social services member, Ray who conducts a needs assessment. During the assessment, Ray asks Frances about her support network – does she have any friends and/or family nearby? Frances says her best friend passed away last year. She has one son but he lives outside Edinburgh with his young family.

When Ray re-visits Frances, he informs her that she is eligible for care and support. He also says, that whilst a number of options exist, it is Ray's opinion, that Frances's severe arthritis now means she is unable to live independently and that a care home may be the best way forward. Frances agrees. She expresses relief that she will not have to return home alone but is anxious at moving to an unfamiliar setting.

Ray asks Frances whether she has considered moving to be nearer her son. Frances says yes, but has previously dismissed the idea because she didn't want to get in the way. Ray asks whether a move to a care home near her son might be attractive. The local authority would take care of the arrangements and her son and his family could visit more easily. Frances is keen to take this further. Ray asks Frances's permission to contact her son. Frances agrees.

Ray contacts Frances's son, Ian. Ian says he wishes he could visit Frances more often but with two young children and a busy job it is hard to do so. Ian phones every few days and says he knows Frances has been feeling down since her friend passed away. Ian's house is too small to accommodate Frances and is empty all day so no-one would be available to support Frances. Ray explains the possibility of a cross-border placement for Frances into a care home close to Ian. Ian says he would find this very attractive. Frances has always enjoyed her visits to Scotland before, especially seeing her grandchildren. Ian agrees to talk to Frances about the possibility.

Ray hears from Frances the next day – she and her son would like to go forward with a cross-border placement. Ray researches possible care homes close to Ian, taking Frances's preferences into account and selects three

---

possibilities which Frances, in conference with Ian, pick from. The preferred home is in a suburban area similar to that in which Frances currently lives and close to a church – Frances is a regular church-goer. Ray contacts the care home provider and confirms availability and fees and informs the provider that this would be a cross-border placement.

Ray phones his opposite number, Rhian, in the Edinburgh local authority where the care home is based. Ray informs Rhian that it appears likely a cross-border placement will take place. Rhian says she knows the care home in question and the standard of care is good based on inspectorate findings. Ray thanks her and follows up in writing with the provisional date when the placement will occur and details of the care provider identified.

Over the next week, arrangements for the placement are firmed up. Ray draws up an agreement as to how Frances's care will be managed on a day-to-day basis with assistance from Rhian's authority. Rhian has agreed that her local authority will take on several roles including providing assistance and information so that the local authority can fulfil its responsibilities. Rhian's team agree to help to carry out regular care reviews by gathering and reporting information back to Ray's local authority as ultimate decision- maker. Rhian also agrees that her local authority will provide support in an emergency situation.

22. SIGHT REGISTERS

This chapter provides guidance on:
- *Section 77 of the Care Act 2014;*
- *The Care and Support (Registers) Regulations 2014.*

This chapter covers:
- Registration;
- Certification;
- Transferring and retaining the Certificate of Vision Impairment (CVI);
- Making contact;
- Continuity of care;
- Care planning;
- Rehabilitation;
- Care and support for deafblind children and adults;
- Other registers.

22.1. Local authorities must keep a register of people who are severely sight impaired and sight impaired.

22.2. Registration is voluntary, however individuals should be encouraged to consent to inclusion on the register as it may assist them in accessing other concessions and benefits. The data which local authorities are provided on registration are also of benefit in service planning for health and care and support. However, individuals' access to care and support is not dependent upon registration, and those with eligible needs for care and support should continue to receive it regardless of whether they consent to inclusion on the register.

22.3. Local authorities should help health and social care organisations to work together to meet the needs of people who have sight loss, for example, ensuring that care and support services know what help somebody needs in their home when they leave hospital. Timely assessment and care and support that is integrated with health care and person-centred offer the potential to make improvements in experience and outcomes of people who are sight impaired, as well as improving system efficiency.

REGISTRATION

22.4. Local authorities must keep a register of people who are severely sight impaired and sight impaired. Local authorities may wish to use this opportunity to bring forward information from existing registers and update details, for example, to check if the information on the register is still current, for example a person may have moved out of the area.

22.5. The Certificate of Vision Impairment (CVI) formally certifies someone as being sight impaired or as severely sight impaired. A copy of the CVI should be sent to the relevant local authority by the hospital staff. However, people in receipt of a CVI should not be added to the local register until they have given their specific consent to the local authority for registration. If the person has given consent he or she may then be registered. Local authorities may take the date of certification given on the CVI as the effective date of registration. However, if consent has not been given, the person should still be offered a needs assessment.

22.6. The CVI is an important source of information for local authorities in relation to their registration duties. Local authorities should satisfy themselves that the CVI is completed correctly and it contains valid signatures as required (currently the consultant ophthalmologist and the patient) when receiving a hard copy of the form. Electronic versions and paper copies of CVIs should be accepted for registration.

22.7. People who agree to be registered may be entitled to some benefits, for example, an increase in personal tax allowance, a reduction in the cost of a TV license, a free bus pass and parking concessions under the Blue Badge Scheme. It is important that strong links exist between local authorities, health services and voluntary organisations to identify those who may benefit from registration. Appendix C of the UK Vision Strategy 2013 contains a tool that offers a pathway, approved by the Strategic Advisory Group of the UK Vision Strategy.

22.8. Schedule 2 of the 1989 Children Act requires local authorities to keep registers of disabled children, which must include children with sight impairments.

Certification

22.9. The CVI is issued by a Consultant Ophthalmologist to the patient certifying as sight impaired or severely sight impaired. The DH guidelines in the "Certificate of Vision Impairment: Explanatory Notes for Consultant Ophthalmologists and Hospital Eye Clinic Staff" states who should be certified as severely sight impaired and sight impaired.

22.10. Certification is not the final stage, but often it is the point when people begin to accept the severity of their sight loss and get access to practical and emotional support.

22.11. It is expected that NHS services will keep the completed certificate, signed by the consultant and the patient, for their records. A copy of the certificate should be sent to the relevant local authority and the patient's GP within five working days of its completion. The "Certificate of Vision Impairment *Explanatory Notes for Consultant Ophthalmologists and Hospital Eye Clinic Staff*" provides information on this.

22.12. The Public Health Outcomes Framework (Domain 4: Healthcare public health and preventing premature mortality) has the overarching objective to reduce numbers of people living with preventable ill health and people dying prematurely and has the "preventable sight loss" indicator. The CVI is the key data source for the preventable sight loss indicator and a copy of the form is also sent to Moorfields Eye Hospital for epidemiological analysis of cases where sight loss is due to age-related macular degeneration, glaucoma, diabetic retinopathy and any other cause.

22.13. The Certifications Office at Moorfields Eye Hospital receives the CVIs from hospitals across England and Wales for anonymised analysis by age, sex, visual status, location and ethnicity. These figures are reported to Public Health England, diabetic screening programmes so that they can monitor the numbers of newly certified people in their areas with potentially avoidable eye disease and to the CVI Committee. The CVI figures are benchmarked against the Health and Social Care Information Centre's (HSCIC) data on numbers of people newly registered so mapping health and social care data. The HSCIC's publication in September 2014 "Registered Blind and Partially Sighted People Year Ending 31 March 2014, provides latest data information.

22.14. Local authorities should note that there will also be people who have a reduced/low vision but do not meet the criteria for certification who may need to be considered in service planning.

Transferring and retaining the CVI

22.15. The CVIs should be kept until the person moves to another area or has passed away. In the event of a person's death, the local authority should keep the CVI for at least three years after the person's death as it may be necessary for tax purposes to establish if a deceased person was registered with a local authority.

Making contact

22.16. Upon receipt of the CVI, the local authority should make contact with the person issued with the CVI (regardless of whether the person has decided to register or not) within two weeks to arrange their inclusion on the local authority's register (with the person's informed consent) and offer individuals a registration card as identified on the CVI registration form. Where there is an appearance of need for care and support, local authorities must arrange an assessment of their needs in a timely manner.

22.17. To minimise unnecessary costs and maximise the ability of people who have sight impairment, they should have early access to information and advice in an accessible format so that they can adapt to their situation as quickly as possible and obtain any aids and support that will help them to manage their lives better.

CONTINUITY OF CARE

22.18. A person may decide to move home and live in another local authority area. In such circumstances local authorities must follow the process which is set out in chapter 20. This is aimed at ensuring that the person's care and support needs will continue to be met during their move. The process requires the original authority to provide the authority the person is moving to with relevant information to support the move such as a copy of the person's care and support plan, their latest assessment, and any other documentation the second authority requests. This should include a copy of their CVI. The second authority should register the person with the person's consent on their register, and the former authority should remove that person's name to avoid duplication.

CARE PLANNING

22.19. *Providing excellent services for blind and partially sighted people – A guide for local authorities,* published by Royal National Institute for Blind People (RNIB) and Action for Blind People, is a good practice guide that helps inform local authorities' understanding of the extent and impact of sight impairment, the main causes and risk factors and the effects on people's lives.

22.20. A vital part of modern care and support is the care and support plan. Having carried out a needs assessment, local authorities must prepare a care and support plan for everyone with eligible needs or other needs which the local authority is going to meet. Where someone has sight loss, this should be recorded in the care and support plan. Further details are set out in chapter 10 of this guidance.

REHABILITATION

22.21. Local authorities should consider securing specialist qualified rehabilitation and assessment provision (whether in- house, or contracted through a third party), to ensure that the needs of people with sight loss are correctly identified and their independence maximised. Certain aspects of independence training with severely sight impaired and sight impaired people require careful risk management and should only be undertaken by professionals with relevant experience and training. This type of rehabilitation should be provided to the person for a period appropriate to meet their needs. This will help the person to gain new skills, for example, when training to use a white cane. As aspects of rehabilitation for people with sight loss are distinct from refer to the Association of Directors of Adults Social Services' (ADASS) position statement of December 2013.164

22.22. This makes it clear that rehabilitation for sight impaired people is a specific form of reablement. However, there are some intrinsic characteristics which define rehabilitation as being distinct from other forms of reablement. It is therefore not appropriate to take a one- size-fits-all approach, and local authorities need to ensure that individual needs are met appropriately.

CARE AND SUPPORT FOR DEAFBLIND CHILDREN AND ADULTS

22.23. This guidance relates to adults with sight impairment only. Guidance in relation to care and support for Deafblind children and adults is issued separately under different legal powers, and should be considered in parallel.

OTHER REGISTERS

22.24. Local authorities may also establish and maintain a register of people living in their area that have a disability (a physical or mental impairment which has a substantial and long- term adverse effect on their ability to carry out normal day-to-day activities) or who need care and support or are likely to do so in the future.

22.25. Inclusion on registers is voluntary and with the individual's informed consent. However local authorities should encourage individual's consent to inclusion on the register as such registers may support the establishment of an accurate and useful local record of people whose needs may change over time, for example:

- someone with a progressive long-term condition whose needs may increase over time; or

- when the person on whom they are mainly dependent for their care has stopped providing care; or

- those who are ordinarily resident but may be receiving temporary care and support out of area, or in-patient treatment in health services, but who are likely to require care and support on their discharge or return.

22.26. For information on ordinary residence and out of area placements see chapter 19 of this guidance. This information can help local authorities to plan and commission services appropriately for those who need or are anticipated in the future to need care and support. This information could be useful, for example, in helping the local authority to meet its obligation to take steps to prevent reduce or delay needs, which requires local authorities to consider the importance of identifying adults whose needs are not being met and to arrange the provision of local preventative services, facilities and resources for its population. It may also support the local authority to undertake its "market shaping" function, which requires the local authority to consider identifying current and future needs and how providers might meet that demand. For further detail see chapter 4 of this guidance.

22.27. Local authorities may wish to link the information collected to the Joint Strategic Needs Assessments (JSNAs) as well as the Joint Health and Wellbeing Strategies. They may also, as part of local JSNA and Health and Wellbeing Strategy development, want to look at this information alongside complementary information from other partners, for example, information drawn appropriately from registers of people with learning disabilities or particular health conditions which are held by GPs, in order to produce a comprehensive and accurate shared local picture.

LINKS TO OTHER RELEVANT GUIDANCE AND DOCUMENTATION
The benefits of registering as blind or partially sighted http://www.nhs.uk/ipgmedia/national/royal%20national%20institute%20of%20blind%20people%20(rnib)/assets/standardsizedversionofthebenefitsofregisteringasblindorpartially sighted.pdf

The Adult UK sight loss pathway is a process map for the Seeing it my way outcomes framework. http://www.vision2020uk.org.uk/ukvisionstrategy/page.asp?section=299&sectionTitle=Adult+UK+sight+loss+pathway

ADASS's position statement of December 2013 http://www.vision2020uk.org.uk/library.asp?libraryID=4329&section=000100050005

The DH guidelines in *Certificate of Vision Impairment: Explanatory Notes for Consultant Ophthalmologists and Hospital Eye Clinic Staff:* https://www.gov.uk/government/uploads/system/uploads/attachment_data/file/127399/CVI-Explanatory-notes-in-DH-template.pdf

The Health and Social Care Information Centre (HSCIC) publishes the number of people registered with councils with Adult Social Services Responsibilities in England. http://www.hscic.gov.uk/media/12854/SSDA902InformationGuidance ProForma2013-14pdf/pdf/SSDA902_InformationGuidanceProForma_2013-14.pdf

23. TRANSITION TO THE NEW LEGAL FRAMEWORK

This chapter provides guidance on transition to the provisions in Part 1 of the Care Act 2014:

This chapter covers:
- Transition to the new legal framework in 2015/16 for people receiving care and support;
- Status of previous assessments and eligibility determinations under the Care Act;
- The role of care planning and review in implementation;
- Preparing for funding reforms in 2016/17;
- Understanding the likely demand;
- Awareness raising;
- Carrying out early assessments and managing capacity;
- Other systems implications.

23.1. The Care Act provides an updated legal framework for care and support, and introduces a number of new rights, responsibilities and processes. It will be crucial to the experience of people who use care and support, carers and their families, as well as those who provide services and work in the system, that the transition to the new legal framework from April 2015 onwards is smooth and effectively-managed by local authorities. How people currently in contact with the care and support system move into the new system will affect their ability to achieve their outcomes, and it will also impact on local authorities' ability to deliver their obligations.

23.2. The additional reforms to the way that care and support is funded, which are to be implemented from 2016/17, will both pose further challenges to local authorities, and provide new opportunities for contact with new groups of people. The steps that local authorities take over 2015/16 to prepare for the reforms in the following year are likely to have a significant impact on their capacity and readiness.

23.3. This chapter of the guidance consider how local authorities should bring people into the new system in the first year, and also how authorities should prepare for the funding reforms of 2016/17. Necessary secondary legislation will be put in place to give effect to the arrangements described in this chapter.

ASSESSMENT

23.4. Where a person has received an assessment under the previous legislation, local authorities will not be required to re-assess their needs purely because of the new duties around assessment coming into force. However, where local authorities identify (whether through a review or otherwise) that a person's needs or circumstances have changed, a needs assessment must be carried out in line with the responsibilities set out in the Care Act.

23.5. Similarly, a carer who has been previously assessed will not automatically require a separate carer's assessment under the Care Act. However, local authorities should consider the fact that the new duty for assessment of carers under the Care Act means that a significant number of carers are likely to have a right to assessment under the Act that have not been assessed previously. Local authorities should consider whether and how they need to increase their expertise and capacity to fulfil this duty.

23.6. Where a local authority has begun or recently completed an assessment under previous legislation, whether for an adult with care and support needs or a carer, it may take this to be the assessment which it is required to carry out under the Care Act, provided that the needs or other circumstances have not changed, and the person concerned agrees.

TRANSITION ASSESSMENTS

23.7. Local authorities may treat a transition assessment conducted before April 2015 as a transition assessment under the Care Act, provided they ensure it complies with the features of a transition assessment set out in Chapter 16.

23.8. From 1 April 2015, the duty will apply to continue children's services where someone reaches the age of 18 and a transition assessment should have been conducted but has not been. This means that where children's services are to be discontinued after that date and a transition assessment has not been conducted, local authorities will need to either assure themselves that a transition assessment was not necessary, or conduct one and act on it before services are discontinued. Similarly, a local authority must ensure that a transition assessment conducted before April 2015 is compliant with the Care Act before discontinuing children's services.

ELIGIBILITY DETERMINATIONS

23.9. The new national minimum eligibility threshold replaces the current guidance on levels of access set out in *Prioritising need in the context of Putting People First.* The minimum threshold, set out in regulations, describes a level of need that has a significant impact on the person's wellbeing (as set out in chapter 6). This is intended to allow for the same level of access to care and support to be maintained in the vast majority of circumstances and local areas.

23.10. Local authorities should review their previous local approach to eligibility, and consider how this relates to the minimum threshold. Local authorities must meet needs at least at this threshold, though they will remain able to meet needs locally at more generous levels. It may be the case that no further action is required, and the authority is satisfied that it will meet needs at the minimum threshold without further change. Where this review indicates that local authorities have not previously met needs which are described in the minimum threshold, they will need to take steps to identify and review the needs of any individuals who may be affected.

23.11. Local authorities should adopt a targeted approach to reviewing the needs of any individuals who may be affected by the implementation of the minimum eligibility threshold. Where the local authority considers that a person whose needs have been met by the local authority in the past will continue to have eligible needs under the Care Act, it need not take any specific steps in relation to that person, if there has been no change. However, where a local authority identifies an individual or a specific cohort who may become eligible, it should target an assessment of needs at those individuals in order to determine whether they now have eligible needs which must be met.

23.12. Local authorities should determine whether and how to use their powers to meet needs beyond the level of the minimum threshold. Where local authorities have previously provided care and support to people with lower level needs, they should consider carefully any proposal to restrict local eligibility to only those needs described within the minimum threshold, and should consult with their local population before making such a change.

23.13. In relation to support for carers, local authorities should review existing local policies in light of the new national minimum eligibility threshold for carers. Where this indicates individuals or groups who may have become eligible as a result, then a carer's assessment should be offered.

FINANCIAL ASSESSMENT

23.14. Local authorities should review the operation of their local charging framework, to ensure that this is consistent with the obligations set out by the Care Act and associated regulations, and the provisions set out in chapter 8. Where local authorities are satisfied that their approach to charging follows the detail required by the Act and regulations, they do not need to take further steps to review funding arrangements for individuals or to carry out new financial assessments, unless other circumstances have changed. Local authorities should consider the need to consult with their local population, but should not be expected to consult formally if their approach to charging has not changed as a result of the Act.

23.15. Where local authorities consider that there will be a change in practice which affects the amount of charges people will pay, for example as a result of changes to the upper capital limits, they must take steps to ensure that individuals concerned are subject to the correct charges. This may include carrying out new financial assessments where circumstances have changed and a new assessment is required.

MEETING NEEDS

23.16. The Care Act's approach to "meeting needs", as opposed to duties to provide specific services, is not intended to place additional requirements on local authorities, and should not give rise to any particular transitional issues to the new system. Where a local authority is providing a service under previous legislation, it should ensure that the person's needs continue to be met through these new arrangements, as part of the usual process of review. "Passporting" people into the new legislation should normally take place at the point of that regular review, when the authority satisfies itself that the needs are being met.

23.17. To ensure that needs continue to be met between the Care Act coming into force and the point of review, existing legislation underpinning service provision will be saved for a period of one year. This means that local authorities will be able to continue with existing arrangements pending the review, to manage capacity issues and to ensure that the review takes place at the right time for the person. However, local authorities must not use existing legislation to underpin care and support planning after April 2015 – the purpose of this saving is only to continue existing provision until a review can take place, at which point the person would transfer under the provisions of the Care Act.

23.18. From April 2015, local authorities will have a duty to meet the eligible needs of people ordinarily resident in their area, which may include those needs identified via previous assessments. The general rules on determining ordinary residence have not changed, and previous ordinary residence determinations will continue to apply. The extension of ordinary residence "deeming" principles to other types of accommodation provided in another authority's area (including shared lives and extra care housing) will be introduced from April 2015 and will not be retrospective. This is described in further detail in chapter 19.

23.19. From April 2015 any adult in a prison, a young offender institution, bail accommodation or an approved premise treated as if they are resident in the local authority area in which that prison, young offender institution, bail accommodation or approved premises is situated, making that local authority area responsible for meeting their care and support needs.

CARE PLANNING AND REVIEW

23.20. Where someone is already receiving care and support under existing legislation, their first review after April 2015 must consider whether their existing plan fulfils the requirements set out in Chapter 10 of this guidance and take any steps necessary to bring it into line. For most people, this review will be the point at which their care and support transfers into the new legislation, but in practice, this should not require any change beyond what might be expected as part of a usual review, where needs or circumstances have changed in some way.

23.21. In particular, the plan will need to include a personal budget for all people whose needs the local authority is meeting, including carers (the only exception to this is set out in chapter 10). Where the person has not previously received a personal budget, this must be provided and explained during the review, to align the plan with the Act's requirements. All existing personal budgets will also need to be reviewed to ensure that they reflect the requirements of the Act, in particular that they are based on meeting needs (delineating eligible needs where appropriate) rather than directly on the costs of particular services.

23.22. At the same point, people should be made aware if they have a right to a direct payment under the Care Act if this has not been discussed before. Where someone is currently receiving a direct payment, the direct payment should continue, but local authorities must use the first review after April 2015 to establish a personal budget and thereafter use this as the basis for the direct payment.

DEFERRED PAYMENT AGREEMENTS

23.23. Where a local authority has entered into a deferred payment agreement (DPA) with a person prior to April 2015, that DPA must remain in place until such a time as it would expire under the existing agreement. The DPA must continue subject to the same terms and conditions as have been agreed between the local authority and the person concerned. Local authorities must not remake an old DPA into a new one via the new regulations, but should use the provisions in the Care Act to make all future agreements after April 2015.

DEBT RECOVERY

23.24. From April 2015, local authorities must only use the debt recovery powers under Section 69 of the Care Act in order to recover any debts from the date the Act comes into force, including for debts that were incurred before that date. Any arrangements that are already in place, or proceedings that are already underway, prior to that may continue to their conclusion, but no new arrangements can be made under those routes. The above includes debts being recovered under Section 22 of HASSASSA (1983).

23.25. As set out in Annex D (para 11), for any debts that have accrued prior to the commencement of the Care Act 2014 the time period for recovering that debt continues to be three years as previously set out under Section 56 of the National

Assistance Act 1948 as any change to this would be retrospective and unfair. For any new debts that occur after the commencement of the Care Act 2014, the time period to recover debts has been extended to six years from the date when the sum became due to the local authority. Where a debt is taking some time to be recovered, provided legal proceedings have issued within the limitation period, enforcement can continue. If it has not, the debt must be written off.

INDEPENDENT LIVING FUND (ILF) TRANSFER

23.26. The Care Act 2014 does not include any provision specifically relating to the Independent Living Fund (ILF) closure and transfer to local authorities. This guidance is aimed at helping authorities to prepare for the transfer of ILF recipients into the new care and support system. Guidance has previously been issued in relation to managing the closure, which this supplements.

23.27. On 30 June 2015, the ILF will close to its users, and both funding and responsibility will transfer to local authorities in England (the devolved governments in Scotland and Wales are making their own arrangements for former ILF users living there). Local authorities will have to meet all former ILF users' eligible needs from 1 July 2015. Funding in respect of former ILF users will be distributed to local authorities on the basis of local patterns of expenditure following transfer, to allow them to meet users' care and support needs.

23.28. Local authorities will need to plan for the transfer of adults currently receiving ILF payments to ensure that their care and support continues and is not interrupted during this period.

23.29. All the duties and obligations under the Care Act 2014 will apply throughout this process. In particular, there must be an ongoing consideration of the person's wellbeing, which begins with the assumption that the individual is best placed to judge their own wellbeing. The concept of 'independent living' is a core part of the wellbeing principle, and is detailed in the requirement to consider the person's control over their day-to-day life, the suitability of their living accommodation and their contribution to society.

Processes in place to support transfer

23.30. A Transfer Review and Support Programme (TRSP), run by the ILF, to support users and local authorities in their preparations will be in place until transfer on 1st July 2015. Under the TRSP, all ILF users receive a face-to-face meeting with an ILF assessor and, where consent has been granted, if possible, a local authority representative. The outcome of this meeting is to provide the adult with an individual, outcome-focused support plan detailing their current level of support and to discuss any concerns about transfer. This Transfer Review and Support Plan will assist adults when discussing with local authorities the outcomes they wish to achieve in their day-to-day lives. As a matter of good practice, local authorities should take the person's Transfer Review and Support Plan into consideration during their assessment.

23.31. The ILF will engage with all local authorities in England to discuss transfer arrangements. Prior to closure, the ILF will hand over to the relevant local authorities the contact details of the ILF users, a comprehensive support plan and information relating to the on-going support arrangements, provided that the users consent has been received. A Code of Practice supporting transition has been agreed with the LGA, ADASS and the ILF to lay down the key principles that underpin partnership working during transfer. It includes a commitment to personalisation, inclusion, and choice and control.

Local authorities preparing for the transfer

23.32. To ensure that the adult's care and support continues uninterrupted during the transfer, local authorities may wish to engage early to offer former ILF users a needs assessment and begin the process of planning for transfer. Local authorities will likely have contact with the majority of ILF users already, as 94% of ILF users already receive care and support from their local authority. The ILF has contacted those users who joined the fund prior to 1993 and who may not be known to their local authority, and will inform the local authority of their details where consent is given.

23.33. The assessment process under the Care Act 2014 is set out in chapter 6 of this guidance, and requires authorities to consider the person's needs, their well-being and their desired outcomes. The adult, their carer and anybody else they wish to involve, must be involved throughout the process, and the local authority must give them a written record of their needs assessment. Further to this, local authority responsibilities surrounding independent advocacy and safeguarding are set out in chapters 7 and 14 of this guidance.

23.34. Local authorities may already know the adult as they are already meeting some of their needs. Authorities will need to consider the adult's need and the outcomes they are looking to achieve but they may decide to carry out the assessment proportionately. They may decide to do this based on the information they already hold about the person and focus on the needs and outcomes that they are not meeting when they carry out an assessment with the person.

23.35. Local authorities must also consider the impact of a person's needs on their family and others in their support network. Many ILF users have multiple and complex needs, and may be receiving care from family members as well as employed Personal Assistants. Where a local authority finds that a person is providing care and has an appearance of needs for support, they must offer a carer's assessment.

23.36. If, on 1 July 2015, a local authority has not carried out an assessment and completed the necessary arrangements for transfer, they will need to consider how the adult's needs can continue to be met. Local authorities could continue to provide the person with the same level of funding, for example as a direct payment, that they were receiving prior to the transfer until a needs assessment has been completed, eligibility determination reached and a care and support plan is in place.

Care and support planning

23.37. Local authorities must involve the person in the care and support planning process, and take steps to agree the final plan with them. Chapter 10 provides guidance on what authorities should consider when developing a care and support plan and to maintain independence.

23.38. Local authorities will need to be aware that the majority of ILF users will already have arrangements in place to meet their needs. For example, many ILF users employ Personal Assistants. Prior to transfer the ILF will provide each user with an information pack regarding the transfer, which will include an 'employer support' leaflet for those users who are employers.

23.39. If the adult's personal budget changes or it is agreed that their needs should be met in a different way, the adult will need to consider how this might impact on any contractual arrangements they have in place. Local authorities should take reasonable steps to make the adult aware of the potential conse-quences of any change in the amount of the adult's personal budget, and any obligations the adult may have as a consequence.

23.40. ILF recipients receive their ILF as a direct payment and the majority of these will also have a direct payment from their local authority to meet their care and support. However, a small number of ILF recipients may not be receiving a direct payment from their local authority. Where an adult within this small group requests a direct payment, local authorities will need to consider if they meet the criteria, and if so, put the necessary processes and arrangements in place (see chapter 12 on direct payments).

PREPARING FOR FUNDING REFORM
Summary of 2016/17 reforms

23.41. April 2016 will see the introduction of the biggest funding reforms to care and support in over 65 years with more people than ever before contacting their local authority. It is vital that every local authority starts to plan and prepare for these changes now to ensure that people are able to benefit immediately.

23.42. The statutory guidance will be updated and re-published in advance of April 2016, to set out how the capped cost system will impact practically on the processes and requirements of the Act, and how the obligations of local auth-orities will change. In summary, the key reforms will be:

- A cap on the care costs which a person pays over their lifetime. This will be set at £72,000 for those over retirement age. How a person progresses towards the cap will be based on what the cost of meeting their eligible needs would be to the local authority. Where a local authority is arranging a person's care, this will be provided through the personal budget. Where they are not, this will be provided through an "independent personal budget".

- Keeping track of how people progress towards the cap and providing a record of progress to the person. Every person with assessed eligible needs will need to have a "care account". This will keep track of what they are paying, what the local authority is paying and what their progress is towards the cap. Local authorities will need to provide regular statements.

- Extending the financial support provided by the local authority, by raising the upper capital limit to £118,000 where someone's property is taken into account. This will mean that more people with modest assets are able to receive financial support to meet their eligible needs.

Understanding the likely demand

23.43. Local authorities should take steps now to understand the additional likely demand for support as a result of the funding reforms. It is anticipated that a significant number of people who would previously have arranged and paid for their own care may approach the local authority for support in accessing care, or for an assessment of their needs. This is needed so that the local authority can record the cost of meeting their eligible needs for the purposes of establishing their care account, and counting costs towards their cap.

23.44. In order to prepare for the implementation of the capped costs system, local authorities should take steps to identify the number of "self-funders" (i.e. people who arrange and pay for their own care and support) in their local area. This group are unlikely to currently be in contact with the local authority, and local authorities should work with other partners who may be better placed to scope the local population, including for example the local NHS, provider organisations and the voluntary sector.

23.45. In identifying people who currently arrange their own care, local authorities should consider specific groups who would benefit most from the introduction of the cap on care costs, and may be most likely to approach the authority – for example:

- People who currently arrange their own care and support, and would be likely to have eligible needs if assessed by the local authority. People already living in care homes who are not funded by the local authority may be most likely to fall into such a category, and may be reasonably estimated using CQC registration data or information available from providers themselves.

- People with modest assets, who would benefit from the rise in the upper capital limit, and may become eligible for financial support from the local authority.

- Working-age adults whose needs for care and support are likely to meet the eligibility criteria.

23.46. In estimating the impact of additional demand, local authorities should take into account other factors in their local population which may influence the likelihood of individuals seeking care and support. For example, information on existing access to universal services by self-funders (e.g. any universal reablement service) may provide a useful indication of the willingness of such groups to contact the local authority. Similarly, information derived from contact centres or existing information and advice services may also indicate the preferences of such groups. Other local services (e.g. local GPs) may also have information and experience with the same groups.

Awareness-raising

23.47. Local authorities should take steps to raise awareness of the reforms, in keeping with their obligations for providing information and advice on the care and support system (see chapter 3). In order to predict and manage additional demand, local authorities should seek out groups, for example those identified above, for targeted communications and the local approach to implementation. Local authorities should consider how to contact any specific groups who may benefit from earlier information, for example individuals who may be at risk of losing mental capacity in the near future. In targeting information and communications, local authorities should follow the same factors of proportionality and appropriateness as in providing any other information and advice.

23.48. Communications which raise awareness of the capped costs system should in particular reflect the aims of the reforms to support people to plan for future care costs and make more informed decisions which reduce needs over time. Earlier contact with professionals who may support financial planning, for example, could support local authorities in managing demand over the longer-term. Information should include helping those targeted to access different types of support, including those options available in the local community, to prevent needs, delay deterioration or prepare for the future wherever possible.

Carrying out early assessments

23.49. Where local authorities have identified groups who would be likely to approach them for support under the capped costs system, they should consider carrying out the relevant processes early in order to manage capacity and workload over a longer period. For example, early needs assessments may be carried out in order to pre-determine eligible needs and record the cost of meeting those needs for people who would benefit.

23.50. Local authorities should consider which groups of individuals may benefit most from such an approach. One such example may be those self-funding people with eligible needs who are in the most settled populations, where needs are least likely to change before April 2016, such as care home residents. However, groups that are difficult to reach or particularly vulnerable may also benefit from early assessment given the potential challenges thereafter; and it may be helpful for local authorities to understand the practicalities of these assessments well in advance of April 2016 to ensure that they have robust processes in place.

23.51. If needs change, the local authority will be required to carry out a further assessment, and authorities should consider how to mitigate such risks in the approach adopted. Local authorities should consider when would be an appropriate time to begin to carry out assessments solely for the purpose of preparing for the capped costs system, bearing in mind the likelihood of needs changing before April 2016. However, this must not lead to a refusal of an assessment where the local authority would be under a duty to carry out an assessment subject to the usual provisions in the Care Act.

23.52. The assessment carried out should meet the same legal obligations as for any other needs assessment (see chapter 6). However, where a local authority carries out such an assessment, this should be assumed to be on the basis that the person does not wish for the authority to meet the person's needs at that time (because the purpose of the assessment is to pre-determine eligible needs and care costs, in advance of April 2016, and not to seek local authority support) and this should be made clear to the person. However, if the person subsequently asks the local authority to meet their eligible needs, then the usual obligations under the Care Act would apply and the local authority would be required to do so. The local authority should make this clear to the individual at the outset.

23.53. Having carried out an assessment, the local authority must determine whether the individual has eligible needs for care and support (see chapter 6). If the person does not have eligible needs, then the authority must provide information and advice. If the person does have eligible needs, then provided the person concerned does not wish for the local authority to meet their needs, the authority will not be required to do so. The local authority should provide the individual with a written record, which includes:

- a record of the assessment and eligibility determination setting out the needs assessed, and of those which needs are eligible;

- the cost to the local authority of meeting the eligible needs. This should use the processes which the local authority will already have in place for calculating indicative personal budgets, in order to provide an interim cost of meeting the needs; and,

- information and advice on how to prevent or delay needs, how to access financial advice, and the anticipated process for confirming their care account from April 2016.

23.54. The cost of meeting the person's eligible needs which is calculated at this point may form their independent personal budget from April 2016, provided that their needs do not change. The costs will not start counting towards the cap and their care account will not begin before this date, and there is no retrospective element. This should be made clear to the person, and if appropriate their family, in the manner in which the information above is provided.

23.55. Where the local authority has carried out an assessment and pre-determined eligible needs, it should contact the person concerned around April 2016 to satisfy itself that the needs or other circumstances (e.g. the person's financial resources) have not changed. The person may ask the local authority to review their needs, and the local authority should respond to such a request. If the needs or circumstances have not changed, or if no request for a review is made, then the authority may take the record of the needs and costs as accurate, and provide an independent personal budget and start the care account on that basis. This must be communicated to the individual in writing.

Managing capacity

23.56. Local authorities should consider the steps that could be taken to manage capacity issues associated with early assessments as described above, as well as additional assessments after April 2016. This could include, for instance, the role of self-assessment in supporting individuals to identify their own needs and make a judgement on eligibility. It may also include adopting a more proportionate approach to the financial assessment for those individuals with assets substantially above the financial limits, or using powers to delegate some or all such assessments to other organisations. Practical guidance has been developed to support local authorities to consider their own capacity and workforce requirements.[1]

23.57. Local authorities should develop a clear understanding of their current workforce and future needs in determining their approach to delivering additional assessments. They may consider a role for strategic partners in the voluntary sector or others who are already in touch with some of the people concerned and who would be open to being trained to carry out assessments on the authority's behalf. Where authorities pursue such an approach, they should consider the effect on other elements of the care and support process and how to manage interactions between the organisations (for example, the audit process put in place by the local authority to assure the assessments carried out on their behalf).

23.58. Where a person carries out a self-assessment, the local authority should consider how the self-assessment is verified and how this links with subsequent steps, such as calculating the cost of meeting eligible needs. Where this is

---

[1] Link to Skills for Care.

delegated to an external organisation there should be clear protocols in place for quality assurance and ongoing monitoring.

SYSTEMS AND TRAINING REQUIREMENTS

23.59. All these changes will place new requirements on local information systems and processes. Local authorities should review the impact on their information systems in conjunction with their suppliers and consider whether new systems and technology is required and carefully consider their procurement approach. In particular, local authorities should take into account the wider health and care technology strategy, including use of open APIs, when making decisions in this area.[1] Local authorities should also consider whether business processes also need to be reviewed and changed in parallel to changes in systems.

23.60. In particular, informatics systems for ongoing case management will need to be revised to incorporate the additional requirements for independent personal budgets, care accounts, deferred payment agreements and changes to charging and assessments (for both people with care and support needs and carers). In addition, authorities should consider how digital approaches can put citizens in control by making systems open and accessible, including online assessment, care planning, access to records and care accounts. Local authorities will also need to consider how systems can be made open and accessible to people where digital internet systems are not accessible, or even not permitted, such as in prison.

23.61. Local authorities should consider the training needs of staff, and in particular the needs of those who carry out the relevant assessments to ensure that there is sufficient understanding of the new system. Where local authorities propose to commission or delegate some activities to other organisations, they should ensure that staff are trained to the same standard. Practical learning and development modules to support the training of staff to implement the technology is required. Local authorities should start early conversations with suppliers to identify the changes required Care Act are under development to support this process.[2]

23.62. Local authorities should also review their provision of financial advice and relationships with existing local independent providers. Local authorities should take steps to identify sources of independent advice which are accessible to local people, and make arrangements for future signposting.

---

[1] See: http://www.local.gov.uk/documents/10180/11411/Social+care+information+and+technology_care+and+support+reform+discussion+paper.pdf/f4dbc387-2106-45f1-8402-56492bdd4cf
[2] Link to Skills for Care L&D plan

ANNEX A: CHOICE OF ACCOMMODATION AND ADDITIONAL PAYMENTS

This annex covers:
- Choice of accommodation when arranging care and support in an accommodation setting;
- Making additional payments for preferred accommodation.

1. A person's ability to make an informed choice is a key element of the care and support system. This must extend to where the care and support planning process has determined that a person needs to live in a specific type of accommodation to meet their care and support needs.

2. The care and support planning process will have determined what type of accommodation will best suit the person's needs. This could be, for example, a care home, shared lives or extra care housing. Where the type of accommodation is one of those specified in regulations, the person will have a right to choose the particular provider or location, subject to certain conditions. Where this is the case, the following guidance should be applied and in doing so, local authorities should have regard to the following principles:

- good communication of clear information and advice to ensure well informed decisions;

- a consistent approach to ensure genuine choice;

- clear and transparent arrangements for choice and any 'top-up' arrangements;

- clear understanding of potential consequences should 'top-up' arrangements fail with clear exit strategies; and

- the choice is suitable to the person's needs.

3. Local authorities **must** also remember that the regulations and guidance on choice of accommodation and additional costs apply equally to those entering care for the first time, those who have already been placed by a local authority, and those who have been self- funders, but because of diminishing resources are on the verge of needing local authority support.

4. Local authorities should also be mindful of their duties under Section 1 of the Care Act 2014 to promote individual wellbeing. Further detail is available in Chapter 1.

CHOICE OF ACCOMMODATION
5. Where a local authority is responsible for meeting a person's care and support needs and their needs have been assessed as requiring a particular type of accommodation in order to ensure that they are met, the person must have the right to choose between different providers of that type of accommodation provided that:

- the accommodation is suitable in relation to the person's assessed needs;

- to do so would not cost the local authority more than the amount specified in the adult's personal budget for accommodation of that type;

- the accommodation is available; and

- the provider of the accommodation is willing to enter into a contract with the local authority to provide the care at the rate identified in the person's personal budget on the local authority's terms and conditions.

6. This choice must not be limited to those settings or individual providers with which the local authority already contracts with or operates, or those that are within that local authority's geographical boundary. It must be a genuine choice across the appropriate provision.

7. If a person chooses to be placed in a setting that is outside the local authority's area, the local authority must still arrange for their preferred care. In doing so, the local authority should have regard to the cost of care in that area when setting a person's personal budget. Local authorities should also read the guidance on ordinary residence in Chapter 20.

SUITABILITY OF ACCOMMODATION

8. In exercising a choice, a local authority must ensure that the accommodation is suitable to meet a person's assessed needs and identified outcomes established as part of the care and support planning process.

9. People are able to express a preference about the setting in which their needs are met through the care and support planning process. This process considers both the person's needs and preferences and detailed guidance is set out in Chapter 10. Once this is agreed, the choice is between different settings, not different types. For example, a person cannot exercise the right to a choice of accommodation to choose a shared lives scheme when the care and support planning process, which involves the person, has assessed their needs as needing to be met in a care home.

COST

10. The care and support planning process will identify how best to meet a person's needs. As part of that, the local authority must provide the person with a personal budget, except in cases or circumstances set out in the Care Act (Personal Budget) Regulations. The Personal Budget is an important tool that provides clear information on the cost of meeting the person's needs. Further guidance on how to undertake care and support planning and calculate a personal budget is set out in Chapters 10 and 11.

11. The personal budget is defined as the cost to the local authority of meeting the person's needs which the local authority chooses or is required to meet. However, the local authority should take into consideration cases or circumstances where this 'cost to the local authority' may need to be adjusted to ensure that needs are met. For example, a person may have specific dietary requirements that can only be met in specific settings. In all cases the local authority must have regard to the actual cost of good quality care in deciding the personal budget to ensure that the amount is one that reflects local market conditions. This should also reflect other factors such as the person's circumstances and the availability of provision. In addition, the local authority should not set arbitrary amounts or ceilings for particular types of accommodation that do not reflect a fair cost of care. Guidance on market shaping and commissioning is set out in Chapter 4. Local authorities **must** also have regard to the

guidance on personal budgets in Chapter 11, and in particular paragraph 11.23 on calculating the personal budget.

12. A person must not be asked to pay a 'top-up' towards the cost of their accommodation because of market inadequacies or commissioning failures and must ensure there is a genuine choice. The local authority therefore **must** ensure that at least one option is available that is affordable within a person's personal budget and should ensure that there is more than one. If no preference has been expressed and no suitable accommodation is available at the amount identified in a personal budget, the local authority must arrange care in a more expensive setting and adjust the budget accordingly to ensure that needs are met. In such circumstances, the local authority must not ask for the payment of a 'top-up' fee. Only when a person has chosen a more expensive accommodation can a 'top-up' payment be sought. Paragraphs 19 and 20 set out guidance on Additional Costs.

AVAILABILITY

13. Local authorities have specific duties to shape and facilitate the market of care and support services locally, including ensuring sufficient supply. As a result, a person should not have to wait for their assessed needs to be met. However, in some cases, a short wait may be unavoidable, particularly when a person has chosen a particular setting that is not immediately available. This may include putting in place temporary arrangements – taking in to account the person's preferences and securing their agreement – and placing the person on the waiting list of their preferred choice of provider for example. It should be remembered however that such arrangements can be unsettling for the person and should be avoided wherever possible.

14. In such cases, the local authority must ensure that in the interim adequate alternative services are provided and set out how long the interim arrangement may last for. In establishing any temporary arrangements, the local authority must provide the person with clear information in writing on the detail of the arrangements as part of their care and support plan. As a minimum this should include the likely duration of the arrangement, information on the operation of the waiting list for their preferred setting alongside any other information that may be relevant. If any interim arrangements exceed 12 weeks, the person may be reassessed to ensure that both the interim and the preferred option are still able to meet the person's needs and that remains their choice.

15. Where a person contributes to the cost of their care following a financial assessment they must not be asked to pay more than their assessment shows they can afford.

16. In some cases a person may decide that they wish to remain in the interim setting, even if their preferred setting subsequently becomes available. If the setting where they are temporarily resident is able to accommodate the arrangement on a permanent basis this should be arranged and they should be removed from the waiting list of their original preferred setting. Before doing so, the local authority must make clear any consequences of that choice, including any financial implications.

CHOICE THAT CANNOT BE MET AND REFUSAL OF ARRANGEMENTS

17. Whilst a local authority should do everything it can to meet a person's choice, inevitably there will be some instances where a choice cannot be met,

for example if the provider does not have capacity to accommodate the person. In such cases, a local authority must set out in writing why it has not been able to meet that choice and should offer suitable alternatives. It should also set out the detail of the local authority's complaints procedure and if and when the decision may be reviewed.

18. A local authority must do everything it can to take into account a person's circumstances and preferences when arranging care. However, in all but a very small number of cases, such as where a person is being placed under guardianship under Section 7 of the Mental Health Act 1983, a person has a right to refuse to enter a setting whether that is on an interim or permanent basis. Where a person unreasonably refuses the arrangements, a local authority is entitled to consider that is has fulfilled its statutory duty to meet needs and may then inform the person in writing that as a result they need to make their own arrangements. This should be a step of last resort and local authorities should consider the risks posed by such an approach, for both the authority itself and the person concerned. Should the person contact the local authority again at a later date, the local authority should reassess the needs as necessary and re-open the care and support planning process.

CONTRACTUAL TERMS AND CONDITIONS

19. In supporting a person's choice of setting, the local authority may need to enter into a contract with a provider that they do not currently have an arrangement with. In doing so, they should ensure that the contractual conditions are broadly the same as those they would negotiate with any other provider whilst taking account of the individual circumstances. Strict or unreasonable conditions should not be used as a means to avoid or deter the arrangement.

ADDITIONAL COSTS OR 'TOP-UP' PAYMENTS

20. In some cases, a person may actively choose a setting that is more expensive than the amount identified for the provision of the accommodation in the personal budget. Where they have chosen a setting that costs more than this, an arrangement will need to be made as to how the difference will be met. This is known as an additional cost or 'top-up' payment and is the difference between the amount specified in the personal budget and the actual cost. In such cases, the local authority must arrange for them to be placed there, provided a third party, or in certain circumstances the person in need of care and support, is willing and able to meet the additional cost.

21. The following sections of guidance only apply where the person has chosen a more expensive setting. Where someone is placed in a more expensive setting solely because the local authority has been unable to make arrangements at the anticipated cost, the personal budget must reflect this amount. The person would then contribute towards this personal budget according to the financial assessment. The additional cost provisions must not apply in such circumstances.

AGREEING A 'TOP-UP' FEE

22. Having chosen a setting that is more expensive, based on good information and advice, the local authority should ensure that the person understands the full implications of this choice, remembering that this is often a point of crisis. This should include for example that a third party, or in certain circumstances the person needing care and support, will need to meet the additional cost of that setting

for the full duration of their stay and that should the additional cost not be met they may be moved to an alternative setting.

23. The local authority must ensure that the person paying the 'top-up' is willing and able to meet the additional cost for the likely duration of the arrangement, recognising that this may be for some time into the future. Therefore it must ensure that the person paying the 'top- up' enters into a written agreement with the local authority, agreeing to meet that cost. The agreement must, as a minimum, include the following:

- the additional amount to be paid;
- the amount specified for the accommodation in the person's personal budget;
- the frequency of the payments;
- to whom the payments are to be made;
- provisions for reviewing the agreement;
- a statement on the consequences of ceasing to make payments;
- a statement on the effect of any increases in charges that a provider may make;
- a statement on the effect of any changes in the financial circumstances of the person paying the 'top-up'.

24. Before entering into the agreement, the local authority must provide the person paying the 'top-up' with sufficient information and advice to ensure that they understand the terms and conditions, including actively considering the provision of independent financial information and advice. Further detail on each of these points is set out below.

25. Ultimately, if the arrangements for a 'top-up' were to fail for any reason, the local authority would need to meet the cost or make alternative arrangements, subject to a needs assessment. Further details are set out below in the consequences of ceasing to make payments. Local authorities should therefore maintain an overview of all 'top-up' agreements and should deter arrangements for 'top-up' payments to be paid directly to a provider.

THE AMOUNT TO BE PAID

26. The amount of the 'top-up' should be the difference between the actual costs of the preferred provider and the amount that the local authority would have set in a personal budget or local mental health after-care limit to meet the person's eligible needs by arranging or providing accommodation of the same type. When considering the cost of care in its area, the local authority is likely to identify a range of costs which apply to different circumstances and settings. For the purposes of agreeing a 'top-up' fee the local authority must consider what personal budget it would have set at the time care and support is needed. It should not automatically default to the cheapest rate or to any other arbitrary figure.

FREQUENCY OF PAYMENTS

27. In agreeing any 'top-up' arrangement, the local authority must clearly set out how often such payments need to be made, e.g. on a weekly or monthly basis.

RESPONSIBILITY FOR COSTS AND TO WHOM THE PAYMENTS ARE MADE

28. When entering into a contract to provide care in a setting that is more expensive than the amount identified in the personal budget, the local authority is responsible for the total cost of that placement. This means that if there is a break down in the arrangement of a 'top-up', for instance if the person making the 'top-up' ceases to make the agreed payments, then the local authority would be liable for the fees until it has either recovered the additional costs it incurs or made alternative arrangements to meet the cared for person's needs.

29. In terms of securing the funds needed to meet the total cost of the care (including the 'top-up' element) a local authority has three options, except where it is being funded by a deferred payment agreement, in which case it is added to the amount owed. In choosing which option to take it will need to consider the individual circumstances of the case, and should be able to assure itself of the security of the arrangements and that there is no undue pressure on the person making the 'top-up' payment to increase the level of payment. Whichever option it chooses, it remains responsible for the total amount. The options are:

- treat the 'top-up' payment as part of the person's income and therefore recover the costs from the person concerned through the financial assessment (where the 'top-up' payments are being made by a third party rather than the cared for person, this is on the assumption that the third party makes the payment to the person with care needs); or

- agree with the person, the third party paying the 'top-up' (if this is not the cared for person) and the provider that payment for the 'top-up' element can be made directly to the provider with the local authority paying the remainder. However, as stated earlier, this is not recommended; or

- the person making the 'top-up' payments pays the 'top-up' amount to the local authority. The local authority then pays the full amount to the provider.

30. In the case of people with eligible needs who pay in full for their own care and support who ask the local authority to arrange their care, refer to paragraph 41.

PROVISIONS FOR REVIEWING THE AGREEMENT

31. As with any financial arrangement, an agreement to make a 'top-up' payment **must** be reviewed. A local authority must set out in writing details of how the arrangements will be reviewed, what may trigger a review, and circumstances when any party can request a review.

32. Local authorities should also consider how often it may be appropriate to review the arrangements. In doing so it should bear in mind how often it reviews other financial arrangements, such as deferred payment agreements. These should take place at least annually and in line with wider reviews of the financial assessment.

CONSEQUENCES OF CEASING TO MAKE PAYMENTS

33. The local authority must make clear in writing the consequences should there be a break down in the arrangement to meet the cost of the 'top-up'. This should include that the person may be moved to an alternative accommodation where this would be suitable to meet their needs and affordable within the personal budget or local mental health after-care limit. As with any change of

circumstance, a local authority must undertake a new assessment before considering this course of action, including consideration of a requirement for an assessment of health needs, and have regard to the person's wellbeing.

PRICE INCREASES

34. Arrangements will need to be reviewed from time to time, for example in response to any changes in circumstances of the cared for person, the person making the 'top-up' payments (if this is different from the cared for person), local authority commissioning arrangements or a change in provider costs. However, these changes may not occur together and a local authority must set out in writing how these changes will be dealt with.

35. The local authority must clearly set out in writing to the person or persons concerned its approach to how any increased costs may be shared. This should also include details of how agreement will be reached on the sharing of any price increases. This should also state that there is no guarantee that these increased costs will automatically be shared evenly should the provider's costs rise more quickly than the amount the local authority would have increased the personal budget or local mental health after-care limit and there is an alternative option that would be affordable within that budget.

36. A local authority may wish to negotiate any future prices rises with the provider at the time of entering into a contract. This can help provide clarity for adults and providers and help ensure that the top up remains affordable.

37. The local authority should also make clear that where the person has a change in circumstances that requires a new financial assessment and this results in a change in the level of contribution the person themself makes, this may not reduce the need for a 'top-up' payment.

CONSEQUENCES OF CHANGES IN CIRCUMSTANCES OF THE PERSON MAKING THE 'TOP-UP' PAYMENT

38. The person making the 'top-up' payment could see an unexpected change in their financial circumstances that will impact their ability to continue to pay the 'top-up' fee. Where a person is unable to continue making 'top-up' payments, the local authority may seek to recover any outstanding debt and has the power to make alternative arrangements to meet a person's needs, subject to a needs assessment. The local authority must set out in writing how it will respond to such a change and what the responsibilities of the person making the 'top-up' payment are in terms of informing the local authority of the change in circumstances.

FIRST PARTY 'TOP UPS'

39. The person whose needs are to be met by the accommodation may themselves choose to make a 'top-up' payment only in the following circumstances:

- where they are subject to a 12-week property disregard (See chapter 8 on Charging);

- where they have a deferred payment agreement in place with the local authority. Where this is the case, the terms of the agreement should reflect this arrangement. For further guidance on deferred payment agreements see Chapter 9; or

- where they are receiving accommodation provided under S117 for mental health aftercare.

PEOPLE WHO ARE UNABLE TO MAKE THEIR OWN CHOICE

40. There will be cases where a person lacks capacity to express a choice for themselves. Local authorities should therefore act on the choices expressed by the person's advocate, carer or legal guardian in the same way they would on the person's own wishes, unless in the local authority's opinion it would be against the best interests of the person.

SELF-FUNDERS WHO ASK THE LOCAL AUTHORITY TO ARRANGE THEIR CARE

41. The Care Act 2014 enables a person who can afford to pay for their own care and support in full to ask the local authority to arrange their care on their behalf. Where the person requires care in a care home to meet their needs, the local authority may choose to respond to the person's request by meeting their needs. Where the person requires some other type of care, including other types of accommodation to which the right to a choice applies, the local authority must meet those needs. In such circumstances, whether because the authority chooses to meet needs in a care home, or is required to meet needs in some other type of accommodation, the same rules on choice **must** apply.

42. In supporting self-funders to arrange care, the local authority may choose to enter into a contract with the preferred provider, or may broker the contract on behalf of the person. Where the local authority is arranging and managing the contract with the provider, it should ensure that there are clear arrangements in place as to how the costs will be met, including any 'top-up' element.

43. Ultimately, the local authority should assure itself that robust contractual arrangements are in place in such circumstances that clearly set out where responsibilities for costs lie and ensure that the person understands those arrangements. Self-funders will have to pay for the costs of their care and support including, in cases where they choose a setting that is more expensive than the amount identified in their personal budget, the top-up element of the costs of that setting.

CHOICE OF ACCOMMODATION AND MENTAL HEALTH AFTER-CARE

44. Regulations made under section 117A of the Mental Health Act 1983 enable persons who qualify for after-care under section 117 to express a preference for particular accommodation if accommodation of the types specified in the regulations is to be provided as part of that after-care. Local authorities are required to provide or arrange the provision of the preferred accommodation if the conditions in the regulations are met.

45. The regulations give people who receive mental health after-care broadly the same rights to choice of accommodation as someone who receives care and support under the Care Act 2014. But some differences arise because after-care is provided free of charge and, as the legislative requirement for a care and support plan under the Care Act 2014 does not apply to section 117 after-care, the care plan should instead be drawn up under guidance on the Care Programme Approach (CPA). Care planning under the CPA should, if accommodation is an issue, include identifying the type of accommodation which is suitable for the person's needs and affording them the right to choice of accommodation set out in the

regulations made under section 117A. The person should be fully involved in the care planning process.

46. An adult has the right to choose accommodation provided that:

- the preferred accommodation is of the same type that the local authority has decided to provide or arrange;

- it is suitable for the person's needs;

- it is available (see guidance in paragraphs 12, 13 and 15; for mental health after-care purposes, "assessed needs" means needs identified in the CPA care plan); and

- where the accommodation is not provided by the local authority, the provider of the accommodation agrees to provide the accommodation to the person on the local authority's terms (see guidance in paragraph 18).

47. The principles in paragraphs, 5, 6, 7 and 40 apply equally where a local authority is providing, or arranging the provision of, accommodation in discharge of its after-care duty. The guidance in paragraphs 17 and 18 applies when the preferred choice cannot be met.

48. Where the cost of the person's preferred accommodation is more than the local authority would provide in a personal budget or local mental health after-care limit to meet the person's needs, then the local authority must arrange for them to be placed there, provided that either the person or a third party is willing and able to meet the additional cost.

49. The guidance in paragraphs 22 to 39 applies where the adult has chosen more expensive accommodation. For the purposes of section 117 after-care, however, references to a third party should be read as including the adult receiving the after-care (because an adult can also meet the additional cost when a local authority is providing, or arranging for the provision of accommodation in discharge of the after-care duty).

50. In securing the funds needed to meet the additional cost, a local authority may:

- Agree with the person and the provider, and in cases where a third party is paying the 'top-up', agree with that third party, that payment for the additional cost can be made directly to the provider with the local authority paying the remainder; or

- The person or the third party pays the 'top-up' amount to the local authority. The local authority then pays the full amount to the provider.

INFORMATION AND ADVICE

51. Under Section 4 of the Care Act 2014 a local authority must establish and maintain a service for providing people in its area with information and advice in relation to care and support. This **must** include information and advice about the different care providers available in the local area to enable choice as well as information and advice to help people to understand care charges, different ways to pay and money management. Local authorities should also have a role in facilitating access to financial information and advice provided independently of the local authority, including regulated information and advice where appropriate; to support people in making informed financial decisions. This may be

particularly appropriate when a person is considering paying a top-up to help them to understand what they would be paying the top-up for and come to a judgment about whether it would represent good value for money.

52. Where a 'top-up' arrangement is being entered in to, all parties should fully understand their responsibilities, liabilities and the consequences of the arrangements. A local authority must provide the third party with sufficient information and advice to support them to understand the terms of the proposed written agreement before entering in to it. Local authorities must also have regard to the general guidance on Information and Advice set out in Chapter 3.

COMPLAINTS

53. Complaints about how choice or any 'top-up' arrangement is exercise by the local authority fall within the scope of the local authority's statutory complaints procedure.

ANNEX B: TREATMENT OF CAPITAL

This annex covers:
- The treatment of capital when conducting a financial assessment in all circumstances.

---

1. This section of the guidance applies where a local authority has chosen to charge a person for the services it is arranging and therefore must undertake a financial assessment. When doing so, it must assess the income and capital of the person. This Annex covers the treatment of capital and should be read in conjunction with Annex C on the treatment of income. The details of the sources capital which local authorities must disregard are set out the regulations.

2. The financial assessment will need to look across all of a person's assets – both capital and income – decide which is capital and which is income, and assess those assets according to the regulations and guidance. A local authority therefore must also refer to Annex C on the treatment of income and Annex E on deliberate deprivation of assets before conducting a financial assessment. The treatment of income will vary depending on the type of setting a person is receiving care in. The treatment of capital, as set out in this annex, is broadly the same for all settings. Where there is a distinction between care homes and all other settings, this is clearly set out.

3. In assessing what a person can afford to contribute a local authority must apply the upper and lower capital limits. The upper capital limit is currently set at £23,250 and the lower capital limit at £14,250.

4. A person with assets above the upper capital limit will be deemed to be able to afford the full cost of their care. Those with capital between the lower and upper capital limit will be deemed as able to make a contribution, known as "tariff income", from their capital. Any capital below the lower capital limit should be disregarded. Further details are set out in paragraphs 24 to 28.

DEFINING CAPITAL
What is capital?
5. Capital can mean many different things and the intention is not to give a definitive definition here as a local authority will need to consult the regulations and consider the individual asset on its merits. In general it refers to financial resources available for use and tends to be from sources that are considered more durable than money in the sense that they can generate a return.

6. The following list gives examples of capital. This list is intended as a guide and is not exhaustive.

(a) Buildings
(b) Land
(c) National Savings Certificates and Ulster Savings Certificates
(d) Premium Bonds
(e) Stocks and shares
(f) Capital held by the Court of Protection or a Deputy appointed by that Court
(g) Any savings held in:
    (i) Building society accounts.

   (ii) Bank current accounts, deposit accounts or special investment accounts. This includes savings held in the National Savings Bank, Girobank and Trustee Savings Bank.

  (iii) SAYE schemes.

  (iv) Unit Trusts.

   (v) Co-operatives share accounts.

  (vi) Cash.

(h) Trust funds

7. It is important that people are not charged twice on the same resources. Therefore, resources should only be treated as income or capital but not both. If a person has saved money from their income then those savings should normally be treated as capital. However they should not be assessed as both income and capital in the same period. Therefore in the period when they are received as income, the resource should be disregarded as capital.

CASES WHERE IT IS NOT CLEAR WHETHER A PAYMENT IS CAPITAL OR INCOME

8. In assessing a person's assets it may not be immediately clear where a resource is capital or income, particularly where a person is due to receive planned payments. In order to guide a local authority's decision, in general, a planned payment of capital is one which is:

(a) not in respect of a specified period; and

(b) not intended to form part of a series of payments.

9. Local authorities should also have regard to the guidance on capital treated as income at paragraph 56.

WHO OWNS THE CAPITAL?

10. A capital asset is normally defined as belonging to the person in whose name it is held, the legal owner. However in some cases this may be disputed and/or beneficial ownership argued. Beneficial ownership is where someone enjoys the benefits of ownership, even though the title of the asset is held by someone else or where they directly or indirectly have the power to vote or influence a transaction regarding a particular asset. In most cases the person will be both the legal and beneficial owner.

11. Where ownership is disputed, a local authority should seek written evidence to prove where the ownership lies. If a person states they are holding capital for someone else, the local authority should obtain evidence of the arrangement, the origin of the capital and intentions for its future use and return to its rightful owner.

Example of capital dispute:

Arlene has £14,000 in a building society account in her own name. She says that £3,000 is set aside for her granddaughter's education. Unfortunately there is no deed of trust or other legal arrangement which would prevent Arlene using the whole amount herself. She is therefore treated as the beneficial owner of the whole amount.

Example of capital dispute:
Lisa has £10,000 in a bank account in her own name and shares valued at £6,500. She provides evidence to show that the shares were purchased on behalf of her son who is abroad and that they will be transferred to her son when he returns to the UK. Although Lisa is the legal owner, she is holding the shares in trust for her son who is the beneficial owner. Only the £10,000 is therefore treated as Lisa's capital.

---

12. Where a person has joint beneficial ownership of capital, except where there is evidence that the person own an unequal share, the total value should be divided equally between the joint owners and the person should be treated as owning an equal share. Once the person is in sole possession of their actual share, they can be treated as owning that actual amount.

13. In some cases a person may be the legal owner of a property but not the beneficial owner of a property. In other words, they have no rights to the proceeds of any sale. In such circumstances the property must not be taken into account.

CALCULATING THE VALUE OF CAPITAL

14. A local authority will need to work out what value a capital asset has in order to take account of it in the financial assessment. Other than National Savings Certificates, valuation must be the current market or surrender value of the capital asset, e.g. property, whichever is higher, *minus*:
   (a) 10% of the value if there will be any actual expenses involved in selling the asset. This must be expenses connected with the actual sale and not simply the realisation of the asset. For example the costs to withdraw funds from a bank account are not expenses of sale, but legal fees to sell a property would be; and
   (b) any outstanding debts secured on the asset, for example a mortgage.

15. A capital asset may have a current market value, for example stocks or shares, or a surrender value, for example premium bonds. The current market value will be the price a willing buyer would pay to a willing seller. The way the market value is obtained will depend on the type of asset held.

16. If the person and the assessing officer both agree that after deducting any relevant amounts set out in paragraph 14 that the total value of the person's capital is more than the upper capital limit of £23,250, or less then the lower capital limit of £14,250, then it is not necessary to obtain a precise valuation. If there are any disputes, a precise valuation should be obtained. However, the local authority should bear in mind how close someone is to the upper capital limit when deciding whether or not to obtain a precise valuation.

17. Where a precise valuation is required, a professional valuer should be asked to provide a current market valuation. Once the asset is sold, the capital value to be taken into account is the actual amount realised from the sale, minus any actual expenses of the sale.

18. Where the value of a property is disputed, the aim should be to resolve this as quickly as possible. Local authorities should try to obtain an independent valuation of the person's beneficial share of the property within the 12-week disregard period where a person is in a care home. This will enable local authorities to work

out what charges a person should pay and enable the person, or their representative, to consider whether to seek a deferred payment agreement.

19. The value of National Savings Certificates (and Ulster Savings Certificates) (Premium Bonds) is assessed in the same way as other capital assets. A valuation for savings certificates can be obtained by contacting the NS&I helpline on 0845 964 5000. An alternative method to get the value of National Savings Certificates is to use the NS&I online calculator.[1] To enable an accurate value for the savings certificates the person must provide details of the:

- certificate issue number(s);

- purchase price;

- date of purchase.

ASSETS HELD ABROAD

20. Where capital is held abroad and all of it can be transferred to the UK, its value in the other country should be obtained and taken into account *less* any appropriate deductions under paragraph 14. Where capital is held jointly, it should be treated the same as if it were held jointly within the UK. The detail will depend on the conditions for transfer to the UK.

21. Where the capital cannot be wholly transferred to the UK due to the rules of that country, for example currency restrictions, the local authority should require evidence confirming this fact. Examples of acceptable evidence could include documentation from a bank, Government official or solicitor in either this country or the country where the capital is held.

22. Where some restriction is in place, a local authority should seek evidence showing what the asset is, what its value is and to understand the nature and terms of the restriction so that should this change, the amount can be taken into account. It should also take into account the value that a willing buyer would pay in the UK for those assets, but be aware that it may be less than the market or surrender value in the foreign country.

CAPITAL NOT IMMEDIATELY REALISABLE

23. Capital which is not immediately realisable due to notice periods, for example National Savings Bank investment accounts or Premium Bonds, should be taken into account in the normal way at its face value. This will be the value at the time of the financial assessment. It may need to be confirmed and adjusted when the capital is realised. If the person chooses not to release the capital, the value at the time of assessment should be used and it should be reassessed at intervals in the normal way.

CAPITAL LIMITS
Upper and lower capital limits
24. The capital limits set out at what point a person is able to access local authority support and how much support they receive. The local authority must apply the capital limits. The capital limits for 2015/16 are:

  (a) Upper capital limit: £23,250;

  (b) Lower capital limit: £14,250.

---

[1] See http://www.nsandi.com/savings-index-linked- savings-certificates#interest-calculator

25. If a person clearly has capital in excess of the upper capital limit, there is no need to make a wider assessment. If a person is near the upper capital limit, the local authority should be mindful of the need to plan ahead for when assets have been spent down and a person may therefore fall below the upper capital limit. This will help reduce burdens on both the local authority and the person from needing to repeat the financial assessment within a short timeframe.

26. The capital which a person has below the lower capital limit must be disregarded in the calculation of tariff income (see below).

TARIFF INCOME

27. Where a person has assets between the lower and upper capital limits the local authority must apply tariff income. This assumes that for every £250 of capital, or part thereof, a person is able to afford to contribute £1 per week towards the cost of their eligible care needs.

Example of tariff income:

Nora has capital of £18,100. This is £3,850 above the lower capital limit of £14,250. Dividing the £3,850 by £250 produces a figure of £15.40. When calculating tariff income, the amount is always rounded up. This therefore gives a tariff income of £16 per week.

NOTIONAL CAPITAL

28. In some circumstances a person may be treated as possessing a capital asset even where they do not actually possess it. This is called notional capital.

29. Notional capital may be capital which:

(a) would be available to the person if they applied for it;
(b) is paid to a third party in respect of the person;
(c) the person has deprived themselves of in order to reduce the amount of charge they have to pay for their care.

30. A person's capital should therefore be the total of both actual and notional capital. However, if a person has actual capital above the upper capital limit, it may not be necessary to consider notional capital.

31. Where a person has been assessed as having notional capital, the value of this must be reduced over time. The rule is that the value of notional capital must be reduced weekly by the difference between the weekly rate the person is paying for their care and the weekly rate they would have paid if notional capital did not apply.

Example of diminishing notional capital:

Hayley is receiving care and support in a care home. She is assessed as having notional capital of £20,000 plus actual capital of £6,000. This means her assets are above the upper capital limit and she needs to pay the full cost of her care and support at £400 per week.

The notional capital should therefore be reduced by the difference between the sum Hayley is paying (£400) and would have paid without the notional capital (£100).

> If she did not have the notional capital it would not affect her ability to pay. This is as she has an income of £120.40 and a personal allowance of £24.40 per week and would therefore be assessed as being able to pay £100.

32. Where a person is benefiting from the 12-week property disregard and has chosen to pay a "top-up" fee from their capital resources between the upper and lower capital limits, the level of tariff income that applies during those 12 weeks is the same as it would be if the person were not using the capital to "top-up".

CAPITAL DISREGARDED

33. The following capital assets must be disregarded:
(a) Property in specified circumstances (see paragraph 34);
(b) The surrender value of any:
  (i) Life insurance policy;
  (ii) Annuity.
(c) Payments of training bonuses of up to £200;
(d) Payments in kind from a charity;
(e) Any personal possessions such as paintings or antiques, unless they were purchased with the intention of reducing capital in order to avoid care and support charges (Schedule 2 Paragraph 13);
(f) Any capital which is to be treated as income or student loans;
(g) Any payment that may be derived from:
  (i) The Macfarlane Trust;
  (ii) The Macfarlane (Special Payments) Trust;
  (iii) The Macfarlane (Special Payment) (No 2) Trust;
  (iv) The Caxton Foundation;
  (v) The Fund (payments to non-haemophiliacs infected with HIV);
  (vi) The Eileen Trust;
  (vii) The MFET Trust;
  (viii) The Independent Living Fund (2006);
  (ix) The Skipton Fund;
  (x) The London Bombings Relief Charitable Fund.
(h) The value of funds held in trust or administered by a court which derive from a payment for personal injury to the person. For example, the vaccine damage and criminal injuries compensation funds;
  (i) The value of a right to receive:
  (i) Income under an annuity;
  (ii) Outstanding instalments under an agreement to repay a capital sum;
  (iii) Payment under a trust where the funds derive from a personal injury;
  (iv) Income under a life interest or a life-rent;
  (v) Income (including earnings) payable in a country outside the UK which cannot be transferred to the UK;
  (vi) An occupational pension;
  (vii) Any rent. Please note however that this does not necessarily mean the income is disregarded. Please see Annex C for guidance on the treatment of income.
(j) Capital derived from an award of damages for personal injury which is administered by a court or which can only be disposed of by a court order or direction;

(k) The value of the right to receive any income under an annuity purchased pursuant to any agreement or court order to make payments in consequence of personal injury or from funds derived from a payment in consequence of a personal injury and any surrender value of such an annuity;

(l) Periodic payments in consequence of personal injury pursuant to a court order or agreement to the extent that they are not a payment of income and area treated as income (and disregarded in the calculation of income);

(m) Any Social Fund payment;

(n) Refund of tax on interest on a loan which was obtained to acquire an interest in a home or for repairs or improvements to the home;

(o) Any capital resources which the person has no rights to as yet, but which will come into his possession at a later date, for example on reaching a certain age;

(p) Payments from the Department of Work and Pensions to compensate for the loss of entitlement to Housing Benefit or Housing Benefit Supplement;

(q) The amount of any bank charges or commission paid to convert capital from foreign currency to sterling;

(r) Payments to jurors or witnesses for court attendance (but not compensation for loss of earnings or benefit);

(s) Community charge rebate/council tax rebate;

(t) Money deposited with a Housing Association as a condition of occupying a dwelling;

(u) Any Child Support Maintenance Payment;

(v) The value of any ex-gratia payments made on or after 1st February 2001 by the Secretary of State in consequence of a person's, or person's spouse or civil partner's imprisonment or internment by the Japanese during the Second World War;

(w) Any payment made by a local authority under the Adoption and Children Act 2002 (under section 2(b)(b) or 3 of this act);

(x) The value of any ex-gratia payments from the Skipton Fund made by the Secretary of State for Health to people infected with Hepatitis C as a result of NHS treatment with blood or blood products;

(y) Payments made under a trust established out of funds provided by the Secretary of State for Health in respect of persons suffering from variant Creutzfeldt-Jakob disease to the victim or their partner (at the time of death of the victim);

(z) Any payments under Section 2, 3 or 7 of the Age-Related Payments Act 2004 or Age Related Payments Regulations 2005 (SI No 1983);

(aa) Any payments made under section 63(6)(b) of the Health Services and Public Health Act 1968 to a person to meet childcare costs where he or she is undertaking instruction connected with the health service by virtue of arrangements made under that section;

(ab) Any payment made in accordance with regulations under Section 14F of the Children Act 1989 to a resident who is a prospective special guardian or special guardian, whether income or capital.

Example of disregarded capital:
Mr T is a former Far East prisoner of war and receives a £10,000 ex-gratia payment as a result of his imprisonment. He now requires care and support and has a total of £25,000 in capital. When calculating how much capital should be taken into account, the local authority must disregard the first £10,000 – the value of the ex-gratia payment. The normal capital rules are then applied to the remaining £15,000. In this case, the first £14,250 would be completely disregarded in addition to the £10,000. Tariff income would therefore only be applied to the remaining £750 giving a charge of £3.

PROPERTY DISREGARDS

34. In the following circumstances the value of the person's *main or only* home must be disregarded:
  (a) Where the person is receiving care in a setting that is not a care home;
  (b) If the person's stay in a care home is temporary and they:
      (i) intend to return to that property and that property is still available to them; or
      (ii) are taking reasonable steps to dispose of the property in order to acquire another more suitable property to return to.
  (c) Where the person no longer occupies the property but it is occupied in part or whole as their main or only home by any of the people listed below, the mandatory disregard only applies where the property has been continuously occupied since before the person went into a care home (for discretionary disregards see below):
      (i) the persons partner, former partner or civil partner, except where they are estranged;
      (ii) a lone parent who is the person's estranged or divorced partner;
      (iii) a relative as defined in paragraph 35 of the person or member of the person's family who is:
          (1) Aged 60 or over, or
          (2) Is a child of the resident aged under 18, or
          (3) Is incapacitated.

35. For the purposes of the disregard a relative is defined as including any of the following:
  (a) Parent (including an adoptive parent)
  (b) Parent-in-law
  (c) Son (including an adoptive son)
  (d) Son-in-law
  (e) Daughter (including an adoptive daughter)
  (f) Daughter-in-law
  (g) Step-parent
  (h) Step-son
      (i) Step-daughter
  (j) Brother
  (k) Sister
  (l) Grandparent
  (m) Grandchild
  (n) Uncle

(o) Aunt
(p) Nephew
(q) Niece
(r) The spouse, civil partner or unmarried partner of a to k inclusive.

36. A member of the person's family is defined as someone who is living with the qualifying relative as part of an unmarried couple, married to or in a civil partnership.

37. For the purposes of the disregard the meaning of "incapacitated" is not closely defined. However, it will be reasonable to conclude that a relative is incapacitated if either of the following conditions apply:

(a) the relative is receiving one (or more) of the following benefits: incapacity benefit, severe disablement allowance, disability living allowance, personal independence payments, armed forces independence payments, attendance allowance, constant attendance allowance, or a similar benefit; or

(b) the relative does not receive any disability related benefit but their degree of incapacity is equivalent to that required to qualify for such a benefit. Medical or other evidence may be needed before a decision is reached.

38. For the purpose of the property disregard, the meaning of "occupy" is not closely defined. In most cases it will be obvious whether or not the property is occupied by a qualifying relative as their main or only home. However, there will be some cases where this may not be clear and the local authority should undertake a factual inquiry weighing up all relevant factors in order to reach a decision. An emotional attachment to the property alone is not sufficient for the disregard to apply.

39. Circumstances where it may be unclear might include where a qualifying relative has to live elsewhere for the purposes of their employment, for example a member of the armed services or the diplomatic service. Whilst they live elsewhere in order to undertake their employment, the property remains their main or only home. Another example may be someone serving a prison sentence. It would not be reasonable to regard the prison as the person's main or only home and they may well intend to return to the property in question at the end of their sentence. In such circumstances the local authority may wish to consider the qualifying relative's length of sentence and the likelihood of them returning to the property. Essentially the qualifying relative is occupying the property but is not physically present.

Example of emotional attachment to a property:

Bea is 62 years' old and lives with her family in Kent. Her father Patrick is a widower who has been living in the family home in Teddington that she and her sister grew up in and where she occasionally stays to help her father. Patrick has been assessed as having eligible care and support needs that are best met by moving into a care home.

Although Bea is over the age of 60, the family home is not her main or only home and the property is therefore not disregarded.

Example of occupying a property when not physically present:
Matt is 60 years old and has been living overseas for the past 10 years due to his job in the diplomatic service. When he is in England, he lives at the family home he grew up in. His father Ken has been assessed as having eligible care and support needs that are best met by moving into a care home.

In Ken's financial assessment, the value of his property is disregarded as his son Matt is a qualifying relative that occupies the property as his main or only home. Although Matt is not physically present at the property at the point Ken moves into the care home, his alternative accommodation is only as a result of his employment and the family home is his main home.

40. The local authority will need to take account of the individual circumstances of each case; however, it may be helpful to consider the following factors in making a decision:

- Does the relative currently occupy another property?
- If the relative has somewhere else to live do they own or rent the property (i.e. how secure/ permanent is it?)
- If the relative is not physically present is there evidence of a firm intention to return to or live in the property
- Where does the relative pay council tax?
- Where is the relative registered to vote?
- Where is the relative registered with a doctor?
- Are the relatives belongings located in the property?
- Is there evidence that the relative has a physical connection with the property?

41. A property must be disregarded where the relative meets the qualifying conditions (i.e. is aged 60 or over or is incapacitated) and has occupied the property as their main or only home since before the resident entered the care home.

DISCRETIONARY DISREGARD
42. A local authority may also use its discretion to apply a property disregard in other circumstances. However, the local authority will need to balance this discretion with ensuring a person's assets are not maintained at public expense. An example where it may be appropriate to apply the disregard is where it is the sole residence of someone who has given up their own home in order to care for the person who is now in a care home or is perhaps the elderly companion of the person.

Example of local authority discretion to apply a property disregard:
Jayne has the early signs of dementia but wishes to continue living in her own home. She is not assessed as having eligible needs, but would benefit from some occasional support. Her best friend Penny gives up her own home to

move in with Jayne. At this point, there is no suggestion that Jayne may need care in a care home.

After 5 years Jayne's dementia has reached the point where she needs a far greater level of care and support and following an assessment it is agreed her needs would best be met in a care home. On moving into the care home, the local authority uses its discretion to apply the property disregard as this has now become Penny's main or only home.

43. A property may be disregarded when a qualifying relative moves into the property after the resident enters a care home. Where this happens the local authority will need to consider all the relevant factors in deciding whether the property must be disregarded. Factors such as the timing and purpose of the move may be relevant to establishing if the property is the relative's main or only home. The purpose of the disregard in these circumstances is to safeguard certain categories of people from the risk of homelessness.

44. The local authority should consider if the principle reason for the move is that it is necessary to ensure the relative has somewhere to live as their main or only home. A disregard would not be appropriate, for example where a person moves into a property solely to protect the family inheritance. Local authorities need to ensure that people are not needlessly maintained at public expense. A local authority will need to take account of the individual circumstances of each case; however, it may be helpful to consider the factors listed above for the mandatory disregard plus the following additional factors in making a decision:

- Was the relative occupying another property as their main or only home at the time of the previous financial assessment?

- Could the relative have reasonably expected to have the property taken into account at the time they moved into the property?

- Would failure to disregard the property result in the eligible relative becoming homeless?

- Would failure to disregard the property negatively impact on the eligible relatives own health and wellbeing?

Example of local authority discretion to apply a property disregard where the qualifying person moves into the property after the resident entered the care home:
Fred's family home is unoccupied because his father has died and his mother is in a care home and Fred and his siblings have their own homes. The property is subject to a deferred payments agreement. Fred has a serious accident and becomes incapacitated.

As a result he unable to work or pay for his existing home. He has nowhere else to live so he moves into the family home which becomes his only home.

In the circumstances, the local authority exercises its discretion to disregard the property.

Example of local authority discretion to apply a property disregard:
Hilda is 63 and lives in a rented flat. Her brother, Stephen, has recently died and his wife, Charlotte, has moved in to a care home. Hilda suddenly loses her job and finds she unable to afford to live in her rented flat. As a result, Hilda moves into Stephen and Charlotte's house and this becomes her only home.

In the circumstances, the local authority exercises its discretion to disregard the property.

12-WEEK PROPERTY DISREGARD

45. A key aim of the charging framework is to prevent people being forced to sell their home at a time of crisis. The regulations under the Care Act 2014 therefore create space for people to make decisions as to how to meet their contribution to the cost of their eligible care needs. A local authority must therefore disregard the value of a person's *main or only* home when the value of their non-housing assets is below the upper capital limit for 12 weeks in the following circumstances:
  (a) when they first enter a care home as a permanent resident; or
  (b) when a property disregard other than the 12-week property disregard unexpectedly ends because the qualifying relative has died or moved into a care home.
46. In addition, a local authority has discretion to choose to apply the disregar when there is a sudden and unexpected change in the person's financial circumstances. In deciding whether to do so, the local authority will want to consider the individual circumstances of the case. Such circumstances might include a fall in share prices or an unanticipated debt. An example is given below.

Example of the end of a property disregard:
Win and Ern have been married for 60 years and brought a home together. 18 months ago, Win moved into a care home as a result of dementia. During her financial assessment, the value of the home she shared with Ern was disregarded as Ern is her husband, was over 60 years old and still lived in the property.

Ern has been in good health and there is no reason to anticipate a sudden change in circumstance. Unfortunately Ern suffers a heart attack and passes away, leaving the property to Win. There is no longer an eligible person living in the property, meaning its value can now be taken into account in what Win can afford to contribute to the cost of her care.

Given this was unplanned for, Win and her family need time to consider what the best option might be. The 12 week disregard would therefore be applied.

Example of an unexpected change in financial circumstances:
Harry is a widower who owns his own home. 10 months ago he moved into a care home as a self-funder. He has been meeting the bulk of his costs from shares he received as part of his redundancy package. Due to an unexpected event, the value of his shared is suddenly reduced by half, meaning he is unable to meet the cost of his care.

Although already in a care home and likely to remain responsible for paying for this care, Harry approaches the local authority for assistance and to seek a Deferred Payment Agreement. During the financial assessment the local authority agrees that the circumstances could not have been foreseen and uses its discretion to disregard the value of his property for the first 12 weeks. This provides Harry with the space he needs to make arrangements for the Deferred Payment Agreement to be put in place and enable him to continue to meet the cost of his care.

26-WEEK DISREGARD

47. The following capital assets must be disregarded for at least 26 weeks in a financial assessment. However, a local authority may choose to apply the disregard for longer where it considers this appropriate. For example where a person is taking legal steps to occupy premises as their home, but the legal processes take more than 26 weeks to complete.
  (a) Assets of any business owned or part-owned by the person in which they were a self- employed worker and has stopped work due to some disease or disablement but intends to take up work again when they are fit to do so. Where the person is in a care home, this should apply from the date they first took up residence. [Schedule 2 Paragraph 9]
  (b) Money acquired specifically for repairs to or replacement of the person's home or personal possessions provided it is used for that purpose. This should apply from the date the funds were received. [Schedule 2 Paragraph 12]
  (c) Premises which the person intends to occupy as their home where they have started legal proceedings to obtain possession. This should be from the date legal advice was first sought or proceedings first commenced. [Schedule 2 Paragraph 22]
  (d) Premises which the person intends to occupy as their home where essential repairs or alterations are required. This should apply from the date the person takes action to effect the repairs. [Schedule 2 Paragraph 21]
  (e) Capital received from the sale of a former home where the capital is to be used by the person to buy another home. This should apply from the date of completion of the sale. [Schedule 2 Paragraph 6]
  (f) Money deposited with a Housing Association which is to be used by the person to purchase another home. This should apply from the date on which the money was deposited. [Schedule 2 Paragraph 11]
  (g) Grant made under a Housing Act which is to be used by the person to purchase a home or pay for repairs to make the home habitable. This should apply from the date the grant is received. [Schedule 4 Paragraph 22]

52-WEEK DISREGARD

48. The following payments of capital must be disregarded for a maximum of 52 weeks from the date they are received.
  (a) The balance of any arrears of or any compensation due to non-payment of:
    (i) Mobility supplement
    (ii) Attendance Allowance
    (iii) Constant Attendance Allowance

(iv) Disability Living Allowance / Personal Independence Payment
(v) Exceptionally Severe Disablement Allowance
(vi) Severe Disablement Occupational Allowance
(vii) Armed forces service pension based on need for attendance
(viii) Pension under the Personal Injuries (Civilians) Scheme 1983, based on the need for attendance
(ix) Income Support/Pension Credit
(x) Minimum Income Guarantee
(xi) Working Tax Credit
(xii) Child Tax Credit
(xiii) Housing Benefit (xiv)Universal Credit
(xv) Special payments to pre-1973 war widows.

As the above payments will be paid for specific periods, they should be treated as income over the period for which they are payable. Any money left over after the period for which they are treated as income has elapsed should be treated as capital. [Schedule 2 Paragraphs 10 and 11]

(b) Payments or refunds for:
(i) NHS glasses, dental treatment or patient's travelling expenses;
(ii) Cash equivalent of free milk and vitamins;
(iii) Expenses in connection with prison visits. [Schedule 2 Paragraph 22]

(c) Personal Injury Payments.

Example of a disregard for 52 weeks:
During his financial assessment it is identified that Colin is eligible for Pension Credit but is not currently claiming the support. He is therefore assessed as being able to pay £75 per week towards the cost of his care.

Colin tells the local authority that he will apply for Pension Credit. It is explained to him that the level of what he can afford to contribute will be reassessed once he started receiving the additional support. If the payments are backdated, his contributions to the cost of his care will also be backdated and he may therefore need to make an additional payment to meet any arrears. Colin therefore chooses to pay £90 per week.

After six weeks, arrears of Pension Credit at £35 per week (£210) are received. What Colin can afford to contribute is reassessed and he is now asked to pay £110 per week. As Colin has been paying £15 a week more than required, he only owes £120 rather than the full £210 of Pension Credit arrears. The remaining £90 of arrears payments should therefore be treated as capital and disregarded

---

2-YEAR DISREGARD
49. Local authorities must disregard payments made under a trust established out of funds by the Secretary of State for Health in respect of vCJD to:
(a) A member of the victim's family for 2 years from the date of death of the victim (or from the date of payment from the trust if later); or
(b) A dependent child or young person until they turn 18. [Schedule 2 Paragraph 27]

OTHER DISREGARDS

50. In some cases a person's assets may be tied up in a business that they own or part- own. Where a person is taking steps to realise their share of the assets, these should be disregarded during the process. However, the person should be required to show that it is their clear intention to realise the asset as soon as practicable. In order to show their intent, the local authority should request the following information:

(a) A description of the nature of the business asset;
(b) The person's estimate of the length of time necessary to realise the asset or their share of it;
(c) A statement of what, if any, steps have been taken to realise the asset, what these were and what is intended in the near future; and
(d) Any other relevant evidence, for example the person's health, receivership, liquidation, estate agent's confirmation of placing any property on the market.

51. Where the person has provided this information to show that steps are being taken to realise the value of the asset, the local authority must disregard the value for a period that it considers to be reasonable. In deciding what is reasonable it should take into account the length of time of any legal processes that may be needed.

52. Where the person has no immediate intention of attempting to realise the business asset, its capital value should be taken into account in the financial assessment. Where a business is jointly owned, this should apply only to the person's share.

TREATMENT OF INVESTMENT BONDS

53. The treatment of investment bonds is currently complex. This is in part because of the differing products that are on offer. As such, local authorities may wish to seek advice from their legal departments.

54. Where an investment bond includes one or more element of life insurance policies that contain cashing-in rights by way of options for total or partial surrender, then the value of those rights must be disregarded as a capital asset in the financial assessment.

CAPITAL TREATED AS INCOME

55. The following capital payments should be treated as income. Local authorities therefore must have regard to Annex C before conducting their assessments.

(a) Any payment under an annuity.
(b) Capital paid by instalment where the total of:
  (i) the instalments outstanding at the time the person first becomes liable to pay for their care, or in the case of a person in temporary care whom the local authority had previously decided not to charge, the first day on which the local authority decided to charge; and
  (ii) the amount of other capital held by the resident is over £16,000. If it is £16,000 or less, each instalment should be treated as capital. [Regulation 16]

EARNINGS

56. Any income of the person derived from employment must be treated as earnings and not taken into account in the financial assessment.

INCOME TREATED AS CAPITAL

57. The following types of income should be treated as capital:

(a) Any refund of income tax charged on profits of a business or earnings of an employed earner; Any holiday pay payable by an employer more than 4 weeks after the termination or interruption of employment;

(b) Income derived from a capital asset, for example, building society interest or dividends from shares. This should be treated as capital from the date it is normally due to be paid to the person. This does not apply to income from certain disregarded capital;

(c) Any advance of earnings or loan made to an employed earner by the employer if the person is still in work. This is as the payment does not form part of the employee's regular income and would have to be repaid;

(d) Any bounty payment paid at intervals of at least one year from employment as:

   (i) A part time fireman;

   (ii) An auxiliary coastguard;

   (iii) A part time lifeboat man;

   (iv) A member of the territorial or reserve forces.

(e) Charitable and voluntary payments which are neither made regularly nor due to be made regularly, apart from certain exemptions such as payments from AIDS trusts. Payments will include those made by a third party to the person to support the clearing of charges for accommodation.

(f) Any payments of arrears of contributions by a local authority to a custodian towards the cost of accommodation and maintenance of a child. [Regulation 18]

CAPITAL AVAILABLE ON APPLICATION

58. In some instances a person may need to apply for access to capital assets but has not yet done so. In such circumstances this capital should be treated as already belonging to the person except in the following instances:

(a) Capital held in a discretionary trust;

(b) Capital held in a trust derived from a payment in consequence of a personal injury;

(c) Capital derived from an award of damages for personal injury which is administered by a court;

(d) Any loan which could be raised against a capital asset which is disregarded, for example the home. [Regulation 21(2)]

59. A local authority should distinguish between:

(a) Capital already owned by the person but which in order to access they must make an application for. For example:

   (i) Money held by the person's solicitor;

   (ii) Premium Bonds;

   (iii) National Savings Certificates;

   (iv) Money held by the Registrar of a County Court which will be released on application; and

(b) Capital not owned by the person that will become theirs on application, for example an unclaimed Premium Bond win. This should be treated as notional capital. [Regulation 21(2)]

60. Where a local authority treats capital available on application as notional capital they should do so only from the date at which it could be acquired by the person. [Regulation 21(2)]

61. April 2015 also sees much greater flexibility introduced regarding how people can access their defined contribution pensions, including enabling them to access their full pension pot. As a result, when applying notional income to a defined contribution pension this should be calculated as the maximum income that would be available if the person had taken out an annuity. Further guidance is provided in paragraph 25 of Annex C.

ANNEX C: TREATMENT OF INCOME

This annex covers:
- The treatment of income when conducting a financial assessment in all circumstances. This is divided into:
- Care homes;
- All other settings;
- The purpose of this annex is to provide local authorities with detailed guidance on how to apply to the Care and Support (Charging and Assessment of Resources) Regulations 2014, in terms of how to treat different types of income when calculating what a person can afford to contribute to the cost of their eligible care needs.

1. This section of the guidance only applies where a local authority has chosen to charge a person for the services it is arranging and therefore must undertake a financial assessment. When doing so, it must assess the income and capital of the person.

2. There are differences in how income is treated in a care home and in all other settings. Charging a person in a care home is provided for in a consistent national framework. When charging a person in all other settings, a local authority has more discretion to enable it to take account of local practices and innovations. The guidance sets out the common issues and then those particular to each setting. Local authorities must read this guidance in all circumstances.

3. This annex covers the treatment of income and should be read in conjunction with Annex B on the treatment of capital. The detail of the sources of income which local authorities must disregard are set out in the regulations which accompany this guidance.

COMMON ISSUES

4. The following section sets out the issues common to charging for all settings.

5. Only the income of the cared-for person can be taken into account in the financial assessment of what they can afford to pay for their care and support. Where this person receives income as one of a couple, the starting presumption is that the cared-for person has an equal share of the income. A local authority should also consider the implications for the cared-for person's partner.

6. Income is net of any tax or National Insurance contributions.

7. Income will always be taken into account unless it is disregarded under the regulations. Income that is disregarded will either be:
(a) Partially disregarded; or
(b) Fully disregarded.

8. In all cases, irrespective of setting, employed and self-employed earnings are fully disregarded. [Regulation 13]

9. Earnings in relation to an employed earner are any remuneration or profit from employment. This will include:
(a) any bonus or commission;
(b) any payment in lieu of remuneration except any periodic sum paid to the person on account of the termination of their employment by reason of redundancy;

(c) any payments in lieu of notice or any lump sum payment intended as compensation for the loss of employment but only in so far as it represents loss of income;

(d) any holiday pay except any payable more than four weeks after the termination or interruption of employment;

(e) any payment by way of a retainer;

(f) any payment made by the person's employer in respect of any expenses not wholly, exclusively and necessarily incurred in the performance of the duties of employment, including any payment made by the person's employer in respect of travelling expenses incurred by the person between their home and the place of employment and expenses incurred by the person under arrangements made for the care of a member of the person's family owing to the person's absence from home;

(g) any award of compensation made under section 112(4) or 117(3)(a) of the Employment Rights Act 1996 (remedies and compensation for unfair dismissal);

(h) any such sum as is referred to in section 112 of the Social Security Contributions and Benefits Act 1992 (certain sums to be earnings for social security purposes);

   (i) any statutory sick pay, statutory maternity pay, statutory paternity pay or statutory adoption pay, or a corresponding payment under any enactment having effect in Northern Ireland;

(j) any remuneration paid by or on behalf of an employer to the person who for the time being is on maternity leave, paternity leave or adoption leave or is absent from work because of illness;

(k) the amount of any payment by way of a non-cash voucher which has been taken into account in the computation of a person's earnings in accordance with Part 5 of Schedule 3 to the Social Security (Contributions) Regulations 2001.

10. Earnings in relation to an employed earner do not include:

(a) any payment in kind, with the exception of any non-cash voucher which has been taken into account in the computation of the person's earnings – as referred to above;

(b) any payment made by an employer for expenses wholly, exclusively and necessarily incurred in the performance of the duties of the employment;

(c) any occupational/personal pension.

11. Earnings in the case of employment as a self-employed earner mean the gross receipts of the employment. This includes any allowance paid under section 2 of the Employment and Training Act 1973 or section 2 of the Enterprise and New Towns (Scotland) Act 1990 to the person for the purpose of assisting the person in carrying on his business.

12. Earnings in the case of employment as a self-employed earner do not include:

(a) any payment to the person by way of a charge for board and lodging accommodation provided by the person;

(b) any sports award.

13. Earnings also include any payment provided to prisoners to encourage and reward their constructive participation in the regime of the establishment, this may include payment for working, education or participation in other related activities.

BENEFITS

14. Local authorities may take most of the benefits people receive into account. Those they must disregard are listed below. However, they need to ensure that in addition to the minimum guaranteed income or personal expenses allowance – details of which are set out below – people retain enough of their benefits to pay for things to meet those needs not being met by the local authority.

15. Any income from the following sources must be fully disregarded:
(a) Direct Payments;
(b) Guaranteed Income Payments made to Veterans under the Armed Forces CompensationScheme;
(c) The mobility component of Disability Living Allowance;
     The mobility component of Personal Independence Payments.

16. Any income from the following benefits must be taken fully into account when considering what a person can afford to pay towards their care from their income:
(a) Attendance Allowance, including Constant Attendance Allowance and Exceptionally Severe Disablement Allowance
(b) Bereavement Allowance
(c) Carers Allowance
(d) Disability Living Allowance (Care component)
(e) Employment and Support Allowance or the benefits this replaces such as Severe Disablement Allowance and Incapacity Benefit
(f) Income Support
(g) Industrial Injuries Disablement Benefit or equivalent benefits
(h) Jobseeker's Allowance
(i) Maternity Allowance
(j) Pension Credit
(k) Personal Independence Payment (Daily Living component)
(l) State Pension
(m) Universal Credit
(n) Working Tax Credit.

17. Where any Social Security benefit payment has been reduced (other than a reduction because of voluntary unemployment), for example because of an earlier overpayment, the amount taken into account should be the gross amount of the benefit before reduction.

ANNUITY AND PENSION INCOME

18. An annuity is a type of pension product that provides a regular income for a number of years in return for an investment. Such products are usually purchased at retirement in order to provide a regular income. While the capital is disregarded, any income from an annuity must be taken fully into account except where it is:
(a) purchased with a loan secured on the person's main or only home; or
(b) a gallantry award such as the Victoria Cross Annuity or George Cross Annuity.

19. For those who have purchased an annuity with a loan secured on their main or only home, this is known as a 'home income plan'. Under these schemes, a person has purchased the annuity against the value of their home – similarly to a Deferred Payment Agreement.

20. Where a person is in a care home and paying half of the value of their occupational pension, personal pension or retirement annuity to their spouse or civil partner the local authority **must** disregard 50% of its value.

21. In order to qualify for the disregard, one of the annuitants must still be occupying the property as their main or only home. This may happen where a couple has jointly purchased an annuity and only one of them has moved into a care home. If this is not the case, the disregard must not be applied.

22. Where the disregard is applied, only the following aspects may be disregarded:

   (a) the net weekly interest on the loan where income tax is deductible from the interest; or

   (b) the gross weekly interest on the loan in any other case.

23. Before applying the disregard, the following conditions must be met:

   (a) The loan must have been made as part of a scheme that required that at least 90% of that loan be used to purchase the annuity;

   (b) The annuity ends with the life of the person who obtained the loan, or where there are two or more annuitants (including the person who obtained the loan), with the life of the last surviving annuitant;

   (c) The person who obtained the loan or one of the other annuitants is liable to pay the interest on the loan;

   (d) The person who obtained the loan (or each of the annuitant where there are more than one) must have reached the age of 65 at the time the loan was made;

   (e) The loan was secured on a property in Great Britain and the person who obtained the loan (or one of the other annuitants) owns an estate or interest in that property; and

   (f) The person who obtained the loan or one of the other annuitant occupies the property as their main or only home at the time the interest is paid.

24. Where the person is using part of the income to repay the loan, the amount paid as interest must be disregarded. If the payments the person makes on the loan are interest only and the person qualifies for tax relief on the interest they pay, disregard the net interest. Otherwise, disregard the gross interest.

25. Reforms to defined contribution pensions come into effect from April 2015. The aim of the reforms is to provide people with much greater flexibility in how they fund later life. This may lead to changes in how people use the money in their pension fund. The rules for how to assess pension income for the purposes of charging are:

   (a) If a person has removed the funds and placed them in another product or savings account, they should be treated according to the rules for that product;

   (b) If a person is only drawing a minimal income, then a local authority can apply notional income choosing not to draw income, or according to the maximum income that could be drawn under an annuity product. If applying maximum notional income, the actual income should be disregarded to avoid double counting;

   (c) If a person is drawing down an income that is higher than the maximum available under an annuity product, the actual income that is being drawn down should be taken into account.

MORTGAGE PROTECTION INSURANCE POLICIES

26. Any income from an insurance policy is usually taken into account. In the case of mortgage protection policies where the income is specifically intended to support the person to acquire or retain an interest in their main or only home or to support them to make repairs or improvements to their main or only home it must be disregarded. However, the income must be being used to meet the repayments on the loan. The amount of income from a mortgage protection insurance policy that should be disregarded is the weekly sum of:

(a) The amount which covers the interest on the loan; plus
(b) The amount of the repayment which reduced the capital outstanding; plus
(c) The amount of the premium due on the policy.

27. It should be remembered that Income Support and Pension Credit may be adjusted to take account of the income from the policy.

OTHER INCOME THAT MUST BE FULLY DISREGARDED

28. Any income from the following sources **must** be fully disregarded:

(a) Armed Forces Independence Payments and Mobility Supplement
(b) Child Support Maintenance Payments and Child Benefit
(c) Child Tax Credit
(d) Council Tax Reduction Schemes where this involves a payment to the person
(e) Disability Living Allowance (Mobility Component) and Mobility Supplement
(f) Christmas bonus
(g) Dependency increases paid with certain benefits
(h) Discretionary Trust
(i) Gallantry Awards
(j) Guardian's Allowance
(k) Guaranteed Income Payments made to Veterans under the Armed Forces CompensationScheme
(l) Income frozen abroad
(m) Income in kind
(n) Pensioners Christmas payments
(o) Personal Independence Payment (Mobility Component) and Mobility Supplement
(p) Personal injury trust, including those administered by a Court
(q) Resettlement benefit
(r) Savings credit disregard
(s) Social Fund payments (including winter fuel payments)
(t) War widows and widowers special payments
(u) Any payments received as a holder of the Victoria Cross, George Cross or equivalent
(v) Any grants or loans paid for the purposes of education; and
(w) Payments made in relation to training for employment.
(x) Any payment from the:
  (i) Macfarlane Trust
  (ii) Macfarlane (Special Payments) Trust
  (iii) Macfarlane (Special Payment) (No 2) Trust
  (iv) Caxton Foundation
  (v) The Fund (payments to non-haemophiliacs infected with HIV)

Example of notional income:
Andrew is 70 and is living in a care home. He has not been receiving his occupational pension to which he would have been entitled to from age 65. After contacting his former employer, they state Andrew will be paid the entire pension due from age 65. The local authority can therefore apply notional income from age 65.

Example of notional income in relation to new pension flexibilities:
Ben has a pension fund worth £30,000. He has taken the opportunity to access this flexibly and as a result is only drawing down £5 a week as income at the point he begins to receive care and support.

The equivalent maximum annuity income would be £120 per week. For the purposes of the financial assessment, the local authority can assume an income £120 per week.

Example of notional income:
Andrew is 70 and is living in a care home. He has not been receiving his occupational pension to which he would have been entitled to from age 65. After contacting his former employer, they state Andrew will be paid the entire pension due from age 65. The local authority can therefore apply notional income from age 65.

---

36. However, there are some exemptions and the following sources of income must not be treated as notional income:
   (a) Income payable under a discretionary trust;
   (b) Income payable under a trust derived from a payment made as a result of a personal injury where the income would be available but has not yet been applied for;
   (c) Income from capital resulting from an award of damages for personal injury that is administered by a court;
   (d) Occupational pension which is not being paid because:
      (i) The trustees or managers of the scheme have suspended or ceased payments due to an insufficiency of resources; or
      (ii) The trustees or managers of the scheme have insufficient resources available to them to meet the scheme's liabilities in full.
   (e) Working Tax Credit.

DISABILITY-RELATED EXPENDITURE
37. Where disability-related benefits are taken into account, the local authority should make an assessment and allow the person to keep enough benefit to pay for necessary disability- related expenditure to meet any needs which are not being met by the local authority.
38. In assessing disability-related expenditure, local authorities should include the following. However, it should also be noted that this list is not intended to be

exhaustive and any reasonable additional costs directly related to a person's disability should be included :

(a) Payment for any community alarm system.

(b) Costs of any privately arranged care services required, including respite care.

(c) Costs of any specialist items needed to meet the person's disability needs, for example:

    iv. Day or night care which is not being arranged by the local authority;

    v. specialist washing powders or laundry;

    vi. additional costs of special dietary needs due to illness or disability (the person may be asked for permission to approach their GP in cases of doubt);

    vii. special clothing or footwear, for example, where this needs to be specially made; or additional wear and tear to clothing and footwear caused by disability;

    viii. additional costs of bedding, for example, because of incontinence;

    ix. any heating costs, or metered costs of water, above the average levels for the area and housing type,

    x. occasioned by age, medical condition or disability;

    xi. reasonable costs of basic garden maintenance, cleaning, or domestic help, if necessitated by the individual's disability and not met by social services;

    xii. purchase, maintenance, and repair of disability-related equipment, including equipment or transport needed to enter or remain in work; this may include IT costs, where necessitated by the disability; reasonable hire costs of equipment may be included, if due to waiting for supply of equipment from the local council;

    xiii. personal assistance costs, including any household or other necessary costs arising for the person;

    xiv. internet access for example for blind and partially sighted people

    xv. other transport costs necessitated by illness or disability, including costs of transport to day centres, over and above the mobility component of DLA or PIP, if in payment and available for these costs. In some cases, it may be reasonable for a council not to take account of claimed transport costs – if, for example, a suitable, cheaper form of transport, e.g. council- provided transport to day centres is available, but has not been used;

    xvi. in other cases, it may be reasonable for a council not to allow for items where a reasonable alternative is available at lesser cost. For example, a council might adopt a policy not to allow for the private purchase cost of continence pads, where these are available from the NHS.

39. The care plan may be a good starting point for considering what is necessary disability- related expenditure. However, flexibility is needed. What is disability-related expenditure should not be limited to what is necessary for care and support. For example, above average heating costs should be considered.

Example of disability related expenditure

Zach is visually impaired and describes the internet as a portal into the seeing world – in enabling him to access information that sighted people take for granted. For example he explains that if a sighted person wants to access information they can go to a library, pick up a book or buy an appropriate magazine that provides them with the information they need.

The internet is also a portal into shopping. For example without the internet if Zach wanted to shop for clothes, food or a gift he would have to wait until a friend or family member could accompany him on a trip out, he would be held by their schedule and they would then have to explain what goods were on offer, what an item looked like, the colour etc and would inevitably be based on the opinion and advice of said friend. A sighted person would be able to go into a shop when their schedule suits and consider what purchase to make on their own. The internet provides Zach with the freedom and independence to do these things on his own.

CARE HOMES

40. The following section deals with those who are receiving care and support in a care home only.

PERSONAL EXPENSES ALLOWANCE

41. The local authority **must** leave the person with a minimum amount of income. This is known as the Personal Expenses Allowance (PEA) and the amount is set out in regulations and updates sent via a local authority circular. Anything above this may be taken into account in determining charges.

42. The PEA is not a benefit but the amount of a person's own income that they **must** be left with after charges have been deducted. However, where a person has no income, the local authority is not responsible for providing one. However, the local authority should support the person to access any relevant state benefits or independent advocacy service.

43. The purpose of the PEA is to ensure that a person has money to spend as they wish. It must not be used to cover any aspect of their care and support that have been contracted for by the local authority and/or assessed as necessary to meet the person's eligible needs. This money is for the person to spend as they wish and any pressure from a local authority or provider to do otherwise is not permitted.

44. There may be some circumstances where it would not be appropriate for the local authority to leave a person only with the personal expenses allowance after charges. For example:

(a) Where a person has a dependent child the local authority should consider the needs of the child in determining how much income a person should be left with after charges. This applies whether the child is living with the person or not.

(b) Where a person is paying half their occupational or personal pension or retirement annuity to a spouse or civil partner who is not living in the same care home, the local authority must disregard this money. This does not automatically apply to unmarried couples although the local authority may wish to exercise its discretion in individual cases.

(c) Where a person is temporarily in a care home and is a member of a couple – whether married or unmarried – the local authority should disregard any Income Support or Pension Credit awarded to pay for home commitments and should consider the needs of the person at home in setting the personal expenses allowance. It should also consider disregarding other costs related to maintain the couple's home (see below).

(d) Where a person's property has been disregarded the local authority should consider whether the PEA is sufficient to enable the person to meet any resultant costs. For example, allowances should be made for fixed payments (like mortgages, rent and Council Tax), building insurance, utility costs (gas, electricity and water, including basic heating during the winter) and reasonable property maintenance costs.

(e) Where a person has moved to local authority support and has a deferred payment agreement (DPA) in place, the local authority **should** ensure the person retains sufficient resources to maintain and insure the property in line with the disposable income allowance (DIA).

ALL OTHER SETTINGS

45. As all earnings must be disregarded, this leaves other sources of income such as benefits, pensions and payments from other products.

MINIMUM INCOME GUARANTEE

46. Local authorities must ensure that a person's income is not reduced below a specified level after charges have been deducted. This must be at least the equivalent of the value of Income Support or the Guaranteed Credit element of Pension Credit plus a minimum buffer of 25%. The amounts are set out in the Care and Support (Charging and Assessment of Resources) Regulations. However, this is only a minimum and local authorities have discretion to set a higher level if they wish. This approach will lead to greater consistency between the charging framework and established income protections under the income support rules. We will keep this under review and seek to update the charging framework in line with the roll-out of Personal Independence Payments and updating/repeal of the income support rules.

47. The purpose of the minimum income guarantee is to promote independence and social inclusion and ensure that they have sufficient funds to meet basic needs such as purchasing food, utility costs or insurance. This must be after any housing costs such as rent and council tax net of any benefits provided to support these costs – and after any disability related expenditure. For example, a council tenant will have water rates as part of a rent service charge whilst a private or housing association tenant will not.

48. Separate guidance applies when determining an appropriate contribution from income under a deferred payment agreement.

- The person or their representative could not reasonably have been aware that the asset in question needed to be included in the financial assessment.

10. It should also consider how different approaches might impact on a person's wellbeing, in line with a local authority's general duty to promote a person's wellbeing.

TIMING OF DEBT RECOVERY

11. The point at which a debt becomes due continues to be the date at which the sum becomes due to the local authority. This means that, for example, if a bill was sent giving 30 days to pay, the payment becomes due on day 30. For any debts that have accrued prior to the commencement of the Care Act 2014 the time period for recovering that debt continues to be three years as previously set out under Section 56 of the National Assistance Act 1948 as any change to this would be retrospective and unfair. For any new debts that occur after the commencement of the Care Act 2014, the time period to recover debts has been extended to six years from the date when the sum became due to the local authority. Where a debt is taking some time to be recovered, provided legal proceedings have issued within the limitation period, enforcement can continue. If it has not, the debt must be written off.

OPTIONS TO RECOVER DEBT

12. Local authorities should consider the full range of options available to recover the debt. This is particularly important as if the claim does end up in the court they are likely to consider what efforts have been made to resolve the issue first. Whilst it is at the discretion of the Court to award costs, if no effort has been made to reach an agreement first a judge may hold this against the local authority when considering making an order for payment of the costs in the case. The greater the person's need, the more effort should be made to resolve the issue positively through the use of effective social work skills. Options may include negotiation, using an advocate to help the person understand the options available to them, supporting the family to gain a power of attorney or deputyship, the local authority itself applying to be a deputy or the use of independent mediation. Local authorities should have regard to *Practice Direction – Pre-Action Conduct* guidance provided by the Ministry of Justice available at http://www.justice.gov.uk/courts/procedure-rules/civil/rules/pd_pre-action_conduct#1.1

13. As a first step, the local authority should contact the person or their representative in an effort to ascertain why the contribution to their care and support costs has not been met. In the first instance this is likely to be by phone, but may also include written communication in an appropriate format or a visit. This should not be a tick box exercise and there should be more than one effort to contact the person by each of these routes in order to simply and quickly address the issue if possible, whilst balancing the need to minimise further delays.

14. In some cases the issue will be easily resolved as a result of the contact, either through the amount being paid or from the offer of a DPA, where appropriate and further detail on this is set out below. However, some cases will be more complex. For example if a person does not meet the eligibility criteria for a DPA, a DPA is refused or there remains a dispute about the amount. Or a person may be unhappy about being placed in a care home and wish to return home, or could be

depressed, have mental health needs or dementia. In many cases, social work assistance may be required.

15. The local authority must establish whether the person has the mental capacity to make financial decisions. This is important as a person who lacks capacity to make financial decisions is in a different legal position from someone who has capacity. While both may be liable for their debt, the way to proceed to recover the debt is different.

16. Where a person has mental capacity to make financial decisions, the local authority can proceed to the County Court but does have alternative options and should consider these. These can include:

- **Negotiating an agreement.** This could be through dealing directly with the person or their representative to broker a solution. This can be done by the local authority which may well support a better outcome, but in some circumstance this may be better led by an independent person such as an advisor or solicitor. In some cases it may be useful to involve an independent advocate to support the person to understand the options available to them.

- **Mediation.** This is where an independent third party assists those involved to reach an agreement. This could be carried out by a professional mediation service, but could also be carried out by anyone who is not involved in the issue, such as an independent social worker or a local voluntary organisation. It is important to understand that it is the people involved, not the mediator, who decide the course of action.

- **Arbitration.** This involves an independent arbitrator hearing both sides of the issue and making a decision on behalf of the parties that will resolve the issue. Local authorities should be aware that arbitration is usually binding on both sides and therefore cannot usually take the case to court after the arbitrator has made a decision.

DIMINISHING OR LACK OF MENTAL CAPACITY

17. In some cases a debt may have accrued as a result of diminishing or a lack of mental capacity. In such cases, the local authority may need to involve their safeguarding teams. It is estimated by the Alzheimer's Society that some 80% of people who enter into care homes have dementia. This means that many of those who are being placed in care homes may lack capacity to make financial decisions, and may have not been able to understand financial assessment forms, or the requests for payments. Social workers should be asked to carry out a decision specific capacity assessment where there is a diagnosis of mental impairment or mental disorder, or where the person's engagement with care planning shows they may lack capacity to make some decisions.

18. The better the local authority's understanding and application of the Mental Capacity Act 2005, the easier it is to prevent debts from building up and the easier it is to recover them. Where people with dementia or with learning disabilities have relevant mental capacity assessments on file, and where they also have appointed attorneys or deputies to make financial decisions with them or for them, or friends to support them in care planning, the local authority will be clearer about who to involve in financial decision making. This should help lead to less debt, and where it does occur, make it easier to recover.

19. Where a person has an attorney for property and financial affairs or a deputy, these roles give the attorney or deputy the legal authority to make financial decisions on behalf of the person, and require them to consider and engage with any debt recovery on behalf of the person. The local authority can use all the above methods with the attorney or deputy. They can negotiate an agreement, they can offer mediation, or they can use arbitration to recover the debt.

20. Where the person lacking capacity has no attorney or deputy and has substantial debts, then an application for a deputy is required. The application has to be made to the Court of Protection. Where there are family involved with the person, they may make the application to become a deputy. Where the local authority has an in house or contracted deputyship service, and there is no family, this service should make the application. Otherwise the social worker can make the application for the Court to appoint a deputy. While this process may take some weeks, it leads to the appointment of someone who has the legal authority both to make financial decisions and also to execute them – i.e. to access bank accounts and make payments. The local authority should also consider the risk of a conflict of interest where it applies to take on a property and financial affairs deputyship.

21. Local authorities should not send threatening letters demanding payment. They should always seek to establish who has the legal authority to make financial decisions and engage with that person.

RECOVERING DEBT AND DEFERRED PAYMENT AGREEMENTS

22. Where a debt has accrued and a person could be offered a deferred payment agreement (DPA), the local authority must offer the person or their attorney or deputy the option of repaying the debt through a DPA as set out in Section 69(2) of the Care Act 2014. A person could be offered a DPA if they are receiving care in a care home or are renting an extra care property, and the person has a form of security adequate to cover the DPA (usually a property).

23. The local authority is only required to offer the DPA for the amount of the accrued debt and is not obliged to defer any future costs;[1] however it may wish to consider allowing the person to defer further payments so as to avoid any further accrual of debts.

24. This option is likely to be attractive to a person as the interest rate for DPAs is set by regulations and is lower than the maximum amount the County Court can apply. It will also avoid the person needing to meet the costs of the local authority if the County Court finds against them. It is also likely to be attractive for a local authority as it will ensure that the debt is secured, is at less risk of default and is likely to be quicker to secure. If a DPA is agreed upon, a local authority must have regard to the guidance set out in Chapter 9.

25. Only where a person refuses the option of a DPA or does not meet the eligibility criteria can a local authority seek to enforce the debt via an application to the County Court. A local authority should therefore make sure a refusal, along with the reason, is recorded appropriately.

26. Where a person lacks capacity to make financial decisions, for example because they have severe dementia, and they have substantial debts to the local

---

[1] The local authority can exercise its discretion under the care act to refuse to agree to defer any further care costs, whilst securing any already-accrued debt. However, if the person meets the criteria governing eligibility for deferred payments, the LA must agree to defer future care costs.

authority or are likely to accrue them, then the local authority should ask the family to apply for a deputyship. Where there is no family or they choose not to, the local authority should apply for one before they proceed to the County Court, bearing in mind the risks of a conflict of interest.

ISSUING A CLAIM AND SUBSEQUENT ENFORCEMENT THROUGH THE COUNTY COURT

27. Where all other reasonable avenues have been exhausted, a local authority may wish to proceed to the County Court in order to recover the debt owed. The County Court has been chosen to enable all the parties involved to have an equal say regarding the debt that has accrued.

GETTING STARTED

28. Before making a claim, local authorities should read the HM Courts and Tribunal Services (HMCTS) leaflet EX302 How do I make a court claim?[1] and comply with the Practice Direction – Pre-Action Conduct provided by the Ministry of Justice[2] The Court will require the local authority to prove the legal basis for their claim. Therefore before applying to the court, local authorities should consult and engage their legal departments and collect the necessary evidence.

29. Issue of claim and other processes, including enforcement, attract a court fee. The level of the fee will vary depending on the amount that is being sought and will vary depending on whether the claim is being issued online or by paper. Details setting out the level of fees can be found in the HMCTS leaflet EX50 Civil and Family Court Fees.[3] Whilst there is an upfront cost to a local authority to meet this fee, if an order or judgment is made in favour of the local authority, the Court may add the fee to the debt recoverable. Any other pre-issue fees the local authority wishes to recover should be included in the claim form. If a solicitor is acting for the local authority, fixed costs may be claimed.

30. In order to make a claim, the local authority will need to fill out the relevant form. This can be done either on paper or online. Conditions apply for claims started online, including that the claim must be for a specified sum of money (under £100,000); that it cannot be against more than two people; and it cannot be against a known protected party or child, this includes a person who lacks capacity. Local authorities will also wish to note that fees are often reduced for online applications. Access to the online service is through https:// www.moneyclaim.gov.uk/web/mcol/welcome and registration for an account with the UK Government Gateway is required. The paper based claim form (N1 and notes for guidance N1A and N1C) can be downloaded at http://hmctsformfinder.justice.gov.uk/HMCTS/ FormFinder.do. It is important that these guidance notes are read carefully. It is at this point that initial fees are required to be paid. If making a paper application this will need to be by cash or cheque and online, by credit or debit card.

31. In order for a local authority to claim interest on the debt, they must include the following text from leaflet EX302: in the section of the form entitled 'Particulars of claim':

---

[1] http://hmctsformfinder.justice.gov.uk/courtfinder/forms/ex302-eng.pdf
[2] http://www.justice.gov.uk/courts/procedure-rules/civil/rules/pd_pre-action_conduct#1.1
[3] http://hmctsformfinder.justice.gov.uk/courtfinder/forms/ex050-eng.pdf

ENFORCING THE JUDGMENT OR ORDER

42. Where there is a court order or judgment for payment, but the person has not complied with it, the local authority may choose to enforce the order. The HMCTS leaflet EX321 *I have a judgment but the defendant hasn't paid*[1] sets out the various options. It is important to note that the court will only issue enforcement proceedings at the request of the local authority.

43. There are various methods of enforcement and local authorities will wish to think carefully about which may be the most appropriate taking into account the person's circumstances and their own responsibilities to the person. The most appropriate are likely to be:

- A warrant or writ of control;

- An attachment of earnings order;

- A third party debt order; or

- A charging order.

44. A warrant or writ of control essentially enables enforcement agents or officers to take control of goods from the person's home or business. If the order is for £5,000 or less, an application for a warrant of control may be made to the County Court. If the order is for over £5,000 the local authority may apply to the High Court for a writ of control.

45. An attachment of earnings order allows for the periodic deduction of monies by the person's employer (where they are known). It cannot be used if a person is unemployed or self-employed. An application may also be made to the court for deductions to be made from other earnings such as a pension. Earnings are disregarded during the financial assessment of what a person can afford to contribute towards the cost of their care so in some instances, this may be an option.

46. A third party debt order will instruct a third party such as a financial institution that holds a bank or building society account for the person to pay out the available funds, less that financial institution's fees, to the local authority. The process will only be successful if there are monies in the account on the day the financial institution receives the court order. Third party debt orders may not be made where the account is held in the name of more than one person. Savings are taken into account in the financial assessment of what someone can afford to contribute towards the cost of their care and this may therefore be a suitable option in some cases.

47. A charging order places a charge on a property or other assets owned by the person in order to secure the debt. This means that, just as with a DPA, payment will only be realised when the property or assets are disposed of. A further claim must be made for an order for sale to enforce the charging order. Where a person owns their own property this is likely to be the most viable option for recovering the debt. It is similar to a DPA in that a charge is secured against the person's property but by order of the court. The charge is usually a first charge unless other charges such as a mortgage are already registered against the property.

48. Further detail on both third party debt and charging orders can be found in the HMCTS leaflet EX325, *Third party debt and charging orders – how do I ask for an order?*[2]

---

[1] http://hmctsformfinder.justice.gov.uk/courtfinder/forms/ex321-eng.pdf
[2] http://hmctsformfinder.justice.gov.uk/courtfinder/forms/ex325-eng.pdf

OTHER ROUTES

49. Local authorities may also want to consider what other options may be available to support them in the recovery of debts. For example, Section 423 of the Insolvency Act 1986 provides additional routes to recover debts where a person may has transferred or sold their assets to a third party at a price that is lower than the market value with the intention of putting those assets out of reach or, or prejudicing the interests of, someone who may wish to bring a claim against that person. In considering the options, a local authority should seek the advice of its legal department.

FURTHER INFORMATION

50. HMCTS have developed a number of leaflets to help guide anyone through the court process, all of which can be found at http://hmctsformfinder.justice.gov.uk/HMCTS/FormFinder.do. A summary of those already referred to in this guidance and others that may be of use are listed below.

- EX301 I'm in a dispute – what can I do?
  http://hmctsformfinder.justice.gov.uk/courtfinder/forms/ex301-eng.pdf

- EX302 How do I make a court claim?
  http://hmctsformfinder.justice.gov.uk/courtfinder/forms/ex302-eng.pdf

- EX304 I've started a claim in court – what happens next?
  http://hmctsformfinder.justice.gov.uk/courtfinder/forms/ex304-eng.pdf

- EX305 The fast and multi-track claims in civil courts
  http://hmctsformfinder.justice.gov.uk/courtfinder/forms/ex305-eng.pdf

- EX306 The small claims track in civil courts
  http://hmctsformfinder.justice.gov.uk/courtfinder/forms/ex304-eng.pdf

- EX321 I have a judgment but the defendant hasn't paid
  http://hmctsformfinder.justice.gov.uk/courtfinder/forms/ex321-eng.pdf

- EX325 Third-party debt and charging orders – how do I ask for an order?
  http://hmctsformfinder.justice.gov.uk/courtfinder/forms/ex325-eng.pdf

- EX342 Coming to a court hearing? Some things you should know
  http://hmctsformfinder.justice.gov.uk/courtfinder/forms/ex342-eng.pdf

- EX50 Civil and family court fees
  http://hmctsformfinder.justice.gov.uk/courtfinder/forms/ex050-eng.pdf

COMPLAINTS

51. A person may wish to make a complaint about any aspect of the way a local authority uses its powers under the Care Act. A local authority must therefore make clear what its complaints procedure is and provide information and advice on how to lodge a complaint and set out details of how to contact the Local Government Ombudsman.

ANNEX E: DEPRIVATION OF ASSETS

This annex covers:
- The deprivation of capital in order to avoid or reduce care and support charges.
- The deprivation of income in order to avoid or reduce care and support charges.

The purpose of this annex is to provide local authorities with detailed guidance on how to respond when they suspect that a person has deliberately deprived themselves of assets in order to avoid or decrease the amount they are asked to pay towards any care and support charges. For the purposes of this section, "assets" means capital and/or income.

SETTING THE CONTEXT

1. A local authority can choose whether or not to charge a person where it is meeting needs. Where it thinks it would charge the person for meeting at least some of the needs, it must carry out a financial assessment which may be a light touch assessment where appropriate.

2. The financial assessment will need to look across all of a person's assets – both capital and income – decide which is which and assess those assets according to the regulations and guidance. A local authority therefore must also refer to Annex C on the treatment of income and Annex B on the treatment of capital before conducting a financial assessment.

3. When undertaking or reviewing a financial assessment a local authority may identify circumstances that suggest that a person may have deliberately deprived themselves of assets in order to reduce the level of the contribution towards the cost of their care. In such circumstances, the local authority should have regard to this guidance. Clearly, local authorities should treat this issue with sensitivity and care.

4. People should be treated with dignity and respect and be able to spend the money they have saved as they wish – it is their money after all. Whilst the Care Act 2014 represents an important step forward in redefining the partnership between the state and the individual, it is important that people pay the contribution to their care costs that they are responsible for. This is key to the overall affordability of the care and support system. A local authority should therefore ensure that people are not rewarded for trying to avoid paying their assessed contribution.

5. But deprivation should not be automatically assumed: there may be valid reasons why someone no longer has an asset and a local authority should ensure it fully explore this first. However, the overall principle should be that when a person has tried to deprive themselves of assets, this should not affect the amount of local authority support they receive.

WHAT IS MEANT BY DEPRIVATION OF ASSETS?

6. Deprivation of assets means where a person has *intentionally* deprived or decreased their overall assets in order to reduce the amount they are charged towards their care. This means that they must have known that they needed

care and support and have reduced their assets in order to reduce the contribution they are asked to make towards the cost of that care and support.

7. Where this has been done to remove a debt that would otherwise remain, even if that is not immediately due, this must not be considered as deprivation.

HAS DEPRIVATION OF CAPITAL OCCURRED?

8. It is up to the person to prove to the local authority that they no longer have the asset. If they are not able to, the local authority must assess them as if they still had the asset. For capital assets, acceptable evidence of their disposal would be:

(a) A trust deed;
(b) Deed of gift;
(c) Receipts for expenditure;
(d) Proof that debts have been repaid.

9. A person can deprive themselves of capital in many ways, but common approaches may be:

(a) A lump-sum payment to someone else, for example as a gift;
(b) Substantial expenditure has been incurred suddenly and is out of character with previous spending;
(c) The title deeds of a property have been transferred to someone else;
(d) Assets have been put in to a trust that cannot be revoked;
(e) Assets have been converted into another form that would be subject to a disregard under the financial assessment, for example personal possessions;
(f) Assets have been reduced by living extravagantly, for example gambling;
(g) Assets have been used to purchase an investment bond with life insurance.

10. However, this will not be deliberate in all cases. Questions of deprivation therefore should only be considered where the person ceases to possess assets that would have otherwise been taken into account for the purposes of the financial assessment or has turned the asset into one that is now disregarded.

Example of where deprivation has not occurred:

Max has moved into a care home and has a 50% interest in a property that continues to be occupied by his civil partner, David. The value of the property is disregarded whilst David lives there, but he decides to move to a smaller property that he can better manage and so sells their shared home to fund this.

At the time the property is sold, Max's 50% share of the proceeds could be taken into account in the financial assessment, but, in order to ensure that David is able to purchase the smaller property, Max makes part of his share of the proceeds from the sale available.

In such circumstance, it would not be reasonable to treat Max as having deprived himself of capital in order to reduce his care home charges.

Example of assets to be considered:

Emma gives her daughter Imogen a painting worth £2,000 the week before she enters care home. The local authority should not consider this as deprivation as the item is a personal possession and would not have been taken into account in her financial assessment.

However, if Emma had purchased the painting immediately prior to entering a care home to give to her daughter with £2,000 previously in a savings account, deprivation should be considered.

11. There may be many reasons for a person depriving themselves of an asset. A local authority should therefore consider the following before deciding whether deprivation for the purpose of avoiding care and support charges has occurred:
  (a) Whether avoiding the care and support charge was a significant motivation;
  (b) The timing of the disposal of the asset. At the point the capital was disposed of could the person have a reasonable expectation of the need for care and support?; and
  (c) Did the person have a reasonable expectation of needing to contribute to the cost of their eligible care needs?

12. For example, it would be unreasonable to decide that a person had disposed of an asset in order to reduce the level of charges for their care and support needs if at the time the disposal took place they were fit and healthy and could not have foreseen the need for care and support.

Example of assets to be considered:
Mrs Kapoor has £18,000 in a building society and uses £10,500 to purchase a car. Two weeks later she enters a care home and gives the car to her daughter Juhie.

If Mrs Kapoor knew when she purchased the car that she would be moving to a care home, then deprivation should be considered. However, all the circumstances must be taken into account so if Mrs Kapoor was admitted as an emergency and had no reason to think she may need care and support when she purchased the car, this should not be considered as deprivation.

HAS DEPRIVATION OF INCOME OCCURRED?
13. It is also possible for a person to deliberately deprive themselves of income. For example, they could give away or sell the right to an income from an occupational pension.

14. It is up to the person to prove to the local authority that they no longer have the income. Where a local authority considers that a person may have deprived themselves of income, they may treat them as possessing notional income.

15. The local authority will need to determine whether deliberate deprivation of income has occurred. In doing so it should consider:
  (a) Was it the person's income?
  (b) What was the purpose of the disposal of the income?
  (c) The timing of the disposal of the income? At the point the income was disposed of could the person have a reasonable expectation of the need for care and support?

16. In some circumstances the income may have been converted into capital. The local authority should consider what tariff income may be applied to the capital and whether the subsequent charge is less or more than the person would have paid without the change.

LOCAL AUTHORITY INVESTIGATIONS

17. In some cases a local authority may wish to conduct its own investigations into whether deprivation of assets has occurred rather than relying solely on the declaration of the person. There is separate guidance under the Regulation of Investigatory Powers Act 2000 that has recently been updated.[1] That sets out the limits to local authority powers to investigate and local authorities should have regard to it before considering any investigations.

WHAT HAPPENS WHERE DEPRIVATION OF ASSETS HAS OCCURRED?

18. If a local authority decides that a person has deliberately deprived themselves of assets in order to avoid or reduce a charge for care and support, they will first need to decide whether to treat that person as still having the asset for the purposes of the financial assessment and charge them accordingly.

19. As a first step, a local authority should seek to charge the person as if the deprivation had not occurred. This means assuming they still own the asset and treating it as notional capital or notional income.

20. If the person in depriving themselves of an actual resource has converted that resource into another of lesser value, the person should be treated as notionally possessing the difference between the value of the new resources and the one which it replaced. For example, if the value of personal possessions acquired is less than the sum spent on them, the difference should be treated as notional resource.

RECOVERING CHARGES FROM A THIRD PARTY

21. Where the person has transferred the asset to a third party to avoid the charge, the third party is liable to pay the local authority the difference between what it would have charged and did charge the person receiving care. However, the third party is not liable to pay anything which exceeds the benefit they have received from the transfer.

22. If the person has transferred funds to more than one third party, each of those people is liable to pay the local authority the difference between what it would have charged or did charge the person receiving care in proportion to the amount they received.

23. As with any other debt, the local authority can use the County Court process to recover debts, but this should only be used after other avenues have been exhausted. When pursing the recovery of charges from a third party, a local authority must read Annex D on debt recovery.

Example of liability of a third party:

Mrs Tong has £23,250 in her savings account. This is the total of her assets. One week before entering care she gives her daughters Louisa and Jenny and her son Frank £7,750 each. This was with the sole intention of avoiding care and support charges.

Had Mrs Tong not given the money away, the first £14,250 would have been disregarded and she would have been charged a tariff income on her assets between £14,250 and £23,250. Assuming £1 for every £250 of assets, this means Mrs Tong should have paid £36 per week towards the cost of her

---

[1] https://www.gov.uk/government/publications/changes-to-local-authority-use-of-ripa

care. After 10 weeks of care, Mrs Tong should have contributed £360. This means Louisa, Jenny and Frank are each liable for £120 towards the cost of their mother's care.

ANNEX F: TEMPORARY AND SHORT-TERM RESIDENTS IN CARE HOMES

This annex covers:
- How to undertake a financial assessment of someone who is temporarily placed in a care home.

SETTING THE CONTEXT

1. Following an assessment of a person's eligible care and support needs a decision may be taken that the person would benefit from a temporary stay in a care home. This could be for a number of reasons such as providing respite care to a carer or to provide a period of more intense support owing to an additional, but temporary, care need.

2. The financial assessment of what they can afford to contribute to the cost of their care and support needs must be undertaken with regard to the following guidance.

3. The financial assessment must be based on the individual resources of the person. However a local authority should give regard to any partner or spouse remaining at home and ensure they are left with a basic level of income support or pension credit to which they may be entitled in their own right.

WHO IS A TEMPORARY RESIDENT?

4. A temporary resident is defined as a person whose need to stay in a care home is *intended* to last for a limited period of time and where there is a plan to return home. The person's stay should be unlikely to exceed 52 weeks, or in exceptional circumstances, unlikely to substantially exceed 52 weeks.

5. A decision to treat a person as a temporary resident must be agreed with the person and/or their representative and written into their care plan.

6. In some cases a person may enter a care home with the intention of a permanent stay but a change in circumstances could result in it being temporary. In such cases the local authority should treat the person as temporary from the date of admission for the purposes of charging.

7. Similarly a stay which was initially intended to be temporary could become permanent. In such cases, the financial assessment of the person as a permanent resident should only be from the date that the care plan is amended and agreed with the person and/or their representative.

CHARGING

8. A local authority can choose whether or not to charge a person where it is arranging to meet needs. In the case of a short-term resident in a care home, the local authority has discretion to assess and charge as if the person were having needs met other than by the provision of accommodation in a care home.

ASSESSING ABILITY TO PAY

9. Once a local authority has decided to charge a person and it has been agreed that they are a temporary resident, the local authority must undertake the financial assessment in accordance with the following guidance.

CAPITAL

10. The person's *main or only* home must be disregarded where the person:
(a) Intends to return to that property as their main or only home and it remains available to them; or
(b) Has taken steps to dispose of the home in order to acquire one that is more suitable and intends to return to that property.

11. Any other capital assets should be treated in the same way as for permanent residents. Guidance is set out in Annex B.

INCOME AND EARNINGS

12. Both income and earnings should be treated in the same way as for permanent residents, as set out in Annex C on income. However, any additional amounts the person may need so they can maintain their home during their temporary stay so that it is in a fit condition for them to return to must be disregarded. Such expenses may include, but are not limited to, ground rent, service charges, water rates or insurance premiums.

13. However, the local authority should also take into account the following additional points.

14. Where Attendance Allowance or Disability Living Allowance is being received, these should be completely disregarded. However, a local authority should note that eligibility for both these benefits ceases after 4 weeks of local authority support and they should make sure they consider the impact on the person's ability to maintain their home.

15. Where a stay in a care home is temporary, the amount of an Income Support or Pension Credit a person receives will usually remain the same as they will be treated as normally residing in their own home. However, any severe disability premium or enhanced disability premium that may have been included will no longer be paid if the Disability Living Allowance or Attendance Allowance has ceased. There are special rules for Income Support and income related Employment Support Allowance where one member of a couple enters a care home for a temporary period. This should be taken into account in considering what a person can afford to pay.

16. If Housing Benefit is paid to the person, this should be disregarded as they will still be responsible for meeting any costs associate with their main or only home.

17. The local authority should also disregard any other payment the person receives in order to meet the cost of their housing and/or to support independent living. For example this may include payments to provide warden support, emergency alarms or the meeting of cleaning costs where the person or someone in the household is unable to do this themselves.

18. The local authority should also consider whether any payments to support the cost of housing and/or independent living are sufficient to cover the person's commitments during their temporary stay. This might be as these costs were met from earnings, which are disregarded, that are not being accrued during the temporary stay. In such cases, the local authority should calculate the additional cost and disregard this amount.

19. Where a person is sub-letting their property, this should be disregarded where the person occupies the property as their main or only home as they intend to return to the property.

20. Alternatively a person may have a boarder living in their property. A boarder is someone for whom at least one cooked meal is provided. Where a person has income from a boarder, the first £20 of the income should be ignored plus half of any balance over £20.

ANNEX G: THE PROCESS FOR MANAGING TRANSFERS OF CARE FROM HOSPITAL FOR PATIENTS WITH CARE AND SUPPORT NEEDS

This annex covers:
- Overview of the requirements of the regulations;
- Legibility of notices;
- Assessment notices (including content, withdrawal and time to carry out assessment);
- Discharge notices (including content, withdrawal and timing of discharge notice);
- Delayed discharge reimbursement;
- Days exempt from payment liability;
- Ordinary residence;
- Dispute resolution;
- Sign-off of data between the NHS and local authority;
- Reporting of all delayed transfers of care days;
- Data and information;
- Patient and carer consultation; and
- Patient choice.

---

1. The Care and Support (Discharge of Hospital Patients) Regulations 2014 set out:

- the details of what the NHS body responsible for a relevant patient must include in the assessment notice that it issues, so that the local authority can then comply with its requirements to undertake assessments and put in place any arrangements necessary for meeting any of the patient's care and support needs or where applicable the carer's needs;

- the minimum period that the local authority has to undertake the assessment;

- the details of what must be included in the discharge notice;

- the minimum period of notice that the NHS must give the local authority in terms of a relevant patient's discharge;

- the circumstances when an assessment notice and a discharge notice must be withdrawn;

- the period and amount of any reimbursement liability which a local authority may be required to pay the NHS for any delayed discharge.

2. The regulations also set out what is to happen when a local authority disputes that the patient is ordinarily resident in its area and to recover expenditure incurred as a result.

LEGIBILITY OF NOTICES

3. All notices issued by the relevant NHS body must be provided in writing to Local Authorities. This means that each notice (whether an assessment notice, discharge notice or withdrawal notice) must be in a legible form capable of being reproduced (e.g. capable of being photocopied, emailed or faxed). Any

notice which is not reasonably legible would therefore not be valid. In order to ensure the legibility of all notification notices, the NHS body who issues the notice should type or print the notices and use a digital format wherever possible. This ensures that the receiving local authority can read the information it requires to comply with its duties and helps to prove that a notice has been issued if ever this was disputed.

4. However, while it is important to establish an audit trail, the system which NHS bodies and local authorities set up around issuing notices should not impede good working practice. Where hospitals and local authorities are already operating joint discharge teams, which are often co-located in the same office with access to a shared database, an update to the database may be all that is required.

ASSESSMENT NOTICES

5. The NHS is required to issue a notice to the local authority where they consider that an NHS hospital patient in receipt of acute care may need care and support as part of supporting a transfer from an acute setting regardless of whether they intend to claim reimbursement. The relevant local authority who the NHS must notify is the one in which the patient is ordinarily resident or, if it is not possible to determine ordinary residence, the local authority area in which the hospital is situated.

6. Not everyone who is admitted to hospital will need care and support after discharge. Indeed, for the majority of hospital discharges, this will not be the case and it is important within this context that NHS organisations do not issue assessment notices in a precautionary and/or routine way without having satisfied itself that there is a reasonable prospect that there may be a need for care and support for which arrangements may need to be made in order to ensure a safe discharge.

7. A locally agreed protocol between the NHS and local authorities which allows NHS staff to identify those likely to need care and support on discharge will provide help and advice as to when a patient should be considered to have possible care and support needs, in order to ensure the NHS issue assessment notices appropriately.

8. However, the relevant NHS body must issue an assessment notice where it considers that a patient may require care and support on discharge and the local authority must or may be required to meet such needs. Before issuing any assessment notice, the NHS must consult with the patient and, where applicable, the carer. This is to avoid unnecessary assessments where, for example, the patient wishes to make private arrangements for care and support without the involvement of the local authority. Before issuing an assessment notice, the NHS body must have also completed any assessment of the potential Continuing Health Care needs of the patient and if applicable made a decision on what services the NHS will be providing.

TIMESCALES FOR NHS TO ISSUE AN ASSESSMENT NOTICE

9. In general, the NHS should seek to give the local authority as much notice as possible of a patient's impending discharge. This is so the local authority has as much notice as possible of its duty to undertake a needs and (where applicable) carer's assessment.

10. However, an assessment notice must not be issued more than 7 days before the patient is expected to be admitted into hospital. This is so the notice is not

provided too far in advance of admission to avoid the risk of wasting preliminary planning in the event that the patient's condition changes. A balance should be struck between giving the local authority early notice of the need to undertake an assessment of the patient and the risk that the patient's condition may change significantly such that any early planning needs to be reviewed.

11. Accordingly, if the NHS is able either to issue an assessment notice up to seven days before the date of the patient's admission into hospital and/or have a good indication of the likely proposed discharge date which is unlikely to change, then the NHS should issue the assessment notice as soon as possible.

CONTENT OF ASSESSMENT NOTICE

12. The information contained in an assessment notification is intended to be minimal, both to reflect patient confidentiality requirements and to minimise bureaucracy – it is only the trigger for assessment and care planning.

13. The assessment notice must state that it is an assessment notice given under paragraph1(1) of Schedule 3 to the Care Act. This is so the local authority is aware of the consequences that could flow from the receipt of the assessment notice (i.e. that it has to take steps to assess the patient and (where applicable) the patient's carer and put in place any arrangements to meet those needs it proposes to meet. Ultimately if the local authority fails to carry out such steps then the local authority may, in certain circumstances, be liable to pay the NHS for any delayed discharge period.

14. The assessment notice must include the following:

- the name of the patient;

- the patient's NHS number;

- if given before the patient's admission, the expected date of admission and the name of the hospital in which the patient is being accommodated;

- an indication of the patient's discharge date, if known

- a statement:

  (a) that the NHS body by whom the assessment notice has been given ("the NHS body") has complied with the requirement to consult the patient and, where feasible, any carer the patient has;
  (b) that the NHS body has considered whether or not to provide the patient with NHS continuing health care and the result of that consideration. So, where the NHS considers that the patient may have needs for continuing health care to be met by the NHS after discharge, then it must have (i) carried out a continuing health care assessment first and(ii) made a decision as to what (if any) services the NHS is to provide to the patient after discharge and (iii) informed the local authority of these details.
  (c) as to whether the patient or carer has objected to the giving of the notice;
  (d) the name and contact details of the person at the hospital who will be responsible for liaising with the local authority in relation to the patient's discharge from that hospital. This must be one or a combination of the person's telephone number and/or their work based E-mail address.

15. The requirements above are intended to make the assessment notice process work more effectively, including the requirements to include the patient's NHS

number and also the contact details of the person at the hospital who will be responsible for liaising with the local authority in relation to the patient's discharge from that hospital.

16. These requirements may be built on at a local level to produce a form that meets the agreed needs of the NHS and local authority. Although not exhaustive, local systems might also want to include on the assessment notice the patient's address and the lead clinician's details. The following template provides a model that the NHS might want to use:

NOTICE OF REQUEST FOR Assessment under The *Care and Support (Discharge of Hospital Patients) Regulations 2014*	
Name	
Date of Birth	
Address*	
NHS Number	
Expected Date Of Admission (where known)	
Name and contact details of the carer (where applicable)*	
Name and contact details of the person at the hospital liaising with the local authority	
Patient's Lead clinician at hospital*	
Please confirm the following	
The patient has been consulted with regarding the assessment	
(Where applicable and feasible) carer has been consulted regarding the assessment	
An assessment of their continuing health care needs has been completed and a decision made	
The patient has not objected to the giving of the assessment notice	
The carer has not objected to the giving of the assessment notice	

*Those marked with an * are not legal requirements but should be included where known as a matter of good practice.*

TIMESCALES FOR LOCAL AUTHORITIES' RESPONSIBILITIES TO CARRY OUT ASSESSMENTS

17. On receiving an assessment notice, the local authority must carry out a need assessment of the patient and (where applicable) a carer's assessment so as to determine, in the first place, whether it considers that the patient and where applicable, carer has needs. If so, the local authority must then determine whether any of these identified needs meet the eligibility criteria and if so, then how it proposes to meet any (if at all) of those needs. The local authority must inform the NHS of the outcome of its assessment and decisions.

18. To avoid any risk of reimbursement liability, the local authority must carry out a needs assessment and put in place any arrangements for meeting such needs that it proposes to meet in relation to a patient and, where applicable, carer, before "the relevant day". The relevant day is either the date upon which the NHS proposes to discharge the patient (as contained in the discharge notice – see below) or the minimum period, whichever is the later.

19. The minimum period is 2 days after the local authority has received an assessment notice or is treated as having received an assessment notice.

20. Any assessment notice which is given after 2pm on any day is treated as being given on the following day.

21. Examples of how these timescales work are set out below:

Scenario 1

- The NHS issue an assessment notice to the local authority at 1pm on Monday. The assessment notice must specify the date of the proposed discharge date. The earliest date which would be permitted is 2 days after the date the assessment notice is given (although a later proposed discharge date could be set out in the discharge notice.) This means that in order to avoid any risk of reimbursement liability, Wednesday would be the earliest day by which the local authority would need to have carried out the assessment and put in place any care and support services and, where applicable, carers' services that it proposes to meet.

Senario 2

- The NHS issue an assessment notice to the local authority at 3pm on Monday. The assessment notice is treated as having been given on the following day, Tuesday. This would mean that if no later discharge notice were given in the assessment notice, then Thursday would be the earliest day by which the local authority would need to have carried out the assessment and put in place any care and support services and, where applicable, carers' services that it proposes to meet if it were to avoid the risk of any reimbursement liability. Again, the assessment notice and later the discharge notice (see below) could set out a proposed discharge date after Thursday, in which case this would be the actual deadline by which the local authority would be required to have carried out the assessment and put in place any care and support and carers' service that is proposes to meet in order to avoid the risk of incurring any reimbursement liability.

ASSESSMENT NOTICE WITHDRAWAL

22. The NHS body which issued the assessment notice may withdraw that assessment notice at any time. Once an assessment notice has been withdrawn by the NHS, this means that the local authority that has been given the assessment notice is no longer required to comply with the requirements to assess or, where an assessment has been carried out, to put in place arrangements to meet some or all of the patient's care and support needs. Once an assessment notice is withdrawn no liability to the local authority can accrue after that date. This is even if a discharge notice has been subsequently issued. But any liability which may have accrued before the withdrawal of the assessment notice is unaffected.

23. There are a number of circumstances when the NHS must withdraw an assessment notice. These are where:

- The NHS body considers that it is likely to be safe to discharge the patient without arrangements being put in place for the meeting of the patient's needs for care and support or (where applicable) the carer's needs for support;

- The NHS body considers that the patient's on-going need is for NHS Continuing Health Care;

- Following the decision as to which (if any) services the relevant local authority will make available to the patient or (where applicable) carer, the NHS body still considers that it is unlikely to be safe to discharge the patient from hospital unless further arrangements are put in place

- for the meeting of the patient's care and support needs or (where applicable) the carer's needs for support;

- The patient's proposed treatment is cancelled or postponed;

- The NHS body has become aware that the relevant authority is not required to carry out any assessment because the patient has refused a needs assessment or (where applicable) the carer has refused a carer's assessment;

- The NHS body becomes aware that either:

  - the patient's ordinary residence has changed since the assessment notice was given; or
  - the notice was given to a local authority other than the one in whose area the patient is ordinarily resident.

24. The regulations do not prescribe what a withdrawal notice must contain. However, it must be in writing, and local systems should be established to ensure that the withdrawal notice provides sufficient information for both the NHS and local authority to be clear as to which patient and assessment notice the withdrawal notice refers to, and the reason(s) as to why the assessment notice is being withdrawn. In the context of identifying the person, mirroring either in full or part what is required for the assessment notice itself should be considered.

DISCHARGE NOTICES

25. Patients and carers should be informed of the discharge date at the same time as or before the local authority. In addition, hospital staff may give the local authority an early indication of when discharge is likely as part of helping their planning.

26. Where the NHS has issued an assessment notice to a local authority (so as to require the local authority to assess a patient's care and support needs to facilitate a transfer of care), it must also give written notice to the local authority of the proposed date of the patient's discharge notwithstanding that it included the proposed discharge date in the assessment notice. This is known as a discharge notice and its purpose is to confirm the discharge date as it either may not have been previously known at the time of the issue of the assessment notice or may have subsequently changed since the assessment notice was issued.

27. The NHS could not seek to recover any reimbursement from the local authority in respect of a patient's delayed transfer of care unless it has first issued both an assessment notice and a discharge notice.

CONTENT OF A DISCHARGE NOTICE

28. A discharge notice must contain:

- The name of the patient;

- The patient's NHS number;

- The name of the hospital in which the patient is being accommodated;

- The name and contact details (telephone and/or email) of the person at the hospital who is responsible for liaising with the relevant authority in relation to the patient's discharge from hospital;

- The date on which it is proposed that the patient be discharged;

- A statement confirming that the patient and, where appropriate, the carer has been informed of the date on which it is proposed that the patient be discharged;

- A statement that the discharge notice is given under paragraph 2(1)(b) of Schedule 3 to the Act. This is to make it clear that the notice is a formal "discharge notice" for the purposes of the Discharge of Hospital Patient provisions.

TIMING OF DISCHARGE NOTICE

29. To ensure that a local authority receives fair advance warning of the discharge, the NHS body must issue a discharge notice indicating the date of the patient's proposed discharge. The minimum discharge notification allowed is at least one day before the proposed discharge date. Again, where the discharge notice is issued after 2pm, it will not be treated as having been served until the next day.

30. Taking the examples above:

Scenario 1

- The NHS issue an assessment notice to the local authority at 1pm on Monday. The assessment notice must specify the date of the proposed discharge date where known. The earliest discharge date which would be permitted to be specified is 2 days after the date the assessment notice is given (although the proposed discharge date can be later than this) i.e. Wednesday. This means that where the minimum period were to apply the discharge notice must be issued no later than Tuesday.

Scenario 2

- The NHS issue an assessment notice to the local authority at 3pm on Monday. The assessment notice is treated as having been given on the following day, Tuesday. This would mean that if the minimum period were to apply then Thursday would be the earliest date by which the local authority would need to have carried out the assessment and put in place any care and support services and, where applicable, carers' services that it proposes to meet if it were to avoid any risk of reimbursement liability. So, this means the discharge notice must be issued no later than Wednesday.

31. The NHS body can issue the discharge notification with a much longer period of advance warning if appropriate and it should continue to seek to provide

the local authority with as much notice of the proposed discharge date as possible. However, it will need to consider the likelihood of such a date being inaccurate and then the potential need to withdraw and reissue the discharge notification in the event the patient's condition changes in the meantime.

32. The NHS body is required to inform the local authority, by way of a withdrawal notice withdrawing the discharge notice, when it considers that it is no longer likely to be safe to discharge the patient on the proposed discharge date for any reason other than the fact that it would be likely to be unsafe to discharge the patient because the local authority has not taken the require steps. So, for example, the NHS must inform the local authority of changes in circumstances affecting the discharge date, for instance if the patient's medical condition changes or the patient dies.

33. The NHS should also consider the appropriateness of issuing the assessment and discharge notices too closely together, as this may result in extremely short time frames for local authorities to put in place what may be complex and comprehensive packages of care, which will also need to be subject to discussion with the patient and/or their carer. This potentially could lead to decisions being made, which while supporting a safe discharge may not be in the best long-term interests of the patient.

WITHDRAWAL OF DISCHARGE NOTICE

34. The NHS body which issued the discharge notice to a local authority may withdraw that discharge notice at any time. Such a withdrawal must also be in writing. It is important that the NHS body informs the local authority as soon as possible of a withdrawal of a discharge notice so that the local authority is not unnecessarily expending resources arranging a discharge on a date, which is no longer correct.

35. A discharge notice must be withdrawn where the NHS body considers that it is no longer likely to be safe to discharge the patient from hospital on the proposed discharge date.

36. However, this does not apply where the reasons for withdrawal are that the local authority has not taken the steps required to inform the NHS body of the outcome of the assessment the needs of the patient (and the carer, where applicable), and whether it Intends to put in place care and support to meet any eligible needs.

37. Local systems should be established to ensure that the withdrawal notice provides sufficient information for both the NHS and local authority to be clear who the person is that the notice refers to, and the reason(s) as to why it is being withdrawn. In the context of identifying the patient, mirroring either in full or part what is required for the discharge notice itself should be considered.

38. Once a discharge notice is withdrawn, no further liability for the local authority to pay the NHS for any delayed transfer of care arises.

DELAYED DISCHARGE REIMBURSEMENT

39. While reimbursement remains available for use by the NHS body, they and local authorities are encouraged to use the provisions on the discharge of hospital patients (such as the issue of assessment and discharge notices) to seek to focus on effective joint working so as to improve the care of those people whose needs span both NHS and local authority care settings. While reimbursement is a potential way of exposing local difficulties in the relationship between the NHS body

and the local authority, NHS bodies should not use reimbursement as the first approach to address any local difficulties around delayed transfers of care.

40. The NHS will only be able to seek any reimbursement from the local authority arising from a delayed transfer of care, if the NHS has first sent both an assessment notice and a discharge notice to the local authority, but the local authority has then either not carried out an assessment or put arrangements in place for the meeting of care and support and, where applicable, carer's needs which it proposes to meet by the end of the relevant day (i.e. the proposed delayed discharge date in the discharge notice or the minimum period and it is for this reason alone that there has been a delay in the patient's delayed transfer of care.

41. In these circumstances, it is then in the NHS's discretion whether to recover payments for reimbursable delayed discharge days. In terms of the level of reimbursement, the regulations provide that:

- for local authorities outside London, the penalty amount per day will be £130 and;

- for London authorities, the penalty amount per day will be £155.

42. The amounts above have risen in line with the CPI measure of inflation since 2003, and the higher rate only applies to local authorities in London.

43. The period for which liability can be sought, if the NHS so chooses, starts on the day after the relevant day i.e. after the date of the proposed discharge date contained in the discharge notice or the minimum period which is, at the earliest, 2 days after the assessment notice is given.

44. It then ends on the earliest date as to when any of the following occurs:

- the NHS withdraws either the assessment notice or the discharge notice;

- the local authority notifies the NHS that it has now carried out the assessment and put in place arrangements for meeting any of the needs it proposes to meet in respect of that patient or where applicable carer;

- the local authority is no longer required to put arrangements in place either because the patient informs the local authority that they have made alternative arrangements for care and support and ,where applicable, the carer informs the local authority that they have made alternative arrangements for their support;

- the patient discharges themselves;

- the NHS decided that the patient now needs to remain in hospital for a further course of treatment; or

- the patient dies.

DAYS EXEMPT FROM PAYMENT LIABILITY

45. It is intended that both the NHS and local authorities should have established systems in place by April 2015 that provide for seven-day coverage. Accordingly, the exemptions that previously existed for weekends and Bank Holidays are no longer to apply and as such all days become potentially reimbursable. However, a day is not to be treated as a day for which a local authority could be liable for reimbursement when the local authority has by 11am that day put in

place arrangements for meeting some or all of the needs that it proposes to meet in relation to the patient and, where applicable, the carer.

46. Also, no liability will arise for any day where the NHS considers that the patient is not able to be discharged because they have suffered a deterioration in their condition on that date so that it would not be safe to discharge them even if the local authority had put in place arrangements for meeting the patient's care and support and, where applicable, the carer's needs.

47. If the patient's deterioration becomes more established such that the patient requires a further course of treatment in hospital, and it would be unsafe to discharge the patient then the NHS body must withdraw the discharge notice and should consider withdrawing the assessment notice.

ORDINARY RESIDENCE

48. The NHS should serve the assessment notice on the local authority where the patient is ordinarily resident or where the patient has no settled address, the local authority in which the hospital is located. Where a local authority disputes the assertion that they are responsible for that individual based on ordinary residence, they must in the period of dispute still comply with the requirements of the Regulations in terms of providing an assessment and any care and support provision which is identified as being needed to secure a safe transfer from one care setting to another.

DISPUTE RESOLUTION

49. Where any dispute arises because a local authority disputes that the patient is ordinarily resident in its area (so that it should not be the local authority to whom an assessment notice is given), then that local authority must accept provisional responsibility and undertake the steps required under the discharge of hospital patient provisions. If no agreement can be reached on ordinary residence, it must then seek a determination as the patient's ordinary residence from the Secretary of State or an appointed representative. Further information on this process can be found within the Ordinary Residence Regulations, which have also been established as part of the Care Act 2014.

50. All other disputes in relation to delayed discharge payments (e.g. whether to seek reimbursement, whether the day should be counted as a day of delayed discharge period etc.) should be resolved between the NHS body and local authority. Where they cannot be resolved then resolution would have to be way of an application for judicial review to the High Court.

SIGN-OFF OF DATA BETWEEN THE NHS AND LOCAL AUTHORITY

51. As set out in existing guidance, the NHS organisation must ensure that before reporting days attributable to care and support that it has verified their accuracy with the local authority, irrespective of whether the NHS body is seeking reimbursement or not. This should happen in advance of them being reported into the formal system so that any errors can be identified and addressed. The system by which this happens is for local determination, although it is expected that it would be the relevant Director of Adult Social Services or their nominated representative who would be the local authority point of contact for this.

ANNEX H: ORDINARY RESIDENCE

ANNEX H1 – PEOPLE WITH "URGENT NEEDS"

1. A person who is ordinarily resident in one local authority area may become in urgent need of accommodation whilst they are in another local authority area. The Care Act provides local authorities with powers[1] to meet the person's needs in such urgent cases, if the adult (or in the case of a carer, the adult for whom they care) is known to be ordinary resident in the area of another local authority.

2. For example, an urgent need for accommodation may arise where a person with severe learning disabilities is on holiday or visiting someone with their carer in another area, and the carer unexpectedly has to be taken to hospital. In this case, the person with learning disabilities may be without assistance and/or unable to care for himself or herself, and may become in urgent need of accommodation, albeit on a short-term basis. Similarly, an urgent need may arise where an older person, who is ordinarily resident in one local authority area, stays with their family in another local authority area during a holiday period, but the caring responsibilities prove too much for the family and they seek assistance from their local authority on the basis that their relative is in urgent need.

3. In circumstances where a person who is ordinarily resident in one local authority area becomes in urgent need in another local authority area, the person's local authority of ordinary residence would have a duty to meet the person's eligible needs. However, since it is unlikely to be practicable for that authority to meet urgent needs, the local authority "of the moment" (i.e. where the person is physically present at the time) should exercise their power to meet the urgent needs and provide the necessary accommodation, even if only on a temporary basis. The local authority of the moment should, in carrying out any assessment of needs and providing any necessary accommodation, inform the local authority where the person is ordinarily resident that it is doing so.

4. The local authority of the moment is not required to seek the consent of the local authority where the person is ordinarily resident, in deciding whether and how to exercise the power to meet urgent needs. However, it should notify the other authority of its intention to do so, to ensure that information is shared on the individual case. The local authorities concerned may come to an agreement about sharing or transferring the costs involved in meeting urgent needs. For instance, the local authority of the moment, which is providing the accommodation, may recover some or all of the costs of the accommodation from the local authority where the person is ordinarily resident (and where the duty to meet needs would otherwise fall).

5. On rare occasions, a person with urgent needs who has been provided with accommodation by the local authority of the moment may be unable to return to their own local authority because of a change in circumstances. In this situation, decisions relating to ordinary residence must be made on an individual basis: the local authority of the moment and the person's local authority of ordinary residence would need to consider all the facts of the case to determine whether the person's ordinary residence had changed.

---

[1] Sections 19(3) and 20(6) provide powers which can be used for meeting urgent needs for adults with care and support needs and carers respectively.

6. A local authority may also meet a person's needs through the provision of accommodation, where the person is not ordinarily resident in that area, even if the needs themselves are not considered to be urgent.

7. For example, a local authority (local authority A) may need to provide accommodation on behalf of another (local authority B) in a situation where a person has been discharged from hospital and needs accommodation but wishes to remain living in the local authority in which he or she received hospital treatment, perhaps to be near family members. In these circumstances, local authority A, where the person was living on discharge from hospital could provide the accommodation, with the notification of his or her local authority of ordinary residence (local authority B). However, if the person subsequently intended to remain in local authority A indefinitely, then their place of ordinary residence would move to local authority A.

ANNEX H2 – PEOPLE WHO ARE PARTY TO DEFERRED PAYMENT AGREEMENTS

8. Deferred payment agreements are designed to prevent people from being forced to sell their home in their lifetime to pay for the costs of their care. They also extend choice, providing people with additional flexibility over how they meet the cost of their care.

9. An individual enters into an agreement with their local authority by which payment for their care and support is 'deferred', being paid in the interim period by the local authority. The money owed to the local authority is subsequently repaid either when the home is sold, from the person's estate, or when the amount due is repaid to the local authority. The local authority could be repaid by either the person with the deferred payment agreement or by a third party. The individual grants the local authority a charge over their property for the purposes of security and to facilitate reclamation of the amount due to the local authority.

10. The regulations and guidance require local authorities to offer deferred payments in certain circumstances, and give local authorities discretion to offer deferred payments in other situations. For further information on deferred payments please see chapter 9 of the guidance.

11. It is the local authority in which the person is ordinarily resident that has responsibility for offering and making arrangements for a deferred payment agreement. That local authority then remains responsible for the deferred payment agreement until the agreement is concluded.

12. Information about deferred payment agreements should be offered when a person approaches a local authority, or at the time the person decides to enter a care home accommodation. Where a person is initially accommodated under the 12-week property disregard, the information should be given and arrangements made during this 12-week period. For details on this please see Annex B and the treatment of capital.

13. For example, where a person who is ordinarily resident in the area of local authority A chooses to meet their care and support needs in a care home in the area of local authority B, and the value of that person's home is being disregarded for 12 weeks, (see Annex H3 – People who are accommodated under the 12 week property disregard), local authority A should offer the person the option of having a deferred payment during the 12-week period. If the person accepts the offer and enters into a deferred payment agreement, local authority A remains responsible

for funding their care (minus any contributions from means-tested income and assets).

ANNEX H3 – PEOPLE WHO ARE ACCOMMODATED UNDER THE 12 WEEK PROPERTY DISREGARD

14. A key aim of the charging framework is to prevent people being forced to sell their home at a time of crisis. The framework therefore creates the space for people who are at risk of needing to sell their home to meet the cost of their care to make informed decisions on how best to do that. This means that a local authority must disregard the value of a person's main or only home when the value of their non-housing assets are below the upper capital limit of £23,250 for a period of 12 weeks from when a person:

- First enters a care home; or

- Where an alternative property disregard is unexpectedly lost.

15. A local authority also has discretion to choose to apply the disregard where a person has a sudden and unexpected change in their financial circumstances. In doing so, it must consider the individual circumstances of the case.

16. This is known as the "12 week property disregard" and full details are set out in Annex B on the Treatment of Capital.

17. During the 12 week disregard period, the person receives local authority support where they are ordinarily resident. The local authority may place the person in a care home in the area of another local authority, for example because they have expressed a desire to be near family members. However, the placing authority remains the responsible authority during this period.

18. At the end of 12 weeks, the value of the person's home is taken into account (unless it is subject of an alternative disregard. See Annex B). This may result in the person becoming liable to pay for all of the costs of their care and choosing to enter into a private contract with the care home for the provision of their care on a permanent basis, rather than continuing to be provided with accommodation by their placing authority. In such a case the person would be likely to acquire an ordinary residence in the new area, in line with the settled purpose test in Shah.

19. If the person's needs or circumstances change and they subsequently require additional or different care and support, including care home support, they should approach the local authority where their care home is situated. However, if they enter into a deferred payment agreement with the original authority or there is another reason such as lack of mental capacity as to why they were unable to enter into a private contract with the care home, they will remain the responsibility of the original authority.

20. If a person arranges for their care and support needs to be met in a care home without regard to the local authority but subsequently contact the local authority in order to receive support, it is likely that they would have acquired ordinary residence in the area in which their care home is situated. If this is the case, it would be the local authority in whose area the care home is situated which would be responsible for funding the person's accommodation.

ANNEX H4 – PEOPLE WHO ARE ARRANGING AND PAYING FOR THEIR OWN CARE

21. When a person moves into permanent accommodation in a new area under private arrangements, and is paying for their own care, they usually acquire an ordinary residence in this new area. If so, and if their needs subsequently change meaning that they require other types of care and support, they should approach the local authority in which their accommodation is situated.

22. A person who has sufficient financial means to pay for their own care, but who has eligible needs, may ask the local authority to meet their needs. This may be, for instance, where a person has capacity, but lacks the skills or confidence to arrange their own care, and would benefit from the local authority's support in managing a contract with a provider. If such a person asks the local authority to do so, then the authority must meet their needs.[1] Where an adult with enough means to pay for their own care and support makes such a request, the adult would still pay for the care and support in full, and the local authority will have a power to charge a fee to cover the additional costs of arranging or brokering that care and support. In such circumstances, the local authority should treat the person in the same manner as it would anyone else whose needs it is meeting – including the agreement of a care and support plan, and the right to a choice of accommodation.

23. Sometimes, a person with sufficient means to pay for their care, who was intending to arrange their own care, may not be able to enter into a private agreement with their care home. This may be because they do not have the mental capacity to do so and have no attorney or deputy to act on their behalf, or it may be that, even though they have the capacity to decide where to live, they are not able to manage the making of the arrangements and have no friends or relatives to assist them. In such cases, the local authority is responsible for making arrangements for the provision of their accommodation, with reimbursement from the person as necessary.[2] The person would remain ordinarily resident in their placing local authority, even where they enter the accommodation in another local authority area.

Scenario: people who are arranging and paying for their care home placement

Wendy is 82 years old and very frail. Following a fall and a stay in hospital, she is assessed as having eligible needs for care and support under the Care Act. A financial assessment undertaken by her local authority, local authority A, concludes that she does not qualify for local authority financial assistance.

Wendy wants to arrange her own care and support, but does want some help in choosing the right care home. Local authority A provides advice to Wendy and her family on care homes in Local authority A and surrounding areas and help her to select a home that best meets her requirements. The care home is located in local authority B, as Wendy has expressed a desire to move closer to her family. Wendy moves into the care home as a self-funder and signs a contract with the care home for the provision of her care.

---

[1] See Section 18(3) of the Care Act.
[2] See Section 18(3) of the Care Act.

A few months after Wendy moves into the care home, her savings fall below the capital limit and she approaches local authority A for support. She is advised by local authority A that she is no longer ordinarily resident in their local authority and that she should seek financial assistance from local authority B. Local authority B agrees to fund Wendy's accommodation costs, but immediately falls into dispute with local authority A over her place of ordinary residence. Local authority B disagrees with A's argument that Wendy has acquired an ordinary residence in their area and contends that she remains the responsibility of local authority A as that is where she has lived for most of her life.

As Wendy is being provided with accommodation, under the Care Act she is deemed to continue to be ordinarily resident in the area in which she was ordinarily resident immediately before her accommodation was provided by a local authority. Immediately before Wendy was provided accommodation, she was living in the same care home, but was responsible for paying for her own care. She had voluntarily left local authority A and moved to the care home in local authority B, which she had adopted voluntarily and for settled purposes. Therefore, Wendy is found to be ordinarily resident in local authority B.

ANNEX H5 – NHS CONTINUING HEALTHCARE

24. NHS Continuing Healthcare (NHS CHC) is a package of ongoing health and care and support that is arranged and funded solely by the NHS where the individual has been found to have a 'primary health need', as set out in The National Framework for NHS Continuing Healthcare and NHS-funded Nursing Care.[1] Such care is provided to people aged 18 or over, to meet needs that have arisen as a result of disability, accident or illness. Eligibility for NHS CHC places no limits on the settings in which the package of support can be offered or on the type of services provided.

25. Where an individual is eligible for NHS CHC, the relevant Clinical Commissioning Group (CCG) is responsible for care planning, commissioning health and care and support services, and for case management. Local authorities will continue to have a wider role, for example in relation to safeguarding responsibilities. However, if a review of a person's care and support needs subsequently determines that the individual is no longer eligible for NHS CHC – perhaps because they needed intensive health and care following an operation and they have now recovered – the NHS ceases to be responsible for the provision of the person's care and support. Instead, the responsibility for the provision of care and support to meet eligible needs falls to the local authority in which the person is ordinarily resident.

26. Where a person has been provided with NHS accommodation as part of a package of NHS CHC, then prior ordinary residence is retained, based on the local authority in which the person had been previously ordinarily resident. Therefore, where a person is placed in a care home (or other accommodation funded by the NHS) in another local authority area for the purpose of receiving

---

[1] https://www.gov.uk/government/uploads/system/uploads/attachment_data/file/213137/National-Framework-for-NHS-CHC-NHS-FNC-Nov-2012.pdf

NHS CHC, they continue to be ordinarily resident in the local authority area in which they were ordinarily resident before entering the NHS accommodation. Where a CCG places a person in such accommodation, it should inform the person's local authority of ordinary residence and, if the person is placed "out of area", it is also good practice for the CCG to inform the local authority in which the care home is located.

27. Where a person is accommodated in a care home as part of their package of NHS CHC, it is possible that they may cease to be eligible for NHS CHC, but still need to remain in their care home, or to be provided with accommodation elsewhere. In such a case, the local authority in whose area the person was ordinarily resident immediately before being provided with NHS accommodation would be the authority responsible for arranging care and support to meet the person's eligible needs, and for funding the person's accommodation, subject to any financial assessment.

Scenario: a person is discharged from NHS Continuing Healthcare

Maureen is 72 years old. Three years ago, she suffered a stroke which left her severely disabled with complex care needs. She was assessed as needing NHS CHC and was moved from hospital to a rehabilitation unit within an independent sector care home in local authority B. This placement was fully funded by Maureen's CCG. Before her stroke, Maureen had lived with her husband in local authority A.

A recent reassessment of Maureen's needs concludes that she is no longer eligible for NHS CHC, but has eligible needs for care and support and requires accommodation under the Care Act 2014 instead. The care home in which Maureen has been living offers her a place on a long-term basis and all those involved in her care agree that this arrangement best meets Maureen's needs.

Local authority B agrees to fund the placement on a 'without prejudice' basis but immediately falls into dispute with local authority A over Maureen's place of ordinary residence. Local authority B contends that Maureen remains ordinarily resident in local authority A, where she had been living with her husband before her placement at the care home began. Local authority A argues that Maureen has acquired an ordinary residence in local authority B due to the length of time she has spent at the care home.

In this situation, when Maureen first enters the care home she is receiving NHS CHC. Therefore, whilst Maureen is receiving NHS CHC at the care home she remains ordinarily resident in local authority A, where she was living before her stroke.

Once Maureen's NHS CHC ceases and she is instead provided with accommodation under the Care Act, she is deemed to be ordinarily resident in the area in which she was ordinarily resident immediately before the accommodation was provided. Immediately before Maureen was provided with accommodation she was living in the care home but was still ordinarily resident in local authority A. Therefore, Maureen remains ordinarily resident in local authority A.

---

28. Under section 9 of the Care Act, local authorities have a duty to assess the needs of any person who appears to have needs for care and support. If it becomes apparent during the course of the assessment that the person has health needs, the local authority should notify the person's CCG and invite them to assist in the assessment.

29. It is the responsibility of the local authority in which the person is ordinarily resident to provide any care and support identified as necessary to meet eligible needs, in the light of the assessment. Any health services identified by the assessment should be met by the person's CCG. CCGs and local authorities should work in partnership to agree their respective responsibilities in relation to the provision of the joint package of care.

30. Where a person is placed in accommodation out of area, they remain ordinarily resident in the area of the placing local authority and the placing authority remains responsible for the provision of any other care and support services required. However, the person's GP may be based in the area in which they are living, and it is this CCG that is responsible for the provision any health services. This may mean that a local authority and a CCG located several miles apart, need to work together to provide a joint package of health and care and support. In the case of a person in receipt of NHS Continuing Healthcare, the placing CCG remains responsible for the provision of care, even where the person changes their GP practice.

ANNEX H6 – BRITISH CITIZENS RESUMING PERMANENT RESIDENCE IN ENGLAND AFTER PERIOD ABROAD

31. British citizens returning to England after a period of residing abroad (who had given up their previous home in this country) are entitled to an assessment as soon as they return if they appear to have needs for care and support.

32. Accordingly, a returning British citizen would usually acquire an ordinary residence in the area in which they chose to locate, if their intention was to stay living there for settled purposes. For example, they may have family in a particular area and choose to settle there for that reason or they may have no particular reason to locate in a given area. As long as they can demonstrate an intention to remain in the place they are living for settled purposes, they are able to acquire an ordinary residence there.

33. However, if a returning citizen presents to a local authority on their return to England but has no particular intention to settle in that area, the local authority may decide they may be found to be of "no settled residence" and/or in "urgent need" (see Annex H1). Each case should be decided on an individual basis.

34. It should be noted that ordinary residence can be acquired as soon as a person moves to an area, if their move is voluntary and for settled purposes. There is no minimum period in which a person has to be living in a particular place for them to be considered ordinarily resident there, because it depends on the nature and quality of the connection with the new place.

ANNEX H7 – ARMED FORCES VETERANS AND THE FAMILIES OF ARMED FORCES PERSONNEL

35. The ordinary residence provisions apply to armed forces veterans and the families of armed forces personnel in active service in the same way as they apply to other people. If veterans have needs for care and support upon leaving the forces, they would usually acquire an ordinary residence in the area to

which they chose to locate. If a veteran does not have a permanent place to live on leaving the forces or does not have a settled purpose in relation to where they are living, they may be found to be of "no settled residence" and/ or in "urgent need". If the person is found to be of no settled residence, then the local authority in which they are physically present will be responsible for meeting their eligible needs for care and support. If the person is determined to have urgent needs, then the same local authority should consider using its powers to meet those needs, in advance of establishing where the person's ordinary residence lies.

36. Where family members (who are 18 or over) of armed forces personnel in active service need care and support, their ordinary residence would fall to be assessed and they would generally be ordinarily resident in the area in which they were living. If the member of the armed forces was subsequently posted to another area of the country, the Shah test would again apply and the family member in need of services would usually acquire an ordinary residence in the area to which they were posted. However, if the family member was in receipt of accommodation, prior to the posting and was placed in accommodation in the new area by their original authority in order to be near their family, they would remain ordinarily resident in the area of the placing authority.

37. In the event of a service family returning from overseas, the ordinary residence of any family members (aged 18 or over) requiring care and support would be assessed and they would usually acquire an ordinary residence in the area in which they chose to reside for settled purposes. If the family had no settled purpose in relation to where they were living, the family member in need of services may be found to be of "no settled residence" and/or in "urgent need".

ANNEX H8 – YOUNG PEOPLE IN TRANSITION FROM CHILDREN'S SERVICES TO ADULT CARE AND SUPPORT

38. Children who are in need of care and support, including children who are 'looked after',[1] are provided with accommodation and/or services under the Children Act 1989 (the "1989 Act"). They may also be provided with care and support under the Chronically Sick and Disabled Persons Act 1970 (the "1970 Act"), though they receive universal services such as access to schools and primary health care in the same way as all other children. When a young person with care and support needs reaches the age of 18, the duty on local authorities to provide accommodation under the 1989 Act ceases and duties to provide other services usually cease. From their 18th birthday, care and support is generally under the Care Act 2014. This is provided by the local authority in which the young person is ordinarily resident as an adult, which may or may not be the same local authority where they were ordinarily resident under the 1989 Act.

DETERMINING ORDINARY RESIDENCE

39. When a young person reaches 18 and has eligible needs for care and support under the Care Act 2014, (the "2014 Act") their ordinary residence should be assessed to determine which local authority is responsible for ensuring these needs are met.

---

[1] A child who is 'looked after' is defined in section 22(1) of the Children Act 1989 and this term means, broadly, that a child is in a local authority's care by virtue of a care order or is provided with accommodation by a local authority in the exercise of their social services functions.

40. Neither the 1989 Act nor the 2014 Act makes provision for how to determine ordinary residence when a young person moves from being eligible under the 1989 Act to being eligible under the 2014 Act. Therefore, when making decisions about the ordinary residence of young people in transition to adult care and support, local authorities should have regard to both Acts. It is important to note that there is no set procedure for determining ordinary residence in this situation: every case must be decided on an individual basis, taking into account the circumstances of the young person and all the facts of their case.

41. Although the provisions of the 1989 Act do not usually apply once a young person reaches 18 (other than the leaving care provisions and the continuity of children's services requirement under section 66 of the 2014 Act, where relevant), local authorities could reasonably have regard to the 1989 Act and start from a preliminary assumption that the young person remains ordinarily resident in the local authority in which the child was ordinarily resident when they turned 18. Section 105(6) of the 1989 Act provides that, in determining the ordinary residence of a child for any purposes of that Act, any period in which a child lives in the following places should be disregarded in determining the child's ordinary residence for certain purposes under the 1989 Act:

- a school or other institution;

- in accordance with the requirements of a supervision order under the 1989 Act;

- in accordance with the requirements of a youth rehabilitation order under Part 1 of the Criminal Justice and Immigration Act 2008; or

- while he or she is being provided with accommodation by or on behalf of a local authority.

42. Therefore, where a local authority in which the child is ordinarily resident has placed a child in accommodation out of area under the 1989 Act, that local authority remains the child's place of ordinary residence for the purposes of the 1989 Act unless the child subsequently acquires a new place of ordinary residence. In such a case, the starting point may be that the young person's place of ordinary residence remains the same for the purposes of the 2014 Act when they turn 18.

43. However, this is only a starting point: the local authority should always consider the circumstances of the individual's case and the application of the [Shah or Vale] tests. Under these tests, a number of factors should be taken into account when considering a person's ordinary residence for the purposes of the 2014 Act. These include: the remaining ties the young person has with the authority where they were ordinarily resident as a child, ties with the authority in which they are currently living, the length and nature of residence in this area and the young person's views in respect of where he or she wants to live (if he or she has the mental capacity to make this decision). If the young person is being provided with care home accommodation under the 2014 Act at the time ordinary residence is assessed, it would be necessary to assess their place of ordinary residence immediately before such accommodation was provided.[1]

---

[1] Vale 1 is currently the subject of litigation and the guidance will be amended in due course.

44. In many cases, establishing a young person's local authority of ordinary residence will be a straightforward matter. However, difficulties may arise where a young person has been placed in residential accommodation out of area as a child under the 1989 Act. In this situation, the young person may be found to be ordinarily resident in the local authority where they were ordinarily resident under the 1989 Act, or they may be found to have acquired a new ordinary residence in the area in which they are living or in the area in which their parents are living,[1] depending on the facts of their case.

45. For example, where a young person (who has been placed out of area) moves out of their residential accommodation under the 1989 Act and into independent living arrangements in their 'host area' on or around their 18th birthday, the starting point would be that they are ordinarily resident in the area where they were ordinarily resident under the 1989 Act. However, in this situation, the starting point is more likely to be displaced than in other situations. By the time the young person reaches the age of 18, they may have been living in another local authority area for several years under the 1989 Act. Shortly before their 18th birthday, they may have a well-established support network outside of their authority of ordinary residence under the 1989 Act which they wish to continue into adulthood. More importantly, they may have made a decision to stay in their host area for settled purposes. In such a case, a consideration of all the facts may lead to the conclusion that, for the purposes of the 2014 Act, the young person is ordinarily resident in the area in which they are living at the time of their 18th birthday. Scenarios 1, 2 and 3 below provide some examples of how ordinary residence is determined when a young person moves from accommodation provided under the 1989 Act to accommodation or other care and support provided under the 2014 Act.

46. Similarly, where a young person is intending to move areas to go to university, the starting point would be that they are ordinarily resident in the same place as they were ordinarily resident under the 1989 Act. Again, this may not always be the case. If the young person moves to the area in which the university is located for settled purposes and has no intention to return to his authority of ordinary residence under the 1989 Act, then the facts of his case may lead to the conclusion that he or she has acquired an ordinary residence in the area of the University.

47. Alternatively, if the young person has a base with his or her parents (or those with parental responsibility for him or her) in the local authority where he or she was ordinarily resident under the 1989 Act, and he or she intends to return to this base during the university holidays (including the long summer holiday) then the facts of his case may lead to the conclusion that he or she remains ordinarily resident in the "base" local authority.

48. It is not possible for a person to be ordinarily resident in two different local authorities under the 2014 Act. Therefore, where a young person goes away to university or college, it is necessary to establish, from all the facts of their case, to which local authority they have the stronger link. If it is the local authority where they were ordinarily resident under the 1989 Act, this local authority would be responsible for meeting eligible needs under the 2014 Act, both during term time at university and during holidays when the young person is staying elsewhere (for example with the parents in the local authority where they are

---

[1] Under the 1989 Act, a child's ordinary residence is by default that of their parents. However, they may acquire an ordinary residence of their own if, for example, they are placed into care.

ordinarily resident). The young person's absence from their local authority of ordinary residence during term time would not result in their ordinary residence being lost: it would be considered a temporary absence. Scenarios 4 and 5 below provide further guidance on how ordinary residence is determined when a young person attends university in a different local authority area.

CARE LEAVERS

49. Where a child's "looked after status" under the 1989 Act ends, the local authority which was formerly responsible for them might retain some duties after they reach the age of 18. These young people are referred to as "young people eligible for care leaving services" or "care leavers".

50. In order to provide care leavers with the assistance they need to achieve their aspirations, local authorities must allocate a personal adviser and work with a care leaver to maintain a pathway plan that sets out the support and services available (which may include assistance with education or training). This support may continue until the young person reaches the age of 21 or for longer if they remain in an approved programme of education or training.[1] Where a young person qualifies for advice and assistance under section 24 of the 1989 Act, the local authority may be required to advise and befriend him or her. They may also be required to give him or her assistance in kind and, exceptionally, by providing accommodation or cash.

51. A local authority which is responsible for providing support to a care leaver is not under a general duty to provide accommodation. Therefore, when a care leaver with assessed care and support needs reaches the age of 18 and requires residential accommodation, their accommodation is usually provided under the 2014 Act, by their local authority of ordinary residence. However, in 2014, the government introduced a duty on local authorities to support those care leavers aged 18 and eligible for care leaving services, who want to stay with their former foster parents until their 21st birthday, known as "Staying Put".

52. There are, however, certain powers and duties to provide accommodation to care leavers in particular cases. Under section 24B(5) of the 1989 Act, local authorities have a duty to provide certain young people who qualify for advice and assistance under section 24 of the 1989 Act[2] with vacation accommodation if they are in full-time further or higher education and their term-time accommodation is not available. They also have a power to provide assistance during term-time, such as expenses to cover travel or equipment costs and expenses incurred by the young person in living near the place where he or she is studying.

53. Local authorities do not have a duty to provide accommodation to care leavers during term time. Such accommodation is funded by whatever mainstream funding sources are available to support higher education students. Nor is there a duty under the 1989 Act to provide care and support in the home to care leavers who are in higher education – such services would be provided under the 2014 Act by the local authority of ordinary residence.

---

[1] See section 23CA of the 1989 Act which was inserted by the Children and Young Persons Act 2008. Where a former relevant child resumes a programme of training up to age 25, they are entitled to continuing support from a leaving care personal adviser allocated by their authority of ordinary residence under the 1989 Act.

[2] That is, a young person who is under the age of 25 and who either (a) had a special guardianship order in force in relation to them when they reached the age of 18, and immediately before the making of that order was a looked after child, or (b) was a looked after child before they were 18.

54. Local authorities also have a power to provide accommodation under section 24A(5) of the 1989 Act to a young person whom they are advising and befriending under section 24A. Such accommodation may only be provided in exceptional circumstances and if, in the circumstances, assistance may not be given under section 24B (vacation accommodation). A young person who is eligible for care home accommodation under the 2014 Act would be unlikely to be regarded as being in "exceptional circumstances".

55. If a care leaver had been placed out of area as a looked after child, and wishes to remain in this area on reaching the age of 18, they may be found to be ordinarily resident there for the purposes of the 2014 Act. In this situation, their accommodation would be provided by the local authority in which they are living but the provision of any leaving care services under the 1989 Act would remain the responsibility of the responsible local authority under the 1989 Act.

56. Where this is the case, the 1989 Act and the 2014 Act would operate in parallel. This means the responsible authority under the 1989 Act and the authority of ordinary residence under the 2014 Act would need to work together to ensure the young person eligible for leaving care services was provided with joined up care and support.

57. It should be noted that where a child has been placed out of area under the 1989 Act and becomes eligible for leaving care services upon reaching the age of 18, this does not automatically mean they are ordinarily resident in the area where they were ordinarily resident under the 1989 Act or in the authority responsible for providing them with the leaving care services under the 1989 Act. Whilst the young person remains entitled to leaving care support from their responsible authority under the 1989 Act, all the circumstances of their case must be considered. Scenarios 3 and 5 below provide examples of how the 1989 Act and the 2014 Act operate in parallel when a young person is eligible to leaving care services under the 1989 Act and accommodation or other care and support under the 2014 Act.

Scenario 1: transition from accommodation under the 1989 Act to accommodation under the 2014 Act

Sunil is 18 years old and has physical and learning disabilities. Since the age of 10 he has been accommodated in a specialist residential school under section 20 of the 1989 Act. The primary purpose of Sunil's placement is to meet his health and education needs. The school is located in local authority B but paid for by local authority A, the local authority where his family live. For the purposes of the 1989 Act, Sunil is the responsibility of local authority A.

Now that Sunil is 18, he is ready to leave school. His needs are assessed and it is decided that he should move in to a house with three other people in a supported living tenancy. As Sunil has capacity to make some decisions for himself, he is able to express a desire to remain living in local authority B, near his friends from school and within the local community to which he feels he now belongs. Therefore, at the end of the school year he moves into his new home in local authority B and his accommodation changes from being provided under the 1989 Act to being provided under the 2014 Act.

At this point, local authority B falls into dispute with local authority A over Sunil's ordinary residence. Local authority B's view is that Sunil should remain the responsibility of local authority A. However, local authority A argues that their duty to Sunil ended when he left school and that he has become ordinarily resident in local authority B.

In these circumstances, the starting point is that Sunil is ordinarily resident in local authority A as this is the local authority in which he was ordinarily resident when he turned 18. However, this is only a starting point and the local authority must go on to consider all the facts of Sunil's case under the 2014 Act.

Sunil has been living in local authority B for 8 years and he has expressed a wish to remain there as he feels part of the local community. Although his family still live in local authority A, their home is not a base to which he returns often, other than for short spells over Christmas and other occasional events. Therefore, in line with the settled purpose test in the [Shah] case, it seems that Sunil has adopted local authority B voluntarily and for settled purposes. As such, the starting point that he remains ordinarily resident in local authority A can be displaced: for the purposes of the 2014 Act, he is ordinarily resident in local authority B.

Scenario 2: transition from accommodation under the 1989 Act to independent living accommodation with care and support provided under the 2014 Act

Rosie is 18 years old and has Down's Syndrome. She has been 'looked after' by local authority E from a young age and has spent the last 5 years living with foster carers "out of area" in local authority F. Although she is living in local authority F, she remains the responsibility of local authority E under the provisions in the 1989 Act.

When Rosie turns 18, she will be ready to leave care and a transition assessment is carried out to determine her future care needs. A move to independent living is agreed in line with Rosie's own wishes. Rosie's support workers in local authority E, together with her foster carers, help her to find a flat share with friends in local authority F. Rosie signs her own tenancy agreement and the move takes place. She receives housing benefit to pay her rent and Supporting People money to fund housing related support. She also receives care and support under the 2014 Act.

Local authority E provides Rosie with care and support but immediately falls into dispute with local authority F. In their view, Rosie has acquired a new ordinary residence in local authority F and any care and support should be its responsibility. However, local authority F argues that local authority E's responsibility towards Rosie has not ended simply because her accommodation status has changed.

As Rosie is in transition from being provided with care and support under the 1989 Act to being provided with care and support under the 2014 Act, the starting point is that her place of ordinary residence is local authority E, the authority where she was ordinarily resident in when she turned 18. However, this is only a starting point and the local authority must go on to look at all the facts of Rosie's case.

Rosie has been 'looked after' from a young age and has lived in local authority F for 5 years by the time she turns 18. She has no contact with her birth parents and no links with anyone in local authority E other than her social workers. She has a well-established support network in local authority F, including her foster parents who she intends to maintain a relationship with. Rosie has chosen to live in local authority F and has a flat share there which indicates that she has a settled purpose to remain there. Therefore, in line with the [Shah] test, Rosie has acquired an ordinary residence in local authority F: the starting point that she is ordinarily resident in local authority E can be displaced.

As Rosie has been 'looked after' by local authority E for the requisite period of time, she is eligible for after-care services under the leaving care provisions in the 1989 Act. Local authority E, the authority that last looked after Rosie, is responsible for the provision of these services, despite the fact that Rosie is now ordinarily resident in local authority F and receiving care and support under the 2014 Act from that authority. Therefore, local authority E and local authority F must work together to ensure that Rosie gets a holistic support package that meets all her eligible needs.

Scenario 3: transition from care and support under the 1989 Act to care and support under the 2014 Act where a young person goes to university
Olu is 18 years old and has a physical disability which requires the use of a wheelchair. He currently lives at home with his parents in local authority G but has a place to study at university in local authority H, which is several miles away from his home town. Olu's disability means that he requires help with his personal care needs and this is currently provided by carers in his parents' home under section 17 of the 1989 Act, in conjunction with section 2 of the Chronically Sick and Disabled Persons Act 1970.

Olu starts his university course at the beginning of term. He lives in university accommodation which has been specially adapted for him by the university in line with their duties under the Equalities Act 2010. His accommodation is funded through mainstream education sources and his personal care is provided by a local domiciliary care agency, arranged by local authority G under the 2014 Act.

However, local authority G immediately falls into dispute with local authority H. It argues that Olu has moved to local authority H for settled purposes and has acquired an ordinary residence there. In the authority's view, local authority H should be providing Olu's care and support under the 2014 Act. By contrast, local authority H argues that Olu is in its local authority on a temporary basis only and has not acquired an ordinary residence there. It believes local authority G remains responsible for the provision of Olu's care and support under the 2014 Act.

As Olu is in transition from receiving care and support under the 1989 Act to receiving them under the 2014 Act, the starting point is that he remains ordinarily resident in local authority G, the local authority where he was ordinarily resident under the 1989 Act. However, this is only a starting point and the local authority must go on to consider all the facts of his case.

Olu has lived in local authority G all his life. He has a close relationship with his parents who provide him with emotional, and some financial, support. He regards their home as his home and plans to return there during his university holidays, and once his course is over. As such, his parents' home can be said to be his "base". Therefore, it does not appear that Olu satisfies the [Shah] settled purpose test as his move to local authority H is not for settled purposes: his home remains with his parents and his absence from their house can said to be temporary. The starting point that Olu is ordinarily resident in local authority G is correct.

As Olu spends a significant amount of time in local authority H, several miles away from his local authority of ordinary residence, local authority G believes it would be more practical for Olu's care and support to be provided and overseen locally. Therefore, it makes arrangements for local authority H to provide care and support to Olu under the 2014 Act on their behalf. Local authority H is able to recover the cost of Olu's care from local authority G.

Scenario 4: transition from care and support under the 1989 Act to care and support under the 2014 Act where a young person goes to university
Marcus is almost 18 years old and has a physical disability which requires the use of a wheelchair. He has been a 'looked after' child since the age of 5 and has been accommodated in several different local authority areas, although his responsible authority is local authority J. For the past two years he has lived in a residential school in local authority K where he has made good progress. He has been offered a university place that he wishes to take up. The university is located in local authority L.

When Marcus turns 18 an assessment is carried out with a view to putting a package of care in place that will support him at university. He is assessed as requiring assistance with personal care tasks such as washing and dressing as his disability means he has difficulty doing these tasks unaided. He plans to live in university accommodation which has been adapted for his use in line with the university's duties under the Equalities Act 2010. This is funded through mainstream education sources.

Local authority J agrees to meet Marcus's personal care needs through care and support provided under the 2014 Act and Marcus's move to university takes place. As Marcus has been a looked after child for the requisite period, he also qualifies for leaving care services under the 1989 Act. Local authority J also arranges these services.

However, local authority J immediately falls into dispute with local authority L over Marcus's place of ordinary residence. In its view, Marcus has moved to local authority L for settled purposes and has acquired an ordinary residence there. As such, Local authority J argues that local authority L should be providing Marcus's care and support under the 2014 Act.

However, in local authority L's view, Marcus remains the responsibility of local authority J, where he was ordinarily resident under the 1989 Act. Local authority L also argues that he may have an ordinary residence in local authority K, the local authority where he last lived. In its view, Marcus's presence in local authority L is temporary in nature and does not amount to a "settled purpose" under the Shah test.

To establish Marcus's ordinary residence, all the facts of his case must be considered. As Marcus is in transition from receiving care and support under the 1989 Act to receiving care and support under the 2014 Act, the starting point is that he is ordinarily resident in local authority J, the local authority where he was ordinarily resident under the 1989 Act. However, this is only a starting point and the local authority must consider all the fact of the case.

Marcus has been looked after by local authority J for most of his life. However, he has only lived within local authority J's boundary for brief periods – most of his care placements have been out of area in neighbouring local authorities. Marcus has no contact with his birth parents, who were originally from local authority J, and no intention to return to the area for settled purposes.

Marcus's only real link to local authority J is the fact that it remains responsible for the provision of his leaving care services. However, this in itself is not enough to affirm that he is ordinarily resident there. In other respects, Marcus has no connection with the local authority area and has no "base" there. Therefore, the starting point that he remains ordinarily resident in local authority J is displaced.

Most recently, Marcus has lived in a residential school in local authority K. However, he only lived there for only 2 years, during which time he remained the responsibility of local authority J. He did not build up any relationships outside his school nor did he establish links within the local community. He has no intention to return there. Therefore, Marcus has not established an ordinary residence in local authority K.

Marcus is, however, in local authority L for a settled purpose. He intends to live there for the duration of his university course and has no other place which can be considered his base. His life is now based in local authority L and he has started to build friendships there and establish links with the local community. Therefore, Marcus acquires an ordinary residence in local authority L. As such, it is local authority L who is responsible for the provision of Marcus's care and support under of the 2014 Act.

As Marcus is eligible for leaving care services under the 1989 Act, local authority J, the local authority that last looked after him, is responsible for the provision of his vacation accommodation. Local authority J is also responsible for providing him with expenses during term time to cover things such as travel and equipment costs, as well as offering him general advice and support. Therefore, local authority J and local authority L need to work together to ensure that Marcus is fully supported during his time at university.

Marcus's situation can be contrasted with that of Olu (above, scenario 4). Olu did not acquire a new ordinary residence in his university town because he had a base to which he was intending to return regularly and at the end of his course, and, as such, his presence in his university town was on a temporary basis only. By contrast, Marcus had been a looked after child and had no base in any local authority. Therefore, when he moved to his university town he intended to live there for settled purposes for the duration of his university course.

ANNEX H9 – OTHER PROVISIONS UNDER WHICH AN ORDINARY RESIDENCE DETERMINATION CAN BE SOUGHT
Schedule 3 to the Care Act 2014
58. Schedule 3 to the Care Act places a duty on local authorities and the NHS to work together to ensure the safe hospital discharge of people with care and support needs. Where a person remains in hospital because a local authority has not carried out an assessment or put in place arrangements to meet the care and support that it proposes to meet in order to ensure that the person can be safely discharged from hospital, the local authority may be liable to pay the relevant NHS body a charge per day of delay.

59. Schedule 3 to the Care Act requires NHS bodies to take reasonable steps to ensure that eligibility for NHS Continuing Healthcare is assessed in all cases where it appears to the NHS body that the person may have a need for such care, in consultation, where it considers it appropriate, with the local authority appearing to the NHS body to be the authority in whose area the patient is ordinarily resident.

60. Where it is not likely to be safe to discharge a hospital patient unless arrangements for meeting their care and support are put in place, the NHS body must notify the patient's local authority of this. Under the Act, it is the local authority in which the patient appears to the NHS body to be ordinarily resident. Or where a person is not ordinarily resident in any local authority, i.e. a person of "no settled residence", the Care Act provides that it is the local authority in which the hospital is situated that the NHS body must notify. Once notification has been received, the local authority must arrange for an assessment of the person's need for care and support to be carried out and for the provision of any services.

61. If a local authority receives notification from the NHS body of a person who it believes is ordinarily resident in another local authority area, it should inform the NHS body that has issued the notification immediately. If the NHS body agrees that the person is ordinarily resident elsewhere, it should withdraw the notification and re-issue it to the correct local authority. If the NHS body does not agree that the person is ordinarily resident elsewhere, the local authority in receipt of the notification must proceed with carrying out the assessment and arranging for the provision of any necessary care and support. A person ready for discharge from hospital should not remain in hospital for longer than necessary because two

or more local authorities have fallen into dispute about the person's place of ordinary residence.

62. Where a local authority has provisionally accepted responsibility for a person discharged from hospital but remains in dispute with one or more local authorities over the person's ordinary residence in relation to which authority should reimburse the NHS body for the person's delayed discharge, a determination from the Secretary of State can be sought under section 40 of the Care Act. Determinations should only be sought as a last resort: local authorities should take all steps necessary to resolve the disputes themselves first.

THE MENTAL CAPACITY ACT 2005 DEPRIVATION OF LIBERTY SAFEGUARDS

63. The Deprivation of Liberty Safeguards ("MCA DoLS")[1] in the Mental Capacity Act 2005 ("the 2005 Act") provide a framework for authorising the deprivation of liberty of people who lack the capacity to consent to arrangements made for their care or treatment (in either a hospital or care home)[2] and who meet the qualifying requirements in Schedule A1, including that they need to be deprived of liberty in their own best interests, and to prevent harm to them, and that the deprivation of liberty is a proportionate response to the likelihood and seriousness of that harm.[3]

64. Under the MCA DoLS, the "managing authority" of a hospital or care home must request a standard authorisation from a local authority (a "supervisory body") if they believe an adult will, or will be likely to be, deprived of their liberty in hospital or care home setting within the next 28 days.

65. In most cases, it should be possible to obtain a standard authorisation in advance of deprivation of liberty occurring. Where this is not possible and a person needs to be deprived of their liberty in their own best interests before the standard authorisation process can be completed, the managing authority must give itself an urgent authorisation and apply to the supervisory body for a standard authorisation to be issued within 7 calendar days.

66. Where a person needs to be deprived of liberty in a care home in England or Wales, the 2005 Act provides that the supervisory body is always the local authority in which the person is ordinarily resident.[4] This remains the case regardless of whether the person has been placed in the care home in another authority's area by the local authority or a CCG.

67. If a person is arranging and paying for their care under private arrangements, they usually acquire an ordinary residence in the area in which their care home is located. Therefore, the local authority in which the care home is located will be the supervisory body.

68. Where a person is not ordinarily resident in any local authority (for example a person of "no settled residence"), the 2005 Act provides that it is the local authority in which the care home is situated that becomes the supervisory body.[5]

---

[1] The Mental Capacity Act Deprivation of Liberty Safeguards were inserted into the Mental Capacity Act 2005 by section 50 and Schedules 7,8 and 9 to the Mental Health Act 2007 which inserted Schedules A1 and 1A into the 2005 Act.

[2] Applications may be made to the Court of Protection under the 2005 Act to authorise deprivation of liberty in settings other than hospital or care homes.

[3] See the best interests requirement paragraph 16 of Schedule A1 to the 2005 Act.

[4] Paragraph 18(2(1) of Schedule A1 to the 2005 Act.

[5] Paragraph 18(2) of Schedule A1 to the 2005 Act.

69. Under paragraph 183 of Schedule A1 to the 2005 Act, the "deeming" provisions in section 39(1) of the Care Act apply for the purposes of determining where a person is ordinarily resident so that the local authority that is the supervisory body can be identified. A person remains ordinarily resident in the area of the local authority (A) in which the person is ordinarily resident before that local authority (A) places the person in the area of authority (B) in an arrangement that amounts to a deprivation of liberty. Therefore the placing local authority remains the supervisory body.

70. If a person needs to be deprived of liberty in a care home upon their discharge from hospital, and the care home applies for a standard authorisation in advance,[1] whilst the person is still in hospital (as would be good practice in this situation), it is the local authority in which the person was ordinarily resident before their admission to hospital which is responsible for acting as the supervisory body. This remains the case even where it is planned that the person will be discharged from hospital to a care home located in another local authority area.

71. If the person arranges and pays for their own care in that care home (usually a deputy appointed by the Court of Protection under the 2005 Act would enter into a contract with the care home on their behalf), they would generally acquire an ordinary residence in the area in which their care home is located (the area of local authority (B). However, if the person does not yet reside in the care home when the care home applies for the standard authorisation, they are not yet ordinarily resident in the area for local authority (B), despite any imminent plans to move there. Whilst the person remains in hospital, they remain ordinarily resident where they were before admission to hospital (the area of local authority A) until they are discharged from hospital. In these circumstances, the supervisory body is local authority (A).

72. Section 39(5) of the Care Act applies to all NHS accommodation and not just hospitals. This means that where a person is placed in a care home "out of area" by a CCG under NHS CHC arrangements, they remain ordinarily resident in the area in which they were ordinarily resident before being provided with NHS CHC. Therefore, if the person in receipt of NHS CHC subsequently needs to be deprived of their liberty, it is the local authority in which they were ordinarily resident immediately before being provided with NHS CHC that is the responsible supervisory body for the purposes of DoLS.

73. Where two or more local authorities dispute the person's ordinary residence for the purpose of identifying which authority is the supervisory body, the 2005 Act provides that disputes may be determined by the Secretary of State or appointed person, or by the Welsh Ministers where they cannot be resolved locally. Disputes between a local authority in England and a local authority in Wales, are determined by the Secretary of State or Welsh Ministers under cross-border arrangements made under paragraph 183(4) of Schedule A1 to the 2.0. Act.

74. A determination under the 2005 Act can only be sought in relation to ordinary residence disputes that arise in connection with which local authority is the responsible supervisory body for the purpose of giving (and potentially reviewing) a standard authorisation. Where ordinary residence disputes occur in

---

[1] A standard authorisation comes into force when it is given, or at any later time specified in the authorisation: paragraph 52 of Schedule A1 to the 2005 Act.

relation to the general provision of care accommodation or services, determinations should be sought under section 40 of the Care Act.

75. Regulations made under the 2005 Act[1] put in place arrangements where there are disputes between local authorities in England over the ordinary residence of a person and who is the supervisory body arising when the managing authority of a care home or hospital requests a standard authorisation from a local authority; or any person requests the local authority to decide whether or not there is an unauthorised deprivation of liberty in a care home or hospital. They set out that, in the event of a dispute occurring, the local authority which receives the request for a standard authorisation must act as the supervisory body until the dispute is resolved, unless another local authority agrees to perform this role.

Scenario: moving from hospital to a care home under a standard authorisation

Geeta is 86 years old and has dementia. She lives on her own in local authority A but receives some care and support at home. She requires a routine operation to remove gallstones and is admitted to hospital in local authority B. During Geeta's stay in hospital she becomes increasingly confused and starts to wander, making various attempts to leave the ward. To ensure that Geeta can continue to receive essential treatment, her doctors and nursing staff feel it would be in her best interests to prevent her from leaving.

As Geeta is having her movements so restricted as to amount to a deprivation of liberty, and does not have capacity to consent to these arrangements, hospital staff place Geeta under an urgent authorisation and apply to local authority B, the local authority for the area in which the hospital is located, for a standard authorisation to last for the remainder of her hospital stay. Local authority B gives the standard authorisation.

Geeta recovers well from her operation but remains very confused. In preparation for her hospital discharge, she is assessed by a multi-disciplinary team; it is found that she does not have capacity to decide where she should live and a best-interests decision is made that concludes she is no longer able to live independently in the community and recommends that she enters a care home. A place in a care home specialising in dementia care is found for Geeta in neighbouring local authority C. Due to Geeta's worsening dementia and the fact that she is unable to consent to living in the care home, the care home manager feels she will need to be deprived of her liberty as soon as she enters the care home, at least for the short-term until she settles in.

The care home manager requests a standard authorisation from local authority B, the area in which the hospital is located, mistakenly believing that local authority B is Geeta's local authority of ordinary residence. Local authority

---

[1] Part 6 of The Mental Capacity (Deprivation of Liberty: Standard Authorisations, Assessments and Ordinary Residence) Regulations 2008 (S.I. 2008/1858) as amended by article 11 of, and paragraph 118 of Schedule 2 of the National Treatment Agency (Abolition) and the Health and Social Care Act 2012 (Consequential, Transitional and Saving Provisions) Order 2013 (S.I. 2013/235). These Regulations apply only to England.

B immediately falls into dispute with local authority A over Geeta's ordinary residence and which authority should act as the supervisory body. Local authority C also becomes involved in the dispute.

Local authority A argues that local authority C should be the supervisory body. Its argument is based on the fact that the standard authorisation would begin as soon as Geeta moves into the care home in local authority C, at which point she will become ordinarily resident there. Local authority B argues that Geeta has not acquired an ordinary residence in their local authority during her hospital stay and, as such, local authority A or C should be the supervisory body. Finally, local authority C argues that, as Geeta is still in hospital and has not yet moved to their local authority area, she cannot be ordinarily resident in local authority C, despite her impending move.

As local authority B has received the request for the standard authorisation, it is obliged to act as the supervisory body until the dispute is resolved, as required by the Mental Capacity (Deprivation of Liberty: Standard Authorisations, Assessments and Ordinary Residence) Regulations 2008. However, local authority C feels strongly that local authority B is not the correct authority to give the standard authorisation and agrees to take on the supervisory body role until the question of Geeta's ordinary residence is decided.

To determine Geeta's ordinary residence for purpose of identifying the responsible supervisory body, paragraph 182 of Schedule A1 to the 2005 Act sets out that the supervisory body is the local authority in which the person is ordinarily resident. Therefore, Geeta's ordinary residence must be established at the point in time when the care home manager requested the standard authorisation.

At the time of the request, Geeta is in hospital in local authority B. Therefore, whilst Geeta is in hospital in local authority B, she remains ordinarily resident in local authority A. When Geeta moves to the care home in local authority C her ordinary residence will not change because local authority A was the area she was living in for settled purposes before she went to the care home. Local authority A is also the supervisory body responsible for considering the request for the standard authorisation.

MCA DoLS authorisations should be given for as short a time as possible. It would be sensible for local authority A to grant a short standard authorisation so her situation can be reviewed once she moves to the care home. If the review concludes that a further standard authorisation is in Geeta's best interests, the care home should request a fresh standard authorisation from the supervisory body, Geeta's local authority of ordinary residence, local authority A. This is because while Geeta remains in receipt of services her ordinary residence does not change and remains with local authority A where she was living immediately before she was admitted to hospital.

ANNEX I: REPEALS AND REVOCATIONS

The following tables summarise some of the key legal provisions and existing statutory guidance which are to be replaced by the Care Act 2014 and the associated regulations and guidance.

Where existing provisions relate to jurisdictions other than England, the provisions will be disapplied so that they no longer relate to English local authorities.Where provisions relate to children as well as adults, they will be disapplied in relation to adults, but will remain in force in relation to children.

The repeals and revocations required will be provided for by Orders under the Care Act. The final detail of which precise provisions are to be replaced is to be confirmed during the consultation process. The tables below are not therefore a final position, but intended to given an indication of the scope of the Act, and the key existing provisions which are to be affected.

PRIMARY LEGISLATION TO BE REPEALED OR DISAPPLIED

Title of legislation to be repealed, in whole or in part
National Assistance Act 1948
Health Services and Public Health Act 1968
Local Authority Social Services Act 1970
Chronically Sick and Disabled Persons Act 1970
Health and Social Services and Social Security Adjudications Act 1983
Disabled Persons (Services, Consultation and Representation) Act 1986
National Health Service and Community Care Act 1990
Carers (Recognition and Services) Act 1995
Carers and Disabled Children Act 2000
Health and Social Care Act 2001
Community Care (Delayed Discharges etc.) Act 2003
Carers (Equal Opportunities) Act 2004
National Health Service Act 2006

SECONDARY LEGISLATION TO BE REVOKED

Title of instruments to be revoked, in whole or in part
Approvals and directions under S.21(1) NAA 1948 (LAC (93)10)
National Assistance (Assessment of Resources) Regulations 1992
National Assistance Act 1948 (Choice of Accommodation) Directions 1992
National Assistance (Residential Accommodation) (Relevant Contributions) Regulations 2001
National Assistance (Residential Accommodation) (Additional Payments and Assessment of Resources) Regulations 2001
Delayed Discharges (Mental Health Care) (England) Order 2003

Delayed Discharges (England) Regulations 2003
National Assistance (Sums for Personal Requirements) Regulations 2003
Community Care (Delayed Discharges etc.) Act (Qualifying Services) Regulations 2003
Community Care Assessment Directions 2004
Community Care, Services for Carers and Children's Services (Direct Payments) (England) Regulations 2009
NHS Continuing Healthcare (Responsibilities) Directions 2009Ordinary Residence Disputes (National Assistance Act 1948) Directions 2010

STATUTORY GUIDANCE TO BE CANCELLED

Title of guidance to be cancelled
Prioritising need in the context of Putting People First: a whole system approach to eligibility for social care (2010)
Fairer Charging Policies for Home Care and other non-residential Social Services (2013) and LAC (2001)32
Charging for residential accommodation guidance (CRAG) (2014)
Guidance on direct payments for community care, services for carers and children's services (2009)
The Personal Care at Home Act 2010 and Charging for Reablement (LAC (2010)6)
Charging for residential accommodation guidance (CRAG) (2014)
Identifying the ordinary residence of people in need of community care services (2013)
Transforming Adult Social Care (LAC (2009)1)
Guidance on National Assistance Act 1948 (Choice of Accommodation) Directions 1992 and National Assistance (Residential Accommodation) (Additional Payments) Regulations 2001 (LAC (2004)20)
The Community Care (Delayed Discharges etc.) Act 2003 guidance for implementation (LAC (2003)21)
Fair Access to Care Services (FACS): Guidance on eligibility criteria for adult social care (2002)
Carers and people with parental responsibility for disabled children (2001)
No secrets: guidance on developing and implementing multi-agency policies and procedures to protect vulnerable adults from abuse (2000)
Caring for people: community care in the next decade and beyond (1990)

GLOSSARY

This glossary refers to key terms used throughout the guidance. More specific terms that are relevant to individual chapters are defined in the section to which they relate.

Definitions of more common terms can be found on Think Local Act Personal's care and support "jargon buster": http://www.thinklocalactpersonal.org.uk/ Browse/ Informationandadvice/CareandSupportJargonBuster

Act of Parliament
If the House of Commons and the House of Lords agree proposals for a new law (called a Bill), and it then receives Royal Assent from the monarch, it becomes an Act of Parliament.

Adult
Any person over the age of 18 years.

Adult with care and support needs
A person over the age of 18 years who has a need for care and support (see below). Depending on the context, this could be an adult receiving a particular care and support service, or an adult who has such needs but are not receiving a service (for example, someone coming forward for an assessment).

Assessment
This is what a local authority does to find out the information so that it can decide whether a person needs care and support to help them live their day-to-day lives. A carer can also have an assessment.

Care and support
The mixture of practical, financial and emotional support for adults who need extra help to manage their lives and be independent – including older people, people with a disability or long-term illness, people with mental health problems, and carers. Care and support includes assessment of people's needs, provision of services and the allocation of funds to enable a person to purchase their own care and support. It could include care home, home care, personal assistants, day services, or the provision of aids and adaptations.

Carer
Somebody who provides support or who looks after a family member, partner or friend who needs help because of their age, physical or mental illness, or disability. This would not usually include someone paid or employed to carry out that role, or someone who is a volunteer.

Commissioners
The people or organisations that arrange the care and support that is available in an area to meet the needs of the population.

Direct payment
Payments made directly to someone in need of care and support by their local authority to allow the person greater choice and flexibility about how their care is delivered.

Domiciliary care
Also known as home care or non-residential care, it enables people to remain independent and living in their own homes.

Duty
This is something that the law says that someone (in this case, usually a local authority) must do, and that if they do not follow may result in legal challenge.

Local authority
An administrative unit of local government.

Person/people
This is used to refer to an individual or individuals. It may include carers as well as adults with care and support needs.

Personal budget
This is a statement that sets out the cost to the local authority of meeting an adult's care needs. It includes the amount that the adult must pay towards that cost themselves (on the basis of their financial assessment), as well as any amount that the local authority must pay.

Primary legislation
This a general term used to describe the main laws passed by Parliament, usually called Acts of Parliament.

Provider
An individual, institution, or agency that provides health, care and/or support services to people.

Provisions
The contents of a legal instrument, like an Act or regulations.

Regulations (see also secondary legislation)
A type of secondary legislation made under an Act of Parliament, setting out extra details that help the Act to be implemented.

INDEX

Index

Index

Index